# THE HANDBOOK OF RESEARCH SYNTHESIS

# THE HANDBOOK

## OF RESEARCH

## SYNTHESIS

Edited by

**HARRIS COOPER and LARRY V. HEDGES**

RUSSELL SAGE FOUNDATION                    NEW YORK

# THE RUSSELL SAGE FOUNDATION

The handbook of research synthesis / edited by Harris Cooper, Larry
  V. Hedges.
     p.  cm.
  Includes bibliographical references and index.
  ISBN 0-87154-226-9
    1. Research—Methodology—Handbooks, manuals, etc.  2. Information
storage and retrieval systems—Research—Handbooks, manuals, etc.
3. Research—Statistical methods—Handbooks, manuals, etc.
I. Cooper, Harris M.  II. Hedges, Larry V.
Q180.M4H35   1994      93-1625
001.4′2—dc20

Text design: JOHN JOHNSTON

RUSSELL SAGE FOUNDATION
112 East 64th Street, New York, New York 10021

10 9 8 7 6 5 4

To the authors of the *Handbook* chapters,
for their remarkable cooperation and commitment
to the advance of science and society

# CONTENTS

# FOREWORD

*The Handbook of Research Synthesis* is an attempt to bring together in a single volume state-of-the-art descriptions of every phase of the research synthesis process, from problem formulation to report writing.

Determining the content of the *Handbook* required us to use multiple decision criteria. First, by relying on personal experience and knowledge of previous books in the area, we identified the central decision points in conducting a research synthesis. This led to the creation of several of the major divisions of the text as well as specific chapters—for example, vote-counting procedures, combining significance levels, and correcting for sources of artificial variation across studies. Next, we examined the issues involved within the major tasks and broke them down so that covering the required information within a single chapter would be manageable. Thus, within the topic of evaluating the literature, separate chapters were given over to judging research quality, evaluating the reliability of coding decisions, and managing meta-analytic databases, among others. We supplemented the resulting list of chapters with others on special topics that cut across the various stages of research synthesis, but were important enough to merit more focused attention. These topics included missing data, publication bias, dependent effect sizes, and using research syntheses to develop theories. Next, for each topic we identified an expert or experts and obtained their agreement to write on the topic. Finally, we held a meeting, in which chapter authors discussed their intended coverage. Ultimately, 32 chapters emerged with 43 authors drawn from at least five distinct disciplines: information science, statistics, psychology, ed-ucation, and social policy analysis. Twenty-two of the authors also served as chapter reviewers along with 31 individuals who took part in the review process only.

In the course of attempting to coordinate such an effort, we were faced with numerous editorial decisions. Perhaps the most critical involved how to handle overlap in coverage across chapters. Because we wanted the *Handbook* to be exhaustive, we defined topics for chapters very narrowly, but anticipated that authors would likely define their domains more broadly. They did. The issue for us, then, became whether to edit out the redundancy or leave it in. We chose to leave it in for several reasons. First, there is considerable insight to be gained when the same issue is treated from multiple perspectives. Second, the repetition of topics helps the reader understand some of the most pervasive problems that confront a research synthesist. Finally, the overlap allows the chapters to stand on their own, as more complete discussions of each topic, thus increasing their individual usefulness for teaching.

Another important editorial issue involved mathematical notation. While some notation in meta-analysis has become relatively standard, few symbols are used universally. In addition, since each statistical chapter would contain some unique mathematical concepts, we had no guarantee that the same symbols might not be used to represent different concepts in different chapters. To minimize these problems, we proposed a notion system and met with the authors to revise and expand it. The system is not perfect, however, and the reader may discover, when moving from one chapter to the next, that the same symbol is used to represent different concepts or that different symbols are used for the same concept. However, each chapter introduces its notation, and we hope that confusion has been minimized.

Not only was finding a common mathematical notation a noteworthy editorial task but, given the number of diverse disciplines contributing to the *Handbook,* we were faced with problems involving more general terminology. Again, we expected that occasionally authors would use different terms for the same concept and the same term for different concepts. Further, some concepts would be new to readers in any particular discipline. Therefore, we asked authors to contribute to a glossary by defining the key terms in their chapter, which we edited for style and overlap. While such an instrument is always flawed and incomplete, we hope it facilitates readers' passage through the book.

Finally, a consideration that arises in any report of quantitative work concerns the conventions for deriving the numerical results given in examples. Specifically, there are several possible ways that numerical results can be rounded for presentation. For example, when final computations involve sums or quotients of intermediate results, the final numerical answer depends somewhat on whether and how the intermediate results are rounded. In the statistical examples, we have usually chosen to round intermediate computations, such as sums, to two decimal places. Thus, hand computations using the intermediate values should yield results corresponding to our examples. If computations are carried out directly with no rounding, the results might differ from those given. Note, however, that this rule is sometimes ambiguous, so readers who obtain slight numerical discrepancies should not be alarmed.

*The Handbook of Research Synthesis* is a joint enterprise that has depended on the efforts of over 100 people. The Russell Sage Foundation provided financial support; more important, the Foundation along with Eric Wanner, its president, dared to think large, divergent thoughts and act on them. In early 1987, it initiated a program designed to improve and disseminate state-of-the-art methods in research synthesis. The program committee included not only ourselves but Thomas Cook, David Cordray, Heidi Hartmann, Richard Light, Thomas Louis, and Frederick Mosteller.

This is the third volume to emerge from the program. The first volume, *The Future of Meta-Analysis,* was published by the Foundation in 1990. It contained the proceedings of a workshop convened by the Committee on National Statistics of the National Research Council. The goal of the workshop was to assess the role of meta-analysis in current policy-relevant research and to identify its strengths and limitations for helping direct future developments in research synthesis methodology.

The second volume, *Meta-Analysis for Explanation: A Casebook,* presented a series of four applications of meta-analysis. The cases were meant to highlight the potential of meta-analysis for generating and testing explanations of social phenomena (i.e., why males and females achieve differently in science) and the effectiveness of social and medical programs (i.e., psycho-educational care with adult surgical patients, juvenile delinquency interventions, and family and marital psychotherapies). Wrapped around the cases were general discussions of issues in research synthesis. The discussions used the cases as examples.

The Russell Sage Foundation Research Synthesis Committee conceived the *Handbook* project, reviewed its execution plan, and provided advice from its implementation to its completion, including the choice of authors and ad hoc chapter reviewers. The chapter reviewers were:

Betsy Jane Becker
College of Education
Michigan State University

Colin B. Begg
Epidemiology and Biostatistics
Memorial Sloan-Kettering Cancer Center

Jesse Berlin
School of Medicine
University of Pennsylvania

Brad J. Bushman
Department of Psychology
Iowa State University

John C. Callender
Proctor & Gamble Company
Cincinnati, OH

Iain Chalmers
The UK Cochrane Centre
Oxford, England

Peter Cohen
School of Dentistry
Medical College of Georgia

Philip Converse
Center for Advanced Study in the Behavioral Sciences
Stanford, CA

Thomas D. Cook
Department of Psychology
Northwestern University

Lee Cronbach
Department of Psychology
Stanford University

Elizabeth Devine
Foundations of Nursing Department
University of Wisconsin

Alice H. Eagly
Department of Psychological Sciences
Purdue University

John D. Emerson
Dean of the College
Middlebury College

Murray Enkin
Department of Obstetrics and Gynecology
McMaster University

Carol Fenichel
Library
Hahnemann University

John Finney
Veterans Administration Medical Center
Menlo Park, CA

Joseph L. Fleiss
Division of Biostatistics
Columbia University

Gene V. Glass
School of Education
Arizona State University

Joel B. Greenhouse
Department of Statistics
Carnegie Mellon University

Judith A. Hall
Department of Psychology
Northeastern University

Monica Harris
Department of Psychology
University of Kentucky

Heidi Hartmann
Institute for Women's Policy Research
Washington, DC

Janet Hyde
Department of Psychology
University of Wisconsin

James Kulik
Center for Research on Teaching and Learning
University of Michigan

Richard J. Light
John F. Kennedy School of Government
Harvard University

Mark W. Lipsey
Department of Human Resources
Vanderbilt University

Roderick Little
Department of Biomathematics
UCLA School of Medicine

Thomas A. Louis
Division of Biostatistics
University of Minnesota

Geoffrey Maruyama
Department of Educational Psychology
University of Minnesota

Norman Miller
Department of Psychology
University of Southern California

Carnot E. Nelson
Department of Psychological Behavior
University of South Florida

Ingram Olkin
Department of Statistics
Stanford University

Bart Osburn
Department of Psychology
University of Texas

Michael Perlman
Department of Statistics
University of Washington

David Pillemer
Department of Psychology
Wellesley College

Stephen W. Raudenbush
College of Education
Michigan State University

Jeffrey G. Reed
Xerox Corporation
Webster, NY

John Rolf
RAND Corporation
Santa Monica, CA

Robert Rosenthal
Department of Psychology
Harvard University

MaryLu C. Rosenthal
OCS America, Inc.
Cambridge, MA

William R. Shadish
Department of Psychology
Memphis State University

Pat Shrout
Department of Biostatistics
Columbia University

Rebecca Der Simonian
National Institute of Child Health
  and Human Development
Washington, DC

Judith D. Singer
School of Education
Harvard University

Robert E. Slavin
Center for Research
  on Elementary and Middle Schools
Johns Hopkins University

Michael Strube
Department of Psychology
Washington University

Eric Wanner
Russell Sage Foundation
New York, NY

Howard D. White
Department of Information Sciences
Drexel University

Thomas Widiger
Department of Psychology
University of Kentucky

John B. Willett
School of Education
Harvard University

Wendy Wood
Department of Psychology
Texas A&M University

Rose Woodsmall
National Library of Medicine
Bethesda, MD

We also received personal assistance from a host of capable individuals. At the University of Missouri, Kathy Craighead provided editorial support. Billye Adams served as administrative executor. At the University of Chicago, Ramona Hartweg and Matthew Beckerman served as editorial assistants and Amy Nowell recomputed all of the examples. At the Russell Sage Foundation, Pauline Jones, Vivian Kaufman, and Camille Yezzi provided secretarial and word processing support. Lisa Nachtigall managed the publication process.

Finally, we thank the chapter authors, to whom this book is dedicated. For both of us, this was our first attempt at book editing. We were forewarned by many about the trials and tribulations that awaited us—more so because of the size of our task and the prestige of our list of contributors. Instead, we experienced remarkable cooperation, flexibility, and good humor from the authors. Not from some, or most, but from all.

*Harris Cooper*
*Larry V. Hedges*
*New York 1993*

# CONTRIBUTORS

Pam M. Baxter
Psychological Sciences Library
Purdue University

Betsy Jane Becker
College of Education
Michigan State University

Colin B. Begg
Epidemiology and Biostatistics
Memorial Sloan-Kettering Cancer Center

Brad J. Bushman
Department of Psychology
Iowa State University

Thomas D. Cook
Department of Psychology
Northwestern University

Harris Cooper
Department of Psychology
University of Missouri

Kay Dickersin
Department of Epidemiology and Preventive Medicine
University of Maryland School of Medicine

Alice H. Eagly
Department of Psychological Sciences
Purdue University

Joseph L. Fleiss
School of Public Health
Columbia University

Leon J. Gleser
Department of Mathematics and Statistics
University of Pittsburgh

Joel B. Greenhouse
Department of Statistics
Carnegie Mellon University

C. Keith Haddock
Willford Hall Medical Center
Lackland AFB Texas

Judith A. Hall
Department of Psychology
Northeastern University

Katherine Taylor Halvorsen
Department of Mathematics
Smith College

Larry V. Hedges
Department of Education
University of Chicago

John E. Hunter
Department of Psychology
Michigan State University

Satish Iyengar
Department of Mathematics and Statistics
University of Pittsburgh

Richard J. Light
John F. Kennedy School of Government
Harvard University

Mark W. Lipsey
Department of Human Resources
Vanderbilt University

Thomas A. Louis
Division of Biostatistics
University of Minnesota

Georg E. Matt
Department of Psychology
San Diego State University

Norman Miller
Department of Psychology
University of Southern California

Frederick Mosteller
School of Public Health
Harvard University

Ingram Olkin
Department of Statistics
Stanford University

Robert G. Orwin
R.O.W. Sciences, Inc.
Rockville, MD

Therese D. Pigott
National-Lewis University
Evanston, IL

Vicki E. Pollock
Department of Psychiatry
University of Southern California

Stephen W. Raudenbush
College of Education
Michigan State University

Jeffrey G. Reed
Document Production Systems Division
Xerox Corporation

MaryLu C. Rosenthal
OCS America, Inc.
Cambridge, MA

Robert Rosenthal
Department of Psychology
Harvard University

Frank L. Schmidt
Department of Management and Organizations
University of Iowa

Christine M. Schram
College of Education
Michigan State University

William R. Shadish
Department of Psychology
Memphis State University

Judith D. Singer
School of Education
Harvard University

William A. Stock
Department of Exercise Science and Physical Education
Arizona State University

Linda Tickle-Degnen
Department of Occupational Therapy
Boston University

Howard D. White
College of Information Studies
Drexel University

John B. Willett
School of Education
Harvard University

Wendy Wood
Department of Psychology
Texas A&M University

George Woodworth
Department of Statistics and Actuarial Sciences
University of Iowa

Paul M. Wortman
Department of Psychology
State University of New York at Stony Brook

Daniel Zelterman
Division of Biostatistics
University of Minnesota

# PART

# I

# INTRODUCTION

Cooper, H. and Hedges, L. V. (Eds.) 1994. *The Handbook of Research Synthesis.* New York: Russell Sage Foundation

# 1

# RESEARCH SYNTHESIS AS A SCIENTIFIC ENTERPRISE

**HARRIS COOPER**
*University of Missouri*

**LARRY V. HEDGES**
*University of Chicago*

## CONTENTS

> . . it is necessary, while formulating the problems of which in our advance we are to find the solutions, to call into council the views of those of our predecessors who have declared an opinion on the subject, in order that we may profit by whatever is sound in their suggestions and avoid their errors.
>
> Aristotle, *De Anima*

## 1. INTRODUCTION

From the moment we are introduced to science we are told it is a cooperative, cumulative enterprise. Like the artisans who construct a building from blueprints, bricks, and mortar, scientists contribute to a common edifice called knowledge. Theorists provide the blueprints and researchers collect the data that are the bricks.

To extend the analogy further, we might say that research synthesists are the bricklayers and hodcarriers of the science guild. It is their job to stack the bricks according to plan and apply the mortar that holds the structure together.

Those who have attempted a research synthesis are entitled to a wry smile as the analogy continues. They know that several sets of theory-blueprints often exist, describing structures that vary in form and function, with no a priori criteria for selecting among them. They also know that the data-bricks are not all six-sided and right-angled. They come in a baffling array of sizes and shapes. Making them fit, securing them with mortar, and seeing whether the resulting construction resembles the blueprint is a challenge worthy of the most dedicated, inspired artisan.

Scientific subliteratures are cluttered with repeated studies of the same phenomena. Repetitive studies arise because investigators are unaware of what others are doing, because they are skeptical about the results of past studies, and/or because they wish to extend (i.e., generalize or search for influences on) previous findings. Experience has shown that even when considerable effort is made to achieve strict replication, results across studies are rarely identical at any high level of precision (even in the physical sciences; see Hedges 1987). No two bricks are exactly alike.

How should science proceed when results differ? First, it is clear how it should *not* proceed: It should not pretend that there is no problem or decide that just one study, perhaps the most recent one, produces the correct finding. If results that are expected to be similar show variability, the scientific instinct should be to account for the variability by further systematic work.

"Research synthesis" or "research integration" in-volves the attempt to discover the consistencies and account for the variability in similar-appearing studies. It is one of a broad array of integrative activities that scientists engage in; its intellectual heritage can be traced back at least as far as Aristotle.

## 2. RESEARCH SYNTHESIS IN CONTEXT

### 2.1 A Definition of the Literature Review

The *ERIC Processing Manual* defines a literature review as an "information analysis and synthesis, focusing on findings and not simply bibliographic citations, summarizing the substance of a literature and drawing conclusions from it" (Educational Resources Information Center 1982, p. 85). Common to all definitions of literature reviews is the notion that they are "not based primarily on new facts and findings, but on publications containing such primary information, whereby the latter is digested, sifted, classified, simplified, and synthesized" (Manten 1973, p. 75).

Cooper (1988) presented a taxonomy that classifies literature reviews based on six characteristics (Table 1.1). The taxonomy can be applied to literature reviews appearing throughout a broad range of behavioral and physical sciences. The six characteristics—focus of attention, goal of the synthesis, perspective on the literature, coverage of the literature, organization of the presentation, and intended audience—and their subordinate categories permit a rich level of distinction among works of synthesis. Of course, nearly all literature reviewers describe their work as having multiple foci and goals.

The role that literature reviews play in the accumulation of knowledge is large and growing larger. Mazela and Malin (1977) reported that literature reviews are among the most highly cited documents in the social sciences. Their importance grows as a direct function of the number of documents on a topic. As early as 1971, Garvey and Griffith wrote, "the individual scientist is . . . overloaded with scientific information and [can] no longer keep up with and assimilate all the

**Table 1.1 A Taxonomy of Literature Reviews**

| Characteristic | Categories |
| --- | --- |
| Focus | Research outcomes |
| | Research methods |
| | Theories |
| | Practices or applications |
| Goal | Integration |
| |     (a) Generalization |
| |     (b) Conflict resolution |
| |     (c) Linguistic bridge-building |
| | Criticism |
| | Identification of central issues |
| Perspective | Neutral representation |
| | Espousal of position |
| Coverage | Exhaustive |
| | Exhaustive with selective citation |
| | Representative |
| | Central or pivotal |
| Organization | Historical |
| | Conceptual |
| | Methodological |
| Audience | Specialized scholars |
| | General scholars |
| | Practitioners or policymakers |
| | General public |

SOURCE: H. M. Cooper (1988).

information being produced that [is] related to his primary specialty'' (p. 350).

In response, specialties in science have narrowed, requiring greater reliance on literature reviews by scholars who wish to remain abreast of developments in collateral fields. Cozzens (1981) reported that 42 percent of the scientists she surveyed said they had read a review in the preceding two weeks. Further, regardless of the cognitive capacities of scholars, expanding literatures require the periodic collecting, evaluating, and integrating of scholarship in order to bring coherence and perspective to a problem area.

## 2.2 A Definition of the Integrative Research Review

The integrative research review can be defined as the conjunction of a particular primary focus and goal: Research syntheses attempt to integrate empirical re-search for the purpose of creating generalizations. Implicit in this definition is the notion that seeking generalizations also involves seeking the limits and modifiers of generalizations. Also, integrative research reviews almost always (a) pay attention to relevant theories, critically analyze the research they cover, (b) try to resolve conflicts in the literature, and (c) attempt to identify central issues for future research. According to Price (1965), integrative research reviews are intended to ''replace those papers that have been lost from sight behind the research front'' (p. 513).

A survey of published literature reviewers by Cooper (1988) indicated that one reviewer in six intended to produce an integrative research review—that is, sought primarily to create research generalizations. We might add to this definition the requirements that the reviewer claims an initially nonjudgmental stance vis-à-vis the outcomes of the synthesis (i.e., neutral representation) and intends to be exhaustive in the coverage of the research base. With this perspective and coverage strategy added to the definition, one literature review in eight still qualifies as integrative research syntheses.

Finally, Glass (1976) coined the term ''meta-analysis'' to refer to ''the statistical analysis of a large collection of analysis results from individual studies for the purpose of integrating the findings'' (p. 3). The authors of the *Handbook* reserve the term to refer specifically to statistical analysis in research synthesis and not to the entire enterprise of research synthesis.

## 3. A BRIEF HISTORY OF RESEARCH SYNTHESIS AS A SCIENTIFIC PROCESS

### 3.1 Early Developments

While Glass gave us the term ''meta-analysis,'' Olkin (1990) pointed out that ways to estimate effect sizes have existed since the turn of the century. For example, Pearson (1904) took the average of estimates from five separate samples of the correlation between inoculation for typhoid fever and mortality. He used this average to better estimate the typical effect of inoculation and to compare this effect with that of inoculation for other diseases. Early work on the methodology for combining estimates across studies includes papers in the physical sciences by Birge (1932) and in the statistical sciences by Cochran (1937) and Yates and Cochran (1938).

Methods for combining probabilities across studies also have a long history, dating at least from procedures suggested in Tippett's *Method of Statistics* (1931) and

Fisher's *Statistical Methods for Research Workers* (1932). The most frequently used probability-combining method was described by Mosteller and Bush (1954) in the first edition of the *Handbook of Social Psychology,* some 40 years ago.

However, the use of quantitative synthesis techniques in the social sciences was rare before the 1970s. Late in the decade, several applications of meta-analytic techniques captured the imagination of behavioral scientists. Included among these were: in clinical psychology, Smith and Glass's meta-analysis of psychotherapy research (1977); in industrial/organizational psychology, Schmidt and Hunter's validity generalization of employment tests (1977); in social psychology, Rosenthal and Rubin's integration of interpersonal expectancy effect research (1978) (also see Rosenthal 1969); and in education, Glass and Smith's synthesis of the literature on class size and achievement (1979).

Several early conceptualizations of the integrative review as a research process occurred independent of the meta-analysis movement. In 1971, Feldman published an article entitled "Using the Work of Others: Some Observations on Reviewing and Integrating," in which he demonstrated remarkable prescience. Feldman wrote, "Systematically reviewing and integrating . . . the literature of a field may be considered a type of research in its own right—one using a characteristic set of research techniques and methods" (p. 86). Feldman described four steps in the reviewing process: sampling topics and studies, developing a scheme for indexing and coding material, integrating the studies, and writing the report.

In the same year, Light and Smith (1971) presented a "cluster approach" to literature reviewing that was meant to redress some of the deficiencies in the existing strategies for integration. These authors argued that if treated properly the variation in outcomes among related studies could be a valuable source of information, rather than a source of consternation, which it appeared to be when treated with traditional reviewing methods.

Three years later, Taveggia (1974) expanded on Light and Smith's approach. He wrote:

A methodological principle overlooked by [reviewers] . . . is that research results are probabilistic. What this principle suggests is that, in and of themselves, the findings of any single research are meaningless—they may have occurred simply by chance. It also follows that, if a large enough number of researches has been done on a particular topic, chance alone dictates that studies will exist that report inconsistent and contradictory findings! Thus, what appears to be contradictory may simply be the positive and negative details of a distribution of findings. (pp. 397–398)

Taveggia went on to describe six common problems in literature reviews: selecting research; retrieving, indexing, and coding studies; analyzing the comparability of findings; accumulating comparable findings; analyzing resulting distributions; and reporting results.

## 3.2 Research Synthesis Comes of Age

The first half of the 1980s witnessed the appearance of four books primarily devoted to meta-analytic methods. The first, by Glass, McGaw, and Smith (1981) presented meta-analysis as a new application of analysis of variance and multiple regression procedures, with effect sizes treated as the dependent variable. In 1982, Hunter, Schmidt, and Jackson introduced meta-analytic procedures that focused on (a) comparing the observed variation in study outcomes with that expected by chance (the statistical realization of Taveggia's point) and (b) correcting observed effect size estimates and their variance for known sources of bias (e.g., sampling error, range restrictions, unreliability of measurements). Rosenthal (1984) presented a compendium of meta-analytic methods covering, among other topics, the combining of significance levels, effect size estimation, and the analysis of variation in effect sizes. Rosenthal's procedures for testing moderators of variation in effect sizes were not based on traditional inferential statistics, but on a new set of techniques involving assumptions tailored specifically for the analysis of study outcomes. Finally, in 1985, with the publication of *Statistical Methods for Meta-Analysis,* Hedges and Olkin helped to elevate the quantitative synthesis of research to an independent specialty within the statistical sciences. This book, summarizing and expanding nearly a decade of programmatic developments by the authors, not only covered the widest array of meta-analytic procedures but also presented rigorous statistical proofs establishing their legitimacy.

Two papers that appeared in the *Review of Educational Research* in the early 1980s brought the meta-analytic and review-as-research perspectives together. The first paper, by Jackson (1980), proposed six reviewing tasks "analogous to those performed during primary research" (p. 441). Jackson portrayed meta-analysis as an aid to the task of analyzing primary studies, but emphasized its limitations as well as its strengths. Also noteworthy about Jackson's paper was his use of a sample of 36 review articles from prestigious social science periodicals to examine the methods used in integrative empirical reviews. For example, Jackson reported that only one of the 36 reviews explicitly reported the indexes or retrieval systems used to locate primary studies. His conclusion was that ''relatively little thought has been given to the methods for doing integrative reviews. Such reviews are critical to science and social policymaking and yet most are done far less rigorously than is currently possible'' (p. 459).

Cooper (1982) drew the analogy between research synthesis and primary research to its logical conclusion. He presented a five-stage model of the integrative review as a research project. For each stage, Cooper codified the research question asked, its primary function in the review, and the procedural differences that might cause variation in review conclusions. In addition, Cooper applied the notion of threats to inferential validity—introduced by Campbell and Stanley (1966; also see Cook & Campbell 1979) for evaluating the utility of primary research designs—to the conduct of research reviews. He identified numerous threats to validity specifically associated with reviewing procedures that might undermine the trustworthiness of the findings of a research synthesis. He also suggested that other threats might exist and that the validity of any particular review could be threatened by consistent deficiencies in the set of studies that formed its database. Table 1.2 presents this schema.

Another text that appeared in 1984 also helped elevate the research review to a more rigorous level. Light and Pillemer focused on the use of research reviews to help decision-making in the social policy domain. Their approach placed special emphasis on the importance of meshing both numbers and narrative for the effective interpretation and communication of synthesis results.

Several other books have appeared on the topic of meta-analysis since the mid 1980s. Some of these treat the topic generally (e.g., Cooper 1989; Eddy, Hasselblad & Shacter 1992; Fricke & Treines 1985; Hunter & Schmidt 1990; Wolf 1986), some treat it from the perspective of particular research design conceptualizations (e.g., Mullen 1989), some are tied to particular software packages (e.g., Johnson 1989), and some look to the future of research synthesis as a scientific endeavor (e.g., Cook et al. 1992; Wachter & Straf 1990).

Since the mid 1980s literally thousands of meta-analyses have been published. The use of meta-analysis spread from psychology and education through many disciplines, especially social policy analysis and the medical sciences. In 1983, the *Evaluation Studies Review Annual* (Light 1983) was devoted to meta-analysis. In 1986, the Workshop on Methodological Issues in Overviews of Randomized Clinical Trials (see *Statistics in Medicine*, 1987, Vol. 6, No. 3), held at the National Institutes of Health, devoted considerable attention to the application of meta-analysis in health and medical research. In 1988, Greenberg and Folger commented that ''if the current interest in meta-analysis is any indication, then meta-analysis is here to stay'' (p. 191).

Meta-analysis has attained particularly distinctive status in research on medicine and health care. At least one textbook—*Effective Care in Pregnancy and Childbirth*, by Chalmers, Enkin, and Keirse (1989)—explicitly uses the results of meta-analyses to derive its clinical recommendations. In addition, federal legislation has recently authorized the creation of an agency for health care policy research to issue guidelines on clinical practice. What is novel about this legislation is that it *requires* the guidelines to be based on a systematic synthesis of research evidence.

Because of the efforts of scholars who chose to apply their skills to how research syntheses might be improved, reviews written in the 1980s and 1990s were held to standards far more demanding than those applied to their predecessors. The process of elevating the rigor of reviews is certain to continue into the twenty-first century. This book may be taken as a case in point.

## 3.3 Rationale for the Handbook

*The Handbook of Research Synthesis* is meant to be the definitive vade mecum for behavioral and medical scientists intent on applying the synthesis craft. It distills the products of 20 years of near-revolutionary developments in how research integrations are conducted. Research synthesis in the 1960s was at best an art, at worst a form of yellow journalism. Today, the summarization and integration of studies is viewed as a research process in its own right; it is held to scientific standards and applies the techniques for data gathering and analysis developed for its unique purpose.

Numerous excellent texts on research synthesis already exist. However, none is as comprehensive as the present volume. Some texts focus on statistical methods. These often emphasize different aspects of statistical integration (e.g., combining probabilities, regression-

**Table 1.2 Research Synthesis as a Research Process**

| Stage Characteristics | Stage of Research | | | | |
|---|---|---|---|---|---|
| | Problem Formulation | Data Collection | Data Evaluation | Analysis and Interpretation | Public Presentation |
| Research question asked | What evidence should be included in the review? | What procedures should be used to find relevant evidence? | What retrieved evidence should be included in the review? | What procedures should be used to make inferences about the literature as a whole? | What information should be included in the review report? |
| Primary function in review | Constructing definitions that distinguish relevant from irrelevant studies | Determining which sources of potentially relevant studies to examine | Applying criteria to separate "valid" from "invalid" studies | Synthesizing valid retrieved studies | Applying editorial criteria to separate important from unimportant information |
| Procedural differences that create variation in review conclusions | (1) Differences in included operational definitions (2) Differences in operational detail | Differences in the research contained in sources of information | (1) Differences in quality criteria (2) Differences in the influence of nonquality criteria | Differences in rules of inference | Differences in guidelines for editorial judgment |
| Sources of potential invalidity in review conclusions | (1) Narrow concepts might make review conclusions less definitive and robust (2) Superficial operational detail might obscure interacting variables | (1) Accessed studies might be qualitatively different from the target population of studies (2) People sampled in accessible studies might be different from target population of people | (1) Nonquality factors might cause improper weighting of study information (2) Omissions in study reports might make conclusions unreliable | (1) Rules for distinguishing patterns from noise might be inappropriate (2) Review-based evidence might be used to infer causality | (1) Omission of review procedures might make conclusions irreproducible (2) Omission of review findings and study procedures might make conclusions obsolete |

SOURCE: H. M. Cooper (1982).

analog models, estimating population effects from sampled effects with known biases) and often approach research accumulation from different perspectives. While these texts are complete within their domains, no single sourcebook describes and integrates all the meta-analytic approaches.

*The Handbook of Research Synthesis* incorporates quantitative statistical techniques from all the synthesis traditions. It brings the leading authorities on the various meta-analytic perspectives together in a single volume. As such, the *Handbook* is an explicit statement by its authors that all the statistical approaches share a common assumptive base. The common base is not only statistical but philosophical as well. Philosophically, all the approaches rest on the presupposition that research syntheses need to be held up to the same standards of rigor and systematicity as the research on which they are based. The second and later users of data must be held as, or perhaps even more, accountable for the validity of their methods as were the first.

Several problems that arise in the course of conducting a quantitative synthesis have not received adequate treatment in any existing text. These include (a) nonindependence of data sets, (b) synthesis of multivariate data sets, (c) Bayesian approaches to research synthesis, and (d) sensitivity analysis, to name just a few. Every integrative reviewer faces these problems and has developed strategies for dealing with them. Some of their solutions are published in widely scattered journals; others are often passed on to colleagues through informal contacts. They have never received complete treatment within the same text. The *Handbook* brings these topics together for the first time.

Further, texts that focus on the statistical aspects of integration tend to give only passing consideration to other aspects of research synthesis, which include (a) the unique characteristics of problem formulation in research integration, (b) the methods of literature search, (c) the coding and evaluation of research reports, (d) the management of meta-analytic data sets, and (e) the meaningful interpretation and effective communication of synthesis results. The existing texts that focus on these aspects of reviewing tend not to be comprehensive in their coverage of statistical issues. Fully half of the chapters in the *Handbook* deal with nonstatistical issues, evidencing the authors' collective belief that high-quality syntheses require considerably more than just the application of quantitative procedures.

Finally, the *Handbook* is meant for those who carry out research syntheses. Discussions of theory and proof are kept to a minimum in favor of descriptions of the practical mechanics needed to apply well the synthesis craft. The chapters present multiple approaches to problem solving and discuss the strengths and weaknesses of each approach. Readers with a comfortable background in analysis of variance and multiple regression who can locate a nearby research library should find the chapters accessible. The *Handbook* authors want to supply the working synthesist with the needed expertise to interpret their blueprints, to wield their mortar hoe and trowel.

## 4. THE STAGES OF RESEARCH SYNTHESIS

The description of the stages of research synthesis presented in Table 1.2 provides the conceptual organization of the *Handbook*. In this section, we will raise the principal issues associated with each stage, which will allow us to briefly introduce the content of the chapters that follow.

### 4.1 The Problem Formulation Stage

There is one major constraint on problem formulation in research synthesis: Primary research on a topic must exist before a synthesis can be conducted. How much research? The methods of meta-analysis can be applied to literatures containing as few as two hypothesis tests. Under certain circumstances—for instance, a researcher synthesizing a pair of replicate studies from her or his own lab—the use of meta-analysis in this fashion might be legitimate. Yet, most scientists would argue that the benefits of such a review would be limited (and its chances for publication even more limited).

A more general answer to "How much research?" is that it varies depending on a number of characteristics of the problem. All else being equal, conceptually broad topics would seem to profit from a synthesis only after the accumulation of a more substantial number of studies than would narrowly defined topics. Similarly, literatures that contain diverse types of operations also would seem to require a relatively large number of studies before firm conclusions could be drawn from a review. Ultimately, the arbiter of whether a review is needed will not be numerical standards, but the fresh insights a review can bring to a field.

Once a sufficient literature on a problem has collected, then the challenge, and promise, of integrative reviews becomes evident. The problems that constrain primary researchers—small and homogeneous samples, limited time and money for operationalizing variables—are less severe for synthesists. They can capitalize on the diversity in methods that has occurred naturally across primary studies. The heterogeneity of methods across studies may permit tests of theoretical hypotheses concerning the mediators of relations that have never been tested in any single primary study. Conclusions about the population and ecological validity of relations uncovered in primary research may also receive more thorough tests in syntheses.

Part II of the *Handbook* focuses on issues in problem formulation. In Chapter 2, Judith Hall, Linda Tickle-Degnen, Robert Rosenthal, and Frederick Mosteller set out the kinds of research questions for which reviews are uniquely suited. They also compare the strengths and weaknesses of primary and meta-analytic research with regard to their relative abilities to rule out different classes of threats to the validity of conclusions about a problem.

In Chapter 3, Larry Hedges looks at the implications of different problem definitions for how study results will be modeled statistically. The major issues involve the population or universe of people and measurements that are the target of a review's inferences, how broadly the treatment construct is defined, especially in terms of whether fixed or random effect models are envisioned, and how choices among models influence the precision of estimates of meta-analytic tests.

### 4.2 The Data Collection Stage: Searching the Literature

The literature search stage in research synthesis is most different from primary research. Still, culling through the literature for relevant studies is not unlike gathering a sample of primary data.

Cooper (1987) found that about half of the reviewers he questioned claimed that they conducted their search with the intention of identifying all or most of the relevant literature. About three quarters of these ambitious searchers said they did not stop searching until they felt they had accomplished their goal. About one third of all reviewers said they stopped their search when they felt their understanding and conclusions about the topic would not be affected by additional material. About one sixth of the reviewers said they stopped searching when retrieval became unacceptably difficult.

Literature searchers considering the problems of access to their population of interest easily can grow envious of their primary research counterparts. In contrast to the (relatively) well-defined sampling frames available to primary researchers, literature searchers confront the fact that any single source of primary reports will lead them to only a fraction of the relevant studies, and a biased fraction at that. For example, the most egalitarian sources of literature are the reference database systems, such as PsycINFO, ERIC, and MEDLINE. Still, these broad, nonevaluative systems exclude the unpublished and most recent literature. Conversely, the least equitable literature survey technique involves accessing one's close colleagues and other like-minded researchers. In spite of the invisible college's obvious biases, there is no single source as likely to yield unpublished and recent works. Further complicating the sampling frame problem is the fact that the relative utility and biases associated with any single source will vary as a function of characteristics of the research problem, including, for example, how long the topic has been the focus of study and whether the topic is interdisciplinary in nature.

These problems imply that research synthesists must carefully consider multiple channels for accessing literature and how the channels they choose complement one another. Part III of the *Handbook* is devoted to helping the synthesist consider and carry out this unique task. In Chapter 4, Howard White presents an overview of searching issues from the viewpoint of an information scientist. In Chapter 5, by Jeffrey Reed and Pam Baxter, Chapter 6, by Kay Dickersin, and Chapter 7, by MaryLu Rosenthal, the practical considerations of how to scour our brickyards and quarries are examined in detail.

### 4.3 The Data Evaluation Stage: Coding the Literature

Once the reviewer has gathered the relevant literature, she or he must extract from each document those bits of information that will help answer the questions that impel research in the field. The problems that can arise at this stage are among the most challenging faced by the synthesist. Put positively, the problems faced during data coding provide a strong test of the synthesist's competence, thoughtfulness, and ingenuity. The solutions found for these problems will have considerable influence on the contribution of the review. Part IV of the *Handbook* focuses on data coding and evaluation.

The aspect of coding that engenders the most discussion involves how to represent differences in primary study designs when carrying out a synthesis. What is meant by "quality" in evaluating research methods?

Should studies be weighted differently if they differ in quality? How does one rate the quality of studies described in incomplete data reports? In Chapter 8, Paul Wortman examines the alternative approaches available to the synthesist.

Beyond quality judgments, synthesists make decisions about the classes of variables that are of potential interest to their review. These can relate to variables that predict outcomes, potential mediators of effects, and the differences in how outcomes are conceptualized (and, therefore, measured). If a synthesist chooses not to code a particular feature of studies, then it cannot be considered in the analysis of results (at least not without going to the expense of recoding studies). Determining guidelines for what information should be extracted from primary research reports is largely a substantive problem; direction will come from the issues that arise in the particular literature, coupled with the synthesist's personal insights into the topic. Still, commonalities emerge in how these decisions are forged. Mark Lipsey, in Chapter 9, and William Stock, in Chapter 10, present complementary templates for what generally should be included in coding frames.

Once decisions on what to code have been made, the synthesist needs to consider how to carry out the coding of the literature and how to assess the trustworthiness with which the coding frame is implemented. There are numerous indexes of reliability available, each with different strengths and weaknesses. In Chapter 11, Robert Orwin describes strategies for reducing and evaluating the amount of error that enters a synthesis during the coding of the literature's features. Orwin's description of reliability assessment focuses on three major approaches: (a) measuring interrater agreement; (b) obtaining confidence ratings from coders; and (c) conducting sensitivity analysis, or using multiple coding strategies to determine whether a review's conclusions are robust across different coding decision rules.

Even the most trustworthy coding frame cannot solve the problem of missing data. Missing data will arise in every research synthesis. The reporting of study features and results, as now practiced, leaves much to be desired. While the ascendancy of meta-analysis has led to many salutary changes, most primary researchers still do not think about a research report in terms of the needs of the next user of the data. Also, problems with missing data would occur even if the needs of the synthesist were the paramount consideration in constructing a report. There is simply no way that primary researchers can anticipate the subtle nuances in their methods and

results that might be identified as critical to piecing together the literature five, ten, or more years later.

The situation is not hopeless, however. In Chapter 12, Theresa Pigott describes how lost information can bear on the results of a research synthesis. She shows how the impact of missing data can be assessed by paying attention to some of its discoverable characteristics. She also describes both simple and complex strategies for handling missing data in research synthesis.

Finally, in Chapter 13, George Woodworth takes on one of the more neglected aspects of conducting quality research syntheses, showing how the synthesist, with a moderate amount of knowledge and forethought, can greatly ease the transition of codings from data sheets to computer files and also can harness the power of the computer to facilitate data analysis and report writing.

## 4.4 The Analysis and Interpretation Stage

As our brief history of research synthesis revealed, techniques for the analysis of accumulated research outcomes has been an area of statistics filled with dramatic developments. Two decades ago, the actual mechanics of integrating research usually involved covert, intuitive processes taking place inside the head of the synthesist. Meta-analysis made these processes public and based them on explicit, shared, statistical assumptions (however well these assumptions were met). We would not accept as valid a primary researcher's conclusion if it were substantiated solely by the statement "I looked at the treatment and control scores and I find the treated group did better." We would demand some sort of statistical test (e.g., a *t* test). Likewise, we should no longer accept "I examined the study outcomes and find the treatment is effective" as substantiation. We should demand meta-analysis.

Part V of the *Handbook* covers the four components of synthesis dealing with combining study results. In Chapter 14, Brad Bushman describes vote-counting procedures in meta-analysis, or those procedures based on viewing the outcomes of studies dichotomously, as either supporting or refuting a hypothesis. In Chapter 15, Betsy Becker covers procedures for combining significance values, the more precise probability levels that are the product of inferential statistics. The next two chapters cover methods for estimating the magnitude of an effect, commonly called the effect size. Cohen (1988) defined an effect size as "the *degree* to which the phenomenon is present in the population, or the degree to which the null hypothesis is false'' (pp. 9–10). In Chapter 16, Robert Rosenthal describes parametric measures of effect size, and in Chapter 17, Joseph Fleiss covers measures of effect size for categorical data, with special attention paid to the estimate of effect called the odds ratio. In Chapter 18, William Shadish and Keith Haddock describe procedures for averaging effects and generating confidence intervals around these population estimates.

To most integrative reviewers, the search for influences on study results is the most exciting and rewarding aspect of the review. Part VI deals with techniques for analyzing whether and why there are differences in the outcomes of studies. As an analog to analysis of variance or multiple regression procedures, effect sizes can be viewed as dependent or criterion variables and the features of study designs as independent or predictor variables. However, because effect size estimates do not all have the same sampling uncertainty, they cannot be inserted into traditional inferential statistics. In Chapter 19, Larry Hedges discusses analysis strategies when fixed effects models are used. In Chapter 20, Stephen Raudenbush describes proper strategies when random effects models are used. Further, effect size estimates may be affected by factors that attenuate their magnitudes. These may include, for example, a lack of reliability in the measurement instruments or restrictions in the range of values in the subject sample. These attenuating biases may be estimated and corrected using the procedures described by John Hunter and Frank Schmidt in Chapter 21.

Part VII focuses on special issues in the statistical treatment of research outcomes. In Chapter 22, Leon Gleser and Ingram Olkin tackle the vexing problem of what to do when the same study (or laboratory, or researcher, if one wishes to push the point) provides more than one effect size to a meta-analysis. Because estimates from the same study may not be independent sources of information about the underlying population value, their contributions to any overall estimates must be adjusted accordingly. Gleser and Olkin describe both simple and more complex strategies for dealing with dependencies among effect sizes.

Sometimes the focus of a research synthesis will not be a simple bivariate relation but a model involving numerous variables and their interrelations. The model could require analysis of more than one simple relation and/or complex partial or second-order relations. In Chapter 23, Betsy Becker and Christine Schram look at what models in meta-analysis are, why they should

be used, and how they affect meta-analytic data analysis.

The next two chapters return to topics introduced earlier in the *Handbook*. Here, however, they are treated more fully as conceptual, data gathering, and, especially, statistical issues. In Chapter 24, Joel Greenhouse and Satish Iyengar present a detailed description of sensitivity analysis and diagnostics. They describe several diagnostic procedures that can be used to assess the sensitivity and robustness of the conclusions of a meta-analysis. Colin Begg, in Chapter 25, examines publication bias. He describes some procedures for identifying whether bias has had an impact on the meta-analytic result. He also details some mathematical adjustments that can help the synthesist estimate what summary effect size estimates might have been in the absence of the selective inclusion of studies.

Finally, in Chapter 26, Thomas Louis and Daniel Zelterman look at Bayesian approaches to effect size estimation. They introduce the conceptual underpinnings of the Bayesian approach, its potential advantages for meta-analysis, and the essential steps in performing such an analysis.

## 4.5 The Public Presentation Stage

All too often, social scientists fall back on the adage ''the data speak for themselves.'' This is an exercise in self-delusion. While the data can tell us that an eight-ounce glass contains four ounces of liquid, it cannot say whether that glass should be viewed as half empty or half full. Such a judgment depends on, among other things, the thirst of the observer, the amount of liquid in glasses nearby, and the nature of the liquid (say, water or bourbon).

Reviewers who believe their task is complete when the statistical synthesis is done shortchange not only their audience but themselves as well. Detailing (with pride, we hope) the procedures used to perform the synthesis and placing the synthesis results in context are the final challenges to the reviewer's intellect.

In Chapter 27, the first of two chapters in Part VIII, Katherine Halvorsen describes the reporting format for research synthesis. Like the coding form, there is no simple schema that fits all reviews. However, certain commonalities do exist, which the author discusses. Not too surprisingly, the organization that emerges bears considerable resemblance to that of a primary research report though, also obviously, the content differs dramatically.

In Chapter 28, Richard Light, Judith Singer, and John Willett present some aids to visual presentation and interpretation of meta-analysis. Charts, graphs, and tables should be used to summarize the numbers in a meta-analysis, along with a careful intertwining of narrative explication to contextualize the summaries. Proper use of interpretive devices can make a complex set of results easily accessible to the intelligent reader. Likewise, inadequate use of these aids can render incomprehensible even the simplest conclusions.

Part IX of the *Handbook* brings us full circle, returning to the nature of the problem that led to undertaking the research synthesis in the first place. The authors attempt to answer the question, ''What can be learned from research synthesis?'' Two separate sets of answers are given. In Chapter 29, Norman Miller and Vicki Pollock examine meta-analytic synthesis for theory development, and in Chapter 30, Alice Eagly and Wendy Wood focus on using research syntheses to plan future research. These chapters are meant to help synthesists think about the substantive questions for which the readers of their reviews will be seeking answers.

## 5. PLACING THE HANDBOOK CHAPTERS IN PERSPECTIVE

The final two chapters of the *Handbook,* Part X, are meant to bring the detailed drawings of the 30 preceding chapters onto a single blueprint. In Chapter 31, Georg Matt and Thomas Cook present an expanded analysis of threats to the validity of research syntheses. They provide an overall appraisal of how inferences from reviews may be restricted or faulty. This chapter brings together many of the concerns expressed throughout the book by the various chapter authors.

Finally, in Chapter 32 we look at some of the potentials and limitations of research synthesis. Special attention is paid to (a) possible future developments in synthesis methodology, (b) the feasibility and expense associated with conducting a sound research synthesis, and (c) a broad-based definition of what makes a literature review good or bad.

No secret will be revealed by stating our conclusion in advance: If procedures for the synthesis of research are held to standards of objectivity, systematicity, and rigor, then our knowledge edifice will be made of bricks and mortar. If not, it will be a house of cards.

## 6. REFERENCES

Birge, R. T. (1932). The calculation of errors by the method of least squares. *Physical Review, 40,* 207–227.

Campbell, D. T., & Stanley, J. C. (1966). *Experimental and quasi-experimental designs for research.* Chicago: Rand McNally.

Chalmers, I., Enkin, M., & Keirse, M. J. N. C. (1989). *Effective care in pregnancy and childbirth.* Oxford: Oxford University Press.

Cochran, W. G. (1937). Problems arising in the analysis of a series of similar experiments. *Journal of the Royal Statistical Society* (Supplement), *4,* 102–118.

Cohen, J. (1988). *Statistical power analysis for the behavioral sciences* (2nd ed.). Hillsdale, NJ: Erlbaum.

Cook, T. D., & Campbell, D. T. (1979). *Quasi-experimentation: Design and analysis issues for field settings.* Chicago: Rand McNally.

Cook, T. D., Cooper, H., Cordray, D. S., Hartmann, H., Hedges, L. V., Light, R. J., Louis, T. A., & Mosteller, F. (1992). *Meta-analysis for explanation: A casebook.* New York: Russell Sage Foundation.

Cooper, H. M. (1982). Scientific guidelines for conducting integrative research reviews. *Review of Educational Research, 52,* 291–302.

Cooper, H. M. (1987). Literature searching strategies of integrative research reviewers: A first survey. *Knowledge: Creation, Diffusion, Utilization, 8,* 372–383.

Cooper, H. M. (1988). Organizing knowledge synthesis: A taxonomy of literature reviews. *Knowledge in Society, 1,* 104–126.

Cooper, H. M. (1989). *Integrating research: A guide for literature reviews* (2nd ed.). Newbury Park, CA: Sage.

Cozzens, S. E. (1981). *User requirements for scientific review* (Report No. IST-7821947). Washington, DC: National Science Foundation.

Eddy, D. M., Hasselblad, V., & Shacter, R. (1992). *The statistical synthesis of evidence: Meta-analysis by the confidence profile method.* New York: Academic Press.

Educational Resources Information Center. (1982). *ERIC processing manual* (Section 5: Cataloging). Washington, DC: Author.

Feldman, K. A. (1971). Using the work of others: Some observations on reviewing and integrating. *Sociology of Education, 4,* 86–102.

Fisher, R. A. (1932). *Statistical methods for research workers* (4th ed.). London: Oliver & Boyd.

Fricke, R., & Treines, G. (1985). *Einführung in die Meta-analyse.* Bern, Switzerland: Hans Huber.

Garvey, W. D., & Griffith, B. C. (1971). Scientific communication: Its role in the conduct of research and the creation of knowledge. *American Psychologist, 26,* 349–361.

Glass, G. V. (1976). Primary, secondary, and meta-analysis. *Educational Researcher, 5,* 3–8.

Glass, G. V., McGaw, B., & Smith, M. L. (1981). *Meta-analysis in social research.* Beverly Hills, CA: Sage.

Glass, G. V., & Smith, M. L. (1978). Meta-analysis of research on the relationship of class size and achievement. *Educational Evaluation and Policy Analysis, 1,* 2–16.

Greenberg, J., & Folger, R. (1988). *Controversial issues in social research methods.* New York: Springer-Verlag.

Hedges, L. V. (1987). How hard is hard science, how soft is soft science? The empirical cumulativeness of research. *American Psychologist, 42,* 443–455.

Hedges, L. V., & Olkin, I. (1985). *Statistical methods for meta-analysis.* Orlando, FL: Academic Press.

Hunter, J. E., & Schmidt, F. L. (1990). *Methods of meta-analysis: Correcting error and bias in research findings.* Newbury Park, CA: Sage.

Hunter, J. E., Schmidt, F. L., & Jackson, G. B. (1982). *Meta-analysis: Cumulating research findings across studies.* Beverly Hills, CA: Sage.

Jackson, G. B. (1980). Methods for integrative reviews. *Review of Educational Research, 50,* 438–460.

Johnson, B. T. (1989). *DSTAT: Software for the meta-analytic review of research literatures.* Hillsdale, NJ: Erlbaum.

Light, R. J. (Ed.). (1983). *Evaluation Studies Review Annual* (Vol. 8). Beverly Hills, CA: Sage.

Light, R. J., & Pillemer, D. B. (1984). *Summing up: The science of reviewing research.* Cambridge, MA: Harvard University Press.

Light, R. J., & Smith, P. V. (1971). Accumulating evidence: Procedures for resolving contradictions among research studies. *Harvard Educational Review, 41,* 429–471.

Manten, A. A. (1973). Scientific literature review. *Scholarly Publishing, 5,* 75–89.

Mazela, A., & Malin, M. (1977). *A bibliometric study of the review literature.* Philadelphia: Institute for Scientific Information.

Mosteller, F., & Bush, R. (1954). Selected quantitative techniques. In G. Lindsey (Ed.), *Handbook of social psychology: Vol. 1. Theory and method.* Cambridge, MA: Addison-Wesley.

Mullen, B. (1989). *Advanced BASIC meta-analysis.* Hillsdale, NJ: Erlbaum.

National Research Council. (1992). *On combining information: Statistical issues and opportunities for research.* Washington, DC: National Academy of Sciences Press.

Olkin, I. (1990). History and goals. In K. W. Wachter & M. L. Straf (Eds.), *The future of meta-analysis* (pp. 3–10). New York: Russell Sage Foundation.

Pearson, K. (1904). Report on certain enteric fever inoculation statistics. *British Medical Journal, 3,* 1243–1246.

Price, D. (1965). Networks of scientific papers. *Science, 149,* 56–64.

Rosenthal, R. (1969). Interpersonal expectations: Effects of the experimenter's hypothesis. In R. Rosenthal & R. L. Rosnow (Eds.), *Artifact in behavioral research* (pp. 181–277). New York: Academic Press.

Rosenthal, R. (1984). *Meta-analytic procedures for social research.* Beverly Hills, CA: Sage.

Rosenthal, R., & Rubin, D. B. (1978). Interpersonal expectancy effects: The first 345 studies. *Behavioral and Brain Sciences, 3,* 377–386.

Schmidt, F. L., & Hunter, J. E. (1977). Development of a general solution to the problem of validity generalization. *Journal of Applied Psychology, 62,* 529–540.

Smith, M. L., & Glass, G. V. (1977). Meta-analysis of psychotherapy outcome studies. *American Psychologist, 32,* 752–760.

Taveggia, T. C. (1974). Resolving research controversy through empirical cumulation: Toward reliable sociological knowledge. *Sociological Methods and Research, 2,* 395–407.

Tippett, L. H. C. (1931). *The methods of statistics.* London: Williams & Norgate.

Wachter, K. W., & Straf, M. L. (Eds.). (1990). *The future of meta-analysis.* New York: Russell Sage Foundation.

Wolf, F. M. (1986). *Meta-analysis: Quantitative methods for research synthesis.* Beverly Hills, CA: Sage.

Yates, F., & Cochran, W. G. (1938). The analysis of groups of experiments. *Journal of Agricultural Science, 28,* 556–580.

# PART
# II

# FORMULATING A PROBLEM
# FOR A RESEARCH SYNTHESIS

Cooper, H. and Hedges, L. V. (Eds.) 1994. *The Handbook of Research Synthesis.* New York: Russell Sage Foundation

# 2

# HYPOTHESES AND PROBLEMS IN RESEARCH SYNTHESIS

**JUDITH A. HALL**
*Northeastern University*

**LINDA TICKLE-DEGNEN**
*Boston University*

**ROBERT ROSENTHAL**
*Harvard University*

**FREDERICK MOSTELLER**
*Harvard University*

CONTENTS

## 1. INTRODUCTION

In the social, behavioral, and medical sciences, investigators wish to strengthen their methods of accumulating evidence. They have been dissatisfied with the classical literature review because these reports of findings are often limited to directions of relationship among variables or to results of significance tests. More and more, reviews of the literature are moving from the traditional literary approaches to the quantitative techniques of research synthesis described in this handbook.

Whenever more than one study has addressed the same conceptual hypothesis, research synthesis can be done. At the simplest level, an investigator might ask whether a study and its replication produce similar or different results, and what the net result is. At the most ambitious extreme, a research synthesis might summarize a very large literature, such as that on psychotherapy outcome studies (Smith & Glass 1977), exploring differences in the effectiveness of psychotherapy for many kinds of therapy and many kinds of outcome.

A quantitative research synthesis requires only that one can identify a set of studies that meet certain criteria regarding the phenomenon in question: The synthesist must be able to define the research question to be summarized and identify which research designs will be considered appropriate and which operational definitions of key constructs (treatments, manipulations, measuring instruments) will be allowed. Two synthesists may not define the domain in the same way even though they want to study the same fundamental hypothesis. For example, one might include only randomized experiments testing the hypothesis in question, whereas another might include nonexperimental studies as well. As another example, one synthesist of clinical drug trials might include patients' self-reports of health and physical functioning, whereas another might include only studies with physiological measures. What is crucial is that the synthesist define the domain clearly and base decisions to include and exclude studies on this definition of constructs.

Research synthesis can accomplish two fundamental tasks: learning from combining studies and learning from comparing studies. "Learning from combining studies" refers to finding, summarizing, and describing the already existing results of research, and "learning from comparing studies" refers to additional analyses that shed new light on variations in the phenomenon under study and on theoretical issues of causation, explanation, and construct validity. Thus, the synthesist

can sometimes make inferences that go well beyond the original results.

In the pages that follow, we identify the kinds of research questions that can be posed, some strengths and weaknesses of primary studies versus research synthesis, and selected problems in practice and interpretation.

## 2. WHAT WE CAN LEARN: COMPARING PRIMARY RESEARCH WITH RESEARCH SYNTHESIS

Research synthesis extends our knowledge through the combination and comparison of primary studies. As with primary research, there are boundaries to how much we can learn from research synthesis. Appreciating these boundaries helps in formulating an appropriate hypothesis or research problem. One way to identify the boundaries of research synthesis is to relate them to the boundaries of primary research. We can define boundaries for both types of research in large part by asking the following questions:

1. Cause and effect: How confident can we be that the independent variable actually affects the dependent or outcome measure?

2. Generalization: How confident can we be that the findings can be generalized beyond a small subset of populations, settings, and procedures?

3. Theory development: Does the research advance the theoretical understanding of a phenomenon?

### 2.1 Cause and Effect

One major role of research is to answer questions of causation. For example, we might want to know whether a treatment is beneficial for patients or whether attitudes affect behavior. Before developing research questions involving causal relationships, the research synthesist must examine the primary research literature. If most of the primary studies have high internal validity (e.g., randomly assigned subjects to conditions), then a synthesist can confidently ask questions of causation. If most of the primary studies have low internal validity (e.g., implement treatments on pre-existing groups), a synthesist can ask whether two variables covary, but cannot confidently address questions of causation. Procedures that enable strong causal inference, like random assignment of subjects to conditions and control over the intervention, are available to the primary researcher but not to the synthesist.

Harris and Rosenthal (1985), for example, discussed the limitation on the causal inference that could be drawn from their meta-analytic study of the mediation of the expectancy effect. They aggregated effects from two types of studies—one set that examined the relationship between teachers' expectations and their emitted behaviors (such as teacher praise) and another set that examined the relationship between emitted behaviors and outcome measures (such as student achievement). Their purpose was to show how teachers' emitted behaviors mediated the expectancy effect. They were limited, however, in their confidence that the emitted behaviors had a causal effect on the outcome measures because many of the behaviors in the second set of studies were not experimentally manipulated. Thus, if we are using research synthesis to learn from combining studies, we are completely dependent on those underlying studies for the decision about the degree of confidence in a causal inference.

If, on the other hand, we are using research synthesis to compare results for different subgroups of studies within our meta-analysis, we will never be able to have great confidence in causal inferences. Although we may attempt to control for the influence of a variety of alternative variables, we cannot randomly assign studies to the different subgroups. Therefore, we cannot be sure that differences in study results are caused by the variable that defines these subgroups (i.e., the moderator variable) and not by some other variable that is correlated with the moderator.

For example, in a meta-analytic study of the relationship between nonverbal behaviors and interpersonal impressions, Tickle-Degnen, Rosenthal, and Harrigan (1991) found 38 studies that had participants interact with a target whose nonverbal behavior was either manipulated or measured. They found 51 studies that had observers not interact with the target. They found only three experimental studies that compared participants' and observers' impressions. For the group of studies that examined either participants' or observers' impressions (but not both), the meta-analysts found that the relationship between nonverbal behavior and impressions was smaller for the participant studies than for the observer studies. The difference between studies remained even when the findings were examined so as to control for several procedural differences in the two types of studies. This evidence supports the conclusion that the observer role causes a person to react more to

nonverbal behavior than does the participant role. However, an analysis of the three primary studies that had subjects randomly assigned to participant or observer conditions failed to find evidence of any effect of the two types of interaction roles.

This example illustrates that we cannot with any confidence ascribe causality to a relationship based on review evidence alone. The boundaries to how much we can learn about causation with research synthesis are defined by the underlying primary studies. Research integrations cannot be used as a substitute for primary studies meant to uncover causal relationships. They may, however, provide guidance for the directions for new primary research (see Chapter 30).

## 2.2 Generalization

**2.2.1 External validity** Much of the work of research depends on how legitimately the findings from one study using particular subjects, situations, and procedures can be generalized to a larger set of results. For example, is treatment A as implemented in study 1 going to demonstrate the same degree of effectiveness under different conditions? Because of practical limitations in selecting subjects, situations, and procedures, primary studies are limited in the breadth of their individual generalizations. By accruing information over a number of primary studies, we can get a sense of the external validity of an effect. Research synthesis directly addresses the issue of generalization during the problem formulation stage as well as during the analysis and interpretation stage of research.

One of the first tasks of the research synthesist is to determine the breadth of the conceptual territory addressed by a prediction or hypothesis. For example, is the researcher interested in the effects of cognitive therapy in particular or psychotherapeutic intervention in general? In depressed patients' responses or all patients' responses? In outcomes related to patients' emotional response alone or to all forms of outcome? The synthesist must decide which studies are legitimate tests of the prediction or hypothesis. The synthesist must determine whether the subject populations, situations, and procedures used in each study are appropriate for the demonstration of a phenomenon. If a phenomenon is conceptually narrow and therefore tied to only a few methodological variations, studies that are close replications may be the only appropriate studies for inclusion in the synthesis. On the other hand, if the phenomenon is conceptually broad and therefore should be demonstrated over a wide variety of contexts, then studies that vary extensively in subjects, situations, and procedures may be appropriate for inclusion.

After a population of studies is identified for inclusion in the synthesis and study results have been recorded, the researcher should again address generalization during the data analysis stage. The researcher examines moderator variables associated with subject populations, situations, and procedures to examine empirically the validity of generalizations. Do the effects of cognitive therapy on beliefs have the same magnitude as the effects of psychodynamic therapy?

A major strength of research synthesis is its reliance on primary studies that, of necessity, involve multiple operationalizations of independent and dependent variables. In this sense it better addresses construct validity (as defined by Cook & Campbell 1979) than any single primary study. Through the aggregation of results from multiple operations of a construct, we learn something essential about it that each operation captures to only a limited extent. For example, to learn about the construct "anxiety," we may use operations such as a self-report anxiety scale, a coding of observed anxiety behavior, or electrodermal skin response. Through aggregation, meta-analysis extracts the essential anxiety effect, while sloughing off residuals due to instrumentation factors.

Paradoxically, meta-analysis has been criticized as "mixing apples and oranges." Such a criticism assumes that the meta-analyst aggregates findings of different phenomena. Sometimes that seems to be done, because the forms of operations are themselves different (e.g., a self-report, a coder's observations, or physiological measurement). The research synthesist, however, judges these various forms as occurring in the context of a constant goal (the measurement of anxiety). Although studies may differ in form, it is appropriate to aggregate them if they measure the same phenomenon. A convergence, or "triangulation," of findings from methodologically varying studies lends credence to the validity of an effect (Campbell & Fiske 1959). When a relationship remains constant though tested under a variety of circumstances, it is clearly robust.

To some degree any synthesis of information from multiple research studies involves an aggregation of studies that are dissimilar. The same is true at the level of repeated observations of the same object. Some degree of mixing apples and oranges must occur in the tidiest of studies. Even when studies are intended to be direct replications, exact replication probably cannot occur.

On the other hand, synthesists must be sensitive to the problem of attempting aggregation of too diverse a sampling of operations and studies. Combining apples and oranges to understand something about fruit may make more sense than combining fruits and humans to understand something about organic matter. Of course, the final criterion for the extensiveness of the sampling of operations is whether the level of generalization is appropriate to the question being asked and scientifically useful. The synthesist must ask, "Does this level of generalization add to our explanation and understanding of a phenomenon?" Too diverse a sampling of studies could obscure useful relationships within subgroupings of the studies and not provide information at the level of the more abstract categorization.

Fields differ somewhat in the generality of their questions. By and large, medicine focuses on specific therapies, procedures, diagnoses, and diseases and does not ask very general questions such as, "Is vitamin X good for patients?" but would want to know how much X and for which patients. In social science, in contrast, we often do ask global questions such as, "Does desegregation improve the education of the pupils?" Part of this difference arises because medicine, as opposed to public health, deals with individuals primarily, whereas much of social science attends to groups.

Research synthesis is the ideal method for confidently answering a question about the generality of an effect. Meta-analytic techniques allow for empirical assessment of external validity to an extent rarely available to a single primary study. In primary research, confidence in the external validity of results is based solely on the judgment that the populations of subjects, situations, and procedures that are of interest are adequately represented by the study.

**2.2.2 Units of analysis** An additional issue associated with generalization relates to the unit of analysis in a primary study. In social psychology, for example, the investigation of a phenomenon may proceed using individuals, dyads, groups, and still higher-order units (like classrooms or hospital wards) as the units of analysis. Each primary study must initially be assumed to allow generalization only to the units that it assesses. In synthesizing research, it is wise to treat the unit of analysis as a potential moderating factor. In that way we can learn whether, for any particular meta-analysis, effect sizes differ in magnitude for studies employing different units of analysis. In one meta-analysis, for example, White (1982) found that the average relation between socioeconomic status and academic achievement more than doubled when the units of analysis were schools or districts rather than individual students. Sometimes this finding may be explained by the greater reliability of a measure based on an aggregate of individuals than a measure based on a single individual. Although it tends to be true that effect sizes are larger for higher-order units, it will not always be the case. For example, in studies such as White's, when the differences between classrooms become very large within each level of the independent variable, relative to the individual differences among students within classrooms, the effect size can actually be smaller for higher-order than for lower-order units. The practical implication is that since the unit of analysis may make an important but unpredictable difference in the effect size obtained, it is wise to record the unit of analysis employed for each primary study.

## 2.3 Theory Development

Both primary studies and meta-analyses can contribute to theory by testing the validity of theoretical relationships. The strength of synthesizing compared to primary research lies in its ability to examine information accrued over multiple replications and several operational definitions. The researcher can aggregate estimates of magnitudes of effects for theorized relations that rarely would or could be tested within one primary study. For example, Harris and Rosenthal (1985) used a ten-arrow model of the expectancy effect to guide their meta-analytic study of how the expectancy effect was mediated. Carlson and Miller (1987) used meta-analysis to compare three theories of why negative affect has a positive relation with helping behavior. Friedman and Booth-Kewley (1987) assembled correlations between five major personality variables and five major diseases in order to test the validity of the theorized relationship between personality and disease.

In these examples, the research synthesists brought together alternative explanations for a phenomenon and compared strengths of theoretical relations that had not been compared previously. These syntheses invoke a broader perspective for the understanding of findings from primary research. Patterns not detected in primary research emerge. The results of these syntheses are not definitive, because of the limitations on cause and effect inference, but they are provocative and can help direct future research.

## 3. THE DIRECTIONALITY OF RESEARCH RESULTS

### 3.1 The Use of Contrasts

What do we mean by the "results of a study?" We like results to give us magnitudes, such as means, and uncertainties associated with those magnitudes, usually a standard error or a set of confidence limits. We prefer results that have some directional orientation (e.g., positive-negative, confirm-disconfirm) so that we can focus on a specific hypothesis and so that similar results can be added, averaged, or compared.

One kind of result that has this property is a contrast. In its simplest form, a contrast deals with two situations and compares them by looking at the difference in performance in these circumstances. For example, how much better do third-graders do on a standardized spelling test than second-graders? If $\bar{x}_3$ is the average score for third-graders and $\bar{x}_2$ for second-graders, a contrast is $\bar{x}_3 - \bar{x}_2$. A feature of a contrast is that the implied coefficients of the variables (here $+1$ and $-1$, i.e., $(+1)\bar{x}_3 + (-1)\bar{x}_2$) add to zero. If we have the same contrasts from several schools, we can average them and get a notion of change associated with the additional year of schooling.

If we had three groups, such as third-, second-, and first-graders, we could test many specific hypotheses; for example, do second-graders fall at the average of third- and first-graders? For this question we use the contrast $(-1)\bar{x}_3 + (+2)\bar{x}_2 + (-1)\bar{x}_1$, and the coefficients $-1$, $+2$, and $-1$ again add to zero. If the contrast is positive or negative, then second-graders do better or worse, respectively, than the average of the first- and third-graders. For example, this contrast was one device used to evaluate the effectiveness of the Salk polio vaccine with grade 2 vaccinated and grades 1 and 3 not vaccinated, and the $\bar{x}$'s were the rates of paralytic polio in the three grades. The results showed that there were 69 fewer cases per 100,000 children in the vaccinated group (Meier 1989).

By suitably forming contrasts with coefficients $+1$ and $-1$, we can answer a variety of questions associated with a two-by-two table of means. For example, does therapy work better when the therapist's sex matches that of the patient? In Table 2.1 the $\bar{x}$'s represent average improvement scores, with the first subscript

**Table 2.1 Performance of Therapists**

|  | Male Therapist | Female Therapist |
|---|---|---|
| Male patient | $\bar{x}_{mm}$ | $\bar{x}_{mf}$ |
| Female patient | $\bar{x}_{fm}$ | $\bar{x}_{ff}$ |

referring to the sex of the patient and the second to the sex of the therapist. We could form the contrast $(+1)\bar{x}_{mm} + (+1)\bar{x}_{ff} + (-1)\bar{x}_{fm} + (-1)\bar{x}_{mf}$ to assess the hypothesis that sex-matching improves therapy. If we wanted to see whether female therapists do better than males, we could use the contrast, written in simplified form, $\bar{x}_{mf} + \bar{x}_{ff} - \bar{x}_{mm} - \bar{x}_{fm}$. If some theory argued that male patients with female therapists would do better than other pairings on the average, we could use the contrast $3\bar{x}_{mf} - \bar{x}_{mm} - \bar{x}_{fm} - \bar{x}_{ff}$. Contrasts can be differentiated from omnibus approaches in that contrasts are always associated with only a single degree of freedom *(df)* whereas omnibus approaches are associated with 2 or more *df*. It is characteristic of research synthesis that only 1 *df* approaches can be combined and compared across studies investigating a common underlying relationship. In the following section we discuss some problems that make omnibus tests essentially unsuitable to the process of research synthesis.

## 3.2 Problems with Omnibus Approaches

If children were tested for spelling performance at ages 4, 6, 8, and 10, the contrast approach might weight performance at these ages by $-1$, $-1$, $+1$, and $+1$, respectively. This contrast would compare "younger" and "older" children. Consider an alternative. We might use an *F* test (with 3 numerator *df*) to test for differences among the four age groups. This *F* test approach gives us a vague result. If we get a significant *F* value, the interpretation is that performance differs among the age groups. But the result does not tell us whether children improved with age (based on the *F* test alone). It merely says that the groups appear to differ in their performance. Do they perform better up to an age and then level off or get worse? Or does some other sequence of outcomes with differing means hold?

In meta-analysis, we try to focus on questions that state a direction of result, and contrasts should point us in specific directions. The *F* tests associated with contrasts have 1 *df* in the numerator. In a similar vein, we

prefer *t* tests and chi-square tests with 1 *df* because they can offer directionality. The *F* tests even with 1 *df* (and the $\chi^2$) need added directional information because the *F* and $\chi^2$ statistics alone do not indicate direction. They lose it in the course of squaring differences. We can retrieve directionality by looking at the relevant differences before they are squared.

## 4. LEARNING FROM COMBINING STUDIES

### 4.1 Combining Effect Sizes

When treatments (or conditions) are evaluated, we speak of their effects or effect sizes. The true effect sizes are what would be found for the entire population of interest, and the observed effects include the fluctuations from sampling plus biases in the investigation. How we measure effect sizes depends on the problem and even the customs in different fields of research. An effect size can be a measure distinguishing the consequences of one treatment (or collection of treatments) from those of one or more other treatments. An effect size can also be thought of as the degree of relationship between two variables. Differences, scaled differences, ratios, logarithms of ratios, and correlation coefficients are among the many kinds of indices that have been found useful. (These are described in Chapters 16 and 17, which also show the various procedures for computing effect sizes.) Note that the statistics listed, like contrasts, include directionality as well as magnitude in their measurement.

One important product of a quantitative research synthesis is a summary of the effect sizes found for all the studies that address the same directional question (e.g., does the treatment help? do older children perform better than younger ones?). We might present the entire set of effect size estimates in a stem-and-leaf display or a similar frequency distribution (Mosteller & Tukey 1977) and include in our summary of this display (a) the unweighted mean of effect size estimates, (b) the weighted-by-sample-size estimate, and (c) the median estimate. These values give us some overall indication of the size and variability of the effect under study. But which of the many possible estimates of the size of the effect or of the relationship shall we choose as our metric?

**4.1.1 Effect sizes based on counts** One broad class of effect size estimates is derived from data that come to us as counts. Table 2.2 provides an example. Each of the women of the study shown was categorized as

**Table 2.2  Preferences for Future Care Among Pregnant Women Who Held Their Own Medical Record Compared with Those Whose Record Was Held by the Clinic**

|  | Held Own Record | Record Held by Clinic | Total |
|---|---|---|---|
| Preferred different care in future | $a = 11$ | $c = 44$ | $a + c = 55$ |
| Preferred same care in future | $b = 112$ | $d = 62$ | $b + d = 174$ |
| Total | $a + b = 123$ | $c + d = 106$ | $n = 229$ |

SOURCE: Elbourne et al. (1987).

belonging in one of the four cells of the study—cells formed by the crossing of the independent variable (experimental vs. control: the medical record held by the patient vs. by the clinic) with the dependent variable (preferring same care vs. preferring different care in the future). In Table 2.2, 8.9 percent of the group holding their own records preferred different care (cell a, $n = 11$), whereas 41.5 percent of the other group preferred different care (cell c, $n = 44$). Three standard approaches to estimating effect sizes in such tables are (a) risk differences or differences in raw percentages for the experimental group and the control group (here, $8.9 - 41.5 = -32.6$), (b) relative risks or ratio of proportions for the experimental group compared with the control group ($8.9/41.5 = 0.21$), and (c) odds ratios: the ratio of the odds in the experimental group to that in the control group (here, $(11/112)/(44/62) = 0.14$). In the example, each index in its own way suggests that women preferred the care that gave them control of their own records. The negative difference and the risk and odds ratios, both less than 1, show that women in the experimental group were less likely to want different care in the future.

A good many other indices are also often found to be useful in such situations—for example, the difference between arcsine transforms of the proportions, the logarithm of the odds ratio, or the Pearson correlation between the independent and dependent variables each coded as 0, 1. (Detailed discussion of effect sizes based on tables of counts can be found in Chapter 17.)

**4.1.2  Effect sizes based on variables taking several values**  When we move from research based on dichotomous outcomes to research based on outcomes that take several numerical values on the same scale, we usually treat the data as if they were interval measurements. For example, the ratings of the effectiveness of psychotherapists made by their supervisors, their peers, their patients, or themselves may range from a score of 1 (not at all effective) to 7 (maximally effective). Whether only the integers are used or intermediate values are permissible, the analysis will be much the same. The blood pressure or cholesterol level of medical patients and the dollars earned by salespersons (or the logarithms of those dollars), although discrete, are the practical representations of continuous measurements.

Some of these metrics have immediate, intrinsic meaning (e.g., blood pressure, cholesterol level, dollars earned) and differences between experimental and control conditions can be usefully indexed by differences in raw units. If the treated group shows a reduction in cholesterol level from 280 to 240 while the control group shows a reduction from 281 to 271, we can summarize the result by saying that the treated group decreased their cholesterol level by 30 points more than did the control group. If this study had been an after-only design, we would say that the treated group showed an average 31-point lower level of cholesterol than did the control group.

In many areas of the social and behavioral sciences, however, the units of measurement lack immediate, intrinsic meaning. In studies employing rating scales—for example, 1 (not at all effective) to 7 (maximally effective)—we cannot tell so clearly what a rating of 5 means unless we know something of the variability of ratings actually employed. A difference of mean ratings of 0.5 implies something quite different in studies with great variation in responses versus studies with little variation (e.g., raters employ all 7 points of the rating scale or only 4 and 5 points). Even IQ points have no intrinsic meaning since their interpretation depends on the variance of the particular test employed. Because of the difficulty in interpretation of many of the measures employed in the social, behavioral, and medical sciences, two families of effect size indices have evolved: the $r$-indices and the $d$-indices. More detailed discussion of these indices is found in Chapter 16, so here we need only illustrate their use.

The $r$-indices include the various product moment correlations (e.g., both variables continuous; one continuous, one dichotomous; both dichotomous; both in ranked form), Fisher's $z$ transformation of the correlation $r$, and a variety of related indices.

The $d$-indices include several magnitudes of effect in

which the difference between the means of two groups is divided by some estimate of standard deviation—for example, the pooled average standard deviation or the standard deviation of the control group only.

The effect size estimates of both the $r$ and the $d$ families can be viewed as indices that give us information about how much we know about a relationship or an effect (i.e., signal) relative to how much we do not know about a relationship or an effect (i.e., noise). Different indices of effect size employ different specific definitions of signal and of noise. However, regardless of the specific index employed, the signal might be increased in future studies by comparing more extreme groups or by employing stronger experimental manipulations (e.g., comparing 10 hours of tutoring to 1 hour rather than comparing 6 hours to 5 hours). Also, regardless of the specific index of effect size employed, the noise, or error, can be decreased by employing more homogeneous groups, more uniformly applied treatment procedures, more valid and more reliably measured dependent variables, and data analytic procedures that minimize error (e.g., analysis of covariance). As we increase the signal and decrease the noise we increase our estimate of the effect size.

Much of the power and flexibility of quantitative research synthesis is owed to the existence of effect size estimators such as $r$ and $d$. Because the synthesist can translate results into a standardized metric of outcome *regardless* of the particular operationalization of research variables within the primary study, it is possible to analyze studies that address the same research hypothesis but use somewhat different manipulations and/or measuring instruments.

The effect size device has the advantage of stripping the original variable of its units and leaving the effects measured in terms of their own standard deviations. When effects are correlated we might suppose that, since length of hospital stay and hospital cost are somewhat related, their effect sizes would have the same sign. Similar arguments may be made for other variables that are proxies for one another. At the same time, it may well be that one of such a pair of variables averaged over many situations will yield an effect size of 0.2 (standard deviations) and its proxy could average 0.5 (standard deviations). So effect size can be of some help in pooling variables, but it does not assure that the variables will have a common average gain. We rarely have enough data to investigate this comparability, and when we do we usually study the proxies separately.

## 4.2  Combining Significance Tests

Although combining or comparing effect sizes is central to the meta-analytic enterprise, we often want also to combine the results of tests of significance from the studies collected to form an overall test of significance for an entire set of studies addressing a common research question. A great many procedures are available for such combining of tests of significance (Mosteller & Bush 1954; Rosenthal 1978; and Chapter 15 of this handbook).

## 5.  LEARNING FROM COMPARING STUDIES

### 5.1  Moderator Variables

In what we have described thus far, the goal of the research synthesist is to summarize the results found by previous investigators. As noted above, these results can be either $p$-values or, especially, estimates of effect magnitude. This alone can be a valuable contribution because one usually wants to know whether the existing literature permits an overall conclusion: Does the new drug speed recovery? Do men excel over women in math? Is social class a predictor of school achievement? And if the answer is yes, by how much do these groups or treatments differ?

We now turn to even more ambitious questions. By comparing results *across* studies of different kinds, we can test hypotheses that were not tested, or tested rarely, in primary studies. Then research synthesis adds as well as summarizes knowledge. Cooper (1984) calls these new findings ''review-generated evidence,'' as distinguished from the ''study-generated evidence'' described above. To uncover these effects one identifies study characteristics that may be *moderator variables:* variables that are associated with effect magnitude. As examples, one can ask whether males' proclivity to be more aggressive than females is greater for physical than verbal aggression (it is; Eagly & Steffen 1986), or whether psychotherapy is equally effective across a range of different outcome variables (it is not; Smith & Glass 1977). The fact that different studies use different forms of aggression and therapy outcomes allows us to relate these variations to differences in effect sizes. Relating results to study characteristics in this way is analogous to a primary study's examination of interaction effects; in both cases, one asks whether the effects are constant across varying circumstances.

The value of the moderator-variable approach is especially evident when relations can be tested *only* by comparing several studies. The effect of the author's sex, the publication year of the study, and the type of publication cannot be tested within a primary study. On the other hand, some moderator variables could be, or have been, tested within primary studies, by examining interaction effects. These primary results and the results of the synthesist's analysis of moderators should be compared whenever possible.

Hall (1978), for example, reviewed sex differences in accuracy of decoding nonverbal cues and found women's advantage to be about the same whether a study had used male or female stimuli; this conclusion was corroborated by ten studies that tested for subject sex × stimulus sex interactions. When such a comparison of between-studies and within-study tests of the same hypothesis point to the same conclusions, one's confidence is greatly increased. If the research literature contains enough instances of within-study interactions involving the same conceptual variables, then a quantitative synthesis could be performed on them. For example, Hall could have treated each subject sex × stimulus sex interaction as a contrast, calculated an effect size for each, and summarized them as in any quantitative synthesis. The larger the average effect size, the more sex of stimulus moderates the relation between subject sex and decoding skill.

Tests of heterogeneity among the estimates of effect size are often performed as a prelude to the search for moderator variables (see Hedges & Olkin 1985; Rosenthal 1991; this volume, Chapter 18). A heterogeneity test asks whether a group of effects is more variable than one would expect based on sampling variation, or, in the words of Hedges and Olkin, "whether the studies can reasonably be described as sharing a common effect size" (p. 122). A significant heterogeneity test means that greater variability than expected by sampling error is present, and one should consider the possibility that one or more moderator variables are at work—in other words, that the effects did not come from a common population but rather from two or more distinct populations (e.g., males and females). When a heterogeneity test is not significant, one can feel more confident that summary statistics, such as the mean effect size, adequately describe the available results. Even so, one should not necessarily conclude that moderators cannot be at work (Hall & Rosenthal 1991). To draw an analogy, a heterogeneity test is comparable to an omnibus $F$ test (more than 1 *df* in numerator), from which a significant contrast can be extracted even when the omnibus $F$ is nonsignificant (Rosenthal & Rosnow 1985). Tests of heterogeneity may have low power against even substantial differences in populations.

## 5.2 Types of Moderator Variables

In practice, moderator variables in research synthesis are of two types: "low-inference" and "high-inference" (as discussed by Cooper 1989, pp. 32–33).

**5.2.1 Low-inference codings** Low-inference codings consist of information that is present in the primary study and that the synthesist can readily transcribe to coding sheets for future analysis. It is impossible to catalog all the variables of this sort that have been used by synthesists, but some examples are characteristics of the publication (e.g., year, journal), type of research design, measuring instruments, subject characteristics, and the kind of setting where the study took place. Sometimes a whole study corresponds to one level of the moderator, as when all subjects are male or all are children under age 12; other times, the study is mixed with respect to a moderator and so must be characterized on a continuum, as in percentage ethnic minority, percentage schizophrenic, or percentage male authors.

These variables can be of methodological or theoretical significance, and such moderators have often led to important new understandings. As examples, analysis employing the year of publication as a moderator has revealed that sex differences in mathematical performance have decreased from one third of a standard deviation to one seventh of a standard deviation from the period 1963–1973 to the period 1974–1988 (Hyde, Fennema & Lamon 1990). Eagly and Carli (1981) uncovered sex-of-author effects in studies of sex differences in persuasion and nonverbal decoding accuracy.

**5.2.2 High-inference codings** The second type of moderator coding, often involving considerable inference by the coder, comes not from the primary study directly, but is rather *added* by the synthesist, usually in the form of ratings of study characteristics. Study quality is often measured in this way, either by giving points for desirable design features (such as keeping experimenters unaware of the hypothesis, randomly assigning subjects to groups, or using double-blind procedures) or by asking raters to apply a global scale of judgment. A more daring purpose is to try to capture the psychological experience of subjects in the primary studies. Miller and Carlson (1990) provide a list of studies that have used this approach. In Eagly and Crowley's review (1986) of sex differences in helping behavior, for example, raters were told about the scenario experienced by the original subjects and were asked to rate how dangerous it would have been to provide the help and how competent and comfortable they would feel if they provided it. Hall and Halberstadt (1986), in reviewing sex differences in smiling and gazing, rated the situations faced by the original subjects in terms of familiarity, comfort, competition, and status vis-à-vis their interaction partner.

Some have argued that such ratings may lack validity because raters' reactions may not parallel those of the original subjects (Cialdini & Fultz 1990). However, most writers seem to agree that such ratings can add valuable insight into psychological processes that may have been operating in the original studies, and therefore have some bearing on theoretical issues. In Eagly and Crowley's work, for example, men were more helpful than women to the extent that women felt the situation was more dangerous than men did. Validity is suggested when, as in this example, the results fit with a priori expectations based on theory. Moreover, Miller, Lee, and Carlson (1991) have added explicit validation for judges' ratings by showing that the ratings are highly correlated with manipulation-check data from the original studies. Research synthesists using high-inference coding should be especially careful to keep raters unaware of a study's results and to evaluate interrater reliability. More than one rater may be required to achieve satisfactory levels of reliability.

**5.2.3 Some cautions about moderators** As all research synthesists know, lists of variables to be tested as moderators can become extremely long. A natural limit often comes from the fact that only a subset of such variables will be codable in all or most studies—for example, year of publication is always available, but the racial composition of a sample often may be unreported. A synthesist may decide to use only the frequently reported study characteristics as moderators. On the other hand, some moderators may be sufficiently important that they should be coded even if they are available for only a portion of the studies; an example would be patient age when considering survival from surgical interventions.

Although it may be tempting to be as complete as possible and to leave the door open for fruitful exploratory analysis, there is a price to be paid for too much "fishing" in terms of both suspect $p$ values (synthesis-wise error rates) and the exhaustion of the synthesist who feels the need to provide an interpretation of all significant effects. As in primary research, the synthesist should establish a basis for selecting moderators to code, using theoretical or practical grounds or sensible prior practice in a particular area of study. For example, in studies of children for the prediction of school achievement from social class, it would be reasonable to look at the moderating effect of age or ethnicity of the child because both may be associated with substantial differences, but it would be impractical to try to use parental IQ because it is rarely available.

To give a notion of the effect of exploring moderators for possible correlations, suppose that a study has 26 subjects and that we have a list of 9 moderators all of which are, unknown to us, actually independent of the response under study and each other. Theory shows that, on average, one moderator will be observed to have a correlation of more than 0.25 with the response and another more negative than $-0.25$. In absolute value the largest correlation will average 0.33, so strong is the power of chance and exploration. Thus, one will likely find correlations of intriguing magnitudes, by accident, between some moderator and the response. Hunting for the best moderator is risky business, though using well-established moderators can be rewarding.

Needless to say, the choice and definition of moderators can profoundly affect the conclusions of a research synthesis. Careful thought should always underlie these decisions, and even then sensible meta-analysts may carve up the pie differently. For example, one meta-analyst might lump into a single category studies that a second meta-analyst sees as crucially different, thereby obscuring a distinction that is crucial to the second meta-analyst's reasoning and research (cf. Johnson & Eagly 1989; Petty & Cacioppo 1990; Johnson & Eagly 1990).

## 5.3 Aggregate Analysis of Descriptive Statistics

Aside from documenting moderator effects, research synthesis can establish new findings in yet another way. This meta-analytic approach, called "aggregate" analysis by one writer (Rosenthal 1991), is based on descriptive statistics from primary studies rather than estimates of effect magnitude. Such statistics might be the percentage of items recalled by subjects, the average number of minutes during which subjects persevered on a task, or the subjects' average score on a scale or test. If these statistics can be put on a common metric so as to be comparable across studies, one can then relate them to coded study characteristics. Underwood's analysis of word recall as a function of the number of lists previously learned (described in Glass, McGaw & Smith 1981) is an early example of this approach. More recently, Hall and Dornan (1988) applied it to the study of patients' satisfaction with their medical care. They converted the mean satisfaction scores of subjects in each of 108 studies to a 0-1 scale and then related these standardized satisfaction scores to study attributes. They found that respondents were more satisfied when the physicians were younger and when the satisfaction instrument asked about the patient's own physician rather than about physicians in general.

## 6. CONCLUSION

Research synthesis aids in accumulating evidence and in generating new evidence. One accomplishes the accumulation task through the aggregation of effect magnitudes, confidence limits, and tests of significance. How new evidence is generated can be as varied as the research synthesist is creative. Methods for generating new evidence described in this chapter include the analysis of moderator variables, both those inherent in the underlying primary studies and those generated by the meta-analyst, and the aggregate analysis of primary descriptive data.

Although research synthesis can be used to determine the associations between variables, questions specifically addressed to cause and effect depend on the inferential strength of the underlying primary data. On the other hand, because the raw data are study replications or at least similar studies, a major strength of research synthesis is its usefulness for studying the generality of effects.

It is not necessary to judge which questions are best addressed by primary research or research synthesis. Obviously syntheses cannot be done without primary research. However, the scientific usefulness of synthesis research flows from its application to the accumulation and synthesis of evidence. Primary and meta-analytic research are complementary. The development of theory emphasizes this complementarity. Together these forms of research direct future research and advance knowledge.

### Authors' Note

The preparation of this chapter was supported in part by the Spencer Foundation and in part by National Science Foundation grant No. SES-8908641 to Harvard University. The content is solely the responsibility of the authors.

## 7. REFERENCES

Bowers, T. G., & Clum, G. A. (1988). Relative contribution of specific and nonspecific treatment effects: Meta-analysis of placebo-controlled behavior therapy research. *Psychological Bulletin, 103,* 315–323.

Campbell, D. T., & Fiske, D. W. (1959). Convergent and discriminant validation by the multitrait-multimethod matrix. *Psychological Bulletin, 56,* 81–105.

Carlson, M., & Miller, N. (1987). Explanation of the relation between negative mood and helping. *Psychological Bulletin, 102,* 91–108.

Cialdini, R. B., & Fultz, J. (1990). Interpreting the negative mood-helping literature via ''mega''-analysis: A contrary view. *Psychological Bulletin, 107,* 210–214.

Cook, T. D., & Campbell, D. T. (1979). *Quasi-experimentation: Design and analysis issues for field settings.* Chicago: Rand McNally.

Cooper, H. M. (1984). *The integrative research review: A systematic approach.* Beverly Hills, CA: Sage.

Cooper, H. M. (1989). *Integrating research: A guide for literature reviews* (2nd ed.). Newbury Park, CA: Sage.

Eagly, A. H., & Carli, L. L. (1981). Sex of researchers and sex-typed communications as determinants of sex differences in influenceability: A meta-analysis of social influence studies. *Psychological Bulletin, 90,* 1–20.

Eagly, A. H., & Crowley, M. (1986). Gender and helping behavior: A meta-analytic review of the social psychological literature. *Psychological Bulletin, 100,* 283–308.

Eagly, A. H., & Steffen, V. J. (1986). Gender and aggressive behavior: A meta-analytic review of the social psychological literature. *Psychological Bulletin, 100,* 308–330.

Elbourne, D., Richardson, M., Chalmers, I., Waterhouse, I., & Holt, E. (1987). The Newbury maternity case study: A randomized controlled trial to evaluate a policy of women holding their own obstetric records. *British Journal of Obstetrics and Gynecology, 94,* 612–619.

Friedman, H. S., & Booth-Kewley, S. (1987). The ''disease-prone personality'': A meta-analytic view of the construct. *American Psychologist, 42,* 539–555.

Glass, G. V., McGaw, B., & Smith, M. L. (1981). *Meta-analysis in social research.* Beverly Hills, CA: Sage.

Hall, J. A. (1978). Gender effects in decoding nonverbal cues. *Psychological Bulletin, 85,* 845–875.

Hall, J. A., & Dornan, M. C. (1988). Meta-analysis of

satisfaction with medical care: Description of research domain and analysis of overall satisfaction levels. *Social Science and Medicine, 27,* 637–644.

Hall, J. A., & Halberstadt, A. G. (1986). Smiling and gazing. In J. S. Hyde & M. C. Linn (Eds.), *The psychology of gender: Advances through meta-analysis.* Baltimore: Johns Hopkins University Press.

Hall, J. A., & Rosenthal, R. (1991). Testing for moderator variables in meta-analysis: Issues and methods. *Communication Monographs, 58,* 437–448.

Harris, M. J., & Rosenthal, R. R. (1985). Mediation of interpersonal expectancy effects: 31 meta-analyses. *Psychological Bulletin, 97,* 363–386.

Hedges, L. V., & Olkin, I. (1985). *Statistical methods for meta-analysis.* Orlando, FL: Academic Press.

Hyde, J. S., Fennema, E., & Lamon, S. H. (1990). Gender differences in mathematics performance: A meta-analysis. *Psychological Bulletin, 107,* 139–155.

Johnson, B. T., & Eagly, A. H. (1989). The effects of involvement on persuasion: A meta-analysis. *Psychological Bulletin, 106,* 290–314.

Johnson, B. T., & Eagly, A. H. (1990). Involvement and persuasion: Types, traditions, and the evidence. *Psychological Bulletin, 107,* 375–384.

Johnson, D. W., Johnson, R. T., & Maruyama, G. (1983). Interdependence and interpersonal attraction among heterogeneous and homogeneous individuals: A theoretical formulation and a meta-analysis of the research. *Review of Educational Research, 53,* 5–54.

Meier, P. (1989). The biggest public health experiment ever: The 1954 field trial of the Salk poliomyelitis vaccine. In J. M. Tanur et al. (Eds.), *Statistics: A guide to the unknown* (3rd ed., pp. 3–14). Pacific Grove, CA: Wadsworth.

Miller, N., & Carlson, M. (1990). Valid theory-testing meta-analyses further question the negative state relief model of helping. *Psychological Bulletin, 107,* 215–225.

Miller, N., Lee, J., & Carlson, M. (1991). The validity of inferential judgments when used in theory-testing meta-analysis. *Personality and Social Psychology Bulletin, 17,* 335–343.

Mosteller, F., & Bush, R. (1954). Selected quantitative techniques. In G. Lindsey (Ed.), *Handbook of social psychology: Vol. 1. Theory and method.* Cambridge, MA: Addison-Wesley.

Mosteller, F., & Tukey, J. W. (1977). *Data analysis and regression.* Reading, MA: Addison-Wesley.

Petty, R. E., & Cacioppo, J. T. (1990). Involvement and persuasion: Tradition versus integration. *Psychological Bulletin, 107,* 367–374.

Rosenthal, R. (1978). Combining results of independent studies. *Psychological Bulletin, 85,* 185–193.

Rosenthal, R. (1991). *Meta-analytic procedures for social research* (rev. ed.). Newbury Park, CA: Sage.

Rosenthal, R., & Rosnow, R. L. (1985). *Contrast analysis: Focused comparisons in the analysis of variance.* New York: Cambridge University Press.

Smith, M. L., & Glass, G. V. (1977). Meta-analysis of psychotherapy outcome studies. *American Psychologist, 32,* 752–760.

Tickle-Degnen, L., Rosenthal, R., & Harrigan, J. (1991). *Nonverbal behavior as determinant of favorableness of impression formed: Eight meta-analyses.* Unpublished manuscript, Boston University.

White, K. R. (1982). The relation between socioeconomic status and academic achievement. *Psychological Bulletin, 91,* 461–481.

Cooper, H. and Hedges, L. V. (Eds.) 1994. *The Handbook of Research Synthesis*. New York: Russell Sage Foundation

# 3

# STATISTICAL CONSIDERATIONS

**LARRY V. HEDGES**
*University of Chicago*

CONTENTS

## 1. INTRODUCTION

Research synthesis is an empirical process. As with any empirical research, statistical considerations have an influence at many points in the process. Some of these considerations, such as how to test particular hypotheses, are narrowly matters of statistical practice. They are considered in detail in subsequent chapters of this handbook. Other issues are more conceptual and might best be considered statistical considerations that impinge on general matters of research strategy or interpretation. This chapter addresses selected issues of the latter type.

## 2. PROBLEM FORMULATION

The formulation of the research synthesis problem has important implications for the statistical methods that may be appropriate and for the interpretation of results. Careful consideration of the questions to be addressed in the synthesis will also have implications for data collection, data evaluation, and presentation of results. In this section I discuss two broad considerations in problem formulation: the universe to which generalizations are made and the number and source of hypotheses addressed.

### 2.1 The Universe to Which Generalizations Are Made

One of the most subtle and difficult aspects of problem formulation is the specification of the universe to which the researcher wishes to generalize. The term "universe" rather than population or hyperpopulation is used to avoid confusion with other uses of these terms in statistics.[1] The basic issue is one of how the results of the synthesis are to be interpreted. One perspective is the fixed effects (conditional) model, perhaps the most frequently used model of generalization in quantitative research synthesis. The other is the random effects (unconditional) model. Both perspectives have their adherents and both can be justified on logical grounds. The choice between them is a matter of choosing between two universes of possible studies that we might wish to know about. In both cases we generalize to

studies "like those that have been conducted," the difference between them is in the precise definition of the term "like" and how uncertainty is treated in the inference process.

To make the distinctions clear we use the terms "universe" and "sample." The universe is the hypothetical collection of studies that could be conducted in principle and about which we wish to generalize. The study sample is the ensemble of studies that are used in the review and that provide the effect size data used in the research synthesis.

**2.1.1 The fixed effects (conditional) model** In the fixed effects, or conditional, model, the universe to which generalizations are made consists of ensembles of studies identical to those in the study sample except for the particular people (or primary sampling units) that appear in the studies. Thus, the studies in the universe differ from those in the study sample only as a result of the sampling of people into the groups of the studies. The only source of sampling error or uncertainty is therefore the variation resulting from the sampling of people into studies.

In a strict sense the universe is structured: It is a collection of *ensembles of studies,* each study in an ensemble corresponding to a particular study in each of the other ensembles. Each of the corresponding studies would have *exactly* the same effect size parameter (population effect size). In fact part of the definition of "identical" (in the requirement that corresponding studies in different ensembles of this universe be identical) is that they have the same effect size parameter.

The model is called the *conditional* model because it can be conceived as a model that conditions (or holds fixed) the characteristics of studies that might be related to the effect size parameter. The conditional model in research synthesis is in the same spirit as the usual regression model and fixed effects analysis of variance in primary research. In the case of regression, the fixed effect refers to the fact that the values of the predictor variables are taken to be fixed (not randomly sampled). The only source of variation that enters into the uncertainty of estimates of the regression coefficients or tests of hypotheses is that due to the sampling of individuals (in particular, their outcome variable scores) *with a given ensemble of predictor variable scores.* Uncertainty due to the sampling of predictor variable scores themselves is *not* taken into account. To put it another way, the regression model is conditional on the particular ensemble of values of the predictor variables in the sample.

---

[1]The use of the term "universe" also suggests a connection with two related problems of generalization in which this terminology has been used: the dependability of behavioral measurements (Cronbach et al. 1972) and generalization in program evaluation (Cronbach 1982).

The situation is similar in the fixed effects analysis of variance. Here the term ''fixed effects'' refers to the fact that the treatment levels in the experiment are considered fixed, and the only source of uncertainty in the tests for treatment effects is a consequence of sampling of a group of individuals (or their outcome scores) within a given ensemble of treatment levels. Uncertainty due to the sampling of treatment levels from a collection of possible treatment levels is not taken into account.

*Inference to other cases.* In conditional models (including regression and analysis of variance) inferences are, in the strictest sense, limited to cases in which the ensemble of values of the predictor variables are represented in the sample. Inferences to other values, for example, typically do not have the correct standard error. Of course, conditional models are widely used in primary research, and the generalizations supported typically are not constrained to predictor values in the sample. For example, generalizations about treatment effects in fixed effects analysis of variance are usually not constrained to apply *only* to the *precise* levels of treatment found in the experiment, but are viewed as applying to ''similar'' treatments as well even if they were not explicitly part of the experiment. How are such inferences justified? Typically they are justified on the basis of an a priori (extra-empirical) decision that other levels (other treatments or ensembles of predictor values) are sufficiently like those in the sample that their behavior will be identical.

There are two variations of the argument. One is that a level not in the sample is sufficiently like a level or levels in the sample that it is essentially judged identical to them (e.g., this instance of behavior modification treatment is essentially the same as the treatment labeled behavior modification in the sample, or this treatment of 20-weeks duration is essentially identical to the treatment of 20-weeks duration in the sample). The other variation of the argument is that a level that is not in the sample ''lies between'' values in the sample on some implicit or explicit dimension and thus it is safe to ''interpolate'' between the results obtained for levels in the sample. For example, suppose we have the predictor values 10 and 20 in the sample; then a new case with predictor value 15 might reasonably have an outcome halfway between that for the two sampled values, or a new treatment might be judged between two others in intensity and therefore its outcome might reasonably be assumed to be between that of the other two. This interpolation between realized values is sometimes formalized as a modeling *assumption* (e.g., in linear regres-

sion, where the assumption of a linear equation justifies the interpolation or even extrapolation to other data provided they are sufficiently similar to fit the same linear model). In either case the generalization to levels not present in the sample requires an assumption that the levels are similar to those in the sample—one not justified by a formal sampling argument.

Inference to studies not *identical* to those in the sample can be justified in meta-analysis by the same intellectual devices used to justify the corresponding inferences in primary research. Specifically, inferences may be justified if the studies are judged a priori to be ''sufficiently similar'' to those in the study sample. It is important to recognize, however, that the inference process has two distinct parts. One part is the generalization from the study sample to a universe of identical studies, which is supported by a sampling theory rationale. The second part is the generalization from the universe of studies that are identical to the sample to a universe of ''sufficiently similar'' (but nonidentical) studies. This second part of the generalization is not strictly supported by a sampling argument but by an extra-statistical one.

**2.1.2 The random effects (unconditional) model** In the random effects, or unconditional, model, the study sample is presumed to be literally a sample from a hypothetical collection (or population) of studies. The universe to which generalizations are made consists of a population of studies from which the study sample is drawn. Studies in this universe differ from those in the study sample along two dimensions. First, the studies differ from one another in study characteristics and in effect size parameter. The generalization is *not*, as it was in the fixed effects case, to a universe consisting of ensembles of studies with corresponding members of the ensembles having identical characteristics and effect size parameters. Instead the studies in the study sample (and their effect size parameters) differ from those in the universe by as much as might be expected as a consequence of drawing a sample from a population. Second, in addition to differences in study characteristics and effect size parameters, the studies in the study sample also differ from those in the universe as a consequence of the sampling of people into the groups of the study. This results in variation of observed effect sizes about their respective effect size parameters.

We can conceive of the two dimensions indicated above as introducing two sources of variability into the observed (sample) effect sizes in the universe; one due to variation in effect size *parameters* and one due to variation in observed (or potentially observable) study effect sizes about their effect size parameters. The latter source of variability is a result of the sampling of people into studies and is the only source of variability conceived as random in the fixed effects model.

This model is called the unconditional model because, unlike the fixed effects model, it does not condition (or hold fixed) the characteristics of studies that might be related to the effect size parameter. The random effects model in research synthesis is in the same spirit as the correlation model or the random effects analysis of variance in primary research. In the correlation model both the values of the predictor variable and those of the dependent variable are considered to be sampled from a population—in this case one with a joint distribution. In the random effects analysis of variance, the levels of the treatment factor are sampled from a universe of possible treatment levels (and consequently the corresponding treatment effect parameters are sampled from a universe of treatment effect parameters). There are two sources of uncertainty in estimates and tests in random effects analyses: one due to the sampling of the treatment effects themselves and the other due to the sampling of individuals (in particular, outcome scores) into each treatment.

*Inference to other cases.* In random effects models, inferences are *not* limited to cases with predictor variables represented in the sample. Instead, the inferences—for example, about the mean or variance of effect size parameter—apply to the universe of studies from which the study sample was obtained. In effect, the warrant for generalization to other studies is via a classical sampling argument. Because the universe contains studies that differ in their characteristics, and those differences find their way into the study sample by the process of random selection, generalizations to the universe pertain to studies that are not identical to those in the study sample.

By utilizing a sampling model of generalization, the random effects model seems to avoid subjective difficulties that plague the fixed effects model in generalizations to studies not identical to the study sample. That is, we do not have to ask, "How similar is similar enough?" Instead we substitute another question, "Is this new study part of the universe from which the study sample was obtained?" If study samples were obtained from well-defined sampling frames via overtly specified sampling schemes, this might be an easy question to answer. This, however, is virtually never the case in meta-analysis (and is unusual in other applications of

random effects models). The universe is usually rather ambiguously specified, and consequently the ambiguity in generalization based on random effects models is that it is difficult to know precisely what the universe is. In contrast, the universe is clear in fixed effects models, but the ambiguity arises in deciding if a new study might be similar enough to the studies already contained in the study sample.

The random effects model does provide the technical means to address an important problem that is not handled in the fixed effects model: namely, the additional uncertainty introduced by the inference to studies that are not identical (except for the sample of people involved) to those in the study sample. Inference to (nonsampled) studies in the fixed effects model occurs outside the technical framework and hence any uncertainty it contributes cannot be evaluated by technical means within the model. In contrast, the random effects model does incorporate between-studies variation into the sampling uncertainty used to compute tests and estimates.

While the random effects model has the advantage of incorporating inferences to a universe of studies exhibiting variation in their characteristics, the definition of the universe may be ambiguous. A tautological universe definition could be derived by using the sample of studies to define the universe as "a universe from which the study sample is representative." Such a population definition remains ambiguous; moreover, it may not be the universe definition desired for the use of the information produced by the synthesis. For example, if the study sample includes many studies of short-duration, high-intensity treatments, but the likely practical applications usually involve low-intensity, long-duration treatments, the universe defined implicitly by the study sample may not be the universe most relevant to *applications*.

One potential solution to this problem might be to explicitly define a structured universe in terms of study characteristics and to consider the study sample as a stratified sample from this universe. Estimates of parameters describing this universe could be obtained by weighting each "stratum" appropriately. For example, if one half of the studies in the universe are long-duration studies, but only one third of the study sample have this characteristic, the results of long-duration studies must be weighted twice as much as the short-duration studies.

**2.1.3 Fixed versus random effects** The choice between fixed (conditional) or random (unconditional) modeling strategies arises in many settings in statistics and has caused lengthy debates because it involves subtleties of how to formulate questions in scientific research and what data are relevant to answering questions. For example, the debate between Fisher and Yates versus Pearson on whether to condition on the marginal frequencies in the analysis of 2 x 2 tables is about precisely this issue (see Camilli 1990), as is the debate concerning whether word stimuli should be treated as fixed or random effects in psycholinguistics (see Clark 1973).

Those who advocated the fixed effects position (e.g., Peto 1987) argue that the basis for scientific inference should be *only* the studies that have actually been conducted and are observed in the study sample. Statistical methods should be employed only to determine the chance consequences of sampling of people into *these* (the observed) studies. Thus, they would emphasize estimation and hypothesis testing for (or conditional on) this collection of studies. If we must generalize to *other studies,* they would argue that this is best done by subjective or extra-statistical procedures.

Those who advocate the random effects perspective argue that the particular studies we observe are, to some extent, an accident of chance. The important inference question is not ''What is true about these studies?'' but ''What is true about studies like these *that could have been done?''* They would emphasize the generalization to other studies or other situations that could have been studied and that these generalizations should be handled by formal statistical methods. In many situations in which research is used to inform public policy by providing information about the likely effects of treatments in situations that have not been explicitly studied, this argument seems persuasive.

## 2.2 The Nature of Parameters

Another fundamental issue in problem formulation concerns the nature of the effect size parameter to be estimated. The issue can best be described in terms of population parameters (although each parameter has a corresponding sample estimate). Consider an actual study in which the effect size parameter represents the true or population relationship between variables measured in the study. This effect size parameter may be systematically affected by artifactual sources of bias such as restriction of range or measurement error in the dependent variable. Corresponding to this actual study, one can imagine a *hypothetical* study in which the biases due to artifacts were controlled or eliminated. The effect

size parameter in this hypothetical study would differ from that of the actual study because the biases from artifacts of design would not be present. A key distinction is between a theoretical effect size (reflecting a relationship between variables in a hypothetical study) and an operational effect size (the parameter that describes the population relationship between variables in an actual study; see Chapter 21). Theoretical effect sizes are often conceived as those corrected for bias or for some aspect of experimental procedure (such as a restrictive sampling plan or use of an unreliable outcome measure) that can systematically influence effect size. Operational effect size parameters, in contrast, are often conceived as affected by whatever bias or aspects of procedure that happen to be present in a particular study.

Perhaps the most prominent example of a theoretical effect size is the population correlation coefficient corrected for attenuation due to measurement error and restriction of range. One can also conceive of this corrected coefficient as the population correlation between true scores in a population in which neither variable is subject to restriction of range. The operational effect size is the correlation parameter between observed scores in the population in which variables have restricted ranges. Because the relation between the attenuated (operational) correlation and disattenuated (theoretical) correlation is known, it is possible to convert operational effect sizes into theoretical effect sizes.

Most research syntheses make use of operational effect size. However, there are two reasons why theoretical effect sizes are sometimes used. One is to enhance the comparability and hence combinability of estimates from studies whose operational effect sizes would otherwise be influenced quite substantially (and differently) by biases or incidental features of study design or procedure. This has sometimes been characterized as ''putting all of the effect sizes on the same metric'' (Glass, McGaw & Smith 1981). For example, in research on personal selection, virtually all studies involve restriction of range, which attenuates correlations. Moreover, the amount of restriction of range typically varies substantially across studies. Hence, correction for restriction of range ensures that each study provides an estimate of the same kind of correlation—the correlation in a population having an unrestricted distribution of test scores. Because restriction of range and many other consequences of design are incidental features of the studies, disattenuation to remove their effects is sometimes called *artifact correction.*

A more controversial reason that theoretical effect

sizes are sometimes used is because they are considered more scientifically relevant. For example, to estimate the benefit of scientific personnel selection using cognitive tests versus selection on an effectively random basis, we would need to compare the performance of applicants with the full range of test scores (those selected at random) with that of applicants selected via the test—applicants who would have a restricted range of test scores. Although a study of the validity of a selection test would compute the correlation between test score and job performance based on the restricted sample, the correlation that reflects the effectiveness of the test in predicting job performance is the correlation that would have been obtained with the full range of test scores—a theoretical correlation. Another example might be the estimation of the standardized mean difference of a treatment intended for a general population of people, but which has typically been investigated with studies using more restricted groups of people. Since the scores in the individual studies have a smaller standard deviation than the general population, the effect sizes will be artifactually large; that is, if the treatment produced the same change in raw score units, dividing by the smaller standard deviations in the study sample would make the standardized difference look too large. Hence a theoretical effect size might be chosen—the effect size that would have been obtained if the outcome scores in each study had the same variation as the general population. This would lead to corrections for sampling variability. (Corrections of this sort are discussed in Chapter 21.)

## 2.3 The Number and Source of Hypotheses

Light and Pillemer (1984) distinguished between two types of questions that might be asked in a research synthesis. One type concerns a hypothesis that is specified precisely in advance (e.g., on average does this treatment work?). The other type is specified only vaguely (e.g., under what conditions does the treatment work best?). This distinction in problem specification is similar to that between planned and post hoc comparisons in the analysis of variance, which is familiar to many researchers. Although either kind of question is legitimate in research synthesis, the calculation of levels of statistical significance may be affected by whether the question was defined in advance or discovered post hoc by examination of the data.

Although it is useful to distinguish the two cases, sharp distinctions are not possible in practice. Some of the research literature is surely known to the reviewer prior to the synthesis, thus putatively a priori hypotheses are likely to have been influenced by the ''data.'' Conversely, hypotheses derived during exploration of the data may have been conceived earlier and proposed for explicit testing because the initial examination of the data suggested that they might be fruitful. Perhaps the greatest ambiguity arises when a very large number of hypotheses are proposed a priori for testing. In this case it is difficult to distinguish between hypotheses selected by searching the data informally and proposing a hypothesis a posteriori and simply proposing all possible hypotheses a priori. For this reason it may be sensible to treat large numbers of hypotheses as if they were post hoc. Despite the difficulty in drawing a sharp distinction, we still believe that the conceptual distinction between cases in which a few hypotheses are specified in advance and those in which there are many hypotheses (or hypotheses not necessarily specified in advance) is useful.

The primary reason for insisting on this distinction is statistical. When testing a hypothesis specified in advance, it is appropriate to consider the test in isolation from other tests that might have been carried out. This is often called the use of a testwise error rate in the theory of multiple comparisons, meaning that the appropriate definition of the significance level of the test is the proportion of the time this test, considered in isolation, would yield a Type I error when the null hypothesis is true.

In contrast, when testing a hypothesis derived after exploring the data, it may not be appropriate to consider the test in isolation from other tests that might have been done. For example, by choosing to test the most ''promising'' of a set of study characteristics (i.e., the one that appears to be most strongly related to effect size), the reviewer has implicitly utilized information from tests that could have been done on other study characteristics. More formally, the sampling distribution of the *largest* relationship is not the same as that of one relationship selected a priori. In cases in which the hypothesis is picked after exploring the data, special post hoc test procedures that take account of the other hypotheses that could have been tested are appropriate (see Chapter 19; Hedges & Olkin 1983, 1985; or, more generally, Miller 1981). This is often called the use of an experimentwise error rate because the appropriate definition of the statistical significance level of the test is the proportion of the time the group of tests would lead to selecting a test that made a Type I error.

Post hoc test procedures are frequently much less

powerful than their a priori counterparts for detecting a particular relationship that is of interest. On the other hand, the post hoc procedures can do something that a priori procedures cannot: detect relationships that are not suspected in advance. The important point is that there is a trade-off between the ability to find relationships that are not suspected and the sensitivity to detect those that are thought to be likely.

## 3. DATA COLLECTION

Data collection in research synthesis is largely a sampling activity that raises all of the concerns attendant on any other sampling activity. Specifically, the sampling procedure must be designed so as to yield studies that are representative of the intended universe of studies. Ideally, the sampling is carried out in a way that reveals aspects of the sampling (like dependence of units in the sample) or selection effects (like publication bias) that might influence the analytic methods chosen to draw inferences from the sample.

### 3.1 Representativeness

Given that a universe has been chosen, so that we know the kinds of studies about which the synthesis is to inform us, a fundamental problem is ensuring that the study sample is selected in such a way that it supports inferences to that universe. Part of the problem is ensuring that search criteria are consistent with the universe definition. Given that search criteria are consistent with the universe definition, an *exhaustive sample* of studies that meet the criteria is often taken to be a representative sample of studies of the universe. However, there are sometimes reasons to view this proposition skeptically.

The concept of representativeness has always been a somewhat ambiguous idea (see Kruskal & Mosteller 1979a, 1979b, 1979c, 1980), but the concept is useful in helping to illuminate potential problems in drawing inferences from samples.

One reason is that some types of studies in the intended universe may not have been *conducted.* The act of defining a universe of studies that *could* be conducted does not guarantee that it will be nonempty. We hope that the sample of studies will inform us about a universe of studies exhibiting variation in their characteristics, but studies with a full range of characteristics may not have been conducted. The types of studies that have been conducted therefore limit the possibility of

generalizations, whatever the search procedures. For example, the universe of studies might be planned to include studies with both behavioral observations and other outcome measures. But if no studies have been conducted using behavioral observations, no possible sample of studies can, strictly speaking, support generalizations to a universe including studies with behavioral observations. The situation need not be as simple or obvious as suggested in this example. Often the limitations on the types of studies conducted arise at the level of the joint frequency of two or more characteristics, such as categories of treatment and outcome. In such situations the limitations of the studies available is evident only in the scarcity of studies with certain joint characteristics and not in the marginal frequency of any type of study.

A second reason that exhaustiveness of sampling may not yield a representative sample of the universe is that although studies may have been *conducted,* they are not *reported* in the forums accessible to the reviewer. This is the problem of missing data, as discussed in Chapter 12. All forms of missing data complicate analyses; a particularly pernicious form of missing data is called publication or reporting bias, which arises when the probability that results are reported depends on the results obtained (e.g., on their statistical significance). (It is discussed at length in Chapter 25 of this volume.) The principal point here is that exhaustive sampling of databases rendered nonrepresentative by publication or reporting bias does not yield a representative sample of the universe intended.

### 3.2 Dependence

Several types of dependence may arise in the sampling of effect size estimates. The simplest form of dependence arises when several effect size estimates are computed from measures from identical or partly overlapping groups of subjects. Methods for handling such dependence are discussed in Chapter 22. While this form of dependence most often arises when several effect size estimates are computed from data reported in the same study, it can also arise when several different studies report data on the same sample of subjects. Failure to recognize this form of dependence and to use appropriate analytic strategies to cope with it can result in inaccurate estimates of effects and their standard errors.

A second type of dependence occurs when studies with similar or identical characteristics exhibit less variability in their effect size parameters than does the entire sample of studies. Such an intraclass correlation of study effects leads to misspecification of random effects models and hence to erroneous characterizations of between-studies variation in effects. This form of dependence would also suggest misspecification in fixed effects models if the study characteristics involved were not part of the formal explanatory model for between-studies variation in effects.

## 4. DATA ANALYSIS

Much of this handbook deals with issues of data analysis in research synthesis. It is appropriate here to discuss two issues of broad application to all types of statistical analyses in research synthesis.

### 4.1 The Unity of Statistical Methods in Meta-Analysis

Much of the literature on statistical methodology for research synthesis is conceived as statistical methods for the analysis of a particular effect size index. Thus, much of the literature on meta-analysis provides methods for combining estimates of odds ratios, or correlation coefficients, or standardized mean differences. Even though the methods for a particular effect size index may be similar to those for another index, they are presented in the literature as essentially different methods. There is, however, a set of underlying statistical theories (see Cochran 1954; Hedges 1983) that provides a common theoretical justification for analyses of the effect size measures in common use (e.g., the standardized mean difference, the correlation coefficient, the log odds ratio, the difference in proportions).

Essentially, all commonly used statistical methods for effect size analyses rely on two facts. The first is that the effect size estimate (or a suitable transformation) is normally distributed in "large samples" with a mean of approximately the effect size parameter. The second is that the standard error of the effect size estimate is a continuous function of the within-study sample sizes, the effect size, and possibly other parameters that can be estimated consistently from within-study data. Statistical methods for different effect size indexes appear to differ primarily because the formulas for the effect size indexes and their standard errors differ.

We are mindful of the variety of indexes of effect size that have been found useful. Chapter 16 treats in detail the variety of effect size indexes that can be applied to studies with continuous outcome measures and gives formulas for their standard errors. Chapter 17 provides a similar treatment of the variety of different effect size measures that are used for studies with categorical outcome variables. However, we have chosen to stress the conceptual unity of statistical methods for different indexes of effect size by describing most methods in terms of a "generic" effect size statistic $T$, its corresponding effect size parameter $\theta$, and a generic standard error $S(T)$. This permits statistical methods to be applied to a collection of any type effect size estimates by substituting the correct formulas for the individual estimates and their standard errors. This procedure not only provides a compact presentation of methods for existing indexes of effect size, but provides the basis for generalization to new indexes that are yet to be used.

### 4.2 Large-Sample Approximations

Virtually all of the statistical methods described in this handbook and used in the analysis of effect sizes in research synthesis are based on so-called large-sample approximations. This means that, unlike some simple statistical methods such as the $t$ test for the differences between means or the $F$ test in analyses of the general linear model, the sampling theory invoked to construct hypothesis tests or confidence intervals is not exactly true in very small samples. The use of large-sample statistical theory is not limited to meta-analysis; in fact, it is used much more frequently in applied statistics than is exact (or small-sample) theory, typically because the exact theory is too difficult to develop. For example, Pearson's chi-square test for simple interactions and log linear procedures for more complex analysis in contingency tables are large-sample procedures, as are most multivariate test procedures, procedures using LISREL models, item response models, or even Fisher's $z$ transformation of the correlation coefficient.

The fact that large-sample procedures are widely used does not imply that they are always without problems in any particular setting. Indeed, one of the major questions that must be addressed in any application of large-sample theory is whether the large-sample approximation is sufficiently accurate in samples of the size available to justify its use. In meta-analysis, large-sample theory is primarily used to obtain the sampling distribution of the sample effect size estimates. The statistical properties of combined estimates or tests depends on the accuracy of the (approximations) to the sampling distributions of these individual effect size estimates. Fortunately, quite a bit is known about the accuracy of these approximations to the distributions of effect size estimates.

In the cases of the standardized mean difference, the large-sample theory is quite accurate for sample sizes as small as 5 to 10 per group (see Hedges 1981, 1982; Hedges & Olkin 1985). In the cases of the correlation coefficient, the large-sample theory is notoriously inaccurate for samples of less than a few hundred, particularly if the population correlation is large in magnitude. However, the large-sample theory for the Fisher $z$-transformed correlation is typically quite accurate when the sample size is 20 or more. For this reason we usually suggest that analyses involving correlation coefficients as the effect size index be performed using the Fisher $z$ transformations of the correlations.

The situation with effect size indexes for experiments with discrete outcomes is more difficult to characterize (see Emerson 1992). The large-sample theory for differences in proportions and for odds ratios usually seems to be reasonably accurate when sample sizes are moderate (e.g., greater than 50) as long as the proportions involved are not too near zero or one. If the proportions are particularly near zero or one, larger sample sizes may be needed to ensure comparable accuracy.

A final technical point about the notion of large-sample theory in meta-analysis concerns the dual meaning of the term. The total sample size $N$ may be thought of as the sum of the sample sizes across $k$ studies included in the synthesis. In studies comparing a treatment group with sample size $n_i^E$ in the $i^{th}$ study and a control group with sample size $n_i^C$ in the $i^{th}$ study, the total sample size is

$$N = \Sigma_{i=1}^{k}(n_i^E + n_i^C).$$

The formal statistical theory underlying most meta-analytic methods is based on large-sample approximations that hold when $N$ is large in such a way that *all* of $n_1^E$, $n_1^C$, $n_2^E$, $n_2^C$, ..., $n_k^E$, $n_k^C$ are also large.

Formally, large-sample theory describes the behavior of the limiting distribution as $N \to \infty$ in such a way that $n_i^E/N$ and $n_i^C/N$ are fixed as $N$ increases. Much of this theory is not true when $N \to \infty$ by letting $k$ increase and keeping the within-study sample sizes $n_i^E$ and $n_i^C$ small (see Neyman & Scott 1948). In most practical situations, this distinction is not important because the within-study sample sizes are large enough to support the assumption that all $n_i^E$ and $n_i^C$ are ''large.'' In unusual cases where all of the sample sizes are very small, real caution is required.

## 5. CONCLUSION

Statistical thinking is important at every stage of research synthesis, as it is in primary research. Statistical issues are part of the problem definition, play a key role in data collection, and are obviously important in data analysis. The careful consideration of statistical issues throughout a synthesis can help assure its validity.

## 6. REFERENCES

Camilli, G. (1990). The test of homogeneity for 2 x 2 contingency tables: A review and some personal opinions on the controversy. *Psychological Bulletin, 108,* 135–145.

Clark, H. H. (1973). The language-as-fixed effect fallacy: A critique of language statistics in psychological research. *Journal of Verbal and Learning Behavior, 12,* 335–359.

Cochran, W. G. (1954). The combination of estimates from different experiments. *Biometrics, 10,* 101–129.

Cronbach, L. J. (1982). *Designing evaluation of educational and social programs.* San Francisco: Jossey-Bass.

Cronbach, L. J., Nanda, H., Rajaratnam, N., & Gleser, G. C. (1972). *The dependability of behavioral measurements.* New York: Wiley.

Emerson, J. D. (1992). Combining estimates of the odds ration in meta-analysis: The state of the art. Unpublished manuscript.

Glass, G. V., McGaw, B., & Smith, M. L. (1981). *Meta-analysis in social research.* Beverly Hills, CA: Sage.

Hedges, L. V. (1981). Distribution theory for Glass's estimator of effect size and related estimators. *Journal of Educational Statistics, 6,* 107–128.

Hedges, L. V. (1982). Estimating effect size from a series of independent experiments. *Psychological Bulletin, 92,* 490–499.

Hedges, L. V. (1983). Combining independent estimators in research synthesis. *British Journal of Mathematical and Statistical Psychology, 36,* 123–131.

Hedges, L. V., & Olkin, I. (1983). Clustering estimates of effect magnitude. *Psychological Bulletin, 93,* 563–573.

Hedges, L. V., & Olkin, I. (1985). *Statistical methods for meta-analysis.* New York: Academic Press.

Kruskal, W., & Mosteller, F. (1979a). Representative sampling I: Non-scientific literature. *International Statistical Review, 47,* 13–24.

Kruskal, W., & Mosteller, F. (1979b). Representative sampling, II: Scientific literature, excluding statistics. *International Statistical Review, 47,* 111–127.

Kruskal, W., & Mosteller, F. (1979c). Representative sampling, III: The current statistical literature. *International Statistical Review, 47,* 245–265.

Kruskal, W., & Mosteller, F. (1980). Representative sampling IV: The history of the concept in statistics, 1895–1939. *International Statistical Review, 48,* 169–195.

Light, R. J., & Pillemer, D. B. (1984). *Summing up: The science of reviewing research.* Cambridge, MA: Harvard University Press.

Miller, R. D. (1981). *Simultaneous statistical inferences,* 2nd ed. New York: Springer-Verlag.

Neyman, J., & Scott, E. L. (1948). Consistent estimates based on partially consistent observations. *Econometrika, 16,* 1–32.

Peto, R. (1987). Why do we need systematic overviews of randomized trials (with discussion)? *Statistics in Medicine, 6,* 233–244.

# PART
# III

# SEARCHING THE LITERATURE

Cooper, H. and Hedges, L. V. (Eds.) 1994. *The Handbook of Research Synthesis.* New York: Russell Sage Foundation

# 4

# SCIENTIFIC COMMUNICATION AND LITERATURE RETRIEVAL

## HOWARD D. WHITE
*Drexel University*

CONTENTS

## 1. THE REVIEWER'S BURDEN

An essential aspect of science is communication of findings (Ziman 1968). Following analysts such as Ackoff et al. (1976), we can conveniently divide scientific communication into four modes: informal oral, informal written, formal oral, and formal written. The first two, exemplified by telephone conversations and letters among colleagues, are relatively free-form and private. They are undoubtedly important, particularly as ways of sharing news and of receiving preliminary feedback on scholarly work (Menzel 1968; Garvey & Griffith 1968; Griffith & Miller 1970). Only through the formal modes, however, can scientists achieve their true goal, which is recognition for claims of new knowledge in a cumulative enterprise. The cost to them is the effort needed to prepare claims for public delivery, especially to critical peers. Of all the modes, formal *written* communication is the most premeditated (even more so than a formal oral presentation, like a briefing or lecture). Its typical products—papers, articles, monographs, and reports—constitute the primary literatures by which scientists lay open their work to permanent public scrutiny in hopes that their claims to new knowledge will be validated and esteemed.

The research review emerges at a late stage in formal written communication, after scores or even hundreds of primary writings have appeared. Among the reviewer's tasks (Woodward 1977), two stand out: reducing the numerous primary works to essentials so as to conserve reading time, and critically evaluating their claims in light of theory. Both tasks require the judgment of one trained in the research tradition (the theory or methodology) under study. As Wilson (1977) put it, "The surveyor must be, or be prepared to become, a specialist in the subject matter being surveyed" (p. 17). But the payoff, he argued, can be rich: "The striking thing about the process of evaluation of a body of work is that, while the intent is not to increase knowledge by the conducting of independent inquiries, the result may be the increase of knowledge, by the drawing of conclusions not made in the literature reviewed but supported by the part of it judged valid" (p. 11). Myers (1991) holds that such activity also serves the well-known rhetorical end of persuasion: ". . . the writer of a review shapes the literature of a field into a story in order to enlist the support of readers to continue that story" (p. 45).

There is little doubt that reviews are useful in Myers's sense, as evidenced by their high citation rates compared with typical papers of the primary literature (Garfield 1989). Nevertheless, while reviews are generally admired as a force for cumulation in science, it may be hard to find people who are both authoritative and dutiful enough to undertake them. "Not enough reviews are written," Bernier and Yerkey (1979) observed, "because of the time required to write them and because of the trauma sometimes experienced during the writing of an excellent critical review" (pp. 48–49). The typical review involves tasks that many scientists find irksome—an ambitious literature search, obtaining of documents, extensive reading, reconciliation of conflicting claims, preparation of citations—and the bulk of effort is centered on the work of others, as if one had to write Chapter 2 of one's dissertation all over again.

Against that backdrop, the present movement in research synthesis is an intriguing development. The new research synthesists, far from avoiding the literature search, encourage consideration of *all* empirical studies on a subject—not only the published but the unpublished ones—so as to capture in their syntheses the full range of reported statistical effects (Rosenthal 1984; Green & Hall 1984). Breaking a long-time gentlemen's agreement, they would actually have scientists return to the library! In short, they are raising the stakes in a game that was already seen as very demanding, and it is tempting to believe that those who criticize meta-analysis on substantive grounds may also be covertly reluctant to see its work ethic become the norm.

## 2. GROWTH DESPITE OVERLOAD

Why did the new style of reviewing appear in the first place? Glass, McGaw, and Smith (1981) suggested that it was a response to one of the most critical problems of formal written communication in science—the massive accumulation of studies on certain topics. At first, such a response seems paradoxical. Faced with too many things to read, the last thing the reviewer might be expected to do is read them all. The expected course (one with years of precedent) would be to limit one's literature search, ignore or exclude as many studies as possible, and focus on theoretically congenial work, such as one's own.

Instead, the overload problem was creatively redefined. What had been merely too many things to read became a population of studies that could be treated like the respondents in survey research. Just as pollsters put questions to people, the new research synthesists could "interview" existing studies (cf. Weick 1970) and sys-

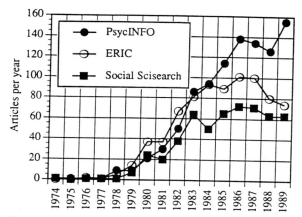

**Figure 4.1** 15-Year Growth of the Meta-Analytic Literature in Three Databases

tematically record their attributes. Moreover, the process could become a team effort, with division and specialization of labor (e.g., a librarian retrieves abstracts of studies; a project director chooses the studies to be read in full and creates the coding sheet; graduate students do the attribute coding). Two other enabling developments were increased computer power for both literature searching and statistical analysis, and the replacement of older, impressionistic reviewing methods ("cognitive algebra") by formal, meta-analytic statistical techniques (Hedges & Olkin 1985; Wolf 1986; Rothstein & Mc-Daniel 1989).

In any case, meta-analyses grew strikingly between 1974 and 1989, as Figure 4.1 shows. Actually the growth is understated. The online literature search used to create the figure was confined to three social science databases and captured only articles labeled "integrative review" or "meta-analy-" (in some form) in their titles. This procedure underestimates the true number of meta-analyses published in the period (compare Bradburn 1990, pp. 135–136). On the other hand, since the databases in Figure 4.1 cover some of the same journals, there would be overlaps in the article counts shown. But whatever the absolute numbers, the pattern is clear for the social sciences and presumably would also hold for biomedicine.

## 3. RECALL AND PRECISION

A task underlying all of these syntheses is the discovery of empirical studies to review: The act of *communing with the literature* is no less a form of scientific com-

munication than talking or writing. In the vocabulary of information science, for which literature retrieval is a main concern, research synthesists are unusually interested in *high recall of documents.* "Recall" is a measure used in evaluating literature searches: It expresses (as a percentage) the ratio of relevant documents retrieved to all those in a collection that should be retrieved. The latter value is, of course, a fiction: If we could identify all existing relevant documents in order to count them, we could retrieve them all, and so recall would always be 100 percent. Difficulties of operationalization aside, recall is a useful fiction in analyzing what users want from document retrieval systems.

Another major desideratum in retrieval systems is *high precision,* where "precision" expresses (as a percentage) the ratio of documents retrieved and judged relevant to all those actually retrieved. Precision measures how many irrelevant documents—false positives—one must go through in order to find the true positives, or "hits."

Precision and recall tend to vary inversely. If one seeks high recall—complete or comprehensive searches—one must be prepared to retrieve many irrelevant documents, thereby degrading precision. Conversely, retrievals can be made highly precise, so as to cut down on false positives, but at the cost of missing many relevant documents scattered through the literature (false negatives), thereby degrading recall.

Most literature searchers actually want high-precision retrievals, preferring relatively little bibliographic output to scan and relatively few items to read at the end of the judgment process. The research synthesists are distinctive in wanting (or at least accepting the need for) high recall. As Jackson (1978) puts it, "Since there is no way of ascertaining whether the set of located studies is representative of the full set of *existing* studies on the topic, the best protection against an unrepresentative set is to locate as many of the existing studies as is possible" (p. 14). Green and Hall (1984) call such attempts "mundane and often tedious," but "of the utmost importance" (p. 46). Some meta-analysts doubt whether comprehensive searches are worth the effort (e.g., Laird 1990), but even they seem to have more rigorous standards for uncovering studies than librarians and information specialists typically encounter. (The only other groups likely to be as driven by a need for exhaustiveness are writers of grant proposals and Ph.D. students in the early stages of their dissertations.)

Given this premise, it is mildly disappointing to see evidence on what synthesists actually do in literature searching. While they are more enterprising than most searchers, they still seem blinkered, exhibiting a kind of tunnel vision toward sources. That is, their search strategies are not wrong (they are efficient and effective as far as they go), but partial: They miss sources that a professional searcher would not miss.

An example appears in Greenhouse et al. (1990, pp. 32–33), a review of the literature on treatment of aphasia. The research team originally estimated that they would find 40 to 50 relevant articles. To their surprise, by consulting their own and a colleague's files, monitoring key journals, following up footnotes, and searching the last ten years of the *Index Medicus* under "Aphasia," they brought the total to 114 items (articles, chapters, grant reports, and conference proceedings). But even the higher total may be too low. While the team thought their search close to exhaustive, numerous other avenues of retrieval remained open: for example, trying additional ways of expressing "Aphasia" in *Index Medicus* or MEDLINE; searching online with "Aphasia" in *Psychological Abstracts, Excerpta Medica, Linguistics and Language Behavior Abstracts,* and *Dissertation Abstracts International;* trying the *Science Citation Index (SCI)* and the *Social Sciences Citation Index (SSCI)* to find writings that cite key papers already known; and looking for a retrospective bibliography of aphasia studies. All of these sources, despite overlaps, are capable of adding unique titles to the population of studies to be considered for review. And while the number of usable aphasia studies may indeed have been around 114 when the meta-analysis began, it is unwise to overlook potential sources, if only to affirm the completeness of the reference list already in hand. (Compare Bates 1992a, on "the fallacy of the perfect 30-item online search.")

## 4. A RATIONALE FOR THE "EXHAUSTIVE" SEARCH

The point is not to track down every paper that is somehow related to the topic. Research synthesists who reject this idea are quite sensible. The point is *to avoid missing a useful paper that lies outside one's regular purview,* thereby ensuring that one's habitual channels of communication will not bias the results of studies obtained by the search. In professional matters, most researchers find it hard to believe that their habitual channels, such as subscriptions to certain journals and conversations with certain colleagues, can fail to keep them fully informed. But the history of science and scholarship is full of examples of mutually relevant specialties that were unaware of each other for years (e.g., Swales 1986) because their members construed their own literatures too narrowly and failed to ask what other researchers—perhaps with different technical vocabularies (Grupp & Heider 1975)—were doing in a similar vein.

More to the point, it is likely that one has missed writings in one's *own* specialty. The experience of the research team reported in Greenhouse et al. (1990) shows that even the sources immediately at hand may produce an unexpectedly large yield. The further lesson to be drawn is that just as known sources can yield unknown items, there may also be whole sources of which one is unaware. A case can be made that research synthesists primarily concerned with substantive and methodological issues should get professional advice in literature retrieval, just as they would in statistics or computing if a problem exceeded their expertise.

Of course, an easy way to protect a search from criticism is simply not to reveal what was done. Jackson (1980) surveyed 36 integrative reviews in which only one stated the indexes (such as *Psychological Abstracts*) used in the search and only three mentioned drawing upon the bibliographies of previous review articles. Jackson believes this to be a failure of reporting rather than of searching, which is very likely true. As he says, however, "The failure of almost all integrative review articles to give information indicating the thoroughness of the search for appropriate primary sources does . . . suggest that neither the reviewers nor their editors attach a great deal of importance to such thoroughness" (p. 444).

This nonchalance is probably changing—but slowly. Cooper (1985, 1987, 1989) presents data on the ways in which 57 authors of empirical research reviews actually conducted literature searches. Table 4.1, adapted from the ranking in Cooper (1985), gives the results, with a space between "majority" and "minority" strategies. It will be seen that most authors prefer to trace the references in review papers, books, and nonreview papers (presumably many of these come from their own files) and to ask colleagues for recommendations. These are classic strategies to minimize work and to maximize payoff in literature retrievals. For those purposes, they are not only not misguided, *they cannot be bettered* (note their rankings in utility and centrality). That is why academics and other intelligent people use them so often. Nevertheless, they are also almost guaranteed to miss relevant writings, particularly if literatures are large and heterogeneous.

**Table 4.1 Use, Utility, and Centrality of Different Sources of References**

| Use[a] | Strategy | Utility[b] | Centrality[c] |
|---|---|---|---|
| 93 | References in review papers written by others | 2.7 | 2.6 |
| 82 | References in books written by others | 3.9 | 3.4 |
| 77 | Communication with people who typically share information with you | 4.8 | 4.3 |
| 70 | References in nonreview papers from journals you subscribe to | 3.3 | 3.4 |
| 61 | Computer search of abstract databases (e.g., ERIC, *Psychological Abstracts*) | 2.6 | 3.1 |
| 56 | Manual search of abstract databases | 4.0 | 4.5 |
| 54 | References in nonreview papers you browsed through at the library | 4.0 | 4.3 |
| 39 | Informal conversations at conferences or with students | 6.1 | 5.6 |
| 35 | Formal requests of scholars you knew were active in field (e.g., solicitation letters) | 5.4 | 4.5 |
| 32 | Topical bibliographies compiled by others | 5.6 | 5.6 |
| 26 | Browsing through library shelves | 6.3 | 5.8 |
| 16 | Comments from readers/reviewers of past work | 7.3 | 5.5 |
| 14 | Manual search of citation index | 4.0 | 3.1 |
| 9 | Computer search of citation index (e.g., *SSCI*) | 4.5 | 3.7 |
| 9 | General requests to government agencies | 7.2 | 5.2 |

SOURCE: Adapted from Cooper (1985).
[a] "Use" is the percentage of reviewers ($n = 57$) who said they used the source to locate references.
[b] "Utility" is the average ranking of the source with regard to the number of references it yielded (only by authors who used the source).
[c] "Centrality" is the average ranking of the source with regard to the significance or centrality of the references it yielded (only by authors who used the source).

## 5. IMPROVING THE YIELD

The most obvious way to improve recall would be for researchers to avail themselves more of bibliographic databases (often called abstracting and indexing, or "A&I," services). Cooper shows only 61 percent of his sample retrieving abstracts by computer, and only 56 percent manually. Moreover, even among those who use these techniques, it is an open question as to whether all likely sources are being consulted; researchers are often unaware of the full range of bibliographic tools available.

The other obvious way to improve recall would be to do what are sometimes called "forward" searches in the citation indexes of the Institute for Scientific Information (ISI). The strategies labeled "References in . . ." in Table 4.1 reflect citation searches that go backward in time; one moves from a known publication to the earlier items it cites. In the contrasting kind of citation search, one moves forward in time by looking up a known publication in the ISI indexes and finding the later items that cite it.

Table 4.1 shows that searches in citation indexes yield documents comparable in utility and centrality to those produced by much higher-ranked strategies. Thus, the percentages of authors who do forward citation searches (manual, 14 percent; computerized, 9 percent) may be seen as disturbingly low. This is not for want of introduction in standard textbooks (e.g., Hunter, Schmidt & Jackson 1982; Cooper 1989). It is more likely the "blinkered" style mentioned earlier, in which one fails to look beyond long-familiar sources. Although the ISI citation indexes will not infallibly yield new items for one's synthesis, it would be foolish to ignore them—roughly equivalent to not keeping abreast of appropriate statistical techniques.

**Table 4.2 Five Major Modes of Searching**

**Footnote Chasing**

References in nonreview papers from journals you
   subscribe to
References in nonreview papers you browsed through at
   the library
References in review papers written by others
References in books written by others
Topical bibliographies compiled by others

**Consultation**

Informal conversations at conferences or with students
Communication with people who typically share
   information with you
Formal requests of scholars you knew were active in the
   field (e.g., solicitation letters)
Comments from readers/reviewers of past work
General requests to government agencies

**Searches in Subject Indexes**

Manual search of abstract databases
Computer search of abstract databases (e.g., ERIC,
   *Psychological Abstracts*)

**Browsing**

Browsing through library shelves

**Citation Searches**

Manual search of citation index
Computer search of citation index (e.g., *SSCI*)

SOURCE: Adapted from Cooper (1985) and Wilson (1992).

The 15 strategies in Table 4.1 pretty well exhaust the possibilities. An independent account from information science—Wilson (1992)—identifies five major modes of searching, and Cooper (1985) illustrates them all. Cooper's results also confirm Wilson's impressions as to academics' preferred means of searching: footnote chasing and consultation.

Table 4.2 regroups the 15 strategies under Wilson's headings (which are further explained below). All 15 ought to be considered—and most tried—by someone striving for high recall of documents. (Strategies can be conducted simultaneously, thus saving time.) Research synthesists disinclined to go beyond their favorite few can still extend their range by delegating searches to information specialists, including librarians. This

would particularly hold for "less favored" strategies, such as searching A&I and citation databases, browsing library collections, and discovering topical bibliographies.

The result of accepting higher retrieval standards would be that rather than veiling one's strategies, one could state them candidly in the final report. Among other benefits, such statements may help prevent unnecessary duplication of effort by later researchers. Whether these statements appear in the main text or as an endnote or appendix, Bates (1992b) has argued that they should include

1. notes on "domain"—all the sources used to identify the studies on which a research synthesis is based (including sources that failed to yield items though they initially seemed plausible);

2. notes on "scope"—subject headings or other search terms used in the various sources; geographic, temporal, and language constraints; and

3. notes on selection principles—editorial criteria used in accepting or rejecting studies to be meta-analyzed.

Since the thoroughness of the search depends on knowledge of the major modes for retrieving studies, a more detailed look at each of Wilson's categories follows. The first two modes, footnote chasing and consultation, are understandably attractive to most scholars, but may be affected by personal biases more than the other three, which involve searching relatively impersonal bibliographies or collections; and so the discussion is somewhat weighted in favor of the latter. It is probably best to assume that all five are needed, although different topics may require them in different proportions.

## 6. FOOTNOTE CHASING

Footnote chasing is the adroit use of other authors' references to the prior literature on a topic. (Because it depends on tracing a document's written "ancestors," it is also known as the ancestry approach.) The reason research synthesists like footnote chasing is that it allows them to find usable primary studies almost immediately. Moreover, the footnotes of a substantive work do not come as unevaluated listings (like those in an anonymous bibliography), but as choices by an author whose critical judgment one can assess in the work itself. They are thus more like "scholarly intelligence" than raw data, especially if one admires the author who provides them.

Footnote chasing is obviously a two-stage process: In order to follow up on someone else's references, the work in which they appear must be in hand. Some reference-bearing works will be already known; others must be discovered. Generally, there will be a strong correlation between familiarity of works and their physical distance from the researcher; known items will tend to be nearby (e.g., in one's office), and unknown items, farther away (e.g., in a local or nonlocal library collection).

The first "chasing" that many researchers do is simply to assemble the publications they already know or can readily discover. Indeed, from the standpoint of efficiency, the best way to begin a search is, first, to pick studies from one's own shelves and files and, second, to follow up leads to earlier work from their reference sections. Cooper's example (1985) was *references in nonreview papers from journals you subscribe to*.

According to Green and Hall (1984, p. 46), meta-analysts doing a literature search should page through the volumes of the best journals for a topic year by year—presumably not only those to which they personally subscribe, but also those in the library. (An alerting service like *Current Contents* can be used as well.) Despite its apparent cost in time, this may actually prove a rather effective way to search, given the small and focused set of titles in any particular table of contents. Items found in this fashion may lead as a bonus to earlier studies, through what Cooper (1985) calls *references in nonreview papers you browsed through at the library*.

Existing syntheses and reviews are probably the types of works most likely to be known to a new synthesist. If not, the first goal in a literature search should be to discover *review papers* or *books written by others* on a topic, since they are likely to be both substantively important in their own right and a rich source of references to earlier studies (Cooper 1989, pp. 29–30).

Another goal should be to discover *topical bibliographies compiled by others*. The entries in freestanding bibliographies are not "footnotes," and they may be harder than footnotes to judge for relevance (especially if abstracts are lacking). Nevertheless, if a bibliography exists, tracking down its "pre-assembled" references may greatly diminish the need for further retrievals (compare Wilson 1992; Bates 1992a).

A way of searching online for reviews and bibliog-

raphies will be given below. A good mind-set at the start of a search assumes the existence of at least one that is unknown. It is also important to ascertain the *nonexistence* of such publications (if that is the case), since one's strategy of presentation will depend on whether one is the first to survey the literature of a topic.

Footnote chasing is an inviting method—so inviting that the danger lies in stopping with it, on the pretext that any other method will quickly produce "diminishing returns." If one is serious about finding primary studies to consider, one will not assume without checking that they do not exist or that diminishing returns begin outside one's office door. The substantive reason for concern is that one may fail to capture the full range of studies—and reported effects—that exist. Just as one's own footnotes reflect personal biases, so does one's collection of books and journals. The authors whose footnotes one pursues will tend to cite works compatible with biases of their own. In journals—the key publications in science—this tendency produces citation networks that link some journals tightly and others loosely or not at all; the result is specialties and disciplines that fail to communicate despite interests in common (see, e.g., Rice 1990). Thus footnote chasing may simply reinforce the homogeneity of one's findings, and other methods are required to learn whether unknown but relevant writings exist. The next strategy is only a partial solution, as we shall see.

## 7. CONSULTATION

Most researchers trust people over bibliographies for answers on what is worth reading. Wilson's "consultation" (1992)—the finding of usable studies by talking and writing to others rather than by literature searching—is illustrated in Table 4.2 with such examples as *informal conversations at conferences or with students*. Actually, one is still searching bibliographies—they are simply inside people's heads. Everyone, including the most learned, does this; there is no more practical or fruitful way of proceeding. The only danger lies in reliance on a personal network to the exclusion of alternate sources—a danger similar to overreliance on a personal library. Bibliographies, however dull, will help one search a literature more thoroughly than colleagues, however responsive. (On authors' relative ignorance of other authors in broad disciplinary areas, see McCain 1990.)

The quality of response that researchers can get depends, of course, on how well connected they are, and also perhaps on their energy in seeking new ties. Regarding the importance of personal connections, a noted author on scientific communication has told his students, "If you have to search the literature before undertaking research, you are not the person to do the research." He is being only slightly ironic. In his view, you may read to get to a research front, but you cannot stay there by waiting for new publications to appear; you should be in personal communication with the creators of the literature and other key informants before your attempt at new research—or synthesis—begins. Some of these *people who typically share information with you* may be local—that is, colleagues in your actual workplace with whom face-to-face conversations are possible every day. Others may be geographically dispersed but linked in your "invisible college" through telephone calls, E-mail, attendance at conferences and seminars, and so on (Cronin 1982; Price 1986).

Crane (1972) described invisible colleges as social circles whose members intercommunicate because they share an intense interest in a set of research problems. While the exact membership of an invisible college may be hard to define, a nucleus of productive and communicative insiders can usually be identified. If one is not actually a member of this elite, one can still try to elicit their advice on the literature by making *formal requests of scholars . . . active in the field (e.g., solicitation letters).* (Scholarly advice in the form of *comments from readers/reviewers of past work* seems less likely unless one is already well published.) The *American Faculty Directory,* the *Research Centers Directory,* and directories of professional organizations are useful when one is trying to find addresses or telephone numbers of persons to contact.

While consultation with people may well bring published writings to light, its unique strength lies in revealing unpublished writings. In order to appreciate this point, one must be clear on the difference between "published" and "unpublished." Writings such as doctoral dissertations and Educational Resources Information Center (ERIC) reports are often called "unpublished." Actually, any document for which copies will be supplied to any requester has been published in the legal sense (Strong 1990), and this would include reports, conference proceedings, and dissertations. It would also include some machine-readable data files. The confusion occurs because people associate publication with a process of editorial quality control; they write "un-

published" when they should write "not independently edited" or "unrefereed." Documents such as reports, dissertations, and data files are published, in effect, by their authors (or other relatively uncritical groups), but they are published nonetheless. Conference proceedings, over which editorial quality control is often slight, have a similar status. "Preprints"—manuscripts sent to requesters after being accepted by an editor—are simply not published *yet.*

Virtually all the printed and computerized bibliographies cover only published documents, in the sense above. Yet meta-analysts place unusual stress on including effects from unpublished studies in their syntheses, to counteract a potential bias among editors and referees for publishing only effects that are statistically significant (see Chapter 25, and, for a broader view, Chalmers et al. 1990).

Documents whose publication status is "lower-grade," such as dissertations and technical reports, are readily available through standard bibliographic services (Dissertation Abstracts International, National Technical Information Service, etc.). To get documents or data that are truly unpublished, one must receive them as a member of an invisible college (e.g., papers in draft form from distant colleagues) or conduct extensive solicitation campaigns (e.g., *general requests to government agencies*). There is no bibliographic control over unreleased writings in file drawers except the human memories one hopes to tap. (Chapters 6 and 7 deal further with these matters.)

Consultation complements footnote chasing in that it may lead to studies not referenced because they have never been published; and, like footnote chasing, it produces bibliographic advice that is selective rather than uncritical. But also like footnote chasing, it may introduce bias into one's search. The problem again is too much homogeneity in the studies that consultants recommend. As Cooper (1989) puts it:

> Relative to all of the research that might be ongoing in a topic area, information from an invisible college is probably more uniformly supportive of the findings of the central researchers than evidence based on more diverse sources. . . . Also, because the participants in an invisible college use one another as a reference group, it is likely that the kinds of operations and measurements employed in the members' research will be more homogeneous than those employed by all researchers who might be interested in a given topic. (p. 41)

These observations should be truer still of groups in daily contact, such as colleagues in an academic department or teachers and their students.

The countermeasure is to seek heterogeneity. The national conferences of research associations, for example, are a kind of trade fair for people with new ideas. Their bibliographic counterparts—big, open, and diversified—are the national bibliographies, the disciplinary abstracting and indexing services, the online library catalogs, the classified library stacks. What many researchers would regard as the weakness of these instruments—that they are so editorially inclusive—may be for research synthesists their greatest strength. We turn now to the ways in which one can use large-scale, critically neutral bibliographies to explore existing subject literatures, as a complement to the more selective approaches of footnote chasing and consultation.

## 8. SEARCHES IN SUBJECT INDEXES

Wilson (1992) calls subject searching "the strategy of approaching the materials we want indirectly by using catalogs, bibliographies, indexes: works that are primarily collections of bibliographical descriptions with more or less complete representations of content" (p. 156). Seemingly straightforward, the retrieval of unknown publications by subject has in fact provided design problems to library and information science for over a century. The main problem, of course, is to effect a match between the searcher's expressed interest and the documentary description.

Only a few practical pointers can be given here. The synthesist wanting to improve recall of publications through a *manual search* or *computer search of abstract databases* (e.g., ERIC, *Psychological Abstracts*) needs to understand the different ways in which topical literatures may be broken out from larger documentary stocks. One gets what one asks for, and so it helps to know that different partitions will result from different ways of asking. What follows is intended to produce greater fluency in the technical vocabulary of document retrieval and to provide a basis for Chapter 5 on computerized searching. (See also the chapter on retrieval in Cooper 1989.)

Different kinds of indexing bind groups of publications into literatures. These are authors' natural-language terms, indexers' controlled-vocabulary terms, names of journals (or monographic series), and authors' citations. While all are usable separately in retrievals

from printed bibliographic tools, it is important to know that they can also be combined, to some degree, in online or CD-ROM searching in attempts to improve recall or precision (or both). If the research synthesist is working with a professional searcher, all varieties of terms should be discussed in the strategy-planning interview. Moreover, the synthesist would do well to try out various search statements personally (e.g., on CD-ROM databases), so as to learn how different expressions perform.

### 8.1 Natural-Language Terms

As authors write, they manifest their topics with terms such as "aphasia," "teacher burnout," or "criterion-referenced education" in titles and abstracts. Since these terms are not assigned from controlled vocabularies by indexers but emerge naturally from the vocabularies of authors, information specialists call them "natural language." Retrieval systems such as DIALOG and BRS are capable of finding any natural-language terms of interest in any or all fields of the record. Thus, insofar as all documents with "teacher burnout" in their titles or abstracts constitute a literature, that entire literature can be retrieved. It is also becoming increasingly possible to retrieve documents on the basis of term occurrence in authors' full texts (although machine-readable full texts, as opposed to bibliographic records, are still in rather limited supply where scholarly and scientific literatures are concerned).

Research synthesists have a special retrieval need in that they generally want to find empirical writings with measured effects and acceptable research designs (compare Cooper & Ribble 1989). This is a precision problem within the larger problem of achieving high recall. That is, given a particular topic, one does not want to retrieve literally *all* writings on it—mainly those with a certain empirical content. Therefore, the strategy should be to specify the topic as broadly as possible (with both natural-language and controlled-vocabulary terms), but then to qualify the search with terms designed to match very specific natural language in abstracts, such as "findings," "results," "ANOVA," "*t* test," "random-," "control-," "*F* test," and "correlat-." Professional searchers can build up large groupings of such terms (called "hedges"), with the effect that if any one of them appears in an abstract, the document is retrieved (Bates 1992a).

This strategy assumes that abstracts of empirical studies state methodologies and results. It would thus be most useful in partitioning a large subject literature into empirical and nonempirical components. Of course, it would also exclude empirical studies that lacked the chosen "signals" in their abstracts, and so would have to be used carefully. Nevertheless, it confers a potentially valuable power not mentioned in meta-analysts' textbooks to date.

## 8.2 Controlled-Vocabulary Terms

Controlled-vocabulary terms are added to the bibliographic record by the employees of A&I services or large research libraries. A major reason for controlled vocabulary in bibliographic files is that authors' natural language in titles and abstracts may scatter related writings rather than bringing them together. Controlled vocabulary is supposed to counteract scattering by re-expressing the content of documents with standard headings, thereby creating literatures on behalf of searchers who would otherwise have to guess how authors might express a subject.

Controlled vocabulary consists of such things as classification codes and subject headings for books, and descriptors for articles and reports. Classification codes reflect a hierarchically arranged subject scheme, such as that of the Library of Congress (almost universal in U.S. academic libraries). They are always assigned one to a book, so that each book will have a single position in collections arranged for browsing. On the other hand, catalogers may assign more than one heading per book from the *Library of Congress Subject Headings*. Usually, however, they assign no more than three, because tables of contents and back-of-the-book indexes are presumed as complements.

Subject headings are generally the most specific terms (or compounds of terms, such as "Reference services—Automation—Bibliographies") that match the scope of an entire work. In contrast, descriptors, taken from a list called a thesaurus, name salient concepts in writings rather than characterizing the work as a whole. Unlike compound subject headings, which are combined by indexers before any search occurs, descriptors are combined by the searcher at the time of a computerized search. Since the articles and reports they describe often lack the internal indexes seen in books, they are applied more liberally than subject headings, eight or ten being common.

Descriptors are important because they are used to index the scientific journal and report literatures that synthesists typically want, and a nodding familiarity with such tools as the *Thesaurus of ERIC Descriptors,* the *Medical Subject Headings,* or the *Thesaurus of Psychological Index Terms* will be helpful in talking with information specialists when searches are to be delegated. Thesauri, created by committees of subject experts, enable one to define research interests in standardized language. They contain definitions of terms ("scope notes"), cues from nonpreferred terms to preferred equivalents ("for 'Criterion-Referenced Education' use 'Competency-Based Education' "), and links between preferred terms ("Aversion Therapy" is related to "Behavior Modification"). Their one drawback is that because the standardization of vocabulary takes time, they are always a bit behind authors' expressions in natural language. (White & Griffith 1987 found that *Medical Subject Headings* did not contain, for example, "Biofeedback" or "Assertiveness Training" for several years after they were current in the psychological literature.) Therefore, anyone doing a search should be able to combine *both* descriptors (or other controlled vocabulary) *and* natural language to achieve the desired fullness of recall. Some online searchers have a fixed style of avoiding descriptor lookups in thesauri and favoring natural language (Fidel 1991). Although sometimes justifiable, this style may be less than optimal for research synthesists' goals.

Supplements to descriptors include *identifiers* (specialized terms not included in the thesaurus) and *document types* (which partition literatures by genres, such as "article" or "book review," rather than content). Being able to qualify an online search by document type allows synthesists to break out one of their favorite forms, past reviews of research, from a subject literature. For example, Bates (1992a) unites descriptors and document types in this statement in an ERIC search on DIALOG:

> Select Mainstreaming AND (Deafness OR Hearing Impairments OR Partial Hearing) AND (Literature Reviews OR State of the Art Reviews)

One could add "Annotated Bibliographies" to the expression if that document type was also wanted. As noted above, relevant review papers and bibliographies are among the first things one should seek in preparing a new synthesis.

## 8.3 Journal Names

When editors accept contributions to journals, or to monographic series in the case of books, they make the journal or series name a part of the writing's standard bibliographic record. Writings so tagged form literatures of a kind. Most A&I services publish lists of journals they cover, and many of the journal titles may be read as if they were broad subject headings.

To insiders, however, names such as *American Sociological Review* or *Psychological Bulletin* connote not only a subject matter but also a level of authority. The latter is a function of editorial quality control, and it can be used to rank journals in prestige, which implicitly extends to the articles appearing in their pages. Above, a manual search through "the best" journals was mentioned—probably for items thought to be suitably refereed before publication. Actually, if one wants to confine a subject search to certain journals, the computer offers an alternative. Journal and series names may be entered into search statements just like other index terms. Thus, one may perform a standard subject or citation search, but restrict the final set to items appearing in specific journals or series. For example:

> Select Aphasia AND JO = Journal of Verbal Learning and Verbal Behavior

One might still have a fair number of abstracts to browse through, but all except those from the desired journal would be winnowed out.

## 9. BROWSING

Book browsing, too, is a form of bibliographic searching. The class-ordered book-spines one scans in library stacks can be construed as a bibliography of collection content (Hyman 1982). Researchers who shun the stacks may often browse journals they subscribe to—that is, they find items not because they were looking for them but because they can recognize titles of interest. Book browsing is exactly similar: Classification codes group books just as journals group articles. One can think of certain class-defined locales in the stacks as "journals" whose slowly growing contents are simply long writings rather than short.

Wilson (1992) calls browsing "a good strategy when one can expect to find a relatively high concentration of things one is looking for in a particular section of a collection; it is not so good if the items being sought are likely to be spread out thinly in a large collection" (p. 156). The Library of Congress (or Dewey) classification codes assigned to books in American libraries are supposed to bring subject-related titles together so that, for example, knowledge of one book will lead to knowledge of others like it. Unfortunately, in the system as implemented—diverse classifiers facing the huge topical complexity of publications over decades—it is common for dissimilar items to be brought together and similar items to be scattered. Indeed, given the multidimensional nature of interrelationships among topics, one needs the ability to tolerate low-precision retrievals at best. Still, serendipitous finds do take place: for example, several textbooks on meta-analysis can be found if one traces the class number of, say, Wachter and Straf (1990) to the H62 section in large academic libraries using the Library of Congress classification scheme. (H62 translates as "Social sciences (general). Study and teaching. Research.")

The charm of browsing is that, as soon as content is recognized, the full text of the book is at hand; other forms of subject searching, which involve surrogates of writings, are less direct. To browsers, it is always surprising that more people do not simply go to the stacks when they want something, but apparently this is a difficult mind-set to acquire. *Browsing through library shelves* is not one of the "majority" strategies in Table 4.1; only about one researcher in four claims to do it. Indeed, propensity to browse bookstacks is probably a trait occurring in a minority of persons; it is not simply one more strategy that researchers in general will adopt. The minority find that browsing—"letting the collection search them"—leads to pleasant discoveries; the majority instinctively avoid it as time-consuming and uncertain (White 1992, pp. 74–75). The latter need not add it to their repertoire if they can find someone who enjoys it, possibly a librarian or information specialist, to do it on their behalf. However, the delegation of browsing is problematical because success depends on recognizing useful books (or other writings) that were not foreknown, and people differ on what they recognize.

## 10. CITATION SEARCHES

The last type of strategy identified by Wilson (1992) and Cooper (1985) is the *manual* or *computer search of a citation index* (e.g., *SSCI*).

Authors' citations make substantive or methodological links between studies explicit, and networks of cited and citing publications may thus constitute literatures. In ISI citation indexes, as noted above, earlier writings become indexing terms by which to trace the later journal articles that cite them. While the earlier writings may be of any sort—books, reports, conference papers, articles, government documents, dissertations, and so on—the later writings retrieved will be drawn solely from the journals (or other serials) covered by ISI; no nonjournal items, such as books, will be retrieved. Nevertheless, forward citation searching, still underutilized, has much to recommend it, since it tends to produce hits different from those produced by retrievals with natural language or controlled vocabulary. In other words, it yields writings related to one's topic that have relatively little overlap with those found by other means (Pao & Worthen 1989).

The reasons for nonoverlap are, first, that authors inadvertently hide the relevance of their work to other studies by using different natural language, which has a scattering effect; and, second, that indexers often fail to remedy this when they apply controlled vocabulary. Luckily, the problems of both kinds of terminology are partly corrected by citation linkages, which are vocabulary-independent. They are also authors' linkages rather than indexers', and so presumably reflect greater subject expertise. Lastly, because of the multidisciplinary nature of ISI databases, they may cut across standard disciplinary lines. (In footnote chasing, we saw, one retrieves *many* writings cited by *one* author, whereas in forward citation searching one starts with *one* writing and retrieves the *many* authors who cited it, which improves the chances for disciplinary diversity.) Hence, forward citation searching should be used with other retrieval procedures by anyone who wants to achieve high recall. Several kinds of forward citation searching are possible in Scisearch and Social Scisearch, available through major U.S. vendors of online databases. (In printed form, these are, respectively, the *Science Citation Index* and the *Social Sciences Citation Index*.) One needs only modest bibliographic data to express one's interests: Retrievable literatures can be defined as all items that cite a known document, a known author, or a known organization. If need be, such data can be discovered by searching initially on natural language from titles (or, recently, abstracts) of citing articles. (ISI databases lack controlled vocabulary.) Title terms may also be intersected with names of cited documents or cited authors to improve precision.

Slightly more avant garde are retrievals of items that cite known *pairs* of papers or *pairs* of authors (White 1986). For example, in Social Scisearch on DIALOG, one might retrieve discussions of the "vote-counting" method of synthesizing research with the following command:

Select CR = Light RJ, 1971, V41? AND CR = Hedges LV, 1980, V88?

This asks the computer to retrieve all writings that include two papers—Light and Smith (1971) and Hedges and Olkin (1980)—among their cited references (CR). In the ISI context, strings consisting of the first author, publication year, journal volume number, and a wildcard character, ?, are sufficient to capture the references as recorded.

In CD-ROM versions of the ISI databases an innovation in software makes it possible to retrieve articles that are "bibliographically coupled"—in other words, that cite identical references. Moreover, ISI now makes entire "research fronts" retrievable online by simply entering a number code. A research front in this sense consists of all papers that cite into a core of heavily co-cited papers. These cores are established algorithmically by proprietary ISI software; the later papers that cite them are dynamically changing subliteratures. There is at least one ISI research front that reflects meta-analysis as a methodology in both social science and biomedicine. It is labeled "Meta-analysis of clinical trials; test validation; validity generalization" and one retrieves on it directly by its RF number, 88-3701-1. Such a retrieval could draw the attention of social scientists to the large biomedical literature on meta-analysis that their own disciplinary A&I services would not capture.

## 11. FINAL OPERATIONS

The synthesist's ideal in gathering primary studies is to have the best possible pool from which to select those finally analyzed. In practice, most would admit that the selection of studies has a large discretionary element. Research syntheses are constructs shaped by individual taste and by expectations about the readership (compare Gilbert 1977). Different synthesists interested in the same topic may differ on the primary studies to be included. If a particular set of studies is challenged as incomplete, a stock defense would claim that it was not "cost-effective" to gather a different set. The degree to which the synthesist has actually tried the various avenues open will determine whether such a defense has merit.

## 11.1 Judging Relevance

The comprehensiveness of a search may be in doubt, but it seems likely that judging the resulting documents for *relevance* will pose no great problems to the research team. Meta-analysis requires comparable, quantified findings. The need for studies with data sharply delineates what is relevant and what is not: The presence or absence of appropriate analytical tables gives an explicit test. Presumably, too, the judges will be scientists or advanced students with high interest in the literature to be synthesized and adequate time in which to make decisions. Further, they will be able to decide on the basis of abstracts or even full texts of documents if titles leave doubts. That limits the potential sources of variation in relevance judgments to factors such as how documents are to be used (Cuadra & Katter 1967), order of presentation of documents (Eisenberg & Barry 1988), and subject knowledge of judges (Cooper & Ribble 1989).

A major remaining cognitive variable is openness to information, as identified by Davidson (1977). Although research synthesists as a group seem highly open to information, considerable variation still exists in their ranks: Some are more open than others. This probably influences not only their relevance judgments, but their relative appetites for multimodal literature searches and their degree of tolerance for studies of less than exemplary quality. Some want to err on the side of inclusiveness, and others want stricter editorial standards. The tension between the two tendencies is felt in their own symposia, sometimes even within the same writer.

## 11.2 Document Delivery

The final step in literature retrieval is to obtain copies of items judged relevant. The online vendors cooperate with document suppliers so that hard copies of items may be ordered as part of an online search. The more "fugitive" publications, such as dissertations, technical reports, and government documents, can often be acquired in less expensive microform editions. Interlibrary loan services are generally reliable for both books and photocopies of articles when local collections fail. The foundation of international interlibrary loan in this country is the Online Computer Library Center (OCLC) system, which has bibliographic records and library holdings data for more than 20 million titles, including a growing number of numeric data files in machine-readable form. Increasingly the transfer of texts, software, and data files is being done between computers, including scholars' personal workstations. Even so, organizations such as OCLC are needed to make resources discoverable in the new electronic wilderness.

The key to availing oneself of these resources is to work closely with librarians and information specialists, whose role in scientific communication has received more emphasis here than is usual, in order to raise their visibility in the synthesist's invisible college. Locating an expert in high recall may take effort; persons with the requisite motivation and knowledge are not at every reference desk. But such experts exist, and it is worth the effort to find them.

## 12. REFERENCES

Ackoff, R. L., et al. (1976). *Designing a national scientific and technological communication system*. Philadelphia: University of Pennsylvania Press.

Bates, M. J. (1992a). Tactics and vocabularies in online searching. In H. D. White, M. J. Bates, & P. Wilson, *For information specialists: Interpretations of reference and bibliographic work* (pp. 201–238). Norwood, NJ: Ablex.

Bates, M. J. (1992b). Rigorous systematic bibliography. In H. D. White, M. J. Bates, & P. Wilson, *For information specialists: Interpretations of reference and bibliographic work* (pp. 117–130). Norwood, NJ: Ablex.

Bernier, C. L., & Yerkey, A. N. (1979). *Cogent communication: Overcoming reading overload*. Westport, CT: Greenwood Press.

Bradburn, N. M. (1990). A survey perspective. In K. W. Wachter & M. L. Straf (Eds.), *The future of meta-analysis* (pp. 135–137). New York: Russell Sage Foundation.

Chalmers, T. C., Frank, C. S., and Reitman, D. (1990). Minimizing the three stages of publication bias. *Journal of the American Medical Association, 263*, 1392–1395.

Cooper, H. M. (1985). Literature searching strategies of integrative research reviewers. *American Psychologist, 40*, 1267–1269.

Cooper, H. M. (1987). Literature searching strategies of integrative research reviewers: A first survey. *Knowledge: Creation, Diffusion, Utilization, 8*, 372–383.

Cooper, H. M. (1989). *Integrating research: A guide for literature reviews* (2nd ed.). Newbury Park, CA: Sage.

Cooper, H. M., & Ribble, R. G. (1989). Influences on the

outcome of literature searches for integrative research reviews. *Knowledge: Creation, Diffusion, Utilization, 10,* 179–201.

Crane, D. (1972). *Invisible colleges: Diffusion of knowledge in scientific communities.* Chicago: University of Chicago Press.

Cronin, B. (1982). Invisible colleges and information transfer: A review and commentary with particular reference to the social sciences. *Journal of Documentation, 38,* 212–236.

Cuadra, C. A., & Katter, R. V. (1967). Opening the black box of relevance. *Journal of Documentation, 23,* 291–303.

Davidson, D. (1977). The effect of individual differences of cognitive style on judgments of document relevance. *Journal of the American Society for Information Science, 28,* 273–284.

Eisenberg, M., & Barry, C. (1988). Order effects: A study of the possible influence of presentation order on user judgments of document relevance. *Journal of the American Society for Information Science, 39,* 293–300.

Fidel, R. (1991). Searchers' selection of search keys: III. Searching styles. *Journal of the American Society for Information Science, 42,* 515–527.

Garfield, E. (1989). Reviewing review literature. (Part 1. Definitions and uses of reviews. Part 2. The place of reviews in the scientific literature.) In *Essays of an Information Scientist* (Vol. 10, pp. 113–122). Philadelphia: ISI Press.

Garvey, W. D., & Griffith, B. C. (1968). Informal channels of communication in the behavioral sciences: Their relevance in the structure of formal or bibliographic communication. In E. B. Montgomery (Ed.), *The foundations of access to knowledge: A symposium* (pp. 129–146). Syracuse, NY: Syracuse University Press.

Gilbert, G. N. (1977). Referencing as persuasion. *Social Studies of Science, 7,* 113–122.

Glass, G. V., McGaw, B., & Smith, M. L. (1981). *Meta-analysis in social research.* Beverly Hills, CA: Sage.

Green, B. F., & Hall, J. A. (1984). Quantitative methods for literature reviews. *Annual Review of Psychology, 35,* 37–53.

Greenhouse, J. B., Fromm, D., Iyengar, S., Dew, M. A., Holland, A. L., & Kass, R. E. (1990). The making of a meta-analysis: A quantitative review of the aphasia treatment literature. In K. W. Wachter & M. L. Straf (Eds.), *The future of meta-analysis* (pp. 29–46). New York: Russell Sage Foundation.

Griffith, B. C., & Miller, J. A. (1970). Networks of informal communication among scientifically productive scientists. In C. E. Nelson & D. K. Pollock (Eds.), *Communication among scientists and engineers* (pp. 125–140). Lexington, MA: Heath Lexington Books.

Grupp, G., & Heider, M. (1975). Non-overlapping disciplinary vocabularies. Communication from the receiver's point of view. In S. B. Day (Ed.), *Communication of scientific information* (pp. 28–36). Basel, Switzerland: S. Karger.

Hedges, L. V., & Olkin, I. (1980). Vote-counting methods in research synthesis. *Psychological Bulletin, 88,* 359–369.

Hedges, L. V., & Olkin, I. (1985). *Statistical methods for meta-analysis.* Orlando, FL: Academic Press.

Hunter, J. E., Schmidt, F. L., & Jackson, G. B. (1982). *Meta-analysis: Cumulating research findings across studies.* Beverly Hills, CA: Sage.

Hyman, R. J. (1982). *Shelf access in libraries.* Chicago: American Library Association.

Jackson, G. B. (1978). *Methods for reviewing and integrating research in the social sciences.* (Final technical report to the National Science Foundation No. PB-283-747). Springfield, VA: National Technical Information Service.

Jackson, G. B. (1980). Methods for integrative reviews. *Review of Educational Research, 50,* 438–460.

Laird, N. M. (1990). A discussion of the aphasia study. In K. W. Wachter & M. L. Straf (Eds.), *The future of meta-analysis* (pp. 47–52). New York: Russell Sage Foundation.

Light, R. J., & Smith, P. V. (1971). Accumulating evidence: Procedures for resolving contradictions among different research studies. *Harvard Educational Review, 41,* 429–471.

McCain, K. W. (1990). Mapping authors in intellectual space: Population genetics in the 1980s. In C. L. Borgman (Ed.), *Scholarly communication and bibliometrics* (pp. 194–216). Newbury Park, CA: Sage.

Menzel, H. (1968). Informal communication in science: Its advantages and its formal analogues. In E. B. Montgomery (Ed.), *The foundations of access to knowledge: A symposium* (pp. 153–163). Syracuse, NY: Syracuse University Press.

Myers, G. (1991). Stories and styles in two molecular biology review articles. In C. Bazerman & J. Paradis (Eds.), *Textual dynamics of the professions: Historical and contemporary studies of writing in professional communities* (pp. 45–75). Madison: University of Wisconsin Press.

Pao, M. L., & Worthen, D. B. (1989). Retrieval effectiveness by semantic and citation searching. *Journal of the American Society for Information Science, 40,* 226–235.

Price, D. J. D. (1986). Invisible colleges and the affluent scientific commuter. In *Little science, big science . . . and beyond* (pp. 56–81). New York: Columbia University Press.

Rice, R. E. (1990). Hierarchies and clusters among communication and library and information science journals, 1977–1987. In C. L. Borgman (Ed.), *Scholarly communication and bibliometrics* (pp. 138–153). Newbury Park, CA: Sage.

Rosenthal, R. (1984). *Meta-analytic procedures for social research.* Beverly Hills, CA: Sage.

Rothstein, H. R., & McDaniel, M. A. (1989). Guidelines for conducting and reporting meta-analyses. *Psychological Reports, 65,* 759–770.

Strong, W. S. (1990). *The copyright book: A practical guide* (3rd ed.). Cambridge, MA: MIT Press.

Swales, J. (1986). Citation analysis and discourse analysis. *Applied Linguistics, 7,* 37–56.

Wachter, K. W., & Straf, M. L. (Eds.). (1990). *The future of meta-analysis.* New York: Russell Sage Foundation.

Weick, K. E. (1970). The twigging of overload. In H. B. Pepinsky (Ed.), *People and information* (pp. 67–129). New York: Pergamon.

White, H. D. (1986). Cocited author retrieval. *Information Technology and Libraries, 5,* 93–99.

White, H. D. (1992). Reference books, databases, and the repertoire. In H. D. White, M. J. Bates, & P. Wilson, *For information specialists: Interpretations of reference and bibliographic work* (pp. 27–78). Norwood, NJ: Ablex.

White, H. D., & Griffith, B. C. (1987). Quality of indexing in online databases. *Information Processing and Management, 23,* 211–224.

Wilson, P. (1977). *Public knowledge, private ignorance: Toward a library and information policy.* Westport, CT: Greenwood Press.

Wilson, P. (1992). Searching: Strategies and evaluation. In H. D. White, M. J. Bates, and P. Wilson, *For information specialists: Interpretations of reference and bibliographic work* (pp. 153–181). Norwood, NJ: Ablex.

Wolf, F. M. (1986). *Meta-analysis: Quantitative methods for research synthesis.* Beverly Hills, CA: Sage.

Woodward, A. M. (1977). The roles of reviews in information transfer. *Journal of the American Society for Information Science, 28,* 175–180.

Ziman, J. (1968). *Public knowledge: The social dimension of science.* Cambridge: Cambridge University Press.

Cooper, H. and Hedges, L. V. (Eds.) 1994. *The Handbook of Research Synthesis.* New York: Russell Sage Foundation

# 5

# USING REFERENCE DATABASES

**JEFFREY G. REED**
*Xerox Corporation*

**PAM M. BAXTER**
*Purdue University*

CONTENTS

## 1. INTRODUCTION

The objective of this chapter is to introduce literature search sources and methods that will be of use to the research synthesist. Our focus is on machine-readable databases relevant to the social, behavioral, and medical sciences. We assume that the reader

1. is familiar with research libraries (e.g., card catalogs, periodical indexes; see Reed & Baxter 1992),

2. is acquainted with the key literature in his/her discipline and the most important sources on the topic of the synthesis, and

3. intends to conduct an exhaustive search of the literature.

The many bibliographic sources that exist take the form of both indexes (providing only bibliographic information) and abstracts (bibliographic citations accompanied by summaries or evaluations). These sources allow access to research literature in many forms; for example, journal articles, books, monographic series, book chapters, unpublished technical reports, conference papers, government publications, and dissertations.

## 2. SERVICE OPTIONS

### 2.1 Intermediary Service Providers

Until the early 1980s, most potential reference database users were limited to search services offered by intermediaries. These intermediaries were of two types: librarians who performed literature searches on behalf of their users and information brokers who provided literature search and document delivery services for a fee. These options still exist. By utilizing the services of large database vendors, information professionals provide access to hundreds of reference databases, covering bibliographic, statistical, directory, and full-text publications. A highly selective list is provided in Table 5.1. Two of the largest vendors, BRS Online Products and DIALOG Information Services, offer a multidisciplinary range of databases providing a wide variety of data: bibliographic (or reference), statistical, directory, and full-text publications.

Other search systems are smaller, but may offer databases in discrete groups of disciplines or may afford exclusive access to specific files. For example, the

ORBIT Online Products is multidisciplinary, but especially strong in the patent literature and engineering. The Human Resource Information Network is intended for human resource professionals and researchers and offers a unique set of statistical, bibliographic, and directory files in organizational and personnel psychology. The German DIMDI service (Deutsches Institut für medizinische Dokumentation und Information) is one of the few vendors providing access to the PSYNDEX bibliographic file. Because of the bewildering array of databases, complex and changing search software and database structures, and competing demands on their time, some researchers choose to have their searching done by information professionals.

### 2.2 End-User Search Systems

The desire of many individuals to conduct their own computerized literature searches and the potential size of the database user market led to the development of user-friendly, menu-driven search software. In addition, the ability of database vendors to provide not only citations to publications but the text of publications themselves has provided an attractive one-stop information source for researchers in many disciplines. In 1983, DIALOG Information Services and BRS Online Products began to offer end-user search systems. Users can conduct their own database searches and are billed directly for services. Customer telephone assistance, user newsletters, and detailed documentation mirror those provided to search intermediaries. However, they are intended for use by the researcher, and their cost can be significantly lower than the more comprehensive database services. For example, BRS After Dark and DIALOG's Knowledge Index each provide access to about 100 reference, statistical, and full-text databases over a broad range of disciplines. Two limitations exist for both systems: (a) Access is limited to evening, early morning, and weekend hours; and (b) some of the more specialized, and therefore low-use, files are not provided. Within these parameters, the systems are an option for those who need frequent access to reference databases.

### 2.3 CD-ROM Search Services

Another option has emerged with the development of user-friendly, readily accessible, and relatively inexpen-

**Table 5.1 Selected Database Vendors**

| Vendor | Subject Emphasis | Approximate Number of Files | End-User Search System | Approximate Number of Files for End-Users |
|---|---|---|---|---|
| BRS Online Products<br>8000 Westpark Drive<br>McLean, VA 22101<br>(307) 442-0900<br>(800) 955-0906 | Multidisciplinary | 200 | BRS After Dark | 100 |
| DIALOG Information Services<br>3460 Hillview Avenue<br>Palo Alto, CA 94304<br>(800) 334-2564 | Multidisciplinary | 380 | Knowledge Index | 80 |
| DIMDI<br>Weisshausstr. 27<br>Postfach 420580<br>D-5000 Cologne 41<br>GERMANY<br>0221-47241 | Multidisciplinary, with emphasis on medicine, agriculture, and the social sciences | 75 | n/a | |
| Human Resource Information Network<br>9585 Valparaiso Court<br>Indianapolis, IN 46268<br>(317) 872-2045<br>(800) 421-8884 | Work-related, social, and policy issues of human resource management | 60 | Intended for end-users | 60 |
| ORBIT Online Products<br>(See BRS for directory information) | Emphasis on environmental science, patent literature, and all areas of engineering | 100 | n/a | |

NOTE: A complete list of vendors and the files available from each is found in *Computer-Readable Databases: A Directory and Data Sourcebook,* 7th ed. (Detroit: Gale Research, 1991).

sive CD-ROM (compact disk–read only memory) technology and its application to information storage and retrieval. CD-ROM media and accompanying search retrieval software allow unlimited search activity with an increasing number of databases. The database and search software are typically mounted on a single user-dedicated microcomputer workstation or on a computer network. Because libraries lease CD-ROM databases for a fixed fee, there is usually no charge to the individual using them. End-user and CD-ROM systems provide researchers with the flexibility to conduct their own literature searches and to download citations for use with word-processing or database management software.

## 3. DATABASE SELECTION

The number and subject coverage of machine-readable files have increased dramatically since 1970. This availability of files has resulted in both expanded access to the published research literature and a bewildering array of small, specialized files. The print and online sources listed in Rosenthal (1985) indicate the wide array of reference sources of potential interest to the research synthesist. An experienced reference or database services librarian can advise on the most appropriate databases. However, an awareness of the scope of relevant files will help the research synthesist to define his or her needs. Conversely, there are lacunae in database subject and publication format coverage. These will be discussed later in the chapter.

Since the 1960s, most of the familiar printed indexes have been generated from machine-readable media. For this reason, the names of many reference databases are familiar to researchers because of experience with their print equivalents. For example, the Sociological Abstracts and Linguistics and Language Behavior files are available as print indexes of the same name. Dissertation Abstracts International currently provides the same records as the print equivalent of parts A (engineering and the sciences), B (the humanities and social sciences), and C (foreign dissertations). The ERIC (Educational Resources Information Center) database, encompassing education and related fields, has from its inception reflected two distinct publications: *Current Index to Journals in Education (CIJE),* covering about 700 journal titles, and *Resources in Education (RIE),* a source of information on unpublished research reports, conference paper presentations, and similar ''fugitive'' literature.

An increasing number of computer files are beginning to show considerable differences in coverage from their print counterparts. Social Scisearch used to correspond to the print *Social Sciences Citation Index (SSCI),* but recently has expanded to include enhanced keyword access. The print index *Psychological Abstracts* used to correspond to its machine-readable parent, PsycINFO, but no longer includes citations to dissertations and foreign language publications, coverage that remains in the online format. The CD-ROM version, PsycLIT, retains foreign-language citations but does not include references to dissertations and research report series. The ABI/Inform and Mental Health Abstracts are examples of databases that have no print equivalents.

## 4. STRUCTURING THE SEARCH

Pfaffenberger (1990) discusses a number of issues that affect the outcome of end-user searches. A critical factor in conducting an effective literature search is planning and executing a logical search strategy. Failure in this area may result in wasted time, excessive costs, and irrelevant or missed citations.

## 4.1 The Selection of Representative Terms

The first step before conducting a search is to identify critical terms descriptive of the topic under investigation. The goal is to use the right set of terms in the right way to accurately describe the topic at the appropriate level of specificity. When done well, this will result in a search of high precision and recall a maximum of ''hits'' (relevant sources), a minimum of ''false positives'' (sources identified but irrelevant), and a very small number of ''false negatives'' (relevant sources not identified). The research synthesist should begin with a crisp, clear definition of the topic, which

1. precisely reflects the scope as well as the limits of the research,
2. includes all important concepts,
3. indicates relationships among concepts, and
4. provides criteria for inclusion/exclusion of materials.

Failure at this early state can result in

1. a search that is too broad and wastes time by requiring review and rejection of the many false positives retrieved;
2. a search that is too narrow and either results in an incomplete synthesis or requires a subsequent search to locate the many false negatives missed in the initial effort; or
3. a research synthesis paper that is poorly focused, neglects important sources, or is too complex because it attempts to accomplish too much.

For the remainder of this chapter, we focus on a sample topic: the impact of teacher expectations on intelligence quotient changes in students of different races.

First, the synthesist should identify each of the key conceptual terms involved in the topic and their likely synonyms. In our example, there are at least three primary concepts: teacher expectancy, IQ, and racial differences. For each, there is a cluster of terms that may be used by different authors or bibliographic services to describe the concept. Relevant terms for this example include teacher expectations, teacher expectancy, instructor expectations, Pygmalion effect, IQ, intelligence, achievement, racial differences, race.

In addition, there is a hypothetical relationship among

these concepts. A computer bibliographic search, however, will not generally deal with the relationship among concepts. Current generation bibliographic searches are limited to Boolean relationships among identified concepts. For example, the search software does not make a distinction between these two topics: (a) the influence of prior knowledge of IQ scores on the expectations of teachers concerning their students' performance and (b) the effect of teachers' expectations on students' performance on intelligence measures.

## 4.2 The Use of Controlled Vocabulary

In most bibliographic services, indexing is done by humans. That is, people select the terms used to describe and index a research report. Because people can err and because judgments differ even among ''experts,'' sometimes what are thought to be the ''right'' conceptual terms to describe a topic are not used in indexing for a particular source.

Many bibliographic sources using a subject indexing approach rely on some type of ''controlled vocabulary,'' a source of standardized terminology. This is the set of terms that the publisher or producer has accepted for use and has defined to describe that area of content contained within its scope. In a print index/abstract, a search is restricted to those terms used in the controlled vocabulary. If a term used to describe a concept is not contained within this vocabulary, it is not used to identify sources covered by the service and would not appear in the subject index for that bibliographic source. Controlled vocabularies are typically defined in a publisher's or producer's thesaurus; for example, the *Thesaurus of Psychological Index Terms,* the *Thesaurus of ERIC Descriptors,* or the *Thesaurus of Sociological Indexing Terms.*

A few printed indexes rely on significant words in document titles to construct their subject indexes. Among these are *Dissertation Abstracts International (DAI)* and *SSCI.* For example, the dissertations listed in the *DAI* teacher expectancy data set are assigned rather unspecific subject headings: ''education psychology'' and ''general education.'' *DAI* also indexes dissertations by important words in their titles and provides more precise indexing. The *SSCI Permuterm Index* serves the same function and is constructed in a similar fashion.

Although *Psychological Abstracts* and ERIC *RIE/CIJE* provide access to different bodies of literature, both cover the area of educational psychology (recall our teacher expectancy topic). Yet, they use different controlled vocabularies. As a result, the set of search terms used for one may yield a different set of hits than the set of terms used for the other. The goal of a search should be to maximize hits while keeping the search strategy as simple as possible. The research synthesist must refer, therefore, to both thesauri to build the list of search terms. In addition to verifying used/unused terms, the thesaurus may also provide additional information such as the frequency of use of a particular term.

A good way to verify a list of search terms is to work with some examples. Most searchers probably know two or three key references within the literature of interest before the search begins. Using an author or article title search approach, the searcher can identify these references in a relevant bibliographic database. The searcher can examine the entry for each source to determine what controlled vocabulary terms have been used to index the reference. For example, searching one of the articles from the teacher expectancy bibliography reveals that in the ERIC database it is assigned the subject headings ''expectation'' and ''intelligence quotient.'' In the PsycINFO database, it is assigned the thesaurus terms ''teacher expectations,'' ''teacher attitudes,'' and ''intelligence quotient.'' A comparison of indexing terms assigned to several other articles should help to identify all important search terms.

## 4.3 Free-Text Searching

Some concepts representing the search topic may not be reflected in a controlled vocabulary or thesaurus, especially in a very new area or in a field that has introduced new concepts and terminology. For example, the term ''teacher expectations'' was not added to the PsycINFO controlled vocabulary until 1978. To locate relevant articles in PsycINFO, as well as the printed *Psychological Abstracts,* prior to 1978 requires the use of the much broader term ''expectations'' and yields results with numerous false positives.

Important concepts that are not contained within the controlled vocabulary may, however, appear in the title of an article or report or in its abstract or summary. An advantage of most computer search services is their ability to search the entire record for a source, a free-text search. If a free-text search term appears anywhere within the record, whether in the list of subject terms, the title, or the abstract, those references would be included in the search output. In our example, only the term "expectation" is used by ERIC as a controlled-vocabulary term. Including both the subject index term "expectation" and the free-text search term "expectancy" would increase the probability of retrieving a high proportion of relevant references contained in the database.

Examples of how the same concepts are represented in three different indexing sources are presented in Table 5.2. The sources used are the *Thesaurus of Psychological Index Terms,* the *Thesaurus of ERIC Descriptors,* and the *Thesaurus of Sociological Indexing Terms.* For each, we illustrate representative controlled vocabulary for three concepts: teacher expectations, intelligence, and racial differences. In some cases, the vocabulary is the same; in others, there are important differences.

## 4.4 Constructing the Search Strategy

Once the appropriate terms have been identified, they must be linked. Services differ in how they handle searches and how searches are constructed (where the Boolean operator is placed, such as before the list or between terms in the list), but they generally follow Boolean rules. For example, using the Boolean OR in "expectation OR expectancy" in a search would identify the union of all sources indexed using either term or both terms. In contrast, the intersection of sets with the Boolean AND in "expectancy AND IQ" would yield only those references indexed by both of these particular terms. Unions are generally used to expand a search and increase the number of references retrieved, whereas intersections created by AND are used to restrict a search.

Figure 5.1 provides an example of a Boolean structure for our search on teacher expectations. Note that in this example, we have linked three concepts with Boolean ANDs (intersections) for our search: teacher expectations of students, intelligence, and racial differences. Because we are doing free-text searching, we will also allow for use of alternative terms within each concept group by using Boolean ORs (unions). Only references addressing all three concepts would be included in the resulting list of references.

Fortunately, there are a number of sources that can assist the online searcher. One may consult such guides as Reed and Baxter (1992) and Vigil (1988) for advice on constructing a search strategy. Many database producers and vendors provide helpful guides to their products and search systems. Some database producers, such as PsycINFO and Sociological Abstracts, set up exhibits at professional meetings and offer workshops. Some libraries also offer this service to researchers.

## 4.5 Hazards of Constructing the Search Strategy

There are a number of problems and pitfalls in conducting a computer search to retrieve references. Searching too broadly can easily overwhelm the user with irrelevant references numbering in the hundreds or even thousands. Structuring the search too narrowly (e.g., only references published between 1980 and 1985) can result in missed references. Performing a narrow search with an incomplete set of search terms (e.g., including only "IQ" as a search term and omitting "intelligence quotient") is guaranteed to miss relevant citations. Some

**Table 5.2 Examples of Descriptors Used in Three Sources**

| Concept | Psychological Abstracts[a] | ERIC[b] | Sociological Abstracts[c] |
|---|---|---|---|
| Teacher expectancy | Teacher expectations | Teacher expectations of students | Expectations/expectancy |
| Intelligence | Intelligence Intelligence quotient | Intelligence Intelligence quotient | Intelligence IQ |
| Race | Race (anthropological) Racial and ethnic differences | Race Racial differences | Race/races |

[a] American Psychological Association, *Thesaurus of Psychological Index Terms,* 6th ed. (Washington, DC: Author, 1991).
[b] J. E. Houston, *Thesaurus of ERIC Descriptors,* 12th ed. (Phoenix: Oryx, 1990).
[c] Sociological Abstracts, *Thesaurus of Sociological Indexing Terms,* 2nd ed. (San Diego: Author, 1989).

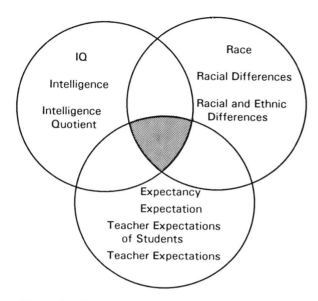

**Figure 5.1** Venn diagram illustrating the intersection of three concepts: teacher expectations of students, IQ, and race

services use a hierarchical search process in which one begins a search with the broadest concept, with each succeeding step narrowing the search results. In this kind of system, beginning with a narrow concept will result in a very restrictive search and missed references.

## 5. CITATION SEARCHING

Citation searching provides an important alternative to subject searching. It allows the researcher to avoid reliance on the subjectivity of indexers. It also avoids the inherent currency lag and biases of controlled vocabularies. For example, many library card catalogs and computer catalogs still index books on intelligence under the subject ''intellect.'' However, two indexes of interest to social and behavioral scientists allow access to current literature by their cited references: the *Social Sciences Citation Index (SSCI)* and the *Science Citation Index (SCI)*.

Printed citation indexes are constructed using the reference lists from the sources indexed. To conduct a

citation search, the searcher begins by identifying several important sources (articles or books) on the topic of interest; for example, the 1968 book by Rosenthal and Jacobson. The citation index will identify, for a specified time period, all articles, reports, or other materials in the body of literature it covers that have cited the reference identified. Thus, by beginning with Rosenthal and Jacobson (1968) in a 1970 volume of *SSCI*, we would find references to journal articles published during the time period covered by the 1970 volume of *SSCI* whose authors cited Rosenthal and Jacobson (1968). One can perform a very effective search by consulting multiple volumes of *SSCI*, using several key sources, and by adding to the list of primary citations on which to search.

Citation searching relies on three important assumptions: (a) one or several key chronologically early sources exist on a topic; (b) these key sources are well known within the field; and (c) these key sources are cited by others reporting subsequent research on the topic.

Several cautions are in order. A key citation need not be the earliest source, nor is it always the most authoritative source. At times, the source that yields the best list of references may be the most well-known source, it may be by a particularly influential author/researcher, or it may have appeared in an influential journal.

Just as indexers and controlled vocabularies have biases, so do researchers. For example, the field of social behavior is studied by both psychologists and sociologists; both consider themselves ''social psychologists.'' However, they have for years maintained separate disciplinary identities, research approaches, journals, societies, and conferences. On some topics, it is not uncommon to find that psychologists fail to cite what some might consider relevant sociological literature, and vice versa. As a result, it is important for a research synthesist to identify key sources reflecting both bodies of social psychological literature, just as it would be important to consult both *Psychological Abstracts* and *Sociological Abstracts* in a literature search.

## 6. ISSUES AND PROBLEMS

Many authors caution those involved in research synthesis on the difficulties involved in an ''exhaustive'' literature search (e.g., Cooper 1989; Glass, McGaw & Smith 1981).

## 6.1 The Need to Search Multiple Databases/ Indexes

Each database or print index is designed for a particular audience and has a particular mission. Sources that overlap in topic, publication format, or source title coverage often have at least as many differences as they do similarities. As a result, especially on topics that are interdisciplinary (e.g., stress, communication, conflict, leadership), it is frequently important to consult multiple databases. Failure to do so will result in an incomplete search and missed sources.

## 6.2 The Limits of Retrospective Searching in Machine-Readable Files

Before computerized reference searches were available, researchers relied on print tools. Even today, many databases limit the time frame of their coverage. For example, if a topic has a body of literature prior to 1967 and is in the field of psychology, one must rely on print indexes since *Psychological Abstracts* does not exist in machine-readable form before this date.

## 6.3 The Limits of Controlled Vocabulary in Print Indexes

We have already addressed a number of limitations associated with print indexes: controlled-vocabulary constraints; biases, skills, and knowledge of indexers; and lack of free-text searching. On the other hand, beginning a search in the print indexes does have the advantage of allowing the researcher to browse citations to the literature. Unlike the results of a highly specific search strategy, browsing titles allows the same serendipitous entrée to the literature as scanning tables of contents in the current journals of one's subject specialty or browsing the shelves of a library's book collection. This is especially important in a field to which one is relatively new and, therefore, unfamiliar with the terminology.

## 6.4 Intermediary Search Services Versus End-User Services

As mentioned earlier in the chapter, in the past the process of initiating a search of reference databases almost always involved an intermediary information professional. The search itself was conducted by this individual, often without the researcher/requester being present. This approach held certain advantages. As Rosenthal (1991) points out, a professional acquainted with a database vendor's retrieval software, myriad sources of controlled vocabulary, and the record structure of relevant databases can take advantage of the nuances of search syntax and the frequently changing software. This can result in a highly tailored, comprehensive list of relevant references. Frequently changing software and file structures make it difficult for researchers who use computerized services infrequently to keep abreast of search techniques.

However, researchers might wonder about the completeness of intermediary-accessed results. The absence of one or two previously identified key references might indicate an incomplete search. A large number of irrelevant references might require a follow-up search with revised terminology or search criteria. In small libraries, where one or two individuals provide computerized literature searching, confidence in the search results might be lower if the intermediary has, for example, a chemistry rather than a social science background and the requester is not present when the search is conducted. There are several ways to counteract the shortcomings involved in relying on an intermediary to conduct a literature search. It is extremely important to share with the intermediary as much information as possible. The synthesist should begin with the carefully defined topic (including constraints and limitations) and the list of proposed search terms, as noted in section 4 of this chapter. Several key sources should be provided to allow verification of proposed search terms. And, if at all possible, the search strategy and proposed databases to be searched should be reviewed in advance with the intermediary.

End-user search systems provide a partial response to these concerns. Most end-user services such as Knowledge Index, After Dark, and CD-ROM are command- or menu-driven, have comprehensible documentation, and offer most of the sophisticated search features available on the more "mature" search systems. Researchers are more likely to be aware of terminology used in their literatures, and search strategies can be altered while the search is in progress. However, researchers still must cope with changes in file structure, search software, and system features. The relatively large number of vendors of CD-ROM reference databases (as well as database producers that act as vendors for their own products with unique retrieval software) compounds the problem. In addition, databases such as the government-produced ERIC and MEDLINE files are made available by several CD-ROM vendors. Other files remain only on systems that are accessed primarily by intermediaries. For example, libraries remain the primary users of the massive OCLC (Dublin, OH: Online Computer Library Center, 1967+) and RLIN (Research Libraries Information Network, Stanford, CA: Research Libraries Group, 1974+) databases of books, nonprint media, and manuscript material because these files were developed by and for libraries.

## 6.5 Underrepresented Research Literature Formats

Some research literature formats are not as well represented bibliographically as others. Certainly research studies in the published journal literature are the most utilized by research synthesists and, fortunately, are by far the most heavily represented format in reference databases. The empirical literature, however, is not restricted to one publication format, so finding research in other formats and procuring the documents can be challenging.

**6.5.1 Books and book chapters** Information on book-length studies has recently been enhanced by subject access to the extensive OCLC database of books, manuscripts, and nonprint media. RLIN offers similar coverage, but to a smaller audience; and its coverage is limited to the holdings of major American research libraries.

Access to individual chapters within edited books in both print and nonprint indexes remains a problem. The publication *PsycBOOKS* (Washington, DC: American Psychological Association, 1987–1990) addressed this deficiency. However, its brief publication history (only four years), annual publication schedule, and print format have made access to this tool more restrictive than journal indexing sources. Fortunately, the four-year contents of *PsycBOOKS* was added to the PsycLIT CD-ROM database in 1992. Subsequent book and book-chapter citations similar to those contained in *PsycBOOKS* are now indexed in PsycLIT and to *Psychological Abstracts*.

**6.5.2 Research and technical reports** Research and technical reports in the social sciences receive only scattered coverage. Report series are most frequently found in databases such as NTIS (National Technical Information Service) and, to a limited extent, PsycINFO and ERIC.

The imprecise definition of ''research report,'' especially in the context of social science research, is partly to blame for poor coverage. For example, PsycINFO indexes the Research Monograph Series published by the National Institute of Drug Abuse, the Society for Research in Child Development Monographs, and several report series produced by branches of the U.S. military. However, large numbers of report series generated by university departments, research institutes, and associations are difficult to locate. Unlike the large body of well-indexed research report literature in the field of economics (such as ''working papers''), papers produced by research institutes in the social sciences are not well indexed by standard bibliographic sources.

**6.5.3 Conference papers** Several authors (Cooper 1989; Glass, McGaw & Smith 1981) discuss both the hazards of omitting unpublished studies and the difficulties of accessing them, bibliographically and physically. In particular, coverage of paper presentations from scholarly conferences remains inadequate, compounded by the fact that a large percentage of papers remain unpublished (McCown & Johnson 1988). Several print indexing tools, such as the *Directory of Published Proceedings: Series SSH-Social Sciences and Humanities Proceedings* (Harrison, NY: Interdok, 1968/71+) and the *Index to Social Sciences and Humanities Proceedings* (Philadelphia: Institute for Scientific Information, 1979+), provide access to individual conference papers but restrict themselves to those published in some form. Neither exists as a publicly accessible reference database. The Conference Papers Index database (Bethesda, MD: Cambridge Scientific Abstracts, 1973+) affords coverage at the paper level and is a publicly available file. It is of primary interest to researchers in the physical and life sciences, engineering, and geosciences with, at best, spotty coverage of the social sciences.

The ERIC database can be a rich source of references to unpublished conference papers, particularly in the areas of educational and developmental psychology, learning and memory, counseling and guidance, and testing. ERIC's document reproduction service makes microfiche copies of these papers available in over 800 libraries or for purchase in paper form. However, because the impetus for submitting papers to ERIC remains with professional organizations and presenters, coverage of this important source of research remains incomplete. The issues associated with obtaining copies of these papers remain, for the most part, unaddressed (Baxter & Sample 1991; McCown & Johnson 1988).

**6.5.4 Errata, letters, and other ''ephemera''** Unfortunately, the amount of text involved in the typical journal article erratum relegates it to the status of ephemera in the view of publishers and, consequently, index producers and indexers. Indeed, some volume indexes to individual journals do not note the existence of an article's erratum.

In similar fashion, few reference databases index such items as letters and "continuing commentary" on previously published research. This is especially true if such a contribution lacks a unique, distinguishing title. MEDLINE, Scisearch, and Social Scisearch represent the few files that include letters and later commentary.

## 7. SOURCES FOR FURTHER INFORMATION

Fortunately, several good directories can keep the researcher current with the burgeoning number of reference databases, database producers, and search services. *Computer-Readable Databases: A Directory and Data Sourcebook* (Detroit: Gale Research, 1991) is currently in its seventh edition and is revised on a regular basis. It provides information on over 6,000 databases worldwide, including bibliographic, statistical, and full-text document files. For reference databases, each entry includes information on its availability, years covered and document type coverage, search aids, cost, and available formats (e.g., CD-ROM, diskette). The biennial *North American Online Directory* (New York: Bowker, 1985+) provides, among other things, information on sources of database search services. The annual *CD-ROMs in Print* (Westport, CT: Meckler, 1987+) is a good source of current knowledge about this relatively new technology.

## 8. CONCLUSION

This chapter provides an introduction to the use of bibliographic (or reference) databases for the research synthesist. Careful database selection is important whether the decision is to rely on an intermediary (information professional) to perform the search or to "do it yourself." Regardless of who does the actual search, critical steps involve clearly defining the topic, identifying several key references, developing a list of search terms, and developing the search strategy. Potential problems in database searching include the limits of controlled vocabulary, the time limitations of database coverage, and the potential need to search multiple database files.

Several topics briefly mentioned in this chapter are dealt with in greater detail elsewhere in this volume. Chapter 7 provides additional information on "fugitive literature": conference papers, unpublished technical

reports, and the like. Chapter 4 discusses researcher and publication biases that make bibliographic research difficult. Chapter 27 provides guidance on reporting results.

The appendix that follows "References" provides an annotated list of 15 of the most widely used and available databases of potential relevance to the social science research synthesist. In addition to basic information, such as producer, years of coverage, and frequency of updates, we have attempted to provide informative notes about the scope and coverage of each database.

## 9. REFERENCES

Baxter, P. M., & Sample, R. A. (1991). Retrieving papers presented at national and regional psychology conferences. *Psychological Reports, 68,* 613–614.

Cooper, H. M. (1989). *Integrating research: A guide for literature reviews* (2nd ed.). Newbury Park, CA: Sage.

Glass, G. V., McGaw, B., & Smith, M. L. (1981). *Meta-analysis in social research.* Beverly Hills, CA: Sage.

McCown, W., & Johnson, J. (1988). Difficulty in securing conference presentation reprints: A need for standardized procedures. *Journal of Social Behavior and Personality, 3,* 155–160.

Pfaffenberger, B. (1990). *Democratizing information: Online databases and the rise of end-user searching.* Boston: G. K. Hall.

Reed, J. G., & Baxter, P. M. (1992). *Library use: A handbook for psychology* (2nd ed.). Washington, DC: American Psychological Association.

Rosenthal, M. C. (1985). Bibliographic retrieval for the social and behavioral scientist. *Research in Higher Education, 22,* 315–333.

Rosenthal, R. (1991). *Meta-analytic procedures for social research* (rev. ed.). Newbury Park, CA: Sage.

Rosenthal, R., & Jacobson, L. (1968). *Pygmalion in the classroom.* New York: Holt, Rinehart & Winston.

Vigil, P. J. (1988). *Online retrieval: Analysis and strategy.* New York: Wiley.

## 10. APPENDIX: Selected Databases in the Behavioral and Social Sciences

The reference databases listed below represent a selection of bibliographic files indexing empirical research studies. Because information on years of coverage, update frequency, and vendor availability change, consult a recent directory of databases or a database vendor directory. Such data as years of coverage and frequency of updates will vary from vendor to vendor; therefore, the maximum number of years and updates for each file are provided below.

## ABI/Inform

Years of coverage: 1970+

Producer: University Microfilms International/Data Courier, Louisville, KY

Updates: Weekly

Format: English-language journal literature, with selected foreign-language coverage

Print equivalent: None

Available in CD-ROM: Yes; 1985+, quarterly updates

Covering approximately 800 periodical titles, this file is of primary interest to those in business management and finance, with coverage of professional, trade, and scholarly publications. However, its coverage of the research literature in human resource management, personnel, management decision-making, and consumer affairs and advertising make this a rich source of empirical research studies.

## Ageline

Years of coverage: 1978+, with selective earlier coverage

Producer: American Association of Retired Persons, National Gerontology Resource Center, Washington, DC

Updates: Bimonthly

Formats: Journal articles, books and book chapters, research reports, government documents

Controlled vocabulary: *Thesaurus of Aging Terminology*, 3rd ed. (1986)

Print equivalent: None

Available in CD-ROM: No

This file includes coverage of social, psychological, economic, and public policy issues associated with the aging process and elderly population.

## Books in Print

Years of coverage: Current

Producer: Bowker, New York

Updates: Monthly

Format: Books

Print equivalents: *Books in Print, Forthcoming Books in Print, Books Out of Print*

Available in CD-ROM: Yes; Book in Print Plus, quarterly updates

Scholarly and popular books currently available for purchase, forthcoming titles, and recently out-of-print titles from U.S. publishers or available from American distributors.

## Current Contents: Social and Behavioral Sciences

Years of coverage: Current 12 months

Producer: Institute for Scientific Information, Philadelphia

Updates: Weekly

Format: Journal articles

Print equivalent: *Current Contents: Social and Behavioral Sciences* and in diskette format

Available in CD-ROM: No

A journal contents current awareness service covering journals in sociology, psychology, psychiatry, rehabilitation, education, social work, public policy and law, and related disciplines and interdisciplinary fields.

## Dissertation Abstracts Online

Years of coverage: 1861+

Producer: University Microfilms International, Ann Arbor, MI

Updates: Monthly

Formats: Doctoral dissertations, master's theses (since 1962)

Print equivalents: *Dissertation Abstracts International, Masters Abstracts, Comprehensive Dissertation Index, American Doctoral Dissertations*

Available in CD-ROM: Yes

Dissertation Abstracts International includes citations to almost every doctoral dissertation accepted in North America since 1861, with abstracts included for those added since 1980. Citations from *Masters Abstracts* were added after 1962, with abstracts included since 1988. Citations to Part C: Worldwide dissertations were added to the file in 1988. A unique access point to an important body of original research literature.

## DRUGINFO/Alcohol Use and Abuse

Years of coverage: 1968+

Producer: University of Minnesota, Drug Information Services, Minneapolis

Updates: Quarterly

Formats: Journal articles, books, conference papers, professional instructional materials

Print equivalent: None

Available in CD-ROM: No

The Alcohol Use and Abuse file terminated coverage with 1978. However, the DRUGINFO segment maintains current coverage. Studies on educational, sociological, and psychological aspects on substance abuse and rehabilitation.

## ERIC (Educational Resources Information Center)

Years of coverage: 1966+

Producer: U.S. Department of Education, Office of Educational Research and Improvement, Washington, DC

Updates: Monthly

Formats: Journal articles, unpublished research reports, conference papers, printed curriculum materials

Print equivalents: *Current Index to Journals in Education, Resources in Education*

Controlled vocabulary: *Thesaurus of ERIC Descriptors,* 12th ed. (1990)

Available in CD-ROM: Yes, 1966+

The primary reference database on all aspects of the educational process, from administration to classroom curriculum, preschool to adult and postdoctoral levels. Because its scope encompasses almost every aspect of the human learning process, the contents of this file are of interest to a broad range of social scientists.

## Family Resources Database

Years of coverage: 1970+

Producer: National Council on Family Relations, St. Paul, MN

Updates: Bimonthly

Formats: Journal articles, books, dissertations, research reports, conference proceedings, government documents, audio-visual material; since 1990, only journal articles and books cited and abstracted

Print equivalent: *Inventory of Marriage and Family Literature,* with some enhanced coverage

Available in CD-ROM: Under investigation

Especially important for coverage on all aspects of marriage and family relations.

## MEDLINE

Years of coverage: 1966+

Producer: National Library of Medicine, Bethesda, MD

Updates: Weekly

Formats: Journal articles, selected published symposia

Controlled vocabulary: *Medical Subject Headings* (annual)

Print equivalents: *Index Medicus, Index to Dental Literature, International Nursing Index,* and additional citations not appearing in print form

Available in CD-ROM: Yes; 1966+ , monthly updates

Exhaustive in its coverage of biomedicine and related fields, MEDLINE provides indexing for approximately 3,600 journals worldwide. It also includes coverage of health care issues and policy, clinical psychology and psychiatry, and interdisciplinary areas such as gerontology. Since 1975, about half of MEDLINE's citations include abstracts.

## Mental Health Abstracts

Years of coverage: 1969+

Producer: IFI/Plenum Data Company, Alexandria, VA (previously produced by National Clearinghouse for Mental Health Information, National Institute of Mental Health, Rockville, MD)

Updates: Monthly

Formats: Journal articles, books, research reports, audio-visual material

Print equivalent: No exact equivalent

Available in CD-ROM: No

Worldwide coverage of all aspects of mental health.

## NTIS (National Technical Information Service)

Years of coverage: 1970+

Producer: U.S. Department of Commerce, National Technical Information Service, Springfield, VA

Updates: Monthly

Format: Unpublished research reports

Print equivalents: *Government Reports Announcements and Index* and other sources

Available in CD-ROM: Yes; 1983+, quarterly updates

An important source of information on reports resulting from government-sponsored research. Although coverage emphasizes engineering, agriculture, energy, and the biological and physical sciences, reports also cover research in personnel and management, public policy, and social attitudes and behavior.

## PsycINFO

Years of coverage: 1967+

Producer: American Psychological Association, Washington, DC

Updates: Monthly

Formats: Journal articles, dissertations, technical reports

Controlled vocabulary: *Thesaurus of Psychological Index Terms,* 6th ed. (1991)

Print equivalent: Approximately *Psychological Abstracts*

Available in CD-ROM: Yes; PsycLIT, 1974+

PsycINFO contains citations and abstracts to approximately 1,300 journal titles worldwide and citations to dissertations. It is the parent file from which the PsycLIT CD-ROM product (containing citations to the journal literature) and *Psychological Abstracts* (English-language journal articles) are generated. In 1992, the contents of *PsycBOOKS* was added to PsycLIT, and book and book-chapter citations are included in PsycLIT and *Psychological Abstracts.*

## Social Scisearch

Years of coverage: 1972+

Producer: Institute for Scientific Information, Philadelphia

Updates: Weekly

Formats: Journal articles, books

Print equivalent: *Social Sciences Citation Index*

Available in CD-ROM: Yes, 1981+, quarterly updates

In addition to keyword-in-title subject indexing, the advantage of Social Scisearch lies in the ability to search by cited reference; that is, using key references to determine other, more recent publications in the journal literature. Worldwide coverage encompasses 1,500 journal titles, with additional relevant journals indexed by its companion file, Scisearch.

## Social Work Abstracts

Years of coverage: 1977+

Producer: National Association of Social Workers, Silver Spring, MD

Updates: Quarterly

Formats: Journal articles and doctoral dissertations

Print equivalent: *Social Work Research and Abstracts*

Available in CD-ROM: Yes, 1977+ semi-annual updates

Despite significant overlap in subject scope with other files, Social Work Abstracts provides supplemental coverage of substance abuse, gerontological, family, and mental health literatures.

## Sociological Abstracts

Years of coverage: 1963+

Producer: Sociological Abstracts, San Diego, CA

Updates: Five times per year

Formats: Journal articles, books, conference publications

Controlled vocabulary: *Thesaurus of Sociological Indexing Terms,* 2nd ed. (1989)

Print equivalent: *Sociological Abstracts*

Available in CD-ROM: Yes; Sociofile, 1974+, quarterly updates

There is some overlapping coverage with such files as PsycINFO and Social Work Abstracts. However, Sociological Abstracts affords excellent coverage of cross-cultural studies in social, developmental, and clinical psychology. BRS and DIALOG provide searching of a combined file containing Sociological Abstracts, Social Planning/Policy and Development Abstracts (1978+) database, and International Review of Publications in Sociology database (1980+) to books, all files created by the same database producer.

Cooper, H. and Hedges, L. V. (Eds.) 1994. *The Handbook of Research Synthesis.* New York: Russell Sage Foundation

# 6

# RESEARCH REGISTERS

**KAY DICKERSIN**
*University of Maryland*
*School of Medicine*

CONTENTS

## 1. INTRODUCTION

Research synthesis would be a far easier task if there were registers of all initiated research projects. A research register can be defined as a database of research studies, either planned, active, or completed (or any combination of these), usually oriented around a common feature of the studies such as subject matter, funding source, or design. This definition is broad enough to include such resources as a database of research projects approved by an institutional review board, an annual report of a funding body, or a comprehensive bibliographic database such as MEDLINE or *Psychological Abstracts*. The registers on which this chapter will focus, however, are those that are specified by their organizers as research registers and that produce regular reports or listings available publicly or on request. Thus, the resources named above will not be considered research registers. MEDLINE, for example, was designed to inventory the contents of journals and is not specifically intended to register reports of research. This type of database is covered in Chapter 5.

All research registers of which this author is aware concentrate, to a large extent, on "prospective" registration of research at the time a project is initiated. Typically, the registration process involves active solicitation of study investigators to obtain descriptive characteristics of research studies, but not study data. For example, the International Committee on Thrombosis and Haemostasis Registry of Clinical Trials (Verstraete 1984) annually surveys known investigators and others who work in related areas to learn of ongoing studies.

A few of the registers also include a component comprising published reports of studies. This component is constructed by the register keepers' reviewing numerous bibliographic sources for articles meeting specific inclusion and exclusion criteria. For example, the Oxford Database of Perinatal Trials (ODPT) includes a register of published reports of randomized trials relevant to the perinatal period. Evidence that this type of bibliographic register is necessary, above and beyond the more general bibliographic database noted earlier, was provided by a study comparing the results of MEDLINE searching by a trained information specialist with the contents of the ODPT (Dickersin et al. 1985). While almost all (92 percent) published reports included on ODPT are also included on the MEDLINE database, the MEDLINE search itself failed to identify 44 percent of known trials of intraventricular hemorrhage and 71 percent of known trials of neonatal hyperbilirubinemia.

Similar results indicating a problem with the process of MEDLINE searching have been found for other areas of medicine (Poynard & Conn 1985; DeNeef 1988; Kirpalani et al. 1989).

Research registers of which this author is aware are described in Table 6.1. This list was not compiled using systematic methods; rather, ad hoc notification by register keepers and other informal methods were used. Therefore, it should not necessarily be considered complete or even representative of the registers actually in existence.

Some registers, such as those containing information on studies of patients with cancer or those who are positive for Human Immunodeficiency Virus (HIV) or have Acquired Immunodeficiency Syndrome (AIDS), were started to provide information to patients and their health care providers on available studies in which they could enroll. Thus, a major impetus behind register development is to motivate recruitment to the ongoing studies. Studies are included either because they are funded by the agency sponsoring the register or because an investigator voluntarily notifies the agency. AIDS research registers are usually designed to include any study approved by an institutional review board for research involving human volunteers, as long as it involves patients who are HIV positive. These registers are largely local or regional and are funded by private donations and local government funds earmarked for AIDS projects. Registration relies mostly on telephone solicitation to past investigators and volunteered information. Dissemination of the register contents is usually through published books containing standardized data on each study. The majority of the cancer and AIDS registers focus on studies actively recruiting patients; when studies cease data collection, they are dropped from the current register. Thus, information on completed studies is available only by way of searching the listings published in the past.

Other registers exist more as a form of recordkeeping. These registers thus serve primarily as an aid to oversight agencies, those performing research syntheses, those looking for similar studies prior to embarking on a new project (either for information on those studies or for possible collaborators), and those performing methodological research. Examples of this type of register are the Computer Retrieval of Information on Scientific Projects (CRISP), DENTALPROJ, the International Committee on Thrombosis and Haemostasis Registry of Clinical Trials, the International Registry of Perinatal Trials, the National Institutes of Health (NIH) Inventory

**Table 6.1 Descriptive Characteristics of Clinical Research and Clinical Trials Registers**

| Register | Subject Matter | Types of Studies | Study Status | Method of Access | Funding Source |
|---|---|---|---|---|---|
| AIDS Clinical Trials Information Service | AIDS/HIV | Clinical trials | Completed Active | By request | Government |
| AIDS/HIV Research Directory | AIDS/HIV | Clinical trials | Active | Printed reports | Private funds |
| AIDS/HIV Treatment Directory | AIDS/HIV | Clinical trials Observational studies | Completed Active Planned | Printed reports Electronic copy | Foundations and charities |
| AIDS/HIV Treatment Directory for New England | AIDS/HIV | Clinical trials | Active Planned | Printed reports Electronic copy Electronic online Telephone | |
| Directory of HIV Clinical Research in the Bay Area | AIDS/HIV | Clinical trials Observational studies | Active | Printed reports | Government |
| International Registry of Clinical Trials of HIV Therapies and Vaccines | AIDS/HIV | Clinical trials | Completed Active Planned | Printed reports Electronic copy Telephone | Government |
| New York State Directory of AIDS/HIV Clinical Trials | AIDS/HIV | Clinical trials Observational studies | Active | Printed reports | Government |
| Philadelphia AIDS Protocol Testing Directory | AIDS/HIV | Clinical trials Observational studies | Active Planned | Printed reports Direct mailings | Government |
| Protocol Registry of HIV Trials Network | AIDS/HIV | Clinical trials (network-funded) | Completed Active Planned | Printed reports Electronic copy Telephone | Government |
| Registry of HIV Clinical Trials in Canada | AIDS/HIV | Clinical trials in Canada | Completed Active Planned | Printed reports Electronic copy Telephone | Government |
| Southern California HIV Treatment Directory | AIDS/HIV | Clinical trials Observational studies | Active | Printed reports | Foundations and charities |
| Washington-Baltimore HIV Research Directory | AIDS/HIV | Clinical trials Observational studies | Active | Printed reports Electronic copy | Industry Foundations and charities |
| ENCLCC Cancer Clinical Trials Registry | Cancer | Clinical trials | Completed Active | Printed reports | Research grant |

**Table 6.1** (*Continued*)

| Register | Subject Matter | Types of Studies | Study Status | Method of Access | Funding Source |
|---|---|---|---|---|---|
| National Cancer Institute, Cancer Control Intervention Studies | Cancer | Clinical trials Observational studies | Completed Active Planned | Printed reports | Government |
| Physician Data Query | Cancer | Clinical trials Observational studies | Completed Active | Electronic copy Electronic online | Government |
| United Kingdom Cancer Trials Register | Cancer | Clinical trials | Completed Active | Printed reports | Government |
| Computer Retrieval of Information on Scientific Projects | NIH-funded studies | Clinical trials Observational studies | Completed Active Planned | By request Electronic online | Government |
| DENTALPROJ | Dentistry | Clinical trials Observational studies | Active Planned | Electronic online | Government |
| International Committee on Thrombosis and Haemostasis Registry of Clinical Trials | Thrombosis, haemostasis | Clinical trials | Active Planned | Published journal | Foundations and charities |
| International Registry of Perinatal Trials | Unpublished perinatal trials | Clinical trials | Active Planned | Printed reports | Government |
| International Registry of Vision Trials | Ophthalmology and optometry trials | Clinical trials | Completed Active | By request | University |
| National Institutes of Health Inventory of Clinical Trials and Studies | NIH clinical studies | Clinical trials Observational studies | Completed Active Planned | Printed reports | Government |
| Neurosurgery Clinical Trials Registry | Neurosurgery | Clinical trials | Completed Active Planned | Printed reports | None |
| Oxford Database of Perinatal Trials | Perinatal trials | Clinical trials | Completed Active Planned | Electronic copy | Government Publisher |
| Spanish Database of Clinical Trials | Clinical trials in Spain | Clinical trials | Completed Active Planned | Electronic online | Government |
| Veterans Administration Cooperative Studies Program Master List | VA clinical research | Clinical trials Observational studies | Completed Active Planned | By request | Government |

of Clinical Trials and Studies, the Neurosurgery Clinical Trials Registry, the Oxford Database of Perinatal Trials, the Spanish Database of Clinical Trials, the Veterans Administration (VA) Cooperative Studies Program Master List, and the International Registry of Vision Trials (Scherer et al. 1992). For the most part, they focus on prospective registration of studies, that is, registration at the time the study is initiated.

Some of the prospective registers, those registering studies at the time they are initiated or while they are ongoing, also include planned studies. For example, the International Registry of Perinatal Trials encompasses planned studies, which it defines as studies having a protocol under review by either an institutional review board or a funding agency. The major purpose of including planned trials is to maximize ascertainment of trials at a later date, when they are initiated.

Two of the prospective registers (ODPT and the International Registry of Vision Trials) also include a separate database of published reports of trials. The primary objective in developing this component is to facilitate research syntheses.

## 2. WHY RESEARCH REGISTERS ARE IMPORTANT

Because registers are designed to contain information on all initiated studies, not just published studies, the effect of publication bias—the tendency to publish selectively study results that are statistically significant (see Chapter 25)—would be more easily detected and thus minimized in associated research syntheses. To date, many, if not most, syntheses have included studies found only in the published literature.

In relying on published reports, investigators have increasingly depended on electronic means of accessing the available literature (see Chapter 5), indexed lists of which are maintained in various databases (e.g., ERIC, *Psychological Abstracts,* MEDLINE). However, these databases are incomplete since it appears that only 50–80 percent of all studies are published (Easterbrook et al. 1991; Dickersin, Min & Meinert 1992). In addition, and perhaps more important, there is now considerable evidence that the published literature these databases represent contains select, perhaps biased, information in that statistically significant results tend to be published more often than nonsignificant results (Dickersin 1990; Easterbrook et al. 1991; Dickersin, Min & Meinert 1992; Dickersin & Min 1993).

Five recent studies have provided consistent and persuasive evidence for the existence of publication bias

(Simes 1986; Dickersin et al. 1987; Easterbrook et al. 1991; Dickersin, Min & Meinert 1992; Dickersin & Min 1993). This bias is consistent across research designs (observational or experimental; Easterbrook et al. 1991; Dickersin, Min & Meinert 1992), subspecialty areas, and geographical boundaries. It appears to be unrelated to investigator characteristics such as faculty rank or sex (Dickersin, Min & Meinert 1992). It is not clear whether research studies receiving industry funding are more likely to be subject to the bias than other studies. Easterbrook and coworkers (1991) found such an association, but Dickersin and coworkers did not (1992).

Although prospective registration of research projects should help those performing research syntheses to detect publication bias, registration per se does not protect against it. Unpublished data still need to be retrieved and integrated into the synthesis. Clearly, registers would simplify this process of gathering available data because investigator names and addresses for all studies would be included on the database, facilitating contact for clarification of published information or for collection of unpublished data. There are other reasons to maintain research registers (these are of less importance to those performing syntheses): to provide a means for patients and their health care providers to learn of ongoing trials (experiments), to provide a basis for methodologic research, to avoid unnecessary duplication of effort by other investigators, and to promote collaboration.

## 3. TYPES OF REGISTERS

In the past, the social sciences have been well ahead of medicine in terms of the development of methods for and use of research synthesis and in terms of the performance of methodologic research related to research synthesis (such as that on the subject of publication bias). Nevertheless, certain areas of medicine may currently be better prepared for performance of meta-analyses because of the existence of registers of clinical research. Table 6.1 summarizes existing clinical research registers and their selected features, and the appendix lists these registers, contact persons, addresses, and telephone numbers.

Many of these registers concentrate on clinical trials, experimental studies designed to test the efficacy of a specified intervention, usually in a setting where the intervention is compared with either a placebo or "standard" medical care. Some trials registers include only randomized trials (experiments), in which the assignment of the patient to test treatment or comparison group has been decided using a randomization process. Other registers include all comparative studies. The large proportion of registers that focus on randomized trials do so because these studies are less likely than studies employing alternative designs to be biased in terms of differential assignment of patients to treatment or control interventions. As far as this author knows, there are no registers of observational studies that examine disease etiology, although they would obviously have many benefits similar to trials registers.

As mentioned earlier, the purposes vary for the 26 registers noted in Table 6.1 and the Appendix. The main goal of some registers is to notify patients and their providers of the existence of ongoing trials (this is almost always the case for the AIDS and cancer studies registers). Other registers are intended to promote research collaboration and systematic literature syntheses (e.g., the Oxford Database of Perinatal Trials).

In general, registers have been started either by funding institutions or by individuals or groups with a particular interest in a subject area. Registers may be oriented around a single common characteristic or a combination of several. Common characteristics include specific diseases or conditions (e.g., AIDS or cancer); institutions where the research is carried out (e.g., the VA Cooperative Studies Program Master List); geographical areas (e.g., the UK Cancer Trials Register); source of funding (e.g., the NIH Inventory of Clinical Trials and Studies); and study design (e.g., the Spanish Database of Clinical Trials).

### 3.1 Reasons for Development

Registers have been developed for a number of reasons, sometimes because the initiators of the register are interested in using it themselves. For example, funding agencies, such as those under the auspices of the NIH, may have been originally interested in developing an inventory system for the clinical studies they fund. Examples of registers supported at least initially as part of an inventory system include the Physician Data Query (PDQ) supported by the National Cancer Institute (NCI) (Hubbard, Henney & DeVita 1987); DENTALPROJ, a register of all clinical research, including clinical trials, supported by the National Institute of Dental Research; the NIH Inventory of Clinical Trials and Studies supported by the Office of the Director; and CRISP, an inventory of all research funded through the NIH Division of Research Grants.

A trials register in Spain originated as a consequence of an inventory system. As a result of laws mandating approval of all trials by a central institutional review board (ethics committee) at the Ministry of Health, all applications for performance of clinical trials and approvals issued by the ministry are inventoried centrally. The register that has evolved from this inventory (Ensayos Clínicos en España 1990) can be viewed as a model for other nations.

In contrast to these examples, the numerous AIDS trials registers were started in order to provide information to patients regarding clinical research in which they might wish to participate. Many of these registers are regional and their aim is to provide information to patients regarding ongoing trials. This aim is an important one: In the case of both the AIDS and cancer registers, the listed studies may be the only means by which a dying patient can find out about and receive an experimental treatment.

Other registers may be outgrowths of an individual register keeper's combined interest in the subject matter and clinical trials. For example, the ODPT originated as an obstetrician-researcher's personal file of randomized perinatal trials. The International Committee on Thrombosis and Haemostasis Registry of Clinical Trials, the Neurosurgery Clinical Trials Registry, and the International Registry of Vision Trials have also been organized by individuals active in research in those areas.

### 3.2 Assessing Quality

No quality evaluation of registers has been performed, perhaps because this field is relatively young, the number of active investigators interested in starting or studying registers is small, and funding for this type of project could prove problematic. One criterion for assessing register quality would be completeness of coverage. In order to assess this, other investigators would need to replicate the activity. Clearly, doing this for an entire register would be difficult, particularly for prospective registers. Estimating completeness for registers of published reports is somewhat easier. For example, the results of a MEDLINE search for trials of intraventricular hemorrhage and neonatal hyperbilirubinemia were compared with the contents of the ODPT. Ninety-two percent of the trials contained in MEDLINE were included in the database (Dickersin et al. 1985), indicating excellent coverage.

Other quality criteria would include use of standardized definitions and data collection instruments by the register, frequency of updating (although the ideal timing has not been demonstrated), and oversight by a responsible individual dedicated to the project.

## 4. EXAMPLES OF HOW REGISTERS HAVE BEEN USED

### 4.1 The Oxford Database of Perinatal Trials (ODPT)

Perhaps the most highly developed register is the ODPT (Chalmers et al. 1986). Started in 1974 as a card file kept in a shoebox, this database is now electronically maintained (Chalmers 1988) and consists of all known randomized controlled trials, both completed and on-going, conducted during the perinatal period (pregnancy through 28 days postpartum). For each trial, the database contains information on study characteristics, key investigators, and publications. The database was originally limited to published reports of trials, but has made a recent effort to identify and register unpublished work through the International Registry of Perinatal Trials (R. Soll, personal communication, June 27, 1991).

The ODPT also includes meta-analyses as an integral part of the register. Data from the trials included on the register have been used to generate a series of over 400 meta-analyses; these comprise both an electronic database and a two-volume book (Chalmers 1988; Chalmers, Enkin & Keirse 1989). The electronic form of the ODPT, which includes the meta-analyses, is updated every six months for subscribers, who include individuals, departments within institutions, and libraries. Currently, there is considerable discussion, both informally and in special conferences arranged for the purpose, as to whether the meta-analyses and book could be the basis for medical practice guideline development.

### 4.2 Physician Data Query (PDQ)

PDQ and its progenitor, CLINPROT, at the International Cancer Research Databank of the NCI, are registers of ongoing cancer trials that include both those trials funded by the NCI, which are registered by an internal inventory system, and those funded by other means, which are registered by the investigators. Any subscriber, such as a library or an individual, can dial into the PDQ database using a computer and modem and search for topics of interest. For example, one could search for ongoing trials of treatments for lung cancer. Currently, updates to the database are made every four months, using mailed questionnaires to principal investigators.

While PDQ and CLINPROT have been used primarily to provide information of direct use to patients, they have also been used as a basis for meta-analyses (Simes 1986; Himel et al. 1986) and methodologic research (Liberati, Himel & Chalmers 1986). Meta-analyses have been performed largely by independent investigators who have used the database as a basis for identification of studies to be included, but also by NCI investigators for ''in-house'' meta-analyses (Editorial 1988).

### 4.3 Studies of Publication Bias

An extremely important use of registers of clinical trials has been for methodological research related to meta-analysis and focusing primarily on the problem of publication bias. Simes (1986) combined the results of registered trials of two types of chemotherapy for ovarian cancer in a meta-analyses, in order to look at the potential effect of publication bias. He found that when data for all registered trials were combined, the difference in effect between the two types of chemotherapy was not statistically significant. When he combined only published data for the registered trials, however, his meta-analysis showed a statistically significant difference between treatments, indicating the existence of a publication bias that could easily affect patient care.

Three additional, related studies of publication bias were conducted using registers or databases of research projects: one following trials listed on the 1979 NIH Inventory of Trials (Dickersin & Min 1993); one following studies reviewed and approved by the Central Oxford Research Ethics Committee, 1984–1987 (Easterbrook et al. 1991); and one following studies reviewed and approved by the institutional review boards of the Johns Hopkins University Health Institutions in 1980 (Dickersin, Min & Meinert 1992). All three studies found that publication of study findings was associated with statistically significant, as opposed to nonsignificant, results.

In a fourth study of publication bias, the ODPT was used to determine the proportion of all trials in the perinatal field initially reported as abstracts that resulted in full publication. A rate of about 36 percent was found (Chalmers et al. 1990). Full publication did not appear to be associated with statistically significant findings or study quality.

### 4.4 Electronic Identification of Trials

Additional methodologic research using research registers has examined the reliability of MEDLINE searching to identify published trials (Dickersin et al. 1985). The number of trials found by a trained information specialist searching MEDLINE was compared with those found in both ODPT and MEDLINE, which was considered to be the "gold standard" database of "all" published perinatal trials. The MEDLINE search yielded only 56 percent of the trials found in ODPT relating to neonatal intraventricular hemorrhage and 29 percent of those relating to neonatal hyperbilirubinemia. Thus, a potentially serious problem can arise by depending solely on electronic literature searches when performing a meta-analysis.

Registers can also be used to provide a "snapshot" of the state-of-the-art or quality of studies or trials in a particular area. Liberati, Himel, and Chalmers (1986) used PDQ, among other databases, to identify all initiated randomized controlled trials of primary treatment for early breast cancer. In preparation for meta-analysis, they evaluated all identified publications for study and report quality. Fewer than half of the available trials could be included in the meta-analysis, because of the poor quality of the report or trial.

One of the concerns of register keepers is whether the registers are or have been useful. Certainly, there is little question regarding usefulness where there have been research projects such as those described above. It is difficult, however, to obtain information as to whether two related reasons to have research registers—to avoid unnecessary duplication of effort and to foster collaboration—have actually been important to investigators.

## 5. CONSIDERATIONS IN THE DEVELOPMENT OF RESEARCH REGISTERS

The major problems faced by all keepers of research registers, and critical to those performing research synthesis without the aid of a register, are inextricably linked: (a) how best to identify studies for inclusion in the register; and (b) once studies are identified, how to estimate the completeness of coverage of the register.

Searching for published trials using MEDLINE or other electronic databases is likely to yield a large number of citations, most of which will either be irrelevant to the research question or not be randomized trials. In an effort not to miss any relevant references, those designing the bibliographic searches have aimed to be exhaustive rather than precise; that is, they have aimed to maximize the number of articles identified as possibly related to the topic rather than to narrow the search such that those probably not relevant are excluded. The result in many cases has been yields of

literally thousands of citations, all of which must have at least the abstract reviewed for a decision regarding possible inclusion in the literature synthesis. This process is expensive, both in terms of database searching and personnel time, and unpredictable, owing to intrinsic differences in the subject matter covered.

If, on the other hand, a register keeper (or other investigator) makes the effort to limit searches somewhat by including search terms having to do with study methodology (e.g., clinical trial), in order to reduce the burden of citation review, many relevant articles may be missed. Several studies, such as one described earlier (Dickersin et al. 1985), have shown this to be true, across a number of different disciplines. In a study in vision research, the authors restricted their search to six prominent journals and compared "hand searching" to MEDLINE searching. In this instance, only 41 percent of the known randomized trials were identified using the MEDLINE search (R. Scherer, personal communication, February 1, 1992).

Searching for unpublished trials conducted in the past is extremely difficult and probably not worth the effort unless one has a lead about an actual trial. An international survey of over 42,000 obstetricians and pediatricians, requesting notification of unpublished randomized trials, resulted in the reporting of only 18 trials completed more than two years previously, while 2,300 are known to have been completed and published during the same time (Hetherington et al. 1989).

On the other hand, searching for current ongoing trials can be fruitful, especially if by way of direct requests to department heads or individuals known to be involved in trials. In the survey noted above of 42,000 physicians, 336 ongoing or recently completed trials were reported to the investigators (Hetherington et al. 1989). In a subsequent effort, Soll and his colleagues directly notified 303 heads of departments of obstetrics and pediatrics and individual investigators, as well as 81 funding organizations, of the existence of the International Registry of Perinatal Trials. In return, he has received notification of 373 planned, ongoing, or recently completed trials (R. Soll, personal communication, June 27, 1991). He found that direct requests to individual investigators resulted in the highest response rate.

## 6. THE ACCESSIBILITY OF REGISTERS

The current trend is to have research registers available electronically. The register may be distributed on regularly updated diskettes (e.g., ODPT), or it may be available online for use by those who connect by modem to the National Library of Medicine or through a vendor (e.g., PDQ, DENTALPROJ). CRISP, like most of the other registers, is computer-based, but cannot be accessed by a user directly. Rather, requests for searches must be made to the register keepers.

Some registers print or publish listings of trials (e.g., the International Committee on Thrombosis and Haemostasis Registry of Clinical Trials); some make information available on request (e.g., CRISP); and some are designed to be used within the institution and not by subscribers (e.g., the NIH Inventory of Clinical Trials and Studies and the VA Cooperative Studies Program Master List).

The cost of searching the registers varies. Fees for searching online databases are applied in the same way as fees for online searching of the literature via MEDLINE or ERIC. ODPT has been available for purchase, either by institutions or individuals. Paper-based registers (e.g., the *AIDS/HIV Experimental Treatment Directory*) are usually free, either being distributed by the register or by publication in a journal (Verstraete 1984). Other registers are small enough that requests are handled individually.

Currently, most people interested in health care research are not aware that research registers exist. Those who are, usually know about a single register, such as an AIDS register, perhaps because they are interested in referring patients to trials; few have thought of additional benefits to research registration. It is important that information about registers be made available and accessible. Several steps have been taken in that direction. First, an International Collaborative Group on Clinical Trial Registries has been formed and is working toward setting guidelines for standardized data collection and forming a network of existing registers (Noticeboard 1991b). Second, the European Regional Office of the World Health Organization, the Spanish Ministry of Health, and the International Society of Drug Bulletins have collaborated to construct a set of guidelines regarding information on pharmaceuticals. One of the guidelines is that government authorities should require that all clinical trials be registered prior to their startup, so that the details of the trial can be available to those interested (Noticeboard 1991a). Third, the journal *Controlled Clinical Trials* has recently instituted a column that will focus on registers and maintain a "register of registers" (Dickersin 1992). Finally, the American Association for the Advancement of Science has announced the startup of a new electronic journal, the Online Journal of Current Clinical Trials, which aims to publish the results of trials and meta-analyses in a continuous and relatively rapid fashion, after peer review and acceptance of the report (Palca 1991). This journal could provide one means of registering trials in health care. While none of these developments ensures that registers are accessible, they do provide a means for those who want to know of the existence of registers specific to their interests.

## 7. FUTURE DIRECTIONS

The research review has evolved sufficiently over the past several years to be considered a research endeavor in and of itself: The evolutionary process has mainly included the rediscovery, development, and testing of related statistical methods. Less attention has been paid during this time to improving the methods used for data collection in a systematic review—that is, the identification of the available research and accession of the data to be analyzed. Areas of particular concern are publication bias and ascertainment of all of the available published literature. Research registers are an obvious system for addressing both problems.

It has been difficult to fund the development of research registers in the various fields of medicine. Clearly, the emergence of an epidemic situation, like AIDS or even cancer, has provided a particular impetus for starting systems of registration. Comparable situations exist that are applicable to the social sciences. For instance, the coverage of psychotherapy by medical insurance and issues related to the education of children have been and continue to be of particular concern in the United States.

As has been noted numerous times (Easterbrook 1987; Dickersin, for the Panel 1988; Meinert 1988), a system for research registration exists internationally, applicable to both medicine and the social sciences: Institutional review boards, or ethics committees, exist in most if not all countries conducting research involving human volunteers. The review board system extends beyond the medical domain and covers social, educational, and psychological research. Harnessing the system to act in this additional capacity will take the cooperation and collaboration of the institutions where the committees reside. This has occurred in Spain, where the mandated cooperation between local and centralized institutional review boards has allowed the concomitant development of a clinical trials register (Ensayos Clínicos en España 1990).

Those in the social sciences can take a lesson from the medical field in initiating research registers, perhaps through review boards, and can chart new territory by networking the individual institution-based registers into a national system. Two decades ago, such a system was unthinkable, given the lack of institutional review boards. A decade ago, it was unmanageable, given the emphasis on paper systems for maintaining databases. Presently, the widespread availability of electronic databases has modified our concept of the role of research registers in literature syntheses: They have evolved from luxury item to necessity.

## 8. REFERENCES

Chalmers, I. (Ed). (1988). *Oxford Database of Perinatal Trials*. Oxford: Oxford University Press.

Chalmers, I., Adams, M., Dickersin, K., Hetherington, J., Tarnow-Mordi, W., Meinert, C., Tonascia, S., & Chalmers, T. C. (1990). A cohort study of summary reports of controlled trials. *Journal of the American Medical Association, 263,* 1401–1405.

Chalmers, I., Enkin, M., & Keirse, M. (Eds.). (1989). *Effective care in pregnancy and childbirth*. Oxford: Oxford University Press.

Chalmers, I., Hetherington, J., Newdick, M., Mutch, L., Grant, A., Enkin, M., Enkin, E., & Dickersin, K. (1986). The Oxford Database of Perinatal Trials: Developing a register of published reports of controlled trials. *Controlled Clinical Trials, 7,* 306–324.

DeNeef, P. (1988). The comprehensiveness of computerized-assisted searches of the medical literature. *Journal of Family Practice, 27,* 404–408.

Dickersin, K. (1990). The existence of publication bias and risk factors for its occurrence. *Journal of the American Medical Association, 263,* 1385–1389.

Dickersin, K. (1992). Keeping posted. Why register clinical trials?—Revisited. *Controlled Clinical Trials, 13,* 170–177.

Dickersin, K., Chan, S., Chalmers, T. C., Sacks, H. S., & Smith, H., Jr. (1987). Publication bias and clinical trials. *Controlled Clinical Trials, 8,* 343–353.

Dickersin, K., Hewitt, P., Mutch, L., Chalmers, I., & Chalmers, T. C. (1985). Perusing the literature: Comparison of MEDLINE searching with a perinatal trials database. *Controlled Clinical Trials, 6,* 306–317.

Dickersin, K., and Min, Y.-I. (1993). NIH Clinical trials and publication bias. *Online Journal of Current Clinical Trials,* Doc. No. 50. *Controlled Clinical Trials, 12,* 634.

Dickersin, K., Min, Y.-I., & Meinert, C. L. (1992). Factors influencing publication of research results: Followup of applications submitted to two institutional review boards. *Journal of the American Medical Association, 267,* 374–378.

Dickersin, K., for the Panel. (1988). Report from the panel on the case for registers of clinical trials. *Controlled Clinical Trials, 9,* 76–81.

Easterbrook, P. J. (1987). Reducing publication bias. *British Medical Journal, 295,* 1347.

Easterbrook, P. J., Berlin, J. A., Gopalan, R., & Matthews, D. R. (1991). Publication bias in clinical research. *Lancet, 337,* 867–872.

Editorial. (1988). Clinical alert from the National Cancer Institute. *Breast Cancer Research and Treatment, 12,* 3–5.

Ensayos Clinícos en España. (1990). *Serie Monografías Técnicas del Ministerio de Sanidad y Consumo* (No. 17), Ed Dirección General de Farmacia y Productos Sanitarios. Madrid.

Hetherington, J., Dickersin, K., Chalmers, I., & Meinert, C. (1989). Retrospective and prospective identification of unpublished controlled trials: Lessons from a survey of obstetricians and pediatricians. *Pediatrics, 84,* 374–380.

Himel, H., Liberati, A., Gelber, R., & Chalmers, T. C. (1986). Adjuvant chemotherapy for breast cancer: A pooled estimate based on published randomized control trials. *Journal of the American Medical Association, 256,* 1148–1159.

Hubbard, S. M., Henney, J. E., & DeVita, V. T., Jr. (1987). A computer database for information on cancer treatment. *New England Journal of Medicine, 316,* 315–318.

Kirpalani, H., Schmidt, B., McKibbon, K. A., Haynes, R. B., & Sinclair, J. C. (1989). Searching MEDLINE for randomized clinical trials involving care of the newborn. *Pediatrics, 83,* 543–546.

Liberati, A., Himel, H., & Chalmers, T. C. (1986). A quality assessment of randomized control trials of primary treatment of breast cancer. *Journal of Clinical Oncology, 4,* 942–951.

Meinert, C. L. (1988). Towards prospective registration of clinical trials. *Controlled Clinical Trials, 9,* 1–5.

Noticeboard. (1991a). Guidelines for drug bulletins. *Lancet, 338,* 1199.

Noticeboard. (1991b). Making clinical trialists register. *Lancet, 338,* 244–245.

Palca, J. (1991). New journal will publish without paper. *Science, 253,* 1480.

Poynard, T., & Conn, H. (1985). The retrieval of randomized clinical trials in liver disease from the medical literature, a comparison of MEDLARS and manual methods. *Controlled Clinical Trials, 6,* 271–279.

Scherer, R., Dickersin, K., Kaplan, E., & Min, Y.-I. (1992). Initiation of a registry of randomized clinical trials in vision research. *Investigative Ophthalmology and Visual Science, 33/34,* 1323.

Simes, R. J. (1986). The case for an international registry of clinical trials. *Journal of Clinical Oncology, 4,* 1529–1541.

Verstraete, M. (1984). Registry of prospective clinical trials, sixth report. *Thrombosis and Haemostasis, 51,* 283–290.

## 9. APPENDIX: Registers of Clinical Research and Clinical Trials

### A. AIDS/HIV

#### AIDS Clinical Trials Information Service

Mr. Ted Karpf, Acting Director
P.O. Box 6421
Bethesda, MD 20849-6421
(301) 251-5750

#### AIDS/HIV Research Directory

Mr. Kenneth Fornaturo
Ms. Patricia Moccia
259 West 30th Street, 9th Floor
New York, NY 10001
(212) 268-4196

#### AIDS/HIV Treatment Directory

Mr. Joseph Guimento
American Foundation for AIDS Research
733 Third Avenue, 12th Floor
New York, NY 10017
(212) 682-7440

#### AIDS/HIV Treatment Directory for New England

Mr. Ramon A. Hernandez
Community Research Institute of New England
338 Newbury Street, 3rd Floor
Boston, MA 02138
(617) 424-1524

#### Directory of HIV Clinical Research in the Bay Area

Mr. Zach Weingart
Directory of HIV Clinical Research in the Bay Area
3180 18th Street, Suite 201
San Francisco, CA 94110
(415) 476-9554

#### International Registry of Clinical Trials of HIV Therapies and Vaccines

Ms. Susan M. Kurucz
Communications Department
Canadian HIV Trials Network
200-1033 Davie Street
Vancouver, BC V6E 1M7
Canada
(604) 631-5327

#### New York State Directory of AIDS/HIV Clinical Trials

Mr. Mitchell Speer
American Foundation for AIDS Research
733 Third Avenue, 12th Floor
New York, NY 10017
(212) 682-7440

#### Philadelphia AIDS Protocol Testing Directory

Dr. Luis J. Morales
Medical Affairs, Policy, and Planning
AIDS Activities Coordinating Office
Department of Public Health
1220 Sansom Street, 6th Floor
Philadelphia, PA 19107
(215) 686-1832

#### Protocol Registry of HIV Trials Network

Ms. Robyn D. Sussel
Communications Department
Canadian HIV Trials Network
200-1033 Davie Street
Vancouver, BC V6E 1M7
Canada
(604) 631-5327

#### Registry of HIV Clinical Trials in Canada

Ms. Robyn D. Sussel
Communications Department
Canadian HIV Trials Network
200-1033 Davie Street
Vancouver, BC V6E 1M7
Canada
(604) 631-5327

#### Southern California HIV Treatment Directory

Jill Glassbrenner, M.Acc.
Southern California HIV Treatment Directory
1800 North Highland Avenue, Suite 610
Los Angeles, CA 90028
(213) 469-5888

## Registers of Clinical Research and Clinical Trials (continued)

### Washington-Baltimore HIV Research Directory

Basil P. Vareldzis, M.D.
Whiteman-Walker Clinic
1407 S Street NW
Washington, DC 20009
(202) 797-3530

## B. Cancer

### ENCLCC Cancer Clinical Trials Registry

Dr. Françoise Bonichon
Biostatistics Unit
Fondation Bergoníe
180 Rue de Saint Genès
Bordeaux 33000
France
33 (56) 92.43.00

### National Cancer Institute Cancer Control Intervention Studies

Brenda K. Edwards, Ph.D.
Associate Director, Surveillance Program
Division of Cancer Prevention and Control
National Cancer Institute
9000 Rockville Pike, EPN Room 343
Bethesda, MD 20892
(301) 496-8506

### Physician Data Query

Dr. Gisele A. Sarosy
International Cancer Research Data Bank
National Cancer Institute
Building 82, Room 113
Bethesda, MD 20892
(301) 496-7403

### United Kingdom Cancer Trials Register

Mrs. Jean Mossman
UKCCCR, Room 1, 2nd Floor
Lincolns in Field
Africa House, 64-78 Kingsway
London WC2B 6BG
UK
44 (71) 269 3249 or 3248

## C. Other

### Computer Retrieval of Information on Scientific Projects

Ms. Seu-Lain Chen, Acting Chief
Research Documentation Section
National Institutes of Health
Westwood Building, Room 148
Bethesda, MD 20892
(301) 496-7543

### DENTALPROJ

Ms. Carla G. Flora
Management Information Section
National Institute of Dental Research
5333 Westbard Avenue, Room 537
Bethesda, MD 20892
(301) 496-7843

### International Committee on Thrombosis and Haemostasis Registry of Clinical Trials

Jean-Pierre Boissel, M.D.
Nadine Bossard, M.D.
ICTH Registry on Clinical Trials
Unité de Pharmacologie Clinique
Hospices Civil de Lyon, Université Claude Bernard
Avenue Lacassagne,
BP 3041 69394 Lyon CEDEX 03
France
33 (78) 53.12.61

### International Registry of Perinatal Trials

Roger F. Soll, M.D.
International Registry of Perinatal Trials
Department of Pediatrics
University of Vermont College of Medicine
Given Building
Burlington, VT 05405
(802) 656-2296

### International Registry of Vision Trials

Kay Dickersin, Ph.D.
Department of Epidemiology
and Preventive Medicine
University of Maryland School of Medicine
660 West Redwood Street
Baltimore, MD 21201
(410) 706-5295

## Registers of Clinical Research and Clinical Trials (continued)

### National Institutes of Health Inventory of Clinical Trials and Studies

John H. Ferguson, M.D.
Director, Office of Medical Applications of Research
National Institutes of Health
7550 Wisconsin Avenue, Room 618
Bethesda, MD 20892
(301) 496-1143

### Neurosurgery Clinical Trials Registry

Stephen J. Haines, M.D.
Department of Neurosurgery
University of Minnesota Medical School
420 Delaware Street SE, Box 96 UMHC
Minneapolis, MN 55455
(612) 624-8651

### Oxford Database of Perinatal Trials

Jini Hetherington
Cochrane Centre

Summertown Pavilion
Middle Way
Oxford OX2 6LG
England
44 (865) 516 300

### Spanish Database of Clinical Trials

Fernando Garcia Alonso, M.D.
Evaluation de Medicamentos
Mijirsterio de Savidad y Consumo
Paseo Prado 18-20
Madrid 28014
Spain
34 (1) 420.2068

### Veterans Administration Cooperative Studies Program Master List

Ping C. Huang, Ph.D.
Cooperative Studies Program (12A4)
Veterans Affairs Central Office
810 Vermont Avenue NW
Washington, DC 20420
(202) 535-7154

NOTES: This list is the product of a project of the author's to "register registers." Goals of the project include providing information to interested parties and forming an international network of registers. Supported in part by grants from the National Eye Institute (No. R21EY07766) and the University of Maryland.

Cooper, H. and Hedges, L. V. (Eds.) 1994. *The Handbook of Research Synthesis.* New York: Russell Sage Foundation

# 7

# THE FUGITIVE LITERATURE

**MARYLU C. ROSENTHAL**
*OCS America, Inc.*

C O N T E N T S

## 1. INTRODUCTION

This chapter describes methods of retrieving hard-to-find ("fugitive") literature and information on particular areas of research. The elusive information may be about a research report that is unpublished or that has been published but cannot be found through traditional, commonly used sources. Indeed, the information on the results of a study or series of studies may not yet be in any formal *written* report but exist instead as data on computer printout along with the researcher's working notes and memos.

### 1.1 Published Literature

Literature may be fugitive in a sense other than being "unpublished." Each year new journals, presenting material in each of the social, behavioral, and medical sciences, are introduced. Each year hundreds of books are published. The costs of subscribing to all of the journals and acquiring all of the books, and providing storage space for them are prohibitive for most academic libraries. When collectors of studies discover that their library does not receive certain publications, the articles they need *seem* "fugitive." In most cases, however, they can be retrieved through the cooperation of another library. For most academic libraries, the alternative to buying every publication and to adding shelf and storage space is membership in a library consortium, a group of libraries sharing resources. Union listing of serials (periodicals and journals), interlibrary loan, cooperative acquisition of materials, and the photocopying and facsimile transmission of single articles for scholarly use are now becoming common practices in large educational institutions.

### 1.2 Completed Research Reports

There are several types of "fugitive" completed research reports. The differences among them are important to the selection of a method for retrieving them. The types of completed research reports are:

1. Technical reports: Many technical reports are prepared for a research-funding government or private agency or organization, but are never published.

2. Interim reports: Some projects require progress reports submitted annually or at regular periods during an ongoing series of studies. An interim report also may be prepared to summarize the results of a study at any stage of its progression.

3. Unsubmitted papers and manuscripts: Some research reports are never submitted for publication because of uninteresting results.

4. Presented papers: This category includes papers presented at international, national, state, and local professional meetings and conventions, including invited conferences and colloquia.

5. Dissertations, theses, and course papers: These range from doctoral dissertations, master's theses, and honors theses to small studies done by undergraduates and graduate students as course work.

6. Rejected papers: Many completed research reports remain unpublished after being rejected for publication. Among a number of authors who discuss the problems of completed science remaining unpublished are Dolby (1979) on the concept of "deviant science" and Lindsey (1978) on publishing in the social sciences.

### 1.3 Uncompleted Research Reports

The eight stages of writing a research report are (a) study plan begun, (b) study plan finished, (c) data collection begun, (d) data collection finished, (e) data analysis begun, (f) data analysis finished, (g) research report begun, and (h) research report finished. Studies that have reached stages (f) and (g) are certain to be of interest to a research synthesis, and studies at stages (d) and (e) may be of interest.

## 2. PRELIMINARY STEPS TO THE RETRIEVAL OF FUGITIVE INFORMATION

### 2.1 Background Experience

The study-collector who is an established contributor in the field to be covered, or one who knows researchers in that field, is probably part of a research network, an "invisible college" (Chubin 1983; Crane 1972). This person, then, may be aware of some completed but unpublished reports, may have heard about a study that a colleague is just finishing, or may have learned from fellow investigators about a conference or colloquium speaker's presentation.

Let us suppose, however, that the collector wants to begin a research synthesis in an unfamiliar area of research, a field in which he or she does not work, has no professional contacts with those who do, and has no names of scientists to contact to begin the search.

## 2.2 Beginning the Search Using Published Literature

Eventually the collector wants to know of the existence of *unpublished* literature and to acquire information about research in progress. To reach those stages of collection, however, the collector first will search for *published* works in order to put together a list of names of investigators who have done, and who may still be doing, research in the area of interest.

Two aids in any search process that the collector should consider before beginning the search are search documentation and professional assistance.

**2.2.1 Search documentation** In their chapter on finding studies, Glass, McGaw, and Smith (1981) stress the importance of documenting the search process. Cooper (1989), in a discussion of validity issues in study retrieval, prescribed a set of guidelines to be followed by the searcher to protect validity: sources that the literature search must be required to include, explanations of how studies were gathered, and presentation of any possible publication bias.

When a search involves gathering a great number of citations, there is often the problem of duplicating titles, especially if they appear in more that one form (e.g., dissertation and journal article). In addition, the process of acquiring papers and articles over long periods of time requires keeping a record of the status of each article—for example, whether it has been requested through interlibrary loan or through a letter to an author.

For the purpose of documenting the search and eliminating duplication of effort during the search process, an aid to the study-collector would be checklists of printed sources and databases searched, and the citations found in each. (See Table 7.1.) Careful documentation might also include checklists of names of libraries used and names of authors contacted (including notes about responses from them).

Another useful tracking procedure can be set up using a computer program that provides a database manage-

ment system, a word-processing system, and a spreadsheet capability. Such an integrated program allows the user to enter data for one of those applications and later use the data for the other applications as well. A researcher could enter the gathered citations into a database (see Table 7.2), later transfer the entries into the word processor to create a list of studies or a reference list, and even use the program's spreadsheet capabilities to enter information (other than bibliographic) to create tables.

**2.2.2 Professional assistance** The wise study-collector seeks the guidance of reference and information librarians in the use of both printed sources and CD-ROM (Compact Disk—Read Only Memory) databases used on the computer. Most academic and research library reference specialists are knowledgeable about new sources of information about scientific research and the frequent changes in online searching techniques (see Chapter 5; Rosenthal 1985). Since online database searches are costly, an experienced searcher aware of the changes and developments in online technology can save the collector time and money. Professional information gatherers can also assist in the retrieval of unpublished papers and reports that *are* attainable.

## 2.3 Search Strategy Using Published Literature

The collector begins at an academic library (or other research library) that can provide the traditional sources for the published work in the new, unfamiliar discipline. He or she searches regular bibliographic works: the library subject catalog, abstracts and indexes, the references in reviews of the literature, and computer-readable bibliographic databases (online and/or CD-ROM). From them the collector learns the titles of a number of relevant published books, articles, and literature reviews.

The collector next retrieves the publications found through the search. The references found in this first set of books, articles, and reviews are used to gather more references, many to older publications authored by earlier researchers. The collector reads more articles and gathers even older references. This retrieval process continues until the same authors' names appear again and again, and there are no references to publications earlier than the ones already found. In addition to many references, this search strategy provides the collector with names of past and present contributors in the field

**Table 7.1 Sample of a Checklist of Sources Searched for Studies Collected for a Research Synthesis**

| Sources | Searched | Not Searched | Years Searched | Search Terms Used |
|---|---|---|---|---|
| Automated library catalog | X | | | Education Schools Homework |
| Card catalog (for older publications) | X | | | Education—United States Schools |
| ERIC | | X | | |
| *Psychological Abstracts* (print) | X | | 1927–present | Children Education |
| PsycINFO | X | | 1967–present | Children Education |
| Child Development Abstracts (print) | | X | | |
| EUDISED (European Education) | X | | 1975–present | Education Children |
| DATRIX II (dissertations) | | X | | |

**Table 7.2 Sample of a Reference and Bibliographic Database Used to Track Studies Collected for a Research Synthesis**

| Sample Database Field | Sample Record 1 | Sample Record 2 | Sample Record 3 |
|---|---|---|---|
| Author 1 Author 2 Author 3 | Cooper, H. M. | Rosenthal, R. | Dolby, R. G. A. |
| Title | Homework | Replication in behavioral research | Reflections on deviant science |
| Information type | Book | Chapter | Journal article |
| In (journal or book title; conference name) | | Replication in research in the social sciences | Sociological Review Monograph 27: On the margins of science |
| Editor | | Neuliep, J. W. | |
| Publication date | 1989 | 1991 | 1970 |
| Publication place | White Plains, NY | Newbury Park, CA | Canterbury, England |
| Publisher name | Longman, Inc. | Sage Publications | University of Kent |
| Retrieval source | ERIC | Library computer catalog | Listed in bibliography |
| Library | Gutman (Harvard Education) | Beatley (Simmons College) | Widener (Harvard) |
| Retrieval status | In circulation; requested | Acquired | Article photocopied |
| Subject word 1 | Education | Social science—methodology | |
| Subject word 2 | Homework | | |
| Keyword 1 | Homework | Replication | |

NOTE: The database can be sorted (arranged) on several fields. For example, keeping track of an author's 65 studies that have similar titles will be an easier task if they can be arranged by date and the title of the journal in which they first appeared.

of interest that can be searched in sources for "fugitive information."

## 3. RETRIEVING FUGITIVE INFORMATION ABOUT COMPLETED PAPERS

### 3.1 Unpublished Papers and Technical Reports

While there are several well-known printed and computer-readable indexes and abstracts that contain references to a few unpublished research papers and reports (see Rosenthal 1985), those indexes and abstracts focus primarily on published works. (See Chapter 5 on using reference databases.) The printed and computer sources listed here contain a greater representation of completed but unpublished material.

*Abstract Newsletter.* Published weekly by the National Technical Information Service (NTIS), an agency of the U.S. Department of Commerce, it provides current information (reviews and surveys, analyses, and planning studies) on 26 research areas.

*ERIC (Educational Resources Information Center).* The ERIC database, in addition to listing published works, includes references to unpublished reports and to papers presented at meetings and conferences. It is online and also available on CD-ROM and magnetic tape. ERIC is the source for many of the reports listed in the database.

*NTIS (National Technical Information Service).* The NTIS bibliographic database (available online and on CD-ROM) announces summaries of completed research sponsored by more than 600 federal agencies and a number of foreign organizations and agencies. Eighty-eight percent of the completed reports cited are available from NTIS (NTIS 1990). Although the NTIS database does contain a disproportionate number of studies sponsored by the Departments of Defense and Energy, studies sponsored by other departments are well represented. NTIS provides a number of useful searching paths such as "document type" (e.g., conference proceedings, thesis, translation) and "sponsoring agency." A well-planned search of this database could be useful to the research synthesist.

When using the NTIS database, as well as the Federal Research in Progress (FEDRIP) database (which will be discussed later), the study-collector should note the name of the sponsoring agency and contact that agency's archives or library for help in retrieving the desired papers.

*Resources in Vocational Education.* This database, produced by the National Center for Research in Vocational Education, lists more that 15,000 citations, from 1978 to date, for ongoing and recently completed federally funded projects. Three hundred records are added each quarter.

*SBSD (Social and Behavioral Science Documents).* Published by the American Psychological Association, it continues *Psychological Documents* (which continued *Catalog of Selected Documents in Psychology*, 1976–1983). It contains abstracts of technical papers, reports, and bibliographies. An introductory page describes the publication role as one providing "an outlet between informal communication networks and conventional journals."

*SOLIS (Social Sciences Literature Information System).* Produced by the Informationzentrum Sozialwissenschaften and sold through STN International or DIMDI (Germany), this database lists monographs, reports, and conference proceedings. Begun in 1976, it contains approximately 111,000 citations on work in the social sciences and the humanities, and 1,000 records are added each month (Cuadra/Elsevier 1991).

*Federal Database Finder: a Directory of Free and Fee-Based Databases and Files Available from the Federal Government.* In its second edition (1987), this reference book, compiled by Information, U.S.A. (Chevy Chase, MD), contains a wealth of sources for data files and reports from all U.S. governmental departments.

*Monthly Checklist of State Publications.* This publication, arranged by state and containing a subject index, lists only those papers that states make available to the publisher, the Library of Congress. The papers cited are often available through the authoring agency.

*Monthly Catalog of United States Government Publications.* This catalog is compiled and published by the Office of the Superintendent of Documents. In addition to the traditional author, title, subject, and keyword indexes, it indexes report series, making it possible to track research updates. It is available on fiche, magnetic tape, and online as the *GPO Monthly Catalog*. Ordering information for specific publications is included in the citations.

### 3.2 Unpublished Dissertations and Master's Theses

The following are print and computer sources for retrieving unpublished dissertations and master's theses.

*DATRIX II (Direct Access to Information).* DATRIX II (a Xerox Service) is an online retrieval system containing citations to more than 800,000 dissertations and more than 20,000 master's theses dating back to 1961. Included in each citation is a reference to the author-prepared abstract to be found in *Dissertation Abstracts International, Masters Abstracts,* or *Research Abstracts.* The information in DATRIX II, in a printed or microfiche form, can also be found in the *Comprehensive Dissertation Index (CDI).* (The database and the printed index and abstracts are all produced by the University Microfilms International (UMI) Dissertation Information Service (Ann Arbor, MI); the publisher is also the source for copies of many of the dissertations and theses cited (UMI 1991). *American Doctoral Dissertations* (published annually) and *Special Subject Bibliographies* (also published by UMI) should, for completeness, be included here as sources for information about dissertations and theses, although that information is also contained in the UMI products mentioned above.

*Index to Theses.* This publication from the Association of Special Libraries and Information Bureaux (AS-LIB), London, contains citations and abstracts to theses written in Great Britain and Ireland. Publication of this volume has been irregular, but beginning in 1991 it will be published annually.

*Guide to Theses and Dissertations: An International Bibliography of Bibliographies* (Phoenix, AZ: Oryx Press, 1985). The author, Michael Reynolds, has compiled a bibliography of reference books that list dissertations and theses. While this guide does not list the titles of dissertations themselves, it is a place to learn about reference books that *do* list them.

## 3.3 Meetings and Conferences

Professional meetings and conferences, particularly national meetings, play an important role in the early dissemination of scientific information about newly completed research (Garvey & Griffith 1979). Attendance at such meetings may enable the study-collector to discover completed studies that may or may not be retrieved otherwise during the first few years following the conference.

The Center for Research in Scientific Communication (1970) conducted a series of studies on national meetings (for nine social and physical sciences) and the role they play in scientific communication. During the two years following those national meetings, follow-up studies were conducted to determine the status of each presented paper—that is, whether it was published, accepted for publication, rejected after being submitted for publication, or never submitted for publication (Garvey et al. 1979; Nelson 1970). From these studies it was concluded that the publication process for scientific papers is a slow one and that many of the papers from these meetings are *never* included in a formal publication. Therefore, many papers presented at professional meetings, conferences, conventions, and colloquia become fugitive literature and remain so.

*Conference programs.* When conference attendance is not possible, printed conference programs may be used as the source of participants' names and the titles and/or abstracts of papers scheduled to be presented. Written requests to authors for copies of their presentation papers are almost always honored (Center for Research in Scientific Communication 1970). This formal communication may also serve as an introduction to incomplete investigations that the author and members of his or her laboratory are conducting.

*Bibliographic Guide to Conference Publications.* Published by G. K. Hall (Boston), this is an annual subject print bibliography of published conference proceedings cataloged by the research libraries of the New York Public Library and the Library of Congress. It includes conference papers published in books and serials, and in all languages.

*BioMeetings.* This database contains 130,000 references to reports of life sciences research projects from meetings, symposia, seminars, and conferences. It also lists some research-in-progress.

*BLL Conference Index.* Compiled by the British Library Lending Division, this index is a cumulation of all citation entries that appeared in the publication *Index of Conference Proceedings* from 1965 through 1973.

*Conference Papers Index.* This index, produced by Cambridge Scientific Abstracts (Bethesda, MD) is available online and in print. It contains approximately 1,290,000 records from 1973 to the present. The information is taken from final programs or abstract publications of conferences. It includes information about the availability, costs, and ordering procedures for preprints, reprints, and proceedings. It is updated with about 8,000 records bimonthly (Cuadra/Elsevier 1991).

*Global Meeting Line Database.* This database was introduced by Global Meeting Line (Oak Ridge, TN) in 1991. It contains information on about 5,000 major upcoming conferences, symposia, and meetings, worldwide. The producer plans an online weekly-updated edition and a quarterly mailing of diskettes.

*Index to Social Sciences and Humanities Proceedings.* The Institute for Scientific Information (Philadelphia) publishes this comprehensive quarterly index with an annual cumulation. It is a guide to *published* conference proceedings and contains a Permuterm subject index that refers the searcher to the appropriate proceedings entry using relevant title words. In addition, there are category, sponsor, meeting location, author/editor, and contents indexes. Information for ordering individual papers is also given.

*Proceedings in Print.* This publication lists citations for proceedings of conferences, congresses, hearings, seminars, courses, institutes, colloquia, meetings, and published symposia. The publications cited are indexed by subject, title of a conference, sponsor, and name of the editor. It is published by Proceedings in Print (Halifax, MA) six times yearly, with an annual cumulative index.

*World Meetings.* Separate volumes for (a) United States and Canada, (b) Outside United States and Canada, (c) Social and Behavioral Sciences, (d) Services Management, and (e) Medicine are published by Macmillan (New York). These publications list conferences and meetings by subject, date, location, and sponsor. They are completely revised and updated quarterly. They are included here as a current awareness source, a place to learn about meetings, and therefore a possible lead to some unpublished materials.

### 3.4 Census and Economic Data Sources

There are several sources for the research synthesist who wishes to locate certain kinds of survey data.

*Census Information Service.* This database is produced by the Public Information Office of the U.S. Census Bureau. It is kept current with periodic updates.

*Economic Bulletin Board.* This online source provides daily updates of economic data and the full text of many unpublished special studies and reports. It is also available on disk and magnetic tape.

*Population Bibliography.* For demographics, worldwide population statistics, and unpublished papers on family planning, this online database provides records from 1966 to the present.

*Statistical Analysis and Retrieval System.* This online database contains all kinds of statistical data, obtained from the Census Bureau and compiled from surveys

conducted by the database producer Glimpse Corporation (Cuadra/Elsevier 1991).

## 4. RETRIEVING INFORMATION ABOUT STUDIES IN PROGRESS

### 4.1 Printed and Computer Sources

The following are sources for information about ongoing series of studies or research in progress.

*FEDRIP (Federal Research in Progress).* FEDRIP is produced by the National Technical Information Service (NTIS). It provides access to information about current and ongoing federally funded research in the FEDRIP database. FEDRIP records consist of the project title, its objectives, starting date, principal investigator, performing and sponsoring organization (all searchable fields), a detailed abstract, and, when available, immediate findings (NTIS 1989, 1990, 1991).

FEDRIP comprises ten subfiles of information derived from ten federal agency sources—for example, the CRISP (Computer Retrieval of Information on Scientific Projects) Subfile, from the U.S. Department of Health and Human Services, Public Health Service; the NSF Subfile, from the National Science Foundation; and the NASA Subfile, from the National Aeronautics and Space Administration. This database lists over 100,400 research projects annually (NTIS 1989, 1990, 1991). FEDRIP partly continues the work of the defunct SSIE (Smithsonian Science Information Exchange) Current Research. SSIE is still available online, but has not been updated since 1982; therefore, it may be useful as a retrospective source (Cuadra/Elsevier 1991).

*UNIVRES (Directory of Federally Supported Research in Universities).* Compiled by the Canada Institute for Scientific and Technical Information, and available through CAN/OLE (Canadian Online Enquiry Service), this database began in 1971 and is updated with 15,000 records annually. It lists 180,000 university-based research projects sponsored by 36 funding agencies in Canada (Cuadra/Elsevier 1991).

*CRIB (Current Research in Britain).* Published by the British Library (Wetherby, England), this database lists 75,000 ongoing research projects currently being conducted in over 500 British universities and public and private research establishments (Cuadra/Elsevier 1991). The information in the database corresponds to the four-volume *Current Research in Britain,* which contains name, study area, and keyword indexes. The book is published yearly (with alternating volumes on the social sciences, physical sciences, biological sciences, and humanities; each appears every four years).

*STRC (Scientific and Technical Research Centers in Australia).* Sponsored by the Commonwealth Scientific Industrial Research Organization, the database lists abstracts of current research in progress in Australia. It is updated irregularly (Cuadra/Elsevier 1991).

*EUDISED (European Documentation and Information System for Education).* Available in print and online since 1975, this database covers recently completed and ongoing research in 16 European countries. The 200 records added quarterly include names of researchers and their institutions, research methods, and results of studies when available.

*FORIS (Information Services on Social Sciences Research).* It is produced by Forschungsinformationssystem Sozialwissenschaften and is available through STN International or DIMDI (Germany). The database citations cover planned, ongoing, and completed research in Austria, Germany, and Switzerland.

*Foundation Grants Index.* Available in print and online, this index, produced by the Foundation Center, began in 1973 and lists recipients' names and project descriptions for more than 300,000 contracts and grants awarded by 500 major U.S. philanthropies and foundations (Cuadra/Elsevier 1991).

### 4.2 Miscellaneous Sources

The following databases list research in progress, but are specialized in their subject coverage. They are included here as other sources that might aid the searcher.

*CRF (Current Research File).* It is compiled by the National Institute for Occupational Health and Safety and contains 5,000 records.

*Family Resources.* Sponsored by the National Council on Family Relations, it contains citations to journal and nonjournal literature from 1970 to the present and is updated monthly with information about work in progress and work planned.

*Rare Disease Database.* Produced and updated weekly by the National Organization for Rare Disorders, it began in 1985 to provide information for researchers working in the area.

*Research-in-Progress Database.* Produced by the Research Libraries Group, it concentrates on women's studies research and is updated daily.

*SPOFOR (SPOrtwissenschaftliche FORschungsprojekte).* Produced by the Sport Council and available

through DIMDI, it contains information about sports psychology, sociology, and medicine with coverage for western Europe from 1978 to date.

*TRIS (Transportation Research Information Services).* Compiled by the National Academy of Science and the National Research Council, its holdings consist of 32,000 government report abstracts and 4,000 ongoing projects on all phases of transportation including user and socioeconomic concerns and safety and environmental issues.

*INROADS.* This Australian version of TRIS is produced by the Australian Road Research Board. It is served online by CSIRO Australi*s* (s, not a) and contains citation to unpublished literature and studies in progress about driver behavior, safety, and accidents.

*USDA.* Prepared by the U.S. Department of Agriculture and its agencies, this database contains information about research in progress sponsored by the department. There are 467 categories of information, updated daily with 700 records per month (Cuadra/Elsevier 1991).

## 5. INFORMAL MEANS FOR RETRIEVING FUGITIVE RESEARCH

There are important quasi-formal and informal methods of retrieving fugitive information about completed and in-progress research.

### 5.1 Informal Communication at Meetings

Meeting and conference attendance provides an opportunity for informal communication between the authors of papers and those attending their presentations (Center for Research in Scientific Communication 1970; Garvey et al. 1979). Such contact may acquaint searchers with scientists conducting ongoing research in their area of interest.

### 5.2 Electronic Networks

Electronic journals, still in their early stages of development, are becoming a vital source of unpublished material and information about research in progress. While the standards, procedures, and technology for formal electronic publishing are still being debated (Estes 1990), many scientists contribute regularly to the more informal electronic publications and bulletin boards known as ''scholarly skywriting.'' This communication is made possible by electronic networks.

BITNET (Because It's Time Network) was initiated by the City University of New York to connect college and university research centers for the purposes of academic and noncommercial exchange of information; the network is now worldwide. It has since been joined by other academic networks: EARN (European Academic and Research Network), connecting institutions in 25 countries; JANET (United Kingdom Joint Academic Network), connecting all UK research centers and universities; NeTNORTH (a private Canadian network), connecting academic and research institutions and organizations in Canada; and ONeT (a North American coast-to-coast network).

INTERNET is a global set of interconnected networks designed to improve resource-sharing within the U.S. scientific and engineering communities. One of its major subnetworks is NSFNeT (National Science Foundation Network), which has three levels to its structure: six super-computer sites that serve smaller networks, which in turn serve even smaller networks. NSFNeT is administered by Bolt Beranek and Neman, Inc. (LaQuey 1990).

Through these networks, via electronic mail (E-mail), formal and informal scientific communication takes place. At this writing some 28,000 E-mail users and their addresses are listed in the online database *National E-Mail White Pages* (Cuadra/Elsevier 1991).

## 5.3 Contact with Public Policy Organizations

A number of quasi-official agencies sponsor research (e.g., the Rand Corporation, the Social Science Research Council, the Woodrow Wilson International Center for Scholars, the Brookings Institution, and the Institute for International Economics). While many of the studies sponsored by these agencies are cited in some of the printed and online sources previously listed, contact with some of them might be useful to the study-collector. Their names, addresses, and other pertinent information may be found in two publications: *The Federal-State-Local Government Directory* (Braddock Communications) and the *U.S. Government Manual* (Office of the Federal Register).

## 5.4 ADVERTISING

In addition to the electronic and print services resources described above, a study-collector may want to gather reprints and preprints about a topic by advertising in widely read journals and newsletters related to the area

of study or by advertising on a bulletin board through an electronic network.

## 5.5 The Invisible College

Earlier, in order to present some basic search procedures, we hypothesized a study-collector who had no prior knowledge of the area of interest. Of course, that is possibly a worst-case scenario. It is usually *not* the case that a searcher knows no one active in the field, therefore excluding him or her from the informal or ''unstructured channels'' of scientific communication.

The ''invisible college'' (see Chapter 4) is the subject of a number of scholarly works (Chubin 1983; Crane 1972; Griffith & Miller 1970). It has been described variously by the scholars who have written about it: as a social system (Garvey & Griffith 1979), or a social organization of research (Crane 1972). It is a research-area community, circle, or network in which scientists appear to develop patterns of communication and a reliance on a membership group of colleagues involved in research and interests similar to their own (Burton 1973; Storer 1968). An invisible college may consist of colleagues a few doors away or a few states away from each other, on the other coast or on the other side of an ocean.

For the established researcher who has access to one of these scientific grapevines, the invisible college may be an efficient path to the collection of needed studies. Many scientists evolve their own ''personal information-handling systems'' (Burton 1973), collecting references and reprints, themselves becoming small special libraries of information about a particular area of research. Association with these scientists becomes invaluable to the study-collector planning a synthesis on that area of research. They have the fugitive information about an ongoing research project known only to a few researchers and their associates. Therefore, it is vital that the study-collector contact these scientists and become a recipient of the information they have to offer.

## 6. CONCLUSION

Many of the sources for ''fugitive'' literature and information cited in this chapter will change during the next few years. Some sources will have changed titles, new sources will be published, and some sources will discontinue publication. In addition, computer technology will provide the searcher with additional options and easier access to both published and unpublished information, through formal electronic journals and informal electronic network communication.

**Author's Note**

I would like to thank Carnot E. Nelson and Norman W. Storer for providing fugitive literature and helpful suggestions for the preparation of this chapter.

## 7. REFERENCES

Burton, H. (1973). Personal information systems. *Special Libraries, 64,* 7–10.

Center for Research in Scientific Communication. (1970). *The role of the national meeting in scientific and technical communication* (Vol. 1). Baltimore: Johns Hopkins University Press.

Chubin, D. E. (1983). *Sociology of sciences: An annotated bibliography on invisible colleges, 1971–1981.* New York: Garland.

Cooper, H. M. (1989). *Integrating research: A guide for literature reviews* (2nd ed.). Newbury Park, CA: Sage.

Crane, D. (1972). *Invisible colleges: Diffusion of knowledge in scientific communities.* Chicago: University of Chicago Press.

Cuadra/Elsevier (1991). *Directory of Online Databases* (Vol. 12). New York: Cuadra/Elsevier.

Dolby, R. G. A. (1979). Reflections on deviant science. In *Sociological Review Monograph 27: On the margins of science: The social construction of rejected knowledge* (pp. 9–47). Canterbury, England: University of Kent.

Estes, W. K. (Ed.). (1990). Special section: Electronic publishing. *Psychological Science: A Journal of the American Psychological Society, 1,* 333–361.

Garvey, W. D., & Griffith, B. C. (1979). Scientific communication as a social system. In W. D. Garvey (Ed.), *Communication: The essence of science* (pp. 148–164). Oxford, England: Pergamon Press.

Garvey, W. D., Lin, N., Nelson, C. E., & Tomita, K. (1979). Research studies in patterns of scientific communication: II. The role of the national meeting in scientific and technical communication. In W. D. Garvey (Ed.), *Communication: The essence of science* (pp. 184–201). Oxford, England: Pergamon Press.

Glass, G. V., McGaw, B., & Smith, M. L. (1981). *Meta-analysis in social research.* Beverly Hills, CA: Sage.

Griffith, B., & Miller, J. A. (1970). Networks of informal communication among scientifically productive scientists. In C. E. Nelson & D. K. Pollock (Eds.), *Communication among scientists and engineers* (pp. 125–140). Lexington, MA: Heath Lexington Books.

LaQuey, T. (1990). *The user's directory of computer networks.* Bedford, MA: Digital Press.

Lindsey, D. (1978). *The scientific publication system in social science.* San Francisco: Jossey-Bass.

National Technical Information Service. (1989). *Search guide to NTIS bibliographic database.* Springfield, VA: U.S. Department of Commerce.

National Technical Information Service. (1990). *The FEDRIP database on DIALOG: Search guide.* Springfield, VA: U.S. Department of Commerce.

National Technical Information Service. (1991). *NTIS 1991 catalog of products.* Springfield, VA: U.S. Department of Commerce.

Nelson, C. E. (1970, March). *The postmeeting journal dissemination of material at the 1968 American Educational Research Association annual meeting.* Paper presented at the annual meeting of the American Educational Research Association, Minneapolis.

Rosenthal, M. C. (1985). Bibliographic retrieval for the social and behavioral scientist. *Research in Higher Education, 22,* 315–333.

Storer, N. W. (1968, February 29–March 1). *Modes and processes of communication among scientists: Theoretical issues and prospects for investigation.* Paper presented at the Conference on Theoretical Issues in the Study of Science, Scientists, and Science Policy, New York.

University Microfilms International. (1991). *Communications: A catalog of current doctoral dissertation research.* Ann Arbor, MI: Author.

# PART
# IV

## EVALUATING THE LITERATURE

Cooper, H. and Hedges, L. V. (Eds.) 1994. *The Handbook of Research Synthesis.* New York: Russell Sage Foundation

# 8

# JUDGING RESEARCH QUALITY

**PAUL M. WORTMAN**

*State University of New York at Stony Brook*

CONTENTS

It is an empirical question whether relatively poorly designed studies give results significantly at variance with those of the best designed studies. . . .

Glass (1976, p. 4)

Eliminate from consideration studies with severe methodological inadequacies. . . .Divide the remaining studies into two categories: those that are reasonably well designed and those that have significant methodological limitations.

Mansfield and Busse (1977, p. 3)

## 1. INTRODUCTION

The discussion about judging research quality in synthesis dates to Glass's unveiling of "meta-analysis" in the November 1976 issue of the *Educational Researcher* (Glass 1976). Prior to that time, the quality of the research studies was considered a major "obstacle" to developing a quantitative synthesis method (Bangert-Drowns 1986). Within a year of Glass's seminal publication critics were debating the merits of his advice on judging the effect of research quality in meta-analysis (Mansfield & Busse 1977). In his rejoinder to his critics Glass (1978) argued, "The sensible course to follow is to describe—in quantitative terms—features of designs and correlate them with the study findings: the obtained relationships will reveal how important matters of design are and precisely what to do about them" (p. 3).

As with many academic debates, there is more agreement than disagreement to be found in the exchange between Glass and his critics. Both agree on the critical issue that research quality should be examined in all meta-analyses. Even on the point of contention involving the elimination of methodologically weak studies, Glass (1978) admitted that he "arbitrarily eliminated 'pretest-posttest' designs from consideration" in his pioneering meta-analysis of psychotherapy (Smith & Glass 1977).

The issue is thus not whether to eliminate studies from a research synthesis since that is almost inevitable, but how to assess or measure the quality of primary studies. The development of such criteria will allow the meta-analyst to decide on which studies to exclude and which studies to include on a consistent and objective basis. Glass's recommendation (1978) to focus on the study and to extract or code information on both the design and its features is still "sensible." In fact, Cooper (1984) has referred to this "mixed-criteria approach" consisting of types of designs and their features as the "optimal strategy for categorizing studies" and judging the quality of research.

The emphasis of this chapter will be primarily, but not exclusively, on methodological issues and criteria for assessing quality in the individual or primary studies that provide the basic data for research synthesis. As will be noted, theoretical and conceptual issues play an important role, which is often overlooked (Durlak & Lipsey 1991), in judging research quality. Examples will be presented illustrating the ability of research synthesis to test theories and their constructs. Such an approach to theory testing in meta-analysis can be viewed as a form of "confirmatory research" (Dooley 1990, p. 292). This confirmatory research approach to synthesis has been advocated by Chalmers and his associates (1987). Alternatively, examples will be presented of using meta-analysis as "exploratory research" (Dooley 1990, p. 293) where theories can only be probed, but neither confirmed nor "falsified." Such exploratory research synthesis has been advocated by Peto and his colleagues at Oxford (Yusuf et al. 1985). This work has led to the design of a number of large individual studies yielding important results.

## 2. TWO APPROACHES TO ASSESSING RESEARCH QUALITY

The research synthesis literature contains two approaches or typologies for coding research quality. The first system, offered by Wortman (1983), applies the validity framework developed by Campbell and his associates (Campbell & Stanley 1966; Cook & Campbell 1979). This approach provides a matrix of designs and their features or "threats to validity." The focus is largely on nonrandomized or "quasi-experimental" designs found in the social science literature, although there is some useful discussion of randomized experiments (see especially, Cook & Campbell 1979, pp. 56–58, 350–366).

The second system was developed by Chalmers and his associates (1981) and later extended by them to a framework for the "quality assessment" of meta-analyses (Sacks et al. 1987). This approach focuses on the "randomized controlled trial" (or "true experiment" in the vernacular of Campbell and Stanley) that is common in the medical literature.

Both systems have been widely used and will be described in detail in the following section. Campbell's validity system encompasses a larger variety of designs, including some randomized ones, as well as a larger number of design features. Chalmers' system provides more in-depth criteria for assessing the quality of randomized designs. Chalmers' approach also provides a specific set of coding forms along with a weighting or scoring system for measuring overall methodological quality.

With respect to meta-analysis, the objective of the Campbell validity system is to assess the "strategic combination argument" (Staines 1974) that design flaws may be self-canceling (i.e., random error) across a set of studies to be synthesized (Wortman 1983). Alternatively, Jackson (1980) has noted that "congruent but invalid findings can occur if one or more methodological flaws are common to all studies" (p. 447). If that is the case, then estimates of the bias in the overall effect size are developed where possible. Several examples of this approach to meta-analysis in both the medical and social sciences will be provided.

The objective of Chalmers' system has been to provide an overall index of quality rather than the estimation of bias. This is true for both individual and meta-analytic studies. While it may prove useful in comparing syntheses (compare Berk & Chalmers 1981, p. 395), it can conceal the presence of systematic bias that pervades the individual studies included in a meta-analysis, even if the synthesis has a high quality index. For example, all the randomized studies included in a synthesis of coronary-artery bypass graft surgery were well done, with a single exception; they all contained a substantial and systematic amount of differential subject attrition (Wortman & Yeaton 1987).

However, this should not deter one from using the features proposed by Chalmers to assess research quality. Although this chapter uses the terminology of the Campbell system, both approaches have much to recommend them. The reader should feel free to be eclectic

in using both of them. Both systems are similar in many respects, as will be discussed below. Where there are differences the terminology used by Chalmers will be cited.

## 3. DEFINING RESEARCH QUALITY

### 3.1 The Validity Framework

The design features developed by Campbell and his collaborators have evolved into a taxonomy containing four distinct categories comprising 33 separate threats to validity. Originally, Campbell and Stanley (1966) proposed just two categories: "internal" and "external" validity. Internal validity is defined as the truthfulness "with which statements can be made about whether there is a causal relationship from one variable to another in the form in which the variables were manipulated or measured" (Cook & Campbell 1979, p. 38). On the other hand, external validity refers to the "approximate" truthfulness "that the presumed causal relationship can be generalized . . . across different types of persons, settings, and times" (p. 37).

In a major revision of this framework, Cook and Campbell (1979) added two additional categories: "statistical conclusion" and "construct" validity. At the same time, five new threats to internal validity were added to the original eight; two were added to external validity while three of its former four threats were placed in construct validity. Statistical conclusion validity is defined as the truthfulness of "conclusions about covariation" between "presumed independent and dependent variables" (Cook & Campbell 1979, p. 37). "Construct validity of putative causes and effects" refers to the approximate truthfulness with which one "can make generalizations about higher-order constructs from research operations" (p. 38).

Statistical conclusion validity consists of seven threats that impair the data analysis and lead (in at least five cases) to null results. Construct validity, on the other hand, consists of ten threats that confound cause and effect variables through problems with their measures. The confounding or confusion occurs when the measures of treatment (i.e., cause) or effect have more than one interpretation, in terms of either other meaningful constructs (e.g., "interaction of different treatments") or other methodological "nuisance factors" (see section 4.2).

## 3.2 Quality = Relevance + Acceptability

**3.2.1 Relevance** Bryant and Wortman (1984) employed the four categories of the Campbell validity framework as "criteria" or a "protocol" (Sacks et al. 1987) for excluding or including studies in a meta-analysis on the effects of desegregation on black achievement. Construct and external validity were used to determine whether a particular study satisfied the meta-analyst's hypothesis with respect to the cause, effect(s), participants, time period, and location. In this case, the synthesis examined the effect of desegregation (i.e., construct of cause) on achievement (i.e., construct of effect) among blacks (i.e., participants) after the 1954 Supreme Court decision outlawing *de jure* segregation (i.e., time period) in U.S. public schools (i.e., location). The first two criteria representing the hypothetical variables relate to construct validity, and the last three criteria are relevant to external validity. If a study met these criteria, it was considered "relevant" for inclusion in the meta-analysis.

A significant, but neglected, part of construct validity is its concern with disconfirming or "falsifying" other theories. Research synthesis is ideally suited for examining the "process of falsification [by] putting our theories into competition with each other" (Cook & Campbell 1979, p. 31). For example, Loher et al. (1985) conducted a meta-analysis to assess a theory relating job characteristics to job satisfaction. Only studies employing the theory-derived measure of job characteristics were included. The synthesis revealed an interaction effect (Light 1984) leading to a proposed modification of the theory (i.e., it was partially falsified).

Similarly, research synthesis can also indicate which operational definition of a theoretical construct is appropriate. Such "subgroup analyses" are viewed as a "quality feature" of synthesis (Sacks et al. 1987). Booth-Kewley and Friedman (1987) conducted a meta-analysis examining the relationship of the Type A behavior pattern and coronary heart disease (CHD). They found that one of two commonly used methods of assessing Type A (i.e., the structured interview diagnosis) was "clearly superior" as a predictor of CHD. The (predictive) validity of this finding was supported in a subsequent meta-analysis employing a different set of methodological exclusion/inclusion criteria (Matthews 1988).

Theoretical considerations are obviously very "relevant" to the proper conduct and quality of research synthesis. Such confirmatory meta-analyses can play a vital role in our understanding of important phenomena.

If either Loher et al. (1985) or Booth-Kewley and Friedman (1987) had not been aware of these important construct validity issues, meaningful findings would have been missed. This has been referred to as "the apples and oranges problem" (Glass, McGaw & Smith 1981) because it confounds constructs. However, Yeaton and Wortman (1992) contend that creating additional strata (i.e., for multiple theories) can adversely affect "the reliability of measures" by creating "data-extraction bias" (see Sacks et al. 1987; and Chapter 11) in the coding process. Fortunately, the approach used by Loher et al. (1985) focused on a single theory, thereby avoiding this coding problem.

**3.2.2 Acceptability** Once the construct and external validity categories are used to determine the set of eligible studies that are relevant to the synthesis, Bryant and Wortman (1984) apply the remaining two categories—internal and statistical conclusion validity—to assess the "acceptability" of the remaining studies for inclusion in the meta-analysis. For example, while Glass (1978) expressed "regret" at not including the "pre-experimental", "one-group pretest-posttest design" studies (compare Campbell & Stanley 1966, p. 8), this design has so many threats to internal validity as to more than justify its omission from the psychotherapy meta-analysis. For these reasons, Cook and Campbell (1979) advise "persons considering the use of this design [to] hesitate before resorting to it" (p. 103). In fact, the studies employing this design in the desegregation synthesis produced an effect size estimate over six times larger ($p < .01$) than those of the best-designed studies (Wortman & Bryant 1985, p. 304). Thus, such weak pre-experimental designs that are subject to numerous threats to internal validity probably should be excluded from a meta-analysis, as Mansfield and Busse (1977) recommended.

Studies will also be unacceptable because of problems related to statistical conclusion validity. For example, they may be excluded because of inappropriate statistical tests (that cannot be corrected by the meta-analyst) and inappropriate grouping (i.e., combining grade levels) or inappropriate comparisons in the analyses (i.e., the use of national norms instead of a control group). On the other hand, low statistical power is not a problem for synthesis since only the actual statistics (i.e., means, standard deviations, or inferential test results), and not the significance levels, are used.

The absence of statistical information needed to calculate an effect size is the most common statistical conclusion validity problem. While technically a problem in reporting quality (compare DerSimonian et al. 1982), it does impair the ability to detect covariation and is thus mentioned under statistical conclusion validity. In some cases, the omission of such information may jeopardize the entire synthesis.

For example, the Loher et al. (1985) study relating job characteristics to job satisfaction involved the synthesis of correlations using the procedures of Hunter, Schmidt, and Jackson (1982). The analysis requires the removal of a number of "statistical artifacts" such as measurement and sampling error. The correction for measurement error is derived from the reported reliabilities of the predictor and criterion variables. If such information is completely unavailable, then this artifact cannot be removed and the synthesist will be unable to determine if a theoretical "moderator" variable is needed.

Fortunately, such information does not have to be reported in every study; Loher et al. found sufficient reporting of the reliabilities to employ the Hunter, Schmidt, and Jackson (1982) "interactive formula" to obtain an estimate of the variance of the correlation parameters corrected for unreliability. If "substantial" variance remains after these corrections, then theoretically derived subgroup analyses are conducted. In Loher et al., one stratum or level of the theoretical variable accounted for the remaining unexplained variation, but it did not in the other strata.

The sequential application of the "relevance" and "acceptability" criteria thus use Campbell's validity framework to define the set of studies to be included in a research synthesis. In the Wortman and Bryant (1985) desegregation meta-analysis, the application of the "relevance" and "acceptability" criteria resulted in the exclusion of 46 and 80 studies, respectively, out of an original set of 157 retrieved studies. These criteria thus eliminated 80 percent of the studies. Moreover, an expert panel recommended even more stringent methodological criteria (i.e., only controlled studies) that excluded 13 of the remaining 31 studies from the meta-analysis (Wortman & Bryant 1985, p. 303).

The specificity or scope of the hypothesis will determine the number of studies included and excluded (Cooper 1982). The final desegregation meta-analysis resulted in the inclusion of 19 studies (since a previously rejected study was added by the expert panel), or 12.1 percent of the original sample. Similarly, Tabak et al. (1991) applied these same two criteria to a meta-analysis of "patient education for preventive health services." From 571 citations only 171 were deemed relevant and 62 acceptable, or only 10.9 percent of the total citations.

Both these examples indicate that few studies will be found worthy of including in many meta-analyses, and in some instances there may be too few studies to synthesize (compare Berk & Chalmers 1981). In either case, Sacks et al. (1987) recommend that the synthesist report both the "list of trials analyzed and log of rejected trials."

## 4. RESEARCH QUALITY AS THE ASSESSMENT OF BIAS

The validity framework provides a useful approach to the first step in the triage strategy proposed by Mansfield and Busse (1977). However, once studies are excluded, it is still necessary to assess the quality of the remaining studies (Jackson 1980). Mansfield and Busse (1977) recommend that they be designated either well-designed or poorly designed, as the final two steps in their triage strategy to assess methodological quality. To accomplish this, the various designs themselves must be coded.

A number of meta-analyses have directly tested the Mansfield and Busse design-effect hypothesis (Wortman 1992). For example, both Devine and Cook (1983) and Wortman and Yeaton (1983) compared randomized or true experiments with nonrandomized, quasi-experiments and found a similar design-effect. In each case, designs that used nonrandom assignment overestimated the effect by at least one third (i.e., .44 vs. .33, p level not reported, and .62 vs. .44, $p < .05$, for nonrandom versus random assignment in the two respective meta-analyses). It should be noted, however, that systematic bias in quasi-experiments can also underestimate effects (compare results for very low birth weight infants in Ozminkowski, Wortman, and Roloff 1988).

It is also possible that a single threat to validity pervades even the randomized studies and systematically biases the estimate of effect (as will be discussed below). In the critical category of internal validity, there are five threats (e.g., "mortality" or "withdrawals") that are not eliminated by random assignment.

The Campbell and Chalmers typologies noted above have been developed and used to provide a more precise coding of design features. The specific elements of each framework are described in the remainder of this section.

### 4.1 Two Systems for Detecting Potential Bias

The features or threats to validity developed by Campbell and Chalmers and their associates (Cook & Campbell 1979; Chalmers et al. 1981) are described in Table

**Table 8.1 Two Frameworks for Describing Design Features**

| Cook & Campbell (1979) | Chalmers et al. (1981) | Definition |
| --- | --- | --- |
| 1. Inadequate preoperational explication of constructs | Description of therapeutic regimens<br>Description of placebo | Adequacy of the definition of the cause and effect variables and their associated measures |
| 2. Mono-operation bias | | A single measure of cause and effect constructs |
| 3. Mono-method bias | | Cause *or* effects measures presented the same way |
| 4. Hypothesis-guessing within experimental conditions | Blinding of patients<br>Testing of blinding | Subjects guess how the experimenters expected them to behave |
| 5. Evaluation apprehension | | Subjects try to obtain a favorable personal evaluation |
| 6. Experimenter expectancies | Randomization blinding<br>Blinding of physicians as to therapy received | Experimenters' knowledge of the hypothesis can affect subject assignment or bias the data obtained |
| 7. Confounding constructs and levels of constructs | Biological equivalent | Different levels of cause-effect variables not measured (e.g., no dose-response) |
| 8. Interaction of different treatments | Description of therapeutic regimens | Respondents experience more than one treatment |
| 9. Interaction of testing and treatment | | Pretest sensitization will limit the generalizability of results |
| 10. Restricted generalizability across constructs | | Related constructs of effect are not measured |
| 11. Interaction of selection and treatment | Retrospective analyses | Generalization of results to other groups of people |
| 12. Interaction of setting and treatment | Source of patients<br>Country | Generalization of results to other settings or locations |
| 13. Interaction of history and treatment | Dates of starting and stopping accession | Generalization of results to other time periods |
| 14. History | | External event between pretest and posttest that affects results |
| 15. Maturation | | Changes in subjects between pretest and posttest that affect results |
| 16. Testing | | Changes in posttest due to pretest |
| 17. Instrumentation | | Change in measure between pretest and posttest that affects results |
| 18. Statistical regression | | Results due to selection of extreme scorers on an unreliable pretest similar to posttest |
| 19. Selection | Selection description | Initial differences between treated and controls account for results |
| 20. Mortality | Withdrawals after randomization | Loss of subjects after the study begins that can account for results |
| 21. Interactions with selection | Distribution of pretreatment variables | Initial subject differences combined with other factors such as maturation can account for results |
| 22. Ambiguity about the direction of causal influence | | Inability to separate cause and effect common in cross-sectional and some retrospective studies |
| 23. Diffusion or imitation of treatments | | Control subjects have access to the treatment or one similar to it |

**Table 8.1** (*Continued*)

| Cook & Campbell (1979) | Chalmers et al. (1981) | Definition |
|---|---|---|
| 24. Compensatory equalization of treatments | | Extra resources provided to control subjects similar to treatment |
| 25. Compensatory rivalry by respondents receiving less desirable treatments | | When controls compare themselves with those treated and are motivated to do as well |
| 26. Resentful demoralization of respondents receiving less desirable treatments | | When controls compare themselves with those treated and feel so helpless or deprived that they do poorly |
| 27. Low statistical power | Sizing the study Posterior B estimates of observed difference for negative trials | Too few subjects to detect a difference |
| 28. Violated assumptions of statistical tests | Appropriate statistical analysis | Inappropriate use of statistics |
| 29. Fishing and error rate problem | The problem of multiple looks | Performing multiple analyses without adjusting the significance level or using sequential designs |
| 30. The reliability of measures | | Amount of error in the outcome or dependent measures |
| 31. The reliability of treatment implementation | Compliance | Amount of error in the treatment |
| 32. Random irrelevancies in the experimental setting | | Amount of error in the experimental setting other than treatment |
| 33. Random heterogeneity of respondents | Ranges of patient characteristics | Variation in subjects can affect results |

8.1. Threats 1–10 deal with construct validity; 11–13 with external validity; 14–26 with internal validity; and 27–33 with statistical conclusion validity. Most of the features of the Chalmers framework fall into the construct and statistical conclusion validity categories. In fact, the framework can be viewed as a more detailed subset of the Campbell threats-to-validity approach.

Chalmers' system provides much more detail on the features concerning "blinding" in construct validity and "power" in statistical conclusion validity. For example, Chalmers et al. (1981) propose five separate features dealing with blinding, including "blinding the statistician." One form of this triple blinding is achieved by "differential photocopying" of the methods section separated from the results and discussion sections of each study. The separate methods sections are then coded first in order to minimize "data-extraction bias" (Sacks et al. 1987), which can affect "the reliability of the measures" (see Table 8.1). This is a useful methodological tactic to consider and is essential when the meta-analyst shares the same type of bias as the experimenter in an original study.

## 4.2 The Threats-to-Validity Approach: An Example

One of the earliest and best examples of the threats-to-validity approach can be found in the meta-analysis of the "effects of psychoeducational interventions on length of post-surgical hospital stay" (Devine & Cook 1983). Research quality was assessed by examining six plausible rival hypotheses or "alternative explanations" that could account for the effects observed. These six alternative explanations and their interpretations within the validity framework are presented in Table 8.2.

The first two plausible alternative explanations deal with the construct validity of the studies. Devine and Cook (1983) reported an effect size estimate of .42 for those 12 studies in which the physician was "explicitly" blinded compared with an effect size of .33 where

**Table 8.2 An Example of the Threats-to-Validity Approach**

| Category | Threat | Description |
|---|---|---|
| Construct | Experimenter expectancies | Physician blinding |
| Construct | Hypothesis guessing within experimental conditions | Hawthorne effect |
| External | Treatment X selection | Publication bias |
| External | Treatment X history | Floor effect |
| Internal | Mortality | Attrition |
| Statistical conclusion | The reliability of treatment implementation | Domains of content |

SOURCE: Adapted from Devine and Cook (1983).

blinding was "questionable." An identical effect size of .42 was obtained from the nine studies employing a placebo condition to control for the attention patients received (i.e., the "Hawthorne effect") compared with the overall effect size of .36 for comparisons using the entire sample of 39 usable studies. Since both of these findings were also comparable to the randomized studies considered high on internal validity (i.e., an effect size of .42; see discussion below on attrition) and were in the opposite direction to predictions (i.e., effects should be larger when the physicians and patients were not blinded), these threats were considered implausible.

The next two potential threats deal with external validity or the generalizability of the findings. The first of these focuses on one of the most serious threats to the validity of a meta-analysis: publication bias. Devine and Cook (1983) describe a "rigorous search" to locate unpublished as well as published studies that included a mail survey of accredited nursing programs. Of the 49 studies relevant to their meta-analysis, 23 were unpublished dissertations or master's theses. The results were consistent with other reports (Cooper 1984, p. 42) showing a higher effect size for published as opposed to unpublished studies (i.e., .41 vs. .31).

The second external validity threat concerns the stability of the results over time (i.e., publication date). For three of the four time periods examined by Devine and Cook (1983) the results were nearly identical (i.e., either .42 or .43). The most recent time period yielded an anomalous −.21, but was based on only four studies and was "confounded by differences in the nature of psychoeducational intervention" (discussed below). Such temporal changes in the "strength" of the treatment (Sechrest et al. 1979) or "confounding constructs and

levels of constructs" are quite common and underline the importance of examining the treatment or independent variables carefully over time (compare Wortman & Yeaton 1987, p. 518).

The last two potential alternative explanations are from the remaining validity categories—internal and statistical conclusion validity, respectively. In addition to the "treatment assignment" (Sacks et al. 1987) or design analysis (random vs. nonrandom that produced effect sizes of .33 and .44, respectively), the amount of attrition was considered in a global assessment of internal validity. Randomized studies that were low in both overall (i.e., 15 percent) and differential (i.e., 10 percent) attrition were considered to have "higher" internal validity. These studies had an effect size of .42 compared with an effect size of .26 for those judged "lower" in internal validity.

The final threat examined concerns the "integrity" of the treatment (Sechrest et al. 1979). Devine and Cook (1983) coded each intervention along three broad dimensions consisting of information, skills training, and psychosocial support. They found that treatments had to include or implement at least two of these "domains of content" to be effective. The effect sizes were .06, .51, and .32 for one, two, or three content domains, respectively.

Of the six plausible rival hypotheses considered, Devine and Cook (1983) concluded that none invalidate the overall result that "it is possible that [psychoeducational] interventions do shorten hospital stay" (p. 271). Nevertheless, it is also clear that three of the threats do influence and potentially bias the results (i.e., publication bias, attrition, and domains of content). A precise estimate of this bias would be desirable given the authors' conclusion that none of these threats "diminish the policy relevance of these findings."

One approach is to select only the subset of studies that are high in methodological quality, such as those whose designs included random assignment. This is the tactic used by Landman and Dawes (1982) in their reanalysis of the seminal meta-analysis of psychotherapy (Smith & Glass 1977). However, many meta-analysts will be unable to employ this technique owing to either small sample sizes or problems affecting the validity of the randomized experiments. For example, the Devine and Cook (1983) meta-analysis was based on a set of 39 studies reporting length of hospital stay. These studies were drawn from a larger population of 105 articles containing a variety of different outcome measures (Devine 1984). The tactic of selecting only the high-quality studies yielded only four out of the 105 studies (Devine 1984, p. 57). For those cases in which there are insufficient high-quality, "well-designed" studies, multivariate statistical analyses may be appropriate (see Chapter 23).

## 4.3 Quality = Relevance + Acceptability − Bias

The final component in judging research quality thus involves the estimation of the bias introduced by plausible validity threats. The estimation of this bias, if possible, will provide a less-biased estimate of the effect size. While such threats are common to quasi-experiments, they are also possible in randomized or true experiments, as was noted earlier. This section will demonstrate how bias can be estimated in meta-analyses of both randomized and quasi-experiments. The approach is illustrated through a series of specific examples drawn from the meta-analytic literature.

**4.3.1 Estimating bias in randomized studies** While randomized experiments are considered to be the "gold standard" of research quality (Chalmers et al. 1987), they are not immune from all threats to validity. In particular, their validity can be seriously impaired by "mortality" or attrition, as was noted above. Moreover, this threat may be both so severe and so widespread as to leave none of the "high-quality" studies unaffected. Such a problem confronted the researchers conducting a meta-analysis of coronary-artery bypass surgery (or CABGS), a well-known surgical procedure to reroute blood around the heart's clogged arteries (Wortman & Yeaton 1983).

The eight randomized clinical trials examining CABGS all suffered from an average 21 percent crossover rate among patients moving from the (medical) control to the (surgical) experimental group. This resulted in a double threat to internal validity consisting of attrition followed by "diffusion." In addition, the crossover patients were typically those most severely ill. These two validity threats thus act to increase the survival rate of the medical controls and to lower that of the CABGS group. As a consequence of this systematic bias, the effectiveness of the surgery will be underestimated.

While it was not possible to determine the exact amount of bias introduced by the patient attrition, it was possible to estimate its size through one simplifying assumption—that only the sickest medical patients crossed over (i.e., those in the tail of the distribution). Based on this reasonable assumption (compare Murphy et al. 1977), Yeaton, Wortman, and Langberg (1983) were able to provide a general solution to the amount of bias in an effect size introduced by a given rate of attrition. For the CABGS meta-analysis the amount of bias was 36 percent, enough to move the result from borderline to clearly beneficial (Wortman 1992). This is an example of the sensitivity analysis (i.e., "varying methods") recommended by Sacks et al. (1987).

**4.3.2 Estimating bias in quasi-experiments** In many research domains there will be no randomized experiments. The meta-analyst can either avoid such areas of research or cope with the problems posed by such quasi-experimental studies. Often the social pressures for informed policy action are so great that it is not possible to ignore these problems (compare Agency for Health Care Policy and Research 1991). This has been the case with school desegregation, carotid endarterectomy, and neonatal intensive care units (NICUs).

For such nonrandomized quasi-experiments the major problem is often the nonequivalence in the "selection" of participants in these studies and the interactions associated with these selection differences. This problem is the mirror image of the attrition threat that can undermine randomized experiments. Three methodological tactics for dealing with selection and some related threats are described in the remainder of this section.

One approach to reducing selection bias is simply to subtract the pretest effect size from the posttest effect size in those studies using such a "nonequivalent control group design" with a pretest and no-treatment control group (Cook & Campbell 1979, pp. 103–108). Wortman and Bryant (1985) employed such a "pretest-adjusted meta-analysis" in synthesizing the quasi-experimental literature dealing with the effect of school desegregation on black achievement. They found that selection bias alone accounted for half of the observed effect (i.e., there was a substantial initial bias found at pretest favoring desegregated students). Studies without pretests or ones that used matching produced comparable effect sizes. Moreover, related problems caused by selection, such as interactions with maturation or regression, were found to be minor.

A second approach to dealing with selection bias involves the use of "pattern matching" (Campbell 1975) to detect "interactions with selection" that are theory-based. Selection-maturation is one of the most common of these interactions. This problem occurs when experimental and control group members are maturing or, in the health area, deteriorating at different rates. If this interaction occurs only within certain maturational levels, then the meta-analyst may be able to predict and match this pattern.

This pattern-matching tactic was employed by Ozminkowski, Wortman, and Roloff (1988) in a meta-analysis of the effect of NICUs on neonatal survival. A differential pattern of selection-maturation interactions was predicted in the lowest and highest birth weight categories, but not in the two middle categories. Thus, selection would bias the results against finding a benefit for NICUs in the lowest birth weight category, whereas the opposite form of selection bias was hypothesized to occur in the highest birth weight category. The pattern of results matched these predictions.

A third methodological tactic can be employed in the synthesis of studies lacking control groups. In this case, important changes in the treatment can be used to create a comparison group. This tactic improves "the reliability of treatment implementation" in statistical conclusion validity. For example, the earlier discussion of the Devine and Cook (1983) meta-analysis noted that the effect depended on there being at least two "domains of content" in the psychoeducational treatment.

This approach was used by Langenbrunner et al. (in press) in a "quantitative synthesis" of carotid endarterectomy (CE) for asymptomatic patients. These investigators retrieved 29 usable studies, of which 28 were uncontrolled. Nearly all of the 13 most recent studies (from 1985 to 1988) employed a new surgical technique that was not widely used in earlier studies. Using a variety of regression models to predict both mortality and morbidity, Langenbrunner et al. found that the change in surgical technique was the only consistent, statistically significant variable. The new surgical method lowered both mortality and morbidity.

These results are provocative, but far from conclu-

sive. They provide another example of an exploratory research synthesis. Such results could be used to improve the construct validity (i.e., the operational definition of CE surgery) in future clinical trials. Unfortunately, this was not done in the randomized trials of CE recently conducted.

## 4.4 Summary: Coding for Quality Assessment

A number of steps have been described that must be taken so that quality can be assessed. These include

1. considering competing theories and measures of theoretical constructs;

2. analyzing for publication bias;

3. creating strata for design types and associated threats to internal validity; and

4. noting important sources of potential heterogeneity such as study participants, setting, time periods, and reliability of measures.

A sample coding scheme coordinated with these four steps is described in Table 8.3 (but also see Figure 10.1, items 2, 22–25, and 27–29). Where applicable, the item codes are drawn from Devine (1984), Wortman and Bryant (1985), and Wortman and Yeaton (1987). The coding scheme captures the quality features (Sacks et al. 1987) of "subgroup analyses" (for theory), "literature search" with respect to "publication bias," "treatment assignment" for design effects, and "measurement" as well as "ranges of patient characteristics, diagnoses, and treatments" for assessing generalizability and heterogeneity (compare DerSimonian & Laird 1986).

## 5. CONCLUSION

In conclusion, six points are worth noting. First, not all of the studies retrieved will be included in a meta-analysis. The validity framework developed by Campbell and his associates provides a useful set of entry criteria or "protocol" for making a precise, objective decision on which studies to exclude and which ones to include in the final meta-analysis. As noted above, these or other "criteria" should be specified along with the set of studies included *and* excluded (Sacks et al. 1987).

Second, the synthesis should include at least two design types. The designs with the fewest threats to internal validity should be considered of highest quality

**Table 8.3 Partial Synthesis Coding Form**

### A. Theory

   1. Specified _____        1 = No    2 = Yes
   2. Inferred _____         1 = No    2 = Yes
   3. Name _____
      1 = Theory A _____
      2 = Theory B _____

### B. Publication Bias

   4. Retrieval from _____
      1 = Computer database (e.g., ERIC, MEDLINE)
      2 = Invisible college (e.g., peers, other experts)
      3 = Reference from other study

   5. Review process _____
      1 = Peer-reviewed
      2 = Not peer-reviewed
      3 = Not known

   6. Type _____
      1 = Journal article     4 = Master's thesis
      2 = Book or chapter    5 = Other
      3 = Doctoral dissertation

   7. Fail-safe $N$'s reported ___   1 = No   2 = Yes

### C. Design

   8. Type _____
      1 = Randomized        4 = Time series
      2 = Nonequivalent with  5 = Other _____
         pretest
      3 = Nonequivalent with
         posttest-only

   9. Control _____
      1 = No treatment     3 = 1 and 2
      2 = Placebo         4 = None

  10. Attrition (%), controls _____

  11. Attrition (%), treated _____

### D. Sources of Heterogeneity

  12. Sex of respondents, % female _____

  13. Location or setting _____
      1 = University 2 = Community 3 = Other ___

---

(e.g., randomized and nonequivalent control group designs in the bypass synthesis). In many cases, only one design type will be considered necessary as in the desegregation meta-analysis (Wortman & Bryant 1985) and Type A-CHD synthesis (Matthews 1988).

Third, the validity framework also provides a comprehensive and useful set of design features for assessing the quality of the studies included in the synthesis. These threats to validity permit a more fine-grained analysis of potential problems than broader design categories. If a design effect is detected, it may often be due to a particular threat.

Fourth, the threats-to-validity approach may allow a more precise effect size estimate to be calculated through the estimation of the bias produced by the validity problem. Such problems can occur in randomized as well as nonrandomized studies. Moreover, a careful validity analysis may allow conceptually important strata to be created in uncontrolled studies, thereby allowing some limited synthesis to be performed. Such exploratory research syntheses can be useful in developing important hypotheses for further examination under more controlled conditions (compare ISIS-2 Collaborative Group 1988, p. 357).

Fifth, one should be selective in using the validity framework. Not all threats to validity will be present in a given content domain to be synthesized. The design can indicate some critical threats to be examined such as attrition or "experimental mortality" for randomized designs and "interactions with selection" for the nonequivalent control group quasi-experimental design (compare Cook & Campbell 1979, pp. 103–112). The determination of other specific threats to be included in the coding scheme, however, must develop from a careful reading of specific studies (e.g., "diffusion" in the bypass graft studies). Often this is an iterative process that evolves as one becomes more familiar with the particular research domain.

Finally, this chapter has focused largely on the methodological problems found in the individual studies being considered for synthesis. As noted above, a global index of quality for the entire research synthesis is provided by Chalmers' system. Both the reliability of this (Wortman 1987) and other global indices (Stock et al. 1982; Yeaton & Wortman in press) have been questioned and found lacking. As was noted in section 4.4, the validity framework may provide a more satisfactory approach to the global assessment of quality.

Each of the four validity categories is associated with a major, global threat to the quality of the overall synthesis. Construct validity requires that the synthesist be aware of both competing theories and competing operational definitions of theoretical constructs. External validity requires the synthesist to address publication bias, either through an extensive literature search or calculation of a "fail-safe $n$" (or more elaborate analytic procedures; see Chapter 25). Internal validity entails the determination of whether certain threats systematically bias the results and estimates of (or adjustments for) the bias. Statistical conclusion validity involves careful attention to the types of treatments, settings, and respondents in the synthesis since they can produce "random heterogeneity" or "irrelevancies." Fortunately, all of these problems can be easily handled and checked with appropriate coding (see Table 8.3). A research synthesis that addresses all of these four potential problems would be considered high in global quality.

### Author's Note

Work on this chapter was partially supported by grant No. HS06264 from the Agency for Health Care Policy and Research.

## 6. REFERENCES

Agency for Health Care Policy and Research. (1991). *Carotid endarterectomy* (rev. ed.) (DHHS Publication No. AHCPR 91-0029). Rockville, MD: Author.

Bangert-Drowns, R. L. (1986). Review of developments in meta-analytic method. *Psychological Bulletin, 99,* 388–399.

Berk, A. A., & Chalmers, T. C. (1981). Cost and efficacy of the substitution of ambulatory for inpatient care. *New England Journal of Medicine, 304,* 393–397.

Booth-Kewley, S., & Friedman, H. S. (1987). Psychological predictors of heart disease: A quantitative review. *Psychological Bulletin, 101,* 343–362.

Bryant, F. B., & Wortman, P. M. (1984). Methodological issues in the meta-analysis of quasi-experiments. *New Directions for Program Evaluation, 24,* 5–24.

Campbell, D. T. (1975). "Degrees of freedom" and the case study. *Comparative Political Studies, 8,* 178–193.

Campbell, D. T., & Stanley, J. C. (1966). *Experimental and quasi-experimental designs for research.* Chicago: Rand McNally.

Chalmers, T. C., Berrier, J., Sacks, H. S., Levin, H., Reitman, D., & Nagalingham, R. (1987). Meta-analysis of clinical trials as a scientific discipline. II. Replicate variability and comparison of studies that agree and disagree. *Statistics in Medicine, 6,* 733–744.

Chalmers, T. C., Smith, H., Jr., Blackburn, B., Silverman, B., Schroeder, B., Reitman, D., & Ambroz, A. (1981). A method for assessing the quality of a randomized control trial. *Controlled Clinical Trials, 2,* 31–49.

Cook, T. D., & Campbell, D. T. (1979). *Quasi-experimentation: Design & analysis issues for field settings.* Boston: Houghton Mifflin.

Cooper, H. M. (1982). Scientific guidelines for conducting integrative research reviews. *Review of Educational Research, 52,* 291–302.

Cooper, H. M. (1984). *The integrative research review: A systematic approach.* Beverly Hills, CA: Sage.

DerSimonian, R., Charette, L. J., McPeek, B., & Mosteller, F. (1982). Reporting on methods in clinical trials. *New England Journal of Medicine, 306,* 1332–1337.

DerSimonian, R., & Laird, N. (1986). Meta-analysis in clinical trials. *Controlled Clinical Trials, 7,* 177–188.

Devine, E. C. (1984). Effects of psychoeducational interventions: A meta-analytic analysis of studies with surgical patients. (Unpublished doctoral dissertation, University of Illinois at Chicago, Health Sciences Center, 1983). *Dissertation Abstracts International, 44,* 3356B. (University Microfilms No. DEQ 84-04400)

Devine, E. C., & Cook, T. D. (1983). A meta-analytic analysis of effects of psychoeducational interventions on length of post-surgical hospital stay. *Nursing Research, 32,* 267–274.

Dooley, D. (1990). *Social research methods* (2nd ed.). Englewood Cliffs, NJ: Prentice-Hall.

Durlak, J. A., & Lipsey, M. W. (1991). A practitioner's guide to meta-analysis. *American Journal of Community Psychology, 19,* 291–332.

Glass, G. V. (1976). Primary, secondary, and meta-analysis. *Educational Researcher, 5,* 3–8.

Glass, G. V. (1978). Reply to Mansfield and Busse. *Educational Researcher, 7,* 3.

Glass, G. V., McGaw, B., & Smith, M. L. (1981). *Meta-analysis in social research.* Beverly Hills, CA: Sage.

Hunter, J. E., Schmidt, F. L., & Jackson, G. B. (1982). *Meta-analysis: Cumulating research findings across studies.* Beverly Hills, CA: Sage.

ISIS-2 Collaborative Group. (1988). Randomised trial of intravenous streptokinase, oral aspirin, both, or neither among 17,187 cases of suspected myocardial infarction: ISIS-2. *Lancet, ii,* 349–360.

Jackson, G. B. (1980). Methods for integrative reviews. *Review of Educational Research, 50,* 438–460.

Landman, J. T., & Dawes, R. M. (1982). Psychotherapy outcome: Smith and Glass; conclusions stand up under scrutiny. *American Psychologist, 37,* 504–516.

Langenbrunner, J. C., Wortman, P. M., Yeaton, W. H., & Holloway, J. J. (in press). Carotid endarterectomy for asymptomatic patients: Assessing results of a quantitative synthesis. *International Journal of Technology Assessment in Health Care.*

Light, R. J. (1984). Six evaluation issues that synthesis can resolve better than single studies. *New Directions for Program Evaluations, 24,* 57–73.

Loher, B. T., Noe, R. A., Moeller, N. L., & Fitzgerald, M. P. (1985). A meta-analysis of the relation of job characteristics to job satisfaction. *Journal of Applied Psychology, 70,* 280–289.

Mansfield, R. S., & Busse, T. V. (1977). Meta-analysis of research: A rejoinder to Glass. *Education Research, 6,* 3.

Matthews, K. A. (1988). Coronary heart disease and Type A behaviors: Update on and alternative to the Booth-Kewley and Friedman (1987) quantitative review. *Psychological Bulletin, 104,* 373–380.

Murphy, M. I., Hultgren, H. N., Detre, K., Thomsen, J., & Takaro, T. (1977). Special correspondence: A debate on coronary bypass. *New England Journal of Medicine, 297,* 1470.

Ozminkowski, R. J., Wortman, P. M., & Roloff, D. W. (1988). Inborn/outborn status and neonatal survival: A meta-analysis of non-randomized studies. *Statistics in Medicine, 7,* 1207–1221.

Rosenthal, R. (1979). The file-drawer problem and tolerance for null results. *Psychological Bulletin, 86,* 638–641.

Sacks, H. S., Berrier, J., Reitman, D., Ancona-Berk, V. A., & Chalmers, T. C. (1987). Meta-analyses of randomized controlled trials. *New England Journal of Medicine, 316,* 450–455.

Sechrest, L., West, S. G., Phillips, M. A., Redner, R., & Yeaton, W. H. (1979). Some neglected problems in evaluation research: Strength and integrity of treatments. In L. Sechrest et al. (Eds.), *Evaluation studies review annual* (Vol. 4) (pp. 15–60). Newbury Park, CA: Sage.

Smith, M. L., & Glass, G. V. (1977). Meta-analysis of psychotherapy outcome studies. *American Psychologist, 32,* 752–760.

Staines, G. L. (1974). The strategic combination argument. In W. Leinfellner & E. Kohler (Eds.), *Developments in the methodology of social science* (pp. 417–430). Dordecht, Holland: Reidel.

Stock, W. A., Okun, M. A., Haring, M. J., Miller, W., Kinney, C., & Ceurvorst, R. W. (1982). Rigor in data synthesis: A case study of reliability in meta-analysis. *Educational Researcher, 11,* 10–20.

Tabak, E. R., Mullen, P. D., Simons-Morton, D. G., Green, L. W., Mains, D. A., Eilat-Greenberg, S., Frankowski, R. F., & Glenday, M. C. (1991). Definition and yield of inclusion criteria for a meta-analysis of patient education studies in clinical preventive services. *Evaluation and the Health Professions, 14,* 388–411.

Wortman, P. M. (1983). Evaluation research: A methodological perspective. *Annual Review of Psychology, 34,* 223–260.

Wortman, P. M. (1987). Meta-analysis (letter to editor). *New England Journal of Medicine, 317,* 575.

Wortman, P. M. (1992). Lessons from the meta-analysis of quasi-experiments. In F. B. Bryant et al. (Eds.), *Methodological issues in applied social psychology* (pp. 65–81). New York: Plenum.

Wortman, P. M., & Bryant, F. B. (1985). School desegregation and black achievement: An integrative review. *Sociological Methods and Research, 13,* 289–324.

Wortman, P. M., & Yeaton, W. H. (1983). Synthesis of results in controlled trials of coronary artery bypass graft surgery. In R. J. Light (Ed.), *Evaluation studies review annual* (Vol. 8, pp. 536–551). Beverly Hills, CA: Sage.

Wortman, P. M., & Yeaton, W. H. (1985). Cumulating quality of life results in controlled trials of coronary artery bypass graft surgery. *Controlled Clinical Trials, 6,* 289–305.

Wortman, P. M., & Yeaton, W. H. (1987). Using research synthesis in medical technology assessment. *International Journal of Technology Assessment in Health Care, 3,* 509–522.

Yeaton, W. H., & Wortman, P. M. (in press). On the reliability of meta-analytic reviews: The role of intercoder agreement. *Evaluation Review.*

Yeaton, W. H., Wortman, P. M., & Langberg, N. (1983). Differential attrition: Estimating the effect of crossovers on the evaluation of a medical technology. *Evaluation Review, 7,* 831–840.

Yusuf, S., Collins, R., Peto, R., Furberg, C., Stampfer, M. J., Goldhaber, S. Z., & Hennekens, C. H. (1985). Intravenous and intracoronary fibrinolytic therapy in acute myocardial infarction: Overview of results on mortality, reinfarction and side-effects from 33 randomized controlled trials. *European Heart Journal, 6,* 556–585.

Cooper, H. and Hedges, L. V. (Eds.) 1994. *The Handbook of Research Synthesis*. New York: Russell Sage Foundation

# 9

# IDENTIFYING POTENTIALLY INTERESTING VARIABLES AND ANALYSIS OPPORTUNITIES

**MARK W. LIPSEY**
*Vanderbilt University*

CONTENTS

# 1. INTRODUCTION

Research synthesis relies on information that is reported in a selection of studies on a topic of interest. The purpose of this chapter is to review the types of variables often available to the synthesist and to outline the kinds of relationships that can be explored in the analysis of the data that results from coding those variables. It will identify a range of opportunities and endeavor to stimulate the synthesist's thinking about what might go into a research integration and what sorts of questions can be addressed.

## 1.1 Potentially Interesting Variables

Research synthesis revolves around one or more statistics, called effect sizes, that summarize the main findings of each study of interest. As detailed elsewhere in this volume, effect sizes come in a variety of forms—correlation coefficients, standardized differences between means, odds ratios, and so forth—depending on the nature of the quantitative study results they represent. Study results embodied in effect sizes, therefore, constitute one major category of variable in research synthesis that is sure to be of interest.

In addition to their results, however, research studies have other characteristics that may be of interest. For instance, they might be described in terms of the nature of the research designs and procedures used, the attributes of the subject samples, and various other features of the settings, personnel, activities, and circumstances involved. These characteristics taken together constitute the second major category of variables of potential concern to the research synthesist. As a group, they will be referred to as study descriptors.

## 1.2 Study Results

Whatever the nature of the issues bearing on study results, one of the first challenges the synthesist faces is the likelihood that those results will be multiple rather than singular. A given study may thus require that a number of effect sizes be coded to fully represent its results. If we define a study to mean a set of observations taken on a subject sample on one or more occasions, there are three possible dimensions of variation in study results. There may be different results for different measures, for different subsamples of people, and for different times of measurement. All of these variations

have implications for conceptualizing and coding effect sizes.

**1.2.1 Results on multiple measures** Each study in a synthesis may report results on more than one measure. These results may represent different constructs, multiple measures of the same construct, or both. A study of predictors of juvenile delinquency, for instance, might report the correlations of age, gender, school achievement, and family structure with a central delinquency measure. Each such correlation can be coded as a separate effect size. Similarly, a study of gender differences in aggression might compare males and females on physical aggression, verbal aggression, and the aggressive content of fantasies, yielding three effect sizes. Moreover, the various studies eligible for a research synthesis may differ among themselves in the type, number, and mix of measures.

The synthesist must decide what categories of measures to define and what effect sizes to code in each. The basic options are threefold. One approach would be to code effect sizes on all constructs and measures in relatively undifferentiated form. This strategy would yield, in essence, a single global category of study results. For example, the outcome measures used in research on the effectiveness of psychotherapy show little commonality from study to study. A synthesist might, for some purposes, treat all these outcomes as the same—that is, as instances of results relevant to some general construct of personal functioning. An average over all the resulting effect sizes addresses the global question of whether psychotherapy has generally positive effects on the mix of measures typical to psychotherapy research (Smith & Glass 1977).

At the other extreme, effect sizes may be coded only when they relate to a single selected construct or measure of specific interest to the synthesist. In the psychotherapy research, for instance, a synthesist might be interested in only the effects of therapy on depression as indexed by Beck's depression inventory. Only effect sizes on that measure would then be coded (Nietzel et al. 1987).

An intermediate strategy is for the synthesist to define a set of constructs or measurement categories of interest and code study results within those categories. Lewis and Vosburgh (1988), for example, distinguished 12 categories of outcome in a synthesis of the effects of kindergarten for preschool children (e.g., language, math, social-emotional development, perceptual-motor skills). These different categories of results were considered distinct and were kept separate in the coding and analysis of effect sizes.

Whether global or highly specific construct categories are defined for coding effect sizes, the synthesist is likely to find that some studies will report results on multiple measures within a given category. In such cases, one of several approaches can be taken. The synthesist can simply code and analyze effect sizes for all the measures in each study. This permits some studies to contribute more effect sizes in a category than others and potentially introduces statistical dependencies among the effect sizes. Alternatively, criteria can be developed for selecting the single most appropriate measure within each construct category and ignoring the remainder. Or multiple effect sizes within a construct category can be coded and then averaged (perhaps using a weighted average) to yield a single mean or median effect size within that category for each study. (This issue is discussed in Chapter 18.)

The most important consideration that must inform the approach a synthesist takes to the matter of study results embodied in multiple measures is the purpose of the synthesis. For some purposes the study results of interest may involve only one construct, as when synthesis of research evaluating educational innovations focuses on achievement test results. For other purposes the synthesist may be interested in a broader range of study results that involves diverse measures and constructs. Having a clear view of the purposes of a research synthesis and adopting criteria for selecting and categorizing study results consistent with those purposes are fundamental requirements of good synthesis. These steps define the effect sizes the synthesist will be able to analyze and, hence, shape the potential findings of the synthesis itself.

**1.2.2 Results for subsamples** In addition to overall results, many studies within a synthesis may report breakdowns for one or more subject subsamples. For example, a validation study of a personnel selection test might report test-criterion correlations for different industries, or a study of the effects of drug counseling for teenagers might report results separately for males and females. Coding effect sizes for each subsample potentially permits a more discriminating analysis of the relationship between subject characteristics and study results than can be obtained from overall study results alone.

Two considerations bear on the potential utility of effect sizes from subsamples in a research synthesis.

First, a given subject breakdown must be reported widely enough to yield a sufficient number of effect sizes to permit meaningful analysis. If most studies do not report results separately for, say, males and females, there is little utility in coding effect sizes for these subsamples. (What constitutes a sufficient number of effect sizes to analyze is a complex issue that depends on the nature of the studies and the reasons for conducting the synthesis.) Second, of course, the variable distinguishing subsamples must represent a dimension of potential interest to the synthesist. Effect sizes computed separately for male and female subsamples, for instance, will be of concern only if there are theoretical, practical, or exploratory reasons to examine whether gender moderates the magnitude of effects.

As with effect sizes from multiple measures within a single study, effect sizes for multiple subsamples within a study may pose issues of statistical dependency. Statistical independence may be compromised, for instance, if an analysis is based on subsamples that are not mutually exclusive—that is, subsamples that share subjects. While the female subsample in a breakdown by gender would not share subjects with the male subsample, it would almost certainly share subjects with the oldest subsample of a breakdown by age. In addition, however, any feature shared in common by subsamples within a study—for example, being studied by the same investigator—can introduce statistical dependencies into the effect sizes computed for those subsamples. Analysis of effect sizes based on subsamples, therefore, must be treated like any analysis that uses more than one effect size from each study and thus potentially violates assumptions of statistical independence (see Chapter 22).

**1.2.3 Results measured at different times** Many studies may report findings on the same variables measured at different times. For example, a study of the effects of a smoking cessation program might report the outcome immediately after treatment and at six-month and one-year follow-ups. Moreover, such results might be reported both for the overall subject sample and for various subsamples. Such time-series information potentially permits an interesting analysis of temporal patterns in outcome—decay curves for the persistence of treatment effects, for example.

As with effect sizes for subsamples, the synthesist must determine whether follow-up results are reported widely enough to yield sufficient data to be worth analyzing. Even in favorable circumstances, only a portion of the studies in a synthesis is likely to provide measures at different points in time. A related problem is that the intervals between times of measurement may vary widely from study to study. If this occurs, one approach is for the synthesist to establish broad categories for follow-up periods and code each result in the category it most closely fits. Another approach is to code the time of measurement for each result as an interval from some common reference point—for instance, the termination of treatment. The synthesist can then analyze the functional relationship between the effect size and the amount of time that has passed since the completion of treatment.

Since the subjects at Time 1 will be much the same (less attrition) as those at follow-up Time 2, the effect sizes for these different occasions will not be statistically independent. As with multiple measures or overlapping subsamples, these effect sizes cannot be included together in an analysis that assumes independent data points unless special adjustments are made.

**1.2.4 The array of study results** As the previous discussion indicates, the quantitative results from a study selected for synthesis may be reported for multiple constructs, for multiple measures of each construct, for the total subject sample, for various subsamples, and for multiple times of measurement. In order to effectively represent key study results and support interesting analyses, the synthesist must establish conceptual categories for each of these dimensions. These categories will group those effect sizes judged to be substantially similar for the purposes of the synthesis, differentiate those believed to be importantly different, and ignore those judged to be irrelevant or uninteresting. Once these categories are developed, it should be possible to classify each effect size that can be coded from any study according to the type of construct, subsample, and time of measurement it represents. When a sufficient number of studies yield comparable effect sizes, that set of results can be separately analyzed. Some studies will contribute only a single effect size (one measure, one sample, one time) to the synthesis. Others will report more differentiated results and may yield a number of useful effect sizes.

It follows that different studies may provide effect sizes for different analyses on different categories of effect sizes. Any analysis based on effect sizes from only a subset of the studies under investigation raises a question of the generalizability of the findings to the entire set, since the studies in that subset may have distinctive characteristics. For instance, in a synthesis of the correlates of effective job performance the subset of studies that break out results by age groups might be those that are conducted in large corporations. What is learned from them about age differences might not apply to employees of small businesses. Studies that report differentiated results, nonetheless, offer the synthesist the opportunity to conduct more probing analyses of the issues of interest. Including such differentiation in a research synthesis can add rich and useful detail to its findings.

## 1.3 Study Descriptors

Whatever the set of effect sizes under investigation, it is often of interest to examine the characteristics of the studies that yield those results. To accomplish this, the synthesist must identify and code information from each study about the particulars of its subjects, methods, treatments, and the like. Research synthesists have shown considerable diversity and ingenuity in the study characteristics they have coded and in the coding schemes they have used. Specific discussion of the development, application, and validation of coding schemes for research synthesis is provided in Chapter 10. What will be reviewed here are the general types of study descriptors that the synthesist might consider in anticipation of conducting certain interesting analyses on the resulting data.

To provide a rudimentary conceptual framework for study descriptors, we first assume that study results are determined conjointly by the nature of the substantive phenomenon under investigation and the nature of the methods used to study it. The variant of the phenomenon selected for study and the particular methods applied, in turn, may be influenced by such factors as the characteristics of the researcher and the research sponsorship and context. These will be labeled extrinsic factors since they are extrinsic to the substantive and methodological factors assumed to directly shape study results. Finally, we recognize that the actual results and characteristics of a study must be fully and accurately reported to be validly coded in a synthesis. Various aspects of study reporting thus constitute a second type of extrinsic factor since they, too, may be associated with study results, as operationalized in a synthesis, but are not assumed to directly shape those results.

This scheme, while somewhat crude, serves to identify four general categories of study descriptor that may interest the synthesist. The most important of these, of course, is the set of features substantively pertinent to characterizing the phenomenon under investigation. In this category are such matters as the nature of the treatment provided; the characteristics of the subjects used; the cultural, geographical, or temporal setting; and those other influences that might mediate or moderate the events or relationships under study. It is these variables that permit the synthesist to identify differences among studies in the substantive characteristics of the situations they investigate that may account for differences in their results. From such information the synthesist may be able to determine that one treatment variation is more effective than another, that a relationship holds for certain types of subjects or circumstances but not for others, or that there is a developmental sequence that yields different results at different time periods. Findings such as these, of course, result in better understanding of the nature of the phenomenon under study in the selected body of research and are the objective of most syntheses.

Those study characteristics not related to the substantive aspects of the phenomenon involve various possible sources of distortion, bias, or artifact in study results as they are operationalized in the original research or in the coding for the synthesis. The most important study features of this sort represent methodological or procedural aspects of the manner in which the studies were actually conducted. These include variations in the designs, research procedures, quality of measures, and forms of data analysis that might yield different study results even if every study were investigating exactly the same phenomenon. A synthesist may be interested in examining the influence of method variables for two reasons. First, analysis of the relationships between method choices and study results provides useful information about which aspects of research procedures make the most difference and, hence, should be most carefully selected by researchers. Second, method differences confound substantive comparisons among study results and must be coded to enable the use of statistical controls in such analyses.

Factors extrinsic to both the substantive phenomenon and the research methods include characteristics of the researcher (e.g., gender, disciplinary affiliation), research circumstances (e.g., nature of study sponsorship), and reporting (e.g., form of publication) that are not believed to directly shape study results but nonetheless may be correlated with coded effect sizes. Whether a researcher is a psychologist or a sociologist, for in-

stance, should not itself directly determine study results. Disciplinary affiliation may, however, influence methodological practices or the selection of variants of the phenomenon to study, which, in turn, could affect study results.

Another type of extrinsic factor involves those aspects of the reporting of study methods and results that might yield different values in the synthesist's coding even if all studies were investigating the same phenomenon with the same methods. For example, studies may not report important details of the procedures, measures, treatments, or results. This requires the coder to engage in guesswork or even to record missing values on items that, with better reporting, could be coded accurately. Insufficiencies in the information reported in a study, therefore, may influence the effect sizes coded or the representation of substantive and methodological features closely related to effect sizes, even though they do not determine actual study effects.

A synthesist who desires a full description of study characteristics will want to make some effort to identify and code all those factors thought to be potentially related to study results as operationalized in synthesis. This will mean giving attention to the substantive features of the studies, to their methodological and procedural arrangements, to the characteristics of researchers and the research circumstances, to certain aspects of study reporting, and to the synthesist's coding of what is reported.

From a practical perspective, the decision about what specific study characteristics to code will have to reconcile two competing considerations. First, synthesis provides a service by documenting in detail the nature of the body of research bearing on a given issue. This consideration motivates a coding of a broad range of study characteristics for descriptive purposes. On the other hand, many codable features of studies have limited value for anything but descriptive purposes. Some potentially interesting study characteristics, for example, may not be widely reported in the literature or may show little variation from study to study and thus have limited value for analysis. Finally, of course, some study characteristics will simply not be germane to the synthesist's purposes (though it is very difficult to specify a priori what will prove relevant and what will not). Documenting study characteristics that are poorly reported, lacking in variation, or irrelevant to present purposes surely has some value, as the next section of this chapter will argue. However, given the time-consuming and expensive nature of coding in research synthesis, the synthesist inevitably must find some balance between coding broadly for descriptive purposes and coding narrowly around the specific target issues of the particular synthesis.

## 2. ANALYSIS OPPORTUNITIES

A researcher embarks on synthesis to answer certain questions. Information pertinent to those questions will emerge from statistical analysis of the data developed by systematically coding the results and characteristics of the studies under consideration. There are, of course, many technical issues involved in such statistical analysis; they are discussed elsewhere in this volume. For present purposes it is more important to obtain some overview of the various types of analysis and the kinds of information they might yield. With such an overview in mind, the synthesist should be in a better position to know what sorts of questions might be answered by synthesis and what data must be coded to address those questions.

Four generic forms of analysis are outlined here. The first, descriptive analysis, uses the coded variables to provide an overall picture of the nature of the research literature included in the synthesis. The other three forms of analysis examine relationships among coded variables. As set out above, variables coded in a synthesis can be divided into those that describe study results (effect sizes) and those that describe study characteristics (study descriptors). Three general possibilities emerge from this scheme: (a) analysis of the relationships among study descriptors, (b) analysis of the relationships between effect sizes and study descriptors, and (c) analysis of the relationships among study effect sizes.

### 2.1 Descriptive Analysis

By its nature research synthesis involves the collection of information describing the key results and various important attributes of the studies under investigation. Descriptive analysis of these data can provide a valuable picture of the nature of a research literature, in terms of both modal characteristics and the distributions of the various features. It can help identify the issues that have already been sufficiently studied and those gaps in the literature that need additional study. It can also highlight common methodological practices and provide a basis for assessing the areas in which improvement is warranted. The descriptive information provided by a syn-

thesis deals with either study effect sizes or study descriptors. Each of these is considered in turn in the following sections.

**2.1.1 Study results** Descriptive information about study results is almost universally reported in research synthesis. The central information, of course, is the distribution of effect sizes across studies. As noted earlier, there may be numerous categories of effect sizes; correspondingly, there may be numerous effect size distributions to describe and compare. (Chapters 16 and 17 explain how to obtain proper means and variances for these distributions, taking into consideration the fact that different effect sizes may have different precision because they are based on different sample sizes.)

A useful illustration of descriptive analysis of effect sizes occurs in Durlak, Fuhrman, and Lampman's synthesis (1991) of 64 studies of the effectiveness of cognitive-behavior therapy for dysfunctional children. They identified and reported descriptive statistics for distributions of effect sizes on eight different types of outcome measures used in these studies (e.g., behavioral observations, peer ratings, achievement tests, and cognitive performance measures). Additionally, they reported effect size means for those outcome variables measured at the conclusion of treatment compared with those measured at some later follow-up time (averaging 15 weeks posttreatment). These reports allow the reader to assess the uniformity of treatment effects across different cognitive and behavioral construct domains (relatively high in this instance). They also allow an appraisal of the extent to which such effects decay in the first several months following treatment (relatively modest in this instance).

Description of effect size distributions may be more than descriptive in the merely statistical sense: Inferential tests also may be reported regarding such matters as the homogeneity of the effect sizes and the confidence interval for their mean value (see Chapter 18). Reporting other information closely related to effect sizes also may be appropriate. Such supplemental information might include the number of effect sizes per study, the basis for computation or estimation of effect sizes, whether effects were statistically significant, what statistical tests were used in the original studies, and coder confidence in the effect size computation.

**2.1.2 Study descriptors** Research synthesists all too often report relatively little information about studies other than their results. It can be quite instructive, however, to provide breakdowns of the coded variables that describe substantive study characteristics, study methods, and extrinsic factors such as publication source. This disclosure accomplishes a twofold purpose. First, it informs readers about the specific nature of the research that has been chosen for the synthesis so that they may judge its comprehensiveness and biases. For example, knowing the proportion of unpublished studies, or studies conducted before a certain date, or studies with a particular type of design might be quite relevant to interpreting the findings of the synthesis. Also, synthesists frequently discover that studies do not adequately report some information that is important to the synthesis. It is informative for readers to know the extent of missing data on various coded variables.

Second, summary statistics for study characteristics provide an overview of the nature of a given field of research. This overview allows readers to ascertain whether researchers have tended to use restricted designs, measures, samples, or treatments. Careful description of the research literature establishes the basis for critique of research practices in a field and helps identify characteristics desirable for future research.

Shapiro and Shapiro (1983) used this descriptive approach to probe the methodological quality of outcome research in psychotherapy. As a framework they adopted Cook and Campbell's validity typology (1979) for experimental and quasi-experimental research: statistical conclusion validity, internal validity, construct validity, and external validity. For each type of validity, Shapiro and Shapiro reported descriptive information on those study features most pertinent to assessing methodological quality on that issue. Internal validity, for instance, is the validity of inferences about the causal relationship between independent and dependent variables. This was examined by considering the extent to which studies employed random assignment to treatment conditions (90 percent did) and the amount of attrition from those conditions subsequent to assignment (which averaged about 10 percent). Additionally, where available, differences among experimental conditions at pretreatment testing were examined to identify any initial nonequivalence on important variables (little was found). From such descriptive information, Shapiro and Shapiro concluded that the internal validity of the studies in this area of research was generally high. By contrast, examination of study features pertinent to the external validity (generalizability) of the results to actual clinical treatments and populations revealed that it was quite low.

It is evident that much can be learned from careful description of study results and characteristics in re-search synthesis. Indeed, it can be argued that providing a broad description and appraisal of the nature and quality of the body of research under examination is fundamental to all other analyses that the synthesist might wish to conduct. Proper interpretation of those analyses depends critically on a clear understanding of the character and limitations of the primary research on which they are based. It follows that conducting and reporting a full descriptive analysis should be routine in research synthesis.

## 2.2 Relationships Among Study Descriptors

The various descriptors that characterize the studies in a synthesis may also have interesting interrelationships among themselves. It is quite unlikely that study characteristics will be randomly and independently distributed over the studies in a given research literature. More likely, they will fall into patterns in which certain characteristics tend to occur together. Many methodological and extrinsic features of studies may be of this sort. We might find, for example, that published studies are more likely to be federally funded and have authors with academic affiliations. Substantive study characteristics may also cluster in interesting ways, as when certain types of treatments are more frequently applied to certain types of subjects. Analysis of across-studies intercorrelations of descriptors that reveals these clusters has not often been explored in research synthesis. Nonetheless, such analysis should be useful both for data reduction—that is, creation of composite predictor variables—and to more fully describe the nature of research practices in the area of inquiry.

Another kind of analysis of relationships among study descriptors focuses on key study features to determine if they are functions of other, temporally or logically prior features. For example, a synthesist might examine whether a particular methodological characteristic, perhaps sample size, is predictable from characteristics of the researcher or the nature of the research setting. Similarly, the synthesist could examine the relationship between the type of subjects in a study and the treatment applied to those subjects.

Pollard (1991) explored the correlates of selected methodological characteristics in this fashion as part of a synthesis of research on juvenile delinquency treatment (Lipsey 1992a, 1992b). One important methodological characteristic in this research, for instance, is whether a study employed random assignment of subjects to experimental conditions. Table 9.1 shows the across-stud-

**Table 9.1 Correlation of Selected Study Characteristics with Method of Subject Assignment (Random vs. Nonrandom) in a Synthesis of Delinquency Treatment Effectiveness Research**

| Variables | Across-Studies Correlation ($n = 263$) |
|---|---|
| Academic author | .17* |
| Funded research | .00 |
| Researcher involved in Tx | .33ᵃ |
| Demonstration project | .27* |
| Program age | −.09 |
| Criminal justice site | .01 |
| Voluntary participation | .18* |

SOURCE: Adapted from Pollard (1991); see also Lipsey (1992b).
NOTE: Random designs coded 1; nonrandom, 0.
*$p < .01$.

ies correlations that proved interesting between method of subject assignment and other coded variables.

The relationships in Table 9.1 and other analyses conducted by Pollard revealed that those studies using random assignment were more likely to have authors with an academic affiliation who were closely involved in the design and implementation of the treatment. Such studies were also more likely to be evaluations of demonstration projects and were more likely to involve voluntary clients. While it is plausible that funded research might be more rigorous and thus more likely to use random assignment, no such relationship was found. Additionally, no relationship was found with criminal justice research sites, despite the generally greater control over subjects characteristic of those sites. From Pollard's analysis of the interrelations among study descriptors, therefore, we learn that innovative projects evaluated by academic researchers who are closely involved in the design or implementation of the treatment are more likely to be conducted as randomized experiments.

A distinctive aspect of analysis of the interrelations of study descriptors is that it does not involve the effect sizes that are central to most other forms of analysis in research synthesis. An important implication of this feature is that the sampling unit for such analyses is the study itself, not the individual subject within a study. The type of design chosen, nature of treatment applied, publication outlet, and other such characteristics describe the study, not the subjects, and thus are not influenced by subject sampling error. This simplifies much of the statistical analysis when investigating these types of relationships since attention need not be paid to the varying number of subjects represented in different studies.

## 2.3 Relationships Between Study Effect Sizes and Study Descriptors

The effect sizes that represent study results often show more variability within their respective categories than would be expected on the basis of sampling error alone (see Chapters 18 and 19). A natural and quite common question for the analyst is whether any study descriptors are associated with the magnitude of the effect. It is almost always appropriate for a synthesis to identify the circumstances under which effect sizes are large and small. This analysis is essentially correlational, examining the covariation of selected study descriptors and effect sizes, though it can be conducted in various statistical formats (see Chapters 19 and 20). In such analysis, the study effect sizes become the dependent variables and the study descriptors become the independent or predictor variables.

The three broad categories of study descriptors identified earlier—those characterizing substantive aspects of the phenomenon under investigation; those describing study methods and procedures; and those dealing with extrinsic matters of research circumstances, reporting, coding, and the like—are all potentially related to study effect sizes. The nature and interpretation of relationships involving descriptors from these three categories, however, is quite different.

**2.3.1 Relationships with extrinsic variables** Extrinsic variables, as defined earlier, are not generally assumed to directly shape actual study results even though they may differentiate studies according to coded effect size. In some instances they may be marker variables that are associated, in turn, with research practices that do exercise direct influence on study results. It is commonly found in synthesis, for example, that published studies have larger effect sizes than unpublished studies (Smith 1980). Publication of a study, of course, does not itself inflate the effect sizes, but it may reflect the selection criteria and reporting proclivities of the authors, reviewers, and editors who decide if and how a study will be published. Analysis of the relationship of extrinsic study variables to effect size, therefore, may reveal interesting aspects of research and publication practices in a field, but is limited in its ability to reveal why those practices are associated with different effect size magnitudes.

A more dramatic example is the discovery that the gender of the authors is a significant predictor of the results of studies of sex differences in conformity. Eagly and Carli (1981) conducted a research synthesis of this literature and found that higher percentages of male authors were associated with findings of greater female conformity. While this may reflect some intentional bias exercised by male researchers, it is also possible that the different results occurred because they tended to use different research methods than female researchers. Indeed, Becker (1986) demonstrated that male authorship was confounded with characteristics of the outcome measures and the number of confederates in the study. Both of these method variables, in turn, were correlated with study effect size.

**2.3.2 Relationships with method variables** The category of predictor variables that has to do with research methods and procedures is particularly important and too often underrepresented in synthesis. Experience has shown that variation in study effect sizes is often associated with methodological variation among the studies (Hedges, Shymansky & Woodworth 1989; Lipsey 1992a; Strube 1988). One reason these relationships are interesting is that much can be learned from synthesis about the connection between a researcher's choice of methods and the results those methods yield. Such knowledge provides a basis for examining research methods to discover which aspects introduce the greatest bias or distortion into study results.

Investigation of method variables, for example, allowed Shapiro and Shapiro (1982) to determine that the manner in which clients were assigned to experimental groups (randomly versus nonrandomly) in psychotherapy studies had no significant relationship to the magnitude of treatment effects found in the study. Attrition from the treatment group, on the other hand, was associated with inflated estimates of treatment effect. Similarly, Eagly et al. (1991) discovered that physical attractiveness stereotype results were stronger when researchers used stimulus pictures in color rather than black and white. On measurement issues, Amato and Keith (1991) found that single-item measures across a range of constructs showed more negative effects of divorce on children's well-being than multiple-item measures of the same constructs. Findings such as these provide invaluable methodological information to re-

searchers seeking to design valid research in their respective areas of study.

Another reason to be concerned about the relationship between methodological features of studies and effect sizes is that method differences may be correlated with substantive differences. In such confounded situations, a synthesist must be very careful not to attribute effect size differences to substantive factors when they are also related to methodological factors.

For example, in her synthesis of institutional treatment for juvenile delinquents, Garrett (1984) found that studies of behavioral therapy resulted in much larger effect sizes than studies of psychodynamic therapy or life skills training (see Table 9.2, first column). However, when she distinguished between studies using more rigorous randomized or matched designs and those using nonequivalent group or pre-post designs, she found that the apparent superiority of behavioral therapy was an artifact resulting from a high proportion of pre-post designs with inflated effect sizes among studies of that particular treatment. Looking only at the results of the more rigorous designs, it appeared that the behavioral and life skills approaches yielded similar results and both were superior to psychodynamic therapy. Still closer inspection, however, revealed that different mixes of outcome measures were used in studies of different therapies. When the key delinquency recidivism outcome measure was examined separately, only life skills training showed positive effects (Table 9.2, fifth column). A synthesist who did not examine the confounding of treatment modality with type of design and type of outcome measure, therefore, could reach quite erroneous conclusions about the relative efficacy of the various therapies.

**2.3.3 Relationships with substantive variables** Once disentangled from method variables, the category of substantive predictor variables is usually of most interest to the synthesist. Determining that effect size is associated with type of subjects, treatments, or settings often has considerable theoretical or practical importance. The Garrett (1984) example of Table 9.2, for instance, after stratification to eliminate design and measurement confoundings, is most important for what it reveals about treatment for institutionalized delinquents. Life skills training, which is relatively less popular than psychodynamic and behavioral therapy, appears far more promising than these traditional approaches in reducing post-release recidivism.

Where there are multiple classes of effect size variables as well as multiple classes of substantive predictor

**Table 9.2 Effect Sizes for Different Delinquency Treatments in Relation to Study Design and Measurement Characteristics**

| Treatment Category | Overall | | Rigorous Designs Only | | Rigorous Designs, Recidivism Outcome Only | |
|---|---|---|---|---|---|---|
| | ES | N | ES | N | ES | N |
| Psychodynamic | .17 | 164 | .17 | 141 | −.01 | 84 |
| Behavioral | .63 | 149 | .30 | 62 | −.08 | 17 |
| Life skills | .31 | 57 | .32 | 35 | .30 | 19 |

SOURCE: Adapted from Garrett (1984).

variables, quite a range of analyses of their interrelations is possible. For instance, investigation can be made of the different correlates of effects on different outcome constructs. Hall and Halberstadt (1986) used this approach in a synthesis of gender differences in nonverbal behavior. They found that situations of low social tension were predictive of gender differences for smiling, but not for gazing. Analogously, examination can be made of the correlates of study results at different times of measurement. Durlak, Fuhrman, and Lampman (1991), for example, attempted to show that the effect of cognitive-behavior therapy for children was moderated by Piagetian developmental level for results measured at treatment termination and also at follow-up. Their efforts were compromised, however, by too few suitable studies using follow-up measures. A third possibility for differentiated analysis is to explore predictor-effect size relationships for different subsamples. This option was illustrated in Becker's synthesis (1992) of models of science achievement separately for male and female students. Discovery of different correlates of achievement for males than for females, had they been found, would have indicated that different factors might be instrumental in determining performance.

The opportunity to conduct systematic analysis of the relationships between study descriptors and study results is one of the most attractive aspects of research synthesis. However, certain limitations must be kept in mind. First, the synthesis can examine only those variables that can be coded from primary studies in essentially complete and accurate form. Second, this aspect of synthesis is a form of observational study, not experimental study. Many of the predictor variables that show relationships with effect size may also be related to each other. As noted above, this is particularly problematic when method variables are confounded with substantive ones. Even without confounded characteristics, the observational nature of synthesis tempers the confidence with which the analyst can describe the causal influence of study characteristics on their findings.

## 2.4 Relationships Among Study Results

In current practice, study results in research synthesis are reported most often either as an overall mean effect size or as means for various categories of results. When multiple classes of effect sizes are available, however, there is potential for informative analysis of the patterns of covariation among the effect sizes themselves. This can be especially fruitful when different results from the same study represent quite different constructs. In that situation, a synthesist can examine whether the magnitude of effects on one construct is associated, across studies, with the magnitude of effects on another construct. Some studies of educational interventions, for instance, may measure effects on both achievement and student attitude toward instruction (e.g., Kulik & Kulik 1989). Under such circumstances, a synthesist might wish to ask whether the effects of the intervention on achievement covaried with the effects on attitude. That is, if an intervention resulted in improved achievement scores for a sample of students, did it also result in improved attitude scores? The across-studies correlation of achievement and attitude effect sizes for studies that report both would provide evidence on this issue. However, this across-studies correlation, while potentially interesting, does not necessarily imply a within-study relationship. Thus, achievement and attitude might covary across studies, but not covary among the students in the samples within the studies.

A broader example is supplied by Lipsey's analysis (1992b) of different categories of findings from a syn-

**Table 9.3** Across-Studies Correlations Between Effect Sizes on Delinquency Outcome and Effect Sizes on Other Outcomes in a Synthesis of Delinquency Treatment Effectiveness Research

| Outcome Category | Weighted Correlation with Delinquency | |
|---|---|---|
| | ES | N |
| Psychological measures | .12 | 80 |
| Interpersonal adjustment | .25 * | 54 |
| School participation | .57 ** | 84 |
| Academic performance | .09 | 40 |
| Vocational accomplishment | .30 ** | 40 |

SOURCE: Adapted from Lipsey (1992b).
$*p < .10.$
$**p < .05.$

thesis of research on treatment of juvenile delinquency. The major outcome variables found in this literature were categorized as delinquency measures, psychological measures (e.g., attitude, self-esteem), interpersonal adjustment (e.g., family, peer relations), school participation (e.g., attendance, dropout), academic performance (e.g., grades), and vocational accomplishment (e.g., holding a job). Many studies reported results in more than one category, which made it possible to ask whether there were any outcome categories that covaried with delinquency outcome. For instance, if treatment reduced delinquency in a juvenile sample, was there also an increase in psychological or interpersonal adjustment, school participation, and so forth?

Table 9.3 reports the across-studies correlations between the effect size for delinquency and those for the other categories of outcome variables. These correlations show that improvement on subsequent delinquency for a treatment group tended to be accompanied by increased school participation and, to a lesser extent, improved vocational accomplishment and interpersonal adjustment. By contrast, change on psychological factors, widely believed to mediate changes in delinquency, showed no significant correlation with change in delinquency. By examining the across-studies covariation of effects on different outcome constructs, therefore, we obtain some insight into the patterning of the change brought about by successful intervention.

An even more ambitious form of synthesis may be used to construct a correlation (or covariance) matrix

that represents the interrelations among different variables in a research literature. Each study in such a synthesis contributes one or more effect sizes representing the correlation between two of the variables of interest. The resulting synthetic correlation matrix can then be used to test multivariate path or structural equation models. An example of such an analysis was provided by Premack and Hunter's synthesis (1988) on factors predictive of employee decisions about unionization. Premack and Hunter proposed a causal model of the decision an individual makes to vote for or against unionization in his or her workplace. In brief, they hypothesized that employees' intended or actual unionization votes would be a complex function of their wage level, dissatisfaction with extrinsic aspects of employment, dissatisfaction with administrative procedures, and perceived instrumentality of unionization for improving conditions. The test of their model with path analysis required a correlation matrix representing the correlation of each of these variables with each other variable.

Premack and Hunter found 14 studies that reported the correlations of at least some of the variables relevant to their path model. These correlational effect sizes were synthesized into a single correlation matrix and corrected for sampling error and measurement unreliability. Their final matrix contained ten correlations, each synthesized from between two and six study estimates. This synthetic matrix, then, became the basis for a path analysis testing their model. A similar example is found in Becker's work (1992) on models of science achievement for males and females.

A potential problem in analyzing multiple categories of study results is that all categories of effects will not be reported by all studies. Thus, each synthesized effect size examining a relationship will most likely draw on a different subset of studies creating uncertainty about their generality and comparability. This and related issues having to do with analyzing synthesized correlation matrices are examined in Chapter 23 and in Becker (1992).

## 3. CONCLUSION

Research synthesis can be thought of as a form of survey research in which the subjects interviewed are not people but research reports (Cordray 1990). The synthesist prepares a questionnaire of items of interest, collects a sample of research reports, interacts with those reports to determine the appropriate coding on each item, and analyzes the resulting data. The kinds of questions that can be addressed by synthesis of a given research literature are thus determined by the variables that the synthesist is able to code and the kinds of analyses that are possible given the nature of the resulting data.

This chapter has reviewed the broad types of variables potentially available from research studies, the kinds of questions that might be addressed using those variables, and the general forms of analysis that investigate those questions. Its purpose has been to provide an overview that will help the prospective research synthesist select appropriate variables for coding and plan a probing and interesting analysis of the resulting database. Contemporary research synthesis often neglects important variables and analysis opportunities. As a consequence, we learn less from such work than we might. Even worse, what we learn may be erroneous if confounds and alternative analysis models have been insufficiently probed. Current practice has only begun to explore the breadth and depth of knowledge that research synthesis can potentially yield.

# 4. REFERENCES

Amato, P. R., & Keith, B. (1991). Parental divorce and the well-being of children: A meta-analysis. *Psychological Bulletin, 110*, 26–46.

Becker, B. J. (1986). Influence again: An examination of reviews and studies of gender differences in social influence. In J. S. Hyde & M. C. Linn (Eds.), *The psychology of gender: Advances through meta-analysis.* Baltimore: Johns Hopkins University Press.

Becker, B. J. (1992). Models of science achievement: Forces affecting male and female performance in school science. In T. D. Cook, H. Cooper, D. S. Cordray, H. Hartmann, L. V. Hedges, R. J. Light, T. A. Louis, & F. Mosteller, *Meta-analysis for explanation: A casebook.* New York: Russell Sage Foundation.

Becker, B. J. (1992). Using the results of replicated studies to estimate linear models. *Journal of Educational Statistics, 17*, 341–362.

Cook, T. D., & Campbell, D. T. (1979). *Quasi-experimentation: Design and analysis issues for field settings.* Chicago: Rand McNally.

Cordray, D. S. (1990). Strengthening causal interpretations of non-experimental data: The role of meta-analysis. In L. Sechrest, E. Perrin, & J. Bunker (Eds.), *Research methodology: Strengthening causal interpretations of non-experimental data* (pp. 151–172). Washington, DC: U.S. Department of Health and Human Services, Agency for Health Care Policy and Research.

Durlak, J. A., Fuhrman, T., & Lampman, C. (1991). Effectiveness of cognitive-behavior therapy for maladapting children: A meta-analysis. *Psychological Bulletin, 110*, 204–214.

Eagly, A. H., Ashmore, R. D., Makhijani, M. G., & Longo, L. C. (1991). What is beautiful is good, but . . . : A meta-analytic review of research on the physical attractiveness stereotype. *Psychological Bulletin, 110*, 109–128.

Eagly, A. H., & Carli, L. L. (1981). Sex of researchers and sex-typed communications as determinants of sex differences in influenceability: A meta-analysis of social influence studies. *Psychological Bulletin, 90*, 1–20.

Garrett, C. J. (1984). *Meta-analysis of the effects of institutional and community residential treatment on adjudicated delinquents.* Unpublished doctoral dissertation, University of Colorado.

Hall, J. A., & Halberstadt, A. G. (1986). Smiling and gazing. In J. S. Hyde & M. C. Linn (Eds.), *The psychology of gender: Advances through meta-analysis.* Baltimore: Johns Hopkins University Press.

Hedges, L. V., Shymansky, J. A., & Woodworth, G. (1989). *A practical guide to modern methods of meta-analysis.* Washington, DC: National Science Teachers Association.

Kulik, J. A., & Kulik, C. L. C. (1989). Meta-analysis in education. *International Journal of Educational Research, 13*, 221–340.

Lewis, R. J., & Vosburgh, W. T. (1988). Effectiveness of kindergarten intervention programs: A meta-analysis. *School Psychology International, 9*, 265–275.

Lipsey, M. W. (1992a). Juvenile delinquency treatment: A meta-analytic inquiry into the variability of effects. In T. D. Cook, H. Cooper, D. S. Cordray, H. Hartmann, L. V. Hedges, R. J. Light, T. A. Louis, & F. Mosteller, (Eds.), *Meta-analysis for explanation: A casebook.* New York: Russell Sage Foundation.

Lipsey, M. W. (1992b). Meta-analysis in evaluation research: Moving from description to explanation. In H. T. Chen & P. H. Rossi (Eds.), *Using theory to improve program and policy evaluations.* New York: Greenwood Press.

Nietzel, M. T., Russell, R. L., Hemmings, K. A., & Gretter, M. L. (1987). Clinical significance of psychotherapy for unipolar depression: A meta-analytic approach to social comparison. *Journal of Consulting and Clinical Psychology, 55*, 156–161.

Pollard, J. A. (1991). *Methodological characteristics of juvenile delinquency treatment evaluations and the reported success of the treatment.* Unpublished doctoral dissertation, Claremont Graduate School.

Premack, S. L., & Hunter, J. E. (1988). Individual unionization decisions. *Psychological Bulletin, 103,* 223–234.

Shapiro, D. A., & Shapiro, D. (1982). Meta-analysis of comparative therapy outcome studies: A replication and refinement. *Psychological Bulletin, 92,* 581–604.

Shapiro, D. A., & Shapiro, D. (1983). Comparative therapy outcome research: Methodological implications of meta-analysis. *Journal of Consulting and Clinical Psychology, 51,* 42–53.

Smith, M. L. (1980). Publication bias and meta-analysis. *Evaluation and Education, 4,* 22–24.

Smith, M. L., & Glass, G. V. (1977). Meta-analysis of psychotherapy outcome studies. *American Psychologist, 32,* 752–760.

Strube, M. J. (1988). Some comments on the use of magnitude-of-effect estimates. *Journal of Counseling Psychology, 35,* 342–345.

Cooper, H. and Hedges, L. V. (Eds.) 1994. *The Handbook of Research Synthesis.* New York: Russell Sage Foundation

# 10

# SYSTEMATIC CODING FOR RESEARCH SYNTHESIS

**WILLIAM A. STOCK**
*Arizona State University*

CONTENTS

## 1. INTRODUCTION

Research synthesists must make many decisions before the actual coding of studies begins: They must choose the study characteristics of interest, and conventions for coding them, and construct coding forms and a code book. They need to develop methods that ensure the reliable and orderly extraction of information from each report. Because these preparations are iterative, they should allocate adequate time for their completion.

Coders locate, reduce, manipulate, and transcribe information. Coders may make judgments about study quality and the adequacy of information in study reports. Because coders can make mistakes, the synthesist should subject their codings to independent verification and should employ tactics to maintain a high level of reliability.

This chapter is a guide to accurate coding. Its content is based on personal experience and the work of others. The sections that follow discuss preparing for coding, designing coding forms and a code book, and ensuring vigilance and accuracy.

## 2. PREREQUISITES TO FULL-SCALE CODING

### 2.1 Decisions About What to Code

A well-designed coding scheme is more likely if the synthesist knows both the research domain and research integration methods, because this knowledge provides the basis for making critical choices. One set of critical choices is the selection of study characteristics to code.

Among authors of books on research synthesis (Cooper 1984; Glass, McGaw & Smith 1981; Hedges & Olkin 1985; Hunter & Schmidt 1990; Hunter, Schmidt & Jackson 1982; Light & Pillemer 1984; Mullen 1989; Mullen & Rosenthal 1985; Rosenthal 1984; Wolf 1986), only Hunter and his colleagues expressed skepticism about the value of coding study characteristics. Hunter, Schmidt, and Jackson (1982) wrote:

> Such coding can be 99 percent of the work in the research integration process. Yet this coding work may be entirely wasted. In our own research in which we have made corrections for sampling error and other artifacts, we have found no significant remaining variation across studies. That is, it is our experience that there is usually no important variation in study results after sampling and other artifacts are removed. (p. 32)

Except for changing "99 percent" to "90 to 95 percent" Hunter and Schmidt (1990) retained the above quotation intact (p. 85).

Total coding time and the likelihood of capitalizing on chance in analyses both increase as coded items are added. For example, an item that takes five minutes per study to code increases total coding time by five hours for every 60 studies. Ultimately, the timeliness of a synthesis is affected if total coding time is too lengthy. For this reason, and because adding items increases the probability of reporting at least one chance relation as significant when studies are statistically analyzed, the meta-analyst needs an item-selection procedure that addresses these costs.

To address their concern about capitalization on chance in statistical analyses, Hunter and his colleagues (1982, 1990) proposed coding an item only when there is theoretical justification for it. There are several reasons for regarding this view as too conservative. First, coded items provide documentation (Kulik & Kulik 1989). Items that describe characteristics of settings, subjects, methodology, treatments, and outcome measures also document the nature of the synthesized research. This documentation is a context for a more complete understanding of the findings and often helps identify where additional research is needed.

Second, although Hunter and Schmidt (1990) claimed that effect size variation is principally accounted for by a finite set of artifacts (e.g., sampling variability, measurement error, deviations from perfect construct validity), their claim is an empirical one that requires verification across substantive domains. Such verification entails coding both artifacts listed by Hunter and Schmidt and additional study characteristics.

Finally, conjecture has a place in science. Requiring formal justification for each coded item can restrict creative conjecture and hunches about a domain because formal justification relies heavily on theory. However, theories in behavioral sciences seldom seem so precise that they reliably provide justification for coding specific features of studies. What is needed is an approach that both addresses concerns about capitalization on chance and supports a reasonable level of conjecture by meta-analysts. A procedure that meets this need is described next.

The meta-analyst should formulate conjectures about covariation between effect size and study characteristics based on his or her knowledge of the research domain. This invites exploration of hunches, speculation, and hypotheses that arise from domain-specific knowledge. Because the synthesist must decide if knowing about a relation between effect size and a coded item is worth the costs, these conjectures should be evaluated with respect to (a) goals of the synthesis, (b) adequacy of information in study reports, (c) whether or not coders can reliably code this information, and (d) costs of coding. Domain-specific knowledge provides a basis for rejecting items (because study characteristics are known to lack potential or are not frequently reported). For each conjecture evaluated favorably on these four criteria, the synthesist should create a coded item and plan to statistically evaluate it.

This procedure may create more coded items than a procedure requiring formal justification, but its goal is to restrict analyses to reasonable conjectures that are constrained by domain-specific knowledge. Its intent is similar to that of Glass, McGaw, and Smith (1981), who wrote, ''the characteristics of studies that are most important in a meta-analysis (apart from the findings, of course) can be roughly classified as either substantive or methodological'' (p. 77).

Categories of frequently coded items, and specific examples within categories, are provided in section 2.2. A few items that are important for methodological reasons have been so identified. There has been no attempt to identify all of the items that might be important for substantive reasons, because these depend on the specific domain of research. Therefore, the meta-analyst should view the material in section 2.2 as guidelines.

## 2.2 A Classification of Items

There are a number of satisfactory classifications of items whose purpose is to provide the prospective meta-analyst with an organized checklist of possible items. Durlak and Lipsey (1991) sorted items into categories related to study context, methodology, subjects/clients, tasks/interventions, and effect sizes. Kulik and Kulik (1989) divided items into categories related to study setting, experimental methodology, treatment, and outcomes. For a synthesis of the effects of class size, Glass, McGaw, and Smith (1981) used categories called report identification, instruction, classroom demographics, study conditions, and outcome variable. For a synthesis of the effects of psychotherapy, they used categories labeled report identification, clients, design, treatment, and effect size.

Adopted here is a set of seven categories labeled report identification, setting, subjects, methodology, treatment, process, and effect size. Each category is described in more detail below.

**2.2.1 Report identification** Items in this category include author, country, year, source of publication, and coder of study. Analyses of effect sizes by these items help spot trends over time, as well as differences associated with authors, publication sources, and coders.

A unique identification number should be assigned to each study report. This ID helps order data before, during, and after coding, and can be used to verify randomly selected studies. Generally, the number of retrieved study reports is larger than the number providing effect sizes, because some retrieved reports lack sufficient information to compute an effect size or because they fail to meet other criteria. Documenting the reasons that study reports are rejected can help during verification of previously coded studies. For example, in a synthesis of subjective well-being research (Stock et al. 1983), one coder failed to code study reports if the effect size had to be calculated from proportions, thinking that insufficient information was given to estimate an effect size. After this error was detected, Stock et al. easily found the reports rejected by this coder and gained a few additional effect sizes.

Synthesists should make two clean copies of each study report (not books, theses, or dissertations, of course) and retain one copy in a master file. This copy is used to provide additional unmarked copies for verification of codings, for items that are coded by multiple coders, and for reliability assessments. The second copy is for the primary coder, who should be encouraged to annotate the copy as information is extracted from it.

**2.2.2 Setting** This category describes general conditions of a study. Possible items include scope of sampling (e.g., local, regional, national), involvement of special populations (e.g., hospital patients, nursing home residents), and ''climate'' characteristics (e.g., SES level of a community, management style in a business). In a synthesis of the effects of class size, Glass, McGaw, and Smith (1981) put the subject matter of instruction in a category labeled instruction. This is a setting variable. Items that describe training and affiliation of primary researchers can be listed here. Not included here are items that describe specific attributes of subjects, methodology, or treatments.

**2.2.3 Subjects** This category includes specific characteristics of sample(s) and subsample(s) of subjects in a study. Subjects are individuals who answer questionnaires or surveys, are observed in field studies, receive therapy, or take part in experiments. Demographic features (e.g., SES, education, age, sex, ethnicity), cognitive abilities (e.g., reading level, IQ), diagnoses (e.g., phobia), and personality traits (e.g., field dependence, extraversion) fall in this category.

**2.2.4 Methodology** Items in this category relate to the conduct of a study. They describe research design, details of sampling and attrition, and presence or absence of threats to internal validity. For experimental research, some items may identify assignment of subjects and those delivering treatments to conditions. For survey research, some items may specify particular techniques used such as type of survey (e.g., mail, phone, interviewer) and number of attempts to contact nonrespondents.

Ratings of study quality (see Chapter 8) are considered to be in this category.

**2.2.5 Treatment** For this category, synthesists should consider items that capture the (a) theoretical orientation that motivated a treatment, (b) specific components of a treatment, (c) nature of control groups, (d) duration of treatment (e.g., per session, number of sessions, span of treatment), and (e) mode of delivery. Also to be considered are items that report whether or not a check of treatment fidelity was conducted.

These items typically pertain to research on experimental or other interventions. Hence, if effect size estimates are indices of association, most items in this category are not relevant.

**2.2.6 Process** This category describes behaviors and dispositions of coders. For example, recording coding times for selected items is particularly useful in preliminary stages of a synthesis. After coding a sample of studies, the meta-analyst may conclude that the time it takes to code an item, relative to the quality of information obtained, does not justify retaining the item.

Confidence ratings are another type of item in this category. In reexamining a meta-analysis of psychotherapy outcomes, Orwin and Cordray (1985) first coded an item and then rated their confidence in the adequacy of the study report with respect to its inclusion of information required to code the item. Reanalyses using these confidence ratings revealed "that deficient reporting injects considerable noise into meta-analytic data and can lead to spurious conclusions" (p. 134). Therefore, synthesists should contemplate using confidence ratings in conjunction with particularly important items.

However, Orwin and Cordray reported that these ratings increased coding time by 3 percent. Further, this estimate is probably optimistic because it was obtained from coders extremely familiar with the methodology and objectives of the study.

**2.2.7 Effect size** In addition to the information required to estimate an effect size, included in this category are items that describe the nature of outcome measures (local or standardized tests). Sample size and reliability information should be routinely coded because analyses of effect sizes are improved by weighting for sample size and by accounting for unreliability in measures. This is a critical methodological improvement. If effect size estimates are indices of association, then reliabilities for both predictor and outcome scales should be coded when the relation of interest involves two measured variables.

**2.2.8 Comments on selecting items** Items selected from these categories should be justified primarily on methodological or substantive grounds. Sample size and reliabilities are routinely coded for methodological reasons. Some sample characteristics, such as gender (e.g., Becker 1989) and age (e.g., Thomas & French 1985), are often justified for substantive reasons. Nevertheless, each item has to be considered carefully.

If many studies report results for samples and subsamples, and across multiple occasions, this circumstance greatly increases total coding time. Say a meta-analyst is interested in gender composition of samples. When a study provides an effect size for a complete sample and for male and female subsamples, each effect size is associated with a different gender composition. Consequently, gender composition has to be coded separately for each effect size. Similar arguments hold for data reported by occasion, by other characteristics (e.g., ethnicity), or by combinations of characteristics. In order to minimize total coding time, the meta-analyst should be convinced that it is important to evaluate each such item before selecting it.

In summary, from these seven categories items should be selected that can be justified on methodological or substantive grounds. Of course, the synthesist can create new items that represent additional conjectures based on knowledge of the research domain, as described in section 2.1. Items can be added that are needed to identify and document study reports or that are used to monitor or modify the coding process. After items are selected, the synthesist should construct a preliminary set of coding forms.

## 3. THE CONSTRUCTION OF CODING FORMS AND A CODE BOOK

Having a set of items to code is an insufficient basis for starting full-scale coding: Coding forms and a code book must be constructed, and coders must be trained in their use. The reliability of coders needs to be examined and raised to an acceptable level. As these preparations go forward, changes in the forms and code book will have to be considered. The entire process is clearly iterative, so the synthesist should remain open to changes and make them when necessary. On this, Rosenthal (1984) proposed: "This form should then be discussed with colleagues and advisors who can suggest other variables to be included. Finally, a revised form might be sent to workers in the area of the meta-analysis, with an invitation to have them suggest other variables that should be coded" (p. 48). Only after coders competently and reliably code items on final versions of coding forms can full-scale coding begin.

Coding is more accurate if the coding forms and code book are designed well. This means that effective coding conventions have to be chosen and implemented on the forms, as well as explained in the code book. The forms should be clear, self-explanatory, and arranged to facilitate data entry.

Although paper is the most frequently used medium for coding forms, direct entry into computers is increasingly feasible using mainframe and microcomputer programs for building relational databases and for doing statistical analyses. (See Chapter 13 for a discussion of these programs.) However, the flexibility needed in computer programs is understood better by examining requirements for constructing good coding forms on paper.

Figure 10.1 contains seven coding forms used to illustrate many of the points made below. These forms have been adapted from the original forms used in a synthesis of subjective well-being research (Stock et al. 1983). A brief description of research on subjective well-being is provided in the appendix to convey the complexity of coding processes and to provide further context for the points made below.

### 3.1 Choosing Conventions for Coding Items

Coding conventions are methods for assigning numbers to information in studies. Some of this information is already numerical, and some is not. One standard that guides the selection of coding conventions is to conserve as much of the original information as possible. The more directly that information is transcribed from study to form, the fewer judgments a coder makes and, consequently, the fewer errors. A second standard stems from the fact that information on forms is transferred to a computer. Preference should be given to those that map nonnumerical information into a numerical format with a mutually exclusive set of categories. Sometimes, these standards conflict with one another. For example, specific manipulations in treatment and comparison groups may be described more effectively by extended verbal descriptions. Although verbal descriptions can be treated as text or string variables in computers, the most likely methods of analysis will require postcoding these descriptions into a system of numerical categories.

Fortunately, tactics exist for conserving descriptive detail in closed coding systems. For example, Guzzetti, Snyder, and Glass (1991) used the following scheme to code the manipulations in treatment and comparison groups in a synthesis of instructional interventions for overcoming misconceptions about science. Common interventions were listed and given code numbers. Coders used as many as six of these code numbers to describe the manipulations administered in treatment and comparison groups. As new interventions were encountered during coding, they were added to the list and given a new code number. The scheme is flexible and open with respect to what appears in studies, but closed with respect to data entry. In Figure 10.1, item 22 on Form 6 and item 26 on Form 7 employ this scheme.

**3.1.1 Direct coding of information that is numerical** The first standard given above counsels that numerical data should be retained intact. There is rarely a point to reducing quantitative data to coding categories. When such items as sample size, ethnic or gender breakdowns (in percentages), and reliability estimates have to be collected into grosser categories, it should be done prior to analyses by using data modification commands in computer packages. In Figure 10.1, items 7, 9, and 10 on Form 2, items 17 and 18 on Form 5, item 24 on Form 6, and item 28 on Form 7 are examples of this type of coding. Item 19 on Form 6 presumes that an index of association is extracted by the coder. (This was the case in the Stock et al. synthesis where almost all effect sizes were Pearson correlation coefficients or other indices of association presented in study reports).

Generally, the preferred approach is to have coders transcribe the information from which effect sizes are

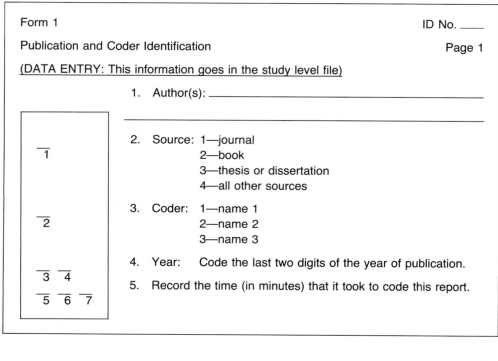

Form 1                                                    ID No. ____

Publication and Coder Identification                      Page 1

(DATA ENTRY: This information goes in the study level file)

    1.  Author(s): _____

                _____

‾1‾

    2.  Source:  1—journal
                 2—book
                 3—thesis or dissertation
                 4—all other sources

‾2‾

    3.  Coder:  1—name 1
                 2—name 2
                 3—name 3

    4.  Year:    Code the last two digits of the year of publication.

‾3‾ ‾4‾

    5.  Record the time (in minutes) that it took to code this report.

‾5‾ ‾6‾ ‾7‾

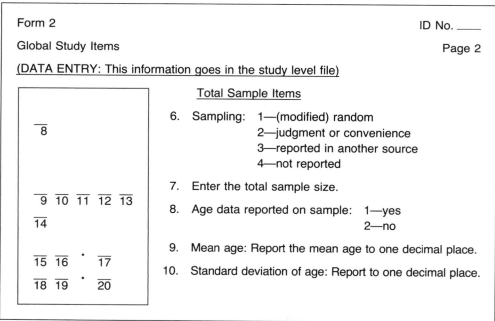

Form 2                                                    ID No. ____

Global Study Items                                        Page 2

(DATA ENTRY: This information goes in the study level file)

                         <u>Total Sample Items</u>

    6.  Sampling:  1—(modified) random
                    2—judgment or convenience
                    3—reported in another source

‾8‾

                    4—not reported

    7.  Enter the total sample size.

‾9‾ ‾10‾ ‾11‾ ‾12‾ ‾13‾

    8.  Age data reported on sample:  1—yes

‾14‾

                                      2—no

    9.  Mean age: Report the mean age to one decimal place.

‾15‾ ‾16‾ · ‾17‾

    10.  Standard deviation of age: Report to one decimal place.

‾18‾ ‾19‾ · ‾20‾

**Figure 10.1** Seven Coding Forms with Abbreviated Annotation

Form 3                                                   ID No. ____

Global Study Items                                       Page 3

(DATA ENTRY: This information goes in the study level file)

<u>Quality of Study Ratings</u>

11.  Item 1:      [Annotation]

$\overline{21}$

12.  Item 2:      [Annotation]

$\overline{22}$

13.  Item 3:      [Annotation]

$\overline{23}$

---

Form 4                                                   ID No. ____

Subsample Identification                                 Page ____

(DATA ENTRY: This information goes in the subsample level file)

$\overline{1}$

14.  Are effect sizes reported for subsamples that are broken down by age ranges?
     1—yes
     2—no

15.  Record a subsample identification number.

$\overline{2}$ $\overline{3}$

Below list the subsamples and give a brief verbal description. List the youngest group first, etc.

Brief verbal description of subsample:

1  _____

2  _____

3  _____

4  _____

5  _____

[Coder adds more as needed.]

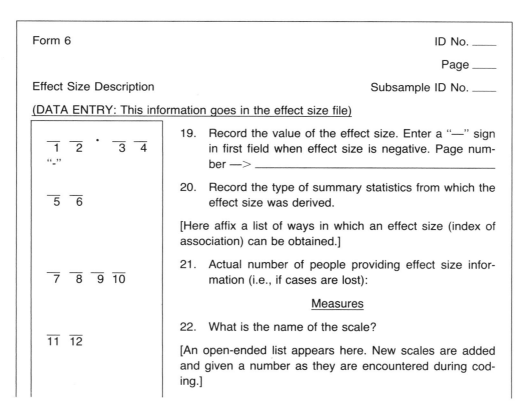

Form 5                                                        ID No. ____

                                                             Page ____

Specific Subsample Description                    Subsample ID No. ____

(DATA ENTRY: This information goes in the subsample level file)

$\overline{4}$

$\overline{5}\ \overline{6}$ $\cdot$ $\overline{7}$

$\overline{8}\ \overline{9}$ $\cdot$ $\overline{10}$

16.  Age data reported on subsample:  1—yes
                                       2—no

17.  Mean age: Report mean age to one decimal place.

18.  Standard deviation of age: Report to one decimal place.

[Add additional subsample characteristics as dictated by substantive and methodological interests.]

---

Form 6                                                        ID No. ____

                                                             Page ____

Effect Size Description                          Subsample ID No. ____

(DATA ENTRY: This information goes in the effect size file)

$\overline{1}\ \overline{2}$ $\cdot$ $\overline{3}\ \overline{4}$
"-"

$\overline{5}\ \overline{6}$

$\overline{7}\ \overline{8}\ \overline{9}\ \overline{10}$

$\overline{11}\ \overline{12}$

19.  Record the value of the effect size. Enter a "—" sign in first field when effect size is negative. Page number —> _____

20.  Record the type of summary statistics from which the effect size was derived.

[Here affix a list of ways in which an effect size (index of association) can be obtained.]

21.  Actual number of people providing effect size information (i.e., if cases are lost):

                          Measures

22.  What is the name of the scale?

[An open-ended list appears here. New scales are added and given a number as they are encountered during coding.]

**Figure 10.1** *(continued)*

<u>Reliability</u>

$\overline{13}$

23. Is reliability reported for this measure on this occasion?   1—yes
    2—no

. $\overline{14}$ $\overline{15}$
$\overline{16}$

24. Record the estimated reliability.

25. Record the type of reliability.
    1—alpha
    2—internal consistency (other)
    3—kappa
    4—percent agreement
    5—split half
    6—test-retest
    7—other (specify below)

_____

Form 7                                          ID No. ____

                                                Page ____

Occasion/Measure Items                          Subsample ID No. ____

<u>(DATA ENTRY: This information goes in the effect size file)</u>

$\overline{17}$ $\overline{18}$

26. What is the predictor variable involved in this effect size?

[An open-ended list, with new scales added and given a number as encountered in coding.]

<u>Reliability of Predictor Variable</u>

$\overline{19}$

27. Is reliability reported for the predictor on this occasion?
    1—yes
    2—no

28. Record the estimated reliability.

$\overline{20}$ . $\overline{21}$ $\overline{22}$
$\overline{23}$

29. Record the type of reliability.

    1—alpha
    2—internal consistency (other)
    3—kappa
    4—percent agreement
    5—split half
    6—test-retest
    7—other (specify below)

_____

estimated and to employ a computer to do the calculations. This decreases the opportunity for errors and increases the time available for other coder tasks. (See Chapter 13 for a detailed description about using computers to calculate effect sizes and for a sample coding form—Figure 13.1—for experimental studies.)

In study reports, a characteristic can be reported in direct or summary numerical form. For example, age can be described by means, medians, or modes, accompanied by standard deviations and ranges. It may also be given as percentages in age-range categories. Sometimes a characteristic is simply described qualitatively (e.g., retirees or college-age students). Because the Stock et al. synthesis dealt primarily with research from social gerontology, six items were coded on age, including whether or not age data were reported, and if so its mean, median, standard deviation, and the upper and lower bounds of the range. Using many items for an important characteristic is acceptable and illustrates that a synthesist allocates resources, here the number of items dealing with age, based on judgments of importance.

**3.1.2 Closed conventions for information that is not numerical** Coding a characteristic that is not numerical requires decisions about how to classify the variations of that characteristic that occur across studies. Here, one should expropriate and capitalize on the work of others whenever possible (Sudman & Bradburn 1989). A critical examination of detailed descriptions of coding conventions that appear in many published syntheses can help reduce the effort required to choose such conventions. However, before adopting them, the synthesist should be convinced that more effective conventions are unlikely to be found.

Fixed and well-defined categories simplify coding. When there is a need for flexibility (e.g., if all manifestations of a characteristic are not known in advance), a scheme should be adopted similar to the one used by Guzzetti, Snyder, and Glass (1991). This scheme permits new categories to be incorporated as coding proceeds, without affecting the data entry task. Selective use of an "other" category can be valuable (see item 25 on Form 6 or item 29 on Form 7). The "other" category works best when the coder appends a verbal description that can be postclassified after all studies have been coded.

Finally, for an item representing a substantive conjecture about variation in effect sizes, it is crucial that categories of the item provide a means of testing a conjecture. That is, the sensitivity of the categories must match the sensitivity of the conjecture. Of course, the

level of sensitivity is constrained by the quality of information presented in the study reports. For two reasons, the meta-analyst should consider employing somewhat more sensitive categories than might be needed. First, finer distinctions can be aggregated into coarser ones by a computer. Second, it can be very time-consuming to have to recode an item whose categories were not sensitive enough. Here again, it is the meta-analyst who must select the most appropriate approach.

After the conventions for coding the items have been selected, the items should be arranged on a preliminary set of forms (the topic of section 3.2.), which are used to provide training to coders and to conduct an assessment of their reliability. Since both of these activities can introduce changes in coding conventions and the forms, they are discussed below.

**3.1.3 Training coders** The object of training is to ensure that coders use the forms, conventions, and procedures of the synthesis in identical ways. Even methodologically sophisticated persons should participate in training if they are among the coders for a synthesis. To prepare them for training, the synthesist should provide coders with a sample of papers to read. The sample should be chosen so as to impart to coders a global sense of the domain to be synthesized.

The training process takes place in group meetings attended by all coders. In these meetings, additions, deletions, or modifications to the set of items can be discussed and perhaps adopted. The forms and code book are revised accordingly. Training includes the following steps:

1. An overview of the synthesis is given by the principal investigator. This step may occur in conjunction with the reading and discussion of the sample of papers described above.

2. Each item on a form and its description in the code book is read and discussed.

3. The process for using the forms is described. This is the method chosen to organize forms so that the transition from coding to data entry and data management is facilitated; it should take into account studies that include reports for subsamples, or multiple occasions or measures.

4. A sample of five-to-ten studies is chosen to "test" the forms.

5. A study is coded by everyone, with each coder recording how long it takes to code each item. These time data are used to estimate how long it

will take to code individual items, entire study reports, and the complete synthesis.

6. Coded forms are compared and discrepancies are identified and resolved.

7. The forms and code book are revised as necessary.

8. Another study is coded and reviewed, and so on. Steps 4–8 are repeated until apparent consensus is achieved. The next step is to obtain empirical evidence of the reliability of coders.

**3.1.4 Establishing the reliability of coders** Chapter 11 describes methods for evaluating coding decisions and ensuring reliability among coders. Therefore, comments here are brief.

The synthesist should consider assigning multiple coders to each study on critical items. An important benefit of this tactic is that composite ratings are more reliable; that is, by using multiple coders, one can accept lower levels of individual reliability (Rosenthal 1984). Using coding times from the training sessions, total coding time for a synthesis can be estimated roughly (average time per study multiplied by the number of studies). Knowing this estimate and the number of coders, one can make selective decisions about the use of multiple coders.

The studies coded as part of an assessment of reliability should be randomly selected. Coders should be given identical instructions, work independently, and be prohibited from discussing studies with one another. Acceptable levels of reliability should be identified before it is assessed, as should a strategy for how to deal with items whose level of reliability remains stubbornly low.

For items with unacceptable levels of reliability, coding discrepancies should be discussed with an eye to revisions of the forms and code book or to alterations in training procedures. If reliability is a problem, the use of multiple coders should be reevaluated. Following revisions, the reliability of coders on these items is examined.

After establishing acceptable levels of reliability, full-scale coding can begin. However, reliability deteriorates over time. Therefore, if the number of studies in the synthesis is large, reliability ought to be rechecked at least once during full-scale coding.

## 3.2 Assembling the Forms

During the steps described in section 3.1 items are assembled on forms. This assembly meets a number of needs, the foremost of which is that information is coded once. In separate groups, forms should gather items at the level of the study, of subsample(s), and of effect size. Items within these groups may be sorted into subgroups for ease of coding, but items in distinct groups are placed on distinct forms. One should not feel compelled to pack items densely onto the fewest possible forms. The physical location and appearance of items on a page affect accuracy, and substantial benefits accrue from focusing on ordering and annotating items.

**3.2.1 Sorting items onto separate forms** Of the items that describe the entire study, the items that document the study reports should be grouped first. Identification items (authors, source and year of publication, and coder) and some process items (date coded and coding time) are included. These items require little annotation and usually fit on a single form that serves as a cover sheet (Form 1).

Next, items should be grouped that describe setting, subjects, and methodology (Forms 2 and 3). Although they may occupy several forms, they are considered a set. Ratings of study quality may require multiple items, which should be placed on a single form if possible and extensively annotated directly on the coding form. This keeps rating criteria in front of the coder (see Chapter 8 for details on coding study quality).

Items collected on subsamples (e.g., sample sizes and gender composition) should be grouped next. These items should be on their own set of forms (Forms 4 and 5). A subsample identification number is useful for linking data files and for collating forms in an orderly way during coding.

Finally, the items that are related to effect size should be gathered together (Forms 6 and 7). This includes effect size information, items describing the context of the particular effect size, and information on measures such as the type of scale and estimates of reliability. When a synthesis entails experimental or intervention research, items should be assembled from the treatment category with effect size items.

Items from the process category most likely will be either estimates of coding time or ratings of the quality of study report information. The process items should appear at the same place on the forms as the corresponding methodological/substantive item. Obviously, both time estimates and ratings should be made immediately following coding of the item.

After these groupings have been determined, thought should be given to arranging items within forms. There are a number of tactics that aid both coders and data entry personnel. Sudman and Bradburn (1989) provide many valuable suggestions (in Chapters 8–11 of their book) that apply to forms as well as to questionnaires.

**3.2.2 Ordering items within forms** The order of items on forms should mirror the order of information in study reports. Thus, related items, like those that describe details of sampling, are grouped together. Synthesists should informally assess the adequacy of this order during training and reliability phases of the synthesis.

With respect to the needs of coders, the placement of items on forms should assist rather than impede coding. A font that is crisp and readable is preferred. Items must be separated from one another. Both items and categories within items should be numbered. For the effect size, a space must be included for recording the page of the study report where the effect size information occurred (item 19 of Form 6). This assists verification.

Annotation is a key aid to coders. For each item, a list of categories should be provided with information that defines and illustrates significant differences between categories. Detailed annotation is important for ratings of study quality because it decreases the rate at which coders turn back and forth between a study and the code book. Because extensive annotation increases the number of forms, spaces are needed at the top of forms for study ID number (an item that is recorded repeatedly) and pagination.

The pattern and placement of coded information affects the accuracy of data entry. Spaces for coded information should be placed systematically along the left (or right) margin of a page to reduce the strain of data entry. The information to be entered in the computer should be enclosed (all forms show this). To assist coders and data entry persons, separate dashes should be used for each digit and preprint decimal points on the form (items 9, 10, 17–19, 24, and 28).

In electronic databases, information often is organized in terms of records and columns. Once items and coding conventions are chosen for a synthesis, and once decisions are made about how many significant digits to record for numerical items, specific columns can be assigned to every item. This column information can then be preprinted on all forms, thereby providing data entry persons with a way of verifying the accuracy of their entries.

Consistently collating forms during coding can be complicated because studies provide different numbers of effect sizes, often with different numbers of subsam-

ples. (Chapter 13 discusses the details of using a relational database for organizing information in computer files.) Here, specific files are defined for different levels of data (study, subsample, effect size) that are linked by relational identifiers. One may adopt a strategy of collating forms in a similar fashion; then data entry persons will deal with each form once.

A quick visual impression of a study can be achieved by using colored paper. For example, white paper can be used for forms at the study level (identification, setting, sample, methodology), blue paper for forms at the subsample level, and yellow paper for forms at the effect size level (treatment, effect size). If these are collated systematically, the pattern of colors gives an immediate visual impression of the study.

**3.2.3 Collating forms during coding** Table 9.1 is a good visual framework for considering the problem of how to systematically collate forms when different subsets of the outcome matrix occur in studies. Since any subset of the outcome matrix can appear in a study, an optimal solution would reflect the pattern of characteristics that occurs most frequently in a particular research literature. There is no single solution to the problem. Therefore, what follows is a method that is conducive to creating the types of computer files described in Chapter 13.

For convenience, forms with items at the study level are labeled a "study" block (Forms 1–3), those at the subsample level a "subsample" block (Forms 4–5), and those at the effect size level an "effect size" block (Forms 6–7). Associated with a study report will be one study block. For each subsample for which effect size information is presented, there will be a subsample block. Finally, for every effect size there will be an effect size block. These blocks should be collated in the following manner: The study block should be placed first, followed by all effect size blocks associated with effect sizes derived from the entire sample. The subsample block for the first subsample should be placed next, followed by all effect size blocks associated with that subsample. Thereafter, the second subsample block and all the effect size blocks for that subsample should follow. Repeat the process as necessary.

Additional organization may be imposed on the collation if necessary. For example, say the synthesist is interested only in subsamples that are either male or female. Rather than allowing coders to haphazardly collate the subsample blocks, one can adopt a convention of placing the same gender subsample block first.

## 3.3 Documenting the Synthesis and Forms in a Code Book

Code books simultaneously satisfy two objectives. They provide detailed guidance to coders, and they furnish a historical record of the synthesis. The first objective is more important when the synthesist contemplates how to organize the code book.

A simple separation of the contents of a code book achieves both objectives without compromising the code book as a guide to coders. That is, the synthesist should separate content that deals with global objectives and descriptions from content that deals with detailed descriptions of the items on the forms.

The description of research synthesis in Part I should be included for inexperienced coders, as well as (a) definitions of primary constructs, (b) descriptions of the general coding categories, and (c) an overview of data entry and data management processes. The need for consistency in extracting and representing information should be emphasized. An overview of the coding forms and their application should appear in the context of a description of the overall coding strategy. The collation procedure should be described.

With respect to defining primary constructs, it is helpful to provide coders with both conceptual and operational definitions. The former are derived from formal definitions of constructs that have appeared in the research literature. One should consider developing a concordance that explicitly links formal definitions of constructs, where alternative definitions exist. Operational definitions provide practical guidelines for making coding decisions. One way to achieve these guidelines is to list verbatim descriptions of the construct(s) that have appeared in primary study reports.

The second part of the code book is organized in the order that forms are used, with an exception noted below. Detailed and extensive descriptions of each item appear in the sequence that items are numbered on the forms. As much as possible, these descriptions dispel all ambiguities in the application of coding conventions. The sole exception to this organization deals with effect size. There should be a separate and detachable section containing an indexed list of the different ways in which effect size information may appear. This list should contain specific examples. If the synthesist chooses to have coders estimate effect sizes, then copies of any tables (e.g., probit tables) used to calculate effect sizes should be attached to this section.

## 4. MAINTAINING VIGILANCE AND OTHER MATTERS

To maintain vigilance during coding, the synthesist should schedule meetings with all coders on a frequent basis. Some meeting time should be set aside for coders to report their progress, to discuss difficulties, and to help one another. The remaining time should be devoted to coding in a group setting. This practice encourages coders to critically appraise their own work and to seek help with difficult coding decisions. More subtly, it fosters a work ethic (we're all in this together and we're going to keep on until it's done).

For times that coders work by themselves, the synthesist should require them to develop strategies for avoiding fatigue. For Stock et al. (1983), one person coded for a fixed period each day (i.e., he coded for 1–2 hours each morning and devoted the rest of the day to other work). Another coder selected a fixed number of studies to code each day.

One or more reliability assessments should be conducted during coding. Before coding begins, the synthesist should inform coders that reliability assessments will occur at unannounced intervals. Also, whenever possible, codings should be independently verified. This can be achieved by assigning each coder a subset of studies from the master list. For verification these subsets are simply shifted to different coders. If coders know that the reliability and accuracy of their work is being systematically evaluated, they maintain their vigilance at higher levels.

In the experience of the author, the best coders approach the task in a persistent, scholarly way. They make an effort to thoroughly understand the domain being synthesized by carefully reading the preparatory materials and the study reports for which they are responsible. They also systematically apply the procedures outlined in the code book and are not afraid to raise issues as the coding process unfolds. Prior knowledge of statistical methods is helpful, but not absolutely necessary, for a coder, especially for those who have the traits described above.

One final word of caution. Even if the recommendations of this chapter are followed, surprises occur. For example, we were at the end of coding studies for the synthesis of subjective well-being literature when we were asked to report on the relation between subjective well-being and health. We agreed, and then examined our coded information. While the information we coded on subjective well-being scales was thorough, information on health features was thin. We ended up creating a new form focused on health scales and features and coded the entire set of 556 studies once again using this form.

### Author's Note

The author gratefully acknowledges the efforts of Morris A. Okun and Herbert J. Walberg, who gave extended preliminary advice on this chapter.

## 5. REFERENCES

Becker, B. J. (1989). Gender and science achievement: A reanalysis of studies from two meta-analyses. *Journal of Research in Science Teaching, 26,* 141–169.

Cooper, H. M. (1984). *The integrative research review: A systematic approach.* Beverly Hills, CA: Sage.

Durlak, J. A., & Lipsey, M. W. (1991). A practitioner's guide to meta-analysis. *American Journal of Community Psychology, 19,* 291–332.

Glass, G. V., McGaw, B., & Smith, M. L. (1981). *Meta-analysis in social research.* Beverly Hills, CA: Sage.

Glass, G. V., & Smith, M. L. (1979). Meta-analysis of research in class size and achievement. *Educational Evaluation and Policy Analysis, 1,* 2–16.

Guzzetti, B. J., Snyder, T. E., & Glass, G. V. (1991, May). *Meta-analysis of instructional interventions from reading education to overcome misconceptions in science.* Paper presented at the meeting of the International Reading Association, Las Vegas, NV.

Hedges, L. V., & Olkin, I. (1985). *Statistical methods for meta-analysis.* Orlando, FL: Academic Press.

Hunter, J. E., and Schmidt, F. L. (1990). *Methods of meta-analysis: Correcting error and bias in research findings.* Newbury Park, CA: Sage.

Hunter, J. E., Schmidt, F. L., & Jackson, G. B. (1982). *Meta-analysis: Cumulating research findings across studies.* Beverly Hills, CA: Sage.

Kulik, J. A., & Kulik, C. L. C. (1989). Meta-analysis in education. *International Journal of Educational Research, 13,* 221–340.

Light, R. J., & Pillemer, D. B. (1984). *Summing up: The science of reviewing research.* Cambridge, MA: Harvard University Press.

Mullen, B. (1989). *Advanced BASIC meta-analysis.* Hillsdale, NJ: Erlbaum.

Mullen, B., & Rosenthal, R. (1985). *BASIC meta-analysis: Procedures and programs.* Hillsdale, NJ: Erlbaum.

Orwin, R. G., & Cordray, D. S. (1985). Effects of deficient reporting on meta-analysis: A conceptual framework and reanalysis. *Psychological Bulletin, 97,* 134–147.

Rosenthal, R. (1984). *Meta-analytic procedures for social research.* Beverly Hills, CA: Sage.

Stock, W. A., Okun, M. A., Haring, M. J., & Witter, R. A. (1983). Age and subjective well-being: A meta-analysis. In R. J. Light (Ed.), *Evaluation studies review annual* (Vol. 8, (pp. 279–302). Beverly Hills, CA: Sage.

Sudman, S., & Bradburn, N. M. (1989). *Asking questions.* San Francisco: Jossey-Bass.

Thomas, J. R., & French, K. E. (1985). Gender differences across age in motor performance: A meta-analysis. *Psychological Bulletin, 98,* 260–282.

Wolf, F. M. (1986). *Meta-analysis: Quantitative methods for research synthesis.* Beverly Hills, CA: Sage.

## 6. APPENDIX: RESEARCH ON SUBJECTIVE WELL-BEING

By 1980, more than 550 study reports dealt with research on subjective well-being in the United States. Most of this research was conducted in the field of social gerontology. Hence, age has been examined extensively as a predictor variable. At least 15 other variables (education, gender, health, housing, income, locus of control, marital status, occupational status, race, religiosity, self-esteem, social activity, socioeconomic status, transportation, work status) also have been examined in the search for predictors of subjective well-being. Each variable is measured in many ways. Further, subjective well-being itself is measured using more than ten scales of the related constructs of happiness, life satisfaction, and morale. Finally, many study reports present data for subsamples based on various combinations of age, gender, and ethnicity, as well as for multiple occasions.

Cooper, H. and Hedges, L. V. (Eds.) 1994. *The Handbook of Research Synthesis*. New York: Russell Sage Foundation

# 11

# EVALUATING CODING DECISIONS

### ROBERT G. ORWIN
*R.O.W. Sciences, Inc.*

CONTENTS

# 1. INTRODUCTION

Coding is a critical part of research synthesis. It represents an attempt to reduce a complex, messy, context-laden, and quantification-resistant reality to a matrix of numbers. Thus, it will always remain a challenge to fit the numerical scheme to the reality, and the fit will never be perfect. Systematic strategies for evaluating coding decisions enable the synthesist to control for much of the error inherent in the process. When used in conjunction with other strategies, they can help reduce error as well. This chapter will discuss strategies to reduce error as well as strategies to control for error and will suggest further research to advance the theory and practice of this particular aspect of the synthesis process. To set the context, however, it will first be useful to describe the sources of error in synthesis coding decisions.

# 2. SOURCES OF ERROR IN CODING DECISIONS

## 2.1 Deficient Reporting in Primary Studies

Reporting deficiencies in original studies present an obvious problem for the synthesist, to whom the research report is the sole documentation of what was done and what was found. Reporting quality of primary research studies has variously been called ''shocking'' (Light & Pillemer 1984), ''deficient'' (Orwin & Cordray 1985), and ''appalling'' (Oliver 1987).[1] In the worst

case, deficient reporting can force the abandonment of a synthesis.[2]

Virtually all write-ups will report some information poorly, but some will be so vague as to obscure what took place entirely. The absence of clear and/or universally accepted norms undoubtedly contributes to the variation, but there are other factors; different emphases in training, scarcity of journal space, statistical mistakes, and poor writing. The consequences are differences in the completeness, accuracy, and clarity with which empirical research is reported.

Treatment regimens and subject characteristics cannot be accurately transcribed by the coder when inadequately reported by the original author. Similarly, methodological features cannot be coded with certainty when research methods are poorly described. The immediate consequence of coder uncertainty is coder error. Smith, Glass, and Miller (1980) recognized the problem and devised guessing conventions as a partial solution. When an investigator was remiss in reporting the length of time the therapist had been practicing, for example, the guessing convention for therapist experience was called on to provide a response. Such a device serves to standardize decisions under uncertainty, and therefore increase intercoder agreement. It is arguable whether it reduces coder error, however, there being no way to externally validate the accuracy of the convention. Furthermore, a guessing convention carries the likelihood of *bias* in addition to error. Unlike pure observational error, which presumably distributes itself randomly around the true value across coders, the convention-generated

---

[1] It should be noted that significant reporting deficiencies, and their deleterious effect on research synthesis, are not confined to social research areas; see, for example, Wortman and Yeaton's synthesis work (1985) on the effectiveness of coronary artery bypass surgery.

[2] For example, Oliver (1987) reports on a colleague who attempted to apply a meta-analytic approach to research on senior leadership, but gave up after finding that only 10 percent of the eligible studies contained sufficient data to sustain the synthesis.

errors may *not* balance out, but consistently over- or underestimate the true value. This would happen, for example, if in reality the average Ph.D. therapist had been practicing eight years, rather than five years as in Smith, Glass, and Miller's guessing convention.

Through its influence on coding accuracy, deficiencies in reporting quality degrade the integrity of later analyses in predictable ways. Errors of observation in dependent variables destabilize parameter estimates and decrease statistical power, whereas errors of observation in independent variables cause parameter estimates to be biased (Kerlinger & Pedhazur 1973). The use of guessing conventions artificially deflates true variance in coded variables, thereby diminishing the sensitivity of the analysis to detect relationships with other variables. Moreover, any systematic over- and underestimation of true values by guessing conventions exacerbates matters further. Specifically, it creates a validity problem (e.g., therapist experience as coded would not be a valid indicator of therapist experience).

## 2.2 Ambiguities in the Judgment Process

Coding difficulty reflects the complexity of the item to be coded, not just the clarity with which it is reported. There is some relationship between reporting quality and the need for judgment calls, in that deficient reporting of study characteristics increases the need for judgment in coding. Many other variables, however, intrinsically require judgment regardless of reporting quality. In fact, more judgment can sometimes be necessary when reporting is thorough, because the coder has more information to weigh.

Numerous variables pose judgment problems for the coder. Consider, for example, treatment integrity: that is, the extent to which the delivered treatment measures up to the intended treatment. In the psychotherapy literature synthesized by Smith, Glass, and Miller (1980), attrition from treatment (but not from measurement), spotty attendance, failure to meet advertised theoretical requirements, and assorted other implementation problems all potentially degraded treatment integrity. Smith, Glass, and Miller did not attempt to code treatment integrity per se, although they did code their degree of confidence that the labels placed on therapies by authors described what actually transpired. In our reanalysis (Orwin & Cordray 1985), we attempted to code integrity more globally, but without much success. The following examples (representing actual cases) point up some of the difficulties:

*Case 1:* The efficacy of ego therapy was tested against a placebo treatment and no-treatment controls. Several participants did not attend every session; only those attending four or more sessions out of seven were posttested.

*Case 2:* The comparative efficacy of therapist-administered desensitization and self-administered desensitization was tested (relative to various control groups) for reducing public speaking anxiety. The therapists were advanced graduate students in clinical psychology who had been trained in the use of desensitization, but were inexperienced in its application.

*Case 3:* The comparative effect of implosive therapy, eclectic verbal therapy, and bibliotherapy was tested for reducing fear of snakes. All eclectic verbal therapy was performed by the second author, who had previously published several articles on implosive therapy.

Case 1 exemplifies by far the most common treatment integrity problem we encountered: the potential dilution of the treatment regimen by nonattendance. Here the coder must judge whether participants with absentee rates up to 43 percent can be said to have received the intended treatment. If not, by how much was it degraded, and how did this degradation affect the estimated effect size (a question made still more difficult by the authors' failure to report the number of participants with nonattendance problems)? In case 2, the treatment as advertised is potentially degraded by the use of inexperienced treatment providers. The coder must judge whether the lack of practice made a difference and, if so, by how much. In case 3, the treatment provider's motivation to maintain the integrity of the treatment comes into question. The coder must judge whether the apparent conflict of interest degraded the treatment and, if so, by how much (e.g., uninspired compliance or outright sabotage).

Theoretically, the need for judgment calls in coding such complex constructs could be eliminated by a coding algorithm that considered every possible contingency and provided the coder with explicit instructions in the event of each one, singly and in every combination. Smith, Glass, and Miller's algorithm for internal validity suggests an attempt at this (1980, pp. 63–64). The components of this decision rule represent generally accepted internal validity concerns. Yet in trying to apply it, we frequently found that it failed to accommodate some important contingencies and thus put our own sense of the study's internal validity in contradiction to the score yielded by the algorithm (see Orwin 1985). But the fault is not with the failure of the algorithm to include and instruct on all contingencies, for in practice that would not be possible. With a construct as complex as treatment integrity or internal validity, no amount of preliminary work on the coding algorithm will eliminate the need for judgment calls. Indeed, the contingency instructions are judgment calls themselves, so at best the point of judgment has only been moved, not eliminated.[3]

Other examples abound. Although Terpstra (1981) reported perfect coding reliability in his synthesis of organization development research, Bullock and Svyantek's replication (1985) reported numerous problems with both reliability and validity. Specifically, they reported that problems occurred in the coding of the dependent variable, where coding required a great deal of subjectivity. Similarly, McGuire et al. (1985) were unable to achieve adequate intercoder agreement on methodological quality despite having methodologically sophisticated coders, written coding instructions, *and* clearly reported study methods. As noted previously, coding difficulty reflects the complexity of the item to be coded, not just the clarity with which it is reported.

Inherent ambiguities affect more fundamental coding decisions than simply what values to code, such as what effect sizes to include. Green and Hall (1984) observed that synthesists are divided as to whether to use multiple outcomes per group comparison. As shown by Orwin and Cordray (1985) and Matt (1989), the so-called conceptual redundancy rule—the process used in the original Smith, Glass, and Miller (1980) psychotherapy synthesis for determining which of multiple effect sizes within a given study should be counted in determining overall effect size—can be interpreted quite differently by different coders.[4] In recoding a 25-study sample from the original Smith, Glass, and Miller (1980) psychotherapy data, four independent coders extracted 81, 159, 172, and 165 effect sizes, respectively (Orwin & Cordray 1985; Matt 1989). The corresponding average effect sizes were .90, .47, .68, and .49. Thus, when

supposedly following the same decision rule for extracting effect sizes, both the number of effect sizes and the resulting findings varied by a factor of 2. Using the same set of printed guidelines on conceptual redundancy, the coders still disagreed substantially. Not surprisingly, coder disagreement on which effect sizes to include led to more discrepant results than coder disagreement on effect size computations once the "set" of effect sizes had been decided on (Matt 1989). Again, more clarity in the decision rule might have better guided the judgment process, but it is unlikely that it could have eliminated the *need* for judgment.

Additional inclusion rules can compensate for the lack of agreement stemming from the conceptual redundancy rule. For instance, the synthesis can be restricted to that subset of nonredundant effect sizes on which all or at least most coders agree (Orwin & Cordray 1985). This has the effect of eliminating potentially questionable effect sizes. In still another variation, Shapiro and Shapiro (1982) retained all measures except those permitting only a "relatively imprecise" effect size estimate. These were discarded if, in the coders' view, the study provided more complete data on enough other measures. Matt (1989) presents additional rules for selecting effect sizes.

## 2.3 Coder Bias

An additional error source is coder bias (e.g., for or against a given therapy). A coder with an agenda is not a good coder. The ideal coder is totally unbiased *and* expert in the content area, but such a coder is difficult to find. (Some would argue that by definition, it is impossible.) Expertise carries the baggage of opinions, and keeping those opinions out of coding decisions—many of which are by definition judgmental—is difficult to do. Ambiguities in the judgment process and coder bias are related in that ambiguity creates a hospitable environment for bias to creep in unnoticed.

Sometimes it is more blatant. In a synthesis of the effects of school desegregation on black achievement (Wortman & Bryant 1985), a panel of six experts convened by the National Institute of Education independently analyzed the same set of studies, obtaining different results and reaching different conclusions. Panelists excluded studies, substituted alternative control groups, and sought missing information from authors in accordance with their prior beliefs on the effectiveness of desegregation. Even after discussion, the panel "disbanded with their initial views intact" (p. 315).

---

[3]That detailed criteria for decisions fail to eliminate coder disagreement should not be surprising, even if all known contingencies are incorporated (see Horwitz & Yu 1984 for an analog from coding patient records in epidemiology).

[4]Specifically, this rule aims to exclude effect sizes based on redundant outcome measures. A measure was judged to be redundant if it matched another in outcome type, reactivity, follow-up time, *and* magnitude of effect.

One approach to reducing bias is to keep coders selectively blind to information that triggers bias. Chalmers et al. (1987) had two coders independently review papers in random order, with the methods sections separated from the results.[5] In addition, papers were photocopied in such a way that the coders could not determine their origins. Sacks et al. (1987) suggest that this is an ideal way to control for this type of bias, but also note that it is rarely done. In the 86 meta-analyses of randomized clinical trials analyzed by Sacks et al., none were successfully blinded (three showed evidence of attempts). The rationale for such blinding is exactly the same as in primary studies: to reduce experimenter expectancy effects and related artifacts. It is consistent with the central theme of this book: that research synthesis is a scientific endeavor subject to the same rigorous standards as primary research.

## 2.4 Coder Mistakes

Of course, coders can be *un*biased in the sense of holding no prior views about the likely outcomes of the research being coded, and still make systematic mistakes—systematic in the statistical sense of nonrandom error. The problem is by no means unique to synthesis coding. In their analysis of errors in the extraction of epidemiological data from patient records, Horwitz and Yu (1984) found that most coding errors occurred because the data extractor simply failed to locate information that was present in the medical record. Additional errors were made when information *was* correctly extracted, but the coding criteria were incorrectly applied.

The synthesis coding process is also subject to the same range of simple coder mistakes as any other coding process, including slips of the pencil and keypunch errors. It is particularly vulnerable to the effects of boredom, fatigue, and so on. In a synthesis of any size, many hours are required, often over a period of months, to code a set of studies. The degradation of coder performance under these conditions is discussed further in section 4.1.6.

## 3. STRATEGIES TO REDUCE ERROR

This section discusses seven strategies that potentially reduce error: contacting original investigators, consulting external literature, training coders, pilot testing the coding protocol, possessing substantive expertise, improving primary reporting, and using averaged ratings.

## 3.1 Contacting Original Investigators

An apparent solution to the problem of missing or unclear information is to contact the original investigators in the hope of retrieving or clarifying it. This becomes a labor-intensive task when the number of studies is large, so it is prudent to consider the odds of successful retrieval: (a) The investigators have to be alive; (b) they have to be located; (c) they have to have collected the information in the first place; (d) they have to have kept it; and (e) they have to be willing and able to provide it. Hyde's synthesis (1981) of cognitive gender differences is informative here. Rather than trying to estimate effect sizes from incomplete information, she wrote to the authors. Of the 53 studies in her database, 18 lacked the necessary means and standard deviations. Although all 18 authors were located, only 7 responded, and only 2 of these were able to supply the information. Furthermore, the successful contact rate may have been atypically high because the topic of cognitive gender differences at that time was relatively young; studies that predated the synthesis by more than 15 years were rare. Of course, Hyde's final success rate could have been still worse had more esoteric information than means and standard deviations been sought. As noted by Light and Pillemer (1984), the chance of success probably depends quite idiosyncratically on the field, the investigators, and other factors such as the dates of the studies.

## 3.2 Consulting External Literature

A subset of the information of interest to the synthesist is theoretically obtainable from other published sources if omitted or obscured in the reports. For one variable, experimenter affiliation (training), this option was exercised by Smith, Glass, and Miller (1980) in their original psychotherapy synthesis, and by others since. When the experimenter's affiliation was not evident from the report, the American Psychological Association directory was consulted. In our reanalysis of the same data (Orwin & Cordray 1985), we attempted to get the reliability of the outcome measure, when not extractable from the report, from the *Mental Measurements Yearbook* (Buros 1938–1978). The strategy was unsuccessful, for a number of reasons: (a) Many measures were

---

[5]The Chalmers et al. (1987) review was actually a review of "replicate" meta-analyses rather than a meta-analysis per se (i.e., the individual studies were meta-analyses), but the principle is equally applicable to meta-analysis proper.

not reviewed (e.g., less-established personality inventories, experimenter-developed convenience scales); (b) when measures were reviewed, a discussion of reliability was frequently omitted; (c) when measures were reviewed and a discussion of reliability included, the range of estimates was sometimes too wide to be useful; and (d) when measures were reviewed, reliability discussed, and an interpretable range of values provided, they were not always generalizable to the population sampled for the psychotherapy study. Contacting test developers directly would provide more information than consulting the *Mental Measurements Yearbook,* but reliabilities of experimenter-developed convenience scales are not obtainable this way. Nor could the problem of generalizing to different populations be resolved.

The use of external sources may be more successful with other variables. However, the proportion of variables that are potentially retrievable via this strategy will typically be small. For example, of the 50+ variables coded in the Smith, Glass, and Miller study, experimenter allegiance appeared to be the only variable other than experimenter affiliation that might be deducible through an external published source.

### 3.3 Training Coders

Given the importance and complexity of the coding task, the need for solid coder training as an error-reduction strategy is self-evident. (This topic is covered in detail in Chapter 10.)

### 3.4 Pilot Testing the Coding Protocol

Piloting the coding protocol for a synthesis is no less essential than piloting any treatment or measurement protocol in primary research. First, it supplies coders with firsthand experience in applying the conventions and decision rules of the process *prior* to coding the main sample, which is necessary to minimize learning effects. Second, it assesses whether a coder's basic interpretations of conventions and decision rules are consistent with the synthesist's intent and with the other coders' intent. This is necessary to preclude underestimation of attainable levels of interrater reliabilities. Third, it can identify inadequacies in the protocol itself, such as the need for additional categories for particular variables or additional variables to adequately map the studies.

The concept of pilot testing was taken a step further by Bullock and Svyantek (1985) in their reanalysis of a prior synthesis of the organization development literature. After dividing the 16-year time period of study in half, each author independently coded the first half so as to develop reliability estimates *as well as* resolve preliminary coding problems. After reviewing their work, along with each instance of disagreement, the authors attempted to improve interrater reliability by developing more explicit decision rules for the same coding scheme. The more explicit rules were then applied to the studies from the second half of the time period. Agreement was higher in the second half on 6 of 7 variables tested, sometimes dramatically so (e.g., agreement on sample size increased from 70 to 94 percent). The distinction between what these authors did from what is typically done is that the preliminary codings were done on a large enough subset of studies to yield reliable quantitative estimates of agreement. This enabled an empirical validation that agreement had indeed improved on the second half. However, it is not clear why the authors halved the sample by time period rather than randomly, since using time period introduced a potential confound into the explanation of improvement. That is, if the quality of reporting improved during the second half of the study period, this alone could account for much of the improvement in interrater reliability.[6]

### 3.5 Possessing Substantive Expertise

Substantive expertise will not reduce the need for judgment calls, but should increase their accuracy. Numerous authors have stressed the need for substantive expertise, and with good reason: The synthesist who possesses it makes more informed and thoughtful judgments at all levels. Still, scholars with comparable expertise disagree frequently on matters of judgment in the social sciences as elsewhere, particularly when they bring pre-existing biases, as noted earlier. Substantive expertise informs judgment, but will not guarantee that the right call was made.

### 3.6 Improving Primary Reporting

While the individual synthesist can do nothing about improving primary reporting, social science publications can do something to reduce error in synthesis coding. There is evidence of progress in this regard. For ex-

---

[6]Such improvement is quite plausible. For example, Orwin (1983b) found that measures of reporting quality were positively correlated with publication date in the Smith, Glass, and Miller (1980) psychotherapy data.

ample, the *Academy of Management Journal* changed its submission requirements to ''improve the accessibility, interest, and scientific usefulness'' of the research published in the *AMJ,* particularly to ensure its utility in future meta-analyses (Beyer 1985). Authors were asked for more uniform and extensive reporting of research procedures and methods than had previously been customary. Detailed specifications were laid out for reporting on the population, sampling, researcher-subject contact, data collection, measurement, analytic methods employed, and basic statistics. On measurement, for example, information was to be provided on each measure used, including all items and their response formats; reliability coefficients; available validity data; details on any techniques used for scale construction, along with results; and similar detail on archival and qualitative measures. Appendices would be permitted for methodological details that would otherwise interrupt the flow of arguments.

The new guidelines also stressed that authors present their research so that scholars *outside their specialized area* (emphasis added) can understand their ideas and data—for example, by making theoretical rationales and linkages explicit and by defining any terms not in general use so that readers from other subfields can follow arguments and procedures. The case might be made that such high-quality reporting would actually reduce the need for substantive expertise on the part of coders (with attendant reduction in bias that such expertise carries with it), in that it reduces the need to ''read between the lines'' in ways only experts can do.

### 3.7 Using Averaged Ratings

It is a psychometric truism that averages of multiple independent ratings will improve reliability (and therefore reduce error) relative to individual ratings. In principle, then, it is desirable for the synthesist to use such averages whenever possible. Two practical problems limit the applicability of this principle: First, the resources required to double- or triple-code the entire set of studies can be substantial, particularly when the number of studies is large and/or the coding form is extensive. Second, many variables of interest in a typical synthesis are categorical, and therefore cannot be readily averaged across raters. For example, ''therapy modality'' from Smith, Glass, and Miller (1980) could be coded as (a) individual, (b) group, (c) family, (d) mixed, (e) automated, or (f) other; it is not clear how an average rating would be possible for such a variable.

The first problem can be ameliorated by targeting for multiple coding only those variables that are known in advance to be both important to the analysis and prone to high error rates (e.g., effect size and internal validity are two variables that would meet both criteria). The foreknowledge to select the variables can frequently be acquired through a targeted review of prior research (Cordray & Sonnefeld 1985), as well as through the synthesist's own pilot test. The second problem is more structural, being a property of the categorical measure itself. A commonsense solution might be, again, to target only those variables that are both important to the analysis and error-prone and have each coded by three raters. Three raters would permit a ''majority rule'' in the event that unanimity was not achieved. (If the three coders selected three different responses—that is, there was no majority—the synthesist should probably reconsider the use of that variable altogether.)

### 4. STRATEGIES TO CONTROL FOR ERROR

It is always better to reduce error than to attempt to control and correct for it after the fact. For example, methods such as the correction for attenuation from measurement error, while useful, tend to *over*correct for error, because the reliability estimates they employ in the denominator often are biased downward. Yet strategies to control for error are necessary because, as documented above, strategies to reduce error can only succeed to a limited degree. Whether due to deficient reporting quality, the limits of coder judgment, or a combination of the two, there will always be a large residual error that cannot be eliminated. The question then becomes how to control for it, and the answer begins with strategies for evaluating coding decisions. Three such strategies will be discussed here: interrater reliability assessment, confidence ratings, and sensitivity analysis.

### 4.1 Reliability Assessment

**4.1.1 Rationale** As in primary research applications, the amount of observer error in research synthesis can be at least partially estimated via one or more forms of interrater reliability (IRR). Our reanalysis of the Smith, Glass, and Miller psychotherapy data (Orwin & Cordray 1985) suggested that failing to assess IRR and to consider it in subsequent analyses can yield misleading results.

In the original synthesis of psychotherapy outcomes,

a 16-variable simultaneous multiple regression analysis was used to predict outcomes. Identical regressions were run within three treatment "classes" and six "sub-classes," as defined through multidimensional scaling techniques with the assistance of substantive experts (see Smith, Glass & Miller 1980). Orwin and Cordray (1985) recoded a sample of studies from the original synthesis, and computed IRRs. They then reran the original regression analyses with corrections for attenuation. Approximately twice per class and twice per subclass, on average, corrections based on one or more reliability estimates caused the sign of an uncorrected predictor's coefficient to reverse.[7] The implication of a sign reversal (when significant) is that interpretation of the uncorrected coefficient would have led to an incorrect conclusion regarding the direction of the predictor's influence on the effect size. In every run in every class and subclass, the reliability correction altered the ranking of the predictors in their capacity to account for variance in effect size.

At least two of the major conclusions of the original study were brought into question by these findings. The first was that the study disconfirmed allegations by critics of psychotherapy that poor-quality research methods have accounted for observed positive outcomes. This conclusion was based on the trivial amount of observed correlation ($r = .03$) between internal validity and effect size, which was taken as evidence that design quality had no effect. Our reanalyses suggested that unreliability may have so seriously attenuated both the bivariate correlation between the two variables and contribution of internal validity to the regression equations that only an unrealistically large relationship could have been detected. Based on our recodings, the reliability of internal validity may have been as low as .36.[8]

The second conclusion by Smith, Glass, and Miller bearing another look in light of these reanalyses was that the outcomes of psychotherapy treatments cannot be very accurately predicted from characteristics of studies. While the reliability-corrected regressions do not account for enough additional variance in effect size to claim "very accurate" prediction, they do improve the situation. It would be likely to improve still more with better-specified models, at least to the extent that re-

porting quality and coder judgment would permit them. The point is that while unreliability *alone* cannot explain the poor performance of the Smith, Glass, and Miller model, it could be part of a larger process that does.

Unreliability in the primary study dependent measure attenuates not only relationships with effect size, but the effect size estimate itself. Under classical test theory assumptions, measurement error has no effect on the means of the treatment and comparison groups, but increases the within-group variance. Hedges and Olkin (1985) have shown that under that model, the true effect size for a given study is equal to the observed effect size over the square root of the reliability of the dependent measure. If the dependent measure had a reliability of .70, for example, the estimated true effect size would equal the observed effect size times $1/.70^{1/2}$, so the observed effect size would underestimate the true effect size by 16 percent. Error in coding effect size estimates then exacerbates the problem by increasing the variance of the effect size distribution at the aggregate level.

Despite wide recognition by writers on research synthesis of the need to assess IRR, in practice addressing coder reliability may still be the exception rather than the rule. For example, only 29 percent of the meta-analyses published in *Psychological Bulletin* from 1986 through 1988 reported a measure of coder reliability (Yeaton & Wortman 1991). Given the high methodological standards of *Psychological Bulletin* relative to many other social research journals that now publish meta-analyses, the field-wide percentage may be significantly lower.

**4.1.2 Across-the-board versus item-by-item agreement** Smith, Glass, and Miller's reliability assessment (1980) consisted of the computation of a simple agreement rate across all variables in an abbreviated coding form, which came to 92 percent. According to Stock et al. (1982), who reviewed the practice of synthesists regarding interrater reliabilities, subsequent synthesists did much the same thing, if that much. That is, a single across-the-board agreement rate, falling somewhere between .7 and 1.0, is the extent of what typically gets reported.

There are at least two major problems with this practice. First, it makes little psychometric sense. The coding form is simply a list of items; it is not a multi-item measure of a trait, such that a total-scale reliability would be meaningful. Some items, such as publication date, will have very high interrater agreement, whereas others, such as internal validity, may not. Particularly if reliabilities are to be meaningfully incorporated into

---

[7]The rationale for using multiple estimates is discussed in section 4.3.3.

[8]There is nothing anomalous about the present coders' relative lack of agreement on internal validity; lack of consensus on ratings of research quality is commonplace (see Stock et al. 1982 for an example within meta-analysis).

subsequent analyses (e.g., by correcting correlation matrices for attenuation), it is this variation that needs to be recognized. In our reanalysis of the Smith, Glass, and Miller (1980) psychotherapy data, we replicated an equivalently high overall agreement rate. However, agreement across individual variables ranged from .24 to 1.00 (other indices of IRR showed similar variability).

Second, an across-the-board reliability fails to inform the synthesist of specific variables needing refinement or replacement. Thus, an opportunity to improve the process is lost. In sum, the synthesist should assess IRR on an item-by-item basis.

**4.1.3 Hierarchical approaches** When synthesists *do* compute item-by-item IRRs, they typically treat the reliability estimate of each item independently. An alternative approach has been suggested by Yeaton and Wortman (1991). In addition to reinforcing the need to examine item-level reliabilities rather than simply overall reliability, the approach recognizes that item reliabilities are hierarchical, in that the correctness of coding decisions at a given level of the hierarchy are contingent on decisions made at higher levels. In such cases, the code given to a particular variable may restrict the possible codes for other variables. In the hierarchical structure, the IRRs of different variables, as well as the codings themselves, are nonindependent. Existing approaches to IRR in research synthesis do not take this into account.

Yeaton and Wortman illustrate the hierarchical approach with three variables from the original Smith, Glass, and Miller (1980) psychotherapy synthesis. Each can be conceived at a different hierarchical level:

Level 1 (condition): Are these treatment or control group data?

Level 2 (type): What type of treatment or control group is used?

Level 3 (measure): For the type of condition, what measure is reported?

Level 1 identifies the group as psychotherapy or control; level 2 involves a choice of ten general types of therapy and control groups; level 3 consists of four general types of outcome measures used in the calculation of effect size measures. The levels of the hierarchy reflect the contingent nature of the coding decisions; that is, agreement at lower levels is conditional on agreement at higher levels. If the variables are strictly hierarchical (and this is an empirical question in each synthesis), then incorrect coding at one level ensures incorrect coding at all lower levels, and, conversely, correct coding at the lowest level indicates that coding was correct at each higher level. The fact that errors can be made at each level adds to the variability of IRR. Without a hierarchical approach, this variability is obscured and results can be misleading. For example, what does it mean to "correctly" code type of control group as placebo (level 2), if in fact that group was actually a treatment group (level 1)?

Yeaton and Wortman examined IRRs by level in several syntheses and found that agreement did indeed decrease as level increased, as predicted by their hierarchical model. The results provide yet another argument against an across-the-board agreement rate; that it overestimates true agreement because of the uneven distribution of items across levels (level 1 items tend to be the most numerous).

While more work is needed on the details of how best to apply a hierarchical approach, it clearly presents a more realistic model of the coding process than one which assumes that IRR for each variable is independent. At minimum, synthesists should understand the hierarchical relationships between their own variables prior to interpreting the IRRs calculated on those variables.

**4.1.4 Specific indices of interrater reliability** Oliver (1987) and others have noted that authorities do not agree on the best index of IRR to use in coding syntheses. This presentation will not attempt to resolve all the controversies, but will hopefully provide enough of a foundation for the synthesist who is not a statistician to make informed choices. Four indices are presented: agreement rate, kappa and weighted kappa, intercoder correlation, and intraclass correlation. The discussion of each will include a description (including formulas), a computational illustration, and a discussion of strengths and limitations in the context of research synthesis. The following section will cover the selection, interpretation, and reporting of IRR indices.

*Agreement rate.* Percent agreement, alternately called agreement rate *(AR),* has been the most widely used index of IRR in research synthesis. The formula for *AR* is as follows:

$$AR = \frac{\text{number of observations agreed upon}}{\text{total number of observations}}$$

Table 11.1 presents a hypothetical data set that might have been created had two coders independently rated 25 studies on a 3-point study characteristic (e.g., the Smith, Glass, and Miller internal validity scale). On this

**Table 11.1 Illustrative Data: Ratings of 25 Studies on a 3-Point Scale by Two Coders**

| Study | Coder 1 | Coder 2 |
|---|---|---|
| 1 | 3 | 2 |
| 2 | 3 | 1 |
| 3 | 2 | 2 |
| 4 | 3 | 2 |
| 5 | 1 | 1 |
| 6 | 3 | 1 |
| 7 | 2 | 2 |
| 8 | 1 | 1 |
| 9 | 2 | 2 |
| 10 | 2 | 1 |
| 11 | 2 | 2 |
| 12 | 3 | 3 |
| 13 | 3 | 1 |
| 14 | 2 | 1 |
| 15 | 1 | 1 |
| 16 | 1 | 1 |
| 17 | 3 | 3 |
| 18 | 2 | 2 |
| 19 | 2 | 2 |
| 20 | 3 | 1 |
| 21 | 2 | 1 |
| 22 | 1 | 1 |
| 23 | 3 | 2 |
| 24 | 3 | 3 |
| 25 | 2 | 2 |

particular characteristic, a rating of 1 = low, 2 = medium, and 3 = high. As shown, the coders agreed in 15 cases out of 25, so $AR = .60$.

$AR$ is computationally simple and intuitively interpretable, being basically a batting average. Yet numerous writers on observational measurement have discussed the pitfalls of its use (Cohen 1960; Hartmann 1977; Light 1971; Scott 1955). When variables are categorical (the usual application), the main problem is chance agreement, particularly when response marginals are extreme. For example, the expected agreement between two raters on a yes-no item in which each rater's marginal response rate is 10–90 percent would be 82 percent *by chance alone* (Hartmann 1977). In other words, these raters could post a respectable (by most standards) interrater reliability simply by guessing without ever having observed an actual case. Extreme marginal response rates are commonplace in many contexts

(e.g., psychiatric diagnosis of low-prevalence disorders), including research synthesis (see, e.g., "historical effects" in Kulik, Kulik & Cohen 1979; "design validity" in Smith 1980). Additional problems arise when marginal response rates differ across raters (Cohen 1960).

When applied to ordinal (as opposed to nominal) categorical variables, $AR$ has an additional drawback: the inability to discriminate between degrees of disagreement. In Smith, Glass, and Miller's 3-point IQ scale, for example, a low-high interrater pattern indicates greater disagreement than does a low-average or average-high pattern, yet a simple $AR$ registers identical disagreement for all three patterns. The situation is taken to the extreme with quantitative variables.

*Cohen's kappa and weighted kappa.* Various statistics have been proposed for categorical data to improve on $AR$ (see Light 1971), particularly with regard to removing chance agreement. Of these, Cohen's (1960) kappa ($\kappa$) has frequently received high marks (Fleiss, Cohen & Everett 1969; Hartmann 1977; Light 1971; Shrout, Spitzer & Fleiss 1987). The parameter $\kappa$ is defined as the proportion of the best possible improvement over chance that is actually obtained by the raters (Shrout, Spitzer & Fleiss 1987). The formula for the estimate $K$ of kappa computed from a sample is as follows:

$$K = \frac{P_o - P_e}{1 - P_e},$$

where $P_o$ and $P_e$ are the observed and expected agreement rates, respectively. The expected agreement rate is the sum of the expected agreement cell probabilities, which are computed exactly as in a chi-square test of association. That is,

$$P_e = \frac{1}{n^2} \sum_{i=1}^{C} n_{i\cdot} n_{\cdot i},$$

where $n$ is the number of observations, $C$ is the number of response categories, and $n_{i\cdot}$ and $n_{\cdot i}$ are the observed row and column marginals for response $i$ for raters 1 and 2, respectively.

The formula for weighted kappa ($K_w$) is as follows:

$$K_w = 1 - \frac{\sum w_i p_{oi}}{\sum w_i p_{ei}},$$

where $w_i$ is the disagreement level assigned to cell $i$, and $p_{oi}$ and $p_{ei}$ are the observed and expected proportions, respectively, in cell $i$. If regular (i.e., unweighted) $K$ is re-expressed as $1 - D_o/D_e$, where $D_o$ and $D_e$ are

**Table 11.2 Illustrative Data: Cell Counts and Marginals**

|  | | Coder 1 | | | |
| --- | --- | --- | --- | --- | --- |
|  | Value | 1 | 2 | 3 | Sum |
|  | 1 | 5 | 3 | 4 | 12 |
| Coder 2 | 2 | 0 | 7 | 3 | 10 |
|  | 3 | 0 | 0 | 3 | 3 |
|  | Sum | 5 | 10 | 10 | 25 |

observed and expected proportion disagreement, it can be seen that $K$ is a special case of $K_w$ in which all disagreement weights equal 1.

Table 11.2 shows the cell counts and marginals from the illustrative data from Table 11.1. Plugging in the values, $P_e = [(12)(5) + (10)(10) + (3)(10)] / (25)^2 = .304$. $K = (.6 - .304) / (1 - .304) = .43$. Thus, chance-corrected agreement in this example is slightly less than half of what it could have been. In order to compute $K_w$, the weights ($w_i$) must be assigned first. Agreement cells are assigned weights of 0. With a 3-point scale such as this one, some logical weights would be 2 for the low-high interrater pattern and 1 for the low-medium and medium-high patterns, although other weights are possible of course. Summing across the $w_i p_{oi}$ products for each cell $i$ yields $\Sigma w_i p_{oi} = .56$. Similarly, summing across the $w_i p_{ei}$ products yields $\Sigma w_i p_{ei} = .912$. Then, $K_w = 1 - .56 / .912 = .39$. In this case, a relatively modest percentage of disagreements (4 of 10) were by two scale points, as one would hope to be the case with a 3-point scale. Consequently, $K_w$ is only slightly lower than $K$. With more scale points, the difference will generally be larger.

As is evident from the formula for $K$, chance agreement is directly removed from both numerator and denominator. Kappa has other desirable properties:

1. It is a "true" reliability statistic, which in large samples is equivalent to the intraclass correlation coefficient (discussed below; Fleiss & Cohen 1973).

2. Because $P_e$ is computed from observed marginals, no assumption of identical marginals across raters (required with certain earlier statistics) is needed.

3. It can be generalized to multiple (i.e., >2) raters (Fleiss 1971; Light 1971).

4. It can be weighted to reflect varying degrees of disagreement (Cohen 1968), for example, for the

Smith, Glass, and Miller IQ variable mentioned earlier.

5. Large-sample standard errors have been derived for both $K$ and $K_w$ (Fleiss, Cohen & Everett 1969), thus permitting the use of significance tests and confidence intervals.

6. It takes on negative values when agreement is less than chance (range is $-1$ to 1), thus indicating the presence of systematic *dis*agreement as well as agreement.

7. It can be adapted to stratified reliability designs (Shrout, Spitzer & Fleiss 1987).

Thus, $K$ is not a single index, but rather a family of indices that can be adapted to various circumstances.

While $K$ and $K_w$ resolve most of the problems of $AR$, potential problems remain if observations are concentrated in only a few cells (Jones et al. 1983). This circumstance increases the probability that a high proportion of scores will be assigned to one or two rating categories while other categories receive small or nonexistent proportions. Jones et al. and others (e.g., Burton 1981) have argued that this distribution violates the assumption on which $K$ and $K_w$ are based, reducing the usefulness of the information. In a similar vein, Whitehurst (1984) noted that $K$ is sensitive to the degree of disagreement between raters, which is desirable, but also remarkably sensitive to the distribution of ratings, which Whitehurst argued was *not* desirable. A highly skewed distribution of ratings will yield high estimates of chance agreement in just those cells in which obtained agreement is also high. This makes for low estimates of true agreement in the face of high levels of obtained agreement and, consequently, low estimates of IRR. As noted earlier, the phenomenon is common in psychiatric diagnosis when prevalence is low and has been termed the base rate problem with $K$ (Carey & Gottesman 1978).

However, others (e.g., Shrout, Spitzer & Fleiss 1987) view this as a case of shooting the messenger. As they see it, the observation that low base rates decrease $K$ is not an indictment of $K$, but rather represents the real problem of making distinctions in increasingly homogeneous populations. Similarly, Zwick (1988) questioned whether the sensitivity of $K$ to the shape of the marginal distributions is necessarily undesirable: If cases are concentrated into a small number of categories, it is less demonstrable that coders can reliably discriminate among *all* $C$ categories, and the IRR coefficient should reflect this. Finally, there is no mathematical necessity for small $K$ values with low base rates (i.e., the maximum value of $K$ remains at 1.0) and high $K$'s have in fact been demonstrated empirically with base rates as low as 2 percent (American Psychiatric Association 1980). However, $K$ was designed for categorical data and is not appropriate for continuous variables, to which we now turn.

*Intercoder correlation.* Numerous statistics have been suggested to assess IRR on continuous variables as well. One of the more popular is the common Pearson correlation coefficient *(r)*, sometimes called the intercoder correlation in this context. Pearson $r$ is as follows:

$$r = \frac{\sum_{i=1}^{n} (X_i - \overline{X})(Y_i - \overline{Y})}{ns_X s_Y},$$

where $(X_i, Y_i)$ are the $n$ pairs of values, and $s_X$ and $s_Y$ are the standard deviations of the two variables computed using $n$ in the denominator. With more than two coders, this index is generally obtained by calculating $r$ across all pairs of coders rating the phenomenon (Jones et al. 1983). The resulting correlations can then be averaged to determine an overall value.

In our example, $\overline{X}$ and $\overline{Y}$ are 2.2 and 1.64, and $s_X$ and $s_Y$ are .75 and .69, respectively, and $n$ is 25. Plugging the values into the above formula, $r = 5.8/12.94 = .45$. In practice, the synthesist will only rarely need to calculate $r$ by hand, as all standard statistical packages and many hand calculators compute it.

The use of Pearson $r$ with observational data to estimate IRRs is analogous to its use in education to estimate test reliabilities when parallel test forms are available (see Stanley 1971). As such, it bears the same relationship to formal reliability theory.[9] The Pearson $r$ also has some drawbacks. First, although it describes the degree to which the scores produced by each coder covary, it says nothing about the degree to which the scores themselves are identical. In principle, this means that coders can produce high $r$'s without actually agreeing on any scores. Conversely, an increase in absolute agreement can actually reduce $r$ if the disagreement had been part of a consistent disagreement pattern (e.g., one

rater rating targets consistently lower than the other).[10] If the IRR estimate will be used only to adjust subsequent analyses, this may not be particularly important. If it will be used to diagnose coder consistency in interpreting instructions (e.g., for extracting effect sizes), it can be quite important. Second, the between-coders variance is always removed in computing the product moment formula. Ebel (1951) noted that this is especially problematic when comparisons are made among single raw scores assigned to different subjects by different coders (in research synthesis, of course, the "subject" is the individual study).

*Intraclass correlation.* Analogous to the concepts of true score and error in classical reliability theory, the intraclass correlation $(r_I)$ is computed as a ratio of the variance of interest over the sum of the variance of interest plus error. Ebel (1951) and others suggested that $r_I$ was preferable to Pearson $r$ as an index of IRR with continuous variables because it permits the researcher to choose whether or not to include the between-raters variance in the error term.

Like $K$, $r_I$ is not a single index but a family of indices that permit great flexibility in matching the form of the reliability index to the reliability "design" used by the synthesist; design in the sense used in Cronbach's generalizability *(G)* theory (Cronbach et al. 1972). Generalizability theory enables the analyst to isolate different sources of variation in the measurement (e.g., forms or occasions) and to estimate their magnitude using the analysis of variance (Shavelson & Webb 1991). The reliability design as discussed here is a special case of the one-facet $G$ study (Shrout & Fleiss 1979), in which coders are the facet.

So far, the running example has been discussed in terms of 25 studies being coded by two coders, but in fact at least three different reliability designs share this description.

*Design 1:* Each study is rated by a different pair of coders, randomly selected from a larger population of coders (one-way random effects model).

*Design 2:* A random pair of coders is selected from a larger population, and each coder rates all 25 studies (two-way random effects model).

*Design 3:* All 25 studies are rated by each of the same pair of coders, who are the only coders of interest (two-way mixed effects model).

---

[9]This desirable characteristic has led some writers (e.g., Hartmann 1977) to advocate extending the use of $r$, in the form of the phi coefficient $(\phi)$, to reliability estimation of dichotomous items: $\phi = (BC - AD) / ((A + B)(C + D)(A + C)(B + D))^{1/2}$, where $A$, $B$, $C$, and $D$ represent the frequencies in the first through fourth quadrants of the resulting $2 \times 2$ table.

[10]This phenomenon is easily demonstrated with the illustrative data; the details are left to the reader as an exercise.

Designs 1 and 2 are common in research synthesis. While actual random selection of coders is rare, the synthesist's usual intent is that those selected represent, at least in principle, a larger population of coders who might have been selected. Whether explicitly stated or not, synthesists typically present their substantive findings as generalizable across that population. The findings will hold little scientific interest if, say, only a particular subset of graduate students at a particular university can reproduce them. Design 3 will hold in rare instances in which the specific coders selected *are* the population of interest and can therefore be modeled as a fixed effect. This could happen if, for example, the coders are a specially convened panel of all known experts in the content area (e.g., the Wortman and Bryant school desegregation synthesis described in section 2 might have met this criterion).

Each design requires a different form of $r_I$, based on a different analysis of variance (ANOVA) structure. These forms for the running example are estimated as follows:[11]

$$r_I(\text{design 1}) = \frac{BMS - WMS}{BMS + WMS},$$

$$r_I(\text{design 2}) = \frac{BMS - EMS}{BMS + EMS + 2(CMS - EMS)/25},$$

$$r_I(\text{design 3}) = \frac{BMS - EMS}{BMS + EMS},$$

where *BMS* and *WMS* are the between-studies and within-study mean squares, respectively, and *CMS* and *EMS* are the between-coders and residual (error) mean square components, resulting from the partitioning of the within-study sum of squares. Note that this partitioning is not possible in design 1; the component representing the coder effect is estimable only when the same pair of coders rated all 25 studies.[12]

The next step is the computation of sums of squares

[11]For a fuller discussion of the statistical models underlying the estimates, see Shrout and Fleiss (1979).

[12]The *general* forms of the equations are

$$r_I(\text{design 1}) = \frac{BMS - WMS}{BMS + (k-1)WMS},$$

$$r_I(\text{design 2}) = \frac{BMS - EMS}{BMS + (k-1)EMS + k(CMS - EMS)/n},$$

$$r_I(\text{design 3}) = \frac{BMS - EMS}{BMS + (k-1)EMS},$$

where *k* is the number of coders rating each study and *n* is the number of studies.

**Table 11.3 Analysis of Variance for Illustrative Ratings**

| Source of Variance | Degrees of Freedom | Mean Squares |
|---|---|---|
| Between-studies (BMS) | 24 | .78 |
| Within-study (WMS) | 25 | .44 |
| Between-coders (CMS) | 1 | 3.92 |
| Residual (EMS) | 24 | .30 |

and mean squares from the coder data (for computational details, see any standard statistics text, e.g., Hayes 1973). Table 11.3 shows the various mean squares and their associated degrees of freedom for the data from Table 11.1. Plugging the values into the above formulae yields the following results:

$$r_I(\text{design 1}) = .28,$$
$$r_I(\text{design 2}) = .35,$$
$$r_I(\text{design 3}) = .44.$$

On average, $r_I(\text{design 1})$ will give smaller values than $r_I(\text{design 2})$ or $r_I(\text{design 3})$ for the same set of data (Shrout & Fleiss 1979).

When its assumptions are met, the $r_I$ family has been mathematically shown to provide appropriate estimates of classical reliability for the IRR case (Lord & Novick 1968). Its flexibility and linkage into *G* theory also argue in its favor.[13] Perhaps most important, its different variants reinforce the idea that a good IRR assessment requires the synthesist to think through the appropriate IRR design, not just calculate reliability statistics. However, because the $r_I$ is ANOVA-based, it fails to produce coefficients that reflect the consistency of ratings when assumptions of normality are grossly violated (Selvage 1976). Furthermore, like *K,* it requires substantial between-items variance to produce a significant indication of agreement. As with *K,* some writers consider $r_I$ to be less useful as an index of IRR when the distributions are concentrated in a small range (e.g., Jones et al. 1983). The arguments and counterarguments on this issue are essentially as described above for *K.*

**4.1.5 Selection, interpretation, and reporting of interrater reliability indices** With the exception of *AR,* the indices presented above have appealing psychometric properties as reliability measures; and when properly

[13]$r_I$ is closely related to the "coefficient of generalizability" and "index of dependability" used in *G* theory (Shavelson & Webb 1991).

applied, they can be recommended for use by synthesists in evaluating coding decisions. The *AR* was included because of its simplicity and widespread use by research synthesis practitioners, but for the reasons discussed earlier, it cannot be recommended as highly. These four indices by no means exhaust all those proposed in the literature for assessing IRR. Most of these, such as Finn's *r* (Whitehurst 1984), Yule's *Y* (Spitznagel & Helzer 1985), Maxwell's *RE* (Janes 1979), and Scott's $\pi$ (Zwick 1988), were proposed to improve on perceived shortcomings of the indices presented here, in particular the $r_I$ and *K* family. Interested readers can explore that literature and draw their own conclusions. They should keep in mind, however, that the prevailing view among statisticians is that, to date, alternatives to $r_I$ and *K* are *not* improvements, but in fact propose misleading solutions to misunderstood problems (see, e.g., Cicchetti 1985 on Whitehurst 1984; and Shrout, Spitzer & Fleiss 1987 on Spitznagel & Helzer 1985). The synthesist who sticks to the appropriate form of *K* for categorical variables, and the appropriate model of $r_I$ for continuous variables, will be on solid ground. Either *AR* or *r* can be used to supplement *K* and $r_I$ for the purpose of computing multiple indices for sensitivity analysis (see section 4.3.3). The synthesist who chooses to rely on one of the less common alternatives would be wise to first become intimately familiar with its strengths and weaknesses and should probably anticipate defending the choice to a journal editor.

Once an index is selected and computed, the obvious question is: How large should it be? The answer is less obvious. For *r*, .80 is considered adequate by many psychometricians (e.g., Nunnally 1978), and at that level correlations between variables are attenuated very little by measurement error. Rules of thumb have also been suggested and used for *K* and $r_I$ (Fleiss 1981; Cicchetti & Sparrow 1981):

$$
\begin{array}{ll}
<.40: & \text{poor} \\
.40-.59: & \text{fair} \\
.60-.74: & \text{good} \\
\geq.75: & \text{excellent}
\end{array}
$$

However, these benchmarks were suggested for the specific context of evaluating IRR of psychiatric diagnoses, and their appropriateness for synthesis coding decisions is not clear.

The issue of how large is large enough is further complicated by distributional variation. The running example showed how the different indices varied for a particular data set, but not how they vary over different conditions. Jones et al. (1983) systematically compared the results obtained when the above indices are applied to a common set of ratings under various distributional assumptions. Four raters rated job descriptions using a questionnaire designed and widely used (and validated) for that purpose. The majority of ratings were on 6-point Likert-type scales with specific anchors for each point; a minority were dichotomous. The *K*, $K_w$, *AR*, *r* (in the form of average pairwise correlations), and $r_I$ were computed on each item. Aggregated across items, *K* and $K_w$ yielded the lowest estimates of IRR, producing median values of .19 and .22, respectively. The *AR* yielded the highest, with a median value of .63; *r* and $r_I$ occupied an intermediate position, with median values of .51 and .39, respectively. For the reasons noted earlier, an overall aggregate agreement index is not very meaningful for evaluating coding decisions, but is still useful for illustrating the wide variation among indices.

To examine the effect of the distributions of individual items on the variation across indices, sample items representing three conditions were analyzed: (a) high variation across ratings and high agreement across raters, (b) high variation across ratings and low agreement across raters, and (c) low variation across ratings and high agreement across raters. As shown in Table 11.4, the effects can be substantial, in particular under the third condition, where *AR* registered 77 percent agreement, but the other indices suggested no agreement beyond chance. With moderate to high variance, it makes far less difference which index is used. Therefore, argued Jones et al., a proper interpretation of the different indices—including whether they are large enough—requires an understanding of the actual distributions of the data.

It should be evident by now that the indices are *not* directly comparable, even though all but *AR* have the same range of possible values. It is therefore essential that synthesists report not only their IRR values, but the indices used to compute them. To give the reader the full picture, it would also be wise to include information about the raters' base rates, as suggested by Grove et al. (1981), particularly when they are very low or very high.

**4.1.6 Assessing coder drift** Whatever index of IRR is chosen, the synthesist cannot assume that IRR will remain stable throughout the coding period, particularly when the number of studies to code is large. As noted by Jackson (1980), coder instability arises because many hours are required, often over a period of months, to

**Table 11.4  Estimates of Interrater Agreement for Different Types of Data Distributions**

| Distributional Conditions | Kappa | Weighted Kappa | Agreement Rate | Average Correlation | Intraclass Correlation |
|---|---|---|---|---|---|
| Variations in ratings across jobs and high agreement among raters | .43 | .45 | .88 | .79 | .74 |
| Variations in ratings across jobs and low agreement among raters | .01 | .04 | .16 | .13 | .05 |
| Little variation in ratings across jobs and high agreement among raters | .04 | .04 | .77 | −.01 | −.03 |

SOURCE: Jones et al. (1983).

code a set of studies. When the coding is lengthy, IRR may change over time, and a single assessment may not be adequate.

We assessed coder drift in our reanalysis of the Smith, Glass, and Miller (1980) psychotherapy synthesis (Orwin & Cordray 1985). Prior to coding, the 25 reports in the main sample were randomly ordered, with coders instructed to adhere to the resulting sequence. It was assumed, given the random ordering, that any trend in IRRs over reports would be due to changes in coders over time (e.g., practice, boredom).[14] Equating for order permits this trend to be detected and, if desired, removed.

Following the completion of coding, a per case agreement rate was computed, consisting of the number of variables agreed on divided by the number of variables coded.[15] In itself, per case agreement rate is not particularly meaningful since it weights observations on all variables equally and is sensitive to the particular subset of variables (considered here as sampled from a larger domain) constituting the coding form. However, change in this indicator over time *is* meaningful, as it speaks to the stability of agreement. Per case agreement rate was plotted against case sequence, and little if any trend was observed. The absence of significant correlation between the two variables substantiated this conclusion. In regression terms, increasing the case sequence by one

resulted in a decrease of the agreement rate by less than one tenth of 1 percent ($b = -.09$). From this exercise it was concluded that further consideration of detrending IRRs was unnecessary in our synthesis. However, we would not presume to generalize this finding to other syntheses. Coder drift will be more of a concern in some syntheses than in others and needs to be assessed on a case-by-case basis.

The drift assessment could also be integrated into the main IRR assessment with a G theory approach. The one-facet G study with coders as the facet could be expanded to a two-facet G study with time (if measured continuously) or occasions (if measured discretely) as the second facet. This would permit the computation of a single IRR coefficient that captured the variance contributed by each facet, as well as by their interaction.

## 4.2 Confidence Ratings

**4.2.1 Rationale**  As a strategy for evaluating coding decisions, IRR is an indirect method of assessment. Directly, it assesses only coder disagreement, which *in turn* is an indicator of coder uncertainty, but a flawed one. High agreement can be forced by a predetermined convention that is little more than a conspiracy to make the same guess. It is desirable, therefore, to seek more direct methods of assessing the accuracy of the numbers gleaned from reports. Tagging each number with a confidence rating is one such method. It is based on the premise that questionable information should not be discarded, nor should it be allowed to freely mingle with less questionable information, as is usually done. The former procedure wastes information, which though

[14]Training and piloting were completed *before* the rater drift assessment began, to avoid picking up obvious training effects.

[15]The term ''case'' is used rather than ''study'' because a study can have multiple cases (one for each effect size). The term ''observation'' refers to the value assigned to a particular variable within a case.

flawed may be the best available on a given variable, while the latter injects noise at best and bias at worst into a system already beset by both problems. With confidence ratings, questionable information can be described as such, and both data point and descriptor entered into the database.

In other contexts, confidence ratings and facsimiles (e.g., adequacy ratings, certainty ratings) have been around for some time. For example, in their international comparative political parties project, Janda and colleagues (Janda 1970) constructed an "adequacy-confidence" scale to evaluate data quality. Similarly, it is not unusual to find interviewer confidence ratings embedded in questionnaires. In the *Addiction Severity Index* (McLellan et al. 1988), for example, interviewers provide confidence ratings of the accuracy of patient responses. Specifically, they coded whether in their view the information was significantly distorted by the patient's misrepresentation or the patient's inability to understand.

Two early meta-analyses, one that integrates the literature on the effects of psychotherapy (Smith & Glass 1977; Smith, Glass & Miller 1980) and another devoted to the influence of class size on achievement (Glass & Smith 1979), are used to illustrate how some of the preceding issues can be assessed. For both meta-analyses, the data files were obtained and subjected to reanalysis (Cordray & Orwin 1981; Orwin & Cordray 1985). In reviewing the primary studies, these authors were careful to note (for some variables) how the data were obtained. For example, in the class size study, the actual number of students enrolled in each class was not always reported directly, so the values recorded in the synthesis were not always based on equally accurate information. In response to this, Glass and Smith included a second variable that scored the perceived accuracy of the numbers recorded. Unfortunately, the accuracy scales were never used in the analysis (G. V. Glass, personal communication, August 1981). Similarly, in the psychotherapy study, source of IQ and confidence of treatment classifications were also coded and not used.

The synthesis of class size and achievement (Glass & Smith 1979) compared smaller class and larger class on achievement. After assigning each comparison an effect size, the authors regressed effect size on three variables: the size of the smaller class $(S)$, the size of the smaller class squared $(S^2)$, and the difference between the larger class and smaller class $(L - S)$. This procedure was done for the total database and for several subdivisions of the

data, one of which was well-controlled versus poorly controlled studies. Cordray and Orwin (1981) reran the regressions as originally reported, except that a dummy variable for overall accuracy was added to the equations. The results are in Table 11.5. Most remarkable is that accuracy made its only nontrivial contribution in well-controlled studies. A possible explanation is that differential accuracy in the reporting of class sizes is only one of many method factors operating in poorly controlled studies (and in the entire sample, as well-controlled studies are a minority) and that these mask the influence of accuracy by interacting with it in unknown ways or by inflating error variance. In any event, the considerable influence of accuracy in well-controlled studies suggested that it does matter, at least under some circumstances.

In the synthesis of psychotherapy outcomes (described earlier), an identical simultaneous multiple regression analysis was run within each treatment "class" and "subclass," but with a different orientation. Rather than specifying the treatment in the model and crosscutting by nontreatment characteristics, as with class size, the nontreatment characteristics (diagnosis, method of client solicitation, etc.) were included in the model. Orwin and Cordray (1985) recoded 20 variables (see Orwin 1983b for selection criteria) and found that across *items,* high confidence proportions ranged from 1.00 for comparison type and location down to .09 for therapist experience. Across *studies,* the proportion of variables coded with certainty or near certainty ranged from 52 to 83 percent. At the opposite pole, the proportion of guesses ranged from 25 to 0 percent.

The effect of confidence on reliabilities was dramatic; for example, the mean *AR* for high-confidence observations more than doubled that for low-confidence observations (.92 vs. .44). As to the effect of confidence on relationships between variables, 82 percent of the correlations increased in absolute value when observations rated with low and medium confidence were removed. Moreover, all correlations with effect size increased. The special importance of these should be self-evident; the relationships between study characteristics and effect size were a major focus of the original study (and are in research synthesis generally). The absolute values of correlations increased by an average of .15 (.21 − .36), or in relative terms, 71 percent.

Questions begged by the above findings include: How credible can the lack of observed relationship between therapist experience and effect size be when therapist experience is extracted from only 1 out of 10 reports

**Table 11.5 Comparison of $R^2$ for Original Glass and Smith (1979) Class Size Regression ($R_1^2$) and Original with Accuracy Added ($R_2^2$)**

|  | $R_1^2$ | $R_2^2$ | $R_2^2 - R_1^2$ |
|---|---|---|---|
| Total sample ($n = 699$) | .1799 | .1845 | .0046, $F_{(1,694)} = 3.94*$ |
| Well-controlled studies ($n = 110$) | .3797 | .4273 | .0476, $F_{(1,105)} = 8.73*$ |
| Poorly controlled studies ($n = 338$) | .0363 | .0369 | .0006, $F_{(1,333)} = 0.65$ |

SOURCE: Cordray and Orwin (1981).
*$p < .05$.

with confidence? Even for variables averaging considerably higher confidence ratings, the depression of IRRs and consequent attenuation of observed relationships between variables is evident. There are plausible alternative explanations for individual variables. For example, the outcome measures that are easiest to classify could also be the most reliable. In such circumstance, the outcome type–effect size relationship should be stronger for high confidence observations simply because the less reliable outcome types have been weeded out. An explanation like this can be plausible for individual variables, but it cannot account for the generally consistent and nontrivial strengthening of observed relationships throughout the system. Each study in the sample has its own pattern of well-reported and poorly reported variables; there was not a particular subset of studies, presumably different from the rest, that chronically fell out when high confidence observations were isolated. Consequently, any alternative explanation must be, like the one above, individually tailored to a particular relationship. Postulating a separate ad hoc explanation for *each* relationship would be unparsimonious to say the least.

**4.2.2 Empirical distinctness from reliability** It was argued previously that confidence judgments provide a more direct method of evaluating coding decisions than does IRR. It is therefore useful to ask whether this conceptual distinctness is supported by an empirical distinctness. If the information provided by confidence judgments simply duplicated that provided by reliabilities, the case for adopting both strategies in the same synthesis would be weakened.

Table 11.6 presents agreement rates by level of confidence for the complete set of variables ($K = 25$) to which confidence judgments were applied. The table indicates that interrater agreement is neither guaranteed by high confidence nor precluded by low confidence. Yet it also shows that confidence and agreement are

associated. Whereas Table 11.6 shows the nonduplicativeness of confidence and agreement on a per variable basis, Table 11.7 shows this nonduplicativeness across variables. To enable this, variables were first rank ordered by the proportion of observations in which confidence was judged as high. As seen in the table, the correlation between the two sets of rankings fell far short of perfect, regardless of the reliability estimate selected. In sum, the conceptual distinctness between reliability and confidence is supported by an empirical distinctness.

**4.2.3 Methods for assessing coder confidence** There is no set method for assessing confidence. Orwin and Cordray (1985) used a single confidence item for each variable. This is not to imply that confidence is unidimensional; no doubt it is a complex composite of numerous factors. These factors can interact in various ways to affect the coder's ultimate confidence judgment, but Orwin and Cordray did not attempt to spell out rules for handling the many contingencies that arise. Confidence judgments reflected the overall pattern of information as deemed appropriate by the coder.

Alternative schemes are of course possible. One might use *two* confidence judgments per data point—one rating confidence in the accuracy and/or completeness of the information as reported and the other rating confidence in the coding interpretation applied to that information. The use of two (or more) such ratings explicitly recognizes multiple sources of error in the coding process (as was described in section 2) and makes some attempt to isolate them. More involved schemes, such as Janda's scheme (1970) might also be attempted, particularly if information is being sought from multiple sources. As noted earlier, Janda constructed an ''adequacy-confidence'' scale to evaluate data quality. The adequacy-confidence scale was designed to reflect four factors considered important in determining the researchers' belief in the accuracy of the coded variable values: (a)

**Table 11.6 Agreement Rate by Level of Confidence for Selected Variables from the Smith, Glass, and Miller (1980) Psychotherapy Meta-Analysis (n = 126) (sample sizes in parenthesis)**

|  | Low | Medium | High |
|---|---|---|---|
| Experimenter affiliation | 1.00 (14) | 1.00 (37) | .95 (75) |
| Blinding | .83 (6) | .91 (66) | .93 (44) |
| Diagnosis | — | 1.00 (12) | .99 (114) |
| Client IQ | 1.00 (11) | .18 (74) | 1.00 (41) |
| Client age | 1.00 (1) | .68 (50) | .83 (75) |
| Client source | — | 1.00 (10) | .89 (116) |
| Client assessment | — | .53 (17) | .98 (103) |
| Therapist assessment | .00 (15) | .67 (18) | .75 (93) |
| Internal validity | — | .52 (27) | .88 (93) |
| Treatment mortality | .00 (4) | 1.00 (1) | .94 (121) |
| Comparison mortality | .00 (4) | 1.00 (1) | .93 (121) |
| Comparison type | — | — | 1.00 (126) |
| Control group type | — | .00 (9) | .69 (114) |
| Experimenter allegiance | .10 (10) | .64 (36) | 1.00 (80) |
| Modality | — | .33 (4) | 1.00 (122) |
| Location | — | — | 1.00 (126) |
| Therapist experience | .55 (55) | .56 (57) | 1.00 (11) |
| Outcome type | .00 (1) | .00 (11) | .92 (114) |
| Follow-up | .00 (2) | .92 (47) | .83 (75) |
| Reactivity | .83 (6) | .28 (65) | .94 (47) |
| Client participation | 1.00 (1) | .67 (3) | 1.00 (122) |
| Setting type | — | .40 (15) | .99 (111) |
| Treatment integrity | .60 (10) | .83 (60) | 1.00 (56) |
| Comparison group contamination | .30 (37) | .32 (50) | 1.00 (39) |
| Outcome Rxx | .13 (150) | .56 (70) | .92 (38) |

SOURCE: Orwin (1983b).

the number of sources providing relevant information for the coding decision, (b) the proportion of agreement to disagreement in the information reported by different sources, (c) the degree of discrepancy among sources when disagreement exists, and (d) the credibility attached to the various sources of information. An adequacy-confidence value was then assigned to each recorded variable value.

Along with the question of what specific indicators of confidence to use is the question of how to scale them. Orwin and Cordray (1985) pilot tested a 5-point scale (1 = low, . . . , 5 = high) for each confidence rating, fashioned after the Smith, Glass, and Miller "confidence of treatment classification" variable. Analysis of the pilot results revealed that five levels of confidence were not being discriminated. Specifically, the choices of 2 versus 3 and 3 versus 4 seemed to be made arbitrarily. The five categories were then collapsed into

three for the main study. In addition, each category was labeled with a verbal descriptor to concretize it and minimize coder drift (see Kazdin 1977): 3 = certain or almost certain, 2 = more likely than not, 1 = guess. Discrepancies were resolved through discussion. The 3-point confidence scale was simple yet adequate for its intended purpose: to establish a mechanism for discerning high-quality from lesser-quality information in the conduct of subsequent analyses.

## 4.3 Sensitivity Analysis

**4.3.1 Rationale** Sensitivity analysis can assess robustness and bound uncertainty. It has been a part of research synthesis at least since the original Smith and Glass (1977) psychotherapy study. Glass's position of including methodologically flawed studies was attacked by his critics as implicitly advocating the abandonment

**Table 11.7 Spearman Rank Order Correlations ($r_{RHO}$) Between Confidence and Interrater Agreement for Selected Variables from the Smith, Glass, and Miller (1980) Psychotherapy Meta-Analysis**

| | $r_{RHO}$ |
|---|---|
| **All Variables ($K = 25$)** | |
| Agreement rate | .71 |
| **Variables for Which Kappa was Computed[a] ($K = 20$)** | |
| Agreement rate | .71 |
| Kappa | .62 |
| **Variables for Which Intercoder Correlation was Computed ($K = 15$)** | |
| Agreement rate | .81 |
| Intercoder correlation | .67 |
| **Variables for Which All Three Estimates Were Computed ($K = 10$)** | |
| Agreement rate | .73 |
| Kappa | .79 |
| Intercoder correlation | .66 |

SOURCE: Orwin (1983b).
[a] $K$ for nominal variables; $K_w$ for ordinal variables.

of critical judgment (e.g., Eyesenck 1978). He rebutted these and related charges on multiple grounds, but the most enduring was the argument that meta-analysis does not ignore methodological quality, but rather presents a way of determining empirically whether particular methodological threats systematically influence outcomes. Glass's indicators of quality (e.g., the 3-point internal validity scale) were crude then and appear even cruder in retrospect, and may not have been at all successful in what they were attempting to do.[16] The *principle,* however—that of empirically assessing covariance of quality and research findings rather than assuming it a priori—was perfectly sensible and consistent with norms of scientific inquiry. In essence, the question was whether research findings were *sensitive* to variations in methodological quality. If not, lesser-quality studies can be analyzed along with high-quality studies, with conse-

[16]Chapter 10 shows how the state of the art has evolved; see also U.S. General Accounting Office (1989), Appendix II.

quent increase in power, generalizability, and so on. The worst-case scenario—that lesser-quality studies produce systematically different results and cannot be used—is no worse than had the synthesist followed the advice of the critics and excluded those studies a priori.

The solutions of Rosenthal (1978) and Orwin (1983a) to the so-called file-drawer problem (for combined probabilities and effect sizes, respectively) are in essence types of sensitivity analysis as well. They test the data's sensitivity to the violation of the assumption that the obtained sample of studies is an unbiased sample of the target population. While some level of sensitivity analysis has always been part of research synthesis, much more could have been done. In their review of 86 meta-analyses of randomized clinical trials, Sacks et al. (1987) found that only 14 presented any sensitivity analyses, defined as "data showing how the results vary through the use of different assumptions, tests, and criteria."

The general issue of sensitivity analysis in research synthesis is discussed in Chapter 24. This chapter focuses on applying the logic of sensitivity analysis to the evaluation of coding decisions.

**4.3.2 Multiple ratings of ambiguous items** The sources of error identified earlier (e.g., deficient reporting, ambiguities of judgment) are not randomly dispersed across all variables. The synthesist frequently knows at the outset which variables will be problematic. If not, a well-designed pilot test will identify them. For those variables, multiple ratings should be considered. Like multiple measures in other contexts, multiple ratings help guard against biases stemming from a particular way of assessing the phenomenon (i.e., monomethod bias) and can set up sensitivity analyses to determine if the choice of rating makes any difference. Smith's synthesis (1980) of sex bias is an example. When an investigator reported only their significant effect, Smith entered an effect size of 0 for the remaining effects. Aware of the pitfalls of this, she alternately (a) used a different procedure and (b) deleted these cases. Neither changed the overall mean effect size by more than a small fraction. In their synthesis of sex differences, Eagly and Carli (1981) took the problem of unreported nonsignificant effects a step further. Noting that the majority of these (15 of 16) tended in the positive (female) direction, they reasoned that setting effect size at 0 would lead to an underestimation of the true mean effect size, whereas deleting them would lead to overestimation. They therefore did both so as to be confident of at least *bracketing* the true value. They also used two indicators of researcher's sex (an important variable in this area), overall percentage of male authors and sex of first author. These were found to differ only slightly in their correlations with outcome. Each of the above are examples of sensitivity analyses directed at specific rival hypotheses. It should be evident that many opportunities exist for thoughtful sensitivity analyses in the evaluation of coding decisions and that these do not require specialized technical expertise; conscientiousness and common sense will frequently suffice.

**4.3.3 Multiple measures of interrater agreement** As described earlier, the choice of IRR index can have a significant effect on the reliability estimate obtained. While the guidelines in section 4.1.5 should narrow the range of choices, they may not uniquely identify the best one. Computing multiple indices is therefore warranted.

In their reanalysis of the Smith, Glass, and Miller (1980) psychotherapy data, Orwin and Cordray (1985) computed multiple estimates of IRR for each variable. For continuous variables, $AR$ and $r$ were computed ($r_I$ was not computed, but should have been). For ordinal categorical variables, $AR$, $r$, and $K_W$ were computed. For nominal categorical variables, $AR$ and $K$ were computed; when nominal variables were dichotomous, $r$ (in the form of phi) was also computed. Four regressions were then run, each using a different set of reliability estimates. The first used the highest estimate available for each variable. Its purpose was to provide a lower bound on the amount of change produced by disattenuation. The second and third runs were successively more liberal (see Orwin & Cordray 1985 for details). A final run, intended as the most liberal credible analysis, disattenuated the criterion variable (effect size) as well as the predictors. The reliability estimates for the four runs are shown in Table 11.8.

**4.3.4 Isolating questionable cases** Average effect sizes remain popular as summary statistics in research synthesis. Like any mean, they are highly sensitive (relative to other measures of central tendency) to the influence of outliers. In a synthesis of German psychotherapy research, it was found that excluding only the 2 most extreme of 426 effect sizes (both were in excess of 7 standard deviation units) produced a 20 percent decrease in the overall average effect size (Matt 1989). As in any research endeavor, good practice suggests that results be computed and presented both including and excluding outliers, so the effect of including or excluding them is readily apparent to authors and readers. While strictly speaking this is an analysis decision rather than a coding decision, the rationale for sensitivity

analysis is the same: to assess robustness and bound uncertainty levels.

**4.3.5 Isolating questionable variables** The same logic can be applied to variables. Both IRRs and confidence ratings are useful tools for flagging such variables. In the Orwin and Cordray (1985) study, for example, the therapist experience variable was coded with high confidence in only 9 percent of the studies, was "guessed" in 45 percent, and had an IRR (using Pearson $r$) of .56. Such numbers would clearly suggest the exercise of caution in further use of that variable. Conducting analyses with and without it, and comparing the results, would be a logical first step.

With regard to both cases *and* variables, the finding of significant differences between inclusion and exclusion does not automatically argue for outright exclusion; rather, it alerts the analyst that mindless inclusion is not warranted. As in primary research, the common practices of dropping cases, dropping variables, and working from a missing-data correlation matrix result in loss of information, loss of statistical power and precision, and biased estimates when (as is frequently the case) the occurrence of missing data is nonrandom (Cohen & Cohen 1975). Therefore, more sophisticated approaches are preferable when feasible. (For more on the treatment of missing data in research synthesis, see Chapter 12.)

## 5. SUGGESTIONS FOR FURTHER RESEARCH

### 5.1 Moving from Observation to Explanation

As Matt (1989) concluded, synthesists need to become more aware, and take deliberate account, of the multiple sources of uncertainty in reading, understanding, and interpreting research reports. But in keeping with the scientific endeavor principle, they also need to begin to move beyond observation of these phenomena and toward explanation. For example, further research on evaluating coding decisions in research synthesis should look beyond how to assess IRR toward better classification and understanding of why coders disagree. Evidence from other fields could probably inform some initial hypotheses. Horwitz and Yu (1984) conducted detailed analyses of errors in the extraction of epidemiological data from patient records and suggested a rough taxonomy of six error categories. Of the six, four were errors in the actual data extraction, and two were errors in the interpretation of the extracted data. The two interpretation errors were (a) incorrect interpretation of criteria and (b) correct interpretation of criteria, but inconsistent

**Table 11.8 Reliability Estimates Used in Four Reliability-Corrected Regression Runs on the Smith, Glass, and Miller (1980) Psychotherapy Data**

| Variable | Run 1 | Run 2 | Run 3 | Run 4 |
|---|---|---|---|---|
| Diagnosis: neurotic, phobic, or depressive | .98 | .98 | .89 | .89 |
| Diagnosis: delinquent, felon, or habituée | 1.00 | 1.00 | 1.00 | 1.00 |
| Diagnosis: psychotic | 1.00 | 1.00 | 1.00 | 1.00 |
| Clients self-presented | .97 | .57 | .71 | .71 |
| Clients solicited | .93 | .86 | .81 | .81 |
| Individual therapy | 1.00 | 1.00 | .85 | .85 |
| Group therapy | .98 | .96 | .94 | .94 |
| Client IQ | .69 | .69 | .60 | .60 |
| Client age [a] | .99 | .99 | .91 | .91 |
| Therapist experience × neurotic diagnosis | .76 | .75 | .70 | .70 |
| Therapist experience × delinquent diagnosis | 1.00 | 1.00 | 1.00 | 1.00 |
| Internal validity | .76 | .71 | .42 | .42 |
| Follow-up time [b] | .99 | .99 | .95 | .95 |
| Outcome type [c] | .87 | .70 | .76 | .76 |
| Reactivity [d] | .57 | .56 | .57 | .57 |
| ES | 1.00 | 1.00 | 1.00 | .78 |

SOURCE: Orwin and Cordray (1985).
[a] Transformed age $= (age - 25)(|age - 25|)^{1/2}$.
[b] Transformed follow-up $= (follow\text{-}up)^{1/2}$.
[c] "Other" category removed for purpose of dichotomization.
[d] Transformed reactivity $= (reactivity)^{2.25}$.

application. Note the similarity between these types of errors and the types of judgment errors described in section 2 with regard to coding in research synthesis.

When the coder must make judgment calls, the rationale for each judgment should be documented. In this way, we can begin to formulate a general theory of the coder judgment process. For complex yet critical variables like effect size, interim codes should be recorded. One code might simply indicate what was reported in the original study. A second code might indicate what decision rule was invoked in further interpretation of the data point. A third code—representing the endpoint and the variable of interest to the synthesis (e.g., effect size)—would be the number that results from the coder's application of that interpretation. Coder disagreement on the third code would no longer be a "black box," but could be readily traced to its source. Coder disagreement could then be broken down to its component parts (i.e., the errors could be partitioned by source), facilitating diagnosis much like a failure analysis in engineering or computer programming. The detailed documentation of coding decision rules could be made available for review and reanalysis by other researchers (much like the list of included studies is currently), including

any estimation procedures used for missing or incomplete data. (See Bullock and Svyantek 1985 for an example.) Theoretical models could also be tested, and most important, more informed strategies for reducing and controlling for error rates would begin to emerge.

## 5.2 Assessing Time and Necessity

The coding stage of research synthesis is time-consuming and tedious, and in many instances additional efforts to evaluate coding decisions further lengthen and complicate it. The time and resources of practicing synthesists is limited, and they would likely want answers to two questions before selecting a given strategy: How much time will it take? How necessary is it?

The time issue has not been systematically studied. Orwin and Cordray (1985) included a small time-of-task side study and concluded that the marginal cost in time of augmenting the task as they did (double codings plus confidence ratings) was quite small given the number of additions involved and the distinct impact they had on the analytic results. In part, this is because while double coding a study approximately doubles the time required to code it, in an actual synthesis only a sample of studies may be double coded. In a synthesis the size of Smith, Glass, and Miller's, the double coding of 25 representative studies would increase the total number of studies coded by only 5 percent. When a particular approach to reliability assessment leads to low occurrence rates or restricted range on key variables—as can happen with Yeaton and Wortman's hierarchical approach (1991)—oversampling techniques can be used. Research that estimated how often oversampling was required would in itself be useful. Other possibilities are easy to envision. In short, this is an area of considerable practical importance that has not been seriously examined to date.

The question of necessity could be studied in the same manner as methodological artifacts of primary research have been studied. For example, a handful of syntheses have used coder blinding techniques, as described in section 2. Keeping coders blind to hypotheses or other information is an additional complication that adds to the cost of the effort and may have unintended side effects. An empirical test of the effect of selective blinding on research synthesis coding would be a useful contribution, as such studies have been in primary research, to determine whether the particular artifact that blinding is intended to guard against (coder bias) is real or imaginary, large or trivial, and so forth. As was the case with pretest sensitization and Hawthorne effects in the evaluation literature (Cook & Campbell 1979), research may show that some suspected artifacts in synthesis coding are only that—perfectly plausible yet not much in evidence when subjected to empirical scrutiny. In reality, few artifacts will be universally present or absent, but rather will interact with the topic area (e.g., coder gender is more likely to matter when the topic is sex differences than when it is acid rain) or with other factors. Research could shed more light on these interactions as well. In sum, additional efforts to assess both the time and need for specific methods of evaluating coding decisions could significantly help the practicing synthesist make cost-effective choices in the synthesis design.

## 6. REFERENCES

American Psychiatric Association, Committee on Nomenclature and Statistics. (1980). *Diagnostic and statistical manual of mental disorders* (3rd ed.). Washington, DC: American Psychiatric Association.

Beyer, J. M. (1985). From the editor. *Academy of Management Journal, 28,* 5–8.

Bullock, R. J., & Svyantek, D. J. (1985). Analyzing meta-analysis: Potential problems, an unsuccessful replication, and evaluation criteria. *Journal of Applied Psychology, 70,* 108–115.

Buros, O. K. (1938–1978). *Mental measurements yearbook.* Highland Park, NJ: Gryphon Press.

Burton, N. W. (1981). Estimating scorer agreement for nominal categorization systems. *Educational and Psychological Measurement, 41,* 953–961.

Carey, G., & Gottesman, I. I. (1978). Reliability and validity in binary ratings: Areas of common misunderstanding in diagnosis and symptom ratings. *Archives of General Psychiatry, 35,* 1454–1459.

Chalmers, T. C., Berrier, J., Sacks, H. S., Levin, H., Reitman, D., & Nagalingham, R. (1987). Meta-analysis of clinical trials as a scientific discipline. II. Replicate variability and comparison of studies that agree and disagree. *Statistics in Medicine, 6,* 733–744.

Cicchetti, D. V. (1985). A critique of Whitehurst's "Interrater agreement for journal manuscript reviews": De omnibus disputandem est. *American Psychologist, 40,* 563–568.

Cicchetti, D. V., & Sparrow, S. S. (1981). Developing criteria for establishing the interrater reliability of specific items in a given inventory. *American Journal of Mental Deficiency, 86,* 127–137.

Cohen, J. (1960). A coefficient of agreement for nominal scales. *Educational and Psychological Measurement, 20,* 37–46.

Cohen, J. (1968). Weighted kappa: Nominal scale agreement with provision for scaled disagreement or partial credit. *Psychological Bulletin, 70,* 213–220.

Cohen, J., & Cohen, P. (1975). *Applied multiple regression/correlation analysis for the behavioral sciences.* Hillsdale, NJ: Erlbaum.

Cook, T. D., & Campbell, D. T. (1979). *Quasi-experimentation: Design and analysis issues for field settings.* Chicago: Rand McNally.

Cordray, D. S., & Orwin, R. G. (1981, September). *Technical evidence necessary for quantitative integration of research and evaluation.* Paper presented at the joint conference of the International Association of Social Science Information Services and Technology and the International Federation of Data Organizations, Grenoble, France.

Cordray, D. S., & Sonnefeld, L. J. (1985). Quantitative synthesis: An actuarial base for planning impact evaluations. In D. S. Cordray (Ed.), *Utilizing prior research in evaluation planning* (New Directions for Program Evaluation No. 27). San Francisco: Jossey-Bass.

Cronbach, L. J., Gleser, G. C., Nanda, H., & Rajaratnam, N. (1972). *Dependability of behavioral measurements.* New York: Wiley.

Eagly, A. H., & Carli, L. L. (1981). Sex of researchers and sex-typed communications as determinants of sex differences in influenceability: A meta-analysis of social influence studies. *Psychological Bulletin, 90*, 1–20.

Ebel, R. L. (1951). Estimation of the reliability of ratings. *Psychometrika, 16*, 407–424.

Eyesenck, H. J. (1978). An exercise in mega-silliness. *American Psychologist, 33*, 517.

Fleiss, J. L. (1971). Measuring nominal scale agreement among many raters. *Psychological Bulletin, 76*, 378–382.

Fleiss, J. L. (1981). *Statistical methods for rates and proportions* (2nd ed.). New York: Wiley.

Fleiss, J. L., & Cohen, J. (1973). The equivalence of weighted kappa and the intraclass correlation coefficient as measures of reliability. *Educational and Psychological Measurement, 33*, 613–619.

Fleiss, J. L., Cohen, J., & Everett, B. S. (1969). Large sample standard errors of kappa and weighted kappa. *Psychological Bulletin, 72*, 323–327.

Glass, G. V., & Smith, M. L. (1979). Meta-analysis of research on the relationship of class size and achievement. *Educational Evaluation and Policy Analysis, 1*, 2–16.

Green, B. F., & Hall, J. A. (1984). Quantitative methods for literature reviews. *Annual Review of Psychology, 35*, 37–53.

Grove, W. M., Andreasen, N. C., McDonald-Scott, P., Keller, M. B., & Shapiro, R. W. (1981). Reliability studies of psychiatric diagnosis: Theory and practice. *Archives of General Psychiatry, 38*, 408–413.

Hartmann, D. P. (1977). Considerations in the choice of interobserver reliability estimates. *Journal of Applied Behavior Analysis, 10*, 103–116.

Hayes, W. L. (1973). *Statistics for the social sciences.* New York: Holt, Rinehart & Winston.

Hedges, L. V., & Olkin, I. (1985). *Statistical methods for meta-analysis.* Orlando, FL: Academic Press.

Horwitz, R. I., & Yu, E. C. (1984). Assessing the reliability of epidemiological data obtained from medical records. *Journal of Chronic Disease, 37*, 825–831.

Hyde, J. S. (1981). How large are cognitive gender differences? A meta-analysis using w and d. *American Psychologist, 36*, 892–901.

Jackson, G. B. (1980). Methods for integrative reviews. *Review of Educational Research, 50*, 438–460.

Janda, K. (1970). Data quality control and library research on political parties. In R. Narall & R. Cohen (Eds.), *A handbook of method in cultural anthropology.* New York: Doubleday.

Janes, C. L. (1979). Agreement measurement and the judgment process. *Journal of Nervous and Mental Disorders, 167*, 343–347.

Jones, A. P., Johnson, L. A., Butler, M. C., & Main, D. S. (1983). Apples and oranges: An empirical comparison of commonly used indices of interrater agreement. *Academy of Management Journal, 26*, 507–519.

Kazdin, A. E. (1977). Artifacts, bias, and complexity of assessment: The ABC's of research. *Journal of Applied Behavior Analysis, 10*, 141–150.

Kerlinger, F. N., & Pedhazur, E. J. (1973). *Multiple regression in behavioral research.* New York: Holt, Rinehart & Winston.

Kulik, J. A., Kulik, C. L. C., & Cohen, P. A. (1979). Meta-analysis of outcome studies of Keller's personalized system of instruction. *American Psychologist, 34*, 307–318.

Light, R. J. (1971). Measures of response agreement for qualitative data: Some generalizations and alternatives. *Psychological Bulletin, 76*, 365–377.

Light, R. J., & Pillemer, D. B. (1984). *Summing up: The science of reviewing research.* Cambridge, MA: Harvard University Press.

Lord, F. M., & Novick, M. R. (1968). *Statistical theories of mental test scores.* Reading, MA: Addison-Wesley.

Matt, G. E. (1989). Decision rules for selecting effect sizes in meta-analysis: A review and reanalysis of psychotherapy outcome studies. *Psychological Bulletin, 105*, 106–115.

McGuire, J., Bates, G. W., Dretzke, B. J., McGivern, J. E., Rembold, K. L., Seabold, D. R., Turpin, B. A., & Levin, J. R. (1985). Methodological quality as a component of meta-analysis. *Educational Psychologist, 20*, 1–5.

McLellan, A. T., Luborsky, L., Cacciola, J., Griffith, J., McGahan, P., & O'Brien, C. (1988). *Guide to the addiction severity index: background, administration, and field testing results.* Philadelphia: Veterans Administration Medical Center.

Nunnally, J. C. (1978). *Psychometric theory* (2nd ed.). New York: McGraw-Hill.

Oliver, L. W. (1987). Research integration for psychologists: An overview of approaches. *Journal of Applied Social Psychology, 17*, 860–874.

Orwin, R. G. (1983a). A fail-safe N for effect size in meta-analysis. *Journal of Educational Statistics, 8*, 157–159.

Orwin, R. G. (1983b). *The influence of reporting quality*

*in primary studies on meta-analytic outcomes: A conceptual framework and reanalysis.* Doctoral dissertation, Northwestern University.

Orwin, R. G. (1985). Obstacles to using prior research and evaluations. In D. S. Cordray (Ed.), *Utilizing prior research in evaluation planning* (New Directions for Program Evaluation No. 27). San Francisco: Jossey-Bass.

Orwin, R. G., & Cordray, D. S. (1985). Effects of deficient reporting on meta-analysis: A conceptual framework and reanalysis. *Psychological Bulletin, 97,* 134–147.

Rosenthal, R. (1978). Combining results of independent studies. *Psychological Bulletin, 85,* 185–193.

Sacks, H. S., Berrier, J., Reitman, D., Ancova-Berk, V. A., & Chalmers, T. C. (1987). Meta-analyses of randomized controlled trials. *New England Journal of Medicine, 316,* 450–455.

Scott, W. A. (1955). Reliability of content analysis: The case of nominal scale coding. *Public Opinion Quarterly, 19,* 321–325.

Selvage, R. (1976). Comments on the analysis of variance strategy for the computation of intraclass reliability. *Educational and Psychological Measurement, 36,* 605–609.

Shapiro, D. A., & Shapiro, D. (1982). Meta-analysis of comparative therapy outcome studies: A replication and refinement. *Psychological Bulletin, 92,* 581–604.

Shavelson, R. J., & Webb, N. M. (1991). *Generalizability theory: A primer.* Newbury Park, CA: Sage.

Shrout, P. E., & Fleiss, J. L. (1979). Intraclass correlations: Uses in assessing rater reliability. *Psychological Bulletin, 86,* 420–428.

Shrout, P. E., Spitzer, R. L., & Fleiss, J. L. (1987). Quantification of agreement in psychiatric diagnosis revisited. *Archives of General Psychiatry, 44,* 172–177.

Smith, M. L. (1980). Sex bias in counseling and psychotherapy. *Psychological Bulletin, 87,* 392–407.

Smith, M. L., & Glass, G. V. (1977). Meta-analysis of psychotherapy outcome studies. *American Psychologist, 32,* 752–760.

Smith, M. L., Glass, G. V., & Miller, T. I. (1980). *The benefits of psychotherapy.* Baltimore: Johns Hopkins University Press.

Spitznagel, E. L., & Helzer, J. E. (1985). A proposed solution to the base rate problem in the kappa statistic. *Archives of General Psychiatry, 42,* 725–728.

Stanley, J. C. (1971). Reliability. In R. L. Thorndike (Ed.), *Educational measurement* (2nd ed.). Washington, DC: American Council on Education.

Stock, W. A., Okun, M. A., Haring, M. J., Miller, W., & Kenney, C. (1982). Rigor in data synthesis: A case study of reliability in meta-analysis. *Educational Researcher, 11,* 10–20.

Terpstra, D. E. (1981). Relationship between methodological rigor and reported outcomes in organization development evaluation research. *Journal of Applied Psychology, 66,* 541–543.

U.S. General Accounting Office (1989). *Prospective evaluation methods: The prospective evaluation synthesis.* (GAO/PEMD Transfer Paper No. 10.1.10). Washington, DC: GAO.

Whitehurst, G. J. (1984). Interrater agreement for journal manuscript reviews. *American Psychologist, 39,* 22–28.

Wortman, P. M., & Bryant, F. B. (1985). School desegregation and black achievement: An integrative review. *Sociological Methods and Research, 13,* 289–324.

Wortman, P. M., & Yeaton, W. H. (1985). Cumulating quality of life results in controlled trials of coronary artery bypass graft surgery. *Controlled Clinical Trials, 6,* 289–305.

Yeaton, W. H., & Wortman, P. M. (1991). *On the reliability of meta-analytic reviews: The role of intercoder agreement.* Unpublished manuscript.

Zwick, R. (1988). Another look at interrater agreement. *Psychological Bulletin, 103,* 374–378.

Cooper, H. and Hedges, L. V. (Eds.) 1994. *The Handbook of Research Synthesis.* New York: Russell Sage Foundation

# 12

# METHODS FOR HANDLING MISSING DATA IN RESEARCH SYNTHESIS

**THERESE D. PIGOTT**
*National-Louis University*

CONTENTS

## 1. INTRODUCTION

Previous chapters of this volume have outlined how to define a research question for a research synthesis, develop a comprehensive search for literature, obtain a representative sample of studies, and design a set of coding procedures. Even after a researcher has carefully planned a research synthesis, problems can emerge when studies do not provide comparable information. The problem of missing data occurs in a research synthesis when studies do not report relevant statistics or adequate descriptions of methods needed for applying quantitative techniques for combining results across studies. This chapter will discuss the problems that missing data cause in a research synthesis, examine the nature of missing data in a research study, and review current strategies for handling missing data, including methods based on the work of Little and Rubin (1987) and Rubin (1987).

Missing data reduce the size of the sample originally gathered for the research synthesis. When a synthesist chooses a representative sample of studies on a given topic, he or she assumes that every study in the sample provides information considered important for the analysis and hopes to use all studies to make inferences about the literature. When important information about methods or relevant statistics are missing from a study, that study may be dropped from further consideration in the synthesis, which changes the nature of the studies used in the synthesis: The studies with complete information may no longer be representative of the population of studies identified.

The problems with using complete cases are compounded in the analysis stage of the synthesis. A synthesist may try several different analyses with the data to determine if any of a study's characteristics relate to the effect magnitude of the study. In each of these analyses, only studies with complete information on relevant variables may be included. Each of these analyses may utilize a different set of studies that may not be representative of the sample originally chosen for the synthesis and may not correspond with each other. The results of each analysis may not generalize to the population of studies on a topic nor to any of the other samples of studies used in other analyses. The next section discusses in more detail the types of missing data in a research synthesis and how they impact the types of generalizations possible for an integrative review.

## 2. TYPES OF MISSING DATA IN A RESEARCH SYNTHESIS

Three kinds of data may be missing in a research synthesis: studies in the identified population, information for estimating effect sizes, and characteristics of studies that may be related to study effects.

### 2.1 Missing Studies in the Sample

Studies that are unavailable for use in a synthesis constitute one form of missing information. For instance, some research studies are unpublished reports or manuscripts that are difficult to locate. (Rosenthal treats the problem of fugitive literature in Chapter 7 of this volume.) In addition, researchers sometimes wish to use only published studies in a synthesis. Since published articles tend to report statistically significant results (Atkinson, Furlong & Wampold 1982), results based on only published literature may not be representative of all studies done on an issue. (Begg discusses publication bias in Chapter 25.) Missing studies in the synthesis affect the representative nature of the sample used. The rest of this chapter will assume that the sample in the research synthesis is representative of the population of studies of interest.

## 2.2 Missing Effect Sizes

In addition to studies missing from an identified population, studies themselves may be missing the relevant information for calculating a measure of the study's effect size. (Chapters 16 and 17 of this volume provide several methods for calculating effect sizes.) A problem arises when studies provide no statistics or an inadequate amount of information about the outcome scores to use the suggestions provided in these chapters.

Missing effect sizes pose a particularly difficult problem in research synthesis. Without a statistical measure for the results of a study, none of the methods for a quantitative review can be implemented. A study with a missing effect size cannot be included in an estimate of average effect size across studies, which jeopardizes the generalizability of the results of a research synthesis. Standard regression programs used to estimate linear models of effect size use only cases with complete information on outcome measures and predictors. Once a study cannot be included in the sample, then potential threats arise to the representativeness of the studies included in the research synthesis.

Frequently in research synthesis studies contain insufficient information to calculate effect sizes. In the collection of research reviews on gender differences edited by Hyde and Linn (1986), four of the five research reviews report a number of studies with missing information on effect sizes. For three of these syntheses, approximately 48, 53, and 92 percent of the originally identified population of studies provide sufficient statistical information to calculate an effect size. If integrative research reviews are thought of as analogous to a sample survey of research literature (Smith 1980), then a 50 percent response rate cannot be thought of as an adequate sampling of a particular population.

Vote-counting is one option for a statistical analysis of results when the direction, if not the magnitude, of the effect size is known. (Bushman treats these procedures in Chapter 14 of this volume.) Some researchers fill in a conservative estimate, such as zero, for missing effect sizes. Imputing a single value for missing observations of effect size may lead to biased results, which may be compounded when those imputed values are used to estimate the variance of the missing effect size. Many research synthesis procedures utilize the variance of the effect size as weights in the estimated mean effect size and in weighted least squares estimation of the linear model of effect size. An example later in the chapter illustrates some of the dangers of imputing values for the effect size.

## 2.3 Missing Information on Study Characteristics

Studies in a research review can also lack information on variables thought to moderate effect size. For instance, a reviewer studying the effects of psychotherapy might be interested in how length of time in therapy relates to the effect size of a study. Not all studies of psychotherapy will provide specific information on the length of time spent in therapy. Studies differ widely in amount of description provided about procedures, measures, and subjects of a study, characteristics commonly used as predictors in models of effect size. Missing predictors in any statistical analysis can cause difficulties. Standard regression programs drop cases missing any variable included in the model. If studies are found to vary in estimates of effect size, then the process of building models of effect size using characteristics of the studies can be hampered when studies fail to provide adequate information about procedures, measures, or subjects. Most quantitative research syntheses may use only studies with complete information on both outcomes and predictors when building models of effect size. The procedures discussed in this chapter for handling missing data will mostly apply to the problem of missing predictors in quantitative analyses of effect sizes.

## 3. REASONS FOR MISSING DATA IN A RESEARCH SYNTHESIS

While studies may be missing for various reasons, data on effect sizes and predictors may be missing because a primary author did not provide information considered essential by the reviewer.

### 3.1 Influences on Researchers' Reporting Practices

Primary authors are influenced by their own preferences as well as outside pressures when deciding what information to report in a research study. The type of publication—for example, dissertation versus journal article—can impact the kinds of information that a primary author can include in the study. Dissertations may require more detailed description of the study than is allowable in a journal article. Although a primary author may have collected the types of information needed by a reviewer, the author may be precluded by the length or type of publication from reporting all details.

Other pressures also influence a primary author's individual decisions about what information to report. Orwin and Cordray (1985) explore reasons why authors either fail to report or underreport facts about a study. They describe customary reporting practices in a particular research area as one set of reasons for incomplete reporting of details of a study. Typical ways of designing studies and describing results exist in certain fields of research. For example, a psychologist studying a juvenile delinquency program may be more apt to report the actual average IQ level of subjects than a sociologist who provides only a general description of the subjects' achievement levels. A report about a juvenile delinquency program written by a psychologist may differ from one by a sociologist in the types of information reported and emphasized. If a reviewer wishes to use the average IQ score of subjects in a linear model of effect size, he or she may encounter missing information on IQ score for many studies written by sociologists. The background of the primary authors can influence the types of information included in a report.

Other reasons that Orwin and Cordray (1985) give for insufficient reporting relate to individual differences between authors in writing style and thoroughness of description. Authors differ in what they view as important information to collect and to provide in a research report and may also vary in their attention to detail and clarity of presentation of results. Information missing in a study may have little to do with conventions of a particular field, but rather an author's preferences, emphases, and interests. For example, some authors may feel that reporting statistically insignificant results is not necessary. Effect sizes are frequently missing in studies in which the difference between the two group means is not significant, and thus the author fails to report the actual values of the means and standard deviations. If an author finds that a delinquency program does not lead to less recidivism compared with a control group, he or she may fail to report the actual levels of recidivism for both groups. The actual value of a variable may be related to whether or not the variable is observed in the study.

Authors' failure to report observations can relate in three different ways to the rest of the information contained in the data. Observations may be missing for reasons unrelated to the data, for reasons related to completely observed variables in the data, or for reasons related to the missing variables themselves. The reasons are important for determining the most appropriate way to handle the missing observations. The following sections discuss these three reasons for missing observations.

## 3.2 Missing for Reasons Unrelated to the Data

Observations missing for reasons unrelated to the data result in a set of complete cases that are representative of the originally identified set of studies. When the reason for missing variables is unrelated to any of the variables in the data, including the actual value of the missing variable itself, the missing observations occur as if they were deleted at random. The cases with complete information can be treated as a random sample of the original set of studies. Little and Rubin (1987) use the term "missing completely at random" (MCAR) to refer to data missing for reasons unrelated to any of the information contained in the data.

A hypothetical example of observations missing for reasons unrelated to the data derives from a review of juvenile delinquency studies that will be discussed later in this chapter. In the juvenile delinquency data, background information about the students' prior arrest history might be missing from some studies owing to lack of adequate funding for extensive research. Some programs may not receive the funds needed to do thorough background checks on all subjects in the study. These funding differences may be a result of differences between the amount of money available in a particular fiscal year and the political climate from year to year. These reasons are not related to the merits of the program, the types of subjects involved, or other characteristics of the study itself. If the reasons for the missing background information are not related to any of the information in the data set, then the complete cases can be considered a random sample of the original set of studies.

## 3.3 Missing for Reasons Related to Completely Observed Variables

Observations may be missing from the data for reasons dependent on one or more completely observed variables in the data set. Missing observations occur because of the value of another completely observed variable, and not because of the value of the missing variable itself.

Little and Rubin (1987) call this type of data "missing at random" (MAR). For example, authors may not report on particular types of information because of differences that operate in the reporting practices in the field of the researcher. Psychologists who conduct studies of juvenile delinquency programs may always report the mean IQ score of the groups, but sociologists may only report on general IQ levels of the groups. An author's theoretical orientation may determine whether certain information is missing in a study. Whether or not an average IQ score is observed is dependent on the theoretical orientation of the author and not on the actual values of these scores.

Analyzing only complete cases when observations are missing for reasons related to completely observed variables may not provide generalizable results. The cases with complete data may not be a random sample of the original set of studies. The methods discussed later in the chapter (Little & Rubin 1987; Rubin 1987) are more appropriate for this reason for missing data.

## 3.4 Missing for Reasons Related to the Missing Values Themselves

Observations may be missing because of the value of the variable itself or because of other unobserved variables. Censoring mechanisms may cause particular observations to be missing because of the value of those observations. Studies may fail to report information needed to calculate effect sizes when the differences between the treatment group and control group are not statistically significant. Small effect sizes may be missing in a research synthesis because they represent insignificant differences between treatment groups. The reason for missing values depends on the value for the observation.

The missing observations may also be related to variables that are not recorded in the data. In the previous example, observing an average IQ score for groups in the study is hypothesized to relate to the theoretical orientation of the researcher. If the reviewer does not include the background of the author in the quantitative review, then missing values for IQ are related to an unobserved variable: orientation of the author. Observations missing because of their unobserved values or because of another unobserved variable result in a set of complete cases that are not representative of the original sample of studies. This reason for missing observations poses one of the more difficult problems in dealing with missing data.

## 4. SIMPLE STRATEGIES FOR DEALING WITH MISSING DATA

Reviewers using meta-analysis commonly employ one of three methods for dealing with missing data: complete cases, ad hoc imputation, or regression imputation. The adequacy of methods for handling missing data depends on the reasons data are missing. This section reviews current procedures for handling missing data and provides two simple examples of the adequacy of these methods.

### 4.1 Analyzing Only Complete Cases

A common method for dealing with missing data is to use only cases that observe all relevant variables. Those cases missing one or more of the variables used in the current model are dropped from further consideration. When large amounts of data are missing, complete case analysis may lead to a much smaller sample of studies than a reviewer originally intended. When analyzing only complete cases, the reviewer generally makes the assumption that the complete cases are representative of the original sample of studies.

### 4.2 Single-Value Imputation

A second method for handling missing data imputes or fills in some reasonable value for the missing information. By filling in missing values, a reviewer does not lose from the analysis all the cases that have missing observations. What values a reviewer imputes for the missing variable may depend on the reviewer's assumptions about how missing data occur. If a reviewer believes that the missing effect sizes in the sample are probably small values, he or she may replace the missing effect sizes with a value of zero. Many researchers fill in missing variables with the mean value of that variable calculated from the cases that observed the variable. Researchers imputing single values for missing observations make the assumption that all missing observations are close to the imputed values.

Imputing single values for missing observations artificially deflates the variability of the variable. Little and Rubin (1987) give the exact formula for the underestimation of the sampling variance that results when the complete case mean is substituted for missing values. Decreasing the variance in important variables in a synthesis has consequences for tests of homogeneity of effect sizes and for estimation of categorical or linear models of effect size. The simple example later in this section illustrates the bias in estimates of sampling variability from single-value imputation procedures.

## 4.3 Regression Imputation: Buck's Method

A third strategy was suggested by Buck (1960). This method uses regression techniques to estimate missing values, replacing missing observations with the conditional mean. For every pattern of missing data, complete cases are used to calculate regression equations predicting a value for each missing variable using the set of completely observed variables. In each study with missing observations, the missing values are replaced by the predicted value. An adjustment can also be made for the underestimation of the sampling variance of a variable with missing values that occurs with Buck's method (Little & Rubin 1987). The assumption inherent in Buck's method is that missing observations can be predicted from a linear regression model estimated from complete cases. The missing variables are assumed to be linearly related to other variables in the data.

While reviewers use the three methods described above to deal with the problems caused by missing data in research synthesis, these methods do not work equally well with every case of missing variables. The adequacy of these methods depends on the reasons data are missing.

## 4.4 Examples of the Use of Simple Strategies for Missing Data

This section examines how each of the methods described earlier work with two different types of missing data. The first example uses missing data created by randomly deleting observations of the effect size, and the second example deletes the largest observations of effect size. In each example, the mean and standard error of the mean will be calculated using complete cases, single-value imputation, and Buck's method.

The meta-analysis data set used to illustrate these strategies is taken from a larger set of studies of the effects of juvenile delinquency programs from a review by Lipsey (1992). A large data set is used to provide a more accurate picture of the adequacy of the methods. The two variables appearing in the example are the estimates of effect size and a code for the type of treatment used in the study. The type of treatment variable takes values from 0 to 7 representing less-

focused treatments such as institutionalization to more-focused treatments such as counseling.

Each example gives the weighted and unweighted mean effect size and its standard error as well as the estimated mean and standard error of mean of the type of treatment variable. Although missing effect sizes are a more difficult problem than missing predictors, the example uses effect size estimates to illustrate some of the problems inherent in using simple strategies for missing observations. Complete case analysis uses only cases with information on both effect size and type of treatment. For the imputation procedures, the weighted mean is calculated by imputing a value for the missing effect size and then using that imputed value to obtain the estimate of the variance of the effect size. The variance of the effect size serves as the weight in the computation of the mean effect. For Buck's method in the weighted analysis, the type of treatment variable serves as the predictor in a weighted least squares regression of effect size. The unweighted analysis uses standard techniques to estimate means and standard errors, and in Buck's method employs ordinary least squares to estimate the regression of effect size on type of treatment.

**4.4.1 Randomly deleting observations of effect size** The example in Table 12.1 shows the results from each method when 56, or 25 percent, of the effect sizes are randomly deleted. The first row of the table gives the estimated weighted and unweighted means and standard error of the means for all 226 studies in the sample. The results from using complete cases, imputing the complete case mean, imputing zero, and using Buck's method are presented in the following rows.

All methods but filling in zero provide estimates of the mean close to the estimate from the original sample. Since the missing effect sizes are deleted at random, the complete cases are a random subsample of the original set of studies. Estimates of the mean based on the complete cases as in complete case analysis, filling in the complete case mean, or using complete cases for obtaining estimates in Buck's method all generalize to the original set of cases. Filling in zero underestimates the mean since the assumption that the missing values are close to zero is incorrect. The effect sizes are missing at random and are not missing because they represent statistically insignificant differences between treatment groups.

The methods differ in estimates of the standard error of the mean. The bias inherent in some of the methods is most apparent in the unweighted analyses. Filling in

**Table 12.1 Randomly Deleting Observations of Effect Size**

| Method | N | Weighted Effect Size | | Unweighted Effect Size | | Treatment Type |
|---|---|---|---|---|---|---|
| | | Mean | SE | Mean | SE | Mean (SE) |
| All cases | 226 | 0.132 | 0.010 | 0.205 | 0.031 | 3.8 (.13) |
| Complete cases | 170 | 0.104 | 0.012 | 0.194 | 0.035 | 3.8 (.15) |
| Fill-in mean | 226 | 0.104 | 0.010 | 0.194 | 0.027 | 3.8 (.13) |
| Fill-in zero | 226 | 0.077 | 0.010 | 0.146 | 0.027 | 3.8 (.13) |
| Buck's method | 226 | 0.127 | 0.010 | 0.204 | 0.031 | 3.8 (.13) |

a single value such as the complete case mean or a conservative estimate of zero underestimates the sampling variance. The standard errors obtained in the unweighted analysis using single-value imputation are based on a sample of 226 studies, as if the imputed values were the true values of the missing effect sizes. No adjustment is made for the uncertainty caused by the missing values.

Buck's method differs from the single-value imputation methods in providing an adjustment to the sampling variance of a variable with missing observations. The sampling variance can be inflated to take into account the imputation of missing values. In the case of two variables, $Y_1$ and $Y_2$, $Y_2$ with missing values, Little and Rubin (1987) show that Buck's method underestimates the sampling variance of $Y_2$ by

$$\frac{\lambda}{(n-1)} \sigma_{22.1}, \qquad (12\text{-}1)$$

where $\lambda$ is the number of missing values of $Y_2$, and $\sigma_{22.1}$ is the residual variance of the regression of $Y_2$ on $Y_1$. Little and Rubin (1987) give a general form of the underestimation from Buck's method for more than two variables. In this example, Buck's method closely approximates the estimate of the mean and standard error of the mean from the original set of cases.

The weighted analysis provides estimates of the standard error of the mean that do not differ significantly from the estimate from all cases. There may be a danger in using the estimates of the standard error of the mean since the imputed effect sizes are used twice in the estimation procedures for both the estimate of effect from an individual study and the estimate of the variance of that individual effect size. The inverse of the estimated variance is then used in calculating the weighted effect size. Studies with large sample sizes will be weighted more heavily in the estimate of the mean effect size even if that study's effect size was imputed. The weighted mean effect size and its standard error do not reflect the uncertainty caused by missing observations and should be used with caution.

**4.4.2 Deleting the largest observations of effect size** The adequacy of the methods changes when missing data result from a censoring mechanism rather than a random deletion. Table 12.2 gives the estimates of the weighted and unweighted means and standard errors when the studies with the 56 largest effect sizes are deleted from the analysis. None of the methods provides an estimate of either the weighted or unweighted mean that is close to the value from the original sample. Imputing either the mean or zero for deleted effect sizes produces essentially the same results since the complete case mean value substituted is close to zero.

None of the methods provides an adequate estimate of the standard error of the mean. The single-value imputation methods provide a standard error that underestimates the uncertainty caused by missing observations in both the weighted and unweighted analyses. Buck's method cannot adjust for the bias caused by imputing values that are not close to the true effect sizes.

## 4.5 A Summary of Simple Strategies

In the simple examples of Tables 12.1 and 12.2, the methods do not work equally well in both situations. When the missing observations are missing randomly, then complete case analysis, mean imputation, and Buck's method provide unbiased estimates of the mean effect size. Both mean imputation and filling in zero underestimate the standard error of the mean.

In the first example, Buck's method provides an estimate of the mean effect size and its standard error

**Table 12.2 Deleting the Largest Observations of Effect Size**

| Method | N | Weighted Effect Size Mean | Weighted Effect Size SE | Unweighted Effect Size Mean | Unweighted Effect Size SE | Treatment Type Mean (SE) |
|---|---|---|---|---|---|---|
| All cases | 226 | 0.132 | 0.010 | 0.205 | 0.031 | 3.8 (.13) |
| Complete cases | 170 | 0.003 | 0.011 | 0.002 | 0.021 | 3.6 (.15) |
| Fill-in mean | 226 | 0.024 | 0.010 | 0.002 | 0.016 | 3.8 (.13) |
| Fill-in zero | 226 | 0.024 | 0.010 | 0.001 | 0.016 | 3.8 (.13) |
| Buck's method | 226 | 0.034 | 0.010 | 0.011 | 0.019 | 3.8 (.13) |

that is close to the value for the whole data set. Since the two variables in the example are linearly related, information about one variable can provide some information on the missing values of the second variable. Deleting the observations at random also ensures that the complete case regressions used to calculate substitutes for the missing values are generalizable to the cases with missing data. The missing cases are similar to the complete cases when variables are deleted at random.

In Table 12.2, in which extreme observations are deleted, no method comes close to the value of the mean effect size estimated from all data. Although Buck's method takes advantage of information from all cases, the estimation procedure cannot adjust for the deletion of extreme values. This censoring mechanism results in cases with incomplete data that are systematically different from the complete cases. Information about variables and their relationship in the complete cases will not generalize to the cases with missing data.

The adequacy of methods for dealing with missing data in a research synthesis depends on the reasons for the missing observations. In order to know how best to analyze a set of data, a reviewer must make a guess about why observations are missing. Complete case analysis and Buck's method produce generalizable results when the complete cases can be considered a random sample of the original set of studies, when the reasons for missing data are unrelated to any variables in the review. Mean imputation can provide an unbiased estimate of the mean, but underestimates the sampling variance of a variable with missing values. If information is missing because of the value of the variable itself or because of other unobserved variables, then none of the simple strategies can provide unbiased results. The next section discusses more sophisticated methods that

can handle data missing for reasons related to completely observed variables in the review. Other strategies also exist for handling observations missing for reasons related to unobserved values.

## 5. MODEL-BASED PROCEDURES FOR HANDLING MISSING DATA

Two different procedures for handling missing data have been developed recently in the statistical literature. These methods—maximum likelihood and multiple imputation—are termed model-based methods since both rely on a model for the hypothetically complete data for estimation purposes. Little and Rubin (1987) and Rubin (1987) describe procedures that can be used when missing observations are related to completely observed variables or to the values of the missing observations. This section will provide a brief overview of both of these methods, concentrating on those that have the potential to apply to current methods for quantitative research reviews. The procedures described by Little and Rubin (1987) and Rubin (1987) have not been used extensively in research synthesis, but have the potential of providing solutions to the difficult problem of missing data.

### 5.1 Maximum Likelihood Models for Missing Data

Little and Rubin (1987) present maximum likelihood methods for analyzing data with missing observations that avoid the problems associated with using complete cases or substituting values for missing observations. The advantage that maximum likelihood has over analyzing only complete cases is that it uses all information contained in the original sample. Maximum likelihood does not require any adjustments to the obtained estimates such as occurs in Buck's method (1960) to allow for the effect of the imputed data on the estimated sampling variance.

One set of maximum likelihood methods applicable to research synthesis requires the assumption that the reasons for missing observations are either unrelated to any variables in the data or are related to completely observed variables in the data. Little and Rubin (1987) call the mechanism that leads to missing observations ignorable when they are either unrelated to information in the data or related to observed information. Ignorable mechanisms governing whether or not variables are observed allow an important simplification of the estimation procedures that is described in the next section.

### 5.1.1 The form of the likelihood function

Maximum likelihood methods for missing data follow the usual steps for complete data maximum likelihood estimation, but also must include a model for the reasons for the missing data in the likelihood of the data. In standard complete data maximum likelihood estimation, the first step is to obtain the likelihood function for the model. The most likely values of the model parameters are found by setting the first derivative of the log-likelihood equal to zero and solving a series of simultaneous equations that in many situations provide a simple form of the estimators for the relevant parameters. The estimation of regression coefficients in linear models is an example of maximum likelihood procedures.

When observations are missing from a data set, the likelihood of the data must include a function that determines if a given observation is or is not observed. The likelihood of a data set with missing information can be thought of as resulting from multiplying the hypothetically complete data likelihood by a function that governs whether a given observation is or is not missing, which can be called the response mechanism. One assumption necessary in one set of maximum likelihood methods for missing data centers on the reasons for missing observations, or, more formally, the response mechanism.

When the probability of observing a variable does not depend on the actual value of that observation, then the response mechanism is considered ignorable. Ignorable response mechanisms allow an important simplification of the likelihood; when the reasons for missing observations are unrelated to the values of the missing variables themselves, then the likelihood of the data is proportional to the likelihood of the observed data only.

The piece of the likelihood pertaining to the response mechanism can be ignored. The estimation process does not rely on information about the response mechanism when that mechanism is ignorable. Reasons for missing observations that are either unrelated to the data or related to completely observed variables are both ignorable response mechanisms.

### 5.1.2 Maximum likelihood procedures for research synthesis

Little and Rubin (1985) describe two methods for ignorable response mechanisms that may apply to problems with missing data in research synthesis. One technique, for mixed normal and nonnormal data, estimates means and cell frequencies when the data contain both continuous and categorical variables, a situation analogous to categorical models of effect size. This method may not be applicable to typical methods of analyzing categorical models of effect size in which the reviewer estimates the mean effect size and the homogeneity of the effect size within cells defined by categorical predictors. The estimation procedure may ensure that studies with incomplete information on categorical predictors end up in cells with mean effect sizes closest to the effect size from that study.

Methods for multivariate normal data described by Little and Rubin (1987) may be more applicable to typical methods for analyzing linear models of effect size. The next section describes the general procedures used to apply maximum likelihood methods for missing data to the case of linear models of effect size.

## 5.2 Maximum Likelihood Methods for Multivariate Normal Data

Procedures that can be adapted to linear models of effect size require the assumption that the variables in the data set are sampled from a multivariate normal distribution. For the case of research synthesis, this assumption requires that the predictors and effect size in the model are jointly distributed as multivariate normal. Strict adherence to this assumption may imply that predictors must be continuous variables in order to estimate a linear model of effect size. In practice, completely observed categorical variables can be included in the model; the procedure is robust to violations of the assumption of multivariate normality (Little 1988a).

Little and Rubin's description (1987) of procedures for multivariate normal data cannot be applied directly to the case of missing data in meta-analysis. Effect size estimates are not distributed identically across studies since the variance of an estimate of effect depends on the sample size employed in the study. In cases in which variables are not distributed identically across cases, others (Chatterjee & Price 1977; Draper & Smith 1981) have suggested the use of weighted least squares to estimate parameters of a linear model. Adjustments are needed to the treatment provided by Little and Rubin (1987) in order to include the use of weighted least squares in the estimation procedure. Space does not permit giving the form of the adapted estimation procedures. The exact form of the algorithm for a linear model of effect size can be obtained in Pigott (1992). The following discussion will outline the process used and describe computer programs that may be adapted to maximum likelihood estimation of linear models of effect size.

**5.2.1 A description of the procedures** Maximum likelihood methods for multivariate normal data differ from the simple strategies discussed earlier in that estimates are not obtained for single missing values. The method instead focuses on estimating the means and covariance matrix of the multivariate normal data by obtaining the expected values of the sufficient statistics of the likelihood. For multivariate normal data, the sufficient statistics are the sums and the sums of the cross-products of the variables in the model, which can be combined to form the means and the covariance matrix of the effect size and the predictors in the model. Once the maximum likelihood estimates of the means and covariance matrix are obtained, then parameters such as regression coefficients of the linear model can be computed and will also be maximum likelihood estimates (Little & Rubin 1987).

The estimation procedures are based on the EM algorithm detailed by Dempster, Laird, and Rubin (1977). Estimation using the EM algorithm consists of two stages: the E-step and the M-step. The E-step calculates the expected values of the sufficient statistics given the model for the data treating the current estimates of the means and covariances as if they were the real values. The M-step then uses the computed sufficient statistics as if they were the true values to obtain the new estimates of the means and covariances of the data. The estimation procedure iterates back and forth between these two steps until the estimates converge.

In order to calculate the expected values of the sufficient statistics (the sums and sums of the cross-products of the variables in the model), the analyst calculates a series of regressions for each pattern of missing data. Missing data can occur on a number of predictor vari-

ables resulting in a series of patterns of missing data. For instance, some cases may be missing only one variable and others a combination of several different variables. Every pattern of missing data has a set of missing variables and a set of completely observed variables. For the E-step, the reviewer estimates the regression predicting the missing variable(s) from the remaining observed variables for each pattern of missing data using current estimates for the means and covariance matrix as in Buck's method (1960). These regressions yield predicted values that will be used to calculate the expected values of the sufficient statistics. The expected values are not exactly the predicted values from Buck's method, but are derived from the model. The M-step then takes the expected values to estimate new values for the means and covariances. The new values of the means and covariance matrix are then used as if they were the true values in re-estimating the sufficient statistics of the model. The process iterates back and forth between estimating the sufficient statistics using current estimates of the means and covariances and re-estimating the means and covariances using current estimates of the sufficient statistics until the estimates converge.

**5.2.2 Standard errors of the estimates** Little and Rubin (1987) show that the second derivative of the log-likelihood of the observed data can yield standard errors of the estimates of parameters of the model in the presence of missing data. The difficulty in applying this method to meta-analysis arises in finding the second derivative of the likelihood and then inverting the matrix of second derivatives. The form of the likelihood in many applications, including research synthesis, can become complex and requires specialized computer programs for numerical differentiation.

Recent work by Meng and Rubin (1991) presents an algorithm that is less difficult than the method described by Little and Rubin (1987) for obtaining the asymptotic variance-covariance matrix. Although the method also requires specialized computer programs, the computation procedures are less complex than the method described by Little and Rubin. A simpler, though less accurate alternative is to use the jackknife (e.g., Mosteller & Tukey 1977) to obtain approximate standard errors of parameters. The jackknife involves computing the estimates several times, dropping a set of cases during each estimation procedure. Meng and Rubin state that in large samples with variables assumed identically and independently distributed, the jackknife can give an approximation of the precision of the estimates.

**5.2.3 Computational procedures** The algorithm described by Little and Rubin (1987) is available in the BMDP statistical package as the BMDPAM program (Dixon 1988). More work is needed to adjust the algorithm as it appears in the BMDP program for estimation of weighted linear models of effect size. Current applications of maximum likelihood methods for multivariate normal data (Pigott 1992) have utilized programs written specifically for particular applications using the SAS PROC IML program (SAS Institute 1985). The BMDPAM program can also describe the pattern of missing values and estimate missing values using both mean imputation and regression imputation.

## 5.3 Maximum Likelihood Methods for Data Missing for Reasons Related to the Missing Values

Little and Rubin (1987) also describe maximum likelihood methods used when observations are missing owing to a nonignorable response mechanism, when observations are missing for reasons related to the missing values themselves. Little and Rubin present two models for the data. One model requires knowledge about the reason for missing data that might occur, for example, when the reviewer knows the exact value for the effect size above which no effect sizes are observed (see Table 12.2). The other model is used most frequently when missing observations occur only on one variable, and the reasons for missing values are unknown. At present, neither model may apply to standard techniques for quantitative research reviews. Most reviewers do not have exact information about the reasons for missing observations, nor are missing values usually confined to only one variable. Continued research in this area may uncover methods more applicable to current research review techniques.

## 5.4 Multiple Imputation Procedures for Missing Data

Multiple imputation, as described by Rubin (1987), represents another model-based procedure developed in the context of large-scale surveys for dealing with missing data. Multiple imputation expands on the idea of filling in values for missing observations by imputing more than one value for each missing value, obtaining a range of possible values for each missing observation. Like maximum likelihood methods, multiple imputation utilizes all the information originally gathered in the

review. This section provides a brief description of multiple imputation methods; more details are available in Rubin (1987) and Little and Rubin (1989). Neither treatment, however, deals specifically with research synthesis.

**5.4.1 A description of the method** With multiple imputation, the analyst makes explicit assumptions about the reasons for missing observations. Multiple imputation allows the researcher to propose several different reasons for the missing data. The reviewer may test the sensitivity of results to assuming that reasons for missing observations are either related to observed variables or to unobserved values (ignorable and nonignorable response mechanisms). These models are then used in the analysis procedures to obtain a set of possible values for the single missing observation. These sets of possible values can be combined to form complete data sets, each of which represents a different model for the reasons for missing observations. Results from these complete data sets can be compared to reveal the sensitivity of results to assumptions about the reasons for missing observations.

Multiple imputation avoids the problems of single-value imputation since it provides a range of possible values for the missing observation. Results from multiple imputation reflect the uncertainty inherent in the data due to missing values and do not treat the imputed values as the true observation.

**5.4.2 The application of the procedures to research synthesis** Although multiple imputation holds promise as a solution to missing data problems, more work needs to be done to adapt the procedures described by Rubin (1987) to the context of research synthesis. The method was also designed for large-scale sample surveys such as the census that researchers other than the original data collector may wish to analyze. The method may be useful for small data sets, though the theory underlying the method is precisely valid only with a large number of cases.

## 6. SUMMARY: SOME PRACTICAL SUGGESTIONS

This chapter describes several methods used for handling missing data in research synthesis. Some of the strategies currently used are easily implemented, but may lead to bias depending on the reasons for missing data. More research is needed to adapt the more complex methods to the context of research synthesis; this effort should be aided by the increasing availability of computer packages applying the techniques described by Little and Rubin (1987).

## 6.1 The Special Problems of Missing Effect Sizes

Missing effect sizes pose a particularly difficult problem in research synthesis. The methods described in this chapter to deal with missing data work best with missing values in variables thought to moderate effect size rather than the effect sizes themselves. The problem lies in the fact that both missing effect sizes and their sampling variances must be estimated when an effect size is unavailable from the study.

Reviewers can also imagine that effect sizes are more likely to be missing from studies in which insignificant differences occur between treatment groups. This situation describes reasons for missing data that are related to the value of the missing variable. At present, few solutions to the problem of nonignorable response mechanisms exist that can be applied to research synthesis. Few methods can be recommended to deal with the problems of missing effect sizes when the reviewer suspects effects are missing for reasons related to the value of the effect size. If a small number of effect sizes are missing and the reason for missing effects is plausibly unrelated to the missing values, then complete case analysis provides unbiased results.

## 6.2 Choosing an Appropriate Method for Analysis

The reasons for missing data determine what method may be most appropriate for analyzing the data. Complete case analysis and Buck's method (1960) may work well when the reasons for missing observations are unrelated to the data. Maximum likelihood methods can handle observations missing for reasons related to observed variables in the data. The difficult problem remaining is determining the reasons for the missing observations.

Many procedures have been proposed to gather evidence about the reasons for missing data. Little (1988b) points out some of the drawbacks of simple strategies and proposes a test of whether data are missing for reasons unrelated to the data. Obtaining information about observations missing because of other observed or unobserved variables may be more difficult. One suggestion involves creating a missing data index variable that takes the value 1 if a variable is observed and

0 if the variable is missing. The missing data index variable can be correlated with other completely observed variables in the data or used as the outcome variable in a logistic regression modeling response as a function of several completely observed variables.

If one finds a correlation between a completely observed variable and the missing data index or a plausible model of the missing values, then some evidence exists that the reasons for missing observations depend on completely observed variables. No relationships between a missing value index variable and other completely observed variables may be a clue that the reasons for missing data depend on the missing values themselves or on some other unobserved variable.

In most situations, reviewers must rely on anecdotal evidence about why primary authors may not report particular information. The reviewer can code studies for variables that may be related to reporting practices such as the type of publication or an author's orientation. Having as much complete information as possible from studies in the sample provides the reviewer with variables that may be related to missing data and thus can be used in methods such as maximum likelihood and multiple imputation to obtain linear models of effect size.

No easy solutions exist for the problems caused by missing data in research synthesis. A reviewer needs to exercise caution in using simple strategies, making the assumptions of the method explicit when reporting results. Maximum likelihood methods and multiple imputation hold promise in handling more complex patterns of missing observations in research synthesis, though more work is needed to adapt these methods for models of effect size. The current development of computer programs that implement the procedures described by Little and Rubin (1987) should advance the development of sensible methods for handling missing data in research synthesis.

## 7. REFERENCES

Atkinson, D. R., Furlong, M. J., & Wampold, B. R. (1982). Statistical significance, reviewer evaluations, and the scientific process: Is there a (statistically) significant relationship? *Journal of Counseling Psychology, 29,* 189–194.

Buck, S. F. (1960). A method of estimation of missing values in multivariate data suitable for use with an electronic computer. *Journal of the Royal Statistical Society, Series B 22,* 302–303.

Chatterjee, S., & Price, B. (1977). *Regression analysis by example.* New York: Wiley.

Dempster, A. P., Laird, N. M., & Rubin, D. B. (1977). Maximum likelihood from incomplete data via the EM algorithm. *Journal of the Royal Statistical Society, Series B 39,* 1–38.

Dixon, W. J. (Ed.). (1988). *BMDP statistical software.* Los Angeles: University of California Press.

Draper, N., & Smith, H. (1981). *Applied regression analysis* (2nd ed.). New York: Wiley.

Hyde, J. S., & Linn, M. C. (Eds.). (1986). *The psychology of gender: Advances through meta-analysis.* Baltimore: Johns Hopkins University Press.

Lipsey, M. (1992). Juvenile delinquency treatment: A meta-analytic inquiry into the variability of effects. In T. D. Cook, H. Cooper, D. S. Cordray, H. Hartmann, L. V. Hedges, R. J. Light, T. A. Louis, & F. Mosteller, *Meta-analysis for explanation: A casebook.* New York: Russell Sage Foundation.

Little, R. J. A. (1988a). Robust estimation of the mean and covariance matrix from data with missing values. *Applied Statistician, 37,* 23–38.

Little, R. J. A. (1988b). A test of missing completely at random for multivariate data with missing values. *Journal of the American Statistical Association, 83,* 1198–1202.

Little, R. J. A., & Rubin, D. B. (1987). *Statistical analysis with missing data.* New York: Wiley.

Little, R. J. A., & Rubin, D. B. (1989). The analysis of social science data with missing values. *Sociological Methods and Research, 18,* 292–326.

Meng, X., & Rubin, D. B. (1991). Using EM to obtain asymptotic variance-covariance matrices: The SEM algorithm. *Journal of the American Statistical Association, 86,* 899–909.

Mosteller, F., & Tukey, J. W. (1977). *Data analysis and regression.* Reading, MA: Addison-Wesley.

Orwin, R. G., & Cordray, D. S. (1985). Effects of deficient reporting on meta-analysis: A conceptual framework and reanalysis. *Psychological Bulletin, 97,* 134–147.

Pigott, T. D. (1992). *The application of maximum likelihood methods to missing data in meta-analysis.* Unpublished doctoral dissertation, University of Chicago.

Rubin, D. B. (1987). *Multiple imputation for nonresponse in surveys.* New York: Wiley.

SAS Institute. (1985). *SAS User's Guide: Statistics* (1985 ed.). Cary, NC: Author.

Smith, M. L. (1980). Publication bias and meta-analysis. *Evaluation in Education, 4,* 22–24.

Cooper, H. and Hedges, L. V. (Eds.) 1994. *The Handbook of Research Synthesis.* New York: Russell Sage Foundation

# 13

# MANAGING META-ANALYTIC DATABASES

**GEORGE WOODWORTH**
*University of Iowa*

## CONTENTS

## 1. INTRODUCTION

This chapter addresses topics of interest to specialists who may be involved in collecting and processing data in research syntheses: data coders, data entry personnel, statisticians, data managers, and project directors. In some cases, one person may fill several if not all of these roles. Nevertheless, different and quite distinct skills are required for each function. In this chapter the central player is the data manager; however, since he or she must rely on the data coders to provide data to be managed and must, in turn, deliver data in a useful form to the statistical analyst, there will be some discussion of these two roles as well.

Not many years ago, data entry was done on punched cards. A good data manager was one who didn't drop the card box on the way to the computer center. Now, however, it is not uncommon for data entry to be done on a personal computer using database management software, which displays a replica of the data coding form with blanks in which to enter data. The data manager translates the resulting database into a data matrix and transfers it electronically to a statistical analysis program.

No matter how sophisticated the software has become, careful planning and organization remain the most important considerations in meta-analytic data management. In this chapter, we will explain how to design a meta-analytic database and how to organize the various tasks involved in data entry, maintenance, and analysis. We will indicate some problems that can be avoided and illustrate our points with specific examples.

The central concept of database management is to create files that can be analyzed from different points of view. By using different linkages, the user can generate different kinds of reports based on the same data files. Although commercial database software systems provide a variety of tools for developing and managing databases, most meta-analyses are comparatively small, involving no more than several hundred effect sizes, and are relatively simple in terms of data linkages. The simple data structures found in most meta-analyses can be efficiently and reliably managed with a variety of types of software, including database management programs such as dBase IV or Paradox; spreadsheets such as Lotus 1-2-3 or Quattro Pro; statistical packages such as SPSS/PC + , SAS/PC, or SYSTAT; or even word processors such as Microsoft Word or Word Perfect.

The three critical steps in acquiring data and preparing it for statistical analysis are data coding, data entry, and data reduction. Data coding involves reading studies and extracting relevant information for further analysis. Data coders require extensive training to be able to extract reliably the statistical information required for a meta-analysis. Statistical training beyond an introductory course is generally required.

The data entry stage involves transferring data from paper data coding forms to a computerized data file. With a well-designed data coding form and a good data entry system, this task can be reliably performed by clerical staff. Although data entry can be done with very simple software (even software as basic as a line editor), the best combination of speed and accuracy is achieved with software specifically designed for data entry.

Two types of software are popular for this purpose: spreadsheets and databases. A spreadsheet program allows data to be entered into a data matrix in which the columns correspond to distinct data items (variables) and the rows correspond to distinct indices of outcome or relation. A database program allows the data manager to set up the computer screen as a form into which data items are entered. The form, which may consist of several screens just as a printed form has several pages, contains a set of entry blanks, called fields, defined by explanatory text displayed on the screen. To fill in a form, a data entry person simply moves the selector to each blank field and types in data. A filled-in form constitutes a record. A database is composed of many such records. Both types of program produce the same end result: a series of records (rows or cases), each containing a set of fields (data items or variables).

## 2. THE INTERFACE BETWEEN DATA CODING AND DATA MANAGEMENT

### 2.1 The Data Coding Form

Data coding (data logging) is the process of reading a study and recording the relevant information on either a printed data coding form or its electronic representation on a laptop computer. Designing data coding forms and collecting data from original studies is covered in other chapters, especially Chapter 10; however, the data manager (who may or may not be the person in charge of designing data coding forms) should be consulted to ensure that the data coding form itself will not create data entry problems.

A poorly designed data coding form can significantly impede data entry and greatly increase the number of data entry errors. Data items on the form should be difficult to overlook, either because they are placed in a consistent, predictable position, such as the right margin, or are boxed or highlighted. If data are to be entered in a spreadsheet or in a text file, the order of entry must be clear and unambiguous.

Figure 13.1 shows a fragment of a data coding form used in a meta-analysis of elementary and secondary science curricula. This data coding form was designed to facilitate reliable data entry into a spreadsheet program such as Lotus 1-2-3, Quattro Pro, or Excel. The spaces where data are to be entered are all at the right margin, making the order of entry unambiguous (top to bottom). Also, the destination of each data item (its column in the spreadsheet) is specified in parentheses.

Figure 13.1 should not be taken as a model for all data coding forms. In fact, when a database management system such as dBase or Paradox is used for data entry, data are entered on electronic forms (screens) that can be made to look like the printed data coding form and can be used to bypass paper forms entirely. Figure 13.2 is a fragment of a data coding form that would be poorly adapted for spreadsheet data entry but would work well with a database program using full-screen data entry. The problem with using a form like Figure 13.2 for spreadsheet data entry is that the order of data items is ambiguous: Are the descriptive statistics to be entered by rows or by columns? Although the ambiguity could be alleviated by indicating the spreadsheet columns on the data coding form, that solution would not be foolproof.

## 2.2 Coding Decisions and Data Entry

Data entry personnel are responsible for entering data into a computer from the data coding forms. The process should be a one-to-one transcription, since interpretations made on the fly are hard to document and are unlikely to be reliable. To avoid the need for interpretation at data entry time, there should be a detailed data coding protocol or manual to guide the data coders (see Chapter 10). The manual should include, among other things, the standard codes to be used for data items. For example, "TOUS" might be listed as the standard code for the Test On Understanding Science. Although most statistical packages can handle such alphanumeric codes, the statistician or data analyst should be consulted to determine if numeric codes are preferable.

The cardinal rule of data entry should be, "What you see is what you enter." Data entry personnel should not be asked to interpret or recode the data. The data coding

staff must be instructed that novel situations are to be dealt with by the project director, not by the invention of new codes or by notes written in the data entry blanks. In particular, if data can be missing in a variety of ways, then a different code should be used for each way. A chronic problem that cannot be dealt with by the data entry staff arises when reported data straddles several coding categories. For example, a study might report combined statistics for students in grades K–2 whereas the data coding form might call for statistics by individual grade levels. Two methods can be used to deal with this problem. If the reported groupings are reasonably standardized, then additional codes can be added to the data protocol. For example, codes K, 1, 2, and so on, could be used to record the exact grade level, if it is reported, and the codes A, B, and so on, could be used for grade groupings, say A = K–2, B = 3–4, C = 5–6, D = 7–8, E = 9–12.

A somewhat more elegant solution is to treat grade as a multiple response ("check all that apply") item. Thus, if a study reported data grouped by K–2, then the data entry person would endorse the responses K, 1, and 2. The data coding form would have a blank for each possible response, to be coded 1 if the response occurred and 0 if it did not. However, this could prove tedious in some cases and should be pilot tested.

Although it is easy to develop data coding forms to handle situations like this, the question of how to use such data in a statistical analysis is not easy to answer. Sometimes the aggregate categories can be used. In other cases missing data will result that can in principle be handled by methods discussed in Chapter 12.

## 2.3 Planning for the Unexpected

Unanticipated situations will inevitably arise, particularly in the early stages of data coding and data entry. For example, in a curriculum study, the type of pupil assignment might initially have been coded as (a) random, (b) matched, or (c) intact classes. A data coder might report finding several studies in which subjects self-selected the treatment or control group, which would require adding a category to this variable and reprinting the data coding form. In some cases it might be necessary to review previously entered studies to determine if the new category had been overlooked. For another example, it might become clear, after the first few studies had been read, that the time of the year the study was conducted is important. The project team might decide to add this to the data coding form as a new data

Subgroup code _____(Q)

       Name (e.g., third-grade boys)_____(R)

Scale code (from code book) _____(S)

       Name (e.g., TOUS) _____(T)

Grade level (1) k–3 (2) 4–6 (3) 7–9 (4) 10–12 _____(U)

Gender (% female) _____(V)

Ability (1) Low (below 95 IQ) (2) Average (95–105) (3) High (above _____(W)
  105)

Homogeneity of IQ (1) Homogeneous (2) Heterogeneous _____(X)

EFFECT SIZE DATA

Treatment

  Mean _____(Y)

  Standard deviation _____(Z)

  Degrees of freedom _____(AA)

  Number of pupils _____(AB)

Control

  Mean _____(AC)

  Standard deviation _____(AD)

  Degrees of freedom _____(AE)

  Number of pupils _____(AF)

Test statistics (treatment vs. control)

  $t$ statistic _____(AG)

  Degrees of freedom _____(AH)

Analysis of variance or covariance

  Treatment

    Sum of squares _____(AI)

    $F$ statistic _____(AJ)

    Degrees of freedom _____(AK)

    Direction (1) control mean larger _____(AL)
          (2) treatment mean larger

  Total

    Sum of squares _____(AM)

    Degrees of freedom _____(AN)

    Includes SS due covariate? (1) = yes _____(AO)
          (2) = no

**Figure 13.1** Fragment of a Science Curriculum Data Form Designed for Spreadsheet Data Entry

Descriptive statistics

|  | Control Group | Treatment Group |
|---|---|---|
| Mean | _____ | _____ |
| Standard deviation | _____ | _____ |
| Degrees of freedom | _____ | _____ |
| N of pupils | _____ | _____ |

Test statistics (treatment vs. control)

| t test | _____ |
|---|---|
| Degrees of freedom | _____ |

Analysis of variance

|  | Sum of Squares | Degrees of Freedom | F |
|---|---|---|---|
| Treatment | _____ | _____ | _____ |
| Total | _____ | _____ | |

**Figure 13.2** Fragment of a Data Coding Form Designed for Full-Screen Entry

item. For a third example, it might become apparent that not enough space had been provided to record a particular data item.

Any data coding effort will encounter situations like this that were not anticipated in the data coding protocol. It is important therefore that the data coding protocol, data entry form, and database design be pilot tested at the beginning of the project. Since several rounds of updating will almost certainly occur, it is important that modifications to the database be comparatively simple. For example, it may be necessary to add a variable, it may be necessary to increase the field width of a vari-

able, or it may prove desirable to rearrange the data coding form. This can be a problem if setting up the database requires the services of a specialized programmer. An important consideration, therefore, is to select software requiring programming that is within the capacity of the data manager.

## 2.4 Managing the Source Documents

Considerable statistical experience is required to extract correct statistical information from a study. Consequently, data coders who are not experienced statisticians will encounter situations beyond their experience and may inadvertently enter data incorrectly. For this reason it is essential that copies of all studies be available to the statistician for review.

A good practice is to have data coders highlight those parts of the study from which data were obtained and make marginal notes to facilitate checking when questions arise. Copies of the original data coding forms should be archived with the studies. Another aspect of this archive is the importance of recording cross-linking information among the studies—for example, cross-referencing studies by the same authors, studies that are part of a series of separately published reports, and secondary or supplementary reports that are used to aid coding of the primary report.

Maintenance of a physical file of copies of studies used in the synthesis is an important component of the data manager's job. Although it is probably not feasible with currently available equipment and software, future meta-analysis databases may well include scanned images of the original studies as part of the database.

With a synthesis of any size, preparation of a bibliography of the studies used is not an easy task. It is a substantial data maintenance task to keep the bibliography of materials identified and considered for inclusion in the synthesis. For this reason, it is useful to computerize this process as well and keep each bibliographic entry coded with regard to its status (e.g., not yet located, declared ineligible, coded, or entered and verified).

### 2.5 Feedback to the Data Coding Team

One of the data manager's most useful tasks is to provide feedback to the data coding team. This feedback should at a minimum include a listing (an echo) of each data form entered, which should be compared with the original forms to ensure accurate data entry. The project manager should arrange to have at least a sample of completed data coding forms reviewed by a statistician against the original studies to ensure that data coders have correctly interpreted the original studies. If a generic problem is identified by the statistician, it may be necessary to review all studies with the suspect code. For example, in a meta-analysis of science curricula the statistician found that numerous studies which had involved testing random *samples* of students from intact classrooms using traditional or experimental curricula had been incorrectly coded as having involved random *assignment* of students to the two curricula.

The data manager should implement consistency checks within and among data items, alerting the data coders to unusual values or combinations of variables that should be checked against original studies. Most data entry software allows the data manager to program consistency checks to be made automatically as data are entered. (Further details can be found in Chapter 11.)

### 2.6 Data for Effect Size Computation

Effect sizes can be computed from a variety of data configurations. For example, some studies report sample sizes, means, and standard deviations, whereas others report sample sizes, means, and an analysis of variance table, and still others only an analysis of variance table. Further variations are possible. A traditional approach to this situation has been to have effect sizes computed by hand under the direction of a statistician. This approach is risky for several reasons. It is difficult to locate errors and difficult to correct errors or try alternate effect size computations. In addition, basic data are kept on paper, not in machine-readable form, and are easily lost or separated from the machine-readable data files.

A better approach is to branch (skip) to a different paragraph on the data coding form and the corresponding data entry screens depending on the particular data configurations. Computation of effect sizes then becomes an aspect of data analysis. While this approach requires more complex programming both for data entry and data analysis, it is feasible in all but the most primitive database and statistical software products.

## 3. DATABASE ORGANIZATION

### 3.1 The Structure of Meta-Analytic Databases

Although the study is the observational unit in a meta-analysis, each study will generally permit several different effect sizes to be computed. For example, Vanek (1974) described a small but elegant experimental study comparing two science curricula, the ESS curriculum and a textbook approach (Laidlaw Science Series):

> Students from two existing third grades and two existing fourth grades were randomly assigned to the two . . . groups (i.e., ESS or traditional) at each grade level, so that approximately equal numbers of boys and girls were in each group. The two teachers at each grade level alternated, by units, teaching the

ESS and the Laidlaw curricula . . . to eliminate teacher variables.

Vanek administered several criterion measures to the pupils, including the Science Attitude Test (SAS) and the Stanford Achievement Test, Science (SATS). She reported descriptive statistics for four subsamples: third-grade girls, third-grade boys, fourth-grade girls, and fourth-grade boys. With these data the meta-analyst was able to compute effect sizes for each subsample for each criterion measure. Thus, this study supported the computation of at least eight effect sizes:

| Subsamples | Criterion Measures |
|---|---|
| Third-grade boys | SAS |
| | SATS |
| Third-grade girls | SAS |
| | SATS |
| Fourth-grade boys | SAS |
| | SATS |
| Fourth-grade girls | SAS |
| | SATS |

This example illustrates how meta-analysis data items fall into a hierarchy of three (or more) levels: first, characteristics of the study as a whole (e.g., author, type of publication, and overall quality of the study design); second, characteristics of each subpopulation within the study (grade level, gender, IQ, etc.); and third, characteristics of each criterion measure and statistics for each measure. This hierarchical data structure adds some complications to the design of the data coding form and database (see Chapter 10).

## 3.2 Flat Files and Relational Databases

Further complexity arises from the fact that statistical packages process ''flat files,'' cases by variables data matrices, in which data items at the top of the hierarchy are stored repeatedly and redundantly. For example, consider a hypothetical data coding form calling for 14 data items: a study identifier; the curriculum area (biology, earth science, general science, etc.); the type of pupil assignment to treatment and control (intact classes, self select, randomization, etc.); the gender, grade level, and average IQ of the subsamples; the name and type of criterion measure (achievement, attitude, etc.); and the means, standard deviations, and sample sizes.

A hypothetical 1974 study by Smith produced the eight rows (records) shown in Figure 13.3. In words, Smith's study was RANDomized, concerned GENeral SCIence curricula, reported data on second- and third-grade girls and boys, but did not report their average IQs. Two criterion measures were used, the Science Attitude Test and the General Science Achievement Test; mean scores were reported as well as standard deviations and sample sizes (not shown).

A relational database would store these data in three linked files: a study file, a subsample file, and a criterion measure file. Each record in each file has identifiers linking it to corresponding records in the other files. The study file contains generic information on each study and is linked to the subsample file by means of the study identification code. The subsample file contains information on subsample demographics within studies and is linked downward to the criterion measure file by means of the study identifier and the subsample identifier. In Figure 13.4 the links shown are for third-grade girls in Smith's hypothetical study.

In a relational database only the link variables are entered more than once in a file, whereas in a flat file, such as the one in Figure 13.3, study variables and subpopulation variables must be entered several times. Drawbacks of relational databases are that data management is more complex and that three (or more) data coding forms are needed—for study data, for subsample data, and for criterion measure data. For the Smith76 study, for example, the data collector would have to complete one study form, four subsample forms, and eight criterion measure forms, taking care to enter the link variable codes so that the forms could be properly merged to form a flat file for statistical analysis.

Most meta-analysis data managers will find it simpler to use a flat file data structure with a single data coding form, one copy per criterion measure per subsample, with some data items entered redundantly. However, for large studies with access to the services of an experienced data manager, a relational database, with its attendant economies of scale, should be considered. This is primarily a decision about how to organize the data files, not a decision about whether to select flat file or relational database software since relational data structures can be implemented as a series of linked flat files. The advantage of relational database software is that record linkage is handled automatically.

It is not essential that the subpopulation and criterion measure link codes be mnemonic, and it is not necessary that they directly suggest the composition of the subpopulation, as this can be handled by means of other

| Study Data | | | Subsample Data | | | | Criterion Data | | |
|---|---|---|---|---|---|---|---|---|---|
| Study | Asgn | Curric | Gndr | Grd | IQ | Measure | Type | CMEAN | TMEAN |
| Smith76 | RAND | GENSCI | M | 2 | ? | SAS | ATT | 226 | 246 |
| Smith76 | RAND | GENSCI | M | 2 | ? | GSAT | ACH | 72 | 75 |
| Smith76 | RAND | GENSCI | F | 2 | ? | SAS | ATT | 241 | 251 |
| Smith76 | RAND | GENSCI | F | 2 | ? | GSAT | ACH | 81 | 83 |
| Smith76 | RAND | GENSCI | M | 3 | ? | SAS | ATT | 213 | 217 |
| Smith76 | RAND | GENSCI | M | 3 | ? | GSAT | ACH | 76 | 79 |
| Smith76 | RAND | GENSCI | F | 3 | ? | SAS | ATT | 216 | 218 |
| Smith76 | RAND | GENSCI | F | 3 | ? | GSAT | ACH | 77 | 78 |

**Figure 13.3** One Study in a Flat File Database

variables or by post-coding. It is essential, however, that the nature of the subgroups be recorded in some form, both by means of subpopulation variables (gender, IQ, grade, urban/rural location, school size, etc.), and in a comment field on the data coding form.

## 4. DATA ENTRY MANAGEMENT

The data manager is responsible for ensuring that data are faithfully entered. It is the data manager's responsibility to select data entry software compatible with his or her programming skills, the data coding form, and the statistical analysis software to be used for data analysis. The data manager must institute quality checks for data entry and see that they are carried out.

Quality checks for data entry may include double entry and comparison or proofreading of entered data. Double entry involves entering each effect in replicate copies of the database, ideally by different personnel. The duplicate copies are compared and discrepancies are resolved by referring to the original data sheets. Proofreading involves printing a copy of the entered data and comparing it with the original data coding form. This task can be performed by any member of the project, but is best performed by the data coder who completed the data form under review.

The data manager and data analyst will also be involved in checking the reliability of the data coders by means of checks of internal consistency of the database. For example, unusually large or small values of a numeric variable are suspicious, as are illegal values of coded variables or unexpected combinations of values of two or more data items. One method of implementing internal consistency checks is to use automated data

checking features available in most database software packages. In this case, the data entry personnel are alerted to possible errors as data are entered.

The importance of regular backups of the database cannot be overemphasized. The data manager must arrange that the database be backed up after each data entry session, preferably on an independent medium such as magnetic tape stored in a different location.

## 5. THE INTERFACE BETWEEN DATA MANAGEMENT AND DATA ANALYSIS

The final duty of the data manager is to deliver data files suitable for processing by a statistical package, along with a printed code book of the data file. Typically, the data manager is also the data analyst, working under the direction of the project manager and a statistician. In any case, the database and code book must be designed to facilitate data analysis.

### 5.1 Database and Statistical Software Compatibility

An important consideration in the selection of data management software is the ease of preparing data files for processing by a statistical package. The selection of incompatible software for data management and statistical analysis is not fatal, but can produce serious delays and inefficiencies. To give an example, one project used commercial database software that was incapable of writing files in any of the standard formats and that had no capacity to perform statistical analyses. To solve the incompatibility problem it was necessary to commission

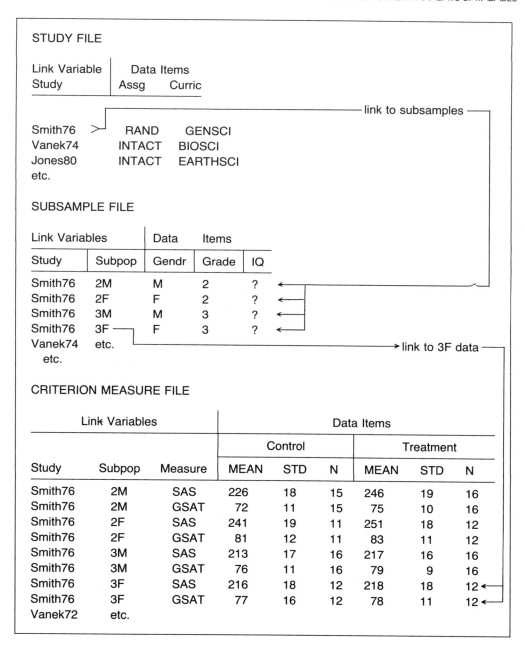

**Figure 13.4** Structure of a Relational Database

custom-written software to convert the comma-delimited ASCII "dump" files produced by the database software into a form that could be read by a statistical package.

Fortunately, it is easy to avoid such problems if certain minimal requirements for smoothly integrating data management and statistical analysis are followed:

1. The data entry system must be capable of displaying variable names as data are entered.

2. It must not require programming skills or other specialized skills on the part of the data entry personnel.

3. It must be capable of writing a file in a standard format: dBase IV, Lotus 1-2-3, or blank-delimited or formatted ASCII.

4. The statistical analysis package must be capable of reading files in a standard format.

5. It must be capable of executing a command file, executing conditional assignment statements involving the four arithmetic operations and the square root function, and writing a file of aggregated data containing several weighted means.

6. It must have a weighted regression or general linear model routine.

7. Several meta-analysis techniques require a statistical package capable of merging two or more files by matching records with the same value of one or more link variables.

8. For the purpose of making heterogeneity plots, the statistical package must be capable of making $x - y$ plots with more than one $y$ variable.

Some software combinations and file formats that meet these requirements are listed in section 5.2. The list is idiosyncratic and by no means complete, so that a project team, in consultation with an expert statistician and an experienced data manager, armed with the following list of minimal requirements should be able to develop other combinations. Indeed, several statistical packages have excellent data entry and data management components and eliminate the need for a separate data management product in small meta-analysis projects.

## 5.2 Selecting Software

Two stand-alone statistical packages that fulfill all these requirements are SPSS/PC+ and SYSTAT. The SPSS/ PC+, package with the Advanced Statistics and DE (data editor) add-on modules, is a very attractive option. The data editor not only allows full-screen spreadsheet-style data entry, but also allows the data manager to set up database-style data entry screens and to implement automatic data consistency checks as data are entered. The SPSS/PC+, package with the Advanced Statistics add-on product, has all the necessary statistical analysis capabilities. More details can be found in the software reviews listed in the appendix at the end of this chapter.

SYSTAT 5.0, another attractive choice, does not need separate data entry software since it has a spreadsheet-style full-screen data editor as standard equipment. However, the data editor does not support database-style data entry screens. SYSTAT has all the necessary statistical analysis capabilities and has outstanding high-resolution graphics.

Another satisfactory strategy is to select a database management system such as dBase IV or Quattro Pro or PARADOX 3.5 for data entry and a statistical package such as SPSS/PC+ with the advanced statistics add-on, SAS/PC with the statistics add-on, or SYSTAT 5.0 for statistical analysis. The advantage of using a separate database management product for data entry is the opportunity it provides to set up data entry screens and automated data-consistency checks.

The statistics package SAS/PC requires a data entry system since, at the time this chapter was written, it has no built-in or add-on data editor; however, it can read dBase files. SAS/PC is strongly recommended for its outstanding data analysis capabilities and, with the SAS GRAPH add-on, its superb graphics. Thus, in conjunction with a separate database package for data entry, it is a strong contender.

A popular, but less attractive alternative is to use a spreadsheet such as Lotus 1-2-3, Excel, or Quattro Pro for flat file data entry and to combine it with one of the above statistics packages for data analysis.

Spreadsheet programs are organized around a rectangular matrix. Cells in the matrix can contain labels, data, or formulas. The advantage of using spreadsheets for data entry is the ease of setting up the data entry system. All that is required is to type in variable names as column heads. Data items for one criterion measure in one subsample are entered in a row of the spreadsheet.

The spreadsheet mode of data entry is simple and direct, but has distinct disadvantages that can slow down data entry and introduce errors. First, with an unstructured data entry form such as the one illustrated in

Figure 13.2, the order of data entry may not be clear. Second, the column heads will necessarily be abbreviated and somewhat cryptic descriptions of the data items. For example, the method by which subjects were allocated to treatment and control groups might be called ''SbjAlloc.'' The combination of ambiguous order of entry of data items and cryptic variable names means that data are more likely to be entered in an incorrect column. In addition, in most spreadsheets, the column labels do not remain on the screen when it scrolls upward. There are ways of working around this problem—for example, indicating the column designator A, B, etc., on the data entry sheet or ''hiding'' rows containing previously entered data. However, the latter generally requires more skilled data entry personnel or frequent intervention by the data manager.

Advanced spreadsheet programs can be made to behave like databases (e.g., in Quattro Pro an area of the data matrix can be set up as a data entry screen). Spreadsheets used this way fall under the category of database software.

Other statistical packages offer data editors either as part of the basic package or as add-on products. Generally, these permit entry and editing of data in a spreadsheet format with the added feature that variable names (column heads) are not lost as the data scrolls. Since this requires the purchase of only one product, it is an attractive option; however, the project planner should check to see that the package has the necessary data management, statistical, and graphics capabilities for conducting a meta-analysis.

Finally, one should not overlook the possibility of using batch-oriented ''mainframe'' computers for data management or data analysis or both. This approach has the advantage that programming consultation is generally available at the computer center.

The principal problem with mainframe data entry is that it must be done with a text editor that will provide no guidance to the data entry person. However, if the meta-analysis project is a one-person operation, then nothing is as powerful and easy to set up and use for data entry and editing as a text editor one is already familiar with.

An intermediate solution that has proved quite successful is to set up data entry screens using a microcomputer database management system, upload data files either in ASCII or, if possible, in a ''portable'' file format compatible with the mainframe statistical package to be used for statistical analysis. A disadvantage of using the ASCII format for file transfer is that variable names are lost in the conversion to ASCII and must be supplied in the data entry step on the mainframe. We have used this approach and have found the major drawback to be the fact that modifications to the database in the form of new or rearranged variables require a parallel modification of the input step in the mainframe statistics package, which may be overlooked if the statistical analyst is not the data manager.

## 6. DATA REDUCTION

Data reduction is the process of preparing database files for statistical analysis. In the context of meta-analysis, this consists of exporting a flat file (data matrix) from the data management system to the statistical software. If a relational database structure is used, it will be necessary to link (merge) corresponding records from the component files of the database. This can be done either within the database or with the statistical software.

Once the data are imported into the statistical software, the first step is to compute effect sizes and their standard errors from basic data, and in some cases to aggregate multiple effect sizes within the same study. Because of the variety of ways in which statistical results are reported, computation of effect sizes requires statistical software capable of conditional (if-then) computations. Although computation and aggregation of effect sizes is generally not a data management responsibility, it is important that the data manager consult with the statistician to determine what data are needed.

## 7. THE CODE BOOK

A frequently overlooked part of the data manager's job is the preparation of a code book, which is a dictionary listing the names, labels, and code values of the variables in a data set. Without a code book, the statistical analyst will have difficulty in identifying the data items. What, for example, is the variable ''TCHPRIEX''? A code book will reveal that this variable reports the teacher's prior experience with the new curriculum and is coded (1) no experience, (2) one year, or (3) two or more years. Most statistical packages provide automated code book creation and maintenance by means of variable labels and value labels.

A fragment of the code book used in a meta-analysis

Code Book for Meta-Analysis Data File

| Item | Name | Description and Codes |
|------|------|----------------------|
| STUDID | Study ID | Three-digit identification number for the study |
| SUBSAMP | Subsample ID | Two-character alphanumeric code identifying a sub-sample of pupils within the study (arbitrary, assigned by data collector) |
| CMNR | Criterion ID | Four-digit code number identifying the criterion measure |
| PUPASSGN | Pupil Assignment | Method of assignment of pupils to treatments<br>(1) Random<br>(2) Matched<br>(3) Intact classes<br>(4) Self-selected |
| TEAASSGN | Teacher Assignment | Method of assignment of teachers to treatments<br>(1) Random<br>(2) Self-selected<br>(3) Crossover<br>(4) Matched<br>(5) Other nonrandom |
| CMTYPE | Criterion Measure Type | Type of criterion measure<br>(1) Cognitive, low<br>(2) Cognitive, high<br>(3) Cognitive, mixed<br>(4) Problem solving<br>(5) Affective, subject<br>(6) Affective, science<br>(7) Affective—procedure/methodology<br>(8) Values<br>(9) Process skills, techniques<br>(10) Methods of science<br>(11) Psychomotor<br>(12) Critical thinking<br>(13) Creativity<br>(14) Decision making<br>(15) Logical thinking, Piagetian<br>(16) Spatial relations, Piagetian<br>(17) Self-concept<br>(18) Classroom behaviors<br>(19) Reading<br>(20) Mathematics<br>(21) Social studies<br>(22) Communication skills |

**Figure 13.5** Science Curricula Meta-Analysis Project

of science curricula is shown in Figure 13.5. The first three data items are link variables.

## 8. SUMMARY

This chapter has outlined the duties of the data manager in a meta-analysis project. They are

1. to participate in the design of the data coding form and protocol;

2. to select data entry software compatible with the layout of the data coding form, appropriate to the skills of the data entry staff and the skills of the data manager, and compatible with the statistical software;

3. to design and maintain the data entry system;

4. to train and oversee the data entry staff and implement procedures for assuring faithful data entry; and

5. to deliver to the statistical analyst a data file containing data sufficient for the computation of effect sizes, data characterizing each study, and a code book describing the contents of the file.

## 9. REFERENCES

Vanek, E. A. P. (1974). *A comparative study of selected science teaching materials (ESS) and a textbook approach on classification skills, science achievement, and attitudes.* Unpublished doctoral dissertation, University of Rochester.

## 10. APPENDIX: Software Reviews

Flat File Databases, *PC Magazine,* June 26, 1990.
Double-Duty Data Managers, *PC World,* May 1991.
Statistics Programs, *Software Digest,* May 1991.
Upgraded Statistics Packages, *Lotus,* May 1991.
Number-Crunching Statistics Software, *Infoworld,* February 26, 1990.
SYSTAT 5.0 Gives Statistics Market Leader a Facelift, *Infoworld,* December 24/31, 1990.
SPSS/PC+ 4.0 Lops Prices, Adds Some Enhancements, *Infoworld,* April 1, 1991.

# PART
# V

# STATISTICALLY DESCRIBING AND COMBINING STUDIES

Cooper, H. and Hedges, L. V. (Eds.) 1994. *The Handbook of Research Synthesis.* New York: Russell Sage Foundation

# 14

## VOTE-COUNTING PROCEDURES IN META-ANALYSIS

**BRAD J. BUSHMAN**
*Iowa State University*

CONTENTS

## 1. INTRODUCTION

The meta-analyst generally has access to at least one of three types of data from research reports: (a) information that can be used to calculate effect size estimates (e.g., means, standard deviations, test statistic values), (b) information about whether the hypothesis tests found statistically significant relations, and (c) information about the direction of the outcomes. These data are rank ordered, from most to least, in terms of the amount of information they contain.[1] If the first type of data are available, the methods described in Chapters 18–20 of this volume are more appropriate than the methods described in this chapter. Vote-counting procedures are useful for the second and third types of data. Often the meta-analyst will want to use both effect size and vote-counting procedures in the same literature review. Effect size procedures can be used for those studies that contain enough information to calculate effect size estimates. Vote-counting procedures can be used for the larger group of studies for which effect size estimates cannot be calculated.

Section 2 of this chapter describes the similarities and differences between the second and third types of data outlined above. Section 3 discusses and illustrates the most common vote-counting procedures. Section 4 applies vote-counting procedures to the problems of publication bias, results all in the same direction, and missing data. Section 5 summarizes the strengths and weaknesses of vote-counting procedures.

## 2. COUNTING POSITIVE AND SIGNIFICANT POSITIVE RESULTS

When primary research reports do not contain enough information to calculate effect size estimates, they may still provide information about the magnitude of the effect. Often the information is in the form of a report of the decision yielded by the significance test (e.g., significant positive[2] relation) or in the form of a direction of the effect without regard to its statistical significance

(e.g., a positive mean difference or a positive correlation). The first of these corresponds to whether the test statistic exceeds a conventional critical value at a given significance level, such as $\alpha = .05$. The second corresponds to whether the test statistic exceeds the rather unconventional critical value at significance level $\alpha = .5$. Both kinds of information indicate whether the test statistic exceeded a critical value $C_\alpha$, the only difference is the value of $\alpha$ used. Thus, with vote-counting procedures, the meta-analyst counts either the number of statistically significant positive results ($\alpha = .05$) or the number of positive results ($\alpha = .5$). We will consider both values of $\alpha$ for the vote-counting procedures described in section 3.

## 3. VOTE-COUNTING PROCEDURES

### 3.1 The Conventional Vote-Counting Procedure

Light and Smith (1971) were among the first to describe formally the ''taking a vote'' procedure:

> All studies which have data on a dependent variable and a specific independent variable of interest are examined. Three possible outcomes are defined. The relationship between the independent variable and the dependent variable is either significantly positive, significantly negative, or there is no specific relationship in either direction. The number of studies falling into each of these three categories is then simply tallied. If a plurality of studies falls into any one of these three categories, with fewer falling into the other two, the modal category is declared the winner. This modal categorization is then assumed to give the best estimate of the direction of the true relationship between the independent and dependent variable. (p. 433)

The conventional vote-counting procedure has been criticized on several grounds. First, as Light and Smith noted, it does not incorporate sample size into the vote. As sample size increases, the probability of obtaining a statistically significant result increases. Second, as Glass, McGaw, and Smith (1981) noted, this method does not allow the meta-analyst to determine whether a treatment ''wins by a nose or in a walkaway'' (p. 95). Although we might know who the ''winner'' is, we do not know what the margin of victory is; it does not provide an effect size estimate. Third, Hedges and Olkin (1980) have shown that it has very low power for the range of

---

[1] Hedges (1986) found that estimators based on the third type of data are, *at most,* only 64 percent as efficient as estimators based on the first type of data. The maximum relative efficiency occurs when the population effect size equals zero for all studies. When the population effect size does not equal zero for all studies, relative efficiency decreases as the population effect size increases and as sample size increases.

[2] I use the term ''positive'' to refer to results in the predicted direction.

sample sizes and effect sizes most common in the social sciences. When effect sizes are medium to small, the conventional vote-counting procedure frequently fails to detect the effects. Moreover, for medium to small effect sizes, the power of the conventional vote-counting procedure tends to zero as the number of studies to be integrated increases.

## 3.2 The Sign Test

The sign test can be used to test the hypothesis that the effect sizes from a collection of $k$ independent studies are all zero. The sign test, the oldest of all nonparametric tests (dating back to 1710), is simply the binomial test with probability $\pi = .5$ (Conover 1980, p. 122). If the effect sizes are all zero, the probability of getting a positive result equals .5. If the treatment has an effect, the probability of getting a positive result is greater than .5. Thus, the appropriate null and alternative hypotheses are

$$H_0: \pi = .5$$
$$H_A: \pi > .5, \qquad (14\text{-}1)$$

where $\pi$ is the proportion of positive results in the population. If $U$ equals the number of positive results in $k$ independent studies, then an estimator of $\pi$ is $p = U/k$.

*Example.* Suppose that a meta-analyst finds exactly 11 positive results in 15 studies. The estimate of $\pi$ is $p = 11/15 \approx .73$. When $\pi = .5$, it is found from a binomial distribution table that the corresponding tail area is .0593 (i.e., $.0417 + .0139 + .0032 + .0005 + .0000$). Thus, we would fail to reject $H_0$ at the .05 significance level because .0593 is greater than .05. If exactly 12 of the 15 studies had positive results, the tail area would be .0176 (i.e., $.0139 + .0032 + .0005 + .0000$), and we would reject $H_0$ at the .05 significance level.

The sign test, like the conventional vote-counting procedure, does not incorporate sample size into the vote and does not provide an effect size estimate. The procedures described in section 3.3 overcome both of these deficiencies.

## 3.3 Confidence Intervals Based on Equal Sample Sizes

The vote-counting procedures described in this section assume that each study in a collection of $k$ independent

studies has an identical sample size $n$. If the independent[3] variable is dichotomous, we assume that the experimental ($E$) and control ($C$) group sample sizes are the same for all $k$ studies. That is, we assume $n_i^E = n_i^C = n$ for all $k$ studies. If the independent variable is continuous, we assume that the number of observations $n$ is the same for all $k$ studies. This assumption is extremely restrictive because studies frequently have different sample sizes. If the sample sizes are not very different, Hedges and Olkin (1980) recommend treating the studies as if all had the same sample size equal to some "average value." There are several "average values" from which to choose, including the arithmetic mean, median, mode, minimum, and maximum values. Hedges and Olkin (1985) offer a general class of means

$$\bar{n}_m = \left( \frac{1}{k} \sum_{i=1}^{k} n_i^{1/m} \right)^m, \ m = 0, 1, 2, \ldots. \qquad (14\text{-}2)$$

When $m = 0$ we have the maximum value; when $m = \infty$ we have the minimum value; and when $m = 1$ we have the arithmetic mean. Gibbons, Olkin, and Sobel (1977) recommend using the square mean root (SMR) for unequal sample sizes, which results when $m = 2$ in equation (14-2),

$$\bar{n}_2 = n_{SMR} = \left( \frac{\sqrt{n_1} + \ldots + \sqrt{n_k}}{k} \right)^2. \qquad (14\text{-}3)$$

The square mean root is not as influenced by extreme values as the arithmetic mean. It is more conservative than the arithmetic mean, but less conservative than the minimum value. If the sample sizes of the studies differ substantially, it may not be reasonable to use an average value like the square mean root. In this case, the methods discussed in section 3.4 should be used instead.

Often a meta-analyst is interested in determining whether a relation exists between the independent variable and the dependent variable for each study in a collection of $k$ independent studies. That is, the meta-analyst wants to determine if the effect size is zero for each study. This situation can be stated in terms of the null and alternative hypotheses. Let $T_1, \ldots, T_k$ be independent effect size estimators from $k$ studies for parameters $\theta_1, \ldots, \theta_k$. If we make the underlying assump-

---

[3] I use the term "independent" to refer to manipulated and nonmanipulated variables. Although this is not technically correct (independent variables are manipulated whereas subject variables are measured), it simplifies the discussion considerably.

tion that the effect sizes are approximately equal, the appropriate null and alternative hypotheses are

$$H_0: \theta_1 = \ldots = \theta_k = 0 \qquad (14\text{-}4)$$
$$H_A: \theta_1 = \ldots = \theta_k = \theta > 0.$$

The test involves rejecting $H_0$ in (14-4) if the estimator $T$ of the common effect size $\theta$ exceeds the one-sided[4] critical value $C_\alpha$. The $100(1 - \alpha)$ percent confidence interval for $\theta$ is given by

$$T - C_{\alpha/2} S_T \le \theta \le T + C_{\alpha/2} S_T, \qquad (14\text{-}5)$$

where $C_{\alpha/2}$ is the two-sided critical value from the distribution of $T$ at significance level $\alpha$, and $S_T$ is the standard error for $T$.

The problem is to obtain an estimate and confidence interval for $\theta$ using the $k$ estimators $T_1, \ldots, T_k$. The essential feature of vote-counting procedures is that the values of $T_1, \ldots, T_k$ are *not* observed. If we do not observe $T_i$, we simply count the number of times $T_i$ exceeded the one-sided critical value $C_\alpha$. For $\alpha = .5$, we count the number of studies with positive results. In this case, the appropriate null and alternative hypotheses are given in (14-1). For $\alpha = .05$, we count the number of studies with *significant* positive results. If $\theta = 0$, the probability of getting a positive result equals .05. Thus, the appropriate null and alternative hypotheses are

$$H_0: \pi = .05 \qquad (14\text{-}6)$$
$$H_A: \pi > .05.$$

In order to test the hypotheses given in (14-1) and (14-6) we need an estimator of $\pi$. The method of maximum likelihood can be used to obtain an estimator of $\pi$. For each study there are two possible outcomes: a "success" if $T_i > C_\alpha$ or a "failure" if $T_i \le C_\alpha$. It is convenient to define an indicator variable $X_i$ that takes on the value 1 if the outcome is a "success" or the value 0 if the outcome is a "failure." That is,

$$X_i = \begin{cases} 1 & \text{if } T_i > C_\alpha \\ 0 & \text{if } T_i \le C_\alpha. \end{cases} \qquad (14\text{-}7)$$

The probabilities associated with each outcome are

[4]I assume that the researcher has a priori predictions about the direction of the treatment effect and is therefore using a one-sided test. For a two-sided test, we let $T_i^2$ be an estimator of $\theta_i^2$. In general, it is not possible to use a two-sided test statistic $T_i^2$ to estimate $\theta$ if $\theta$ can be either positive or negative (Hedges & Olkin 1985, p. 52).

$$\Pr(X_i = 1) = \Pr(T_i > C_\alpha) = \pi \qquad \text{and}$$
$$\Pr(X_i = 0) = \Pr(T_i \le C_\alpha) = 1 - \pi. \qquad (14\text{-}8)$$

Each $X_i$ has a Bernoulli distribution with parameter $\pi$. The maximum likelihood estimator (MLE) of $\pi$ is

$$p = \sum_{i=1}^{k} x_i \Big/ k. \qquad (14\text{-}9)$$

The numerator in (14-9) is simply the number of studies with positive or significant positive results. Thus, $p$ is the proportion of positive or significant positive results for the $k$ studies. That is, $p = U/k$, where $U = \Sigma_{i=1}^{k} x_i$.

We can also construct a confidence interval for $\pi$. It is well known that if the random variables $X_1, \ldots, X_k$ form $k$ Bernoulli trials with parameter $\pi$, and if $X = X_1 + \ldots + X_k$, then $X$ has a binomial distribution with parameters $k$ and $\pi$ (e.g., DeGroot 1986). Note that the observed value of $X$ is the total number of positive or significant positive results, $\Sigma_{i=1}^{k} x_i = U$. Clopper and Pearson (1934) have published nomographs for obtaining exact confidence intervals for binomial proportions (also see Hedges & Olkin 1985, pp. 337–340). In addition, methods exist for obtaining confidence intervals for $\pi$ based on large-sample binomial approximations to the normal distribution. The binomial distribution provides a good approximation to the normal distribution if $k\pi \ge 5$ *and* $k(1 - \pi) \ge 5$. When these conditions are met, $p$ is approximately normally distributed with mean $\pi$ and variance $\pi(1 - \pi)/k$. That is,

$$z = \frac{p - \pi}{\sqrt{\dfrac{\pi(1 - \pi)}{k}}} \qquad (14\text{-}10)$$

has a standard normal distribution.

Using $p(1 - p)/k$ to estimate the variance $\pi(1 - \pi)/k$, we obtain a $100(1 - \alpha)$ percent confidence interval $[\pi_L, \pi_U]$ for $\pi$:

$$\pi_L = p - z_{\alpha/2} \sqrt{\frac{p(1 - p)}{k}} \le \pi \le p + z_{\alpha/2} \sqrt{\frac{p(1 - p)}{k}} = \pi_U, \qquad (14\text{-}11)$$

where $z_{\alpha/2}$ is the two-sided critical value of the standard normal distribution. The critical value for a 95 percent confidence interval is $z_{.025} = 1.96$.

It is well known that the square of a standard normal variate has a chi-square distribution with 1 degree of freedom (e.g., DeGroot 1986). If we square both sides of equation (14-10), we have

$$z^2 = \left[ \frac{p - \pi}{\sqrt{\frac{\pi(1-\pi)}{k}}} \right]^2 = \frac{k(p-\pi)^2}{\pi(1-\pi)}. \quad (14\text{-}12)$$

Thus, $z^2$ has a chi-square distribution with 1 degree of freedom. Equation (14-12) provides an alternative method for obtaining a confidence interval for $\pi$. The upper and lower $[\pi_L, \pi_U]$ bounds for the $100(1-\alpha)$ percent confidence interval are obtained by solving the quadratic equation (Hedges & Olkin 1985)

$$\frac{(2p + b) \pm \sqrt{b^2 + 4bp(1-p)}}{2(1+b)}, \quad (14\text{-}13)$$

where $b = \chi_\alpha^2(1)/k$. For a 95 percent confidence interval, the upper critical value of the chi-square distribution with 1 degree of freedom is $\chi_{.05}^2(1) = 3.841$.

Therefore, two methods are available for constructing confidence intervals for the proportion of positive or significant positive results. Both methods are based on large-sample approximations to the normal distribution. The meta-analyst should use the method that gives the narrowest confidence interval.

Once a confidence interval $[\pi_L, \pi_U]$ has been calculated for $\pi$ it can be transformed to a confidence interval $[\theta_L, \theta_U]$ for $\theta$ by finding the value of $\theta$ such that $\Pr(T > C_\alpha) = \pi$. If $T$ is approximately normally distributed with mean $\theta$ and variance $S^2(\theta)$, then the probability $\pi$ can be expressed as an explicit function of $\theta$,

$$
\begin{aligned}
\pi &= \Pr(T > C_\alpha) \\
&= \Pr\{(T - \theta)/S(\theta) > (C_\alpha - \theta)/S(\theta)\} \quad (14\text{-}14) \\
&= 1 - \Phi[(C_\alpha - \theta)/S(\theta)],
\end{aligned}
$$

where $\Phi(.)$ is the standard normal cumulative distribution function. Solving equation (14-14) for $\theta$ we obtain

$$\theta = C_\alpha - S(\theta)\Phi^{-1}(1 - \pi). \quad (14\text{-}15)$$

Equation (14-15) provides a general large-sample approximate relation between a proportion and an effect size. It is applicable to effect size indexes that are normally distributed in large samples. More accurate (but more complicated) results can be obtained for specific effect size indexes by using their exact distributions. This chapter includes tables based on the exact distributions of the two most common effect sizes indexes: the standardized mean difference and the correlation coefficient.

If the independent variable is dichotomous and the dependent variable is continuous, one common effect size for the $i$th study is the population standardized mean difference

$$\delta_i = \frac{\mu_i^E - \mu_i^C}{\sigma_i}, \quad i = 1, \ldots, k, \quad (14\text{-}16)$$

where $\mu_i^E$ is the population mean for the experimental group in the $i$th study, $\mu_i^C$ is the population mean for the control group in the $i$th study, and $\sigma_i$ is the common population standard deviation in the $i$th study. The sample estimator of $\delta_i$ is

$$d_i = \frac{\overline{Y}_i^E - \overline{Y}_i^C}{S_i}, \quad i = 1, \ldots, k, \quad (14\text{-}17)$$

where $\overline{Y}_i^E$ is the sample mean for the experimental group in the $i$th study, $\overline{Y}_i^C$ is the sample mean for the control group in the $i$th study, and $S_i$ is the pooled within-group sample standard deviation in the $i$th study.

If both the independent variable $X$ and the dependent variable $Y$ are continuous, one common effect size for the $i$th study is the population coefficient of correlation between $X$ and $Y$:

$$\rho_i = \frac{\text{Cov}(X_i, Y_i)}{\sigma_{X_i}\sigma_{Y_i}}, \quad i = 1, \ldots, k, \quad (14\text{-}18)$$

where $\text{Cov}(X_i, Y_i)$ is the population covariance of $X$ and $Y$ for the $i$th study, $\sigma_{X_i}$ is the population standard deviation of $X$ for the $i$th study, and $\sigma_{Y_i}$ is the population standard deviation of $Y$ for the $i$th study. The sample estimator of $\rho_i$ is the Pearson product moment correlation coefficient

$$r_i = \frac{\sum_{j=1}^{n_i}(X_j - \overline{X})(Y_j - \overline{Y})}{\sqrt{\left[\sum_{j=1}^{n_i}(X_j - \overline{X})^2\right]\left[\sum_{j=1}^{n_i}(Y_j - \overline{Y})^2\right]}}, \quad i = 1, \ldots, k.$$

$$(14\text{-}19)$$

Procedures for transforming a confidence interval for $\pi$ to a confidence interval for $\delta$ are described in sections 3.3.1 (equal sample sizes) and 3.4.1 (unequal sample sizes). Procedures for transforming a confidence interval for $\pi$ to a confidence interval for $\rho$ are described in section 3.3.2 (equal sample sizes) and 3.4.2 (unequal sample sizes).

**3.3.1 Confidence interval for the population standardized mean difference $\delta$** If the independent vari-

**Table 14.1 Probability That the Sample Mean of the Experimental Group Exceeds the Sample Mean of the Control Group When the Common Sample Size per Group Is $n$ and the Population Standardized Mean Difference Is $\delta$**

| | Population Standardized Mean Difference $\delta$ | | | | | | | | | | |
|---|---|---|---|---|---|---|---|---|---|---|---|
| $n$ | 0.00 | 0.01 | 0.02 | 0.03 | 0.04 | 0.05 | 0.06 | 0.07 | 0.08 | 0.09 | 0.10 |
| 1 | 0.500 | 0.503 | 0.506 | 0.508 | 0.511 | 0.514 | 0.517 | 0.520 | 0.523 | 0.525 | 0.528 |
| 2 | 0.500 | 0.504 | 0.508 | 0.512 | 0.516 | 0.520 | 0.524 | 0.528 | 0.532 | 0.536 | 0.540 |
| 3 | 0.500 | 0.505 | 0.510 | 0.515 | 0.520 | 0.524 | 0.529 | 0.534 | 0.539 | 0.544 | 0.549 |
| 4 | 0.500 | 0.506 | 0.511 | 0.517 | 0.523 | 0.528 | 0.534 | 0.539 | 0.545 | 0.551 | 0.556 |
| 5 | 0.500 | 0.506 | 0.513 | 0.519 | 0.525 | 0.532 | 0.538 | 0.544 | 0.550 | 0.557 | 0.563 |
| 6 | 0.500 | 0.507 | 0.514 | 0.521 | 0.528 | 0.534 | 0.541 | 0.548 | 0.555 | 0.562 | 0.569 |
| 7 | 0.500 | 0.508 | 0.515 | 0.522 | 0.530 | 0.537 | 0.545 | 0.552 | 0.560 | 0.567 | 0.574 |
| 8 | 0.500 | 0.508 | 0.516 | 0.524 | 0.532 | 0.540 | 0.548 | 0.556 | 0.564 | 0.571 | 0.579 |
| 9 | 0.500 | 0.508 | 0.517 | 0.525 | 0.534 | 0.542 | 0.551 | 0.559 | 0.567 | 0.576 | 0.584 |
| 10 | 0.500 | 0.509 | 0.518 | 0.527 | 0.536 | 0.544 | 0.553 | 0.562 | 0.571 | 0.580 | 0.588 |
| 11 | 0.500 | 0.509 | 0.519 | 0.528 | 0.537 | 0.547 | 0.556 | 0.565 | 0.574 | 0.584 | 0.593 |
| 12 | 0.500 | 0.510 | 0.520 | 0.529 | 0.539 | 0.549 | 0.558 | 0.568 | 0.578 | 0.587 | 0.597 |
| 13 | 0.500 | 0.510 | 0.520 | 0.530 | 0.541 | 0.551 | 0.561 | 0.571 | 0.581 | 0.591 | 0.601 |
| 14 | 0.500 | 0.511 | 0.521 | 0.532 | 0.542 | 0.553 | 0.563 | 0.574 | 0.584 | 0.594 | 0.604 |
| 15 | 0.500 | 0.511 | 0.522 | 0.533 | 0.544 | 0.554 | 0.565 | 0.576 | 0.587 | 0.597 | 0.608 |
| 16 | 0.500 | 0.511 | 0.523 | 0.534 | 0.545 | 0.556 | 0.567 | 0.578 | 0.590 | 0.600 | 0.611 |
| 17 | 0.500 | 0.512 | 0.523 | 0.535 | 0.546 | 0.558 | 0.569 | 0.581 | 0.592 | 0.604 | 0.615 |
| 18 | 0.500 | 0.512 | 0.524 | 0.536 | 0.548 | 0.560 | 0.571 | 0.583 | 0.595 | 0.606 | 0.618 |
| 19 | 0.500 | 0.512 | 0.525 | 0.537 | 0.549 | 0.561 | 0.573 | 0.585 | 0.597 | 0.609 | 0.621 |
| 20 | 0.500 | 0.513 | 0.525 | 0.538 | 0.550 | 0.563 | 0.575 | 0.588 | 0.600 | 0.612 | 0.624 |
| 21 | 0.500 | 0.513 | 0.526 | 0.539 | 0.552 | 0.564 | 0.577 | 0.590 | 0.602 | 0.615 | 0.627 |
| 22 | 0.500 | 0.513 | 0.526 | 0.540 | 0.553 | 0.566 | 0.579 | 0.592 | 0.605 | 0.617 | 0.630 |
| 23 | 0.500 | 0.514 | 0.527 | 0.540 | 0.554 | 0.567 | 0.581 | 0.594 | 0.607 | 0.620 | 0.633 |
| 24 | 0.500 | 0.514 | 0.528 | 0.541 | 0.555 | 0.569 | 0.582 | 0.596 | 0.609 | 0.622 | 0.636 |
| 25 | 0.500 | 0.514 | 0.528 | 0.542 | 0.556 | 0.570 | 0.584 | 0.598 | 0.611 | 0.625 | 0.638 |
| 50 | 0.500 | 0.520 | 0.540 | 0.560 | 0.579 | 0.599 | 0.618 | 0.637 | 0.655 | 0.674 | 0.692 |
| 100 | 0.500 | 0.528 | 0.556 | 0.584 | 0.611 | 0.638 | 0.664 | 0.690 | 0.714 | 0.738 | 0.760 |
| 200 | 0.500 | 0.540 | 0.579 | 0.618 | 0.655 | 0.692 | 0.726 | 0.758 | 0.788 | 0.816 | 0.841 |
| 400 | 0.500 | 0.556 | 0.611 | 0.664 | 0.714 | 0.760 | 0.802 | 0.839 | 0.871 | 0.898 | 0.921 |

SOURCE: Hedges and Olkin (1985).

able is dichotomous and the dependent variable is continuous, an effect size for the $i$th study is the population standardized mean difference $\delta_i$ given in (14-16). If we assume that the effect sizes are homogeneous, the hypotheses in (14-14) can be written as

$$H_0: \delta_1 = \ldots = \delta_k = 0$$
$$H_A: \delta_1 = \ldots = \delta_k = \delta > 0. \qquad (14\text{-}20)$$

To estimate the common population effect size $\delta$, we simply count the number of times $t_i$ exceeds $t_\alpha$, where $t_i$ is defined as

$$t_i = \frac{\overline{Y}_i^E - \overline{Y}_i^C}{S_i \sqrt{\dfrac{2}{n}}}, \quad i = 1, \ldots, k, \qquad (14\text{-}21)$$

and $t_\alpha$ is obtained from the $t$ distribution with $2n - 2$ degrees of freedom, at significance level $\alpha$. For $\alpha = .5$, we count the number of studies with positive mean differences $\overline{Y}_i^E - \overline{Y}_i^C$. For $\alpha = .05$, we count the number of studies with *significant* positive mean differences.

Hedges and Olkin (1985) have produced tables (see

| | | | | Population Standardized Mean Difference $\delta$ | | | | | | | | |
|---|---|---|---|---|---|---|---|---|---|---|---|---|
| 0.2 | 0.3 | 0.4 | 0.5 | 0.6 | 0.7 | 0.8 | 0.9 | 1.0 | 1.1 | 1.2 | 1.3 | 1.4 |
| 0.556 | 0.584 | 0.611 | 0.638 | 0.664 | 0.690 | 0.714 | 0.738 | 0.760 | 0.782 | 0.802 | 0.821 | 0.839 |
| 0.579 | 0.618 | 0.655 | 0.692 | 0.726 | 0.758 | 0.788 | 0.816 | 0.841 | 0.864 | 0.885 | 0.903 | 0.920 |
| 0.597 | 0.643 | 0.688 | 0.730 | 0.769 | 0.804 | 0.836 | 0.865 | 0.890 | 0.911 | 0.929 | 0.944 | 0.957 |
| 0.611 | 0.664 | 0.714 | 0.760 | 0.802 | 0.839 | 0.871 | 0.898 | 0.921 | 0.940 | 0.955 | 0.967 | 0.976 |
| 0.624 | 0.682 | 0.736 | 0.785 | 0.829 | 0.866 | 0.897 | 0.923 | 0.943 | 0.959 | 0.971 | 0.980 | 0.986 |
| 0.636 | 0.698 | 0.756 | 0.807 | 0.851 | 0.887 | 0.917 | 0.940 | 0.958 | 0.972 | 0.981 | 0.988 | 0.992 |
| 0.646 | 0.713 | 0.773 | 0.825 | 0.869 | 0.905 | 0.933 | 0.954 | 0.969 | 0.980 | 0.988 | 0.992 | 0.996 |
| 0.655 | 0.726 | 0.788 | 0.841 | 0.885 | 0.919 | 0.945 | 0.964 | 0.977 | 0.986 | 0.992 | 0.995 | 0.997 |
| 0.664 | 0.738 | 0.802 | 0.856 | 0.898 | 0.931 | 0.955 | 0.972 | 0.983 | 0.990 | 0.994 | 0.997 | 0.998 |
| 0.673 | 0.749 | 0.814 | 0.868 | 0.910 | 0.941 | 0.963 | 0.978 | 0.987 | 0.993 | 0.996 | 0.998 | 0.999 |
| 0.680 | 0.759 | 0.826 | 0.880 | 0.920 | 0.950 | 0.970 | 0.983 | 0.990 | 0.995 | 0.998 | 0.999 | 1.000 |
| 0.688 | 0.769 | 0.836 | 0.890 | 0.929 | 0.957 | 0.975 | 0.986 | 0.993 | 0.996 | 0.998 | 0.999 | 1.000 |
| 0.695 | 0.778 | 0.846 | 0.899 | 0.937 | 0.963 | 0.979 | 0.989 | 0.995 | 0.998 | 0.999 | 1.000 | |
| 0.702 | 0.786 | 0.855 | 0.907 | 0.944 | 0.968 | 0.983 | 0.991 | 0.996 | 0.998 | 0.999 | 1.000 | |
| 0.708 | 0.794 | 0.863 | 0.914 | 0.950 | 0.972 | 0.986 | 0.993 | 0.997 | 0.999 | 1.000 | | |
| 0.714 | 0.802 | 0.871 | 0.921 | 0.955 | 0.976 | 0.988 | 0.994 | 0.998 | 0.999 | 1.000 | | |
| 0.720 | 0.809 | 0.878 | 0.928 | 0.960 | 0.979 | 0.990 | 0.996 | 0.998 | 0.999 | 1.000 | | |
| 0.726 | 0.816 | 0.885 | 0.933 | 0.964 | 0.982 | 0.992 | 0.996 | 0.999 | 1.000 | | | |
| 0.731 | 0.822 | 0.891 | 0.938 | 0.968 | 0.984 | 0.993 | 0.997 | 0.999 | 1.000 | | | |
| 0.736 | 0.829 | 0.897 | 0.943 | 0.971 | 0.987 | 0.994 | 0.998 | 0.999 | 1.000 | | | |
| 0.742 | 0.834 | 0.902 | 0.947 | 0.974 | 0.988 | 0.995 | 0.998 | 0.999 | | | | |
| 0.746 | 0.840 | 0.908 | 0.951 | 0.977 | 0.990 | 0.996 | 0.999 | 1.000 | | | | |
| 0.751 | 0.846 | 0.912 | 0.955 | 0.979 | 0.991 | 0.997 | 0.999 | 1.000 | | | | |
| 0.756 | 0.851 | 0.917 | 0.958 | 0.981 | 0.992 | 0.997 | 0.999 | 1.000 | | | | |
| 0.760 | 0.856 | 0.921 | 0.962 | 0.983 | 0.993 | 0.998 | 0.999 | 1.000 | | | | |
| 0.841 | 0.933 | 0.977 | 0.994 | 0.999 | 1.000 | 1.000 | 1.000 | | | | | |
| 0.921 | 0.983 | 0.998 | 1.000 | 1.000 | | | | | | | | |
| 0.977 | 0.999 | 1.000 | | | | | | | | | | |
| 0.998 | 1.000 | | | | | | | | | | | |

Tables 14.1 and 14.2) that can be used to transform a confidence interval for $\pi$ to a confidence interval for $\delta$ by finding the values $[\delta_L, \delta_U]$ that correspond to the lower and upper confidence limits $[\pi_L, \pi_U]$. The following two examples will use the results from Data Set II on the effects of teacher expectancy on pupil IQ (see Appendix A) to illustrate these procedures. Example 1 uses the proportion of positive results to estimate $\delta$, whereas Example 2 uses the proportion of *significant* positive results to estimate $\delta$. It should be noted, however, that Data Set II severely violates the equal sample size assumption. Studies 3, 10, 11, 13, and 16 are the only ones with equal experimental and control group sample sizes. In addition, the total number of subjects per study ranges from 33 to 746. Nevertheless, Data Set II will suffice for purposes of illustration.

*Example 1.* Suppose that we wish to obtain an estimate and confidence interval for $\delta$ based on the proportion of positive results in Data Set II. The square mean root for the 19 studies was calculated by substituting the mean of the experimental and control group sample sizes in (14-3),

**Table 14.2 Probability That a Two-Sample *t* Test Is Significant at the 5 Percent Level When the Common Sample Size Is *n* per Group and the Population Standardized Mean Difference Is δ**

| | Population Standardized Mean Difference δ | | | | | | | | | | |
|---|---|---|---|---|---|---|---|---|---|---|---|
| *n* | 0.00 | 0.01 | 0.02 | 0.03 | 0.04 | 0.05 | 0.06 | 0.07 | 0.08 | 0.09 | 0.10 |
| 2 | 0.050 | 0.051 | 0.052 | 0.052 | 0.053 | 0.054 | 0.055 | 0.056 | 0.056 | 0.057 | 0.058 |
| 3 | 0.050 | 0.051 | 0.052 | 0.053 | 0.054 | 0.056 | 0.057 | 0.058 | 0.059 | 0.060 | 0.062 |
| 4 | 0.050 | 0.051 | 0.053 | 0.054 | 0.055 | 0.057 | 0.058 | 0.060 | 0.061 | 0.063 | 0.064 |
| 5 | 0.050 | 0.052 | 0.053 | 0.055 | 0.056 | 0.058 | 0.060 | 0.061 | 0.063 | 0.065 | 0.067 |
| 6 | 0.050 | 0.052 | 0.053 | 0.055 | 0.057 | 0.059 | 0.061 | 0.063 | 0.065 | 0.067 | 0.069 |
| 7 | 0.050 | 0.052 | 0.054 | 0.056 | 0.058 | 0.060 | 0.062 | 0.064 | 0.066 | 0.069 | 0.071 |
| 8 | 0.050 | 0.052 | 0.054 | 0.056 | 0.058 | 0.061 | 0.063 | 0.065 | 0.068 | 0.070 | 0.073 |
| 9 | 0.050 | 0.052 | 0.054 | 0.057 | 0.059 | 0.061 | 0.064 | 0.066 | 0.069 | 0.072 | 0.075 |
| 10 | 0.050 | 0.052 | 0.055 | 0.057 | 0.060 | 0.062 | 0.065 | 0.068 | 0.070 | 0.073 | 0.076 |
| 11 | 0.050 | 0.052 | 0.055 | 0.057 | 0.060 | 0.063 | 0.066 | 0.069 | 0.072 | 0.075 | 0.078 |
| 12 | 0.050 | 0.052 | 0.055 | 0.058 | 0.061 | 0.064 | 0.066 | 0.070 | 0.073 | 0.076 | 0.080 |
| 13 | 0.050 | 0.053 | 0.055 | 0.058 | 0.061 | 0.064 | 0.067 | 0.071 | 0.074 | 0.078 | 0.081 |
| 14 | 0.050 | 0.053 | 0.056 | 0.058 | 0.062 | 0.065 | 0.068 | 0.072 | 0.075 | 0.079 | 0.083 |
| 15 | 0.050 | 0.053 | 0.056 | 0.059 | 0.062 | 0.065 | 0.069 | 0.072 | 0.076 | 0.080 | 0.084 |
| 16 | 0.050 | 0.053 | 0.056 | 0.059 | 0.062 | 0.066 | 0.070 | 0.073 | 0.077 | 0.081 | 0.086 |
| 17 | 0.050 | 0.053 | 0.056 | 0.060 | 0.063 | 0.066 | 0.070 | 0.074 | 0.078 | 0.083 | 0.087 |
| 18 | 0.050 | 0.053 | 0.056 | 0.060 | 0.063 | 0.067 | 0.071 | 0.075 | 0.079 | 0.084 | 0.088 |
| 19 | 0.050 | 0.053 | 0.057 | 0.060 | 0.064 | 0.068 | 0.072 | 0.076 | 0.080 | 0.085 | 0.090 |
| 20 | 0.050 | 0.053 | 0.057 | 0.060 | 0.064 | 0.068 | 0.072 | 0.077 | 0.081 | 0.086 | 0.091 |
| 21 | 0.050 | 0.053 | 0.057 | 0.061 | 0.065 | 0.069 | 0.073 | 0.078 | 0.082 | 0.087 | 0.092 |
| 22 | 0.050 | 0.054 | 0.057 | 0.061 | 0.065 | 0.069 | 0.074 | 0.078 | 0.083 | 0.088 | 0.094 |
| 23 | 0.050 | 0.054 | 0.057 | 0.061 | 0.065 | 0.070 | 0.074 | 0.079 | 0.084 | 0.089 | 0.095 |
| 24 | 0.050 | 0.054 | 0.058 | 0.062 | 0.066 | 0.070 | 0.075 | 0.080 | 0.085 | 0.090 | 0.096 |
| 25 | 0.050 | 0.054 | 0.058 | 0.062 | 0.066 | 0.071 | 0.076 | 0.081 | 0.086 | 0.092 | 0.098 |
| 50 | 0.050 | 0.055 | 0.061 | 0.067 | 0.074 | 0.081 | 0.089 | 0.097 | 0.106 | 0.116 | 0.125 |
| 100 | 0.050 | 0.058 | 0.066 | 0.076 | 0.086 | 0.098 | 0.111 | 0.125 | 0.140 | 0.156 | 0.174 |
| 200 | 0.050 | 0.061 | 0.074 | 0.089 | 0.106 | 0.126 | 0.148 | 0.172 | 0.199 | 0.228 | 0.259 |
| 400 | 0.050 | 0.066 | 0.087 | 0.111 | 0.140 | 0.174 | 0.213 | 0.256 | 0.304 | 0.355 | 0.408 |

SOURCE: Hedges and Olkin (1985).

$$n_{SMR} = \left\{ \left[ \left( \sqrt{\frac{(77+339)}{2}} \right) + \dots \right. \right.$$

$$\left. \left. + \left( \sqrt{\frac{(65+67)}{2}} \right) \right] \middle/ 19 \right\}^2 = 83.515 \text{ or } 84.$$

The estimate of $\pi$ is $p = U/k = 11/19 = 0.579$. Because there is no entry for $n = 84$ in Table 14.1, we must interpolate between the entries for $n = 50$ and $n = 100$. The two-point equation of the line can be used to obtain linear interpolations

$$(Y - Y_1) = \left( \frac{Y_2 - Y_1}{X_2 - X_1} \right)(X - X_1). \qquad (14\text{-}22)$$

For $n = 50$, $p = 0.579$ corresponds to the value $\delta = 0.04$. For $n = 100$, $p = 0.579$ falls between 0.556 ($\delta = 0.02$) and 0.584 ($\delta = 0.03$). Linear interpolation using equation (14-22) yields

$$(\hat{\delta} - 0.02) = \left( \frac{0.03 - 0.02}{0.584 - 0.556} \right)(0.579 - 0.556).$$

Solving for $\hat{\delta}$ we obtain 0.028. Therefore, our estimate of $\delta$ for $n = 84$ is between 0.028 ($n = 100$) and 0.04 ($n = 50$). Using the point-slope equation of the line given in (14-22) once more yields

$$(\hat{\delta} - 0.028) = \left( \frac{0.04 - 0.028}{50 - 100} \right)(84 - 100),$$

or $\hat{\delta} = 0.032$.

| | | | | Population Standardized Mean Difference $\delta$ | | | | | | | | |
|---|---|---|---|---|---|---|---|---|---|---|---|---|
| 0.2 | 0.3 | 0.4 | 0.5 | 0.6 | 0.7 | 0.8 | 0.9 | 1.0 | 1.1 | 1.2 | 1.3 | 1.4 |
| 0.067 | 0.077 | 0.088 | 0.099 | 0.112 | 0.126 | 0.141 | 0.157 | 0.174 | 0.191 | 0.210 | 0.229 | 0.250 |
| 0.075 | 0.091 | 0.109 | 0.129 | 0.152 | 0.177 | 0.205 | 0.235 | 0.267 | 0.301 | 0.337 | 0.374 | 0.413 |
| 0.082 | 0.103 | 0.127 | 0.155 | 0.187 | 0.222 | 0.261 | 0.304 | 0.348 | 0.396 | 0.444 | 0.493 | 0.543 |
| 0.088 | 0.113 | 0.144 | 0.179 | 0.219 | 0.264 | 0.313 | 0.366 | 0.422 | 0.478 | 0.536 | 0.592 | 0.647 |
| 0.093 | 0.123 | 0.159 | 0.201 | 0.250 | 0.304 | 0.362 | 0.424 | 0.488 | 0.552 | 0.614 | 0.674 | 0.730 |
| 0.098 | 0.132 | 0.174 | 0.223 | 0.279 | 0.341 | 0.408 | 0.477 | 0.548 | 0.616 | 0.681 | 0.741 | 0.795 |
| 0.103 | 0.142 | 0.189 | 0.244 | 0.308 | 0.377 | 0.451 | 0.527 | 0.602 | 0.673 | 0.738 | 0.796 | 0.845 |
| 0.108 | 0.150 | 0.203 | 0.265 | 0.335 | 0.412 | 0.492 | 0.573 | 0.650 | 0.722 | 0.786 | 0.840 | 0.884 |
| 0.112 | 0.159 | 0.217 | 0.285 | 0.362 | 0.445 | 0.530 | 0.615 | 0.694 | 0.765 | 0.825 | 0.875 | 0.914 |
| 0.117 | 0.167 | 0.230 | 0.304 | 0.388 | 0.476 | 0.566 | 0.653 | 0.732 | 0.801 | 0.858 | 0.903 | 0.936 |
| 0.121 | 0.176 | 0.244 | 0.324 | 0.413 | 0.507 | 0.600 | 0.688 | 0.767 | 0.833 | 0.885 | 0.925 | 0.953 |
| 0.125 | 0.184 | 0.257 | 0.342 | 0.437 | 0.536 | 0.632 | 0.720 | 0.797 | 0.860 | 0.908 | 0.942 | 0.966 |
| 0.130 | 0.192 | 0.270 | 0.361 | 0.461 | 0.563 | 0.661 | 0.750 | 0.824 | 0.883 | 0.926 | 0.956 | 0.975 |
| 0.133 | 0.200 | 0.282 | 0.379 | 0.483 | 0.589 | 0.689 | 0.776 | 0.848 | 0.902 | 0.941 | 0.966 | 0.982 |
| 0.138 | 0.207 | 0.295 | 0.396 | 0.506 | 0.614 | 0.714 | 0.800 | 0.868 | 0.918 | 0.953 | 0.974 | 0.987 |
| 0.141 | 0.215 | 0.307 | 0.414 | 0.527 | 0.638 | 0.738 | 0.822 | 0.886 | 0.932 | 0.962 | 0.981 | 0.991 |
| 0.145 | 0.223 | 0.320 | 0.431 | 0.547 | 0.660 | 0.760 | 0.842 | 0.902 | 0.944 | 0.970 | 0.985 | 0.993 |
| 0.149 | 0.230 | 0.332 | 0.447 | 0.567 | 0.682 | 0.781 | 0.859 | 0.916 | 0.954 | 0.976 | 0.989 | 0.995 |
| 0.153 | 0.238 | 0.344 | 0.463 | 0.586 | 0.702 | 0.799 | 0.875 | 0.928 | 0.962 | 0.981 | 0.992 | 0.997 |
| 0.157 | 0.245 | 0.356 | 0.479 | 0.605 | 0.721 | 0.817 | 0.889 | 0.938 | 0.968 | 0.985 | 0.994 | 0.998 |
| 0.161 | 0.253 | 0.367 | 0.495 | 0.623 | 0.739 | 0.833 | 0.902 | 0.947 | 0.974 | 0.988 | 0.995 | 0.998 |
| 0.164 | 0.260 | 0.379 | 0.509 | 0.640 | 0.756 | 0.848 | 0.913 | 0.955 | 0.979 | 0.991 | 0.996 | 0.999 |
| 0.168 | 0.267 | 0.390 | 0.525 | 0.656 | 0.772 | 0.861 | 0.923 | 0.961 | 0.982 | 0.993 | 0.997 | 0.999 |
| 0.172 | 0.275 | 0.401 | 0.539 | 0.672 | 0.787 | 0.874 | 0.932 | 0.967 | 0.986 | 0.994 | 0.998 | 0.999 |
| 0.257 | 0.438 | 0.634 | 0.799 | 0.909 | 0.966 | 0.990 | 0.998 | 1.000 | 1.000 | 1.000 | 1.000 | 1.000 |
| 0.407 | 0.681 | 0.880 | 0.970 | 0.995 | 1.000 | 1.000 | 1.000 | | | | | |
| 0.637 | 0.911 | 0.990 | 1.000 | 1.000 | | | | | | | | |
| 0.881 | 0.995 | 1.000 | | | | | | | | | | |

The binomial distribution should provide a good approximation to the normal distribution for this example because $k\pi = k(1 - \pi) = 19(.5) = 9.5 > 5$. We have two methods available for calculating a confidence interval for $\pi$. The 95 percent confidence interval based on the standard normal distribution given in (14-11) is

$$0.579 - 1.96 \sqrt{\frac{0.579(1 - 0.579)}{19}} \leq \pi$$

$$\leq 0.579 + 1.96 \sqrt{\frac{0.579(1 - 0.579)}{19}},$$

or simplifying, [0.357, 0.801]. The 95 percent confidence interval based on the chi-square distribution given in (14-13) is

$$\frac{(2(0.579) + 0.202) \pm \sqrt{0.202^2 + 4(.202)(0.579)(1 - 0.579)}}{2(1 + 0.202)},$$

where $b = 3.841/19 = 0.202$. Simplifying we have [0.363, 0.769].

For this example, the confidence interval based on the chi-square distribution is slightly narrower $(0.769 - 0.363 = 0.406)$ than the confidence interval based on the standard normal distribution $(0.801 - 0.357 = 0.444)$. Table 14.1 can be used to transform the chi-square distribution confidence interval for $\pi$ to a confidence interval for $\delta$. The lower limit of the confidence interval

**Table 14.3 Probability That a Correlation Coefficient from a Sample of Size $n$ Will Be Positive When the Population Correlation Coefficient Is $\rho$**

| $n$ | Population Correlation Coefficient $\rho$ | | | | | | | | | | | |
|---|---|---|---|---|---|---|---|---|---|---|---|---|
| | 0 | 0.01 | 0.02 | 0.03 | 0.04 | 0.05 | 0.06 | 0.07 | 0.08 | 0.09 | 0.10 | 0.20 |
| 3 | 0.500 | 0.505 | 0.510 | 0.515 | 0.520 | 0.525 | 0.530 | 0.535 | 0.540 | 0.545 | 0.550 | 0.600 |
| 4 | 0.500 | 0.506 | 0.513 | 0.519 | 0.525 | 0.532 | 0.538 | 0.545 | 0.551 | 0.557 | 0.564 | 0.626 |
| 5 | 0.500 | 0.508 | 0.515 | 0.522 | 0.530 | 0.537 | 0.545 | 0.552 | 0.560 | 0.567 | 0.575 | 0.648 |
| 6 | 0.500 | 0.508 | 0.517 | 0.525 | 0.534 | 0.542 | 0.551 | 0.559 | 0.568 | 0.576 | 0.584 | 0.666 |
| 7 | 0.500 | 0.509 | 0.519 | 0.528 | 0.537 | 0.547 | 0.556 | 0.565 | 0.575 | 0.584 | 0.593 | 0.683 |
| 8 | 0.500 | 0.510 | 0.520 | 0.531 | 0.541 | 0.551 | 0.561 | 0.571 | 0.581 | 0.591 | 0.601 | 0.697 |
| 9 | 0.500 | 0.511 | 0.522 | 0.533 | 0.544 | 0.555 | 0.565 | 0.576 | 0.587 | 0.598 | 0.608 | 0.710 |
| 10 | 0.500 | 0.512 | 0.523 | 0.535 | 0.546 | 0.558 | 0.570 | 0.581 | 0.592 | 0.604 | 0.615 | 0.722 |
| 11 | 0.500 | 0.512 | 0.525 | 0.537 | 0.549 | 0.561 | 0.573 | 0.586 | 0.598 | 0.610 | 0.621 | 0.733 |
| 12 | 0.500 | 0.513 | 0.526 | 0.539 | 0.552 | 0.564 | 0.577 | 0.590 | 0.602 | 0.615 | 0.627 | 0.744 |
| 13 | 0.500 | 0.514 | 0.527 | 0.541 | 0.554 | 0.567 | 0.581 | 0.594 | 0.607 | 0.620 | 0.633 | 0.754 |
| 14 | 0.500 | 0.514 | 0.528 | 0.542 | 0.556 | 0.570 | 0.584 | 0.598 | 0.612 | 0.625 | 0.639 | 0.763 |
| 15 | 0.500 | 0.515 | 0.529 | 0.544 | 0.558 | 0.573 | 0.587 | 0.602 | 0.616 | 0.630 | 0.644 | 0.771 |
| 16 | 0.500 | 0.515 | 0.530 | 0.546 | 0.561 | 0.576 | 0.590 | 0.605 | 0.620 | 0.634 | 0.649 | 0.779 |
| 17 | 0.500 | 0.516 | 0.531 | 0.547 | 0.563 | 0.578 | 0.593 | 0.609 | 0.624 | 0.639 | 0.654 | 0.787 |
| 18 | 0.500 | 0.516 | 0.532 | 0.549 | 0.565 | 0.581 | 0.596 | 0.612 | 0.628 | 0.643 | 0.658 | 0.794 |
| 19 | 0.500 | 0.517 | 0.533 | 0.550 | 0.566 | 0.583 | 0.599 | 0.615 | 0.631 | 0.647 | 0.663 | 0.801 |
| 20 | 0.500 | 0.517 | 0.534 | 0.551 | 0.568 | 0.585 | 0.602 | 0.618 | 0.635 | 0.651 | 0.667 | 0.808 |
| 21 | 0.500 | 0.518 | 0.535 | 0.553 | 0.570 | 0.587 | 0.605 | 0.622 | 0.638 | 0.655 | 0.671 | 0.814 |
| 22 | 0.500 | 0.518 | 0.536 | 0.554 | 0.572 | 0.590 | 0.607 | 0.625 | 0.642 | 0.659 | 0.675 | 0.820 |
| 23 | 0.500 | 0.518 | 0.537 | 0.555 | 0.574 | 0.592 | 0.610 | 0.627 | 0.645 | 0.662 | 0.679 | 0.826 |
| 24 | 0.500 | 0.519 | 0.538 | 0.557 | 0.575 | 0.594 | 0.612 | 0.630 | 0.648 | 0.666 | 0.683 | 0.831 |
| 25 | 0.500 | 0.519 | 0.539 | 0.558 | 0.577 | 0.596 | 0.615 | 0.633 | 0.651 | 0.669 | 0.687 | 0.836 |
| 50 | 0.500 | 0.528 | 0.555 | 0.583 | 0.610 | 0.636 | 0.662 | 0.687 | 0.712 | 0.735 | 0.757 | 0.920 |
| 100 | 0.500 | 0.540 | 0.579 | 0.617 | 0.654 | 0.690 | 0.724 | 0.757 | 0.787 | 0.815 | 0.840 | 0.978 |
| 200 | 0.500 | 0.556 | 0.611 | 0.664 | 0.714 | 0.760 | 0.801 | 0.838 | 0.871 | 0.898 | 0.921 | 0.998 |
| 400 | 0.500 | 0.579 | 0.655 | 0.725 | 0.788 | 0.841 | 0.885 | 0.919 | 0.945 | 0.964 | 0.977 | 1.000 |

SOURCE: Olkin (1973).

for $\pi$ is $p = 0.363$. Note that Table 14.1 contains only proportions greater than or equal to 0.500. Proportions less than 0.500 correspond to *negative* values of $\delta$. Because the binomial distribution is symmetrical when $\pi = 0.500$, we can use $1 - p$ for values of $p$ less than 0.500. Therefore, we use $1 - 0.363 = 0.637$ for the lower limit. Because there is no row for $n = 84$ in Table 14.1, we must interpolate between rows $n = 50$ and $n = 100$. Entering Table 14.1 we find that $p = 0.637$ corresponds to $\delta = -0.07$ for $n = 50$ and to $\delta = -0.05$ for $n = 100$. Linear interpolation between these two values yields the lower limit $\delta_L = -0.056$ for $n = 84$. The upper limit of the confidence interval for $\pi$ is $p = 0.769$. Entering Table 14.1 for $n = 50$, we find that $p = 0.769$ is between 0.692 ($\delta = 0.1$) and 0.841 ($\delta = 0.2$). Linear interpolation between these values gives 0.152. Entering Table 14.1

for $n = 100$, we find that $p = 0.769$ is between 0.760 ($\delta = 0.1$) and 0.921 ($\delta = 0.2$). Linear interpolation between these values gives 0.106. Thus, the upper limit $\delta_U$ must be between 0.106 ($n = 100$) and 0.152 ($n = 50$). Linear interpolation yields the upper limit $\delta_U = 0.121$ for $n = 84$. Because the $\delta$ confidence interval $[-0.056, 0.121]$ contains the value zero, we fail to reject the null hypothesis in (14-20) and conclude that all the effect sizes equal zero.

*Example 2.* Suppose that we wish to obtain an estimate and confidence interval for $\delta$ based on the proportion of *significant* positive results in Data Set II. From Table 1 in Raudenbush and Bryk (1985) we find that 3 of the 19 results are statistically significant at the 0.05 level. The estimate of the proportion of *significant* positive results in the population is $p = U/k = 3/19 = 0.158$.

| 0.30 | 0.40 | 0.50 | 0.60 | 0.70 | 0.80 | 0.90 |
|------|------|------|------|------|------|------|
| 0.650 | 0.700 | 0.750 | 0.800 | 0.850 | 0.900 | 0.950 |
| 0.688 | 0.748 | 0.805 | 0.858 | 0.906 | 0.948 | 0.981 |
| 0.718 | 0.784 | 0.844 | 0.896 | 0.939 | 0.972 | 0.993 |
| 0.743 | 0.813 | 0.873 | 0.923 | 0.960 | 0.985 | 0.997 |
| 0.765 | 0.837 | 0.896 | 0.942 | 0.973 | 0.991 | 0.998 |
| 0.784 | 0.857 | 0.915 | 0.956 | 0.982 | 0.995 | 1.000 |
| 0.800 | 0.874 | 0.929 | 0.967 | 0.988 | 0.997 | 1.000 |
| 0.815 | 0.889 | 0.941 | 0.975 | 0.992 | 0.998 | 1.000 |
| 0.828 | 0.901 | 0.951 | 0.980 | 0.994 | 0.999 | 1.000 |
| 0.840 | 0.912 | 0.959 | 0.985 | 0.996 | 0.999 | 1.000 |
| 0.851 | 0.922 | 0.966 | 0.988 | 0.997 | 1.000 | |
| 0.861 | 0.930 | 0.971 | 0.991 | 0.998 | 1.000 | |
| 0.871 | 0.938 | 0.976 | 0.993 | 0.999 | 1.000 | |
| 0.879 | 0.944 | 0.980 | 0.995 | 0.999 | 1.000 | |
| 0.887 | 0.950 | 0.983 | 0.996 | 0.999 | 1.000 | |
| 0.894 | 0.955 | 0.985 | 0.997 | 1.000 | | |
| 0.901 | 0.960 | 0.988 | 0.997 | 1.000 | | |
| 0.907 | 0.964 | 0.990 | 0.998 | 1.000 | | |
| 0.913 | 0.967 | 0.991 | 0.998 | 1.000 | | |
| 0.918 | 0.971 | 0.992 | 0.999 | 1.000 | | |
| 0.923 | 0.974 | 0.994 | 0.999 | 1.000 | | |
| 0.927 | 0.976 | 0.995 | 0.999 | 1.000 | | |
| 0.932 | 0.979 | 0.995 | 0.999 | 1.000 | | |
| 0.984 | 0.998 | 1.000 | 1.000 | | | |
| 0.999 | 1.000 | | | | | |
| 1.000 | | | | | | |

Linear interpolation in Table 2 yields the estimate $\hat{\delta} = 0.103$.

Checking the assumptions for the normal distribution we have $k\pi = 19(.05) = 0.95$, and $k(1 - \pi) = 19(.95) = 18.05$. If $\delta = 0$, the binomial distribution probably will *not* provide a good approximation to the normal distribution because $k\pi < 5$. I will finish the example, however, for illustration.[5] The confidence interval for $\pi$ based on standard normal distribution theory given in (14-11) is $[-0.006, 0.322]$, and the confidence interval

---

[5]If $\pi = .05$, $k\pi \geq 5$ if and only if $k \geq 100$. Thus, if the effect size is near zero, the assumptions for the normal approximation will *not* be met for meta-analyses that include fewer than 100 studies. If the effect size is greater than zero, then $\pi$ will be larger than .05, and the assumptions for the normal approximation might be met for meta-analyses that include fewer than 100 studies.

for $\pi$ based on chi-square distribution theory given in (14-13) is $[0.055, 0.376]$. Because the latter confidence interval is narrower than the former, we will use it to obtain a confidence interval for $\delta$. For $p = 0.263$ and $n = 84$ we obtain the $\delta$ confidence interval $[0.032, 0.212]$ by linear interpolation in Table 14.2. Because the confidence interval for $\delta$ does *not* include the value zero, we reject the null hypothesis and conclude that the common effect size $\delta$ is significantly greater than zero.

It is of interest to note that the estimate of $\delta$ based on effect size procedures was $d. = 0.058$, with confidence interval $[-0.014, 0.130]$. The confidence intervals based on the proportion of positive results is similar to the confidence interval based on effect sizes. Both confidence intervals contain the value zero and have similar end points. The confidence interval based on the proportion of significant positive results, in contrast, does not contain the value zero. This difference may be due to the fairly severe violation of the expected number of studies needed for adequacy of the normal approximation.

### 3.3.2 Confidence interval for the population correlation coefficient $\rho$

If both the independent and dependent variables are continuous, the effect size for the $i$th study is the population coefficient of correlation $\rho_i$ given in (14-18). If we assume that the effect sizes are homogeneous, the hypotheses in equation (14-4) can be written as

$$H_0: \rho_1 = \ldots = \rho_k = 0$$
$$H_A: \rho_1 = \ldots = \rho_k = > 0. \quad (14\text{-}23)$$

The sample estimate of $\rho_i$ is the Pearson product moment correlation coefficient $r_i$ given in (14-19). To estimate the common population correlation $\rho$, we count the number of times $r_i$ exceeds the critical value $r_\alpha$ from the $r$ distribution at significance level $\alpha$. For $\alpha = .5$, we count the number of studies with positive correlations. For $\alpha = .05$, we count the number of studies with *significant* positive correlations.

Olkin (1973) produced a table (see Table 14.3) for obtaining an estimate and confidence interval for $\rho$ given the proportion of positive results.[6] For this chapter, we produced a table (Table 14.4) for obtaining an estimate

---

[6]As with Table 14.1, Table 14.3 contains only proportions greater than or equal to 0.500. Proportions less than 0.500, which correspond to negative values of $\rho$, can be obtained by using $1 - p$ instead of $p$. For example, if we found 9 positive correlations in 20 studies, the estimate of $\pi$ would be $p = 9/20 = 0.450$. Since this estimate is less than 0.500, we use $1 - p = 0.550$, which corresponds to $\rho = -.03$.

**Table 14.4 Probability That a Correlation Coefficient from a Sample of Size n Will Be Significant at the 5 Percent Level When the Population Correlation Coefficient Is ρ**

| n | \multicolumn{12}{c}{Population Correlation Coefficient $\rho$} |
|---|---|---|---|---|---|---|---|---|---|---|---|---|
|   | 0 | 0.01 | 0.02 | 0.03 | 0.04 | 0.05 | 0.06 | 0.07 | 0.08 | 0.09 | 0.10 | 0.20 |
| 3 | 0.050 | 0.051 | 0.052 | 0.052 | 0.053 | 0.054 | 0.055 | 0.056 | 0.057 | 0.057 | 0.058 | 0.068 |
| 4 | 0.050 | 0.051 | 0.052 | 0.054 | 0.055 | 0.056 | 0.058 | 0.059 | 0.061 | 0.062 | 0.064 | 0.080 |
| 5 | 0.050 | 0.052 | 0.053 | 0.055 | 0.057 | 0.058 | 0.060 | 0.062 | 0.064 | 0.066 | 0.068 | 0.092 |
| 6 | 0.050 | 0.052 | 0.054 | 0.056 | 0.058 | 0.060 | 0.062 | 0.065 | 0.067 | 0.069 | 0.072 | 0.102 |
| 7 | 0.050 | 0.052 | 0.054 | 0.057 | 0.059 | 0.062 | 0.064 | 0.067 | 0.070 | 0.073 | 0.076 | 0.112 |
| 8 | 0.050 | 0.052 | 0.055 | 0.058 | 0.060 | 0.063 | 0.066 | 0.069 | 0.072 | 0.075 | 0.079 | 0.121 |
| 9 | 0.050 | 0.053 | 0.055 | 0.058 | 0.061 | 0.064 | 0.068 | 0.071 | 0.074 | 0.078 | 0.082 | 0.130 |
| 10 | 0.050 | 0.053 | 0.056 | 0.059 | 0.062 | 0.066 | 0.069 | 0.073 | 0.077 | 0.081 | 0.085 | 0.138 |
| 11 | 0.050 | 0.053 | 0.056 | 0.060 | 0.063 | 0.067 | 0.071 | 0.075 | 0.079 | 0.083 | 0.088 | 0.146 |
| 12 | 0.050 | 0.053 | 0.057 | 0.060 | 0.064 | 0.068 | 0.072 | 0.076 | 0.081 | 0.086 | 0.091 | 0.154 |
| 13 | 0.050 | 0.053 | 0.057 | 0.061 | 0.065 | 0.069 | 0.073 | 0.078 | 0.083 | 0.088 | 0.093 | 0.162 |
| 14 | 0.050 | 0.054 | 0.057 | 0.061 | 0.065 | 0.070 | 0.075 | 0.079 | 0.085 | 0.090 | 0.096 | 0.170 |
| 15 | 0.050 | 0.054 | 0.058 | 0.062 | 0.066 | 0.071 | 0.076 | 0.081 | 0.086 | 0.092 | 0.098 | 0.178 |
| 16 | 0.050 | 0.054 | 0.058 | 0.062 | 0.067 | 0.072 | 0.077 | 0.082 | 0.088 | 0.094 | 0.101 | 0.185 |
| 17 | 0.050 | 0.054 | 0.058 | 0.063 | 0.068 | 0.073 | 0.078 | 0.084 | 0.090 | 0.096 | 0.103 | 0.192 |
| 18 | 0.050 | 0.054 | 0.059 | 0.063 | 0.068 | 0.074 | 0.079 | 0.085 | 0.092 | 0.098 | 0.106 | 0.200 |
| 19 | 0.050 | 0.054 | 0.059 | 0.064 | 0.069 | 0.075 | 0.080 | 0.087 | 0.093 | 0.100 | 0.108 | 0.207 |
| 20 | 0.050 | 0.054 | 0.059 | 0.064 | 0.070 | 0.075 | 0.082 | 0.088 | 0.095 | 0.102 | 0.110 | 0.214 |
| 21 | 0.050 | 0.055 | 0.059 | 0.065 | 0.070 | 0.076 | 0.083 | 0.089 | 0.097 | 0.104 | 0.112 | 0.221 |
| 22 | 0.050 | 0.055 | 0.060 | 0.065 | 0.071 | 0.077 | 0.084 | 0.091 | 0.098 | 0.106 | 0.115 | 0.228 |
| 23 | 0.050 | 0.055 | 0.060 | 0.066 | 0.072 | 0.078 | 0.085 | 0.092 | 0.100 | 0.108 | 0.117 | 0.235 |
| 24 | 0.050 | 0.055 | 0.060 | 0.066 | 0.072 | 0.079 | 0.086 | 0.093 | 0.101 | 0.110 | 0.119 | 0.242 |
| 25 | 0.050 | 0.055 | 0.061 | 0.066 | 0.073 | 0.080 | 0.087 | 0.095 | 0.103 | 0.112 | 0.121 | 0.249 |
| 50 | 0.050 | 0.058 | 0.066 | 0.075 | 0.085 | 0.097 | 0.109 | 0.123 | 0.137 | 0.153 | 0.170 | 0.405 |
| 100 | 0.050 | 0.061 | 0.074 | 0.089 | 0.106 | 0.125 | 0.147 | 0.171 | 0.197 | 0.226 | 0.257 | 0.642 |
| 200 | 0.050 | 0.066 | 0.086 | 0.111 | 0.140 | 0.173 | 0.212 | 0.255 | 0.303 | 0.354 | 0.408 | 0.887 |
| 400 | 0.050 | 0.074 | 0.106 | 0.148 | 0.199 | 0.259 | 0.328 | 0.403 | 0.482 | 0.562 | 0.640 | 0.992 |

and confidence interval for $\rho$ given the proportion of *significant* positive results.[7] Examples 1 and 2 that follow illustrate how to use Tables 14.3 and 14.4, respectively.

*Example 1.* Suppose that we wish to obtain an estimate and confidence interval for $\rho$ based on the proportion of positive results in Data Set III on the validity of student evaluations of teachers (see Appendix A). Like Data Set II, Data Set III severely violates the equal sample size assumption (sample sizes range from 10 to 121), but it will suffice for purposes of illustration.

Using equation (14-3) we obtain the square mean root for the 20 studies,

$$n_{SMR} = \left( \frac{\sqrt{10} + \ldots + \sqrt{20}}{20} \right)^2 = 25.878 \text{ or } 26.$$

The estimate of $\pi$ is $p = U/k = 18/20 = 0.9$. Because there is no entry for $n = 26$ in Table 14.3, we must interpolate between the entries for $n = 25$ and $n = 50$. Linear interpolation yields the estimate $\hat{\rho} = 0.264$.

The binomial distribution will probably provide a good approximation to the normal distribution in this example because $k\pi = k(1 - \pi) = 20(.5) = 10 > 5$. The approximate 95 percent confidence interval based on the standard normal distribution given in (14-11) is

$$0.9 - 1.96 \sqrt{\frac{0.9(1 - 0.9)}{20}} \le \pi \le$$

[7] I would like to thank Morgan Wang for writing the computer program that was used to generate the results in Tables 14.4 and 14.12.

| 0.30 | 0.40 | 0.50 | 0.60 | 0.70 | 0.80 | 0.90 |
|------|------|------|------|------|------|------|
| 0.079 | 0.093 | 0.110 | 0.132 | 0.163 | 0.211 | 0.311 |
| 0.102 | 0.130 | 0.167 | 0.219 | 0.295 | 0.416 | 0.629 |
| 0.123 | 0.166 | 0.224 | 0.305 | 0.419 | 0.583 | 0.809 |
| 0.143 | 0.200 | 0.277 | 0.383 | 0.524 | 0.705 | 0.900 |
| 0.162 | 0.232 | 0.327 | 0.453 | 0.612 | 0.791 | 0.947 |
| 0.181 | 0.263 | 0.375 | 0.517 | 0.684 | 0.853 | 0.970 |
| 0.198 | 0.293 | 0.419 | 0.573 | 0.744 | 0.897 | 0.981 |
| 0.215 | 0.322 | 0.460 | 0.624 | 0.793 | 0.928 | 0.984 |
| 0.232 | 0.350 | 0.499 | 0.669 | 0.833 | 0.950 | 1.000 |
| 0.248 | 0.377 | 0.536 | 0.710 | 0.866 | 0.965 | 1.000 |
| 0.264 | 0.403 | 0.570 | 0.746 | 0.892 | 0.976 | 1.000 |
| 0.280 | 0.428 | 0.603 | 0.778 | 0.914 | 0.984 | 1.000 |
| 0.295 | 0.452 | 0.633 | 0.806 | 0.931 | 0.989 | 1.000 |
| 0.311 | 0.475 | 0.661 | 0.831 | 0.945 | 0.992 | 1.000 |
| 0.325 | 0.498 | 0.687 | 0.853 | 0.957 | 0.995 | 1.000 |
| 0.340 | 0.520 | 0.712 | 0.872 | 0.966 | 0.996 | 1.000 |
| 0.354 | 0.541 | 0.735 | 0.889 | 0.973 | 0.997 | 1.000 |
| 0.369 | 0.561 | 0.756 | 0.904 | 0.978 | 0.998 | 1.000 |
| 0.382 | 0.581 | 0.775 | 0.916 | 0.983 | 0.999 | 1.000 |
| 0.396 | 0.600 | 0.793 | 0.928 | 0.987 | 0.999 | 1.000 |
| 0.410 | 0.618 | 0.810 | 0.938 | 0.989 | 0.999 | 1.000 |
| 0.423 | 0.635 | 0.826 | 0.946 | 0.992 | 0.999 | 1.000 |
| 0.436 | 0.652 | 0.840 | 0.953 | 0.994 | 1.000 | |
| 0.692 | 0.902 | 0.984 | 0.999 | 0.999 | 1.000 | |
| 0.922 | 0.994 | 1.000 | 1.000 | 1.000 | | |
| 0.997 | 1.000 | | | | | |
| 1.000 | | | | | | |

$$0.9 + 1.96 \sqrt{\frac{0.9(1 - 0.9)}{20}},$$

or simplifying, [0.769, 1.031], where the right-hand value is truncated to one, the maximum possible value of a proportion. The approximate 95 percent confidence interval based on the chi-square distribution given in (14-13) is

$$\frac{(2(0.9) + 0.192) \pm \sqrt{0.192^2 + 4(.192)(0.9)(1 - 0.9)}}{2(1 + 0.192)},$$

where $b = 3.841/20 = 0.192$. Simplifying we have [0.699, 0.972]. For this example, the confidence interval based on standard normal distribution theory provides no information about the upper confidence limit for $\rho$ because $\pi_U > 1$. Thus, we will use the confidence interval based

on chi-square distribution theory to obtain a confidence interval for $\rho$. Linear interpolation in Table 14.3 yields the $\rho$ confidence interval [0.107, 0.381]. Because the confidence interval does not contain the value zero, we reject $H_0$ and conclude that there is a positive correlation between student ratings of the instructor and student achievement.

*Example 2.* Suppose that we wish to obtain an estimate and confidence interval for $\rho$ based on the proportion of *significant* positive results in Data Set III. From Table 1 in Cohen (1983) we see that 12 of the 20 results are statistically significant at the .05 level. Our estimate of the proportion of *significant* positive results is $p = U/k = 12/20 = 0.6$. Linear interpolation in Table 14.4 yields the estimate $\hat{\rho} = 0.372$.

Checking the assumptions for the normal distribution we have $k\pi = 20(.05) = 1$ and $k(1 - \pi) = 20(.95) = 19$. Thus, if $\rho = 0$, the binomial distribution probably will *not* provide a good approximation to the normal distribution because $k\pi < 5$. The confidence interval for $\pi$ based on standard normal distribution theory given in (14-11) is [0.385, 0.815], and the confidence interval based on chi-square distribution theory given in (14-13) is [0.387, 0.781]. For this example, the confidence interval computed using (14-13) is narrower than the confidence interval computed using (14-11). By linear interpolation in Table 14.4 we obtain the $\rho$ confidence interval [0.271, 0.464]. Because the confidence interval does not include the value zero, we reject $H_0$ and conclude that there is a significant positive correlation between student ratings of the instructor and student achievement.

It is interesting to compare the confidence intervals for vote-counting and effect size procedures. The estimate of $\rho$ based on effect size procedures is $r = 0.363$, with confidence interval [0.286, 0.434]. The confidence interval based on effect sizes is narrowest $(0.434 - 0.286 = 0.148)$, followed by the confidence interval based on *significant* positive results $(0.464 - 0.271 = 0.193)$ and the confidence interval based on positive results $(0.381 - 0.107 = 0.274)$. None of the confidence intervals includes the value zero.

## 3.4 Confidence Intervals Based on Unequal Sample Sizes

The vote-counting methods described in section 3.3 can be extended to handle unequal sample sizes (Hedges & Olkin 1985). For each study we observe whether $T_i$ exceeds some critical value $C_{\alpha_i}$. Note that the critical value has a subscript $i$. Because the sample sizes for the studies may differ, the critical values may also differ. For each study there are two possible outcomes: $T_i > C_{\alpha i}$ or $T_i \leq C_{\alpha i}$. Let $X_i$ be an indicator variable that takes on the value 1 if $T_i > C_{\alpha i}$, or the value 0 if $T_i \leq C_{\alpha i}$. That is,

$$X_i = \begin{cases} 1 & \text{if } T_i > C_{\alpha i} \\ 0 & \text{if } T_i \leq C_{\alpha i} \end{cases}. \qquad (14\text{-}24)$$

The probabilities associated with each outcome are

$$\Pr(X_i = 1) = \Pr(T_i > C_{\alpha i}) = \pi_i \quad \text{and}$$
$$\Pr(X_i = 0) = \Pr(T_i \leq C_{\alpha i}) = 1 - \pi_i. \qquad (14\text{-}25)$$

If $T_i$ is approximately normally distributed with mean $\theta$ and variance $S^2(\theta)$, then the probability $\pi_i$ can be expressed as an explicit function of $\theta$,

$$\begin{aligned} \pi_i &= \Pr(T_i > C_{\alpha i}) \\ &= \Pr\{(T_i - \theta)/S(\theta) > (C_{\alpha i} - \theta)/S(\theta)\} \quad (14\text{-}26) \\ &= 1 - \Phi[(C_{\alpha i} - \theta)/S(\theta)]. \end{aligned}$$

The method of maximum likelihood can be used to estimate $\theta$ by observing whether $T_i > C_{\alpha i}$ in each of the $k$ studies. Unfortunately, there is generally no closed form expression for the MLE $\hat{\theta}$, and $\hat{\theta}$ must be obtained numerically. The simplest way to obtain $\hat{\theta}$ is to calculate log-likelihood function $L(\theta)$ for a coarse grid of $\theta$ values and use the maximum value of $L(\theta)$ to determine the region where $\hat{\theta}$ lies. Then a finer grid of $\theta$ values can be used to obtain a more precise estimate of $\hat{\theta}$.

When the number of studies combined is large, $\hat{\theta}$ is approximately normally distributed, and the large-sample variance of $\hat{\theta}$ is given by (Hedges & Olkin 1985, p. 70)

$$\text{Var}(\hat{\theta}) = \left[ \sum_{i=1}^{k} \frac{[D_i^{(1)}]^2}{\pi_i(1 - \pi_i)} \right]^{-1}, \qquad (14\text{-}27)$$

where $D_i^{(1)} = \partial \pi_i / \partial \theta = \{[S_i(\theta) - \theta S_i'(\theta)]/[S_i^2(\theta)\sqrt{2\pi}]\}$ exp $\left\{ -\frac{1}{2}(C_{\alpha i} - \theta)^2/S_i^2(\theta) \right\}$, where $S_i'(\theta) = \partial S_i(\theta)/\partial \theta$, evaluated at $\hat{\theta}$. The $100(1 - \alpha)$ percent confidence interval $[\theta_L, \theta_U]$ is given by

$$\hat{\theta} - C_{\alpha/2}\sqrt{\text{Var}(\hat{\theta})} \leq \theta \leq \hat{\theta} + C_{\alpha/2}\sqrt{\text{Var}(\hat{\theta})}. \qquad (14\text{-}28)$$

**Table 14.5 Experimental and Control Group Sample Sizes, Standardized Mean Differences, and Indicator Variable Values from 19 Studies of the Effects of Teacher Expectancy on Pupil IQ**

| Study | $n^E$ | $n^C$ | $\bar{n}$ | $d$ | $X$ |
|---|---|---|---|---|---|
| 1 | 77 | 339 | 62.748 | 0.03 | 1 |
| 2 | 60 | 198 | 46.047 | 0.12 | 1 |
| 3 | 72 | 72 | 36.000 | −0.14 | 0 |
| 4 | 11 | 22 | 7.333 | 1.18 | 1 |
| 5 | 11 | 22 | 7.333 | 0.26 | 1 |
| 6 | 129 | 348 | 94.113 | −0.06 | 0 |
| 7 | 110 | 636 | 93.780 | −0.02 | 0 |
| 8 | 26 | 99 | 20.592 | −0.32 | 0 |
| 9 | 75 | 74 | 37.248 | 0.27 | 1 |
| 10 | 32 | 32 | 16.000 | 0.80 | 1 |
| 11 | 22 | 22 | 11.000 | 0.54 | 1 |
| 12 | 43 | 38 | 20.173 | 0.18 | 1 |
| 13 | 24 | 24 | 12.000 | −0.02 | 0 |
| 14 | 19 | 32 | 11.922 | 0.23 | 1 |
| 15 | 80 | 79 | 39.748 | −0.18 | 0 |
| 16 | 72 | 72 | 36.000 | −0.06 | 0 |
| 17 | 65 | 255 | 51.797 | 0.30 | 1 |
| 18 | 233 | 224 | 114.206 | 0.07 | 1 |
| 19 | 65 | 67 | 32.992 | −0.07 | 0 |

NOTE: $n^E$ = experimental group sample size; $n^C$ = control group sample size; $\bar{n}_i = n_i^E n_i^C / (n_i^E + n_i^C)$; $d$ = sample standardized mean difference given in (14–17); and $X$ = indicator variable given in (14–24).

**Table 14.6 Log-Likelihood Function Values for $\delta$ Based on Data from 19 Studies of the Effects of Teacher Expectancy on Pupil IQ**

| Coarse Grid | | Fine Grid | |
|---|---|---|---|
| $\delta$ | $L(\delta)$ | $\delta$ | $L(\delta)$ |
| −0.50 | −52.430 | −0.10 | −15.259 |
| −0.40 | −39.135 | −0.09 | −14.912 |
| −0.30 | −28.409 | −0.08 | −14.596 |
| −0.20 | −20.387 | −0.07 | −14.311 |
| −0.10 | −15.259 | −0.06 | −14.056 |
| 0.00 | −13.170 | −0.05 | −13.831 |
| 0.10 | −14.082 | −0.04 | −13.638 |
| 0.20 | −17.733 | −0.03 | −13.475 |
| 0.30 | −23.813 | −0.02 | −13.343 |
| 0.40 | −32.149 | −0.01 | −13.241 |
| 0.50 | −42.657 | 0.00 | −13.170 |
| | | 0.01 | −13.129 |
| | | 0.02 | −13.118 |
| | | 0.03 | −13.136 |
| | | 0.04 | −13.185 |
| | | 0.05 | −13.263 |
| | | 0.06 | −13.370 |
| | | 0.07 | −13.505 |
| | | 0.08 | −13.669 |
| | | 0.09 | −13.862 |
| | | 0.10 | −14.082 |

Section 3.4.1 illustrates how to obtain an estimate and confidence interval for the standardized mean difference $\delta$, and section 3.4.2 illustrates how to obtain an estimate and confidence interval for the population coefficient of correlation $\rho$.

**3.4.1 Confidence interval for the population standardized mean difference $\delta$** Suppose that we observe whether the mean difference $\overline{Y}_i^E - \overline{Y}_i^C$ is positive for each study in a collection of $k$ independent studies. If we assume that the effect sizes are homogeneous, then the mean difference $\overline{Y}_i^E - \overline{Y}_i^C$ is approximately normally distributed with mean $\delta\sigma_i$ and variance $\sigma_i^2/\bar{n}_i$, where $\bar{n}_i = n_i^E n_i^C/(n_i^E + n_i^C)$. Note that the sample sizes for the experimental and control groups may differ across studies. The probability of a positive result is

$$\pi_i = \Pr(T_i > C_{\alpha i}) = \Pr(\overline{Y}_i^E - \overline{Y}_i^C > 0)$$
$$= 1 - \Phi(-\sqrt{\bar{n}_i}\delta). \quad (14\text{-}29)$$

Note that $\pi_i$ is a function of both $\delta$ and $\bar{n}_i$. The log-likelihood function is given by

$$L(\delta) = \sum_{i=1}^{k} [x_i \log(1 - \Phi(-\sqrt{\bar{n}_i}\delta)) \\ + (1 - x_i)\log\Phi(-\sqrt{\bar{n}_i}\delta)], \quad (14\text{-}30)$$

and the derivative $D_i^{(1)}$ is given by

$$D_i^{(1)} = \frac{\partial \pi_i}{\partial \delta} = \sqrt{\frac{\bar{n}_i}{2\pi}}\exp\left(-\frac{1}{2}\bar{n}_i\hat{\delta}^2\right). \quad (14\text{-}31)$$

The large-sample variance of $\hat{\delta}$ is obtained by substituting equation (14-29) for $\pi_i$, and equation (14-31) for $D_i^{(1)}$ in equation (14-27).

*Example.* The proportion of positive results in Data Set II will be used to illustrate how to obtain an estimate and confidence interval for $\delta$. Table 14.5 gives the values of $n^E$, $n^C$, $\bar{n}$, $d$, and $X$ for the 19 studies in Data Set II. Inserting these values in equation (14-30), for values of $\delta$ ranging from −0.50 to 0.50, gives the log-likelihood function values on the left-hand side of Table 14.6. This coarse grid of $\delta$ values reveals that the maximum value of $L(\delta)$ lies between $\delta = -0.10$ and $\delta = 0.10$. To obtain an estimate of $\delta$ to two decimal

**Table 14.7 Computations for Obtaining the Large-Sample Variance of $\hat{\delta}$ from 19 Studies of the Effects of Teacher Expectancy on Pupil IQ**

| Study | $p_i$ | $D_i^{(1)}$ | $[D_i^{(1)}]^2/[p_i(1-p_i)]$ |
|---|---|---|---|
| 1 | 0.563 | 3.121 | 39.583 |
| 2 | 0.554 | 2.682 | 29.119 |
| 3 | 0.548 | 2.376 | 22.799 |
| 4 | 0.522 | 1.079 | 4.664 |
| 5 | 0.522 | 1.079 | 4.664 |
| 6 | 0.577 | 3.798 | 59.100 |
| 7 | 0.577 | 3.792 | 58.893 |
| 8 | 0.536 | 1.803 | 13.070 |
| 9 | 0.549 | 2.417 | 23.585 |
| 10 | 0.532 | 1.591 | 10.162 |
| 11 | 0.526 | 1.320 | 6.992 |
| 12 | 0.536 | 1.785 | 12.805 |
| 13 | 0.528 | 1.379 | 7.626 |
| 14 | 0.528 | 1.374 | 7.576 |
| 15 | 0.550 | 2.495 | 25.159 |
| 16 | 0.548 | 2.376 | 22.799 |
| 17 | 0.557 | 2.842 | 32.728 |
| 18 | 0.585 | 4.167 | 71.507 |
| 19 | 0.546 | 2.276 | 20.903 |
| | | | 473.734 |

places, we calculate the log-likelihood function values between $\delta = -0.10$ and $\delta = 0.10$ in steps of 0.01. The fine grid of $\delta$ values is given on the right-hand side of Table 14.6. Because the log-likelihood function value is largest at $\delta = 0.02$, the MLE is $\hat{\delta} = 0.02$.

Substituting the values in Table 14.7 in equation (14-27), we obtain the large-sample variance $\text{Var}(\hat{\delta}) = 1/473.734 = 0.00211$. The 95 percent confidence interval for $\delta$ given in (14-28) is

$$0.02 - 1.96\sqrt{0.00211} \le \delta \le 0.02 + 1.96\sqrt{0.00211},$$

or simplifying, $[-0.070, 0.110]$. It is interesting to note that the confidence interval based on the equal sample size methods was $[-0.056, 0.121]$ (see example 1 in section 3.3.1). Both confidence intervals contain the value zero and have similar end points.

**3.4.2 Confidence interval for the population correlation coefficient $\rho$** Suppose that we observe whether $r_i$ is positive for each study in a collection of $k$ independent studies. If we assume that the effect sizes are

**Table 14.8 Sample Sizes, Correlations, and Indicator Variable Values from 20 Studies of the Relation Between Student Ratings of the Instructor and Student Achievement**

| Study | $n$ | $r$ | $X$ |
|---|---|---|---|
| 1 | 10 | .68 | 1 |
| 2 | 20 | .56 | 1 |
| 3 | 13 | .23 | 1 |
| 4 | 22 | .64 | 1 |
| 5 | 28 | .49 | 1 |
| 6 | 12 | −.04 | 0 |
| 7 | 12 | .49 | 1 |
| 8 | 36 | .33 | 1 |
| 9 | 19 | .58 | 1 |
| 10 | 12 | .18 | 1 |
| 11 | 36 | −.11 | 0 |
| 12 | 75 | .27 | 1 |
| 13 | 33 | .26 | 1 |
| 14 | 121 | .40 | 1 |
| 15 | 37 | .49 | 1 |
| 16 | 14 | .51 | 1 |
| 17 | 40 | .40 | 1 |
| 18 | 16 | .34 | 1 |
| 19 | 14 | .42 | 1 |
| 20 | 20 | .16 | 1 |

NOTE: $n$ = sample size; $r$ = Pearson product moment correlation coefficient given in (14–19); and $X$ = indicator variable given in (14–24).

**Table 14.9 Log-Likelihood Function Values for $\rho$ Based on Data from 20 Studies of the Relation Between Student Ratings of the Instructor and Student Achievement**

| Coarse Grid | | Fine Grid | |
|---|---|---|---|
| $\rho$ | $L(\rho)$ | $\rho$ | $L(\rho)$ |
| −0.50 | −159.677 | 0.10 | −8.961 |
| −0.40 | −95.780 | 0.11 | −8.640 |
| −0.30 | −59.089 | 0.12 | −8.346 |
| −0.20 | −36.659 | 0.13 | −8.079 |
| −0.10 | −22.568 | 0.14 | −7.837 |
| 0.00 | −13.863 | 0.15 | −7.621 |
| 0.10 | −8.961 | 0.16 | −7.430 |
| 0.20 | −6.900 | 0.17 | −7.263 |
| 0.30 | −7.108 | 0.18 | −7.119 |
| 0.40 | −9.552 | 0.19 | −6.998 |
| 0.50 | −14.990 | 0.20 | −6.900 |
| | | 0.21 | −6.824 |
| | | 0.22 | −6.770 |
| | | 0.23 | −6.738 |
| | | 0.24 | −6.727 |
| | | 0.25 | −6.737 |
| | | 0.26 | −6.769 |
| | | 0.27 | −6.821 |
| | | 0.28 | −6.895 |
| | | 0.29 | −6.991 |
| | | 0.30 | −7.108 |

homogeneous, then $r_i$ is approximately normally distributed with mean $\rho$ and variance $(1 - \rho^2)^2/n_i$, where the sample sizes $n_i$ for the studies may differ. The probability of a positive result is

$$\pi_i = \text{Pr}(T_i > C_{\alpha_i}) = \text{Pr}(r_i > 0) = 1 - \Phi[-\sqrt{n_i}\rho/(1 - \rho^2)].$$

$$(14\text{-}32)$$

The log-likelihood function is given by

$$L(\rho) = \sum_{i=1}^{k} \{x_i \log(1 - \Phi[-\sqrt{n_i}\rho/(1 - \rho^2)])$$

$$+ (1 - x_i)\log\Phi[-\sqrt{n_i}\rho/(1 - \rho^2)]\}, \quad (14\text{-}33)$$

and the derivative $D_i^{(1)}$ is given by

$$D_i^{(1)} = \frac{\partial \pi_i}{\partial \rho} = \sqrt{\frac{n_i}{2\pi}}\left[\frac{1 + \rho^2}{(1 - \rho^2)^2}\right]\exp\left[-\frac{1}{2}\frac{n_i\rho^2}{(1 - \rho^2)^2}\right].$$

$$(14\text{-}34)$$

The large-sample variance of $\hat{\rho}$ is obtained by substituting equation (14-32) for $\pi_i$, and equation (14-34) for $D_i^{(1)}$ in equation (14-27).

*Example.* The proportion of positive results in Data Set III will be used to illustrate how to obtain an estimate and confidence interval for $\rho$. Table 14.8 gives the values of $n$, $r$, and $X$ for the 20 studies in Data Set III. Inserting these values in equation (14-33), for values of $\rho$ ranging from $-0.50$ to $0.50$, gives the log-likelihood function values on the left-hand side of Table 14.9. This coarse grid of $\rho$ values reveals that the maximum value of $L(\rho)$ lies between $\rho=0.10$ and $\rho=0.30$. To obtain an estimate of $\rho$ to two decimal places, we calculate the log-likelihood function values between $\rho=0.10$ and $\rho=0.30$ in steps of 0.01. The fine grid of $\rho$ values is given on the right-hand side of Table 14.9. Because the log-likelihood function value is largest at $\rho=0.24$, the MLE is $\hat{\rho}=0.24$.

Substituting the values in Table 14.10 in equation (14-27), we obtain the large-sample variance $\text{Var}(\hat{\rho}) = 1/$

2026.900 = 0.000493. The 95 percent confidence interval for $\rho$ given in (14-28) is

$$0.24 - 1.96\sqrt{0.000493} \leq \rho \leq 0.24 + 1.96\sqrt{0.000493},$$

or simplifying, $[0.196, 0.283]$. It is interesting to note that the confidence interval based on the equal sample size methods was $[0.107, 0.381]$ (see example 1 in section 3.3.2). The confidence interval based on unequal sample sizes is narrower $(0.283 - 0.196 = 0.087)$ than the confidence interval based on equal sample sizes $(0.381 - 0.107 = 0.274)$. Neither confidence interval contains the value zero.

## 4. APPLICATIONS OF VOTE-COUNTING METHODS

### 4.1 Publication Bias

Chapter 25 of this volume is devoted to publication bias, so I will not discuss this topic in great detail. I will, however, show how vote-counting procedures can be used to examine the extent of publication bias. If studies with significant results are more likely to be published than studies with nonsignificant results, then published studies may reflect only a biased subsample of the total collection of studies in the population. This problem can be minimized if the meta-analyst counts both positive and negative significant results, as Hedges and Olkin (1980) state:

> When both positive and negative significant results are counted, it is possible to dispense with the requirement that the sample available is representative of all studies conducted. Instead, the requirement is that the sample of positive and negative *significant* results is representative of the population of positive or negative *significant* results. If only statistically significant findings tend to be published, this requirement is probably more realistic. (p. 366; italics in original)

Suppose that we wish to obtain an estimate and confidence interval for $\theta$ using the $k$ estimators $T_1, \ldots, T_k$. In this case, because the values $T_1, \ldots, T_k$ are *not* observed, we count the number of times $T_i > C_{\alpha/2}$, and the number of times $T_i < -C_{\alpha/2}$. That is, we count the number of *two-sided* tests that found significant positive or significant negative results. To obtain a confidence interval for $\theta$ we find the values $[\theta_L, \theta_U]$ that correspond to the upper and lower confidence limits for $\pi$ $[\pi_L, \pi_U]$,

**Table 14.10 Computations for Obtaining the Large-Sample Variance of $\hat{\rho}$ from 20 Studies of the Relation Between Student Ratings of the Instructor and Student Achievement**

| Study | $p_i$ | $D_i^{(1)}$ | $[D_i^{(1)}]^2/[p_i(1-p_i)]$ |
|---|---|---|---|
| 1 | 0.790 | 3.413 | 70.118 |
| 2 | 0.873 | 3.489 | 109.552 |
| 3 | 0.821 | 3.530 | 84.708 |
| 4 | 0.884 | 3.430 | 114.607 |
| 5 | 0.911 | 3.185 | 125.273 |
| 6 | 0.811 | 3.503 | 80.133 |
| 7 | 0.811 | 3.503 | 80.133 |
| 8 | 0.937 | 2.787 | 131.041 |
| 9 | 0.867 | 3.513 | 106.710 |
| 10 | 0.811 | 3.503 | 80.133 |
| 11 | 0.937 | 2.787 | 131.041 |
| 12 | 0.986 | 1.136 | 95.356 |
| 13 | 0.928 | 2.940 | 129.840 |
| 14 | 0.997 | 0.325 | 41.491 |
| 15 | 0.939 | 2.735 | 131.219 |
| 16 | 0.830 | 3.547 | 89.008 |
| 17 | 0.946 | 2.580 | 131.152 |
| 18 | 0.846 | 3.553 | 96.821 |
| 19 | 0.830 | 3.547 | 89.008 |
| 20 | 0.873 | 3.489 | 109.552 |
| | | | 2026.900 |

Table 14.11 Conditional Probability $p(\delta, n) = P\{t > 0 | |t| > c_t\}$ That a Two-Sample $t$ Statistic with $n$ Subjects per Group Is Positive Given That the Absolute Value of the $t$ Statistic Exceeds the $\alpha = 0.05$ Critical Value

| | Population Standard Mean Difference $\delta$ | | | | | | | | | | | | |
|---|---|---|---|---|---|---|---|---|---|---|---|---|---|
| $n$ | 0.00 | 0.02 | 0.04 | 0.06 | 0.08 | 0.10 | 0.15 | 0.20 | 0.25 | 0.30 | 0.40 | 0.50 | 0.70 |
| 2 | 0.500 | 0.516 | 0.531 | 0.547 | 0.562 | 0.577 | 0.615 | 0.651 | 0.685 | 0.718 | 0.777 | 0.827 | 0.900 |
| 4 | 0.500 | 0.528 | 0.556 | 0.584 | 0.611 | 0.638 | 0.700 | 0.756 | 0.805 | 0.845 | 0.906 | 0.945 | 0.982 |
| 6 | 0.500 | 0.537 | 0.573 | 0.609 | 0.643 | 0.676 | 0.751 | 0.814 | 0.863 | 0.901 | 0.950 | 0.976 | 0.994 |
| 8 | 0.500 | 0.544 | 0.586 | 0.628 | 0.668 | 0.706 | 0.788 | 0.852 | 0.899 | 0.932 | 0.971 | 0.988 | 0.998 |
| 10 | 0.500 | 0.549 | 0.598 | 0.644 | 0.689 | 0.729 | 0.816 | 0.879 | 0.923 | 0.952 | 0.982 | 0.993 | 0.999 |
| 12 | 0.500 | 0.555 | 0.608 | 0.659 | 0.706 | 0.750 | 0.838 | 0.900 | 0.940 | 0.964 | 0.988 | 0.996 | 1.000 |
| 14 | 0.500 | 0.559 | 0.617 | 0.672 | 0.722 | 0.767 | 0.857 | 0.916 | 0.952 | 0.973 | 0.992 | 0.998 | 1.000 |
| 16 | 0.500 | 0.564 | 0.625 | 0.683 | 0.736 | 0.783 | 0.872 | 0.929 | 0.961 | 0.979 | 0.994 | 0.998 | 1.000 |
| 18 | 0.500 | 0.568 | 0.633 | 0.694 | 0.749 | 0.796 | 0.886 | 0.939 | 0.968 | 0.984 | 0.996 | 0.999 | 1.000 |
| 20 | 0.500 | 0.572 | 0.640 | 0.704 | 0.760 | 0.809 | 0.897 | 0.947 | 0.974 | 0.987 | 0.997 | 0.999 | 1.000 |
| 22 | 0.500 | 0.575 | 0.647 | 0.713 | 0.771 | 0.820 | 0.907 | 0.954 | 0.978 | 0.990 | 0.998 | 1.000 | |
| 24 | 0.500 | 0.579 | 0.654 | 0.721 | 0.781 | 0.830 | 0.915 | 0.960 | 0.982 | 0.992 | 0.998 | 1.000 | |
| 50 | 0.500 | 0.614 | 0.716 | 0.800 | 0.864 | 0.910 | 0.970 | 0.991 | 0.997 | 0.999 | | | |
| 100 | 0.500 | 0.659 | 0.789 | 0.878 | 0.933 | 0.964 | 0.993 | 0.999 | 1.000 | 1.000 | | | |

SOURCE: Hedges and Olkin (1980).

where $\pi$ denotes the proportion of the total number of significant results that were positive. That is,

$$\pi = \frac{\pi^+}{\pi^+ + \pi^-}, \qquad (14\text{-}35)$$

where $\pi^+ = \Pr(T_i > C_{\alpha/2})$, and $\pi^- = \Pr(T_i < -C_{\alpha/2})$. The MLE of $\pi$ is

$$p = \frac{p^+}{p^+ + p^-}, \qquad (14\text{-}36)$$

where $p^+$ is the number of significant positive results and $p^-$ is the number of significant negative results in $k$ independent studies.

Hedges and Olkin (1980) produced a table (see Table 14.11) for obtaining an estimate and confidence interval for $\delta$ given the proportion of the total number of significant mean differences that were positive. For this chapter, we produced a table (Table 14.12) for obtaining an estimate and confidence interval for $\rho$ given the proportion of the total number of significant correlations that were positive. Examples 1 and 2 that follow illustrate how to use Tables 14.11 and 14.12, respectively.

*Example 1.* Suppose that all the results in Data Set II were significant; then we would have 11 significant positive results and 8 significant negative results. Recall from example 1 in section 3.3.1 that the square mean root for Data Set II is 84. Our estimate of $\pi$ given by equation (14-36) is $p = 11/(11 + 8) \approx 0.579$. Linear interpolation in Table 14.11 yields the estimate $\hat{\delta} = 0.011$. Recall that the confidence interval for $\pi$ given by (14-13) was [0.363, 0.769]. Linear interpolation in Table 14.11 yields a confidence interval for $\delta$, [−0.020, 0.042].

*Example 2.* Suppose that all the results in Data Set III were significant; then we would have 18 significant positive results and 2 significant negative results. Recall from example 1 in section 3.3.2 that the square mean root for Data Set III is 26. Our estimate of $\pi$ given by (14-36) is $p = 18/(18 + 2) = 0.9$. Linear interpolation in Table 14.12 yields the estimate $\hat{\rho} = 0.101$. Recall that the confidence interval for $\pi$ given by (14-13) was [0.699, 0.972]. Linear interpolation in Table 14.12 yields a confidence interval for $\rho$, [0.038, 0.180].

### 4.2 Results All in the Same Direction

The method of maximum likelihood cannot be used if the MLE of $\pi$ given in (14-9) is unity or zero because there is not a unique value of $p$. If all of the results are in the same direction, we can obtain a Bayes estimate

of $\pi$ (Hedges & Olkin 1985, p. 300). For example, we can assume that $\pi$ has a truncated uniform prior distribution. That is, we assume that there is a value $\pi_0$ such that any value of $\pi$ in the interval $[\pi_0, 1]$ is equally likely. The Bayes estimator of $\pi$ is

$$p = (k+1)(1 - \pi_0^{k+2})/(k+2)(1 - \pi_0^{k+1}). \qquad (14\text{-}37)$$

*Example.* Suppose that all of the studies in Data Set II found positive results and that it is reasonable to assume that the true value of $\pi$ is in the interval [0.5, 1]. Thus, we believe that the proportion of significant results is at least 0.5, and that any value 0.5 or greater is equally likely. The Bayes estimate given in (14-37) is

$$p = (19+1)(1 - 0.50^{(19+2)})/(19+2)(1 - 0.50^{(19+1)})$$
$$= 0.952.$$

### 4.3 Missing Data

Generally, not all studies collected by a meta-analyst report test statistics. Rather than discarding those studies that do not, the meta-analyst may want to compare the effect size results, based on the smaller group of studies that report test statistics, with the vote-counting results, based on all studies. For example, suppose that the first 10 studies in Data Set II report enough information to calculate effect sizes but the last 9 studies report only the direction of the effects. Using the standardized mean differences from the first 10 studies, we find that $d_. = 0.047$ with 95 percent confidence interval $[−0.049, 0.143]$. Using the direction of effects from all 19 studies, we find that $\hat{\delta} = 0.032$ with 95 percent confidence interval $[−0.056, 0.120]$. Both confidence intervals contain the value zero and have similar end points. The confidence interval for $\hat{\delta}$, however, is slightly narrower than the confidence interval for $d_. = 0.047$. This example illustrates the advantage of using both vote-counting and effect size analyses in the same literature review.

## 5. CONCLUSION

Vote-counting is not the method of choice when test statistic values are reported for each study. Estimators based on vote-counting methods are less efficient than estimators based on effect sizes (Hedges 1986). If $U = 0$ or $U = k$, vote-counting methods cannot be used to estimate $\theta$ because the estimate of $p$ is zero or one, but a Bayes estimate might still be calculated. Another

**Table 14.12 Conditional Probability $p(\rho, n) = P\{r>0 \| |r|>C_r\}$ That a Correlation Coefficient $r$ from a Sample of Size $n$ Is Positive Given That the Absolute Value of $r$ Exceeds the $\alpha = .05$ Critical Value for Effect Size $\rho$**

| | Population Correlation Coefficient $\rho$ | | | | | | | | | | | |
|---|---|---|---|---|---|---|---|---|---|---|---|---|
| $n$ | 0 | 0.01 | 0.02 | 0.03 | 0.04 | 0.05 | 0.06 | 0.07 | 0.08 | 0.09 | 0.10 | 0.20 |
| 3 | 0.500 | 0.508 | 0.516 | 0.524 | 0.531 | 0.539 | 0.547 | 0.555 | 0.563 | 0.570 | 0.578 | 0.654 |
| 4 | 0.500 | 0.512 | 0.525 | 0.537 | 0.550 | 0.562 | 0.574 | 0.586 | 0.598 | 0.610 | 0.622 | 0.732 |
| 5 | 0.500 | 0.516 | 0.533 | 0.549 | 0.565 | 0.581 | 0.597 | 0.613 | 0.628 | 0.644 | 0.659 | 0.790 |
| 6 | 0.500 | 0.520 | 0.540 | 0.559 | 0.578 | 0.598 | 0.617 | 0.635 | 0.654 | 0.671 | 0.689 | 0.832 |
| 7 | 0.500 | 0.523 | 0.546 | 0.568 | 0.590 | 0.612 | 0.634 | 0.655 | 0.675 | 0.695 | 0.714 | 0.864 |
| 8 | 0.500 | 0.526 | 0.551 | 0.576 | 0.601 | 0.625 | 0.649 | 0.672 | 0.694 | 0.715 | 0.736 | 0.887 |
| 9 | 0.500 | 0.528 | 0.556 | 0.583 | 0.610 | 0.637 | 0.662 | 0.687 | 0.711 | 0.733 | 0.755 | 0.906 |
| 10 | 0.500 | 0.530 | 0.560 | 0.590 | 0.619 | 0.647 | 0.674 | 0.701 | 0.725 | 0.749 | 0.771 | 0.920 |
| 11 | 0.500 | 0.532 | 0.565 | 0.596 | 0.627 | 0.657 | 0.686 | 0.713 | 0.739 | 0.763 | 0.786 | 0.932 |
| 12 | 0.500 | 0.534 | 0.569 | 0.602 | 0.635 | 0.666 | 0.696 | 0.724 | 0.751 | 0.776 | 0.799 | 0.942 |
| 13 | 0.500 | 0.536 | 0.572 | 0.607 | 0.642 | 0.674 | 0.706 | 0.735 | 0.762 | 0.788 | 0.811 | 0.950 |
| 14 | 0.500 | 0.538 | 0.576 | 0.613 | 0.648 | 0.682 | 0.714 | 0.745 | 0.773 | 0.799 | 0.822 | 0.956 |
| 15 | 0.500 | 0.540 | 0.579 | 0.618 | 0.655 | 0.690 | 0.723 | 0.754 | 0.782 | 0.808 | 0.832 | 0.962 |
| 16 | 0.500 | 0.542 | 0.582 | 0.622 | 0.661 | 0.697 | 0.731 | 0.762 | 0.791 | 0.818 | 0.841 | 0.966 |
| 17 | 0.500 | 0.543 | 0.586 | 0.627 | 0.666 | 0.704 | 0.738 | 0.770 | 0.800 | 0.826 | 0.850 | 0.970 |
| 18 | 0.500 | 0.545 | 0.589 | 0.631 | 0.672 | 0.710 | 0.745 | 0.778 | 0.807 | 0.834 | 0.857 | 0.974 |
| 19 | 0.500 | 0.546 | 0.591 | 0.635 | 0.677 | 0.716 | 0.752 | 0.785 | 0.815 | 0.841 | 0.865 | 0.977 |
| 20 | 0.500 | 0.548 | 0.594 | 0.639 | 0.682 | 0.722 | 0.759 | 0.792 | 0.822 | 0.848 | 0.871 | 0.979 |
| 21 | 0.500 | 0.549 | 0.597 | 0.643 | 0.687 | 0.728 | 0.765 | 0.798 | 0.828 | 0.854 | 0.877 | 0.981 |
| 22 | 0.500 | 0.550 | 0.600 | 0.647 | 0.692 | 0.733 | 0.771 | 0.804 | 0.834 | 0.861 | 0.883 | 0.983 |
| 23 | 0.500 | 0.552 | 0.602 | 0.651 | 0.696 | 0.738 | 0.776 | 0.810 | 0.840 | 0.866 | 0.889 | 0.985 |
| 24 | 0.500 | 0.553 | 0.605 | 0.654 | 0.701 | 0.743 | 0.782 | 0.816 | 0.846 | 0.872 | 0.894 | 0.986 |
| 25 | 0.500 | 0.554 | 0.607 | 0.658 | 0.705 | 0.748 | 0.787 | 0.821 | 0.851 | 0.877 | 0.898 | 0.988 |
| 50 | 0.500 | 0.579 | 0.654 | 0.723 | 0.782 | 0.832 | 0.872 | 0.904 | 0.928 | 0.947 | 0.961 | 0.998 |
| 100 | 0.500 | 0.613 | 0.715 | 0.799 | 0.863 | 0.909 | 0.941 | 0.962 | 0.976 | 0.985 | 0.990 | 1.000 |
| 200 | 0.500 | 0.658 | 0.788 | 0.877 | 0.933 | 0.964 | 0.981 | 0.990 | 0.995 | 0.997 | 0.999 | 1.000 |
| 400 | 0.500 | 0.717 | 0.866 | 0.943 | 0.977 | 0.991 | 0.996 | 0.999 | 0.999 | 1.000 | 1.000 | 1.000 |

limitation of the simplest vote-counting procedures is that they are based on the assumption that each study has an identical sample size $n$. When the study sample sizes are similar, this problem can be overcome by using an ''average value'' such as the square mean root. When study sample sizes are not similar, however, more complicated procedures are required.

Although vote-counting is not always the method of choice, in some cases the meta-analyst might not have a choice. If one or more of the studies do not report test statistics, but do report the direction and/or statistical significance of results, vote-counting procedures can be

quite useful. The meta-analyst can supplement effect size analyses with vote-counting analyses for the larger group of studies for which effect size estimates cannot be calculated. In addition, vote-counting procedures can be used to examine problems such as publication bias.

**Author's Note**

The computer programs used for most of the examples given in this chapter can be obtained by writing to Brad J. Bushman.

| 0.30 | 0.40 | 0.50 | 0.60 | 0.70 | 0.80 | 0.90 |
|------|------|------|------|------|------|------|
| 0.725 | 0.790 | 0.848 | 0.897 | 0.937 | 0.968 | 0.989 |
| 0.823 | 0.891 | 0.938 | 0.968 | 0.986 | 0.995 | 0.999 |
| 0.883 | 0.940 | 0.972 | 0.988 | 0.996 | 0.999 | 1.000 |
| 0.920 | 0.965 | 0.986 | 0.995 | 0.999 | 1.000 |  |
| 0.943 | 0.978 | 0.993 | 0.998 | 0.999 | 1.000 |  |
| 0.958 | 0.986 | 0.996 | 0.999 | 1.000 |  |  |
| 0.969 | 0.991 | 0.997 | 0.999 |  |  |  |
| 0.976 | 0.994 | 0.998 | 1.000 |  |  |  |
| 0.981 | 0.995 | 0.999 | 1.000 |  |  |  |
| 0.985 | 0.997 | 0.999 | 1.000 |  |  |  |
| 0.988 | 0.998 | 1.000 |  |  |  |  |
| 0.991 | 0.998 | 1.000 |  |  |  |  |
| 0.992 | 0.999 | 1.000 |  |  |  |  |
| 0.994 | 0.999 | 1.000 |  |  |  |  |
| 0.995 | 0.999 | 1.000 |  |  |  |  |
| 0.996 | 0.999 | 1.000 |  |  |  |  |
| 0.997 | 1.000 |  |  |  |  |  |
| 0.997 | 1.000 |  |  |  |  |  |
| 0.998 | 1.000 |  |  |  |  |  |
| 0.998 | 1.000 |  |  |  |  |  |
| 0.998 | 1.000 |  |  |  |  |  |
| 0.999 | 1.000 |  |  |  |  |  |
| 0.999 | 1.000 |  |  |  |  |  |
| 1.000 |  |  |  |  |  |  |

## 6. REFERENCES

Clopper, C. J., & Pearson, E. S. (1934). The use of confidence or fiducial limits illustrated in the case of the binomial. *Biometrika, 26,* 404–413.

Cohen, J. (1988). *Statistical power analysis for the behavioral sciences* (2nd ed.). Hillsdale, NJ: Erlbaum.

Cohen, P. A. (1983). Comment on ''A selective review of the validity of student ratings of teaching.'' *Journal of Higher Education, 54,* 448–458.

Conover, W. J. (1980). *Practical nonparametric statistics* (2nd ed.). New York: Wiley.

DeGroot, M. H. (1986). *Probability and statistics* (2nd ed.). Reading, MA: Addison-Wesley.

Gibbons, J. D., Olkin, I., & Sobel, M. (1977). *Selecting and ordering populations: A new statistical methodology.* New York: Wiley.

Glass, G. V., McGaw, B., & Smith, M. L. (1981). *Meta-analysis in social research.* Newbury Park, CA: Sage.

Hedges, L. V. (1986). *Estimating effect sizes from vote counts or box score data.* Paper presented at the annual meeting of the American Educational Research Association, San Francisco.

Hedges, L. V., & Olkin, I. (1980). Vote-counting methods in research synthesis. *Psychological Bulletin, 88,* 359–369.

Hedges, L. V., & Olkin, I. (1985). *Statistical methods for meta-analysis.* New York: Academic Press.

Light, R. J., & Smith, P. V. (1971). Accumulating evidence: Procedures for resolving contradictions among different research studies. *Harvard Educational Review, 41,* 429–471.

Olkin, I. (1973). *Do positive population correlation coefficients yield positive sample correlation coefficients.* Technical Report No. 73, Stanford University, Department of Statistics, Stanford, CA.

Raudenbush, S. W., & Bryk, A. S. (1985). Empirical Bayes meta-analysis. *Journal of Educational Statistics, 10,* 75–98.

Cooper, H. and Hedges, L. V. (Eds.) 1994. *The Handbook of Research Synthesis.* New York: Russell Sage Foundation

# 15

# COMBINING SIGNIFICANCE LEVELS

### BETSY JANE BECKER
*Michigan State University*

CONTENTS

## 1. INTRODUCTION

This chapter discusses methods for combining probability values (or significance levels) from independent significance tests. These ''combined significance'' methods have a long history (e.g., Fisher 1932; Tippett 1931) and have been studied extensively by statisticians. Several of the methods are closely related to the vote-counting techniques described in the preceding chapter.

The first sections of the chapter describe significance levels and briefly introduce the combined significance methods, differentiating them from parametric methods. Next, the hypotheses tested by the combined significance methods are examined and compared with those tested by the parametric methods. The methods are introduced, with a focus on four exemplars. Their application is illustrated using two data sets. Related statistical issues are briefly treated, as are other applications of probability values in research synthesis. Recommendations for the use of combined significance techniques conclude the chapter.

## 2. DEFINING THE $p$ VALUE

Simply stated, a significance level is a probability. Significance levels arise in the context of testing statistical hypotheses. Such hypotheses may concern relationships between variables, the effects of some treatment(s), or more complex phenomena. On the basis of knowledge about the effects of interest the researcher formulates a *research hypothesis*. This hypothesis is ''translated'' into a statistical model or *null hypothesis*,

also referred to as $H_0$, which can be tested. The test statistics and their significance levels indicate the appropriateness of the statistical model for the population from which the data are obtained.

### 2.1 The $p$ from a Single Test

More precisely, a significance level is the probability of finding a test statistic (i.e., a set of sample data) as unusual or extreme as that calculated *given* that the null hypothesis is true. Consider a one-sided test involving an unknown parameter $\theta$. A common formulation of a directional hypothesis about $\theta$ would be $H_0$: $\theta \le 0$ versus $H_a$: $\theta > 0$. Hypotheses can be tested about fixed values by defining $\theta$ as a difference. For example, to test whether a population mean $\mu$ is greater than 100 we can test

$$H_0: \theta = \mu - 100 \le 0.$$

When the directional test of significance about $\theta$ is computed for a sample statistic $t_0$, the upper-tail one-sided probability is

$$p_0 = \int_{t_0}^{\infty} f(t)\ dt = 1 - F(t_0) = P(t > t_0), \quad (15\text{-}1)$$

where $f(t)$ is the probability density function for the statistic $t$, and $F(t)$ is the cumulative distribution function for $t$ given that $H_0$ is true. Significance levels are sometimes called Type I error probabilities, or simply just $p$ values or $p$'s.

Significance levels range from zero to one, and values near zero show that the probability of obtaining the calculated test statistic value (or a more unusual value) would be small *if* the null hypothesis model were correct. Large *p* values are generally taken to mean that the data are accurately described by the statistical null condition. Large *p* values usually do not indicate that the researcher's *substantive* (research) hypothesis is confirmed, since the null and research hypotheses are often chosen to be incompatible.

## 2.2 The Misuse of *p* Values

Much of the criticism of significance testing has been aimed at the misuse and misinterpretation of *p* values. Carver (1978) discussed many common misconceptions about *p*, as have others (e.g., Bakan 1966; Duggan & Dean 1968). Common misinterpretations of *p* values are that they represent confidence in the replicability of results, that they indicate the probability that the research hypothesis is true, that *p* values measure how predictable the behavior of a population will be, and that they represent the probability that the study results are due to chance.

The last of these misinterpretations plagues the literature on tests of combined significance. Numerous references state that combined significance tests provide the probability that the results of a series of studies are due to chance. Carver (1978, p. 383) has explicated the error in this statement. The *p* value describes the probability of obtaining a particular sample result given the hypothesis that chance (i.e., random sampling variation) caused the results. Carver stated that *p* cannot represent the probability that chance *causes* the pattern of results because *p* is calculated "by assuming that the probability was 1.00 that chance did cause [the results]." The *p* is then used to decide whether to accept the idea that the "probability is 1.00 that chance caused the [results]" (1978, p. 383). The *p* value is the probability of obtaining certain results, given a hypothesis, not the probability that the hypothesis is true, given the results. The misconceptions covered by Carver, however, are not flaws or weaknesses of *p* values but rather of how they have been used.

## 2.3 Null Hypothesis Testing

Other criticisms of significance testing relate to the choice between the null and alternative hypotheses. Many authors contend that this choice is unrealistic. In much significance testing the null hypothesis is not initially believed to be true (see, e.g., Bakan 1966) and is set up as what Carver (1978) called a "straw man" to be knocked down. Rozeboom (1960) felt that the aim of a study was "not to precipitate decisions, but to make an appropriate adjustment in the degree to which one accepts, or believes, the hypothesis or hypotheses being tested" (p. 420). This aim is more consonant with the effect-magnitude approach to research synthesis. (See also Pillemer 1992.)

These criticisms are relevant to the use of significance level summaries. The problem that the null hypothesis is not initially believed is compounded when a series of hypotheses is tested. The process of deciding between the null hypothesis, which is typically that the treatment effect or relationship between variables is completely absent, and *all other* outcomes is usually neither required of, nor informative for, the researcher or research synthesist. This is a weakness of all tests of significance, including *p* value summaries.

## 2.4 Bayesian Perspectives

The idea of summarizing studies via tests of combined significance is fundamentally at odds with a strict Bayesian perspective on evidence. This conflict is evident in part because decisions based on individual *p* values can conflict with decisions suggested by Bayesian analyses (see, e.g., Edwards, Lindman & Savage 1963). Also, because *p* value summaries are nonparametric they do not provide the detailed evidence about the nature of population parameters sought by Bayesians.

Many authors have studied the correspondence (or lack of it) between significance levels and Bayesian posterior probabilities in the context of individual significance tests. Often in the case of tests of point null hypotheses, significance levels have been found to overstate the evidence against the null hypothesis compared with posterior probabilities (e.g., Berger & Sellke 1987).

Casella and Berger (1987) examined *p* values and posterior probabilities in the case of one-sided individual tests of $\theta \le 0$ versus $\theta > 0$. Prior distributions that placed all or most of their mass on a single parameter value (or in a narrow interval) produced discrepancies. However, Casella and Berger reported considerable agreement between *p* values and posterior probabilities for several large classes of prior densities having monotone likelihood ratio (e.g., for distributions symmetric about zero). Thus, *p* values may not always be in conflict with Bayesian assessments of evidence for single studies.

(See also the commentary following Casella and Berger 1987 and Berger and Sellke 1987.)

The effect of incorporating parametric evidence into the combined significance tests has not been well studied. This topic has most often been considered in discussions of the use of weighting in particular summaries and is discussed under that heading below. A fundamental problem is that information about sample size, study design, and the like is intertwined with parametric information in each $p$ value. Thus, it is difficult to use combined significance methods to make inferences about particular patterns of parameter values.

## 2.5 The Probability Density Function of $p$

Under the null hypothesis the density of a $p$ from a continuously distributed test statistic—that is, $p$ as defined in (15-1)—is uniform on the interval from zero to one. Thus, $p$'s from diverse tests can be combined because under $H_0$ they are identically distributed.

Some statistical tests, such as binomial tests for small samples, take on a limited set of values. Such tests are called "discrete" tests. Probability values based on discrete test statistics do not share the common (uniform) distribution, even under $H_0$. Therefore, they are not interchangeable with $p$'s from continuous tests and should not be treated equivalently in computing $p$ value summaries. Adjustments designed for discrete $p$ values are discussed below.

The densities of $p$'s under alternative models are much more complicated. The density of $p$ depends on the distribution of the test statistic used, the values of relevant parameters (under the alternative), and the sample size.

Although two-sided tests (e.g., tests of $H_0$: $\theta = 0$ versus $\theta \neq 0$) are common in primary research, most summaries of $p$ values are meant to be computed based on one-sided $p$'s. Two-sided $p$ values are problematic because they do not convey information about the direction of deviations from $H_0$. Birnbaum (1954) and George (1977) have examined the problem of two-sided $p$ values.

## 3. SUMMARIZING $p$ VALUES

The nonparametric (distribution-free) form of the null hypothesis densities of continuous $p$ values leads naturally to the idea of combining probabilities. The $p$ values from individual studies contain information about the effects (parameters) of interest and are identically distributed when the series of null hypotheses holds. Because $p$ values from diverse statistical tests are identically distributed under $H_0$, $p$ value summaries are sometimes labeled nonparametric tests. Also, these summaries, like $F$ tests and chi-square tests for degrees of freedom larger than one, are called omnibus procedures.

Summaries of $p$ values represent one of two major approaches to research synthesis (Hedges & Olkin 1982). The other approach is represented by analyses of effect sizes, as discussed in many other chapters of this handbook.

Because $p$ values contain information about precision (via the sample size or degrees of freedom), they do not provide pure measures of treatment effects or relationships. That is, small $p$ values may arise in part because of large effects and in part because of large samples or experimental-design advantages. Thus, analyses based on effect-magnitude measures are usually preferable to combined significance procedures. (This idea is discussed below.) However, some situations require the use of nonparametric procedures. When study outcomes are not on commensurate scales, or when studies have examined different parametric representations of a single phenomenon, nonparametric procedures can be preferable.

## 3.1 The Null Hypothesis for Combined Significance Tests

Because all studies to be combined ask the same *substantive* question, some synthesists believe that $p$ value summaries must test a common statistical null hypothesis. This assumption can be untrue, because the studies need not all test the same *statistical* null model for $p$ value summaries to be applicable. Sometimes the differences in models are small: One study may report a $t$ test of a sex difference, whereas another may examine sex as one factor in a multi-way analysis of variance. But even in this case the parametric models differ under the null hypothesis.

The null hypothesis for the test of combined significance is that the substantive effects or phenomena of interest *are not present* in *any* of the populations studied. Let $\theta_i$ represent the effect of interest in the population examined in the $i$th study. The value $\theta_i$ can represent any population effect or outcome of interest. For example, $\theta_i$ may represent a population correlation value $\rho_i$ or a difference between two population means $\mu_{i1} - \mu_{i2}$.

Different parameters may be represented by $\theta_i$ and $\theta_j$ (from studies $i$ and $j$), as mentioned above. For example, study 1 might examine the correlation between socio-economic status (SES) and mathematics achievement, whereas study 2 may consider the correlation of SES and reading achievement. Judd and Harackiewicz (1980) used a test of combined significance to summarize $p$'s from a regression coefficient representing an interaction effect and an analysis-of-variance main effect. Both parameters represented ''contrast effects'' in attitude judgment.

Let $k$ be the number of studies to be summarized. The statistical model for the null hypothesis for the series of $k$ studies is

$$H_0: \theta_i = 0, \text{ for } i = 1, \ldots, k. \quad (15\text{-}2)$$

This null hypothesis is the intersection of the individual null hypotheses from all $k$ studies. For the joint null hypothesis of the series to be true, *all* the individual null hypotheses must be true. All null hypotheses need not refer to the same statistical parameters, but each null model in the series must be valid.

Van Zwet and Oosterhoff (1967) noted that in some cases the null model $H_0$ can be extended as $H_0: \theta_i \leq 0$, for $i = 1, \ldots, k$, but they argued that the possibility of having both positive and negative $\theta_i$ values should be ''simply ruled out in advance'' (p. 660) in classical applications of one-sided combination procedures.

### 3.2 Alternative Hypotheses

The assumption that a $p$ value summary answers the same question as the tests in the individual studies can be misleading for another reason. Even if all the studies in a series test the same statistical null hypothesis, the possible patterns of population outcomes under alternatives for series of studies are more complex than those for a single study. Blommers and Forsyth (1977, p. 245) argued that specifying *both* a null model and a list of alternatives is necessary in selecting a statistical test.

In a single study the null and alternative hypotheses are relatively simple. Rejection of the one-sided null hypothesis in a single study implies that $\theta_i$ is positive. The null hypothesis for the combined significance test given in (15-2) is also simple and well defined. However, rejection of the null model can imply many different possible patterns of population parameters.

**3.2.1 The complement to $H_0$** The comprehensive alternative (the formal logical negation) to the hypothesis $H_0$ shown in (15-2) is that *at least one* study is of

a population in which $\theta_i$ is nonzero. This alternative, which can be written as

$$H_A: \theta_i \neq 0, \text{ for at least one } i, i = 1, \ldots, k, \quad (15\text{-}3)$$

was discussed in detail by George (1977). Oosterhoff (1969) stated earlier that testing $H_0$ against $H_A$ is ''not a combination problem at all'' (p. 2). Under this alternative the population parameters are not required to have the same sign.

Only very general substantive conclusions can be based on a test of the alternative given in (15-3). If $H_0$ is rejected, one can only say that at least one population studied has a nonzero parameter $\theta_i$. Without further analysis the synthesist cannot discern how many studies or which studies sample populations with nonnull effects. Also the summaries provide no information about the directions of differences. Tests of (15-3) are much like the overall $F$ test for a multilevel factor in analysis of variance. Both these tests and the $F$ test indicate whether there is greater than random variability in outcomes, but neither test informs about the specific structure of that variability.

Often the synthesist is not interested in the complete set of alternatives to $H_0$, defined by $H_A$. Prior information may suggest that certain values of $\theta_i$ are implausible or impossible. For example, $\theta_i$ may represent the squared multiple correlation coefficient or a variance, which can be only zero or positive. A directional test may also be used when the reviewer is not interested in negative $\theta_i$ values. Negative estimates of the parameter $\theta_i$ are taken as evidence that $\theta_i = 0$. This is common practice, for example, in the estimation of variance components. Alternately, a range of values of $\theta_i$ might be equivalent in terms of decisions to be based on a summary of outcomes. Alternatives more specific than $H_A$ can be examined.

**3.2.2 The one-sided alternative** This alternative, known as the classical one-sided combination problem, has been the focus of almost all of the literature on combining $p$ values. Within each study, a directional test of $\theta_i = 0$ versus $\theta_i > 0$ is conducted. The one-sided alternative for the series of $k$ studies is

$$H_1: \theta_i \geq 0, \text{ for } i = 1, \ldots, k, \text{ with}$$
$$\theta_j > 0, \text{ for at least one } j.$$

This alternative specifies not that all parameters are positive, but that *at least* one is positive.

$H_1$ should be tested when the meta-analyst is willing to assume that the population effects represented by the

$\theta_i$ values all have the same sign (are in the same direction). The one-sided test can also be used to detect evidence of individual contrary findings in a mass of support for a treatment or theory. The direction of the outcome expected of the treatment would be treated as the null condition. For example, consider a summary of evidence regarding the effects of a seemingly efficacious medical treatment, such as aspirin therapy for heart disease. The goal might be to locate evidence of any shortcoming or deleterious effect of the therapy. Thus, we could define $\theta_i \leq 0$ to represent successful medical outcomes (e.g., decreased blood pressure), which could be ignored if deleterious effects are sought. Then $\theta_i > 0$ would represent health problems or detrimental outcomes of the treatment.

Confusion can result if one-sided summaries are applied when it is possible that there are both positive and negative $\theta$ values. Some summaries support *both* one-sided alternatives—that is, indicate both "at least one $\theta_i > 0$" *and* "at least one $\theta_i < 0$" (Adcock 1960; Rosenthal 1978). Others are more likely to fail to reject $H_0$ at all.

### 3.3 Misunderstandings of the Hypotheses

The hypotheses tested by $p$ value summaries have received little explicit attention in the literature, especially in the social sciences. (An exception is Becker 1987.) However, the hypotheses that synthesists think they are testing can sometimes be inferred. Considerable confusion is evidenced in accurate and inaccurate comments about what $p$ value summaries are testing.

Tests of combined significance have been described as providing an overall level of significance for series of studies. One might assume from this statement that a significant $p$ value summary would indicate that, overall, the set of studies examined does not support the null hypothesis. Another interpretation might be that one population parameter which represents (underlies) all the studies is not equal to the null hypothesis value. Neither of these conclusions can be based on a $p$ value summary alone because the summaries examine the hypothesis that *at least one* population parameter differs from the proposed null hypothesis value.

Many users of combined significance tests have misinterpreted the overall $p$ value from the summary as the probability that the results reviewed are "due to chance." This misconception is discussed above. Another misinterpretation of the summary $p$ is the belief that the summary will show whether the effects of a treatment

are robust across two (or more) methodologies (i.e., data collection or analysis procedures).

A last fallacious interpretation is that $p$ value summaries assess how well a given set of results fits the predictions of a theory. This would be true only if that theory predicted the results portrayed in the null hypothesis ($H_0$), which is probably rare. Problems associated with this approach to testing theory are discussed by Grant (1962) and others.

Some interpretations of $p$ value summaries are based on the belief that the summaries are parametric tests. When all studies being summarized examine a single parametric model, the null model $H_0$ in (15-2) is a special case of the situation in which $\Sigma\theta_i = 0$, or in which $\bar{\theta} = \Sigma\theta_i/k = 0$. If it is sensible to interpret the average $\theta_i$ value, then the classical tests of combined significance also provide a test of

$$H_{0M}: \bar{\theta} = 0. \qquad (15\text{-}4)$$

However, if it is reasonable to expect both positive and negative values of $\theta_i$, and if it is *acceptable* for negative and positive $\theta_i$ values to "balance" each other, then the classical, one-sided summaries are *not* the most appropriate tests to use in testing $H_{0M}$ because they are designed to reject $H_{0M}$ if any $\theta_i$ is greater than zero. That is, positive and negative $\theta_i$ values (represented by large and small $p$'s) should not cancel each other out. However, inspection of the formulas for the combined significance tests shows that several of the tests (i.e., the sum of $z$'s, logit, and weighted versions of these tests) do operate in this fashion. Such summaries are still reasonable tests of the $H_0$ shown in (15-2), but they can also be used to examine the hypothesis $H_{0M}$, shown in (15-4). However, for the test of (15-4) to be sensible, it must be possible to interpret the value of $\bar{\theta}$. In other words, all $\theta_i$ must represent the *same* parameter.

Some confusion results when meta-analysts *are* testing a parametric hypothesis, but they do not understand the alternative they are testing. Some authors have interpreted rejection of the null hypothesis (based on a test of combined significance) as an indication of *consistency* in research results. However, a significant $p$ value summary may indicate inconsistent rather than consistent findings.

### 3.4 Advantages and Disadvantages of the Combined Significance Methods

The primary advantage of the omnibus combined significance methods is their broad applicability. The $p$

values can be drawn from any test statistic representing a substantive hypothesis of interest. Even if studies use dissimilar sampling designs and analyses, under the null hypothesis the resultant $p$ values (from continuous tests) are identically distributed. Consequently, evidence from a variety of studies can be synthesized.

The limitation of the methods is that they do not provide very detailed information. An omnibus test does not give information about the average effect, except to suggest whether it is nonzero. In fact, if negative outcomes can occur (but simply are not of interest), we cannot even safely conclude from rejection of $H_0$ that the average effect is positive. One-tailed omnibus tests indicate simply whether *any* population seems to have a positive effect. We do not know how many studies may have arisen from such populations, whether any arise from populations with opposing results (if they are possible); nor do we know which studies most likely represent the populations with nonzero effects.

## 4. METHODS FOR SUMMARIZING SIGNIFICANCE LEVELS

The numerous methods for summarizing significance levels are derived from a few general principles. All of the summary methods are based on the assumption that the $p$ value is a continuous variable (i.e., is from a continuous test statistic). For discrete $p$ values these summaries, or the terms of these summaries that are associated with discrete $p$'s, are adjusted. This is discussed briefly below.

Summaries for continuous $p$'s are of two types: those based directly on the uniform distribution and those based on statistical theory for other random variables (i.e., for transformed uniform variables). Counting methods (related to the vote-counting techniques discussed by Hedges & Olkin 1980 and in Chapter 14) and linear combinations of $p$'s constitute the uniform summaries.

In the probability-transformation summaries the $k$ significance levels are transformed through inverse probability distribution functions. Each new variable is denoted as $F^{-1}(p)$, where F is some cumulative probability distribution function. Any legitimate distributional form may be used for $F^{-1}$. The normal, $t$, and chi-square are simple and familiar and thus are used often, though Liptak (1958) illustrated a transformation to the Cauchy distribution (i.e., the $t$ distribution with 1 degree of freedom). A summary of the transformed $p$ values is

then calculated. Liptak (1958) presented a comprehensive treatment of this idea.

### 4.1 Notation

Define $k$ as the number of independent statistics (or studies) to be summarized, and $p_i$ as the upper-tail probability from the $i$th study, based on a sample of size $n_i$. Then the $p_i$, $i = 1, \ldots, k$, are the $k$ $p$ values to be summarized. The $i$th significance level $p_i$ from a continuous test statistic $t_i$ is defined as the upper-tail probability

$$p_i = \int_{t_{i0}}^{\infty} f_i(t)\, dt, \qquad (15\text{-}5)$$

where $f_i(t)$ is the probability density function for the statistic $t$ under $H_0$ and $t_{i0}$ is the sample $t$ value in the $i$th study. Equivalently $p_i$ may be written as $p_i = 1 - F_i(t_{i0})$, where $F_i(t)$ is the cumulative distribution function of $t$ in the $i$th study under $H_0$. Neither the distributions of the $k$ test statistics nor the sample sizes $n_i$, $i = 1$ to $k$ need to be identical.

### 4.2 Obtaining Exact $p$ Values

Computation of the combined significance summaries requires exact $p$ values. Often research reports present only general statements such as "$p < .05$" or "the test was significant" at a preset $\alpha$ level.

Exact probabilities can be obtained for most test statistics either computationally or from extended tabulations of distribution functions (e.g., Smirnov 1961), which are documented by Johnson and Kotz (1970a, 1970b). Some computer packages such as SAS (Statistical Analysis System) and Minitab now provide probability values for the more common (central) distributions such as $F$, $t$, and $z$. Researchers with access to the International Mathematical and Statistical Libraries (IMSL) FORTRAN subroutines can obtain very precise $p$ values with call statements to the probability distribution functions and subroutines. And, finally, some of the more sophisticated statistical calculators also offer probability computations.

### 4.3 Summary Methods

The methods for summarizing significance values are listed in Table 15.1, in which summaries derived by a common approach are classed together. Formulas are

**Table 15.1 Methods for Summarizing Significance Values**

**Uniform Distribution Methods**

Counting methods
  Wilkinson
  Brozek and Tiede
  Minimum $p$
  Sign test
  Chi-square
Linear combinations
  Sum of $p$'s
  Mean $p$

**Probability – Transformation Methods**

Inverse normal methods
  Sum of $z$'s (Stouffer)
  Weighted sum of $z$'s
  Mean $z$
Inverse $t$ methods
  Inverse $t$ (Winer)
  Weighted inverse $t$
Inverse chi-square methods
  Inverse chi-square
  Weighted inverse chi-square
  Sum of logs (Fisher)
  Weighted sum of logs
Logistic methods
  Logit
  Weighted logit

shown in Table 15.2. In this table, $\alpha_*$ is the preset Type I error rate for the series of studies, that is, for the combined significance test itself. The value $\alpha$ represents the level of significance to be attained within a single study.

## 4.4 Four Exemplary Summaries

Below four summaries are used to illustrate the application of tests of combined significance. Formulas for the minimum $p$, sum of $z$'s, sum of logs, and logit summaries are described in detail. A small set of data is used in examples of the computations. For more detail on the other summaries, see Becker (1985), Hedges and Olkin (1985), and Rosenthal (1978).

**4.4.1 Minimum $p$ method** Tippett's minimum $p$ test (1931) rejects the null hypothesis in (15-2) if any of the $k$ $p$ values is less than $\alpha$, where $\alpha$ is computed as $1 - (1 - \alpha_*)^{1/k}$ and $\alpha_*$ is the preset significance level for the combined significance test. The rejection region for

this test is explicitly defined as the union of the rejection regions from all $k$ separate studies (Littell & Folks 1971). We reject $H_0$ if

$$\text{Min}(p_1, \ldots, p_k) = p_{[1]} < \alpha = 1 - (1 - \alpha_*)^{1/k}.$$
(15-6)

This method is a special case of Wilkinson's method (1951), for $r = 1$ and $\alpha = 1 - (1 - \alpha_*)^{1/k}$ (Birnbaum 1954). Also the beta distribution with 1 and $k$ degrees of freedom can be used to obtain a level $\alpha_*$ test based on the minimum $p$ ($p_{[1]}$).

Consider the following set of probabilities, which are ordered

$$.016, .067, .250, .405, .871.$$

The minimum $p$ value is $p_{[1]} = .016$. If we desire an error rate of $\alpha_* = .05$ for the combined significance test, we reject $H_0$ if $p_{[1]}$ is less than

$$\alpha = 1 - (1 - .05)^{1/5} = 1 - .9898 = .0102.$$

Since $p_{[1]} = .016 > \alpha = .0102$, the minimum $p$ test fails to reject $H_0$ for this set of data.

**4.4.2 Sum of $z$'s method** This method, first described by Stouffer and his colleagues (Stouffer et al. 1949) is widely used in the social sciences. It was highly recommended by Rosenthal in his influential 1978 article as well as by Mosteller and Bush (1954). The combined significance test is based on the sum of $z(p_i)$ values. This sum, which has a normal distribution under the null hypothesis, is divided by its standard deviation, $\sqrt{k}$. The statistic

$$\sum_{i=1}^{k} z(p_i) / \sqrt{k}$$
(15-7)

can be compared with critical values in the standard normal table.

We can compute the value of the sum of $z$'s test for our small data set. First, we obtain the standard normal deviates for the five $p$ values, specifically,

$$z(.016) = 2.149, \ z(.067) = 1.495, \ z(.250) = 0.674,$$
$$z(.405) = 0.240, \ z(.871) = -1.131.$$

The $z$ values are summed, giving $\Sigma z(p_i) = 3.427$. The sum is divided by the square root of $k = 5$, leading to the normal test statistic $z = 1.533$. This value is compared with the critical value for a one-tailed test at $\alpha_* = .05$, or 1.645. The sum of $z$'s test also fails to reject $H_0$ for this data set.

**4.4.3 Sum of logs method** A special case of the inverse chi-square summary was described by Fisher

**Table 15.2 Decision Rules for Significance Level Summaries**

| Method | Reject $H_0$ if |
|---|---|
| Wilkinson | $p_* = \Sigma_{s=r}^k \binom{k}{s}\alpha^s(1-\alpha)^{k-s} < \alpha_*$ |
| Brozek and Tiede | $(r - k\alpha)/\sqrt{k\alpha(1-\alpha)} > z(\alpha_*)$ |
| Minimum $p$ | $\text{Min}(p_1, \ldots, p_k) = p_{[1]} < \alpha = 1 - (1 - \alpha_*)^{1/k}$ |
| Sign test | $(r - r')^2/(r + r') > \chi_1^2(\alpha_*)$ |
| Chi-square | $\Sigma_{j=1}^J (O_j - E_j)^2/E_j > \chi_{r-1}^2(\alpha_*)$ |
| Sum of $p$'s | $P[S \le \Sigma_{i=1}^k p_i] = (k!)^{-1}\Sigma_{r=0}^{S'}\binom{k}{r}([\Sigma_{i=1}^k p_i] - r)^k,$ where $\Sigma_{i=1}^k p_i \ge S' \in$ integers |
| Mean $p$ | $\sqrt{12k}\,(.5 - \Sigma p_i/k) = \sqrt{12k}\,(.5 - \bar{p}) > z(\alpha_*)$ |
| Sum of $z$'s | $\Sigma_{i=1}^k z(p_i)/\sqrt{k} = \Sigma\Phi^{-1}(1 - p_i)/\sqrt{k} > z(\alpha_*)$ |
| Weighted sum of $z$'s | $\Sigma_{i=1}^k w_i z(p_i)/\sqrt{\Sigma_{i=1}^k w_i^2} > z(\alpha_*)$ |
| Mean $z$ | $\Sigma_{i=1}^k z(p_i)/k)/(s_z/\sqrt{k}) = \bar{z}/s_{\bar{z}} > t_{k-1}(\alpha_*)$ |
| Inverse $t$[a] | $\Sigma_{i=1}^k t_{f_i}(p_i)/\sqrt{\Sigma_{i=1}^k [f_i/(f_i - 2)]} > z(\alpha_*)$ |
| Inverse chi-square[a] | $\Sigma_{i=1}^k \chi_{f_i}^2(p_i) > \chi_{\Sigma f_i}^2(\alpha_*)$ |
| Sum of logs | $\Sigma_{i=1}^k -2\log(p_i) = -2\log(\Pi_{i=1}^k p_i) > \chi_{2k}^2(\alpha_*)$ |
| Weighted sum of logs | $-\log(\Pi_{i=1}^k p_i^{w_i}) = -\Sigma_{i=1}^k w_i \log(p_i) > C(\alpha_*)$ |
| Logit | $-(k\pi^2(5k+2)/3(5k+4))^{-1/2}\,\Sigma_{i=1}^k \log(p_i/1-p_i) > t_{5k+4}(\alpha_*)$ |
| Weighted logit | $-\Sigma_{i=1}^k w_i \log(p_i/1-p_i) > C_v\,t_v(\alpha_*)$ |

[a]Weighted inverse $t$ and chi-square summaries are computed by selecting different degrees of freedom $f_i$ than those used in the unweighted summaries.
NOTES: $r$ is the count of $p$ values less than .5, $r'$ the number greater than .5, and $O_j$ and $E_j$ are the observed and expected numbers of $p$ values in the $j$th of $J$ classes, based on the assumption of uniformly distributed $p$s. The mean $p$ is $\bar{p} = \Sigma_{i=1}^k p_i/k$. Also $z(a)$ is the standard normal deviate associated with upper-tail probability $a$, and $\chi^2(a)$ is the $100(1-a)$ percentile point of the chi-square distribution with $f_i$ degrees of freedom.

The computed variance for the $k$ $z(p_i)$ values is $s_z^2$. The $t$ value with $f_i$ degrees of freedom associated with upper-tail probability $a$ is $t_{f_i}(a)$, and for the weighted sum of logs and weighted logit methods, C, $C_v$, and $v$ depend on the values of $w_1$ through $w_k$.

(1932). The method is based on the fact that the variable $-2\log(u)$ will be distributed as a chi-square variable with 2 degrees of freedom if $u$ is uniformly distributed on the unit interval. The sum of $k$ of these values is a chi-square with $2k$ degrees of freedom under the null hypothesis. Fisher noted that under the null hypothesis $p$ values are uniformly distributed between zero and one, and thus could be transformed to chi-squares using the above function. Thus, the test is accomplished by comparing

$$-2 \Sigma_{i=1}^k \log(p_i) \qquad (15\text{-}8)$$

with the $100(1 - \alpha_*)$ percent critical value of the chi-square distribution with $2k$ degrees of freedom.

We compute the sum of logs statistic for the sample data set. First, we compute the natural logarithm of each $p$ value, specifically,

$$\log(.016) = -4.135, \log(.067) = -2.703,$$
$$\log(.250) = -1.386,$$
$$\log(.405) = -0.904, \log(.871) = -0.138.$$

These values are summed and multiplied by $-2$. The test statistic is $-2 \times (-9.267) = 18.533$, which is a chi-square statistic with $2k = 10$ degrees of freedom under $H_0$. We compare the value with the $\alpha_* = .05$ upper-tail critical value, which is 18.307 for the chi-square distribution with 10 degrees of freedom. Therefore, we reject $H_0$ using the sum of logs procedure. This test suggests that at least one population has a population parameter that is nonzero.

**4.4.4 Logit method** George (1977) proposed using the statistic

$$-\sum_{i=1}^{k} \log(p_i/1 - p_i) \, [k \, \pi^2 \, (5k+2)/3(5k+4)]^{-1/2}$$
(15-9)

as another combined significance technique. He noted that the logit (i.e., $\log(p/(1-p))$) is distributed as a logistic variable under $H_0$. George capitalized on the similarity of the distribution of the sum of the logits to the $t$ distribution. He proposed to approximate the distribution of (15-9) with the $t$ distribution on $5k+4$ degrees of freedom. (George also noted that under $H_0$, $\Sigma \log(p_i/(1-p_i))$ could be viewed as approximately normal with a zero mean and variance of $k \, \pi^2/3$.) The test (using the $t$ approximation) is accomplished by comparing (15-9) with the $100(1-\alpha_*)$ percent critical value of the $t$ distribution with $5k+4$ degrees of freedom.

The logit statistic requires that we compute the natural logarithm of $(p/(1-p))$ for each $p$ value. The values are

$$\log(.016/.984) = -4.119, \log(.067/.933) = -2.634,$$
$$\log(.250/.750) = -1.099, \log(.405/.595) = -0.385,$$
$$\log(.871/.129) = 1.910.$$

These values are summed, which gives $\Sigma \log(p_i/1 - p_i) = -6.327$. The sum is multiplied by $-[5 \, \pi^2 \, (27)/(3 \times 29)]^{-1/2}$ or $-0.256$. The test statistic is 1.620, which is compared with the $100(1-\alpha_*)$ percentile point of the $t$ distribution with 29 degrees of freedom. That critical value is 1.699; thus, we fail to reject $H_0$ on the basis of the logit summary.

## 4.5 Methods for *p* Values from Discrete Statistics

The methods shown in Table 15.2 assume that all $p$ values arise from continuously distributed test statistics. Significance levels that arise from discrete statistics (e.g., binomial tests) will have distributions (even under $H_0$) that reflect the discrete distributions of those tests. That is, such $p$'s are not uniformly distributed even when the null hypothesis is true. Adjustments for discrete $p$'s, proposed by Lancaster (1949), Pearson (1950),

and Wallis (1942), have been reviewed by Kincaid (1962). Mosteller and Bush (1954) also discuss this issue.

## 5. APPLICATIONS OF TESTS OF COMBINED PROBABILITY

To illustrate the use of the combined significance tests, the four methods just described are applied to two of the handbook data sets. The minimum $p$, sum of $z$'s, sum of logs, and logit summaries have been computed for the studies of teacher-expectancy effects given in Data Set II and the studies of student ratings of their college instructors given in Data Set III (see Appendix A).

## 5.1 Teacher-Expectancy Effects

Both Raudenbush (1984) and Raudenbush and Bryk (1985) have analyzed these studies of the effects of teacher-expectancy inductions on later IQ scores of students. The effect magnitude for each sample represents the mean IQ score of an expectancy group minus the mean of a control group, divided by a pooled standard deviation. Data from 19 samples, including $p$ values and transformed $p$ values, are shown in Table 15.3.

**Table 15.3 Data from Teacher-Expectancy Studies**

| Sample | $p$ | $-2\log(p)$ | $z(p)$ | $\log(p/(1-p))$ |
|---|---|---|---|---|
| 1 | 0.405 | 1.808 | 0.240 | −0.385 |
| 2 | 0.208 | 3.140 | 0.813 | −1.337 |
| 3 | 0.799 | 0.449 | −0.837 | 1.380 |
| 4 | 0.002 | 12.429 | 2.948 | −6.213 |
| 5 | 0.243 | 2.829 | 0.696 | −1.136 |
| 6 | 0.720 | 0.657 | −0.582 | 0.944 |
| 7 | 0.577 | 1.100 | −0.194 | 0.310 |
| 8 | 0.926 | 0.154 | −1.443 | 2.527 |
| 9 | 0.051 | 5.952 | 1.637 | −2.924 |
| 10 | 0.001 | 13.816 | 3.062 | −6.907 |
| 11 | 0.040 | 6.438 | 1.747 | 3.178 |
| 12 | 0.211 | 3.112 | 0.804 | −1.319 |
| 13 | 0.528 | 1.277 | −0.069 | 0.112 |
| 14 | 0.216 | 3.065 | 0.787 | −1.289 |
| 15 | 0.871 | 0.277 | −1.131 | −1.910 |
| 16 | 0.640 | 0.893 | −0.359 | 0.575 |
| 17 | 0.016 | 8.270 | 2.149 | −4.119 |
| 18 | 0.227 | 2.966 | 0.747 | −1.225 |
| 19 | 0.656 | 0.843 | −0.401 | 0.646 |
| Sums | | 69.473 | 10.615 | −21.627 |

**Table 15.4  Values of Test Statistics and Combined $p$= Values for Four Combined Significance Tests**

| Data set | Minimum $p$ | Sum of $z$'s | Sum of logs | Logit |
|---|---|---|---|---|
| Teacher expectancy | .0011 | 2.435 | 69.473, $df=38$ | 2.763, $df=99$ |
| ($k=19$) | $p=.0207$ | $p=.0074$ | $p=.0014$ | $p=.0034$ |
| Validity | .00001 | 8.191 | 159.820, $df=40$ | 9.521, $df=104$ |
| ($k=20$) | $p=1.99\times10^{-4}$ | $p=1.25\times10^{-16}$ | $p=2.91\times10^{-16}$ | $p=3.89\times10^{-16}$ |

Analyses by Raudenbush (1984) and Raudenbush and Bryk (1985) showed that the 19 samples do not appear to share a common population effect magnitude. A test of homogeneity of effect sizes (see Chapter 18) gives $Q=35.85$ ($df=18$, $p<.01$). The average effect magnitude was estimated to be 0.08 ($SE=0.05$), which does not differ from zero at the .05 level. However, the lack of consistency in the data indicates that some populations seem to have effects that deviate from the average.

We would expect the combined significance tests to reject the overall null hypothesis, and they do. Table 15.4 shows that all four tests are significant at or beyond the .05 level.

Further analyses of the effect magnitudes have shown that the amount of teacher-pupil contact before the expectancy induction accounts for the considerable variation in study outcomes. Becker's analysis (1987) was a simplification of that conducted by Raudenbush and Bryk (1985). Becker found two internally consistent yet distinct groups of samples: those having no teacher-pupil contact and those with a week or more of contact. Five samples that had no contact shared a common effect of 0.36 standard deviations. The other samples showed a difference of only 0.02.

## 5.2  Validity Studies

The data from Cohen (1983) comprise correlations from a set of studies of the relationship between student ratings of their college instructors and student achievement levels. Classes covered a variety of topics ranging from introductory math, psychology, and biology to aircraft mechanics. Most, however, were introductory classes. Analyses described below are based on Fisher's $z$ transformation of the sample correlations shown in Table 15.5. The significance level for study $i$ is based on the $t$ test of the hypothesis that $\rho_i=0$.

The results for the 20 samples show mostly positive correlations, with an average correlation of .36. (The average was obtained as the weighted average Fisher $z$ value, transformed to the scale of $r$.) The results are consistent, with a nonsignificant homogeneity test value of $Q=20.98$ ($df=19$, $p>.25$; again see Chapter 18). The 95 percent confidence interval for the population correlation, which extends from 0.29 to 0.43, indicates that the common correlation differs from zero. That is, all studies appear to be of populations with a correlation of .36 between student achievement and student ratings of their instructors.

Assuming that these sample results accurately depict the populations studied, it would be desirable for all tests of combined significance to reject the hypothesis of a zero population correlation across all studies. Table 15.3 shows that the four tests are significant at even the stringent .001 level.

## 5.3  An Evaluation of the Analyses

The results of the combined significance tests were as predicted on the basis of analyses of the effect magnitudes for each data set. Additionally, all of the combined significance tests were significant. Slight differences in sensitivity were apparent, in that some tests reached more stringent levels of significance. Thus, as tests of the overall null hypothesis of ''no effect'' across all studies, the four exemplary summaries performed well.

However, in each case the analyses of effect magnitudes revealed more information about the study outcomes than did the combined significance summaries. Specifically, effect-magnitude analyses revealed that two different patterns of population parameters were studied. The validity studies were relatively consistent, with an estimated common population correlation of .36. The results of the teacher-expectancy studies were not homogeneous at first analysis. Grouping the teacher-expectancy studies according to the amount of teacher-

**Table 15.5 Data from Validity Studies**

| Sample | $n$ | $r$ | $t$ | $p$ | $-2 \log(p)$ | $z(p)$ | $\log(p/(1-p))$ |
|---|---|---|---|---|---|---|---|
| 1 | 10 | 0.68 | 2.623 | 0.015223 | 8.370 | 2.164 | −4.170 |
| 2 | 20 | 0.56 | 2.868 | 0.005117 | 10.550 | 2.568 | −5.270 |
| 3 | 13 | 0.23 | 0.784 | 0.224837 | 2.985 | 0.756 | −1.238 |
| 4 | 22 | 0.64 | 3.725 | 0.000669 | 14.619 | 3.208 | −7.309 |
| 5 | 28 | 0.49 | 2.866 | 0.004063 | 11.012 | 2.647 | −5.502 |
| 6 | 12 | −0.04 | −0.127 | 0.549106 | 1.199 | −0.123 | 0.197 |
| 7 | 12 | 0.49 | 1.778 | 0.052925 | 5.878 | 1.617 | −2.885 |
| 8 | 36 | 0.33 | 2.038 | 0.024674 | 7.404 | 1.966 | −3.677 |
| 9 | 19 | 0.58 | 2.936 | 0.004618 | 10.756 | 2.603 | −5.373 |
| 10 | 12 | 0.18 | 0.579 | 0.287803 | 2.491 | 0.560 | −0.906 |
| 11 | 36 | −0.11 | −0.645 | 0.738475 | 0.606 | −0.639 | 1.038 |
| 12 | 75 | 0.27 | 2.396 | 0.009563 | 9.300 | 2.343 | −4.640 |
| 13 | 33 | 0.26 | 1.499 | 0.071971 | 5.263 | 1.461 | −2.557 |
| 14 | 121 | 0.40 | 4.761 | 0.000003 | 25.434 | 4.545 | −12.717 |
| 15 | 37 | 0.49 | 3.325 | 0.001040 | 13.737 | 3.078 | −6.867 |
| 16 | 14 | 0.51 | 2.054 | 0.031221 | 6.933 | 1.863 | −3.435 |
| 17 | 40 | 0.40 | 2.690 | 0.005274 | 10.490 | 2.557 | −5.240 |
| 18 | 16 | 0.34 | 1.353 | 0.098791 | 4.629 | 1.288 | −2.211 |
| 19 | 14 | 0.42 | 1.603 | 0.067441 | 5.393 | 1.495 | −2.627 |
| 20 | 20 | 0.16 | 0.688 | 0.250210 | 2.771 | 0.674 | −1.097 |
| Sums | | | | | 159.820 | 36.632 | −76.485 |

pupil contact, however, explained the between-studies differences in that population.

Effect-magnitude analyses allowed us to formulate two different explanations for the patterns of outcomes in these data sets. Yet in both cases the combined significance tests rejected the null hypothesis, indicating only that at least one sample was from a population with a nonzero effect. The two different patterns of results cannot be distinguished on the basis of the tests of combined significance.

This is a serious drawback if the studies have actually examined data arising from a single parametric model. However, sometimes series of studies examine the same *substantive* effect (or very similar effects) via different parametric formulations. In such cases the effect-magnitude analyses described above could not be justified, and it would be impossible to derive a single parametric model encompassing the results.

For instance, a series of medical studies may investigate possible deleterious effects of a drug or other intervention. Different side effects may be examined in each study, since by definition the research is aimed at finding unintended outcomes of the intervention. The existence of a single significant deleterious effect of any

kind would warrant attention. Also, it may not be possible or necessary to understand why one kind of side effect appears stronger than another. In such cases, the combined significance summaries may be the only summaries that can be applied to the full series of studies.

## 6. STATISTICAL ISSUES REGARDING TESTS OF COMBINED SIGNIFICANCE

The summaries known as tests of combined significance differ in a variety of ways. Even in situations wherein the use of combined significance methods is reasonable, selection of a test is not straightforward. In this section two aspects that differentiate the tests are discussed: the weighting of the $p$ values (or transformed $p$'s) and the power of the statistical tests.

### 6.1 Weighting $p$ Values

Reviewers may consider weighting $p$ values to account for prior information about the sizes of effects (when parametric data are available), to allow for subjective differences (e.g., in judged quality) between the studies or statistical tests being summarized, or to account for differences in sample size or degrees of freedom (including the extreme situation in which data are missing).

The first procedure is easily justifiable. Weighting according to prior knowledge about effect magnitude is equivalent to using Bayesian analyses. Such weighting can greatly improve the power of the combination procedure, as might be expected (Koziol & Perlman 1976, 1978). The idea of weighting $p$ values on the basis of test efficiency in interblock and intrablock analyses was proposed by Zelen (1957). However, Zelen and Joel (1959) showed that *improper* weighting of such $p$ values can reduce the power of the combination. Weighting according to study quality or other subjective differences has been debated in the meta-analysis literature (e.g., Rosenthal 1984, p. 55; Slavin 1986), but is more of a conceptual than statistical issue.

Differential weighting on the basis of sample size in the sum of $z$'s formula was suggested by Mosteller and Bush (1954), and weighted versions of every test are possible. However, Perlman (1978) has commented that $p$ values ''are already weighted'' (p. 4). In fact, Hedges, Cooper, and Bushman (1992) showed that, in some cases, the sum of $z$'s statistic corresponds exactly to a weighted combination of effect sizes. Since the $p$ value depends on the sample size for which it is calculated, for any given effect size or outcome a larger study will have a smaller $p$ than a smaller study. Giving larger studies even more weight would be inappropriate and might adversely affect the power of the methods. Weighting has also been discussed by Liptak (1958), Oosterhoff (1969), and Pape (1972).

## 6.2 Power

Power is the likelihood that a test correctly rejects a false null hypothesis. Many of the tests we use in analyses in primary research can be shown to be ''most powerful,'' under a wide range of conditions because they are more likely to reject $H_0$ than other competing tests. In the case of the combined significance tests, however, no test is most powerful (e.g., Oosterhoff 1969). Studies of the power of the tests show that the nature of the alternative model greatly influences which test (or group of tests) will have high power.

Many authors have investigated the power of the combined significance methods, using methods ranging from proof in a very simple case (Pearson 1938) to numerical integration (e.g., Oosterhoff 1969; Zelen & Joel 1959) to simulation (e.g., Becker 1985; George

1977; Koziol & Perlman 1978; Koziol, Perlman, & Rasmussen 1988). Although the complete results of the power studies for the combined significance methods are too detailed for presentation in this chapter, a few broad conclusions can be made about the most familiar tests.

Many of the most familiar tests do not vary greatly in their levels of power across a number of different situations. Becker (1985) reported, though, that the mean $p$ test was considerably less powerful than others for a number of common patterns of outcomes. (Presumably the sum of $p$'s, based on the same sufficient statistic, would perform similarly.) Fisher's sum of logs has been widely recommended as the test of choice when the reviewer is interested in single deviant outcomes. However, for summaries of $p$'s from chi-square tests, Koziol and Perlman (1978) reported that Tippett's minimum $p$ test was more powerful than even the sum of logs summary for detecting single unusual populations.

The sum of $z$'s test, which is equivalent to the likelihood ratio test in certain cases (see Liptak 1958), is more powerful than the sum of logs summary at rejecting $H_0$ when sample sizes and effect magnitudes are equal. Similarly, the logit method seems effective at detecting patterns of equal population parameters. The advantage in power of the sum of $z$'s test is not great, however, which has led a number of researchers to recommend the sum of logs test as a general purpose summary.

Finally, the mean $z$ procedure has the peculiar property that it becomes large when there is little variation in the $p$ values (i.e., in the $z(p)$ values). Thus, this test can reject $H_0$ when it is exactly true (e.g., if all $p$'s are close to .5), as well as when it is false. The power of this test has not been formally investigated, however.

## 7. OTHER USES OF $p$ VALUES IN RESEARCH SYNTHESIS

The omnibus $p$ value summaries are related to several other sets of procedures used in meta-analysis. Those procedures are briefly reviewed here.

## 7.1 Vote-Counting

The $p$ value summaries known as counting methods are closely related to the vote-counting methods discussed in Chapter 14. As noted earlier by Hedges and Olkin (1980), decisions based on simple counts can be misleading, especially as the number of studies increases.

Other techniques based on counts, such as the estimation of effect magnitudes based on counts of probabilities, are somewhat more informative. However, the vote-count methods all fail to provide information about the values of individual population parameters for the studies under review.

## 7.2 File-Drawer (Fail-Safe) Numbers

The "file-drawer problem" is one aspect of the more general problem of publication bias. Considerable evidence suggests that the set of available studies does not mirror the set of all studies ever conducted, for a number of reasons. One reason is that researchers may have unpublished reports "in their file drawers," reports not submitted because their results were not statistically significant.

Rosenthal (1979) has promoted the use of a statistic derived from the sum of $z$'s summary as an estimate of the number of such nonsignificant studies. The estimate represents the number of additional studies having on average no effect (i.e., having effect magnitudes averaging zero) that would be needed to reduce the sum of $z$'s test to nonsignificance. Similar estimates can be derived for other combined test statistics.

Rosenthal (1984) noted that there were "no firm guidelines . . . as to what constitutes an unlikely number of unretrieved and/or unpublished studies" (p. 110). However, the behavior of these so-called fail-safe numbers relates to the behavior of the summaries from which they are derived. Loosely, a large fail-safe number lends credence to the finding of significance even under the assumption of a biased collection of studies, and in many cases this number will be reasonably large. However, in domains in which *contrary* results are more likely to have been withheld from publication, the fail-safe number may be an overestimate of the number of filed studies. That is, fewer negative or opposing results would be needed to reduce the sum of $z$'s test to nonsignificance. Thus, if the literature is one in which a large number of unreported studies with opposing results may exist, then the usual fail-safe number may add unwarranted confidence to the interpretation of the reported (but potentially biased) results.

## 7.3 Tests and Contrasts Based on $p$ Values

An extension of the combination of probability values is the use of transformed $p$'s to represent study results

in their own right. Rosenthal (1984; Rosenthal & Rubin 1979) has suggested the use of the function $z(p)$, the standard normal deviate for the $p$ value, as an effect-magnitude measure. He describes "focused and diffuse tests" based on $z(p)$ values, to be used when the reviewer "cannot do any better than comparing [the] $p$ values" from the studies (1984, p. 65).

The tests are based on the assumption that $z(p)$ will have a standard normal distribution. (This is also the basis for the sum of $z$'s test.) This assumption is exactly true when the null hypothesis is true and may be reasonable for small effects. However, Becker (1992) has shown that for moderate to large effects ($t$ test effect magnitudes of 0.5 or more) and larger samples ($n \geq 25$) the standard normal approximation to the distribution of $z(p)$ may deviate considerably from (have much larger variance than) the actual distribution. Thus, procedures based on the standard normal approximation may tend to overlook real differences in effects when the null hypothesis is false.

## 8. CONCLUSION

Tests of combined significance provide a nonparametric alternative to the parametric analyses of effect magnitudes outlined elsewhere in this handbook. Many of the tests are easy to compute, and most require little more than the obtained $p$ values from the studies under review. Because the combined significance tests are nonparametric, they can be applied to sets of data that do not satisfy the stricter assumptions needed to justify parametric tests.

However, when the studies under consideration provide data that meet the assumptions of a parametric model, the combined significance methods are relatively uninformative, redundant with analyses of effect-magnitude data, and potentially misleading when misinterpreted. The dependence of the combined significance tests with effect-magnitude analyses is clear from the direct relationship between the individual effect magnitude and $p$.

Analyses of effect magnitudes thus are more highly recommended than combinations of $p$ values when inferences about the size and strength of effects are sought. When studies have examined a common substantive issue, but are represented by a variety of different effect-magnitude measures, combined significance tests may be the best summaries available.

**Author's Note**

This chapter was written while the author was a visiting scholar at the Department of Education, University of Chicago.

# 9. REFERENCES

Adcock, C. J. (1960). A note on combining probabilities. *Psychometrika, 25,* 303–305.

Bakan, D. (1966). The test of significance in psychological research. *Psychological Bulletin, 66,* 423–437.

Becker, B. J. (1985). *Applying tests of combined significance: Hypotheses and power considerations.* Unpublished doctoral dissertation, University of Chicago.

Becker, B. J. (1987). Applying tests of combined significance in meta-analysis. *Psychological Bulletin, 102,* 164–171.

Becker, B. J. (1992). Small-sample accuracy of approximate distributions of functions of observed probabilities from *t* tests. *Journal of Educational Statistics, 16,* 345–369.

Berger, J. O., & Sellke, T. (1987). Testing a point null hypothesis: The irreconcilability of *p* values and evidence. *Journal of the American Statistical Association, 82,* 112–122.

Birnbaum, A. (1954). Combining independent tests of significance. *Journal of the American Statistical Association, 49,* 559–574.

Blommers, P. J., & Forsyth, R. A. (1977). *Elementary statistical methods in psychology and education* (2nd ed.). Boston: Houghton Mifflin.

Carver, R. P. (1978). The case against statistical significance testing. *Harvard Educational Review, 48,* 378–399.

Casella, G., & Berger, R. L. (1987). Reconciling Bayesian and frequentist evidence in the one-sided testing problem. *Journal of the American Statistical Association, 82,* 106–112.

Cohen, P. A. (1983). Comment on a selective review of the validity of student ratings of teaching. *Journal of Higher Education, 54,* 449–458.

Duggan, T. J., & Dean, C. W. (1968). Common misinterpretations of significance levels in sociology journals. *American Sociologist, 3,* 45–46.

Edwards, W., Lindman, H., & Savage, L. J. (1963). Bayesian statistical inference for psychological research. *Psychological Review, 70,* 193–242.

Fisher, R. A. (1932). *Statistical methods for research workers* (4th ed.). London: Oliver & Boyd.

George, E. O. (1977). *Combining independent one-sided and two-sided statistical tests: Some theory and applications.* Unpublished doctoral dissertation, University of Rochester.

Grant, D. A. (1962). Testing the null hypothesis and the strategy and tactics of investigating theoretical models. *Psychological Review, 69,* 54–61.

Hedges, L. V., Cooper, H. M., & Bushman, B. J. (1992). Testing the null hypothesis in meta-analysis: A comparison of combined probability and confidence interval procedures. *Psychological Bulletin, 111,* 188–194.

Hedges, L. V., & Olkin, I. (1980). Vote-counting methods in research synthesis. *Psychological Bulletin, 93,* 563–573.

Hedges, L. V., & Olkin, I. (1982). Analyses, reanalyses and meta-analysis. *Contemporary Education Review, 1,* 157–165.

Hedges, L. V., & Olkin, I. (1985). *Statistical methods for meta-analysis.* Orlando, FL: Academic Press.

Johnson, N. L., & Kotz, S. (1970a). *Distributions in statistics: Continuous univariate distributions* (Vol. 1). New York: Wiley.

Johnson, N. L., & Kotz, S. (1970b). *Distributions in statistics: Continuous univariate distributions* (Vol. 2). New York: Wiley.

Judd, C. M., & Harackiewicz, J. M. (1980). Contrast effects in attitude judgment: An examination of the accentuation hypothesis. *Journal of Personality and Social Psychology, 38,* 390–398.

Kincaid, W. M. (1962). The combination of $2 \times m$ contingency tables. *Biometrics, 18,* 224–228.

Koziol, J. A., & Perlman, M. D. (1976). *Combining independent chi-squared tests* (Tech. Rep. No. 19). Chicago: University of Chicago, Department of Statistics.

Koziol, J. A., & Perlman, M. D. (1978). Combining independent chi-squared tests. *Journal of the American Statistical Association, 73,* 753–763.

Koziol, J. A., Perlman, M. D., & Rasmussen, U. A. (1988). *Combining independent F tests* (Tech. Rep. No. 129). Seattle: University of Washington, Department of Statistics.

Lancaster, H. O. (1949). The combination of probabilities arising from data in discrete distributions. *Biometrika, 36,* 370–382.

Liptak, T. (1958). On the combination of independent tests. *Magyar Tudomanyos Akademia Matematikai Kutato Intezetenek Kozlemenyei, 3,* 171–197.

Littell, R. C., & Folks, J. L. (1971). Asymptotic optimality of Fisher's method of combining independent tests. *Journal of the American Statistical Association, 66*, 802–806.

Mosteller, F., & Bush, R. R. (1954). Selected quantitative techniques. In G. Lindsey (Ed.), *Handbook of social psychology: Vol. 1. Theory and method.* Cambridge, MA: Addison-Wesley.

Oosterhoff, J. (1969). Combination of one-sided statistical tests. *Mathematical Center Tracts, 28.* Amsterdam: Mathematische Centrum.

Pape, E. S. (1972). A combination of *F*-statistics. *Technometrics, 14*, 89–99.

Pearson, E. S. (1938). The probability integral transformation for testing goodness of fit and combining independent tests of significance. *Biometrika, 30*, 134–148.

Pearson, E. S. (1950). On questions raised by the combination of tests based on discontinuous distributions. *Biometrika, 37*, 383–398.

Perlman, M. D. (1978, October 27). Letter to Frederick Mosteller.

Pillemer, D. B. (1992). One- versus two-tailed hypothesis tests in contemporary educational research. *Educational Researcher, 20*, 13–17.

Raudenbush, S. W. (1984). Magnitude of teacher expectancy effects on pupil IQ as a function of the credibility of expectancy induction: A synthesis of findings from 18 experiments. *Journal of Educational Psychology, 76*, 85–97.

Raudenbush, S. W., & Bryk, A. S. (1985). Empirical Bayes meta-analysis. *Journal of Educational Statistics, 10*, 75–98.

Rosenthal, R. (1978). Combining results of independent studies. *Psychological Bulletin, 85*, 185–193.

Rosenthal, R. (1979). The "file drawer problem" and tolerance for null results. *Psychological Bulletin, 86*, 638–641.

Rosenthal, R. (1984). *Meta-analytic procedures for social research.* Beverly Hills, CA: Sage.

Rosenthal, R., & Rubin, D. B. (1979). Comparing significance levels of independent studies. *Psychological Bulletin, 86*, 1165–1168.

Rozeboom, W. W. (1960). The fallacy of the null-hypothesis significance test. *Psychological Bulletin, 57*, 416–428.

Slavin, R. E. (1986). Best evidence synthesis: An alternative to meta-analytic and traditional reviews. *Educational Researcher, 15*, 5–11.

Smirnov, N. V. (1961). *Tables for the distribution and density functions of t-distribution ("Student's" distribution).* Oxford, England: Pergamon Press.

Stouffer, S. A., Suchman, E. A., DeVinney, L. C., Star, S. A., & Williams, R. M., Jr. (1949). *The American soldier: Adjustment during army life* (Vol. 1). Princeton, NJ: Princeton University Press.

Tippett, L. H. C. (1931). *The methods of statistics* (1st ed.). London: Williams & Norgate.

van Zwet, W. R., & Oosterhoff, J. (1967). On the combination of independent test statistics. *Annals of Mathematical Statistics, 38*, 659–680.

Wallis, W. A. (1942). Compounding probabilities from independent significance tests. *Econometrica, 10*, 229–248.

Wilkinson, B. A. (1951). A statistical consideration in psychological research. *Psychological Bulletin, 48*, 156–158.

Zelen, M. (1957). The analysis of incomplete block designs. *Journal of the American Statistical Association, 52*, 204–217.

Zelen, M., & Joel, L. (1959). The weighted compounding of two independent significance tests. *Annals of Mathematical Statistics, 30*, 885–895.

Cooper, H. and Hedges, L. V. (Eds.) 1994. *The Handbook of Research Synthesis*. New York: Russell Sage Foundation

# 16

# PARAMETRIC MEASURES OF EFFECT SIZE

**ROBERT ROSENTHAL**
*Harvard University*

CONTENTS

# 1. DEFINING RESEARCH RESULTS

## 1.1 Effect Size and Tests of Significance

The heart of the enterprise of synthesizing research consists of comparing and combining the results of individual studies of a particular, focused research question. In Chapter 15, the emphasis was on one type of result of an individual study—the test of significance. In the present chapter, the emphasis will be on a different type of result of an individual study—the size of the effect of an independent variable on a dependent variable, or, more generally, the size of the relationship between any two variables (Rosenthal 1991).

These two types of results, the test of significance (test statistic) and the size of the effect (effect size estimate), are related to each other in a simple, direct way:

Test of significance = size of effect × size of study.

Table 16.1 gives useful specific examples of this general equation. Equation (16-1) shows that $\chi^2$ on $df = 1$ is the product of the size of the effect expressed by $\phi^2$, the squared product moment correlation, multiplied by $N$, the number of subjects or other sampling units. (It should be noted that $\phi$ is merely Pearson's $r$ applied to dichotomous data, i.e., data coded as taking on only two values such as 0 and 1, 1 and 2, or $-1$ and $+1$; in section 1.2.1, other product moment correlations are described.)

Equation (16-2) is simply the square root of equation (16-1). It shows that the standard normal deviate $Z$ (i.e., the square root of $\chi^2$ on 1 $df$) is the product of $\phi$ (the product moment correlation) and $\sqrt{N}$. Equation (16-3) shows that $t$ is the product of the effect size $r\sqrt{1-r^2}$ and $\sqrt{df}$, an index of the size of the study. The denominator of this effect size ($\sqrt{1-r^2}$) is also known as the coefficient of alienation, or $k$, an index of the degree of noncorrelation (Guilford & Fruchter 1978). This effect size, therefore, can be rewritten as $r/k$, the ratio of correlation to noncorrelation, a kind of signal-to-noise ratio. Equations (16-4) and (16-5) share the same effect size, Hedges's $g$, the difference between the means of the two compared groups divided by, or standardized by, the approximately unbiased estimate of the population standard deviation.

This latter effect size $(M_1 - M_2)/S$ is the one typically employed by Glass, McGaw, and Smith (1981) with the $S$ computed as $[\Sigma(X - \overline{X})^2/(n_c - 1)]^{1/2}$ employing only the subjects or other sampling units from the *control group*. When this computation is employed, the index is called Glass's $\Delta$. The pooled $S$—that is, the one computed from both groups—tends to provide a better estimate, in the long run, of the population standard deviation (Hedges & Olkin 1985, p. 79). However, when the $S$'s based on the two different conditions differ greatly from each other, choosing the control group $S$ as the standardizing quantity is a very reasonable alternative. That is because it is always possible that the experimental treatment itself has made the $S$ of the experimental group too large or too small relative to the $S$ of the control group.

**Table 16.1 Examples of the Relationship Between Statistics Used in Tests of Significance and Effect Size Estimates**

| Equation | Test Statistic | = | Size of Effect | × | Size of Study |
|---|---|---|---|---|---|
| 16-1 | $\chi^2(1)$ | = | $\Phi^2$ | × | $N$ |
| 16-2 | $Z$ | = | $\Phi$ | × | $\sqrt{N}$ |
| 16-3 | $t$ | = | $\dfrac{r}{\sqrt{1-r^2}}$ | × | $\sqrt{df}$ |
| 16-4 | $t$ | = | $\left(\dfrac{M_1-M_2}{S}\right)^a$ | × | $\dfrac{1}{\sqrt{\dfrac{1}{n_1}+\dfrac{1}{n_2}}}$ |
| 16-5 | $t$ | = | $\left(\dfrac{M_1-M_2}{S}\right)^a$ | × | $\sqrt{\dfrac{n_1 n_2}{n_1+n_2}}$ |
| 16-6 | $t$ | = | $\left(\dfrac{M_1-M_2}{\sigma}\right)^b$ | × | $\left[\dfrac{\sqrt{n_1 n_2}}{(n_1+n_2)}\times\sqrt{df}\right]$ |
| 16-7 | $t$ | = | $d$ | × | $\dfrac{\sqrt{df}}{2}$ |
| 16-8 | $F^c$ | = | $\dfrac{r^2}{1-r^2}$ | × | $df$ error |
| 16-9 | $F^d$ | = | $\dfrac{\text{eta}^2}{1-\text{eta}^2}$ | × | $\dfrac{df\ \text{error}}{df\ \text{means}}$ |
| 16-10 | $F^d$ | = | $\dfrac{s^2\ \text{means}}{s^2}$ | × | $n$ |
| 16-11 | $t^e$ | = | $\dfrac{r}{\sqrt{1-r^2}}$ | × | $\sqrt{df}$ |
| 16-12 | $t^e$ | = | $\dfrac{\overline{D}}{S_D}$ | × | $\sqrt{n}$ |
| 16-13 | $t^e$ | = | $d$ | × | $\sqrt{df}$ |

NOTE: $N$ = total study sample size, $n$ = sample size for each condition, and $df=N-2$ for most applications.
[a] Also called $g$ (Hedges 1981, 1982).
[b] Also called $d$ (Cohen 1969, 1977, 1988).
[c] Numerator $df=1$.
[d] Numerator $df$ may take on any value.
[e] Correlated observations.

Another alternative when the $S$'s of the two groups differ greatly is to transform the data to make the $S$'s more similar. Such transformations (e.g., logs, square roots) of course require our having access to the original data, but that is also often required to compute $S$ separately for the control group. When only a mean square error from an analysis of variance is available, we must be content to use its square root ($S$) as our standardizing denominator in any case. Or if only the results of a $t$ test are given, we are similarly forced to compute the effect size using a pooled estimate of $S$. (We could use equations 16-4 or 16-5 to solve for $(M_1-M_2)/S$.) Thus, in many real-life meta-analytic applications it may not be possible to employ Glass's $\Delta$. If, for a subset of the studies to be combined and/or compared, it is possible to compute both Glass's $\Delta$ and Hedges's $g$, it will be instructive to compare the results. In reporting the results of the entire set of studies, however, it is advisable to report the index that can be computed for a greater proportion of the studies retrieved, usually an index such as Hedges's $g$ or $r$.

Before leaving the topic of whether to compute $S$ only from the control group or from both groups, a cautionary note about significance testing is in order. When $S$'s differ greatly for the two groups so that we are inclined to compute $S$ only from the control group, ordinary $t$ tests may give misleading results. Such problems can be approached by approximate procedures (Snedecor & Cochran 1989, pp. 96–98), but are perhaps best dealt with by appropriate transformation of the data (Tukey 1977).

Equation (16-6) shows an effect size only slightly different from that of equations (16-4) and (16-5). The only difference is that the standardizing quantity for the difference between the means is the sample standard deviation $\sigma$ (pooled sums of squares divided by $N$) rather than $S$ (pooled sums of squares divided by $N - k$ for $k$ groups). This is one of the effect sizes employed by Cohen (1969, 1977, 1988) and by Friedman (1968). Basically this index, Cohen's $d$, is the difference between the means of the groups being compared given in standard score units or $z$ scores. Equation (16-7) shows $(M_1 - M_2)/\sigma$ expressed as $d$ and the size of study term simplified considerably for those situations in which it is known, or in which it can be reasonably assumed, that the sample sizes ($n_1$ and $n_2$) are equal.

Equation (16-8) shows that $F$ with one $df$ in the numerator is the product of the squared ingredients of the right-hand side of equation (16-3). That is just as it should be, of course, given that $t^2 = F$ when $df = 1$ in the numerator of $F$.

Equation (16-9) is the generalization of equation (16-8) to the situation of $df > 1$ in the numerator. Thus, eta$^2$ refers to the proportion of variance accounted for just as $r^2$ does, but eta$^2$ carries no implication that the relationship between the two variables in question is linear. Equation (16-10) shows the effect size for $F$ as the ratio of the variance of the condition means to the pooled within-group variance, while the size of the study is indexed by $n$, the number of observations in each of the groups. Because we rarely employ fixed effect $F$

tests with $df > 1$ in the numerator in meta-analytic work, equations (16-9) and (16-10) are used infrequently in summarizing domains of research.

Table 16.1 gives only a small sample of the many effect size estimates that could be employed and is designed primarily to show that significance tests can be usefully viewed as simple products of effect size estimates and sample sizes. Any nonzero effect size will reach statistical significance given a sufficiently large sample size.

## 1.2 Two Families of Effect Sizes

**1.2.1 The $r$ family** Table 16.1 also suggests that most effect size estimates may fall into one of two families of effect sizes: the $r$ family and the $d$ family. The $r$ family includes the Pearson product moment correlation in any of its popular incarnations with labels:

$r$    when both variables are continuous;

$\phi$    when both variables are dichotomous;

$r_{pb}$    when one variable is continuous and one variable is dichotomous; and

$\rho$    when both variables are in ranked form.

The $r$ family also includes $Z_r$ the Fisher transformation of $r$ (described in more detail in section 3.1.1); $r/k$, a little used ratio that was referred to earlier, and the various squared indices of $r$ and $r$-like quantities including $r^2$, $r^2/k^2$, $\omega^2$ (omega-squared), $\xi^2$ (epsilon-squared), and eta$^2$. Because squared indices of effect size lose their directionality (Is the treatment helping or hurting? Is the correlation positive or negative?), they are of little use in meta-analytic work for which information on directionality is essential. Another reason to avoid the use of the squared indices of effect size is that the practical magnitude of these indices is likely to be seriously misinterpreted (Rosenthal & Rubin 1979, 1982; Rosenthal 1990; Rosenthal & Rosnow 1991).

**1.2.2 The $d$ family** The $d$ family of effect sizes includes Hedges's $g$, Glass's $\Delta$, and Cohen's $d$ as described above and such other indices of differences as the raw difference in proportions $d^1$ (see Chapter 17), and the difference between two proportions after each has been transformed to (a) radians (Cohen's $h$, case 1; Cohen 1988, p. 200) (b) probits, or (c) logits (Glass, McGaw & Smith 1981).

## 1.3 Effect Sizes for the One-Sample Case

The effect size estimates discussed so far have applied to situations in which we wanted to index the magnitude of a linear relationship between two variables by means of a correlation or by means of a comparison between the means of two conditions—say, by $g$, $\Delta$, or $d$. There are situations, however, in which there is only a single sample in our experiment, perhaps with each sampling unit exposed to two different experimental conditions. For example, teachers' favorableness of nonverbal behavior is recorded toward children for whom they hold more versus less favorable expectations. One test of significance of this effect of teachers' expectations on their nonverbal behavior could be the $t$ for correlated observations. Equations (16-11), (16-12), and (16-13) of Table 16.1 show three effect sizes that can be employed in such situations: $r/\sqrt{1-r^2}$, the same index as that of equation (16-3); $\overline{D}/S_D$, the mean difference divided by the sample $S$ analogous to Hedges's two-sample $g$; and $\overline{D}/\sigma$, the mean difference divided by the sample $\sigma$ analogous to Cohen's two-sample $d$. Thus, both the $r$ family and the $d$ family of effect size estimates can be employed in the one sample case.

When the data are dichotomous rather than continuous, a number of $d$ family indices are available including Cohen's $g$, Cohen's $h$ (case 2), and a newer index, $\Pi$.

The index Cohen's $g$ is simply the difference between an observed proportion and .50. For example, the magnitude of an electoral victory is given directly by $g$. If .60 of the electorate voted for the winner, then $g = .60 - .50 = .10$. Such an effect size might be regarded as enormous in the case of an election result, but as far less noteworthy as the result of a true-false test! The index Cohen's $h$ (case 2) is the difference between an observed proportion and a theoretically expected proportion after each of these proportions has been transformed to radians (an arcsine transformation). For example, in a multiple-choice examination in which one of four alternatives is correct and the position of the correct alternative has been assigned at random, guessing alone should yield an accuracy rate of .25. If the actual performance on this examination were found to be .75, we would compute $h$ by transforming the actual (.75) and the expected (.25) proportions by means of 2 arcsin $\sqrt{P}$ yielding

$$h = 2 \text{ arcsin } \sqrt{.75} - 2 \text{ arcsin } \sqrt{.25}$$
$$= 2.09 - 1.05 = 1.04.$$

The reason for employing the arcsin transformation is to make all $h$'s comparable in the sense of having variances independent of the parameter. Differences between raw proportions are not at all comparable, for example, with respect to statistical power. Thus, a difference between proportions of .95 and .90 yields an $h$ of .19, whereas a difference between proportions of .55 and .50 yields an $h$ of only .10 (Cohen 1988).

The one-sample effect size index, $\Pi$, is expressed as the proportion of correct guesses if there had been only two choices. When there are more than two choices, $\Pi$ converts the proportion of hits to the proportion of hits made if there had been only two equally likely choices:

$$\Pi = \frac{P(k-1)}{P(k-2)+1}, \tag{16-14}$$

where $P$ is the raw proportion of hits and $k$ is the number of alternative choices available. The standard error of $\Pi$ is

$$SE_{(\Pi)} = \frac{1}{\sqrt{N}} \left( \frac{\Pi(1-\Pi)}{\sqrt{P(1-P)}} \right). \tag{16-15}$$

This index would be especially valuable in evaluating performance on a multiple-choice-type examination in which the number of alternatives varied from item to item. The index $\Pi$ allows us to summarize the overall performance so that we can compare performances on tests made up of varying numbers of alternatives per item. Further details can be found in Rosenthal and Rubin (1989, 1991), and in Schaffer (1991).

## 1.4 Effect Sizes for Comparing Effect Sizes

**1.4.1 The two-sample case** Sometimes the basic research question concerns the difference between two effect sizes. For example, a developmental psychologist might hypothesize that two cognitive performance measures will be more highly correlated in preschool children than in fifth-graders. The degree to which the hypothesis is supported will depend on the difference between the correlations obtained from preschoolers and fifth-graders, $r_1 - r_2$. Cohen's $q$ is just such an index, one in which each $r$ is transformed to Fisher's $Z_r$ (see section 3.1.1) before the difference is computed so that

$$\text{Cohen's } q = Z_{r1} - Z_{r2}. \tag{16-16}$$

**1.4.2 The one-sample case** Cohen's $q$ can also be employed when an obtained effect size is to be compared with a theoretical value of $r$. In this case, we simply take the difference between the $Z_r$ associated with our observed sample and the $Z_r$ associated with our theoretical value of $r$ (Cohen 1988).

### 1.5 Comparing the *r* and *d* Families

It seems natural to employ $r$-type effect size estimators when the original effect size estimates are reported in $r$-type indices such as in meta-analyses of validity coefficients for test instruments (e.g., Hunter & Schmidt 1990). Similarly, it seems natural to employ $d$-type effect size estimates when the original studies have compared two groups so that the difference between their means and their within-group $S$'s or $\sigma$'s are available. In actual meta-analytic work, however, it is often the case that the effect size estimates will be a mixture of $r$-type and $d$-type indices. Because $r$-type and $d$-type estimates can readily be converted to one another, as we shall see later in this chapter, obtaining both types of estimates in our meta-analytic work will produce no hardship. However, it will be necessary to make a decision to convert all our effect size estimates to one particular index, usually $r$ or $Z_r$ for the $r$ family or Hedges's $g$ (or Cohen's $d$) for the $d$ family.

Although any of these effect size estimates can be employed, there are some reasons to view $r$ as the more generally useful effect size estimate.

**1.5.1 Generality of interpretation** If our data came to us as $r$'s, it would not make much sense to convert $r$'s to $d$'s because the concept of a mean difference index makes little sense in describing a linear relationship over a great many values of the independent variable. On the other hand, given a $d$-type effect size estimate, $r$ makes perfectly good sense in its point biserial form, that is, just two levels of the independent variable.

Suppose that our theory calls for us to employ at least three levels of our independent variable because we predict a quadratic trend in the relationship between level of arousal and subsequent performance. The magnitude of the effect associated with our quadratic trend contrast is quite naturally indexed by $r$, but not so naturally indexed by $d$-type indices.

**1.5.2 Consistency of meaning in the one-sample case** The $r$-type index requires no computational adjustment in going from the two-sample or multi-sample case to the one-sample case. This is most easily seen by consulting Table 16.1, in which $r$ is identically related to $t$ for the two-sample or multi-sample case of

equation (16-3) and for the one-sample case of equation (16-11). That is not the case for the $d$-type indices, however. For example, a comparison of equations (16-7) and (16-13) shows that the definition of the size of the study changes by a factor of 2 in going from a $t$ test for two samples to a $t$ test for one sample.

**1.5.3 Simplicity of interpretation** Finally, $r$ is more simply interpreted in terms of practical importance than are the usual $d$-type indices such as Hedges's $g$ and Cohen's $d$. In section 5 the details are given.

## 2. THE COMPUTATION OF EFFECT SIZES

In this section four major approaches to the computation of effect sizes will be described: Computation from (a) definitions, (b) significance test statistics, (c) significance levels, and (d) other effect size estimates.

### 2.1 Direct Computation

Table 16.2 gives the definitions for 11 of the effect size estimates used most frequently in meta-analytic work and also describes the population values (parameters) estimated by each effect size estimate; Table 16.3 gives the estimated variance of each effect size estimate. In practice, it often happens that the primary research study to be included in a research synthesis has computed or reported no effect size estimate at all. When that is the case, we can compute our own effect size estimate from the results of the test of significance reported in the research study. The following section describes such computational procedures for three of the most frequently used effect size estimates: $r$, Cohen's $d$, and Hedges's $g$.

### 2.2 From Significance Tests

In computing effect size estimates from significance tests (or from significance levels or various effect size estimates), it is essential to be thoughtful about the sign attached to each effect size estimate. The convention is to attach a plus sign to effect size estimates obtained in the predicted direction (e.g., the treatment is better than the control) and a minus sign to effect size estimates obtained in the unpredicted direction (e.g., the treatment is worse than the control). We are reminded of the need for a thoughtful decision about the sign in those equations where we must take a square root, since both a positive and a negative root are possible. But we must also be alert to questions of sign where the square root of a test statistic is not taken. The reason is that many

**Table 16.2 Effect Size Estimates, Their Definitions, and the Parameters They Estimate**

| Effect Size Estimate | = | Definition | Parameter Estimated |
|---|---|---|---|
| $r$ | = | $\dfrac{\Sigma Zx Zy}{N}$ | Population correlation between variables $X$ and $Y$ |
| $Z_r$ | = | $\frac{1}{2} \log_e \left[ \dfrac{1+r}{1-r} \right]$ | Population Fisher $Z_r$ transformation of population correlation |
| Cohen's $q$ | = | $Z_{r1} - Z_{r2}$ | Difference between Fisher $Z_r$ transformations of population correlation |
| Cohen's $d$ | = | $\dfrac{M_1 - M_2}{\sigma \text{ pooled}}$ | Difference between population means divided by average population standard deviation |
| Glass's $\Delta$ | = | $\dfrac{M_1 - M_2}{S \text{ control group}}$ | Difference between population means divided by the standard deviation of the population control group |
| Hedges's $g$ | = | $\dfrac{M_1 - M_2}{S \text{ pooled}}$ | Difference between population means divided by average population standard deviation |
| Cohen's $g$ | = | $p^a - .50$ | Population proportion $-$ .50 |
| $d'$ | = | $p_1 - p_2$ | Difference between population proportions |
| Cohen's $h$ | = | $\arcsin p_1 - \arcsin p_2$ | Difference between arcsin transformed population proportions |
| Probit $d'$ | = | $Z_{p1} - Z_{p2}$ | Difference between standard normal deviate transformed population proportions |
| Logit $d'$ | = | $\log_e\left(\dfrac{p_1}{1-p_1}\right) - \log_e\left(\dfrac{p_2}{1-p_2}\right)$ | Difference between logit transformed population proportions |

[a]The symbol $p$ refers to the proportion of cases.

investigators report all $t$ tests as positive, that is, regardless of whether the $t$ supports the superiority or inferiority of the treatment condition compared with the control.

**2.2.1 For $r$** The following formulas can be found by rearranging equations given in Table 16.1 (Cohen 1965; Friedman 1968):

$$r = \phi = \sqrt{\frac{\chi^2(1)}{N}} = \sqrt{\frac{Z^2}{N}} \qquad (16\text{-}17)$$

and

$$r = \sqrt{\frac{t^2}{t^2 + df}}, \qquad (16\text{-}18)$$

where $df = n_1 + n_2 - 2$. In equation (16-18) we can replace $t^2$ by $F$ so long as the $F$ is based on only a single $df$ in the numerator. The $df$ term in the denominator is then the $df$—that is, $n - 1$—collected from all conditions entering into the contrast being evaluated. Usually, this collection of $df$ will be the $df$ error. It may be a smaller

**Table 16.3 Estimated Variances for Effect Size Estimates of Table 16.2**

| Effect Size Estimate | Estimated Variance |
|---|---|
| $r$ | $(1 - r^2)^2/(N-2)$ |
| $Z_r$ | $1/(N-3)$ |
| Cohen's $q$ | $1/(N_1 - 3) + 1/(N_2 - 3)$ |
| Cohen's $d$ | $\left(\dfrac{n_1 + n_2}{n_1 n_2} + \dfrac{d^2}{2(n_1 + n_2 - 2)}\right)\left(\dfrac{n_1 + n_2}{n_1 + n_2 - 2}\right)$ |
| Glass's $\Delta$ | $\dfrac{n_1 + n_2}{n_1 n_2} + \dfrac{\Delta^2}{2(n_2 - 1)}$ |
| Hedges's $g$ | $\dfrac{n_1 + n_2}{n_1 n_2} + \dfrac{g^2}{2(n_1 + n_2 - 2)}$ |
| Cohen's $g$ | $p(1-p)/N$ |
| $d'$ | $p_1(1-p_1)/n_1 + p_2(1-p_2)/n_2$ |
| Cohen's $h$ | $1/n_1 + 1/n_2$ |
| Probit $d'$ | $\dfrac{2\pi p_1(1-p_1)e^{(Z_{p1}^2)}}{n_1} + \dfrac{2\pi p_2(1-p_2)e^{(Z_{p2}^2)}}{n_2}$ |
| Logit $d'$ | $\dfrac{1}{p_1(1-p_1)n_1} + \dfrac{1}{p_2(1-p_2)n_2}$ |

number of *df* than that, however, if some of the conditions are of no substantive interest and have been given zero weight in the contrast.

**2.2.2 For Cohen's d** We can obtain $d$ from

$$d = \frac{t(n_1 + n_2)}{\sqrt{df}\,\sqrt{n_1 n_2}} \,. \qquad (16\text{-}19)$$

When we can (or must, for lack of information) consider the two sample sizes to be equal, equation (16-19) simplifies to

$$d = \frac{2t}{\sqrt{df}} \,. \qquad (16\text{-}20)$$

In equations (16-19) and (16-20) we can replace $t$ by $\sqrt{F}$ so long as the $F$ is based on only a single $df$ in the numerator and $df$ is defined as in section 2.2.1.

**2.2.3 For Hedges's g** We can obtain $g$ from

$$g = \frac{t\sqrt{n_1 + n_2}}{\sqrt{n_1 n_2}} \,; \qquad (16\text{-}21)$$

and when $n_1$ is assumed to equal $n_2$ we can employ

$$g = \frac{2t}{\sqrt{N}} \,, \qquad (16\text{-}22)$$

where $N = n_1 + n_2$.

**2.2.4 When $\chi^2$ $df > 1$ or $F$ $df > 1$ in the numerator** A special word of caution should be entered here since meta-analysts often find that a primary research report has interpreted a $\chi^2$ with $df > 1$ or an $F$ with $df > 1$ in the numerator as though it were a contrast. For example, a psychologist may note that, for five age groups, performance shows a steady increase with age with $F(4,95) = 2.47$, $p = .05$. That $F$ and that $p$ may then be reported as representing the test statistic for the hypothesis that performance grows linearly with age. However, it would be incorrect since the omnibus $F$ would be the same even if the five age groups were scrambled randomly. The proper test requires the computation of a linear trend in the five means. These procedures are detailed elsewhere (Rosenthal & Rosnow 1985, 1991).

## 2.3 From Significance Levels

Sometimes the meta-analyst will find that a primary research report gives neither an effect size estimate nor a test of significance, but will give a significance level. When that happens the $p$ level reported is likely to be not very accurate, given perhaps only as "significant at .05" (or .01, or .001, etc.). Still, we can use the information to get a lower limit effect size estimate from

$$r = \phi = \frac{Z}{\sqrt{N}} . \qquad (16\text{-}23)$$

All we need to employ equation (16-23) is a table of the standard normal deviates so that we can find $Z$ for any reported $p$ level. There are also inexpensive hand-held calculators that will give $Z$ (or $t$, or $F$, or $\chi^2$) directly for any entered level of significance. Using these equivalences of $p$ values and $t$ we can readily obtain $r$ from equation (16-18), Cohen's $d$ from equations (16-19) and (16-20), and Hedges's $g$ from equations (16-21) and (16-22), as shown in the following examples.

**2.3.1 $r$ from $t$** Suppose that an article compares a treatment with a control condition and tells us only that $p$ was significant at .05, two-tailed, and $n_1 = n_2 = 16$, so that $N = 32$, and $df = 30$. From a $t$ table we learn that for $p = .05$, two-tailed and $df = 30$, $t = 2.04$. Then from equation (16-18) we find

$$r = \sqrt{\frac{t^2}{t^2 + df}} = \sqrt{\frac{(2.04)^2}{(2.04)^2 + 30}} = .349.$$

Had we not had a $t$ table but only a table of standard normal deviates, we could have used equation (16-17) to find

$$r = \sqrt{\frac{\chi^2(1)}{N}} = \sqrt{\frac{Z^2}{N}} = \sqrt{\frac{(1.96)^2}{32}} = .346.$$

**2.3.2 Cohen's $d$ from $t$** For the example of $p = .05$, two-tailed, based on $n_1 = n_2 = 16$, we found $t = 2.04$. To obtain $d$ we employ equation (16-20) to find

$$d = \frac{2t}{\sqrt{df}} = \frac{2(2.04)}{\sqrt{30}} = .745.$$

**2.3.3 Hedges's $g$ from $t$** For the same example of $p = .05$, $t = 2.04$, we find $g$ from equation (16-22) as

$$g = \frac{2t}{\sqrt{N}} = \frac{2(2.04)}{\sqrt{32}} = .721,$$

a slightly smaller, and less biased, estimate of the population effect than $d$.

## 2.4 From Other Effect Size Indices

It often happens in meta-analytic work that we obtain different effect size indices for different studies, which must then all be converted to a single index before we begin the task of comparing and combining effect size indices. In this section procedures are shown for converting any of our three primary indices $r$, Cohen's $d$, and Hedges's $g$ to either of the other two.

**2.4.1 $r$ from $d$ and $g$** We can obtain $r$ from $d$ as follows:

$$r = \sqrt{\frac{d^2}{d^2 + 4}}. \qquad (16\text{-}24)$$

Equation (16-24) is always applicable in experimental contexts in which we think of the populations (e.g., treated versus controls) as equally numerous, or when the populations are otherwise to be regarded as essentially equal in size. If the populations are clearly different in size (patients with a rare disease vs. all others), the following equation is preferred (Cohen 1988, p. 24):

$$r = \sqrt{\frac{d^2}{d^2 + \frac{1}{PQ}}}, \qquad (16\text{-}25)$$

where $P = $ proportion of A's in the combined $A + B$ populations and $Q = 1 - P$.

We can obtain $r$ from $g$ as follows:

$$r = \sqrt{\frac{g^2 n_1 n_2}{g^2 n_1 n_2 + (n_1 + n_2)df}} . \qquad (16\text{-}26)$$

**2.4.2 Cohen's $d$ from $r$ and $g$** We can obtain Cohen's $d$ from $r$ as follows:

$$d = \frac{2r}{\sqrt{1 - r^2}} ; \qquad (16\text{-}27)$$

and from $g$:

$$d = g\sqrt{\frac{n_1 + n_2}{df}} . \qquad (16\text{-}28)$$

**2.4.3 Hedges's $g$ from $r$ and $d$** We can obtain Hedges's $g$ from $r$ as follows:

$$g = \frac{r}{\sqrt{1 - r^2}} \sqrt{\frac{df(n_1 + n_2)}{n_1 n_2}} ; \qquad (16\text{-}29)$$

and from $d$:

$$g = \frac{d}{\sqrt{\dfrac{n_1 + n_2}{df}}} . \qquad (16\text{-}30)$$

## 2.5 Choosing an Approach

Four major approaches to the computation of effect sizes have been described and none is intrinsically better than the others. Meta-analytic experience suggests, however, that most often our computation of effect sizes will be based on significance tests, because many studies retrieved in a meta-analysis do not report the ingredients required to compute effect sizes directly nor do they report effect sizes of any kind from which we could compute our own preferred index. Tests of significance and significance levels are usually reported, however; and between those two pieces of information, tests of significance are usually reported more accurately than are levels of significance, so their use is preferred.

## 3. ADJUSTING EFFECT SIZE ESTIMATES

### 3.1 The Fisher and Hedges Adjustments

**3.1.1 Adjusting $Z_r$ and $r$**  One of the most important effect size estimates in meta-analytic work is $r$. However, as the population value of $r$ gets further and further from zero, the distribution of $r$'s sampled from that population becomes more and more skewed. This fact complicates the comparison and combination of $r$'s, a complication addressed by Fisher (1928). He devised the transformation ($Z_r$), referred to earlier, that is distributed nearly normally. In virtually all meta-analytic procedures, whenever we are interested in $r$ we actually carry out most of our computations not on $r$ but on its transformation $Z_r$. The relationship between $r$ and $Z_r$ is given by

$$Z_r = \tfrac{1}{2} \log_e \left[ \frac{1+r}{1-r} \right]. \qquad (16\text{-}31)$$

Fisher (1928, p. 172) noted that there was a small and often negligible bias in $Z_r$, each being too large by $r$-population/$[2(N-1)]$. Only when $N$ is very small while at the same time the $r$-population (the actual population value of $r$) is very substantial is the bias of any conse-

quence. For practical purposes, therefore, it can safely be ignored (Snedecor & Cochran 1989).

Although we are more likely to work with $Z_r$ than with $r$ itself in our meta-analytic work, it should be noted that there is also a bias in $r$, $r$ being too *small* by $r(1 - r^2)/2(N - 3)$. This bias is serious only when $N$ is small and $r$ is not far from .5 (Hedges & Olkin 1985).

**3.1.2 Adjusting $g$ and $\Delta$**  There are analogous biases in other effect size estimates, such as Glass's $\Delta$, Hedges's $g$, and Cohen's $d$; Hedges (1981, 1982) has provided both exact and approximate correction factors. Hedges's unbiased estimator $g^U$ is given by

$$g^U = c(m)g, \qquad (16\text{-}32)$$

where $g$ is the effect size estimate computed as $(M_1 - M_2)/S$ (with $S$ computed from both the experimental and the control groups), and $c(m)$ is given approximately by

$$c(m) \approx 1 - \frac{3}{4m - 1}, \qquad (16\text{-}33)$$

where $m$ is the $df$ computed from both the experimental and control groups or $n_1 + n_2 - 2$ (see also Hedges & Olkin 1985). Building on Hedges's work Glass, McGaw, and Smith (1981) also describe corrections for bias in Glass's $\Delta$ requiring only that $\Delta$ be multiplied by $c(m)$ as shown in equation (16-33).

### 3.2 The Hunter and Schmidt Adjustments

The most elaborate set of adjustments has been proposed by Hunter and Schmidt (1990; see also Hunter, Schmidt & Jackson 1982). They recommend adjustment for unreliability of the independent and dependent variables, dichotomization of continuous variables, restriction of range of the independent and dependent variables, imperfection of construct validity of the independent and dependent variables, and even employment of unequal sample sizes for the experimental and control groups. The Hunter and Schmidt work is valuable for reminding us that there are many sources of noise that may serve to lower obtained effect sizes. Their work is also valuable for providing us with procedures for adjusting for these sources of noise. The application of these procedures gives us some estimate of what effect size we might expect to find in the best of all possible worlds. However, these adjustments (described in Chapter 21) must be applied with great caution (Guilford 1954; Johnson 1944; Rosenthal 1991; Spearman 1910).

## 3.3 The Glass, McGaw, and Smith Adjustments

Studies entering into a meta-analysis differ in the precision of the statistical procedures employed in their analysis. Thus, repeated measures designs (of which gain score analyses are a special case), analysis of covariance designs, and designs employing blocking will tend to produce larger effect sizes and more significant test statistics than would the analogous unblocked posttest-only designs. Glass and his colleagues have shown how we might convert the results of various designs onto a common scale of effect size (e.g., $\Delta$ or $g$) based on the unblocked posttest only. For example, if our study compares the gain scores of the experimental and control groups, the standard deviation of the gain scores ($S_g$) is often substantially smaller than the standard deviation of the post scores ($S_p$), leading to a substantially larger $\Delta$ or $g$. To convert the $S_g$ to $S_p$, we employ equation (16-34):

$$S_p = \frac{S_g}{\sqrt{2(1-r)}}, \qquad (16\text{-}34)$$

where $r$ is the correlation between pre- and post-measure for the control group only ($\Delta$) or for the average of both the control and experimental groups ($g$) (Glass, McGaw, & Smith 1981).

To make an analogous adjustment in the context of an analysis of covariance, we employ equation (16-35):

$$S_p = \sqrt{\frac{MS_{\text{error}}}{1-r^2}\left(\frac{df_{\text{error}}-1}{df_{\text{error}}-2}\right)}, \qquad (16\text{-}35)$$

where $MS_{\text{error}}$ is the pooled within-group mean square after adjusting for the covariate, $r$ is the correlation between the outcome variable and the covariate, and $df_{\text{error}}$ is the $df$ for the $MS_{\text{error}}$. Other adjustments are described as well by Glass, McGaw, and Smith (1981, pp. 114–123). These adjustments cannot always be made for the results of other people's studies, but can often be quite usefully employed. However, when they are employed, it seems best to report both the adjusted and unadjusted statistics.

Just as repeated measures, covariance, and blocking designs tend to increase power, the use of nonparametric tests of significance may tend to decrease power, and Glass, McGaw, and Smith (1981) provide adjustment procedures. As in the case of adjustments described earlier, it seems wise to report both unadjusted and adjusted statistics.

## 4. EFFECT SIZES FOR CORRELATED DEPENDENT VARIABLES

Many of the studies entering into our meta-analyses will have more than one test of significance relevant to our hypothesis; and since for every test of significance there is an effect size estimate, these studies will have more than one effect size estimate as well. The various dependent variables employed in a study should all be examined for clues as to the types of dependent variable that seem most affected and least affected by the independent variable of interest. If there are many studies using several of the same dependent variables, we could perform a separate meta-analysis for each different type of dependent variable involved. For example, if we were studying the effects of alcoholism treatment programs, preliminary separate analyses could be performed for the dependent variables of sobriety, number of days of employment, number of arrests, general medical health, personal and social adjustment, and so on, to reveal the variation in effect sizes. Each of these types of dependent variable could be operationalized in several ways. For example, for each of them we could obtain self-reports, family reports, and institutional reports (from hospitals, clinics, courts, police departments, etc.). A preliminary separate meta-analysis could be conducted for each of these three sources of information as well, so we might further investigate variation associated with information source.

It seems wise in most cases to have each independent primary study contribute only a single estimate of some overall effect size estimate to each meta-analysis to which that study is to contribute. There are many procedures available for reducing multiple effect sizes for a study to a single effect size. Simple, conservative procedures include using the mean or median effect size. More accurate procedures are also available and have been described elsewhere in more detail (Hedges & Olkin 1985; Rosenthal 1984, 1991; Rosenthal & Rubin 1986; and, especially, in Chapter 22 of this handbook). These more accurate procedures tend to yield somewhat larger effect size estimates than do the simpler methods of employing the mean or median effect sizes and are generally to be preferred.

## 5. THE INTERPRETATION OF EFFECT SIZES

Despite the growing awareness of the importance of estimating effect sizes, there is a problem in evaluating various effect size estimators from the point of view of practical usefulness (Cooper 1981). Rosenthal and Rubin (1979, 1982) found that neither experienced behavioral researchers nor experienced statisticians had a good intuitive feel for the practical meaning of common effect size estimators and that this was particularly true for such squared indices as $r^2$, omega$^2$, epsilon$^2$, and similar estimates.

## 5.1 The Physicians' Aspirin Study

At a special meeting held on December 18, 1987, it was decided to end, prematurely, a randomized double blind experiment on the effects of aspirin in reducing heart attacks (Steering Committee of the Physicians' Health Study Research Group 1988). The reason for this unusual termination of such an experiment was that it had become so clear that aspirin prevented heart attacks (and deaths from heart attacks) that it would be unethical to continue to give half the physician research subjects a placebo. And what was the magnitude of the experimental effect that was so dramatic as to call for the termination of this research? Was $r^2$ .80 or .60, so that the corresponding $r$'s would have been .89 or .77? Was $r^2$ .40 or even .20, so that the corresponding $r$'s would have been .63 or .45? No, none of these. Actually $r^2$ was .0011, with a corresponding $r$ of .034.

**Table 16.4  Effects of Aspirin on Heart Attacks Among 22,071 Physicians**

|  | Heart Attack | No Heart Attack | Total |
|---|---|---|---|
| **Raw Counts** | | | |
| Aspirin | 104 | 10,933 | 11,037 |
| Placebo | 189 | 10,845 | 11,034 |
| Total | 293 | 21,778 | 22,071 |
| **Percentages** | | | |
| Aspirin | 0.94 | 99.06 | 100 |
| Placebo | 1.71 | 98.29 | 100 |
| Total | 1.33 | 98.67 | 100 |
| **Binomial Effect Size Display** | | | |
| Aspirin | 48.3 | 51.7 | 100 |
| Placebo | 51.7 | 48.3 | 100 |
| Total | 100 | 100 | 200 |

## 5.2 The Binomial Effect Size Display

Table 16.4 shows the results of the aspirin study in terms of raw counts, percentages, and as a Binomial Effect Size Display (BESD). This display is a way of showing the practical importance of any effect indexed by a correlation coefficient. The correlation is shown to be the simple difference in outcome rates between the experimental and control groups in this standard table, column and row totals of which always add up to 100 (Rosenthal & Rubin 1982). We obtain the BESD from any obtained effect size $r$ by computing the treatment condition success rate as .50 plus $r/2$ and the control condition success rate as .50 minus $r/2$. Thus, an $r$ of .20 yields a treatment success rate of $.50 + .20/2 = .60$ and a control success rate of $.50 - .20/2 = .40$, or a BESD of:

|  | Success | Failure | $\Sigma$ |
|---|---|---|---|
| Treatment | 60 | 40 | 100 |
| Control | 40 | 60 | 100 |
| $\Sigma$ | 100 | 100 | 200 |

Had we been given the BESD to examine before knowing $r$, we could easily have calculated it mentally for ourselves; $r$ is simply the difference between the success rates of the experimental versus the control group $(.60 - .40 = .20).$[1]

The type of result seen in the physicians' aspirin study is not at all unusual in biomedical research. Some years earlier, on October 29, 1981, the National Heart, Lung, and Blood Institute discontinued its placebo-controlled study of propranolol because results were so favorable to the treatment that it would have been unethical to continue withholding the life-saving drug from the control patients. Once again, the effect size $r$ was .04, and the $r^2$ was zero to two decimal places. As behavioral researchers we are not used to thinking of $r$'s of .04 as reflecting effect sizes of practical importance. But when

---

[1]Long before the introduction of the BESD, Cohen (1969) proposed several measures to aid in the interpretation of his effect size index $d$. These measures, called $u_1$, $u_2$, and $u_3$, are measures of percentage overlap. For example, $u_3$ gives the percentage of the control population that the upper half of the experimental population exceeds. When $d = .00$, $u_3 = 50$ percent since the upper half of the experimentals exceeds only 50 percent of the controls. When $d = .50$, $u_3 = 69$ percent because the upper half of the experimentals exceeds 69 percent of the controls.

we think of an $r$ of .04 as reflecting a 4 percent decrease in heart attacks, the interpretation given $r$ in a BESD, the $r$ does not appear to be quite so small (Rosenthal 1984, 1991).

## 5.3 Additional Results

Table 16.5 gives three further examples of BESDs. In a recent study of 4,462 army veterans of the Vietnam War era (1965–1971), the correlation between having served in Vietnam (rather than elsewhere) and having suffered from alcohol abuse or dependence was .07 (Centers for Disease Control 1988). The top display of Table 16.5 shows that the difference between the problem rates of 53.5 and 46.5 per 100 is equal to the correlation coefficient of .07.

The center display of Table 16.5 shows the results of a study of the effects of AZT on the survival of 282 patients suffering from AIDS or AIDS-related complex (ARC) (Barnes 1986). This result of a correlation of .23 between survival and receiving AZT (an $r^2$ of .054) was so dramatic as to lead to the premature termination of the clinical trial on the ethical grounds that it would be improper to continue to give a placebo to the control group patients.

The bottom display of Table 16.5 shows the results of a famous meta-analysis of psychotherapy outcome studies reported by Smith and Glass (1977). An eminent critic believed that the results of their analysis sounded the ''death knell'' for psychotherapy because of the modest size of the effect. This modest effect size was an $r$ of .32, accounting for ''only'' 10 percent of the variance.

Examination of the bottom display of Table 16.5 shows that it is not very realistic to label as ''modest indeed'' an effect size equivalent to increasing a success rate from 34 to 66 percent (e.g., reducing a death rate or a failure rate from 66 to 34 percent). Indeed, as we have seen, the dramatic effects of AZT were substantially smaller ($r = .23$).

### Table 16.5 Other Examples of Binomial Effect Size Displays

**Vietnam Service and Alcohol Problems ($r = .07$)**

|  | Problem | No Problem | Total |
| --- | --- | --- | --- |
| Vietnam Veteran | 53.5 | 46.5 | 100 |
| Non-Vietnam Veteran | 46.5 | 53.5 | 100 |
| Total | 100 | 100 | 200 |

**AZT in the Treatment of AIDS ($r = .23$)**

|  | Death | Survival | Total |
| --- | --- | --- | --- |
| AZT | 38.5 | 61.5 | 100 |
| Placebo | 61.5 | 38.5 | 100 |
| Total | 100 | 100 | 200 |

**Benefits of Psychotherapy ($r = .32$)[a]**

|  | Less Benefit | Greater Benefit | Total |
| --- | --- | --- | --- |
| Psychotherapy | 34 | 66 | 100 |
| Control | 66 | 34 | 100 |
| Total | 100 | 100 | 200 |

[a]The analogous $r$ for 443 studies of interpersonal expectancy effects was .30 (Rosenthal 1993).

**Author's note**

Preparation of this chapter was supported in part by the Spencer Foundation. The content of this chapter is solely the responsibility of the author, though it was greatly improved by the suggestions of Donald Rubin.

## 6. REFERENCES

Barnes, D. M. (1986). Promising results halt trial of anti-AIDS drug. *Science, 234,* 15–16.

Centers for Disease Control, Vietnam Experience Study. (1988). Health status of Vietnam veterans: 1. Psychosocial characteristics. *Journal of the American Medical Association, 259,* 2701–2707.

Cohen, J. (1965). Some statistical issues in psychological research. In B. B. Wolman (Ed.), *Handbook of clinical psychology.* New York: McGraw-Hill.

Cohen, J. (1969). *Statistical power analysis for the behavioral sciences.* New York: Academic Press.

Cohen, J. (1977). *Statistical power analysis for the behavioral sciences* (rev. ed.). New York: Academic Press.

Cohen, J. (1988). *Statistical power analysis for the behavioral sciences* (2nd ed.). Hillsdale, NJ: Erlbaum.

Cooper, H. M. (1981). On the significance of effects and the effects of significance. *Journal of Personality and Social Psychology, 41,* 1013–1018.

Fisher, R. A. (1928). *Statistical methods for research workers* (2nd ed.). London: Oliver & Boyd.

Friedman, H. (1968). Magnitude of experimental effect and a table for its rapid estimation. *Psychological Bulletin, 70,* 245–251.

Glass, G. V, McGaw, B., & Smith, M. L. (1981). *Meta-analysis in social research.* Beverly Hills, CA: Sage.

Guilford, J. P. (1954). *Psychometric methods* (2nd ed.). New York: McGraw-Hill.

Guilford, J. P., & Fruchter, B. (1978). *Fundamental statistics in psychology and education* (6th ed.). New York: McGraw-Hill.

Hedges, L. V. (1981). Distribution theory for Glass's estimator of effect size and related estimators. *Journal of Educational Statistics, 6,* 107–128.

Hedges, L. V. (1982). Estimation of effect size from a series of independent experiments. *Psychological Bulletin, 92,* 490–499.

Hedges, L. V., & Olkin, I. (1985). *Statistical methods for meta-analysis.* New York: Academic Press.

Hunter, J. E., & Schmidt, F. L. (1990). *Methods of meta-analysis: Correcting error and bias in research findings.* Newbury Park, CA: Sage.

Hunter, J. E., Schmidt, F. L., & Jackson, G. B. (1982). *Meta-analysis: Cumulating research findings across studies.* Beverly Hills, CA: Sage.

Johnson, H. G. (1944). An empirical study of the influence of errors of measurement upon correlation. *American Journal of Psychology, 57,* 521–536.

Rosenthal, R. (1984). *Meta-analytic procedures for social research.* Beverly Hills, CA: Sage.

Rosenthal, R. (1990). How are we doing in soft psychology? *American Psychologist, 45,* 775–777.

Rosenthal, R. (1991). *Meta-analytic procedures for social research* (rev. ed). Newbury Park, CA: Sage.

Rosenthal, R. (1993). Cumulating evidence. In G. Keren & C. Lewis (Eds.), *A handbook for data analysis in the behavioral sciences: Methodological issues.* Hillsdale, NJ: Erlbaum.

Rosenthal, R., & Rosnow, R. L. (1985). *Contrast analysis: Focused comparisons in the analysis of variance.* New York: Cambridge University Press.

Rosenthal, R., & Rosnow, R. L. (1991). *Essentials of behavioral research: Methods and data analysis* (2nd ed.). New York: McGraw-Hill.

Rosenthal, R., & Rubin, D. B. (1979). A note on percent variance explained as a measure of the importance of effects. *Journal of Applied Social Psychology, 9,* 395–396.

Rosenthal, R., & Rubin, D. B. (1982). A simple, general purpose display of magnitude of experimental effect. *Journal of Educational Psychology, 74,* 166–169.

Rosenthal, R., & Rubin, D. B. (1986). Meta-analytic procedures for combining studies with multiple effect sizes. *Psychological Bulletin, 99,* 400–406.

Rosenthal, R., & Rubin, D. B. (1989). Effect size estimation for one-sample multiple-choice-type data: Design, analysis, and meta-analysis. *Psychological Bulletin, 106,* 332–337.

Rosenthal, R., & Rubin, D. B. (1991). Further issues in effect size estimation for one-sample multiple-choice-type data. *Psychological Bulletin, 109,* 351–352.

Schaffer, J. P. (1991). Comment on "Effect size estimation for one-sample multiple-choice-type data: Design, analysis, and meta-analysis" by Rosenthal and Rubin (1989). *Psychological Bulletin, 109,* 348–350.

Smith, M. L., & Glass, G. V (1977). Meta-analysis of psychotherapy outcome studies. *American Psychologist, 32,* 752–760.

Snedecor, G. W., & Cochran, W. G. (1989). *Statistical methods* (8th ed.). Ames: Iowa State University Press.

Spearman, C. (1910). Correlation calculated from faulty data. *British Journal of Psychology, 3,* 271–295.

Steering Committee of the Physicians' Health Study Research Group. (1988). Preliminary report: Findings from the aspirin component of the ongoing physicians' health study. *New England Journal of Medicine, 318,* 262–264.

Tukey, J. W. (1977). *Exploratory data analysis.* Reading, MA: Addison-Wesley.

Cooper, H. and Hedges, L. V. (Eds.) 1994. *The Handbook of Research Synthesis.* New York: Russell Sage Foundation

# 17

# MEASURES OF EFFECT SIZE FOR CATEGORICAL DATA

**JOSEPH L. FLEISS**
*Columbia University*

CONTENTS

## 1. INTRODUCTION

In many studies measurements are made on binary rather than numerical scales. Examples include studies of attitudes or opinions (the two categories for the response variable being agree or disagree with some statement), case-control studies in epidemiology (the two categories being exposed or not exposed to some hypothesized risk factor), and intervention studies (the two categories being improved or unimproved). In this chapter we present and analyze four popular measures of association or effect that are appropriate for categorical data: the difference between two probabilities, the ratio of two probabilities, the phi coefficient, and the odds ratio. The odds ratio is shown to be the measure of choice according to several statistical criteria, and the major portion of the chapter is devoted to methods for making inferences about this measure under a variety of study designs.

Consider a comparative study in which two groups are compared with respect to the frequency of a binary characteristic. Let $\Pi_1$ and $\Pi_2$ denote the probabilities in the two underlying populations of a subject's being classified into one of the two categories, and let $P_1$ and $P_2$ denote the two sample proportions based on samples of sizes $n_1$ and $n_2$. Three of the four parameters to be studied in this chapter are the simple *difference* between the two probabilities,

$$\Delta = \Pi_1 - \Pi_2; \qquad (17\text{-}1)$$

the ratio of the two probabilities, or the *rate ratio* (referred to as the risk ratio or relative risk in the health sciences),

$$RR = \Pi_1/\Pi_2; \qquad (17\text{-}2)$$

and the *odds ratio,*

$$\omega = (\Pi_1/(1-\Pi_1))/(\Pi_2/(1-\Pi_2)). \qquad (17\text{-}3)$$

The fourth measure, $\varphi$ (the phi coefficient), will be defined later.

The parameters $\Delta$ and $\varphi$ are such that the value 0 indicates no association or no difference. For the other two parameters, $RR$ and $\omega$, the logarithm of the measure is typically analyzed in order to overcome the awkward features that the value 1 indicates no association or no difference, and that the finite interval from 0 to 1 is available for indexing negative association, but the infinite interval from 1 on up is available for indexing positive association. With the parameters transformed if necessary so that the value 0 separates negative from positive association, we present for each the formula for its maximum likelihood estimator, say $L$, and for its non-null standard error, say $SE$. (A non-null standard error is one in which no restrictions are imposed on the parameters—in particular, no restrictions that are associated with the null hypothesis.)

We assume throughout this chapter that the sample sizes within each individual study are large enough for classical large-sample methods assuming normality to be valid. The quantities $L$, $SE$, and

$$w = 1/SE^2 \qquad (17\text{-}4)$$

are then sufficient for making the following important inferences about the parameter being analyzed within each individual study, and for pooling a given study's results with the results of others. Let $C_\alpha$ denote the value cutting off the fraction $\alpha$ in the upper tail of the standard normal distribution. The interval $L \pm C_\alpha SE$ is, approximately, a $100(1-2\alpha)$ percent confidence interval for the parameter that $L$ is estimating. The given study's contribution to the numerator of the pooled estimate of the parameter of interest is, under the model of fixed effects, $wL$, and its contribution to the denominator is $w$. (In a so-called fixed effects model for $k$ studies, the assumption is made that there is interest in only these studies. In a random effects model, the assumption is made that these $k$ studies are a sample from a larger population of studies. We restrict attention in this chapter to fixed effects analyses.) If $\bar{L}$. is the pooled estimate across the several studies, that is, $\bar{L}. = \Sigma\, w_i L_i / \Sigma w_i$, the given study's contribution to the statistic for testing for heterogeneity (i.e., differences between studies in their underlying parameter values) is $w_i(L_i - \bar{L}.)^2$.

## 2. THE DIFFERENCE BETWEEN TWO PROBABILITIES

### 2.1 A Critique of the Difference

The straightforward difference, $\Delta = \Pi_1 - \Pi_2$, is the simplest parameter for estimating the effect on a binary variable of whatever characteristic or intervention distinguishes group 1 from group 2. Its simplicity is perhaps its only virtue, though, especially in the context of research syntheses. A technical difficulty with $\Delta$ is that its range of variation is limited by the magnitudes of $\Pi_1$ and $\Pi_2$: The possible values of $\Delta$ when $\Pi_1$ and $\Pi_2$ are close to 0.5 are greater than when $\Pi_1$ and $\Pi_2$ are close to 0 or to 1. If the values of $\Pi_1$ and $\Pi_2$ vary across the

**Table 17.1 Mortality Rates from Lung Cancer by Smoking History and by Occupational Exposure to Asbestos (per 100,000 person-years)**

| Smoker | Exposed to Asbestos | |
|--------|------|------|
| | Yes | No |
| Yes | 601.6 | 122.6 |
| No | 58.4 | 11.3 |

$k$ studies whose results are being synthesized, the associated values of $\Delta$ may also vary. There might then be the appearance of heterogeneity (i.e., nonconstancy in the measure of effect) in this scale of measurement owing to the mathematical constraints imposed on probabilities rather than to substantive reasons.

The example in Table 17.1 illustrates this phenomenon. The values are mortality rates from lung cancer in four groups of workers: exposed or not to asbestos in the workplace cross-classified by cigarette smoker or not (Hammond, Selikoff & Seidman 1979). The asbestos–no asbestos difference in lung cancer mortality rates for cigarette smokers is $601.6 - 122.6$, or approximately 500 deaths per 100,000 person-years. Given the mortality rate of 58.4 per 100,000 person-years for nonsmokers exposed to asbestos, it is obviously impossible for the asbestos–no asbestos difference between lung cancer mortality rates for nonsmokers to come anywhere near 500 per 100,000 person-years. Heterogeneity—a difference between smokers and nonsmokers in the effect of exposure to asbestos, with effect measured as the difference between two rates—exists, but it is difficult to assign biological meaning to it.

## 2.2 Inference about the Difference

In spite of the possible inappropriateness for a meta-analysis of the difference between two probabilities, the investigator might nevertheless choose to employ $\Delta$ as the measure of effect. The factor $w$ by which a study's estimated difference, $D = P_1 - P_2$, is to be weighted in a fixed effects meta-analysis is equal to the reciprocal of its estimated squared standard error,

$$w = 1/SE^2 = \left( \frac{P_1(1-P_1)}{n_1} + \frac{P_2(1-P_2)}{n_2} \right)^{-1}. \quad (17\text{-}5)$$

## 2.3 An Example

Consider as an example a comparative study in which one treatment was applied to a randomly constituted sample of $n_1 = 80$ subjects and the other was applied to a randomly constituted sample of $n_2 = 70$ subjects. If the proportions unimproved are $P_1 = 0.60$ and $P_2 = 0.80$, the value of $D$ is $-0.20$ and the standard error of $P_1 - P_2$ is

$$SE = \left( \frac{0.60 \times 0.40}{80} + \frac{0.80 \times 0.20}{70} \right)^{1/2} = 0.0727.$$

The resulting weighting factor is $w = 1/SE^2 = 189.2$. An approximate 95 percent confidence interval for $\Delta$ is $D \pm 1.96 \cdot SE$. In the present example, the interval is $-0.20 \pm 1.96 \times 0.0727$, or the interval from $-0.34$ to $-0.06$.

## 3. THE RATIO OF TWO PROBABILITIES

### 3.1 The Rate Ratio

The ratio of two probabilities, $RR = \Pi_1/\Pi_2$, is another popular measure of the effect of an intervention. Its use requires that one be able to distinguish between the two outcomes so that one is in some sense undesirable and the other is in some sense preferred. The names given to this measure in the health sciences, the *risk* ratio or relative *risk,* reflect the fact that the measure is not symmetric (i.e., $\Pi_1/\Pi_2 \neq (1-\Pi_1)/(1-\Pi_2)$), but is the ratio of the first group's probability of an undesirable outcome to the second's probability. $RR$ is a natural measure of effect for those investigators who are accustomed to comparing two probabilities in terms of their proportionate difference. If $\Pi_1$ is the probability of an untoward outcome in the experimental group and if $\Pi_2$ is the same in the control or comparison group, the proportionate reduction in the likelihood of such an outcome is

$$\frac{\Pi_2 - \Pi_1}{\Pi_2} = 1 - RR. \quad (17\text{-}6)$$

Inferences about a proportionate reduction may therefore be based on inferences about the associated relative risk.

### 3.2 Inferences about the Rate Ratio

The estimator of $RR$ is simply

$$rr = P_1/P_2.$$

The range of variation of $rr$ is an inconvenient one for drawing inferences. Only the finite interval from 0 to 1 is available for indexing a lower risk in population 1, but the infinite interval from 1 up is, theoretically, available for indexing a higher risk in population 1. A corollary is that the value 1 (rather than the more familiar and convenient value 0) indexes no differential risk. It is standard practice to undo these inconveniences by carrying out one's statistical analysis on the logarithms of the rate ratios and transforming point and interval estimates back to the original units by taking antilogarithms of the results. An important by-product is that the sampling distribution of the logarithm of $rr$ is more nearly normal than the sampling distribution of $rr$.

The large-sample standard error of $\ln(rr)$, the natural logarithm of $rr$, may be estimated as

$$SE = \left(\frac{1-P_1}{n_1 P_1} + \frac{1-P_2}{n_2 P_2}\right)^{1/2}. \tag{17-7}$$

An approximate two-sided $100(1-\alpha)$ percent confidence interval for $RR$ is obtained by taking the antilogarithms of the limits

$$\ln(rr) - C_{\alpha/2} \cdot SE \tag{17-8}$$

and

$$\ln(rr) + C_{\alpha/2} \cdot SE. \tag{17-9}$$

Consider again the numerical example in section 2.3: $n_1 = 80$, $P_1 = 0.60$; $n_2 = 70$ and $P_2 = 0.80$. The estimated rate ratio is $rr = 0.60/0.80 = 0.75$, so group 1 is estimated to be at a risk that is 25 percent less than group 2's risk. Suppose that a confidence interval for $RR$ is desired. One first obtains the value $\ln(rr) = -0.2877$ and then obtains the value of its estimated standard error,

$$SE = \left(\frac{0.40}{80 \times 0.60} + \frac{0.20}{70 \times 0.80}\right)^{1/2} = 0.0119^{1/2} = 0.1091$$

(the associated weighting factor is $w = 1/SE^2 = 84.0$). An approximate 95 percent confidence interval for $\ln(RR)$ has as its lower limit

$$\ln(RR_L) = -0.2877 - 1.96 \times 0.1091 = -0.5015$$

and as its upper limit

$$\ln(RR_U) = -0.2877 + 1.96 \times 0.1091 = -0.0739.$$

The resulting interval for $RR$ extends from $RR_L = \exp(-0.5015) = 0.61$ to $RR_U = \exp(-0.0739) = 0.93$. The corresponding interval for the proportionate reduction in risk, finally, extends from $1 - RR_U = 0.07$ to $1 - RR_L = $ 0.39, or from 7 to 39 percent. Notice that the confidence interval is not symmetric about the point estimate of 25 percent.

## 3.3 Problems with the Rate Ratio

Thanks to its connection with the intuitively appealing proportionate reduction in the probability of an undesirable response, the rate ratio continues to be a popular measure of the effect of an intervention in controlled studies. It is also a popular and understandable measure of association in nonexperimental studies. There are at least two technical problems with this measure, however. If the chances are good, in the two groups being compared (experimental treatment versus control or exposed versus not exposed), that a subject will experience the outcome under study, many values of the rate ratio are mathematically impossible. For example, if the probability $\Pi_2$ in the comparison group is equal to 0.40, only values for $RR$ in the interval $0 \leq RR \leq 2.5$ are possible. The possibility therefore exists that the appearance of study-to-study heterogeneity will emerge in the value of $RR$ only because the studies differ in their values of $\Pi_2$. As we will see in section 5, this kind of constraint does not characterize the odds ratio, a measure related to the rate ratio.

A second difficulty with $RR$, one that is especially important in epidemiological studies, is that it is not estimable from data collected in retrospective studies. Let $E$ and $\overline{E}$ denote exposure or not to the risk factor under study, and let $D$ and $\overline{D}$ denote the development or not of the disease under study. The rate ratio may then be expressed as the ratio of the two conditional probabilities of developing disease,

$$RR = \frac{P(D|E)}{P(D|\overline{E})}.$$

Studies that rely on random, cross-sectional sampling from the entire population and those that rely on separate random samples from the exposed and unexposed populations permit $P(D|E)$ and $P(D|\overline{E})$, and thus $RR$, to be estimated. In a retrospective study, subjects who have developed the disease under investigation as well as subjects who have not are evaluated with respect to whether or not they had been exposed to the putative risk factor. Such a study permits $P(E|D)$ and $P(E|\overline{D})$ to be estimated, but these two probabilities are not sufficient to estimate $RR$. We will see in section 5 that, unlike $RR$, the odds ratio is estimable from all three kinds of studies.

## 4. THE PHI COEFFICIENT

### 4.1 Inference about $\varphi$

Consider a series of cross-sectional studies in each of which the correlation coefficient between a pair of binary random variables, $X$ and $Y$, is the measure of interest. Table 17.2 presents notation for the underlying parameters and Table 17.3 presents notation for the observed frequencies in the 2 x 2 table cross-classifying subjects' categories on the two variables. Let the two levels of $X$ be coded numerically as 0 or 1, and let the same be done for $Y$. The product moment correlation coefficient in the population between the two numerically coded variables is equal to

$$\varphi = \frac{\Pi_{11}\Pi_{22} - \Pi_{12}\Pi_{21}}{\sqrt{\Pi_{1.}\Pi_{2.} \cdot \Pi_{.1}\Pi_{.2}}}, \qquad (17\text{-}10)$$

and its maximum likelihood estimator (assuming random, cross-sectional sampling) is equal to

$$\hat{\varphi} = \frac{n_{11}n_{22} - n_{12}n_{21}}{\sqrt{n_{1.}n_{2.}n_{.1}n_{.2}}}. \qquad (17\text{-}11)$$

Note that $\hat{\varphi}$ is closely related to the classical chi-square statistic for testing for association in a fourfold table: $\chi^2 = n_{..}\hat{\varphi}^2$. If numerical values other than 0 or 1 are

#### Table 17.2 Underlying Probabilities Associated with Two Binary Characteristics

| X | Y | | Total |
|---|---|---|---|
| | Positive | Negative | |
| Positive | $\Pi_{11}$ | $\Pi_{12}$ | $\Pi_{1.}$ |
| Negative | $\Pi_{21}$ | $\Pi_{22}$ | $\Pi_{2.}$ |
| Total | $\Pi_{.1}$ | $\Pi_{.2}$ | 1 |

#### Table 17.3 Observed Frequencies in a Study Cross-Classifying Subjects on Two Binary Characteristics

| X | Y | | Total |
|---|---|---|---|
| | Positive | Negative | |
| Positive | $n_{11}$ | $n_{12}$ | $n_{1.}$ |
| Negative | $n_{21}$ | $n_{22}$ | $n_{2.}$ |
| Total | $n_{.1}$ | $n_{.2}$ | $n_{..}$ |

#### Table 17.4 Hypothetical Frequencies in a Fourfold Table

| X | Y | | Total |
|---|---|---|---|
| | Positive | Negative | |
| Positive | 135 | 15 | 150 |
| Negative | 40 | 10 | 50 |
| Total | 175 | 25 | 200 |

assigned to the categories of $X$ or $Y$, the sign of $\hat{\varphi}$ may change but not its absolute value.

The value of $\hat{\varphi}$ for the frequencies in Table 17.4 is

$$\hat{\varphi} = \frac{135 \times 10 - 15 \times 40}{\sqrt{150 \times 50 \times 175 \times 25}} = 0.130931,$$

a modest association. Bishop, Fienberg, and Holland (1975, pp. 381–382) ascribe the following formula for the large-sample standard error of $\hat{\varphi}$ to Yule:

$$SE = \frac{1}{\sqrt{n_{..}}} \left( 1 - \hat{\varphi}^2 + \hat{\varphi}(1 + \frac{\hat{\varphi}^2}{2}) \frac{(p_{1.} - p_{2.})(p_{.1} - p_{.2})}{\sqrt{p_{1.}p_{.1}p_{2.}p_{.2}}} \right.$$
$$\left. - \frac{3}{4} \hat{\varphi}^2 \left[ \frac{(p_{1.} - p_{2.})^2}{p_{1.}p_{2.}} + \frac{(p_{.1} - p_{.2})^2}{p_{.1}p_{.2}} \right] \right)^{1/2}. \qquad (17\text{-}12)$$

For the data under analysis,

$$SE = \frac{1}{\sqrt{200}} (1.245388)^{1/2} = 0.079. \qquad (17\text{-}13)$$

### 4.2 The Jackknife

A straightforward large-sample procedure known as the jackknife (Quenouille 1956; Tukey 1958) provides an excellent approximation to the standard error of $\hat{\varphi}$ (as well as the standard errors of other functions of frequencies; Fleiss & Davies 1982) without the necessity for memorizing or programming a formula as complicated as the one in expression (17-12).

Suppose, in general, that one has classified a random sample of $n$ experimental or study units into $k$ mutually exclusive and exhaustive categories, and that the numbers of units assigned to the respective categories are $n_1, \ldots, n_k$, with $\Sigma n_i = n$. Consider some function $\hat{F} = \hat{F}(n_1, \ldots, n_k)$ of these multinomial frequencies that is to serve as an estimator of a parameter $F$, but suppose that $\hat{F}$ is such that its expected value is equal to $F$ plus a term of order $1/n$. The jackknifed estimator, obtained

**Table 17.5 Jackknifing the Phi Coefficient for the Frequencies in Table 17.4**

| Category | Frequency | $\hat{\varphi}_{-i}$ |
|----------|-----------|----------------------|
| + + | 135 | 0.129990 |
| + − | 15 | 0.141229 |
| − + | 40 | 0.135292 |
| − − | 10 | 0.110690 |

by applying the following algorithm, will, for virtually all functions $\hat{F}$ used in practice, have an expected value equal to $F$ plus a term of order $1/n^2$, and will thus be less biased.

Define $\hat{F}_{-i}$ to be the value of the estimator when one unit is deleted from category $i$—so that $\hat{F}_{-1} = \hat{F}(n_1 - 1, n_2, \ldots, n_k)$, $\hat{F}_{-2} = \hat{F}(n_1, n_2 - 1, \ldots, n_k)$, etc.—and define

$$\hat{F}_{(-)} = \Sigma n_i \hat{F}_{-i}/n. \quad (17\text{-}14)$$

The jackknifed estimator of $F$, denoted $\bar{F}$, is then given by

$$\bar{F} = n\hat{F} - (n-1)\hat{F}_{(-)}, \quad (17\text{-}15)$$

and the jackknifed estimator of the variance of $\bar{F}$ is given by

$$\text{Var}(\bar{F}) = \frac{n-1}{n} \Sigma n_i(\hat{F}_{-i} - \hat{F}_{(-)})^2. \quad (17\text{-}16)$$

$\text{Var}(\bar{F})$ also provides a good approximation to the variance of $\hat{F}$.

The arithmetic required to apply the jackknife to the frequencies in Table 17.4 is shown in Table 17.5. The value of $\hat{\varphi}_{(-)}$ is

$$\hat{\varphi}_{(-)} = \frac{1}{200}(135 \times 0.129990 + \ldots$$
$$+ 10 \times 0.110690) = 0.130928,$$

and thus the jackknifed estimate of $\varphi$ is, by (17-15),

$$\bar{\varphi} = 200 \times 0.130931 - 199 \times 0.130928 = 0.131463.$$

The jackknifed estimate is only slightly larger than the maximum likelihood estimate of 0.130931. By (17-16), the jackknifed estimate of the variance of $\bar{\varphi}$ is

$$\text{Var}(\bar{\varphi}) = \frac{199}{200}(135 \times (0.129990 - 0.130928)^2 + \ldots$$
$$+ 10 \times (0.110690 - 0.130928)^2) = 0.006535,$$

and the jackknifed estimate of the standard error is

$$SE(\bar{\varphi}) = 0.081,$$

trivially larger than the value in (17-13) obtained using classical large-sample methods.

### 4.3 Problems with the Phi Coefficient

A number of theoretical problems with the phi coefficient limit its usefulness as a measure of association between two random variables. If the binary random variables $X$ and $Y$ result from dichotomizing one or both of a pair of continuous random variables, the value of $\varphi$ depends strongly on where the cut points are set (Carroll 1961). A second problem is that two studies with populations having different marginal distributions (e.g., $\Pi_1$. for one study different from $\Pi_1$. for another) but otherwise identical conditional probability structures (e.g., equal values of $\Pi_{11}/\Pi_1$. in the two study populations) may have strongly unequal phi coefficients. An untoward consequence of this phenomenon is that there will be the appearance of study-to-study heterogeneity (i.e., unequal correlations across studies), even though the associations defined in terms of the conditional probabilities are identical.

Finally, the phi coefficient shares with other correlation coefficients the characteristic that it is an invalid measure of association when a method of sampling other than cross-sectional (multinomial and simple random sampling are synonyms) is used. The two fourfold tables in Table 17.6 (plus the original one in Table 17.4) illustrate this problem as well as the previous one. The

**Table 17.6 Hypothetical Fourfold Tables Illustrating Problems with the Phi Coefficient**

| **Second Study** | | | |
|------------------|----------|----------|-------|
| | | $Y$ | |
| $X$ | Positive | Negative | Total |
| Positive | 45 | 5 | 50 |
| Negative | 120 | 30 | 150 |
| Total | 165 | 35 | 200 |
| **Third Study** | | | |
| Positive | 90 | 10 | 100 |
| Negative | 80 | 20 | 100 |
| Total | 170 | 30 | 200 |

NOTE: Data for the original study are in Table 17.4.

associations are identical in the three tables in the sense that the estimated conditional probabilities that $Y$ is positive, given that $X$ is positive, are all equal to 0.90, and the estimated conditional probabilities that $Y$ is positive, given that $X$ is negative, are all equal to 0.80. If these tables summarized the results of three studies in which the numbers of subjects positive on $X$ and negative on $X$ were sampled in the ratio 150:50 in the first study, 50:150 in the second, and 100:100 in the third, the problem becomes apparent when the three phi coefficients are calculated. Unlike the other three measures of association studied in this chapter, the values of $\hat{\varphi}$ vary across the three studies, from 0.13 to 0.11 to 0.14. The important conclusion is not that the values of $\hat{\varphi}$ are nearly equal one to another, but that the values are not identical.

The reader is referred to Bishop, Fienberg, and Holland (1975, pp. 380–383) for further discussion of the phi coefficient.

## 5. THE ODDS RATIO

### 5.1 Introduction

We have seen that the phi coefficient is estimable only from data collected in a cross-sectional study and that the simple difference and the rate ratio are estimable only from data collected using a cross-sectional or prospective study. The odds ratio, however, is estimable from data collected using any of the three major study designs: cross-sectional, prospective, or retrospective. Consider a bivariate population with underlying multinomial probabilities given in Table 17.2. The odds ratio (sometimes referred to as the cross-product ratio) associating $X$ and $Y$ is equal to

$$\omega = \frac{\Pi_{11}\Pi_{22}}{\Pi_{12}\Pi_{21}} . \tag{17-17}$$

If the observed multinomial frequencies are as displayed in Table 17.3, the maximum likelihood estimator of $\omega$ is

$$o = \frac{n_{11}n_{22}}{n_{12}n_{21}} . \tag{17-18}$$

Suppose that the study design calls for $n_{1.}$ units to be sampled from the population positive on $X$, and for $n_{2.}$ units to be sampled from the population negative on $X$. Then $P(Y+|X+)$, the conditional probability that $Y$ is positive given that $X$ is positive, is equal to $\Pi_{11}/\Pi_{1.}$,

and the *odds* for $Y$ being positive, conditional on $X$ being positive, are equal to

$$\text{Odds } (Y+|X+) = P(Y+|X+)/P(Y-|X+)$$
$$= (\Pi_{11}/\Pi_{1.})/(\Pi_{12}/\Pi_{1.}) = \Pi_{11}/\Pi_{12}.$$

Similarly,

$$\text{Odds } (Y+|X-) = P(Y+|X-)/P(Y-|X-)$$
$$= (\Pi_{21}/\Pi_{2.})/(\Pi_{22}/\Pi_{2.}) = \Pi_{21}/\Pi_{22}.$$

The *odds ratio* is simply the ratio of these two odds values (see equation 17-3),

$$\omega = \frac{\text{Odds } (Y+|X+)}{\text{Odds } (Y+|X-)} = \frac{\Pi_{11}/\Pi_{12}}{\Pi_{21}/\Pi_{22}} = \frac{\Pi_{11}\Pi_{22}}{\Pi_{12}\Pi_{21}} . \tag{17-19}$$

The odds ratio is therefore estimable from a study in which prespecified numbers of units positive on $X$ and negative on $X$ are selected for a determination of their status on $Y$.

A similar analysis shows that the same is true for the odds ratio associated with a study in which prespecified numbers of units positive on $Y$ and negative on $Y$ are selected for a determination of their status on $X$. Because the latter two study designs correspond to prospective and retrospective sampling, it is clear that the odds ratio is estimable using data from either of these two designs (as well as from a cross-sectional study). Other properties of the odds ratio are discussed in the final subsection of this section.

Unlike the meanings of the measures $\Delta$ and $RR$, the meaning of the odds ratio is not intuitively clear—perhaps because the odds value itself is not. Consider, for example, the quantity

$$\text{Odds } (Y+|X+) = \Pi_{11}/\Pi_{12}.$$

The odds value is thus the ratio, in the population of individuals who are positive on $X$, of the proportion who are positive on $Y$ to the proportion who are negative. Given the identities

$$P(Y+|X+) = \text{Odds } (Y+|X+)/(1+\text{Odds } (Y+|X+))$$

and the complementary

$$\text{Odds } (Y+|X+) = P(Y+/X+)/(1-P(Y+|X+)),$$

it is clear that the information present in Odds $(Y+|X+)$ is identical to the information present in $P(Y+|X+)$. Nevertheless, the impact of "for every 100 subjects negative on $Y$ (all of whom are positive on $X$), $100 \times \text{Odds}$ $(Y+|X+)$ is the number expected to be positive on $Y$" may be very different from the impact of "for every

100 subjects (all of whom are positive on $X$), $100 \times P(Y+|X+)$ is the number expected to be positive on $Y$.'' Once the reader develops an intuitive understanding of an odds value, it will quickly become obvious that two odds values are naturally contrasted by means of their ratio—the odds ratio.

The functional form of the maximum likelihood estimator of $\omega$ is the same for each study design; see equation (17-18). Remarkably, the function form of the estimated standard error is also the same for each study design. For reasons similar to those given in section 3.2, it is customary to perform one's statistical analyses on $\ln(o)$, the natural logarithm of the sample odds ratio, rather than on $o$ directly. (Sato 1990, however, obtained a valid confidence interval for the population odds ratio without transforming to logarithms.) The large-sample standard error of $\ln(o)$ (see Woolf 1955) is given by the equation

$$SE = \left( \frac{1}{n_{11}} + \frac{1}{n_{12}} + \frac{1}{n_{21}} + \frac{1}{n_{22}} \right)^{1/2} \quad (17\text{-}20)$$

for each of the study designs considered here.

### 5.2 A Single Fourfold Table

For data arrayed as in Table 17.3, equations (17-18) and (17-20) provide the point estimate of the odds ratio and the estimated standard error of its logarithm. To reduce the bias caused by one or more small cell frequencies (note that neither $\ln(o)$ nor $SE$ is defined when a cell frequency is equal to zero), it is good practice to add 0.5 to each cell frequency before proceeding with the analysis (Gart & Zweifel 1967). For the frequencies in Table 17.4, the values of the several statistics calculated with (vs. without) the adjustment factor are $o = 2.2500$ (versus 2.2664), $\ln(o) = 0.81$ (versus 0.82), and $SE = 0.4462$ (vs. 0.4380). The effect of adjustment is obviously minor in this example.

### 5.3 An Alternative Analysis: $(O - E)/V$

In their meta-analysis of randomized clinical trials of a class of drugs known as beta blockers, Yusuf et al. (1985) used an approach that has become popular in the health sciences. It may be applied to a single fourfold table as well as to several tables (such as in a study incorporating stratification). Consider the generic table displayed in Table 17.3 and select for analysis any of its four cells (the upper left-hand cell is traditionally the

one analyzed). The observed frequency in the selected cell is

$$O = n_{11}, \quad (17\text{-}21)$$

the expected frequency in that cell, under the null hypothesis that $X$ and $Y$ are independent and conditional on the marginal frequencies being held fixed, is

$$E = \frac{n_1 . n_{.1}}{n_{..}}, \quad (17\text{-}22)$$

and the exact hypergeometric variance of $n_{11}$, under the same restrictions as above, is

$$V = \frac{n_1 . n_2 . n_{.1} n_{.2}}{n_{..}^2 (n_{..} - 1)}. \quad (17\text{-}23)$$

When $\omega$ is close to unity, a good estimator of $\ln(\omega)$ is

$$L = \frac{O - E}{V}, \quad (17\text{-}24)$$

with an estimated standard error of

$$SE = 1/\sqrt{V}. \quad (17\text{-}25)$$

For the frequencies in Table 17.4,

$$L = \frac{135 - 131.25}{4.1222} = 0.9097$$

(which corresponds to an estimated odds ratio of exp $(0.9097) = 2.48$), with an estimated standard error of

$$SE = 1/\sqrt{4.1222} = 0.49.$$

In this example, what has become known in the health sciences as "the Peto method" or as "the $(O - E)/V$ method" produces overestimates of the point estimate and its standard error.

The method is capable of producing underestimates as well as overestimates of the underlying parameter. For the frequencies from the two studies summarized in Table 17.6, the respective values of $L$ are 0.6892 (yielding 1.99 as the estimated odds ratio) and 0.7804 (yielding 2.18 as the estimated odds ratio). The latter estimate, coming from a study in which one of the two sets of marginal frequencies was uniform, comes closest of all (for the frequencies in Tables 17.4 and 17.6) to the correct value of 2.25. Greenland and Salvan (1990) showed that the $(O - E)/V$ method may yield biased results when there is serious imbalance on both margins. Furthermore, they showed that the method may yield biased results when the underlying odds ratio is large, even when there is balance on both margins. Earlier, Mantel, Brown, and Byar (1977) and Fleiss (1981, pp. 178–180) pointed out flaws in a measure of association identical to $(O - E)/V$, the *standardized difference*.

Given the simplicity and theoretical superiority of the more traditional methods described in section 5, there is no compelling reason for the $(O - E)/V$ method to be employed.

## 5.4 Inference in the Presence of Covariates

Covariates (i.e., variables predictive of the outcome measure) are frequently incorporated into the analysis. In randomized intervention studies, they are adjusted for in order to improve the precision with which key parameters are estimated and to increase the power of significance tests. In nonrandomized studies, they are adjusted for in order to eliminate the bias caused by confounding—that is, the presence of characteristics associated with both the exposure variable and the outcome variable. There are three major classes of methods for controlling for the effects of covariates: regression adjustment, stratification, and matching. Each will be considered.

**5.4.1 Control by regression analysis** Let $Y$ represent the binary response variable under study ($Y = 1$ when the response is positive and $Y = 0$ when it is negative), let $X$ represent the binary exposure variable ($X = 1$ when the study unit was exposed and $X = 0$ when it was not), and let $Z_1, \ldots, Z_p$ represent the values of $p$ covariates. A popular statistical model for representing the conditional probability of a positive response as a function of $X$ and the $Z$'s is the *linear logistic regression model*,

$$\Pi = P(Y = 1 | X, Z_1, \ldots, Z_p)$$

$$= \frac{1}{1 + e^{-(\alpha + \beta X + \gamma_1 Z_1 + \ldots + \gamma_p Z_p)}} . \quad (17\text{-}26)$$

This model is such that the *logit* or *log odds* of $\Pi$,

$$\text{logit } (\Pi) = \ln \frac{\Pi}{1 - \Pi} , \quad (17\text{-}27)$$

is linear in the independent variables:

$$\text{logit } (\Pi) = \alpha + \beta X + \gamma_1 Z_1 + \ldots + \gamma_p Z_p \quad (17\text{-}28)$$

(see Hosmer & Lemeshow 1989 for a thorough review of logistic regression analysis).

The coefficient $\beta$ is the difference between the log odds for the population coded $X = 1$ and the log odds for the population coded $X = 0$, adjusting for the effects of the $p$ covariates (i.e., $\beta$ is the logarithm of the adjusted odds ratio). The antilogarithm, exp $(\beta)$, is therefore the odds ratio associating $X$ with $Y$. Every major package of computer programs has a program for carrying out a linear logistic regression analysis using maximum likelihood methods. The program produces $\hat{\beta}$, the maximum likelihood estimate of the adjusted log odds ratio, and $SE$, the standard error of $\hat{\beta}$. Inferences about the odds ratio itself may be drawn in the usual ways.

**5.4.2 Control by stratification: The Mantel-Haenszel estimator** When the $p$ covariates are categorical (e.g., sex, social class, and ethnicity), or are numerical but may be partitioned into a set of convenient and

**Table 17.7 Stratified Comparison of Two Treatments**

| | Treatment | Outcome Success | Failure | Total |
|---|---|---|---|---|
| **Stratum 1** | Experimental | 4 | 0 | 4 |
| | Control | 0 | 1 | 1 |
| | Total | 4 | 1 | 5 |
| **Stratum 2** | Experimental | 7 | 4 | 11 |
| | Control | 3 | 8 | 11 |
| | Total | 10 | 12 | 22 |
| **Stratum 3** | Experimental | 1 | 0 | 1 |
| | Control | 4 | 9 | 13 |
| | Total | 5 | 9 | 14 |

familiar categories (e.g., ages 20–34, 35–49, and 50–64), their effects may be controlled for by stratification. Each subject is assigned to the stratum defined by his or her combination of categories on the $p$ prespecified covariates, and, within each stratum, a fourfold table is constructed cross-classifying subjects by their values on $X$ and $Y$. If $c_1, c_2, \ldots, c_p$ are the numbers of categories for the $p$ covariates, the total number of strata is, say, $S = c_1.c_2 \ldots c_p$. Let the frequencies within the fourfold table for stratum $s$ be denoted by the superscript $(s)$, so that $n_{ij}^{(s)}$ represents a typical frequency in that table.

The frequencies in Table 17.7 are adapted from a comparative study reported by Armitage (1971, p. 266). The associated relative frequencies are tabulated in Table 17.8. Within each of the $S = 3$ strata, the success rate for the subjects in the experimental group is greater than the success rate for those in the control group. Two algebraically identical formulas for the summary odds ratio proposed by Mantel and Haenszel (1959) are popular. One is a function of the frequencies,

$$o_{MH} = \frac{\sum_{s=1}^{S} n_{11}^{(s)} n_{22}^{(s)} / n_{..}^{(s)}}{\sum_{s=1}^{S} n_{12}^{(s)} n_{21}^{(s)} / n_{..}^{(s)}}, \qquad (17\text{-}29)$$

and the other is a function of the relative frequencies,

$$o_{MH} = \frac{\sum_{s=1}^{S} W^{(s)} p_1^{(s)} (1 - p_2)^{(s)}}{\sum_{s=1}^{S} W^{(s)} p_2^{(s)} (1 - p_1)^{(s)}}, \qquad (17\text{-}30)$$

where

$$W^{(s)} = \frac{n_1.^{(s)} n_2.^{(s)}}{n_{..}^{(s)}}. \qquad (17\text{-}31)$$

By either formula, the value of the Mantel-Haenszel odds ratio is

$$o_{MH} = 7.31.$$

Robins, Breslow, and Greenland (1986) (see also Robins, Greenland, & Breslow 1986) derived the non-null standard error of $\ln(o_{MH})$. Its formula is

$$SE = \frac{1}{\sum A^{(s)} \sqrt{2}} \Big( \sum A^{(s)} B^{(s)} + \qquad (17\text{-}32)$$
$$o_{MH} \sum (B^{(s)} C^{(s)} + A^{(s)} D^{(s)}) + o^2_{MH} \sum C^{(s)} D^{(s)} \Big)^{1/2},$$

where

$$A^{(s)} = \frac{n_{11}^{(s)} n_{22}^{(s)}}{n_{..}^{(s)}}, \qquad (17\text{-}33)$$

$$B^{(s)} = \frac{1}{n_{..}^{(s)}} (n_{11}^{(s)} + n_{22}^{(s)}), \qquad (17\text{-}34)$$

$$C^{(s)} = \frac{n_{12}^{(s)} n_{21}^{(s)}}{n_{..}^{(s)}}, \qquad (17\text{-}35)$$

and

$$D^{(s)} = \frac{1}{n_{..}^{(s)}} (n_{12}^{(s)} + n_{21}^{(s)}). \qquad (17\text{-}36)$$

For the data under analysis (see Tables 17.8 and 17.9),

$$\sum A^{(s)} = 3.9884,$$
$$\sum C^{(s)} = 0.5455,$$
$$\sum A^{(s)} B^{(s)} = 2.9947,$$
$$\sum B^{(s)} C^{(s)} = 0.3719,$$
$$\sum A^{(s)} D^{(s)} = 0.9937,$$

and

$$\sum C^{(s)} D^{(s)} = 0.1736.$$

**Table 17.8 Relative Frequencies for the Stratified Comparison of Two Treatments**

| | Treatment 1 | | Treatment 2 | |
|---|---|---|---|---|
| Stratum | Sample Size $(n_1^{(s)})$ | Success Rate $(p_1^{(s)})$ | Sample Size $(n_2^{(s)})$ | Success Rate $(p_2^{(s)})$ |
| 1 | 4 | 1.0000 | 1 | 0.0000 |
| 2 | 11 | 0.6364 | 11 | 0.2727 |
| 3 | 1 | 1.0000 | 13 | 0.3077 |

**Table 17.9 Quantities Needed for the Calculation of the Standard Error of ln ($o_{MH}$) for the Values in Table 17.8**

| Stratum | $A^{(s)}$ | $B^{(s)}$ | $C^{(s)}$ | $D^{(s)}$ |
|---------|-----------|-----------|-----------|-----------|
| 1 | 0.8000 | 1.0000 | 0 | 0 |
| 2 | 2.5455 | 0.6818 | 0.5455 | 0.3182 |
| 3 | 0.6429 | 0.7143 | 0 | 0.2857 |

With $o_{MH} = \Sigma A^{(s)} / \Sigma C^{(s)} = 7.3115$,

$$SE = \frac{1}{3.9884\sqrt{2}}(2.9947 + 7.3115(0.3719 + 0.9937)$$
$$+ 7.3115^2 \times 0.1736)^{1/2} = 0.8365,$$

and the weighting factor for a fixed effects meta-analysis is $w = 1/0.8365^2 = 1.4291$. An approximate 95 percent confidence interval for $\ln(\omega)$ is

$$\ln(7.3115) \pm 1.96 \times 0.8365,$$

or the interval from 0.35 to 3.63. The corresponding interval for $\omega$ extends from 1.42 to 37.7.

Note that $o_{MH}$ is actually a weighted average of the $S$ stratum-specific odds ratios. Within stratum $s$, the odds ratio is equal to

$$o_s = \frac{n_{11}^{(s)} n_{22}^{(s)}}{n_{12}^{(s)} n_{21}^{(s)}}.$$

Define the multiplicative weight for $o_s$ to be

$$W_s = \frac{n_{12}^{(s)} n_{21}^{(s)}}{n_{..}^{(s)}}.$$

Then

$$o_{MH} = \frac{\Sigma W_s o_s}{\Sigma W_s}. \tag{17-37}$$

**5.4.3 Control by stratification: Combining log odds ratios** The pooling of log odds ratios across the $S$ strata is a widely used alternative to the Mantel-Haenszel method of pooling. Define

$$L_s = \ln \frac{(n_{11}^{(s)} + 0.5)(n_{22}^{(s)} + 0.5)}{(n_{12}^{(s)} + 0.5)(n_{21}^{(s)} + 0.5)} \tag{17-38}$$

and

$$W_s^* = \left(\Sigma\Sigma \frac{1}{n_{ij}^{(s)} + 0.5}\right)^{-1}. \tag{17-39}$$

The pooled log odds ratio is equal to

$$\bar{L}_\bullet = \frac{\Sigma W_s^* L_s}{\Sigma W_s^*}, \tag{17-40}$$

with a standard error of

$$SE = \frac{1}{(\Sigma W_s^*)^{1/2}}. \tag{17-41}$$

For a fixed effects meta-analysis, the weighting factor associated with $\bar{L}_\bullet$ is, as usual, the squared reciprocal of $SE$.

The reader will note, for the frequencies in Table 17.7, that the additive adjustment factor of 0.5 must be applied in order for the log odds ratios and their standard errors to be calculable in strata 1 and 3. Summary values appear in Table 17.10. They yield a point estimate for the log odds ratio of

$$\bar{L}_\bullet = 3.1326/1.8560 = 1.6878,$$

and a point estimate for the odds ratio of

$$o_L = \exp(1.6878) = 5.41.$$

This estimate is appreciably less than the Mantel-Haenszel estimate of $o_{MH} = 7.31$. As all sample sizes increase, the two estimates converge to the same value.

The estimated standard error of $\bar{L}_\bullet$ is equal to

$$SE = \left(\frac{1}{1.8560}\right)^{1/2} = 0.7340,$$

and the corresponding weighting factor is equal to $w_L = 1.8560$. The (grossly) approximate 95 percent confidence interval for $\omega$ derived from these values extends from 1.28 to 22.8.

**5.4.4 Control by stratification: A comparison of the two methods** When the cell frequencies within the $S$ strata are all large, the Mantel-Haenszel estimate will be close in value to the estimate obtained by pooling

**Table 17.10 Quantities Needed to Calculate the Pooled Log Odds Ratio for the Frequencies in Table 17.7**

| Stratum | $L_s$ | $SE_s$ | $L_s/SE_s^2$ | $1/SE_s^2$ |
|---------|-------|--------|--------------|------------|
| 1 | 3.2958 | 2.2111 | 0.6741 | 0.2045 |
| 2 | 1.3981 | 0.8712 | 1.8421 | 1.3175 |
| 3 | 1.8458 | 1.7304 | 0.6164 | 0.3340 |
| Total | | | 3.1326 | 1.8560 |

the log odds ratios (see Fleiss 1981, pp. 168 and 173), and either method may be used. As seen in the preceding subsection, close agreement may not be the case when some of the cell frequencies are small. In such a circumstance, the Mantel-Haenszel estimator is superior to the log odds ratio estimator (Hauck 1989). Note that there is no need to add 0.5 (or any other constant) to a cell frequency of zero in order for a stratum's frequencies to contribute to the Mantel-Haenszel estimator. In fact, it would be incorrect to add any constant to the cell frequencies when applying the Mantel-Haenszel method. The method must be applied to the $n_{ij}^{(s)}$ values directly.

Others have compared competing estimators of the odds ratio in the case of a stratified study (Agresti 1990, pp. 235–237; Gart 1970; Kleinbaum, Kupper & Morgenstern 1982, pp. 350–351; McKinlay 1975). The consensus is that the Mantel-Haenszel procedure is, uniformly, the method of choice.

**5.4.5 Control by matching** Matching, the third and final technique considered for controlling for the effects of covariates, calls for the creation of sets of subjects similar to one another on the covariates. Unlike stratification, in which the total number of strata, $S$, is specifiable in advance of collecting one's sample, with matching one generally cannot anticipate the number of matched sets one will end up with. Consider a study with $p = 2$ covariates, sex and age, and suppose that the investigators desire close matching on age—say, ages no more than one year apart. If the first subject enrolled in the study is, for example, a 12-year-old male, then the next male aged between 11 and 13, whether from group 1 or group 2, will be matched to the first subject. If one or more later subjects are also males within this age span, they should be added to the matched set that was already constituted and should not form the bases for new sets. If $M$ represents the total number of matched sets, and if the frequencies within set $m$ are represented as in Table 17.11, all that is required for the inclusion

of this set in the analysis is that $t_{m1} \geq 1$ and $t_{m2} \geq 1$. The values $t_{m1} = t_{m2} = 1$ for all $m$ correspond to pairwise matching, and the values $t_{m1} = 1$ and $t_{m2} = r$ for all $m$ correspond to $r$:1 matching. Here, such convenient balance is not necessarily assumed. The reader is referred to Kleinbaum, Kupper, and Morgenstern (1982, Chapter 18) for a discussion of matching as a strategy in study design.

The Mantel-Haenszel estimator of the odds ratio is given by the adaptation of the equation in formula (17-29) to the notation in Table 17.11:

$$o_{\text{MH,matched}} = \frac{\Sigma a_m d_m / t_m.}{\Sigma b_m c_m / t_m.} . \tag{17-42}$$

Breslow (1981), Connett et al. (1982), Fleiss (1984), Robins, Breslow, and Greenland (1986), and Robins, Greenland, and Breslow (1986) have all derived estimators of the standard error of $\ln(o_{\text{MH,matched}})$ in the case of matched sets. Remarkably, the formula in expression (7-32), with the appropriate changes in notation, applies to the case of matched sets as well as to the case of stratified samples. That is, with

$$U_m = (a_m d_m) / t_m., \tag{17-43}$$

$$V_m = (a_m + d_m) / t_m., \tag{17-44}$$

$$W_m = (b_m c_m) / t_m., \tag{17-45}$$

**Table 17.11 Notation for Observed Frequencies Within a Typical Matched Set**

| Group | Outcome Characteristic | | Total |
|-------|--------|--------|-------|
| | Positive | Negative | |
| 1 | $a_m$ | $b_m$ | $t_{m1}$ |
| 2 | $c_m$ | $d_m$ | $t_{m2}$ |
| Total | $a_m + c_m$ | $b_m + d_m$ | $t_m.$ |

and

$$X_m = (b_m + c_m)/t_{m.}, \qquad (17\text{-}46)$$

the estimated standard error of $\ln(o_{\text{MH,matched}})$ (see Robins, Breslow & Greenland 1986), and identical to the formula in (17-32), is

$$SE = \frac{1}{\Sigma U_m \sqrt{2}} (\Sigma U_m V_m +$$
$$o_{\text{MH,matched}} \Sigma (V_m W_m + U_m X_m) + o^2_{\text{MH,matched}} \Sigma W_m X_m)^{1/2}. \qquad (17\text{-}47)$$

The frequencies in Table 17.12 have been analyzed by Mack et al. (1976), Breslow and Day (1980, pp. 176–182), and Fleiss (1984). For example, there were nine matched sets consisting of one exposed case, no unexposed cases, three exposed controls, and one unexposed control. For the frequencies in the table,

$$\Sigma U_m = 21.85,$$
$$\Sigma W_m = 3.80,$$
$$\Sigma U_m V_m = 16.595,$$
$$\Sigma V_m W_m = 1.320,$$
$$\Sigma U_m X_m = 5.255,$$

and

$$\Sigma W_m X_m = 2.480.$$

Thus,

$$o_{\text{MH,matched}} = \Sigma U_m / \Sigma W_m = 5.75,$$
$$\ln(o_{\text{MH,matched}}) = 1.75,$$

and the estimated standard error of $\ln(o_{\text{MH,matched}})$ is

$$SE = 0.3780.$$

The resulting approximate 95 percent confidence interval for the value in the population of the adjusted odds ratio extends from $\exp(1.75 - 1.96 \times 0.3780) = \exp(1.0091) = 2.74$ to $\exp(1.75 + 1.96 \times 0.3780) = \exp(2.4909) = 12.07$.

An important special (and simple) case is that of matched pairs. The above analysis simplifies to the following. Let $D$ represent the number of matched pairs that are discordant in the direction of the case having been exposed and the control not, and let $E$ represent the number of matched pairs that are discordant in the other direction. Thus, $D = 2U$ and $E = 2W$. The Mantel-Haenszel estimator of the underlying odds ratio is simply

$$o_{\text{MH,matched}} = \frac{D}{E}, \qquad (17\text{-}48)$$

**Table 17.12 Results of a Matched-Sets Case-Control Study of the Association Between Use of Estrogens and Endometrial Cancer**

| $a_m$ | $b_m$ | $c_m$ | $d_m$ | $t_{m.}$ | Number of Matched Sets with Given Pattern |
|---|---|---|---|---|---|
| 1 | 0 | 0 | 3 | 4 | 1 |
| 1 | 0 | 1 | 2 | 4 | 3 |
| 1 | 0 | 0 | 4 | 5 | 4 |
| 1 | 0 | 1 | 3 | 5 | 17 |
| 1 | 0 | 2 | 2 | 5 | 11 |
| 1 | 0 | 3 | 1 | 5 | 9 |
| 1 | 0 | 4 | 0 | 5 | 2 |
| 0 | 1 | 0 | 4 | 5 | 1 |
| 0 | 1 | 1 | 3 | 5 | 6 |
| 0 | 1 | 2 | 2 | 5 | 3 |
| 0 | 1 | 3 | 1 | 5 | 1 |
| 0 | 1 | 4 | 0 | 5 | 1 |

and the estimated standard error of $\ln(o_{\text{MH,matched}})$ simplifies to

$$SE = \left(\frac{D+E}{DE}\right)^{1/2}. \qquad (17\text{-}49)$$

## 5.5 Reasons for Analyzing the Odds Ratio

The odds ratio is the least intuitively understandable measure of association of those considered in this chapter, but it has a great many practical and theoretical advantages over its competitors. One important practical advantage—that it is estimable from data collected according to a number of different study designs—was demonstrated in section 5.1. A second, illustrated in section 5.4.1, is that the logarithm of the odds ratio is the key parameter in a linear logistic regression model, a widely used model for describing the effects of predictor variables on a binary response variable. Other important features of the odds ratio will now be pointed out.

If $X$ represents group membership (coded 0 or 1), and if $Y$ is a binary random variable obtained by dichotomizing a continuous random variable $Y^*$ at the point $y$, then the odds ratio will be independent of $y$ if $Y^*$ has the cumulative logistic distribution,

$$P(Y^* \leq y^* | X) = \frac{1}{1 + e^{-(\alpha + \beta X + \gamma y^*)}}, \qquad (17\text{-}50)$$

for all $y^*$. If, instead, a model specified by two cumulative normal distributions with the same variance is assumed, the odds ratio will be nearly independent of $y$ (Edwards 1966; Fleiss 1970).

Many investigators automatically compare two proportions by taking their ratio, $rr$. When the proportions are small, the odds ratio provides an excellent approximation to the rate ratio. Assume, for example, that $P_1 = 0.09$ and $P_2 = 0.07$. The estimated rate ratio is

$$rr = P_1/P_2 = 0.09/0.07 = 1.286,$$

and the estimated odds ratio is nearly equal to it,

$$O = \frac{P_1(1 - P_2)}{P_2(1 - P_1)} = \frac{0.09 \times 0.93}{0.07 \times 0.91} = 1.314.$$

A practical consequence is that the odds ratio estimated from a retrospective study—the kind of study from which the rate ratio is not directly estimable—will, in the case of relatively rare events and in the absence of bias, provide an excellent approximation to the rate ratio.

Two theoretically important properties of the odds ratio pertain to underlying probability models. Consider first the sampling distribution of the frequencies in Table 17.3, conditional on all marginal frequencies being held fixed at their observed values. When $X$ and $Y$ are independent, the sampling distribution of the obtained frequencies is given by the familiar hypergeometric distribution. When $X$ and $Y$ are not independent, however, the sampling distribution, referred to as the *noncentral hypergeometric distribution,* is more complicated. This exact conditional distribution depends on the underlying probabilities only through the odds ratio:

$$Pr(n_{11}, n_{22}, n_{21}, n_{22} | n_{1.}, n_{2.}, n_{.1}, n_{.2}, \omega) = \frac{n_{1.}!}{n_{11}! n_{12}!}$$
$$\cdot \frac{n_{2.}!}{n_{21}! n_{22}!} \, \omega^{n_{11}} \Big/ \sum_x \frac{n_{1.}!}{x!(n_{1.} - x)!} \qquad (17\text{-}51)$$
$$\cdot \frac{n_{2.}!}{(n_{.1} - x)!(n_{..} - n_{1.} - n_{.1} + x)!} \, \omega^x,$$

where the summation is over all permissible integers in the upper left-hand cell (Agresti 1990, pp. 66–67).

The odds ratio also plays a key role in *loglinear models.* The simplest such model is for the fourfold table. When the row and column classifications are independent, the linear model for the natural logarithm of the expected frequency in row $i$ and column $j$ is

$$\ln\big(E(n_{ij})\big) = \mu + \alpha_i + \beta_j, \qquad (17\text{-}52)$$

with the parameters subject to the constraints $\alpha_1 + \alpha_2 = \beta_1 + \beta_2 = 0$. In the general case, dependence is modeled by adding additional terms to the model:

$$\ln\big(E(n_{1j})\big) = \mu + \alpha_i + \beta_j + \gamma_{ij}, \qquad (17\text{-}53)$$

with $\Sigma \gamma_{1j} = \Sigma \gamma_{2j} = \Sigma \gamma_{i1} = \Sigma \gamma_{i2} = 0$. Let $\gamma = \gamma_{11}$. Thanks to these constraints, $\gamma = -\gamma_{12} = -\gamma_{21} = \gamma_{22}$, and the association parameter $\gamma$ is related to the odds ratio by the simple equation

$$\gamma = \frac{1}{4} \ln(\omega). \qquad (17\text{-}54)$$

Odds ratios and their logarithms represent descriptors of association in more complicated loglinear models as well (Agresti 1990, Chapter 5).

A final property of the odds ratio with great practical importance is that it can assume any value between 0 and $\infty$, no matter what the values of the marginal frequencies and no matter what the value of one of the two probabilities being compared. As we learned earlier in this chapter, neither the simple difference nor the rate ratio nor the phi coefficient is generally capable of assuming values throughout its possible range. We saw for the rate ratio, for example, that the parameter value was restricted to the interval $O \leq RR \leq 2.5$ when the probability $\Pi_2$ was equal to 0.40. The odds ratio can assume any nonnegative value, however. Given that

$$\omega = \frac{\Pi_1(1 - \Pi_2)}{\Pi_2(1 - \Pi_1)} = 1.5 \, \frac{\Pi_1}{1 - \Pi_1}$$

when $\Pi_2 = 0.40$, $\omega = 0$ when $\Pi_1 = 0$ and $\omega \to \infty$ when $\Pi_1 \to 1$.

Consider, as another example, the frequencies in Table 17.4. With the marginal frequencies held fixed, the simple difference may assume values only in the interval $-0.17 \leq D \leq 0.50$ (and not $-1 \leq D \leq 1$); the rate ratio with "positive" as the untoward outcome may assume values only in the interval $0.83 \leq rr \leq 2.0$ (and not $0 \leq rr \leq \infty$); and the phi coefficient may assume values only in the interval $-0.22 \leq \hat{\varphi} \leq 0.65$ (and not $-1 \leq \hat{\varphi} \leq 1$); but the odds ratio may assume values throughout the interval $0 \leq o \leq \infty$. (To be sure, the rate ratio may assume values throughout the interval $0 \leq rr \leq \infty$ when "negative" represents the untoward outcome.)

The final example brings us back to Table 17.1. We saw earlier that there was heterogeneity in the association between exposure to asbestos and mortality from lung cancer, when association was measured by the simple difference between two rates:

$$D_{\text{smokers}} = 601.6 - 122.6 = 479.0 \text{ deaths per } 100,000$$
$$\text{person-years}$$

and

$$D_{nonsmokers} = 58.4 - 11.3 = 47.1 \text{ deaths per } 100,000 \text{ person-years.}$$

This appearance of heterogeneous association essentially vanishes when association is measured by the odds ratio:

$$o_{smokers} = \frac{601.6 \times (100,000 - 122.6)}{122.6 \times (100,000 - 601.6)} = 4.93$$

and

$$o_{nonsmokers} = \frac{58.4 \times (100,000 - 11.3)}{11.3 \times (100,000 - 58.4)} = 5.17.$$

Whether one is considering smokers or nonsmokers, the odds that a person exposed to asbestos will die of lung cancer are approximately five times the odds that a person not so exposed will die of lung cancer.

As a result, we see that the odds ratio is not prone to the artifactual appearance of interaction across studies due to the influence on other measures of association or effect of varying marginal frequencies or to constraints on one or the other sample proportion. On the basis of this and all of its other positive features, the odds ratio is recommended as the measure of choice for measuring effect or association when the studies contributing to the research synthesis are summarized by fourfold tables.

### Author's Note

Drs. Melissa Begg and Bruce Levin provided valuable criticisms of an earlier version of this chapter. This work was supported in part by grant No. MH45763 from the National Institute of Mental Health.

## 6. REFERENCES

Agresti, A. (1990). *Categorical data analysis*. New York: Wiley.

Armitage, P. (1971). *Statistical methods in medical research*. New York: Wiley.

Bishop, Y. M. M., Fienberg, S. E., & Holland, P. W. (1975). *Discrete multivariate analysis: Theory and practice*. Cambridge, MA: MIT Press.

Breslow, N. E. (1981). Odds ratio estimators when the data are sparse. *Biometrika, 68,* 73–84.

Breslow, N. E., & Day, N. E. (1980). *Statistical methods in cancer research: Vol. 1. The analysis of case-control studies*. Lyon, France: International Agency for Research on Cancer.

Carroll, J. B. (1961). The nature of the data, or how to choose a correlation coefficient. *Psychometrika, 26,* 347–372.

Connett, J., Ejigou, A., McHugh, R., & Breslow, N. (1982). The precision of the Mantel-Haenszel estimator in case-control studies with multiple matching. *American Journal of Epidemiology, 116,* 875–877.

Edwards, J. H. (1966). Some taxonomic implications of a curious feature of the bivariate normal surface. *British Journal of Preventive and Social Medicine, 20,* 42–43.

Fleiss, J. L. (1970). On the asserted invariance of the odds ratio. *British Journal of Preventive and Social Medicine, 24,* 45–46.

Fleiss, J. L. (1981). *Statistical methods for rates and proportions* (2nd ed.). New York: Wiley.

Fleiss, J. L. (1984). The Mantel-Haenszel estimator in case-control studies with varying numbers of controls matched to each case. *American Journal of Epidemiology, 120,* 1–3.

Fleiss, J. L., & Davies, M. (1982). Jackknifing functions of multinomial frequencies, with an application to a measure of concordance. *American Journal of Epidemiology, 115,* 841–845.

Gart, J. J. (1970). Point and interval estimation of the common odds ratio in the combination of 2 × 2 tables with fixed marginals. *Biometrika, 57,* 471–475.

Gart, J. J., & Zweifel, J. R. (1967). On the bias of various estimators of the logit and its variance, with application to quantal bioassay. *Biometrika, 54,* 181–187.

Greenland, S., & Salvan, A. (1990). Bias in the one-step method for pooling study results. *Statistics in Medicine, 9,* 247–252.

Hammond, E. C., Selikoff, I. J., & Seidman, H. (1979). Asbestos exposure, cigarette smoking and death rates. *Annals of the New York Academy of Sciences, 330,* 473–490.

Hauck, W. W. (1989). Odds ratio inference from stratified samples. *Communications in Statistics, 18A,* 767–800.

Hosmer, D. W., & Lemeshow, S. (1989). *Applied logistic regression*. New York: Wiley.

Kleinbaum, D. G., Kupper, L. L., & Morgenstern, H. (1982). *Epidemiologic research: Principles and quantitative methods*. Belmont, CA: Lifetime Learning.

Mack, T. M., Pike, M. C., Henderson, B. E., Pfeffer, R. I., Gerkins, V. R., Arthur, B. S., & Brown, S. E. (1976). Estrogens and endometrial cancer in a retirement community. *New England Journal of Medicine, 294,* 1262–1267.

Mantel, N., Brown, C., & Byar, D. P. (1977). Tests for homogeneity of effect in an epidemiologic investigation. *American Journal of Epidemiology, 106,* 125–129.

Mantel, N., & Haenszel, W. (1959). Statistical aspects of the analysis of data from retrospective studies of disease. *Journal of the National Cancer Institute, 22,* 719–748.

McKinlay, S. M. (1975). The effect of bias on estimators of relative risk for pair-matched and stratified samples. *Journal of the American Statistical Association, 70,* 859–864.

Quenouille, M. H. (1956). Notes on bias in estimation. *Biometrika, 43,* 353–360.

Robins, J., Breslow, N. E., & Greenland, S. (1986). Estimators of the Mantel-Haenszel variance consistent in both sparse data and large-strata limiting models. *Biometrics, 42,* 311–323.

Robins, J., Greenland, S., & Breslow, N. E. (1986). A general estimator for the variance of the Mantel-Haenszel odds ratio. *American Journal of Epidemiology, 124,* 719–723.

Sato, T. (1990). Confidence limits for the common odds ratio based on the asymptotic distribution of the Mantel-Haenszel estimator. *Biometrics, 46,* 71–80.

Tukey, J. W. (1958). Bias and confidence in not-quite-large samples. *Annals of Mathematical Statistics, 29,* 614.

Woolf, B. (1955). On estimating the relation between blood group and disease. *Annals of Human Genetics, 19,* 251–253.

Yusuf, S., Peto, R., Lewis, J., Collins, R., & Sleight, P. (1985). Beta blockade during and after myocardial infarction: An overview of the randomized trials. *Progress in Cardiovascular Diseases, 27,* 335–371.

Cooper, H. and Hedges, L. V. (Eds.) 1994. *The Handbook of Research Synthesis.* New York: Russell Sage Foundation

# 18

# COMBINING ESTIMATES OF EFFECT SIZE

**WILLIAM R. SHADISH**
*Memphis State University*

**C. KEITH HADDOCK**
*Wilford Hall Medical Center*

CONTENTS

## 1. INTRODUCTION

In 1896, Sir Almroth Wright developed a vaccine to protect against typhoid (Susser 1977; Wright, incidentally, was a colleague and mentor of Sir Alexander Fleming, who later discovered penicillin; see Roberts 1989). The typhoid vaccine was tested in several settings, and on the basis of these tests the vaccine was recommended for routine use in the British army for soldiers at risk for the disease. In that same year, Karl Pearson, the famous biometrician, was asked to review the empirical evidence bearing on the decision. To do so, he reviewed evidence from five studies reporting data about the relationship between inoculation status and typhoid immunity, and six studies reporting data on inoculation status and fatality among those who contracted the disease. He computed tetrachoric correlations for each of these 11 cases, and then averaged these correlations (separately for incidence and fatality) to describe average inoculation effectiveness (see Table 18.1). In his subsequent report of this research, Pearson (1904b) concluded that the average correlations were too low to warrant adopting the vaccine, since other accepted vaccines at that time routinely produced correlations at or far above .20 to .30: "I think the right conclusion to draw would be not that it was desirable to inoculate the whole army, but that improvement of the serum and method of dosing, with a view to a far higher correlation, should be attempted" (p. 1245).

We tell this story for three reasons. First, it is the earliest example we have found of what we would now call a meta-analysis, so it is historically interesting (Pearson alludes in the 1904b article to possible earlier examples). Second, we will use the data in Table 18.1 to illustrate how to combine results from fourfold tables. Finally, the study illustrates some conceptual and methodological issues involved in combining estimates of effect size across studies, points we return to in the conclusion of this chapter. In many ways, of course, this capacity to combine results across studies is the defining feature of meta-analysis. Hence, the conceptual and statistical issues involved in computing these combined estimates must receive extremely careful attention.

### 1.1 Dealing with Differences Among Studies

Combining estimates of effect size from different studies would be easy if studies were perfect replicates of each other—if they made the same methodological choices about such matters as within-study sample size, measures, or design, and if they all investigated exactly the same conceptual issues and constructs (see Chapter 19). Under the simplest fixed effects models of a single population effect size $\theta$, all these replicates would differ from each other only by virtue of having used just a sample of observations from the total population, so that observed studies would yield effect sizes that differed from the true population effect size only by sampling error (henceforth we refer to the variance of these sampling errors as conditional variance, for reasons explained in section 3). The unbiased estimate of the population effect would then be the simple average of observed study effects; and its standard error would allow computation of confidence intervals around that average. Under random effects models, one would not assume that there is just one population effect size; rather a distribution of population effect sizes would exist generated by a distribution of possible study realizations (see Chapter 3). Hence, observed outcomes in studies would differ from each other not just because of sampling error, but also because they reflect these true, underlying population differences.

It is rarely (if ever) the case that studies are perfect replicates of each other, however, because they almost always differ from each other in many methodological and substantive ways. Hence, most research syntheses must grapple with certain decisions about the kinds of combinations of studies that are justified when studies differ from each other in multiple ways. For example, it may seem at first glance that the 11 samples in Table 18.1 are perfect replicates. Compared with many sets of studies currently submitted to meta-analytic procedures, they may well be. But still, many sources of differences remain. For instance, the 11 samples obviously differ dramatically in within-study sample size. They also differ in other ways that were extensively and acrimoniously debated by Pearson and Wright (Susser

**Table 18.1 Effects of Typhoid Inoculations on Incidence and Fatality**

| Incidence | Inoculated | | Not Inoculated | | | |
|---|---|---|---|---|---|---|
| | N | Cases | N | Cases | r | Odds Ratio |
| **Sample** | | | | | | |
| Hospital staffs | 297 | 32 | 279 | 75 | .373 | 3.04 |
| Ladysmith garrison | 1,705 | 35 | 10,529 | 1,489 | .445 | 7.86 |
| Methuen's column | 2,535 | 26 | 10,981 | 257 | .191 | 2.31 |
| Single regiments | 1,207 | 72 | 1,285 | 82 | .021 | 1.07 |
| Army in India | 15,384 | 128 | 136,360 | 2,132 | .100 | 1.89 |
| Average | | | | | .226 | |
| **Fatality Among Those Contracting Typhoid** | | | | | | |
| | Lived | Died | Lived | Died | | |
| Hospital staffs | 30 | 2 | 63 | 12 | .307 | 2.86 |
| Ladysmith garrison | 27 | 8 | 1,160 | 329 | −.010 | .96 |
| Single regiments | 63 | 9 | 61 | 21 | .300 | 2.41 |
| Special hospitals | 1,088 | 86 | 4,453 | 538 | .119 | 1.53 |
| Various military hospitals | 701 | 63 | 2,864 | 510 | .194 | 1.98 |
| Army in India | 73 | 11 | 1,052 | 423 | .194 | 2.67 |
| Average | | | | | .248 | |
| | | | | | .193 | |

SOURCE: Adapted with permission from Susser (1977), who adapted the data from Pearson (1904b).

1977). For example, both Wright and Pearson recognized that unreliability of inoculation history and typhoid diagnosis attenuated sample correlations. Further, clinical diagnoses of typhoid were less reliable than autopsy diagnoses, and studies differed in which diagnostic measure they used. One might reasonably consider, therefore, whether and how to take these differences into account.

## 1.2 Weighting Studies Prior to or While Combining Them

In general, one could deal with such study differences *either* prior to or while combining results *or* subsequent to combining results. Weighting schemes that are applied at the earlier points seem to be based on three assumptions: (a) Theory or evidence suggests that studies with some characteristics are more accurate or less biased with respect to the desired inference than studies with other characteristics, (b) the nature and direction of that bias can be estimated prior to combining, and (c) appropriate weights to compensate for the bias can be constructed and justified. Examples of such weighting schemes are described in the following three sections.

**1.2.1 Variance and within-study sample size schemes** Everyone who has had an undergraduate statistics course will recognize the principle underlying these schemes: Studies with larger within-study sample sizes will give more accurate estimates of population parameters than studies with smaller sample sizes. They will be more accurate in the sense that the variance of the estimate around the parameter will be smaller, allowing greater confidence in narrowing the region in which the population value falls. Pearson noted this dependence of confidence on within-study sample size in the typhoid inoculation data, stating that ''many of the groups . . . are far too small to allow of any definite opinion being formed at all, having regard to the size of the probable error involved'' (1904b, p. 1243; see Cowles 1989 for explanation of probable error). In Table 18.1, for example, estimates of typhoid incidence from the army-in-India sample were based on over 150,000 subjects, more than 200 times as many subjects as the hospital staff sample of less than 600. The large sample used in the army-in-India study greatly reduced the role of sampling error in determining the outcome. Hence, all things being equal, such large-sample studies should be weighted more heavily; doing so would improve

Pearson's estimates. To implement this scheme, one must have access to the within-study sample sizes used in each of the studies being reviewed. Fortunately, this information is almost always available to meta-analysts. This is by far the most widely accepted a priori weighting scheme, and the only one to be discussed in detail in this chapter.

This weighting scheme fulfills all three assumptions outlined previously. First, our preference for studies with large within-study sample sizes is based on strong, widely accepted statistical theory. To wit, large-sample studies tend to produce sample means that are closer to the population mean, and estimating that population mean is (often) the desired inference. Second, the nature and direction of uncertainty in studies that have small within-study sample sizes is clear—greater variability of sample estimates symmetrically around the population parameter. Third, statistical theory suggests very specific weights (to be described shortly) that are known to maximize the chances of correctly making the desired inference to the population parameter. We know of only one other weighting scheme that so unambiguously meets these three conditions, which we now describe.

**1.2.2 Reliability and validity of measurement** If studies were perfect replicates, they would measure exactly the same variables. This is rarely the case. As a result, each different measure, both within and between studies, can have different reliability and validity. For example, some studies in Table 18.1 used incidence, some used mortality, and others used both measures; and incidence and mortality were measured different ways in different studies. The differential reliability and validity of these measures was one of the sources of controversy between Pearson and Wright. Fortunately, the effects of reliability and validity on assessments of study outcomes are well specified in classical measurement theory. In the simplest case, for example, unreliability of measurement attenuates relationships between two variables, so that univariate correlation coefficients and standardized mean difference statistics are smaller than they would be with more reliable measures. In multivariate cases, the effects of unreliability and invalidity can be more complex (Bollen 1989), but even then they are well known, and very specific corrections are available to maximize the chances of making the correct population inference (Hedges & Olkin 1985; Hunter & Schmidt 1990).

However, unlike within-study sample sizes, information about reliability and validity coefficients will often not be available or easily accessible in reports of primary studies. Neither Pearson nor Wright, for example, reported these coefficients in the articles in which they debated the issues. Sometimes relevant coefficients can be borrowed from test manuals or reports of similar research. Even when no reasonable reliability or validity estimates can be found, however, procedures exist for integrating effect size estimates over studies when some studies are corrected and others are not (Hunter & Schmidt 1990). These and related matters are addressed by Schmidt and Hunter in Chapter 21; hence we do not discuss them further in this chapter. However, those procedures can be applied concurrently with the variance-based weighting schemes illustrated in this chapter (Hedges & Olkin 1985).

**1.2.3 Other weighting schemes** No schemes other than those discussed above seem clearly to meet the three conditions previously outlined. Hence, they should be applied with caution and viewed as primarily exploratory in nature (Boissel et al. 1989). Perhaps the most frequent contender for an alternative scheme is weighting by study ''quality'' (e.g., Chalmers et al. 1981). The latter term, of course, means different things to different people, so more specific examples are required. When treatment effectiveness is an issue, one of the most informative examples would be to weight treatment outcome studies according to aspects of design that, presumably, facilitate causal inference. Of all such design features, random assignment of units to conditions has the strongest justification, so it is worth examining it against our three assumptions. Strong theory buttresses the preference we give to random assignment in treatment outcome studies, so it meets the first criterion. But it does not clearly meet the other two. We know only that estimates from nonrandomized studies may be biased; we rarely know the direction or nature of the bias. In fact, the latter can vary from study to study, in mostly unpredictable ways (Cook & Campbell 1979; Freedman 1987). Further, theory does not suggest a very specific weighting scheme that makes it more likely we will obtain a better estimate of the population parameter. We might choose to assign all randomized studies ''somewhat greater weight'' than all quasi-experiments. But even this is arguable since it may be that we should assign all-or-none weights to this dichotomy: If quasi-experiments are biased, allowing them any weight at all may bias the combined result in unknown ways. But this dichotomous (1,0) weighting scheme is not really a weighting scheme at all because applying it is equivalent to excluding all quasi-experiments in the first place. Given our present lack of knowledge about random assignment pertaining to our second and third conditions for using weighting schemes, we think it is best to examine differences between randomized and quasi-experiments after combining effect sizes rather than before. Other "quality" measures, such as whether the experimenter is blind to conditions, can be even more equivocal than random assignment; and combining such diverse quality measures into quality scales can compound such problems if the scales are not carefully constructed.

### 1.3 Examining the Effects of Study Quality After Combining Results

Weighting schemes that are a function of either within-study sample size or reliability and validity can routinely be used prior to combining studies. However, we cannot recommend that other weighting schemes be used routinely prior to combining results: We currently do not know if they generate more accurate inferences, and they can generate less accurate inferences. However, they should be freely explored *after* combining results; and results with and without such weighting can be compared. In fact, such explorations are one of the few ways to generate badly needed information about the nature and direction of biases introduced by the many ways in which studies differ from each other. Methods for such explorations are the topics of many other chapters in this book.

## 2. FIXED EFFECTS MODELS

Suppose that the data to be combined arise from a series of $k$ independent studies, in which the $i$th study reports one observed effect size $T_i$, with population effect size $\theta_i$ and variance $v_i$. Thus, the data to be combined consist of $k$ effect size estimates $T_1, \ldots, T_k$ of parameters $\theta_1, \ldots, \theta_k$, and variances $v_1, \ldots, v_k$. Under the fixed effects model, we assume $\theta_1 = \ldots = \theta_k = \theta$, a common effect size. Then a general formula for the weighted average effect size over those studies is

$$\overline{T}_{\bullet} = \frac{\sum_{i=1}^{k} w_i T_i}{\sum_{i=1}^{k} w_i}, \quad (18\text{-}1)$$

where $w_i$ is a weight assigned to the $i$th study that is defined in equation (18-2). Equation (18-1) can be adapted, if desired, to include a "quality" index for each study, where $q_i$ is the $i$th study's score on the index, perhaps scaled from 0 to 1:

$$\overline{T}_{\bullet} = \frac{\sum_{i=1}^{k} q_i w_i T_i}{\sum_{i=1}^{k} q_i w_i}.$$

When all observed effect size indicators estimate a single population parameter, as is hypothesized under a fixed effects model, then $\overline{T}_{\bullet}$ is an unbiased estimate of the population parameter $\theta$. In equation (18-1), $T_i$ may be estimated by any specific effect size statistic, including the standardized mean difference statistic $d$ (for which the relevant population parameter is $\delta$), the correlation coefficient $r$ (population parameter $\rho$) or its Fisher $z$ transformation (population parameter $\zeta$), the odds ratio $o$ (population parameter $\omega$), the log odds ratio $l$ (population parameter $\lambda$), the difference between proportions $D$ (population parameter $\Delta$), or even differences between outcomes measured in their original metric.

The weights that minimize the variance of $\overline{T}_{\bullet}$ are inversely proportional to the conditional variance (the square of the standard error) in each study:

$$w_i = \frac{1}{v_i}. \quad (18\text{-}2)$$

Formulas for the conditional variances, $v_i$, vary for different effect size indices, so we present them separately for each index in later sections. However, they share in common the fact that conditional variance is inversely proportional to within-study sample size—the larger the sample, the smaller the variance, so the more precise the estimate of effect size should be. Hence, larger weights are assigned to effect sizes from studies with smaller variances and larger within-study sample sizes.

Given the use of weights as defined in (18-2), the average effect size $\overline{T}_{\bullet}$ has conditional variance $v_{\bullet}$, which is itself a function of the conditional variances of each effect size being combined:

$$v_{\bullet} = \frac{1}{\sum_{i=1}^{k} (1/v_i)}. \quad (18\text{-}3)$$

If the quality-weighted version of (18-1) is used to compute the weighted average effect size, where the weights $w_i$ are defined in (18-2), then the conditional variance of the quality-weighted average effect size is

$$v_{\bullet} = \frac{\left(\sum_{i=1}^{k} q_i^2 w_i\right)}{\left(\sum_{i=1}^{k} q_i w_i\right)^2}.$$

Note that this simplifies to (18-3) if $q_i = 1$ for all $i$, in effect, not weighting for quality.

The square root of $v_{\bullet}$ is the standard error of estimate of the combined effect size. Multiplying the standard error by an appropriate critical value $C_\alpha$ (most commonly, the unit normal $C_\alpha = 1.96$, the $Z$ statistic for a two-tailed test at $\alpha = .05$; but see Chapter 20 for some exceptions), and adding and subtracting the resulting product to $\overline{T}_{\bullet}$, yields the (95 percent) confidence interval $(\theta_L, \theta_U)$ for $\theta$:

$$\theta_L = \overline{T}_{\bullet} - C_\alpha(v_{\bullet})^{1/2}, \quad \theta_U = \overline{T}_{\bullet} + C_\alpha(v_{\bullet})^{1/2}. \quad (18\text{-}4)$$

If the confidence interval does not contain zero, we reject the null hypothesis that the population effect size $\theta$ is zero. Equivalently, we may test the null hypothesis that $\theta = 0$ with the statistic

$$Z = \frac{|\overline{T}_{\bullet}|}{(v_{\bullet})^{1/2}}, \quad (18\text{-}5)$$

where $|\overline{T}_{\bullet}|$ is the absolute value of the weighted average effect size over studies (given by equation 18-1). Under (18-5), $\overline{T}_{\bullet}$ differs from zero if $Z$ exceeds 1.96, the 95 percent two-tailed critical value of the standard normal distribution.

Finally, a test of the assumption of equation (18-1) that studies do, in fact, share a common population effect size uses the following homogeneity test statistic:

$$Q = \sum_{i=1}^{k} [(T_i - \overline{T}_{\bullet})^2/(v_i)]. \quad (18\text{-}6)$$

A computationally convenient form of (18-6) is

$$Q = \sum_{i=1}^{k} w_i T_i^2 - \frac{\left(\sum_{i=1}^{k} w_i T_i\right)^2}{\sum_{i=1}^{k} w_i}.$$

In general, if $Q$ exceeds the upper-tail critical value of chi-square at $k - 1$ degrees of freedom, the observed variance in study effect sizes is significantly greater than

what we would expect by chance if all studies shared a common population effect size. When within-study sample sizes in each study are very large, however, $Q$ may be rejected even when the individual effect size estimates do not really differ much; in such cases, it may be reasonable to pool effect size estimates anyway. In either case, if homogeneity is rejected, $\overline{T}_{\bullet}$ should not be interpreted as an estimate of a single effect parameter $\theta$ that gave rise to the sample observations, but rather simply as describing a mean of observed effect sizes, or as estimating a mean $\theta$—which may, of course, be of practical interest in particular research syntheses. If $Q$ is rejected, the researcher may wish to disaggregate study effect sizes by grouping studies into appropriate categories until $Q$ is not rejected within those categories, or may use regression techniques to account for variance among the $\theta_i$. These latter techniques are discussed in subsequent chapters, as are methods for conducting sensitivity analyses that help examine the influence of particular studies on combined effect size estimates and on heterogeneity.

Alternatively, we will see later in this chapter that one can incorporate this heterogeneity into one's model using random effects rather than fixed effects models. For example, when the heterogeneity cannot be explained as a function of known study-level covariates (e.g., characteristics of studies such as type of treatment or publication status, or some aggregate characteristic of patients within studies such as average age), or when fixed effects covariate models are not feasible because sufficient information is not reported in primary studies, random effects models help take heterogeneity into account when estimating the average size of effect and its confidence interval (Hedges 1983; DerSimonian & Laird 1986). Essentially, in the presence of unexplained heterogeneity, the random effects test is more conservative than the fixed effects test (Berlin et al. 1989), for reasons explained later. Finally, sometimes a move to random effects models is suggested for purely theoretical reasons, as when levels of the variable are thought to be sampled from a larger population to which one desires to generalize (Hunter & Schmidt 1990).

In both the fixed and random effects cases, however, $Q$ is a diagnostic tool to help researchers know whether they have, to put it in the vernacular, "accounted for all the variance" in the effect sizes they are studying. Experience has shown that $Q$ is usually rejected in most simple, fixed effects univariate analyses—for example, when the researcher simply lumps all studies into one category or contrasts one category of studies, such as randomized experiments, with another category of studies, such as quasi-experiments. In such simple category systems, rejection of homogeneity makes eminent theoretical sense! Each simple categorical analysis can be thought of as the researcher's theoretical model about what variables account for the variance in effect sizes. We would rarely expect that just one variable, or even just two or three variables, would be sufficient to account for all observed variance. The phenomena we study are usually far more complex than that. Often, extensive multivariate models are required to model these phenomena successfully. In essence, then, the variables that a researcher uses to categorize or predict effect sizes can be considered to be the model that the researcher has specified about what variables generated study outcome. The $Q$ statistic tells whether that model specification is statistically adequate. Thus, while homogeneity tests are not without problems (Boissel et al. 1989; Fleiss & Gross 1991; Sackett, Harris & Orr 1986; Spector & Levine 1987), they can serve a valuable diagnostic function.

In the following subsections, we use the equations just developed to show how to combine standardized mean differences, correlations, various results from fourfold tables, and raw mean differences. A sample computer program for implementing such analyses in the case of the standardized mean difference statistic is presented in the appendix, and similar programs for other effect size indicators are available from the first author. The subsections in both sections 2 and 3 hinge on definitions of the conditional variance of the effect size estimates to be combined, for use in equations (18-2) and (18-3). Sometimes alternative estimators of conditional variance are available that might be preferable in some situations to those we use (Hedges & Olkin 1985; DerSimonian & Laird 1986); the estimates we present should prove satisfactory in most situations, however.

## 2.1 Combining Standardized Mean Differences

Suppose that the effect size statistic to be combined is the standardized mean difference statistic $d$:

$$d_i = \frac{\overline{X}^t_i - \overline{X}^c_i}{s_i} ,$$

where $\overline{X}^t_i$ is the mean of the treatment group in the $i$th study, $\overline{X}^c_i$ is the mean of the control group in the $i$th study, and $s_i$ is the pooled standard deviation of the two groups [see Chapter 16; a correction for small sample bias can also be applied (Hedges & Olkin 1985, p. 81)].

**Table 18.2 Computational Details of Standardized Mean Difference Example**

| Study | $d_i$ | $v_i$ | $w_i$ | $w_i d_i$ | $w_i d_i^2$ |
|---|---|---|---|---|---|
| 1 | 0.03 | 0.01563 | 64.000 | 1.9200 | 0.0576 |
| 2 | 0.12 | 0.02161 | 46.277 | 5.5532 | 0.6664 |
| 3 | −0.14 | 0.02789 | 35.856 | −5.0199 | 0.7028 |
| 4 | 1.18 | 0.13913 | 7.188 | 8.4813 | 10.0080 |
| 5 | 0.26 | 0.13616 | 7.344 | 1.9095 | 0.4965 |
| 6 | −0.06 | 0.01061 | 94.260 | −5.6556 | 0.3393 |
| 7 | −0.02 | 0.01061 | 94.260 | −1.8852 | 0.0377 |
| 8 | −0.32 | 0.04840 | 20.661 | −6.6116 | 2.1157 |
| 9 | 0.27 | 0.02690 | 37.180 | 10.0387 | 2.7104 |
| 10 | 0.80 | 0.06300 | 15.873 | 12.6982 | 10.1586 |
| 11 | 0.54 | 0.09120 | 10.964 | 5.9208 | 3.1972 |
| 12 | 0.18 | 0.04973 | 20.109 | 3.6196 | 0.6515 |
| 13 | −0.02 | 0.08352 | 11.973 | −0.2395 | 0.0048 |
| 14 | 0.23 | 0.08410 | 11.891 | 2.7348 | 0.6290 |
| 15 | −0.18 | 0.02528 | 39.555 | −7.1200 | 1.2816 |
| 16 | −0.06 | 0.02789 | 35.856 | −2.1514 | 0.1291 |
| 17 | 0.30 | 0.01932 | 51.757 | 15.5271 | 4.6581 |
| 18 | 0.07 | 0.00884 | 113.173 | 7.9221 | 0.5545 |
| 19 | −0.07 | 0.03028 | 33.029 | −2.3121 | 0.1618 |
| Sum | | | 751.206 | 45.3300 | 38.5606 |

If the underlying data are normal, the conditional variance of $d_i$ is estimated as

$$v_i = \frac{n^t_i + n^c_i}{n^t_i n^c_i} + \frac{d_i^2}{2(n^t_i + n^c_i)} , \qquad (18\text{-}7)$$

where $n^t_i$ is the within-study sample size in the treatment group of the $i$th study, $n^c_i$ is the within-study sample size in the comparison group of the $i$th study, and $d_i$ estimates the population parameter $\delta$.

Consider how this applies to the 19 studies of the effects of teacher expectancy on pupil IQ in Data Set II (see Appendix A). Table 18.2 presents details of this computation (throughout this chapter, results will vary slightly depending on the number of decimals carried through computations; this can particularly affect odds ratio statistics, especially when some proportions are small). The weighted average effect size $\bar{d}_\cdot = 45.3303/751.2075 = .06$ with a variance of $v_\cdot = 1/751.2075 = .00133$, and standard error $= (1/751.2075)^{1/2} = .03649$. We test the significance of this effect size in either of two equivalent ways: by computing 95 percent confidence intervals, which in this case range from $\delta_L = [(.06) - 1.96(.036)] = -.01$ to $\delta_U = [(.06) + 1.96(.036)] = .13$, which includes zero in the confidence interval, and the statistic $Z = |\bar{d}_\cdot|/(v_\cdot)^{1/2} = |.06|/.036 = 1.65$, which does not exceed the 1.96 critical value at $\alpha = .05$. Hence we conclude that teacher expectancy has no significant effect on student IQ. However, homogeneity of effect size is rejected in this data, with the computational version of equation (18-6) yielding $Q = [38.56 - (45.33)^2/751.21] = 35.83$, which exceeds 34.81, the 99 percent critical value of the chi-square distribution for $k - 1 = 19 - 1 = 18$ degrees of freedom, so we reject homogeneity of effect sizes at significance level .01. Hence, we might assume that other variables could be necessary to explain fully the variance in these effect sizes; subsequent chapters in this book will explore such possibilities.

## 2.2 Combining Correlations

**2.2.1 Combining $z$-transformed correlations** For the correlation coefficient $r$, some authors recommend first converting each correlation by Fisher's (1925) variance stabilizing $z$ transform:

$$z_i = .5\{\ln[(1 + r_i)/(1 - r_i)]\},$$

where $\ln$ is the natural (base $e$) logarithm. The correlation parameter corresponding to $z_i$ is

$$\zeta_i = .5\{\ln[(1 + \rho_i)/(1 - \rho_i)]\}.$$

If the underlying data are bivariate normal, the conditional variance of $z_i$ is

$$v_i = \frac{1}{(n_i - 3)} , \qquad (18\text{-}8)$$

where $n_i$ is the within-study sample size of the $i$th study. Note that this variance depends only on within-study sample size and not on the correlation parameter itself, a desirable property; and when correlations are small (e.g., $|r| < .5$), $z_i$ is close to $r_i$ so the variance of $r_i$ is close to the variance of $z_i$. Using this variance estimate in equations (18-1) through (18-6), an estimate $\bar{z}_\cdot$ and a confidence interval bounded by $\zeta_L$ and $\zeta_U$ are obtained directly. Interpretation of results is facilitated if $\bar{z}_\cdot$, $\zeta_L$, and $\zeta_U$ are converted back again to the metric of a correlation, $\bar{\rho}_\cdot$, via the inverse of the $r$ to $z$ transform given by

$$\rho(z) = (e^{2z} - 1)/(e^{2z} + 1), \qquad (18\text{-}9)$$

yielding both an estimate of $\rho$ and also upper and lower bounds ($\rho_L$, $\rho_U$) around that estimate.

As an example, Data Set III (see Appendix A) reported correlations from 20 studies between overall student ratings of the instructor and student achievement. We obtain an average $z$ transform of $\bar{z}_\cdot = 201.13/530.00 = .38$, and a variance $v_\cdot = (1/530.00) = .0019$, the square root of which (.044) is the standard error. This average effect size is significantly different from zero since $Z = |\bar{z}_\cdot|/(v_\cdot)^{1/2} = .38/.044 = 8.64$, which exceeds the critical value of 1.96 for $\alpha = .05$ in the standard normal distribution. The limits of the 95 percent confidence interval are $\zeta_L = [.38 - 1.96(.044)] = .294$ and $\zeta_U = [.38 + 1.96(.044)] = .466$. For interpretability, we can use equation (18-9) transform the $z$'s back into estimates of correlations; since $2\bar{z}_\cdot = 2(.38) = .76$, $\bar{\rho}_\cdot = (e^{.76} - 1)/(e^{.76} + 1) = .36$, where $e^{.76} \approx 2.14$. Transforming the upper and lower bounds using the same equation yields $\rho_L = .287$ and $\rho_U = .434$. Hence, we conclude that the better the ratings of the instructor, the better is student achievement. Homogeneity of correlations is not rejected [$Q = 97.27 - (201.13)^2/530.00 = 20.94$, $df = 19$, prob $= .338$]; a $Q$ value this large would be expected between 30 and 35 percent of the time if all the population correlations were identical.

**2.2.2 Combining correlation coefficients directly** Hunter and Schmidt (1990) argue that the average $z$ transform is positively biased, so they prefer combining correlations without $z$ transform. In that case, if the underlying data are bivariate normal, the variance of the correlation coefficient, $r$, is approximately

$$v_i = (1 - r_i^2)^2/(n_i - 1), \qquad (18\text{-}10)$$

where $r_i$ is the single study correlation and $n_i$ is the within-study sample size in that same study. Note that this variance now depends not only on within-study sample size, but also on the size of the original correlation. Use of (18-1) to (18-6) is straightforward. Using Data Set III, we obtain an estimate of the common correlation of $\bar{r}_\bullet = 337.00/847.180 = .40$, with a variance of $v_\bullet = 1/847.18 = .0012$, yielding a standard error of .0344. This average correlation is significantly different from zero $[Z = |\bar{r}_\bullet|/(v_\bullet)^{1/2} = .40/.035 = 11.43]$, with the limits of the 95 percent confidence interval being $\rho_L = .40 - (1.96).035 = .33$ and $\rho_U = .3978 + (1.96).035 = .47$. Homogeneity of effect size is not rejected $[Q = 159.687 - (337.00)^2/847.18 = 25.63; \ df = k - 1 = 19; \ \text{prob} = .14]$; a value of $Q$ this large would be expected about 15 percent of the time if all the population correlations were identical.

Two points should be noted in comparing these two methods of combining correlations. First, both methods yield roughly the same point estimate of the average correlation. However, few statisticians would advocate the use of untransformed correlations unless sample sizes are very large because standard errors, confidence intervals, and homogeneity tests can be quite different. The present data illustrate this, where the probability associated with the $Q$ test for the untransformed correlations was only 40 percent as large as the probability associated with the z-transformed correlations. The reason is the poor quality of the normal approximation to the distribution of $r$, particularly when the population correlation is relatively large. Second, the approximate variances in (18-8) and (18-10) assume bivariate normality to the raw measurements; however, there should be a good deal of robustness of the distribution theory, just as there is for the $t$ distribution. A similar argument applies to the robustness of variance of the standardized mean difference statistic under nonnormality.

## 2.3 Combining Fourfold Tables: Rates, Proportions, and Odds Ratios

Fourfold tables report data concerning the relationship between two dichotomous factors—say, a risk factor and a disease or treatment-control status and successful outcome at posttest. The dependent variable in such tables is always either a frequency of the number of subjects falling into a cell or the percentage of subjects in the cell. Table 18.3 presents such a fourfold table

**Table 18.3 A Fourfold Table from Pearson's Hospital Staff Incidence Data**

| Group | Condition of Interest | | |
| --- | --- | --- | --- |
| | Immune | Diseased | All |
| Inoculated | $A = 265$ | $B = 32$ | $M_1 = 297$ |
| Not Inoculated | $C = 204$ | $D = 75$ | $M_0 = 279$ |
| Total | $N_1 = 469$ | $N_0 = 107$ | $T = 576$ |

constructed from the data in the first row of Table 18.1—the incidence data for the hospital staff sample. In Table 18.3, the risk factor is immunization status and the disease is typhoid incidence. We could construct a similar fourfold table for each row in Table 18.1. From such primary data, various measures of effect size can be computed.

One measure that is often used is the odds ratio, which may be defined several equivalent ways (see Chapter 17 of this volume). One formula depends only on the four cell sizes A, B, C, and D (see Table 18.3):

$$o_i = \frac{AD}{BC} \ .$$

If any cell size is zero, then .5 should be added to all cell sizes for that sample; however, if the total sample size is small, this correction may not work well. This version of the odds ratio is sometimes called the cross-product ratio since it depends on the cross-products of the table cell sizes. Computing this odds ratio based on the data in Table 18.3 yields $o_i = 3.04$, suggesting that the odds that inoculated subjects were immune to typhoid were three times the odds for subjects not inoculated. The same odds ratio can also be computed from knowledge of the proportion of subjects in each condition of a study who have the disease:

$$o_i = \frac{p_{i1}(1 - p_{i2})}{p_{i2}(1 - p_{i1})}, \qquad (18\text{-}11)$$

where $p_{ij}$ is the proportion of individuals in condition $j$ of study $i$ who have the disease. In the incidence data in Table 18.1, for example, if one wants to assess the odds of being immune to typhoid depending on whether or not the subject was inoculated, $p_{11}$ is the proportion of subjects in the inoculation condition of the hospital staff study who were immune to typhoid ($p_{11} = 265/297 = .8923$); and $p_{32}$ is the proportion of subjects in the noninoculated condition of the Methuen's column study who remained immune to typhoid ($p_{32} = 10724/10981 = .9766$). Computing the odds ratio using this formula for the data in Table 18.3 yields $o_i = (.892/1.08)/(.731/.269) = 3.04$, the same as before.

From either odds ratio we may also define the log odds ratio $l_i = \ln(o_i)$, where $\ln$ is the natural logarithm and is equal to $l_i = \ln(3.04) = 1.11$ for the data in Table 18.3. An advantage of the log odds ratio is that it takes on a value of zero when no relationship exists between the two factors, yielding a similar interpretation of a zero effect size as $r$ and $d$.

We may also compute the difference between proportions $D_i = p_{i1} - p_{i2}$, which in Table 18.3 yields $D_i = .892 - .731 = .161$, interpretable as the actual gains expected in terms of the percentage of patients treated. DerSimonian and Laird (1986) and Berlin et al. (1989) discuss the relative merits of these various indicators. Use of these statistics in meta-analysis has been largely limited to medicine and epidemiology, but should apply more widely. For example, psychotherapy researchers often report primary data about percentage success or failure of clients in treatment or control groups. Analyzing the latter data as standardized mean difference statistics or correlations can lead to important errors that the methods presented in this section avoid (Fleiss 1981).

**2.3.1 Combining differences between proportions** Some studies report the proportion of the treatment (exposed) group with a condition (a disease, treatment success, status as case or control) and the proportion of the comparison (unexposed) group with that condition. The difference between these proportions, sometimes called a rate difference, is $D_i = p_{i1} - p_{i2}$. The rate difference has a variance of

$$v_i = \frac{p_{i1}(1 - p_{i1})}{n_{i1}} + \frac{p_{i2}(1 - p_{i2})}{n_{i2}}, \qquad (18\text{-}12)$$

where all terms are defined as in equation (18-11) and $n_{ij}$ is the number of subjects in condition $j$ of study $i$. Use of (18-1) to (18-6) is again straightforward.

Using these methods to combine rate differences for the incidence data in Table 18.1, we find that the average rate difference $\overline{D}_{\bullet} = 18811.91/1759249 = .011$, with a variance of $v_{\bullet} = 1/1759249 = 5.7 \times 10^{-7}$, yielding a standard error of .00075. The significance test $Z = |\overline{D}_{\bullet}|/(v_{\bullet})^{1/2} = 14.67$, which exceeds the 1.96 critical value at $\alpha = .05$. The 95 percent confidence interval is bounded by $\Delta_L = .011 - 1.96(.00075) = .0095$ and $\Delta_U = .011 + 1.96(.00075) = .012$; that is, about 1 percent more of the inoculated soldiers would be expected to be immune to typhoid compared with the noninoculated soldiers.

However, homogeneity of effect size is rejected, with $Q = 763.00 - (18812)^2/1759249 = 561.84$, which exceeds 14.86 the 99.5 percent critical value of the chi-square distribution with $5 - 1 = 4$ $df$, so we reject homogeneity of rate differences over these five studies at significance level .005.

This example points to an interesting corollary problem with the weighting scheme used in this chapter (this problem and its solutions apply equally to combining other effect size indicators such as $d$ or $r$). The incidence data in Table 18.1 come from studies with vastly discrepant within-study sample sizes. In an analysis in which weights are dependent on within-study sample size, the influence of the one study with over 150,000 subjects can dwarf the influence of the other studies, even though some of their sample sizes—at over 10,000 subjects—are large enough that these studies may also provide reliable estimates of effect. One might bound weights to some a priori maximum to avoid this problem; but bounding complicates the variance of the weighted mean, which is no longer equation (18-3), and bounding produces a less efficient (more variable) estimator. An alternative is to compute estimates separately for "big" and "other" studies, an option we do not pursue here only because the number of studies in Table 18.1 is small. One might also redo analyses excluding one or more studies—say, the study with the largest sample size, or the smallest, or both—to assess stability of results. So, for example, if we eliminate the samples with the largest (army in India) and smallest (hospital staffs) number of subjects, the rate difference increases somewhat to $\overline{D}_{\bullet} = .034$, still significantly different from zero and heterogeneous.

**2.3.2 Combining log odds ratios** Fleiss (1981) distinguishes two different cases in which we might want to combine odds ratios from multiple fourfold tables. In the first case, the number of studies to be combined is small, but the within-study sample sizes per study are large, as with the incidence data in Table 18.1. In this case, the proper measure of association to be combined is the log odds ratio $l_i$, the variance of which is

$$v_i = \frac{1}{A_i} + \frac{1}{B_i} + \frac{1}{C_i} + \frac{1}{D_i},$$

or alternatively

$$v_i = \frac{1}{n_{i1}p_{i1}(1 - p_{i1})} + \frac{1}{n_{i2}p_{i2}(1 - p_{i2})}, \qquad (18\text{-}13)$$

where all terms are defined in equation (18-11), and $n_{ij}$ is the number of subjects in condition $j$ of study $i$. In

Table 18.1, for example, $n_{11} = 297$ is the number of subjects in the inoculated condition of the hospital staff study; and $n_{32} = 10,981$ is the number of subjects in the noninoculated condition of the Methuen's column study. Using this variance estimate in equations (18-1) through (18-6) is again straightforward. Subsequently, it may aid interpretation to report final results in terms of the mean odds ratio over studies. This is done by transforming the average log odds ratio, $\bar{l}_{\cdot}$, back into an average odds ratio $\bar{o}_{\cdot} = \text{antilog}(\bar{l}_{\cdot})$, and similarly by reporting upper and lower bounds as odds ratios, $\omega_L = \text{antilog}(\lambda_L)$ and $\omega_U = \text{antilog}(\lambda_U)$.

For example, using the incidence data in Table 18.1, we find the average log odds ratio $\bar{l}_{\cdot} = 188.005/230.937 = .814$, with variance $v_{\cdot} = 1/230.937 = .0043$, yielding a standard error of .066. The significance test $Z = |\bar{l}_{\cdot}|/(v_{\cdot})^{1/2} = 12.33$, which exceeds the 1.96 critical value at $\alpha = .05$; and the 95 percent confidence interval is bounded by $\lambda_L = .814 - 1.96(.066) = .685$ and $\lambda_U = .814 + 1.96(.066) = .943$. Returning the log odds ratios to their original metrics via the antilog transformation yields a common odds ratio of $\bar{o}_{\cdot} = \text{antilog}(.814) = 2.26$ with bounds of $\omega_L = \text{antilog}(.685) = 1.98$ and $\omega_U = \text{antilog}(.943) = 2.57$. The common odds ratio of 2.26 suggests that the odds that inoculated soldiers were immune to typhoid were twice the odds for soldiers not inoculated; and this improvement in the odds over groups is statistically significant. However, homogeneity of effect size is rejected, with $Q = 230.317 - (188.005)^2/230.937 = 77.26$, substantially larger than 14.86, the 99.5 percent critical value of the chi-square distribution with $5 - 1 = 4$ $df$; that is, the odds ratios do not seem to be consistent over these five studies.

**2.3.3 Combining odds ratios with Mantel-Haenszel** The second case that Fleiss distinguishes is when one has many studies to combine, but the within-study sample size in each study is small. In this case, the general logic of equations (18-1) to (18-6) does not dictate analysis. Instead, we compute the Mantel-Haenszel summary estimate of the odds ratio:

$$\bar{o}_{MH} = \frac{\sum_{i=1}^{k}(w_i)[p_{i1}(1 - p_{i2})]}{\sum_{i=1}^{k}(w_i)[p_{i2}(1 - p_{i1})]}, \quad (18\text{-}14)$$

where the proportions are as defined for (18-11) and where

$$w_i = \frac{n_{i1}n_{i2}}{n_{i1} + n_{i2}}.$$

A formula that is equivalent to (18-14), but computed from cell sizes as indexed in Table 18.3, is

$$\bar{o}_{MH} = \frac{\sum_{i=1}^{k}A_iD_i/T_i}{\sum_{i=1}^{k}B_iC_i/T_i}, \quad (18\text{-}15)$$

where $T_i$ is the total number of subjects in the sample. Note that in the case of $k = 1$ (i.e., when there is just one study), the $T_i$'s cancel from the numerator and denominator of (18-15), which then reduces to the odds ratio defined in (18-11). An estimate of the variance of the log of $\bar{o}_{MH}$ (Robins, Breslow & Greenland 1986; Robins, Greenland & Breslow 1986) is

$$v_{\cdot} = \frac{\sum_{i=1}^{k}P_iR_i}{2\left(\sum_{i=1}^{k}R_i\right)^2} + \frac{\sum_{i=1}^{k}(P_iS_i + Q_iR_i)}{2\left(\sum_{i=1}^{k}R_i\right)\left(\sum_{i=1}^{k}S_i\right)} + \frac{\sum_{i=1}^{k}Q_iS_i}{2\left(\sum_{i=1}^{k}S_i\right)^2}, \quad (18\text{-}16)$$

where $P_i = (A_i + D_i)/T_i$, $Q_i = (B_i + C_i)/T_i$, $R_i = A_iD_i/T_i$, and $S_i = B_iC_i/T_i$. When $k = 1$, (18-16) reduces to the standard equation for the variance of a log odds ratio in a study as defined in (18-13). Then, the 95 percent confidence interval is bounded by $\omega_L = \text{antilog}[\log(\bar{o}_{\cdot}) - 1.96(v_{\cdot})^{1/2}]$ and $\omega_U = \text{antilog}[\log(\bar{o}_{MH}) + 1.96(v_{\cdot})^{1/2}]$.

To test the significance of the overall Mantel-Haenszel odds ratio, we can compute the Mantel-Haenszel chi-square statistic:

$$\chi^2_{MH} = \frac{\left\{\left|\sum_{i=1}^{k}[(n_{i1}n_{i2})/(n_{i1} + n_{i2})](p_{i1} - p_{i2})\right| - .5\right\}^2}{\sum_{i=1}^{k}\{[(n_{i1}n_{i2})/(n_{i1} + n_{i2} - 1)]p_i(1 - p_i)\}}, \quad (18\text{-}17)$$

where

$$p_i = \frac{n_{i1}p_{i1} + n_{i2}p_{i2}}{n_{i1} + n_{i2}}.$$

Alternatively, (18-17) can be written in terms of cell frequencies and marginals as

$$\chi^2_{MH} = \frac{\left[\left|\sum_{i=1}^{k}(O_i - E_i)\right| - .5\right]^2}{\sum_{i=1}^{k}V_i},$$

where $O_i = A_i$, $E_i = [(A_i + C_i)/T_i](A_i + B_i)$, and $V_i = E_i[(T_i - (A_i + C_i))/T_i][(T_i - (A_i + B_i))/(T_i - 1)]$. The difference

$(O_i - E_i)$ in the numerator is simply the difference "between the observed number of treatment patients who experienced the outcome event, $O$, and the number expected to have done so under the hypothesis that the treatment is no different from the control, $E$" (Fleiss & Gross 1991, p. 131). In the denominator, $V_i$ is the variance of the difference $(O_i - E_i)$, which can also be expressed as the product of the four marginal frequencies divided by $T_i^2(T_i - 1)$, or $[(A_i + C_i)(A_i + B_i)(B_i + D_i)(C_i + D_i)]/[T_i^2(T_i - 1)]$. The result of this chi-square is compared with the critical value of chi-square with 1 $df$. Homogeneity may be tested using the same test developed for the log odds ratio. However, better homogeneity tests, although computationally complex, are available (Jones et al. 1989; Paul & Donner 1989); one of these, the Breslow-Day test, may be obtained as part of the output from the FREQ procedure in SAS (SAS Institute 1985; see also Kuritz, Landis & Koch 1988), although not necessarily accessible in a way that is convenient for use in meta-analysis.

We illustrate the Mantel-Haenszel technique by applying it to the fatality data in Table 18.1. The Mantel-Haenszel common odds ratio is $218.934/123.976 = 1.77$; that is, the odds that inoculated subjects who contracted typhoid would survive were almost two times the odds that noninoculated subjects who contracted typhoid would survive. The variance of the log of this ratio is $v_* = 63.996/[2(218.934)^2] + 190.273/[2(218.934)(123.976)] + 88.64/[2(123.976)^2] = .00706$, and the 95 percent confidence interval is bounded by $\omega_L = \text{antilog}[\log(1.77) - 1.96(.007)^{1/2}] = 1.50$ and $\omega_U = \text{antilog}[\log(1.77) + 1.96(.007)^{1/2}] = 2.08$. The Mantel-Haenszel $\chi^2 = (94.96 - .5)^2/191.31 = 46.64$, $p < .00001$, suggesting that inoculation significantly increases the odds of survival among those who contracted typhoid. Finally, homogeneity of odds ratios is not rejected over these six studies, $Q = 50.88 - [(78.97)^2/141.46] = 6.80$, $df = 5$, prob $= .24$); a $Q$ value this large would be expected between 20 and 25 percent of the time if all the population correlations were identical.

The results of a Mantel-Haenszel analysis are valid whether one is analyzing many studies with small sample sizes or few studies with large sample sizes; but the results of the log odds ratio analysis in section 2.3.2 are valid only in the latter case. Therefore, we can reanalyze the incidence data in Table 18.1 using Mantel-Haenszel techniques and compare the results to the log odds ratio analysis. The Mantel-Haenszel common odds ratio for the incidence data is $537.007/205.823 = 2.61$; that is, the odds that inoculated subjects who contracted typhoid

would survive were two and a half times the odds that noninoculated subjects who contracted typhoid would survive. The variance of the log of this ratio is $v_* = 125.355/[2(537.007)^2] + 459.181/[2(537.007)(205.823)] + 158.294/[2(205.823)^2] = .00416$, and the 95 percent confidence interval is bounded by $\omega_L = \text{antilog}[\log(2.61) - 1.96(.004)^{1/2}] = 2.30$ and $\omega_U = \text{antilog}[\log(2.61) + 1.96(.004)^{1/2}] = 2.96$. The Mantel-Haenszel $\chi^2 = (331.185 - .5)^2/462.879 = 236.244$, $p < .00001$, suggesting that inoculation significantly increases the odds of survival among those who contracted typhoid. Finally, homogeneity of odds ratios is rejected over these five studies, $Q = 230.373 - [(188.188)^2/231.173] = 77.18$, which greatly exceeds 14.86, the 99.5 percent critical value of the chi-square distribution at $5 - 1 = 4$ $df$. Under the Mantel-Haenszel techniques, therefore, the odds ratio was somewhat larger than under the log odds approach; but the variance and $Q$ test results were very similar, and the confidence interval was about as wide under both approaches.

**2.3.4 Further developments in combining odds ratios** Our presentation of methods for combining odds ratios is complex and, unfortunately, incomplete. The interested reader is referred to further readings on the following topics: The variance of the Mantel-Haenszel log odds ratio estimate is further examined by Phillips and Holland (1987); exact confidence intervals for the common odds ratio in $2 \times 2$ tables are described by Mehta, Patel, and Gray (1985); inadequacies of the Peto-modified Mantel-Haenszel method described by Berlin et al. (1989) and Yusuf et al. (1985) are elaborated by Fleiss (1981), Fleiss and Gross (1991), and Greenland and Salvan (1990); and power and sample size issues for a variety of different situations are discussed by Lubin and Gail (1990) and Mantel and Fleiss (1980).

## 2.4 Combining Data in Their Original Metric

On some occasions, the researcher may wish to combine outcomes over studies in which the metric of the outcome variable is exactly the same across studies. Under such circumstances, converting outcomes to the various effect size indicators might be not only unnecessary but also distracting since the meaning of the original variable may be obscured. An example might be a review of the effects of treatments for obesity compared with control conditions, where the dependent variable is always weight in pounds or kilograms; in this case computing a standardized mean difference score for each study might be less clear than simply reporting outcomes as weight in pounds. Even so, the researcher should still weight each study by a function of sample variance. If $T_i$ is a mean difference between treatment and control group means, $T_i = \overline{X}^t_i - \overline{X}^c_i$, then an estimate of the variance of $T_i$ is

$$v_i = \sigma_i^2(1/n^t_i + 1/n^c_i), \qquad (18\text{-}18)$$

where $n^t$ is the within-study sample size in the treatment group, $n^c$ is the within-study sample size for the control group, and $\sigma_i^2$ is the assumed common variance (note that this assumes the two variances *within* each study are homogeneous, but *different* studies need not have the same variances). The latter can be estimated by the pooled within-group variance if the within-study sample sizes and standard deviations of each group are reported:

$$s_{pi}^2 = [(n^t_i - 1)s^t_i{}^2 + (n^c_i - 1)s^c_i{}^2]/[n^t_i + n^c_i - 2],$$

where $s^t_i{}^2$ is the variance of the treatment group in the $i$th study, and $s^c_i{}^2$ is the variance of the control group or the comparison treatment in the $i$th study. The pooled variance can sometimes be estimated other ways (see Chapter 16). Squaring the pooled standard deviation yields an estimate of the pooled variance. Lacking any estimate of the pooled variance at all, one cannot use (18-1) to (18-6); but then one cannot compute a standardized mean difference, either.

As an example, Mumford et al. (1984) reviewed studies of the effects of mental health treatment on reducing costs of medical utilization, the latter measured by the number of days of hospitalization. From their Table 1, we extract eight randomized studies comparing treatment groups that received psychological interven-

tion with control groups, which report means, within-study sample sizes, and standard deviations (see Table 18.4). The weighted average of the difference between the number of days the treatment groups were hospitalized versus the number of days the control groups were hospitalized was $\overline{T}_\bullet = -14.70/27.24 = -.54$ days; that is, the treatment group left the hospital about half a day sooner than the control group. The variance of this effect is $v_\bullet = 1/27.24 = .037$, yielding a standard error of .19. The 95 percent confidence interval is bounded by $T_L = -.54 - 1.96(.19)^{1/2} = -.91$ and $T_U = -.54 + 1.96(.19)^{1/2} = -.17$, and $Z = |\overline{T}_\bullet|/v_\bullet^{1/2} = |-.54|/.19 = 2.84$ (prob = .0048), both of which indicate that the effect is significantly different from zero. However, the homogeneity test closely approaches significance, with $Q = [21.85 - (-14.70)^2/27.24] = 13.92$, $df = 7$, p = .053, suggesting that mean differences may not be similar over studies.

## 3. RANDOM EFFECTS MODELS

Under a fixed effects model, the effect size statistics, $T_i$, from $k$ studies estimate a population parameter $\theta_i$ that is fixed at a particular value so that $\theta_1 = \ldots = \theta_k = \theta$. The estimate $T_i$ in any given study differs from $\theta$ due to sampling error, or what we have been referring to as conditional variability; that is, because a given study used a *sample* of subjects from the population, the estimate of $T_i$ computed for that sample will differ somewhat from $\theta$ for the population.

**Table 18.4 Effects of Psychological Intervention on Reducing Hospital Length of Stay (in days)**

| Study | Psychotherapy Groups | | | Control Group | | | Mean Difference |
|---|---|---|---|---|---|---|---|
| | N | Mean Days | SD | N | Mean Days | SD | |
| 1 | 13 | 5.00 | 4.70 | 13 | 6.50 | 3.80 | −1.50 |
| 2 | 30 | 4.90 | 1.71 | 50 | 6.10 | 2.30 | −1.20 |
| 3 | 35 | 22.50 | 3.44 | 35 | 24.90 | 10.65 | −2.40 |
| 4 | 20 | 12.50 | 1.47 | 20 | 12.30 | 1.66 | .20 |
| 5 | 10 | 3.37 | .92 | 10 | 3.19 | .79 | .18 |
| 6 | 13 | 4.90 | 1.10 | 14 | 5.50 | .90 | −.60 |
| 7 | 9 | 10.56 | 1.13 | 9 | 12.78 | 2.05 | −2.22 |
| 8 | 8 | 6.50 | .76 | 8 | 7.38 | 1.41 | −.88 |

SOURCE: Adapted from Mumford et al. (1984), Table 1, including only randomized trials that reported means and standard deviations.

Under a random effects model, $\theta_i$ is not fixed, but is itself random and has its own distribution. Hence, total variability of an observed study effect size estimate $v_i^*$ reflects *both* conditional variation $v_i$ of that effect size around each population $\theta_i$ *and* random variation, $\sigma_\theta^2$, of the individual $\theta_i$ around the mean population effect size:

$$v_i^* = \sigma_\theta^2 + v_i. \qquad (18\text{-}19)$$

In this equation, we will refer to $\sigma_\theta^2$ as either the between-studies variance or the variance component (Chapter 20 refers to this as random effects variance); to $v_i$ as either within-study variance or the conditional variance of $T_i$ (i.e., the variance of an observed effect size conditional on $\theta$ being fixed at the value $\theta_i$; Chapter 20 calls this estimation variance); and to $v_i^*$ as the unconditional variance of an observed effect size $T_i$ (Chapter 20 calls this the variance of estimated effects). If the between-studies variance is zero, then the equations of the random effects model reduce to those of the fixed effects model, with unconditional variability of an observed effect size $[v_i^*]$ hypothesized to be due entirely to conditional variability $[v_i]$ (i.e., to sampling error).

The reader may wonder how to make the choice between a fixed versus random effects model. The answer is partly statistical, partly conceptual, and rarely indisputable. Statistically, the presence of a variance component estimate that is significantly different from zero might indicate the presence of random effects to be accounted for. However, this finding is not definitive because the test for significance of the variance component might have inadequate power under some circumstances, and because the addition of fixed effects covariates are sometimes sufficient to produce a nonsignificant variance component. Conceptually, some rationales can be advanced for adopting a random effects model a priori (see Chapter 20). For example, sometimes the researcher has sampled some facet of the research from a population and desires inference to that population. So the choice between models must be made after careful review of the applicability of all these matters to the particular meta-analysis being done.

In any case, once the researcher decides to proceed with a random effects analysis, a first task is to determine whether or not the variance component differs significantly from zero and, if it does, then to estimate its magnitude. The significance of the variance component is known if the researcher has already conducted a fixed effects analysis—if the $Q$ test for homogeneity of effect size (equation 18-6) was rejected, the variance component differs significantly from zero. In that case, the remaining task is to estimate the magnitude of the variance component. If the investigator has not conducted a fixed effects analysis already, $Q$ must be calculated in addition to estimating the variance component magnitude.

Estimating the variance component can be done in either of two ways. The first method begins with the ordinary *(unweighted)* sample estimate of the variance of the effect sizes, $T_1, \ldots, T_k$, computed as

$$s^2(T) = \sum_{i=1}^{k} [(T_i - \overline{T})^2/(k-1)], \qquad (18\text{-}20)$$

where $\overline{T}$ is the *unweighted* mean of $T_1$ through $T_k$. A computationally convenient form of (18-20) is

$$s^2(T) = \left[ \sum_{i=1}^{k} T_i^2 - \left( \sum_{i=1}^{k} T_i \right)^2 / k \right] / (k-1).$$

The expected value of $s^2(T)$—that is, the unconditional variance we would expect to be associated with any particular effect size—is

$$E[s^2(T)] = \sigma_\theta^2 + (1/k) \sum_{i=1}^{k} \sigma^2(T_i | \theta_i). \qquad (18\text{-}21)$$

The observed variance $s^2(T)$ from equation (18-20) is an unbiased estimate of $E[s^2(T)]$ by definition. To estimate $\sigma^2(T_i | \theta_i)$, we use the $v_i$ from equations (18-7), (18-8), (18-10), (18-12), (18-13), (18-16), or (18-18), depending on which effect size indicator is being aggregated (although other, more exact estimates of conditional variability under the random effects model exist—Hedges & Olkin 1985—their use makes little practical difference). With these estimates, equation (18-21) can be solved to obtain an estimate of the variance component:

$$\hat{\sigma}_\theta^2 = s^2(T) - (1/k) \sum_{i=1}^{k} v_i. \qquad (18\text{-}22)$$

This sample estimate of the variance component will sometimes be negative, even though the population variance component must be a positive number. In these cases, it is customary to fix the component to zero.

The second method for estimating the variance component begins with $Q$ as defined in equation (18-6), which we now take as an estimate of the *weighted* sample estimate of the unconditional variance $\sigma^2(T_i)$. The expected value of $Q$ is

$$E[Q] = c(\sigma_\theta^2) + (k-1),$$

where

$$c = \sum_{i=1}^{k} w_i - \left[ \sum_{i=1}^{k} w_i^2 / \sum_{i=1}^{k} w_i \right].$$

Solving for $\sigma_\theta^2$ and substituting $Q$ for its expectation gives another estimator of the variance component:

$$\hat{\sigma}_\theta^2 = [Q - (k-1)]/c. \qquad (18\text{-}23)$$

Hence (18-22) and (18-23) are two competing estimators for the variance component (see Chapter 20 for additional estimators). The relative merits of the two estimators have not been widely studied. However, an important property of (18-23) is that it gives a nonzero estimate of the variance component only if the homogeneity statistic $Q$ is larger than its expected value under the null hypothesis that $\sigma_\theta^2 = 0$. The variance component differs significantly from zero if $Q$ as defined in (18-6) exceeds the relevant critical value of chi-square at $k-1$ $df$. Note that we have now used $Q$ as defined in (18-6) for three purposes: to test for homogeneity of effect size, to test for the significance of the variance component, and to estimate the unconditional variance of effect sizes.

When the variance component is significant, one may also compute $\overline{T}_*$, the random effects weighted mean of $T_1, \ldots, T_k$, as an estimate of $\mu_\theta$, the average of the random effects in the population; $v_*$, the variance of $\overline{T}_*$ (the square root of $v_*$ is the standard error of $\overline{T}_*$); and random effects confidence limits $\theta_L$ and $\theta_U$ for $\mu_\theta$ by multiplying the standard error by an appropriate critical value (often, 1.96 at $\alpha = .05$), and adding and subtracting the resulting product from $\overline{T}_*$. In general, the computations follow (18-1) to (18-5), except that the following unconditional variance estimate is used in (18-2) through (18-5) in place of the conditional variances outlined in the fixed effects models:

$$v_i^* = \hat{\sigma}_\theta^2 + v_i, \qquad (18\text{-}24)$$

where $\hat{\sigma}_\theta^2$ is the variance component estimate yielded by (18-22) or (18-23) and $v_i$ is defined by (18-7), (18-8), (18-10), (18-12), (18-13), (18-16), or (18-18), as appropriate. The square root of the variance component describes the standard deviation of the distribution of effect parameters. Multiplying that standard deviation by 1.96, and adding and subtracting the result from the average random effect size $\overline{T}_*$, yields the limits of an approximate 95 percent confidence interval within which the population effect sizes are likely to fall. All these random effects analyses assume that the random effects are normally distributed with constant variance, an as-

sumption that is particularly difficult to assess when the number of studies is small (see Chapter 20).

Earlier in this chapter, we noted that the random effects model provided more conservative estimates of the significance of average effect sizes over studies *in the presence of unexplained heterogeneity*. Given the preceding paragraphs, we can now see why. Under both fixed and random effects models, significant unexplained heterogeneity results in rejection of $Q$, since $Q$ is exactly the same under both models. The variance component is an index of how much variance remained unexplained. But in the fixed effects model, this unexplained variance is ignored in the computation of standard errors and confidence intervals. By contrast, in the random effects model the unexplained heterogeneity represented by the variance component is added to the conditional variance, and the sum of these is then used in computing standard errors and confidence intervals. Obviously, with more variance, the latter will be larger, providing a more conservative test of the significance and distribution of combined effects size estimators. In addition, because the weights in equation (18-1) and (18-2) under the random effects model are computed using the unconditional variance in equation (18-24), these weights will tend toward equality over studies— no matter how unequal their within-study sample size— as study heterogeneity, and thus the variance component, increases.

## 3.1 Combining Standardized Mean Differences

Estimating the conditional variance of $d_i$ with (18-7) allows us to solve equations (18-20) through (18-24) to estimate the variance component $\sigma_\delta^2$. If the variance component is significant (i.e., if $Q$ in 18-6 is rejected), then the weighted average of the random effects is computed using (18-1) with weights as computed by (18-2), but where the variance for the denominator of (18-2) is estimated as (18-24):

$$v_i^* = \hat{\sigma}_\delta^2 + v_i,$$

where $v_i$ is defined as (18-7). Similarly, the variance of the estimate of $\mu_\delta$ is given by (18-3) but using the above estimate of the unconditional variance, $v_i^*$; using the resulting variance estimate yields the 95 percent confidence intervals and $Z$ test as defined in (18-4) and (18-5). If the variance component exceeds zero, the random effects unconditional variance $v_i^*$ will be larger than the fixed effects variance $v_i$, so the variance of the estimate and the confidence intervals will both be larger under random effects models, and $Z$ will always be smaller, reflecting the greater variability of effect sizes under that model.

We apply these procedures to Data Set II, using the data from 19 studies on the effects of teacher expectancy on student IQ. Equation (18-20) yields a sample estimate of the variance of $s^2(d) = [2.8273 - (3.11)^2/19]/18$ $= .1288$. We then estimate $(1/k)\sum_{i=1}^{k} \sigma^2(d_i|\delta_i)$ by averag-

ing the $v_i$ as defined by (18-7) to obtain $(1/k)\sum_{i=1}^{k} v_i$ $= .04843$, and solve (18-22) for a variance component estimate of $\hat{\sigma}_\delta^2 = .1288 - .04843 = .082$, which is significantly different from zero because $Q = 35.83$ exceeds 34.81, the 99 percent critical value of the chi-square distribution for $k - 1 = 19 - 1 = 18$ $df$ (note that this is the same $Q$ for homogeneity under a fixed effects model). Recomputing the aggregate statistics under the random effects model then yields an average population effect size of $\bar{d}_* = 18.22/159.36 = .114$, with a standard error $= (1/159.36)^{1/2} = .079$. The limits of the 95 percent confidence intervals are $\delta_L = .114 - 1.96(.079) = -.04$ and $\delta_U = .114 + 1.96(.079) = .27$, and $Z = |\bar{d}_*|/(v_*^{1/2}) = .114|/.079 = 1.44$, which does not exceed 1.96, so we do not reject the hypothesis that the average effect size in the population is zero. These results suggest that although the central tendency over the 19 studies is rather small at .114, population effect sizes do vary significantly from that tendency. Note the much wider confidence interval relative to the fixed effects model analysis, reflecting the greater inherent variability of effect sizes under the random effects model.

Finally, the square root of the variance component in this data is .34, which we can take (under the untestable assumption of a normal distribution of effect sizes in the population) as the standard deviation of the population effect sizes. Multiplying it by 1.96 yields a 95 percent confidence interval bounded by $-.55$ to .78, suggesting that most effect sizes in the population probably fall into this range. Indeed, this mirrors the data in the sample, with all but two study effect sizes falling within this range.

Alternatively, using the weighted variance model of equation (18-23), we obtain $c = 751.2075 - 47697.39/751.2075 = 687.71$; and then the variance component is $\hat{\sigma}_\delta^2 = [(35.83 - 18)/687.71] = .026$, somewhat smaller than the variance component estimated using (18-21). Recomputing the aggregated statistics yields an average population effect size of $\bar{\delta}_* = 28.68/321.08 = .0893$, with

a standard error $= (1/321.08)^{1/2} = .0558$. The limits of the 95 percent confidence interval are $\delta_L = .089 - 1.96(.0558) = -.020$ and $\delta_U = .089 + 1.96(.0558) = .199$, and $Z = |.0893|/.0558 = 1.60$. Note that these results are similar, both in order of magnitude and in inference, to those resulting from the analysis that began with the ordinary, unweighted sample estimate of the variance reported earlier in this section.

## 3.2 Combining Correlations

### 3.2.1 Combining z-transformed correlations
If we follow the z-transform procedure outlined in section 2.2.1, then equation (18-8) defines the conditional variance of the individual $z$ statistics, allowing us to solve equations (18-20) to (18-24). We apply this procedure to Data Set III, which reported correlations from 20 studies between overall student ratings of the instructor and student achievement. Equation (18-20) yields a sample estimate of the variance of $s^2(z) = .0604$. We then estimate $(1/k)\sum_{i=1}^{k} \sigma^2(z_i|\zeta_i)$ by averaging the $v_i$ as defined by (18-8) to obtain $(1/k)\sum_{i=1}^{k} v_i = .0640$, and solve (18-22) for a variance component estimate of $\hat{\sigma}_\zeta^2 = .0604 - .0640 = -.0036$, $Q = 20.94$ (the same $Q$ for homogeneity under a fixed effects model), which at $k - 1 = 19$ $df$ is not significant (prob = .34). Since this variance component is negative, we set it equal to zero by convention. The weighted variance method (equation 18-23) yields $c = 530 - 27334/530 = 478.43$, and then the variance component is $\hat{\sigma}_\zeta^2 = [20.94 - 19]/478.43 = .0041$, also not significantly different from zero by the same $Q$ test. As in section 3.1, the unweighted and weighted analyses yield similar results. When the variance component is not significantly different from zero, we do not recompute average effect sizes, standard errors, and confidence intervals; but the reader should recall our previous comments that some analysts would choose to compute all these random effect statistics even though the variance component is not significantly different from zero.

### 3.2.2 Combining correlation coefficients directly
If we choose to combine correlation coefficients, the conditional variance of $r_i$ is defined in (18-10), allowing us to use equations (18-20) to (18-24). We apply this procedure to Data Set III. Equation (18-20) yields a sample estimate of the variance of $s^2(r) = (1/19)$ $[3.4884 - (7.28)^2/20] = .0441$. Using equation (18-22),

we then obtain a variance component of $\hat{\sigma}_\rho^2 = .0441 - .0374 = .0067$, which is not significantly different from zero $Q = 25.631$, prob $= .14$. Using equation (18-23), the weighted variance method yields $c = 847.18 - (60444.68/847.18) = 775.83$, which then yields a variance component of $\hat{\sigma}_\rho^2 = (25.631 - 19)/775.83 = .0085$, also nonsignificant by the same $Q$ test and similar to that produced by the unweighted analysis.

## 3.3 Combining Fourfold Tables: Rates, Proportions, and Odds Ratios

### 3.3.1 Combining differences between proportions
In the case of rate differences $D_i = p_{i1} - p_{i2}$, the conditional variance is defined in (18-12). As an example, we apply equations (18-20) to (18-24) to the incidence data in Table 18.1. Equation (18-20) yields a sample estimate of the variance of $s^2(D) = (1/4)[.0408 - (.3065)^2/5) = .0055$. Using equation (18-22), we then obtain a variance component of $\hat{\sigma}_\Delta^2 = .0055 - .0002 = .0053$, which at $k - 1 = 4$ $df$ is significantly different from zero, $Q = 562.296$. Recomputing the aggregate effect size statistics yields an average rate difference $\overline{D}_* = 53.00/912.49 = .058$, a variance $v_* = 1/912.49 = .0011$, standard error $= .033$, with a 95 percent confidence interval bounded by $\Delta_L = .058 - (1.96)(.033) = -.0069$ and $\Delta_U = .058 + (1.96)(.033) = .12$.

Using equation (18-23), the weighted variance method yields $c = 393167.45$, which then yields a variance component estimate of $\hat{\sigma}_\Delta^2 = (562.296 - 4)/c = .0014$, also significant by the same $Q$ test. Recomputing the average effect size statistics yields an average difference between proportions of $\overline{D}_* = 166.75/3170.42 = .053$, a variance $v_* = 1/3170.42 = .0003$, standard error $= .018$, and a 95 percent confidence interval bounded by $\Delta_L = .053 - (1.96)(.018) = .018$ and $\Delta_U = .053 + (1.96)(.018) = .087$. Again, the weighted and unweighted methods yield very similar results.

### 3.3.2 Combining odds and log odds ratios
The methods outlined in this section can be used to test random effects models in both cases discussed by Fleiss—combining log odds ratios, and combining odds ratios using Mantel-Haenszel methods. We use (18-13) to estimate the conditional variance of the log odds ratio and then use (18-20) to (18-24) with the incidence data in Table 18.1. Equation (18-20) yields a sample estimate of variance of $s^2(l) = (1/4)[6.604 - (4.72)^2/5] = .537$. Using equation (18-22), we then obtain a variance component estimate of $\hat{\sigma}_\lambda^2 = .537 - .032 = .505$, which at $k - 1 = 4$ $df$ is significantly different from zero,

$Q = 77.2626$. Recomputing the average effect size statistics yields an average log odds ratio $\overline{l}_* = 8.75/9.32 = .94$, a variance $v_* = 1/9.32 = .107$, standard error $= .328$, and a 95 percent confidence interval bounded by $\lambda_L = .94 - (1.96)(.328) = .30$ and $\lambda_U = .94 + (1.96)(.328) = 1.58$. As in section 2.3, we then reconvert the common log odds ratios into the more interpretable common odds ratio as $\overline{o}_* = \text{antilog}(\overline{l}_*) = 2.56$, and $\omega_L = \text{antilog}(\lambda_L) = 1.35$ and $\omega_U = \text{antilog}(\lambda_U) = 4.85$ are the bounds of the 95 percent confidence interval.

Using equation (18-23), the weighted variance method yields again yields similar results, with $c = 230.94 - (17566.09/230.94) = 154.88$, which then yields a variance component estimate of $\hat{\sigma}_\lambda^2 = (77.26 - 4)/154.88 = .473$, also significant by the same $Q$ test. Recomputing the average effect size statistics yields an average log odds ratio $\overline{l}_* = 9.30/9.90 = .94$, a variance $v_* = 1/9.90 = .102$, standard error $= .319$, and a 95 percent confidence interval bounded by $\lambda_L = .94 - (1.96)(.319) = .32$ and $\lambda_U = .94 + (1.96)(.319) = 1.56$. As in section 2.3, we then reconvert the common log odds ratio into the more interpretable common odds ratio as $\overline{o}_* = \text{antilog}(\overline{l}_*) = 2.56$, and the 95 percent confidence interval is then bounded by $\omega_L = \text{antilog}(\lambda_L) = 1.37$ and $\omega_U = \text{antilog}(\lambda_U) = 4.73$.

## 3.4 Combining Differences Between Raw Means

Equation (18-18) gives the conditional variance for differences between two independent means. Using that estimate in equations (18-20) to (18-24) yields the random effects solution. For the data in Table 18.4, equation (18-20) yields a sample estimate of the variance of $s^2(T) = (1/7)[15.59 - (8.42)^2/8] = .96$. Using equation (18-22), we then obtain a variance component of $\hat{\sigma}_{\theta T}^2 = .96 - 1.01 = -.05$, which by convention we round to zero; since $Q = 13.92$, and prob $= .053$, however, this is very close to significance. Using equation (18-23), the weighted variance method yields $c = 27.24 - (138.75/27.24) = 22.15$, which then yields $\hat{\sigma}_\theta^2 = (13.92 - 7)/22.15 = .31$, which is clearly higher than the unweighted estimate and makes more sense given the $Q$ test. Recomputing the average effect size statistics under the random effects model for the unweighted variance estimate yields an average mean difference of $\overline{T}_* = -18.41/37.94 = -.49$ days, with $v_* = 1/37.94 = .027$, standard error $= .16$, and a 95 percent confidence interval bounded by $\theta_L = -.49 - 1.96(.16) = -.80$ and $\theta_U = -.49 + 1.96(.16) = -.13$. Recomputing these same statistics under the weighted variance model yields $\overline{T}_* = -7.66/$

$11.25 = -.68$ days, with $v_* = 1/11.25 = .09$, standard error $= .30$, and a 95 percent confidence interval bounded by $\theta_L = -.68 - 1.96(.30) = -1.27$ and $\theta_U = -.68 + 1.96(.30) = -.09$.

## 4. CONCLUSION

We opened this chapter with a discussion of the debate between Pearson and Wright about the effectiveness of the typhoid vaccine. Hence, it is fitting to return to this topic as we conclude. If we were to apply the methods outlined in section 2.2.1 to the data in Table 18.1, we would find that the typhoid vaccine is even *less* effective than Pearson concluded. For example, the weighted average tetrachoric correlation between immunity and inoculation is $\bar{\rho}_\bullet = .132 (Z = 56.41)$ and the weighted average tetrachoric correlation between inoculation and survival among those who contract typhoid is $\bar{\rho}_\bullet = .146 (Z = 17.199)$. Both these averages are smaller than the unweighted averages reported by Pearson of .23 and .19, respectively. It is ironic in retrospect, then, that Wright was right: Subsequent developments showed that the vaccine works very well indeed.

Yet this possibility was not lost on Pearson. Anticipating informally the results of the formal $Q$ tests, which reject homogeneity of effect size for this data ($Q = 1740.36$, and $Q = 76.833$, respectively), Pearson (1904b) said early in his report that "the material appears to be so heterogeneous, and the results so irregular, that it must be doubtful how much weight is to be attributed to the different results" (p. 1243). He went on to outline a host of possible sources of heterogeneity. For example, some of the data came from army units located in India, and others located in South Africa, which for a variety of reasons he thought "seem hardly comparable" (p. 1243); for example, "the efficiency of nursing . . . must vary largely from hospital to hospital under military necessities" (1904a, p. 1663). He also noted that the samples differed in ways that might affect study outcome: "the single regiments were very rapidly changing their environment . . . the Ladysmith garrison least, and Methuen's column more mobile than the Ladysmith garrison, but far less than the single regiments" (1904b, p. 1244). Since "it is far more easy to be cautious under a constant environment than when the environment is nightly changing," it might be that "the apparent correlation between inoculation and immunity arose from the more cautious and careful men volunteering for inoculation" (1904b, p. 1244). Hence, he

called for better-designed "experimental inquiry," using "volunteers, but while keeping a register of all men who volunteered, only to inoculate every second volunteer" (p. 1245); recall that Fisher's work (1925, 1926) on randomized experiments had not yet been published.

Wright (1904a), too, cited various sources of heterogeneity, noting that the validity of typhoid diagnosis was undoubtedly highly variable over units, partly because "under ordinary circumstances the only practically certain criterion of typhoid fever is to be found in the intestinal lesions which are disclosed by *post-mortem* examination" (p. 1490). Such autopsies were not routine in all units, so measurements of fatality in some units were probably more valid than in others. Moreover, autopsy diagnosis is definitive, whereas physician diagnosis of incidence of typhoid was very unreliable. For these and other reasons, Wright (1904b) questioned the validity of measurement in these studies, chiding Pearson for neglecting "to make inquiry into the trustworthiness of . . . the comparative value of a death-rate and an incidence-rate of the efficacy of an inoculation process" (p. 1727).

Methods for exploring such sources of heterogeneity are the topic of the next several chapters of this book. Unfortunately, neither Pearson nor Wright provided more precise information about which studies were associated with which sources of heterogeneity in the data they argued about. Hence, use of the Pearson-Wright example ends here. But the issues are timeless. Pearson and Wright understood them nearly a century ago; they lacked only the methods to pursue them. We turn to those methods now.

### Authors' Note

This research was supported in part by a Centers of Excellence grant awarded to the Department of Psychology, Memphis State University, by the State of Tennessee. The authors wish to thank Joseph Fleiss for providing very helpful reviews and statistical consultation. Correspondence should be sent to the first author at Memphis State University.

## 5. REFERENCES

Berlin, J. A., Laird, N. M., Sacks, H. S., & Chalmers, T. C. (1989). A comparison of statistical methods for combining event rates from clinical trials. *Statistics in Medicine, 8,* 141–151.

Boissel, J. P., Blanchard, J., Panak, E., Peyrieux, J. C., & Sacks, H. (1989). Considerations for the meta-analysis of randomized clinical trials. *Controlled Clinical Trials, 10,* 254–281.

Bollen, K. A. (1989). *Structural equations with latent variables.* New York: Wiley.

Chalmers, T. C., Smith, H., Blackburn, B., Silverman, B., Schroeder, B., Reitman, D., & Ambroz, A. (1981). A method for assessing the quality of a randomized control trial. *Controlled Clinical Trials, 2,* 31–49.

Cook, T. D., & Campbell, D. T. (1979). *Quasi-experimentation: Design and analysis issues for field settings.* Chicago: Rand McNally.

Cowles, M. (1989). *Statistics in psychology: An historical perspective.* Hillsdale, NJ: Erlbaum.

DerSimonian, R., & Laird, N. (1986). Meta-analysis in clinical trials. *Controlled Clinical Trials, 7,* 177–188.

Fisher, R. A. (1925). *Statistical methods for research workers.* Edinburgh: Oliver & Boyd.

Fisher, R. A. (1926). The arrangement of field experiments. *Journal of the Ministry of Agriculture of Great Britain, 33,* 505–513.

Fleiss, J. L. (1981). *Statistical methods for rates and proportions* (2nd ed.). New York: Wiley.

Fleiss, J. L., & Gross, A. J. (1991). Meta-analysis in epidemiology, with special reference to studies of the association between exposure to environmental tobacco smoke and lung cancer: A critique. *Journal of Clinical Epidemiology, 44,* 127–139.

Freedman, D. A. (1987). As others see us: A case study in path analysis. *Journal of Educational Statistics, 12,* 101–128.

Greenland, S., & Salvan, A. (1990). Bias in the one-step method for pooling study results. *Statistics in Medicine, 9,* 247–252.

Hedges, L. V. (1983). A random effects model for effect sizes. *Psychological Bulletin, 93,* 388–395.

Hedges, L. V., & Olkin, I. (1985). *Statistical methods for meta-analysis.* Orlando, FL: Academic Press.

Hunter, J. E., & Schmidt, F. L. (1990). *Methods of meta-analysis: Correcting errors and bias in research findings.* Newbury Park, CA: Sage.

Jones, M. P., O'Gorman, T. W., Lemke, J. H., & Woolson, R. F. (1989). A Monte Carlo investigation of homogeneity tests of the odds ratio under various sample size configurations. *Biometrics, 45,* 171–181.

Kleinbaum, D. G., Kupper, L. L., & Morgenstern, H. (1982). *Epidemiologic research: Principles and quantitative methods.* New York: Van Nostrand Reinhold.

Kuritz, S. J., Landis, J. R., & Koch, G. G. (1988). A general overview of Mantel-Haenszel methods: Applications and recent developments. *Annual Review of Public Health, 9,* 123–160.

Lubin, J. H., & Gail, M. H. (1990). On power and sample size for studying features of the relative odds of disease. *American Journal of Epidemiology, 131,* 552–566.

Mantel, N., & Fleiss, J. L. (1980). Minimum expected cell size requirements for the Mantel-Haenszel one-degree-of-freedom chi-square test and a related rapid procedure. *American Journal of Epidemiology, 112,* 129–134.

Mehta, C. R., Patel, N. R., & Gray, R. (1985). Computing an exact confidence interval for the common odds ratio in several 2 x 2 contingency tables. *Journal of the American Statistical Association, 80,* 969–973.

Mumford, E., Schlesinger, H. J., Glass, G. V., Patrick, C., & Cuerdon, T. (1984). A new look at evidence about reduced cost of medical utilization following mental health treatment. *American Journal of Psychiatry, 141,* 1145–1158.

Paul, S. R., & Donner, A. (1989). A comparison of tests of homogeneity of odds ratios in *k* 2 x 2 tables. *Statistics in Medicine, 8,* 1455–1468.

Pearson, K. (1904a). Antityphoid inoculation. *British Medical Journal, 2,* 1667–1668.

Pearson, K. (1904b). Report on certain enteric fever inoculation statistics. *British Medical Journal, 2,* 1243–1246.

Phillips, A., & Holland, P. W. (1987). Estimators of the variance of the Mantel-Haenszel log-odds-ratio estimate. *Biometrics, 43,* 425–431.

Roberts, R. M. (1989). *Serendipity: Accidental discoveries in science.* New York: Wiley.

Robins, J., Breslow, N., & Greenland, S. (1986). Estimators of the Mantel-Haenszel variance consistent in both sparse data and large-strata limiting models. *Biometrics, 42,* 311–323.

Robins, J., Greenland, S., & Breslow, N. (1986). A general estimator for the variance of the Mantel-Haenszel odds ratio. *American Journal of Epidemiology, 124,* 719–723.

Sackett, P. R., Harris, M. M., & Orr, J. M. (1986). On seeking moderator variables in the meta-analysis of correlational data: A Monte Carlo investigation of statistical power and resistance to Type I error. *Journal of Applied Psychology, 71,* 302–310.

SAS Institute. (1985). *SAS User's Guide: Statistics (1985 ed).* Cary, NC: Author.

Spector, P. E., & Levine, E. L. (1987). Meta-analysis for integrating study outcomes: A Monte Carlo study of its susceptibility to Type I and Type II errors. *Journal of Applied Psychology, 72,* 3–9.

Susser, M. (1977). Judgment and causal inference: Criteria in epidemiologic studies. *American Journal of Epidemiology, 105,* 1–15.

Wright, A. E. (1904a). Antityphoid inoculation. *British Medical Journal, 2,* 1489–1491.

Wright, A. E. (1904b). Antityphoid inoculation. *British Medical Journal, 2,* 1727.

Yusuf, S., Peto, R., Lewis, J., Collins, R., & Sleight, P. (1985). Beta blockade during and after myocardial infarction: An overview of the randomized trials. *Progress in Cardiovascular Disease, 27,* 335–371.

## 6. APPENDIX: SAS Program to Combine Standardized Mean Difference Statistics

The following program illustrates how SAS can be used to combine standardized mean difference statistics. This program shows the general structure needed first to compute necessary effect-size-level statistics and then to combine data for both fixed and random effects modes. Following the formulas in this chapter, the program can be adapted to combining other effect size estimates (in fact, trying to make the required changes and then comparing results with those in the present chapter is a good teaching device). More simply, the programs used in computing examples in the present chapter for combining raw and $z$-transformed correlations, odds ratios using Mantel-Haenszel techniques, log odds ratios, and raw mean differences are available from the first author. These programs can be sent as hard copy or as an ASCII file if a blank, formatted floppy diskette is enclosed with the request.

The following program computes relevant statistics for combining standardized mean difference statistics under both fixed and random effects models. The specific example used is Data Set II. In addition to a study identification number, key input includes the standardized mean difference statistic ($D$) and its variance ($V$). Prior to analyzing new data, it may be useful for the reader to execute this program using Data Set II to ensure proper replication of results. Once the program runs correctly, the user should make appropriate changes to the title, data, and input lines, and substitute the data set to be analyzed. Note that when the probability associated with a test statistic is smaller than $10^{-16}$, SAS prints the probability as exactly zero. Note also

that in some data sets, variances of $D$ will not be available but sample sizes will be available. If so, the following input line may be substituted:

```
INPUT STUDYID 1–2 N1 4–7 N2 9–12 D 14–17 .2;
```

where $N1$ is the within-study sample size in the first group and $N2$ is the within-study sample size in the second group. In addition, the following line should be inserted immediately after the INPUT line to compute the variance:

$$V = ((N1 + N2)/(N1* N2)) + ((D**2)/(2*(N1 + N2)));$$

```
TITLE 'COMBINING STANDARDIZED MEAN
     DIFFERENCES';
DATA SETI;
INPUT STUDYID 1–2 D 4–6 .2 V 8–14 .6;
  W = 1/V;
  WD = W*D;
  DSQ = D**2;
  WDSQ = W*DSQ;
  QVARCONE = D/V;
  QVARCTWO = 1/V;
  QVARCTHR = (D**2)/V;
  WSQ = W**2;
LINES;
 1  003  0015625
 2  012  0021609
 3  −14  0027889
 4  118  0139129
 5  026  0136161
 6  −06  0010609
 7  −02  0010609
 8  −32  0048400
 9  027  0026896
10  080  0063001
11  054  0091204
12  018  0049729
13  −02  0083521
14  023  0084100
15  −18  0025281
16  −06  0027889
17  030  0019321
18  007  0008836
19  −07  0030276
;
PROC PRINT;
  TITLE 'SUMMARY STATISTICS FOR D';
  VAR STUDYID D V W WD WDSQ WSQ;
PROC MEANS SUM MEAN N;
  VAR V WD W WDSQ WSQ D DSQ QVARCONE
     QVARCTWO QVARCTHR;
```

```
  OUTPUT OUT=COMBINE SUM=SV SWD SW
    SWDSQ SWSQ SD SDSQ SUMQVC1 SUMQVC2
    SUMQVC3 MEAN=MNV MNWD MNW MNWDSQ
    MNWSQ MND MNDSQ MNQVC1 MNQVC2
    MNQVC3 N=N1 N2 N3 N4 N5 N6 N7 N8 N9 N10;
DATA COMBINE;
  SET COMBINE;
  DPLUS=SWD/SW;
  STANDERR=SQRT (1/SW);
  DLOWBND=DPLUS-(1.96*(STANDERR));
  DUPPBND=DPLUS+(1.96*(STANDERR));
  ZTEST=(ABS(DPLUS))/STANDERR;
  ZPROB=2*(1-(PROBNORM(ZTEST)));
  Q=SWDSQ-((SWD**2)/SW);
  POFQ=1-PROBCHI(Q,N1-1);
  S2D=(1/(N1-1))*((SDSQ)-((SD**2)/N1));
  SIG2DELT=S2D-MNV;
  QVARC=SUMQVC3-((SUMQVC1**2)/SUMQVC2);
  POFQVC=1-PROBCHI(QVARC,N1-1);
  C=(SW-((SWSQ)/SW));
  VARCOMP2=(Q-(N1-1))/C;
PROC PRINT;
  TITLE 'COMBINING STANDARDIZED MEAN
    DIFFERENCES IN FIXED EFFECTS MODELS';
  VAR DPLUS STANDERR DLOWBND DUPPBND
    ZTEST ZPROB Q POFQ;
PROC PRINT;
  TITLE 'COMBINING STANDARDIZED MEAN
    DIFFERENCES UNDER RANDOM EFFECTS
    MODEL';
  VAR SIG2DELT VARCOMP2 QVARC POFQVC;
DATA NEW2;
  IF _N_=1 THEN SET COMBINE;
  SET SETI;

  DELTANUM=D/(SIG2DELT+V);
  DELTADEN=1/(SIG2DELT+V);
  DELTANU2=D/(VARCOMP2+V);
  DELTADE2=1/(VARCOMP2+V);
PROC MEANS SUM;
  VAR    DELTANUM    DELTADEN    DELTANU2
    DELTADE2;
  OUTPUT    OUT=RESULTS    SUM=SUMDNUM
    SUMDDEN SUMDNUM2 SUMDDEN2;
DATA RESULTS;
  SET RESULTS;
  AVGDELTA=SUMDNUM/SUMDDEN;
  SDVDELTA=SQRT(1/SUMDDEN);
  UPPDELTA=AVGDELTA+(1.96*SDVDELTA);
  LOWDELTA=AVGDELTA-(1.96*SDVDELTA);
  AVGDELT2=SUMDNUM2/SUMDDEN2;
  SDVDELT2=SQRT(1/SUMDDEN2);
  UPPDELT2=AVGDELT2+(1.96*SDVDELT2);
  LOWDELT2=AVGDELT2-(1.96*SDVDELT2);
  ZTEST=(ABS(AVGDELTA))/SDVDELTA;
  ZPROB=2*(1-(PROBNORM(ZTEST)));
  ZTEST2=(ABS(AVGDELT2))/SDVDELT2;
  ZPROB2=2*(1-(PROBNORM(ZTEST2)));
PROC PRINT;
  TITLE 'COMPUTING AVERAGE D UNDER
    RANDOM    EFFECTS    MODEL,    UNWTD
    VARIANCE'; VAR AVGDELTA SDVDELTA
    LOWDELTA UPPDELTA ZTEST ZPROB;
PROC PRINT;
  TITLE 'COMPUTING AVERAGE D UNDER
    RANDOM EFFECTS MODEL, WTD VARIANCE';
    VAR    AVGDELT2    SDVDELT2    LOWDELT2
    UPPDELT2 ZTEST2 ZPROB2;
RUN;
```

# PART
# VI

## STATISTICALLY
## ANALYZING EFFECT SIZES

Cooper, H. and Hedges, L. V. (Eds.) 1994. *The Handbook of Research Synthesis.* New York: Russell Sage Foundation

# 19

# FIXED EFFECTS MODELS

**LARRY V. HEDGES**
*University of Chicago*

CONTENTS

## 1. INTRODUCTION

A central question in research synthesis is whether methodological, contextual, or substantive variations in research studies are related to variations in effect size parameters. Both fixed and random effects methodologies are available for studying the variation in effects. In this chapter, two general classes of fixed effects models are presented. One class of models is appropriate when the independent (study characteristic) variables are categorical. This class of models is analogous to the analysis of variance, but is adapted to the special characteristics of effect size estimates. The second class of models is appropriate for either discrete or continuous independent variables and therefore technically includes the first class as a special case. This second class is analogous to multiple regression analysis for effect sizes. In both cases we describe the models along with procedures for estimation and hypothesis testing. Although some formulas for hand computation are given, we stress computation via widely available packaged computer programs.

Tests of goodness of fit are given for each fixed effect model. They test the notion that there is no more variability in the observed effect sizes than would be expected if all (100 percent) of the variation in effect size *parameters* is "explained" by the data analysis model. These tests can be conceived as tests of "model specification." That is, if a fixed effects model explains all of the variation in effect size parameters, the (fixed effect) model is unquestionably appropriate. Models that are well specified can provide a strong basis for inference about effect sizes in fixed effects models, but are not essential for inference from them. If differences between studies that lead to differences in effects are *not* regarded as random (e.g., if they are regarded as consequences of purposeful design decisions), then fixed effects methods are appropriate for the analysis. Similarly, fixed effects analyses are appropriate if the inferences desired are regarded as *conditional*—applying only to studies like those under examination.

## 2. AN ANALYSIS OF VARIANCE FOR EFFECT SIZES

One of the most common situations in research synthesis arises when the effect sizes can be sorted into independent groups according to one or more characteristics of the studies generating them. The analytic question is whether the groups' (average) population effect size varies across groups of effects and whether the groups are internally homogeneous—that is, whether the effect sizes vary within the groups. Alternatively, we can describe the situation as one of exploring the relationship between a categorical independent variable (the grouping variable) and effect size.

Many experimental social scientists have encountered the statistical method of analysis of variance (ANOVA) as a way of examining the relationship between categorical independent variables and continuous dependent variables in primary research. The purpose of this section is to describe an analogue to the analysis of variance for effect sizes. We first consider the one-factor analysis in detail: outlining the logic of the procedure, illustrating the computations, and demonstrating the analogy to one-factor analysis of variance. Then we demonstrate the extension of the methodology to more than one factor and illustrate the use of computer programs for (weighted) ANOVA to carry out computations. Finally, we discuss the use of contrasts or comparisons to explore differences among group means. Methods for analyses of both planned comparisons and post hoc (data-driven) comparisons are described. Technical details are given in Hedges (1982b) and Hedges and Olkin (1985).

### 2.1 The One-Factor Model

Situations frequently arise in which we wish to determine whether a particular discrete characteristic of studies is related to effect size. For example, we may want to know if the type of treatment is related to its effect or if all variations of the treatment produce essentially the same effect. The analogue to one-factor analysis of variance for effect sizes is designed to answer just such questions. We present this analysis in somewhat greater detail than its multifactor extensions because it illustrates the logic of more complex analyses and because it is among the simplest and most frequently used methods for analyzing variation in effect sizes.

**2.1.1 Notation** In the discussion of the one-factor model, we will employ a notation emphasizing that the independent effect size estimates fall into $p$ groups, defined a priori by the independent (grouping) variable. Suppose that there are $p$ disjoint groups of effects with $m_1$ effects in the first group, $m_2$ effects in the second group, . . . , and $m_p$ effects in the $p$th group. Denote the $j$th effect parameter in the $i$th group by $\theta_{ij}$ and its estimate by $T_{ij}$ with (conditional) variance $v_{ij}$. That is, $T_{ij}$ estimates $\theta_{ij}$ with standard error $\sqrt{v_{ij}}$. In most cases, $v_{ij}$ will actually be an estimated variance that is a func-

**Table 19.1 Effect Size Estimates and Sampling Variances for $p$ Groups of Studies**

| | Effect Size Estimates | Variances |
|---|---|---|
| **Group 1** | | |
| Study 1 | $T_{11}$ | $v_{11}$ |
| Study 2 | $T_{12}$ | $v_{12}$ |
| . | . | . |
| . | . | . |
| . | . | . |
| Study $m_1$ | $T_{1m_1}$ | $v_{1m_1}$ |
| **Group 2** | | |
| Study 1 | $T_{21}$ | $v_{21}$ |
| Study 2 | $T_{22}$ | $v_{22}$ |
| . | . | . |
| . | . | . |
| . | . | . |
| Study $m_2$ | $T_{2m_2}$ | $v_{2m_2}$ |
| **Group $p$** | | |
| Study 1 | $T_{p1}$ | $v_{p1}$ |
| Study 2 | $T_{p2}$ | $v_{p2}$ |
| . | . | . |
| . | . | . |
| . | . | . |
| Study $m_p$ | $T_{pm_p}$ | $v_{pm_p}$ |

tion of the within-study sample size and the effect size estimate. However, unless the within-study sample size is exceptionally small we can treat $v_{ij}$ as known. Therefore, in the rest of this chapter we assume that $v_{ij}$ is known for each study. The sample data from the collection of studies can be represented as in Table 19.1.

**2.1.2 Means** Making use of the ''dot notation'' from the analysis of variance, define the group mean effect estimate for the $i$th group $\overline{T}_{i\bullet}$ by

$$\overline{T}_{i\bullet} = \frac{\sum_{j=1}^{mi} w_{ij} T_{ij}}{\sum_{j=1}^{mi} w_{ij}} , \qquad i = 1, \ldots, p, \quad (19\text{-}1)$$

where the weight $w_{ij}$ is simply the reciprocal of the variance of $T_{ij}$,

$$w_{ij} = 1/v_{ij}. \quad (19\text{-}2)$$

The grand weighted mean $\overline{T}_{\bullet\bullet}$ is

$$\overline{T}_{\bullet\bullet} = \frac{\sum_{i=1}^{p} \sum_{j=1}^{mi} w_{ij} T_{ij}}{\sum_{i=1}^{p} \sum_{j=1}^{mi} w_{ij}} . \quad (19\text{-}3)$$

The ground mean $\overline{T}_{\bullet\bullet}$ can also be seen as the weighted mean of the group means $\overline{T}_{1\bullet}, \ldots, \overline{T}_{p\bullet}$.

$$\overline{T}_{\bullet\bullet} = \frac{\sum_{i=1}^{p} w_{i\bullet} \overline{T}_{i\bullet}}{\sum_{i=1}^{p} w_{i\bullet}} ,$$

where the weight $w_{i\bullet}$ is just the sum of the weights for the $i$th group

$$w_{i\bullet} = w_{i1} + w_{i2} + \ldots + w_{imi} .$$

Thus, $\overline{T}_{i\bullet}$ is simply the weighted mean that would be computed by applying formula (18-1) from Chapter 18 to the studies in group $i$, and $\overline{T}_{\bullet\bullet}$ is the weighted mean that would be obtained by applying formula (18-1) to all of the studies. If all of the studies in group $i$ estimate a common effect size parameter $\theta_{i\bullet}$—that is, if $\theta_{i1} = \theta_{i2} = \ldots = \theta_{imi} = \theta_{i\bullet}$—then $\overline{T}_{i\bullet}$ estimates $\theta_{i\bullet}$. If the studies within the $i$th group do *not* estimate a common effect parameter, then $\overline{T}_{i\bullet}$ estimates the weighted mean of the effect size parameters $\theta_{ij}$ given by

$$\bar{\theta}_{i\bullet} = \frac{\sum_{j=1}^{mi} w_{ij} \theta_{ij}}{\sum_{j=1}^{mi} w_{ij}} , \quad i = 1, \ldots, p. \quad (19\text{-}4)$$

Similarly, if all of the studies in the collection estimate a common parameter $\theta_{\bullet\bullet}$—that is, if $\theta_{11} = \ldots = \theta_{1m1} = \theta_{21} = \ldots = \theta_{pmp} = \theta_{\bullet\bullet}$—then $\overline{T}_{\bullet\bullet}$ estimates $\theta_{\bullet\bullet}$. If the studies do *not* all estimate the parameter, then $\overline{T}_{\bullet\bullet}$ can be seen as an estimate of a weighted mean $\bar{\theta}_{\bullet\bullet}$ of the effect parameters given by

$$\bar{\theta}_{\bullet\bullet} = \frac{\sum_{i=1}^{p} \sum_{j=1}^{mi} w_{ij} \theta_{ij}}{\sum_{i=1}^{p} \sum_{j=1}^{mi} w_{ij}} . \quad (19\text{-}5)$$

Alternatively, $\bar{\theta}_{\bullet\bullet}$ can be viewed as a weighted mean of the $\bar{\theta}_{i\bullet}$:

$$\bar{\theta}_{\bullet\bullet} = \frac{\sum_{i=1}^{p} w_{i\bullet} \bar{\theta}_{i\bullet}}{\sum_{i=1}^{p} w_{i\bullet}} ,$$

where $w_{i\bullet}$ is just the sum of the weights $w_{ij}$ for the $i$th group as in the alternate expression for $\overline{T}_{\bullet\bullet}$ above.

**2.1.3 Standard errors** The sampling variances $v_{1\bullet}, \ldots, v_{p\bullet}$ of the group mean effect estimates $\overline{T}_{1\bullet}, \ldots, \overline{T}_{p\bullet}$ are given by the reciprocal of the sum of the weights in each group, that is,

$$v_{i\bullet} = \frac{1}{\sum_{j=1}^{mi} w_{ij}} , \quad i = 1, \ldots, p. \quad (19\text{-}6)$$

Similarly, the sampling variance $v_{..}$ of the grand weighted mean is given by the reciprocal of the sum of all the weights or

$$v_{..} = \frac{1}{\sum_{i=1}^{p} \sum_{j=1}^{mi} w_{ij}} . \qquad (19\text{-}7)$$

The standard errors of the group mean effect estimates $\bar{T}_{i.}$ and the grand mean $\bar{T}_{..}$ are just the square roots of their respective sampling variances.

**2.1.4 Tests and confidence intervals** The group means $\bar{T}_{1.}, \ldots, \bar{T}_{p.}$ are normally distributed about the respective effect size parameters $\theta_{1.}, \ldots, \theta_{p.}$ that they estimate. The fact that these means are normally distributed with the variances given in (19-6) leads to rather straightforward procedures for constructing tests and confidence intervals. For example, to test whether the $i$th group mean effect $\theta_{i.}$ differs from a predefined constant $\theta_{o}$ (e.g., to test if $\theta_{i.} - \theta_{o} = 0$) by testing the null hypothesis

$$H_o: \theta_{i.} = \theta_o,$$

use the statistic

$$Z = \frac{\bar{T}_{i.} - \theta_o}{(v_{i.})^{1/2}}, \qquad (19\text{-}8)$$

and reject $H_o$ at level $\alpha$ (i.e., decide that the effect parameter differs from $\theta_o$) if the absolute value of $Z$ exceeds the $100\alpha$ percent critical value of the standard normal distribution. For example, for a two-sided test that $\theta_{i.} = 0$ at $\alpha = .05$ level of significance, reject the null hypothesis if the absolute value of $Z$ exceeds 1.96. Note that when there is only one group of studies, this test is identical to that described in Chapter 18 using the statistic $Z$ given in (18-5).

Confidence intervals for the group mean effect $\theta_{i.}$ can be computed by multiplying the standard error ($\sqrt{v_{i.}}$) by the appropriate two-tailed critical value of the standard normal distribution ($C_{\alpha} = 1.96$ for $\alpha = .05$ and 95 percent confidence intervals) and then adding and subtracting this amount from the weighted mean effect size $\bar{T}_{i.}$. Thus, the $100(1-\alpha)$ percent confidence interval for $\theta_{i.}$ is given by

$$\bar{T}_{i.} - C_{\alpha}(v_{i.})^{1/2} \le \theta_{i.} \le \bar{T}_{i.} + C_{\alpha}(v_{i.})^{1/2}. \qquad (19\text{-}9)$$

*Example.* Eagly and Carli (1981) reported a synthesis of ten studies of gender differences in conformity using the so-called fictitious norm group paradigm (See Data Set I, Appendix A). The effect sizes were standardized mean differences, which were separated into three groups on the basis of the percentage of the authors of the research report who were male. Group 1 consisted of two studies in which 25 percent of the authors were male, group 2 consisted of a single study in which 50 percent of the authors were male, and group 3 consisted of seven studies in which all authors were male. The effect size estimate $T_{ij}$ for each study, its variance $v_{ij}$, the weight $w_{ij} = 1/v_{ij}$, $w_{ij} T_{ij}$, and $w_{ij} T_{ij}^2$ (which will be used later) are given in Table 19.2. Using the sums for each group from Table 19.3, the weighted mean effect sizes for the three classes $\bar{T}_{1.}$, $\bar{T}_{2.}$, and $\bar{T}_{3.}$ are given by

$$\bar{T}_{1.} = -9.395/64.505 = -.15,$$
$$\bar{T}_{2.} = -13.640/45.466 = -.30,$$
$$\bar{T}_{3.} = 57.458/169.417 = .34,$$

and the weighted grand mean effect size is

$$\bar{T}_{..} = 34.423/279.388 = .123.$$

**Table 19.2 Data for the Male-Authorship Example**

| Study | % Male Authors | Group | No. of Items | $T$ | $v$ | $w$ | $wT$ | $wT^2$ |
|-------|------|-------|------|-------|------|--------|---------|--------|
| 1 | 25 | 1 | 2 | −.33 | .029 | 34.775 | −11.476 | 3.787 |
| 2 | 25 | 1 | 2 | .07 | .034 | 29.730 | 2.081 | .146 |
| 3 | 50 | 2 | 2 | −.30 | .022 | 45.466 | −13.640 | 4.092 |
| 4 | 100 | 3 | 38 | .35 | .016 | 62.233 | 21.782 | 7.624 |
| 5 | 100 | 3 | 30 | .70 | .066 | 15.077 | 10.554 | 7.388 |
| 6 | 100 | 3 | 45 | .85 | .218 | 4.586 | 3.898 | 3.313 |
| 7 | 100 | 3 | 45 | .40 | .045 | 22.059 | 8.824 | 3.529 |
| 8 | 100 | 3 | 45 | .48 | .069 | 14.580 | 6.998 | 3.359 |
| 9 | 100 | 3 | 5 | .37 | .051 | 19.664 | 7.275 | 2.692 |
| 10 | 100 | 3 | 5 | −.06 | .032 | 31.218 | −1.873 | 0.112 |

**Table 19.3 Sums of Quantities Used to Compute the Male-Authorship Example Analysis**

|  | $w$ | $wT$ | $WT^2$ |
|---|---|---|---|
| Group 1 (25% studies) | 64.505 | −9.395 | 3.933 |
| Group 2 (50% studies) | 45.466 | −13.640 | 4.092 |
| Group 3 (100% studies) | 169.417 | 57.458 | 28.015 |
| Overall groups | 279.388 | 34.423 | 36.040 |

The variances $v_{1\bullet}$, $v_{2\bullet}$, and $v_{3\bullet}$ of $\bar{T}_{1\bullet}$, $\bar{T}_{2\bullet}$, and $\bar{T}_{3\bullet}$ are given by

$$v_{1\bullet} = 1/64.505 = .015,$$
$$v_{2\bullet} = 1/45.466 = .022,$$
$$v_{3\bullet} = 1/169.417 = .006,$$

and the variance $v_{\bullet\bullet}$ of $\bar{T}_{\bullet\bullet}$ is

$$v_{\bullet\bullet} = 1/279.388 = .00358.$$

Using formula (19-9) with $C_{.05} = 1.96$, the limits of the 95 percent confidence interval for the group mean parameter $\bar{\theta}_{1\bullet}$ are given by

$$-.15 \pm 1.96\sqrt{.015} = -.15 \pm .24.$$

Thus, the 95 percent confidence interval for $\bar{\theta}_{1\bullet}$ is given by

$$-.39 \le \bar{\theta}_{1\bullet} \le .09.$$

Because this confidence interval contains zero or, alternately, because the test statistic

$$Z = |-.15|/\sqrt{.015} < 1.96,$$

we cannot reject the hypothesis that $\bar{\theta}_{1\bullet} = 0$ at the $\alpha = .05$ level of significance. Similarly, 95 percent confidence intervals for the group mean parameters $\bar{\theta}_{2\bullet}$ and $\bar{\theta}_{3\bullet}$ are given by

$$-.59 = -.30 - 1.96\sqrt{.022} \le \bar{\theta}_{2\bullet} \le -.30 + 1.96\sqrt{.022}$$
$$= -.01$$
$$.19 = .34 - 1.96\sqrt{.006} \le \bar{\theta}_{3\bullet} \le .34 + 1.96\sqrt{.006} = .49.$$

Thus, we see that the effect size for group 2 is significantly less than zero, whereas the group mean effect size for group 3 is significantly greater than zero and the group mean effect size for group 1 was not different from zero.

**2.1.5 Tests of heterogeneity** In the analysis of variance, tests for systematic sources of variance are con-structed from sums of squared deviations from means. The fact that the effects due to different sources of variance partition the sums of squares leads to the interpretation that the total variation about the grand mean is partitioned into parts that arise from between-groups and within-group sources. The analysis of variance for effect sizes has a similar interpretation. The total heterogeneity statistic $Q = Q_T$ (the weighted total sum of squares about the grand mean) is partitioned into a between-groups-of-studies part $Q_{BET}$ (the weighted sum of squares of group means about the grand mean) and a within-groups-of-studies part $Q_W$ (the total of the weighted sum of squares of the individual effect estimates about the respective group means). These statistics $Q_{BET}$ and $Q_W$ yield direct omnibus tests of variation across groups in mean effects and variation within groups of individual effects.

*An omnibus test for between-groups differences.* To test the hypothesis that there is no variation in group mean effect sizes, that is, to test

$$\mathrm{H_0}\colon \theta_{1\bullet} = \theta_{2\bullet} = \ldots = \theta_{p\bullet},$$

we use the between-groups heterogeneity statistic $Q_{BET}$ defined by

$$Q_{BET} = \sum_{i=1}^{p} w_{i\bullet}(\bar{T}_{i\bullet} - \bar{T}_{\bullet\bullet})^2, \qquad (19\text{-}10)$$

where $w_{i\bullet}$ is the reciprocal of the variance of $\bar{T}_{i\bullet}$. Note that $Q_{BET}$ is just the weighted sum of squares of group mean effect sizes about the grand mean effect size. When the null hypothesis of no variation across group mean effect sizes is true, $Q_{BET}$ has a chi-square distribution with $p-1$ degrees of freedom. Hence, we test $\mathrm{H_0}$ by comparing the obtained value of $Q_{BET}$ with the upper-tail critical values of the chi-square distribution with $(p-1)$ degrees of freedom. If $Q_{BET}$ exceeds the $100(1-\alpha)$ percent point of the chi-square distribution (e.g., $C_{.05} = 18.31$ for 10 degrees of freedom and $\alpha = .05$), $\mathrm{H_0}$ is rejected at level $\alpha$ and between-groups differences are significant.

This test is analogous to the omnibus $F$ test for variation in group means in one-way ANOVA. It differs in that $Q_{\text{BET}}$, unlike the $F$ test, incorporates an estimate of unsystematic error in the form of the weights. Thus, no separate error term is needed and the sum of squares can be used directly as a test statistic.

*An omnibus test for within-group variation in effects.* To test the hypothesis that there is no variation of population effect sizes within the groups of studies, that is, to test

$$H_0: \begin{array}{ccc} \theta_{11} = \ldots = & \theta_{1m1} = & \theta_{1\bullet} \\ \theta_{21} = \ldots = & \theta_{2m2} = & \theta_{2\bullet} \\ \cdot & \cdot & \cdot \\ \cdot & \cdot & \cdot \\ \cdot & \cdot & \cdot \\ \theta_{p1} = \ldots = & \theta_{pmp} = & \theta_{p\bullet}, \end{array}$$

use the within-group heterogeneity statistic $Q_{\text{W}}$ given by

$$Q_{\text{W}} = \sum_{i=1}^{p} \sum_{j=1}^{mi} w_{ij}(T_{ij} - \overline{T}_{i\bullet})^2, \quad (19\text{-}11)$$

where the $w_{ij}$ are the reciprocals of the $v_{ij}$, the sampling variances of the $T_{ij}$. When the null hypothesis of perfect homogeneity of effect size parameters is true, $Q_{\text{W}}$ has a chi-square distribution with $(k-p)$ degrees of freedom where $k = m_1 + m_2 + \ldots + m_p$ is the total number of studies. Therefore, within-group homogeneity at significance level $\alpha$ is rejected if the computed value of $Q_{\text{W}}$ exceeds the $100(1-\alpha)$ percent point (the upper-tail critical value) of the chi-square distribution with $(k-p)$ degrees of freedom.

Although $Q_{\text{W}}$ provides an overall test of within-group variability in effects, it is actually the sum of $p$ separate (and independent) within-group heterogeneity statistics, one for each of the $p$ groups of effects. Thus,

$$Q_{\text{W}} = Q_{\text{W}1} + Q_{\text{W}2} + \ldots + Q_{\text{W}p}, \quad (19\text{-}12)$$

where each $Q_{\text{W}i}$ is just the heterogeneity statistic $Q$ given in formula (18-6) of Chapter 18. In the notation used here, $Q_{\text{W}i}$ is given by

$$Q_{\text{w}i} = \sum_{j=1}^{mi} w_{ij}(T_{ij} - \overline{T}_{i\bullet})^2. \quad (19\text{-}13)$$

These individual within-group statistics are often useful in determining which groups are the major sources of within-group heterogeneity and which groups have relatively homogeneous effects. For example, in analyses of the effects of study quality, study effect estimates might be placed into two groups: those from randomized experiments and those from quasi-experiments. The effect sizes within the two groups might be quite heterogeneous overall, leading to a large $Q_{\text{W}}$, but most of that heterogeneity might arise within the groups of quasi-experiments so that $Q_{\text{W}1}$ (the statistic for quasi-experiments) would indicate great heterogeneity, but $Q_{\text{W}2}$ (the statistic for randomized experiments) would indicate relative homogeneity.

If the effect size parameters within the $i$th group of studies are homogeneous—that is, if $\theta_{i1} = \ldots = \theta_{imi}$—then $Q_{\text{W}i}$ has the chi-square distribution with $m_i - 1$ degrees of freedom. Thus, the test for homogeneity of effects within the $i$th group at significance level $\alpha$ consists of rejecting the hypothesis of homogeneity if $Q_{\text{W}i}$ exceeds the $100(1-\alpha)$ percent point of the chi-square distribution with $(m_i - 1)$ degrees of freedom.

It is often convenient to summarize the relationships among the heterogeneity statistics via a table analogous to an ANOVA source table (see Table 19.4).

*The partitioning of heterogeneity.* There is a simple relationship among the total homogeneity statistic $Q$

**Table 19.4 Heterogeneity Summary Table**

| Source | Statistic | | Degrees of Freedom |
|---|---|---|---|
| Between groups | | $Q_{\text{BET}}$ | $p-1$ |
| Within groups | | | |
|     Within group 1 | $Q_{\text{W}1}$ | | $m_1 - 1$ |
|     Within group 2 | $Q_{\text{W}2}$ | | $m_2 - 1$ |
|     · | · | | · |
| · | | | |
| · | | | |
|     Within group $p$ | $Q_{\text{W}p}$ | | $m_p - 1$ |
|     Total within groups | | $Q_{\text{W}}$ | $k-p$ |
| Overall | | $Q$ | $k-1$ |

NOTE: Here $k = m_1 + m_2 = \ldots + m_p$.

given in formula (18-6) and the between-groups and within-group fit statistics discussed in this section. This relationship corresponds to the partitioning of the sums of squares in ordinary analysis of variance. That is,

$$Q = Q_{BET} + Q_W.$$

One interpretation is that the "total heterogeneity" about the mean $Q$ is partitioned into between-groups heterogeneity $Q_{BET}$ and within-group heterogeneity $Q_W$. The ideal is to select independent (grouping) variables that explain variation (heterogeneity) so that most of the total heterogeneity is between-groups and relatively little remains within-group. Of course, the grouping variable must, in principle, be chosen a priori (i.e., before examination of the effect sizes) to assure that tests for the significance of group effects do not capitalize on chance.

### 2.1.6 Computing the one-factor analysis

Although $Q_{BET}$ and $Q_W$ can be computed via a computer program for weighted ANOVA, the weighted cell means and their standard errors cannot generally be obtained this way. Computational formulas can greatly simplify direct calculation of $Q_{BET}$ and $Q_W$ as well as the cell means $\overline{T}_{i.}$ and their standard errors. These formulas are analogous to computational formulas in the analysis of variance, and they enable the computation of all of the statistics in one pass through the data (e.g., by a packaged computer program). The formulas are expressed in terms of totals (sums) across cases of the weights, of the weights times the effect estimates, and of the weights times the squared effect estimates. Define

$$TW_i = \sum_{j=1}^{m_i} w_{ij}, \qquad TW_{\bullet} = \sum_{i=1}^{p} TW_i,$$

$$TWD_i = \sum_{j=1}^{m_i} w_{ij} T_{ij}, \qquad TWD_{\bullet} = \sum_{i=1}^{p} TWD_i,$$

$$TWDS_i = \sum_{j=1}^{m_i} w_{ij} T_{ij}^2, \qquad TWDS_{\bullet} = \sum_{i=1}^{p} TWDS_i,$$

where $w_{ij} = 1/v_{ij}$ is just the weight for $T_{ij}$. Then the overall heterogeneity statistic $Q$ is

$$Q = TWDS_{\bullet} - (TWD_{\bullet})^2 / TW_{\bullet}.$$

Each of the within-group heterogeneity statistics is given by

$$Q_{Wi} = TWDS_i - (TWD_i)^2 / TW_i, \quad i = 1, \ldots, p.$$

The overall within-group statistic is obtained as $Q_W = Q_{W1} + \ldots + Q_{Wp}$. The between-groups heterogeneity statistic is obtained as $Q_{BET} = Q - Q_W$. The weighted overall mean effects and its variance are

$$\overline{T}_{\bullet\bullet} = TWD_{\bullet} / TW_{\bullet}, \qquad v_{\bullet\bullet} = 1/TW_{\bullet}.$$

and the weighted group means and their variance are

$$\overline{T}_{i\bullet} = TWD_i / TW_i, \quad i = 1, \ldots, p,$$
$$v_{i\bullet} = 1/TW_i, \quad i = 1, \ldots, p.$$

The omnibus test statistics $Q$, $Q_{BET}$, and $Q_W$ can also be computed using a weighted ANOVA program. The grouping variable is used as the "factor" in the weighted ANOVA, the effect size estimates are the observations, and the weight given to effect size $T_{ij}$ is just $w_{ij}$. The weighted between-groups or model *sum* of squares is exactly $Q_{BET}$, the weighted within-group or residual *sum* of squares is exactly $Q_W$, and the corrected total *sum* of squares is exactly $Q$.

*Example.* We now continue the analysis of the standardized mean differences from studies of gender differences in conformity of Data Set I (see Appendix A). Using formula (18-6) from Chapter 18, and the sums given in Table 19.3, the overall heterogeneity statistic $Q$ is

$$Q = 36.040 - (34.423)^2 / 279.388 = 31.799.$$

Using the sums given in Table 19.3 in formula (19-13), the within-group heterogeneity statistics $Q_{W1}$, $Q_{W2}$, and $Q_{W3}$ are

$$Q_{W1} = 3.933 - (-9.395)^2 / 64.505 = 2.565,$$
$$Q_{W2} = 4.092 - (13.640)^2 / 45.466 = 0.0,$$
$$Q_{W3} = 28.015 - (57.458)^2 / 169.417 = 8.528.$$

The overall within-group heterogeneity statistic is therefore

$$Q_W = 2.565 + 0.0 + 8.528 = 11.093.$$

Because 11.093 does not exceed 14.07, the 95 percent point of the chi-square distribution with $10 - 3 = 7$ degrees of freedom, we do not reject the hypothesis that the effect size parameters are homogeneous within the groups. In fact, a value this large would occur between 10 and 25 percent of the time owing to chance even with perfect homogeneity of effect *parameters*. Thus, we conclude that the effect sizes are relatively homogeneous within groups.

The between-groups heterogeneity statistic is calculated as

$$Q_{BET} = Q - Q_W = 31.799 - 11.093 = 20.706.$$

Because 20.706 exceeds 5.99, the 95 percent point of the chi-square distribution with $3 - 1 = 2$ degrees of freedom, we reject the null hypothesis of no variation in effect size across studies with different proportions of male authors. In other words, there is a statistically significant relationship between the percentage of male authors and effect size.

**2.1.7. Comparisons or contrasts among mean effects** Omnibus tests for the difference among group means can reveal that the mean effect parameters are not all the same, but they are not useful for revealing the specific pattern of mean differences that might be present. For example, the $Q_{BET}$ statistic might reveal that there was variation in mean effects when the effects were grouped according to type of treatment, but the omnibus statistic gives no insight about *which* types of treatment (which groups) were associated with the largest effect size. In other cases, the omnibus test statistic may not be significant, but we may wish to test for a specific difference that the omnibus test may not have been powerful enough to detect. In conventional ANOVA, contrasts or comparisons are used to explore the differences among group means. Contrasts can be used in precisely the same way to examine patterns among group mean effect sizes in meta-analysis. In fact all of the strategies used for selecting contrasts in ANOVA (such as orthogonal polynomials to estimate trends or Helmert contrasts to discover discrepant groups) are also applicable in meta-analysis.

A contrast (parameter) is just a linear combination of group means

$$\gamma = c_1 \, \bar{\theta}_{1\bullet} + \ldots + c_p \, \bar{\theta}_{p\bullet}, \qquad (19\text{-}14)$$

where the coefficients $c_1, \ldots, c_p$ (called the contrast coefficients) are known constants that satisfy the constraint $c_1 + \ldots + c_p = 0$ and are chosen so that the value of the contrast will reflect a particular comparison or pattern of interest. For example, the coefficients $c_1 = 1$, $c_2 = -1$, $c_3 = \ldots = c_p = 0$ might be chosen so that the value of the contrast is the difference between the mean $\bar{\theta}_{1\bullet}$ of group 1 and the mean $\bar{\theta}_{2\bullet}$ of group 2. Sometimes we refer to a contrast among population means as a population contrast or a contrast parameter to emphasize that it is a function of population parameters and to distinguish it from *estimates* of the contrast. The contrast parameter specified by coefficients $c_1, \ldots, c_p$ is usually estimated by a sample contrast

$$g = c_1 \overline{T}_{1\bullet} + \ldots + c_p \overline{T}_{p\bullet}. \qquad (19\text{-}15)$$

The estimated contrast $g$ has a normal sampling distribution with variance $v_g$ given by

$$v_g = c_1^2 v_{1\bullet} + \ldots + c_p^2 v_{p\bullet}. \qquad (19\text{-}16)$$

Note that while the notation used here for contrasts suggests that they compare group mean effects, they can

be used to compare individual studies (groups consisting of a single study) or to compare a single study with a group mean. All that is required is the appropriate definition of the "groups" involved.

*Confidence intervals and tests of significance.* Because the estimated contrast $g$ has a normal distribution with known variance $v_g$, confidence intervals and tests of statistical significance are relatively easy to construct. Note, however, that just as with contrasts in ordinary ANOVA, test procedures differ depending on whether the contrasts were planned or *were selected using information from the data.* Procedures for testing planned comparisons and for constructing nonsimultaneous confidence intervals are given in this section. Procedures for testing post hoc contrasts (contrast selected using information from the data) are given in the next section.

Confidence intervals for the (planned) contrast parameter $\gamma$ are computed by multiplying the standard error of $g$, $(v_g)^{1/2}$ by the appropriate two-tailed critical value of the standard normal distribution ($C_\alpha = 1.96$ for $\alpha = .05$ and 95 percent confidence intervals) and adding and subtracting this amount from the estimated contrast $g$. Thus, the $100(1-\alpha)$ percent confidence interval for the contrast parameter $\gamma$ is

$$g - C_\alpha(v_g)^{1/2} \le \gamma \le g + C_\alpha(v_g)^{1/2}. \qquad (19\text{-}17)$$

Alternatively, a (two-sided) test of the null hypothesis that $\gamma = 0$ uses the statistic

$$X^2 = g^2 / v_g. \qquad (19\text{-}18)$$

If $X^2$ exceeds the $100(1-\alpha)$ percent point of the chi-square distribution with 1 degree of freedom, reject the hypothesis that $\gamma = 0$ and declare the contrast to be significant at the level of significance $\alpha$.

*Post hoc contrasts and simultaneous tests.* Situations often occur in which several contrasts among group means will be of interest. If several tests are made at the same nominal significance level $\alpha$, the chance that *at least one* of the tests will reject (when all of the relevant null hypotheses are true) is generally greater than $\alpha$ and can be considerably greater if the number of tests is large. Similarly, the probability that tests will reject may also be greater than the nominal significance level for contrasts that are selected because they "appear to stand out" when one is examining the data. Simultaneous and post hoc testing procedures are designed to address these problems by assuring that the probability of at least one Type I error is controlled at a preset significance level $\alpha$. Many simultaneous test procedures have been developed (see Miller 1981). We now discuss the application of two of these procedures to contrasts in meta-analysis (see also Hedges & Olkin 1985).

The simplest simultaneous test procedure is called the Bonferroni method. It exacts a penalty for simultaneous testing by requiring a higher level of significance from each individual contrast for it to be declared significant in the simultaneous test. If a number $L \geq 1$ of contrasts are to be tested simultaneously at level $\alpha$, the Bonferroni test requires that any contrast be significant at (nonsimultaneous) significance level $\alpha/L$ in order to be declared significant at level $\alpha$ in the simultaneous analysis. For example, if $L = 5$ contrasts were tested at simultaneous significance level $\alpha = .05$, any one of the contrasts would have to be *individually* significant at the $.01 = .05/5$ level (i.e., $X^2$ would have to exceed 6.635, the 99 percent point of the chi-square distribution) in order to be declared significant at $\alpha = .05$ level by the simultaneous test.

The Bonferroni method can be used as a post hoc test if the number of contrasts $L$ is chosen as the number of contrasts that *could* have been conducted. This procedure works well when all contrasts conducted are chosen from a well-defined class of contrasts. For example, if there are four groups, six pairwise contrasts are possible, so the Bonferroni method is applied to any pairwise contrast chosen post hoc by treating it as one of six contrasts examined simultaneously. If number $L$ of comparisons (or possible comparisons) is large, the Bonferroni method can be quite conservative since it rejects only if a contrast has a very high level of significance.

An alternative test procedure that is a generalization of the Scheffé method from the analysis of variance can be used for both post hoc and simultaneous testing (see Hedges & Olkin 1985). This procedure for testing contrasts at simultaneous significance level $\alpha$ consists of computing the statistic $X^2$ given in (19-18) for each contrast and rejecting the null hypothesis whenever $X^2$ exceeds the $100(1 - \alpha)$ percent point of the chi-square distribution with $L'$ degrees of freedom, where $L'$ is the smaller of $L$ (the number of contrasts) or $p - 1$ (the number of groups minus one).

When the number of contrasts (or potential contrasts) is small, simultaneous tests based on the Bonferroni method will usually be more powerful. When the number of contrasts is large, the Scheffé method will usually be more powerful.

*Example.* Continuing the analysis of standardized mean difference data on gender difference in conformity, recall that there are three groups of effects: those in which

25 percent, 50 percent, and 100 percent, respectively, of the authors are male. To contrast the mean of the effects of group 1 (25 percent male authors) with those of group 3 (100 percent male authors), use the contrast coefficients

$$c_1 = -1.0, \ c_2 = 0.0, \ c_3 = 1.0.$$

The value of the contrast estimate $g$ is

$$g = -1.0(-.15) + 0.0(-.30) + 1.0(.34) = .49,$$

with an estimated variance of

$$v_g = (-1.0)^2(.015) + (0.0)^2(.022) + (1.0)^2(.006) = .021.$$

Hence, a 95 percent confidence interval for $\gamma = \bar{\theta}_{3 \bullet} - \bar{\theta}_{1 \bullet}$ is

$$.21 = .49 - 1.96\sqrt{.021} \leq \gamma \leq .49 + 1.96\sqrt{.021} = .77.$$

Because this confidence interval does not contain zero or, alternatively, because

$$X^2 = (.49)^2/(.021) = 11.43$$

exceeds 3.84, we reject the hypothesis that $\gamma = 0$ and declare the contrast statistically significant at the $\alpha = .05$ level.

## 2.2 Multifactor Models

A multifactor ANOVA for effect sizes exists and has the same relationship to conventional multifactor ANOVA as the one-factor ANOVA for effect sizes has to one-factor ANOVA. The principal difference is that, because of the weighting involved, multifactor analyses for effect sizes are essentially always unbalanced. Hence, the details of the computations are rather involved and the formulas for the omnibus test statistics are not intuitively appealing. Consequently, they will not be presented here. Computations of multifactor analyses for effect sizes, like unbalanced analyses of variance in primary research, will almost always be carried out via packaged computer programs. Thus, this section will describe how to use computer programs that can compute weighted multiway ANOVA to produce the computations required to obtain omnibus test statistics. Procedures for estimating group means and contrasts are exactly the same in the multifactor case as in the one-factor case.

**2.2.1 The two-factor model** Suppose that there are two categorical independent variables $A$ and $B$, where $A$ has $a$ distinct values and $B$ has $b$ distinct values, so that each effect can be simultaneously classified according to both variable $A$ and variable $B$. In conventional terminology used in the analysis of variance, we would say that $A$ and $B$ are crossed factors with $a$ and $b$ levels, respectively. We extend the notation used in the one-factor model to incorporate an additional subscript to reflect the level of the second factor. Thus, the individual effect size estimate and parameter for the $k$th study at the $i$th level of factor $A$ and the $j$th level of factor $B$ are denoted $T_{ijk}$ and $\theta_{ijk}$, respectively. Let $m_{ij}$ be the number of effects at level $i$ of factor $A$ and level $j$ of factor $B$, and denote the variance of $T_{ijk}$ by $v_{ijk}$.

The weighted mean effect size parameter for the $i$th level of factor $A$, $\bar{\theta}_{i..}$, is

$$\bar{\theta}_{i..} = \frac{\sum_{j=1}^{b} \sum_{k=1}^{mij} w_{ijk} \theta_{ijk}}{\sum_{j=1}^{b} \sum_{k=1}^{mij} w_{ijk}}, \qquad (19\text{-}19)$$

where the $w_{ijk}$ are the reciprocals of the sampling variances: $w_{ijk} = 1/v_{ijk}$. The weighted mean effect size parameter for the $j$th level of factor $B$, $\bar{\theta}_{.j.}$, is

$$\bar{\theta}_{.j.} = \frac{\sum_{i=1}^{a} \sum_{k=1}^{mij} w_{ijk} \theta_{ijk}}{\sum_{i=1}^{a} \sum_{k=1}^{mij} w_{ijk}}. \qquad (19\text{-}20)$$

The weighted mean effect size parameter for the group defined by the $i$th level of factor $A$ and the $j$th level of factor $B$, $\bar{\theta}_{ij.}$, is

$$\bar{\theta}_{ij.} = \frac{\sum_{k=1}^{mij} w_{ijk} \theta_{ijk}}{\sum_{k=1}^{mij} w_{ijk}}. \qquad (19\text{-}21)$$

The structural model for the two-factor analysis is analogous to that in two-factor ANOVA. It can be expressed as

$$\bar{\theta}_{ij.} = \mu + \alpha_i + \beta_j + \alpha\beta_{ij}, i = 1, \dots, a; j = 1, \dots, b, \qquad (19\text{-}22)$$

where $\mu$ is the "grand mean effect" parameter, $\alpha_1, \dots, \alpha_a$ are the "main effect" parameters for factor $A$, $\beta_1, \dots, \beta_b$ are the "main effect" parameters for factor $B$, and $\alpha\beta_{11}, \dots, \alpha\beta_{ab}$ are the "$AB$ interaction effect" parameters. The omnibus tests in the model have the same interpretation here as in conventional ANOVA.

There are four omnibus tests connected with the two-factor model: one for the main effect of $A$, one for the main effect of $B$, one for the $AB$ interaction, and one that tests homogeneity of effects within groups. The test for the main effect of factor $A$ is a test of the null hypothesis that there is no variation in the factor level mean effects across levels of factor $A$. This null hypothesis can be expressed in terms of factor level means as

$$H_{0A} : \bar{\theta}_{1..} = \dots = \bar{\theta}_{a..},$$

or, in terms of treatment effect parameters, the null hypothesis is that $\alpha_1 = \dots = \alpha_a$. The test statistic is $Q_A$, the weighted sum of squares for factor $A$. The test for the main effect of $A$ at significance level $\alpha$ involves rejecting $H_{0A}$ if the statistic $Q_A$ is larger than the $100(1 - \alpha)$ percent point of the chi-square distribution with $(a - 1)$ degrees of freedom.

The tests for the main effect of factor $B$ is a test of the null hypothesis that there is no variation in the factor level mean effects across levels of factor $B$. This null hypothesis can be expressed in terms of factor level mean parameters as

$$H_{0B}: \bar{\theta}_{.1.} = \dots = \bar{\theta}_{.b.},$$

or, in terms of treatment effect parameters, the null hypothesis is that $\beta_1 = \dots = \beta_b$. The test statistic is $Q_B$, the weighted sum of squares for factor $B$. The test for the main effect of $B$ at significance level $\alpha$ involves rejecting $H_{0B}$ if the statistic $Q_B$ is larger than the $100(1 - \alpha)$ percent point of the chi-square distribution with $(b - 1)$ degrees of freedom.

The test for the $AB$ interaction is a test of the null hypothesis that the effects of factor $A$ and the effects of factor $B$ are additive. One might also describe the null hypothesis of no interaction by saying that the effects of factor $A$ are the same at every level of factor $B$ or, equivalently, that the effects of factor $B$ are the same at every level of factor $A$. In terms of treatment effect parameters the null hypothesis of no interaction is

$$H_{0AB}: \begin{matrix} \alpha\beta_{11} = \dots = \alpha\beta_{1b} \\ \cdot \quad\quad \cdot \quad\quad \cdot \\ \cdot \quad\quad \cdot \quad\quad \cdot \\ \cdot \quad\quad \cdot \quad\quad \cdot \\ \alpha\beta_{a1} = \dots = \alpha\beta_{ab}. \end{matrix}$$

The test statistic is $Q_{AB}$, the weighted sum of squares for the $AB$ interaction. The test for the $AB$ interaction at significance level $\alpha$ involves rejecting $H_{0AB}$ if $Q_{AB}$ is larger than the $100(1 - \alpha)$ percent point of the chi-square distribution with $(a - 1)(b - 1)$ degrees of freedom.

The test for heterogeneity of effect size parameters within cells is a test of the null hypothesis that there is no variation of effect size parameters within the cells defined by the cross-classification of effects via factors $A$ and $B$. The null hypothesis can be stated in terms of effect parameters as

$$H_{0w}: \theta_{ijk} = \bar{\theta}_{ij.}, i = 1, \dots, a; j = 1, \dots, b; k = 1, \dots, m_{ij}.$$

The test statistic is $Q_W$, the weighted sum of squares "within groups." The test for within-group homogeneity of effect parameters at significance level $\alpha$ consists of rejecting $H_{OW}$ if $Q_W$ is larger than the $100(1 - \alpha)$ percent point of the chi-square distribution with

$$\sum_{i=1}^{a} \sum_{j=1}^{b} (m_{ij} - 1)$$

degrees of freedom.

**2.2.3 Computing omnibus test statistics** Each of the omnibus test statistics is carried out by computing a weighted ANOVA on the effect estimates (e.g., by using SAS, SPSSX, or BMDP computer programs), where the weight given to the effect estimate is the reciprocal of its sampling variance $v_{ijk}$. Thus, the weight $w_{ijk}$ for corresponding to the estimate $T_{ijk}$ is

$$w_{ijk} = 1/v_{ijk}.$$

The omnibus test statistics used in the analysis are the weighted *sums* of squares. When the corresponding null hypotheses are true, these weighted sums of squares have chi-square distributions with the number of degrees of freedom indicated by the computer program. Thus, $Q_A$, $Q_B$, $Q_{AB}$, and $Q_W$ are the weighted sums of squares for factor $A$, factor $B$, the $AB$ interaction, and the within-cell (or residual), respectively. The mean squares and $F$ test statistics *are not used in this analysis*. Similarly, the cell means and standard deviations reported by the computer program are generally not useful. Thus, the ANOVA computer program is used exclusively to compute the weighted sums of squares that are the omnibus test statistics. Weighted means for each cell and for each factor level should be computed separately using the methods discussed in connection with the one-factor analysis.

**2.2.4 Multifactor models with three or more factors** Procedures for multifactor models with more than two factors are analogous to those in two-factor models. Omnibus tests for main effects, interactions, and within-cell variation are carried out using the weighted *sums* of squares as the test statistics with appropriate degrees of freedom as indicated by the computer program. The interpretation of main effects and interactions is analogous to that in conventional analyses of variance in primary research.

# 3. A MULTIPLE REGRESSION ANALYSIS FOR EFFECT SIZES

In many case it is desirable to represent the characteristics of research studies by continuously coded variables or by a combination of discrete and continuous variables. In such cases the reviewer often wants to determine the relationship between these continuous variables and effect size. One very flexible analytic procedure for investigating these relationships is an analogue to multiple regression analysis for effect sizes (see Hedges 1982c, 1983; and Hedges & Olkin 1985). These methods share the generality and ease of use of conventional multiple regression analysis; and like their conventional counterparts, they can be viewed as including ANOVA models as a special case.

## 3.1 Models and Notation

Suppose that we have $k$ independent effect size estimates $T_1, \ldots, T_k$ with (estimated) sampling variances $v_1, \ldots, v_k$. The corresponding effect size parameters are $\theta_1, \ldots, \theta_k$. Suppose also that there are $p$ known predictor variables $X_1, \ldots, X_p$ which are believed to be related to the effects via a linear model of the form

$$\theta_i = \beta_0 + \beta_1 x_{i1} + \ldots + \beta_p x_{ip}, \qquad (19-23)$$

where $x_{i1}, \ldots, x_{ip}$ are the values of the predictor variables $X_1, \ldots, X_p$ for the $i$th study (i.e., $x_{ij}$ is the value of $X_j$ for study $i$), and $\beta_0, \beta_1, \ldots, \beta_p$ are unknown regression coefficients.

## 3.2 Estimation and Significance Test for Individual Coefficients

Estimation is usually carried out via weighted least squares algorithms. The formulas for estimators and test statistics can be expressed most succinctly in matrix notation and are given, for example, in Hedges and Olkin (1985). The analysis can be conducted using standard computer programs (e.g., in SAS, SPSSX, or BMDP) that compute weighted multiple regression analyses. The regression should be run with the effect estimates as the dependent variable and the predictor variables as independent variables with weights defined by the reciprocal of the sampling variances. That is, the weight for $T_i$ is $w_i = 1/v_i$.

Standard computer programs for weighted regression analysis produce the correct (asymptotically efficient) estimates $b_0, b_1, \ldots, b_p$ of the unstandardized regression coefficients $\beta_0, \beta_1, \ldots, \beta_p$. (Note that unlike the SPSS computer program, we use the symbols $\beta_0, \beta_1, \ldots, \beta_p$ to refer to the population value of the unstandardized regression coefficients *not* to the standardized regression coefficients.) While these standard computer programs give the correct *estimates* of the regression coefficients, the standard errors and significance computed by the programs are based on a slightly different model than that used for fixed effects meta-analysis and are *incorrect* for the meta-analysis model. Calculating the correct significance tests for individual regression coefficients requires some straightforward hand computations from information given in the computer output.

The correct standard error $S_i$ of the estimated coefficient estimate $b_j$ is simply

$$S_j = SE_j / \sqrt{MS_{\text{ERROR}}}, \qquad (19\text{-}24)$$

where $SE_j$ is the standard error of $b_j$ *as given by the computer program* and $MS_{\text{ERROR}}$ is the "error" or "residual" mean square from the analysis of variance for the regression as given by the computer program. Alternatively, the correct standard errors of $b_0, b_1, \ldots, b_p$ are the square roots of the diagonal elements of the inverse of the $(X'WX)$ matrix, which is sometimes called the inverse of the weighted sum of squares and cross-products matrix. Many regression analysis programs (such as SAS Proc GLM) will print this matrix as an option. The (correct) standard errors obtained from both methods are, of course, identical. They are simply alternative ways to compute the same thing.

The regression coefficient estimates (the $b_j$'s) are normally distributed about their respective parameter ($\beta_j$) values with standard deviations given by the standard errors (the $S_j$'s). Hence, a $100(1 - \alpha)$ percent confidence interval for each $\beta_j$ can be obtained by multiplying $S_j$ by the two-tailed critical value $C_\alpha$ of the standard normal distribution (for $\alpha = .05$, $C_\alpha = 1.96$) and then adding and subtracting this product from $b_j$. Thus, the $100(1 - \alpha)$ percent confidence interval for $\beta_j$ is

$$b_j - C_\alpha S_j \leq \beta_j \leq b_j + C_\alpha S_j. \qquad (19\text{-}25)$$

A two-sided test of the null hypothesis that the regression coefficient is zero,

$$H_0: \ \beta_j = 0, \qquad (19\text{-}26)$$

at significance level $\alpha$ consists of rejecting $H_0$ if

$$Z_j = |b_j| / S_j$$

exceeds the $100\alpha$ percent critical value of the standard normal distribution.

*Example.* Consider the example of the standardized mean differences for gender differences in conformity given in Data Set I. In this analysis we fit the linear model suggested by Becker (1986), who explained variation in effect sizes by a predictor variable that was the natural logarithm of the number of items on the con-

formity measure (Table 19.2, column 4). This predictor variable is highly correlated with the percentage of male authors used as a predictor in the example given for the categorical model analysis. Using SAS Proc GLM with effect sizes and weights given in Table 19.3, we computed a weighted regression analysis. The estimates of the regression coefficients given were $b_0 = -.323$ for the intercept and $b_1 = .210$ for the effect of the number of items. The standard errors of $b_0$ and $b_1$ could be computed in either of two ways. The $(X'WX)$ inverse matrix computed by SAS was

$$\left\{ \begin{array}{cc} .01219 & -.00406 \\ -.00406 & .00191 \end{array} \right\},$$

and hence the standard errors could be computed as

$$S_0 = \sqrt{.01291} = .110,$$

$$S_1 = \sqrt{.00191} = .044.$$

Alternatively, we could have obtained the standard errors by correcting the standard errors printed by the program (which are incorrect for our purposes). The standard errors printed by the SAS program were $SE(b_0) = .1151$ and $SE(b_1) = .0456$, and the residual mean square from the analysis of variance for the regression is $MS_{\text{ERROR}} = 1.086$. Using formula (19–24) gives

$$S_0 = .1151 / \sqrt{1.086} = .110,$$

$$S_1 = .0456 / \sqrt{1.086} = .044.$$

A 95 percent confidence interval for the effect $\beta_1$ of the number of items using $C_{.05} = 1.96$, $S_1 = .044$, and formula (19-25) is given by $.210 \pm 1.96(.044)$

$$.12 \leq \beta_1 \leq .30.$$

Since the confidence interval does not contain zero or, alternatively, because the statistic

$$Z_1 = .210 / .044 = 4.77$$

exceeds 1.96, we reject the hypothesis that there is no relationship between number of items and effect size. Thus, the number of items on the response measure has a statistically significant relationship to effect size.

### 3.3 Omnibus Tests

It is sometimes desirable to test hypotheses about groups or blocks of regression coefficients. For example, stepwise regression strategies may involve entering one block of predictor variables (e.g., a set of variables reflecting methodological characteristics) and then entering another block of predictor variables (e.g., a set of variables reflecting treatment characteristics) to see if the second block of variables explained any of the variation in effect size not accounted for by the first block of variables. Formally we need a test of the hypothesis that all of the regression coefficients for predictor variables in the second block are zero.

Suppose that the $a$ predictor variables $X_1, \ldots, X_a$ have already been entered and we wish to test whether the regression coefficients for a block of $b$ additional predictor variables $X_{a+1}, X_{a+2}, \ldots, X_{a+b}$ are simultaneously zero. That is, we wish to test

$$H_0: \; \beta_{a+1} = \ldots = \beta_{a+b} = 0.$$

The test statistic is the weighted *sum* of squares for the addition of this block of variables. It can be obtained directly as the difference in the weighted error sum of squares for the model with $a$ predictors and the weighted error sum of squares of the model with $a+b$ predictors. Alternatively, it can be computed from the output of the weighted stepwise regression as

$$Q_{\text{CHANGE}} = b \, F_{\text{CHANGE}} \, MS_{\text{ERROR}}, \quad (19\text{-}27)$$

where $F_{\text{CHANGE}}$ is the value of the $F$ test for the significance of the addition of the block of $b$ predictor variables and $MS_{\text{ERROR}}$ is the weighted error or residual mean square from the ANOVA for the regression. The test at significance level $\alpha$ consists of rejecting $H_0$ if $Q_{\text{CHANGE}}$ exceeds the $100(1-\alpha)$ percent point of the chi-square distribution with $b$ degrees of freedom.

If the number $k$ of effects exceeds $(p+1)$, the number of predictors plus the intercept, then a test of goodness of fit or model specification is possible. The test is formally a test of the null hypothesis that the population effect sizes $\theta_1, \ldots, \theta_k$ are exactly determined by the linear model

$$\theta_i = \beta_0 + \beta_1 x_{i1} + \ldots + \beta_p x_{ip}, \; i = 1, \ldots, p,$$

versus the alternative that some of the variation in the $\theta_i$'s is not fully explained by $X_1, \ldots, X_p$. The test statistic is the weighted residual sum of squares $Q_E$ about the regression ''line,'' and the test can be viewed as a test for greater than expected residual variation. This statistic is given in the analysis of variance for the regression and is usually called the error or residual sum of squares on computer printouts. The test at significance level $\alpha$ consists of rejecting the null hypothesis of model fit if $Q_E$ exceeds the $100(1-\alpha)$ percent point of the chi-square distribution with $(k-p-1)$ degrees of freedom.

Note that the tests of homogeneity of effect given in Chapter 18 and tests of homogeneity of effects within groups of independent effects described in connection with the analysis of variance for effect sizes are special cases of the test of model fit given here. That is, the statistic $Q_E$ reduces to the statistic $Q$ given in formula (18-6) of Chapter 18 when there are no predictor variables, and $Q_E$ reduces to the statistic $Q_{\text{WITHIN}}$ given in formula (19-11) when the predictor variables are dummy-coded to represent group membership.

*Example.* Continue the example of the regression analysis of the standardized mean differences for gender differences in conformity, using SAS Proc GLM to compute a weighted regression of effect size on the logarithm of the number of items on the conformity measure. Although we can illustrate the test for the significance of blocks of predictors, there is only one predictor. We start with $a = 0$ predictors and add $b = 1$ predictor variables. The weighted sum of squares for the regression in the analysis of variance for the regression gives $Q_{\text{CHANGE}} = 23.11$. We could also have computed $Q_{\text{CHANGE}}$ from the $F$ test statistic $F_{\text{CHANGE}}$ for the $R$-squared change and the $MS_{\text{ERROR}}$ for the analysis of variance for the regression. Here $F_{\text{CHANGE}} = 21.29$ and $MS_{\text{ERROR}} = 1.086$; thus, using formula (19-27),

$$Q_{\text{CHANGE}} = 1(21.29)(1.086) = 23.12,$$

identical to the result obtained directly (note that the two values disagree because of rounding). Comparing 23.12 with 3.84, the 95 percent point of the chi-square distribution with 1 degree of freedom, we reject the hypothesis that the (single) predictor is unrelated to effect size. This is, of course, the same result that was obtained by a test for the significance of the regression coefficient.

We also test the goodness of fit of the regression model. The weighted residual sum of squares was computed by SAS Proc GLM as $Q_E = 8.69$. Comparing this value with 15.51, the 95 percent point of the chi-square distribution with $10 - 2 = 8$ degrees of freedom, we see that we cannot reject the fit of the linear model. In fact chi-square values as large as 8.43 would occur between 25 and 50 percent of the time *owing to chance* if the model fit exactly.

## 3.4 Colinearity

All of the problems that arise in connection with multiple regression analysis can also arise in meta-analysis. Colinearity may degrade the quality of estimates of regression coefficients, wildly influencing their values and increasing their standard errors. The same procedures that are used to safeguard against excessive colinearity in multiple regression analysis in primary research are useful in meta-analysis. Examination of the correlation matrix of the predictors and the exclusion of some predictors that are too highly intercorrelated with the others can often be helpful. In some cases predictor variables derived from critical study characteristics may be too highly correlated for any meaningful analysis using more than a very few predictors. It is important to recognize, however, that colinearity is a limitation of the data (reflecting little information about the independent relations among variables) and not an inadequacy of statistical method. Thus, highly colinear predictors based on study characteristics imply that the studies simply do not have the array of characteristics that might make it possible to ascertain precisely their joint relationship with study effect size.

*Quantifying explained variation.* While the $Q_E$ statistic (or the $Q_W$ statistic for models with categorical independent variables) is a useful *test statistic* for assessing whether there is *any* statistically reliable unexplained variation, it is not a useful descriptive statistic for quantifying the *amount* of unexplained variation. A descriptive statistic $R_B$ (called the Birge ratio) is often used in the physical sciences. It is the ratio of $Q_E$ (or $Q_W$) to its degrees of freedom, that is,

$$R_B = Q_E/(k - p - 1)$$

(for a regression model with intercept) or

$$R_B = Q_W/(k - p)$$

(for a categorical model). The expected value of $R_B$ is exactly one when the effect parameters are determined exactly by the linear model. When the model does not fit exactly, $R_B$ tends to be larger than one. The Birge ratio has the interpretation that it estimates the ratio of the between-studies variation in effects to the variation in effects due to (within-study) sampling error. Thus, a Birge ratio of 1.5 suggests that there is 50 percent more between-studies variation than might be expected given the within-study sampling variance.

The squared multiple correlation between the observed effect sizes and the predictor variables is sometimes used as a descriptive statistic. However, the multiple correlation may be misinterpreted in this context because the maximum value of the population multiple correlation is always less than one, and can be much less than one. The reason is that the squared multiple correlation is a measure of "variance (in the observed effect size estimates) accounted for" by the predictors. But there are two sources of variation in the effect size

estimates: between-studies (systematic) effects and within-study (nonsystematic or sampling) effects. Only between-studies effects are systematic and therefore only they *can* be explained via predictor variables. Variance due to within-study sampling errors cannot be explained. Consequently, the maximum proportion of variance that can be explained is determined by the proportion of total variance that is due to between-studies effects. Thus, the maximum possible value of the squared multiple correlation can be expressed (loosely) as

$$\frac{\text{Variance (between)}}{\text{Variance (between)} + \text{Variance (within)}}.$$

Clearly, this ratio can be quite small when the between-studies variance is small relative to the within-study variance. For example, if the between-studies variance (component) is 50 percent of the (average) within-study variance, the maximum squared multiple correlation would be

$$\frac{.5}{.5 + 1.0} = .33.$$

In this example, predictors that yielded an $R^2$ of .30 would have explained 90 percent of the *explainable* variance even though they explain only 30 percent of the *total* variance in effect estimates.

## 4. CONCLUSION

Fixed effects approaches to meta-analysis provide a variety of techniques for statistically analyzing effect sizes. These techniques are analogous to fixed effects statistical methods commonly used in the analysis of primary data: the analysis of variance and multiple regression analysis. Consequently, familiar analysis strategies (such as contrasts from analysis of variance) or coding methods (such as dummy or effect coding from multiple regression analysis) can be used in meta-analysis just as they are in primary analyses.

## 5. REFERENCES

Becker, B. J. (1986). Influence again: An examination of reviews and studies of gender differences in social influence. In J. S. Hyde & M. C. Linn (Eds.), *The psychology of gender: Advances through meta-analysis.* Baltimore: Johns Hopkins University Press.

Eagly, A. H., & Carli, L. L. (1981). Sex of researchers and sex typed communication as determinants of sex differences in influenceability: A meta-analysis of social influence studies. *Psychological Bulletin, 90,* 1–20.

Hedges, L. V. (1982a). Estimating effect size from a series of independent experiments. *Psychological Bulletin, 92,* 490–499.

Hedges, L. V. (1982b). Fitting categorical models to effect sizes from a series of experiments. *Journal of Educational Statistics, 7,* 119–137.

Hedges, L. V. (1982c). Fitting continuous models to effect size data. *Journal of Educational Statistics, 7,* 245–270.

Hedges, L. V. (1983). Combining independent estimators in research synthesis. *British Journal of Mathematical and Statistical Psychology, 36,* 123–131.

Hedges, L. V., & Olkin, I. (1985). *Statistical methods for meta-analysis.* Orlando, FL: Academic Press.

Miller, R. G., Jr. (1981). *Simultaneous statistical inference* (2nd ed.). New York: Springer-Verlag.

Rosenthal, R., & Rubin, D. B. (1982). Comparing effect sizes of independent studies. *Psychological Bulletin, 92,* 500–504.

Cooper, H. and Hedges, L. V. (Eds.) 1994. *The Handbook of Research Synthesis.* New York: Russell Sage Foundation

# 20

# RANDOM EFFECTS MODELS

**STEPHEN W. RAUDENBUSH**
*Michigan State University*

CONTENTS

## 1. INTRODUCTION

A skilled researcher who wishes to assess the generalizability of findings from a single study will try to select a sample that represents the target population. The researcher will examine interaction effects—for example, by asking whether a new medical treatment depends on the age of the patient; whether the effectiveness of a new method of instruction depends on student aptitude; whether men are as responsive as women to nonverbal communication. If such interactions are null—if treatment effects do not depend on the age, aptitude, or sex of the subject—a finding is viewed as generalizing across these subject characteristics. If, on the other hand, such interactions are significant, the researcher can clarify the limits of generalization.

Inevitably, however, the capacity of a single study to clarify the generalizability of a finding is limited. Of necessity, many conditions that might affect a finding will be constant in any given study. The manner in which the treatment is implemented, the geographic or cultural setting, the particular instrumentation used, and the historical era during which a particular experiment is implemented are all potential moderators of study findings. Such moderators can rarely be examined in the context of a single study because rarely do these factors vary within a single study.

Across a series of replicated or similar studies, however, such moderators will naturally tend to vary. For example, later in this chapter we shall reanalyze data from 19 experiments testing the effect of teacher expectancy on pupil IQ. Several factors widely believed to influence results in this type of study varied across those studies: the timing and duration of the treatment, the conditions of pupil testing, and the age of the subjects. Using methods described in Chapter 19, we can test hypotheses about the effect of such potential moderators on study outcomes, thereby clarifying the conditions under which a positive effect of treatment appears. However, many other characteristics of the studies varied: the year the study was conducted, its geographic location and administrative context, the characteristics of the teachers expected to implement the treatment, and the socioeconomic status of the communities providing the setting. Although no theory was available a priori to suggest that such characteristics would influence the outcome of the studies, it is at least possible that these characteristics are also related to differences between studies in effect size. For any synthesis, a long list of *possible* moderators of effect size can be enumerated, many of which cannot be ascertained even by the most careful reading of each study's report.

The multiplicity of potential moderators underlies the concept of a study's true effect size as random. Indeed, the concept of randomness in nature arises from a belief that the outcome of a process cannot be predicted in advance, precisely because the sources of influence on the outcome are both numerous and unidentifiable.

The concept of a *true* effect size as random must clearly be distinguished from that of an effect size *estimate* as random. Suppose that a random sample of subjects is selected from a well-defined population and that half of the resulting sample are assigned at random to receive a new medical treatment; a second random sample is then selected from the same population and the experimental procedure is replicated exactly, so that the assignment of subjects to conditions, the implementation of the treatment, the setting, instrumentation, and so on, are the same in every detail. In this case, the two *true* treatment effects will be identical. However, the *estimates* of the treatment effect will vary as a result of chance differences between the two samples. Such variation is conventionally termed "sampling variance". However, we shall refer to this variation as "estimation variance" because chance differences in the two samples will lead to chance differences in the sample estimates of the common true effect size shared by the two studies.

On the other hand, suppose that despite determined efforts at exact replication, a large number of uncontrollable factors influence the implementation of the treatment, the setting, and the measurement procedures in the two studies and that these differences have some effect on the outcome of the experiment. We say then that the "true" effect size itself varied, in addition to the "estimation variance" that arose because the two studies used different random samples of subjects. We refer to the variance of the true effect sizes as "random effects variance." Hence, the variance of the estimated effect sizes has two components:

$$
\begin{matrix}
\text{Variance of} \\ \text{estimated} \\ \text{effects}
\end{matrix}
=
\begin{matrix}
\text{random} \\ \text{effects} \\ \text{variance}
\end{matrix}
+
\begin{matrix}
\text{estimation} \\ \text{variance.}
\end{matrix}
\quad (20\text{-}1)
$$

In the notation used throughout this handbook, $T_i$ is an estimate of effect size, $\theta_i$ is the true effect size, and the relation between them may be written as

$$T_i = \theta_i + e_i, \quad (20\text{-}2)$$

where $e_i$ is the error with which $T_i$ estimates $\theta_i$. Hence, the variance described in equation (20-1) may be written as

$$\mathrm{Var}(T_i) = \nu_i^* = \sigma_\theta^2 + v_i, \quad (20\text{-}3)$$

where

$\nu_i^*$ is the total variance of the estimated effect size $T_i$,

$\sigma_\theta^2$ is the random effects variance, and

$v_i$ is the estimation variance.

It should be clear that if every study had exactly the same true effect size, ($\theta_i = \theta$ for $i = 1, \ldots, k$), $\sigma_\theta^2$ would be zero. In that case, all of the variation across the $k$ estimates $T_i$ would be attributable to estimation variance. Similarly, if these true effect sizes varied strictly as a result of a few identifiable study characteristics, we would view such variation as nonrandom. That is, once those study characteristics were identified and taken into account, no additional variation among the true effect sizes remains to be explained. In either case—true effect sizes invariant or true effect sizes varying predictably—the fixed effects approaches described in detail in the previous chapter would apply. On the other hand, if it were more reasonable to assume that true effect sizes vary at least in part as a function

of multiple, unidentifiable sources, the random effects approaches described in this chapter will be appropriate.

We first consider more formally alternative conceptual frameworks that underlie random effects models for effect size. To illuminate essential principles, we then illustrate a random effects approach to research synthesis in the comparatively simple context of parallel randomized experiments with balanced designs. We then turn our attention to more realistic unbalanced effect size data and introduce a weighted least squares regression approach, which enables us to use study characteristics to predict study outcomes and to estimate the component of the effect size variance unexplained by the model. Our numerical examples reveal similarities and contrasts between results obtained via fixed effects and random effects approaches. Finally, we discuss several threats to valid inference that arise uniquely in the applications of the random effects approach. Appendices at the end of the chapter provide details of alternative estimation procedures and a simple computing code for implementing these procedures.

## 2. ALTERNATIVE CONCEPTUAL BASES OF RANDOM EFFECTS MODELS FOR EFFECT SIZE

Two alternative rationales—classical and Bayesian—provide quite different justifications for a random effects approach. According to the classical approach, the true effect sizes under study are sampled from a larger population of effect sizes, and their randomness reflects the resulting sampling variability. According to the Bayesian approach, the randomness of the true effect size represents the investigator's subjective uncertainty about the process that produces them.

### 2.1 The Classical View

We may conceive of the set of studies in a synthesis as constituting a random sample from a larger "population" of studies. For some syntheses, this assumption may literally be true. For example, because Rosenthal and Rubin (1978) located far more studies of interpersonal expectancy effects than they could code in any detail with available resources, they drew a random sample of studies for intensive analysis. In this case, an exhaustive search yielded a list or sampling frame of the population of studies, from which a random sample was selected. In other syntheses, one might wish to view the studies obtained through a literature search as a sample from the complete set or population of studies.

A reasonable question is whether the sample is representative of the population (see Chapter 25 on publication bias).

One might also view the set of studies under synthesis as constituting a realization from a universe of "possible" studies—studies that realistically could have been conducted or that might be conducted in the future. Because one wishes to generalize to this larger universe of possible implementations of a treatment or observations of a relationship, one conceives of the true effect size of each available study as one item from a random sample of all possible effect sizes. The notion of a hypothetical universe of possible observations is standard in measurement theory. Cronbach et al. (1972) wrote: "A behavioral measurement is a sample from the measurements that might have been made, and interest attaches to the obtained score only because it is representative of the whole collection or universe" (p. 18).

Once the set of studies under investigation is conceived as a random sample, it is clear that a meta-analysis can readily be viewed as a survey having a two-stage cluster sampling procedure. One first obtains a random sample of studies from a larger population of studies. Within each study or "cluster" one then obtains a random sample of subjects from the population of subjects "in that cluster." This population is the universe of persons who might have participated in the particular study. Of course, many studies are not actually based on random samples of subjects from well-defined populations. Nevertheless, the investigators use standard inferential statistical procedures. By doing so, each investigator is implicitly viewing his or her sample as a random sample from a hypothetical population or universe of possible observations that supply the target of any generalizations that arise from the statistical inferences.

The two-stage sampling design implies a model with two components of variance, as in equation (20-1). The first component ("random effects variance") represents the variance that arises as a result of the sampling of studies. The second component ("estimation variance") arises because, for any given study, the effect size estimate is based on a sample of subjects. At either stage, it is conceivable to view the population as either finite or infinite. Of course, it is hard to imagine that an infinite number of studies have been conducted on a particular topic. Nevertheless, in practice, populations at both levels are viewed as infinite. This simplifies analysis because one need not use finite population

correction factors. Perhaps more important, the view of populations as infinite is consistent with the notion of generalizing to a universe of possible observations (Cronbach et al. 1972) and is therefore consistent with standard scientific aims.

## 2.2 The Bayesian View

The Bayesian view, described in detail in Chapter 26 of this volume, avoids the specification of any sampling mechanism as a justification for the random effects model.[1] Instead, the random variation of the "true" effect sizes represents the investigator's lack of knowledge about the process that generates them. Imagine that one could have observed the true effect size for a very large number, $k$, of highly similar studies. A Bayesian might say that these studies are "exchangeable" (De Finetti 1964) if she or he has no a priori reason to believe that one study's effect size should be any larger than any other study's effect size. In this context, $\mu_\theta$ represents the investigator's belief about the mean of the effect sizes from the $k$ studies and $\sigma_\theta^2$ represents the degree of uncertainty associated with that belief. Such beliefs could be informed by the data, by prior knowledge or opinion, or by both.

Given a particular effect size $\theta_i$, the investigator might also consider the computed effect size $T_i$. The conditional variance of $T_i$ given $\theta_i$— that is, the variance of a particular computed effect size given knowledge of the true effect size—is equal to $v_i$. To the classical statistician, the estimation variance $v_i$ represents sampling variance. To the Bayesian statistician, the same quantity, $v_i$, represents the investigator's degree of uncertainty regarding the proposition that $T_i$ is near $\theta_i$.

Just as the classical statistician might envision a synthesis as a two-stage sampling process, the Bayesian statistician envisions two components of uncertainty. At one level, there is the uncertainty that a particular true effect size, $\theta_i$, will be near $\mu_\theta$, the central tendency of all true effect sizes. At another stage, there is the uncertainty that a computed effect size, $T_i$, will be near $\theta_i$. Either way, one perceives two components of variation, represented in equation (20-3) by $\sigma_\theta^2$ and $v_i$. The notion that the true effect sizes are exchangeable is functionally equivalent to the classical statistician's as-

---

[1] In fact, Bayesians tend to avoid distinctions between fixed and random effects approaches (Dempster, Rubin & Tsutakawa 1981). The conception of a study's effect size as probabilistic fits naturally within the Bayesian viewpoint whereas the fixed effects approach does not.

sumption that the true effect sizes constitute a random sample from a population of studies.

In many cases, however, there will be a priori reason to believe that some studies will have larger effects than others. For example, a treatment may have a longer duration in one set of studies than in another, and one may hypothesize that longer durations are associated with larger effect sizes. In this case, the Bayesian may view the effect sizes as *conditionally exchangeable*. Given a set of studies sharing the same duration, their effect sizes are exchangeable. The differences in effect size that are predicted by knowing duration reflect the investigator's knowledge about the process that produces effect sizes; the remaining variance, $\sigma_\theta^2$, of the effect sizes reflects the investigator's lack of knowledge, so that a large value of $\sigma_\theta^2$ implies that much remains unknown about this process even after accounting for duration.

Our discussion reveals that classical and Bayes approaches to random effects meta-analysis assign different definitions to quantities like $\theta_i$, $T_i$, $\mu_\theta$, $\sigma_\theta^2$, and $v_i$, but use those quantities in functionally similar ways. In interpreting the results presented here, the reader is free to employ either the classical conception (that the variance of the computed effect sizes represents a two-stage sampling process) or the Bayesian interpretation (that the variance of the computed effects reflects two sources of the investigator's uncertainty).

## 3. APPLICATION TO PARALLEL RANDOMIZED EXPERIMENTS

Key conceptual issues in synthesizing study results become quite clear in the context of parallel randomized experiments in which every study uses the same outcome variable. In this case, well-known analysis of variance (ANOVA) procedures apply.

### 3.1 A Hypothetical Example: No Between-Studies Predictors

Suppose that investigators have conducted $k = 6$ replications of a randomized experiment using outcomes $Y_{ij}^T$ and $Y_{ij}^C$ for subject $j$ in study $i$ of the treatment and control groups, respectively. Suppose, further, that in every study, exactly $n = 30$ subjects have been assigned to each group, so that each study has a sample size of 60, with 360 subjects in the entire set of six studies. Summary statistics for this hypothetical synthesis are presented in Table 20.1. The table gives the treatment group means (column 2), the control means (column 3), each study's overall mean (column 4), and the treatment-control mean difference (column 5).

Readers familiar with basic experimental design will recognize our synthesis as having a randomized blocks design with replications (see Kirk 1982, p. 293). Studies are blocks; within each block subjects are assigned at random to treatments; and there are 30 replications per cell. The standard analysis for such a design is a two-way ($6 \times 2$) ANOVA. Many analysts would consider blocks random and treatments fixed, though both factors could be considered fixed. The model with blocks random and treatments fixed has been termed a "mixed model" analysis of variance because the model contains both fixed and random effects.

Inspection of Table 20.1 shows a tendency for treatment means to be larger than control means. However, the differences between treatment and control means seem to vary from study to study. For example, the benefit of the experimental treatment relative to the control looks greater in study 1 than in study 6. Of course, some variation in such sample statistics is expected purely as a result of chance. To facilitate further interpretation, we construct an ANOVA source table (Table 20.2). The results of hypothesis testing depend on the conception of studies as either fixed or random.

**3.1.1 Fixed effects analysis** The fixed effects analysis tests the treatment main effect by means of the statistic

$$F(1,348) = MS(\text{treatment})/MS(\text{within-cell}) = 9.0,$$

$p < .01$ implying that experimental subjects, on average, scored significantly higher than did the controls. However, we know that main effects must be interpreted with extreme caution in the presence of interactions. Indeed, the results in Table 20.2 reveal a significant interaction:

$$F(5,348) = MS(\text{treatment-by-studies})/MS(\text{within-cell}) = 3.0,$$

$p < .01$, implying that the effect of treatment does vary across studies. The overall mean difference $\bar{Y}^T - \bar{Y}^C$ is therefore a poor summary of the results. The usual procedure in the fixed effects ANOVA is to follow the finding of a significant omnibus test with a post hoc analysis of specific comparisons. For example, one could follow up the finding of a significant treatment-by-studies $F$ test by comparing $T - C$ contrasts of particular pairs of studies. However, it is doubtful that such an analysis would lead to insights of much value without

**Table 20.1 Hypothetical Data from Six Parallel Randomized Experiments**

| Study | Treatment Mean, $\bar{Y}_i^T$ | Control Mean, $\bar{Y}_i^C$ | Study Mean, $\bar{Y}_i$ | Mean Difference $T_i = \bar{Y}_i^T - \bar{Y}_i^C$ |
|---|---|---|---|---|
| 1 | 12.5 | 9.5 | 11.0 | 3.0 |
| 2 | 13.0 | 11.0 | 12.0 | 2.0 |
| 3 | 10.5 | 9.5 | 10.0 | 1.0 |
| 4 | 10.0 | 10.0 | 10.0 | 0.0 |
| 5 | 11.5 | 10.5 | 11.0 | 1.0 |
| 6 | 8.5 | 9.5 | 9.0 | $-1.0$ |
| Overall | $\bar{Y}_{\bullet}^T = 11.0$ | $\bar{Y}_{\bullet}^C = 10.0$ | $\bar{Y}_{\bullet\bullet} = 10.5$ | $T = \bar{Y}_{\bullet}^T - \bar{Y}_{\bullet}^C = 1.0$ |

NOTE: The pooled, within-cell standard deviation is 3.16 based on 30 subjects per cell, 60 per study, 360 overall studies.

**Table 20.2 Analysis of Variance Source Table for Data in Table 20.1**

| Source | df | Sum of Squares | Mean Square | $F$ [a] (Studies Fixed) | $F$ [a] (Studies Random) |
|---|---|---|---|---|---|
| Studies | 5 | 330 | 66 | 6.6 [b] | 6.6 [b] |
| Treatments | 1 | 90 | 90 | 9.0 [b] | 3.0 |
| Treatment-by-studies | 5 | 150 | 30 | 3.0 [b] | 3.0 [b] |
| Within-cell | 348 | 3,480 | 10 | | |

[a] Treatments are viewed as fixed in each case.
[b] $p < .01$.

more information about how the studies varied in design, implementation, setting, and so on. In particular, knowing that the treatment effect was larger in study 1 than in study 6 is not much help without knowing more about those studies.

**3.1.2 Random effects analysis** When studies are conceived as random, the appropriate $F$ test for the treatment main effect is different from the analysis that conceived of studies as fixed.[2] Now the appropriate test is

$$F(1,5) = MS(\text{treatment}/MS(\text{treatment-by-studies}) = 3.0,$$

$p > .05$. Notice that the denominator of the $F$ test is different from that used in a fixed effects analysis and has only 5 degrees of freedom rather than 348. The resulting $F$ test is more conservative than that used in the fixed effects analysis because the random effects $F$

[2] Choice of appropriate $F$ tests is based on an analysis of expected mean squares. In the case of the present two-way design, these are presented, for example, by Kirk (1982, p. 296). In general, conceiving effects as random rather than fixed adds components of variance to the expected means squares.

test incorporates the additional uncertainty that arises from the randomness of the true effect sizes. The result of the random effects $F$ test leads one to conclude that there is no evidence of a significant treatment main effect.

Note that the test for the treatment-by-studies interaction is identical to that in the fixed effects analysis. However, the interpretation is a bit different. Let us label the "true" $T - C$ contrast for study $i$ as $\theta_i$, that is,

$$\theta_i = \mu_i^T - \mu_i^C.$$

In the fixed effects context, the null hypothesis of the treatment-by-studies interaction may be written as

$$\text{H}_0\text{: } \theta_1 = \theta_2 = \ldots = \theta_k.$$

However, in the random effects context, each $\theta_i$ is typically viewed as random, having a normal distribution with mean $\mu_\theta$ and variance $\sigma_\theta^2$. Hence, the null hypothesis may be written as

$$\text{H}_0\text{: } \sigma_\theta^2 = 0.$$

In the present case, we have rejected this null hypothesis and inferred that $\sigma_\theta^2 > 0$. As in the fixed effects case, the test for treatment main effects must be interpreted with caution in the presence of significant interactions. In particular, the nonsignificant treatment main effect should not be interpreted as evidence that the treatment is utterly inefficacious in light of evidence that the treatment effect varies from study to study. Having found a significant treatment-by-studies interaction, the follow-up procedure in the random effects analysis is different from that used in the fixed effects case. Recall that in the fixed effects case, the usual procedure is to test specific post hoc comparisons. In a random effects analysis, the usual procedure is to estimate the treatment-by-studies variance component. We shall call this variance $\sigma_\theta^2$ because it represents the variance of the $T - C$ contrasts across studies. In the present case, the usual estimate (see Appendix A at the end of this chapter) is

$$\hat{\sigma}_\theta^2 = 1.33.$$

A random effects summary might then be a "two-number" summary. Our point estimate of the mean of the six treatment contrasts is 1.0 (not significantly different from zero), and the estimated standard deviation of the treatment effects is $\sqrt{(1.33)} = 1.15$. Hence, we estimate that a study with an effect one SD below average would have a treatment − control contrast of $1.00 - 1.15 = -0.15$, and a study with an effect one SD above average would have a treatment − control contrast of $1.00 + 1.15 = 2.15$. These numbers may be standardized to $-0.05$ and $0.68$, respectively, in units of the pooled standard deviation of 3.16. This is a large range indeed.

In supplying both a central tendency and a range of likely treatment effects, the random effects approach provides a more interpretable summary than does the fixed effects approach. Most important, this summary is constructed to apply to a larger universe of possible implementations of the treatment and therefore may be viewed as more generalizable than is the fixed effects summary. However, assertions about the range of likely effects (e.g., statements about the likely value of effect sizes one SD above or below average) are fragile in two regards. First, they depend on the accuracy of estimation of $\sigma_\theta^2$, and this estimate will be imprecise in syntheses of small numbers of studies. Second, they apply to a universe or population of studies "like those" in our sample; when studies are not sampled from a well-

defined population, the target of such a generalization is unclear.

### 3.1.3 The influence of $k$ on the choice between fixed and random effects models

Our discussion suggests that the choice between a conception of study effects as fixed versus random depends in part on the number of studies available. In the extreme case of a synthesis of only two studies, the fixed effects approach seems most sensible. If two experiments produced different $T - C$ contrasts, interest would tend to focus on the particular studies and possible explanations for the discrepant findings in light of those particularities. The magnitude of each $T - C$ contrast would constitute the key numerical evidence. With only two studies, a random effects analysis would supply a poor summary. The variance $\sigma_\theta^2$ would be estimated with extremely poor precision based on only two studies, and, correspondingly, the notion of generalizing to a larger population of studies with a sample of size two would seem ludicrous.

At the other extreme, with several hundred studies, the fixed effects approach would make little sense. The treatment-by-studies interaction $F$ would be tested with great power, virtually ensuring rejection of the null hypothesis of no difference in $T - C$ contrasts across studies. Particular studies and their $T - C$ contrasts would tend to be of relatively little interest, and post hoc pairwise comparisons among hundreds of levels of a factor might not be illuminating. In contrast, the random effects approach would supply a parsimonious and interpretable summary. Both the mean and variance of the true $T - C$ contrasts would be estimated with precision, and the notion of generalizing to a large population of studies with such a large sample could make good sense.

Regardless of the choice of fixed versus random effects conceptualization, a finding of significant treatment-by-studies interaction invites investigation of the possible explanations for discrepancies in study results. We now turn to the question of incorporating information about study differences into the analysis of our hypothetical data from six parallel randomized experiments.

## 3.2 A Hypothetical Example: Incorporating Between-Studies Predictors

Suppose now that our investigators, having conducted six experiments whose results are listed in Table 20.1, neglected to tell us that the studies differed in a crucial regard: The first set of three studies had a long treatment duration, whereas the second set of three studies had a short treatment duration. The ANOVA results are illustrated in Table 20.3.

Readers familiar with basic experimental design will now recognize our synthesis as having a split-plot design with replications. Again, the six studies may be viewed as blocks; duration is the between-blocks factor. Within each block, subjects are assigned at random to treatments. Hence, treatment is the within-blocks factor. There are 30 replications per cell. The standard analysis for such a design is a three-factor ANOVA in which studies are nested within levels of duration and crossed with treatments (see Winer 1971, p. 363). Many analysts would consider blocks random, and we illustrate that approach here.

Inspection of Table 20.1 shows a tendency for studies of long duration to have more positive treatment effects than do studies of brief duration. There is little evidence that, within levels of duration, $T - C$ differences vary much. Of course, such inferences are quite speculative without utilizing appropriate hypothesis testing procedures, and so we have constructed an ANOVA source table (Table 20.3).

We first consider whether effect sizes depend on the duration of the treatment. When studies are conceived as random, the appropriate $F$ test is

$$F(1,4) = MS(\text{treatment-by-duration})/MS(\text{treatment-by-studies}) = 6.0,$$

$.05 < p < .10$, leaving in doubt the reliability of the proposition that duration of treatment is related to the magnitude of the experimental effect. A fixed effects

analysis would have found a result significant at the .01 level. Either analysis would test the significance of the treatment-by-studies interaction by

$$F(4, 348) = MS(\text{treatment-by-studies})/MS(\text{within-cell}) = 1.5,$$

$p > .10$. Given the nonsignificance of this test, investigators have differed about the appropriate course of action (Fabian 1991). Some would drop the treatment-by-studies interaction from the model, effectively concluding that the $T - C$ differences are invariant across studies once duration is controlled. They would then retest treatment-by-duration interaction, and (in this case) find a significant effect. Other researchers favor a more conservative approach of leaving the treatment-by-studies variation in the model. The example reveals how the conception of treatment contrasts as random can lead to more conservative results than those based on a fixed effects conception. Using the random effects analysis, the error mean square reflects the extra uncertainty associated with the variance in the true $T - C$ contrasts in the population of studies; and the reduced error degrees of freedom reflects the sense in which studies rather than subjects serve as the units of analysis.

## 4. STATISTICAL INFERENCE FOR EFFECT SIZE DATA

The case of parallel randomized experiments illustrates in the familiar context of ANOVA the logic of research synthesis based on the conception that study effect sizes are random. The data from most research syntheses have

**Table 20.3 Analysis of Variance Source Table for Data in Table 20.1 (duration included as a factor)**

| Source | df | Sum of Squares | Mean Square | $F$[a] (Studies Fixed) | $F$[a] (Studies Random) |
|---|---|---|---|---|---|
| **Between-Studies** | | | | | |
| Duration | 1 | 90 | 90 | 9.0[b] | 1.5 |
| Studies | 4 | 240 | 60 | 6.0[b] | 6.0[b] |
| **Within-Study** | | | | | |
| Treatments | 1 | 90 | 90 | 9.0[b] | 6.0 |
| Treatment-by-duration | 1 | 90 | 90 | 9.0[b] | 6.0 |
| Treatment-by-studies | 4 | 60 | 15 | 1.5 | 1.5 |
| Within-cell | 348 | 3,480 | 10 | | |

[a] Treatment and duration are viewed as fixed in each case.
[b] $p < .01$.

two characteristics, however, that increase the complexity of research synthesis and render the usual ANOVA inapplicable.

First, the data from research syntheses will nearly always be unbalanced. The number of subjects per study will vary, and, if the studies involve treatment conditions, the proportion of subjects in each condition will vary across studies. The unbalanced character of the data guarantees that study effect sizes will be estimated with unequal precision. The precision of a study's effect size estimate will depend both on the sample size in that study and on the degree of heterogeneity among the true effect sizes. In this context, standard ANOVA procedures for mixed models are not applicable.

Second, the outcome variables will differ across studies. Because each outcome will likely be measured on a different scale, the investigator will need to construct a standardized measure of effect for each study prior to synthesis. Such standardization introduces some complexity into distribution theory for the effect size estimate $T_i$ as an estimate of the true effect size $\theta_i$. This complexity is described in detail in Chapter 18 for a variety of measures of effect size. The discussion shows that conventional ANOVA and regression procedures will be inapplicable.

Both of these difficulties are readily overcome owing to recent developments in statistical methods for effect size analysis. Estimation and hypothesis testing for such data are discussed in detail in Chapter 19 on fixed effects analysis. Chapter 18 indicates how to estimate the mean and variance of true effect sizes under the random effects conceptualization.

In this section we introduce a fairly general analytic approach for effect size data based on the random effects conceptualization. The approach utilizes a regression model and weighted least squares estimation. It provides a generalization of previously considered analytic approaches in three ways:

1. When the model has no predictors other than an intercept, it duplicates the random effects approach to combining effect sizes in Chapter 18.

2. In the case of parallel randomized experiments with studies classified into categories (e.g., high- versus low-duration, as in section 3), the results duplicate the mixed model ANOVA described in section 3 of this chapter, as we shall illustrate.

3. When the random effects variance is null ($\sigma_\theta^2 = 0$), the results will duplicate the results of the fixed

effects regression approach introduced in Chapter 19.

We first present the model and describe procedures for estimation. Three examples illustrate analysis and interpretation and demonstrate the generalizations described above.

## 4.1 The Model

Suppose that we have calculated an effect size estimate $T_i$ of the true effect size $\theta_i$ for each of $k$ studies, $i = 1, \ldots, k$. Recall from equation (20-2) the linkage between the estimated and true effect size

$$T_i = \theta_i + e_i, \qquad (20\text{-}4)$$

where we assume that the errors of estimation, $e_i$, are statistically independent, each with a mean of zero and estimation variance $v_i$. We now formulate a prediction model for the true effects as depending on a set of study characteristics plus error:

$$\theta_i = \beta_0 + \beta_1 X_{i1} + \beta_2 X_{i2} + \ldots + \beta_p X_{ip} + u_i, (20\text{-}5)$$

where

$\beta_0$ is the model intercept;

$X_{i1}, \ldots, X_{ip}$ are coded characteristics of studies hypothesized to predict the study effect size $\theta_i$;

$\beta_1, \ldots, \beta_p$ are regression coefficients capturing the association between study characteristics and effect sizes; and

$u_i$ is the random effect of study $i$, that is, the deviation of study $i$'s true effect size from the value predicted on the basis of the model. Each random effect, $u_i$, is assumed independent with a mean of zero and variance $\sigma_\theta^2$.

Equation (20-5) is identical to the fixed effects regression model given in equation (19-23), with one exception: the addition of the random effect $u_i$. Under the fixed effects specification, the study characteristics $X_{i1}, \ldots, X_{ip}$ are presumed to account completely for variation in the true effect sizes. In contrast, the random effects specification assumes that part of the variability in these true effects is unexplainable by the model. The statistical literature describes equation (20-5) as a mixed effects linear model with fixed effects $\beta_0, \beta_1, \ldots, \beta_p$ and random effects $u_i$, $i = 1, \ldots, k$.

## 4.2 Estimation

Estimating the parameters of the mixed effects regression model for effect sizes (20-5) is more complicated than estimation in standard regression models and even a bit more complicated than in the fixed effects regression model for effect sizes (19-23). To understand why, it helps to substitute equation (20-5) into equation (20-4), yielding the regression model for the effect size estimate $T_i$:

$$T_i = \beta_0 + \beta_1 X_{i1} + \beta_2 X_{i2} + \ldots + \beta_p X_{ip} + u_i + e_i. \tag{20-6}$$

Equation (20-6) has two components in its error term, $u_i + e_i$, and so the variance of $T_i$, controlling for the $X$'s, is

$$v_i^* = \text{Var}(u_i + e_i) = \sigma_\theta^2 + v_i. \tag{20-7}$$

It would clearly be inappropriate to use ordinary least squares regression for equation (20-6) because ordinary least squares assumes that every residual has the same variance (homoscedasticity). In contrast, the residual variances of our model, $v_i^*$, will be unequal (heteroscedastic) so long as $v_i$ varies across studies. In this regard, our model is similar to the fixed effects regression model in Chapter 19. As in Chapter 19, a weighted least squares approach is needed, and the optimal weights will be the inverse of each study's variance:

$$w_i^* = 1/v_i^* = 1/(\sigma_\theta^2 + v_i), \tag{20-8}$$

which differ from weights in the fixed effects analysis

$$w_i = 1/v_i. \tag{20-9}$$

In many research syntheses, $v_i$ will be computed with a high degree of accuracy based on each study's data, and so the calculation of $w_i = 1/v_i$ for use in a fixed effects analysis is quite straightforward. Chapter 18 provides expressions for $v_i$ in the case of several measures of effect including standardized means differences, correlations, log odds ratios, and others. Those computations are also useful in the random effects case, but, as equation (20-8) shows, the weights $w_i^*$ needed in the random effects analysis also depend on $\sigma_\theta^2$, which is generally unknown and must be estimated from the data.

In fact, an estimate of the regression coefficients (the $\beta$'s in equation 20-6) is required in order to obtain estimates of $\sigma_\theta^2$ and hence $w_i^*$. The dilemma posed for us, then, is that estimation of the regression coefficients depends on the unknown values of $\sigma_\theta^2$ and estimation of

$\sigma_\theta^2$ depends on the unknown values of the $\beta$'s. We consider two approaches to solving this problem: a three-step "method of moments" solution and an iterative maximum likelihood approach.

**4.2.1 The method of moments** Using the method of moments, the researcher computes provisional estimates of the $\beta$'s in equation (20-6). Based on these estimates, he or she can then estimate $\sigma_\theta^2$ and, therefore, the weights, $w_i^*$. These weights are then employed in a weighted least squares regression to obtain new (and final) estimates of the $\beta$'s. The process works in three steps:

*Step 1.* Compute estimates $\hat{\beta}_0, \ldots, \hat{\beta}_p$ using ordinary least squares regression. This analysis will yield as a by-product the residual sum of squares

$$RSS = \Sigma (T_i - \hat{\beta}_0 - \hat{\beta}_1 X_{i1} - \ldots - \hat{\beta}_p X_{ip})^2. \tag{20-10}$$

*Step 2.* Estimate $\sigma_\theta^2$. It can readily be shown that the expected value of the residual sum of squares is given by

$$E(RSS) = \text{constant}(1) + \text{constant}(2)*\sigma_\theta^2 \tag{20-11}$$

The appendix provides general expressions for the two constants, which involve matrix notation. Equation (20-11) is now solved for $\sigma_\theta^2$ by substituting the observed sum of square residuals, $RSS$ for its expectation $E(RSS)$, leading to the estimate

$$\hat{\sigma}_\theta^2 = [RSS - \text{constant}(1)]/\text{constant}(2). \tag{20-12}$$

When equation (20-12) produces a negative number, $\sigma_\theta^2$ is set to zero.

*Step 3.* New estimates of the regression coefficients are now computed by means of weighted least squares regression with weights given by

$$w_i^* = 1/(v_i + \hat{\sigma}_\theta^2). \tag{20-13}$$

A variant of the above utilizes a similar three-step approach. However, rather than starting with ordinary least squares regression at step 1, one starts with the weighted least squares method described in Chapter 19 for the fixed effects model. At step 2, one again computes the residual sum of squares, $RSS$, but $RSS$ from the weighted least squares approach will differ from $RSS$ from the ordinary least squares approach, yielding different values of the two constants in equations (20-11) and (20-12) (see Appendix A at the end of this chapter for details). The two approaches exactly parallel equations (18-22) and (18-23) when the goal is simply to estimate the mean and the variance of the effect sizes.

*The balanced case.* If every study's estimate $T_i$ had the same sampling variance, $v_i$, that is, $v_i = v$ for every study, equation (20-12) simplifies. Noting that $p + 1$ is the total number of regression parameters including the intercept, shows that

$$\hat{\sigma}_\theta^2 = [RSS/(k - p - 1)] - v, \qquad (20\text{-}14)$$

which is the mean square residual from the regression minus the estimation variance, $v$. This formula is not practically useful because the balanced case rarely if ever arises in research synthesis. However, substituting

$$\bar{v} = \Sigma\, v_i / k \qquad (20\text{-}15)$$

for $v$ in equation (20-14) yields an approximation to the method of moments estimator that tends to be quite accurate. The simplicity of equation (20-14) makes this approximation attractive. An alternative simple approximation is

$$\hat{\sigma}_\theta^2 = k\{[Q_E/(k - p - 1)] - 1\}/\Sigma w_i, \qquad (20\text{-}16)$$

where $Q_E$ is the weighted residual sum of squares from the weighted least squares regression using $w_i = 1/v_i$ as weights.

*Hypothesis testing.* Conventional hypothesis testing closely parallels the procedure specified in Chapter 19 (sections 3.2 and 3.3). The normality assumption is required for the random effects, $u_i$, and the errors, $e_i$. The usual null hypothesis for the regression coefficient $\beta_q$ for any $q = 0, \ldots, p$ is

$$H_0\colon \beta_q = 0.$$

This hypothesis may be tested by computing the ratio of the estimate to its standard error, that is,

$$t = \hat{\beta}_q / S(\hat{\beta}_q),$$

where $S(\hat{\beta}_q)$ is the estimated standard error of $\hat{\beta}_q$. The needed statistics $\hat{\beta}_q$ and $S(\hat{\beta}_q)$ are produced by the weighted least squares regression procedure (see Appendix A at the end of this chapter). The $t$ ratio is approximately normally distributed, with the approximation improving as the number of studies increases. However, experience shows that it is sensible to compare $t$ with the critical values of $t$ with $k - p - 1$ degrees of freedom rather than with critical values of the unit normal distribution. Indeed, in the balanced parallel randomized case, $t$ is exactly distributed as a central $t$ under the null hypothesis.

One may also wish to test the hypothesis that the random effects variance is null, that is,

$$H_0\colon \sigma_\theta^2 = 0.$$

If this hypothesis is retained, the inference is that the $X$'s in the model (equation 20-5) fully account for the variation in the random effects. Rejection of the hypothesis implies, in contrast, that significant variation among the random effects (the values of $u_i$) remain unexplained after controlling for those $X$'s. This hypothesis is tested exactly as in the fixed effects case: One computes a weighted least squares regression with weights equal to $w_i = 1/v_i$. The weighted residual sum of squares is the test statistic, to be compared with the critical values of a chi-square distribution with $k - p - 1$ degrees of freedom.

**4.2.2 The method of maximum likelihood** So far we have assumed the values of $T_i$ to be independent with variance $v_i^* = v_i + \sigma_\theta^2$, with $v_i$ assumed known and $\sigma_\theta^2$ to be estimated from the data. If we are willing to assume further that each $T_i$ is normally distributed, a very simple iterative procedure can be used to compute maximum likelihood estimates of the fixed effects ($\beta_0$, $\beta_1, \ldots, \beta_p$) and $\sigma_\theta^2$. Maximum likelihood estimates have certain desirable properties: In large samples they are efficient and normally distributed with known standard errors, facilitating statistical inference. Appendix B at the end of this chapter provides formulas and a simple computing code needed to produce maximum likelihood estimates, including a standard error estimate for $\sigma_\theta^2$.[3]

## 4.3 Illustrative Examples

**4.3.1 Example 1: Balanced data with no predictors** To illustrate the logic of estimation and hypothesis testing in a computationally simple setting, we return to our simple data from six hypothetical parallel randomized experiments (Table 20.1), now organized for effect size analysis in Table 20.4. Results are in Table 20.5. Our goal in this analysis is simply to estimate the mean and variance of true effect sizes and to test hypotheses about these two parameters. Each effect size is the true mean difference between treatment means, so that

$$\theta_i = \mu_i^T - \mu_i^C,$$

and each estimate is the corresponding sample mean difference

---

[3] A distinction can be made between "full" and "restricted" maximum likelihood estimates. The restricted maximum likelihood estimates are identical to the method of moments estimates in the balanced case. See Appendix A at the end of this chapter for details.

**Table 20.4  Effect Size Data from Six Hypothetical Parallel Randomized Experiments**

| Study | $T_i$ | $v_i$ | $X_i$ |
|-------|-------|-------|-------|
| 1 | 3.0 | 0.667 | .5 |
| 2 | 2.0 | 0.667 | .5 |
| 3 | 1.0 | 0.667 | .5 |
| 4 | 0.0 | 0.667 | −.5 |
| 5 | 1.0 | 0.667 | −.5 |
| 6 | −1.0 | 0.667 | −.5 |

$$T_i = \overline{Y}_i^T - \overline{Y}_i^C.$$

Notice that there is no need to standardize the mean difference because each randomized experiment employs the same outcome variable and because we assume homogeneity of variance across studies. Given the balanced nature of the data, the estimation variance $v_i$ is the same across studies, that is, $v_i = v$ for every study $i$, where

$$v = 2\hat{\sigma}^2/n = MSW/15 = .667$$

and $MSW$ is the mean square within cell (see Table 20.2).

Our "prediction model" for $T_i$ is equation (20-6) devoid of all predictors ($X$'s), so that the only regression parameter is the intercept:

$$T_i = \beta_0 + u_i + e_i.$$

Clearly, the intercept is just the grand mean, that is, $\beta_0 = \mu_\theta$. We shall assume $u_i$ and $e_i$ to be independently, normally distributed, that is,

$$u_i \sim N(0, \sigma_\theta^2), \ e_i \sim N(0, v)$$

with $v = .667$. Employing our three-step method of moments estimation procedure yields at step 1

$$\hat{\beta}_0 = \overline{T} = \Sigma \ T_i/6 = 1.0,$$

that is, the ordinary least squares estimate of $\beta_0$ is just the arithmetic mean of the effect size estimates. The residual sum of squares needed for step 2 is the sum of squared deviations of $T_i$ about $\overline{T}$:

$$RSS = \Sigma \ (T_i - \overline{T})^2,$$

and for step 2 we derive the expectation

$$E(RSS) = (k-1)v + (k-1)\sigma_\theta^2,$$

so that the method of moments estimator is

$$\hat{\sigma}_\theta^2 = [RSS/(k-1)] - v = (10/5) - .667 = 1.33.$$

Step 3, which computes weighted least squares estimates, is unnecessary in this case because, when the data are balanced, weighted least squares and ordinary least squares produce the same results.

*Hypothesis testing.* We first test the null hypothesis

$$H_0: \beta_0 = 0,$$

that is, the hypothesis that the mean effect size is null, by the means of the statistic

$$t = \hat{\beta}_0 / S(\hat{\beta}_0) = 1.00/.577 = 1.73,$$

$p$ (two-tailed) $> .05$, implying that there is insufficient evidence to reject the null hypothesis.[4] Of course, this result does not imply that the treatment effect is always null. One needs also to consider the variance $\sigma_\theta^2$ of the random effects. A positive variance implies that the treatment effect size varies from study to study.

[4]In this case, $S(\hat{\beta}_q) = \sqrt{[(v + \hat{\sigma}_\theta^2)/k]}$, a simplification that occurs in the balanced case.

**Table 20.5  Results of Effect Size Analysis for Six Hypothetical Parallel Randomized Experiments**

| Parameter | Estimate | Standard Error | $t$ | Chi-square | $df$ |
|-----------|----------|----------------|-----|------------|------|
| **No Predictors** | | | | | |
| $\mu_\theta$ | 1.000 | 0.577 | 1.73 | | |
| $\sigma_\theta^2$ | 1.333 | | | 15.00[a] | 5 |
| **Duration as a Predictor** | | | | | |
| $\beta_0$ | 1.000 | 0.408 | 2.45[a] | | |
| $\beta_1$ | 2.000 | 0.816 | 2.45[a] | | |
| $\sigma_\theta^2$ | 0.333 | | | 61.00 | 4 |

[a]$p < .05$.

To test the hypothesis that the random effects variance is null, that is,

$$H_0:\ \sigma_\theta^2 = 0,$$

we first recognize that if this null hypothesis were true, the fixed effects model

$$T_i = \beta_0 + e_i,\ e_i \sim N(0,\ v_i)$$

would be true. Under this model, Chapter 18 (equation 18-6) provides a test statistic

$$Q = \Sigma\ w_i(T_i - \overline{T})^2,\ \text{with}\ \overline{T} = \Sigma\ w_i T_i/\Sigma\ w_i,\ w_i = 1/v_i,$$

which has an approximate chi-square distribution with $k - 1 = 5$ degrees of freedom. Notice that our balanced case ($v_i = v = .667$ for every $i$), $Q$ simplifies:

$$Q = RSS/v = 10/.667 = 15,$$

which, when compared with the critical values of chi-square with 5 degrees of freedom is significant, $p < .01$, and implies the existence of significant variation in effect size across studies.

*Comparison with analysis of variance results.* The results using the three-step weighted least squares regression approach exactly duplicate the results of the mixed model ANOVA (Table 20.2). Point estimates for $\hat{\beta}_0 = \hat{\mu}_\theta$ and for $\sigma_\theta^2$ are identical. The square of the $t$ test for the mean effect size ($t = 1.73$) equals computed $F(1, 5)$ for testing the treatment main effect in Table 20.2. And the interested reader will note that $Q/(k - 1) = Q/5$ is exactly equivalent to the computed $F(5, 348)$ in Table 20.2 as a test of the treatment-by-studies interaction. The duplication is not accidental. The more general weighted least squares approach will always duplicate the more limited balanced ANOVA approach when the assumptions for the ANOVA apply. We note also that the weighted least squares formulas duplicate the results of Chapter 18 for combining effect sizes in random effects models when the regression model contains only an intercept, $\beta_0$, whether the data are balanced or unbalanced.

**4.3.2 Example 2: Balanced data with one predictor** We now consider a case in which the regression model (equation 20-6) has an intercept and one predictor, but the data remain balanced. We return to our data from six hypothetical parallel randomized experiments, but now we take into account the duration of treatment as predictor of effect size.

Our prediction model for $T_i$ is equation (20-6) with a single $X$:

$$T_i = \beta_0 + \beta_1 X_i + u_i + e_i,$$

where

$X_i$ takes on a value of 1/2 for studies with long duration and -1/2 for studies with short duration;

$\beta_0$ remains the grand mean effect size;

$\beta_1$ is the expected mean difference in effect sizes between studies having long duration and studies having short duration;

$e_i$ remains the error of estimation with variance $v = .667$ for every study; and

$u_i$ is now a residual, that is, the component of the true effect size not explained by duration of treatment, $X$.

Employing our three-step method of moments estimation procedure yields at step 1

$$\hat{\beta}_0 = \overline{T} = \Sigma\ T_i\ /6 = 1.0,$$
$$\hat{\beta}_1 = \Sigma\ X_i T_i\ /\ \Sigma\ X_i^2 = 2.0,$$

indicating that the grand mean effect size is again estimated to be 1.0 and that the mean difference in effect sizes between studies of long duration and studies of short duration is estimated to be 2.0.

The residual sum of squares needed for step 2 is the sum of squared deviations of $T_i$ about the regression line $1.0 + 2.0*X_i$

$$RSS = \Sigma\ (T_i - 1.0 - 2.0*X_i)^2 = 4.00$$

and for step 2 we derive the expectation

$$E(RSS) = (k - 2)v + (k - 2)\hat{\sigma}_\theta^2,$$

so that the method of moments estimator is

$$\hat{\sigma}_\theta^2 = [RSS/(k - 2)] - v = 1.00 - .667 = .33.$$

Recall that, without including duration as a predictor, our estimate of $\sigma_\theta^2$ was 1.33 (Table 20.5). We may now define the proportion of true effect size variance explained by the model as

$$R^2 = [\hat{\sigma}_\theta^2\ (\text{no predictors}) - \hat{\sigma}_\theta^2\ (X\ \text{as predictor})]/\hat{\sigma}_\theta^2\ (\text{no predictors})$$
$$= (1.33 - .33)/1.33 = .75, \text{ or } 75 \text{ percent};$$

that is, incorporating duration as a predictor reduced $\hat{\sigma}_\theta^2$ by 75 percent. Because the data are balanced, ordinary least squares and weighted least squares are equivalent and step 3, which computes the weighted least squares estimates, is not needed.

*Hypothesis testing.* We first test the null hypothesis

$$H_0: \beta_0 = 0,$$

that is, the hypothesis that the mean effect size is null, by means of the statistic

$$T = \hat{\beta}_0/S(\hat{\beta}_0) = 1.00/0.408 = 2.45,$$

which, when compared with the critical value of $t$ with 4 degrees of freedom, fails to achieve the two-tailed critical value at the 5 percent level. (Note that $t^2 =$ the $F$ for the main effect of treatment in Table 20.3.) Perhaps more important is the test of the effect of duration, that is, the test of

$$H_0: \beta_1 = 0,$$

which can be tested by the statistic

$$t = \hat{\beta}_1/S(\hat{\beta}_1) = 2.00/0.816 = 2.45,$$

again to be compared with the critical values of $t$ with $df = 4$. (Notice again that $t^2 =$ the $F$ for the treatment-by-duration interaction in Table 20.3).

To test the hypothesis that the random effects variance is null, that is,

$$H_0: \sigma_\theta^2 = 0,$$

we recognize that if this null hypothesis were true, the fixed effects model

$$T_i = \beta_0 + \beta_1 X_i + e_i, \; e_i \sim N(0, \, v_i)$$

would be true, where $v_i = .667$ for each study $i$ in our case. Under this model, equation (18-6) provides the test statistic

$$Q_E = \Sigma w_i (T_i - \hat{\beta}_0 - \hat{\beta}_1 X_i)^2,$$

which has an approximate chi-square distribution with $k - 2 = 4$ degrees of freedom. In our balanced case, $Q$ simplifies:

$$Q_E = RSS/v = 4/.667 = 6.00,$$

which, when compared with the critical values of chi-square with 4 degrees of freedom, is not significant at the 5 percent level. (Note that $Q_E/4$ equals the $F$ for treatments-by-studies in Table 20.3.)

The results imply that this model, which includes three parameters, $\beta_0$, $\beta_1$, and $\sigma_\theta^2$, is hard to defend, since none of these parameters can be shown significantly different from zero. The earlier model, representing the treatment effect distribution as having a grand mean and a variance (example 20-1) is perhaps a good choice. That model has just two parameters, $\beta_0$ and $\sigma_\theta^2$. A plausible alternative is a model that includes $\beta_0$ and $\beta_1$, but sets $\sigma_\theta^2$ to 0. This is equivalent to a fixed

**Table 20.6 Effect Size Data from 19 Experiments Testing the Effect of Teacher Expectancy on Pupil IQ**

| Study | $T_i$ | $v_i$ | $X_i$ |
|---|---|---|---|
| 1 | 0.03 | 0.015625 | 2 |
| 2 | 0.12 | 0.021609 | 3 |
| 3 | −0.14 | 0.027889 | 3 |
| 4 | 1.18 | 0.139129 | 0 |
| 5 | 0.26 | 0.136161 | 0 |
| 6 | −0.06 | 0.010609 | 3 |
| 7 | −0.02 | 0.010609 | 3 |
| 8 | −0.32 | 0.048400 | 3 |
| 9 | 0.27 | 0.026896 | 0 |
| 10 | 0.80 | 0.063001 | 1 |
| 11 | 0.54 | 0.091204 | 0 |
| 12 | 0.18 | 0.049729 | 0 |
| 13 | −0.02 | 0.083521 | 1 |
| 14 | 0.23 | 0.084100 | 2 |
| 15 | −0.18 | 0.025281 | 3 |
| 16 | −0.06 | 0.027889 | 3 |
| 17 | 0.30 | 0.019321 | 1 |
| 18 | 0.07 | 0.008836 | 2 |
| 19 | −0.07 | 0.030276 | 3 |

effects model; with $\sigma_\theta^2$ set to zero, the duration effect would be found significant (see Table 20.3). The problem is that the test of significance of $\sigma_\theta^2$ is unpowerful, and to build the case for a significant duration effect on the failure to reject $H_0: \sigma_\theta^2 = 0$ when that test has so little power seems questionable. The essential difficulty is that this case presents too little data to distinguish among interpretations that are substantively different. In essence, inferences are sensitive to assumptions about the effects being fixed or random, and more data are needed to resolve the dilemma. In contrast, the next example, based on real data, produces results that are insensitive to the specification of the effects as fixed or random.

**4.3.3 Example 3: Data from teacher-expectancy experiments** We now illustrate a mixed model regression analysis for the more realistic case in which the investigator has identified $k$-related studies that compare an experimental group and a control group; sample sizes are unequal across studies; and outcome variables are measured on a different scale across the studies, so that standardization is required prior to synthesis. We take our data from Raudenbush's (1984) synthesis of 19 experimental tests of the effect of teacher expectancy on pupil IQ (see Appendix A Data Set II). The data are described in Table 20.6.

Early commentary on teacher-expectancy experiments suggested that the experimental treatment is difficult to implement if teachers and their students know each other well at the time of the experiment. Essentially, the treatment depends on deception: Researchers attempt to convince teachers that certain children can be expected to show dramatic intellectual growth. In fact, those designated children are assigned at random to this "high-expectancy" condition, so that if the deception is successful, the only difference between experimental and control children is in the minds of the teachers. Early studies provided anecdotal evidence that the deception will fail if the teachers have had sufficient prior contact to form their own judgments of the children's capabilities.

For these reasons, we hypothesize that the length of time that teachers and children knew each other at the time of the experiment will be negatively related to a study's effect size. The model for testing this prediction is

$$\theta_i = \beta_0 + \beta_1 X_i + u_i,$$

where $X_i = 0$, 1, 2, or 3 depending on whether prior teacher-pupil contact occurred for 0, 1, 2, or more than two weeks prior to the experiment;

$\beta_0$ is the intercept of the model, and because $X$ is zero for studies having no prior teacher-pupil contact, $\beta_0$ represents the expected effect size for such studies;

$\beta_1$ is a regression coefficient indicating the expected difference in effect size between studies differing by one week in prior contact; and

$u_i$ is the "random effect," that is, the random deviation of study $i$'s effect $\theta_i$ from the predicted value $\beta_0 + \beta_1 X_i$. We assume that $u_i$ has a mean of zero and a variance $\sigma_\theta^2$.

*Estimation.* We again employ the method of moments. Results are collected in Table 20.7.
Step 1 yields ordinary least squares estimate

$$\hat{\beta}_0 = 0.506, \ \hat{\beta}_1 = -0.197.$$

To implement step 2, we apply the formula for the expected sum of squares residuals given in Appendix A at the end of this chapter and solve for $\sigma_\theta^2$, yielding

$$\hat{\sigma}_\theta^2 = .021.$$

Alternatively, applying the simpler approximation (equations 20-14 and 20-15) yields

$$\hat{\sigma}_\theta^2 = RSS/(k-2) - \bar{v} = .020.$$

Now, to implement step 3, we compute weights

$$w_i^* = 1/(v_i + \hat{\sigma}_\theta^2) = 1/(v_i + .021)$$

and utilize weighted least squares regression. Our estimate $\hat{\beta}_0 = .434$, $S(\hat{\beta}_0) = .110$, $t = 3.93$ suggests that the expected effect size for studies having no prior teacher-pupil contact is .434 or about 43 percent of a standard deviation, certainly an effect of nontrivial magnitude. Our point estimate of $\hat{\beta}_1 = -.168$, $SE = S(\hat{\beta}_1) = .047$, $t = -3.60$, implies that, for each week of additional prior contact, we expect a decrement of about .17 points in effect size (up to two weeks). Our estimate of $\hat{\sigma}_\theta^2 = .021$ implies that, once prior contact is taken into account, considerable variance in the true effect sizes has been explained: the estimate of $\sigma_\theta^2$ without including prior contact was .080 (see top panel of Table 20-7), so that about 75 percent of the unconditional variance (.080) is accounted for by prior contact.

One might wonder whether including prior contact as a predictor in the model eliminates the unexplained variance in the true effects. To test the hypothesis that the random effects variance is null, that is,

$$H_0: \sigma_\theta^2 = 0,$$

we re-estimate the model setting $\sigma_\theta^2$ to zero and compute

$$Q_E = \Sigma w_i (T_i - \hat{\beta}_0 - \hat{\beta}_1 X_i)^2 = 16.57,$$

which, when compared with the critical values of the chi-square distribution with $k - 2 = 17$ degrees of freedom, implies that the random effects variance is not significantly different from zero. Point estimates and standard errors for the regression coefficients $\beta_0$ and $\beta_1$ estimated under the fixed effects model are very similar to those estimated under the random effects model. Hence, the substantive inferences to be drawn from the analysis are not sensitive to specification of the effects as fixed or random.

We also estimated the model using the method of maximum likelihood. The maximum likelihood estimate of $\sigma_\theta^2$ was zero, and the maximum likelihood approach based on the random effects specification produces exactly the same point estimates and standard errors for $\beta_0$ and $\beta_1$ as does the fixed effect analysis using the methods of Chapter 19. This result illustrates that the fixed effects specification may be viewed as a special case of the random effects specification in which $\sigma_\theta^2 = 0$.

**Table 20.7  Results of Effect Size Analysis for 19 Teacher-Expectancy Experiments**

| Parameter | Estimate | Standard Error | $t$ | Chi-square | $df$ |
|---|---|---|---|---|---|
| **No Predictors** | | | | | |
| $\mu_\theta$ | 0.114 | 0.079 | 1.44 | | |
| $\sigma_\theta^2$ | 0.080 | | | 35.82[a] | 18 |
| **Prior Teacher-Student Contact as a Predictor** | | | | | |
| $\beta_0$ | 0.434 | 0.110 | 3.93[a] | | |
| $\beta_1$ | −0.168 | 0.047 | −3.60[a] | | |
| $\sigma_\theta^2$ | 0.021 | | | 16.57 | 17 |

[a] $p < .01$.

## 5. SUMMARY

### 5.1  Advantages of the Random Effects Approach

This chapter has described several potential advantages in using a random effects approach to quantitative research synthesis, especially when the number of studies is large. First, the random effects conceptualization is consistent with standard scientific aims of generalization: Studies under synthesis can be viewed as representative of a larger population or universe of implementations of a treatment or observations of a relationship. The statistical methods described in this chapter allow the investigator to account for the extra uncertainty that arises when the studies under synthesis are viewed as a representative sample from a larger universe rather than themselves constituting the universe of scientific interest. This uncertainty arises because, despite concerted attempts at replication, study contexts, treatments, and procedures will inevitably vary in many ways that may influence results. This feature of the random effects approach was illustrated in examples in which the standard errors for important model parameter estimates were shown to be appropriately larger under the random effects approach than under the fixed effects approach.

Second, the random effects approach allows a parsimonious summary of results when the number of studies is very large. In such large-sample syntheses it may be impossible to formulate fully adequate explanatory models for effects of study characteristics on study outcomes. Estimation of the random effects variance enables the investigator to make summary statements about the range of likely effects in a particular area of research even when the sources of discrepancies in study results are poorly understood. In addition, the re-estimation of the random effects variance after adding explanatory variables make possible a kind of "percentage of variance explained" criterion for assessing the adequacy of the explanatory models. In our illustrative examples the estimate of $\sigma_\theta^2$ with no predictors in the model defined "the maximum explainable variance" and served as a baseline for evaluating the explanatory power of subsequent models that included predictors of effect size.

### 5.2  Threats to Valid Statistical Inference

The problem is that the advantages of the random effects conceptualization are purchased at the price of two extra assumptions. First, the approach we have presented treats the random effects variance $\sigma_\theta^2$ as if it were known, when, in fact, it must be estimated from the data. Second, to allow for hypothesis testing, we have assumed that the random effects are normally distributed. These assumptions are unique to the random effects approach and can be avoided by employing a fixed effects approach. In addition, we shall briefly discuss certain threats to inference that the random effects approach shares with the fixed effects approach. These include problems of model misspecification, multiple effect sizes, and the need to make inferences about particular study effects. When the extra assumptions are met, the random effects approach enjoys certain advantages in coping with these difficulties.

**5.2.1 Uncertainty about the variance** In standard practice and in the methods presented in this chapter, estimation of grand means or regression coefficients requires the assumption that the random effects variance is known whenever the data are unbalanced.[5] The truth is that this variance is uncertain, especially in small-sample syntheses. Failure to account for this source of uncertainty can lead to errors of inference. Rubin (1981) describes this problem and approaches to addressing it in the context of parallel randomized experiments. Raudenbush and Bryk (1985) describe a procedure for sensitivity analysis in research synthesis that allows the investigator to gauge the likely consequences of uncertainty about the variance for inferences about means and regression coefficients in effect size analyses. In Chapter 26 of this handbook, Louis and Zelterman describe Bayesian methods that enable the analyst to account for uncertainty about variances in drawing inferences.

**5.2.2 Failure of parametric assumptions** Standard practice requires the assumption that the random effects are normally distributed with constant variance. This assumption is difficult to assess when the number of studies is small. It should be emphasized that this assumption is in addition to the usual assumption that the error of $T_i$ as an estimate of $\theta_i$ is normal. Hedges (1981) has intensively investigated this latter assumption. Seltzer (1991) has developed a robust estimation procedure that allows the analyst to assume that the random effects are $t$-distributed rather than normal. As the degrees of freedom of the $t$ increase, the results converge to those based on normal assumptions. The robust estimates are resistant to influence by outlier values of the random effects. Raudenbush and Bryk (1987) describe techniques for assessing the validity of the normality assumption when the number of studies is reasonably large. The method is built into the "HLM" software they describe—software that can be used for random effects meta-analysis.

**5.2.3 Problems of model misspecification and capitalizing on chance** As in any linear model analysis, estimates of regression coefficients will be biased if confounding variables—exogenous predictors related both to the explanatory variables in the model and to the outcome variable—are not included in the model. This is the classic problem of "underfitting." The opposite problem is that of "overfitting," wherein the investigator includes a large number of candidate explanatory variables as predictors, some of which may seem to improve prediction strictly as a result of chance. The best solutions to the problems of under- and overfitting seem to be to (a) develop strong a priori theory about study characteristics that might affect outcomes and (b) include as many studies as possible. Hunter, Schmidt, and Jackson (1982) and Hunter and Schmidt (1990) have warned especially against the overfitting that occurs when investigators carry out an extensive fishing expedition for explanatory variables even when there may be little "true" variance in the effect sizes. In the absence of strong a priori theory, they advocate simple summaries using a random effects approach where the key parameters are the mean and variance of the true effect sizes. Raudenbush (1983) describes a method for deriving a priori hypotheses by carefully reading discussion sections of early studies to find speculations testable on the basis of later studies.

**5.2.4 Multiple effect sizes** Most studies employ several outcome variables. Such variables will tend to be correlated, and syntheses that fail to account for the resulting dependency may commit statistical errors (see Hedges & Olkin 1985, Chapter 10; Rosenthal & Rubin 1986; Raudenbush, Becker & Kalaian 1988). Becker (1988) employed a random effects approach to multiple effect sizes. These issues are discussed by Gleser and Olkin in Chapter 22 of this handbook.

**5.2.5 Inferences about particular effect sizes** In some cases, the investigator may wish to conceive of the effect sizes as random and yet make inferences about particular effects. For example, it may be of interest to assess the largest effect size in a series of studies or to identify for more intensive investigation effect sizes that are somehow unusual. The need to make such inferences, however, poses a problem: On the one hand, each particular study's data may yield an imprecise estimate of that study's effect, especially if samples are small. In that case, an effect size may appear impressive based on chance alone. On the other hand, the grand mean effect or the value predicted on the basis of a regression model may produce a poor indicator of the effect of any particular study. DerSimonian and Laird (1983), Rubin (1981), and Raudenbush and Bryk (1985) describe methods for combining data from all studies to strengthen inferences about the effects in each particular

---

[5]When the data are unbalanced, estimates of regression coefficients rely on the weights $w_i^* = 1/v_i^* = 1/(v_i + \sigma_\theta^2)$ where $w_i^*$ are known constants. In fact, each $w_i^*$ must be estimated by $1/(v_i + \hat{\sigma}_\theta^2)$. In unbalanced designs, no weighting is needed so the regression coefficient estimates do not depend on the estimate $\hat{\sigma}_\theta^2$.

study and to create a reasonably accurate picture of the effects of a collection of studies.

## 6. REFERENCES

Becker, B. J. (1988). Synthesizing standardized mean change measures. *British Journal of Mathematical and Statistical Psychology, 41,* 257–278.

Bryk, A. S., Raudenbush, S. W., Seltzer, M., & Congdon, R. T. (1988). *An introduction to HLM: Computer program and users' guide.* Chicago: University of Chicago, Department of Education.

Cronbach, L. J., Gleser, G. C., Harinder, N., & Rajaratnam, N. (1972). *The dependability of behavioral measurements: Theory of generalizability for scores and profiles.* New York: Wiley.

De Finetti, B. (1964). Foresight: Its logical laws, its subjective sources. In H. E. Kyburg, Jr., and H. E. Smokler (Eds.), *Studies in subjective probability* (pp. 93–158). New York: Wiley.

Dempster, A. P., Rubin, D. B., & Tsutakawa, R. K. (1981). Estimation in covariance components models. *Journal of the American Statistical Association, 76,* 341–353.

DerSimonian, R., & Laird, N. M. (1983). Evaluating the effect of coaching on SAT scores: A meta-analysis. *Harvard Educational Review, 53,* 1–15.

Fabian, V. (1991). On the problem of interactions in the analysis of variance. *Journal of the American Statistical Association, 86,* 362–367.

Goldstein, H. I. (1987). *Multilevel models in educational and social research.* London: Oxford University Press.

Hanushek, E. A. (1974). Efficient estimators for regressing regression coefficients. *American Statistician, 28,* 66–67.

Hedges, L. V. (1981). Distribution theory for Glass's estimator of effect size and related estimators. *Journal of Educational Statistics, 6,* 107–128.

Hedges, L. V. (1983). A random effects model for effect size. *Psychological Bulletin, 93,* 388–395.

Hedges, L. V., & Olkin, I. (1985). *Statistical methods for meta-analysis.* Orlando, FL: Academic Press.

Henderson, C. R. (1953). Estimation of variance and covariance components. *Biometrics, 9,* 226–310.

Hunter, J. E., & Schmidt, F. L. (1990). *Methods of meta-analysis: Correcting error and bias in research findings.* Beverly Hills, CA: Sage.

Hunter, J. E., Schmidt, F. L., & Jackson, G. B. (1982). *Meta-analysis: Cumulating research findings across studies.* Beverly Hills, CA: Sage.

Kirk, R. E. (1982). *Experimental design: Procedures for the behavioral sciences* (2nd ed.). Belmont, CA: Brooks/Cole.

Longford, N. T. (1987). A fast scoring algorithm for maximum likelihood estimation in unbalanced mixed models with nested effects. *Biometrica, 74,* 817–827.

Raudenbush, S. W. (1983). Utilizing controversy as a source of hypotheses for meta-analysis: The case of teacher expectancy on pupil IQ. In R. J. Light (Ed.), *Evaluation Studies Review Annual.* Beverly Hills, CA: Sage.

Raudenbush, S. W. (1984). Magnitude of teacher expectancy effects on pupil IQ as a function of the credibility of expectancy induction: A synthesis of findings from 18 experiments. *Journal of Educational Psychology, 76,* 85–97.

Raudenbush, S. W., Becker, B. J., & Kalaian, S. (1988). Modeling multivariate effect sizes. *Psychological Bulletin, 103,* 111–120.

Raudenbush, S. W., & Bryk, A. S. (1985). Empirical Bayes meta-analysis. *Journal of Educational Statistics, 10,* 75–98.

Raudenbush, S. W., & Bryk, A. S. (1987). Examining correlates of diversity. *Journal of Educational Statistics, 12,* 241–269.

Rosenthal, R., & Rubin, D. B. (1978). Interpersonal expectancy effects: The first 345 studies. *Behavioral and Brain Sciences, 3,* 377–386.

Rosenthal, R., & Rubin, D. B. (1986). Meta-analytic procedures for combining studies with multiple effect sizes. *Psychological Bulletin, 99,* 400–406.

Rubin, D. B. (1981). Estimation in parallel randomized experiments. *Journal of Educational Statistics, 6,* 337–401.

Seltzer, M. (1991). *The use of data augmentation in fitting hierarchical models to educational data.* Unpublished doctoral dissertation, University of Chicago.

Winer, B. J. (1971). *Statistical principles in experimental design.* New York: McGraw-Hill.

## 7. APPENDIX A: Estimation Procedures

### 7.1 The Method of Moments

In our examples we have utilized simple method of moments estimators. These are described by Hanushek (1974) and by Hedges (1983) and Hedges and Olkin (1985) in the context of effect size data. One first computes ordinary least squares (OLS) estimates of the fixed effects. The expected value of the sum of squared residuals about these OLS estimators is then equated to its observed value and the resulting equation solved for

$\sigma_\theta^2$. Once $\sigma_\theta^2$ is estimated, the weights $w_i^* = 1/v_i^* = 1/(v_i + \hat{\sigma}_\theta^2)$ are computed and a weighted least squares regression is performed.

To derive the expected mean square residual, we first rewrite equation (20-6) in matrix notation as

$$\mathbf{T} = \mathbf{X}\boldsymbol{\beta} + \mathbf{u} + \mathbf{e}, \quad \text{Var}(\mathbf{u} + \mathbf{e}) = \sigma_\theta^2 \mathbf{I} + \mathbf{V}, \quad \text{(A20-1)}$$

where $\mathbf{T}$ is a $k$ by 1 vector of effect size estimates with elements $\{T_i\}$, $\mathbf{X}$ is a $k$ by $P$ matrix of predictors ($P = p + 1$), $\mathbf{u}$ is a $k$ by 1 vector of random effects with elements $\{u_i\}$, e is a $k$ by 1 vector of estimation errors with elements $\{e_i\}$, $\mathbf{I}$ *is a* $k$ *by* $k$ identity matrix, and $\mathbf{V}$ is a $k$ by $k$ diagonal matrix with elements $\{v_i\}$. Then the ordinary least squares estimator of $\boldsymbol{\beta}$ is

$$\hat{\boldsymbol{\beta}}_{\text{ols}} = (\mathbf{X}'\mathbf{X})^{-1}\mathbf{X}'\mathbf{T}, \quad \text{(A20-2)}$$

the residual sum of squares is

$$RSS = \mathbf{T}'(\mathbf{I} - \mathbf{M})\mathbf{T}, \quad \text{(A20-3)}$$

with $\mathbf{M} = \mathbf{X}(\mathbf{X}'\mathbf{X})^{-1}\mathbf{X}'$. The expected residual sum of squares is

$$E(RSS) = \text{constant}(1) + \text{constant}(2) * \sigma_\theta^2, \text{(A20-4)}$$

where

$$\text{Constant}(1) = \text{tr}(\mathbf{I} - \mathbf{M})\mathbf{V} = \Sigma \, v_i - \text{tr}[\mathbf{X}'\mathbf{V}\mathbf{X}(\mathbf{X}'\mathbf{X})^{-1}] \quad \text{(A20-5)}$$

and

$$\text{Constant}(2) = k - P. \quad \text{(A20-6)}$$

Equation (20-12) follows. One may wish to begin with weighted least squares estimates

$$\hat{\boldsymbol{\beta}}_{\text{wls}} = (\mathbf{X}'\mathbf{V}^{-1}\mathbf{X})^{-1}\mathbf{X}'\mathbf{V}^{-1}\mathbf{T} \quad \text{(A20-7)}$$

instead of ordinary least squares, in which case the *RSS* becomes

$$RSS = (\mathbf{T} - \mathbf{X}\hat{\boldsymbol{\beta}}_{\text{wls}})\mathbf{V}^{-1}(\mathbf{T} - \mathbf{X}\hat{\boldsymbol{\beta}}_{\text{wls}}) \quad \text{(A20-8)}$$

and *E[RSS]* has the same form as equation (A20-4), but now

$$\text{Constant}(1) = k - P \quad \text{(A20-9)}$$

$$\text{Constant}(2) = \Sigma v_i^{-1} - \text{tr}[\mathbf{X}'\mathbf{V}^{-2}\mathbf{X}(\mathbf{X}'\mathbf{V}^{-1}\mathbf{X})^{-1}]. \quad \text{(A20-10)}$$

Appendix B gives a simple Minitab code used for examples 2 and 3 (having one predictor). The method of moments code, based on equations (A20-4, A20-5, and A20-6), can be extended to cases with more predictors, but the user must be familiar with matrix notation.

However, the code for implementing the approximation (equations 20-14 and 20-15) readily generalizes. Also, the code for the maximum likelihood method, which uses the code for the approximation to generate starting values, generalizes readily. We caution that to obtain correct standard errors for the regression coefficients (conditional model) for method of moments or maximum likelihood requires a transformation of the Minitab code:

Correct standard error = Minitab standard error/
(Minitab mean squared error)$^{1/2}$.

## 7.2 The Method of Maximum Likelihood

Assuming $T_i - \theta_i \sim N(0, v_i)$, where $v_i$ is known, simple iterative maximum likelihood estimators are readily available. Bryk et al.'s HLM program (1988) computes restricted likelihood estimates for univariate or multivariate models. Appendix B provides a simple code for full information likelihood estimation. The restricted approach is a bit more satisfactory, especially when numbers of studies are small, because it adjusts variance estimates for the uncertainty associated with estimation of the fixed effects. However, since the full information method is simpler, we present it here. In the case of univariate meta-analysis, the Fisher scoring approach (see Longford 1987) and the iterative generalized least squares approach (see Goldstein 1987) are identical. Given an initial estimate of $\sigma_\theta^2$ (e.g., from the approximate method of moments approach), one computes the weighted least squares regression as usual. Then $\sigma_\theta^2$ is re-estimated by means of the weighted average

$$\sigma_\theta^2 \, (\text{new}) = \Sigma w_i^{*2}(r_i^2 - v_i)/\Sigma \, w_i^{*2}, \quad \text{(A20-11)}$$

where $r_i$ is the residual from the weighted regression and $w_i^* = 1/(v_i + \hat{\sigma}_\theta^2)$ is based on the initial estimate of $\sigma_\theta^2$. One recomputes the weighted regression based on the new estimate of $\sigma_\theta^2$, and the process iterates until the estimates converge. One should check each estimate of $\sigma_\theta^2$, converting negative estimates to zero. The procedure naturally produces an estimate of the standard error of the $\hat{\sigma}_\theta^2$ at convergence:

$$S(\hat{\sigma}_\theta^2) = \sqrt{(2/\Sigma \, w_i^{*2})}. \quad \text{(A20-12)}$$

This standard error estimate, not available in the method of moments case, is most useful when the number of studies is quite large.

## 8. APPENDIX B: Computing Code

### 8.1 Method of Moments (Approximation)

(Comment: The code first reads the data.)

```
read 'pyg2.dat' c1-c4
name c1 'id'
name c2 'ti'
name c3 'vi'
name c4 'x'
```

(Step 1: Compute the ordinary least squares regression and save the mean squared error.)

```
regress 'ti' on 1 predictor, 'x';
mse into k1.
```

(Step 2: $\sigma_\theta^2$ is estimated and printed as k4.)
```
let k2=mean('vi')
let k4=k1 − k2
print k4
```

(Step 3: The weighted least squares estimates are computed.)

```
let c5=1/ (k4+'vi')
name c5 'w'
regress 'ti' on 1 predictor, 'x';
weights 'w';
resids in c6.
name c6 'resid'
```

(Comment: The next lines compute the fixed effects weighted least squares analysis described in Chapter 19 and needed here to test $H_0$: $\sigma_\theta^2 = 0$. The residual mean square is the test statistic, $Q$.)

```
let c7 = 1/'vi'
regress 'ti' on 1 predictor, 'x';
weights c7.
save 'iter2.mtw'
```

### 8.2 Maximum Likelihood

Notice that this code starts by reading 'iter2.mtw,' which was the result of the approximation method.

```
retr 'iter2.mtw'
let c10=1/('vi'+k4)**2
```

```
name c10 'w2'
let k4=sum ('w2'*('resid'**2 − 'vi'))/sum('w2')
let k13=sqrt (2/sum('w2'))
print k4 k13
let c5=1/ ('vi'+k4)
name c5 'w'
regress 'ti' on 1 predictor, 'x';
weights 'w'.
save 'iter2.mtw'
```

(Comment: The user re-executes the above code until the estimates are essentially unchanged across iterations. Just a few iterations are typically needed; k4 will contain $\hat{\sigma}_\theta^2$ and k13 will contain its standard error estimate.)

### 8.3 Methods of Moments (One Predictor)

The code needed for the method of moments is considerably more complex than that needed either for the approximation or for the maximum likelihood method.

```
(The code below reads the teacher-expectancy data.)
Read 'pyg2.dat' c1-c4
name c1 'id'
name c2 'ti'
name c3 'vi'
name c4 'x'
```

(Now we compute ordinary least squares residuals and save them.)

```
regress 'ti' on 1 predictor, 'x';
mse into k1.
```

(The next section of code computes the constants needed to estimate $\sigma_\theta^2$.)
```
let k2=sum('vi')
let c10=c1/c1
copy c10 c4 m1
let c9=sqrt(c3)
multiply c9 c4 c11
copy c9 c11 m2
transpose m1 store in m3
multiply m3 m1 store in m4
invert m4 store in m5
transpose m2 store in m6
multiply m6 m2 store in m7
```

multiply m7 m5 store in m8
diagonals of m8 in c12

(Comment: The next section of code computes $\hat{\sigma}_{\theta}^2$.)

let k3=k1−(k2−sum(c12))/(sum(c10)−2)
print k3

(Comment: The next section of code computes the weighted least squares regression.)

let c5 = 1/(k3 + 'vi')
name c5 'w'
regress 'ti' on 1 predictor 'x';
weights in 'w';
resids in c6.

Cooper, H. and Hedges, L. V. (Eds.) 1994. *The Handbook of Research Synthesis.* New York: Russell Sage Foundation

# 21

## CORRECTING FOR SOURCES
## OF ARTIFICIAL VARIATION ACROSS STUDIES

**JOHN E. HUNTER**
*Michigan State University*

**FRANK L. SCHMIDT**
*University of Iowa*

CONTENTS

## 1. ARTIFACTS OF STUDY IMPERFECTIONS

Every study has imperfections. In some cases we can define precisely what a perfect study might be, and thus we can say that the effect size value obtained from any real study will differ to some extent from the value that would have been obtained had the study been done perfectly. While it is important to control and estimate bias in isolated studies, it is even more important to reduce such errors in cumulative research reviews such as meta-analysis.

Some authors have argued that meta-analysts should not correct for study imperfections because the purpose of meta-analysis is only to provide a description of study findings, not an estimate of what would have been found in a perfect study. But we argue that the errors that stem from study imperfections are artifactual in character; they stem from imperfections in our research methods, not from facts of nature. Thus, most scientific questions are better addressed by results from perfect studies than by results distorted by artifacts. For example, in correlation research the results most relevant to evaluation of a scientific theory are those that would be obtained from a study employing an *infinitely large* sample from the *relevant* population (i.e., the population itself) and employing measures of the independent and dependent variables that are *free of measurement error* and are *perfectly construct valid*. Such a study would be expected to provide a perfectly accurate estimate of the relation between constructs in the population of interest; such an estimate is maximally relevant to the testing and evaluation of scientific theories (and also to theory *construction*). We believe that corrections for errors in study findings due to study imperfections (which we call "artifacts") is essential to the development of cumulative knowledge. Most artifacts with which we are concerned have been studied in the field of psychometrics. If possible, we search for methods of measuring the artifact and correcting for its influence.

### 1.1 Unsystematic Artifacts

Some artifacts produce a systematic effect on the study effect size and some cause unsystematic effects. Even within a single study, it is sometimes possible to correct for a systematic effect, though it usually requires special information to do so. Unsystematic effects usually cannot be corrected in isolated studies and may or may not be correctable at the level of meta-analysis. The two

unsystematic artifacts currently identified are sampling error and bad data.

**1.1.1 Sampling error** It is impossible to correct for the effect of sampling error in an isolated study. The confidence interval gives an idea of the potential size of the sampling error, but the magnitude of the sampling error in any one study is unknown and hence cannot be corrected. The effects of sampling error can be measured and eliminated in meta-analysis if the number of studies is large enough to produce a very large total sample size. If the total sample size in the meta-analysis is not large enough, one can still correct for the effects of sampling error, though the correction is less precise and some smaller amount of sampling error will remain in the final meta-analysis results (second-order sampling error; see Hunter & Schmidt 1990b, Chapter 9). A meta-analysis that corrects for only sampling error has sometimes been called a "bare-bones" meta-analysis (e.g., in validity generalization studies).

**1.1.2 Bad data** Bad data in meta-analysis stem from a variety of errors in handling data: (a) Primary data may be erroneous owing to transcription error, coding error, and so on; (b) primary study results may be incorrect owing to computational error, transcriptional error, double correction for error, and so on; (c) the secondary results may have errors caused by transcriptional error by the investigator, by a typist, or by a printer; (d) a meta-analyst may miscopy a result or make a computational error in correction, though this source of error probably occurs very infrequently.

### 1.2. Systematic Artifacts

Many artifacts have a systematic influence on study effect size parameters and their estimates. If such an effect can be measured and quantified, often there is an algebraic formula for the effect of the artifact. Most algebraic formulas can be inverted. Thus, for most systematic artifacts, there is a "correction" formula. Since the correction often increases the study effect size estimate, some people are suspicious of such corrections because they appear to "inflate" the value. However, what appears in one light as "inflation" can also be seen as estimating the values that would have been obtained had the researcher carried out a study without the corresponding imperfection.

Correction for an artifact requires knowledge about the size and extent of the effect of that artifact. Correction for each new artifact usually requires at least one new piece of information. For example, to correct for sampling error in meta-analysis, we need to know the sample sizes of the studies. To correct for the effects of random error of measurement in the dependent variable, we need to know the reliability of the dependent variable in the studies. The main limitation to correction in current meta-analysis is that many study authors do not collect and present information on study artifacts in the primary study. Thus, artifact information is sometimes quite sparse. Furthermore, even when artifact information is available, it is not always of the required type. For example, in correcting for the influence of measurement error, it is important to use an estimate of the appropriate type of reliability coefficient. Use of an inappropriate coefficient will lead to erroneous correction (see Hunter & Schmidt 1990b, pp. 123–125).

The remainder of this chapter is devoted to nine systematic artifacts that can be corrected if the artifact information is available. The correction can be within each study individually if artifact information is available for all (or nearly all) studies individually. If this is not the case, the correction can be made at the level of the meta-analysis if the *distribution* of artifact values across studies is known. As pointed out elsewhere in this volume, study effect sizes can be expressed in a variety of ways, with the two most frequently used indices being the correlation coefficient and the standardized mean difference (*d* value and variations thereof). For ease of explication, artifact effects and corrections are discussed in this chapter in terms of correlations. The same principles apply to standardized mean differences, although it is often more difficult to make appropriate corrections for artifacts affecting the independent variable in true experiments (see Hunter & Schmidt 1990b, Chapters 6 and 7).

**1.2.1 Single artifacts** Most artifacts attenuate the population correlation $\rho$. The extent of attenuation depends on the artifact. For each artifact, it is possible to present a conceptual definition that makes it possible to quantify the influence of the artifact on effect size. For example, the reliability of the dependent variable measures the extent to which there is random error of measurement in the measure of the dependent variable. The reliability, and hence the artifact parameter that determines the influence of measurement error on effect size, can be empirically estimated. We believe that journal editors should require authors to furnish those artifact values. Most of the artifacts presently known cause a systematic attenuation of the correlation. That

is, the study correlation is lower than the actual correlation by some amount. This attenuation is usually most easily expressed as a product in which the actual correlation is multiplied by an "artifact multiplier" usually denoted $a$.

Denote the actual (unattenuated) population correlation by $\rho$, and denote the (attenuated) study population correlation by $\rho_o$. Because we cannot do the study perfectly (e.g., without measurement error), this study imperfection produces an artifact that systematically reduces the actual correlation parameter. Thus, the study correlation $\rho_o$ is smaller than the actual correlation $\rho$. Denote by $a_i$ the artifact value for the study expressed in the form multiplier. If the artifact parameter is expressed by a multiplier $a_i$, then

$$\rho_o = a_i \rho,$$

where $a_c$ is some fraction, $0 < a_i < 1$. The size of $a_c$ depends on the artifact—the greater the error, the smaller the value of $a_i$. In the developments that follow, these artifacts are described as they occur in cross-sectional correlation studies. However, each artifact has a direct analogue in experimental studies; these analogues are explored in some detail in Hunter and Schmidt (1990b, Chapters 6–8).

Attenuation artifacts and the corresponding multiplier are as follows:

1. Random error of measurement in dependent variable $Y$:
   $a_i = \sqrt{r_{yy}}$,
   where $r_{yy}$ is the reliability of the $Y$ measure.
   Example: $r_{yy} = .49$ implies $a_1 = .70$,
   $\rho_o = .70\,\rho$, a 30 percent reduction.

2. Random error of measurement in independent variable $X$:
   $a_2 = \sqrt{r_{xx}}$,
   where $r_{xx}$ is the reliability of the measure of $X$.
   Example: $r_{xx} = .81$ implies $a_2 = .90$,
   $\rho_o = .90\,\rho$, a 10 percent reduction.

3. Artificial dichotomization of continuous dependent variable split into proportions $p$ and $q$:
   $a_3 =$ biserial constant
   $= \phi(c)/\sqrt{(pq)}$,
   where $\phi(x) = e^{-x^2}/\sqrt{2\pi}$ is the unit normal density function and where $c$ is the unit normal distribution cut point corresponding to a split of $p$. That is, $c = \Phi^{-1}(p)$, where $\Phi(x)$ is the unit normal cumulative distribution function.

Example: $Y$ is split at the median, $p = q = .5$, $a_3 = .80$, $\rho_o = .80\, \rho$, a 20 percent reduction.

4. Artificial dichotomization of continuous independent variable split into proportions $p$ and $q$:
$a_4 = $ biserial constant
$= \phi(c)/\sqrt{(pq)}$,
where $c$ is the unit normal distribution cut point corresponding to a split of $p$ and $\phi(x)$ is the unit normal density function. That is, $c = \Phi^{-1}(p)$.
Example: $X$ is split such that $p = .9$ and $q = .1$. Then $a_4 = .60$,
$\rho_o = .60\, \rho$, a 40 percent reduction.

5. Imperfect construct validity of the dependent variable $Y$. Construct validity is the correlation of the dependent variable *measure* with the *actual* dependent variable:
$a_5 = $ the construct validity of $Y$.
Example: supervisor ratings of job performance, $a_5 = .52$,
$\rho_o = .52\, \rho$, a 48 percent reduction.

6. Imperfect construct validity of the independent variable $X$. Construct validity is defined as in (5) above:
$a_6 = $ the construct validity of $X$.
Example: use of a speeded test to assess general cognitive ability, $a_6 = .65$,
$\rho_o = .65\, \rho$, a 35 percent reduction.

7. Range restriction on the independent variable $X$. Range restriction results from systematic exclusion of certain scores on $X$ from the sample compared with the relevant (or reference) population:
$a_7$ depends on the standard deviation ratio,
$u = (SD_X$ study population$)/(SD_X$ reference population$)$.
Example: The average level of range restriction for general cognitive ability in job incumbent populations is $u = .67$.
Complication: The size of the multiplier $a$ depends on the size of $\rho$ (Hunter & Schmidt 1990b, pp. 125–133).
Formula: $a = \sqrt{(u^2 + \rho^2 - u^2\rho^2)}$.
Example: For $\rho = .20$ and $u = .67$, $a_7 = .69$.
$\rho_o = .69\, \rho$, a 31 percent reduction.

8. Range restriction on the dependent variable $Y$. Range restriction results from systematic exclusion of certain scores on $Y$ from the sample in comparison to the relevant population:
$a_8$ depends on the standard deviation ratio,
$u = (SD_Y$ study population$)/(SD_Y$ reference population$)$.
Example: Some workers are fired early for poor performance and are hence underrepresented in the incumbent population. Assume that exactly the bottom 20 percent are fired. Then from normal curve calculations, $u = .83$.
Complication: The size of the multiplier $a$ depends on the size of $\rho$.
Formula: $a_8 = \sqrt{(u^2 + \rho^2 - u^2\rho^2)}$.
Example: For $\rho = .20$ and $u = .83$, $a_8 = .84$,
$\rho_o = .84\, \rho$, a 16 percent reduction.
Note: Correction of the same correlation for range restriction on both the independent and dependent variables is complicated and requires special formulas. (See Hunter & Schmidt 1990b, pp. 49–52, for a discussion of this problem.)

9. Bias in the correlation coefficient:
$a_9 = 1 - (1 - \rho^2)/(2N - 2)$.
Comment: For sample sizes of 20 or more, bias is smaller than rounding error. Thus, bias is trivial in size, but is worth computing a time or two to see that it is in fact trivial.
Example: For $\rho = .20$ and $N = 68$, $a_9 = .9997$,
$\rho_o = .9997\, \rho$, a .03 percent reduction.

10. Study-caused variation.
Example: Concurrent validation studies conducted on ability tests evaluate the job performance of workers who vary in job experience, whereas applicants all start with zero job experience. Job experience correlates with job performance, even holding ability constant.
Formula: partial correlation to remove the effects of unwanted variation in experience.
Specific case: study done in new plant with very low mean experience (e.g., mean = 2 years). Correlation of experience with ability is zero. Correlation of job experience with job performance is .50. Comparison of the partial correlation to the zero order correlation shows that $a_{10} = \sqrt{1 - .50^2} = .87$,
$\rho_o = .87\, \rho$, a 13 percent reduction.
Of the artifacts enumerated here, this one is the most difficult conceptually and mathematically.

**1.2.2 Multiple artifacts** Suppose that the study correlation is affected by several artifacts with parameters $a_1, a_2, a_3, \ldots$ . The first artifact reduces the actual correlation from $\rho$ to

$$\rho_{o1} = a_1\, \rho.$$

The second artifact reduces that correlation to

$$\rho_{o2} = a_2\, \rho_{o1} = a_2\, (a_1\, \rho) = a_1\, a_2\, \rho.$$

The third artifact reduces that correlation to

$$\rho_{o3} = a_3 \, \rho_{o2} = a_3 \, (a_1 \, a_2 \, \rho) = a_1 \, a_2 \, a_3 \, \rho,$$

and so on.

Thus, the joint effect of the artifacts is to multiply the population correlation by all the multipliers

$$\rho_o = a_1 \, a_2 \, a_3 \, \ldots \, \rho$$

or

$$\rho_o = A \, \rho,$$

where $A$ is the compound artifact multiplier equal to the product of the individual artifact multipliers

$$A = a_1 \, a_2 \, a_3 \, \ldots \, .$$

**1.2.3 A numerical illustration** Here we illustrate the impact of some of these artifacts using actual data from studies of personnel selection. The quantitative impact is large: Typical observed correlations are only about half the size of the estimated population correlations based on perfect measures and computed on the relevant (reference) population. We give two illustrations: (a) the impact on the average correlation between general cognitive ability and job performance ratings and (b) the impact of variation in artifacts across studies.

A meta-analysis of 425 validation studies conducted by the U.S. Employment Service shows that for medium-complexity jobs, the average applicant population correlation between true scores on general cognitive ability and true scores on job performance ratings is .57 (Hunter 1980). We now show how this value is reduced by study artifacts to an observed mean correlation of .24.

*The ideal study.* Ideally, each worker would serve under a population of judges (raters), so that idiosyncrasy of judgment could be eliminated by averaging ratings across judges.

Let $P$ = consensus (average) rating of performance by a population of judges, and let $A$ = actual cognitive ability.

The correlation $r_{AP}$ would then be computed on an extremely *large* sample of applicants hired *at random* from the applicant population. Hence, there would be no unreliability in either measure, no range restriction, and virtually no sampling error. Previous experience suggests that the obtained correlation should be .57.

*The actual study.* In the actual study, $x$ = score on an imperfect test of general cognitive ability, and $y$ = rating by one immediate supervisor.

The correlation $r_{xy}$ is computed on a small sample of

workers (incumbents) hired by the company using the best information available at the time of hire.

*Impact of error of measurement.* Because of error in the independent variable, $r_{AP}$ is reduced to

$$r_{XP} = \sqrt{r_{xx}} \, r_{AP}.$$

Because of error in the dependent variable, $r_{AP}$ is reduced to

$$r_{Ay} = \sqrt{r_{yy}} \, r_{AP}.$$

When there is error in both, $r_{AP}$ is reduced to

$$r_{xy} = \sqrt{r_{xx}} \sqrt{r_{yy}} \, r_{AP}.$$

No test can be long enough to be a perfect measure of general cognitive ability. For example, the General Aptitude Test Battery (GATB) of the U.S. Employment Service has a reliability (generalizability) coefficient of .80 (Hunter 1980). Thus, even with a relatively reliable test such as the GATB, the correlation is reduced from $r_{AP} = .57$ to

$$r_{xP} = \sqrt{.80} \, (.57) = .51.$$

For ratings by a single supervisor, a meta-analysis of performance rating studies (Hunter & Hirsh 1987; see also Rothstein 1990) shows the reliability is at most .47. Thus, the validity is reduced from .51 to

$$r_{xy} = \sqrt{r_{yy}} \, r_{xP} = \sqrt{.47} \, (.51) = .35.$$

Because of error of measurement, the correlation is reduced from .57 to .35, a reduction of 39 percent.

*Impact of restriction in range.* All studies by the U.S. Employment Service were conducted in settings in which the GATB had not been used to select workers. Even so, the average extent of restriction in range for general cognitive ability was found to be (Hunter 1980) $u = (SD \text{ incumbents})/(SD \text{ applicants}) = .67$. This reduces the validity from

.35 to $r_{xy} = (.67)(.35)/[.67^2(.35^2) - .35^2 + 1]^{1/2} = .24.$

*Study correlations.* The total impact of study limitations was to reduce the mean population correlation from .57 to .24, a reduction of 58 percent. This was followed by the blurring effect of sampling error in individual studies, that is, $r_i = .24 + e_i$.

The average sample size was 76. Even if there had been no variation across study population correlations, the middle 95 percent of observed correlations would have ranged across studies from .03 to .45. Only about 55 percent of these correlations would have been statistically significant, for a Type I error rate of about 45 percent. That is, the average statistical power was approximately .55.

We now present numerical examples of the effects of variation in artifacts across studies. Assume a correlation of .57 in the applicant population for perfectly measured variables. Even if there was no variation in this value across studies (i.e., employers), variation in artifact values would produce substantial variation in observed correlations.

*Predictor reliability.* Suppose that each study is conducted using either a long or a short ability test. Assume that the reliability for the long test is $r_{xx} = .81$ and that for the short test is .49. The corresponding correlations would be

$$\text{Long test } r_{xy} = \sqrt{.81} \ (.57) = .51,$$

and

$$\text{Short test } r_{xy} = \sqrt{.49} \ (.57) = .40.$$

*Criterion reliability: one rater versus multiple raters.* Suppose that some studies use one rater and other studies use two raters. Reliability would then be either $r_{yy} = .47$ or $r_{yy} = .60$.

The correlations would be

1. Long test and two raters: $r_{xy} = \sqrt{.81} \ \sqrt{.60} \ (.57)$ = .40;
2. Long test and one rater: $r_{xy} = \sqrt{.81} \ \sqrt{.47} \ (.57)$ = .35;
3. Short test and two raters: $r_{xy} = \sqrt{.49} \ \sqrt{.60} \ (.57)$ = .33;
4. Short test and one rater: $r_{xy} = \sqrt{.49} \ \sqrt{.47} \ (.57)$ = .27.

*Direct range restriction.* Suppose that some firms hire from the top half of applicants and some firms hire only from the top tenth. The degree of range restriction will be $u = .60$ for those hiring from the top half and $u = .40$ for those hiring from the top tenth.

The correlations would then be (left, $u = .60$; right, $u = .40$)

1. Long test and two raters: $r_{xy} = .25, .17$;
2. Long test and one rater: $r_{xy} = .22, .15$;
3. Short test and two raters: $r_{xy} = .21, .14$;
4. Short test and one rater: $r_{xy} = .17, .11$.

Thus, variation in artifacts produces variation in study population correlations. Instead of one population correlation of .57, we have a distribution of population correlations: .11, .14, .15, .17, .17, .21, .22, and .25. One of these values would be the population correlation underlying each study. To that value sampling error would then be added to yield the correlation observed in the study. If there was variation in population correlations prior to the introduction of these artifacts, that variance would be expanded because the process illustrated here applies to each value in the prior distribution.

## 2. CORRECTING FOR ATTENUATION

### 2.1 The Population Correlation: Attenuation and Disattenuation

The population correlation can be exactly corrected for the effect of any artifact. Since

$$\rho_o = A \ \rho,$$

we can reverse the equation algebraically to obtain

$$\rho = \rho_o / A.$$

That is, if we correct the attenuated population we estimate it to what its value would have been had it been possible to do the study perfectly.

Note that to divide by a fraction is to increase the value. That is, if artifacts reduce the study population correlation in size, then to estimate the disattenuated correlation must increase it.

### 2.2 The Sample Correlation

The sample correlation can be corrected using the same formula as for the population correlation. This eliminates the systematic error in the sample correlation, but it does not eliminate the sampling error.

The sample study correlation relates to the population correlation by

$$r_o = \rho_o + e,$$

where $e$ is the sampling error in $r_o$. To within a close approximation, the average error is zero (Hedges 1989) and the error variance is

$$\text{Var}(e) = (1 - \rho^2)^2 / (N - 1)$$

The corrected sample correlation is

$$r = r_o / A,$$

where $A$ is the compound artifact multiplier. The sampling error in the corrected correlation is related to the population correlation by

$$r = r_o/A = (\rho_o + e)/A$$
$$= \rho_o/A + e/A$$
$$= \rho + e'.$$

That is, the corrected correlation differs from the actual effect size correlation by only sampling error $e'$, where the new sampling error $e'$ is given by

$$e' = e/A.$$

Since $A$ is less than 1, the sampling error $e'$ is larger than the sampling error $e$. This shows in the sampling error variance

$$\text{Var}(e') = \text{Var}(e)/A^2.$$

However, since the average error $e$ is essentially zero, the average error $e'$ is also essentially zero.

## 3. META-ANALYSIS OF CORRECTED CORRELATIONS

Suppose that the extent of artifact interference is reported for each study (as we believe should be required in published research reports). Then for each study, we have three numbers.

For study $i$ we have

$r_{oi} =$ the $i$th study correlation,
$A_i =$ the compound artifact multiplier for study $i$, and
$N_i =$ the sample size for study $i$.

We then compute for each study the disattenuated correlation:

$r_i =$ the disattenuated correlation for study $i$.

Two meta-analyses can be done: one on the attenuated study correlations (the "bare-bones" meta-analysis) and one on the attenuated correlations.

### 3.1 The Mean Correlation

As Schmidt and Hunter (1977) noted, large-sample studies contain more information than small-sample studies and thus should be given more weight. This corresponds to certain theorems in statistics that are stated explicitly elsewhere (e.g., in Hedges & Olkin 1985). Our approach (Hunter & Schmidt 1990b) recommends a more complicated weighting formula that takes into account the other artifact values for the study—for example, the

poorer the measurement of the dependent variable, the less the information in the study. Thus, a low-reliability study should be given less weight than a high-reliability study.

Hunter and Schmidt (1990b) recommended that the weight for study $i$ should be

$$w_i = N_i A_i^2,$$

where $A_i$ is the compound artifact multiplier for study $i$.

In all cases, the average correlation can be written

$$\text{Ave}(r) = \Sigma w_i r_i / \Sigma w_i,$$

where

$w_i = 1$      for unweighted average,
$w_i = N_i$    for sample size weighted average, and
$w_i = N_i A_i^2$ for full artifact weighted average.

An analysis with any of the sets of weights is correct. If the number of studies was infinite so that sampling error was totally eliminated, the resulting mean would be the same regardless of which weights were used. But for a finite number of studies, meta-analysis does not totally eliminate sampling error. There is still some sampling error left in the mean correlation. If the full artifact weights are not used, then the meta-analysis has more residual sampling error in the mean correlation.

### 3.2 Corrected Versus Uncorrected Correlations

In some research domains, the artifact values for each study are not known. Thus, some published meta-analyses do not correct for artifacts. Failure to correct means that the mean uncorrected correlation will differ from the actual (unattenuated) correlation. The error in a meta-analysis of uncorrected correlations will depend on the extent of error caused by artifacts in the average study. This average extent of systematic error is measured by the average compound multiplier, $\text{Ave}(A)$.

To a close approximation, the mean corrected correlation $\text{Ave}(r)$ relates to the mean uncorrected correlation $\text{Ave}(r_o)$ in much the same way as does an individual corrected correlation. Just as

$$r = r_o/A,$$

so to a close approximation we have

$$\text{Ave}(r) = \text{Ave}(r_o)/\text{Ave}(A).$$

Thus, to a close approximation, the difference in findings of an analysis that does not correct for artifacts and one that does is the difference between the uncorrected mean $\text{Ave}(r_o)$ and the corrected mean correlation $\text{Ave}(r)$ (Hunter & Schmidt 1990b, Chapter 4).

### 3.3 Variance of Correlations: Procedure

The variance of observed correlations greatly overstates the variance of population correlations. This is just as true for corrected correlations as for uncorrected correlations. From the fact that the corrected correlation is

$$r_i = \rho_i + e'_i,$$

where $r_i$ and $\rho_i$ are the corrected sample and population correlations and $e'_i$ is the sampling error, we have the decomposition of variance

$$\text{Var}(r) = \text{Var}(\rho) + \text{Var}(e').$$

Thus, by subtraction, we have the desired variance

$$\text{Var}(\rho) = \text{Var}(r) - \text{Var}(e').$$

The variance of study corrected correlations is the weighted squared deviation of the $i$th correlation from the mean correlation. If we denote the average correlation by $\bar{r}$, then

$$\bar{r} = \text{Ave}(r) = \Sigma \, w_i \, r_i / \Sigma \, w_i,$$
$$\text{Var}(r) = \Sigma \, w_i \, (r_i - \bar{r})^2 / \Sigma \, w_i.$$

The sampling error variance is computed by averaging the error variances of the individual studies. The error variance of the individual study depends on the size of the uncorrected population correlation. To estimate that number, we first compute the average uncorrected correlation $\bar{r}_o$, where

$$\bar{r}_o = \text{Ave}(r_o) = \Sigma \, w_i \, r_{oi} / \Sigma \, w_i.$$

For study $i$, we have

$$\text{Var}(e_i) = v_i = (1 - \bar{r}_o^2)^2 / (N_i - 1),$$

and

$$\text{Var}(e_i') = \text{Var}(e_i)/A_i^2 = v_i/A_i^2.$$

For simplicity, denote the study error variance $\text{Var}(e'_i)$ by $v'_i$. The weighted average error variance for the meta-analysis is the average

$$\text{Var}(e') = \Sigma \, w_i \, v'_i / \Sigma \, w_i.$$

*Procedure.* The specific computational procedure involves six steps:
1. Given for each study
   $r_{oi} =$ uncorrected correlation,
   $A_i =$ compound artifact multiplier, and
   $N_i =$ sample size,

2. Compute for each study
   $r_i =$ corrected correlation, and
   $w_i =$ the proper weight to be given to $r_i$.
3. In order to estimate the effect of sampling error, compute the average *uncorrected* correlation $\bar{r}_o$. This is done using weights $w_i$.
4. For each study compute the sampling error variance $v'_i =$ sampling error variance.
5. The meta-analysis of disattenuated correlations has four steps:
   (a) Compute the mean corrected correlation using weights $w_i$:
   Mean correlation $= \text{Ave}(r)$.
   (b) Compute the variance of corrected correlations using $w_i$:
   Variance of corrected correlations $= \text{Var}(r)$.
   (c) Compute the sampling error variance $\text{Var}(e')$ by averaging the individual study sampling error variances:
   $\text{Var}(e') = \text{Ave}(v'_i)$.
   (d) Now compute the estimate of the variance of population correlations by correcting for sampling error:
   $\text{Var}(\rho) = \text{Var}(r) - \text{Var}(e')$.
6. The final fundamental estimates are
   $\text{Ave}(\rho) = \text{Ave}(r)$
   and
   $SD\rho = \sqrt{\text{Var}(\rho)}.$

Simplified examples of application of this approach to meta-analysis can be found in Hunter and Schmidt (1990b), Chapter 3. Meta-analyses in which each correlation is corrected individually are not frequent because in most study domains there is much missing artifact information. An example of an extensive published meta-analyses of this sort is Rothstein et al. (1990). In this study, a previously developed weighted biodata form was correlated with the job performance ratings of 11,288 first-line supervisors in 79 organizations. Thus, there were 79 studies, with a mean $N$ per study of 143. The reliability of the dependent variable— the job performance ratings––was determined in each organization as the correlation between two raters, adjusted by the Spearman-Brown formula to reflect the fact that the rating used was the average across the two raters. The standard deviation (SD) of the independent variable was computed in each organization, and the SD of *applicants* for the position of first-line supervisors was known, allowing each individual correlation to be corrected for range variation. In this meta-analysis, there was no between-studies variation in correlations due to variation in measurement error in the *independent* variable—because the same biodata scale was used in all 79 studies. Thus, no correction to the variance of study outcomes was needed for this source of variation. Also, in this meta-analysis, the interest was in the effectiveness of this particular biodata scale in predicting job performance. Hence, mean $\rho$ was not corrected for unreliability in the independent variable.

The results were as follows:

$$\text{Ave } (r_{oi}) = .30,$$
$$\text{Ave } (\rho) = .36,$$
$$\text{Var } (\rho) = \text{Var } (r_i) - \text{Var } (e')$$
$$= .015876 - .00925$$
$$= .006626, \text{ and}$$
$$\text{SD}\rho = \sqrt{\text{Var}(\rho)} = .081.$$

Thus, the mean "true validity" of this scale across organizations is estimated as .36, with a standard deviation of .081. After correcting for measurement error, range variation, and sampling error, there is still some apparent variability across organizations in this correlation. (Only 58 percent of the observed variance of the $r_i$ was found to be due to artifacts.) If we assume a normal distribution for $\rho$, and assume that our estimates were perfectly accurate, the value at the 10th percentile is $.36 - 1.28 (.081) = .26$. Thus, we conclude that the correlation is at least .26 in 90 percent of these (and comparable) organizations.

## 4. ARTIFACT DISTRIBUTIONS

In most contemporary research domains, the artifact values are not known for every study. Instead, artifact values are given only for a sporadic subset of studies, usually a different subset for each individual artifact. It is still possible to do meta-analysis in such a domain, though the formulas are more complicated.

Simplified examples of application of artifact distribution meta-analysis can be found in Hunter and Schmidt (1990b, Chapter 3). Most published (and unpublished) meta-analyses based on these meta-analysis methods have been artifact distribution meta-analyses. These analyses have often been conducted on correlation coefficients representing the validities of various kinds of predictors of job performance—usually tests, but also interviews, ratings of education and job experience, assessment centers, and so on. Examples include Schmidt, Gast-Rosenberg, and Hunter (1980); Schmidt et al. (1979); Pearlman, Schmidt, and Hunter (1980); Schmidt, Hunter,

and Kaplan (1981); Hirsh, Northroup, and Schmidt (1986); McDaniel, Schmidt, and Hunter (1988); Gangler et al. (1987); and McDaniel et al. (1990). The implications of the findings of these meta-analyses for personnel selection practices have been quite profound and are described in Schmidt, Hunter, and Pearlman (1980); Schmidt and Hunter (1981); Schmidt et al. (1985); Schmidt (1988); and Schmidt, Ones, and Hunter (1992). Artifact distribution meta-analyses have also been conducted in a variety of research areas outside personnel selection, such as role conflict and leadership. About 40 such meta-analyses have appeared in the literature to date (Schmidt, 1992).

The key assumption made in considering artifact distributions is independence of artifact values across artifacts. We believe that this assumption is plausible for the currently known artifacts in all research domains that we have considered. The basis for independence is the fact that the resource limitations that produce problems with one artifact are generally different and hence independent of those that produce problems with another.

Use the following notation for the correlations associated with the $i$th study:

$\rho_i =$ the true (unattenuated) study population correlation;

$r_i =$ the study sample corrected correlation that can be computed if artifact information is available for the study so that corrections can be made;

$r_{oi} =$ uncorrected (observed) study sample correlation; and

$\rho_{oi} =$ uncorrected (attenuated) study population correlation.

In the previous section, we assumed that artifact information is available for each study individually. Thus, an estimate $r_i$ of the true correlation $\rho_i$ can be computed for each study and meta-analysis can be done on these estimates. In this section, we assume that artifact information is missing for many or most studies. However, we assume that the distribution (or at least the mean and variance) of artifact values is known for each artifact. The meta-analysis then proceeds in two steps:

1. An analysis is conducted, yielding estimates of the mean and standard deviation of attenuated study population correlations.

2. The mean and standard deviation from the above analysis are then corrected for the effects of artifacts other than sampling error.

## 4.1 The Mean Correlation

The attenuated study population correlation $\rho_{oi}$ is related to the actual study population correlation $\rho_i$ by the formula

$$\rho_{oi} = A_i\,\rho_i,$$

where

$A_i$ = the compound artifact multiplier for study $i$ (which is unknown for most studies).

The sample attenuated correlation $r_{oi}$ for each study is related to the attenuated population correlation for that study by

$$r_{oi} = \rho_{oi} + e_{oi},$$

where

$e_{oi}$ = the sampling error in study $i$ (which is unknown).

**4.1.1 Meta-analysis on attenuated correlations** The meta-analysis uses the additivity of means to produce

$$\mathrm{Ave}(r_{oi}) = \mathrm{Ave}(\rho_{oi} + e_{oi}) = \mathrm{Ave}(\rho_{oi}) + \mathrm{Ave}(e_{oi}).$$

If the number of studies is large, the average sampling error will tend to zero and hence

$$\mathrm{Ave}(r_{oi}) = \mathrm{Ave}(\rho_{oi}) + 0 = \mathrm{Ave}(\rho_{oi}).$$

Thus, the bare-bones estimate of the mean attenuated study *population* correlation is the expected mean attenuated study *sample* correlation.

**4.1.2 Correction of the mean** The attenuated population correlation for the study $i$ is related to the disattenuated correlation for study $i$ by

$$\rho_{oi} = A_i\,\rho_i,$$

where

$A_i$ = the compound artifact multiplier for study $i$.

Thus, the mean attenuated correlation is given by

$$\mathrm{Ave}(\rho_{oi}) = \mathrm{Ave}(A_i\,\rho_i).$$

Because we assume that artifact values are independent of the size of the true correlation, the average of the product is the product of the averages:

$$\mathrm{Ave}(A_i\,\rho_i) = \mathrm{Ave}(A_i)\,\mathrm{Ave}(\rho_i).$$

Hence, the average attenuated correlation is related to the average unattenuated correlation by

$$\mathrm{Ave}(\rho_{oi}) = \mathrm{Ave}(A_i)\,\mathrm{Ave}(\rho_i),$$

where

$\mathrm{Ave}(A_i)$ = the AVERAGE compound multiplier across studies.

Note that we need not know all the individual study artifact multipliers; we need only know the average. If the average multiplier is known, then the corrected mean correlation is

$$\mathrm{Ave}(\rho_i) = \mathrm{Ave}(r_{oi})/\mathrm{Ave}(A_i).$$

**4.1.3 The mean compound multiplier** In order to estimate the average compound multiplier, it is sufficient to be able to estimate the average for each single artifact multiplier separately. This follows from the independence of artifacts. In order to avoid double subscripts, let us denote the separate artifact multipliers by $a$, $b$, $c$, . . . . The compound multiplier $A$ is then given by the product

$$A = a\,b\,c\,\ldots$$

Because of independence, the average product is the product of averages:

$$\mathrm{Ave}(A) = \mathrm{Ave}(a)\,\mathrm{Ave}(b)\,\mathrm{Ave}(c)\,\ldots$$

Thus, the steps in estimating the compound multiplier are as follows:

1. Consider the separate artifacts.
   (a) Consider the first artifact $a$. For each study that includes a measurement of the artifact magnitude, denote the value $a_i$. Average those values to produce $\mathrm{Ave}(a_i)$ = average of attenuation multiplier for first artifact.
   (b) Consider the second artifact $b$. For each study that includes a measurement of the artifact magnitude, denote the value $b_i$. Average those values to produce $\mathrm{Ave}(b_i)$ = average of attenuation multiplier for second artifact.
   (c) Similarly, consider the other separate artifacts $c$, $d$, and so on, that produce estimates of the averages $\mathrm{Ave}(c)$, $\mathrm{Ave}(d)$, . . . .

The accuracy of these averages depends on the assumption that the available artifacts are a reasonably representative sample of all artifacts. This assumption is discussed in Hunter and Schmidt (1990b).

2. Compute the product

$$\mathrm{Ave}(A) = \mathrm{Ave}(a)\,\mathrm{Ave}(b)\,\mathrm{Ave}(c)\,\mathrm{Ave}(d)\,\ldots$$

## 4.2 Correcting the Standard Deviation

The meta-analysis of uncorrected correlations provides an estimate of the variance of study population correlations. However, these study population correlations are themselves uncorrected. They have been attenuated by the study artifacts and are thus systematically reduced in magnitude. Furthermore, the variation in artifact extremity across studies causes the study correlations to be attenuated by different amounts in different studies. This produces variation in the size of the study correlation that could be confused with variation due to a real moderator variable, as we saw in our earlier numerical example. Thus, the variance of population study correlations computed from a meta-analysis of uncorrected correlations is affected in two different ways. The systematic artifact-induced reduction in the magnitude of the study correlations tends to decrease variability, and variation in artifact magnitude tends to increase variability across studies. Both sources of influence must be addressed in order to accurately estimate the standard deviation of the disattenuated correlations across studies.

Let us begin with notation. The study correlation free of study artifacts (the disattenuated correlation) is denoted $\rho_i$, and the compound artifact attenuation factor for study $i$ is denoted $A_i$. The attenuated study correlation $\rho_{oi}$ is computed from the disattenuated study correlation by

$$\rho_{oi} = A_i \rho_i.$$

The study sample correlation $r_{oi}$ departs from the disattenuated study population correlation $\rho_{oi}$ by sampling error $e_i$ defined by

$$r_{oi} = \rho_{oi} + e_i = A_i \rho_i + e_i.$$

Consider now a bare-bones meta-analysis on the uncorrected correlations. We know that the variance of sample correlations is the variance of population correlations added to the sampling error variance. That is,

$$\mathrm{Var}(r_{oi}) = \mathrm{Var}(\rho_{oi}) + \mathrm{Var}(e_i).$$

Since the sampling error variance can be computed by statistical formula, we can subtract it to yield

$$\mathrm{Var}(\rho_{oi}) = \mathrm{Var}(r_{oi}) - \mathrm{Var}(e_i).$$

That is, the meta-analysis of uncorrected correlations produces an estimate of the variance of attenuated study population correlations, the actual study correlations after they have been reduced in magnitude by the study imperfections.

At the end of a meta-analysis of uncorrected (attenuated) correlations, we have the variance of attenuated study population correlations $\mathrm{Var}(\rho_{oi})$, but we want the variance of actual disattenuated correlations $\mathrm{Var}(\rho_i)$. The relationship between them is

$$\mathrm{Var}(\rho_{oi}) = \mathrm{Var}(A_i \rho_i).$$

We assume that $A_i$ and $\rho_i$ are independent. Can we use this assumption to compute the variance of the product? A formula for the variance of this product is given in Hunter and Schmidt (1990b, Chapter 4). Here we simply use this formula. Let us denote the average disattenuated study correlation by $\bar{\rho}$ and denote the average compound attenuation factor by $\bar{A}$. The variance of the attenuated correlations is given by

$$\mathrm{Var}(A_i \rho_i) = \bar{A}^2 \mathrm{Var}(\rho_i) + \bar{\rho}^2 \mathrm{Var}(A_i) + \mathrm{Var}(\rho_i)\mathrm{Var}(A_i).$$

Because the third term on the right is negligibly small, then to a close approximation

$$\mathrm{Var}(A_i \rho_i) = \bar{A}^2 \mathrm{Var}(\rho_i) + \bar{\rho}^2 \mathrm{Var}(A_i).$$

We can then rearrange this equation algebraically to obtain the desired equation for the variance of actual study correlations free of artifact effects:

$$\mathrm{Var}(\rho_i) = [\mathrm{Var}(A_i \rho_i) - \bar{\rho}^2 \mathrm{Var}(A_i)]/\bar{A}^2.$$

That is, starting from the meta-analysis of uncorrected correlations, we have

$$\mathrm{Var}(\rho_i) = [\mathrm{Var}(\rho_{oi}) - \bar{\rho}^2 \mathrm{Var}(A_i)]/\bar{A}^2.$$

The right-hand side of this equation has four numbers:

1. $\mathrm{Var}(\rho_{oi})$: the population correlation variance from the meta-analysis of uncorrected correlations;

2. $\bar{\rho}$: the mean of disattenuated study population correlations whose estimate was derived in the preceding section;

3. $\bar{A}$: the mean compound attenuation factor that was estimated as part of the process of estimating the mean disattenuated correlation $\rho$;

4. $\mathrm{Var}(A_i)$: the variance of the compound attenuation factor that has not yet been estimated.

**4.2.1 Variance of the artifact multiplier**  How do we compute the variance of the compound attenuation factor $A_i$? We are given the distribution of each component attenuation factor, which must be combined to produce the variance of the compound attenuation factor. The key to this computation lies in two facts: (a) that the compound attenuation factor is the product of the component attenuation factors and (b) that the attenuation factors are assumed to be independent. That is, since

$$A_i = a_i b_i c_i \ldots ,$$

the variance of $A_i$ is

$$\mathrm{Var}(A_i) = \mathrm{Var}(a_i b_i c_i \ldots).$$

The variance of the compound attenuation factor is the variance of the product of independent component attenuation factors. The formula for the variance of this product is given in Hunter and Schmidt (1990b, Chapter 4). Here we simply use the result.

For each separate artifact, we have a mean and a standard deviation for that component attenuation factor. From the mean and the standard deviation, we can compute the "coefficient of variation," which is the standard deviation divided by the mean. For our purposes here, we need a symbol for the *squared* coefficient of variation:

$$cv = [\mathrm{SD/Mean}]^2.$$

For each artifact, we now compute the *squared* coefficient of variation. For the first artifact attenuation factor $a$, we compute

$$cv_1 = \mathrm{Var}(a)/[\mathrm{Ave}(a)]^2.$$

For the second artifact attenuation factor $b$, we compute

$$cv_2 = \mathrm{Var}(b)/[\mathrm{Ave}(b)]^2.$$

For the third artifact attenuation factor $c$, we compute

$$cv_3 = \mathrm{Var}(c)/[\mathrm{Ave}(c)]^2,$$

and so on. Thus, we compute a squared coefficient of variation for each artifact. These are then summed to form a total

$$CVT = cv_1 + cv_2 + cv_3 + \ldots .$$

Recalling that $\overline{A}$ denotes the mean compound attenuation factor, we write the formula for the variance of the compound attenuation factor (to a close approximation) as the product

$$\mathrm{Var}(A_i) = \overline{A}^2 CVT.$$

We now have all the elements needed to estimate the variance in actual study correlations $\mathrm{Var}(\rho_i)$. The final formula is

$$\mathrm{Var}(\rho_i) = [\mathrm{Var}(\rho_{oi}) - \bar{\rho}^2 \mathrm{Var}(A_i)]/\overline{A}^2$$
$$= [\mathrm{Var}(\rho_{oi}) - \bar{\rho}^2 \overline{A}^2 CVT]/\overline{A}^2.$$

**4.2.2 Decomposition of the variance** Buried in the derivation above is a decomposition of the variance of uncorrected correlations. Let us pull that decomposition together here:

$$\mathrm{Var}(r_{oi}) = \mathrm{Var}(\rho_{oi}) + \mathrm{Var}(e_i),$$
$$\mathrm{Var}(\rho_{oi}) = \mathrm{Var}(A_i \rho_i) = \overline{A}^2 \mathrm{Var}(\rho_i) + \bar{\rho}^2 \mathrm{Var}(A_i),$$

and

$$\mathrm{Var}(A_i) = \overline{A}^2 CVT.$$

That is,

$$\mathrm{Var}(r_{oi}) = \overline{A}^2 \mathrm{Var}(\rho_i) + \bar{\rho}^2 \overline{A}^2 CVT + \mathrm{Var}(e_i)$$
$$= \quad S1 \quad + \quad S2 \quad + \quad S3.$$

where $S1$ is the variance in uncorrected correlations produced by the variation in actual unattenuated effect size correlations, $S2$ is the variance in uncorrected correlations produced by the variation in artifact extremity, and $S3$ is the variance in uncorrected correlations produced by sampling error.

In this decomposition, the term $S1$ contains the estimated variance of effect size correlations. This estimated variance is corrected for those artifacts that were corrected in the meta-analysis (in the typical case, this means nothing but sampling error). This is usually not all the artifacts that affect the study value. Thus, $S1$ is an upper-bound estimate of the component of variance in uncorrected correlations due to real variation in the strength of the relationship and not due to artifacts of the study design. To the extent that there are uncorrected artifacts, $S1$ will overestimate the real variation; it may greatly overestimate that variation.

Consider the null hypothesis that there is no real variance in unattenuated correlations, that all of the observed variance is due to variation in artifacts and due to sampling error. A chi-square test can be used to test the hypothesis. If there was no real variance in unattenuated correlations, then the observed variance of uncorrected study correlations would equal that due to artifacts and sampling error alone—that is, terms $S2$ and $S3$ in the decomposition above. Denote the predicted variance by $S$ where

$$S = S2 + S3 = \bar{\rho}^2 \bar{A}^2 V + \text{Var}(e_i).$$

Define the test statistic $Q$ by

$$Q = k \text{Var}(r_{oi})/S,$$

where $k$ is the number of studies. Then under the null hypothesis, $Q$ will have an approximately chi-square distribution with $k - 1$ degrees of freedom. This chi-square test is discussed in more detail in Hunter and Schmidt (1990b, Chapters 3 and 4) and Hunter and Schmidt (1990a). In both these sources, we warn that there are many disadvantages to relying on statistical significance tests in meta-analysis, just as there are in the analysis of primary research data (Hunter & Schmidt 1990b, Chapters 1 and 2). Thus, use of this chi-square test is by no means a required or essential component of the meta-analysis methods presented here.

Note, however, that if there are uncorrected artifacts, then the null hypothesis of no variation in the $\rho_{oi}$ will be false even if there is no variation in the $\rho_i$ values. As long as there are uncorrected artifacts, there will be artifactual variation in study correlations produced by variation in those uncorrected artifacts. Further, this uncorrected artifactual variance will cause the chi-square test to reject the null hypothesis even when the unattenuated correlations (the $\rho_i$) are identical.

**4.2.3 The "75 percent rule"** Schmidt and Hunter (1977) noted this problem and recommended that if the term $S1$ is less than 25 percent of the total variance, then it is probably true that the remaining variance is also due to uncorrected artifacts. This is the often cited "75 percent rule." Our argument was that in any given meta-analysis it is probably the case that uncorrected artifacts account for 25 percent of the variance. If the real variance estimate is not at least this high, it suggests that there may be no real variance (See Hunter & Schmidt 1990b, pp. 68 and 440).

The 75 percent rule has been widely misinterpreted. Many authors have taken this to be a rule for judging whether or not the variance is explained by second-order sampling error. Consider a meta-analysis in a research domain where the number of studies is small. If the number of studies in the meta-analysis is small, there is sampling error in the observed variance of sample correlations, that is, second-order sampling error (Hunter & Schmidt 1990b, Chapter 9). Thus, by chance the observed value of Var ($r_{oi}$) may be larger than that predicted by the sampling error variance formula. Many authors have incorrectly assumed that the 75 percent

rule is intended to be a statistical test for such chance fluctuation.

# 5. REFERENCES

Gangler, B. B., Rosenthal, D. B., Thornton, G. C., & Bentson, C. (1987). Meta-analysis of assessment center validity. *Journal of Applied Psychology, 72,* 493–511.

Hedges, L. V. (1989). An unbiased correction for sampling error in validity generalization studies. *Journal of Applied Psychology, 74,* 469–477.

Hedges, L. V., & Olkin, I. (1985). *Statistical methods for meta-analysis.* Orlando, FL: Academic Press.

Hirsh, H. R., Northroup, L., & Schmidt, F. L. (1986). Validity generalization results for law enforcement occupations. *Personnel Psychology, 39,* 432–439.

Hunter, J. E. (1980). Validity generalization for 12,000 jobs: An application of synthetic validity and validity generalization to the General Aptitude Test Battery (GATB). Washington, DC: U.S. Employment Service, U.S. Department of Labor.

Hunter, J. E., & Hirsh, H. R. (1987). Applications of meta-analysis. In C. L. Cooper & I. T. Robertson (Eds.), *International Review of Industrial and Organizational Psychology 1987.* London: Wiley.

Hunter, J. E., & Schmidt, F. L. (1990a). Dichotomization of continuous variables: The implications for meta-analysis. *Journal of Applied Psychology, 75,* 334–349.

Hunter, J. E., & Schmidt, F. L. (1990b). *Methods of meta-analysis: Correcting error and bias in research findings.* Beverly Hills, CA: Sage.

Hunter, J. E., Schmidt, F. L., & Jackson, G. B. (1982). *Meta-analysis: Cumulating research findings across studies.* Beverly Hills, CA: Sage.

McDaniel, M. A., Schmidt, F. L., & Hunter, J. E. (1988). A meta-analysis of the validity of methods for rating training and experience in personnel selection. *Personnel Psychology, 41,* 283–314.

McDaniel, M. A., Whetzel, D. L., Schmidt, F. L., Hunter, J. E., Mauer, S., & Russell, J. (1990). The validity of employment interviews: A review and meta-analysis. Unpublished paper.

Pearlman, K., Schmidt, F. L., & Hunter, J. E. (1980). Validity generalization results for tests used to predict job proficiency and training criteria in clerical occupations. *Journal of Applied Psychology, 65,* 373–407.

Rothstein, H. R. (1990). Interrater reliability of job performance ratings: Growth to asymptote with increasing opportunity to observe. *Journal of Applied Psychology, 75*, 322–327.

Rothstein, H. R., Schmidt, F. L., Erwin, F. W., Owens, W. A., & Sparks, C. P. (1990). Biographical data in employment selection: Can validities be made generalizable? *Journal of Applied Psychology, 75*, 175–184.

Schmidt, F. L. (1988). Validity generalization and the future of criterion-related validity. In H. Wainer and H. I. Braun (Eds.), *Test validity* (pp. 173–190). Hillsdale, NJ: Erlbaum.

Schmidt, F. L. (1992). What do data really mean? Research findings, meta-analysis, and cumulative knowledge in the social sciences. *American Psychologist, 47*, 1173–1181

Schmidt, F. L., Gast-Rosenberg, I. F., & Hunter, J. E. (1980). Validity generalization results for computer programmers. *Journal of Applied Psychology, 65*, 643–661.

Schmidt, F. L., & Hunter, J. E. (1977). Development of a general solution to the problem of validity generalization. *Journal of Applied Psychology, 62*, 529–540.

Schmidt, F. L., & Hunter, J. E. (1981). Employment testing: Old theories and new research findings. *American Psychologist, 36*, 1128–1137.

Schmidt, F. L., & Hunter, J. E. (1988). Validity general-ization and situational specificity: A second look at the 75% rule and the Fisher Z transformation. *Journal of Applied Psychology, 73*, 665–672.

Schmidt, F. L., Hunter, J. E., & Caplan, J. R. (1981). Validity generalization results for two job groups in the petroleum industry. *Journal of Applied Psychology, 66*, 261–273.

Schmidt, F. L., Ones, D. S., & Hunter, J. E. (1992). Personnel selection. *Annual Review of Psychology, 43*, 627–670.

Schmidt, F. L., Hunter, J. E., & Pearlman, K. (1980). Task differences and validity of aptitude tests in selection: A red herring. *Journal of Applied Psychology, 66*, 166–185.

Schmidt, F. L., Hunter, J. E., Pearlman, K., & Hirsh, H. R. (1985). Forty questions about validity generalization and meta-analysis. *Personnel Psychology, 38*, 697–798.

Schmidt, F. L., Hunter, J. E., Pearlman, K., & Shane, G. S. (1979). Further tests of the Schmidt-Hunter Bayesian validity generalization model. *Personnel Psychology, 32*, 257–281.

# PART
# VII

## SPECIAL STATISTICAL ISSUES AND PROBLEMS

Cooper, H. and Hedges, L. V. (Eds.) 1994. *The Handbook of Research Synthesis.* New York: Russell Sage Foundation

# 22

## STOCHASTICALLY DEPENDENT EFFECT SIZES

**LEON J. GLESER**
*University of Pittsburgh*

**INGRAM OLKIN**
*Stanford University*

CONTENTS

## 1. INTRODUCTION

Much of the literature on meta-analysis deals with analyzing effect sizes obtained from $k$ independent studies in each of which a single treatment is compared with a control (or with a standard treatment). Because the studies are statistically independent, so are the effect sizes.

Studies, however, are not always so simple. Thus, some studies may compare multiple variants of a treatment against a common control. For example, in a study of the beneficial effects of exercise on blood pressure, independent groups of subjects may each be assigned one of several types of exercise: running for 20 minutes daily, running for 40 minutes daily, running every other day, brisk walking, and so on. Each of these exercise groups is to be compared with a common sedentary control group. In consequence, such a study will yield more than one exercise versus control effect size. Because of the common control group, the estimates of these effect sizes will be correlated. Studies of this kind are called *multiple-treatment studies*.

In other studies, the single-treatment, single-control paradigm may be followed, but multiple measures will be used as endpoints for each subject. Thus, exercise can be compared with nonexercise on systolic blood pressure, diastolic blood pressure, pulse rate, cholesterol concentration, and so on. Similarly, studies on the use of carbon dioxide for storage of apples can include measures on flavor, appearance, firmness, and resistance to disease. A treatment versus control effect size estimate may be calculated for each endpoint measure. Because measures on each subject are correlated, corresponding estimated effect sizes for these measures will be correlated within studies. Studies of this type are called *multiple-endpoint studies*.

A special, but common, kind of multiple-endpoint study is that in which the measures (endpoints) used are subscales of a psychological test. For study-to-study comparisons, or to have a single effect size for treatment versus control, we may want to combine the effect sizes obtained from the subscales into an overall effect size. Because subscales have differing accuracies, it is well known that weighted averages of such effect sizes are required. Weighting by inverses of the variances of the estimated subscale effect sizes is appropriate when these effect sizes are independent, but may not produce the most precise estimates when the effect sizes are correlated.

In each of the above situations, the existence of possible correlations among the estimated effect sizes needs to be accounted for in the analysis. To do so, additional information has to be obtained from the various studies. For example, in the multiple-endpoint studies, correlations between the endpoint measures lead to correlations between the corresponding estimated effect sizes; thus, values for these between-measures correlations will be needed for any analysis. Fortunately, as will be seen, in most cases this is all the extra information that will be needed. When the studies themselves fail to provide this information, the correlations can often be imputed from test manuals (e.g., when the measures are subscales of a test) or from published literature on the measures used.

Before discussing how to deal with correlated estimated effect sizes, we need to find formulas for the correlations. Note that the dependency between estimated effect sizes in multiple-endpoint studies is intrinsic to such studies, arising from the relationships between the measures used, whereas the dependency between estimated effect sizes in multiple-treatment studies is an artifact of the design (the use of a common control). This implies that formulas for the correlations between estimated effect sizes will differ between these two types of studies, thus requiring separate consideration of each type. On the other hand, the variances of the estimated effect sizes have the same form in both types of study—namely, that obtained from considering each effect size in isolation (Chapters 16 and 17). Recall that such variances depend on the true effect size, the sample sizes for treatment and control, and (possibly) the treatment-to-control variance ratio (when the variance of a given measurement is assumed to be affected by the treatment). As is often the case in analyses in other chapters, the results obtained are large-sample approximations based on normality assumptions for the original measured data.

In section 2 we present formulas for large-sample variances and correlations related to estimated effect sizes in multiple-treatment studies under various assumptions and show how to combine estimates of common effect sizes across studies using a regression model. In section 3 we give similar formulas and results for multiple-endpoint studies, and in section 4 provide a discussion of when one can ignore correlations among estimated effect sizes, at the cost of being conservative, and use univariate approaches, and when such univariate approaches are not advisable. We conclude that univariate approaches can be used for certain across-studies inferences on individual effect sizes, but that multivar-

## Table 22.1 Example of Six Studies with Five Experimental (Treatment) Groups and a Single Control Group

| Study | C | $E_1$ | $E_2$ | $E_3$ | $E_4$ | $E_5$ |
|-------|---|-------|-------|-------|-------|-------|
| 1 | * | * | * | * | | |
| 2 | * | | * | * | * | |
| 3 | * | | * | | * | |
| 4 | * | | * | | | * |
| 5 | * | * | * | * | * | |
| 6 | * | * | | | | |

iate methods are needed for most within-study inferences on effect sizes. A special case of within-study inference is when one wishes to combine effect sizes within a study into a composite or overall effect size; we consider this problem in section 5. Finally, in section 6 we briefly mention and reference some extensions of the general regression methods used in this chapter.

## 2. MULTIPLE-TREATMENT STUDIES

As indicated in the introduction, multiple-treatment studies assign independent groups of subjects to one of $p$ treatments or a control. Let the control group be denoted $C$ and the $p$ treatment (experimental) groups $E_1, \ldots, E_p$. Not all studies will involve the same treatments, because investigators may have different research goals. Part of the task of the meta-analysis will be to identify comparable treatments across studies (these are assigned a common index $j$). Table 22.1 gives an example of six studies, each of which involves a control and some, but not all, of five treatments. Asterisks indicate when a particular treatment is included in a study. Thus, for example, study 2 involves the control and treatments $E_2$, $E_3$, and $E_4$, whereas study 6 has a control and only treatment $E_1$.

An observation on the $t$th subject from the control group is denoted $y_{0t}$, whereas an observation from the $t$th subject from treatment group $E_j$ is $y_{jt}$; $j = 1, \ldots, p$. We assume that $y_{jt}$ is normally distributed, with mean $\mu_j$ and standard deviation $\sigma_j$, $j = 0, 1, 2, \ldots, p$. The corresponding effect sizes for the treatments are

$$\delta_j = \frac{\mu_j - \mu_0}{\sigma_0}, j = 1, \ldots, p. \quad (22\text{-}1)$$

In each study, the sample size for the control is denoted $n_0$. When the experimental group $E_j$ is included

in a study, the sample size for this group is denoted $n_j$, $j = 1, 2, \ldots, p$. For example, study 2 in Table 22.1 has sample sizes $n_0$, $n_2$, $n_3$, and $n_4$, but not $n_1$ and $n_5$. Although sample sizes for the control, or any particular experimental group, may vary from study to study, it will not be necessary to index sample sizes by the study number $i$ because the sample size to use will be clear from the context.

From the sample means $\bar{y}_0, \bar{y}_1, \ldots, \bar{y}_p$, and sample standard deviations $s_0, s_1, \ldots, s_p$, the effect sizes $\delta_j$ can be estimated by

$$d_j = \frac{\bar{y}_j - \bar{y}_0}{s_0}, j = 1, \ldots, p. \quad (22\text{-}2)$$

Note that $d_1, \ldots, d_p$ have $\bar{y}_0$ and $s_0$ in common. It is this repetition that creates the dependency between any two estimates of effect size within a study.

When the sample sizes are all large, the large-sample variance of $d_j$ is

$$\Psi_{jj} = \frac{1}{n_j} + \frac{1 + \frac{1}{2} \delta_j^2}{n_0}, \quad (22\text{-}3)$$

whereas the covariance between the $j$th and $j^*$th effect sizes $d_j$ and $d_{j*}$ is

$$\Psi_{jj*} = \frac{1 + \frac{1}{2} \delta_j \delta_{j*}}{n_0}, j^* \neq j. \quad (22\text{-}4)$$

The asymptotic variance (22-3) is obtained under the assumption of homogeneity of variances; that is, when $\sigma_0^2 = \sigma_1^2 = \ldots = \sigma_p^2$. This assumption is made implicitly when the primary analysis is conducted by an analysis of variance (ANOVA), because it is required for the validity of the statistical tests.

The large-sample variances and covariances, (22-3) and (22-4), of the estimated effect sizes are functions of the true unknown effect sizes, and hence must be estimated; the large-sample variances and covariances of $d_1, \ldots, d_p$ are estimated by

$$\hat{\Psi}_{jj} = \frac{1}{n_j} + \frac{1 + \frac{1}{2} d_j^2}{n_0}, \hat{\Psi}_{jj*} = \frac{1 + \frac{1}{2} d_j d_{j*}}{n_0}, \quad (22\text{-}5)$$

$$j^* \neq j, j = 1, \ldots, p.$$

When the homogeneity of variance hypothesis prevails, more precise estimates of effect sizes can be obtained by using a pooled standard deviation in place of $s_0$. In this case, the formula (22-3) for the asymptotic variance of $d_j$ requires modification. It is important to note, however, that the use of a pooled variance when there is heterogeneity of variance can lead to biased estimates of the effect sizes. When the homogeneity of variance hypothesis does not hold, a slightly more complicated formula replaces (22-3). Both of these modifications are briefly discussed later in this section.

To keep our notation simple, each study is represented by vectors of estimated effect sizes of dimension $p$ ($p = 5$ for our example), but we leave blank components corresponding to treatments not included in the study. For example, study 3 in Table 22.1 would be represented by the vector

$$\mathbf{d}_3 = (-, d_{32}, -, d_{34}, -).$$

Similarly, the estimated covariance matrix $\hat{\boldsymbol{\psi}}_3$ for study 3 is

$$\hat{\boldsymbol{\psi}}_3 = \begin{bmatrix} - & - & - & - & - \\ - & \hat{\psi}_{322} & - & \hat{\psi}_{324} & - \\ - & - & - & - & - \\ - & \hat{\psi}_{342} & - & \hat{\psi}_{344} & - \\ - & - & - & - & - \end{bmatrix}.$$

Note that the first subscript 3 refers to the study, and the remaining two subscripts indicate the estimated effect sizes for which the variance or covariance is given.

## 2.1 An Example

To illustrate the methodology, we consider a simulated set of data in which there are six studies of five treatments as in Table 22.1. The treatments are various modes of exercise; the control is no regular exercise. The dependent variable is systolic blood pressure. Summary information for this data set is given in Table 22.2.

Note that, as expected, average blood pressure is always less for the treatments than for the control. To avoid having to deal with negative effect sizes, we will define effect sizes and estimated effect sizes to be $\delta_j = (\mu_0 - \mu_j)/\sigma_0$ and $d_j = (\bar{y}_0 - \bar{y}_j)/s_0$ instead of by (22-1) and (22-2). This redefinition does not affect the covariance matrices $\boldsymbol{\psi}$ or their estimates.

The following are then the vectors of estimated effect sizes:

| Study | $\mathbf{d} = (d_1, d_2, d_3, d_4, d_5)$ |
|---|---|
| 1 | $\mathbf{d}_1 = (0.808, 1.308, 1.379, -, -)$ |
| 2 | $\mathbf{d}_2 = (-, 1.266, 1.828, 1.962, -)$ |
| 3 | $\mathbf{d}_3 = (-, 1.835, -, 2.568, -)$ |
| 4 | $\mathbf{d}_4 = (-, 1.272, -, -, 2.038)$ |
| 5 | $\mathbf{d}_5 = (1.171, 2.024, 2.423, 3.159, -)$ |
| 6 | $\mathbf{d}_6 = (0.681, -, -, -, -)$ |

The computation, using (22-2), of the estimated effect size $d_{32}$ for treatment 2 in study 3 is illustrated below:

$$d_{32} = \frac{152.45 - 140.80}{6.35} = 1.835.$$

The corresponding estimated large-sample covariance matrices, computed using (22-5), are given below. Only entries on and above the diagonal are given because of the symmetry of covariance matrices.

$$\hat{\boldsymbol{\psi}}_1 = \begin{bmatrix} .0985 & .0611 & .0623 & - & - \\ & .1142 & .0761 & - & - \\ & & .1215 & - & - \\ & & & - & - \\ & & & & - \end{bmatrix}, \quad \hat{\boldsymbol{\psi}}_2 = \begin{bmatrix} - & - & - & - & - \\ & .0713 & .0539 & .0561 & - \\ & & .0938 & .0698 & - \\ & & & .0981 & - \\ & & & & - \end{bmatrix},$$

$$\hat{\boldsymbol{\psi}}_3 = \begin{bmatrix} - & - & - & - & - \\ & .1228 & - & .1119 & - \\ & & - & - & - \\ & & & .1790 & - \\ & & & & - \end{bmatrix}, \quad \hat{\boldsymbol{\psi}}_4 = \begin{bmatrix} - & - & - & - & - \\ & .0562 & - & - & .0459 \\ & & - & - & - \\ & & & - & - \\ & & & & .0815 \end{bmatrix},$$

$$\hat{\boldsymbol{\psi}}_5 = \begin{bmatrix} .0895 & .0729 & .0806 & .0950 & - \\ & .1350 & .1151 & .1394 & - \\ & & .1669 & .1609 & - \\ & & & .2381 & - \\ & & & & - \end{bmatrix}, \quad \hat{\boldsymbol{\psi}}_6 = \begin{bmatrix} .0223 & - & - & - & - \\ & - & - & - & - \\ & & - & - & - \\ & & & - & - \\ & & & & - \end{bmatrix}.$$

For illustrative purposes, we provide details for the computation, using (22-5), of $\hat{\boldsymbol{\psi}}_3$:

$$\hat{\psi}_{322} = \frac{1}{30} + \frac{1 + \frac{1}{2}(1.835)^2}{30} = .1228,$$

$$\hat{\psi}_{344} = \frac{1}{28} + \frac{1 + \frac{1}{2}(2.568)^2}{30} = .1790,$$

$$\hat{\psi}_{324} = \frac{1 + \frac{1}{2}(1.835)(2.568)}{30} = .1119.$$

The vectors $\mathbf{d}_i$ of estimated effect sizes and the estimated large-sample covariance matrices $\hat{\boldsymbol{\psi}}_i$ of the $\mathbf{d}_i$

**Table 22.2 Summary Information for Studies of the Effect of Exercise on Systolic Blood Pressure**

| Study | C | $E_1$ | $E_2$ | $E_3$ | $E_4$ | $E_5$ |
|---|---|---|---|---|---|---|
| **Sample Sizes** | | | | | | |
| 1 | 25 | 22 | 25 | 23 | — | — |
| 2 | 40 | — | 38 | 37 | 40 | — |
| 3 | 30 | — | 30 | — | 28 | — |
| 4 | 50 | — | 50 | — | — | 50 |
| 5 | 30 | 30 | 30 | 28 | 26 | — |
| 6 | 100 | 100 | — | — | — | — |
| **Means** | | | | | | |
| 1 | 150.96 | 144.14 | 139.92 | 139.32 | — | — |
| 2 | 149.94 | — | 141.23 | 137.36 | 136.44 | — |
| 3 | 152.45 | — | 140.80 | — | 136.14 | — |
| 4 | 149.49 | — | 140.69 | — | — | 135.39 |
| 5 | 150.36 | 144.55 | 140.32 | 138.34 | 134.69 | — |
| 6 | 150.19 | 145.62 | — | — | — | — |
| **Standard Deviations** | | | | | | |
| 1 | 8.44 | 4.25 | 5.06 | 3.60 | — | — |
| 2 | 6.88 | — | 5.11 | 5.29 | 3.34 | — |
| 3 | 6.35 | — | 4.52 | — | 3.35 | — |
| 4 | 6.92 | — | 5.33 | — | — | 3.35 |
| 5 | 4.96 | 5.58 | 4.16 | 5.76 | 4.05 | — |
| 6 | 6.71 | 5.06 | — | — | — | — |

form the basis for statistical inference about the effect sizes $\delta_{ij}$. Such inferences are guided by fitting or testing linear regression models for the estimated effect size vectors $\mathbf{d}_i$, treating the estimated large-sample covariance matrices $\hat{\boldsymbol{\psi}}_i$ of these vectors as if they were equal to the true large-sample covariance matrices $\boldsymbol{\psi}_i$. Fitting such models requires use of statistical computer packages that provide generalized least squares estimators of the regression coefficients. Because not all statistical packages are programmed to deal with vectors $\mathbf{d}_i$ that have missing or blank entries and corresponding co-variance matrices $\boldsymbol{\psi}_i$ that do not have inverses, and to save unnecessary effort in inputting blanks and zeroes, it is useful to provide an alternative summary. This is done by combining all estimated effect sizes that actually appear in the studies into a single column vector $\mathbf{d}$, where the first components of $\mathbf{d}$ are the estimated effect sizes from study 1, the next components are from study 2, and so on. The resulting vector $\mathbf{d}$ for the data of Table 22.2, transposed to form a row vector is

$$\mathbf{d}' = (0.808, 1.308, 1.379; 1.266, 1.828, 1.962;$$
$$1.835, 2.568; 1.272, 2.038; 1.171, 2.024,$$
$$2.423, 3.159; 0.681).$$

Here, semicolons have been used to separate estimated effect sizes from the different studies. The vector $\mathbf{d}$ serves as the vector of dependent variables for any regression model. The dimension $f$ of $\mathbf{d}$ is equal to the number of effect sizes actually observed in the studies being analyzed. For our example, $f = 15$.

Let $\boldsymbol{\delta}$ be the vector of true effect sizes $\delta_{ij}$ corresponding to the elements of $\mathbf{d}$; this vector is the expected value of $\mathbf{d}$ in large samples. Because estimated effect sizes from different studies are independent, whereas estimated effect sizes within a study may be dependent, the covariance matrix $\hat{\boldsymbol{\psi}}$ of $\mathbf{d}$ has the block diagonal form illustrated for our example in Table 22.3.

The blocks in $\hat{\boldsymbol{\psi}}$ are matrices of the variances and covariances for the estimated effect sizes calculated in a given study.

**Table 22.3 Covariance Matrix $\hat{\Psi}$ of d in Example 2.1**

| | | | | | | | |
|---|---|---|---|---|---|---|---|
| 0.0985 | 0.0611 | 0.0623 | 0.0000 | 0.0000 | 0.0000 | 0.0000 | 0.0000 |
| 0.0611 | 0.1142 | 0.0761 | 0.0000 | 0.0000 | 0.0000 | 0.0000 | 0.0000 |
| 0.0623 | 0.0761 | 0.1215 | 0.0000 | 0.0000 | 0.0000 | 0.0000 | 0.0000 |
| 0.0000 | 0.0000 | 0.0000 | 0.0713 | 0.0539 | 0.0561 | 0.0000 | 0.0000 |
| 0.0000 | 0.0000 | 0.0000 | 0.0539 | 0.0938 | 0.0698 | 0.0000 | 0.0000 |
| 0.0000 | 0.0000 | 0.0000 | 0.0561 | 0.0698 | 0.0481 | 0.0000 | 0.0000 |
| 0.0000 | 0.0000 | 0.0000 | 0.0000 | 0.0000 | 0.0000 | 0.1228 | 0.1119 |
| 0.0000 | 0.0000 | 0.0000 | 0.0000 | 0.0000 | 0.0000 | 0.1119 | 0.1790 |
| 0.0000 | 0.0000 | 0.0000 | 0.0000 | 0.0000 | 0.0000 | 0.0000 | 0.0000 |
| 0.0000 | 0.0000 | 0.0000 | 0.0000 | 0.0000 | 0.0000 | 0.0000 | 0.0000 |
| 0.0000 | 0.0000 | 0.0000 | 0.0000 | 0.0000 | 0.0000 | 0.0000 | 0.0000 |
| 0.0000 | 0.0000 | 0.0000 | 0.0000 | 0.0000 | 0.0000 | 0.0000 | 0.0000 |
| 0.0000 | 0.0000 | 0.0000 | 0.0000 | 0.0000 | 0.0000 | 0.0000 | 0.0000 |
| 0.0000 | 0.0000 | 0.0000 | 0.0000 | 0.0000 | 0.0000 | 0.0000 | 0.0000 |
| 0.0000 | 0.0000 | 0.0000 | 0.0000 | 0.0000 | 0.0000 | 0.0000 | 0.0000 |

The most general model for the vector **d** of estimated effect sizes has the familiar form

$$\mathbf{d} = \boldsymbol{\delta} + \mathbf{e}, \qquad (22\text{-}6)$$

where the error vector **e** has mean vector **0** and covariance matrix $\hat{\boldsymbol{\psi}}$. Regression models linearly relating the elements of $\boldsymbol{\delta}$ to each other, or to specified covariates measured for the studies, can now be substituted for $\boldsymbol{\delta}$ in (22-6), yielding models of the regression form

$$\mathbf{d} = \mathbf{X}\,\boldsymbol{\beta} + \mathbf{e}. \qquad (22\text{-}7)$$

## 2.2 A Regression Model

One regression model of the form (22-7) represents the null hypothesis that effect sizes $\delta_{ij}$ for a given treatment $j$ have a common value $\beta_j$ across those studies $i$ where treatment $j$ was observed, $j = 1, \ldots, p$. The design matrix **X** and slope vector for such a regression model applied to our example are

$$\mathbf{X} = \begin{bmatrix} 1 & 0 & 0 & 0 & 0 \\ 0 & 1 & 0 & 0 & 0 \\ 0 & 0 & 1 & 0 & 0 \\ \hline 0 & 1 & 0 & 0 & 0 \\ 0 & 0 & 1 & 0 & 0 \\ 0 & 0 & 0 & 1 & 0 \\ \hline 0 & 1 & 0 & 0 & 0 \\ 0 & 0 & 1 & 0 \\ \hline 0 & 1 & 0 & 0 & 0 \\ 0 & 0 & 0 & 0 & 1 \end{bmatrix}, \; \boldsymbol{\beta} = \begin{bmatrix} \beta_1 \\ \beta_2 \\ \beta_3 \\ \beta_4 \\ \beta_5 \end{bmatrix}$$

$$\begin{bmatrix} 1 & 0 & 0 & 0 & 0 \\ 0 & 1 & 0 & 0 & 0 \\ 0 & 0 & 1 & 0 & 0 \\ 0 & 0 & 0 & 1 & 0 \\ 1 & 0 & 0 & 0 & 0 \end{bmatrix}$$

Note, for example, that the third block in **X**, corresponding to study 3, picks up the common effect sizes $\beta_2$ and $\beta_4$ for the second and fourth treatments, which are the only treatments observed in study 3.

The general theory of least squares applied to a model of the form (22-7) yields the estimator

$$\hat{\boldsymbol{\beta}} = (\mathbf{X}'\hat{\boldsymbol{\psi}}^{-1}\mathbf{X})^{-1}\mathbf{X}'\hat{\boldsymbol{\psi}}^{-1}\mathbf{d} \qquad (22\text{-}8)$$

for the vector $\boldsymbol{\beta}$. For our example, the estimate of the vector $\boldsymbol{\beta}$ of common effect sizes is

$$\hat{\boldsymbol{\beta}}' = (0.746, 1.379, 1.764, 1.846, 2.125).$$

In general, the estimated large-sample covariance matrix of the estimator (22-8) is

$$\text{Cov}\,(\hat{\boldsymbol{\beta}}) = (\mathbf{X}'\hat{\boldsymbol{\psi}}^{-1}\mathbf{X})^{-1}, \qquad (22\text{-}9)$$

which for our example is

$$\text{Cov}\,\hat{\boldsymbol{\beta}} = \begin{bmatrix} .0131 & .0038 & .0052 & .0037 & .0031 \\ .0038 & .0159 & .0114 & .0113 & .0130 \\ .0052 & .0114 & .0270 & .0193 & .0093 \\ .0037 & .0113 & .0193 & .0005 & .0092 \\ .0031 & .0130 & .0093 & .0092 & .0546 \end{bmatrix}.$$

Because $\hat{\boldsymbol{\beta}}$ is approximately normally distributed, an approximate $100(1 - \alpha)$ percent confidence interval for

| | | | | | | |
|---|---|---|---|---|---|---|
| 0.0000 | 0.0000 | 0.0000 | 0.0000 | 0.0000 | 0.0000 | 0.0000 |
| 0.0000 | 0.0000 | 0.0000 | 0.0000 | 0.0000 | 0.0000 | 0.0000 |
| 0.0000 | 0.0000 | 0.0000 | 0.0000 | 0.0000 | 0.0000 | 0.0000 |
| 0.0000 | 0.0000 | 0.0000 | 0.0000 | 0.0000 | 0.0000 | 0.0000 |
| 0.0000 | 0.0000 | 0.0000 | 0.0000 | 0.0000 | 0.0000 | 0.0000 |
| 0.0000 | 0.0000 | 0.0000 | 0.0000 | 0.0000 | 0.0000 | 0.0000 |
| 0.0000 | 0.0000 | 0.0000 | 0.0000 | 0.0000 | 0.0000 | 0.0000 |
| 0.0000 | 0.0000 | 0.0000 | 0.0000 | 0.0000 | 0.0000 | 0.0000 |
| 0.0562 | 0.0459 | 0.0000 | 0.0000 | 0.0000 | 0.0000 | 0.0000 |
| 0.0459 | 0.0815 | 0.0000 | 0.0000 | 0.0000 | 0.0000 | 0.0000 |
| 0.0000 | 0.0000 | 0.0895 | 0.0729 | 0.0806 | 0.0950 | 0.0000 |
| 0.0000 | 0.0000 | 0.0729 | 0.1350 | 0.1151 | 0.1399 | 0.0000 |
| 0.0000 | 0.0000 | 0.0806 | 0.1151 | 0.1669 | 0.1609 | 0.0000 |
| 0.0000 | 0.0000 | 0.0950 | 0.1399 | 0.1609 | 0.2381 | 0.0000 |
| 0.0000 | 0.0000 | 0.0000 | 0.0000 | 0.0000 | 0.0000 | 0.0223 |

any linear combination $\mathbf{a}'\boldsymbol{\beta} = a_1\beta_1 + a_2\beta_2 + \cdots + a_q\beta_q$ of the elements of $\boldsymbol{\beta}$ is

$$\mathbf{a}'\hat{\boldsymbol{\beta}} \pm z_{\alpha/2}(\mathbf{a}'\mathrm{Cov}(\hat{\boldsymbol{\beta}})\mathbf{a})^{1/2}, \qquad (22\text{-}10)$$

where $z_{\alpha/2}$ is the $100(1-\alpha/2)$th percentile of the standard normal distribution. For example, a 95 percent confidence interval for $\beta_2$, the common effect size for treatment 2, in our example is $1.279 \pm (1.96)(.0159)^{1/2}$ or [1.132, 1.626]. Similarly, a 95 percent confidence interval for $\beta_2 - \beta_1 = (-1,1,0,0,0)$ $\boldsymbol{\beta}$ is

$$1.379 - 0.746 \pm (1.96)[.0159 - 2(.0038) + .0131]^{1/2}$$

or [.346, .920]. Recall that the null hypothesis that any particular linear combination $\mathbf{a}'\boldsymbol{\beta}$ of $\boldsymbol{\beta}$ has specified value $c$ can be tested at level of significance $\alpha$ by determining whether or not the value $c$ falls within the confidence limits (22-10); this is a two-sided test of the null hypothesis. Thus, because 0 is not included within the limits of the 95 percent confidence interval derived for $\beta_2 - \beta_1$, we reject the null hypothesis $H_0$ that $\beta_1 = \beta_2$ at the 5 percent level of significance.

Simultaneous $100(1-\alpha)$ percent confidence intervals for all linear combinations $\mathbf{a}'\boldsymbol{\beta}$ of $\boldsymbol{\beta}$ can be obtained by replacing $z_{\alpha/2}$ in (22-10) by $(\chi_q^2(\alpha))^{1/2}$, where $\chi_q^2(\alpha)$ is the $100(1-\alpha)$th percentile of the chi-square distribution with $q$ degrees of freedom and $q$ is the dimension of $\boldsymbol{\beta}$. For our example, $q = 5$.

A level $\alpha$ test of goodness-of-fit for a regression model (22-7) versus the most general model (22-6) is based on the test statistic

$$Q = \mathbf{d}'\hat{\boldsymbol{\psi}}^{-1}\mathbf{d} - \hat{\boldsymbol{\beta}}'(\mathbf{X}'\hat{\boldsymbol{\psi}}^{-1}\mathbf{X})^{-1}\hat{\boldsymbol{\beta}} \qquad (22\text{-}11)$$

and rejects the model (22-6) when $Q \geq \chi_{f-q}^2(\alpha)$. Recall that $f$ is the dimension of the vector $\mathbf{d}$ and $q$ is the dimension of the vector $\boldsymbol{\beta}$. In our example, testing the regression model (22-7) corresponds to a test of the null hypothesis $H_0$ that the effect sizes are homogeneous over studies for all treatments, and

$$Q = 170.10 > \chi_{15-5}^2(.05) = 18.30.$$

Consequently, $H_0$ is rejected at the .05 level of significance. Because a model of common effect sizes over studies fails to hold, the tests and confidence intervals obtained above for linear combinations of the elements of $\boldsymbol{\beta}$ are not meaningful. These procedures have been presented here only as illustrations of computations and inferences that would be appropriate if the model (22-7) had adequately fit the data.

## 2.3 Modifications of Formulas

It was noted earlier that the formulas (22-3) and (22-4) for the large-sample variances and covariances of estimated effect sizes are based on the assumption of homogeneity of control and treatment standard deviations within each study. If such an assumption holds, greater accuracy can be obtained in the estimation of the effect sizes by replacing the control sample standard deviation $s_0$ in (22-2) with the pooled estimate of the common standard deviation:

$$s_{\text{pooled}} = \left[ \frac{(n_0 - 1)s_0^2 + \sum_j (n_j - 1)s_j^2}{n_0 - 1 + \sum_j (n_j - 1)} \right]^{1/2},$$

where the summation is over the indices $j$ of all treatments observed in the study. For study 3 in our example,

$$s = \left[ \frac{(29)(6.35)^2 + (29)(4.52)^2 + (27)(3.35)^2}{29 + 29 + 27} \right]^{1/2} = 4.93,$$

and our modified estimate of $\delta_{32}$ is

$$d_{32} = (152.45 - 140.80)/4.93 = 2.363.$$

Because of the change in how the effect sizes are estimated, new formulas for the large-sample variances and covariances of the estimated effect sizes are needed. In place of (22-3) and (22-4) we have

$$\psi_{jj} = \frac{1}{n_j} + \frac{1}{n_0} + \frac{\frac{1}{2}\delta_j^2}{n^*}, \tag{22-12}$$

$$\psi_{jj*} = \frac{1}{n_0} + \frac{\frac{1}{2}\delta_j \delta_{j*}}{n^*}, \quad j^* \neq j,$$

and these are estimated by

$$\hat{\psi}_{jj} = \frac{1}{n_j} + \frac{1}{n_0} + \frac{\frac{1}{2}d_j^2}{n^*}, \tag{22-13}$$

$$\hat{\psi}_{jj*} = \frac{1}{n_0} + \frac{\frac{1}{2}d_j d_{j*}}{n^*}, \quad j^* \neq j, j = 1, \ldots, p,$$

where $n^* = n_0 + \sum_j n_j$ is the total sample size in the study in which the effect size is calculated. (For study 3 in our example, $n^* = 88$.) Observe that because $n^* > n_0$, the variances and covariances of the modified estimators of effect size are smaller than the variances and covariances of the original estimators (22-2). Note, however, the warning given in the remark following equation (22-5).

What if the assumption of homogeneity of control and treatment variances in each study fails to hold? In this case, the estimated effect sizes $d_j$ given in (22-2) no longer have the large-sample variance (22-3); the correct formula for this large-sample variance is now

$$\psi_{jj} = \frac{1}{n_j} \left[ \frac{\sigma_j}{\sigma_0} \right]^2 + \frac{1 + \frac{1}{2}\delta_j^2}{n_0}. \tag{22-14}$$

On the other hand, the formula (22-4) for the large-sample covariances between estimated effect sizes in a study remains unchanged. To estimate the large-sample variances (22-14) of the effect sizes $d_j$ in a study, estimates of the ratios $\sigma_j^2/\sigma_0^2$ of the treatment variances to the control variances must be available. If the sample variances are published for the study, the ratios $s_j^2/s_0^2$ may be used as estimates, yielding the estimated large-sample variance

$$\hat{\psi}_{jj} = \frac{1}{n_j} \left[ \frac{s_j^2}{s_0^2} \right] + \frac{1 + \frac{1}{2}d_j^2}{n_0}. \tag{22-15}$$

Otherwise, the variance ratios must be imputed either from prior knowledge or by borrowing available estimates from other studies.

The modified estimates of effect sizes and/or their estimated large-sample variances and covariances can be used for inference about the true effect sizes, using appropriate regression models, in the manner previously illustrated in this section.

## 3. MULTIPLE-ENDPOINT STUDIES

Multiple-endpoint studies involve a treatment group E and an independent control group C. (In some studies, another treatment may be used in place of a control.) On every subject in the study, $p$ variables (endpoints) are measured.

To serve as an example, we have selected seven published studies that deal with the effect of coaching on SAT-Math and SAT-Verbal scores. Here, the control is "no coaching" and the treatment or experimental group is "coaching." There are $p = 2$ measures. The data are given in Table 22.4.

Consider any particular study. Because we are focusing on this one study, we can for simplicity of notation omit the study index $i$ temporarily. Thus, let $y_{jt}^C$ and $y_{jt}^E$ be the measurement on variable $j$ of the $t$th subject in groups C and E, respectively. It is assumed that the vector of measurements $y_t = (y_{1t}, \ldots, y_{pt})'$ on a subject $t$ has a multivariate normal distribution with vector of means either

$$\boldsymbol{\mu}^C = (\mu_1^C, \ldots, \mu_p^C)' \text{ or } \boldsymbol{\mu}^E = (\mu_1^E, \ldots, \mu_p^E)'$$

and matrix of variances and covariances either

$$\boldsymbol{\Sigma}^C = (\sigma_{jj*}^C) \text{ or } \boldsymbol{\Sigma}^E = (\sigma_{jj*}^E),$$

**Table 22.4  Effect of Coaching on SAT Scores**

| | | Uncoached | | | Coached | | |
|---|---|---|---|---|---|---|---|
| Study | | Sample Size | Math | Verbal | Sample Size | Math | Verbal |
| **Means** | | | | | | | |
| 1 | | 34 | 510 | 503 | 21 | 620 | 561 |
| 2 | | 17 | 383 | 385 | 16 | 446 | 375 |
| 3 | | 52 | 475.32 | 451.15 | 52 | 469.32 | 462.12 |
| 4 | | 14 | 431.43 | 393.57 | 13 | 423.31 | 436.15 |
| 5 | | 47 | 512 | 462 | 93 | 540 | 443 |
| 6 | | 45 | 630.44 | 597.47 | 45 | 641.94 | 607.22 |
| 7 | | 8 | 342.5 | 250 | 8 | 290 | 293.75 |
| **Standard Deviations** | | | | | | | |
| 1 | | | 83.6 | 102.4 | | 102.5 | 78.5 |
| 2 | | | 82.9 | 73.3 | | 104.7 | 56.7 |
| 3 | | | 88.97 | 86.19 | | 96.38 | 89.62 |
| 4 | | | 83.47 | 102.48 | | 115.48 | 100.04 |
| 5 | | | 72 | 78 | | 76 | 76 |
| 6 | | | 70.02 | 72.86 | | 56.94 | 72.1 |
| 7 | | | 65.19 | 29.28 | | 35.05 | 92.42 |

NOTE: The seven studies are reported in Zuman (1988); Whitla (1962), which reports two studies; Laschewer (1985); Reynolds and Oberman (1987); Frankel (1960); and Coffin (1987).

depending on whether the subject comes from the control group C or the experimental group E. Let $n_C$ be the sample size for the control group and $n_E$ be the sample size for the experimental group.

The effect size for the $j$th endpoint (variable) is defined to be

$$\delta_j = \frac{\mu_j^E - \mu_j^C}{\sqrt{\sigma_{jj}^C}}, \quad j = 1, \ldots, p. \quad (22\text{-}16)$$

If

$$\bar{\mathbf{y}}^C = (\bar{y}_1^C, \ldots, \bar{y}_p^C)', \quad \bar{\mathbf{y}}^E = (\bar{y}_1^E, \ldots, \bar{y}_p^E)',$$

are the vectors of sample means for the control and treatment groups, respectively, and if

$$\mathbf{S}^C = (s_{jj*}^C), \quad \mathbf{S}^E = (s_{jj*}^E)$$

are matrices of sample variances and covariances for these two groups, then

$$d_j = \frac{\bar{y}_j^E - \bar{y}_j^C}{\sqrt{s_{jj}^C}} \quad (22\text{-}17)$$

is the estimated effect size for the $j$th endpoint, $j = 1, \ldots, p$. For example, using the data in Table 22.4, the effect sizes for the effect of coaching are given in Table 22.5.

**Table 22.5  Effect Sizes for Coaching**

| Study | Math | Verbal |
|---|---|---|
| 1 | 1.316 | .566 |
| 2 | .760 | −.136 |
| 3 | −.029 | .127 |
| 4 | −.109 | .415 |
| 5 | .389 | −.244 |
| 6 | .169 | .134 |
| 7 | −.805 | 1.494 |

Because the measurements $y_{1t}, \ldots, y_{pt}$ for any subject are correlated, so will be the differences of means $\bar{y}_j^E - \bar{y}_j^C$ (and also $s_{jj}^C$), $j = 1, \ldots, p$. Consequently, the estimates $d_1, d_2, \ldots, d_p$ will be correlated, and intuitively the correlations among the $d_j$'s will depend on the correlations $\rho_{jj*}^C$ and $\rho_{jj*}^E$ between the measurements for subjects in the control and experimental groups, respectively.

Unfortunately, not all studies will report sample correlations, forcing us to impute values for the population correlations from other sources (other studies or, in the case where the endpoints are subscores of a psychological test, published test manuals). In the present instance, the correlation between SAT-Math and SAT-Verbal scores is obtained from the test manual; its value is $r = 0.66$.

The assumption of homogeneity of covariance matrices is usually needed when imputing values for the population variances and covariances. Under the assumption of homogeneity of control and experimental covariance matrices, the asymptotic variances and covariances of the estimated effect sizes are

$$\psi_{jj} = \frac{1}{n_E} + \frac{1 + \frac{1}{2}\delta_j^2}{n_C}, \quad j = 1, \ldots, p, \quad (22\text{-}18)$$

$$\psi_{jj*} = \left(\frac{1}{n_E} + \frac{1}{n_C}\right)\rho_{jj*} + \frac{\frac{1}{2}\delta_j\delta_{j*}\rho_{jj*}^2}{n_C}, \quad j^* \neq j, \quad (22\text{-}19)$$

where $\rho_{jj*}$ is the common value of the control and experimental correlations.

Estimating $\boldsymbol{\psi}$ requires us to replace the effect sizes $\delta_j$ by their estimates $d_j$ and to use either sample or imputed values $r_{jj*}$ of the correlations in place of $\rho_{jj*}$. Thus,

$$\hat{\psi}_{jj} = \frac{1}{n_E} + \frac{1 + \frac{1}{2}d_j^2}{n_C}, \quad j = 1, \ldots, p, \quad (22\text{-}20)$$

$$\hat{\psi}_{jj*} = \left(\frac{1}{n_E} + \frac{1}{n_C}\right)r_{jj*} + \frac{\frac{1}{2}d_jd_{j*}r_{jj*}^2}{n_C}, \quad j^* \neq j. \quad (22\text{-}21)$$

Although the data in Table 22.4 appear to contradict the assumption of equal population covariance matrices, for illustrative purposes we carry out the necessary computations as if the population covariance matrices are equal. At the end of this selection, modifications needed to account for unequal population covariance matrices will be presented.

Using (22-20) and (22-21):

$$\hat{\boldsymbol{\psi}}_1 = \begin{bmatrix} .1025 & .0048 \\ & .0817 \end{bmatrix}, \quad \hat{\boldsymbol{\psi}}_2 = \begin{bmatrix} .1283 & .0788 \\ & .1219 \end{bmatrix},$$

$$\hat{\boldsymbol{\psi}}_3 = \begin{bmatrix} .0395 & .0254 \\ & .0386 \end{bmatrix}, \quad \hat{\boldsymbol{\psi}}_4 = \begin{bmatrix} .1488 & .0972 \\ & .1545 \end{bmatrix},$$

$$\hat{\boldsymbol{\psi}}_5 = \begin{bmatrix} .0337 & .0208 \\ & .0327 \end{bmatrix}, \quad \hat{\boldsymbol{\psi}}_6 = \begin{bmatrix} .0447 & .0294 \\ & .0446 \end{bmatrix},$$

$$\hat{\boldsymbol{\psi}}_7 = \begin{bmatrix} .2905 & .1323 \\ & .3895 \end{bmatrix}.$$

As in section 2, every study will produce a (column) vector

$$\mathbf{d}_i = (d_{i1}, \ldots, d_{ip})', \quad i = 1, \ldots, k,$$

of estimated effect sizes. Here, $i$ indexes the study, and $\mathbf{d}_i$ estimates the (column) vector

$$\boldsymbol{\delta}_i = (\delta_{i1}, \ldots, \delta_{ip})'$$

of population effect sizes. Also from every study an estimate

$$\hat{\boldsymbol{\psi}}_i = (\hat{\psi}_{ijj*})$$

of the large-sample variance-covariance matrix of $\mathbf{d}_i$ will be calculated, $i = 1, 2, \ldots, k$.

Again, as in section 2, it will often be the case that not every endpoint (variable) will be measured in every study. For summary purposes, the convention of leaving blank the $j$th coordinate of the estimated effect size vector $\mathbf{d}_i$ if endpoint $j$ is not observed in the $i$th study and of inserting blanks into the $j$th row and column of the corresponding estimated covariance matrix $\hat{\boldsymbol{\psi}}_i$ will be followed. For purposes of statistical inference, the estimated effect sizes can be arrayed in a single column vector $\mathbf{d}$, and a corresponding covariance matrix $\hat{\boldsymbol{\psi}}$ can be formed from the estimated covariance matrices $\hat{\boldsymbol{\psi}}_i$ as discussed in section 2. Appropriate regression models for the effect sizes can then be fit by generalized least squares. A special case of such modeling is discussed in section 5.

Studies may mention the existence of missing observations on certain measured variables. This is different from the situation described above, in which an entire variable is missing in a study (not merely some observations on that variable). Rarely will the meta-analyst have access to the raw data in such studies, so that whatever methodology used by the studies to adjust for missing observations will have to be accepted without adjustment by the meta-analyst. Unless a high proportion of observations on any variable is missing, this will not seriously bias the large-sample methods described here. Nevertheless, this is a potential problem of which the meta-analyst should be aware.

## 3.1 Pooled Estimates of Variance

Formulas (22-18) and (22-19) for the large-sample variances and covariances are based on the assumption, $\Sigma^C = \Sigma^E$, of homogeneous covariance matrices within studies. If this is the case, $s_{jj}^C$ can be replaced in (22-17) by a pooled estimator formed from $s_{jj}^C$ and $s_{jj}^E$. In this case, the large-sample variances and covariances of the estimated effect sizes $d_j$ are

$$\psi_{jj} = \frac{1}{n_E} + \frac{1}{n_C} + \frac{\frac{1}{2}\delta_j^2}{n_C + n_E} , \quad (22\text{-}22)$$

$$\psi_{jj*} = \left(\frac{1}{n_E} + \frac{1}{n_C}\right)\rho_{jj*} + \frac{\frac{1}{2}\delta_j\delta_{j*}\rho_{jj*}^2}{n_C + n_E} ,$$

for $j, j^* = 1, 2, \ldots, p, j \neq j^*$. As usual, these large-sample variances and covariances are estimated by substituting sample estimates for the unknown population parameters.

## 3.2 Nonhomogeneous Covariance Matrices

When complete homogeneity of the control and experimental covariance matrices does not prevail, there may still be partial homogeneity, as, for example, when there is homogeneity of variances, but not of correlations:

$$\sigma_{jj}^C = \sigma_{jj}^E, j = 1, \ldots, p. \quad (22\text{-}23)$$

In this case we require knowledge of the correlations in both the control and experimental groups. The large-sample covariances of $d_j$ and $d_{j*}$ given in (22-21) are replaced by

$$\psi_{jj*} = \frac{1}{n_E}\rho_{jj*}^E + \frac{\rho_{jj*}^C(1 + \frac{1}{2}\delta_j\delta_{j*}\rho_{jj*}^C)}{n_C} , \quad (22\text{-}24)$$

which are estimated by

$$\hat{\psi}_{jj*} = \frac{1}{n_E}r_{jj*}^E + \frac{1}{n_C}r_{jj*}^C(1 + \frac{1}{2}d_jd_{j*}r_{jj*}^C), j \neq j^*. \quad (22\text{-}25)$$

In some instances the correlations $\rho_{jj*}^E$, $\rho_{jj*}^C$ may be known from published results. For example, correlations between SAT-Verbal and SAT-Math tests are generally known.

When no homogeneity assumptions prevail, the large-sample covariances of $d_j$ and $d_{j*}$ are

$$\psi_{jj*} = \frac{1}{n_E}\tau_j\tau_{j*}\rho_{jj*}^E + \frac{\rho_{jj*}^C\left(1 + \frac{1}{2}\delta_j\delta_{j*}\rho_{jj*}^C\right)}{n_C}, j \neq j^*, \quad (22\text{-}26)$$

where $\tau_j^2 = \sigma_{jj}^E/\sigma_{jj}^C$, $j = 1, \ldots, p$. These covariances are estimated by inserting sample values for the corresponding population parameters.

## 4. UNIVARIATE APPROACHES

The effect sizes $\delta_{ij}$, the estimates $d_{ij}$, and the large-sample variances $\psi_{ijj}$ of the estimates are the same regardless of whether $j$ is the only treatment or endpoint measure considered in study $i$ or is part of a multiple-treatment or multiple-endpoint study. The temptation thus exists to ignore correlations between the effect size estimates and pretend that they are independent. In this case, one can view the effect size estimates $d_{jj}$, $i = 1, \ldots, k, j = 1, \ldots, p$, as arising from $pk$ independent studies of the treatment versus control type and use univariate methods to compare the corresponding effect sizes $\delta_{ij}$ either across studies (over $i$) or across treatments or endpoints (over $j$).

### 4.1 Across-Studies Inferences

Using univariate methods to compare effect sizes $\delta_{ij}$ across studies for a particular treatment or endpoint $j$ is a valid approach. That is, the statistical tests (or confidence regions) used have desired probabilities of error (or coverage probabilities). The validity of these procedures follows because the studies $i$ are independent. Even so, such procedures may not be optimally accurate (efficient) because they do not use statistical information about the errors $d_{ij} - \delta_{ij}$ of estimation, $i = 1, \ldots, k$, contained in the other estimated effect sizes $d_{ij*}$, $j^* \neq j$ in study $i$. That is, the errors $d_{ij} - \delta_{ij}$ could be regressed on the remaining estimated effect sizes $d_{ij*}$, $j^* \neq j$, in each study $i$ to improve accuracy of estimation. Multivariate procedures take account of such information and thus can be more statistically efficient.

Examples of across-studies inferences for specified treatments or endpoints $j$ that can be validly performed using univariate methods are

1. tests of the null hypotheses: $H_{0j}:\delta_{1j} = \delta_{2j} = \ldots = \delta_{kj}$ of homogeneity of effect sizes over studies for

**Table 22.6 Probabilities of Type I Error for Various Values of $\Psi_{i12}$**

| $\Psi_{i12}$ | $-0.1$ | $-0.2$ | $-0.3$ | $-0.4$ |
|---|---|---|---|---|
| P (Type I error) | .063 | .073 | .085 | .097 |

$j = 1, \ldots, p$, and follow-up multiple comparisons;

2. assuming homogeneity of effect sizes over studies, either tests of the null hypothesis that the common effect size $\delta_j$ is 0 or confidence intervals for $\delta_j$;

3. if homogeneity of effect sizes is not believed (or rejected), goodness-of-fit tests for models

$$\delta_{ij} = \beta_{0j} + \sum_{u=1}^{r} x_{iu}\beta_{uj}$$

relating effect sizes to certain study characteristics $x_{i1}, \ldots, x_{ir}$, $r + 1 < k$.

On the other hand, using univariate methods to compare effect sizes $\delta_{ij}$, $j = 1, 2, \ldots, p$, *within* studies $i$ can lead to serious error. To see this, suppose that we wish to test that the effect sizes $\delta_{i1}$ and $\delta_{i2}$ are equal. An obvious way to make this comparison is to construct the test statistic

$$Z = \frac{d_{i1} - d_{i2}}{\text{Var}(d_{i1} - d_{i2})} = \frac{d_{i1} - d_{i2}}{\sqrt{\psi_{i11} + \psi_{i22} - 2\psi_{i12}}}, \quad (22\text{-}27)$$

which has approximately a standard normal, N(0, 1), distribution (assuming large sample sizes) when the null hypothesis $H_0: \delta_{i1} = \delta_{i2}$ is true. Large values of the absolute value $|z|$ of $Z$ would lead to rejection of the hypothesis $H_0$. If $d_{i1}$ and $d_{i2}$ are assumed to be independent, then one would use $\text{Var}(d_{i1} - d_{i2}) = \psi_{i11} + \psi_{i22}$ in place of $\psi_{i11} + \psi_{i22} - 2\psi_{i12}$ in (22-27). This substitution would lead to inflated values of $|Z|$ when $\psi_{i12} < 0$, and thus lead to a higher probability of Type I error than desired. To illustrate, Table 22.6 gives the probability of Type I error for a level $\alpha = .05$ test when $Z$ is calculated using an assumption of independence, $\psi_{i11} = \psi_{i22} = 1$, and $\psi_{i12}$ takes on the values shown.

Another univariate procedure that is adversely affected by ignoring correlation among estimated effect sizes is that of estimating a combined within-study effect size such as $\delta_i = (1/2)(\delta_{i1} + \delta_{i2})$, which might be used as a summary effect size for study $i$. An approximate

$100(1 - \alpha)$ percent confidence interval for $\delta_i$ has the form:

$$\frac{1}{2}(d_{i1} + d_{i2}) \pm z_{(\alpha/2)}\sqrt{\text{Var}\left(\frac{1}{2}(d_{i1} + d_{i2})\right)}, \quad (22\text{-}28)$$

where $z_{(\alpha/2)}$ is the $100(1 - (\alpha/2))$th percentile of the standard normal distribution. The correct value of the large-sample (asymptotic) variance of $(d_{i1} + d_{i2})/2$ is

$$\text{Var}\left(\frac{1}{2}(d_{i1} + d_{i2})\right) = \frac{1}{4}(\psi_{i11} + \psi_{i22} + 2\psi_{i12}).$$

If instead of the correct value, we assumed independence of $d_{i1}$ and $d_{i2}$ ($\psi_{i12} = 0$), then if $\psi_{i12}$ were actually positive, the resulting confidence interval would be too narrow and the coverage probability of this interval would be smaller than the stated confidence $1 - \alpha$. For example, if $\alpha = .05$, $\psi_{i11} = \psi_{i22} = 1$, and $\psi_{i12} = 0.3$, then the true coverage probability of a confidence interval (22-28) constructed assuming independence would be 0.915 rather than the desired 0.950.

Walsh (1947) studied the effects of ignoring correlations between observations on standard statistical procedures, such as the $t$ test, the chi-square test, and the $F$ test. As a simple illustration, suppose that $x_1$, $x_2$, $\ldots$, $x_p$ have a joint normal distribution with each $x_i$ having mean $\mu$ and variance $\sigma^2$; but rather than being independent each pair $x_j$, $x_{j*}$ has correlation $\rho$. Suppose that the usual 95 percent confidence interval for $\mu$, based on assuming that the $x_i$'s are independent (a sample from the N($\mu$, $\sigma^2$) distribution) is constructed. Then if $p = 16$ and $\rho$ is as small as 0.05, the actual coverage probability of this interval is only 0.865 (rather than 0.950). For $\rho = 0.20$, the coverage probability is 0.640, and for $\rho = 0.50$ the coverage probability is 0.515. These examples, and Walsh's results, show that it is dangerous to ignore correlational effects when comparing or combining effect sizes within studies. Alternative methods for within-study inferences about effect sizes are illustrated in section 5.

Note that the crucial difference between across-studies inferences and within-study inferences about effect sizes is that in the former case asymptotic variances of the estimated effect sizes are those implied by independence, while assumptions of independence yield incorrect variances for within-study comparisons or combinations of estimated effect sizes, leading to possibly invalid methods of inference.

Although the univariate procedures for the types of across-studies inference described in (22-27) are valid individually for each treatment or endpoint $j$, what do we do if we wish to combine across-studies inferences for all treatments or endpoints into a comprehensive conclusion? The statistics used for inference on each treatment or endpoint are correlated, making it difficult to determine error probabilities for the combined inference.

Fortunately, there are methods of simultaneous inference (Miller 1981) that allow us to ignore these correlations, at the cost of being somewhat conservative. One of the most useful of these procedures is based on the Boole-Bonferroni inequality. This method is also used to compute simultaneous tests and confidence intervals for post hoc contrasts among effect sizes.

## 4.2 Boole-Bonferroni Inequality

Suppose that $R_1, R_2, \ldots, R_p$ are rejection regions for tests of hypotheses (see 22-27) about the effect sizes for treatments or endpoints 1, 2, $\ldots$, $p$, respectively. Suppose that the null hypotheses tested by these hypotheses are all true. Then $\alpha_j = P(R_j)$, $j = 1, \ldots, p$, are probabilities of Type I error for these tests. However, when we combine the conclusions of these tests into an overall assertion, we need to worry about *experiment-wise Type I error*, which occurs if one or more of these tests falsely rejects its null hypothesis. This is given by the probability of the union $R_1 \cup R_2 \cup \cdots \cup R_p$ of the rejection regions $R_j$, calculated assuming that all null hypotheses are true. The Boole-Bonferroni inequality states that

$$P(R_1 \cup R_2 \cup \cdots \cup R_p) \leq \sum_{j=1}^{p} P(R_j) = \sum_{j=1}^{p} \alpha_j. \quad (22\text{-}29)$$

Consequently, if we desire the probability of an experiment-wise Type I error to be no greater than some prespecified value $\alpha$ (e.g., $\alpha = .05$), then we can choose the levels of significance $\alpha_j$ for the individual across-studies tests so that they sum to $\alpha$; that is,

$$\sum_{j=1}^{p} \alpha_j = \alpha.$$

It is customary to choose $\alpha_1 = \alpha_2 = \cdots = \alpha_p = \alpha/p$. Note that if a large number of treatments or endpoints are involved in the studies, then $\alpha/p$ will be relatively small, thereby making it difficult to reject the individual treatment-specific null hypotheses.

By choosing differing $\alpha_j$ values, we can emphasize treatments (endpoints) of greatest interest (larger $\alpha_j$'s are given to these treatments). Thus, if $\alpha = .10$, $p = 5$ and treatment 1 is to be emphasized, the choice $\alpha_1 = .06$, $\alpha_2 = \alpha_3 = \alpha_4 = \alpha_5 = .01$ might be used in place of the more conventional $\alpha_j = .10/5 = .02$, $j = 1, \ldots, 5$. The larger value of $\alpha_1$ gives the test for treatment 1 greater power to detect violations of the null hypothesis tested for that treatment.

Similarly, $100(1 - \alpha_j)$ percent confidence intervals might be used for a common (over studies) effect size $\delta_j$ for treatment $j$, $j = 1, \ldots, p$. Let $A_j$ be the event that the confidence interval for $\delta_j$ covers the correct population value of this parameter. Then $P(A_1 \cap A_2 \cap \cdots \cap A_p)$ is the probability that all $p$ intervals simultaneously cover their respective true parameter values. However, by the Boole-Bonferroni inequality,

$$P(A_1 \cap A_2 \cap \cdots \cap A_p) = 1 - P(A_1^c \cup A_2^c \cup \cdots \cup A_p^c)$$

$$\geq 1 - \sum_{j=1}^{p} P(A_j^c) = 1 - \sum_{j=1}^{p} \alpha_j,$$

where $A_j^c$ is the complementary event to $A_j$ and $P(A_j^c) = 1 - P(A_j) = 1 - (1 - \alpha_j) = \alpha_j$. Thus, if we want the probability that all confidence intervals simultaneously cover their respective true parameter values to be at least $1 - \alpha$, we can select $\alpha_1, \alpha_2, \ldots, \alpha_p$ so that

$$\sum_{j=1}^{p} \alpha_j = \alpha.$$

If the customary choice $\alpha_j = \alpha/p$, $j = 1, \ldots, p$, is used and $p$ is large, this will force the individual confidence intervals to be fairly wide.

A comparison of the ratio of the univariate (Boole-Bonferroni) expected length to that of the appropriate multivariate (Roy-Bose) expected length is favorable to the conservative univariate method. However, this is unfair to the multivariate procedure, which is designed to allow one to estimate not only the population means, but also all possible linear combinations thereof. If one studied the case in which one seeks simultaneous confidence intervals for a large number of linear combinations, then similar comparisons of expected lengths would favor the multivariate approach.

## 5. COMBINING EFFECT SIZES WITHIN STUDIES

In multiple-treatment studies, the treatments may all be regarded as instances or aspects of a common treatment construct. Thus, in the example of section 2 the various forms of exercise are various aspects of the construct "exercise." Instead of effect sizes for the individual treatment aspects $j$, we may wish to determine an overall (composite) effect size $\delta_i$ for the treatment construct in each study $i$. These effect sizes can then be compared across studies using a regression model.

Similarly, in multiple-endpoint studies, the endpoints may be similar measures at each of several times or may be subscales of a psychological test (for which an overall summary score may not have been given). Here, there is strong reason a priori to believe that the effect sizes $\delta_{ij}$, $j = 1, \ldots, p$, for the endpoints are relatively homogeneous, and that a composite effect size $\delta_i$ obtained by combining these endpoint effect sizes would adequately summarize the effect of treatment. Once an estimate of $\delta_i$ and its asymptotic variance can be obtained, the effect sizes $\delta_i$ can be compared across studies.

### 5.1 Obtaining Composite Effect Sizes

To obtain a composite effect size, we may begin by modeling the individual effect sizes $\delta_{ij}$, $j = 1, \ldots, p$, in each study. For the multiple-endpoint study, it might be thought that

$$\delta_{ij} = \delta_i, \quad j = 1, \ldots, p. \qquad (22\text{-}30)$$

On the other hand, as exemplified by a multiple-treatment study in which the treatments are various degrees of exercise, it might be thought that

$$\delta_{ij} = \delta_i w_j, \quad j = 1, \ldots, p, \qquad (22\text{-}31)$$

where $w_j$ represents the strength (degree) of treatment and is specified by the meta-analyst for each treatment $j$. For example, if the treatments $j$ are running for various lengths of time, the $w_j$'s might be the time spent running. (Brisk walking would then have to be equated to an equivalent running time, if brisk walking was one of the exercises considered in the studies.) Note that (22-30) is a special case of (22-31) with $w_j = 1$ for all $j$, and that (22-31) is a regression model for effect sizes corresponding (see 22-1) to the regression model

$$\mu_{ij} = (\sigma_{i0}\delta_i)w_j + \mu_{i0}, \quad j = 1, \ldots, p,$$

for the treatment or endpoint means $\mu_{ij}$.

Given the estimated effect sizes $d_{ij}$, the model (22-31) yields a regression model

$$d_{ij} = \delta_i w_j + e_{ij}, \quad j = 1, \ldots, p, \qquad (22\text{-}32)$$

where the errors $e_{ij}$, $j = 1, 2, \ldots, p$, have approximately a multivariate normal distribution with mean vector $\mathbf{0}$ and covariance matrix $\boldsymbol{\psi}_i = (\psi_{ijj^*})$. A separate regression (22-32) estimates the parameter $\delta_i$ in each study $i$, $i = 1, \ldots, k$. Assuming that $\boldsymbol{\psi}_i = \hat{\boldsymbol{\psi}}_i$ is known, the estimate of $\delta_i$ can be obtained from the theory of linear regression. It is known that this estimate $\hat{\delta}_i$ is a linear combination

$$\hat{\delta}_i = \sum_{j=1}^{p} a_{ij} d_{ij}$$

of the estimated effect sizes, with

$$\sum_{j=1}^{p} a_{ij} w_j = 1,$$

and thus is unbiased for $\delta_i$, $i = 1, \ldots, k$. For the model (22-30), the weights $a_{ij}$ sum to 1; that is,

$$\sum_{j=1}^{p} a_{ij} = 1.$$

There has been considerable interest in finding optimal (minimum variance) unbiased linear combinations of estimated effect sizes in the context of the model (22-30). Solutions that have been given, however, have treated the $d_{ij}$, $j = 1, \ldots, p$, as independent. In this case, the optimal weights are

$$a_{ij} = \frac{1/\psi_{ijj}}{\sum^{k} 1/\psi_{ijj}}, \quad j = 1, \ldots, p. \qquad (22\text{-}33)$$

These weights not only sum to 1, but are also nonnegative (as one might intuitively expect).

However, in multiple-treatment and multiple-endpoint studies, we have seen that the $d_{ij}$, $j = 1, \ldots, p$, are correlated. Here, the optimal weights are given in vector-matrix form by

$$(a_{i1}, \ldots, a_{ip}) = \left[\frac{1}{\mathbf{e}'\boldsymbol{\psi}_i^{-1}\mathbf{e}}\right]\mathbf{e}'\boldsymbol{\psi}_i^{-1} \qquad (22\text{-}34)$$

where $\mathbf{e} = (1, 1, \ldots, 1)'$. We estimate these weights by replacing $\boldsymbol{\psi}_i$ with its estimate $\hat{\boldsymbol{\psi}}_i$. The variance of this optimal minimum variance estimator

$$\hat{\delta}_i = \sum_{j=1}^{p} a_{ij} d_{ij}$$

is given by $(\mathbf{e}'\boldsymbol{\psi}_i^{-1}\mathbf{e})^{-1}$, which is 1 divided by the sum of the elements in $\boldsymbol{\psi}_i^{-1}$. It should be noted that although the weights $a_{ij}$ defined in (22-34) sum to 1, they need not all be nonnegative. In consequence, $\hat{\delta}_i$ can be smaller (or larger) than the minimum (maximum) of the $d_{ij}$, $j = 1, \ldots, p$. This may seem nonintuitive, but is explained by the fact that $\hat{\delta}_i$ is a sum of the $d_{ij}$'s each corrected for its regression on the other estimated effect sizes.

For the general model (22-31),

$$\hat{\delta}_i = \sum_{j=1}^{p} a_{ij} d_{ij}, \qquad (22\text{-}35)$$

where

$$(a_{i1}, \ldots, a_{ip}) = \left[ \frac{1}{\mathbf{w}' \boldsymbol{\psi}_i^{-1} \mathbf{w}} \right] \mathbf{w}' \boldsymbol{\psi}_i^{-1}, \qquad (22\text{-}36)$$

and $\mathbf{w} = (w_1, \ldots, w_p)'$. The variance of $\hat{\delta}_i$ is given by $(\mathbf{w}' \boldsymbol{\psi}_i^{-1} \mathbf{w})^{-1}$.

## 5.2 An Example

Very (1967) describes an experiment conducted to establish sex differences in mathematical ability, in which a total of 30 mathematical and verbal ability tests were given to 193 males and 162 females. To illustrate the methods, we have chosen a subset of four tests: addition, subtraction, division, and arithmetic computation. We treat the differences of the means between sexes on these tests, after division by 100, as if they were estimated effect sizes:

$$(d_1, d_2, d_3, d_4) = (.345, .536, .364, .109).$$

Note that only one study is being considered ($k = 1$), so that the study subscript $i = 1$ has been omitted. We assume that the model (22-30) holds and seek to estimate the common effect size $\delta$. The standard deviations corresponding to $d_1, d_2, d_3, d_4$ are .088, .154, .124, .029, and the correlations are

$$\begin{bmatrix} 1.00 & .78 & .70 & .39 \\ & 1.00 & .72 & .45 \\ & & 1.00 & .59 \\ & & & 1.00 \end{bmatrix},$$

from which the covariance matrix $\boldsymbol{\psi}$ can be determined:

$$\boldsymbol{\psi} = \begin{bmatrix} .0774 & .0106 & .0076 & .0010 \\ .0106 & .0237 & .0137 & .0020 \\ .0076 & .0137 & .0154 & .0021 \\ .0010 & .0020 & .0021 & .0008 \end{bmatrix}.$$

To determine the weights we require the inverse matrix

$$\boldsymbol{\psi}^{-1} = \begin{bmatrix} 369.29 & -121.57 & -83.65 & 64.49 \\ -121.57 & 127.75 & -48.43 & -39.24 \\ -83.65 & -48.43 & 184.48 & -250.70 \\ 64.49 & -39.24 & -250.70 & 1838.95 \end{bmatrix}$$

The column (or row) sums of $\boldsymbol{\psi}^{-1}$ are 228.57, −81.49, −198.30, and 1613.51. The total of all elements in $\boldsymbol{\psi}^{-1}$ is 1562.3. Thus the weights, which are the column sums divided by the total, are

$$(a_1, a_2, a_3, a_4) = (.146, -.052, -.127, 1.033).$$

Note that the weights sum to unity, but that some of the weights are negative.

The final composite score is then

$$\hat{\delta} = (.146)(.345) + (-.052)(.536) + (-.127)(.364) + (1.033)(.109) = .0889,$$

which is smaller than each of $d_1, d_2, d_3, d_4$.

If we compute the weights as if the four arithmetic tests are independent, the weights obtained from (22-33) are (.09, .03, .05, .83), with resulting estimate $\hat{\delta} = .156$. Although the sets of weights obtained from (22-33), ignoring correlations, and (22-34), taking correlations into account, both give more weight to the arithmetic computation test (endpoint 4), accounting for the correlations removes some of the redundancy among the tests. As a consequence, the variance of the estimator based on the weights (22-34) is $1/1562.3 = .00064$, whereas the variance of the estimator based on the weights (22-33) is $1/1425.39 = .00070$.

The formulas (22-34) and (22-36) assume that all studies observe the same treatments or endpoints. We have already given an example in section 1 where this is not the case and also have noted that a computationally convenient way of dealing with this problem is to array the estimated effect sizes from all studies into a vector $\mathbf{d}$ of estimated effect sizes and create a corresponding block diagonal estimated covariance matrix $\hat{\boldsymbol{\psi}}$. Models for the effect sizes $\delta_{ij}$, such as the ones presented in this section, can then be put into regression form by constructing a design matrix $\mathbf{X}$ and a vector $\boldsymbol{\beta}$ of slopes. Here, the components of the vector $\boldsymbol{\beta}$ are the composite effect sizes $\delta_1, \delta_2, \ldots, \delta_k$. For example, $\mathbf{X}$ and $\boldsymbol{\beta}$ corresponding to the data of Table 22.2 and based on the model (22-32) are

$$\mathbf{X} = \begin{bmatrix} w_1 & 0 & 0 & 0 & 0 & 0 \\ w_2 & 0 & 0 & 0 & 0 & 0 \\ w_3 & 0 & 0 & 0 & 0 & 0 \\ \hline 0 & w_2 & 0 & 0 & 0 & 0 \\ 0 & w_3 & 0 & 0 & 0 & 0 \\ 0 & w_4 & 0 & 0 & 0 & 0 \\ \hline 0 & 0 & w_2 & 0 & 0 & 0 \\ 0 & 0 & w_4 & 0 & 0 & 0 \\ \hline 0 & 0 & 0 & w_2 & 0 & 0 \\ 0 & 0 & 0 & w_5 & 0 & 0 \\ \hline 0 & 0 & 0 & 0 & w_1 & 0 \\ 0 & 0 & 0 & 0 & w_2 & 0 \\ 0 & 0 & 0 & 0 & w_3 & 0 \\ 0 & 0 & 0 & 0 & w_4 & 0 \\ \hline 0 & 0 & 0 & 0 & 0 & w_1 \end{bmatrix}, \quad \boldsymbol{\beta} = \begin{bmatrix} \delta_1 \\ \delta_2 \\ \delta_3 \\ \delta_4 \\ \delta_5 \\ \delta_6 \end{bmatrix}.$$

To fit the model (22-30) instead, simply let $w_1 = \cdots = w_5 = 1$. For the example based on the data from Very (1967), $w_1 = w_2 = \cdots = w_5 = 1$, and $\boldsymbol{\beta}$ is the single composite effect size $\delta_1$.

Once $\mathbf{X}$ and $\boldsymbol{\beta}$ have been constructed, fit the regression model

$$\mathbf{d} = \mathbf{X}\boldsymbol{\beta} + \mathbf{e}, \quad \text{Cov}(\mathbf{e}) = \hat{\boldsymbol{\psi}}, \qquad (22\text{-}37)$$

by generalized least squares regression. When all treatments are present in all studies, the components $\hat{\delta}_i$ of the generalized least squares estimator

$$\hat{\boldsymbol{\beta}} = (\hat{\delta}_1, \ldots, \hat{\delta}_k)' = (\mathbf{X}'\hat{\boldsymbol{\psi}}^{-1}\mathbf{X})^{-1}\mathbf{X}'\hat{\boldsymbol{\psi}}^{-1}\mathbf{d}$$

can be shown to be exactly equal to the optimal weighted estimators defined by the weights (22-34) or (22-36), depending on whether model (22-30) or (22-31) is fit. When some treatments are missing in some studies, the estimator $\hat{\delta}_i$ is the optimal weighted estimator applied only to those effect sizes actually observed in study $i$, $i = 1, \ldots, k$.

As in section 2, let $f$ be the dimension of the vector $\mathbf{d}$. That is, $f$ is the total number of estimated effect sizes in all studies. Note that the dimension of $\boldsymbol{\beta}$ here is the number, $k$, of studies. A level-$\alpha$ goodness-of-fit test of the model (22-32) against the most general model (22-6) for $\mathbf{d}$ is based on the test statistics

$$Q = \mathbf{d}'\hat{\boldsymbol{\psi}}^{-1}\mathbf{d} - \hat{\boldsymbol{\beta}}'(\mathbf{X}'\hat{\boldsymbol{\psi}}^{-1}\mathbf{X})\hat{\boldsymbol{\beta}}. \qquad (22\text{-}38)$$

To test the model (22-30), simply recall that this is a special case of the model (22-32) with $w_1 = \cdots = w_k = 1$.

If model (22-32) holds, $Q$ has a chi-square distribution with $f - k$ degrees of freedom, so the null hypothesis $H_0$ that model (22-32) holds is rejected when $Q \geq \chi^2_{f-k}(\alpha)$. Recall that a test of similar form, but with different degrees of freedom, was presented in section 2 for a different model for the effect sizes.

If all treatments or endpoints are present in all studies, then $f = kp$,

$$Q = \sum_{i=1}^{k} Q_i = \sum_{i=1}^{k}\left[\sum_{j=1}^{p}\sum_{j^*=1}^{p}(d_{ij} - \hat{\delta}_i w_j)\hat{\psi}^{ijj^*}(d_{ij^*} - \hat{\delta}_i w_{j^*})\right],$$

$$(22\text{-}39)$$

where $\hat{\boldsymbol{\psi}}_i^{-1} = (\psi^{ijj^*})$, and the null hypothesis $H_0$ is rejected if $Q \geq \chi^2_{k(p-1)}(\alpha)$. In the case of the data taken from Very (1967), $k = 1$, $p = 4$, $w_1 = \cdots = w_4 = 1$, and

$$Q = .113 > \chi^2_{1(4-1)}(.05) = 7.81,$$

so that we cannot reject the model (22-30) at the .05 level of significance.

## 6. CONCLUSION

The generalized regression approach used in this chapter applies not only to meta-analysis, but also to a wide variety of multivariate statistical problems. It can be used to fit and test a wide variety of models and hypotheses of interest in meta-analysis, both across studies (section 2) and within studies (section 5). Other models that might be considered include

$$\delta_{ij} = \beta_{0j} + \sum_{u=1}^{r} x_{iu}\beta_{uj}, \quad i = 1, \ldots, k, \qquad (22\text{-}40)$$

where $x_{i1}, x_{i2}, \ldots, x_{ir}$ are $r$ measured characteristics for the $i$th study. Such models can be fitted and tested for fit separately for each treatment or endpoint. If a study $i$ does not involve treatment or endpoint $j$, then such a study can be excluded from the model (22-40). The advantage of such an approach is simplicity; whereas a possible disadvantage is a loss of efficiency, in that correlations between estimated effect sizes within studies are ignored. Note that different collections of study characteristics can be used to model different treatment or endpoint effect sizes; thus, it might be thought that certain study characteristics (such as duration of treatment) influence treatment or endpoint 1, but not treatment or endpoint 2.

For example, if there are $k = 5$ studies in each of which $p = 2$ treatments or endpoints are of interest, and if each such treatment or endpoint is assumed to depend on a common set of $r = 2$ study characteristics through the model (22-40), then

$$\mathbf{X} = \begin{bmatrix} 1 & x_{11} & x_{12} & 0 & 0 & 0 \\ 0 & 0 & 0 & 1 & x_{11} & x_{12} \\ 1 & x_{21} & x_{22} & 0 & 0 & 0 \\ 0 & 0 & 0 & 1 & x_{21} & x_{22} \\ \cdot & \cdot & \cdot & \cdot & \cdot & \cdot \\ \cdot & \cdot & \cdot & \cdot & \cdot & \cdot \\ \cdot & \cdot & \cdot & \cdot & \cdot & \cdot \\ 1 & x_{51} & x_{52} & 0 & 0 & 0 \\ 0 & 0 & 0 & 1 & x_{51} & x_{52} \end{bmatrix}, \quad \boldsymbol{\beta} = \begin{bmatrix} \beta_{01} \\ \beta_{11} \\ \beta_{21} \\ \beta_{02} \\ \beta_{12} \\ \beta_{22} \end{bmatrix}$$

On the other hand, treatments (or endpoints) 1 and 2 might depend on different, but possibly overlapping, sets of study characteristics. For example, treatment (or endpoint) 1 might depend on $x_{i1}$, $x_{i2}$ (in study $i$), and treatment 2 on $x_{i1}$, $x_{i2}^*$, where $x_{i2}^*$ is different from $x_{i2}$. In this case, $\boldsymbol{\beta}$ would have the same form, but

$$\mathbf{X} = \begin{bmatrix} 1 & x_{11} & x_{12} & 0 & 0 & 0 \\ 0 & 0 & 0 & 1 & x_{12} & x_{12}^* \\ 1 & x_{21} & x_{22} & 0 & 0 & 0 \\ 0 & 0 & 0 & 1 & x_{21} & x_{22}^* \\ \cdot & \cdot & \cdot & \cdot & \cdot & \cdot \\ \cdot & \cdot & \cdot & \cdot & \cdot & \cdot \\ \cdot & \cdot & \cdot & \cdot & \cdot & \cdot \\ 1 & x_{51} & x_{52} & 0 & 0 & 0 \\ 0 & 0 & 0 & 1 & x_{51} & x_{52}^* \end{bmatrix}$$

Still other regression models and examples are given by Raudenbush, Becker, and Kalaian (1988). A general discussion of multivariate models for meta-analysis is given in Hedges and Olkin (1985). It should be mentioned that equation (6) in the Raudenbush, Becker, and Kalaian paper repeats an error in Hedges and Olkin in asserting that the large-sample correlation between two estimated effect sizes $d_{ij}$ and $d_{ij*}$ in a given multiple-endpoint study is equal to the correlation $\rho_{jj*}$. From the results given in section 3, it can be shown that this is not the case.

Finally, we remark that a more detailed discussion of the effects of coaching on Scholastic Aptitude Test performance (section 3) is given in Becker (1990).

## 7. REFERENCES

Becker, B. J. (1990). Coaching for the Scholastic Aptitude Test: Further synthesis appraisal. *Review of Educational Research, 60,* 373–417.

Coffin, G. C. (1987, February). *Computer as a tool in SAT preparation.* Paper presented at the annual meeting of the Florida Instructional Computing Conference, Orlando. (ERIC Document Reproduction Service No. ED 286 932)

Frankel, E. (1960). Effects of growth, practice, and coaching on Scholastic Aptitude Test scores. *Personnel and Guidance Journal, 38,* 713–719.

Hedges, L. V., & Olkin, I. (1985). *Statistical methods for meta-analysis.* New York: Academic Press.

Laschewer, A. D. (1985). *The effect of computer assisted instruction as a coaching technique for the Scholastic Aptitude Test preparation of high school juniors.* Unpublished doctoral dissertation, Hofstra University. (University Microfilms No. 86-06936)

Miller, R. G., Jr. (1981). *Simultaneous statistical inference* (2nd ed.). New York: Springer-Verlag.

Raudenbush, S. W., Becker, B. J., & Kalaian, H. (1988). Modeling multivariate effect sizes. *Psychological Bulletin, 103,* 111–120.

Reynolds, A. J., & Oberman, G. O. (1987, April). *An analysis of a PSAT preparation program for urban gifted students.* Paper presented at the annual meeting of the American Educational Research Association. Washington, D.C.

Roy, S. N., & Bose, R. C. (1953). Simultaneous confidence interval estimation. *Annals of Mathematical Statistics, 24,* 513–536.

Very, P. S. (1967). Differential factor structures in mathematical ability. *Genetic Psychology Monographs, 75,* 169–207.

Walsh, J. E. (1947). Concerning the effect of intraclass correlation on certain significance tests. *Annals of Mathematical Statistics, 18,* 88–96.

Whitla, D. K. (1962). Effect of tutoring on Scholastic Aptitude Test scores. *Personnel and Guidance Journal, 41,* 32–37.

Zuman, J. P. (1988, April). *The effectiveness of special preparation for the verbal section of the SAT: An evaluation of a commercial coaching school.* Paper presented at the annual meeting of the American Educational Research Association, New Orleans. (ERIC Document Reproduction Service No. ED 294 900)

Cooper, H. and Hedges, L. V. (Eds.) 1994. *The Handbook of Research Synthesis.* New York: Russell Sage Foundation

# 23

# EXAMINING EXPLANATORY MODELS THROUGH RESEARCH SYNTHESIS

**BETSY JANE BECKER**
*Michigan State University*

**CHRISTINE M. SCHRAM**
*Michigan State University*

CONTENTS

# 1. INTRODUCTION

This chapter describes a way to bring substantive theory directly into the process of research synthesis, something that critics of quantitative research synthesis have claimed is missing from it. We begin with a discussion of models and a rationale for incorporating models into research synthesis. A brief history of explanatory modeling in meta-analysis follows. Then we describe three approaches to the analysis of data in a "model-driven" synthesis. Finally, we mention some of the problems that the reviewer faces in conducting a model-driven synthesis and the factors that limit inferences based on models derived from quantitative reviews.

## 1.1 Models

The term "model" implies a set of postulated interrelationships among constructs or variables. Models allow and encourage the simultaneous examination of multiple relationships. In many fields it is no longer sufficient to examine only a few bivariate relationships, or differences on a few outcomes. For example, studies of gender differences in science examine more complicated questions than simply whether males outperform females on standardized tests of achievement (e.g., Smith 1966). They also explore under what circumstances one group excels, and what factors predict performance.

However, most meta-analyses focus on questions of main effects (see, e.g., Shadish & Sweeney, 1991). Critics of meta-analysis mention its failure to attend to possibly important moderator variables (e.g., Presby 1978) and the excessive simplicity of the questions that have been addressed (e.g., the criticism that interactions have been ignored). Thus, another reason for using models in research synthesis is in response to the growing complexity of primary research. To make sense of studies that are complex and multivariate requires an inherently multivariate approach. Such an approach is exemplified by the use of models in meta-analysis.

We will use as one illustrative example a model of achievement-behavior development proposed and elaborated by Eccles and her colleagues (Eccles et al. 1983). The model postulates relationships among many variables relating to math achievement (Figure 23.1) and is a product of both theoretical and empirical work. The model, originally developed as a general model of academic choice, can also be used to organize and analyze existing research, as we will show throughout this chapter.

A second example of a much simpler model is drawn from the work of Friedman (in press). Her interest is in the relationships among spatial, verbal, and mathematical abilities. A model of the relationships she has investigated is represented in Figure 23.2.

Primary studies may have examined one or more paths in such a model, with or without an explicit theoretical orientation. Like the blind man's description of the

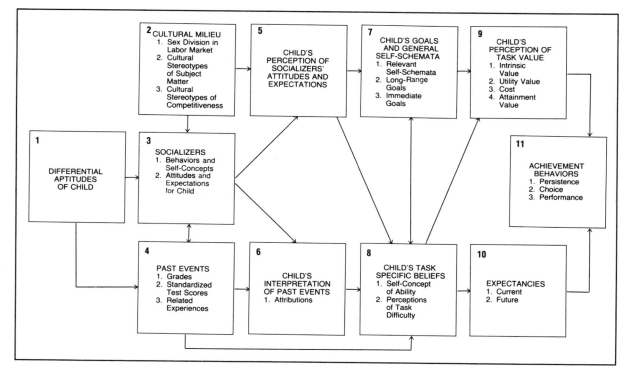

**Figure 23.1** Eccles's Model. Adapted from Eccles et al. (1983).

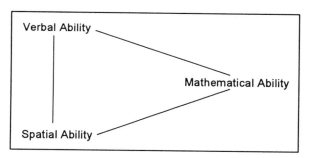

**Figure 23.2** Model of relationships among mathematical, spatial, and verbal abilities. After Friedman (in press).

elephant, these primary studies may provide many conclusions, but little understanding of the big picture that is explicit in the model (Eccles et al. 1983).

## 1.2 Explanation and Models

The nature of explanation in meta-analysis is discussed by Cook and his coauthors (1992). They detail four types of explanation, three of which are derived largely from Collingwood (1940). Two types of explanation are particularly relevant to the examination of explanatory models: Collingwood's "scientific explanation" and "explanation through predicting variation" in study outcomes.

The ideal of scientific explanation is to identify all contingencies or circumstances that lead to an event or relationship. Good scientific explanations may enable very accurate prediction of outcomes, but they depend on (near) complete specification of the chain of events to be explained. Cook et al. point out that such complete specification can be difficult to achieve in practice, especially in the social sciences.

Explanatory models that aspire to provide scientific explanations should outline all mediating variables that figure in the causal process or relationships of interest. Additionally, other contingencies (such as setting or subject factors) should be included in these explanatory models.

Examination of the two illustrative models indicates that neither is likely to provide a completely satisfactory "scientific explanation" of the phenomenon under study.

Eccles's model, which outlines factors important to the development of achievement behaviors, does not explicitly account for the impact of schooling (or instruction). Similarly, the model implicit in Friedman's work ignores any influence on mathematics performance outside of verbal and spatial skills. If we believe in any of the relationships outlined by Eccles's model, we will find Friedman's simple framework inadequate.

The second type of explanation that is relevant to our consideration of explanatory models in meta-analysis is "explanation through predicting variation" in outcomes (see also Bridgeman 1927). The premise is that we come to understand a phenomenon by accounting for or explaining variation in measures of the phenomenon. Thus, in meta-analysis we would begin to explain a relationship between two variables by first accounting for variation in the strength of the relationship due to "methodological and substantive irrelevancies." Explanation is achieved by attributing remaining variation in the strength of the relationship to substantively important factors such as types of treatment or treatment dosages. According to this view of explanation, the more variation that can be explained, the better is the explanation.

In our approach to the study of explanatory models we combine these two views. To begin, if a proposed model of relationships is to be plausible, the most important mediating variables in the model must be specified. The methods of analysis we develop below enable the reviewer to assess the explanatory power of the proposed mediating variables by examining outcome variability. We also discuss methods for assessing the impact of setting, subject, and measure characteristics on the proposed relationships and for quantifying the uncertainty that remains after methodological irrelevancies and substantive factors (moderator variables) have been examined.

## 1.3 Rationale for Incorporating Models in Research Synthesis

A first reason to examine theoretical models through research synthesis is the *importance of theory* and theoretical models in primary research. One of the goals of much primary research is to build explanations by verifying and refuting theories that claim to specify how or why events are related. Research syntheses can help build stronger bases of explanation if they can address those same issues in an explicit way (see also Becker 1991).

Any research synthesis should allow the researcher to see *patterns across studies* that are not apparent when studies are examined individually or serially. However, understanding simple differences or relationships (main effects) is rarely the sole research objective. Models provide a context for examining more complex systems of interrelationships and thereby increasing prediction. Although no single study may investigate all aspects of a process, by piecing together parts of the process studied by different researchers or studied using different samples, we may be able to form a picture of the whole that would not be available from any one study. A "synergy" among existing studies may lead to a kind of Gestalt in which the synthesized model is greater than the sum of its separate parts.

Working models of processes often help guide the conduct of primary research, and they *can guide the conduct of reviews* as well. A priori consideration of theoretical models can suggest which studies should be included in a review. Eccles and her colleagues (e.g., Eccles et al. 1983; Meece et al. 1982) have written extensively on the role of social and psychological factors in the development of achievement behaviors. The inclusion of aptitudes, past-achievement behaviors, and expectancies in Eccles's model implies that these factors are probably important to children's achievement. The model suggests that primary research on achievement *and* reviews of the literature on the process of achievement should consider these factors.

## 1.4 Objectives of a Model-Driven Meta-Analysis

We consider three possible objectives of a model-driven quantitative synthesis. First, the reviewer may want to determine the extent to which the existing research has addressed all or parts of a theoretical model or models. Next, he or she will usually want to know what the existing research says about paths in the model or models. Assessing variation in research results due to different experimental procedures or operations will be an important part of this task. Finally, the reviewer might want to create an empirical model with the existing data and to use it to make predictions based on real or hypothetical predictor values.

## 1.5 A History of the Use of Models in Meta-Analysis

In recent years a number of authors have attempted to synthesize studies pertinent to systems of relationships or interrelated collections of findings. In this section we mention several notable efforts in this domain.

**1.5.1 Harris and Rosenthal** Harris and Rosenthal (1985) examined a multivariate causal model of the mediation of interpersonal expectancy effects by using, in effect, eight univariate meta-analyses. They located 135 studies from which they extracted correlations between expectancies and mediators and between mediators and outcome. Four types of mediators were represented: climate, feedback, input, and output. Relationships of each type of mediator with expectancy and with outcome were of interest. Harris and Rosenthal calculated average correlations and tested the combined significance for each of these eight relationships or paths. The eight aggregated correlations were significant, though small to moderate in size ($\bar{r} = .07$ to $\bar{r} = .36$).

Harris and Rosenthal noted that their analysis did not account for dependencies between the paths, in part because the intercorrelations needed to assess dependence were generally not available. If a study reported more than one correlation representing a particular path, an average (median) correlation was used, eliminating potential within-path dependence. As has been true in other examinations of models in meta-analytic research, Harris and Rosenthal found that some paths were well studied (48 correlations measured the expectancy-output path), whereas others were not (only 6 output-outcome correlations were found).

**1.5.2 Premack and Hunter** Another review that demonstrates the potential of multivariate meta-analysis is a recent synthesis on employee decisions about unionization. Premack and Hunter (1988) proposed a causal model involving five predictors of the unionization decision. They used evidence from 14 studies to estimate and test that model. None of these studies had examined all six variables in the model, and between two and six studies had examined each pair of variables. However, by synthesizing correlations from subsets of the studies, Premack and Hunter estimated a single correlation matrix, which they then used to test their causal model.[1] This work demonstrates the potential for a multivariate synthesis across studies, when none of the studies have investigated all of the variables important to the research problem.

**1.5.3 Shadish** Recent work by Shadish (1992) shows the potential for building models to explain treatment effects in marital and family psychotherapies. He reviewed randomized controlled studies in which treatment and control subjects were compared on a variety of therapeutic outcomes. Shadish hypothesized that the elusive effects of theoretical orientation (i.e., the difference between behavioral and nonbehavioral therapies) would be mediated by other variables. Specifically, he examined type of outcome (behavioral versus nonbehavioral) and a series of setting and treatment variables.

Shadish and Sweeney (1991) showed that the indirect effects of theoretical orientation were significant, whereas the direct effect (assessed in a model without mediators) was nonsignificant. University setting, treatment standardization and implementation, and publication status provided a model that fit the meta-analytic data extremely well. Further commentary on Shadish's review can be found in Cook et al. (1992).

**1.5.4 Becker** Finally, Becker (1992b) has conducted a synthesis to examine Eccles's model of achievement behavior development as applied to the domain of science achievement. This analysis more closely resembles the approach we describe below than the reviews just described, but differs in how moderating variables are treated. Becker gathered over 400 correlations among predictors of science achievement and science outcomes, from studies that had examined male and female students separately. Becker asked whether the same variables were important in the prediction of science achievement for the sexes, and also whether such differences existed after accounting for setting and study characteristics. Finding that the data were inadequate to address most aspects of Eccles's model, Becker also examined a simpler model involving those relationships that were most thoroughly studied.

## 2. DATA EVALUATION

Elsewhere Becker (1989) has described how models can be incorporated throughout the research-synthesis process and the sources of invalidity that arise in doing so. That discussion is based on Cooper's five stages of the review (1982), which are problem formulation, data collection, data evaluation, data analysis and interpretation, and public presentation. Here we briefly discuss the retrieval of study outcomes and evaluation of data. We focus on the analysis of those data for the examination of explanatory models.

---

[1]The particular synthesis methods used by Premack and Hunter are problematic because they ignore dependencies among the correlations synthesized. However, the general idea behind their synthesis appears sound and is consonant with the present conception of model-driven meta-analysis.

Data evaluation in research synthesis involves gathering data on study outcomes and coding study features such as characteristics of samples, study design, and measures. Validity and reliability of measures, treatment fidelity, representativeness of samples, and other aspects of the adequacy of research methods must be evaluated.

The coding of study quality may be even more important in a theory-based synthesis than in a typical meta-analysis because of the role that evaluation of methodology plays in the evolution of theory. Chow (1987) has argued that the evaluation of study validity is the basis of the rigor of traditional reviews. Model-based synthesis methods depend (as would any synthesis) on the existing research in a field. If the research is truly inadequate, no new approach to synthesis will help. Additionally, when models are a focus, information relevant to the model or models in question should be coded. For instance, Becker (1992b) classified 192 measures from 32 studies according to the construct in Eccles's model that best described how each had been used.

At this stage the synthesist also retrieves study outcomes, typically data on relationships such as correlations or regression results. In some cases the desired data will relate to treatment effects. Eventually, it may be possible to make predictions on the basis of data about group differences in performance (e.g., a synthesized model might predict the extent of gender differences on achievement from information about aptitude differences). However, at the model-building stage, correlational data are often the primary focus.

Correlational results may be presented in a variety of ways—for instance, as simple correlations or in the context of regression or structural-equation models. The reviewer's challenge is to find ways to incorporate information presented in such disparate ways into a cohesive presentation. It may not be possible to achieve this in only one analysis. However, a proper assessment and fair comparison of research on different models must somehow include all of this information.

Primary research provides several kinds of data that may be incorporated into models. The simplest statistic used to express the relationship between variables is the correlation coefficient. Related indices (e.g., phi coefficients, contingency tables) are also common, as are biserial correlations calculated from subsample statistics.

Regression analyses, path analyses, canonical correlations, and factor analyses also yield data on relationships, but these are not as easily synthesized. Such analyses provide measures of partial relationships, via partial coefficients (e.g., partial $r$'s or partial slopes). In primary research, one way to control for the effect of a variable is to include it in a multipredictor regression equation. The slopes or partial regression coefficients in the equation represent the effect of each predictor on the outcome, while holding the other predictors constant. Similarly, path coefficients can be estimated to represent both the direct and indirect effects of each variable on the others.

When different studies have examined different regression models, they provide information about *different* partial relationships. That is, though two studies may use, say, math scores on the California Achievement Test (CAT) as predictors of science achievement, if the other predictors in the two equations are different, the slopes for the CAT math scores will not have the same meaning and do not estimate the same parameter. Furthermore, exact replication studies are rare. Thus, it is quite unusual to find partial slopes that examine exactly the same partial relationships in different studies.

It is not sensible to combine statistics that do not estimate the same parameter; thus, we focus only on the synthesis of zero-order relationships. In this chapter we discuss recent methodological developments in the synthesis of zero-order correlation matrices. Partial relationships can still be examined in the research synthesis, through the estimation of regression models based on synthesized zero-order correlations.

Such synthetic models allow for the study not only of individual paths, but also interrelationships among paths. We may believe, for example, that attitude and aptitude both influence achievement. Each predictor affects the outcome, and they may also interact. Ignoring interrelationships among predictors may lead to problems. Determining the extent of interrelationship among all three variables, and examining the individual effects of each predictor after controlling the effects of the others, is desirable.

In each case, we examine both the effect of the variable on the outcome, and the effect of each predictor on every other predictor. One goal of synthesizing models in research synthesis is to examine each path while allowing for some form of statistical control on extraneous variables—in this case, the other paths. Controlling for moderating variables allows the statistical model to more accurately represent the empirical model we wish to assess.

Synthesized models also may allow tests of fit crucial to generalization. Once the synthesis of paths is complete, examining the extent to which the relationships proposed in the model are observed in the data will provide an indication of the model's validity. If more than one model is consistent with the data, we can compare their results.

## 3. DATA ANALYSIS

A major challenge in incorporating models in research synthesis is to develop an appropriate and feasible method of data analysis. The objectives listed above focus on the existence of (or quantity of) research, analysis of the existing results, and construction of a synthetic model based on those results. Our analyses must attempt to produce information for these three objectives. Determining whether any studies have examined paths in the models is a simple job of counting. But the question of how to best analyze the existing data is harder.

### 3.1 The Form of Data and Notation

Before discussing possible data analyses, we consider what the data from a model-driven synthesis might look like. We will deal here with a case in which each primary study has presented data in the form of a set of zero-order correlations. If $p$ is the total number of variables examined across all studies, then $p^* = p(p-1)/2$ is the total number of unique correlations possible in any study. If all variables are examined in study $i$, the correlations for that study can be denoted as $r_{i1}$ through $r_{ip^*}$. For Eccles's model, for example, if a study had one measure of every aspect of the model, plus one demographic variable, the correlation matrix from that study would be a 12 x 12 matrix, and it would have 11 $\times$ 12/2 = 66 unique correlations. Usually, however, few studies will have that much data, with the exception of large-scale studies such as the National Longitudinal Study or High School and Beyond.

In a real synthesis, any study might have any number of correlations (denoted $m_i$) representing any number of relations among the components in some model. Usually $m_i$ will be less than $p^*$, but $m_i$ could be larger than $p^*$ if a study had measured the same components of the model with more than one variable. For our examples we consider a case in which most studies have examined the same number of correlations. If study $i$ has not reported a correlation for the $j$th relationship, we consider $r_{ij}$ to be unobserved. The pattern of unobserved correlations is indexed by the variable $m_{ij}$, where $m_{ij}$ is

1 if $r_{ij}$ is observed and 0 otherwise. Note that $\Sigma_j m_{ij} = m_i$.

The form of the data for a series of $k$ studies, each of which examines $m_i$ relationships, is shown in Table 23.1. The simplest case occurs when every study reports results for all $p^*$ relationships. Then $p^* = m_i$, for $i = 1$ to $k$. More often, however, most studies do not report all correlations. We denote the number of observed correlations that represent relationship $j$ as $k_j = \Sigma_i m_{ij}$.

### 3.2 The Sampling Distribution of the Correlation Coefficient

The basis of the analyses described below is a result reported by Olkin and Siotani (1976) and others. The limiting distribution of the set of correlations from each sample is multivariate normal, with variances and covariances typically estimated by substituting sample values for the population correlations in the following formulas (adapted from Olkin & Siotani). For a single sample, the asymptotic variance and covariance are

$$\text{Var}(r_{ab}) = (1 - \rho^2_{ab})^2/n \tag{23-1}$$

$$\text{Cov}(r_{ab}, r_{cd}) = [0.5\, \rho_{ab}\, \rho_{cd}\, (\rho^2_{ac} + \rho^2_{ad} + \rho^2_{bc} + \rho^2_{bd}) + \rho_{ac}\, \rho_{bd} + \rho_{ad}\, \rho_{cb} - (\rho_{ab}\, \rho_{ac}\, \rho_{ad} + \rho_{ba}\, \rho_{bc}\, \rho_{bd} + \rho_{ca}\, \rho_{cb}\, \rho_{cd} + \rho_{da}\, \rho_{db}\, \rho_{dc})]/n, \tag{23-2}$$

where $r_{xy}$ is the sample correlation between variables $x$ and $y$, $\rho_{xy}$ is the corresponding parameter, and $n$ is the sample size. We assume that correlations from different samples are independent, except as discussed below. The matrix of variance and covariance values for study $i$ is denoted as $\Sigma_i$ and the full covariance matrix is denoted $\Sigma$.

Other transformations of the correlation coefficient (e.g., Fisher's $z$ transformation) can also be used, but their covariances are somewhat more complicated than those of the simple zero-order correlation.

### 3.3 Data for Examples

The data for our example are from the work of Friedman (in press), who is interested in gender differences in correlations among measures of spatial, verbal, and mathematical ability. The five studies in our example measured verbal and mathematical abilities via the Scholastic Aptitude Test (SAT). Three different measures of

**Table 23.1 Correlational Data in a Model-Driven Synthesis**

| Study | Correlation | | | | | |
|---|---|---|---|---|---|---|
| | 1 | 2 | · | $j$ | · | $p*$ |
| 1 | $r_{11}$ | $r_{12}$ | · | $r_{1j}$ | · | $r_{1p*}$ |
| 2 | $r_{21}$ | $r_{22}$ | · | $r_{2j}$ | · | $r_{2p*}$ |
| | · | · | · | · | · | |
| $i$ | $r_{i1}$ | $r_{i2}$ | · | $r_{ij}$ | · | $r_{ip*}$ |
| | · | · | · | · | · | |
| $k$ | $r_{k1}$ | $r_{k2}$ | · | $r_{kj}$ | · | $r_{kp*}$ |

spatial ability were used. All five studies provided separate correlations for independent male and female samples. Also, although all studies reported all correlations, we have eliminated the correlations between SAT-Math and spatial ability reported by Rosenberg (1981), to illustrate the more common situation in which data are incomplete. The correlations and sample sizes are shown in Table 23.2.

Variances and covariances for all of the studies were computed using formulas (23-1) and (23-2) above. Table 23.3 shows the covariance matrices for the two samples from the study by Berry (1957). The covariances represent positive correlations between $r$'s ranging from .16 (for Corr($r_{F1}$, $r_{F2}$)) to .44 (for Corr($r_{F2}$, $r_{F3}$)).

## 3.4 Requirements of a Data Analysis

Both between-studies and within-study sources of variation contribute to differences in the magnitudes of correlational data in a review; we must attempt to account for those sources of variation in our analysis. Some differences in outcomes may arise because of between-studies differences, in samples, study design, or the relationships being studied.

Other differences will result from within-study differences. Size of correlations may vary for different relationships within a study (e.g., for relationship 1 versus 2 in our example). When more than one relationship is studied for each sample, dependencies arise because these multiple study results are correlated. It may be difficult to justify the assumption that the dependencies are minimal enough to be overlooked. In Becker's science synthesis (1992b) some intercorrelations between $r$'s (i.e., computed using formulas 23-1 and 23-2) were as high as .80, for $r$'s representing the same path, and the median intercorrelation across all relationships was .60. The intercorrelations among the $r$'s in our example range from $-.14$ to .70, with a median value of .29.

**Table 23.2 Sample Correlations for Examples**

| Study | Sample ($n$) | Correlation | | |
|---|---|---|---|---|
| | | SAT-Math–Spatial | SAT-Math–SAT-Verbal | SAT-Verbal–Spatial |
| Becker (1978) | Females (74) | .47 | $-.21$ | $-.15$ |
| | Males (153) | .28 | .19 | .18 |
| Berry (1957) | Females (48) | .48 | .41 | .26 |
| | Males (55) | .37 | .40 | .27 |
| Rosenberg (1981) | Females (51) | .42* | .48 | .23 |
| | Males (18) | .41* | .74 | .44 |
| Weiner A (1984) | Females (27) | .26 | .72 | .36 |
| | Males (43) | .32 | .52 | .10 |
| Weiner B (1984) | Females (35) | .58 | .64 | .40 |
| | Males (34) | .34 | .28 | $-.03$ |

SOURCE: Data from Friedman (in press). Starred values are treated as missing in all analyses.

**Table 23.3 Example of a Variance-Covariance Matrix for Correlations**

| | Correlation | | | | | |
|---|---|---|---|---|---|---|
| | $r_{F1}$ | $r_{F2}$ | $r_{F3}$ | $r_{M1}$ | $r_{M2}$ | $r_{M3}$ |
| $r_{F1}$ | 0.012339 | 0.002164 | 0.005302 | 0 | 0 | 0 |
| $r_{F2}$ | 0.002164 | 0.014418 | 0.007050 | 0 | 0 | 0 |
| $r_{F3}$ | 0.005302 | 0.007050 | 0.018112 | 0 | 0 | 0 |
| $r_{M1}$ | 0 | 0 | 0 | 0.013544 | 0.002604 | 0.005175 |
| $r_{M2}$ | 0 | 0 | 0 | 0.002604 | 0.012829 | 0.004542 |
| $r_{M3}$ | 0 | 0 | 0 | 0.005175 | 0.004542 | 0.015628 |

SOURCE: From Berry (1957).

Finally, though the samples are technically independent, results for subsamples (e.g., males and females) often appear correlated across studies. Such intercorrelations can arise because of similarities in sample characteristics and from the fact that the same measures are usually administered to subjects within studies. An optimal analysis would deal with both between-studies and within-study sources of variation in the correlations.

Even if our analysis is capable of accounting for both between-studies and within-study sources of variation, we may find that some variation in the correlations cannot be explained. In some cases we may *expect* that the relationships studied will vary in strength across different types of subjects, settings, or measures used. When a series of sample correlations does not seem to arise from a single population, we may wish to estimate the extent of variability in the population parameters. It may also be desirable to incorporate this estimate of parameter variation into the uncertainties of the individual correlation estimates and into analyses based on them. That is, we may wish to assume that a random effects model underlies the data.

### 3.5 Univariate Data Analysis

Once data have been gathered for the paths in the model, they can be analyzed in several different ways. One possible method of examining a set of relationships from several studies is to perform a univariate analysis on each relationship or path. Traditional research-synthesis techniques can be used to calculate an average effect for each path and to test for homogeneity (Hedges & Olkin 1985; also Chapters 18 and 19). Each study may provide more than one correlation per path, or several correlations, each representing a different path. In the example data each sample has three correlations (one per path).

A univariate analysis of Friedman's data appears in Table 23.4. The table shows average correlations, standard errors, and a homogeneity test for each path. The statistics are calculated using formulas described in Chapter 18.

When the homogeneity statistic for each path (i.e., $Q$ for each path), is compared with a chi-square distribution with $k_j - 1$ degrees of freedom, we accept the null hypothesis that the correlations are homogeneous for two of the three paths. The results indicate that the ten samples do not share a common population correlation for the relationship between SAT-Math and SAT-Verbal scores ($Q = 67.13$, $df = 9$). The weighted average correlations are .39 for the spatial–SAT-Math path; .42 for the SAT-Verbal–SAT-Math relationship, and .18 for the spatial–SAT-Verbal path.

When correlations appear inconsistent, potential moderating variables (e.g., gender, publication date, type of spatial-ability measure) can be examined. Different variables may explain the variability in the correlations along different paths (e.g., type of spatial ability tested may explain differences in the spatial-math and spatial-verbal correlations). Table 23.5 shows the results when correlations for each gender are considered separately. These results suggest differences by sex for the SAT-Math–spatial ability relationship ($Q_{Between} = 4.63$, $df = 1$, $p = .03$) but not for the other two relationships.

The univariate data-analysis approach requires that each path be examined individually rather than treating the model as a whole. Essentially, several different but related meta-analyses are produced when the intent was to do one analysis, representing the entire model.

*Limitations.* The univariate analysis overlooks several dependencies in the data. First, the paths are treated as independent, and covariances within studies that have investigated more than one path are ignored. Second, within-study covariation due to the use of multiple

**Table 23.4  Results from the Univariate Analysis of Friedman's Data for Each Path**

| Relationship | df | r. | SE(r.) | Q |
|---|---|---|---|---|
| SAT-Math–spatial | 7 | 0.391 | 0.039 | 7.41 |
| SAT-Math–SAT-Verbal | 9 | 0.422 | 0.033 | 67.13 |
| SAT-Verbal–spatial | 9 | 0.182 | 0.041 | 16.65 |

**Table 23.5  Results from the Univariate Analysis by Gender for Each Path**

| Relationship | Females | | | | Males | | | |
|---|---|---|---|---|---|---|---|---|
| | df | r. | SE(r.) | Q | df | r. | SE(r.) | Q |
| SAT-Math–spatial | 3 | 0.480 | 0.056 | 2.31 | 3 | 0.312 | 0.053 | 0.47 |
| SAT-Math–SAT-Verbal | 4 | 0.443 | 0.047 | 47.56 | 4 | 0.400 | 0.047 | 19.17 |
| SAT-Verbal–spatial | 4 | 0.176 | 0.060 | 12.48 | 4 | 0.187 | 0.055 | 4.16 |

samples is also ignored, though subsample correlations may be related because of similarities in sample and design characteristics. Each study from Friedman (in press) provided correlations for males and for females, and the analysis above treated them as independent. Also, two of the four studies are by the same author (Weiner 1984) and may be interrelated because sample characteristics are similar (e.g., the two gifted samples studied by Weiner may be more similar than other unselected samples) or because of other similarities in methods. All of these features may yield moderate to severe dependencies. Modeling within-sample dependencies should lead to more accurate error rates and ensure that samples that provide more data do not overinfluence the results. In addition, the analysis exhibited thus far has not explicitly addressed the question of between-studies differences. Further univariate analyses (e.g., as described in Chapter 19) can be conducted to investigate between-studies differences.

### 3.6  Random Effects and Mixed Model Analyses

Random effects and mixed model analyses are appropriate when the reviewer expects the patterns of *population* correlations among a set of variables to differ across studies. When different subject groups have been sampled and different measures used, it may be more reasonable to expect random *parameter* variation, which may not be completely "explained" by a set of fixed predictor variables.

The simplest random effects model consists of models at two levels or stages. The first (within-study) level might describe each sample correlation as being composed of the population correlation for the study plus some random variation ($e_{ij}$). Specifically, in study $i$,

$$r_{ij} = \rho_{ij} + e_{ij}, \text{ for } j = 1 \text{ to } m_i \text{ and } i = 1 \text{ to } k. \quad (23\text{-}3)$$

The index $j$ represents the relationship or path examined. (More complicated within-study models are possible.)

The second-stage model shows the population correlation for each study varying around a mean population correlation for the $j$th relationship, across studies. We write

$$\rho_{ij} = \rho_j + u_{ij}, \text{ for } j = 1 \text{ to } p^* \text{ and } i = 1 \text{ to } k. \quad (23\text{-}4)$$

Combining models (23-3) and (23-4) we obtain

$$r_{ij} = \rho_j + u_{ij} + e_{ij}, \text{ for } j = 1 \text{ to } p^* \text{ and } i = 1 \text{ to } k. \quad (23\text{-}5)$$

In this model the correlation $r_{ij}$ differs from a common correlation $\rho_j$ for the $j$th relationship because of two factors: within-study variation (represented by $e_{ij}$) and between-studies *parameter* variability (represented by $u_{ij}$). The goal, if the random effects model is deemed appropriate, is to estimate both components of variation.

Much of the literature about analysis of random effects models in the social sciences deals with the case of normally distributed outcomes. Since the sampling distribution of the correlation is asymptotically normal, when the data are complete, standard methods for hierarchical analysis can be applied directly. Sampling error in the individual correlations (the $e_{ij}$ error components) and covariances among relationships within the same study are estimated via the formulas given in (23-1) and (23-2) above and incorporated into the analysis via the variance-covariance matrix for the $r$'s.

The goal is to estimate the variation and covariation among the $u_{ij}$'s. We typically assume that parameter variation is constant across studies; thus we have

$$\text{Var}\,(u_{ij}) = \tau_{jj}, \qquad \text{for } j = 1 \text{ to } p^*, \text{ and}$$
$$\text{Cov}\,(u_{ij}, u_{ij'}) = \tau_{jj'}, \qquad \text{for } j, j' = 1 \text{ to } p^*.$$

The elements, $\tau_{jj'}$, for $j, j' = 1$ to $p^*$ thus form the matrix **T**, which is the variance-covariance matrix of the vector $\mathbf{u_i}$.

Among random effects and mixed model analyses, hierarchical linear models have received considerable attention. Hierarchical data analyses have an advantage over univariate analyses because they allow for the modeling of variation and covariation both between and within studies (see, e.g., Raudenbush & Bryk 1985). The results (e.g., from Bryk et al.'s 1989 HLM or Longford's 1988 VARCL) typically display estimates of the average correlation matrix containing all relationships or paths, as well as estimates of the **T** matrix. Sampling variation can be acknowledged by specifying that the within-study or conditional variances of the observations (i.e., study outcomes) are known. Tests of fit for the paths can be obtained using estimates of sampling variation and parameter variation and covariation. Additional variation in the correlations can be modeled by specifying predictors at either of the stages of the hierarchical model.

However, current software limits hierarchical analyses to data with a strict multivariate structure. Each study must report the same number of correlations and must examine every path in the model. Most collections of study outcomes will probably not conform to the required multivariate structure; thus, hierarchical analysis (i.e., without any modification) will currently be impossible in most cases. (This is also discussed in Becker 1992b.)

**3.6.1 Other random effects analyses** Becker (1992c) has presented two method of moments estimators of the random effects **T** matrix that do not require complete data. Also, these estimators do not require distributional assumptions for the correlations. However, the estimators have a weakness: They can produce values that are out of range (e.g., negative $\tau_{jj}$ estimates), which can occur fairly frequently when the numbers of correlations being synthesized are small. Consequently, these esti-

mators can also produce estimated **T** matrices that are not positive definite.

A preferable estimate of **T** is obtained through use of the EM algorithm. This approach also provides an estimate of the average correlation matrix and improved estimates of the individual study parameters (the $\rho_{ij}$'s). Additionally, the EM estimation procedure can accommodate situations in which some correlations have not been observed.

**3.6.2 The EM estimation of $\rho_j$ and T** The EM approach first requires initial estimates of **T** and $\rho_1$ through $\rho_{p^*}$ (the average correlations). Because these are starting values, simple estimators are typically all that is needed. Here we use weighted method of moments estimators of $\rho_j$ and $\tau_{jj'}$, as described in the appendix. These estimators are superscripted with the index zero to indicate that they are starting values.

The estimation of **T** using the EM algorithm next requires the imputation (substitution) of values for any unobserved correlations (see, e.g., Little & Rubin 1987). Values of the missing $r$'s are predicted based on a regression model derived from the observed correlations. (Technically, we substitute the expected value of each missing correlation, conditional on the observed data and parameters estimated from the complete data.) Thus, since two values of $r_{i1}$ are missing in our example, we predict $r_{i1}$ from $r_{i2}$ and $r_{i3}$ for the eight samples in which data are complete. The regression model (obtained via generalized least squares regression) is

$$\hat{r}_{i1} = 0.388 - 0.024\,r_{i2} + 0.062\,r_{i3},$$

which produces predicted values for the Rosenberg samples of $r_{51} = .391$ and $r_{61} = .398$. These values are then used to compute the needed variances and covariances. Becker (1992a) proposed variances adjusted for the fact that the values were predicted (not observed). However, for our example we use formulas (23-1) and (23-2) to compute the variances and covariances involving $r_{51}$ and $r_{61}$. The imputed $r_{ij}$ values are thereby viewed as no more imprecise than if they had been observed for a sample of size $n_i$.

The posterior distribution of the values $\rho_{11}, \ldots,$ $\rho_{1p^*}, \ldots, \rho_{k1}, \ldots, \rho_{kp^*}$ (given the data) is then used to obtain estimates of the study parameters. These are essentially weighted combinations of the original data (the $r$'s) and the "prior" values of the mean correlations $\rho_1$ through $\rho_{p^*}$. Then a new estimate of **T** is obtained from the sufficient statistics for the study-parameter estimates. This process of estimation and maximization is repeated until the likelihood function is maximized (i.e., until the values of **T** and $\rho_1$ through $\rho_{p^*}$ do not change much from one iteration to the next). Further details of the EM estimation procedure and a computer routine are given in the technical appendix to the chapter.

Also, if initial values for the missing data have been imputed (and their standard errors computed), the augmented data set can then be submitted to analysis by one of the standard hierarchical analysis programs that uses the EM algorithm in its estimation (such as HLM). Once missing data have been "filled in" to produce a complete multivariate data set, a program that employs the EM algorithm can be used because the prediction of the missing $r$ values does not need to be repeated on each iteration.

*Example.* As mentioned above, in our example the initial estimates of the **T** matrix and the mean correlations computed from the original data set were

$$\mathbf{r.} = (.39, .42, .18)',$$

and

$$\hat{\mathbf{T}}^{(0)} = \begin{bmatrix} .0007 & -.0002 & -.0044 \\ -.0002 & .0723 & .0396 \\ -.0044 & .0396 & .0146 \end{bmatrix}.$$

The two unobserved correlations were then replaced by $r_{51} = .391$ and $r_{61} = .398$. The estimation of **T** and the mean correlations $\rho_1$ through $\rho_3$ was accomplished using the matrix utilities (PROC IML) of the Statistical Analysis System (SAS). After 40 iterations the estimates of the mean correlations were

$$\rho_1 = .394, \; \rho_2 = .424, \text{ and } \rho_3 = .226,$$

and the final $\hat{\mathbf{T}}$ matrix was

$$\hat{\mathbf{T}} = \begin{bmatrix} .0011 & .0006 & .0002 \\ .0006 & .0620 & .0329 \\ .0002 & .0329 & .0181 \end{bmatrix}.$$

Inspection of the standard errors shows the parameter variation to be the greatest for the values of $\rho_{i2}$, that is, for the relationship between SAT-Math and SAT-Verbal. This is consistent with the results of the univariate analyses in Table 23.3.

## 3.7 Generalized Least Squares

Generalized least squares (GLS) regression is a more feasible and flexible approach to analyzing data from a model-based synthesis than the computationally intensive EM algorithm. GLS estimation can be used regardless of whether all correlations are observed. It provides estimates of a common set of correlations across studies, and the resulting estimated $r$'s (and their variance-covariance matrix) can be used to obtain a "synthetic" standardized regression equation for predicting some variable from the others. GLS estimation also can be applied whether a fixed or random effects model is assumed to underlie the series of studies. GLS estimation techniques are described in detail by Becker (1992c).

Another procedure available with GLS is a test of whether the pooled correlation matrix is a good representation of a common population matrix for all of the studies (i.e., a test for homogeneity). Also, more complicated models on the correlations can be estimated (e.g., separate matrices for subgroups such as the sexes). The only variation that the GLS approach ignores is the within-study correlation between results for subsamples.

To accomplish the GLS analysis the correlations in Table 23.1 would be written as a single vector of correlations. Correlations from different samples are considered independent, but within samples they are dependent. The dependencies among the correlations are represented by their variance-covariance matrix. When two correlations arise from independent samples, their covariance (an off-diagonal element in the $\mathbf{\Sigma}$ matrix) is zero. If a random effects model is assumed to underlie the series of studies (e.g., model 23-5 above), the variance-covariance matrix of the correlations would be $\mathbf{T} + \mathbf{\Sigma}$. (Note that an estimate of **T** is still needed for this random effects model.)

### 3.7.1 A model of a common population correlation matrix
We begin the GLS analysis by writing a fixed effects model for the correlation vector. The simplest model shows a population correlation for each relationship, or

$$r_{ij} = \rho_j + e_{ij}, \text{ for } i = 1 \text{ to } k \text{ and } j = 1 \text{ to } p^*. \quad (23\text{-}6)$$

This model can be written as a multiple regression model, in which the product of a matrix **X** (of zeros and ones) and a set of population correlations $\rho_1$ through $\rho_{p^*}$ predicts the values of the sample correlations.

We begin by considering the case in which all samples have reported all correlations of interest (here, all $p^* = 3$ correlations). The **X** matrix would be a stack of $k = 10$ $p^* \times p^*$ (here, 3 x 3) identity matrices, one for each sample. Within the GLS framework many other models (and corresponding **X** matrices) are possible. (For example, we also estimate separate sets of correlations for males and females in section 3.7.3.) The model for a single underlying correlation matrix is

$$\mathbf{r} = \mathbf{X}\boldsymbol{\rho}_{\boldsymbol{\cdot}} + \mathbf{e} = \begin{bmatrix} 1 & 0 & 0 \\ 0 & 1 & 0 \\ 0 & 0 & 1 \\ - & - & - \\ 1 & 0 & 0 \\ 0 & 1 & 0 \\ 0 & 0 & 1 \\ & \cdot & \\ & \cdot & \\ & \cdot & \\ 1 & 0 & 0 \\ 0 & 1 & 0 \\ 0 & 0 & 1 \end{bmatrix} \begin{bmatrix} \rho_1 \\ \rho_2 \\ \rho_3 \end{bmatrix} + \mathbf{e}.$$

As above, $\rho_1$ is the SAT-Math–spatial ability population correlation, $\rho_2$ is the SAT-Math–SAT-Verbal population correlation, and $\rho_3$ is the SAT-Verbal—spatial ability correlation.

Becker (1992a) has discussed a number of ways to estimate the common correlation vector when some studies do not report all $p*$ correlations. In the GLS approach, the vector $\mathbf{r}$ and the matrix $\mathbf{X}$ are reduced by removing the rows that represent unobserved correlations. The covariance matrix for the vector $\mathbf{r}$ is reduced by removing rows and columns that correspond to unobserved $r$'s. Also, other covariances involving unobserved $r$'s will be missing. To compute the covariance between correlations $r_{ab}$ and $r_{bc}$ in a study, for example, we need $r_{ac}$. Thus, even when all the correlations *of interest* are available, it may still be impossible to estimate a covariance matrix for them. In our GLS analyses we estimate covariances involving unobserved correlations by replacing those missing $r$'s with the corresponding mean estimated via the univariate analysis (i.e., $r_1 = .391$).

The usual GLS formulas,

$$\hat{\boldsymbol{\rho}}_{\boldsymbol{\cdot}} = (\mathbf{X}' \; \boldsymbol{\Sigma}^{-1} \; \mathbf{X})^{-1} \; \mathbf{X}' \; \boldsymbol{\Sigma}^{-1} \; \mathbf{r} \qquad (23\text{-}7)$$

and

$$\hat{\mathbf{V}}(\hat{\boldsymbol{\rho}}_{\boldsymbol{\cdot}}) = (\mathbf{X}' \; \boldsymbol{\Sigma}^{-1} \; \mathbf{X})^{-1}, \qquad (23\text{-}8)$$

give the pooled correlations and their standard errors, which for our example are shown in the first columns of Table 23.6. These computations can be accomplished using SAS PROC IML or any other matrix utility, or via some spreadsheets. Our examples were computed using matrix operations in SAS and in the PlanPerfect 5.0 spreadsheet program (from WordPerfect Corporation).

Each of the correlations differs from zero at very stringent alpha levels. SAT-Math and SAT-Verbal scores are positively correlated, as are spatial skills and scores on both sections of the Scholastic Aptitude Test. The full variance-covariance matrix for the mean correlations is

$$\hat{\mathbf{V}}(\hat{\boldsymbol{\rho}}_{\boldsymbol{\cdot}}) = \begin{bmatrix} .0014 & .0001 & .0004 \\ .0001 & .0011 & .0004 \\ .0004 & .0004 & .0015 \end{bmatrix}$$

An overall test of the significance of the correlation vector (a test of $H_0$: $\boldsymbol{\rho} = \mathbf{0}$) is given by

$$Q_B = \hat{\boldsymbol{\rho}}_{\boldsymbol{\cdot}}' \; (\mathbf{X}' \; \boldsymbol{\Sigma}^{-1} \; \mathbf{X}) \; \hat{\boldsymbol{\rho}}_{\boldsymbol{\cdot}}, \qquad (23\text{-}9)$$

which under $H_0$ is a chi-square with $p*$ degrees of freedom. For this example $Q_B = 254.57$, which under $H_0$ is a chi-square with $p* = 3$ degrees of freedom. As expected, the value is highly significant.

**3.7.2 A test of homogeneity** We next test the hypothesis that this single correlation matrix adequately describes all of our sample results. When such a "test of fit" of the proposed model is applied to these data, they do not appear consistent with a single underlying correlation matrix. The test for residual variation, described by Becker (1992c), is

$$Q_E = \mathbf{r}' \; \boldsymbol{\Sigma}^{-1} \; \mathbf{r} - Q_B, \qquad (23\text{-}10)$$

where $Q_B$ is defined in (23-9). The statistic $Q_E$ has a chi-square distribution under the null model that a single population matrix underlies all studies (i.e., explains all of the variation in the observed correlations). For our example the statistic is $Q_E = 81.84$, which is a chi-square with $m - p* = 25$ degrees of freedom. The value is significant, suggesting that all samples do not share a common population correlation matrix ($p \leq .001$).

**3.7.3 Modeling between-studies differences in correlation matrices** Sometimes a single correlation matrix will not adequately describe the results of all populations studied. At other times a synthesist may wish to estimate separate correlation matrices for some groups of studies even when a single matrix adequately characterizes all studies. In the case of Friedman's data, there is strong motivation to examine the correlation matrices separately by sex.

Thus, a second GLS analysis was conducted to examine the model of separate correlations for males and females. The model for this case was

**Table 23.6 Correlations Estimated via Generalized Least Squares: Pooled and by Gender**

|  | Pooled | By Gender | |
|---|---|---|---|
|  |  | Females | Males |
| SAT-Math–spatial | .373 (.037) | .407 (.053) | .341 (.052) |
| SAT-Math–SAT-Verbal | .436 (.033) | .467 (.046) | .405 (.047) |
| SAT-Verbal–spatial | .226 (.039) | .258 (.055) | .196 (.054) |

NOTE: Estimated standard errors are in parentheses.

$$\mathbf{r} = \mathbf{X}\boldsymbol{\rho}_S + \mathbf{e} = \begin{bmatrix} 1\,0\,0\,0\,0\,0 \\ 0\,1\,0\,0\,0\,0 \\ 0\,0\,1\,0\,0\,0 \\ 0\,0\,0\,1\,0\,0 \\ 0\,0\,0\,0\,1\,0 \\ 0\,0\,0\,0\,0\,1 \\ .\qquad. \\ .\qquad. \\ .\qquad. \\ 0\,0\,0\,1\,0\,0 \\ 0\,0\,0\,0\,1\,0 \\ 0\,0\,0\,0\,0\,1 \end{bmatrix} \begin{bmatrix} \rho_{F1} \\ \rho_{F2} \\ \rho_{F3} \\ \rho_{M1} \\ \rho_{M2} \\ \rho_{M3} \end{bmatrix} + \mathbf{e}.$$

As above, rows of $\mathbf{r}$ and $\mathbf{X}$ corresponding to the unobserved correlations from Rosenberg's study were eliminated from the matrices. The correlations pooled across the five female samples are in column 2 and those for the five male samples are in the last column of Table 23.6.

Again, for this model we can conduct tests of model adequacy and of the hypothesis that the average correlations differ from zero. For the model that estimates separate correlations for the sexes we compute $Q_B = 256.21$ ($df = 6$), which again suggests that at least one population correlation differs from zero (and the standard errors in Table 23.6 show that indeed all of the population correlations appear different from zero). Also, $Q_E = 80.19$ ($df = 22$), and is significant, indicating remaining unexplained variation.

**3.7.4 Random effects models** We can also use the GLS approach when it is assumed that a random effects model (such as 23-5) underlies the series of correlations. If we assume that $r_{ij} = \rho_j + u_{ij} + e_{ij}$ for all $i$ and $j$, then estimation of an average correlation matrix (and its variance matrix) would proceed as above with the exception that we would use the matrix $(\boldsymbol{\Sigma} + \mathbf{T})$ as the variance of $\mathbf{r}$, in place of $\boldsymbol{\Sigma}$ in (23-7) through (23-10) above.

In our example data we use the estimate of $\mathbf{T}$ obtained via the EM algorithm in combination with the standard GLS formulas in (23-7) and (23-8) to obtain the average correlation matrix under the random effects model as

$$(.397, .422, .225),$$

with variance-covariance matrix

$$\hat{\mathbf{V}}(\hat{\rho}_{\cdot}) = \begin{bmatrix} .0016 & .0002 & .0004 \\ .0002 & .0074 & .0038 \\ .0004 & .0038 & .0034 \end{bmatrix}.$$

The mean correlations are similar to those from the fixed effects analysis, but the estimated variances are larger, especially for the second and third correlations. The variance of the SAT-Math–SAT-Verbal correlation (the second variance) is more than six times larger than the variance estimated under the fixed effects model. The variance of the SAT-Verbal–spatial ability correlation approximately doubles when parameter variation is incorporated into the estimate. Because the homogeneity test indicates that the series of correlation matrices does not seem to arise from a single population, the random effects model is more appropriate for our data.

### 3.8 Estimating a Synthesized Model

Once we have a synthesized correlation matrix that gives a reasonable description of the correlations for our population(s), we might want to derive a predictive model for some outcome variable in the matrix. Such a model might provide one way of accomplishing the third objective of the model-driven meta-analysis—the creation of an empirical model. Additionally, such a model provides the reviewer with a means for exploring various partial and indirect relationships among variables, at the synthesis level.

We can estimate a standardized regression equation for one variable (the outcome) based on the other variables (the predictors) in the pooled matrix. The limiting distribution of the estimated regression coefficients can then be used to compute confidence intervals or conduct significance tests, as desired. In Friedman's data the outcome variable is the SAT-Math. Thus, we can derive a regression equation for predicting performance on SAT-Math on the basis of knowledge of the correlations of spatial ability scores and of SAT-Verbal scores with SAT-Math.

The pooled matrix is partitioned as shown in Figure 23.3 so that the correlations of the predictors with the outcome (here, SAT-Math) are contained in $\mathbf{R}_{01}$ (and $\mathbf{R}_{10}$), and the correlations among the predictors are in $\mathbf{R}_{11}$. Since there are only two predictors in this example, $\mathbf{R}_{11}$ contains only a single correlation. The estimator of the regression slope is the vector $\mathbf{b} = \mathbf{R}_{11}^{-1} \mathbf{R}_{01}$. This is analogous to the formula for standardized regression in a single sample given, for instance, by Cooley and Lohnes (1971).

The variance matrix of the slope estimates is obtained via the formula

$$\hat{\mathbf{V}}(\mathbf{b}) = \mathbf{J} \ \hat{\mathbf{V}}(\hat{\boldsymbol{\rho}}_{\bullet}) \ \mathbf{J}',$$

where $\mathbf{J}$ is the matrix of the first derivatives of the formulas for the $b_j$ values (see Becker 1992c for more details).

**3.8.1 A fixed effects example** For Friedman's data, under the assumption of a fixed effects model we use the estimated correlations from the first column of Table 23.6. The standardized regression slopes (the $b$'s) are $b_1 = .29$ for predicting SAT-Math from spatial ability and $b_2 = .37$ for the SAT-Verbal predictor. The variance matrix for $\mathbf{b}$ is estimated as

$$\hat{\mathbf{V}}(\mathbf{b}) = \begin{bmatrix} .0015 & -.0005 \\ -.0005 & .0011 \end{bmatrix} .$$

Thus, the standard errors of both slopes are small; each is less than .04.

With these results we can compute large-sample tests and confidence intervals for the slope parameters or differences between them. (These techniques are described in more detail in Becker 1992c.) For instance, we can test the hypothesis that the two standardized slopes are equal. The $z$ test value

$$z = (b_1 - b_2)/\sqrt{\hat{\mathbf{V}}(b_1) + \hat{\mathbf{V}}(b_2) - 2 \ \hat{\mathrm{Cov}}(b_1, \ b_2)} = -1.33$$

indicates that the two ability variables contribute roughly equally to the prediction of SAT-Math.

Confidence intervals for the slope parameters are based on the standard errors and the normal distribution. Ninety-five percent confidence intervals are

$$0.21 = b_1 - 1.96 \ \sqrt{\hat{\mathbf{V}}(b_1)} \leq \beta_1 \leq$$
$$b_1 + 1.96 \ \sqrt{\hat{\mathbf{V}}(b_1)} = 0.37$$

for spatial ability and

$$0.30 = b_2 - 1.96 \ \sqrt{\hat{\mathbf{V}}(b_2)} \leq \beta_2 \leq$$
$$b_2 + 1.96 \ \sqrt{\hat{\mathbf{V}}(b_2)} = 0.44$$

for SAT-Verbal. These intervals suggest that verbal ability as measured by the SAT-Verbal is somewhat more important to the prediction of SAT-Math scores than spatial ability, with a one standard deviation change in SAT-Verbal leading to between a third and a half of a standard deviation change in SAT-Math. The amount of change expected for spatial aptitude is slightly less than that amount.

| Notation for a General Matrix | | Pooled Matrix from Friedman Data | | | |
|---|---|---|---|---|---|
| | | | M | S | V |
| 1 | $\mathbf{R}_{10}$ | M | 1 | .37 | .44 |
| $\mathbf{R}_{01}$ | $\mathbf{R}_{11}$ | S | .37 | 1 | .23 |
| | | V | .44 | .23 | 1 |

**Figure 23.3** Partitioning the Pooled Correlation Matrix

**3.8.2 A random effects example** We can also use the average correlations estimated under the random effects model and their variance matrix to compute the standardized regression coefficients and their standard errors. The slopes based on the random effects model are similar to those obtained under the fixed effects assumptions, but are slightly closer to each other. The slope for predicting SAT-Math from spatial ability is .32 and the slope is .35 for the SAT-Verbal predictor. The standard errors of the slopes are both larger than those obtained above, with values of .051 for $b_1$ and .080 for $b_2$. The standard error of $b_2$ (the slope for SAT-Verbal) for the random effects model is more than twice as large as that for the fixed effects model. Consequently, the confidence intervals for the two slopes are also wider, with

$$0.22 = b_1 - 1.96 \sqrt{\widehat{V}(b_1)} \leq \beta_1 \leq$$
$$b_1 + 1.96 \sqrt{\widehat{V}(b_1)} = 0.42$$

for spatial ability and

$$0.19 = b_2 - 1.96 \sqrt{\widehat{V}(b_2)} \leq \beta_2 \leq$$
$$b_2 + 1.96 \sqrt{\widehat{V}(b_2)} = 0.51$$

for SAT-Verbal. By including the estimates of uncertainty in the *parameters* into the analysis we increase our uncertainty about the slope estimates and about the importance of each of the two predictors to SAT-Math performance.

**3.8.3 Summary** These examples show how we can synthesize zero-order correlations across studies and estimate a synthetic regression equation that can inform us about higher-order relationships. Even though the information from each study was in the form of zero-order relationships among the three variables, we were able to assess the importance of each predictor of SAT-Math performance while controlling for the other.

## 4. STATISTICAL PROBLEMS IN SYNTHESIZING MODELS

### 4.1 Missing Data

One of the most pernicious problems in this kind of synthesis is missing data. Complicated models, with many components or paths between components, will be more likely to be associated with missing data at the synthesis level. Synthesis-level missing data arise when a reviewer finds one or more paths between model components that have not been examined by any study in the synthesis. Such missing data can make estimation of certain synthetic regressions difficult or impossible.

However, lack of data at the synthesis level can also lead to insights into what aspects of a process bear further study. Conversely, an abundance of data can indicate what parts of a process are well researched. Also, as discussed above, data missing at the study level can be problematic for a model-based synthesis.

Table 23.7 shows counts of the correlations among the variables representing components in Eccles's model from the 32 studies in Becker's synthesis (1992b). Correlations that represent paths in the model are underlined. Only 4 of the 18 relationships specified by the model have been studied (for females and males separately).

The table also shows a number of relationships that appear to have been very thoroughly studied for males and females. For instance, 100 correlations between various measures of aptitudes and measures of science achievement were gathered. These relationships may provide substantial information about the roles of moderator variables (e.g., sample characteristics) because it is likely that more variation in the settings and samples examined will occur for larger sets of studies.

This kind of display can also indicate what kinds of inquiry have most often been pursued in a domain. Table 23.7 suggests that the most fundamental, and perhaps the most simplistic, pieces of the science-achievement process have received the most attention. These include the direct relationships to achievement of several kinds of predictors, such as past events (past achievement), and perceptions of task value (e.g., liking of science), as well as aptitudes.

The display also makes concrete an underlying fact about a model-based synthesis. The information available about different paths in the model may be based on greatly different numbers of studies and results. To some extent the uncertainty that results from having smaller amounts of data is reflected in the variance estimates that are computed for the pooled or average correlations. However, smaller numbers of studies are typically associated with less diversity in the samples, settings, measures, and the like that form the context for the study of each relationship. The uncertainty associated with contexts that have not been studied is more difficult to assess. Consequently it may be more difficult to make generalizations about relationships studied less thoroughly.

### 4.2 Assumptions of the Analysis

We make a number of assumptions in using models in research synthesis. Violations of these assumptions may affect the inferences we can make. For example, as

**Table 23.7 Number of Correlations for Paths in Eccles's Model**

| First Component | Second Component | | | | | | | | | | | |
|---|---|---|---|---|---|---|---|---|---|---|---|---|
| | Dem 0 | Apt 1 | Cul 2 | Soc 3 | Pas 4 | Pe3 5 | In4 6 | Goa 7 | Sel 8 | Tas 9 | Exp 10 | Ach 11 |
| Demographics | 0 | 4 | | | 2 | | | | | 6 | | 6 |
| Aptitudes | | 54 | | — | 12 | | | 3 | | 26 | | 100 |
| Culture | | | 0 | — | 2 | — | | 4 | 2 | 20 | | 18 |
| Socializers | | | | 0 | — | — | — | | | 6 | | 2 |
| Past events | | | | | 2 | | — | 8 | — | 2 | | 28 |
| Perceptions of 3 | | | | | | 0 | | — | — | 16 | | |
| Interpretations of 4 | | | | | | | 0 | | — | | | |
| Goals/self-schemata | | | | | | | | 0 | — | — | | 5 |
| Self-concept | | | | | | | | | 0 | 14 | 2 | 12 |
| Perception of task value | | | | | | | | | | 26 | | 44 |
| Expectations | | | | | | | | | | | 0 | — |
| Achievement behaviors | | | | | | | | | | | | 20 |

NOTE: Labels are 0, demographics; 1, aptitudes; 2, culture; 3, socializers; 4, past events; 5, perceptions of socializers; 6, student's interpretations of past events; 7, goals/self-schemata; 8, student's self-concept; 9, student's perception of task value; 10, expectations; and 11, achievement behaviors.

mentioned above, ignoring dependencies in the data can lead to severe error-rate problems. Also sufficient sample sizes (within studies) are needed to justify the application of the normal approximation to the distribution of the correlation coefficient. We examine several other less technical assumptions in this section.

**4.2.1 The operationalization of constructs** An assumption of analyses of models in research synthesis is that all of the studies classified as having examined a particular relationship or path actually study that path. However, it is clear that primary researchers conceptualize and measure constructs differently from study to study. Including studies that mistakenly appear to measure the same constructs may lead to inconsistent results for a relationship or path. For example, a model may posit a strong relationship between academic self-esteem and math achievement, but only a weak relation between general self-esteem and achievement. Several studies may examine general self-esteem, whereas others may examine academic self-esteem. If the nature of the measured variables is not considered, results from the two kinds of studies may be analyzed together, and heterogeneity may be found. Careful examination of each study is crucial, and gathering detailed information on the measures used can help with this problem. The question of how to assess how much uncertainty in our knowledge of relationships between *constructs* arises because of differences between *measures* is a subject of ongoing research.

**4.2.2 Variation in synthetic models** A related issue concerns between-studies and within-study variation in synthetic correlations and regressions. The synthesist must carefully consider whether the average correlation matrix is a good estimate for the population correlation matrix it is meant to represent. The test for the homogeneity of the correlation matrices that produce each pooled (or average) correlation matrix provides evidence on this issue. The GLS approach fortunately is flexible enough so that separate matrices for groups such as the two sexes can be estimated. If we had found gender differences in the correlations among SAT-Math, SAT-Verbal, and spatial ability, to finish the analysis we might have also wanted to estimate separate synthetic regressions (predicting SAT-Math from the other two variables).

Alternately, a finding of heterogeneous correlation matrices could lead us to adopt a random effects model and to estimate the amount of uncertainty due to variation in the correlation parameters. Here we would acknowledge the variation by estimating uncertainty and incorporating it into our analysis, rather than trying to ''explain'' variation as described above (e.g., by estimating separate models for subgroups of studies).

Another related problem in synthesizing models occurs when evidence linking predictors and outcomes is based on multiple, widely differing populations. In other words, it may be possible (or even likely) that no common subject group has been studied for all relationships or paths in a model. For instance, the relationship between science aptitudes and attitudes may have been studied using high school samples, whereas the attitude–achievement relationship may have been studied using elementary school samples.

If the patterns of relationships differ across the populations studied, distinct models may be appropriate for those populations. A single synthesized model may overlook such group differences. Whenever possible, the appropriateness of distinct models should be examined. However, if the populations studied and the relationships studied are "confounded," it may be difficult to fully understand the patterns of interrelationships.

**4.2.3 Sources of artifactual variation** The analyses presented above have also assumed that the correlations contain no important sources of artifactual variation. Sources of artifactual variation including range restriction and differential unreliability give rise to other potential problems in synthesizing correlations. For instance, even when the subjects of different studies appear to be from a single population the samples used may differ. One study may examine high-scoring students, while a second study samples an unrestricted population. Results based on these two samples may differ even if they are truly drawn from the same population.

Corrections for these artifacts are readily available for series of single (bivariate) correlations (see, e.g., Chapter 21). However, applying bivariate corrections sequentially to the entries in a correlation matrix, or correcting only some correlations in a matrix, may produce correlation matrices that are not positive definite (Bock & Petersen 1975). Resulting intercorrelations may be out of range (i.e., greater than one), which could jeopardize the integrity of the analysis. Remedies for differential selection and unreliability in dependent correlations are available for some cases (e.g., Bock & Petersen 1975; Lawley 1943). The effects of multiple corrections and of correcting for artifacts in some but not all of the relationships in a correlation matrix have yet to be examined. Work on these issues is ongoing.

Finally, in both the univariate and multivariate cases reliability and selection data may be reported sparingly. Even within studies, selection and attenuation information may be presented selectively. Ways of handling data missing at the study level may help in imputing values for these study and measure characteristics (see, e.g., Chapter 12).

**4.2.4 A lack of data and model misspecification** In structural-equation modeling, a model is identified if

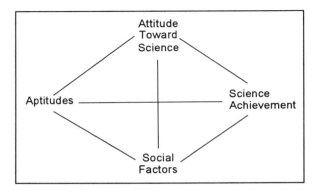

**Figure 23.4** Model of relationships among science aptitudes, attitudes, social factors, and science achievement. After Steinkamp and Maehr (1983).

sufficient data exist to estimate the parameters. In a model-driven synthesis, if a proposed path has not been studied, a correlation for that path simply cannot be estimated and the model may be misspecified. If an unstudied path is critical to the model, the effects (e.g., standardized regression slopes) estimated for the variables that *were* studied may be over- or underestimated and the results biased. Such model misspecification can lead to incorrect conclusions, but is hard to avoid when using existing data. This problem underscores the importance of thoroughly searching for and collecting relevant studies.

One potential solution to the lack of data for a path is to combine several paths or eliminate model components and consider a less complex theoretical model. Becker (1992b) considered two models in her synthesis of gender differences in science. One model (adapted from Steinkamp and Maehr 1983), which contained only six paths, is shown in Figure 23.4. The other model (Eccles et al. 1983), which contained 18 paths, is shown in Figure 23.1. (See also Table 23.7.) The smaller, less complex model had been studied more thoroughly, though it too had one path that had not been investigated. The simpler model appears to be better understood, though it may be at the price of oversimplifying the process of science achievement.

Clearly, in our example Friedman's data allow for the estimation of all three relationships in her very simple model. However, if one wanted to use her model to fully "explain" student performance in math, it would be necessary to ask whether other important variables had been overlooked. If other critical variables (e.g., career goals, value of mathematics) are important for explaining or predicting math performance, Friedman's model may be misspecified.

**4.2.5 The issue of causality** One precept of causality is temporal precedence. Even in primary studies, determining temporal precedence can be somewhat judgmental. In research synthesis the synthesist can rarely infer temporal precedence within the individual studies, especially when results have been presented as correlation matrices with no clearly defined outcome. Without temporal precedence, strong statements of causality are impossible.

However, our view of explanation for ''explanatory models'' does not require strict causal inferences to be made. Rather, we use explanatory models to examine mediating processes via examination of the relationships between proposed mediators and outcome variables. By explaining variation in the relationships observed, we reduce our uncertainty about the nature of those relationships. Attributing differences in observed relationships to substantively important variables (such as types of treatment or types of subjects) and eliminating irrelevant factors as explanatory variables help us to build a case for possible causal relationships.

### 4.3 A Problem-free Model-based Synthesis?

Under what conditions can a problem-free model-based synthesis be accomplished? First, the literature should be sufficiently large so that all paths have been studied. Second, if dependent data exist, sufficient statistics for modeling that dependency are necessary. And third, in most syntheses the synthesist must be willing to explore random effects and mixed model analyses to successfully account for the variation in study outcomes.

For such a literature, correlations for paths can be successfully estimated and prediction equations formed. Both zero-order and partial relationships can be explored. Also inspection of the amounts and kinds of evidence gathered for the different paths in a model can inform us about both what we know and what we do not know about the process represented by our model. Generalizations of results must be carefully made, on the basis of examinations of model fit and in light of the uncertainty in our estimates.

Documenting assumptions, discussing potential problems, and qualifying generalizations must be part of the reporting process. Conventions are still being developed for the presentation of more standard research syntheses. For syntheses involving models, no conventions exist. Cooper (1989) recommends giving enough information so that the review can be replicated, which may require much information in the case of a model-based synthesis.

## 5. CONCLUSION

In spite of its limitations, the use of models in meta-analysis represents an interesting attempt to connect volumes of data to explanatory models in a direct and explicit way. This approach has the potential of helping to identify patterns in research findings that probably would not be found using more traditional methods of research synthesis or narrative reviewing. It should provide a basis for more comprehensive explanations than is available with traditional synthesis approaches.

Even if individual research efforts in an area have not been formed in terms of models, when people need to use that research they need good explanations. Many areas of research can no longer be characterized by simple main effects and bivariate relationships. Research-synthesis techniques will not be applied in more complicated areas unless they provide ways to deal with that complexity.

**Author's note**

This research was supported in part by a grant from the Russell Sage Foundation. Parts of this work were presented at the annual meeting of the American Educational Research Association March 27, 1989, in San Francisco.

## 6. REFERENCES

Becker, B. J. (1978). *The relationship of spatial ability to sex differences in the performance of mathematically precocious youths on the mathematical sections of the Scholastic Aptitude Test.* Unpublished master's thesis, Johns Hopkins University.

Becker, B. J. (1989). *Model-driven meta-analysis: Possibilities and limitations.* Paper presented at the annual meeting of the American Educational Research Association, San Francisco.

Becker, B. J. (1991). *Examining theoretical models through research synthesis.* Manuscript submitted for publication.

Becker, B. J. (1992a). *Missing data and the synthesis of correlation matrices.* Paper presented at the annual meeting of the American Educational Research Association, San Francisco.

Becker, B. J. (1992b). Models of science achievement: Factors affecting male and female performance in school science. In T. D. Cook, H. Cooper, D. S. Cordray, H. Hartmann, L. V. Hedges, R. J. Light, T. A. Louis, & F. Mosteller, *Meta-analysis for explanation: A casebook.* New York: Russell Sage Foundation.

Becker, B. J. (1992c). Using results from replicated studies to estimate linear models. *Journal of Educational Statistics, 17,* 341–362.

Berry, P. C. (1957). *An exploration of the interrelations among some nonintellectual predictors of achievement in problem solving* (Tech. No. 4). New Haven: Yale University, Department of Industrial Administration and Psychology.

Bock, R. D., & Petersen, A. C. (1975). A multivariate correction for attenuation. *Biometrika, 62,* 673–678.

Bridgeman, P. W. (1927). *The logic of modern physics.* New York: Macmillan.

Bryk, A. S., Raudenbush, S. W., Seltzer, M., & Congdon, R. (1989). *An introduction to HLM: Computer program and user's guide* (2nd ed.). Chicago: University of Chicago, Department of Education.

Chow, S. L. (1987). Meta-analysis of pragmatic and theoretical research: A critique. *Journal of Psychology, 121,* 259–271.

Collingwood, R. G. (1940). *An essay on metaphysics.* Oxford, England: Clarendon Press.

Cook, T. D., Cooper, H., Cordray, D. S., Hartmann, H., Hedges, L. V., Light, R. J., Louis, T. A., & Mosteller, F. (1992). *Meta-analysis for explanation: A casebook.* New York: Russell Sage Foundation.

Cooley, W. W., & Lohnes, P. R. (1971). *Multivariate data analysis.* New York: Wiley.

Cooper, H. M. (1982). Scientific guidelines for conducting integrative research reviews. *Review of Educational Research, 52,* 291–302.

Cooper, H. M. (1989). *Integrating research: A guide for literature reviews.* Beverly Hills, CA: Sage.

Eccles, J., Adler, T. F., Futterman, R., Goff, S., Kaczala, C., Meece, J. L., & Midgley, C. (1983). Expectancies, values, and academic behaviors. In J. T. Spence (Ed.), *Achievement and achievement motives: Psychological and sociological approaches* (pp. 76–146). San Francisco: Freeman.

Friedman, L. (in press). Meta-analytic contributions to the study of gender differences in mathematics. *International Journal of Education.*

Harris, M. J., & Rosenthal, R. (1985). Mediation of interpersonal expectancy effects: 31 meta-analyses. *Psychological Bulletin, 97,* 363–386.

Hedges, L. V., & Olkin, I. (1985). *Statistical methods for meta-analysis.* New York: Academic Press.

Lawley, D. N. (1943). A note on Karl Pearson's selection formulae. *Royal Society of Edinburgh Proceedings,* Section A, *62,* 28–30.

Little, R. J. A., & Rubin, D. B. (1987). *Statistical analysis with missing data.* New York: Wiley.

Longford, N. T. (1988). *VARCL Manual: Software for variance component analysis of data with hierarchically nested random effects (maximum likelihood).* Princeton, NJ: Educational Testing Service.

Meece, J. L., Parsons, J. E., Kaczala, C. M., Goff, S. B., & Futterman, R. (1982). Sex differences in math achievement: Toward a model of academic choice. *Psychological Bulletin, 91,* 324–348.

Olkin, I., & Siotani, M. (1976). Asymptotic distribution of functions of a correlation matrix. In S. Ideka (Ed.), *Essays in probability and statistics.* Tokyo: Sinko Tsusho.

Premack, S. L., & Hunter, J. E. (1988). Individual unionization decisions. *Psychological Bulletin, 103,* 223–234.

Presby, S. (1978). Overly broad categories obscure important differences between therapies. *American Psychologist, 33,* 514–515.

Raudenbush, S. W., & Bryk, A. S. (1985). Empirical Bayes meta-analysis. *Journal of Educational Statistics, 10,* 75–98.

Rosenberg, J. H. (1981). *The ability of selected cognitive, affective, and educational variables to predict the presence of anxiety related to mathematics.* Unpublished doctoral dissertation, University of Connecticut.

Shadish, W. R. (1992). Marital and family psychotherapies. In T. D. Cook, H. Cooper, D. S. Cordray, H. Hartmann, L. V. Hedges, R. J. Light, T. A. Louis, & F. Mosteller, *Meta-analysis for explanation: A casebook.* New York: Russell Sage Foundation.

Shadish, W. R., & Sweeney, R. B. (1991). Mediators and moderators in meta-analysis: There's a reason we don't let dodo birds tell us which psychotherapies should have prizes. *Journal of Consulting and Clinical Psychology, 59,* 883–893.

Smith, I. R. (1966). *Factors in chemistry achievement among eleventh-grade girls and boys.* Unpublished doctoral dissertation, Catholic University of America.

Steinkamp, M. W., & Maehr, M. L. (1983). Affect, ability, and science achievement: A quantitative synthesis of correlational research. *Review of Educational Research, 53,* 369–396.

Weiner, N. C. (1984). *Cognitive aptitudes, personality variables, and gender difference effects on mathematical achievement for mathematically gifted students.* Unpublished doctoral dissertation, Arizona State University.

## 7. APPENDIX: The Posterior Distribution of $\rho$, the EM Algorithm, and Missing Data

### 7.1 The Posterior Distribution of $\rho$

The estimation of the mean vector $\boldsymbol{\rho}.$ and the variance-covariance matrix $\mathbf{T}$ requires the posterior distribution of the vector of study parameters $\rho_{11}$ through $\rho_{kp*}$ (i.e., $\boldsymbol{\rho}$). From model (23-3) in the text, and the distribution of the sample correlation in (23-1) and (23-2) we know that within-study sampling error ($e_{ij}$) is normally distributed. Since

$$r_{ij} = \rho_{ij} + e_{ij}, \qquad \text{for } j = 1 \text{ to } p^* \text{ and } i = 1 \text{ to } k,$$

then if $N = \Sigma_i \, n_i$ and $\pi_i = n_i/N$ remain fixed as $N$ approaches $\infty$, we can write

$$\sqrt{N}(\mathbf{r} - \boldsymbol{\rho}) \sim N(\mathbf{0}, \boldsymbol{\Sigma}^*),$$

where $\boldsymbol{\Sigma}^*$ is defined via $\boldsymbol{\Sigma}^* = \sqrt{N}\, \boldsymbol{\Sigma}$, and the elements of $\boldsymbol{\Sigma}$ are given by (23-1) and (23-2) in the text. Thus, the approximate density of the vector $\mathbf{r}$, conditional on the vector of study-parameters $\boldsymbol{\rho}$ is given by

$$\text{f}(\mathbf{r} \mid \boldsymbol{\rho}) = |\boldsymbol{\Sigma}|^{-1/2}(2\pi)^{-kp^*/2} \exp\{-\tfrac{1}{2}\,(\mathbf{r}-\boldsymbol{\rho})'\boldsymbol{\Sigma}^{-1}(\mathbf{r}-\boldsymbol{\rho})\}.$$

The second-stage model (23-4) in the text shows the population correlation for each study varying around the mean population correlation for the $j$th relationship, across studies. Specifically,

$$\rho_{ij} = \rho_j + u_{ij}, \qquad \text{for } j = 1 \text{ to } p^* \text{ and } i = 1 \text{ to } k.$$

We define $\tau_{jj'} = \text{Cov}(\rho_{ij}, \rho_{ij'})$ for $i = 1$ to $k$ and $j, j' = 1$ to $p^*$. If we are willing to assume that the study-parameters $\rho_{ij}$ are normally distributed about the means $\rho_j$, then we can write the density of the vector of study-parameters $\boldsymbol{\rho}$ as

$$\text{f}(\boldsymbol{\rho}) = |\mathbf{T}|^{-1/2}\,(2\pi)^{-kp^*/2}\exp\{-\tfrac{1}{2}\,(\boldsymbol{\rho}-\boldsymbol{\rho}.)'\mathbf{T}^{-1}(\boldsymbol{\rho}-\boldsymbol{\rho}.)\},$$

where $\mathbf{T}$ is a $kp^*$ x $kp^*$ blockwise diagonal matrix containing $k$ ($p^*$ x $p^*$) blocks of $\tau_{jj'}$ values and $\boldsymbol{\rho}.$ is a $kp^*$ x 1 vector defined as

$$\boldsymbol{\rho}. = (\rho_1, \rho_2, \ldots, \rho_{p^*}, \ldots, \rho_1, \rho_2, \ldots, \rho_{p^*}).'$$

That is, $\boldsymbol{\rho}.$ is a concatenation of $k$ sets of the average population correlations $\rho_1$ through $\rho_{p^*}$.

The posterior distribution of $\boldsymbol{\rho}$ given $\mathbf{r}$ is then

$$
\begin{aligned}
\text{f}(\boldsymbol{\rho}|\mathbf{r}) &\propto \text{f}(\mathbf{r}|\boldsymbol{\rho})\,\text{f}(\boldsymbol{\rho}) = |\boldsymbol{\Sigma}\;\mathbf{T}|^{-1/2}\,(2\pi)^{-kp^*} \\
&\quad \exp\{-\tfrac{1}{2}(\mathbf{r}-\boldsymbol{\rho})'\boldsymbol{\Sigma}^{-1}(\mathbf{r}-\boldsymbol{\rho})\} \times \\
&\quad \exp\{-\tfrac{1}{2}(\boldsymbol{\rho}-\boldsymbol{\rho}.)'\mathbf{T}^{-1}(\boldsymbol{\rho}-\boldsymbol{\rho}.)\} \\
&\propto \exp\{-\tfrac{1}{2}(\mathbf{r}-\boldsymbol{\rho})'\boldsymbol{\Sigma}^{-1}(\mathbf{r}-\boldsymbol{\rho}) + \\
&\quad -\tfrac{1}{2}(\boldsymbol{\rho}-\boldsymbol{\rho}.)'\mathbf{T}^{-1}(\boldsymbol{\rho}-\boldsymbol{\rho}.)\}. \quad (A23\text{-}1)
\end{aligned}
$$

By expanding the quadratic forms in (A23-1) and eliminating terms that do not depend on $\boldsymbol{\rho}$ we obtain

$$
\begin{aligned}
\text{f}(\boldsymbol{\rho}|\mathbf{r}) &\propto \\
&\exp\{-\tfrac{1}{2}[\boldsymbol{\rho}'\,\boldsymbol{\Sigma}^{-1}\,\boldsymbol{\rho} - 2\boldsymbol{\rho}'\boldsymbol{\Sigma}^{-1}\,\mathbf{r} + \\
&\boldsymbol{\rho}'\,\mathbf{T}^{-1}\,\boldsymbol{\rho} - 2\boldsymbol{\rho}'\,\mathbf{T}^{-1}\,\boldsymbol{\rho}.]\} = \\
&\exp\{-\tfrac{1}{2}[\boldsymbol{\rho}'\,(\boldsymbol{\Sigma}^{-1}+\mathbf{T}^{-1})\,\boldsymbol{\rho} \\
&-2\boldsymbol{\rho}'\,(\boldsymbol{\Sigma}^{-1}\,\mathbf{r}+\mathbf{T}^{-1}\,\boldsymbol{\rho}.)]\}. \quad (A23\text{-}2)
\end{aligned}
$$

We next define the matrices

$$\boldsymbol{\psi} = (\boldsymbol{\Sigma}^{-1}+\mathbf{T}^{-1})^{-1}$$

and

$$
\begin{aligned}
\boldsymbol{\rho}_1 &= (\boldsymbol{\Sigma}^{-1}+\mathbf{T}^{-1})^{-1}(\boldsymbol{\Sigma}^{-1}\,\mathbf{r}+\mathbf{T}^{-1}\,\boldsymbol{\rho}.) = \\
&\boldsymbol{\psi}\,(\boldsymbol{\Sigma}^{-1}\,\mathbf{r}+\mathbf{T}^{-1}\,\boldsymbol{\rho}.).
\end{aligned}
$$

Note that although $\boldsymbol{\rho}_1$ is a one-dimensional vector, we will denote its elements as $\rho_{1ij}$ in order to identify the study and relationship associated with each element. The elements of $\boldsymbol{\rho}_1'$ are thus arrayed as ($\rho_{111}$, $\rho_{112}$, $\ldots$, $\rho_{11p^*}$, $\ldots$, $\rho_{1k1}$, $\rho_{1k2}$, $\ldots$, $\rho_{1kp^*}$).

Next multiply (A23-2) by the term $\exp\{-\tfrac{1}{2}\,\boldsymbol{\rho}_1'\,\boldsymbol{\psi}^{-1}\,\boldsymbol{\rho}_1\}$, which is independent of $\boldsymbol{\rho}$. Substituting $\boldsymbol{\psi}^{-1}$ for $(\boldsymbol{\Sigma}^{-1} + \mathbf{T}^{-1})$ and $\boldsymbol{\psi}^{-1}\,\boldsymbol{\rho}_1$ for $(\boldsymbol{\Sigma}^{-1}\,\mathbf{r} + \mathbf{T}^{-1}\,\boldsymbol{\rho}.)$ produces

$$
\begin{aligned}
\text{f}(\boldsymbol{\rho}|\mathbf{r}) &\propto \exp\{-\tfrac{1}{2}[\boldsymbol{\rho}'\,(\boldsymbol{\Sigma}^{-1}+\mathbf{T}^{-1})\,\boldsymbol{\rho} - 2\boldsymbol{\rho}'\,(\boldsymbol{\Sigma}^{-1}\,\mathbf{r} + \\
&\mathbf{T}^{-1}\,\boldsymbol{\rho}.) + \boldsymbol{\rho}_1'\,\boldsymbol{\psi}^{-1}\,\boldsymbol{\rho}_1]\} \\
&= \exp\{-\tfrac{1}{2}[\boldsymbol{\rho}'\,\boldsymbol{\psi}^{-1}\boldsymbol{\rho} - 2\boldsymbol{\rho}'\,\boldsymbol{\psi}^{-1}\,\boldsymbol{\rho}_1 + \\
&\boldsymbol{\rho}_1'\,\boldsymbol{\psi}^{-1}\,\boldsymbol{\rho}_1]\} \\
&= \exp\{-\tfrac{1}{2}(\boldsymbol{\rho}-\boldsymbol{\rho}_1)'\,\boldsymbol{\psi}^{-1}(\boldsymbol{\rho}-\boldsymbol{\rho}_1)\}, \quad (A23\text{-}3)
\end{aligned}
$$

which is the kernel of the multivariate normal distribution. Thus, the posterior distribution of $\boldsymbol{\rho}$ (given $\mathbf{r}$) is normal with mean $\boldsymbol{\rho}_1$ and variance $\boldsymbol{\psi}$.

### 7.2 The EM Algorithm

The EM algorithm makes use of the distribution defined by (A23-3) in the E, or estimation, step of the process. The EM approach requires initial estimates of $\mathbf{T}$ and $\rho_1$ through $\rho_{p*}$ (the average correlations). Because these are starting values, simple estimators are typically all that is needed. The starting values $\hat{\mathbf{T}}^{(0)}$ and $\hat{\boldsymbol{\rho}}.^{(0)}$ are used to compute the posterior mean of $\boldsymbol{\rho}$ and its variance, that is, $\hat{\boldsymbol{\rho}}_1^{(1)}$ and $\hat{\boldsymbol{\psi}}^{(1)}$. New estimates of $\mathbf{T}$ and $\boldsymbol{\rho}.$ (i.e., $\hat{\mathbf{T}}^{(1)}$ and $\hat{\boldsymbol{\rho}}.^{(1)}$) are then computed based on the sufficient statistics from the $\hat{\rho}_1^{(1)}$ values. (The specific forms of the estimates are given below.) The cycle continues until the likelihood in (A23-3) is maximized or, practically speaking, until the differences between parameter estimates from one iteration to the next are small.

*Starting values.* For starting values we use weighted method of moments estimators $\hat{\rho}_{.j}^{(0)}$ for $j = 1$ to $p^*$ and $\hat{\mathbf{T}}^{(0)} = (\hat{\tau}_{jj'}^{(0)})$ for $j, j' = 1$ to $p^*$, specifically,

$$\hat{\rho}_{.j}^{(0)} = r_{.j} = \Sigma_i w_{ij} r_{ij},$$

and

$$\tau_{jj'}^{(0)} =$$
$$\frac{S^*_{jj'} - \Sigma_i w_{ijj'} \cdot \sigma_{ijj'} (1 - w_{ij} - w_{ij'}) - (\Sigma_i w_{ijj'})(\Sigma_i w_{ij} w_{ij'} \cdot \sigma_{ijj'})}{\Sigma_i w_{ijj'} (1 - w_{ij} - w_{ij'} + \Sigma_s w_{sj} w_{sj'})},$$

for

$$S^*_{jj'} = \Sigma w_{ijj'} (r_{ij} - r_{.j})(r_{ij'} - r_{.j'}),$$

where $w_{ijj'} = (w_{ij} w_{ij'})^{1/2}$ is a weight associated with correlations $r_{ij}$ and $r_{ij'}$, $w_{ij} = [1/\hat{\sigma}_{ijj}]/\Sigma_s[1/\hat{\sigma}_{sjj}]$ (i.e., $w_{ij}$ is the usual inverse-variance weight used in univariate analyses), and where the values of $\hat{\sigma}_{ijj'}$ are given by (23-1) and (23-2) in the text. These estimators are superscripted with the index zero to indicate that they are starting values.

When the amount of variation in the sample correlations for the $j$th relationship is quite small the variance estimate $\hat{\tau}_{jj}^{(0)}$ can frequently be negative. By convention, negative values are set to zero, as would be any other covariance estimates involving the $j$th relationship (i.e., values of $\hat{\tau}_{jj'}^{(0)}$ for that value of $j$).

*Expectation step.* The posterior distribution of the values $\rho_{11}, \ldots, \rho_{1p^*}, \ldots, \rho_{k1}, \ldots, \rho_{kp^*}$ (given the data) is then used to obtain estimates of the study parameters. These are essentially weighted combinations of the original data (the $r$'s) and the starting values of the mean correlations $\rho_1$ through $\rho_{p^*}$. We compute

$$\hat{\psi}^{(0)} = (\mathbf{\Sigma}^{-1} + [\hat{\mathbf{T}}^{(0)}]^{-1})^{-1}$$

and

$$\hat{\rho}_1^{(0)} = \hat{\psi}^{(0)} (\mathbf{\Sigma}^{-1} \mathbf{r} + [\hat{\mathbf{T}}^{(0)}]^{-1} \hat{\rho}_{.}^{(0)}).$$

*Maximization step.* In this step new estimates of $\mathbf{T}$ (i.e., $\hat{\mathbf{T}}^{(1)}$) and the mean correlation vector are obtained from the sufficient statistics for the study-parameter estimates. The estimates of the elements of $\mathbf{T}$ and $\boldsymbol{\rho}_.$ on iteration $(t + 1)$ are given by

$$\hat{\tau}_{jj'}^{(t+1)} = (1/k)[\Sigma_i (\hat{\psi}_{ijj'}^{(t)} + \hat{\rho}_{1ij}^{(t)} \hat{\rho}_{1ij'}^{(t)}) - k \hat{\rho}_{.j}^{(t)} \hat{\rho}_{.j'}^{(t)}],$$

and

$$\hat{\rho}_{.j}^{(t+1)} = [\Sigma_i \hat{\rho}_{1ij}^{(t)}]/k,$$

where $\hat{\psi}_{ijj'}^{(t)}$ is an element of the matrix $\hat{\psi}^{(t)}$, $\hat{\rho}_{1ij}^{(t)}$ is an element of $\hat{\rho}_1^{(t)}$, and

$$\hat{\rho}_1^{(t)} = \hat{\psi}^{(t)} (\mathbf{\Sigma}^{-1} \mathbf{r} + [\hat{\mathbf{T}}^{(t)}]^{-1} \hat{\rho}_{.}^{(t)}).$$

*Iteration.* The process of estimation and maximization is repeated until the likelihood function is maximized—that is, until the parameter estimates (e.g., the estimates of $\mathbf{T}$ and $\rho_1$ through $\rho_{p^*}$) do not change much from one iteration to the next. Note, however, that the program below stops after iterating for a fixed number of cycles rather than stopping after a convergence criterion has been met.

## 7.3 Missing Data

The EM algorithm can be applied when all correlations have been observed or when some correlations are missing. When data are missing at random (i.e., when the reason that correlations are unobserved is unrelated to the actual values of the unobserved correlations), then it is possible to get maximum likelihood estimates by ignoring the missing-data mechanism. Little and Rubin (1987, Chapter 8) discuss this problem in detail for multivariate normal examples with unknown covariance matrices. The present case is similar, but involves normal data with a known covariance matrix.

Application of Little and Rubin's methodology for handling missing data adds only one step to the estimation process described above. After obtaining starting values $\hat{\mathbf{T}}^{(0)}$ and $\hat{\rho}_.^{(0)}$ we must impute values of the unobserved correlations.

The value imputed is the expected value of the missing correlation, conditional on the observed data. In practice, this means substituting the best estimate available for any missing value, using all observed data. If correlation $r_{ij}$ is missing, one would regress the observed correlations for the $j$th relationship on the other $(p^* - 1)$ correlations for all available cases. The resulting regression equation would be used to predict a value of $r_{ij}$ for study $i$. When some studies are missing more than one correlation, missing values would be estimated for each pattern of missing data, using an approach similar to that described in Little and Rubin (1987,

Chapter 6). See Becker (1992a) for further discussion of imputing conditional means for missing correlations.

After the imputed values have been obtained, they are substituted into the data set and analysis proceeds as if the data were complete.

## SAS Program for EM Estimation of T

```
CMS FILEDEF INDATA DISK CORR2 DAT A;
DATA IN;      INFILE INDATA;      INPUT R1 RBAR V1-V30 T1-T30;

*HERE THE INITIAL VALUES ARE READ IN: R1 IS THE VECTOR OF CORRELA-
TIONS, R BAR IS A VECTOR OF MEAN CORRELATIONS USED FOR STARTING VAL-
UES, V1-V30 IS THE VARIANCE-COVARIANCE MATRIX AND T1-T30 IS THE INITIAL
TAU;

DATA RS; SET IN; KEEP R1;
DATA RD; SET IN; KEEP RBAR;
DATA VS; SET IN; KEEP V1-V30;
DATA TS; SET IN; KEEP T1-T30;
PROC IML;
USE RS; READ ALL INTO R;
USE RD; READ ALL INTO RDOT;
USE VS; READ ALL INTO VR;
USE TS; READ ALL INTO T;

*THE MATRICES ARE INITIALIZED;
M = J(3,1,0);      T3 = J(3,3,0);      S = J(3,3,0);

*M IS A MATRIX CONTAINING THE ESTIMATED MEAN CORRELATIONS;
*T3 IS A 3X3 MATRIX CONTAINING THE TAU VALUES, AND S CONTAINS RELATED
SUMS;

*HERE WE COMPUTE THE MATRIX PSI AND THE ESTIMATED POSTERIOR MEAN
(RHO1) FROM THE DATA AND THE INITIAL TAU AND MEAN ESTIMATES;
VRI = INV(VR);      TI = INV(T);      PSI = INV (VRI + TI);
RHO1 = PSI*(VRI*R + TI*RDOT);

*THE LOOP OVER THE INDEX IT DEFINES ITERATIONS OF THE EM ALGORITHM;
    IT = 1;      DO      WHILE (IT< = 40);

*THE LOOP OVER I SUMS THE ELEMENTS THAT GO INTO THE NEW MEAN AND
TAU MATRICES;

    I = 1;   DO WHILE (I< = 30);
        S(|1,1|) = S(|1,1|) + PSI(|I,I|) + RHO1(|I,1|)##2;
        S(|2,2|) = S(|2,2|) + PSI(|I+1,I+1|) + RHO1(|I+1,1|)##2;
        S(|3,3|) = S(|3,3|) + PSI(|I+2,I+2|) + RHO1(|I+2,1|)##2;
        S(|1,2|) = S(|1,2|) + PSI(|I,I+1|) + RHO1(|I,1|)#RHO1(|I+1,1|);
```

```
      S(|1,3|) = S(|1,3|) + PSI(|I,I + 2|) + RHO1(|I,1|)#RHO1(|I + 2,1|);
      S(|2,3|) = S(|2,3|) + PSI(|I + 1,I + 2|) + RHO1(|I + 1,1|)#RHO1(|I + 2,1|);
      M(|1,1|) = M(|1,1|) + RHO1(|I,1|);
      M(|2,1|) = M(|2,1|) + RHO1(|I + 1,1|);
      M(|3,1|) = M(|3,1|) + RHO1(|I + 2,1|);
   I = I + 3;     END;
```

*THIS IS THE END OF THE SUMMING LOOP. BELOW, THE MEAN (M) AND TAU ARE COMPUTED;

```
   S(|2,1|) = S(|1,2|);      M(|1,1|) = M(|1,1|)/10;
   S(|3,1|) = S(|1,3|);      M(|2,1|) = M(|2,1|)/10;
   S(|3,2|) = S(|2,3|);      M(|3,1|) = M(|3,1|)/10;
```

*THESE ARE THE ELEMENTS OF THE NEW ESTIMATED TAU MATRIX;

```
   T3(|1,1|) = .10#(S(|1,1|) − 10#M(|1,1|)#M(|1,1|));
   T3(|1,2|) = .10#(S(|1,2|) − 10#M(|1,1|)#M(|2,1|));
   T3(|2,1|) = .10#(S(|2,1|) − 10#M(|2,1|)#M(|1,1|));
   T3(|1,3|) = .10#(S(|1,3|) − 10#M(|1,1|)#M(|3,1|));
   T3(|3,1|) = .10#(S(|3,1|) − 10#M(|3,1|)#M(|1,1|));
   T3(|2,2|) = .10#(S(|2,2|) − 10#M(|2,1|)#M(|2,1|));
   T3(|2,3|) = .10#(S(|2,3|) − 10#M(|2,1|)#M(|3,1|));
   T3(|3,2|) = .10#(S(|3,2|) − 10#M(|3,1|)#M(|2,1|));
   T3(|3,3|) = .10#(S(|3,3|) − 10#M(|3,1|)#M(|3,1|));

   J = 1;
```

*THIS LOOP REDEFINES THE T MATRIX TO CONTAIN THE NEW TAU ELEMENTS;

```
   DO WHILE (J < = 30);
   T(|J,J|) = T3(|1,1|);
   T(|J + 1,J + 1|) = T3(|2,2|);
   T(|J + 2,J + 2|) = T3(|3,3|);
   T(|J,J + 1|) = T3(|1,2|);
   T(|J,J + 2|) = T3(|1,3|);
   T(|J + 1,J + 2|) = T3(|2,3|);
   T(|J + 1,J|) = T3(|1,2|);
   T(|J + 2,J|) = T3(|1,3|);
   T(|J + 2,J + 1|) = T3(|2,3|);
   J = J + 3;
   END;
```

*ON THE LAST ITERATIONS THE MEAN, TAU, AND POSTERIOR MEAN ARE PRINTED;
```
IF IT>35 THEN DO;
```

```
     PRINT  IT  M  T3  RHO1;
     END;
```

*NEW VALUES OF THE MEAN, PSI, AND RHO1 ARE COMPUTED FOR THE NEXT ITERATION;
*ALSO THE SUM AND MEAN MATRICES ARE REINITIALIZED;

*THE VECTOR RDOT IS THE VECTOR RHO-DOT, AS DEFINED ABOVE FORMULA (A23-1);

```
RDOT = M//M//M//M//M//M//M//M//M//M;
S = J(3,3,0);     M = J(3,1,0);
TI = INV(T);      PSI = INV (VRI + TI);     RHO1 = PSI*(VRI*R + TI*RDOT) ;

IT = IT + 1;
END;
ENDSAS;
```

Cooper, H. and Hedges, L. V. (Eds.) 1994. *The Handbook of Research Synthesis.* New York: Russell Sage Foundation

# 24

# SENSITIVITY ANALYSIS AND DIAGNOSTICS

**JOEL B. GREENHOUSE**
*Carnegie Mellon University*

**SATISH IYENGAR**
*University of Pittsburgh*

CONTENTS

# 1. INTRODUCTION

At every step in a research synthesis decisions are made that can affect the conclusions and inferences drawn from the analysis. Sometimes, a decision is easy to defend, such as the decision to omit a poor-quality study from the meta-analysis or to use a weighted average instead of an unweighted one to estimate an effect size. At other times, a decision is less defendable, such as the decision to use only the published literature, to omit a study with an unusual effect size estimate, or to use a fixed effects model instead of a random effects model. When the basis for a decision is tenuous, it is important to check whether reasonable alternatives to the decision appreciably affect the conclusions. In other words, it is important to check how sensitive the conclusions are to the method of analysis or to changes in the data. Sensitivity analysis is a systematic approach to the question, "What happens if some aspect of the data or the analysis is changed?" Since little has been written on the subject of sensitivity analysis, our aim is to discuss its role in research synthesis and to introduce methods for doing sensitivity analysis.

A sensitivity analysis need not be quantitative. For instance, the first step in a research synthesis is the formulation of the research question. Although a quantitative sensitivity analysis is not appropriate here, it is, nevertheless, useful to entertain variations of the research question before proceeding further—that is, to ask the "what if" question. Since different questions will require different types of data and data analytic methods, it is important to state clearly the aims of the research synthesis at the outset in order to collect the relevant data and to explain why certain questions (and not others) were addressed. At another step in a meta-analysis decisions are made concerning the identification and retrieval of studies. Here the investigator must choose which studies to include. Should only peer-reviewed, published studies be included? What about conference proceedings or Ph.D. dissertations? Should only randomized controlled studies be considered? These decisions can affect the generalizability of the conclusions of the meta-analysis. We view the process of asking these questions as part of sensitivity analysis since it encourages the meta-analyst to reflect on decisions that are made and to consider the consequences of those decisions in terms of the subsequent interpretation and generalizability of the results. In this chapter our focus will be primarily on quantitative methods for sensitivity analysis. However, it is important to keep in mind that these early decisions about the nature of the research question and the identification and retrieval of the literature can have a profound impact on the usefulness of the meta-analysis.

We will use a rather broad brush to discuss sensitivity analysis. Since, as we have suggested, sensitivity analysis is potentially applicable at every step of a research synthesis, we will touch on many topics covered in greater detail elsewhere in this volume. Our aim here is to provide a unified approach to the assessment of the robustness, or cogency, of the conclusions of a research synthesis. The key element to this approach is simply the recognition of the importance of asking the "what if" question. While a research synthesis need not concern itself with every issue discussed below, our point of view and the technical tools we describe in this chapter should be useful generally. Many of these tools come from the extensive statistical literature on exploratory data analysis; others have been developed largely in the context of meta-analysis itself, such as those for assessing the effects of publication bias.

To illustrate some of the quantitative approaches to research synthesis, we will use two data sets throughout this chapter. The first is a subset of studies from a larger study of the effectiveness of open education programs (Hedges, Giaconia & Gage 1981). The objective of the meta-analysis was to examine the effects of open education on student outcomes by comparing students in experimental open classroom schools with students from traditional schools. Specifically, in Table 24.1 we look at the studies presented in Hedges and Olkin (1985, Table 8, pp. 25 and 111), which consist of the randomized experiments and other well-controlled studies of the effects of open education on self-concept. The table presents the students' grade levels, the sample size for each group, a weight for each study, and an unbiased estimate, $d$ (called $g^u$ in Chapter 16), of the standardized mean difference for each study. The second data set is from Hedges and Olkin (1985, Table 7, p. 24) on the effects of open education on student independence and self-reliance. These data are presented in Table 24.2. Unbiased estimates of the standardized mean differences are shown for seven studies, all of which have the same sample sizes. No covariate information, such as grade level, was given in Hedges and Olkin (1985) for this data set.

The plan for the chapter is as follows. We will review the steps in doing a research synthesis from the point of

**Table 24.1  Studies of the Effects of Open Education on Student Self-Concept**

| Study | Grade Level | Open Education Group, $n^E$ | Traditional School Group, $n^C$ | Weights $w_i$ | Standardized Mean Difference $d$ |
|---|---|---|---|---|---|
| 1 | 4–6 | 100 | 180 | 0.115 | 0.100 |
| 2 | 4–6 | 131 | 138 | 0.120 | −0.162 |
| 3 | 4–6 | 40 | 40 | 0.036 | −0.091 |
| 4 | 4–6 | 40 | 40 | 0.036 | −0.049 |
| 5 | 4–6 | 97 | 47 | 0.057 | −0.046 |
| 6 | K–3 | 28 | 61 | 0.034 | −0.010 |
| 7 | K–3 | 60 | 55 | 0.051 | −0.434 |
| 8 | 4–6 | 72 | 102 | 0.076 | −0.262 |
| 9 | 4–6 | 87 | 45 | 0.053 | 0.135 |
| 10 | K–3 | 80 | 49 | 0.054 | 0.019 |
| 11 | K–3 | 79 | 55 | 0.058 | 0.176 |
| 12 | 4–6 | 40 | 109 | 0.052 | 0.056 |
| 13 | 4–6 | 36 | 93 | 0.046 | 0.045 |
| 14 | K–3 | 9 | 18 | 0.011 | 0.106 |
| 15 | K–3 | 14 | 16 | 0.013 | 0.124 |
| 16 | 4–6 | 21 | 22 | 0.019 | −0.491 |
| 17 | 4–6 | 133 | 124 | 0.115 | 0.291 |
| 18 | K–3 | 83 | 45 | 0.052 | 0.344 |

SOURCE: Hedges and Olkin (1985), Table 8.

**Table 24.2  Studies of the Effects of Open Education on Student Independence and Self-Reliance**

| Study | $n^E = n^C$ | $d$ |
|---|---|---|
| 1 | 30 | 0.699 |
| 2 | 30 | 0.091 |
| 3 | 30 | −0.058 |
| 4 | 30 | −0.079 |
| 5 | 30 | −0.235 |
| 6 | 30 | −0.494 |
| 7 | 30 | −0.587 |

SOURCE: Hedges and Olkin (1985), Table 7.

view of sensitivity analysis. In other words, at each decision point of a research synthesis we consider what questions could be asked and what methods could be used to assess the effect of different decisions on the results of the meta-analysis. In section 2, we discuss

issues related to the selection of studies and examine the various decisions that are made at this stage of a research synthesis. In section 3, we introduce relatively simple data analytic methods, such as stem-and-leaf plots and box plots, that help reveal features of the data that could have a large impact on the choice of and the interpretation of more formal statistical procedures for the actual synthesis. Issues concerned with how to combine and summarize effect size estimates are taken up in section 4. Here we discuss various strategies for sensitivity analysis related to the choice of the underlying statistical model used to combine effect sizes, that is, the use of fixed effects and random effects models. Finally in section 5, we introduce methods for assessing the presence and the impact of publication bias in research synthesis.

## 2. THE RETRIEVAL OF LITERATURE

The discussions in Part III of this volume clearly demonstrate that the retrieval of papers that describe relevant studies for a research synthesis is not as straightforward as it might seem. Some questions that arise at the outset of this time-consuming yet essential component of a meta-analysis are: Should a single person search the literature, or should (time and resources permitting) at least two people conduct independent searches? Should the search concentrate on the published literature only (i.e., from peer-reviewed journals), or should it attempt to retrieve all possible studies? Which time period should be covered by the search? The first two questions deal with the concern that the studies missed by a search may arrive at qualitatively different conclusions than those retrieved. The third question is more subtle: It is possible that within a period of time studies yield homogeneous results, but that different periods of time show considerable heterogeneity. For instance, initial enthusiastically positive reports may be followed by a sober period of null, or even negative, results. Rosenthal has called this a "publication cycle." Light and Pillemer (1984) also discuss the use of graphic displays to see how research results in a variety of fields change with the passage of time.

The use of more than one investigator to search the literature is a type of sensitivity analysis. It is especially helpful when the central question in a research synthesis spans several disciplines and the identification of relevant studies requires subject-matter expertise in these disciplines (see, e.g., Greenhouse et al. 1990). It is intuitively clear that if the overlap between the searches is large, we will be more confident that a thorough retrieval has been done. (A formal approach for assessing the completeness of a literature search might involve capture-recapture calculations of population size estimation; see, for example, Bishop, Fienberg & Holland 1975). Clearly, the more comprehensive a search, the better, for then the meta-analysis can use all of the available data. However, a thorough search may not be feasible owing to practical constraints. To decide whether a search limited, for example, to the published literature can lead to biased results, it is worthwhile to do a small search of the unpublished literature (e.g., dissertations, conference proceedings, and abstracts) and compare the two. For a more complete discussion of other issues related to the question of the thoroughness of a search, see Wachter and Straf (1990, Chapter 15).

When a substantial group of studies is retrieved, and data from them gleaned, it is useful to investigate the relationship between study characteristics and study results. The following are some of the questions that can be addressed using the exploratory data analytic tools discussed in section 3: Do published and unpublished studies yield different results? If the studies are rated according to quality, do the lower-quality studies show greater variability or systematic bias? When two disciplines touch on the same issue, how do the results of studies done in one compare with those in the other? When these issues arise early in the literature search, it is possible to alter the focus of the retrieval process to ensure a more comprehensive database.

## 3. EXPLORATORY DATA ANALYSIS

Once the literature has been searched and studies have been retrieved, the next step in a meta-analysis is the analysis of effect size. Formal statistical procedures for determining the significance of an effect size summary usually are based on assumptions about the probabilistic process generating the observations. Violations of these assumptions could have an important impact on the validity of the conclusions drawn from the research synthesis. In this section, we discuss relatively simple methods for investigating features of a data set and the validity of the statistical assumptions. We consider these methods to be a part of a sensitivity analysis since they help reveal features of the data that could have a large impact on the choice of more formal statistical procedures and the interpretation of their results.

The approach described here, known as exploratory data analysis, is based on the premise that the more that is known about the data, the more effectively it can be used to develop, test, and refine theory. Methods for exploratory data analysis should be relatively easy to use with or without a computer, quick to use so that a data set may be explored from different points of view, and robust in the sense that they are not adversely influenced by such misleading phenomena as extreme cases, measurement errors, or unique cases that need special attention. Two methods to be discussed here, the stem-and-leaf plot and the box plot, are graphic methods that satisfy these requirements and are powerful tools for developing insights and hypotheses about the data in a meta-analysis.

### 3.1 Stem-and-Leaf Plots

In a stem-and-leaf plot, the data values are sorted into numerical order and brought together quickly and effi-

```
-4 | 83
-3 |
-2 | 6
-1 | 6
-0 | 9441
 0 | 145
 1 | 00237
 2 | 9
 3 | 4
```

**Figure 24.1** Stem-and-leaf plot of the standardized mean differences, *d*, for the studies reported in Table 24.1 ($n = 18$; leaf unit $= 0.010$).

ciently in the form of a graphic display. The stem-and-leaf plot uses all of the data and illustrates the shape of a distribution; that is, it shows whether it is symmetric or skewed, how many peaks it has, and whether it has outliers (atypical extreme values) or gaps within the distribution. Figure 24.1 shows the stem-and-leaf plot for the distribution of the standardized mean differences, *d*, for the 18 studies given in Table 24.1. Here, for ease of exposition, we have rounded the values of the standardized mean differences in the last column of Table 24.1 to two significant digits. The first significant digit of *d* is designated the *stem* and the second digit the *leaf*. For example, the rounded standardized mean difference for study 2 is $-0.16$. Therefore, the stem is $-1$ and the leaf is 6. The possible stem values are listed vertically in increasing order from top (negative stems) to bottom (positive stems) and a vertical line is drawn to the right of the stems. The leaves are recorded directly from Table 24.1 onto the lines corresponding to their stem value to the right of the vertical line. Within each stem the leaves should be arranged in increasing order away from the stem.

In Figure 24.1 we can begin to see some important features of the distribution of *d*.

1. *Typical values.* It is not difficult to locate by eye the typical values or central location of the distribution of *d* by finding the stem or stems where most of the observations fall. For the distribution in Figure 24.1, we see that the center of the distribution seems to be in the stems corresponding to values of *d* in a range between $-0.01$ to 0.17.

2. *Shape.* Does the distribution have one peak or several peaks? Is it approximately symmetric or is it skewed in one direction? We see that the distri-

bution in Figure 24.1 may have two peaks and seems to have a longer lower tail (i.e., skewed toward negative values).

3. *Gaps/atypical values.* The stem-and-leaf plot is useful for identifying atypical observations that are usually highlighted by gaps in the distribution. For example, there is a gap between study 8 with a *d* of $-0.26$ and the next two studies, study 7 with a *d* of $-0.43$ and study 16 with a *d* of $-0.49$, suggesting that these two studies might be unusual observations.

For generalizations and modifications of the stem-and-leaf plot for other sorts of data configurations, see Koopmans (1987, pp. 19–22).

At this stage of a meta-analysis, the stem-and-leaf plot is a useful tool to help the data analyst become more familiar with the sample distribution of the effect size. From the point of view of sensitivity analysis, we are particularly interested in (a) identifying unusual or outlying studies, (b) deciding whether the assumptions of more formal statistical procedures for making inferences about the population effect size are satisfied, and (c) investigating whether there are important differences in the sample distributions of effect size for different values or levels of an explanatory variable. The stem-and-leaf plot and the box plot (described in the next section) are both useful exploratory data analytic techniques for carrying out these aspects of a sensitivity analysis.

## 3.2 Box Plots

As noted earlier, major features of a distribution include the central location of the data, the spread of the data, the shape of the distribution, and the presence of any unusual observations, called outliers. The box plot is a visual display of numerical summaries, based in part on sample percentiles, that highlights such major features of the data. A box plot differs from a stem-and-leaf plot in several ways. It is constructed from numerical summaries of the distribution and does not simply display every observation, as is the case with the stem-and-leaf plot; it provides a much clearer picture of the tails of the distribution and is more useful for identifying outliers than the stem-and-leaf plot. Sample percentiles are used to construct the box plot because percentiles, such as the median (50th percentile), are robust measures of location. The mean, in contrast, is not a robust measure of central location because it is influenced by atypical observations, or outliers.

Figure 24.2 presents a box plot of the sample distribution of $d$ produced by the statistical software package Minitab (Ryan, Joiner & Ryan 1985). The box itself is drawn from the first quartile ($Q_1 = -0.109$) to the third quartile ($Q_3 = 0.127$). The "plus" inside the box denotes the median ($m = 0.032$). The difference or distance between the third quartile and the first quartile ($Q_3 - Q_1 = 0.127 - (-0.109) = .236$) is called the interquartile range (IQR) and is a robust measure of variability. The IQR is the length of the box in Figure 24.2. The lines going in either direction from the ends of the box (i.e., away from $Q_1$ and $Q_3$, respectively) denote the tails of the distribution. These lines extend to an observed data point within 1.5 times the IQR from each respective quartile to establish regions far enough from the center of the distribution to highlight observations that may be outliers (see Koopmans 1987, pp. 51–57). The two asterisks in Figure 24.2 denote outliers, $-0.491$ and $-0.434$, and are so defined because they are located a distance more than 1.5 times the IQR from the nearest quartile. Note that the sample mean of $d$ is $-0.008$ and is smaller than the median because of the inclusion of the two negative atypical values.

From the viewpoint of sensitivity analysis, awareness of unusual features of the data, such as outliers or skewness, can guide the analyst with respect to the choice of statistical methods for synthesis and alert the analyst to the potential for erroneous conclusions based on a few influential observations. Furthermore, it is often the aim of a research synthesis to compare the sample distribution of effect size at different values of an explanatory variable—that is, to characterize how studies differ and why. Box plots are particularly useful for comparing distributions because they so clearly highlight important features of the data. For example, we might be interested in seeing whether the effects of open education on student self-concept are different for students in grades K–3 versus grades 4–6. The investigation of such questions using exploratory data analysis techniques is a form of sensitivity analysis. As an illustration, we present in Figure 24.3, a pair of box plots displaying the distribution of $d$ in each grade range. Table 24.3 gives the relevant numerical summary measures for each grade level. A comparison of the two distributions reveals:

1. *Central location.* The sample distribution of $d$ for the studies of children in grades K–3 is shifted to the right relative to the distribution for the studies of children in grades 4–6, suggesting a potentially greater effect of open education on self-concept in the younger students. Even though the median effect size for the studies of children in grades 4–6 is smaller than the median effect size for the studies of children in grades K–3, the two distributions have a great deal of overlap.

2. *Spread.* Judging by the IQRs for each distribution—that is, the length of the boxes in Figure 24.3—the spread of the sample distribution of $d$ is a little larger for the studies of children in grades 4–6, 0.262, than for the studies of children in grades K–3, 0.186.

3. *Shape.* The shape of the middle 50 percent of the sample distribution of $d$ for the studies of children in grades K–3 is skewed to the left. Note that the median is closer to $Q_3$ than to $Q_1$. Yet, we see that the right tail is longer than the left. The shape of the middle 50 percent of the distribution for the studies of children in grades 4–6 is approximately symmetric, though the median is a little closer to $Q_1$ than to $Q_3$ and the right tail is a little longer than the left, suggesting a slight skewness to the right.

4. *Outliers.* We see that each distribution has an outlier. The open circle in the box plot for the studies of children in grades K–3 indicates that the outlier in this group of studies, study 5, is very far away from $Q_1$, whereas the outlier in the group of studies for children in grades 4–6 is not quite as far out.

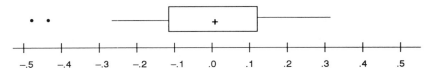

**Figure 24.2** Box plot of the standardized mean differences, *d,* for the studies reported in Table 24.1

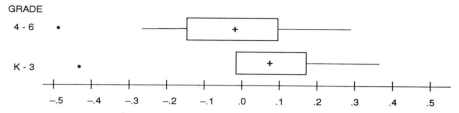

**Figure 24.3** Comparative box plots of the distribution of the standardized mean differences for studies of grades K–3 versus grades 4–6

**Table 24.3** Numerical Summary Measures for the Distribution of *d* for Grade Levels K–3 and 4–6 and for the Grade Levels Combined

|        | K–3    | 4–6    | Total  |
|--------|--------|--------|--------|
| $N$    | 7      | 11     | 18     |
| Median | 0.106  | −0.046 | 0.032  |
| Mean   | 0.046  | −0.043 | −0.008 |
| $Q_1$  | −0.010 | −0.162 | −0.109 |
| $Q_3$  | 0.176  | 0.100  | 0.127  |
| IQR    | 0.186  | 0.262  | 0.236  |

Having identified the outliers in each group, it is necessary to make some decisions about how to handle these potentially anomalous studies in subsequent analyses. Nevertheless, because of the use of robust measures of central location in the box plots displayed in Figure 24.3, we have a relatively good feeling for the amount of overlap of the distributions for the two grade ranges. As a result, for example, we might be wary of a single summary measure of effect size obtained by pooling across the two grade ranges. In summary, informal exploratory analyses from the perspective of sensitivity analysis have been useful in highlighting features of the data that we need to be aware of, sources of heterogeneity, and situations in which pooling across a stratification variable might be inappropriate.

## 4. COMBINING EFFECT SIZE ESTIMATES

Based on the exploratory analysis, we will have a better understanding of the interesting features of the data set, the effect on the research synthesis of studies that are outliers, and issues related to distributional assumptions. In the next step of a meta-analysis, decisions must be made about how to combine and summarize the effect size estimates. For example, do we assume a fixed effects model, in which studies in our research synthesis represent a random sample from the same population with a common but unknown population effect? Or do we assume a random effects model, in which there is a distribution of true effects? Should we use a weighted or unweighted summary measure of effect size? Should we use parametric or nonparametric procedures for assessing the statistical significance of our combined results? In this section we consider some of these questions as issues in sensitivity analysis.

### 4.1 Fixed Effects

Hedges and Olkin (1985) provide a catalog of effect size estimates from a single study and methods of combining them across studies. In practice, when there is a choice between two analyses or between two summary measures, it is prudent to do both analyses to see how the conclusions differ and to understand why they differ (Greenhouse et al. 1990). For example, the average of the standardized mean difference for the studies of the effect of open education on student self-concept given in Table 24.1 is $\bar{d} = -.008$ with an approximate 95 percent confidence interval of $(-0.111, 0.023)$. Since zero is contained in this interval we can conclude that there is not a statistically significant difference between the effect of open education and traditional education on student self-concept. If we are concerned with the effect of the different sample sizes in the primary studies, we can calculate a nearly optimally weighted average of the standardized mean difference, $\bar{d}_w$, using the weights given in Table 24.1, where $w_i = \tilde{n}_i / \sum_{i=1}^{k} \tilde{n}_i$ and $\tilde{n}_i = (n_i^T \cdot n_i^C)/(n_i^T + n_i^C)$. From Table 24.1 we find the weighted average of the standardized mean difference to be

**Table 24.4 The Values of $\overline{d}(i)$ for the Studies in Table 24.1**

| Study Left Out $i$ | $d$ | Unweighted $\overline{d}(i)$ | Weighted $\overline{d}_w(i)$ |
|---|---|---|---|
| 1 | 0.100 | −0.015 | −0.001 |
| 2 | −0.162 | 0.001 | 0.030 |
| 3 | −0.091 | −0.003 | 0.013 |
| 4 | −0.049 | −0.006 | 0.012 |
| 5 | −0.046 | −0.006 | 0.013 |
| 6 | −0.010 | −0.008 | 0.011 |
| 7 | −0.434 | 0.017 | 0.032 |
| 8 | −0.262 | 0.008 | 0.030 |
| 9 | 0.135 | −0.017 | 0.003 |
| 10 | 0.019 | −0.010 | 0.009 |
| 11 | 0.176 | −0.019 | 0.000 |
| 12 | 0.056 | −0.012 | 0.007 |
| 13 | 0.045 | −0.011 | 0.008 |
| 14 | 0.106 | −0.015 | 0.009 |
| 15 | 0.124 | −0.016 | 0.009 |
| 16 | −0.491 | 0.020 | 0.020 |
| 17 | 0.291 | −0.026 | −0.023 |
| 18 | 0.344 | −0.029 | −0.008 |
| Median | 0.032 | −0.011 | 0.009 |

$$\overline{d}_w = w_1 \cdot d_1 + \ldots + w_k \cdot d_k = 0.010.$$

with an approximate 95 percent confidence interval of $(-0.073, 0.093)$. We see that our conclusions about the population effect size in this case do not depend on whether we use a weighted or unweighted estimate.

At this stage, it is of interest to see whether any individual studies or groups of studies have a large influence on the effect size estimate. For example, recall that in section 3 we identified several studies as potential outliers. A relatively simple method for doing this is to hold one study out, calculate the average effect size by combining the remaining studies, and compare the results with the overall combined estimate. Here we are interested in assessing how sensitive the combined measure of the effect size is to any one particular study. In other words, how large is the influence of each study on the overall estimate of effect size. Let $\overline{d}(i)$ be the unweighted average standardized mean difference computed from all the studies except study $i$. Table 24.4 presents the values of $\overline{d}(i)$ for the studies in Table 24.1. We see that the effect of leaving study 7 or 16 out of the unweighted average of the standardized mean difference, respectively, is an increase in the summary estimate. Since we identified these two studies earlier

as outliers, this is not a surprising result. We also see from Table 24.4 that studies 17 and 18 have the largest values of $d$ among all of the studies and the effect of leaving each of these studies out of the combined estimate, respectively, is a decrease in the average standardized mean difference. In summary, the results in this analysis are as we might expect: Remove a study that has a smaller-than-the-mean effect size, and the overall summary measure increases.

In Table 24.4, we also report the analysis of leaving one study out using the weighted average, $\overline{d}_w(i)$. We see similar results for the analysis with the unweighted average. However, in addition, we now see that studies 2 and 8 are fairly influential studies, respectively. Because they are larger studies, removing them one at a time from the analysis causes the weighted average effect size to increase.

Leaving out more than one study at a time can become very complicated. For instance, if we leave out all pairs, all triplets, and so on, the number of cases to consider would be too large to give any useful information. It is better to identify beforehand covariates that are of interest and leave out studies according to levels of the covariates. In our example, the only covariate provided is the grade level (K–3 and 4–6); thus, leaving out one level of that covariate is equivalent to the box plot analysis given in Table 24.3 and Figure 24.3 above. Finally, we note that the leave-one-out method can be used for other combining procedures. For instance, maximum likelihood estimation is common when we have a specific model for the effect sizes. In that case, the sensitivity of each case can be assessed as shown above; of course, the computational burden involved will be much greater.

### 4.2 Random Effects

In the previous sections, the covariate information (grade level) was useful in accounting for some of the variability among the effect size estimates. There are times, though, when such attempts fail to find "consistent relationships between study characteristics and effect size" (Hedges & Olkin 1985, p. 190). In such cases, random effects models provide an alternative framework for combining effect sizes. These models regard the population effect sizes themselves as random variables, sampled from a distribution of possible effect sizes. Chapters 3 and 20 of this volume and Chapter 9 of Hedges and Olkin (1985) provide a discussion of the distinction between random and fixed effect models, the conceptual bases underlying random effects models, and their application to research synthesis. The discussion below assumes familiarity with those chapters. The development of methods for sensitivity analysis for random effects models is an important, open research area. In fact, Hedges and Olkin (1985) do not refer to random effects models in their chapter on diagnostic procedures for research synthesis. In this section we will briefly outline the most common random effects model and then mention one notable example of the use of sensitivity analysis for random effects models in meta-analysis.

In the random effects approach, the true effect sizes $\{\delta_i : i = 1, \ldots, k\}$ are considered to be realizations of a random variable $\Delta$; that is, they are a random sample from a population of effect sizes, which is governed by some distribution with mean $\mu_\Delta$ and variance $\sigma_\Delta^2$, a measure of the between-studies variability. Given sample estimates, $d_i$, of $\delta_i$ for $i = 1, \ldots, k$, the analysis proceeds by estimating these parameters or performing tests on them. For instance, a common starting point is the test of the hypothesis that the between-studies variance component is zero, that is, $\sigma_\Delta^2 = 0$, which is also a test of the fixed effects model with complete homogeneity of the effect sizes across the $k$ studies; $\delta_1 = \ldots = \delta_k = \delta$. Note that this common effect size, $\delta$, in the fixed effects model has a different interpretation than $\hat{\mu}_\Delta$: Even if $\hat{\mu}_\Delta$ is positive, there may be realizations $\delta_i$ that are negative. For more discussion, see Hedges (1983), Hedges and Olkin (1985), and DerSimonian and Laird (1986).

An important example of sensitivity analysis is the comparison of the results of fixed and random effects models for a particular data set. The output from a fixed effects analysis includes an estimate of the common effect size, $\hat{\delta}$, and its estimated standard error, $SE$. The output from a random effects analysis includes an estimate of the mean of the distribution of effect sizes, $\hat{\mu}_\Delta$, its estimated standard error, $SE(\hat{\mu}_\Delta)$, an estimate of the variance of the distribution of random effects, $\hat{\sigma}_\Delta^2$, and the value of the chi-square test of the hypothesis of complete homogeneity. Confidence intervals for the mean effect sizes ($\delta$ and $\hat{\mu}_\Delta$) are also provided. All calculations below are based on the technical details provided by Hedges and Olkin (1985).

Tables 24.5 and 24.6 contain the results of the two analyses for the data in Tables 24.1 and 24.2. Recall that Table 24.1 consists of studies that measured the effects of open education on self-concept and included grade level as a covariate. Table 24.2 consists of studies

that measured the effects of open education on student independence and self-reliance, but provided no covariate information. For Table 24.2, the estimates of (common or mean) effect size are virtually the same ($\hat{\delta} = -0.095$, $\hat{\mu}_\Delta = -0.095$), but the $SE$ for the random effects model, 0.161, is greater than that for the fixed effects model, 0.099. Next, the estimate $\hat{\sigma}_\Delta^2 = 0.113$ is significantly different from zero, as the corresponding chi-square value is 15.50, which exceeds the 5 percent critical value of 12.59 for 6 degrees of freedom. Since this test of complete homogeneity rejects, the conservative (in the sense of having wider confidence intervals) random effects analysis is deemed more valid. In this case, the substantive conclusions may well be the same under both models, since both confidence intervals contain zero. On the other hand, when the two methods differ, it is important to use the analysis of $\hat{\sigma}_\Delta^2$ to help choose between the two.

The rest of Tables 24.5 and 24.6 compare the two analyses for the data in Table 24.1. In section 3 above, we saw that grade level, the one covariate provided, helped to explain variability among the effect size estimates. Thus, neither the fixed effects nor the random effects models should be applied to these data without modification. We present these data to illustrate several points. First, we can compare the two on subsets of the data defined by the levels of the covariate (in this case, grades K–3 and 4–6). Next, making inferences about $\sigma_\Delta^2$ can be difficult, because a large number of primary studies are needed, and strong distributional assumptions must be satisfied in order to use the procedures described in Hedges and Olkin (1985). In fact, for the K–3 data, the unbiased estimate of $\sigma_\Delta^2$ is negative. While it is tempting to interpret this as supporting the hypothesis that $\sigma_\Delta^2 = 0$ and then to use the fixed effects analysis, more research is needed to find better methods of estimating $\sigma_\Delta^2$ for such cases. (See Chapter 20 in this volume for further discussion as well as Hill 1965.) Of course, the methods from exploratory data analysis discussed earlier are also useful for sensitivity analysis. For instance, the leave-one-out method can be readily used in a random effects context to informally investigate the influence of studies.

Random effects models typically assume the normal distribution for the effect sizes (for continuous data), so one concern is how sensitive the analysis is to this assumption. The two main steps in addressing this concern are to detect departures from normality of the random effects and then to assess the impact of nonnormality on the combined estimates of interest. The weighted

**Table 24.5  Results of the Analysis of the Fixed Effects Model for the Studies in Tables 24.1 and 24.2**

| Data Set | (Table) | $k$ | $\hat{\delta}$ | $SE(\hat{\delta})$ | 95% CI for $\delta$ |
|---|---|---|---|---|---|
| Independence | (24.2) | 7 | $-0.095$ | 0.099 | $(-0.288, 0.099)$ |
| Self-concept | (21.1, K–3) | 7 | 0.034 | 0.081 | $(-0.125, 0.192)$ |
| Self-concept | (24.1, 4–6) | 11 | 0.001 | 0.050 | $(-0.096, 0.099)$ |

**Table 24.6  Results of the Analysis of the Random Effects Model for the Studies in Tables 24.1 and 24.2**

| Data Set | (Table) | $k$ | $\hat{\mu}_\Delta$ | $SE(\hat{\mu}_\Delta)$ | 95% CI for $\hat{\mu}_\Delta$ | $\hat{\sigma}^2_\Delta$ | chi-square $H_0: \sigma^2_\Delta = 0$ |
|---|---|---|---|---|---|---|---|
| Independence | (24.2) | 7 | $-0.095$ | 0.161 | $(-0.411, 0.220)$ | 0.113 | 15.50 |
| Self-concept | (24.1, K–3) | 7 | 0.037 | 0.066 | $(-0.093, 0.167)$ | 0.0* | 9.56 |
| Self-concept | (24.1, 4–6) | 11 | 0.004 | 0.057 | $(-0.116, 0.107)$ | 0.007 | 13.96 |

*The unbiased estimate, $-0.012$, is inadmissible.

normal plot (Dempster & Ryan 1985) is a graphic procedure designed to check the assumption of normality of the random effects in linear models. This diagnostic plot has been used by Carlin (1992) in his study combining the log of odds ratios from several $2 \times 2$ tables. If the normality of the random effects is found to be inappropriate, several new problems arise. For instance, the usual parameters (such as $\mu_\delta$) are no longer easily interpretable. For example, if the distribution of effect sizes is sufficiently skewed, it is possible for the mean effect size to be positive (indicating on average an efficacious result), but for more than half of all the effect sizes to be negative. One way to assess the sensitivity of the analysis to this kind of departure from the normal assumption is to use skewed densities, such as the gamma or log-normal families. Carrying out this kind of sensitivity analysis is not easy, however, because appropriate software is not yet available.

The random effects models described above are closely related to a Bayesian approach to meta-analysis; see Chapter 26 for more detailed discussion of Bayesian methods. Many of the techniques described here can be adapted for use in this context also. For instance, DuMouchel and Harris (1983) provide an example of sensitivity analysis for a meta-analysis using Bayesian methods. Their aim is to combine information from studies of the effects of carcinogens on humans and various animal species. Their data set consists of a matrix (rows for species, columns for carcinogens) of

the estimated slope of the dose-response lines given from each experiment. They postulate a linear model for the logarithm of these slopes. In addition, they adopt a hierarchical model for the parameters of the linear model. That is, the parameters of the linear model are themselves random variables that have certain specified prior distributions. In this context, they vary the prior distribution to see how the inferences are affected. They also use a variant of the leave-one-out method by leaving out an entire row or an entire column from their data matrix to investigate the fit of their model.

### 4.3 Other Methods

There are, of course, many other analytic methods used in research synthesis that we could consider from the viewpoint of sensitivity analysis. Two commonly used methods are the combination of $p$ values and regression analysis. Our aim in this section is to alert the reader to the need for sensitivity analysis at the data-combining stage of a research synthesis. The details of the sensitivity analysis depend on the methods used to combine data. For $p$ values many of the techniques described above are directly applicable. For regression analysis a number of diagnostic tools, such as residual analysis and case analysis (Weisberg 1985; Hedges & Olkin 1985, Chapter 12), can be applied. In addition, as we have indicated in this section, there are open research opportunities for the development of new methods for sensitivity analysis.

## 5. PUBLICATION BIAS

One criticism of meta-analysis is that the available studies may not be representative of all studies addressing the research question. Publication bias occurs when studies reporting statistically significant results are published and studies reporting less significant results are not. Rosenthal (1979) imagined that these unpublished studies ended up in investigators' files, and dubbed this phenomenon the file-drawer problem. At least two variations of this problem have been identified. One is reporting bias (Hedges 1988), which arises in published studies in which authors do not report results that are statistically nonsignificant or provide insufficient information about them. The other is retrieval bias (Rosenthal 1990), which is due to the inability to retrieve all of the research, whether published or not.

In this section we discuss methods for assessing the presence of publication bias and for assessing the impact of publication bias from the point of view of sensitivity analysis. The steps we follow are first to consider a graphic display for the detection of publication bias called a "funnel plot." Then, having used the funnel plot as a diagnostic tool to indicate the presence of publication bias, we would next decide how to adjust the observed combined effect size estimate for this bias. Suppose, for the moment, that an adjustment method is agreed on. Then a sensitivity analysis would find the adjusted values for a variety of possible selection mechanisms. If these values are not far from the unadjusted average, the latter is deemed robust, or insensitive to publication bias; otherwise, the unadjusted average should not be trusted unless a subsequent search for more studies still supports it. In practice, the use of a single adjustment method is usually not warranted. It is better to apply a range of plausible adjustment methods to see how robust the observed value is.

Another approach to sensitivity analysis for dealing with publication bias is the "fail-safe sample size" approach of Rosenthal (1979). This approach uses combined significance levels rather than effect size estimates. For a critique of this and other approaches to publication bias, see Iyengar and Greenhouse (1988) and Chapter 25 in this volume. For a Bayesian approach to this problem, see Bayarri (1988). In summary, the role of sensitivity analysis with respect to publication bias is twofold: to assess its presence and to assess its impact. We next turn to the details of these two roles.

### 5.1 Assessing the Presence of Publication Bias

Light and Pillemer (1984) introduced the "funnel plot" for the graphic detection of publication bias. A funnel plot is a scatterplot of sample size versus estimated effect size for a group of studies. Since small studies will typically show more variability among the effect sizes than larger studies, and there will typically be fewer of the latter, the plot should look like a funnel, hence its name. When there is publication bias against, say, studies showing small effect sizes, a bite will be taken out of a part of this plot. Figure 24.4 shows a funnel plot for a meta-analysis where there is no publication bias: It is a plot of 100 simulated studies that compare treatment and control. For the $i$th study there are $n_i$ observations per group, where $n_i$ span the range 10 to 100; the population effect size was set at 0.50. Because of its shape, the funnel plot is a useful visual diagnostic for an informal assessment of the file-drawer problem.

Two simple biasing mechanisms are depicted in Figures 24.5 and 24.6. The data in both of these figures are derived from data in Figure 24.4. In Figure 24.5, all 70 studies that report statistically significant results at the 0.05 level are shown; in Figure 24.6, significant results have an 80 percent chance of being reported, while the rest have only a 10 percent chance of being reported. Note in Figure 24.5 that the plot is skewed to the right, and there appears to be a sharp cutoff of effect sizes at 0.30. Thus, it is reasonable to suspect publication bias against small or negative effect sizes. These two selection mechanisms are presented here for illustration, but others are possible (see Chapter 25). It is interesting to note how much more difficult it is to detect publication bias in Figure 24.6 than in Figure 24.5. This is partly because there are fewer cases overall, but also because detection of the pattern requires detection of variation in the density of points, not simply the absolute presence or absence of points in the lower lefthand corner of the plot.

### 5.2 Assessing the Impact of Publication Bias

There are several ways of dealing with publication bias once it has been detected or suspected. One approach explicitly incorporates the biasing or selection mechanism into the model to get an adjusted overall estimate

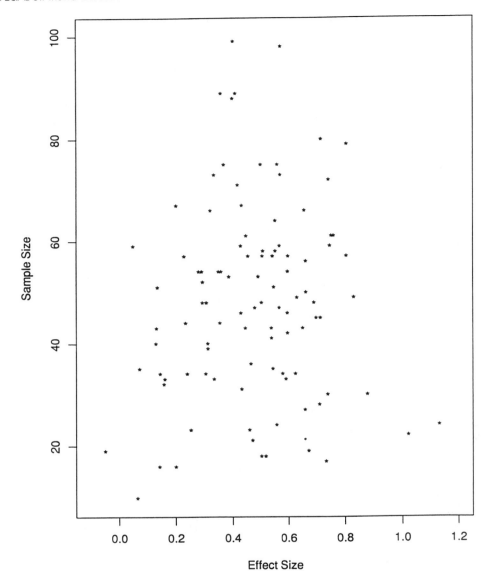

**Figure 24.4** Funnel plot for all studies

of the effect size. For instance, suppose that the biasing mechanism favors publication of results that are statistically significant and that the primary studies report one-sided $z$ tests using the 0.05 level, which has a cutoff of $z = 1.645$. That is, the probability, $w(z)$, of publication of a study's results increases with its $z$ value. An extreme case is the situation in which only the statistically significant results are published, so that

$$w(z) = \begin{cases} 0 \text{ if } z < 1.645 \\ 1 \text{ if } z \geq 1.645. \end{cases}$$

The probability $w(z)$ is known as a weight function (Rao 1985). In this approach, the weight function is used to

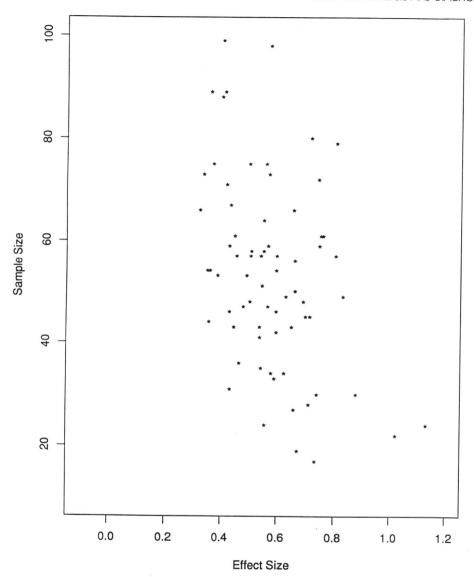

**Figure 24.5** Funnel plot when only studies statistically significant at the 0.05 level are reported

construct the likelihood function based on the published studies. Adjusted estimates of the effect size are then derived using standard maximum likelihood or Bayesian methods. See the appendix and Chapter 25 for technical details.

Several comments about this approach are in order. First, it is flexible in the sense that it can also be used to model other types of bias, such as retrieval bias. For example, if $p_1$ and $p_2$ are the probabilities of retrieving a published study and an unpublished study, respectively, then the probability of a study entering a meta-analysis at all may be modeled as $p_1 w(z)$ for a published study and as $p_2 w(z)$ for an unpublished study. Several empirical studies (Chalmers, Frank & Reitman 1990;

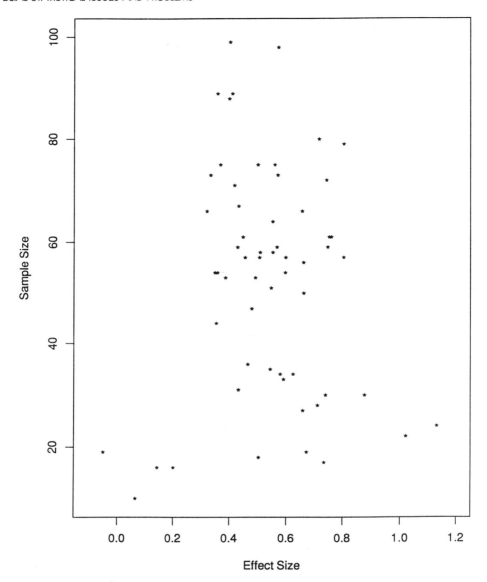

**Figure 24.6** Funnel plot when studies statistically significant at the 0.05 level have an 80 percent chance of being reported and insignificant results have a 10 percent chance of being reported.

Dickersin et al. 1985) of the retrieval process have been done, and they may be useful in providing rough guidelines for determining ranges for $p_1$ and $p_2$. Next, since the weight function is typically not known, it is useful to do the analysis of the weighted models with various plausible families of weight functions. If the resulting effect size estimates do not change much, such a sensitivity analysis will give more credence to the inferences based on the retrieved studies (Iyengar & Greenhouse 1988).

We end this discussion with a numerical example illustrating the use of weighted distributions for the data in Table 24.1. Suppose that all studies use a two-sided $z$ test at the 0.05 level, which has cutoffs $-1.96$ and $1.96$. Suppose further that the bias is such that a study with a significant result will definitely be published, whereas other studies will be published with some probability less than 1. A weight function that models this situation is

$$w(z; \beta) = \begin{cases} e^{-\beta} & \text{if } -1.96 < z < 1.96 \\ 1 & \text{else.} \end{cases}$$

This choice of $w$ is actually a member of a family of weight functions parameterized by a nonnegative quantity $\beta$, indicating uncertainty about the probability of publication when an effect size is not significant; the larger the value of $\beta$, the greater the degree of publication bias. Maximum likelihood estimation of the two parameters $\delta$, the true effect size, and $\beta$, the bias parameter yields $\hat{\delta} = -0.006$ ($SE = 0.033$) and $\hat{\beta} = 0.17$ ($SE = 0.192$), respectively. Since the unweighted estimate of the true effect size is $-0.008$, we conclude that the result is not sensitive to this choice of publication bias mechanism. The estimate of $\beta$ indicates that the probability of publishing a statistically nonsignificant result is about 0.85; note, however, that the standard error for the estimate of $\beta$ is relatively large, indicating that the data provide little information about that parameter.

## 6. SUMMARY

Sensitivity analysis is a systematic approach to address the question, "What happens if some aspect of the data or the analysis is changed?" Since at every step of a research synthesis decisions and judgments are made that can affect the conclusions and generalizability of the results, we believe that sensitivity analysis has an important role to play in research synthesis. In order for the results of a meta-analysis to be convincing to a wide range of readers, it is important to assess the effects of these decisions and judgments. One way to do this is to demonstrate that a broad range of viewpoints and statistical analyses yield substantially the same conclusions. Sensitivity analysis and diagnostics as described in this chapter provide a conceptual framework and some technical tools for doing just that. On the other hand, a meta-analysis is useful even if the conclusions are sensitive to such alternatives, for then the sensitivity analysis points to the features of the problem that deserve further attention.

## 7. REFERENCES

Bayarri, M. J. (1988). Discussion. *Statistical Science, 3,* 109–135.

Begg, C., & Berlin, J. (1988). Publication bias: A problem in interpreting medical data (with discussion). *Journal of the Royal Statistical Society,* Series A, *151,* 419–463.

Bishop, Y., Fienberg, S., & Holland, P. (1975). *Discrete multivariate analysis: Theory and practice.* Cambridge, MA: MIT Press.

Carlin, J. (1992). Meta-analysis for 2 × 2 tables: A Bayesian approach. *Statistics in Medicine, 11,* 141–158.

Chalmers, T., Frank, C., & Reitman, D. (1990). Minimizing the three stages of publication bias. *Journal of the American Medical Association, 263,* 1392–1395.

Cronbach, L. (1980). *Toward reform of program evaluation.* San Francisco: Jossey-Bass.

Dempster, A., & Ryan, L. (1985). Weighted normal plots. *Journal of the American Statistical Association, 80,* 845–850.

DerSimonian, R., & Laird, N. (1986). Meta-analysis in clinical trials. *Controlled Clinical Trials, 7,* 177–188.

Dickersin, K., Hewitt, P., Mutch, L., Chalmers, I., & Chalmers, T. (1985). Perusing the literature: Comparison of MEDLINE searching with a perinatal trials database. *Controlled Clinical Trials, 6,* 306–317.

DuMouchel, W., & Harris, J. (1983). Bayes methods for combining the results of cancer studies in humans and other species. *Journal of the American Statistical Society, 78,* 293–315.

Greenhouse, J. B., Fromm, D., Iyengar, S., Dew, M. A., Holland, A., and Kass, R. (1990). The making of a meta-analysis: A quantitative review of the aphasia treatment literature. In K. W. Wachter & M. L. Straf (Eds.), *The future of meta-analysis.* New York: Russell Sage Foundation.

Hedges, L. V. (1983). A random effects model for effect sizes. *Psychological Bulletin, 93,* 388–395.

Hedges, L. V. (1990). Directions for future methodology. In K. W. Wachter & M. L. Straf (Eds.), *The future of meta-analysis.* New York: Russell Sage Foundation.

Hedges, L. V., Giaconia, R., and Gage, N. (1981). *The empirical evidence on the effectiveness of open education.* Stanford, CA: Stanford University, School of Education.

Hedges, L. V., and Olkin, I. (1985). *Statistical methods for meta-analysis.* New York: Academic Press.

Hill, B. M. (1965). Inference about variance components in the one-way model. *Journal of the American Statistical Association, 60,* 806–825.

Iyengar, S., and Greenhouse, J. B. (1988). Selection models and the file-drawer problem (with discussion). *Statistical Science, 3,* 109–135.

Koopmans, L. (1987). *Introduction to contemporary statistical methods.* Boston: Duxbury Press.

Light, R. J., and Pillemer, D. B. (1984). *Summing up: The science of reviewing research.* Cambridge, MA: Harvard University Press.

Rao, C. R. (1985). Weighted distributions arising out of methods of ascertainment: What population does a sample represent? In A. C. Atkinson & S. E. Fienberg (Eds.), *A Celebration of Statistics* (pp. 543–569). New York: Springer-Verlag.

Rosenthal, R. (1979). The ''file-drawer'' problem and tolerance for null results. *Psychological Bulletin, 86,* 638–641.

Rosenthal, R. (1984). *Meta-analytic procedures for social research.* Beverly Hills, CA: Sage.

Rosenthal, R. (1988). An evaluation of procedures and results. In K. W. Wachter & M. L. Straf (Eds.), *The future of meta-analysis.* New York: Russell Sage Foundation.

Ryan, B., Joiner, B., and Ryan, T. (1985). *Minitab handbook.* Boston: Duxbury Press.

Wachter, K. W., & Straf, M. L. (Eds.). (1990). *The future of meta-analysis.* New York: Russell Sage Foundation.

Weisberg, S. (1985). *Applied linear regression 2nd ed.* New York: Wiley.

## 8. APPENDIX: A Selection Model for the File-Drawer Problem

Suppose that $w(z)$ is interpreted as the probability of publishing a study when the effect size estimate from that study is $z$. If an effect size estimate is normally distributed, then the published effect size estimate from a study is a random variable from the weighted normal probability density

$$f(z;\delta,w) = \frac{\phi(z - \delta;\ \sigma^2/n)w(x)}{A(\delta,\sigma^2/n;\ w)},$$

where $\phi(z;\sigma^2)$ is the density of the normal distribution with mean zero and variance $\sigma^2$,

$$A(\delta,\sigma^2;w) = \int_{-\infty}^{\infty} \phi(t - \delta;\sigma^2)w(t)dt$$

is the normalizing constant, and $n$ and $\delta$ are the sample size and the true effect size for that study, respectively. Inference about the effect size can then be based on this weighted model, using maximum likelihood or Bayesian estimates. Since the weighted model is also a member of an exponential family, an iterative procedure for computing the estimate is relatively easy. Often, primary studies report $t$ statistics with their degrees of freedom; in that case, a noncentral $t$ density replaces the normal density above, and the computations become considerably more difficult. For an example involving the combination of $t$ statistics, see Iyengar and Greenhouse (1988). When the degrees of freedom within each primary study are fairly large, however, the normal approximation is quite accurate.

Cooper, H. and Hedges, L. V. (Eds.) 1994. *The Handbook of Research Synthesis.* New York: Russell Sage Foundation

# 25

## PUBLICATION BIAS

**COLIN B. BEGG**
*Memorial Sloan-Kettering Cancer Center*

CONTENTS

## 1. BACKGROUND

The style of reporting the results of a research study in a journal article is governed as much by human nature as by the tradition of scientific objectivity. That is, research studies are commonly reported in an advocacy style. Statistical significance, if it is achieved, may be used as "proof" of a theory. Moreover, the statistical analysis may be subjectively influenced by the use of a variety of statistical tests, excluding certain categories of subjects, performing analyses in selected subgroups, or adjusting the analysis for covariates, all with the goal of presenting the data in such a way as to provide the greatest support for the preferred theory under study. Of course, the fact that the published article does not accurately reflect the true research process is not limited to the purely statistical aspects of the paper, and indeed Medawar (1963) has suggested that most scientific articles are essentially fraudulent in that they systematically misrepresent the process by which the conclusions have been reached. This entire phenomenon is a kind of publication bias, which one might refer to as subjective publication bias, and it is a bias that is well recognized throughout the scientific community.

Another widely recognized bias, and one that is very important for meta-analysis, is the one that is induced by selective publication, in which the decision to publish is influenced by the results of the study. This is what meta-analysts refer to as publication bias, and one might refer to it as objective publication bias, since it is the "objective" data reported that are subject to the bias. That is, if one can extract the raw data or relevant summary data from the paper, stripping away the attendant subjective interpretations, these seemingly objective data are still subject to bias owing to the selective publication.

How does this bias occur? One way of conceptualizing the problem is to consider the scenario in which a number of investigators are independently conducting identical studies to estimate some effect. After the studies are completed the estimates will differ owing to random variation. The investigator who happened to perform the study that produced the largest effect (i.e., the most significant effect) is the most likely to publish the results. However, selecting the largest of a random sample of estimates will provide a positively biased estimate of the true (mean) effect, and the magnitude of this bias is a function of the sample size of the study and the number of concurrent studies from which the largest estimate is selected. For example, if five identical studies are conducted, each with a sample size of 20, the largest mean effect size is positively biased by 0.26 standard deviations. A study of this phenomenon shows that the magnitude of the bias is inversely related to sample size and positively associated with the number of concurrent studies (Begg 1985). In other words, we should be especially concerned about publication bias in settings in which lots of small studies are being conducted.

In many cases the decision to publish will be influenced by the presence or absence of a statistically significant effect, with significant results more likely to be published. Such a phenomenon produces a preponderance of statistically significant publications and increases the chance that any single publication is a false positive. That is, the nominal 5 percent chance of a false positive is an underestimate. Editorial policy can potentially accentuate this problem by discouraging the publication of negative studies (Melton 1962).

There have been a number of empirical investigations of the magnitude of publication bias, most of which demonstrate the potentially serious implications for meta-analysis. The following review is not intended to be comprehensive, but merely highlights a few of the studies that have been conducted. For a more detailed exposition, see Begg and Berlin (1988).

The earliest studies of publication bias were concentrated in the social science literature. In a pioneering study, Sterling (1959) examined a consecutive series of published articles involving significance testing in four psychology journals and found that 286 of the 294 articles (97 percent) reported statistically significant findings, providing strong indirect evidence of publication bias. Greenwald (1975) studied the issue conceptually, distinguishing the roles of authors and editors in selective publication. In more recent investigations Smith (1980) demonstrated that effect sizes in studies of educational innovations were smaller for unpublished studies than for published studies. Coursol and Wagner (1986) have shown in a survey of psychological researchers that both the decision to submit an article and the editorial decision to accept or reject were correlated with positive results of the studies.

In the past few years researchers have been examining these issues in the medical literature. Two recent follow-up studies in which lists of research studies from hospital ethics committees have been used as a sampling frame provide strong direct evidence for publication bias. The study by Easterbrook et al. (1991) showed that studies demonstrating statistical significance had an increased chance of publication (odds ratio = 2.3), a result that has been verified in an independent study by Dickersin, Min, and Meinert (1992), who also show that the strength of the bias is greater in clinical research (odds ratio = 3.4) than in public health research (odds ratio = 1.8). Both of these studies also showed that larger studies are more likely to be published, and the Easterbrook study also demonstrated a greater propensity for publication bias in observational studies versus randomized trials, a result that was inferred indirectly in earlier studies by Sacks, Chalmers, and Smith (1983) and Berlin, Begg, and Louis (1989).

These results underscore the importance of publication bias for the meta-analyst. If the meta-analysis is restricted to published studies, then there is a risk that it will lead to biased conclusions. This is especially problematic in that one of the major advantages of meta-analysis is that the aggregation of data can lead to effect size estimates with very small variance, giving the impression of conclusiveness in circumstances where the summary estimate is biased. That is, the resulting inferences may not only be wrong but appear convincing.

To summarize, most studies of the issue have consistently demonstrated that positive (statistically significant) studies are more likely to be published, leading to bias. (Note: Some authors have studied circumstances in which negative studies are more likely to be reported; see, e.g., Kotelchuck 1974 and Hemminki 1980.) A feature of a study that is likely to be positively associated with bias, both from theoretical and empirical evidence, is (small) sample size. It is possible that other features of study design, such as failure to use randomization or the absence of a control group may also be associated with bias. As we shall see, these factors provide the main levers for identifying publication bias prior to embarking on a meta-analysis.

## 2. METHODS FOR IDENTIFYING PUBLICATION BIAS

When the component studies have been assembled for the meta-analysis, a preliminary analysis should be undertaken to assess the chances that publication bias could be playing a role in the selection of the studies. Such an exploratory analysis is the only type of analysis of those presented in this chapter that is widely accepted and in common usage. However, this methodology represents an essential component in the methodological

armamentarium, and should be used routinely, prior to developing a more formal statistical analysis.

### 2.1 Preliminary Analysis

The general technique for detecting the possibility of bias is to correlate the observed effect sizes (or any primary measure of efficacy) with important design features of the studies that are risk factors for publication bias. As we saw in the previous section, the most important such factor is sample size, with other likely correlates of bias being the presence or absence of randomization, and prospective versus retrospective study design. Assuming that the effect sizes are commensurate in each of the studies, and the populations of subjects are similar, then ostensibly there should exist no association between effect size and any of these design factors. Consequently, the presence of an association is indicative of the possibility of publication bias, in which case one would want to either abandon the meta-analysis as being unreliable or focus on a subset of the studies believed to be unbiased, or least biased. (Note that an association of this nature could be due to other reasons than publication bias.) For example, in a meta-analysis of a treatment intervention that consists of a mixture of randomized and nonrandomized studies, if randomization status appears to be associated with the effect sizes one might choose to eliminate all the nonrandomized studies from the analysis, on the grounds that they lead to less reliable data. Empirical evidence supporting the elimination of nonrandomized studies is provided by Sacks, Chalmers, and Smith (1983), who showed that in six prominent issues the published nonrandomized trials were predominantly positive, while very few of the randomized trials showed a positive effect. A similar approach could be used in meta-analyses involving prospective and retrospective studies, or indeed any group of studies that can be classified on objective methodological criteria.

### 2.2 Sample Size

The most important leverage for identifying publication bias is, however, sample size. Part of the rationale for sample size being strongly associated with publication bias, if it exists, was described in the previous section. Briefly, small studies produce highly variable effect size estimates. Therefore, the most aberrant values that occur by chance are much farther from the true mean effect size than the aberrant values for large studies. Therefore,

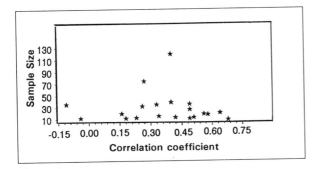

**Figure 25.1** Funnel-Graph: Data Set III

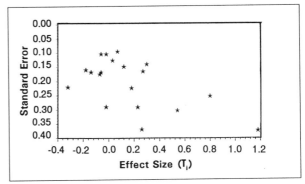

**Figure 25.2** Funnel-Graph: Data Set II

if selective publication causes the more extreme effect sizes to be selected for publication, regardless of the sample size, then the effect sizes from the small studies will be more extreme than those from the larger studies, leading to an induced association. It is also possible that small studies may be less likely to be published because of *perceived* unreliability, and so authors may feel that statistical significance is necessary to justify publication to a greater extent than for larger studies.

This effect can be examined informally by using a "funnel graph," a plot of sample size versus effect size (Light & Pillemer 1984). If no bias is present, this plot should be shaped like a funnel, with the spout pointing up—that is, with a broad spread of points for the highly variable small studies at the bottom and decreasing spread as the sample size increases. However, the mean effect size should be the same regardless of sample size. That is, one should be able to draw a vertical line through the mean effect size, and the points should be distributed on either side for all sample sizes. In other words, the funnel should not be skewed. A funnel graph consistent with this pattern is obtained from Data Set III (see Appendix A), in which students ratings of their instructor are correlated with achievement (Figure 25.1). However, the range of sample sizes for all but two of the studies is so narrow that the demonstration of a trend would be unlikely. Nonetheless, this plot provides reassuring evidence that publication bias is unlikely to be a problem for this meta-analysis.

By contrast the funnel graph for Data Set II does not display the characteristic funnel shape (Figure 25.2). This is a meta-analysis of the effects of teacher expectancy on pupil IQ (Raudenbush 1984), in which the standard error of the effect size replaces sample size on the vertical axis. (For our purposes these two terms are essentially equivalent.) In this case the large studies (i.e., small standard error) at the top seem to be clustered

around the null value, whereas the small studies at the bottom are skewed toward a positive effect. This demonstrates the classic publication bias pattern, the speculation being that there really are a number of small studies with effect sizes distributed around the null value, but most of these remain unpublished.

## 2.3 Statistical Significance Test

A formal statistical significance test can be constructed to provide quantitative evidence against the hypothesis that no publication bias exists. Probably the best approach is to use a rank correlation test, such as the test based on Kendall's tau (Armitage & Berry 1987). Such an approach involves no modeling assumptions, but suffers from a lack of power, a topic we shall return to momentarily. One might alternatively use the test based on Spearman's rho, which is somewhat simpler to compute (see Colton 1974).

The test involves determining the ranks of the two factors and constructing the rank-ordered sample on the basis of one of them, say effect size. Since the test is based on the assumption that the effect sizes are statistically independent and identically distributed, under the null hypothesis of no bias, it is necessary to standardize the effect sizes prior to performing the test. That is, if $\{T_i\}$ and $\{v_i\}$ are the individual effect sizes and sampling variances, respectively, we perform a rank correlation of $\{T_i^*\}$ versus $\{n_i\}$, where

$$T_i^* = (T_i - \overline{T}.)/(\hat{v}_i^*)^{1/2}$$

$$\overline{T}. = (\sum_{j=1}^{k} v_i^{-1} T_j)/ \sum_{j=1}^{k} v_i^{-1},$$

and where

$$\bar{v}_i = v_i - (\sum_{j=1}^{k} v_j^{-1})^{-1}$$

is the variance of $(T_i - \bar{T}.)$. Note that for Data Set II this is equivalent to correlating $\{T_i^*\}$ versus $\{v_i\}$ since there is a one-to-one correspondence between $\{n_i\}$ and $\{v_i\}$. The test involves evaluating $P$, the number of all possible pairings in which one factor is ranked in the same order as the other, and $Q$, the number in which the ordering is reversed. A normalized test statistic ($z$ score) is then obtained using

$$Z = (P - Q)/[k(k-1)(2k+5)/18]^{1/2},$$

where $k$ is the number of studies in the meta-analysis, and a $p$ value can be obtained from tables of the normal distribution. A worked example of Data Set II is provided in Table 25.1. The components of $P$ are determined by counting the number of elements of rank $(T_i^*)$ lower in the table that are of greater rank than the index element, excluding ties. For example, determining the first element of $P$ involves comparing the first ranked value of $T_i^*$, 10, with all the subsequent ranks and counting the numbers that are larger than 10, that is, 9. Calculation of the second element, 13, involves counting the number of subsequent ranks that are larger than 4, excluding the tied rank in brackets. Then $Q$ is conversely determined by counting lower ranks. In the example the test statistic is $Z = 1.78$, leading to $p = 0.08$.

I believe that this example highlights the need for using this test with a very liberal significance level. In the context of meta-analysis the adverse consequences of a false negative test are much more profound than those of a false positive test. In other words, any evidence of publication bias should make us cautious about proceeding with the analysis. For meta-analyses with relatively small numbers of studies we should rely on an informal assessment of the funnel graph as an "eyeball" test for bias.

The use of the standardized effect sizes $\{T_i^*\}$ for the preceding test suggests that a graph of $T_i^*$ versus $v_i^{1/2}$ (or sample size) might be preferable to the funnel graph, since one would not have to judge the anticipated increase in spread at the base of the graph. That is, if no publication bias is present there should be no funneling effect in this graph, and one is simply looking for correlation in the data points. This graph is presented in Figure 25.3.

An alternative but complementary way to study the

**Table 25.1 Rank Correlation Test Computations**

| $v_i$ | $v_i^{-1}$ | $\bar{v}_i$ | $T_i$ | $T_i^*$ | Rank $v_i$ | Rank $T_i^*$ | $P$ | $Q$ |
|---|---|---|---|---|---|---|---|---|
| .094 | 10.6 | .085 | .07 | −.103 | 1 | 10 | 9 | 9 |
| .103 | 9.7 | .094 | −.06 | −.522 | [2] | [4] | 13 | 3 |
| .103 | 9.7 | .094 | −.02 | −.391 | [2] | [7] | 11 | 5 |
| .125 | 8.0 | .116 | .03 | −.206 | 4 | 9 | 9 | 6 |
| .139 | 7.2 | .130 | .30 | .555 | 5 | 16 | 3 | 11 |
| .147 | 6.8 | .138 | .12 | .054 | 6 | 11 | 7 | 6 |
| .159 | 6.3 | .150 | −.18 | −.723 | 7 | 2 | 11 | 1 |
| .164 | 6.1 | .155 | .27 | .432 | 8 | 15 | 3 | 8 |
| .167 | 6.0 | .158 | −.14 | −.604 | [9] | [3] | 8 | 1 |
| .167 | 6.0 | .158 | −.06 | −.403 | [9] | [6] | 7 | 2 |
| .174 | 5.7 | .165 | −.07 | −.419 | 11 | 5 | 7 | 1 |
| .220 | 4.5 | .211 | −.32 | −.914 | 12 | 1 | 7 | 0 |
| .223 | 4.5 | .214 | .18 | .173 | 13 | 12 | 5 | 1 |
| .251 | 4.0 | .242 | .80 | 1.423 | 14 | 18 | 1 | 4 |
| .289 | 3.5 | .280 | −.02 | −.227 | 15 | 8 | 4 | 0 |
| .290 | 3.4 | .281 | .23 | .245 | 16 | 13 | 3 | 0 |
| .302 | 3.3 | .293 | .54 | .813 | 17 | 17 | 1 | 1 |
| .369 | 2.7 | .360 | .26 | .267 | 18 | 14 | 1 | 0 |
| .373 | 2.7 | .364 | 1.18 | 1.790 | 19 | 19 | 0 | 0 |
| | | | | | | | 110 | 59 |

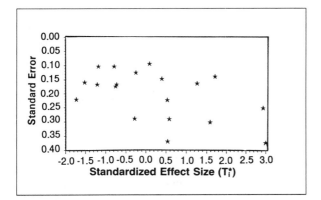

**Figure 25.3** Standardized Funnel-Graph: Data Set II

data is to examine the trend in mean effect sizes as a function of sample size. The mean effect size has been computed for three sample size groupings and the results are summarized in Table 25.2. This table shows that it is in the studies with small sample sizes (i.e., $v_i > 0.25$) that the large effect sizes occur, a fact that is evident on examination of Figure 25.2.

The construction of the preceding test is based on the premise that if publication bias is present, it is induced by a mechanism in which studies with large effect sizes are more likely to be published. This is why we correlate effect size versus sample size, since larger effect sizes are increasingly likely for small sample sizes. The test is sensitive against one-sided alternatives—that is, situations in which, say, only large positive effect sizes have an increased chance of publication. An alternative premise is that the decision to publish is based primarily on the $p$ value rather than the absolute value of the effect size. This kind of selection will also induce a negative correlation between effect size and sample size, in circumstances where the true effect size is not at its null value. However, if the true effect size is at the null value, then the standardization of the effect sizes prior

to performing the test will remove the "nuisance" effect of sample size and will create a scale in which the distribution of effect sizes is independent of sample size. In other words, if the $p$ value is the only determinant of selective publication then the test should demonstrate no correlation between effect size and sample size. (In fact, the empirical standardization is based on the *estimated* mean effect, which will be positively biased, and so this will produce small correlation. However, this is not of great concern since the test will generally have very low power.)

In the next section we will discuss recently developed models that characterize publication bias as a function of the $p$ value and that permit a corresponding test for publication bias. In fact, it seems plausible that in practice selective publication will be influenced by both the magnitude of the effect size and the $p$ value, and it would be desirable to develop a test that is sensitive to either of these influences, but at present no such methodology is available.

## 3. METHODS FOR CORRECTING PUBLICATION BIAS

We consider two general strategies: sampling methods and analytic methods. Sampling methods are designed to circumvent publication bias by directly addressing the manner in which the studies are selected for inclusion in the meta-analysis. In principle these are preferable to analytic methods, which are based on the premise that all we have available are the published studies, and we must identify and correct the bias by examining the internal consistency of the data.

### 3.1 Sampling Methods

Since publication bias is caused by the preferential decision to publish based on the results of the studies, we can circumvent the problem by restricting the meta-analysis to those studies selected on the basis of a

**Table 25.2 Trend in Estimated Effect Size**

| Standard Error | ($\equiv$ Sample Size) | Mean Effect Size ($\pm$ SE) |
|---|---|---|
| $v_i < 0.15$ | ($k = 6$) | $0.06 \pm 0.14$ |
| $0.15 < v_i < 0.25$ | ($k = 7$) | $-0.04 \pm 0.16$ |
| $v_i > 0.25$ | ($k = 6$) | $0.49 \pm 0.23$ |
| All studies combined ($k = 19$) | | $0.10 \pm 0.10$ |

sampling frame that cannot be affected by the results of the studies. Such sampling frames exist in special circumstances. For example, in some areas of medical research there are registries of prospective trials. (See Chapter 6 of this book.) New trials are registered before they are started, and so clearly the decision to register a trial cannot be affected by the result of the study, which is not yet known. One of the earliest registries was the registry of perinatal trials at Oxford University (Chalmers et al. 1986), which has been used as a resource for numerous meta-analyses. A compendium of registries has recently been assembled by Easterbrook (1991). There are other possible sources for developing an unbiased sampling frame in this way, such as the lists of studies approved by hospital ethics committees. Indeed, these were used for the empirical studies of publication bias described in the previous section (Easterbrook et al. 1991; Dickersin, Min & Meinert 1991). However, the logistical obstacles involved in using these for a specific meta-analysis would be formidable, and nobody has attempted to recruit studies for a meta-analysis in this way, to my knowledge.

Registries have, however, been used for this purpose. Simes (1986) employed the International Cancer Research Data Bank to identify comparative trials of single alkylating agent therapy versus combination chemotherapy in the treatment of advanced ovarian cancer; he found that an analysis restricted to published studies demonstrated a significant effect, whereas an analysis restricted to registered trials showed no appreciable advantage for combination chemotherapy. Of course, this approach requires the inclusion of data from the registered studies that are unpublished, and these data may be difficult to obtain and/or unreliable. Nonetheless, at a minimum, the use of a registry as a sampling frame provides hard data on the number of unpublished studies.

A more commonly used method is the one advocated by Peto and colleagues at Oxford. This involves attempting by all reasonable means to track down relevant unpublished studies on the topic (Collins et al. 1987). Techniques used to identify the missing studies include following up on published abstracts and contacting knowledgeable investigators in the field for leads on studies known to have been conducted. Clearly, the success of this method will be directly proportional to the assiduousness of the search, but even with great care we can never be sure that we have identified all, or even most, of the studies. This method has been criticized by Chalmers et al. (1987), who feel that the accuracy of

the unpublished data may often be suspect, and the quality of the studies may be inferior.

## 3.2 Analytic Methods

For many meta-analysts, evidence of selective publication will render the analysis unreliable, leading to an unwillingness to proceed further and complete the analysis by providing a correction for publication bias. For others, the appropriate response will be to exclude the groups of studies deemed unreliable—for example, nonrandomized studies—if these are observed to be systematically different from randomized studies. However, there has been research on methods that make use of all the data while simultaneously correcting for bias. For the most part these methods are very new, and their statistical properties have not been subjected to rigorous scrutiny. Therefore, the material in this section must be considered as experimental rather than standard methodology.

**3.2.1 The file-drawer method** The most well-known technique is Rosenthal's ''file-drawer'' method (Rosenthal 1979). This approach is designed to provide a simple qualification on a summary $p$ value from a meta-analysis. The idea is as follows. Suppose that the meta-analysis results in a statistically significant effect, using a test based on combining the $z$ scores of the individual (published) studies (see section 4.4.2 of Chapter 15). Then the overall $z$ score is

$$Z = \sum_{i=1}^{k} Z_i / \sqrt{k}.$$

This is significant at the $\alpha$-level of significance if $Z > Z_{1-\alpha/2}$ (two-sided). The goal of the method is to determine the number of unpublished studies with an average observed effect of zero that there would need to be in order that the overall $z$ score is no longer significant. In other words, if $k_0$ is the number of additional studies required, we need $k_0$ such that

$$\sum_{i=1}^{k} Z_i / \sqrt{k + k_0} < Z_{1-\alpha/2},$$

that is,

$$k_0 > -k + (\sum_{i=1}^{k} Z_i)^2 / (Z_{1-\alpha/2})^2.$$

The rationale behind the method is as follows: Considering the relevant research domain, if $k_0$ is judged to be sufficiently large that it is unlikely that so many unpublished studies exist, then we can conclude that the significance of the observed effects is unchallengeable.

We can apply this method to Data Set II. The individual $z$ scores are computed by dividing the effect sizes by the corresponding standard errors, leading to $\Sigma Z_i = 11.03$, that is, $Z = 2.53$. Clearly, this is significant at the 5 percent level. Using the preceding formula we have $k_0 > -19 + (11.03/1.96)^2$, that is, $k_0 \geq 13$. In other words, if there are at least 13 unpublished studies, with average effect size at the null value, the apparent statistical significance of the analysis would be reversed. The plausibility of there being this number of unpublished studies is necessarily a judgment in the context of the analysis under consideration, including the search techniques used by the synthesist.

The advantage of the file-drawer method is that it is very simple and easily interpretable. A disadvantage is the assumption that the results of the missing studies are centered on the null hypothesis, an assumption that seems artificial and is basically a device to permit an interpretable correction. Also, the method is not influenced in any way by the evidence in favor of bias in the data. That is, it is not influenced by the shape of the funnel graph, for example. The correction is entirely based on the conclusiveness of the $p$ value and the number of component studies in the meta-analysis, relative to the number that might be missing. An analogous method for assessing the impact of missing studies on the summary estimate of effect size has been developed by Orwin (1983).

**3.2.2 Weighted distribution theory** More sophisticated methods for adjusting the meta-analysis for publication bias have recently been developed using weighted distribution theory. This leads to a much more complex analysis, with attendant methodological problems.

Weighted distribution theory is based on the premise that an item (in our case a study) is included in the analysis with a probability that is determined by the outcome; in our case the observed $p$ value (Patil & Rao 1977). These selection probabilities are related to different possible outcomes via a weight function. If $T$ is the observed effect size, and if $f(T;\theta)$ is the "face value" probability density of $T$ irrespective of whether or not the study is published, $\theta$ is the true mean effect size, and $w(T)$ is the weight function, then the probability density of $T$ given that the study is published, $g(T;\theta)$, is given by

$$g(T;\theta) = \frac{f(T;\theta)w(t)}{A(\theta)}, \qquad (25\text{-}1)$$

where

$$A(\theta) = \int_{-\infty}^{\infty} f(t;\theta)w(t)dt.$$

Using these expressions it is possible to construct a likelihood function and make inferences about the true distribution of $T$, that is, $f(T\theta)$, provided that models for $f(\bullet)$ and $w(\bullet)$ are specified. This kind of analysis has the additional merit that the estimated weight function is a direct reflection of the selection probabilities that are giving rise to publication bias. That is, if the weight function is constant there is no bias. Conversely, if the weight function is small for effect sizes close to the null and large for effect sizes distant from the null, then the bias will be substantial. In other words, by examining the estimated weight function we can assess directly the chances of bias being present in the meta-analysis.

All of the authors who have studied this model have made the assumption that the weight function is determined by the $p$ value of the study rather than the effect size. (Note: These two factors would be equivalent "metrics" for this purpose only if all studies in the meta-analysis have the same variance, i.e., sample size.) Consequently, in terms of $T_i$ the weight function, denoted $w_i(T_i)$, is different for each study.

The simplest version of this model has been examined in detail by Hedges (1984) following an earlier investigation by Lane and Dunlap (1978). This involves the assumption that the weight function is 1 if the test is significant and 0 otherwise. That is,

$$w_i(T_i) = \begin{bmatrix} 1 & if & T_i > C_\alpha(v_i) \\ 0 & if & T_i < C_\alpha(v_i), \end{bmatrix}$$

where $C_\alpha(v_i)$ is the critical value of the $\alpha$-level test for the $i$th study, and $v_i$ is the standard error of the $i$th effect size. Hedges examined the properties of this model and showed that small studies provide a greater contribution to bias. In a recent paper Hedges (1992) has generalized this model to permit the weight function to take different values in different regions of the $p$ value scale. For example, the probability of publication may be greater if $p < 0.01$ than if $0.01 < p < 0.05$, and likewise the latter may be greater than the probability of publication if $p > 0.05$. In general the weight function takes the form

$$w_i(T_i) = \begin{bmatrix} w_1 & if & 0<|T_i|< C_{\alpha(1)}\ (v_i) \\ w_2 & if & C_{\alpha(1)}\ (v_i)<|T_i|< C_{\alpha(2)}\ (v_i) \\ \vdots \\ w_l & if & C_{\alpha(l-1)}\ (v_i)<|T_i|<\infty \end{bmatrix}$$

for a two-sided test, where the critical values $\alpha(1)$ . . . $\alpha(l-1)$ are selected a priori. Iyengar and Greenhouse (1988) have elected to use a much simpler parametric model in which the weight function is 1 for $p<0.05$, but either declines exponentially for $p>0.05$ or is constant (but not 1). However, this model has a monotonically decreasing weight function by design and is therefore based on the presupposition that publication bias is operating in a specified direction, that is, publication bias is assumed to be more likely if the results are more significant. Finally, Dear and Begg (1992) have studied the most model-free form of the weight function, in which the weight function is entirely determined by the empirical distribution of the $p$ values. In this case, assuming that the effect sizes are normally distributed with standard deviation $\{v_i\}$, then

$$w_i(T_i) = \begin{bmatrix} w_1 & if & \infty>|T_i|\geq -v_i\Phi^{-1}(p_{2l-2}/2) \\ \vdots \\ w_j & if & -v_i\Phi^{-1}(p_{2j}/2)>|T_i|\geq -v_i\Phi^{-1}(p_{2j-2}/2) \\ \vdots \\ w_l & if & -v_i\Phi^{-1}\ (p_2/2)>|T_i|\geq 0. \end{bmatrix}$$

Here the $p$ values $p_1$, . . . , $p_{2l}$ are ranked and grouped in twos, since the parameters of the model would be nonidentifiable if the weight function were allowed to vary between adjacent, ranked $p$ values.

The parameters characterizing the effect size distribution and the weight function can be estimated using maximum likelihood for any of the preceding models. In general the weighted likelihood has the form

$$L(\theta,\{w_i\}) = \prod_{i=1}^{k} \frac{f_i(T_i;\theta)\ w_i(T_i)}{A_i(\theta)}.$$

If a random effects model is employed, $f(\bullet)$ and $A_i(\bullet)$ will also depend on the random effects variance. The difficulty of obtaining maximum likelihood estimates increases with the complexity of the weight function.

The preceding methodology can be applied in the context of either one-sided or two-sided tests, but not a mixture of both in the same analysis. However, the distinction between these two contexts does not refer to whether or not a one-sided or two-sided test was employed in the published articles, but rather whether or

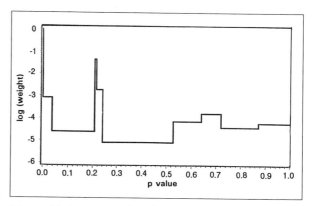

**Figure 25.4**  Weight Function: Data Set II

not the weight function can be assumed to be the same for negative and positive effect sizes of similar magnitude. For example, the funnel graph for Data Set II suggests a selection model in which large positive effect sizes for small studies are selectively published, but not large negative effect sizes. Consequently, a one-sided weight model would appear to be appropriate in this case. The empirical weight function derived from the method of Dear and Begg for this data set using the one-sided model is displayed in Figure 25.4. The significance of the trend toward higher weights for smaller $p$ values can be tested by performing a rank correlation test of the ten estimated weights, ranked by $p$ values as in the graph. This test has a $p$ value of 0.13, two-sided. This is an alternative test for publication bias to the one presented in the previous section.

As indicated earlier, this entire line of research is in an early stage of development, and there is as yet no commercially available software. Also, the properties of these methods require further research before they can be recommended for widespread use.

## 4. DISCUSSION

Publication bias presents possibly the greatest methodologic threat to validity of a meta-analysis. It can be caused by the biased and selective reporting of the results of a given study, or, more seriously, by the selective decision to publish the results of the study in the first place. Undetected publication bias is especially serious owing to the fact that the meta-analysis may not only lead to a spurious conclusion, but the aggregation of data may give the impression, with standard statistical methodology, that the conclusions are very precise.

How should we respond to this problem in practice? In my view, the appropriate global response is to be conservative in interpreting data from meta-analyses. That is, we should not as a general rule be using a criterion such as $p < 0.05$ in this context, or better still we should not use statistical significance testing at all. The results of the meta-analysis should be very compelling before we regard them as definitive. For the individual meta-analysis, it is important to be aware of the problem and to perform some standard exploratory analyses before proceeding with any conventional statistical analyses. Specifically, a funnel graph should be mandatory, possibly augmented with an examination of the association between the effect sizes and other relevant design criteria.

As indicated earlier there has been relatively little research on techniques for identifying and correcting publication bias. Most of the methods discussed are still under development. There are many important unresolved questions. For instance, what are the most sensitive approaches for detecting bias? What are the relative merits of methods based on the funnel graph versus methods based on weighted distribution theory? What are the chances of failing to detect a bias that would have a profound effect on the meta-analysis? How many component studies must there be before one has reasonable power to detect bias?

Perhaps analytic approaches to the problem of publication bias should be considered as merely a temporary expedient, the real solution requiring a major reassessment of the manner in which the results of scientific studies are disseminated. Currently, the journals play a prominent role. A possible solution is for funding agencies, such as the National Institutes of Health, to take responsibility for ensuring the collection and dissemination of the results of the studies they fund (Begg & Berlin 1989). This could be accomplished in concert with the development of prospective registries of research studies and would ideally be accessed electronically, in an analogous manner to MEDLINE and various other computerized databases. An online system of this sort would enormously facilitate the conduct and the validity of meta-analyses, by standardizing the format for reporting results as well as ensuring that all prospective studies are represented. Indeed, efforts to standardize the reporting of clinical research studies have led to significant progress in the past few years (Huth 1987; Ad Hoc Working Group for Critical Appraisal of the Medical Literature 1987).

In summary, publication bias is a serious problem for

the meta-analyst. Some analytic techniques are available to identify and correct the bias, but there remain significant questions about the properties of these methods. In general, effective circumvention of this problem will require an evolution of the way in which the results of scientific studies are reported toward a system in which results of research studies are linked to the original research plan (e.g., via registries of prospective studies). It is likely that the continued expansion and complexity of scientific research will further emphasize the critical role of meta-analysis in the synthesis of the results of the research.

### Author's Note

I am grateful to May Nah Ho for assistance with this chapter.

## 5. REFERENCES

Ad Hoc Working Group for Critical Appraisal of the Medical Literature. (1987). A proposal for more informative abstracts of clinical trials. *Annals of Internal Medicine, 106,* 598–604.

Armitage, P., & Berry, G. (1987). *Statistical methods in medical research* (2nd ed.). Oxford, England: Blackwell.

Begg, C. B. (1985). A measure to aid in the interpretation of published clinical trials. *Statistics in Medicine, 4,* 1–9.

Begg, C. B., & Berlin, J. A. (1988). Publication bias: A problem in interpreting medical data. *Journal of the Royal Statistical Society,* Series A, *151,* 419–463.

Begg, C. B., and Berlin, J. A. (1989). Publication bias and the dissemination of clinical research. *Journal of the National Cancer Institute, 81,* 107–115.

Berlin, J. A., Begg, C. B., & Louis, T. A. (1989). An assessment of publication bias using a sample of published clinical trials. *Journal of the American Statistical Association, 84,* 381–392.

Chalmers, I., Hetherington, J., Newdick, M., Mutch, L., Grant, A., Enkin, M., Enkin, E., & Dickersin, K. (1986). The Oxford database of perinatal trials: Developing a register of published reports of controlled trials. *Controlled Clinical Trials, 7,* 306–324.

Chalmers, T. C., Levin, H., Sacks, H. S., Reitman, D., Berrier, J., & Nagalingam, R. (1987). Meta-analysis of clinical trials as a scientific discipline. I: Control of bias and comparison with large cooperative trials. *Statistics in Medicine, 6,* 315–325.

Cohen, P. A. (1983). Comment on "A selective review of the validity of student ratings of teachers." *Journal of Higher Education, 54*, 449–458.

Collins, R., Gray, R., Godwin, J., & Peto, R. (1987). Avoidance of large biases and large random errors in the assessment of moderate treatment effects: The need for systematic overviews. *Statistics in Medicine, 6*, 245–250.

Colton, T. (1974). *Statistics in medicine*. Boston: Little, Brown.

Coursol, A., & Wagner, E. E. (1986). Effect of positive findings on submission and acceptance rates: A note on meta-analysis bias. *Professional Psychology, 17*, 136–137.

Dear, K. B. G., & Begg, C. B. (1992). An approach for assessing publication bias prior to performing a meta-analysis. *Statistical Science, 7*, 237–245.

Dickersin, K., Min, Y.-I., & Meinert, C. L. (1992). Factors influencing publication of research results: Follow-up of applications submitted to two institutional review boards. *Journal of the American Medical Association, 267*, 374–378.

Easterbrook, P. J. (1992). Directory of registries of clinical trials. *Statistics in Medicine, 11*, 345–359.

Easterbrook, P. J., Berlin, J. A., Gopalan, R., & Mathews, D. R. (1991). Publication bias in clinical research. *Lancet, 337*, 867–872.

Greenwald, A. G. (1975). Consequences of prejudice against the null hypothesis. *Psychological Bulletin, 82*, 1–12.

Hedges, L. V. (1984). Estimation of effect size under nonrandom sampling: The effects of censoring studies yielding statistically insignificant mean differences. *Journal of Educational Studies, 9*, 61–85.

Hedges, L. V. (1992). Modelling publication selection effects in meta-analysis. *Statistical Science, 7*, 246–255.

Hemminki, E. (1980). Study of information submitted by drug companies to licensing authorities. *British Medical Journal, 280*, 833–836.

Huth, E. J. (1987). Structured abstracts for papers reporting clinical trials. *Annals of Internal Medicine, 106*, 626–627.

Iyengar, S., & Greenhouse, J. B. (1988). Selection models and the file drawer problem. *Statistical Science, 3*, 109–117.

Kotelchuck, D. (1974). Asbestos research: Winning the battle but losing the war. *Health/PAC Bulletin, 61*, 1–27.

Lane, D. M., & Dunlap, W. P. (1978). Estimating effect-size bias resulting from the significance test criterion in editorial decisions. *British Journal of Mathematical and Statistical Psychology, 31*, 107–112.

Light, R. J., & Pillemer, D. B. (1984). *Summing up: The science of reviewing research*. Cambridge, MA: Harvard University Press.

Medawar, P. B. (1963). Is the scientific paper a fraud? *Listener, 70*, 377–378.

Melton, A. (1962). Editorial. *Journal of Experimental Psychology, 64*, 553–557.

Orwin, R. G. (1983). A fail-safe N for effect size in meta-analysis. *Journal of Educational Statistics, 8*, 157–159.

Patil, G. P., & Rao, C. R. (1977). The weighted distributions: A survey of their applications. In P. R. Krishiaiah (Ed.), *Applications of statistics* (pp. 383–405). Amsterdam: North Holland.

Raudenbush, S. W. (1984). Magnitude of teacher expectancy effects of pupil IQ as a function of the credibility of expectancy induction: A synthesis of findings from 18 experiments *Journal of Educational Psychology, 76*, 85–97.

Rosenthal, R. (1979). The "file-drawer problem" and tolerance for null results. *Psychological Bulletin, 86*, 638–641.

Sacks, H. S., Chalmers, T. C. & Smith, H. (1983). Sensitivity and specificity of clinical trials: Randomized versus historical controls. *Archives of Internal Medicine, 143*, 753–755.

Simes, R. J. (1986). Confronting publication bias: A cohort design for meta-analysis. *Statistics in Medicine, 6*, 11–30.

Smith, M. L. (1980). Publication bias and meta-analysis. *Evaluation in Education, 4*, 22–24.

Sterling, T. D. (1959). Publication decisions and their possible effects on inferences drawn from tests of significance—or vice versa. *Journal of the American Statistical Association, 54*, 30–34.

Cooper, H. and Hedges, L. V. (Eds.) 1994. *The Handbook of Research Synthesis.* New York: Russell Sage Foundation

# 26

# BAYESIAN APPROACHES TO RESEARCH SYNTHESIS

**THOMAS A. LOUIS**
*University of Minnesota*

**DANIEL ZELTERMAN**
*University of Minnesota*

CONTENTS

**411**

## 1. INTRODUCTION

As in other scientific studies, efficient design, conduct, and analysis of a research synthesis requires that investigators use expert opinion and empirical evidence from previous studies. Design and analysis decisions are made at every stage of the process; these should be based on a combination of subjective and objective inputs. For example, statistical models are based on assumptions that require justification, but the analyst can never prove that the models are correct.

The Bayesian approach provides a formal structure for incorporating such uncertainties. All unknown parameters are treated as random variables that are governed by a joint probability distribution specified prior to viewing data. These prior distributions are based on subjective opinion and objective evidence, such as the results of previous experiments. Bayesian analysis uses ''Bayes's rule'' to update the prior distribution in the light of the data, producing the posterior distribution. All statistical inferences (point estimates, confidence intervals, etc.) are based on this posterior distribution. Furthermore, the posterior distribution acts as the prior for the next investigation. Berger (1985), Breslow (1990), and Lindley (1990) extensively discuss Bayesian theory and practice.

The Bayesian approach documents expert opinion and objective evidence on the likelihood of different values for parameters of interest such as the effect size. The approach provides a structure that can incorporate evidence and opinion on the bias, quality, and other features of each candidate study. After this specification, the Bayes approach provides automatic bias correction and weighting of the individual studies to produce a posterior distribution for the effect size of interest. This posterior distribution can be summarized by its mean, variance, interquartile range, and so on. These summaries and the entire distribution can be used to communicate the current evidence on the relative likelihood of different values of the effect size. Thus, Bayesian confidence intervals (called tolerance or prediction intervals) are cast in a natural language: ''Given the data, there is a 95 percent probability that the effect size falls in the interval (.44, .96).'' This statement cannot be made unless the effect size is considered a random variable.

Importantly, a meta-analysis is not conducted to inform a single individual, but to communicate the current state of information to a broad community of consumers. If the prior distributions differ substantially for different consumers, then the related Bayesian analyses can produce qualitatively as well as quantitatively different results. Therefore, it is important to perform a sensitivity analysis over the range of opinions. If conclusions are stable, then we have ''findings.'' If they are not, the collection of Bayesian analyses underscores the finding that the data are not sufficiently compelling to bring a group of relevant consumers to consensus. This situation should motivate additional primary studies.

Despite its many attractive features, the Bayesian approach has failed to gain acceptance in settings in which a large and diverse group of ''consumers'' constitute the target audience for the results of the experiment. Prior distributions (and therefore posterior distributions and conclusions) may vary a great deal among consumers. A broadly convincing Bayesian analysis must not depend too strongly on the prior. Granting these problems, the Bayesian approach can still be effective and convincing, especially if coupled with exploration of the impact of the prior distribution through sensitivity analysis (see Chapter 24 as well as Du-Mouchel & Harris 1983; Laird 1987; McCann, Horn & Kaldor 1984; Mosteller & Wallace 1964; Raudenbush & Bryk 1985) or use of other robust Bayesian methods (Berger 1985; Chaloner et al. 1993; Kadane 1986). The ''what if'' sensitivity analysis approach communicates clearly and should always accompany analyses based on specific prior opinions.

Much has been written about the virtues of the Bayesian approach to inference, showing its superiority, in principle, over other approaches (Lindley 1990). By modeling all unknowns as random variables, the probability calculus can be used to knit together diverse sources of information in a complex model. Once the probability structure has been developed, inferences can be made about population quantities (features of prior distributions), individual studies, the effects of covariates that influence study results, and complex combinations of these. Importantly, the posterior distribution reports an honest level of uncertainty that captures all relevant sources of variability in a complex structure (Lane et al. 1987). Achieving this unification requires specifying prior distributions, frequently a difficult task.

In this chapter we outline Bayes and empirical Bayes approaches, showing the basic computations and identifying their strengths and weaknesses. We show how the Bayesian approach can be used to bolster classical analyses and document the decisions and assumptions necessary for an effective meta-analysis. We analyze Data Set II on teacher expectancy and produce a variety of estimates based on different models and opinions. Our intent is to provide a basic introduction to the concepts and formalism; we leave many details to be found in the references.

## 2. BASIC BAYESIAN METHODS

### 2.1 Two Motivating Examples

**2.1.1 Example 1: Subjective opinion** "We are all inherently Bayesian, but usually it is difficult to behave as one." Consider a situation in which you are about to submit an article (possibly a meta-analysis) to a journal (possibly the *American Sociological Review*). You are asked to assess your chances of publication in that journal. Any number in the interval [0,1] is fair game, and, depending on your knowledge of the journal's policies and acceptance rate, you will be more or less confident in your prediction. Whatever your level of knowledge, the true acceptance probability for your paper (or a sequence of papers) is unknown and has a distribution of possible values; it is a random variable. Of course, it may be extremely difficult for you to come up with the full distribution, but you may be able to specify a "best guess" (mean, median, mode) and some measure of uncertainty (standard deviation, interquartile range, a tail probability).

You submit your article and it is accepted. Congratulations! What is your revised opinion on the acceptance probability for papers like yours? (We know that it is 1 for this specific paper.) The "classical" estimate would indeed be 1, for you have one success in one trial, but that estimate seems overly optimistic. You are likely to come up with a number that pulls back from 1 toward your prior opinion. The amount you pull back will depend on the "trust" you had in our prior opinion. You are a Bayesian!

**2.1.2 Example 2: Objective prior evidence** Now consider two experiments conducted in sequence. In one experiment you observe Gaussian data $(X_1, \ldots, X_m)$ with mean $\overline{X}_m$ and standard error of the mean $\sigma/\sqrt{m}$ (the variance of the mean is $\sigma^2/m$). (Gaussian data are distributed according to the well-known normal or bell-shaped curve.) In the second experiment you observe $(T_1, \ldots, T_n)$ with mean $\overline{T}_n$ and variance of the mean $= \sigma^2/n$. Note that the variability of each individual observation ($X_i$ or $T_i$) is $\sigma^2$. You assume that all data come from the same Gaussian distribution and want to make inference on the mean ($\theta$) of that distribution.

Since all data are assumed to have the same expec-

tation and variability, they can be pooled, producing the overall inference:

$$\hat{\theta} = \frac{m\overline{X}_m + n\overline{T}_n}{m + n},$$

with

$$\text{Var}(\hat{\theta}) = \frac{\sigma^2}{(m + n)}.$$

If we think of the $X$ data as providing prior information on $\theta$ that is updated by the $T$ data, we can write the inference for the combined analysis as follows:

$$\hat{\theta} = B\,\overline{X}_m + (1 - B)\overline{T}_n$$
$$= \overline{X}_m + (1 - B)(\overline{T}_n - \overline{X}_m),$$
$$\text{Var}(\hat{\theta}) = (1 - B)\frac{\sigma^2}{n},$$

where

$$B = \frac{m}{m + n}.$$

Notice that by the first representation, $\hat{\theta}$ is a weighted average of the two sample means with weights ($B$ and $1 - B$) proportional to sample size, since the inherent variabilities are equal. The second representation shows that the estimate takes $\overline{T}_n$ and shrinks it toward $\overline{X}_m$. The variance of $\hat{\theta}$ is lower than that produced by the $T$'s alone by a factor $(1 - B)$. If $n$ is much larger than $m$, then $B$ is close to zero and almost all weight is given to the $T$ data. If you think of the $X$ data as forming the prior distribution, then inferences from the current data ($T$) are modified by the prior by an amount that depends on the relative information in the two data sets.

### 2.2 The Formalism

These two examples can be formalized by developing a variance components model (see Chapter 20 of this handbook and Begg & Pilote 1991; DerSimonian & Laird 1983; Morris & Normand 1991; and Raudenbush & Bryk 1985; in addition to references cited previously). For ease of presentation, we shall use Gaussian distributions. Consider the basic model where the parameter of interest ($\theta$) comes from a Gaussian distribution with mean ($\mu$) and variance ($\tau^2$) (analogous to the distribution created by the $X$ data). Once the $\theta'^s$ have been generated, the observed effect size estimates ($T_1, \ldots, T_n$) arise as a sample from a Gaussian distribution with mean $\theta$

and variance $\sigma^2$. In this example, $\mu$ is the best a priori estimate of the effect size and $\tau$ measures the spread of possible values for the effect size. More formally, we have

$$\theta \sim N(\mu, \tau^2) \quad (26\text{-}1)$$
$$T_1, \ldots, T_n | \theta \sim N(\theta, \sigma^2)$$

This model is equivalent to the regression model:

$$T_i = \mu + b + \epsilon_i,$$

where $\theta = \mu + b$, $b \sim N(0, \tau^2)$ and the $\epsilon_i \sim N(0, \sigma^2)$. The symbol "$\sim$" denotes "behaves as" or "is distributed according to." Notice that the marginal distribution for any $T_i$ is Gaussian with mean $\mu$ and variance $\sigma^2 + \tau^2$, and $\text{Var}(\overline{T}_n) = \dfrac{\sigma^2}{n} + \tau^2$. These distributions are "overdispersed" relative to the usual model with no prior variation ($\tau^2 = 0$).

Having observed $\overline{T}_n$, the Bayesian calculation updates the prior distribution by computing the posterior distribution (e.g., $\theta$ conditional on $T_1, \ldots, T_n$). For this Gaussian/Gaussian case the posterior distribution is also Gaussian with mean:

$$E[\theta | \overline{T}_n] = B\mu + (1 - B)\overline{T}_n \quad (26\text{-}2)$$
$$= \mu + (1 - B)(\overline{T}_n - \mu),$$

and the posterior variance is

$$V[\theta | \overline{T}_n] = (1 - B)\frac{\sigma^2}{n}, \quad (26\text{-}3)$$

where,

$$B = \frac{\sigma^2/n}{\sigma^2/n + \tau^2}.$$

Notice that the posterior distribution depends on the data only through the sample mean ($\overline{T}_n$). As in our second example, the posterior mean is a weighted average of the prior mean and the data mean with weights inversely proportional to the respective variances. The other representation shows that the posterior mean is closer to the prior mean than is the data mean. This relation is similar to a regression to the mean adjustment (see Efron & Morris 1977; Laird & Louis 1987; Morris 1983). The posterior variance is smaller than the usual sampling variance ($\sigma^2/n$) by the factor $(1 - B)$. As $n$ increases, $B$ decreases and inferences become less dependent on the prior, an intuitively appealing property.

The variance reduction in equation (26-3) is called

the Bayes advantage over the classical approach. For example, classical confidence intervals would add and subtract a multiple of $\sigma/\sqrt{n}$, whereas the Bayesian interval (a posterior region) will be shorter by the factor $\sqrt{1-B}$. For $\tau$ close to 0 (an informative prior and therefore $B$ close to 1), the posterior variance decreases to 0. That is, if you are certain of the value a priori you will be certain a posteriori. For $\tau$ very large (an "ignorance prior" and therefore $B$ close to 0), the Bayesian formulas converge to the classical, but interpretations differ. The classical confidence coefficient (say 95 percent) measures the long-term relative frequency of covering the true parameter in repetitions of the experiment (fix the parameter, repeatedly generate data). The Bayesian posterior coverage reports that *for this data set* the probability is .95 that the parameter (itself a random variable) is in the interval.

These two interpretations of intervals show a principal difference between the Bayesian and classical approaches. The classical inference must make reference to replications of the original experiment with the parameters of interest fixed. Since replications may be impossible (we cannot replicate submitting our first meta-analysis for publication or the conceptualization and conduct of primary studies similar to those in the synthesis), this construct can appear inappropriate. A Bayesian statistician conditions on the data at hand and computes probabilities for possible values of the unknown parameters.

Although there are exceptions, the Gaussian model displays features common to a wide class of Bayesian analyses. The posterior mean for this model lies between the prior mean and the data-based estimate (shrinkage). As in equation (26-3), the posterior variance is smaller than the classical sampling variance (producing the Bayes advantage). In the Bayes approach, uncertainty about parameters is represented by probability distribution for them, the prior and then the posterior. These distributions can be summarized in a variety of ways. We have mentioned confidence intervals, but other summaries such as the posterior probability that the parameter of interest is below zero ($\text{pr}[\theta < 0 | \text{data}]$) may be more relevant in some applications.

## 2.3 The General (Basic) Model

In the general case we have a prior distribution ($G$) and a sampling distribution ($F$). Taking the case of a single observation, we have

$$\theta \sim G,$$
$$T | \theta \sim F(t | \theta)$$

To avoid mathematical details, consider the case in which both $\theta$ and $T$ can take on only a finite number of values and let $g$ be the mass function for $\theta$ [i.e., $g(\theta)$ is the probability that the random variable $\Theta$ equals the specific value $\theta$], and let $f$ be the same for $T$.

Using Bayes's theorem, the posterior distribution mass function $[g(\theta | T = t)]$ is proportional to the prior times the sampling mass functions. That is, the relative posterior probability for $\theta$ versus $\theta*$ (posterior odds) is

$$\frac{g(\theta | T = t)}{g(\theta* | T = t)} = \left[ \frac{g(\theta)}{g(\theta*)} \right] \cdot \left[ \frac{f(t | \theta)}{f(t | \theta*)} \right].$$

Notice that the posterior odds is the product of the prior odds (the first term in square brackets) times the relative likelihood of the data under $\theta$ and $\theta*$ (the likelihood ratio). The prior odds bring in prior opinion and the likelihood ratio brings in information from the data.

To get the actual posterior distribution, these relative probabilities must be normalized so that the total mass is one. We have

$$g(\theta | T = t) = \frac{f(t | \theta) g(\theta)}{f_G(t)}$$

$$f_G(t) = \sum_u f(t | u) g(u),$$

where $f_G$ is the marginal distribution of the data (the distribution describing the observed data). Similar computations hold when $\theta$ and/or $T$ are continuous random variables.

In general, producing the posterior distribution and computing with it (especially in complex models) can be difficult. In the continuous case, one needs to evaluate complicated integrals that replace the summations in the preceding formulas, and only the most basic models are mathematically tractable. Until recently, more complex but still quite basic models were handled by approximating the posterior mean and variance. However, recent advances in computational approaches (Carlin & Gelfand 1990; Gelfand & Smith 1990; Tanner 1991) allow the analyst to produce full posterior distributions for complicated models.

All statistical analyses depend either explicitly or implicitly on sampling distributions ($F$). In addition, the Bayesian approach requires a prior ($G$). Although we may "all think like Bayesians," it can be extremely difficult to evaluate and communicate prior opinions,

and considerable research continues on this aspect of Bayesian analysis. (See Chaloner et al., 1993; Freedman & Spiegelhalter 1983; Garthwaite & Dickey 1990, 1991; and Winkler 1967 for a sampling of this work.)

## 3. THE COMPOUND MODEL

### 3.1 Basics

To see how the foregoing fits into the meta-analysis framework, we must generalize further. Suppose that we plan to synthesize $K$ studies, each with an estimated effect size ($T_k$) and a true, unobserved effect size ($\theta_k$). We assume that the $\theta_k$ are sampled from a common prior distribution. The $T_k$ can have different sampling variances (and so different standard errors). This structure is similar to the previous one except that we sample $K$ times from the prior distribution.

Specifically, assume that the underlying effect sizes ($\theta_k$) are a random sample from a Gaussian distribution with mean $\mu$ and variance $\tau^2$. Then, conditional on underlying effect size $\theta_k$, the estimated effect size, $T_k$, for the $k$th study is Gaussian with mean equal to the underlying effect size and sampling variance $\sigma_k^2$. More formally:

$$\theta_1 \ldots \theta_K \sim N(\mu, \tau^2)$$
$$T_k | \theta_k \sim N(\theta_k, \sigma_k^2), \qquad (26\text{-}4)$$
$$k = 1, \ldots, K.$$

For given values of $\mu$ and $\tau$, the analysis proceeds as previously, study by study. We compute a posterior distribution for each $\theta_k$ as in equations (26-2) and (26-3), where the shrinkage parameter $B_k$ equals $\sigma_k^2 / (\sigma_k^2 + \tau^2)$. A study with a smaller $\sigma_k$ is adjusted less (has a smaller $B_k$) than one with a larger $\sigma_k$.

In a meta-analysis we are primarily interested in making inferences on the population effect size ($\mu$) and on the heterogeneity among studies ($\tau$). In the foregoing we have assumed these parameters to be known, but in a meta-analysis they will be unknown, otherwise there is no need to perform the meta-analysis. Before introducing the Bayesian analysis for these parameters, let us look at a classical (empirical Bayes) approach.

Combining the two stages in (26-4) produces a *marginal distribution* for $T_k$ that is Gaussian with mean $\mu$ and variance $\sigma_k^2 + \tau^2$, the sum of the two variance components. Therefore, each $T_k$ is unbiased for $\mu$ and the $T_k$ provide information on $\mu$ and $\tau$. When all of the $\sigma_k$ are equal to $\sigma$, we have direct estimates of these parameters by equating the sample mean and variance of the $T_k$ to those from the model. We obtain

$$\hat{\mu} = \overline{T} = \frac{1}{K} \sum_{k=1}^{K} T_k$$

$$\hat{\tau}^2 = \left[ \frac{1}{K-1} \sum_{k=1}^{K} (T_k - \overline{T})^2 - \sigma^2 \right]^+ , \tag{26-5}$$

where the "+" indicates that if the estimate is negative, we should replace it by zero. Chapter 18 develops similar estimates. When the $\sigma_k^2$ vary from study to study, the computations are more complicated and full Bayesian methods generally require an iterative approach (Gelfand & Smith 1990; Tanner 1991).

If we substitute the values from (26-5) into formula (26-2) with $\overline{T}_n$ replaced by $T_k$, we see that inferences for individual studies depend on the characteristics of all studies through the sample mean and sample variance of the effect size estimates. Posterior means are shrunk toward the sample mean by an amount that depends on the observed heterogeneity ($\hat{\tau}^2$). The estimate of $\tau^2$ depends on the between-studies sum of squares used in the numerator of the $F$ statistic to test the null hypothesis that all of the $\theta$'s are equal (equivalently that $\tau = 0$). Traditionally, we might choose to estimate all effect sizes by the pooled mean, if the $F$ test were not statistically significant and use the individual $T_k$, if the test were statistically significant. An empirical Bayes analysis (and some forms of Bayesian analysis) strikes a compromise between overall pooling and complete splitting. Such "borrowing strength" can be very effective in improving estimates of individual effect sizes (Efron & Morris 1977; Morris 1983).

When the sampling variances ($\sigma_k^2$) are not all equal, we use the following estimates for the population effect size ($\mu$) and its standard error:

$$\hat{\mu} = \sum_{k=1}^{K} w_k T_k / (\sum_{1}^{K} w_k),$$

$$V[\hat{\mu}] = 1/(\sum_{1}^{K} w_k), \tag{26-6}$$

where

$$w_k = \frac{1}{\sigma_k^2 + \tau^2}.$$

The population overall effect size estimate ($\hat{\mu}$) is a weighted average of the study-specific estimates ($T_k$), with weights inversely proportional to their total variance ($\sigma_k^2 + \tau^2$). In contrast, the analysis based on fixed effects ($\tau = 0$) uses weights inversely proportional to $\sigma_k^2$. Thus, the random effects analysis makes the weights more nearly equal and gives relatively less weight to large or high-precision studies than they would have received under the traditional fixed effects model.

### 3.2 Data Analysis

We shall first consider the non-Bayesian random effects approach to analyzing Data Set II on teacher expectancy. Raudenbush and Bryk (1985) give a more technical and extensive analysis. Appendix Table A.2 gives the basic data; Table 26.1 and Figure 26.1 present our analyses (the $Z$ notation is explained below). The standard fixed effects analysis (model 0 in Table 26.1 with $\tau = 0$ in equation 26-6) produces $E(\mu|\text{data}) = .060$ with posterior standard deviation .036. This pair is the Bayesian analogue of a point estimate and standard error. The basic empirical Bayes analysis (model 1; $\hat{\tau}$ used in equation 26-6) produces $E(\mu|\text{data}) = .080$ with posterior standard deviation .049, and $\hat{\tau} = .120$. If the Gaussian assumption is approximately correct and if we ignore the sampling uncertainty in estimating $\mu$ and $\tau$, then the random effects analysis (model 1) indicates that studies such as these have *true* underlying means centered at .080 with standard deviation .120. It is quite possible for a study sampled from this population to have a true effect size that is negative. Taking the difference of the models 0 and 1 entries in the "−2LL" (minus two times the log-likelihood) column in Table 26.1, we obtain 0.6, which is not statistically significant compared with a chi-square distribution with 1 degree of freedom. This comparison indicates that the fixed effects model ($\tau = 0$) cannot be rejected.

The estimates for $\mu$ are different for models 0 and 1, since they are based on different weighted averages of the $T_k$. For example, using equation (26-6) with $\tau = 0$, in model 0 studies 6, 7, 11, and 13 have weights 12.7, 12.7, 1.5, and 1.6 percent. In model 1 (with $\tau = .120$) these weights are 8.9, 8.9, 2.5, and 2.6 percent, showing the flattening of weights relative to the fixed effects analysis. The random effects analysis (model 1) produces a posterior standard deviation 36 percent larger than that for the fixed effects. This variance inflation accommodates broadening the inference from "these specific studies" to a "reference population of studies." Choosing the appropriate variance depends on inferential goals and can generate considerable controversy (Colton, Freedman & Johnson 1987). Chapter 20 of this handbook discusses these points in more detail.

**Table 26.1  Models and Estimated Parameters for Studies of Effects of Teacher Expectancy**

| Model | $E(\mu)$ $E(\alpha)$ | $SD(\mu)$ | $P$ value* | $\tau$ | $-2LL$ |
|---|---|---|---|---|---|
| 0 $X_k=1, Z_k=0$ | .060 | .036 | .098 | 0 | 70.7 |
| 1 $X_k=1, Z_k=1$ | .080 | .049 | .103 | .120 | 70.1 |
| 2 $X_k=(1, WEEKS*)$ | .088 | .044 | .046 | .086 | 62.4 |
|   $Z_k=1$ | −.015 | .005 | .005 | | |
| 3 $X_k=1, Z_k=c_k$ | .087 | .046 | .059 | .097 | 69.7 |
| 4 $X_k=1, Z_k=1/c_k$ | .062 | .051 | .221 | .137 | 67.4 |
| 5 $T'_k=T_k-d_k$ | .060 | .045 | .180 | .092 | 64.7 |
|   $X_k=Z_k=1$ | | | | | |
| 6 $T'_k=T_k-(-d_k)$ | .124 | .066 | .058 | .213 | 80.7 |
|   $X_k=Z_k=1$ | | | | | |
| 7 $X_k=(1, WEEKS*)$ | .085 | .041 | .039 | .064 | 62.9 |
|   $Z_k=c_k$ | −.014 | .005 | .008 | | |
| 8 $T'_k=T_k-(-d_k)$ | .084 | .047 | .074 | .109 | 60.0 |
|   $X_k=(1, WEEKS*)$ | −.016 | .006 | .006 | | |
|   $Z_k=1/c_k$ | | | | | |
| 9 $T'_k=T_k-d_k$ | .070 | .045 | .120 | .090 | 64.1 |
|   $X_k=1, Z_k=c_k$ | | | | | |
| 10 $T'_k=T_k-d_k$ | .071 | .041 | .082 | .060 | 58.4 |
|   $X_k=(1, WEEKS*)$ | −.012 | .005 | .016 | | |
|   $Z_k=c_k$ | | | | | |

NOTES: The $-2LL$ column reports $-2$ log-likelihood. Statistical comparisons for nested models can be made by taking differences and comparing the statistic with a chi-square distribution with degrees of freedom equal to the difference in the number of model parameters. The regressor $WEEKS* = WEEKS - 6.42$, the mean number of weeks. In models 3, 5, 9, and 10, $c_4=.3$, $c_8=c_{15}=2$, and all other $c$'s $=1$. In models 4 and 6 reciprocal $c$'s are used. In models 7, 9, and 10 $d_4=d_5=.5$ and all other $d$'s $=0$. In model 8 negative $d$'s are used.

*We report the usual two-sided $p$ value. It can be thought of as twice the smaller of $pr(\mu>0|data)$ and $pr(\mu<0|data)$.

Figure 26.1 presents the raw effect sizes ($T$), the empirical Bayes estimated effect sizes (the $\hat{\theta}^B$), and ensemble estimates (the $\hat{\theta}^E$) to be discussed in section 6. As we presented in section 2, study-specific effect size estimates with larger standard errors (see Appendix Table A.2) shrink more toward the common mean than do relatively precisely estimated effects. Mathematical and data analyses have shown that in a broad range of settings these empirical Bayes estimates produce better study-specific inferences than do the unadjusted $T_k$ (Efron & Morris 1977; Louis 1991).

The random effects variance ($\tau^2$) accounts for unexplained variation over and above $\sigma_k^2$, which is the sampling variation of $T_k$ conditional on $\theta_k$. Additional statistical modeling using between-studies attributes can help explain some of this unexplained variation. For example, in the teacher-expectancy synthesis the studies

are not identical. They differ in many ways, including the estimated number of weeks of teacher-student contact prior to expectancy induction. To incorporate this effect we can include a regression model for the mean of the prior. Specifically, assume that the unobserved effect size for study $k$ comes from a prior distribution with mean: $\mu + \alpha WEEKS_k^*$ and variance $\tau^2$, where $WEEKS_k^*$ is the number of WEEKS of prior contact minus 6.42 (the mean prior contact over all studies). Centering the regressor in this way allows interpretation of the intercept ($\mu$) as the population effect size.

To find estimates we used BMDP5V (Dixon 1990) along with a modification by Grandits, Grambsch, and Louis (1992) that allows the $\sigma_k$ to vary from study to study. In standard notation we have model 2:

$$T_k = \mu + \alpha WEEKS_k^* + Z_k b_k + e_k, \quad (26\text{-}7)$$

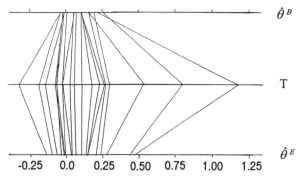

**Figure 26.1** Unadjusted and adjusted effect size estimates from Data Set II on teacher expectancy. The middle line displays unadjusted estimates ($T$), the top line standard empirical Bayes estimates ($\hat{\theta}^B$), and the bottom line ensembled estimates ($\hat{\theta}^E$).

where $b_k \sim N(0, \tau^2)$ and $e_k \sim N(0, \sigma_k^2)$ and all of the $Z_k$ equal 1. Notice that if we set $\alpha = 0$ we are back to the basic model with $\theta_k = \mu + Z_k b_k$. The standard regression structure (the intercept and slope on WEEKS*) models variation in the prior means, the $b$'s model unexplained variation around the prior mean, and the $e$'s bring in sampling variation.

Our regression produces:

| Parameter | Posterior Mean | Posterior SD |
|-----------|---------------|--------------|
| $\mu$ | .088 | .044 |
| $\alpha$ | −0.015 | .005 |
| $\tau$ | .086 | |

We see that the greater the number of weeks, the lower is the effect of expectancy ($\alpha$ is negative). The estimated population effect size is .088, and the model predicts an effect size of 0.184 ($= .088 - .015 \times (-6.42)$ for 0 weeks of prior teacher-student contact. The difference in the "−2LL" column of Table 26.1 is 7.7, which is statistically significant. Including the regressor reduces the estimate of prior variation from .120 for model 1 to .086 for model 2. The regression structure explains some of the previously unexplained variation.

## 4. PRIOR OPINION FOR THE COMPOUND MODEL

For a Bayesian approach to the model in (26-4) we introduce an additional conceptual stage of sampling by assuming that $(\mu, \tau)$ come from a distribution called the hyperprior. Only *one* unobservable draw is made from this distribution, and then the sampling described in equation (26-4) takes place. This structure includes a third stage of sampling, but our goal is similar to that for the two-stage model. We still need to compute the posterior distribution of $(\mu, \tau)$ given the observed data $(T_1, \ldots, T_K)$. This computation can be quite difficult except in the most basic cases.

To see how this three-stage model behaves, consider the model where $\tau$ is known to equal $\tau_0$ and $\mu$ has a Gaussian distribution with mean $m$ and variance $A$. The posterior distribution for $\mu$ is Gaussian with mean and variance:

$$E[\mu \mid T_1, \ldots, T_K] = w \cdot m + (1-w) \cdot \overline{T}$$

$$V[\mu \mid T_1, \ldots, T_K] = (1-w) \cdot \frac{\sigma^2 + \tau_0^2}{K},$$

where

$$w = \frac{\sigma^2 + \tau_0^2}{\sigma^2 + \tau_0^2 + K \cdot A}.$$

The same shrinkage phenomenon as in (26-2) occurs. To wit, the estimated effect size ($E[\mu \mid T_1, \ldots, T_K]$) is shrunk toward the hyperprior mean ($m$). The amount of shrinkage and variance reduction depends on variance components and sample size. When $A$ is very large, the above formulas equal the standard random effects estimates (equation 26-5 or 26-6). If $\tau_0$ is unknown, the Bayesian analysis is more complicated. (See Carlin & Gelfand 1990; Gelfand & Smith 1990; Laird & Louis 1987; Morris 1983; and Tanner 1991.)

To implement this Bayesian approach we need to specify distributions for the population effect size ($\mu$) and the between-studies standard deviation ($\tau$) in true, underlying effect sizes. Generally, this elicitation is done by asking the respondent for a "best guess" for the mean or median. Using this measure of center to anchor the distribution, the respondent is asked for additional percentiles of the distribution. An individual who has "no idea" of values for these parameters would specify that $A$ (the prior variance of $\mu$) is extremely large and that the distribution for $\tau$ also has a large variance. Such priors are called "noninformative." Generally, reasonable ranges can be specified for parameters, even if one cannot produce much detail of relative probabilities within the range. (See Chaloner & Duncan 1983; Chaloner et al., 1993; Freedman & Spiegelhalter 1983; Garthwaite & Dickey 1990, 1991; Kadane et al. 1980; and Winkler 1967.)

## 4.1 Including Study Ratings

In meta-analysis we are rarely dealing with studies whose effect sizes can be considered to come from a common prior distribution. The true effect is influenced by study attributes such as type and quality of design, details of conduct, target population, date of conduct, type of intervention, methods of measurement, and methods of analysis. Some of these influences can be modeled as we have done in the previous section by including the covariate "WEEKS*" in the prior distribution. Adjusting for other features may benefit from a more opinion-based approach.

We consider formal inclusion of prior opinions relating quality and study bias. Including such opinions requires ratings of quality and bias provided by one or several "experts." Analyses can be performed for each set of ratings to study the dependence of conclusions on individual opinion. If conclusions are stable over this "community of opinion," then the meta-analysis is likely to have substantial impact. If conclusions are sensitive to the range of opinions, then no consensus has been reached. Quantifying the degree of sensitivity is itself important.

Chalmers (1991) and Emerson et al. (1990) discuss and reference formal methods for producing study quality and bias ratings. These ratings might be used in a model-based adjustment, to select studies to include in the synthesis or simply to present as additional information. Evaluators of study quality and bias must not know study results. Such knowledge can result in conscious or unconscious bias where studies that support preconceived conclusions are given better ratings than are those that go against preconceptions. Evaluators may come to the enterprise with inherent biases for or against specific researchers, sources of funding, research designs, outcome measures, and the like. These a priori biases are precisely what the Bayesian analysis is attempting explicitly to measure and incorporate, rather than have them operate in an undocumented manner. But the results of the studies being evaluated should not be allowed to influence the assessments.

Research is required on where to draw the line between "inputs" and "results." We propose that all information available on study attributes and baseline characteristics of participants (i.e., gender distributions, characteristics of organizational settings) be made available to those rating the studies. At issue is whether information such as follow-up rates should be allowed to inform the assessment. High follow-up rates indicate both a well-designed and well-conducted study, but also may indicate an effective treatment (Lipsey 1992).

## 4.2 Structuring the Evaluation

In section 3 we discussed the compound model where the true effect size for each study is sampled from a common prior distribution. Here, we incorporate quality and bias ratings by broadening the basic model to include study-specific prior means and variances. Staying with the Gaussian model, consider elicitation of study-specific prior means ($\mu_k$) and standard deviations ($\tau_k$). If the study-specific means and variances have no relation across the studies, then each study stands on its own and we have no synthesis. There is no shared parameter on which to combine evidence. We need to formulate a relation and propose:

$$\mu_k = \mu + d_k \qquad (26\text{-}8)$$
$$\tau_k = c_k \tau.$$

The parameters ($\mu$, $\tau^2$) are the prior mean and variance for a "typical" study. The constant $d_k$ measures bias; $d_k > 0$ indicates a study with positive bias. The constant $c_k$ relates to the likelihood that studies "like" study $k$ will have a true underlying effect size relatively close to the population effect size. A value of $c_k > 1$ indicates a study with true effect size sampled from a prior distribution that is more dispersed than that of the typical study. A larger $c_k$ will down-weight a study. This structure is one example of Rubin's idea (1990) of relating all studies to an archtype. Estimates for $\mu$ and $\tau$ apply to this archtypical ($c = 1$, $d = 0$) study, and the $c$'s and $d$'s must be elicited with this in mind. Different interpretations of $\mu$ and $\tau$ result from different normalizations and interpretations of the $c$'s and $d$'s.

We estimated $\mu$ and $\tau$ using BMDP5V (Dixon 1990). We use equation (26-7) (initially without "WEEKS*"), but use $T_k' = T_k - d_k$ instead of $T_k$ as dependent variable and set $Z_k = c_k$. If all $d_k = 0$ and all $c_k = 1$, the model produced by (26-8) reduces to that produced by (26-7).

## 5. DATA ANALYSIS

We have not performed a formal elicitation of the $d$'s and $c$'s, but present the results of a few "what if's" to show the influence of various choices. Suppose that study 4 is of good quality and studies 8 and 15 are of relatively poor quality. Other studies are similar to each other in quality and will serve as the baseline. To quantify these ratings we set: $c_4 = .3$, $c_8 = c_{15} = 2$ and all other $c$'s $= 1$. Studies with small values of $c$ will be given relatively more weight in the analysis. We consider all studies to be from unbiased prior distributions (the $d$'s $= 0$). These inputs produce model 3 in Table 26.1.

Compared with model 1, the estimated effect size in model 3 has slightly increased because study 4 has a relatively large effect size and is given increased weight. The posterior standard deviation is slightly reduced. Model 4 uses reciprocals of the $c$'s from model 3 (study 4 gets relatively less weight and studies 8 and 15 get relatively more weight than in models 1 and 3). The change in the estimated effects size is substantial.

Models 5 and 6 present the effects of nonzero $d$'s. Suppose we believe that studies 4 and 5 have a large, positive bias. For model 5, we set $d_4 = d_5 = .5$ and all other $d$'s $= 0$. This specification reduces the extremely large effect sizes from studies 4 and 5 and thereby produces an effect size smaller than that from model 1. Model 6 gives studies 4 and 5 negative bias, and the resulting effect size estimate is increased. Also, by inducing changes in $\hat{\tau}$ these models produce quite dramatic changes in posterior standard deviations.

Models 7 through 10 report on other analyses using the $d$'s and $c$'s to show the effects of formally including opinions. One could continue producing such "what if" analyses over a range of $d$'s and $c$'s to determine the sensitivity of results. Ideally, we would elicit the $d$'s and $c$'s from several experts and potential consumers of the meta-analysis and see how results vary over this collection of prior opinions. If the posterior distributions of parameters change little over this collection of prior distributions, we have a stable and credible set of findings. If results vary a great deal over the collection of priors, we have to explain why certain deviant opinions (priors) should be discounted or need to bring in (possibly to conduct) additional primary research that will settle the controversy.

## 6. ENSEMBLE ESTIMATES

Commonly, reports of research synthesis display a histogram of study-specific effect size estimates. Ideally, we would like to display a histogram of the true underlying effect sizes, but of course we do not have that luxury. Because of the within-study sampling variation, displaying the raw effect size estimates produces a histogram that is too spread out. A histogram based on a collection of large studies will be more concentrated than one based on small studies even if the underlying effect size distribution is the same. For an accurate depiction of the distribution of study-specific effect sizes, the histogram needs to be adjusted. A histogram of the standard empirical Bayes estimates (see section 2) overadjusts and produces a display with too little spread. Louis (1984, 1991) shows that a compromise between these two based (approximately) on

$$\hat{\theta}^E = \mu + \sqrt{1 - B_k}\,(T_k - \mu)$$

produces a valid display. These values appear at the bottom of Figure 26.1. Notice that they shrink toward the common mean, but not as far as the empirical Bayes estimates. We recommend displaying these values in a histogram.

## 7. DISCUSSION

This chapter concentrates on Bayesian meta-analysis. We can turn things around and consider performing a meta-analysis to help in developing objective prior distributions for a Bayesian design or analysis of the "next" study or sequence of studies. For example, we could use the output of model 1 and use a Gaussian prior distribution with $\mu = 0.085$, $\tau = 0.142$ in designing (and possibly in analyzing) the next study. The National Institutes of Health have recognized the value of such an approach by their encouragement of a meta-analysis to precede a consensus conference.

We have presented basic models and analyses in order to highlight concepts. The Bayesian paradigm can handle complex models relating many parameters and several stages of random variation. Recent developments in computing (Carlin & Gelfand 1990; Gelfand & Smith 1990; Laird & Louis 1987; Morris 1983; and Tanner 1991) make analysis of such models possible. The principal challenges concern structuring the models and the elicitation process (Lane et al. 1987).

The Bayesian approach requires that the meta-analyst make explicit structural relations and personal opinions. Even if these were to be used only informally, they are valuable in evaluating the meta-analysis. Using them in a formal manner allows the probability calculus to combine evidence in a coherent manner and to produce assessments (posterior distributions, confidence intervals, etc.) that incorporate the influence of all relevant sources of variation. Coupled with some form of sensitivity analysis, the Bayesian approach clearly identifies the stable findings and those that require further investigation. The approach is likely to be controversial because it depends on opinions, and frequently they will vary considerably. To implement credible Bayesian analyses additional development in eliciting priors and conducting robust analyses is needed.

The Bayesian approach is by no means a panacea. For example, it cannot solve the problems of developing an effective search for studies, deciding which studies to include, dealing with poor reporting of primary studies, and a host of other problems and challenges. Historically, the Bayesian approach has been criticized in part because it depends on a single prior distribution and in part because it usually makes explicit uncertainties and assumptions left implicit or buried in other approaches. Using a community of priors and reporting sensitivity analyses removes dependence on a single prior. The reporting of an honest level of uncertainty should be seen as a virtue and used to improve the design and analysis of primary and meta-analytic studies. With advances in computing that facilitate a Bayesian analysis of complicated and relevant models, we predict that its influence on meta-analysis will grow.

### Authors' Note

We thank Marjorie Ireland for technical assistance. Partial support was provided by contract No. NO1-AI05073 from the National Institute of Allergy and Infectious Diseases.

## 8. REFERENCES

Begg, C. B., & Pilote, L. (1991). A model for incorporating historical controls into a meta-analysis. *Biometrics, 47*, 899–906.

Berger, J. O. (1985). *Statistical decision theory and Bayesian analysis* (2nd ed.). New York: Springer-Verlag.

Breslow, N. (1990). Biostatistics and Bayes. *Statistical Science, 5*, 269–298.

Canner, P. L. (1983). Aspirin in coronary heart disease: Comparison of six clinical trials. *Israel Journal of Medical Science, 19*, 413–423.

Carlin, B. P., & Gelfand, A. E. (1990). Approaches for empirical Bayes confidence intervals. *Journal of the American Statistical Association, 85*, 105–114.

Chalmers, T. C. (1991). Problems induced by meta-analysis. *Statistics in Medicine, 10*, 971–980.

Chaloner, K., Church, T., Louis, T. A., & Matts, J. (in press). Bayesian monitoring for clinical trials: With a case study in AIDS. *Applied Statistics.*

Chaloner, K. M., & Duncan, G. T. (1983). Assessment

of a beta prior distribution: PM elicitation. *Statistician, 32*, 174–180.

Colton, T., Freedman, L. S., & Johnson, A. L. (eds.). (1987). Proceedings of the workshop on methodologic issues in overviews of randomized clinical trials, May 1986. *Statistics in Medicine, 6*, no. 3.

DerSimonian, R. & Laird, N. M. (1983). Evaluating the effect of coaching in SAT scores: A meta-analysis. *Harvard Educational Review, 53*, 1–15.

Dixon, W. J. (Ed.). (1990). *BMDP statistical software manual* (Vol. 2). Los Angeles: UCLA Press.

DuMouchel, W. H. & Harris, J. E. (1983). Bayes methods for combining the results of cancer studies in humans and other species (with discussion). *Journal of the American Statistical Association, 78*, 293–315.

Efron, B., & Morris, C. (1977). Stein's paradox in statistics. *Scientific American, 72*, 119–127.

Emerson, J. D., Burdick, E., Hoaglin, D. C., Mosteller, F., & Chalmers, T. C. (1990). An empirical study of the possible relation of treatment differences to quality scores in controlled randomized clinical trials. *Controlled Clinical Trials, 11*, 339–352.

Freedman, L. S., & Spiegelhalter, D. J. (1983). The assessment of subjective opinion and its use in relation to stopping rules for clinical trials. *Statistician, 32*, 153–160.

Garthwaite, P. H., & Dickey, J. M. (1990). Quantifying expert opinion in linear regression models. *Journal of the Royal Statistical Society*, Series B, *50*, 462–474.

Garthwaite, P. H., & Dickey, J. M. (1991). An elicitation method for multiple linear regression models. *Journal of Behavioral Decision Making, 4*, 17–31.

Gelfand, A. E., & Smith, A. F. M. (1990). Sampling-based approaches to calculating marginal densities. *Journal of the American Statistical Association, 85*, 398–409.

Grandits, G., Grambsch, P., & Louis, T. A. (1992). A SAS macro for performing analyses of random effects models of longitudinal data using the IML procedure. *Proceedings of the Seventeenth Annual SAS Users Group International Conference* (pp. 1145–1150). Carey, NC: SAS Institute.

Kadane, J. B. (1986). Progress toward a more ethical method for clinical trials. *Journal of Medicine and Philosophy, 11*, 385–404.

Kadane, J. B., Dickey, J. M., Winkler, R. L., Smith, W. S., & Peters, S. C. (1980). Interactive elicitation of opinion for a normal linear model. *Journal of the American Statistical Association, 75*, 845–854.

Laird, N. M. (1987). Thyroid cancer risk from exposure to ionizing radiation: A case study in the comparative potency model. *Risk Analysis, 7*, 299–309.

Laird, N. M., & Louis, T. A. (1987). Empirical Bayes confidence intervals based on bootstrap samples (with discussion). *Journal of the American Statistical Association, 82,* 739–757.

Lane, D., Kramer, M., Hutchinson, T., Jones, J., & Naranjo, C. (1987). The causality assessment of adverse drug reactions using a Bayesian approach. *Pharmaceutical Medicine, 2,* 265–283.

Lindley, D. V. (1990). Bayesian statistics. *Statistical Science, 5,* 44–89.

Lipsey, M. W. (1992). Juvenile delinquency treatment: A meta-analytic inquiry into the variability of effects. In T. D. Cook, H. Cooper, D. S. Cordray, H. Hartmann, L. V. Hedges, R. J. Light, T. A. Louis, & F. Mosteller, *Meta-analysis for explanation: A casebook.* New York: Russell Sage Foundation.

Louis, T. A. (1984). Estimating a population of parameter values using Bayes and empirical Bayes methods. *Journal of the American Statistical Association, 79,* 393–398.

Louis, T. A. (1991). Using empirical Bayes methods in biopharmaceutical research. *Statistics in Medicine, 10,* 811–829.

McCann, J., Horn, L., & Kaldor, J. (1984). An evaluation of salmonella (ames) test data in the published literature: Application of statistical procedures and analysis of mutagenic potency. *Mutation Research, 134,* 1–47.

Morris, C. (1983). Parametric empirical Bayes inference: Theory and applications. *Journal of the American Statistical Association, 78,* 47–59.

Morris, C. N., & Normand, S. L. (1991). *Hierarchical models for combining information and for meta-analysis.* Paper presented at the fourth international meeting on Bayesian Statistics, Valencia, Spain.

Mosteller, F., & Wallace, D. L. (1964). *Inference and disputed authorship: The Federalist.* Reading, MA: Addison-Wesley.

Raudenbush, S. W., & Bryk, A. S. (1985). Empirical Bayes meta-analysis. *Journal of Educational Statistics, 10,* 75–98.

Rubin, D. B. (1990). A new perspective on meta-analysis. In K. W. Wachter & M. L. Straf (Eds.), *The future of meta-analysis.* New York: Russell Sage Foundation.

Tanner, M. A. (1991). *Tools for statistical inference: Observed data and data augmentation methods.* Lecture Notes in Statistics No. 67. New York: Springer-Verlag.

Tukey, J. W. (1977). *Exploratory data analysis.* Reading, MA: Addison-Wesley.

Wachter, K. W., & Straf, M. L. (Eds.). (1990). *The future of meta-analysis.* New York: Russell Sage Foundation.

Winkler, R. L. (1967). The assessment of prior distributions in Bayesian analysis. *Journal of the American Statistical Association, 62,* 1105–1120.

# PART
# VIII

## REPORTING THE RESULTS
## OF RESEARCH SYNTHESIS

Cooper, H. and Hedges, L. V. (Eds.) 1994. *The Handbook of Research Synthesis*. New York: Russell Sage Foundation

# 27

# THE REPORTING FORMAT

## KATHERINE TAYLOR HALVORSEN
*Smith College*

CONTENTS

# 1. INTRODUCTION

Several articles examining the quality of published research syntheses or meta-analyses have appeared in journals in both the behavioral sciences and medicine (Beaman 1991; Sacks et al. 1987; Jackson 1980). Through these articles and others like them the scientific community has begun to establish guidelines concerning what information about a research synthesis should be made public. It is important to note that a reader's judgment of the quality of research depends entirely on the clarity of writing and the thoroughness of reporting in the published research report. Becker (1991), in her interviews with review journal editors, found that they "overwhelmingly seek clarity in review manuscripts . . . clarity of purpose and problem definition . . . clarity of arguments . . . clarity of writing and presentation . . . clarity of the review's conclusions" (p. 268). This chapter provides guidelines for preparing a clear and thorough report of a research synthesis that gives readers the information they need to evaluate and interpret its results.

Because the research synthesis presents technical material, we encourage authors to use the standard presentation format for scientific studies: introduction, methods, results, and discussion. The following sections of this chapter examine the issues that should be addressed under each of these headings.

# 2. INTRODUCING THE RESEARCH

The introduction describes the broad scientific question that the research synthesis addresses. Often it explains the importance of this field of inquiry within the wider context of the history of the field. For example, Giaconia and Hedges (1982) introduce their study of open education by identifying the two major problems that investigators encounter when they attempt to characterize the features of effective open education.

> The identification of general effects for open education is complicated by the fact that open education is not a single, well-defined treatment. . . . These naturally occurring variations in open education programs would not hinder efforts to draw general

conclusions about the efficacy of open education if a consistent treatment could be identified across all the empirical studies of open education programs. (p. 579)

A few paragraphs later they place the question of effectiveness of open education in a historical context and explain why they believe the problem is an important one:

> Over the years, a plethora of terms has emerged for innovative educational programs that all seem to share some common philosophical assumptions and observable features of open education, for example, progressive education, informal education, free school, open space school, open corridor school, integrated day plan, alternative school, and so on. . . . The persistence of the open education debate and the large number of empirical studies that have been generated by this debate both suggest the importance of attempts to search for meaningful ways to summarize the empirical findings. (p. 580)

## 2.1 The Need for the Review

The introduction to a research synthesis should also specify why a quantitative review of the field is needed: The field may never have been reviewed, and there may be so many studies that only meta-analysis makes sense (if earlier syntheses exist, the current authors should review them and give a convincing argument for doing another one); there may be controversy in a field unresolved by previous reviews; there may be narrative reviews but no quantitative reviews; only a portion of the literature may have been reviewed; the goal of the review may be to produce an overall estimate of effect size, and important new primary studies have appeared in the literature since the existing reviews were published; the goal, from the start, may be to look at one or more moderators of effect that have not been examined across studies previously.

Lytton and Romney (1991), in their study of parents' differential socialization of boys and girls, identify clearly what their review contributes to the field.

> No quantitative review of studies of sex-differentiated socialization has, however, to our knowledge

appeared, and this is the gap that our study attempts to fill. Such a meta-analysis at this time is able to take note of the many studies in this domain published since Maccoby and Jacklin's book (1974), and it can also benefit from and take account of the criticisms of the review noted previously here [Maccoby and Jacklin's]. (p. 268)

## 2.2 Describing the Research Question in Detail

After giving a broad outline of the research question, the introduction should formulate the problem in greater detail. What particular aspect of the scientific question does the current research investigate? In the area of social science research, this frequently includes defining the concepts under study and their contexts. For example, in an article concerned with "prosocial behavior" (Eisenberg 1991) the author defines prosocial behavior as "voluntary behavior intended to benefit another" (p. 273) and states that one aspect of her research explores the relationship between empathy and prosocial behavior.

## 2.3 What the Reader Gains from This Review

Finally, the introduction tells the reader what he or she can expect to gain from reading the research synthesis, and, perhaps, use in his or her own work. The last section of the introduction should provide an overview of the structure of the review report itself, stating what will be discussed first, second, and so on.

## 2.4 An Example

An introduction by Becker (1990) accomplishes all these objectives. The article contains a long introduction covering several pages, but the first few paragraphs include all the pertinent information: that her research addresses the broad question of effectiveness of coaching for the Scholastic Aptitude Test (SAT) and that because SAT scores are widely used in college admission decisions there is strong interest in both academic circles and the general public in this topic. She points out that the question of whether coaching helps has not been resolved. Her work addresses four aspects of this issue:

1. What are the relative contributions of characteristics of the subjects, the coaching interventions, and the studies themselves to the magnitudes of coaching effects, and which of these characteristics are confounded with one another?

2. Is the effect of coaching the same for the math and verbal sections of the SAT?

3. Can a "model" or set of predictors be found that explains the variation in the results of these coaching studies?

4. Have any studies produced coaching effects that appear unusual or extreme in light of the outcomes predicted by models of coaching-study results?

The reader can expect to gain new information from her work, she tells us, because she uses statistical methods that make possible analysis of these questions and because these questions have not been directly addressed in previous reviews.

She does not provide a definition of "coaching" in the introductory paragraphs, but devotes an entire section to it immediately following these paragraphs because an understanding of coaching involves the question of coaching for what kind of skills, and this additional complexity is important to her work. In all other respects her introduction adheres to the recommended pattern.

## 3. PRESENTING THE STUDY METHODS

Like other scientific research, a synthesis should begin with the development of a study protocol. This written document defines concepts used in the synthesis and describes study procedures in as much detail as investigators can provide before beginning the research. These procedures include specifying operational definitions used to relate concepts to observable events, describing the literature search methods and scope, defining eligibility criteria for primary studies included in the research synthesis, describing methods for carrying out an evaluation of these criteria for each primary study located in the search, determining what data will be extracted from each primary study and how this will be accomplished accurately, describing which statistical methods will be used for comparing or combining results from the primary studies, and specifying methods for presenting the results. The methods section of the research report should outline the definitions and procedures discussed in the protocol and should report, either in the text or in a footnote, the sources of funding for the research synthesis. If earlier meta-analyses exist, differences between the current study and the earlier ones, especially in study selection, should be discussed in detail.

## 3.1 Specifying Operational Definitions

Readers want to know how the investigators defined the outcome variable extracted from each primary study and how that variable was measured. Cooper (1982) has pointed out that operational definitions vary and that the inclusivity of the definitions used and the level of detail specified in the definitions can affect the outcome of a research synthesis.

Examples of these two effects of the operationalization of concepts can be seen in Halvorsen's (unpublished) research synthesis of rates of kidney damage caused by toxic levels of the drug Gentamicin. The definition of kidney toxicity used in the meta-analysis may be more or less inclusive. The investigator might define kidney damage by the rise in blood levels of an organic acid, creatine (serum creatine), by the increase in concentration of urea nitrogen in the blood (BUN), by an increase in the excretion of creatine (creatine clearance), or by other indicators. If we include in the meta-analysis primary studies that use any of these definitions of kidney toxicity, we find 18 published studies. Restricting the meta-analysis to studies that define kidney toxicity as "an increase in serum creatine" limits the analysis to 14 studies.

The level of detail specified in the definition may also vary, and its variation can affect the outcome of this analysis. For example, suppose that we use "increase in serum creatine" as evidence for kidney toxicity, and we measure the change in the serum creatine level by subtracting the initial creatine level, measured just before therapy begins, from the highest creatine level measured during therapy or within 48 hours after therapy ends. We specify further that in order to be classified as having kidney toxicity due to drug treatment, a patient must show either that

1. the initial serum creatine level before treatment with the drug is less than 3 milligrams per deciliter (mg/dL) of blood and the increase is at least 0.5 mg/dL after treatment is administered for greater than or equal to 72 hours, or

2. the initial serum creatine level before treatment with the drug is greater than or equal to 3 milligrams per deciliter (mg/dL) of blood and the increase is at least 1.0 mg/dL after treatment is administered for greater than or equal to 72 hours.

Such a definition would allow only 3 studies to be used in the research synthesis.

The study by Giaconia and Hedges (1982) provides an example from the social sciences in which the investigation focuses on a concept—open education—that is not well defined. The investigators define the concept implicitly in their study by using the inclusion criterion developed in an earlier research synthesis (Horowitz 1979). That investigation included primary studies in the review ". . . if the educational treatment had either been explicitly labeled by the term 'open' or if it had been described as having characteristics generally ascribed to open education, such as flexibility of space, student choice of activity, richness of learning materials, integration of curriculum areas, and more individual and small-group than large-group instruction" (p. 581).

## 3.2 Describing the Literature Search

Readers want to know the population of research reports from which authors drew their samples. By specifying the methods they used to search for relevant studies, authors implicitly define the research population. If computerized databases were searched, the names of the databases, the keywords used to define the search fields, and the years of publication included in the search should be reported. Other methods—such as personal communications with colleagues working in the field; identifying articles in bibliographies given in primary studies already identified or in review articles; or searches of the Science Citation Index, Social Sciences Citation Index, or *Current Contents*—should also be specified in the research report.

Goldstein et al. (1989) provide a good example of reporting the base of research reports they used for their meta-analysis of progestational agents used during pregnancy:

A preliminary list of papers was provided by the Oxford Database of Perinatal Trials (Chalmers et al. 1987). Papers were also searched for through the Bibliographic Retrieval Service (BRS) and the National Library of Medicine (NLM) computer systems based on medical subject heading keywords (e.g., pregnancy, clinical trials, random allocation, double-blind method, progesterone, sex hormones), by routine searching of *Current Contents* (a weekly publication listing recently published articles by journal), and by searching the references of studies and review articles as they were obtained. (p. 266)

## 3.3 Specifying the Eligibility Criteria

The eligibility criteria for studies determine which primary studies among those retrieved in the literature search phase will be used in the research synthesis. These criteria usually define characteristics of a primary study's subjects, the treatments that subjects receive, the study design, and the study results that allow a study's inclusion in the synthesis. For example, eligibility criteria that use characteristics of a study's subjects might specify that only studies using female subjects aged 5 or younger are eligible for the meta-analysis. Eligibility criteria might also be based on treatment type or duration, or on design features such as minimum sample size, presence of a control group, or random allocation of subjects to treatments. Aspects of study results that may affect eligibility often involve the type of results reported. Studies might be excluded from a meta-analysis if they do not report sufficient information about the outcome to allow computation of an effect size. Characteristics of the article that describes the primary study, such as date of publication or language in which the article is written, also may be used to define eligibility criteria. Retrieved studies that fail to meet at least one of the eligibility criteria might be excluded from the meta-analysis.

Sometimes authors use ineligibility criteria rather than eligibility criteria for determining which articles will be included in their research synthesis. For example, Cohn (1991) reports the characteristics that would exclude a study from his synthesis of research on sex differences in the course of personality development. He lists the following reasons that studies were excluded from the analysis (the numbers shown in parentheses are the number of studies excluded for each reason):

1. Subjects were all of the same gender ($n = 88$).
2. Subjects were drawn from clinical populations (e.g., hospitalized psychiatric patients or drug addicts; $n = 10$).
3. Findings were reported in previously published articles ($n = 11$).
4. Sampling procedures were inappropriate for male and female comparisons (e.g., subjects were chosen to represent a range of ego levels within each sex; $n = 8$).
5. Protocols were not rated with the scoring manuals ($n = 1$).
6. Age differences between boys and girls were present . . . or might have been present ($n = 3$). This criterion was not applied to adults older than

22 because ego development appears to stabilize by the early 20's, making age differences between males and females an unlikely confound when examining gender differences in ego development.
7. Sampling demographics were not provided ($n = 23$). (p. 257)

Cohn describes the "protocols" mentioned in item 5 before he gives this list of exclusion criteria. Thus, with the exception of item 7, each item is so well defined that a research assistant could apply them without further instruction. To clarify item 7, the author could list the particular aspects of the demographics required for eligibility.

To reassure readers that the eligibility criteria were applied uniformly to all retrieved studies, authors should report how they checked the eligibility status of these papers. For instance, two researchers, working independently, might determine the eligibility status of each paper retrieved. They might compare their results and discuss differences, coming to a consensus on each paper. The research synthesis report should state the agreement rate between researchers and how differences among the researchers were resolved.

To avoid selection bias, some investigators (Sacks et al. 1987; Cooper 1982) recommend that the researchers who determine study eligibility status should not know the authors, journal sources, and results of the primary studies. This can be done by giving researchers only the methods sections of the primary papers to use for determining study eligibility. The research report should say if such a method has been used in the synthesis.

## 3.4 Reporting Data Collection Methods

To assure readers that data were collected from the primary studies accurately and consistently from study to study, authors should report the methods used to code primary study data. If a data coding form was developed to assure greater accuracy in the data collection process, it should be reported. If two or more investigators independently coded the data, the number of coders and measures of coder agreement (see Chapter 11) should be reported, as well as the methods used to adjudicate differences between data coders.

Data extraction bias may occur when data coders have to interpret the information they gather. Different coders may have different interpretations, and their interpretations could be influenced by knowledge of the authors or of the treatments that were used in the various treatment groups. This bias may be controlled by having more than one reader extract the data and by masking the names identifying authors and treatments in the copies of the papers the data coders read. Some investigators recommend this practice strongly (Sacks et al. 1987), and when it has been used the research report should say so.

## 3.5 Reporting Statistical Methods

The statistical methods section might begin by reporting the criteria used to decide which studies were similar enough to be combined. If a test was performed to determine the homogeneity of study results, it should be reported. The issue of pooling results is a sensitive one, and authors should report sufficient detail of the statistical analysis to convince readers that a useful result will be obtained.

Readers want to know the specific statistical procedures used so that they can interpret a combined significance test or estimate. Authors should provide sufficient information about their statistical analyses, including the names of computing programs if they used widely available packages, so that readers can perform similar analyses.

Authors should consider the probabilities of Type I statistical errors (concluding that there is a significant result when none exists) and Type II errors (concluding that the result is not statistically significant when it is). They should report standard errors for estimates and the appropriate $p$ values (one- or two-sided) and the power of statistical tests they use, when these are known.

Methods for examining relationships between study outcomes and features of the study subjects, treatments, study design, or publication characteristics of the primary studies should be reported. Features that may be important include age, gender, or ethnicity of study subjects; duration or type of treatment; type of control; method of allocation of subjects to treatments; or year of publication.

Clinical studies in medicine often report analyses of subgroups of study subjects because investigators want to find the best treatment for each subgroup of patients. Subgroups are usually defined by patient or disease characteristics evident at the time of diagnosis. If subgroup analyses are reported, authors should carefully report how the subgroups were determined. Evaluation of treatment effects for subgroups pooled across several studies may provide stronger evidence than could be obtained in any individual study. There may be, however, subtle

or not-so-subtle differences found among subgroup definitions across studies, and these should be made clear. Gelber and Goldhirsch (1987) point out that inconsistent subgroup definitions from study to study may limit the value of these analyses.

## 3.6 Reporting Sources of Funding

Readers need to know the source of financial support for a research synthesis to be able to evaluate its conclusions. As stated by Sacks et al. (1987), ''Potential conflicts of interest do not necessarily disqualify a research synthesis, but they should be clearly acknowledged'' (p. 452).

## 4. REPORTING THE RESULTS

The results section of the research synthesis reports the findings for each aspect of the study. These include the results of the literature search and of the selection of eligible studies; the results of the data collection, including descriptive statistics for various characteristics of the primary studies; the results of the tests for homogeneity, of the pooling, and of any subgroup or other analyses made.

## 4.1 The Primary Studies Analyzed and Those Omitted

We recommend that the references section of the report of a research synthesis consist of two separate lists: one giving the primary studies used in the synthesis and the other giving the methodological or other articles referenced in the text that do not belong to the population of research reports from which authors drew their sample. This makes very clear which articles were used as data sources for the research synthesis. Although we prefer to have the list of primary studies published with the the research synthesis, it may be too long for a journal to print. When the list is omitted, the author should certainly tell readers where they can write to obtain a complete bibliography.

Additionally, investigators should enumerate the primary studies retrieved at the literature search stage of the research, but excluded from the analysis, and they should give the reasons for their exclusion. Authors could provide this information in the form of a table that lists the reasons for excluding studies from the synthesis and gives the numbers of studies excluded for each reason. Readers want to be told about papers that were retrieved but not used because the inclusion or exclusion of particular papers may have large effects on the results of the meta-analysis. Also, knowledge of which papers were included and which excluded may help readers understand the author's definitions of concepts used in the research synthesis. Authors should make the bibliography of retrieved-but-excluded studies available to readers on request.

## 4.2 The Experimental Conditions Used in the Primary Studies

Authors should give as many characteristics of the experimental conditions used in primary studies as are relevant to the broad scientific question addressed by the research synthesis. Readers find summary tables of primary study characteristics important to their understanding of the research synthesis database.

The amount of information that authors present may depend to some extent on the amount of journal space that editors allow. A table format that gives extensive information about primary study characteristics reports each primary study in a separate row and each study characteristic in a separate column. Lytton and Romney's research synthesis of parents' differential socialization of boys and girls (1991) provides an unusually lengthy example of this kind of table. The table covers slightly more than ten pages in their article. For each of 17 socialization areas, the table reports values of six study characteristics and gives the effect size for each primary study that reports results for the socialization area. Thus, a primary study appears in the table several times, once in each socialization area for which an effect size could be computed. Table 27.1 shows part of the table. This particular part lists articles in the "warmth, nurturance, responsiveness" socialization area.

Another table format—one that requires less journal space—reports frequency data for various study attributes. Groups of rows in the table give levels of each study characteristic and the number of primary studies with that level of the characteristic. Lytton and Romney's research synthesis also provides an example of a frequency table of primary study characteristics (see Table 27.2). The table lists primary study characteristics and characteristics of the written reports that describe the studies, including whether the report was published, year of publication, and sex of first author. The table also lists "quality rating" as a primary study characteristic.

The table has one troublesome aspect. The numbers of studies reported for each age group within the characteristic "age of children" add to 175 studies, and the numbers reported for the various methods within "data-collection method" add to 174. Elsewhere the article states that the total sample size for the meta-analysis is 172 studies, and the article does not explain why these differences occur.

Another example of a frequency table that reports primary study characteristics comes from Becker's study of effectiveness of coaching for the SAT (1990). She reports two characteristics of the samples used in the primary studies and one characteristic of the treatments.

**Table 27.1 Effect Sizes by Study and Socialization Area: Warmth, Nurturance, Responsiveness**

| Study | N | Age (Years) | Data Collection Method | Sex of First Author | Country | Parent | d |
|---|---|---|---|---|---|---|---|
| Armentraut 1975 | 126 | >12 | Report by child | Male | North America | PC | −.02 |
| Armentraut & Burger 1972 | 635 | 6–12 | Report by child | Male | North America | PC | −.19 |
| Barnes 1986 | 16 | 0–5 | Observation, experiment | Female | North America | PC | −1.80 |
| Barnett et al. 1980 | 72 | 6–12 | Report by child | Male | North America | PC | −.56 |
| Baumrind 1971 | 149 | 0–5 | Observation, experiment | Female | North America | PC | −.08 |

SOURCE: Lytton and Romney (1991).

NOTE: These studies marked PC (parents combined) looked at both parents. Some other studies reported in this article looked at fathers only or mothers only.

**Table 27.2 Characteristics of Sample of Studies**
**(n = 172)**

| Characteristic | Studies (n) |
|---|---|
| Sample size | |
| ≤ 50 | 70 |
| 50–150 | 60 |
| > 150 | 42 |
| Parent sex | |
| Mother only | 60 |
| Father only | 11 |
| Both parents | 101 |
| Age of children | |
| 0–5 years | 95 |
| 6–12 years | 44 |
| 13–adulthood | 25 |
| Not stated, mixed | 11 |
| Data collection method | |
| Report by child | 34 |
| Interview/questionnaire for parent | 56 |
| Reaction to video/story | 8 |
| Observation/experiment | 76 |
| Source of study | |
| Published (journal, book) | 140 |
| Unpublished (dissertation, etc.) | 32 |
| Year of publication | |
| ≤ 1973 | 42 |
| 1974–1980 | 59 |
| > 1980 | 71 |
| Sex of first author | |
| Male | 80 |
| Female | 92 |
| Quality rating | |
| Low (2 and 3) | 67 |
| High (4 and 5) | 105 |

SOURCE: Lytton and Romney (1991).

Each characteristic has several levels. The table reports the number of primary studies found at each level of each characteristic. In this example, the numbers of studies summed over the levels of a characteristic add to 48 for each characteristic, and the article states that the meta-analysis used results from 48 studies. Table 27.3 shows these results.

## 4.3 The Results Observed in Primary Studies

Authors often report, in a single table, study characteristics and study results for each primary study. Readers, however, may find a statistical summary of primary study results more useful. In particular, the meta-analysis could include a display of the distribution of study outcomes. An example of a clear presentation of the distribution of primary study results comes from Wood, Wong, and Chachere (1991). In a study of the effects of media violence on viewers' aggression in unconstrained social interaction, these authors present a stem-and-leaf display of the effect sizes obtained in the 12 studies in which exact effect sizes could be computed. Readers can scan the distribution and see that it is fairly symmetric, ranging from −0.34 to +1.04, and contains no obvious outliers. Table 27.4 gives their stem-and-leaf plot. Chapter 28 discusses other graphical methods for displaying the results from primary studies.

## 4.4 Homogeneity of Results in Primary Studies

Additionally, readers want to know whether the variation in primary study outcomes may be attributed to sampling alone or if other sources contribute to the variation. Thus, authors should report the results of tests for homogeneity among primary study outcomes. These tests determine which of two possible models for combining study results should be used. In one model, usually called a fixed effects model, all effect sizes from studies are treated as if they estimate the same parameter. Differences among estimates from different studies are due to sampling error. The second model, usually called a random effects model, assumes that the effect size in each study is a sample estimate from a different population, and it estimates the parameter for that population. The estimates differ from study to study owing to differences among the study population parameters (between-studies variation) and to sampling of different subjects within the study populations (within-study variation). Methods for pooling results differ depending on which model is assumed (see Chapters 3 and 18).

A variance-component estimate is often used as a supplement to the homogeneity test, particularly for random effects models. Essentially, the homogeneity test tests the null hypothesis that the between-studies variance in effects is no greater than would be expected due to sampling error alone. The variance-component estimate is the point estimate of the between-studies variance in effect size parameters. In the event that the null hypothesis is rejected for the homogeneity test—that is, the test indicates that between-studies variance is nonzero—authors should give readers an estimate of the variance component.

**Table 27.3 Characteristics of Coaching Studies**

| Characteristic | Category | Studies (n) | (%) |
|---|---|---|---|
| Selectivity of sample | Low achievers | 6 | (12) |
| | Mix of students | 18 | (38) |
| | Selective sample | 24 | (50) |
| Voluntariness of sample | Compulsory coaching | 3 | (6) |
| | Elective/free coaching | 19 | (40) |
| | Voluntary/costly coaching | 26 | (54) |
| Content of instruction | Math and verbal | 27 | (56) |
| | Math only | 4 | (8) |
| | Verbal only | 15 | (31) |
| | Neither math nor verbal | 2 | (4) |

SOURCE: Becker (1990).

**Table 27.4 Distribution of Effect Size Outcomes on a Stem-and-Leaf Plot**

| Stem | Leaf |
|---|---|
| +1.0 | 4 |
| +.9 | |
| +.8 | 3 |
| +.7 | 8 |
| +.6 | 3, 5 |
| +.5 | 6 |
| +.4 | |
| +.3 | 2, 5 |
| +.2 | |
| +.1 | |
| +.0 | |
| −.0 | 7 |
| −.1 | 7 |
| −.2 | |
| −.3 | |

SOURCE: Wood, Wong, and Chachere (1991).
NOTE: Each effect size estimate is composed of one stem and one leaf. The numbers in the left column represent the stems or first numerals (the ones and the one-tenths places) in the estimates, and the numbers in the right column represent the leaves or second numerals (the one-hundredths place) in the estimates. Multiple entries in a row indicate that more than one estimate is composed of a given stem. Positive numbers reflect greater aggressiveness of subjects exposed to violent media, and negative numbers reflect greater aggressiveness of control subjects.

## 4.5 The Pooled Results

Research syntheses do not differ from primary studies in their need to report estimates of the precision of their results together with the pooled results. An estimate of the precision of a population mean effect size might be an estimate of its standard error or it might be a 95 percent confidence interval for the mean effect size. A pooled estimate of a correlation coefficient may be accompanied by a confidence interval or by the $p$ value for a test of the hypothesis that the pooled estimate does not differ significantly from zero. The $p$ values should be included in reports of the results of pooled significance tests as well as the test's associated degrees of freedom.

When the pooling involves moderate numbers of primary results, the pooled result might be displayed most effectively in a graph or a table accompanied by the results from each primary study on which the pooled result depends. A tabular summary might give effect size estimates for each primary study, their standard errors, and 95 percent confidence bounds along with the pooled result, its standard error, and its confidence bounds. A graphical summary of the same information might show the point estimate of the effect size from each primary study and a 95 percent confidence interval together with the pooled estimate and a 95 percent confidence interval. This kind of presentation allows readers to easily compare the results from primary studies with the pooled summary measure. Chapter 28 describes charts and graphs for effective presentations of results in more detail.

**4.5.1 Subgroup analyses** A format that works well for analyses that include results for subgroups of studies is shown in Table 27.5. The statistics reported in the table follow the recommendations of Hedges and Olkin (1985). The first row of the table (A) gives the analysis pooled across groups: the homogeneity statistic $Q_T$, its degrees of freedom, a variance component estimate or its square root (for random effects models only), the mean effect size, its standard error, and a confidence interval for the mean effect size. Rows B through Z of the table give the results of analyses that are relevant for subgroup studies. Row B gives the between-groups statistic $Q_{BET}$ for testing the hypothesis that different groups have the same mean effect. Row C gives the within-group homogeneity statistic $Q_W$. Rows D through Z give the results of analyses for each subgroup. These results include a homogeneity statistic, variance component (for random effects analyses), subgroup mean effect size, its standard error, and a confidence interval.

Johnson and Eagly (1989), in their research synthesis of the effects of involvement on persuasion, use an abbreviated version of Table 27.5 to report the results from an analysis of the type of involvement used in the primary studies. Table 27.6 shows their results. The authors classify studies into three groups by type of involvement examined in each study. The first column in Table 27.6 gives the three types of involvement. The second column reports the between-groups fit statistic $Q_{BET}$, which follows a chi-square distribution on 2 degrees of freedom. The reported statistic is significant at the .001 level, and the authors reject the hypothesis that the average effect sizes are equal across classes.

The third column gives the numbers of studies in each group. The next three columns give the weighted mean effect size and lower and upper confidence bounds for the group mean in each group. The final column reports the within-group fit statistic $Q_{Wi}$. Each follows a chi-square distribution on degrees of freedom equal to the number of studies in the group minus one. Each tests for homogeneity of effect size within group. The values reported in Table 27.6 indicate that the hypothesis of homogeneity of effect size within group should be rejected for the value-relevant and outcome-relevant groups.

**4.5.2 Sensitivity analysis** Readers want to know whether the results of a research synthesis are sensitive to the inclusion or exclusion of particular studies and whether the results are sensitive to the method of analysis. If there is doubt about whether some primary studies should be included in the combined analysis, then investigators should report the combined results when the studies are included and when they are omitted. In clinical experiments the results may depend to a greater or lesser degree on whether data from subjects who withdraw from treatment before the end of the experiment are included in the analysis. If this situation occurs, then the results should be reported both with and without these data. The principle extends to meta-analyses. If the primary studies report results with and without the withdrawals, the combined result should do so also.

## 5. DISCUSSING THE RESULTS

The discussion sections of research syntheses may differ widely. Not all papers address all of the issues presented here. Certainly, some issues are more important than others. Authors should give an assessment of the potential for bias in the retrieved literature, and they should

**Table 27.5 A Table Format for Reporting Statistical Results**

|   | Source | $Q$ | $df$ | Variance Component | ES | (SE) | 95% CI |
|---|--------|-----|------|--------------------|-----|------|--------|
| A | Total | $Q_T$ | | | | | |
| B | Between Groups | $Q_{BET}$ | | | | | |
| C | Within Groups | $Q_W$ | | | | | |
| D | Group 1 | $Q_{W1}$ | | | | | |
| E | Group 2 | $Q_{W2}$ | | | | | |
| . | . | | | | | | |
| . | . | | | | | | |
| . | . | | | | | | |
| Z | Group $L$ | $Q_{WL}$ | | | | | |

**Table 27.6 Test of Categorical Model for Type of Involvement**

| Variable and Class | Between-Classes Effect ($Q_{BET}$) | N | Mean $d_{i+}$ | 95% CI for $d_{i+}$ Lower | Upper | Homogeneity within Each Class ($Q_{Wi}$)[a] |
|---|---|---|---|---|---|---|
| Type of involvement | 68.68** | | | | | |
| Value relevant | | 15 | −0.48 | −0.57 | −0.40 | 73.17** |
| Outcome relevant | | 20 | 0.02 | −0.06 | 0.10 | 40.68* |
| Impression relevant | | 5 | −0.17 | −0.33 | −0.01 | 6.57 |

SOURCE: Johnson and Eagly (1989).
NOTE: Effect sizes are positive for differences in the high-involvement direction and negative for differences in the low-involvement direction.
[a]Significance indicates rejection of the hypothesis of homogeneity.
*$p < .01$; **$p < .001$.

tell readers what inferences can be drawn from the results as well as the limitations of the findings.

The economic impact of the results may be quite important for some research syntheses and of little importance for others. If, for example, coaching for the SAT was found to be ineffective, it would have an economic impact on the coaching industry. However, this effect may not be of any interest to either the researcher or reader oriented toward education or psychology. The implications of the results for future research may be of importance to the academically oriented researcher or reader. Meta-analyses summarize the accumulated evidence in a scientific field, and many meta-analyses are undertaken with the goal of finding the current status of knowledge within a particular field.

## 5.1 Potential Biases in the Retrieved Literature

The subjects who participate in an experiment or in an observational study may be referred to as "experimental units" or, more simply, as "units." Cox (1958) defines them as the smallest division of the experimental (or observational) material such that any two units may receive different treatments. The population of units for which we wish to draw inference is called the target population; the accessible population is that subset of the target population from which we draw the experimental units. The accessible population and the target population may be identical, but the former is more likely to be some subset of the latter.

In research synthesis the smallest division of the experimental material, the experimental unit, is a study. The target population may be viewed as all research (both completed studies and potential studies) that meets

the eligibility criteria used for including studies in the synthesis, and the accessible population is the subset of the target population that the investigator is able to obtain.

The report of the research synthesis should contain some discussion of the target population and of the accessible population of studies, and it should attempt to account for the discrepancies between the two. The accessible population can differ from the target population for two reasons: the retrieval techniques failed to find some of the available studies or the studies completed in the area may not represent all units in the target population (Cooper 1982). Failure to find all completed studies may be due to the difficulty of finding unpublished material or to a less-than-thorough literature search. However, the failure to represent all possible units in the target population may also be due to the fact that the needed studies have not yet been conducted.

There is great concern among some investigators over the potential for publication bias: the belief that more studies with statistically nonsignificant results remain unpublished than studies with significant results, and that these studies could, if they were included in the analysis, negate the findings of a research synthesis based only on published work. However, Laird and Mosteller (1990) comment:

The shortcomings of meta-analysis are often the shortcomings of primary studies or of science in general that have been highlighted by the meta-analytic context. A good example of this is the concern for publication bias. Reading a meta-analysis, we worry about this. But the reader reading a single article in a journal rarely says, "I wonder how many unpublished articles produced the opposite effect.'' It is the thinking about populations of studies that produces such concerns. (pp. 27–28)

Some authorities on research synthesis recommend that the initial pooling be conducted only with the results of published studies because these reports have the advantage of having undergone peer review (Chalmers et al. 1987; and L'Abbe, Detsky & O'Rourke 1987). They believe that peer review ensures a basic level of quality in published studies that cannot be counted on in unpublished studies. This concern may be addressed, however, by examining the variation in results between published and unpublished studies. Additionally, study quality might be quantified and the variation in study results with study quality measured. Given the divergence of opinions about the importance of including unpublished material in the research synthesis, investigators should discuss sources of potential bias as thoroughly as possible.

## 5.2 Drawing Inferences from the Results

The discussion section, rather than the results section, is the place for making generalizations based on the findings. In medicine what is needed is an assessment of the clinical significance of the statistical findings in addition to their theoretical implications. Similarly, in the social sciences some readers want to know the practical meaning of the results, and others want to know the theoretical implications of the statistical findings.

If other reviews of the field exist, investigators should make clear any similarities or differences in their findings and why these occur. Findings from key primary studies should also be compared with the results of the synthesis. Readers want these similarities and differences pointed out and explained.

When drawing inferences from the results of research synthesis, authors should point out the limitations of their findings. Gaps in the accessible population of units due to the lack of primary studies present the most obvious limitations on the generalization of the meta-analysis' findings.

## 5.3 The Economic Impact of the Results

Readers want to know whether improvements in treatments identified by research synthesis have economic consequences. The benefits of new methods may look less appealing when we evaluate their costs. Savings may result when newer, cheaper methods supplant old methods. Levin, Glass, and Meister (1987) use the results from research synthesis to investigate the cost-effectiveness of four educational interventions: computer-assisted instruction, cross-age tutoring, reductions in class size, and increasing instructional time. They employ estimates of effect sizes obtained from Glass (1984) to compute the effect sizes for each $100 of cost per pupil and use these ratios to compare the interventions.

Although such a detailed analysis of the economic implications of their findings is beyond the scope of most research syntheses, a brief discussion of the costs of new methods, when they are known, would be useful. For example, in health care, with the increasing concern for escalating costs, it could be considered irresponsible to recommend adopting new methods of treatment or diagnosis without also considering their economic impact.

## 5.4 Implications for Future Research

Authors should pay particular attention to one of the most important benefits from research synthesis, the implications of its results for future research. Research syntheses attempt to locate all available previous research and provide a quantitative summary. The process that gives us this summary also highlights places where there are gaps in the research record and places where the research to date allows us to state with some confidence that a result is ''well known'' and further research in the area is not needed.

## 6. SUMMARY AND CONCLUSION

We cannot overestimate the importance of careful attention to the writing of the research synthesis report. We would like the report to describe results both fully and simply. Cooper (1982) has pointed out two threats to the validity of the research review's conclusions that occur when the report does not describe the research fully. These threats come from, first, the omission of details about how the review was conducted, because an incomplete report reduces the replicability of the review conclusions, and, second, the omission of evidence about characteristics of study subjects or about relations among study characteristics, in the primary studies, because ''as research on a specific behavior [or treatment] progresses, more details concerning the experimental conditions are found to be relevant'' (Matheson, Bruce & Beauchamp 1978, p. 265).

Even the most carefully conducted research runs the risk of being discounted if the reporting is sloppy and incomplete. Careful research merits equally careful writing. Both research and writing should be held to the same high standards.

# 7. REFERENCES

Beaman, A. L. (1991). An empirical comparison of meta-analytic and traditional reviews. *Personality and Social Psychology Bulletin, 17,* 252–257.

Becker, B. J. (1990). Coaching for the Scholastic Aptitude Test: Further synthesis and appraisal. *Review of Educational Research, 60,* 373–417.

Becker, B. J. (1991). The quality and credibility of research reviews: What the editors say. *Personality and Social Psychology Bulletin, 17,* 267–272.

Chalmers, T. C., Levin, H., Sacks, H. S., Reitman, D., Berrier, J., & Nagalingham, R. (1987). Meta-analysis of clinical trials as a scientific discipline. I. Control of bias and comparison with large co-operative trials. *Statistics in Medicine, 6,* 733–744.

Cohn, L. D. (1991). Sex differences in the course of personality development: A meta-analysis. *Psychological Bulletin, 109,* 252–266.

Cooper, H. M. (1982). Scientific guidelines for conducting integrative research reviews. *Review of Educational Research, 52,* 291–302.

Cox, D. R. (1958). *Planning of experiments.* New York: Wiley.

Eisenberg, N. (1991). Meta-analytic contributions to the literature on prosocial behavior. *Personality and Social Psychology Bulletin, 17,* 273.

Gelber, R. D., & Goldhirsch, A. (1987). Interpretation of results from subset analyses within overviews of randomized clinical trials. *Statistics in Medicine, 6,* 371–378.

Giaconia, R. M., & Hedges, L. V. (1982). Identifying features of effective open education. *Review of Educational Research, 52,* 579–602.

Glass, G. V. (1984). *The effectiveness of four educational interventions* (IFG Project Paper No. 84-A19). Palo Alto, CA: Stanford University, Institute for Research on Educational Finance and Governance.

Goldstein, P., Berrier, J., Rosen, S., Sacks, H. S., & Chalmers, T. C. (1989). A meta-analysis of randomized control trials of progestational agents in pregnancy. *British Journal of Obstetrics and Gynecology, 96,* 265–274.

Halvorsen, K. T. *Renal, auditory, and vestibular toxicity in aminoglycoside use.* Unpublished manuscript.

Hedges, L. V., & Olkin, I. (1985). *Statistical methods for meta-analysis.* Orlando, FL: Academic Press.

Horowitz, R. A. (1979). Psychological effects of the "open classroom." *Review of Educational Research, 49,* 71–86.

Jackson, G. B. (1980). Methods for integrative reviews. *Review of Educational Research, 50,* 438–460.

Johnson, B. T., & Eagly, A. H. (1989). Effects of involvement on persuasion: A meta-analysis. *Psychological Bulletin, 106,* 290–314.

L'Abbe, K. A., Detsky, A., & O'Rourke, K. (1987). Meta-analysis in clinical research. *Annals of Internal Medicine, 107,* 224–233.

Laird, N. M., & Mosteller, F. (1990). Some statistical methods for combining experimental results. *International Journal of Technology Assessment in Health Care, 6,* 5–30.

Levin, H. M., Glass, G. V., & Meister, G. R. (1987). Cost-effectiveness of computer-assisted instruction. *Evaluation Review, 11,* 50–72.

Lytton, H., & Romney, D. M. (1991). Parents' differential socialization of boys and girls: A meta-analysis. *Psychological Bulletin, 109,* 267–290.

Maccoby, E. E., & Jacklin, C. N. (1974). *The psychology of sex differences.* Stanford, CA: Stanford University Press.

Matheson, D., Bruce, R., & Beauchamp, K. (1978). *Experimental psychology* (3rd ed.). New York: Holt, Rinehart & Winston.

Sacks, H. S., Berrier, J., Reitman, D., Ancona-Berk, V. A., & Chalmers, T. C. (1987). Meta-analyses of randomized controlled trials. *New England Journal of Medicine, 316,* 450–455.

Wood, W., Wong, F. Y., & Chachere, J. G. (1991). Effects of media violence on viewers' aggression in unconstrained social interaction. *Psychological Bulletin, 109,* 371–383.

Cooper, H. and Hedges, L. V. (Eds.) 1994. *The Handbook of Research Synthesis*. New York: Russell Sage Foundation

# 28

# THE VISUAL PRESENTATION AND INTERPRETATION OF META-ANALYSES

**RICHARD J. LIGHT**
*Harvard University*

**JUDITH D. SINGER**
*Harvard University*

**JOHN B. WILLETT**
*Harvard University*

CONTENTS

## 1. INTRODUCTION

A large proportion of meta-analyses in education and the social sciences, including many that we consider excellent, pose a surprising challenge. The reader must struggle to figure out exactly what the researchers found!

How are the results of meta-analyses currently presented? Typically, and especially in the social sciences and education, readers are offered two types of summary table. The first table gives a lengthy list of the actual studies that were included in the meta-analysis, together with their date of publication, sample size, effect size, and so forth. The second table presents the overall average effect size for the entire meta-analysis. This is often accompanied by an extended breakdown giving the mean effect sizes for important subgroups of studies that were defined by the values of various critical predictors (such as whether the original studies had a randomized or nonrandomized design, or whether the studies were published recently or not so recently). The material in these tables is not necessarily presented in any particular order.

We have found it surprising that after expending great energy carrying out their research syntheses, authors of meta-analyses do not fully capitalize on these efforts. They do not display their results in ways that enhance the clarity of their conclusions. Indeed, when we examine a group of meta-analyses published in the 1990s, we ask: In this innovative age, where are the interesting displays and creative graphics? Where are the pictures and plots? It seems as though meta-analytic findings are still presented using display methods that were popular before the age of computers, graphics, and exploratory data analysis.

It is helpful to readers of meta-analyses for authors to report the individual "data points," each of which is actually the outcome of a single study, in their integrative review; and that reports of research syntheses contain overall effect sizes, along with breakdowns of mean effect size along important and interesting dimensions. But is it necessary, or even advantageous, to publish these summaries as simple lists? What can be done with these lists to communicate more information? Are there more easily comprehensible and attractive ways of displaying collections of effect sizes? How can meta-analyses be reported in ways that emphasize their substantive findings?

In this chapter, we give several concrete suggestions for improving the reporting and interpretation of meta-analytic findings. Our emphasis is to report findings

with clarity and simplicity, and most of our suggestions can be implemented easily. In section 2 we briefly review how displays are currently used in the reporting of meta-analyses. We also illustrate how simple displays can dramatically enhance an author's presentation of findings. Since a critical problem for most meta-analyses is how to summarize all the effect sizes that were computed during the research synthesis, our section 3 focuses on constructive ways to display univariate distributions of effect size. Section 4 offers suggestions for displaying relationships between effect size and study characteristics. Included in this discussion are suggestions about how to use carefully constructed tables to present these relationships. Our theme is that simple techniques, such as ordering, or boldfacing entries in a single table, can be used to communicate critical information. And in a similar spirit, we argue that, by adopting the basic principles of exploratory data analysis, important relationships between effect size and study characteristics can be presented easily and constructively.

Finally, in section 5, we suggest five guidelines for displaying results. Our broad purpose is to provide ways of ensuring that meta-analytic findings are presented accurately and simply in order to help the consumer of a meta-analysis grasp the "big picture" quickly.

## 2. DISPLAYING EFFECT SIZES: SOME EXAMPLES

### 2.1 Current Presentations of Meta-Analytic Findings

As we prepared to write this chapter, we wondered how frequently (and how well) graphics and displays have been used to communicate the findings of recent meta-analyses. So we carried out a small-scale empirical exploration, examining recent books on meta-analysis published by the Russell Sage Foundation and all the issues published between 1985 and 1991 of *Psychological Bulletin*, a journal that publishes meta-analyses in the social sciences and psychology.

Our examination revealed a great paucity of graphic displays in published meta-analyses. While these examples are somewhat limited in their detail and coverage, our own experience suggests that the conclusions about the scarcity of good displays reflect the reporting of meta-analyses generally in the 1980s and early 1990s. For instance, in 1990, the Russell Sage Foundation published a discussion of six different meta-analyses on the effects of desegregation on the school achievement of African-American students (Wachter & Straf 1990). Each of them had integrated a large set of empirical studies (and yet they came to different conclusions). The conclusions are described clearly in the text, but in neither the original meta-analyses nor the discussions are graphs or displays used to summarize them. These were critical research syntheses whose impact on public policy could have been enhanced by a few well-chosen graphics designed to appeal to the school superintendent and to the state and federal policymaker.

In 1992, the Russell Sage Foundation published a casebook called *Meta-Analysis for Explanation* (Cook et al. 1992). In this volume, meta-analyses by Becker, Devine, Lipsey, and Shadish were presented as exemplary research syntheses. And, indeed, their analytic work is exemplary. However, none of these authors chose to use tabular displays to communicate their findings, and none used any sort of graphic to supplement or aid their presentation. All explained their findings with textual discussion alone.

To assess more broadly how the results of meta-analyses are reported, we examined all issues in the 13 most recent volumes of *Psychological Bulletin*. Our examination was most instructive. Of course, we cannot assert that what we found generalizes exactly to other journals or domains of research, but we believe that our main conclusions are broadly applicable. In Table 28.1, we summarize what we saw: column 1 contains the volume number of the journal, column 2 displays the number of meta-analyses that were published in each volume, and columns 3–8 record the frequency with which a variety of tabular and graphic displays were used in the meta-analyses.

First, notice that meta-analyses play a large role in the journal. Several meta-analyses were published in every volume—from a minimum of 2 in Volume 99 to a maximum of 10 in Volume 101. In fact, a total of 74 meta-analyses were published in *Psychological Bulletin* between 1985 and 1991. Among these meta-analyses, the most common format for presenting the findings of the research synthesis is a simple summary table of mean effect size, broken down by critical characteristics of the studies (column 4): 57 meta-analyses, or 80 percent, present such a summary table. In addition, more than half of the meta-analyses (41 of the 74, or 58 percent) present summary tables of raw data—a listing of the studies included in the synthesis along with a brief description of each study, their sample size and effect sizes. These lists are usually ordered alphabeti-

cally by author name. The raw data lists are similar to the three small sets of studies that have been used as examples throughout this book—the collections of studies of gender differences, studies of teacher expectancy, and studies of student ratings of instructors.

Only 19 percent of the meta-analyses (14 out of 74) contain at least one graph (column 8). Just 11 percent (8 out of 74) make use of a simple histogram or stem-and-leaf display to show the distribution of the effect sizes across studies (column 5). Only 11 percent (8 out of 74) use some other type of graphic display, such as a bivariate plot of the relationship between effect size and an important study characteristic (column 7), although these tend to be the same meta-analyses that have already displayed the effect size distributions (compare columns 5 and 7). Only one of the 74 meta-analyses uses a funnel plot to relate effect size to sample size (column 6).

From Table 28.1 we conclude that graphic displays are not yet a routine part of the presentation of meta-analyses, especially in education and the social sciences. Yet it is clear from the several reports that do use graphics how such a presentation can be extraordinarily helpful. We will try to make this point clearer by examining displays from two meta-analyses that use graphics.

## 2.2 Two Examples of the Strength of Well-Designed Displays

Light and Pillemer (1984) suggest a simple graphic for examining pictorially whether a set of effect sizes from a large group of studies is "well behaved." The idea is to plot each study's effect size, whether it is a standardized mean difference, a correlation coefficient, or some other measure, against its sample size. If the sample of studies is well behaved (i.e., if all studies are estimating a single underlying population effect size parameter), then the plot should look roughly like a funnel because studies with smaller samples sizes will display more variability in effect size than the investigations with larger sample sizes.

As an example, in a synthesis of studies exploring the psychological factors underlying heart disease, Booth-Kewley and Friedman (1987) make good use of this funnel idea to plot effect size (in this case, correlation coefficients) against sample size for 83 studies reported between 1945 and 1984. An important motivation for this plot is their concern that aggregating studies over

**Table 28.1 Types of Graphic and Tabular Summaries Used in All Meta-Analyses Published in *Psychological Bulletin* Between 1985 and 1991**

| Volume | Meta-Analyses (n) | Type of Display (n) | | | | | |
|---|---|---|---|---|---|---|---|
| | | Raw Data | Summary Effect Size | Stem-and-Leaf | Funnel Plot | Other Graphs | Any Graphs |
| 97 | 7 | 4 | 7 | | | | |
| 98 | 4 | | 4 | | | 1 | 1 |
| 99 | 2 | | 2 | | | | |
| 100 | 9 | 5 | 9 | 1 | | | 1 |
| 101 | 10 | 9 | 4 | 2 | 1 | 1 | 2 |
| 102 | 6 | 3 | 5 | | | 1 | 1 |
| 103 | 3 | 1 | 2 | | | | |
| 104 | 4 | 3 | 3 | | | | |
| 105 | 5 | 4 | 2 | | | 1 | 1 |
| 106 | 7 | 4 | 5 | 1 | | 1 | 2 |
| 107 | 6 | 3 | 5 | | | 1 | 1 |
| 108 | 5 | 1 | 5 | 2 | | 1 | 2 |
| 109 | 6 | 4 | 4 | 2 | | 1 | 3 |
| **TOTAL** | **74** | **41** | **57** | **8** | **1** | **8** | **14** |

such a long period of time may result in combining "apples and oranges." We reproduce Booth-Kewley and Friedman's plot as Figure 28.1.[1] Notice how easy it is to appreciate the central tendency and spread of the effect sizes in this plot, and imagine how much more difficult it would be to reach the same understanding from text or from a simple list of the effect sizes. The plot looks very much like a horizontal funnel, tending to a single "spout" on the right (at an effect size just slightly greater than zero). Booth-Kewley and Friedman can easily argue from this plot that the effect sizes do appear to be sampled from a population with a single, underlying parameter. Their plot also provides a perspective on the confidence that the reader can attach to the findings of a single study with small sample size.

In a similar vein, meta-analysts can also display their study-by-study effect sizes (the raw data of a meta-analysis) not just as single points, but as confidence intervals. This way, the reader sees the range of uncertainty for each study's effect size, as well as the overall distribution of effect sizes. Medical researchers have paved the way in creating such displays. In a superb discussion of methods for combining results from randomized clinical trials, Demets (1987) reports on an

exemplary meta-analysis by Yusuf et al. (1985). Yusuf and colleagues aggregated 24 investigations of the effects of fibrinolytic treatment on patient mortality. We reproduce their summary display as Figure 28.2, in which the effect sizes (in this case, each reported as an odds ratio) are displayed graphically, each with an attached 95 percent confidence interval.

Notice how much information is succinctly conveyed by Figure 28.2 First, we see that, overall, the 24 studies taken as a group demonstrate a significant reduction in mortality for fibrinolytic treatment because the limits of the 95 percent confidence interval associated with the "overall result" do not include an odds ratio of 1.0 within their borders. Second, examining the outcome of the 24 studies separately, we see that while for 7 studies the odds ratio is greater than 1.0 (indicating an increase in mortality) and for several individual studies the upper bound of the confidence interval exceeds 1.0, not one of these studies has an odds ratio that can be distinguished statistically from 1.0 because, in every case, the individual 95 percent confidence intervals include a value of 1.0 for the odds ratio. Do we believe that fibrinolytic treatment reduces mortality in cases of acute myocardial infarction? Yes, we do. Yusuf and his colleagues have summarized many valuable quantities in a single display, simultaneously giving the reader information about each study in the research synthesis and about the overall integrated finding.

[1]Theoretical and empirical follow-ups to these findings can be found in Friedman (1990, 1991).

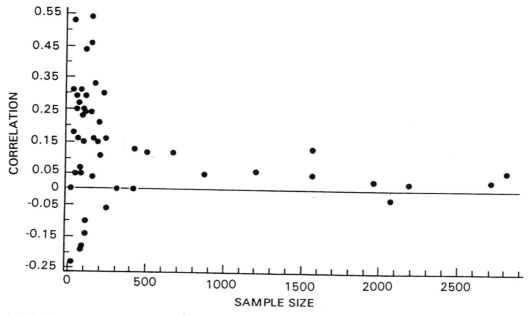

**Figure 28.1** Effect size (estimated bivariate correlation between Type A behavior and all disease outcomes) displayed as a function of sample size ($n = 49$). Adapted from Booth-Kewley and Friedman (1987). Reproduced by permission of the American Psychological Association and Professor Howard S. Friedman.

## 3. SIMPLE METHODS FOR DISPLAYING UNIVARIATE EFFECT SIZES

Along with many other authors and methodologists, we believe that it is important to display the distribution of the effect sizes obtained in a research synthesis. Then readers will be able to assess the shape of the distribution and draw their own conclusions about the overall size and variability of the effects being integrated. Whether a table or a figure is used to contain the display, there are strategies available for enhancing such displays in substantively interesting and methodologically meaningful ways. In this section, we review several ways to achieve this.

To begin, we think that providing readers with the raw data (the study-by-study effect sizes) is a good idea for several reasons: (a) It allows them to verify statements made by the authors of the synthesis; (b) it facilitates the "tacking on" and integration of information from additional studies into the synthesis; (c) it permits the incorporation of these data into a new synthesis without need to recompute (though recomputing is a good reliability check); (d) it permits the reader to cross-check the data with other syntheses; (e) it helps the reader to develop a sense of the variation in effect

size from study to study. Unfortunately, "raw data lists" as currently published in the literature do little to enhance their own value. For instance, entries in these tables are rarely ordered in an informative way. Most of them are simply ordered alphabetically or chronologically, by date of publication, at best. Very few are ordered with the intention of conveying a substantive message. We have some concrete suggestions.

### 3.1 Sorting Raw Data Lists by Effect Sizes

Table 28.2 presents a list of studies sorted by effect size from the meta-analysis of the multisection validity study of students' ratings reported earlier in this book as Data Set III, Appendix A, Column 1 provides a reference to the original study, the column 2 identifies the academic discipline from which the sample of students was drawn, column 3 provides information on the research design (see the following section), and columns 4 and 5 provide the sample size and effect size. In this meta-analysis, the effect sizes are correlations between student ratings of the teacher and student grades.

We have simply resorted the 20 studies in order of decreasing effect size. This strategy emphasizes the extent of the variation in effect size from study to study,

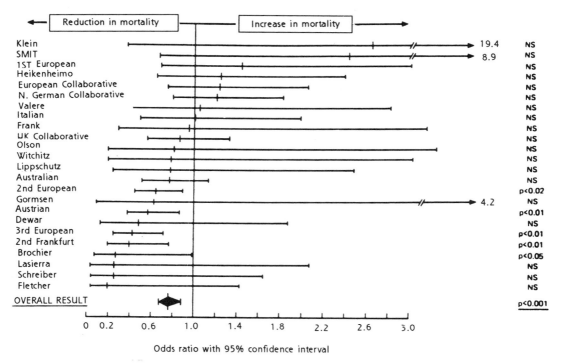

**Figure 28.2** Effect sizes (and 95 percent confidence intervals) illustrating the apparent effects of fibrinolytic treatment on mortality in the randomized trials of intravenous treatment of acute myocardial infarction. Reproduced by permission of *Statistics and Medicine,* the *European Heart Journal,* and Dr. S. Yusuf.

which ranges from +.68 to −.11. Resorting causes atypical studies that demand a careful examination to stand out more. Also notice that there are only two negative entries, that approximately 80 percent of the studies have an effect size greater than .2, and that more than half of the studies have an effect size greater than .4. Just by examining this ordered table instead of the original, unordered table, we can easily appreciate the approximate magnitude of the effect being integrated. We quickly discover that there is a positive relationship between students' ratings and student achievement. This "eyeball" conclusion is less easily retrieved from the original table.

Eagly and Crowley (1986) use a sorting strategy effectively in their display of effect sizes from 99 studies relating gender and helping behavior. They sorted by the magnitude of the effect sizes, which were standardized mean differences, ranging from −1.48 to +.71. Positive effect sizes indicated differences in helping behavior favoring males; negative effect sizes indicated differences favoring females. To ensure that the reader

could link specific effect sizes to the original study citations in the bibliography, the authors used citation codes in their display.

## 3.2 Converting Raw Data Lists into Graphic Displays

Instead of simply listing the effect sizes in a table, a meta-analyst can easily plot them on the number line, study by study. When confidence intervals for effect sizes are available, they can be included, too. We have already used the "confidence interval" display by Yusuf and his colleagues (1985) to illustrate the effectiveness of this strategy in Figure 28.2.

## 3.3 Graphic Summaries of Effect Size Distributions

Examining graphic displays of the distribution of all the effect sizes helps readers appreciate where the distribution is *centered* and how far it *spreads*. They can also

**Table 28.2 List of Effect Sizes in 20 Multisection Validity Studies, in Order of Decreasing Magnitude**

| Study | Sample | Ability Control | $n$ | $r$ |
|---|---|---|---|---|
| Bolton et al. 1979 | General psychology | Random assignment | 10 | .68 |
| Centra 1977 [2] | General psychology | Prior final exam | 22 | .64 |
| Ellis & Richard 1977 | General psychology | Random assignment | 19 | .58 |
| Bryson 1974 | College algebra | CIAT pretest | 20 | .56 |
| Sullivan & Skanes 1974 [1] | First-year science | Random assignment | 14 | .51 |
| Remmer et al. 1949 | General chemistry | Orientation test | 37 | .49 |
| Crooks & Smock 1974 | General physics | Math pretest | 28 | .49 |
| Doyle & Whitely 1974 | Beginning French | Minnesota SAT | 12 | .49 |
| Sullivan & Skanes 1974 [4] | First-year biology | Random assignment | 14 | .42 |
| Marsh et al. 1956 | Aircraft mechanics | Hydraulics pretest | 121 | .40 |
| Sullivan & Skanes 1974 [2] | Introductory psychology | Random assignment | 40 | .40 |
| Sullivan & Skanes 1974 [3] | First-year math | Random assignment | 16 | .34 |
| Elliot 1950 | General chemistry | College entrance exam | 36 | .33 |
| Hoffman 1978 | Introductory math | SAT math | 75 | .27 |
| McKeachie et al. 1971 | General psychology | Intelligence test | 33 | .26 |
| Centra 1977 [1] | General biology | Prior final exam | 13 | .23 |
| Frey, Leonard & Beatty 1975 | Introductory calculus | SAT math | 12 | .18 |
| Wherry 1952 | Introductory psychology | Ability test | 20 | .16 |
| Doyle & Crichton 1978 | Introductory communications | PSAT verbal | 12 | −.04 |
| Greenwood et al. 1976 | Analytic geometry and calculus | Achievement pretest | 36 | −.11 |

ascertain the *shape* of the distribution: Is it skewed? Is it bimodal? Are there outliers, or any especially popular or unpopular values? The answers to all of these questions can be very informative in terms of the overall research integration.

Two simple displays that summarize all these attributes of a distribution in a single picture are the *stem-and-leaf display* and the *schematic plot*. These graphics can be easily constructed by hand, and we have found them useful in summarizing lists of effect sizes. Figures 28.3 and 28.4 present a stem-and-leaf plot and a schematic plot, respectively, for the students' rating validity meta-analysis.

The stem-and-leaf plot is created by typing out the effect sizes for each study with, in this case, (a) the first decimal place in each effect size appearing in the "stem" to the left of the vertical line and (b) the second decimal place appearing as a "leaf" to the right. Thus, the top line of the stem-and-leaf plot records two effect sizes, .64 and .68, corresponding to the studies by Bolton et al. (1979) and Centra (1977) in the top two rows of Table 28.2. The schematic plot records (a) the maximum and minimum effect sizes (at the extreme ends of the

```
.6  | 48
.5  | 168
.4  | 002999
.3  | 34
.2  | 367
.1  | 68
.0  |
-.0 | 4        Doyle & Crichton 1978
-.1 | 1        Greenwood et al. 1976
```

**Figure 28.3** Stem-and-leaf plot displaying the sample distribution of effect size in 20 multisection validity studies

vertical "whiskers"), (b) the upper and lower quartile values of effect size (the narrow ends of the central "box"), and (c) the median effect size (the central horizontal line). See Tukey (1977) for more details of these two summary plots.

From both of the displays, we learn that the sample distribution of effect sizes is centered at approximately .4 and that most of the effect sizes fall between +.2 and +.6. Two modest outliers are low, negative values

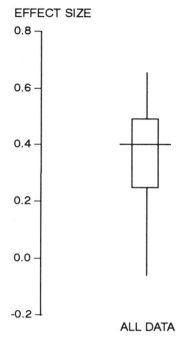

EFFECT SIZE

**Figure 28.4** Schematic plot displaying the sample distribution of effect size in 20 multisection validity studies.

from the studies by Doyle and Crichton (1978) and Greenwood et al. (1976). With only 20 studies, it is difficult to make concrete claims about the shape of their distribution.[2] But from the schematic plot, we see that they are unimodal and approximately symmetrical, suggesting that they have been sampled from a homogeneous population. Particularly ingenious authors might design ways to integrate both tables and plots into the same graphic; for instance, it would be possible to create an ordered list of effect sizes (such as Table 28.2) and then attach the schematic plot of Figure 28.4, suitably scaled, in the right or left margin. Other ideas will no doubt suggest themselves to the reader.

Stem-and-leaf displays are the most popular graphic tool used currently by meta-analysts. But their popularity is modest: Only 7 of the 74 meta-analyses we

[2]An anonymous reviewer suggested caution in interpreting the observed variability displayed in the plots of Figure 28.3, and in subsequent figures, stating that "much of this variability may be a result of sampling error. Because sampling-error variance is determined by sample size, comparisons of groups of studies may reveal only differences in sample size from study to study (see Chapter 18)."

examined in the 13 volumes of *Psychological Bulletin* included even this most basic display. Schematic plots are even rarer.

Yet when these displays are used, meta-analysts have found them to be an effective way to convey results. Rubonis and Bickman (1991), in their meta-analysis of psychological impairment in the wake of disaster, present a stem-and-leaf display of 31 effect sizes (their Figure 1, p. 391), with each effect size describing the bivariate correlation between exposure to a disaster and psychopathology. The authors use their display in two ways. First, they note that there are very few negative effect sizes, whereas there are many small nonsignificant positive effect sizes, causing the authors to explore the possibility that their data are an example of Rosenthal's "file drawer" dilemma (1979, 1984). Second, they identify several studies with unusually high or low effect sizes and explicitly explore the design details of these studies. For the largest outlying effect size (on the upside), they write:

> Part of the reason for such a high estimate may be that the data are representative of only the hardest hit village in Sri Lanka (Paddirupu), where a reported 77% of the disaster sample manifested psychological impairment; only 4% of the control sample experienced any evident dysfunction. In this case, the severity of destruction in this one village may be taking an unusually high toll on the mental health of victims. (p. 391)

Turning to the other end of the distribution, the authors comment on how the one large, negative effect size, arising from a study of the Beverly Hills Sizzler Club fire, in which the control subjects were more impaired than the victims, has a simple explanation. They write:

> This study used a control group comprised of rescue workers and a victim's family member who did not experience the disaster. With such a control population, it is not unusual to expect equally high or higher pathology estimates when compared with the victim group. (p. 392)

The key idea is that by using graphic techniques to examine the sample distribution of effect size across studies, and by seeing where the distribution is centered and noting extreme values, meta-analysts can learn much about the variation in their data. Indeed, when these displays are used in conjunction with the more formal tests of homogeneity that are described elsewhere in this

**Table 28.3 List of Effect Sizes in 20 Multisection Validity Studies, by Type of Ability Control and in Order of Decreasing Magnitude**

| Study | Sample | Ability Control | $n$ | $r$ |
|---|---|---|---|---|
| **Random Assignment** | | | | |
| Bolton et al. 1979 | General psychology | Random assignment | 10 | .68 |
| Ellis & Richard 1977 | General psychology | Random assignment | 19 | .58 |
| Sullivan & Skanes 1974 [1] | First-year science | Random assignment | 14 | .51 |
| Sullivan & Skanes 1974 [4] | First-year biology | Random assignment | 14 | .42 |
| Sullivan & Skanes 1974 [2] | Introductory psychology | Random assignment | 40 | .40 |
| Sullivan & Skanes 1974 [3] | First-year math | Random assignment | 16 | .34 |
| **Covariate Adjustment** | | | | |
| Centra 1977 [2] | General psychology | Prior final exam | 22 | .64 |
| Bryson 1974 | College algebra | CIAT pretest | 20 | .56 |
| Remmer et al. 1949 | General chemistry | Orientation test | 37 | .49 |
| Crooks & Smock 1974 | General physics | Math pretest | 28 | .49 |
| Doyle & Whitely 1974 | Beginning French | Minnesota SAT | 12 | .49 |
| Marsh et al. 1956 | Aircraft mechanics | Hydraulics pretest | 121 | .40 |
| Elliot 1950 | General chemistry | College entrance exam | 36 | .33 |
| Hoffman 1978 | Introductory math | SAT math | 75 | .27 |
| McKeachie et al. 1971 | General psychology | Intelligence test | 33 | .26 |
| Centra 1977 [1] | General biology | Prior final exam | 13 | .23 |
| Frey, Leonard & Beatty 1975 | Introductory calculus | SAT math | 12 | .18 |
| Wherry 1952 | Introductory psychology | Ability test | 20 | .16 |
| Doyle & Crichton 1978 | Introductory commu-nications | PSAT verbal | 12 | −.04 |
| Greenwood et al. 1976 | Analytic geometry and calculus | Achievement pretest | 36 | −.11 |

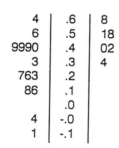

```
      4 | .6 | 8
      6 | .5 | 18
   9990 | .4 | 02
      3 | .3 | 4
    763 | .2 |
     86 | .1 |
        | .0 |
      4 | -.0 |
      1 | -.1 |
```

Covariate          Random
Adjustment         Assignment

**Figure 28.5** Back-to-back stem-and-leaf plots displaying the sample distribution of effect size, by type of ability control.

book, they can help meta-analysts decide whether a single, average effect size is an effective summary of the data or whether they need to go further and explore variation in effect size as a function of study characteristics. We turn now to several graphic strategies for examining such relationships.

## 4. DISPLAYING SOURCES OF VARIATION IN EFFECT SIZE

Often there is *systematic* variation in effect size from study to study: In other words, across studies, effect size is related to critical design features of the original studies. Meta-analysts' favorite way of displaying this systematic variation in effect size is to present summary tables giving mean effect sizes estimated for different subgroups of studies. To be effective, the subgroups in these displays must be defined by interesting values of

EFFECT SIZE

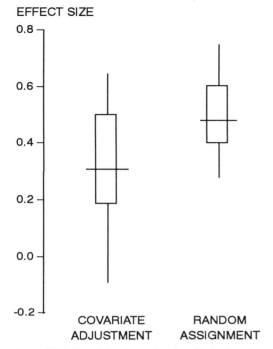

**Figure 28.6** Parallel schematic plots displaying the sample distribution of effect size, by type of ability control.

those study characteristics that have been shown to be systematically related to effect size. A raw data list can be improved dramatically by resorting along substantively important dimensions. Research synthesists must identify their central message and then devise a way of reordering the table to facilitate the communication of this message.

Rubonis and Bickman (1991), for example, followed up their single stem-and-leaf display of 31 effect sizes by testing for the homogeneity of effect size in their sample. They concluded that their 31 effect sizes were statistically heterogeneous, and they therefore broke them down by the type of psychopathological impairment measured in the original study. They discovered that effect sizes were largest in those studies in which anxiety, alcohol addiction, or nontraditional outcomes were the measures of psychopathology used. About four fifths of the meta-analyses summarized in Table 28.1 used this type of approach.

We are convinced that such "breakdowns" are a valuable component of any meta-analysis. We also believe that these displays and the information they com-

municate can be enhanced. This is easily done by extending the exploratory data-analytic strategies introduced in the previous section. The goal is to restructure the effect size displays, such as that presented in Figure 28.3, to communicate more clearly any relationship between effect size and critical study characteristics. In this spirit, we offer three concrete suggestions.

### 4.1 Sorting Raw Data Lists by Important Study Characteristics

Let us return to the multisection validity data presented in Table 28.3. Column 3 of Table 28.2 indicates whether students in the original studies were randomized into teaching sections ("random assignment") or, if they were not, identifies the covariate that was used to control for student ability when effect sizes were computed. A central question in the original meta-analysis was whether effect size varied by the design of a study. Specifically, we can ask whether effect sizes are generally larger or smaller when a randomized study was carried out—this is about the relationship between effect size and a categorical predictor describing study design. To answer our question, we sorted the studies by design characteristic ("random assignment" or "covariate adjustment") and by the magnitude of effect size (see Table 28.3).

Table 28.3 shows that only 6 of the 31 effect sizes come from studies that used random assignment, with 4 being derived from a single study by Sullivan and Skanes (1974). Yet inspection of the double-sorted raw data shows that effect sizes from the randomized studies are uniformly high and homogeneous, varying within a fairly narrow range (.34 to .68). The effect sizes from studies using covariate adjustment, on the other hand, are smaller in magnitude and far more heterogeneous.

Although this double-sorting format is rarely found in the literature, it has been used occasionally in at least a partial way. For example, Lytton and Romney (1991), in a meta-analysis of parents' differential socialization of boys and girls, sorted effect sizes from 172 studies by the 17 areas of socialization they investigated (such as warmth, discipline, and achievement). Their display could be enhanced even further, of course, if the collection of studies were also sorted by effect size. The double-sorting strategy can easily be extended to triple and quadruple sorting to create "subgroups within subgroups." Unfortunately, this strategy rapidly becomes unwieldy, but can be applied as long as there are sufficient effect sizes in the meta-analysis to cover all

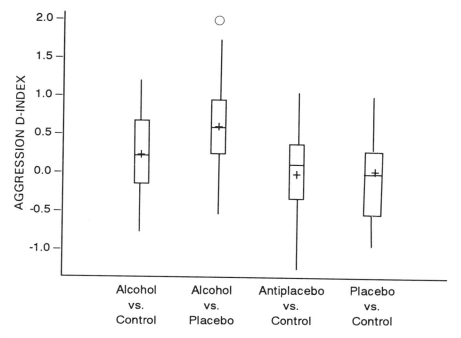

**Figure 28.7** Side-by-side schematic plots of effect sizes describing aggression resulting from alcohol consumption, displayed by the type of comparison used in the original studies. Reproduced by permission of the American Psychological Association and Dr. Brad J. Bushman.

possible permutations of the study characteristics that have been selected.

## 4.2 Converting Double-Sorted Lists into Graphic Displays

We can easily extend the ideas of exploratory data analysis introduced in the previous section to produce simple yet powerful graphic displays of the relationships between effect size and study characteristics. In Figures 28.5 and 28.6 we use the multisection student validity data to illustrate the utility of double-sorted graphics. These panels illustrate the effectiveness of back-to-back stem-and-leaf displays and side-by-side schematic plots in displaying the relationship between effect size and study design.

Figures 28.5 and 28.6 clarify further the patterns that first appeared in the ordered listing of Table 28.3. The difference between findings from randomized versus nonrandomized studies becomes especially sharpened. The back-to-back stem-and-leaf plots clearly illustrates

how effect sizes from randomly assigned studies are clustered tightly and generally have high values. In contrast, nonrandomized studies contribute effect sizes that are far more widely dispersed, including two potential negative outliers. Similar conclusions emerge from comparing the parallel schematic plots in Figure 28.6. These graphics lead us to the conclusion that the correlation between students' ratings of teachers and student grades are generally higher in randomized studies.

How common are side-by-side displays like these? Our review of the 74 *Psychological Bulletin* meta-analyses turned up only one review that presented a back-to-back stem-and-leaf display (Okun, Olding & Cohn 1990). In a meta-analysis of interventions designed to enhance the subjective well-being of elderly people, these authors used such a graphic. Their figure demonstrated convincingly that effect sizes from studies in which well-being is measured immediately after treatment are larger than effect sizes from studies in which measurement is delayed. The advantage of using the side-by-side stem-and-leaf displays is that in an "eye-

**Table 28.4  List of Effect Sizes in 19 Studies of the Effect of Teacher Expectancy on Pupil IQ, in Order of Weeks of Teacher-Student Contact Prior to Expectancy Induction**

| Study | Estimated Weeks of Teacher-Student Contact Prior to Expectancy Induction | $d$ |
| --- | --- | --- |
| Pelligrini & Hicks 1972 [1] | 0 | 1.18 |
| Carter 1970 | 0 | .54 |
| Pelligrini & Hicks 1972 [2] | 0 | .26 |
| Kester 1969 | 0 | .27 |
| Flowers 1966 | 0 | .18 |
| Maxwell 1970 | 1 | .80 |
| Rosenthal & Jacobsen 1968 | 1 | .30 |
| Keshock 1970 | 1 | −.02 |
| Henrikson 1970 | 2 | .23 |
| Fleming & Anttonen 1971 | 2 | .07 |
| Rosenthal et al. 1974 | 2 | .03 |
| Evans & Rosenthal 1968 | 3 | −.06 |
| Greiger 1970 | 5 | −.06 |
| Ginsburg 1970 | 7 | −.07 |
| Fielder et al. 1971 | 17 | −.02 |
| Fine 1972 | 17 | −.18 |
| Jose & Cody 1971 | 19 | −.14 |
| Conn et al. 1971 | 21 | .12 |
| Claiborn 1969 | 24 | −.32 |

ball'' analysis the reader can easily discount the potential influence of several outlying effect sizes.

Parallel schematic plots are also helpful, yet underutilized. Our review of the 74 meta-analyses turned up only two examples of this type of plot. One particularly good example appears in a review of the effects of alcohol on human aggression by Bushman and Cooper (1990). We reproduce their results as Figure 28.7. It displays standardized mean differences in aggression as a function of the different groups being compared in the original studies.

Figure 28.7 reveals the influence of research design among a group of studies on aggressiveness resulting from alcohol consumption. Some studies compare men who consume alcohol with men who consume a placebo; other studies compare drinkers with a control group. The authors viewed the set of parallel schematic plots as more informative than simply offering the reader an average effect size in each subgroup of studies ''because extreme, unrepresentative values can seriously distort tests on estimates of parameters'' (p. 344). Such an

unusual value is immediately identified in the second schematic plot from the left in Figure 28.7 and is represented by a circle. Figure 28.7 shows clearly that, in general, drinkers appear more aggressive compared with men who consume a placebo than compared with simply a control group.

### 4.3 The Power of Graphs

While inferential techniques for exploring relationships are covered elsewhere in this volume, we believe that the *results* of those procedures are communicated particularly well through the use of sorted tables and well-plotted graphs. Table 28.4 and Figure 28.8 illustrates some possibilities.

In Table 28.4, we present the set of effect sizes from the teacher-expectancy meta-analysis used in this volume as an example. Notice that in this list the effect sizes are sorted not in order of their magnitude, but rather by the value of a critical ''question'' variable: the estimated number of weeks of teacher-student contact prior to expectancy induction. When several studies have identical values on this predictor, effect sizes have been ordered by magnitude within that predictor value.

Just by examining this ordered table of raw effect sizes, one can detect an interesting trend. Effect sizes are larger in studies in which there was little teacher-student contact prior to expectancy induction and smaller in those in which there was more teacher-student contact. This relationship is clarified further by the graph in Figure 28.8. Here we plot effect size against the number of weeks of prior teacher-student contact. Where multiple effect sizes are available at a given value of the predictor (e.g., at 0, 1, and 2 weeks), we display the median effect size as a horizontal line. In addition, we indicate the variation among effect sizes by providing short horizontal bars denoting the range of values at each value of the predictor. (Consequently, where there is only a single effect size at a given value of the predictor—such as at 3, 5, and 7 weeks—this single effect size is represented by a horizontal line.) Finally, the dashed line superimposed on the plot presents running medians of length 3 (Tukey 1977; Velleman & Hoaglin 1981). It is this latter ''smooth'' that summarizes the ''big picture,'' capturing the declining relationship between effect size and prior weeks of contact.

Several authors have used this type of approach effectively (Cohn 1991; Glass & Smith 1979; Raz & Raz 1990). A particularly good example is provided by Thomas and French 1985 in their meta-analysis of 64

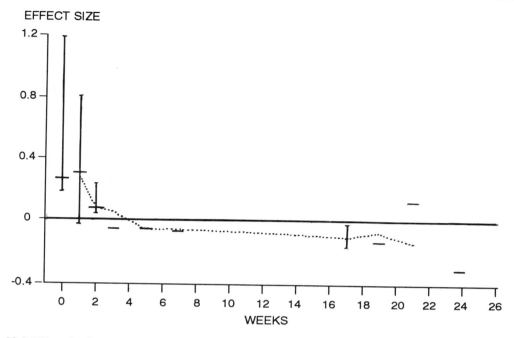

**Figure 28.8** Effect size in 19 studies of the effect of teacher expectancy on pupil IQ, plotted against the number of weeks of teacher-student contact prior to expectancy induction.

studies of gender differences in motor performance for children between ages 3 and 19. They present a sequence of plots depicting the standardized mean differences between boys and girls on several measures of motor performance. Their plots not only illustrate how the gender differential consistently favors boys (the effect size being positive when boys outperform girls), but how the difference becomes larger among children who are older. Figure 28.9 reproduces their graphs for the outcomes ''long jump,'' ''shuttle run,'' and ''grip strength.'' We especially admire their use of 95 percent confidence intervals to bracket average effect size at each age.

## 5. CONCLUSION

Our main point is that *simple graphic displays of effect sizes in a meta-analysis can impose order onto what at first may seem like a morass of data.* Especially when the meta-analyst faces hundreds of effect sizes from a large sample of studies, a tabular list of effect sizes will sometimes not reveal the pattern that becomes clear in

a simple, descriptive graph. For those who want to follow our advice, we offer the following:

1. *The spirit of good graphics can even be captured in a table of raw effect sizes, providing they are presented in a purposeful way.* Many meta-analyses provide a table of the original studies and their effect sizes. While we believe that graphic summaries are especially helpful for interpreting collections of raw data, a solid second choice is to present a table, a list, organized in a purposeful way to help readers grasp important trends in the data. However, to achieve this, tables of effect sizes must be ordered meaningfully—perhaps by the magnitude of the constituent effect sizes, perhaps by the values of an important study characteristic, or perhaps by both. Such a reordering can convey much useful information.

2. *Graphic displays should be used to emphasize the big picture.* Readers come to a report of meta-analytic findings with many questions in mind. Graphics can help to answer them. But the first order of business is to make the main point clear.

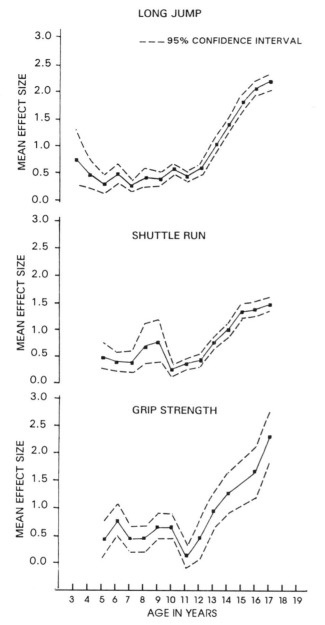

With this framework established, the reader can move ahead to answer some of the more detailed and more precise questions.

3. *Graphics are especially valuable for communicating findings from a meta-analysis when each individual study outcome is accompanied by a confidence interval.* It is not routine for each effect size in a meta-analysis to be surrounded by a confidence interval. But where such limits are available, incorporating them into a visual display is often worth many pages of verbal description. It then becomes possible, in a single picture, to summarize not only the effect of each study, but also whether that effect size is statistically distinguishable from its null value.

4. *Graphic displays should encourage the eye to compare different pieces of information.* An emphasis on comparison is especially appropriate in meta-analysis. A criticism that meta-analysts face, more than occasionally, is that results of their "objective" integration depend heavily on which studies were sampled in the review or which statistical method was used to carry out the meta-analysis. The side-by-side presentation of the meta-analytic findings from several different samples of studies, or from several analyses of the same sample of studies, quickly clarifies the impact of different analytic plans.

5. *Stem-and-leaf plots and schematic plots are especially efficient for presenting the big picture that emerges in a research synthesis.* These two graphic displays are easy to interpret and offer two strong pluses for meta-analysis. They display simple and straightforwardly the distribution of a large group of study outcomes, and they facilitate the immediate identification of strange or atypical effect sizes. They are particularly valuable for comparing the distributions of effect size in subgroups of studies.

Finally, we advise anyone planning to use graphics and displays for interpreting and communicating their meta-analytic findings to pay heed to the excellent advice that can be found in the works of Tufte (1983), Wainer (1981, 1984), Cleveland (1985), and Ehrenberg (1977).

**Figure 28.9** Average standardized gender differential in long jump, shuttle run, and grip strength, plotted against the age of the children. Reproduced by permission of the American Psychological Association and Professor Jerry J. Thomas.

**Authors' Note**

The three authors contributed equally to this chapter. Their names are listed alphabetically.

# 6. REFERENCES

Booth-Kewley, S., & Friedman, H. S. (1987). Psychological predictors of heart disease: A quantitative review. *Psychological Bulletin, 101,* 343–362.

Bushman, B. J., & Cooper, H. M. (1990). Effects of alcohol on human aggression: An integrative research review. *Psychological Bulletin, 107,* 341–354.

Cleveland, W. S. (1985). *The elements of graphing data.* Monterey, CA: Wadsworth.

Cohn, L. D. (1991). Sex differences in the course of personality development: A meta-analysis. *Psychological Bulletin, 104,* 252–266.

Cook, T. D., Cooper, H., Cordray, D. S., Hartmann, H., Hedges, L. V., Light, R. J., Louis, T. A., & Mosteller, F. (1992). *Meta-analysis for explanation: A casebook.* New York: Russell Sage Foundation.

Demets, A. L. (1987). Methods for combining randomized clinical trials: Strengths and limitations. *Statistics and Medicine, 6,* 341–348.

Eagly, A. H., & Crowley, M. (1986). Gender and helping behavior: A meta-analytic review of the social psychological literature. *Psychological Bulletin, 100,* 283–308.

Ehrenberg, A. S. C. (1977). Rudiments of numeracy. Journal of the Royal Statistical Society, Series A, 140, 277–297.

Friedman, H. S. (Ed.). (1990). *Personality and disease.* New York: Wiley.

Friedman, H. S. (1991). *The self-healing personality.* New York: Holt.

Glass, G. V., & Smith, M. L. (1979). Meta-analysis of the relationship between class size and achievements. *Educational Evaluation and Policy Analysis, 1,* 2–16.

Light, R. J., & Pillemer, D. B. (1984). *Summing up: The science of reviewing research.* Cambridge, MA: Harvard University Press.

Lytton, H., & Romney, D. M. (1991). Parents' differential socialization of boys and girls: A meta-analysis. *Psychological Bulletin, 104,* 267–290.

Okun, M. A., Olding, R. W., & Cohn, C. M. G. (1990). A meta-analysis of subjective well-being interventions among elders. *Psychological Bulletin, 103,* 257–265.

Raz, S., & Raz, N. (1990). Structural brain abnormalities in the major psychoses: A quantitative review of the evidence from computerized imaging. *Psychological Bulletin, 103,* 93–108.

Rosenthal, R. (1979). The file-drawer problem and tolerance for null results. *Psychological Bulletin, 86,* 638–641.

Rosenthal, R. (1984). *Meta-analytic procedures for social research.* Beverly Hills, CA: Sage.

Rubonis, A. V., & Bickman, L. (1991). Psychological impairments in the wake of disaster: The disaster-psychopathology relationship. *Psychological Bulletin, 109,* 384–399.

Thomas, J. R., & French, K. E. (1985). Gender differences across age in motor performance: A meta-analysis. *Psychological Bulletin, 98,* 260–282.

Tufte, E. R. (1983). *The visual display of quantitative information.* Cheshire, CT: Graphics Press.

Tukey, J. W. (1977). *Exploratory data analysis.* Reading, MA: Addison-Wesley.

Velleman, P. F., & Hoaglin, D. C. (1981). *Applications, basics, and computing of exploratory data analysis.* Boston: Duxbury Press.

Wachter, K. W., & Straf, M. L. (Eds.). (1990). *The future of meta-analysis.* New York: Russell Sage Foundation.

Wainer, H. (1981). Graphical data analysis. *Annual Review of Psychology, 32,* 191–241.

Wainer, H. (1984). How to display data badly. *American Statistician, 38,* 137–147.

Yusuf, S., Peto, R., Lewis, J., Collins, R., & Sleight, P. (1985). Beta blockage during and after myocardial infarction: An overview of the randomized trials. *Progress in Cardiovascular Diseases, 27,* 335–371.

# PART
# IX

## TYING RESEARCH SYNTHESIS
## TO SUBSTANTIVE ISSUES

Cooper, H., and Hedges, L. V. (Eds.) 1994. *The Handbook of Research Synthesis.* New York: Russell Sage Foundation

# 29

# META-ANALYTIC SYNTHESIS FOR THEORY DEVELOPMENT

**NORMAN MILLER**
*University of Southern California*

**VICKI E. POLLOCK**
*University of Southern California*

CONTENTS

**457**

## 1. INTRODUCTION

In this chapter we contend that some of the features of meta-analysis make it superior to individual studies for testing and formulating theories. In section 2 we discuss the ambiguous use of the term "theory." In section 3 we discuss what we mean by "testing theory." In section 4 we review the potential roles of meta-analysis in developing and evaluating theory, which include assessing causal relationships as well as fulfilling other explanatory tasks. In this section we also consider its advantages relative to single empirical studies. In section 5 we discuss three types of meta-analysis that differ in the way and degree to which they promote theoretical advance. Finally, we discuss issues that confront the meta-analyst who undertakes *comparative* theory testing.

## 2. DEFINING THEORY

A *hypothesis* is a guess at an empirical relationship that links two theoretical concepts. An empirical *law* is a confirmed hypothesis—a relationship between two concepts that has been (relatively) well established by research. A scientific *theory* is a framework for interpreting a conceptually related set of empirical laws. As an abstract nomological network, a theory also provides a basis for deriving new hypotheses from its more general postulates, which can then be tested by research. In Lewin's metaphor (1951): "The ultimate goal is to establish a network of highways and superhighways, so that any important point may be linked with any other. This network of highways will have to be adapted to the natural topography of the country and will thus itself be a mirror of its structure and of the position of its resources" (p. 3; compare Hempel 1952 for a similar description).

In addition, a theory must have scope. In principle, the collection of laws describing the behavior of a lever as a function of various magnitudes of weights, placed at different distances from the fulcrum on which the lever is positioned, can be termed a theory. Innumerable individual laws, including the law of equilibrium, each based on a specific combination of weights, and distances, will predict the direction and speed of the lever's rotation and can be derived from more general principles. Most scientists, however, would balk at terming all this "the general theory of the lever," objecting that it lacks sufficient scope. Instead, they might prefer to view the effects of the specific combinations of weights and distances as a single general law.

To scientifically *explain* something is to state the laws known about it. When one theory is said to provide more or less explanation or understanding than another, what is being referred to is the relative number and scope of the laws that constitute each theory. When *process understanding* (knowledge of why or how *a* and *g* are related, as, for instance, by linking each to *b*, *c*, *d*, *e*, and *f*), *reductionism* (relating a theoretical concept at a more molar level to a concept or set of concepts at a more molecular level), or *axiomatization* (converting the constructs of a theory to abstract symbols and formally specifying the logical relations among them) are discussed as ingredients of an explanation or a theory, this more general definition of explanation still applies. Greater explanation simply means knowing more laws about the substantive area of concern (Bergmann 1957; Simon 1992).

In sum, theories differ in scope (Merton 1949), subject matter, origin of their postulates, and precision (Marx & Hillix 1963), but also in their utility and in the validity of their predictions. Theories are, in Popper's terms (1976), World 3 entities—part of an objective world of knowledge and problems that contains interpretations of facts.[1]

Nevertheless, the term "theory" is ambiguous for several reasons. One ambiguity stems from the ontological distinction between the realist and the instrumentalist (e.g., Casti 1989; Rohrlich 1987) or constructivist views of science (e.g., McGuire 1983). In the realist view, theories describe an external reality that exists

---

[1]In Popper's categorization, World 1 entities are physical, palpable objects; World 2 entities are subjective mental states.

independently of our observations. By contrast, in the currently more accepted instrumentalist or constructivist view, although theories continue to be viewed as useful tools for describing and organizing data, their constructs are not interpreted as necessarily depicting external reality or mapping it in a simple isomorphic manner.

A second ambiguity arises from variation among substantive areas of investigation. Different disciplines (e.g., biology, psychology, chemistry, physics) present unique challenges and complexities. Theories are more elaborated in some fields than in others. Concepts in physics often can be defined mathematically, but such definitions are not as frequent in the social sciences. It has been argued that social science differs in principle from physical science in terms of its fundamental nature (Winch 1967), its complexity (Cronbach 1982), its measures (Demming 1975; Rossi 1971), its need to be emic and view its research problems from the perspective of participant observers (Geertz 1973), and its system properties (e.g., Bandura 1977); or that it differs on the basis of the hermeneutical criticism that unlike physical processes, which are causally determined by forces, people act in response to *reasons to act* or because they follow *rules or scripts* (e.g., Harré & Secord 1977). Nevertheless, few working social scientists explicitly adopt a post-positivist (namely, a Popperian) position (Popper 1959, 1974). Instead, it is recognized that most psychologists (e.g., Gergen 1982), educational researchers

[2]Although there are important nuances of distinction in the meanings of positivism (logical empiricism), for our purpose here we refer to the oversimplified view that a straightforward application of the procedures of science will provide a clear path to a single truth or understanding about the nature of that aspect of the external world with which the individual scientist is concerned. (Other simplified views of positivism include "If you can measure it, it has meaning; if you can't, it doesn't." "Science produces 'the answer.' ") In contrast, post-positivists have a much keener awareness of the potential catastrophes that lie along the path, including an awareness that multiple "right answers" may lie at its end. In McGuire's metaphor for the constructivist (or, in his term, contextualist) view of theory construction, a scientific theorist is like "a rope-walker who, on arriving at a precipice of ignorance, ties one end of a chain of inferences to a stake on its brink, and flinging the free end as far as possible out over the abyss, runs quickly along the thrown chain to get the maximum distance before plunging to disaster" (1983, p. 3).

Perhaps most extreme (and nihilistic for science) are the deconstructionists (e.g., Foucault 1972; Parker & Shotter 1990), who view the products (empirical laws) that the scientist discovers (or produces) as holograms that (solely) reflect unconscious motives, perceptions, or political agendas of the scientist or scientific community.

(e.g., Giroux 1981), and sociologists (e.g., Halfpenny 1982) are positivists at heart.[2] At the same time, however, social scientists may agree that some of these issues are problems. For instance, despite Hedges's disclaimers (1987), many may continue to believe that social science is indeed more complex and less cumulative than physical science.

A third source of ambiguity is that in the social sciences the term "theory" is sometimes used rather loosely. As in Blalock's theory of conflict and conflict reduction (1989), its use can conform to the depiction above—an abstract nomologically linked network of conceptual variables. Other times, it provides a structural analysis of a concept or process, as in Sternberg's three-component theory of love (1987). In some instances, (mistakenly, we think) it is even used as synonymous with a simple, empirically derived hypothesis linking two variables, as in Bass's "theory" of participant leadership (1949).

There are numerous typologies for classifying theories. For example, Marx (1970) describes *deductive, inductive,* and *functional* theories and adds *models* as a fourth category. Deductive and inductive theories lie at opposite ends of a continuum in which functional theories exist in some middle ground between the two. Most theories in social science fall into this latter category. The term "model" typically refers to theorizing that is built on an analogy as, for instance, when the operation of a flashlight is said to be a model for human attention. Usually, models tend to have a narrow focus.

## 3. DEFINING THEORY TESTING

Apart from nuances in the meaning of the term "theory," variation in the philosophical positions of scientists, or where a theory lies within a particular typology of theories, all scientific theories are, in part, developed inductively from prior evidence. The working scientist then tests a theory by gathering data to assess the inductively and deductively derived propositions that constitute it. Better tests will not only use new operationalizations of the concepts that enter the theory (rather than those initially used to provide an inductive basis for it), but also assess new hypotheses that link the concepts of the theory in ways not previously examined (Blalock 1969). From this simplified perspective, testing theory means testing hypotheses. The degree to which research has assessed all of the hypothesized lawful relations that can be derived from a theory defines the degree to which it has been tested. When a theory predicts interactions, its confirmation requires more tests than one that contains an identical number of conceptual variables but does not posit interactions. Empirical assessments of single relationships or sets of relationships can test a theory, albeit with differing comprehensiveness.

Philosophers of science recognize that this is a very oversimplified view. They note that, generally, theories are underdetermined by evidence.

> Non-laboratory social science is precariously scientific at best. *But even for the strongest sciences,* the theories believed to be true are radically underjustified and have, at most, the status of ''better than'' rather than ''proven'' [emphasis added]. All common-sense and scientific knowledge is presumptive. In any setting in which we seem to gain new knowledge, we do so at the expense of many presumptions. . . . Single presumptions or small subsets can in turn be probed, but the total set of presumptions is not of demonstrable validity, is radically underjustified. Such are the pessimistic conclusions of the most modern developments in philosophy of science. (D. T. Campbell 1978, p. 185)

Consequently, there is more to a theory than its confirmed laws: ''. . . it would be more accurate to say that we believe our laws because they are consequences of our theories than to say that we believe our theories because they predict and explain true laws'' (N. Campbell 1928, p. 91). Put differently, theory adds more to the validity of a law than confirmation of a law adds to the validity of a theory. And a reliable failure to confirm a theoretical prediction rarely disqualifies or requires rejection of a theory (Phillips 1987, p. 13; see also the Duhem-Quine thesis: Duhem 1962; Quine 1953). Thus, judgments about a theory's adequacy depend on criteria other than the reliability of the empirical facts of concern. Instead, theory preference or theory acceptance rests on criteria such as simplicity, elegance, mathematical representation, provision of process understanding, familiarity or appeal of its concepts, and values.

Nevertheless, even within the post-positivist scientific view, it is the persistence of ''confirmations''—the inductive fallacy notwithstanding (Popper 1959, 1976)—that prompts retention and elaboration of a theory. Similarly, a growing accumulation of disconfirmations in part leads to modification of a theory or a turn toward an alternative theory. Reliable evidence contrary to a theory creates pressure for theoretical adjustment or

innovation (Phillips 1987). Consequently, as previously indicated, we interpret ''testing a theory'' as synonymous with testing the individual hypotheses that constitute it or can be deduced from it.

Other chapters in the *Handbook* focus on issues that overlap with those implied by our title. Chapter 2 concerns using research synthesis to test hypotheses and Chapter 30 discusses its use as a source of hypotheses for future experimental research. Although opposite sides of the same cloth, these chapters overlap with our focus in this chapter in that hypotheses attempt to link the conceptual patches that, when connected, form a theoretical quilt. Because a model can be viewed as a theory (Kaplan 1964), Chapter 23, which focuses on model testing in research syntheses, also conceptually overlaps with this one. Chapter 31, concerned with threats to the validity of research syntheses, discusses the strength of meta-analytically based inferences about relationships and thereby attempts to assess the strength of the thread that ties the patches of the quilt together. Other chapters also contain material that, with a little imagination, can be forced into this metaphor.

## 4. META-ANALYSIS FOR THEORY TESTING

The things one might want to know prior to making a scientific knowledge claim are much the same whether it is to be based on a single study or a meta-analysis.

### 4.1 Cause and Effect

A key goal with respect to a knowledge claim that two variables ($a$ and $b$) are related is to determine whether that relationship is causal. The complexity of this issue cannot be treated adequately here. To say that a cause *produces* an effect oversimplifies. Three ingredients commonly accepted as criteria for causality (see Mill 1874) are covariation, temporal ordering, and isolation. Covariation means that when $a$ is present, $b$ is present; and when $a$ is absent, $b$ is absent. Common observations, such as the covariation between hair length and marijuana use in the sixties, suggest that covariation yields weak causal evidence. Temporal ordering means that when $b$ is present, $a$ must have temporally preceded it. But further, there should be no instances of the reverse ordering. Boyles's laws about gases, relating pressure, temperature, and volume, fail this latter requirement. Finally, isolation, the most difficult feature, requires showing that other variables are not causes of $b$. Rarely does a single study provide much evidence on isolation. Considerations of the degree of temporal and spatial proximity of *a* to *b* also enter into evaluations of causality. Finally, causal explanation will frequently consist of a string of relationships linking multiple variables, rather than just a single pair. Cook and Campbell (1979) provide a more detailed and sophisticated discussion of causation.

A key feature for inferring a causal relation is control over the occurrence of the alleged causal factor, rather than the mere passive observance of the sequencing or the presence or absence of covariation between two events. Consequently, it is not surprising that the working scientist accepts the experimental method as the sine qua non vehicle for inferring cause. In applying it, researchers might also be urged to use it to rule out alternative explanations—Popper's falsification principle. However, even after many tests to eliminate rival accounts, conclusions will remain fallible. Nevertheless, this advice applies to the meta-analyst as well. Critical to causal explanation is the ruling out of competing alternatives.

**4.1.1 When meta-analysis can provide causal evidence** A causal interpretation of meta-analytic results depends on the design strategies used in primary studies, in conjunction with the procedures used in the meta-analysis. If meta-analytic procedures are used to aggregate the effects of a particular experimental manipulation present in all members of a set of primary-level studies (by, for instance, computing a mean effect size and determining whether its confidence interval excludes zero), then the meta-analytic result speaks on the causal relation between that experimental manipulation and the dependent variable. For example, because Bushman and Cooper (1990) restricted their meta-analysis to experimental studies of the effect of alcohol on human aggression and the confidence interval surrounding the obtained mean effect size did not include zero, their results support the conclusion that alcohol ingestion *causes* an increase in aggression.[3]

**4.1.2 Why most meta-analytic results do not provide causal evidence** Clearly, when applied to integrate the outcomes of individual *experimental* studies, a meta-analysis can provide evidence concerning causal relationships. As most often applied, however, there are two reasons why it does not. First, if the studies at the

primary level use correlational designs, no causal inference appropriately can be made. Quasi-experimental designs fall in some middle ground, some being close to experiments in their ability to rule out rival interpretations and others not. Thus, the nature of the designs used in the primary research constrains the degree to which a causal interpretation of a meta-analytic integration is justified. Second, however, many meta-analyses do not merely integrate the results of individual studies. In addition, they compare subsets of studies. Even if the designs in the primary literature all used experimental manipulation, no meta-analytic comparisons of subsets of studies (from the larger set) allow a causal inference because the subsets cannot be randomly assigned by the meta-analyst to examine the issue of interest. Such comparisons can only assess whether the variable represented by the partitioning of studies *moderates* the magnitude of effect sizes. A moderator variable tells us about circumstances under which effect size magnitudes vary, but it does not tell us why. Meta-analytic results based on comparisons of subsets of studies are analogous to the application of post hoc internal analyses across (nonrandomized) levels of a blocking factor within a single experiment. The following discussion will clarify this issue.

Consider a fictitious experiment on the effectiveness with which a fear-eliciting persuasive message about heart disease changes the behavior of men "at risk." Our researcher suspects that anxiety mediates the effectiveness of fear-eliciting persuasive appeals, hypothesizing that only when a low to moderate level of anxiety is elicited by the fear-arousing message will it be effective in changing the behavior of men at risk. A mediating variable is one that causally lies between the independent and dependent variables; the mediator is *caused by* the independent variable and *causes* the dependent variable. To test the mediating role of anxiety, our (unsophisticated) researcher performs an internal analysis, aggregating subjects within the experimental condition on the basis of self-reported anxiety assessed immediately after exposure to the persuasive appeal. As anticipated, only for subjects below the median on anxiety does the fear-arousing message produce more behavior change (in terms of diet, increased exercise, preventative use of aspirin, etc.) than the neutral control message.

Although intriguing, this outcome would not establish that anxiety *mediated* the effect of the fear appeal. Instead, pre-experimental specific knowledge about appropriate actions to reduce risk of heart attack might produce both the behavioral changes of the men in the

---

[3]For this point we put aside other factors that may compromise the acceptance of a causal relation: for example, the ruling out of expectation effects (as shown by Hull & Bond 1986) or the ruling out of demand as an alternative explanation (e.g., Berkowitz & Donnerstein 1982; Carlson, Marcus-Newhall & Miller 1990).

experimental condition and their self-reported anxiety. Specifically, those more knowledgeable might not only take more actions after hearing the fear-arousing message (because it makes the need for action more salient), but also report less anxiety after hearing it (because they knew what to do). If so, anxiety had no necessary causal or mediational role in changing behavior. The message itself directly produced behavior change (particularly among those who were knowledgeable), whereas the anxiety outcomes were ancillary. If, prior to the experiment, an anxiety-reducing drug had been administered to those (unknowledgeable) subjects who were made anxious by the fear appeal, they still would not have exhibited more behavior change than control subjects.[4]

When a meta-analyst observes that variability in a distribution of effect sizes exceeds that expected from sampling error, or has a specific a priori hypothesis about a variable that moderates or mediates variation among effect sizes, a common "next step" is to partition studies into sets respectively high and low (or order them) on the potential explanatory variable. Comparisons of the mean effect sizes of the subsets, or correlation between the ordering on the moderator and the effect sizes, correspond to the internal correlational analysis described above. Even when the explanatory variable hypothesized to play a mediational (causal) role is shown to be related to the key dependent variable, this type of meta-analytic test only provides associational or correlational evidence.

To illustrate, the meta-analyst might group studies of the effect of fear-arousing messages on men "at risk" into sets based on ancillary information in each study about the mean level of subjects' anxiety. A contrast that demonstrates a greater effect of the fear-arousing message in the low-anxiety set than in the high-anxiety set will not establish that anxiety plays a causal role in mediating the effect of fear-arousing messages. Again, a third variable may account for the meta-analytic result of greater effectiveness when anxiety was low. In studies in which subjects' mean anxiety scores were lower, researchers may have unintentionally selected (or recruited) subjects higher in social class and hence, owing

to their better education, also more knowledgeable about appropriate actions to take when "at risk". Thus, in this meta-analytic example, too, anxiety was merely a moderator variable. Moreover, it was a proxy moderator for the knowledge differences correlated with social class.[5]

To propose that anxiety plays a causal or mediating role, as distinct from a moderating one, requires experimental manipulation of anxiety and random assignment of subjects from each anxiety-level group to the high-fear and low-fear message conditions. To propose a meta-analytic causal effect requires aggregating studies that experimentally manipulated subjects' anxiety levels and examining the interaction between this manipulation (of anxiety) and the manipulation of type of persuasive message (high-fear vs. low-fear) to which subjects were exposed.

We return to this issue in the next section.

## 4.2 Explanatory Tasks Within Meta-Analysis

In *Meta-Analysis for Explanation* (Cook et al. 1992), a number of explanatory tasks are enumerated. We condense them into six related, but distinguishable, activities: (a) assessing evidence that a relationship, or law, exists and that it is (relatively) nonartifactual; (b) examining the form of a relationship; (c) analyzing the causal or key conceptual components of the independent variable (treatment) and the key components of the dependent (outcome) variable; (d) assessing the scope of a relationship; and (e) analyzing the mediating processes that underlie a relationship. A sixth task, (f) developing a model that accounts for the variance among study outcomes, conceptually corresponds to tasks (c) and (d) to some degree. However, whereas tasks (c) and (d) can be undertaken successfully in the sense that they account for some additional variance among effect sizes, task (f) emphasizes the completeness with which variance has been explained. Nevertheless, all six qualify as contributing to theoretical explanation. And, as indicated, they apply as much to knowledge claims based on a single study as to those based on a meta-

---

[4]Clearly, a blocking design would be a better design. It would administer an anxiety measure prior to the treatment and then, separately for each of the two groups created by a median split on the anxiety measure, randomly assign subjects to the two persuasive message conditions. Parenthetically, a second anxiety measure, administered after the message manipulation, might usefully be retained in this latter design. Further discussion of causal mediation appears in section 3.1.5.

[5]In line with some theorizing (e.g., Leventhal 1970), meta-analysis of the effects of fear-arousing messages on persuasion (Boster & Mongeau 1985) suggests increased persuasion as a function of fear arousal, though prior theory has also suggested the inverse (e.g., Janis & Feshbach 1953) as well as inverted-U (e.g., McGuire 1968) relationships. As B. Johnson (1991) notes, however, by failing to examine the moderators specified in prior theorizing, this meta-analysis was not as theoretically incisive as it might have been.

analysis. We discuss these six components of explanation in sequence.

**4.2.1 Assessing a relationship and ruling out artifactuality** Assessing evidence that a relationship exists and that it is nonartifactual is a first step in determining its validity. Within meta-analysis, this consists of quantitative aggregation of the outcome of individual studies that examined variables *a* and *b* in order to assess the existence of a relationship. Alternatively, or additionally, it might consist of comparing two subsets of studies that assessed *b,* one of which contained studies coded or judged as high on *a* and the other of which contained studies low on *a* (or regressing *b* on a continuous ordering of studies based on their level on *a*). It also consists of evaluating the contribution of nontheoretical implementation or methodological factors that bear on whether the meta-analytic outcome is valid or artifactual. Thus, the meta-analyst might compare study outcomes when treatments and assessments were or were not administered blind, with or without placebo controls, with or without fully automated machine- or computer-controlled procedures, and so on. The assessment might also consist of direct comparison of strong and weak methodological tests of the relation, such as comparing experimental versus correlational studies, confounded versus conceptually pure independent and dependent variables, and so on.

Raz and Raz (1990) provide an example of this explanatory task. One theoretical perspective on mental disorders emphasizes biological factors involved in their etiology. Both computer-assisted tomography and magnetic resonance imaging can be used to visualize gross features of brain anatomy. In a meta-analysis of neuroimaging research on schizophrenia, Raz and Raz (1990) showed that schizophrenics exhibit lateral ventricular enlargement compared with control subjects. Methodological factors—such as variation in the resolution of the brain-scanning devices that were used, or whether the control groups contained healthy, normal volunteers or medical patients—appeared unrelated to this result. Thus, the meta-analysis seemingly confirms a nonartifactual relationship.

**4.2.2 Assessing the form of a relationship** Assessing the form of a relationship is to state its nature with greater precision. In meta-analysis, this may consist of determining differences on the outcome measure as a function of the magnitude of treatments within primary-level studies. Even when no single study within a literature explores such features, if there is sufficient variation among studies in their treatments or conditions,

they can be grouped for application of trend analysis or curve-fitting techniques, or to assess whether the relationship is continuous or discontinuous.

Steinberg and colleagues (1991) provide an example. They derived dose-response curves from a series of studies to assess the relation between breast cancer risk and duration of estrogen use. Breast cancer risk did not appear to increase until at least five years of estrogen use. But after 15 years of estrogen use, women who had experienced menopause for any reason had a 30 percent increased risk of developing breast cancer.[6] Thus, meta-analysis enabled a more precise, quantitative statement of the form of the theoretical relation than was previously available.

**4.2.3 Assessing the critical components of theoretical concepts** Often, researchers will operationalize a single theoretical concept in slightly different ways. Analyzing which components of an independent or a dependent variable are more or less critical to their relationship with another variable refines our understanding of the law. Within a meta-analysis it may be possible to show that subsets of studies which vary in their operationalization of a concept produce different outcomes, thereby differentiating what was initially conceptualized as a unitary concept. Alternatively, it may be possible to show that a set of allegedly distinct concepts all share the same functional relationships with each of an array of other variables, thereby challenging such meaningless conceptual proliferation. We discuss theoretical differentiation and integration in turn.

*Theoretical differentiation.* In education, it is now well established that use of cooperative team learning procedures not only improves mastery of curriculum materials (Maruyama 1991), but also, when there is racial/ethnic heterogeneity among students, increases intergroup acceptance (Johnson, Johnson, & Maruyama 1984). The distinct procedures that have been developed share common features. For instance, all divide the class into subgroups, each of which is given responsibility for the mastery of the lesson materials. Nevertheless, across individual experimental studies, there is variation in

---

[6]The relationship between estrogen use and risk of breast cancer remains a controversial topic. As is true in other substantive areas of study, the conclusions drawn from single meta-analyses of comparable research literatures may not always coincide (e.g., Cooper 1990; Dillard 1991). And, irrespective of its ability to document the form of the relationship, it is important to emphasize, once again, that meta-analyses of research literatures such as this do not provide a firm foundation for forming causal inferences. More primary-level research on estrogen replacement therapy is needed to establish its role in breast cancer.

implementation procedures with respect to key theoretical components. For example, the relative numerosity of minority and majority students on teams varies (e.g., numbers are equal in some studies, whereas Anglo students are in a numerical minority or majority in others); some studies use reward interdependence (e.g., all team members get the same grade), whereas others retain individual performance measures. Meta-analytic examination of such variations in implementation showed that cooperative team learning procedures that contained some ingredients (e.g., task interdependence, equal numerical representation) increased intergroup acceptance, whereas those that contained other components (e.g., interdependent reward structures, publicized performance) did not (Miller & Davidson-Podgorny 1987). Thus, the research synthesis provides suggestive evidence about components of cooperative interaction that may be more important than others or may be irrelevant to its beneficial effects on intergroup social acceptance. Similarly, Johnson and Eagly (1989, 1990) used meta-analytic procedures to differentiate three types of attitude involvement in research on persuasion, whereas narrative reviewers (Petty & Cacioppo 1990) concluded that only two types are needed. Carlson & Miller (1987) conceptually differentiated three meanings of self-focus and provided meta-analytic evidence for their discriminative construct validity.

Of course, the outcome of such attempts at conceptual refinement will in part reflect differences in the reliabilities of specific measures. In addition, when attempting conceptual refinement of an experimentally manipulated independent variable, differences in the implementation strength of the distinct components of the independent variable will muddle attempts to assess the components as critical or superfluous unless the meta-analyst applies procedures to control such variation. For instance, in the previously described meta-analytic attempt to assess critical components of cooperation, if, in the comparison of individual and team rewards, the individual-reward studies had used amounts ranging from $10 to $50 per person and the team-reward studies had used amounts ranging from $1 to $10 per team, the disparity of implementation strengths would preclude meaningful comparison. Had the primary-level studies used random effects designs in selecting reward levels, implementation strength would not be an issue. Unfortunately, for practical reasons, few experiments do. One approach to this problem is to use expert judges' ratings to assess implementation strength within each study. The selection of sets of studies that differ in the key components

contained in their manipulation of the independent variable and for which the components of interest are judged to have been strongly and equivalently implemented will allow more meaningful comparison.

When the meta-analytic database contains multiple measures of each of several conceptually distinct dependent variables, confirmatory factor-analytic procedures or measurement models (LISREL, EQS) can be applied to assess coherence among specific measures and their distinctiveness from other sets. Bushman, Cooper, and Lemke (1991) discuss meta-analytic integration of factor-analytic studies, describing procedures to synthesize information about the factor structures found in independent studies.

The need for conceptual differentiation, however, will also depend on the empirical development of the science. Whereas early Italian physicists in the hilltop universities of Parma, Bologne, and Perugia argued about the proper definition of the concept *force,* subsequent empirical work showed all three rival definitions to be "correct." That is, empirical research revealed distinct laws that separately involved kinetic energy, momentum, and force. Future meta-analytic efforts might reveal that although the cognitive, affective, and behavioral components of attitudes are related, the circumstances in which each best predicts behavior vary. This might push theorists away from a unitary conceptualization of attitude (e.g., Cacioppo & Tassinary 1989) toward a more differentiated conceptualization (e.g., McGuire 1985). Clearly, such conceptual refinement advances the science.

*Theoretical integration.* Our preceding discussion emphasized the contribution of conceptual differentiation to theory. Conceptual integration can also serve a useful theoretical function. Social science is plagued by instances of distinct terms for what may be a common underlying concept. Researchers seek distinctive labels for what they study. Rosenthal (1991) has labeled this inclination concept capture. In personality research on cognitive styles Bogen (1975) lists 39 scholars, each of whom use a distinct pair of terms to describe a dichotomization of cognitive styles into two opposing types—the focused and narrow-minded versus the general and broad-minded. Miller and Pollock (in press) have questioned whether there is discriminative construct validity for the concepts dissonance (Festinger 1957), self-affirmation (Steele 1988), responsibility for a negative event (Scher & Cooper 1989), and guilt (Carlson & Miller 1987)—all prominent and allegedly distinct concepts in psychological research. They raise similar concern about the dozen-plus terms used to refer to exaggerated perceptions of similarity between self and other, such as assumed similarity (e.g., Cronbach 1955), false consensus (e.g., Ross 1977), social projection (e.g., Allport 1924), and so on. Erdelyi (1990) questions the conceptual distinctions between repression (Freud 1915), selective inattention (Sullivan 1956), thought stopping (Dollard & Miller 1950), and cognitive avoidance (Eriksen & Pierce 1968). Proliferation of nonmeaningful conceptual distinctions undermines the cumulative approach to knowledge integration and illustrates one way in which theory can impede scientific progress.

When a single study contains multiple dependent measures of a single conceptual variable, the researcher can determine whether specific dependent measures are affected equivalently by an independent variable. Similarly, meta-analysis can be used to evaluate such alleged discriminative construct validity by assessing the relation of theoretically relevant variables to each of the apparent synonyms of the concept in question. If all of ten variables exhibit the same functional relationship with concept 1a and 1b, then there is little reason to view 1a and 1b as distinct. If, instead, some of the ten interact disordinally with (show different directions of effect on) 1a and 1b, that is evidence for viewing 1a and 1b as distinct constructs (i.e., as 1 and 2, rather than 1a and 1b). This general principle applies whether or not the suspected conceptual proliferation has occurred with respect to the independent or the dependent variable.

This strategy was used in conjunction with meta-analytic procedures to assess the functional relation between indices of verbal and written aggression and each of four relevant independent variables (Carlson, Marcus-Newhall & Miller 1990). Tedeschi and his colleagues had suggested that these two measures of aggression reflect distinct theoretical concepts rather than an underlying single concept (e.g., Tedeschi, Smith & Brown 1974; Tedeschi 1983). Contrary to this view, measures of verbal and written aggression were affected similarly by anger, frustration, personal attack, and directness of aggression, implying that both of the measures of aggression assess the same underlying construct. Used in this way, meta-analysis might serve as Occam's razor, slashing out unneeded theoretical terms.

**4.2.4 Assessing the scope or limits of a relationship** The fourth explanatory goal assesses the generality or limits of a law. Individual studies address this by examining how situation, person, or temporal variables moderate the outcome. This approach can be applied

within meta-analysis. When studies vary in the type of subject (male or female; old or young) or situation in which a phenomenon is studied (inpatient or outpatient facility; court-ordered or voluntary school desegregation), the meta-analyst can perform moderator analyses to examine the effect of such variation.

If a meta-analytic contrast shows less conformity among studies that assessed male compared with female subjects, can we conclude that females are more compliant than males? Not necessarily, because studies that used female subjects may have differed in important ways from those that used male subjects. Studies that used female subjects may have used female confederates more frequently as well. Conformity may depend more on sex of the target persons whose judgments form the standard against which conformity is assessed than on sex of the subject. Male sources of influence may elicit more psychological resistance or reactance (Brehm 1966) than female sources. If so, and if sex of subject is typically matched to sex of confederates, the misleading outcome of greater conformity among females would erroneously emerge. Conformity research paradigms may covary with the sex of subjects in numerous other ways. Studies that used female subjects may have used a paradigm that contains more surveillance (Eagly & Carli 1981). Thus, more generally, a meta-analytic contrast which indicates that a variable such as sex of subject moderates a relationship can be misleading. It may rest instead on some other correlated variable.[7]

There are many specific methods for testing whether a given moderator variable qualifies a meta-analytic relationship (see Hall & Rosenthal, in press). In addition, Hull, Tedlie, and Lehn (1992) discuss misapplication of multiple regression procedures in primary-level studies concerned with moderators in personality theory

---

[7]In many substantive areas results are reported separately for males and females. In such instances the meta-analysis can be conducted directly on the separate gender effects reported within each study. Here, too, however, when the outcome of a contrast in mean effect sizes shows females to be more compliant, this result is no less likely to be artifactual than in the first instance. Continuing with our earlier example, if experimenters routinely match sex of subject with sex of influence source, one cannot tell whether the outcome is due to the subject, the target, or the interaction between the two. Since sex of subject cannot be assigned randomly to subjects, it can only function as a moderator variable. This remains true irrespective of how it is studied— whether in single experimental studies or in meta-analytic syntheses. In any meta-analytic contrast that involves a partitioning of a set of studies, the fact that studies cannot be randomly assigned to the subsets precludes any causal statement about the obtained effect.

research. Their concerns also apply to meta-analytic use of regression. Others have noted the insensitivity of the omnibus $F$ test for interaction (e.g., Bobko 1986) or of multivariate interaction tests (Morris, Sherman & Mansfield 1986). Sackett, Harris, and Orr (1986) show that these concerns apply to meta-analyses as well. For these reasons, when theory can specify the manner in which a moderator variable will modify a relationship, the use of planned comparisons is recommended (Hall & Rosenthal, in press). At the same time, however, to whatever degree we gain knowledge of variables that moderate (modify) a causal or correlational relation, the more complete is our understanding or explanation.

**4.2.5 Specifying mediating processes** Judd and Kenny (1981) outline steps necessary for inferring that within a given experimental study a measured (but nonmanipulated) variable serves a mediating function. In addition to confirming that the independent and dependent variables are related, they include showing that (a) manipulation of the independent variable produces the hypothesized change on the mediating variable; (b) the mediating and dependent variables are correlated; and (c) when the relation between the mediating variable and the dependent variable is controlled (e.g., by using the mediator as a covariate in analysis of covariance), the relation between the independent and dependent variables vanishes.

In experimental research, the use of such mediational analysis is increasing (e.g., Gaertner et al. 1990; Sanna 1992), but still remains rare. Moreover, it does not overcome completely the difficulties of establishing causal or mediational process laws because the causal link between the mediator and the dependent variable is assessed correlationally and because, as in most research, evidence regarding isolation of the causal mediator (or antecedent) is weak. Furthermore, its application to meta-analysis, though in principle feasible, seems unlikely because few literatures will contain multiple studies, all of which assess a given potential mediator. A more feasible approach would be three separate meta-analyses examining the link between the independent and dependent variables, the link between the independent and mediating variables, and the link between the mediating and dependent variables. Separate from the advantages of aggregation ordinarily conferred by meta-analysis, if all three literatures were *experimental,* an additional advantage over the Judd and Kenny (1981) procedure (prescribed for a single experiment) would accrue. The causal link between the mediator and

the dependent variable would be more strongly established.

Becker (1992), Driskell and Mullen (1990), Premack and Hunter (1988), and Shadish (1992) provide examples of the application of path analysis procedures to meta-analytic data in order to assess mediational models of the relations among conceptual variables. Although such efforts provide plausible models of relations among variables, our earlier discussion of the requirements for inferring causation stands.

**4.2.6 Accounting for the variance among study outcomes** A final explanatory task is to account for the variability among a set of study outcomes. Although the explanatory tasks discussed in the two preceding sections (namely, the examination of moderating and mediating variables) also account for variability, here the task is framed in the manner in which it is addressed in studies that use multiple regression procedures: What is the multiple $R^2$, or how much of the variance in the dependent measure has been explained? When a variable conceptualized as a moderator or mediator typically is measured on a continuous dimension, rather than categorically, multiple regression procedures (with appropriate weighting by sample size) can be applied to meta-analytic data (e.g., Lipsey 1992a). When the residual variance among effect sizes is sufficiently small, as determined by a homogeneity test, the model—whether containing methodological variables, theoretical variables, or a combination of both—is viewed as successful.

Although this approach to explanation is likely to see increasing use in meta-analyses, more explained variance is not isomorphic with better theory. Usually, as more variables are added, more variance can be accounted for in a multiple regression solution. Such proliferation may be the antithesis of elegant theory. Also, counter to the goal of developing ''good theory,'' the increasing addition of methodological factors may do better at explaining variance than does the addition of theoretical variables (e.g., Lipsey 1992b). Finally, good theory typically contains process or mediational laws. A multivariate accounting of effect size variance may be successful, but it may not increase knowledge about the process or mediators involved in producing the phenomenon of interest.

## 4.3 Advantages of Using Meta-Analysis to Test Theory

The preceding section discussed the use of meta-analytic procedures to perform the major explanatory tasks required for testing components of a theory. This section describes additional advantages of meta-analysis.

### 4.3.1 The power of quantitative integration

The most obvious advantage of meta-analytic tests of theory is the additional power that quantitative integration can bring to bear on the substantive issue. Low reliability always reduces statistical power (Cohen 1988) and low validity can reduce it, too. For the narrative reviewer, this contributes to a perception that studies within a set "differ in kind." To a degree, meta-analysis can overcome these sources of variation. Thus, as indicated, its foremost quality is that it provides greater precision, objectivity, and replicability in the assessment of relationships than can a single study or a narrative review.

### 4.3.2 Avoiding the logistical constraints of the single study

Logistical problems constrain the testing of theory within a single study. Examination of more than three or four theoretical variables in a single experiment may not be cost-effective or even feasible. With meta-analysis, the empirical database sometimes can be expanded by coding or rating studies on many theoretical dimensions, and thereby permitting examination of all, or many, of the variables that bear on a particular theory. Carlson and Miller (1987) meta-analytically compared three theoretical explanations of the relation between bad mood and helping behavior by using judges' ratings of each experimental study to assess the contextual levels of about a dozen and a half theoretical variables relevant to the three theories. They then regressed helping effect sizes on the judged variables. The empirical relationships posited by two explanations, attentional focus and objective self-awareness, were supported, but for negative state relief (Cialdini, Baumann & Kenrick 1981), the most well-differentiated and well-established theory, none of 17 tests provided support for any of its postulated relationships (Carlson & Miller 1987; Miller & Carlson 1990). Although these meta-analytic effects are compromised by the fact that they are correlational, a single experiment testing the effects of 18 or so variables would be infeasible.

### 4.3.3 Expanding temporal horizons

When time, in units of decades, enters theoretical formulations it may pose a serious obstacle to testing theory within a single study (Cronbach 1975). Sometimes, however, temporal effects that would have been difficult to assess in primary research can be examined effectively with meta-analytic procedures. Raudenbush (1984) used meta-analysis to test a hypothesis about temporal effects that, although not extended over decades or years, would not

be easily testable in primary research and, in fact, had not been tested experimentally.

The teacher-expectancy hypothesis argues that teachers' knowledge about a child's prior academic performance or IQ creates an expectancy about that child's future performance. Such expectancies then lead the teacher to see confirming evidence and to act toward each child in a manner that will cause the child to confirm the intellectual performance outcome implicit in the expectancy. Recently Jussim (1991) has empirically challenged the view that expectancy effects are large in magnitude. Anticipating such work, Raudenbush (1984) hypothesized that knowledge or reality can confer strong resistance to the manipulation of expectancies. The logistics of testing this hypothesis within a single experimental study require that the information relevant to creating an expectancy be introduced to different teachers at successively longer intervals after the start of a school year. Practical problems need to be solved in order to implement such a design (e.g., providing teachers within a school a plausible explanation of why the school records containing IQ information were available to one teacher four, six, or eight months before they were available to another). Approaching the problem meta-analytically, Raudenbush found a strong negative correlation between the number of weeks of teacher-student contact prior to the teachers' exposure to the expectancy experimental treatment and the magnitude of its effect on the teachers' judgments of students' IQ.

### 4.3.4 Avoiding the constraints imposed by changes in ethical and institutional standards

Changes in ethical standards or institutional policy may preclude the study of a phenomenon well studied at an earlier point. For example, institutional review boards currently are more reluctant to approve studies of human aggression that include the administration of electric shock, as in Milgram (1963); with changes in federal policy during the 1980s there are no longer new instances of court-ordered school desegregation to be studied by those interested in factors that govern its effective implementation. Moreover, new theory may implicate new variables whose effects had not been assessed at the time when such phenomena could be easily studied. In such cases it might be illuminating if old data could be used to assess the effects of new variables. As is implicit in the discussion in section 4.3.2, in meta-analysis this might be achieved in some instances by coding studies or having judges rate studies on the theoretical variables of interest. Using these procedures, meta-analysts (e.g.,

Carlson, Marcus-Newhall & Miller 1990; Eagly & Steffen 1986) have added to our understanding of human aggression despite the dramatic recent decline in primary-level aggression research.

## 5. THREE TYPES OF META-ANALYTIC EVIDENCE IN TESTS OF THEORY

This section organizes the types of meta-analyses found in recent published work into three categories that differentiate the manner in which they contribute to theory. Type A meta-analyses have as their sole purpose the integration of individual studies that all examined a single empirical relation. The meta-analytic goal is to establish an empirical fact or association. Type B meta-analyses (typically, in addition to achieving the Type A goal) assess the generality of empirical relationships or associations. They emphasize the conceptual goal of identifying theory-relevant conditions or constraints that modify the relationship. The theoretical variables examined, however, are ones that have been invoked in prior individual studies of the substantive issue. Type C meta-analyses (typically, in addition to achieving Type A and Type B goals) examine the effect of new theoretical concepts that had not been considered in the primary-level studies.

### 5.1 Type A Tests: Aggregation of Study-Level Evidence

As indicated, Type A meta-analysis aggregates the relation examined between variables studied previously within individual studies to assess the validity of a relationship. Is it meta-analytically upheld and is it nonartifactual? Hence, its major focus is to obtain a mean effect size, provide evidence that it differs from zero, offer evidence that the phenomenon is not artifactual, and, thereby, evaluate the validity of a theoretical prediction.

In terms of the six explanatory tasks previously enumerated, it does not move beyond the first goal of assessing evidence for a reliable relationship. The example provided in section 4.1.1, Bushman and Cooper's synthesis of experimental research on alcohol and aggression (1990), illustrates a Type A meta-analysis. There are stages at which data, in the form of facts and lawful associations between variables, are needed in order for theory development to progress (e.g., Teitelbaum & Pellis 1992). Once established, they are the basic ingredients that theories are constructed to explain. Thus, a

Type A meta-analysis can serve an important role for theory, albeit a limited one.

### 5.2 Type B Tests: Differentiation and Generalization

The major purpose of a Type B meta-analysis is to examine variables that moderate a theory's range of utility or its scope. It does so by examining sources of variability among individual study outcomes as a function of theoretically relevant categories. Thus, it can provide evidence on both theoretical differentiation and theoretical generalization. As in Type A meta-analysis, a Type B meta-analysis may examine variability in study outcomes due to methodological features, but such analyses are secondary to the major purpose, which is to examine theoretical variables. Type B meta-analyses use the procedures and perform the explanatory tasks discussed in sections 4.1.2–4.1.6. However, although they can make valuable theoretical contributions, they do not require high theoretical creativity because the variables they examine as moderators of a basic theoretical law are ones that have been invoked in prior, primary-level research.

Mullen, Brown, and Smith (1992) provide an example of a Type B meta-analysis. They examined experimental studies of intergroup bias—the tendency to evaluatively favor one's ingroup over an outgroup. Evidence for such bias is pervasive and had been reported in prior narrative reviews. Not surprisingly, the meta-analytic integration confirmed it, a Type A result. In addition, they performed moderator analyses to assess the effects of variables that might qualify its magnitude: relative size of the ingroup and outgroup, the relative status of the two groups, and the relevance or importance of the evaluative dimension on which bias was assessed. Because these variables had been manipulated previously in primary-level research, their study was a Type B meta-analysis. Their results showed that bias was stronger in relatively smaller groups. In addition, higher-status groups displayed stronger bias on relevant (important) evaluative dimensions whereas lower-status groups displayed it more strongly on irrelevant dimensions. Although theoretical analysis had predicted this interaction, it had lacked strong support in primary research.

### 5.3 Type C Tests: Evidence Bearing on New Theories

A third use of meta-analysis is to test new theoretical hypotheses that had not been considered previously in primary-level research. The degree to which one can perform such tests depends in part on the ingenuity of the researcher, but probably also depends on the nature of primary-level data and on the level of prior theoretical development in the area. Like Type B meta-analyses, the basic strategy relies on coding information reported in the method or result sections of individual studies in theoretically relevant ways. Alternatively, judges can be used to rate the contextual levels of theoretically relevant variables, within experimental and control conditions (compare Miller, Lee & Carlson 1991). Sometimes, however, theoretically relevant data can be obtained from external sources. In a meta-analysis that examined how crowding moderated the effects of a model's behavior on the frequency of jaywalking, Mullen, Cooper, and Driskell (1990) located archival data on pedestrian traffic flow as a function of time of day. They then coordinated it with the time of day in which the primary study data were collected, as reported in their method sections. Crowded sidewalks increased the tendency for a disobedient model to augment jaywalking and undermined the tendency for an obedient model to decrease jaywalking.

Instances of Type C meta-analyses are infrequent, but Steele and Southwick (1985) reported an early example. They theorized that alcohol increases the extremity of social responses as a function of the magnitude of inhibitory conflict, defined as the simultaneous occurrence of incompatible response tendencies. When both strong instigating and inhibiting cues are present, as when peers urge a teenager to commit a delinquent act for which the severe consequences that might later be imposed are highly salient, alcohol is hypothesized to increase the extremity of any type of social response (e.g., antisocial behavior, responsiveness to humor). When inhibitory conflict is weak, alcohol should have little influence on social response extremity. No primary-level study had examined this theoretical view. Thus, at least in alcohol research, inhibitory conflict was a new theoretical variable.

The authors dichotomously coded the degree of inhibitory conflict in the conditions of the primary studies as either high or low, after having first developed coding rules relevant to the 12 social behaviors studied (e.g., aggression, self-disclosure, risk-taking). As predicted, under conditions of high inhibitory conflict the influence of alcohol on social behaviors substantially exceeded that which occurred under the placebo conditions ($d = 1.06$; 95 percent confidence interval excludes zero), but under low inhibitory conflict it did not ($d = .14$; 95

percent confidence interval includes zero). Additional analyses of these conflict ratings suggested that expectancies did not moderate their effects, nor did other study characteristics, such as subjects' age, sex, and drinking habits.

## 5.4 Type A, B, and C Tests in Published Meta-Analyses

To examine the frequency with which Type A, B, and C tests have been used in psychological research in recent years, all articles published in *Psychological Bulletin* in 1984, 1986, 1988, and 1990 were examined and considered to be a meta-analysis if cumulations of effect sizes were reported. Hence, some studies seemingly justifiable as a meta-analysis were excluded by this criterion (e.g., Flynn 1984; Matthews 1988). Among the 32 meta-analyses identified, most were of Type B ($n = 26$). Almost all of these also reported information contained in a Type A meta-analysis, but only five fell solely in the Type A category. Finally, only one fell into the Type C category (Watson & Clark 1984).

Thus, in contemporary psychological research the frequency of Type C meta-analyses appears quite low relative to those that only provided Type B tests. Perhaps this is due to the historical or consensual perception of meta-analysis as a tool for integration rather than as a tool for testing new theoretical ideas. These goals are not incompatible. With greater awareness of its potential to contribute in novel or creative ways to theory construction, perhaps future meta-analysts will more frequently attempt to assess the role of new concepts, as well as examining those posited to be important by primary-level researchers. The relative infrequency of Type A tests in psychological research is also striking. Although we have made no systematic examination, inspection of medical journals leads us to suspect that Type A tests are more frequent in medical research. If so, the explanation is unclear. Differences in the nature of the data in each domain, the level of theoretical development, and the normative standards that guide application of meta-analytic procedures may all contribute.

## 6. OTHER ISSUES IN TESTING THEORY VIA META-ANALYSIS

More general perspectives on the use of meta-analysis to develop and test theory are considered in this section.

**Table 29.1 Studies Using Meta-Analysis**

| Author | Title (Paraphrased) and Topic | Reliability of Coding |
|---|---|---|
| **1990** | | |
| Hyde, Fennema, & Lamon | Gender differences in mathematics<br>Does gender difference in performance vary in the types of samples studied? | .88–1.00 |
| McCartney, Harris, & Bernieri | Developmental twin studies<br>Does age influence twins' intelligence and personality test scores? | NR |
| Bushman & Cooper | Alcohol and human aggression<br>What is the interaction between provocation and alcohol effects on aggression? | .85–1.00 subset of 15 studies, 4 raters |
| Robinson, Berman, & Neimeyer | Psychotherapy in depression treatment<br>Do differences in authors' preference for certain types of therapies influence their outcomes? | NR |
| Mathieu & Zajac | Organizational commitment<br>Does type of organizational commitment—attitudinal vs. calculative—influence outcomes obtained? | 1.00 for a subset of 30 studies, two raters |
| Eagly & Johnson | Gender and leadership<br>Do gender-stereotypic qualities of leadership roles relate to sex differences in the styles that persons use carrying them out? | Median 97% over 162 studies two raters |
| Okun, Olding, & Cohn | Subjective well-being interventions among elders<br>Does the length of time elapsed between an intervention and completion of a posttest designed to tap well-being influence self-ratings? | .93–1.00 over 29 studies, 3 raters |

| Level of Inference | Theoretical Meta-Analytic Hypothesis Test | | | Novel Meta-Analytic Theoretical Hypothesis? (Type C) |
| | Variable | Reliability of Theoretical Variable | Construct Validity (Type B) | |
| --- | --- | --- | --- | --- |
| Low | Type of subject sample: general (e.g., classrooms) vs. moderately select (e.g., college) vs. highly select (e.g., precocious math ability) or those selected for poor performance (5 categories) | .90 | Gender differences were more pronounced in moderately and highly select samples than in general samples | No |
| Low | Age (continuous) | NR | As twins age, their intelligence and personality test scores became more dissimilar | No |
| High | Level of provocation (75 undergraduates indicated how angry or provoked they would feel on an 11-point scale after reading descriptions of experimental procedures) | NR | NR | No |
| High | Five-point scale used to categorize authors' attitudes toward therapies, based on reading the published articles | Intraclass correlations .85 and .95 for two raters, respectively | Judgments of authors' therapy preferences correlated with favorable outcomes for them ($r = +.58, p < .001$) | No |
| Low | Most studies were categorized as attitudinal vs. calculative organizational commitment | 100% for two raters over 30 studies | Different moderators were positively associated with each type of commitment, but the mean ES for attitudinal (.45) did not differ significantly from calculative ($r = .50$) | No |
| High | Male ($n = 181$) and female ($n = 125$) undergraduates rated 119 leadership roles according to how interesting they were, how much competence they required, and how much ability was needed for them on 15-point scales | NR | Judgments of the leadership roles were significantly related to sex differences in task style | No |
| Low | Dichotomized time between cessation of intervention and posttest completion as within or greater than zero days | NR | Mean effect size of immediate posttests exceeded those of delayed posttests | No |

**Table 29.1 (continued)**

| Author | Title (Paraphrased) and Topic | Reliability of Coding |
|---|---|---|
| **1988** | | |
| Premack & Hunter | Unionization decisions by individuals<br>Used a path model to examine the relationship among relevant job-related indicators (e.g., wages, dissatisfaction) and assessed its conformance to multiple theories | NR |
| Bowers & Clum | Treatment effects in behavior therapy<br>Is the credibility of placebo conditions used in behavior therapy studies related to the placebo effect size? | NR |
| Miller & Eisenberg | The relation of empathy to aggression<br>From a theoretical perspective which posited that aggressive behavior was negatively related to empathy, the authors hypothesized that low levels of empathy would characterize child abuse victims | NR |
| Hyde & Linn | Gender differences in verbal ability<br>Are certain specific cognitive processes, such as the ability to generate words, related to sex differences in performance? | NR |
| Feingold | Attractiveness in romantic partners and same-sex friends<br>Does the attractiveness-matching hypothesis apply to same-sex friends, in addition to romantic partners? | NR |
| Matthews | Coronary heart disease and Type A behaviors<br>Is anxiety one of the negative emotions that is related to risk for coronary heart disease in prospective research? | NR |
| **1986** | | |
| Ford, Kraiger, & Schechtman | Race effects and performance<br>Do objective and subjective criteria distinguish job performance of blacks and whites? | Differences were resolved through consensus or recalculation by three authors |

| | Theoretical Meta-Analytic Hypothesis Test | | | Novel Meta-Analytic Theoretical Hypothesis? (Type C) |
|---|---|---|---|---|
| Level of Inference | Variable | Reliability of Theoretical Variable | Construct Validity (Type B) | |
| Low | Aggregated study outcomes | NR | None of the theories accounted for the results obtained | No |
| High | The credibility of each placebo condition was rated on a scale from 1 to 7 | .88 for two raters by Spearman-Brown formula | Results were quite varied, but credibility ratings tended to be greater in studies that yielded higher placebo effect sizes | No |
| Low | Capacity for empathy in physical child abuse victims was evaluated in a group of studies | NR | Empathy levels among child abuse victims were, as hypothesized, low | No |
| High | Each type of verbal ability measure used in single studies was coded | .94 agreement by two raters | The ability to generate words was related to sex differences in performance on verbal tests | No |
| Low | Compared groups of studies that assessed romantic partners and pairs of male and female friends | NR | Moderate relationships between romantic partners and pairs of male, but not female, friends were observed for physical attractiveness ratings | No |
| Low | Analyzed results from a subset of studies that assessed anxiety | NR | Anxiety was a significant predictor of coronary heart disease | No |
| High | Categorization of job criteria as objective vs. subjective and as performance vs. absenteeism vs. cognitive | .91 for five categories | There were not significant race differences in objective performance indicators or in objective or subjective absenteeism, but blacks were rated lower than whites on subjective performance indicators and on objective and subjective cognitive criteria | No |

**Table 29.1** (continued)

| Author | Title (Paraphrased) and Topic | Reliability of Coding |
|---|---|---|
| Hull & Bond | Alcohol effects and expectancies on behavior<br>Do the effects, expectancies, or their interactions influence subjects social and nonsocial responses to alcohol? | NR |
| Eaton & Enns | Human sex differences in motor activity level<br>Do factors such as subject age, situation, type of measurement, or investigator characteristics influence estimates of sex differences in motor activity level? | NR |
| Powers | Practice effects and types of test items<br>Are test items with complex task directions more susceptible to coaching or test preparation than others? | NR |
| Shapiro & Penrod | Facial identification<br>Is the type of study—facial recognition vs. eyewitness identification—related to subjects' accuracies of target identification? | .96 for 23 randomly selected studies |
| Weiss, Weisz, & Bromfield | Information processing in mental retardation<br>Does extant evidence favor a developmental or a difference perspective in theoretical accounts of mental retardation? | NR |
| Falbo & Polit | Only children<br>Compares empirical studies that yield data bearing on three theories of only children | NR |
| Eagly & Crowley | Gender and helping behavior<br>One prediction from a social-role theory of gender and helping, that stereotypic sex differences in helping would be positively related to actual sex differences in helping behavior, was examined | .92–1.00 for one author's ratings of two other raters' classification of 25 studies |

| Theoretical Meta-Analytic Hypothesis Test | | | | Novel Meta-Analytic Theoretical Hypothesis? (Type C) |
|---|---|---|---|---|
| Level of Inference | Variable | Reliability of Theoretical Variable | Construct Validity (Type B) | |
| Low | Social behaviors were indexed by sexual arousal, aggression, and alcohol consumption; nonsocial behaviors were indexed by memory, internal sensations, mood, physiology, and performance | NR | Effects and expectancies of alcohol influenced subjects' responses; specific results depended on the response measures used | No |
| Low and high | Multiple measures for situation, type of measurement, and investigator characteristics were obtained | Range of Cohen's kappa for 12 measures, .44–.99 | Sex differences in motor activity level increased with age and tended to be higher in certain situations (e.g., when peers were present) such that males exceeded females | No |
| High | Complexity of directions and/or task was rated on a scale from 1 to 5 by reviewing individual tests | .67 for two independent raters | Test items with more complex directions and/or tasks were more likely to be influenced by coaching or practice than other items | No |
| Low | Studies were categorized according to whether their procedures used facial recognition or eyewitness identification | NR | Reliable differences in hits, false alarms, and $d'*$ depended on whether data were obtained in facial recognition or eyewitness identification studies | No |
| Low | Studies were grouped according to theoretically meaningful predictions derived from each perspective | NR | No single theory appears to explain the outcomes | No |
| Low | Five types of outcome data—achievement, adjustment, character, intelligence, and sociability—were examined | NR | The results were consistent with one of three theories, but not the other two | No |
| High | Stereotypic sex differences in helping were estimated by the standardized scores computed by subtracting the ratings (15-point scale) of 146 female undergraduates from those of 158 male undergraduates in response to specific examples of how likely it was that the average man or woman would render help in such situations | Reports 95% confidence intervals for undergraduates ratings | The magnitude of the undergraduates' stereotypic sex differences in ratings of helping behaviors were moderately related to actual sex difference effect sizes of helping behaviors in empirical studies | No |

**Table 29.1 (continued)**

| Author | Title (Paraphrased) and Topic | Reliability of Coding |
|---|---|---|
| Eagly & Steffen | Gender and aggression<br>One prediction derived from a social role theory is that the magnitude of sex differences in aggression are correlated with women's tendencies to perceive their own aggressive behaviors as more dangerous to themselves than do men | .85–1.00 for two raters |
| **1984** | | |
| Kulik, Bangert-Drowns, & Kulik | Coaching effectiveness for aptitude tests<br>Do coaching effects vary depending on the aptitude tests? | NR |
| Tanford & Penrod | Majority and minority social influence process<br>Three theories of the influence of target and source members were examined by using predictions derived from each model in relation to the empirical data. | NR |
| Hattie, Sharpley, & Rogers | Effectiveness of professionals and paraprofessionals<br>Among paraprofessionals, do variations in experience account for effectiveness of counselors? | Coding of study data was checked by two authors and errors were corrected |
| Watson & Clark | Negative affectivity<br>The authors theorize that negative affectivity constitutes a stable personality trait | NR |

NOTES: Studies using meta-analysis to aggregate outcomes that were published in the review section of *Psychological Bulletin* in 1990, 1988, 1986, and 1984 are listed in chronological order under the authors' names. As mentioned in the text, studies were considered to be meta-analyses if cumulations of effect sizes (i.e., $r$, $d$, or $z$) were reported in them. If any information on coding of the meta-analysis
*In signal detection, $d'$ refers to the ability to discriminate signal from noise.

## 6.1 Procedures for Comparative Meta-Analytic Theory Testing

Global comparative assessment of theories depends on a combination of factors. In addition to those named in section 3 in regard to theory preference or theory acceptance, one might include the extent to which theories provide differentiated predictions, the relative proportions of the theoretical propositions of each theory that are supported, and the relative scope of the circumstances under which each theory's supported hypotheses are found to "hold true". If all of the propositions of one theory fail to receive any support, whereas those of another receive partial or full support, there is little difficulty in reaching a conclusion about their comparative validity. Short of such clear-cut results, however, the problem becomes more difficult. Theories that generate more hypotheses (or, with number constant, more

| | | Theoretical Meta-Analytic Hypothesis Test | | Novel Meta-Analytic Theoretical Hypothesis? (Type C) |
|---|---|---|---|---|
| Level of Inference | Variable | Reliability of Theoretical Variable | Construct Validity (Type B) | |
| High | Standardized scores were computed by subtracting the ratings of 97 female from 103 male undergraduates, elicited by responding to a question concerning how much danger they would face if they enacted specific behaviors in certain situations | Reports 95% confidence intervals for undergraduates ratings | Results showed that sex differences in ratings of how much danger males and females would face if they aggressed exhibited one of the highest magnitude relationships with effect sizes in the hypothesized direction | No |
| Low | Studies coded as SAT vs. other aptitude tests | NR | Increases in SAT scores as a result of coaching were not as large as those for other aptitude tests (.15 vs. .51, respectively) | No |
| Low | Model parameters vs. Latane's social impact vs. social influence model vs. simple linear | NR | Support for social influence model was $R^2 = .62$, for social impact model, $R^2 = .59$, and for linear model, $R^2 = .52$ | No |
| Low | Paraprofessionals with experience (e.g., medical students, speech pathologists) vs. those without (e.g., volunteers, college students) | NR | More experienced para-professionals were significantly more effective (.75) than those who were less experienced (.21) | No |
| Low | Allows grouping multiple state and trait inventories as measures of the negative affectivity construct | NR | Reliability and validity data attest to theoretical existence of the negative affectivity construct | Yes |

variables were reported, the reliabilities are shown. The level of inference required for scoring the variable of theoretical interest was judged low or high. The variable of theoretical interest is described, and its reliability is specified if it was reported in the meta-analysis. The final two columns indicate whether it was categorized as Type B or C and its outcome. NR denotes not reported.

differentiated hypotheses) are more open to disconfirmation. How do we compare Theory A, for which its only two general propositions receive support, with Theory B, for which five of its eight major hypotheses receive support? Although the latter is inferior in terms of instances of failure to confirm (three), it is superior not only in its greater capacity for disconfirmation, but also in its absolute number of confirmations. In addition, when assessing disconfirmations, a distinction needs to

be made between failure to support the meta-analytic hypothesis versus an effect directionally opposite to that predicted. Clearly, the latter threatens the theory more than the former.

Since evidence suggests that variables created by having judges make inferential codings are useful for theoretical meta-analytic tests (e.g., Bowers & Clum 1988; Carlson, Charlin & Miller 1988; Miller & Carlson 1990; Miller, Lee, & Carlson 1991), the use of such codes might be extended to address some of these issues. For example, scientists who are independent of a particular research area might be asked to make judgments about competing theories. Theories could be rated with respect to their comparative number of propositions, their level of generality, the precision with which their propositions are stated, the number of distinct constructs that enter the theory, and so on. Such ratings could then be used to modify an assessment of the theories that is based solely on the extent to which hypotheses derived from each are meta-analytically confirmed.

Multicollinearity among the variables within and between competing theories also warrants consideration. To the degree that there is more multicollinearity among the variables of theory A than among those of theory B, if any single hypothesis of A receives support, the total number of supported hypotheses of A is also likely to be exaggerated. This suggests that in evaluating each of several theories, when testing the effect of any single variable of a theory, the effects of its other variables should be partialed out. A second suggestion, partialing out the effects of variables from other theories when testing those of any one theory, controls for differential conceptual overlap between theories. It will increase the meaningfulness of comparisons between the relative numbers of confirmations within all pairings of theories. The problems introduced by multicollinearity among variables in primary research (e.g., Cronbach 1987; Dunlap & Kemery 1987) no doubt apply to meta-analysis as well.

## 6.2 Meta-Analysis and the Psychology of Science

Those concerned with the psychology or history of science, but scientists as well, will want to examine comparisons among research laboratories, teams, or scientific programs. For instance, the number of meta-analytically confirmable findings produced by one laboratory (and its descendants) might be compared with that of another. It seems likely, however, that laboratory or program comparisons will be confounded not only with differences in preference for one or another methodological paradigm, but also with differences in theoretical allegiance (e.g., Miller & Davidson-Podgorny 1987).

Some critics of the positivist position (e.g., Lakatos 1972) argue that evaluation of theories requires judging them on the basis of their heuristic value, their programmatic impact, their historic context, and their sociocultural functions. It is difficult to imagine how meta-analysis might contribute to these goals. Presumably, however, even from this broader perspective, the relative degree of confirmation that is found for each theory's hypotheses would contribute to its evaluation. If one is interested in assessing the relative empirical confirmation of rival theories, however, confirmation bias is a problem. A variety of cognitive biases (e.g., Higgins, Herman, & Zanna 1981; Nisbett & Ross 1980) may contribute to the operation of confirmation bias in theory testing (Greenwald et al. 1986). Among these are expectancy effects (e.g., Harris 1991), which can influence the outcomes of experiments in the direction of confirming experimental hypotheses, thus leading to bias in tests of theory. Contemporary psychology may exaggerate the degree to which perceiver characteristics (e.g., expectancies) intrude in evaluations of external events (e.g., Funder 1987). Nevertheless, even a weak constructivist position suggests that in any substantive area the relative number or magnitude of confirmed hypothesis tests that support one theoretical camp over another may reflect instead the proportion of effects that each camp has contributed to the entire literature. Furthermore, confirmation bias is not likely to function as a constant error across different laboratories. The psychology of groups suggests that distinct laboratory ''cultures'' will develop, reflecting differences between them with respect to their norms about how research is conducted and reported. This will add to the murkiness of comparisons among laboratories. Finally, the bias of journal editors against reporting null results further undermines the meaningfulness of comparisons of the relative number of theoretical confirmations and failures between rival theoretical camps: Only the confirmations of each get published. A more informative comparison might examine the relative number of confirmations by scientists who are not members of the rival camps being compared. Relevant to these concerns, meta-analysis has been used to compare the relative numbers of confirmed hypotheses produced by primary researchers within and outside specific theoretical camps (e.g., Carlson & Miller 1987; Johnson & Eagly 1989, 1990).

Can meta-analysis be responsive to other new approaches in science such as those that are explicitly constructivist in their view of knowledge formation? For instance, McGuire (1989) advocates perspectivism—that for every theoretically derived hypothesis one should attempt to develop not only a theoretical account of it, but also an opposing account that suggests a contrary hypothesis. Perspectivism emphasizes a consideration of the explanations for the subsets of circumstances under which a hypothesis and its alternative receive support. Because meta-analysis is ideal for generating and testing comparisons within subsets of a research literature, it seems well suited to the goals of perspectivism.

### Authors' Note

We thank Dr. Mitchell Earleywine for his thoughtful comments on an earlier version of this chapter. This work was supported, in part, by National Science Foundation grant No. BNS-8719439 to Norman Miller and National Institute on Alcohol Abuse and Alcoholism grant No. K02AA0146 to Vicki Pollock.

## 7. REFERENCES

Allport, F. H. (1924). *Social psychology*. Boston: Houghton Mifflin.

Bandura, A. (1977). *Social learning theory*. Englewood Cliffs, NJ: Prentice-Hall.

Bass, B. M. (1949). An analysis of the leaderless group discussion. *Journal of Applied Psychology, 33*, 527–533.

Becker, B. J. (1992). Models of science achievement: Forces affecting male and female performance in school science. In T. D. Cook, H. Cooper, D. F. Cordray, H. Hartmann, L. V. Hedges, R. J. Light, T. A. Louis, & F. Mosteller, *Meta-analysis for explanation: A casebook*. New York: Russell Sage Foundation.

Bergmann, G. (1957). *Philosophy of science*. Madison: University of Wisconsin Press.

Berkowitz, L., & Donnerstein, E. I. (1982). External validity is more than skin deep: Some answers to criticisms of laboratory experiments. *American Psychologist, 37*, 245–257.

Blalock, H. M., Jr. (1969). *Theory construction: From verbal to mathematical formulations*. Englewood Cliffs, NJ: Prentice-Hall.

Blalock, H. M., Jr. (1989). *Power and conflict: Toward a general theory*. Newbury Park, CA: Sage.

Bobko, P. (1986). A solution to some dilemmas when testing hypotheses about ordinal interactions. *Journal of Applied Psychology, 71*, 323–326.

Bogen, J. E. (1975). Some educational aspects of hemispheric specialization. *UCLA Educator, 17*, 24–32.

Boster, F. J., & Mongeau, P. (1985). Fear-arousing persuasive messages. In R. N. Bostram (Ed.), *Communication yearbook* (Vol. 8, pp. 330–375). Beverley Hills, CA: Sage.

Bowers, T. G., & Clum, G. A. (1988). Relative contribution of specific and nonspecific treatment effects: A meta-analysis of placebo-controlled behavior therapy research. *Psychological Bulletin, 103*, 315–323.

Brehm, J. W. (1966). *A theory of psychological reactance*. New York: Academic Press.

Bushman, B. J., & Cooper, H. M. (1990). Effects of alcohol on human aggression: An integrative research review. *Psychological Bulletin, 107*, 341–354.

Bushman, B. J., Cooper, H. M., & Lemke, K. M. (1991). Meta-analysis of factor analyses: An illustration using the Buss-Durkey hostility inventory. *Personality and Social Psychology Bulletin, 17*, 344–349.

Cacioppo, J. T., & Tassinary, L. G. (1989). The concept of attitude: A psychophysiological analysis. In H. Wagner & A. Manstead (Eds.), *Handbook of psychophysiology: Emotion and social behavior*. Chichester, England: Wiley.

Campbell, D. T. (1978). Qualitative knowing and action research. In M. Brenner, P. Marsh, and M. Brenner (Eds.), *The social context of method*. London: Croom Helm.

Campbell, N. (1928). *Measurement and calculation*. New York: Cambridge University Press.

Carlson, M., Charlin, V., & Miller, N. (1988). Positive mood and helping behavior: A test of six hypotheses. *Journal of Personality and Social Psychology, 55*, 211–229.

Carlson, M., Marcus-Newhall, A., & Miller, N. (1989). Evidence for a general construct of aggression. *Personality and Social Psychology Bulletin, 15*, 377–389.

Carlson, M., Marcus-Newhall, A., & Miller, N. (1990). Effects of situational aggression cues: A quantitative review. *Journal of Personality and Social Psychology, 58*, 622–633.

Carlson, M., & Miller, N. (1987). Explanation of the relation between negative mood and helping. *Psychological Bulletin, 102*, 91–108.

Casti, J. L. (1989). *Paradigms lost: Images of man in the mirror of science*. New York: Morrow.

Cialdini, R. B., Baumann, D. J., & Kenrick, D. T. (1981). Insights from sadness: A three-step model of the development of altruism as hedonism. *Developmental Review, 1*, 207–223.

Cohen, J. (1988). *Statistical power analysis for the behavioral sciences* (2nd ed.). Hillsdale, NJ: Erlbaum.

Cook, T. D., & Campbell, D. T. (1979). *Quasi-experimentation: Design and analysis issues for field settings*. Chicago: Rand McNally.

Cook, T. D., Cooper, H., Cordray, D. F., Hartman, H., Hedges, L. V., Light, R. J., Louis, T. A., & Mosteller,

F. (1992). *Meta-analysis for explanation: A casebook.* New York: Russell Sage Foundation.

Cooper, H. M. (1990). On the social psychology of using research reviews. In K. W. Wachter and M. L. Straf (Eds.), *The future of meta-analyses.* New York: Russell Sage Foundation.

Cronbach, L. J. (1955). Processes affecting scores on "understanding of others" and "assumed similarity." *Psychological Bulletin, 52,* 177–193.

Cronbach, L. J. (1975). Beyond the two disciplines of scientific psychology. *American Psychologist, 12,* 116–127.

Cronbach, L. J. (1982). Prudent aspirations for social inquiry. In W. Kruskal (Ed.), *The social sciences: Their nature and uses.* Chicago: Chicago University Press.

Cronbach, L. J. (1987). Statistical tests for moderator variables: Flaws in analyses recently proposed. *Psychological Bulletin, 102,* 414–417.

Demming, W. E. (1975). The logic of evaluation. In E. L. Struening and M. Guttentag (Eds.), *Handbook of evaluation research.* Beverly Hills, CA: Sage.

Dillard, J. P. (1991). The current status of research on sequential-request compliance techniques. *Personality and Social Psychology Bulletin, 17,* 283–288.

Dollard, J., & Miller, N. (1950). *Personality and psychotherapy.* New York: McGraw-Hill.

Driskell, J. E., & Mullen, B. (1990). Status, expectations, and behavior: A meta-analytic review and test of the theory. *Personality and Social Psychology Bulletin, 16,* 541–553.

Duhem, P. (1962). *The aim and structure of physical theory.* New York: Atheneum. (Original work published 1908)

Dunlap, W. P., & Kemery, E. R. (1987). Failure to detect moderating effects: Is multicollinearity the problem? *Psychological Bulletin, 102,* 418–420.

Eagly, A. H., & Carli, L. L. (1981). Sex of researchers and sex-typed communications as determinants of sex differences in influenceability: A meta-analysis of social influence studies. *Psychological Bulletin, 90,* 1–20.

Eagly, A. H., & Steffen, V. J. (1986). Gender and aggressive behavior: A meta-analytic review of the social psychological literature. *Psychological Bulletin, 100,* 308–330.

Erdelyi, M. H. (1990). Repression, reconstruction and defense: History and integration of the psychoanalytic and experimental frameworks. In J. L. Singer (Ed.), *Repression and dissociation: Implications for personality theory, psychopathology, and health.* Chicago: University of Chicago Press.

Eriksen, C., & Pierce, J. (1968). Defense mechanisms. In E. Borgatta and W. Lambert (Eds.), *Handbook of personality theory and research.* Chicago: Rand McNally.

Festinger, L. (1957). *A theory of cognitive dissonance.* Stanford, CA: Stanford University Press.

Flynn, J. R. (1984). The mean IQ of Americans: Massive gains 1932 to 1978. *Psychological Bulletin, 95,* 29–51.

Foucault, M. (1972). *The archaeology of knowledge.* London: Tavistock.

Freud, S. (1915). The unconscious. In J. Strachey (Ed. and Trans.), *The standard edition of the complete psychological works of Sigmund Freud* (Vol. 14). London: Hogarth Press and Institute of Psycho-analysis.

Funder, D. C. (1987). Errors and mistakes: Evaluating the accuracy of social judgment. *Psychological Bulletin, 101,* 75–90.

Gaertner, S. L., Dovidio, J. F., Mann, J. A., Murrell, A. J., & Pomare, M. (1990). How does cooperation reduce intergroup bias? *Journal of Personality and Social Psychology, 59,* 692–704.

Geertz, C. (1973). *The interpretation of cultures.* New York: Basic Books.

Gergen, K. (1982). *Toward transformation in social knowledge.* New York: Springer-Verlag.

Giroux, H. (1981). *Ideology, culture, and the process of schooling.* Philadelphia: Temple University Press.

Greenwald, A. G., Pratkanis, A. R., Leippe, M. R., & Baumgardner, M. H. (1986). Under what conditions does theory obstruct research progress? *Psychological Review, 93,* 216–229.

Halfpenny, P. (1982). *Positivism and sociology.* London: Allen & Unwin.

Hall, J. A., & Rosenthal, R. (1992). Testing for moderator variables in meta-analysis: Issues and methods. *Communication Monographs, 58,* 437–462.

Harré, R., & Secord, P. (1977). *The explanation of social behavior.* Totowa, NJ: Littlefield.

Harris, M. J. (1991). Controversy and cumulation: Meta-analysis and research on interpersonal expectancy effects. *Personality and Social Psychology Bulletin, 17,* 316–322.

Hedges, L. V. (1987). How hard is hard science, how soft is soft science? The empirical cumulativeness of research. *American Psychologist, 42,* 443–455.

Hempel, C. (1952). *Fundamentals of concept formation in empirical science.* Chicago: University of Chicago Press.

Higgins, E. T., Herman, C. P., & Zanna, M. P. (1981). *The Ontario symposium.* Hillsdale, NJ: Erlbaum.

Hull, J. G., & Bond, C. F. (1986). Social and behavioral consequences of alcohol consumption and expectancy: A meta-analysis. *Psychological Bulletin, 99,* 347–360.

Hull, J. G., Tedlie, J. C., & Lehn, D. A. (1992). Moderator variables in personality research: The problem of controlling for plausible alternatives. *Personality and Social Psychology Bulletin, 18,* 115–117.

Janis, I. L., & Feshbach, S. (1953). Effects of fear-arousing communications. *Journal of Abnormal and Social Psychology, 48,* 78–92.

Johnson, B. T. (1991). Insights about attitudes: Meta-analytic perspectives. *Personality and Social Psychology Bulletin, 17,* 289–299.

Johnson, B. T., & Eagly, A. H. (1989). Effects of involvement on persuasion: A meta-analysis. *Psychological Bulletin, 104,* 290–314.

Johnson, B. T., & Eagly, A. H. (1990). Involvement and persuasion: Types, traditions, and the evidence. *Psychological Bulletin, 107,* 375–384.

Johnson, D. W., Johnson, R., & Maruyama, G. (1984). Goal interdependence and interpersonal attraction in heterogeneous classrooms: A meta-analysis. In N. Miller and M. B. Brewer (Eds.), *Groups in contact: The psychology of desegregation.* Orlando, FL: Academic Press.

Judd, C. M., & Kenny, D. A. (1981). *Estimating the effects of social interventions.* New York: Cambridge University Press.

Jussim, L. (1991). Social perception and social reality: A reflection-construction model. *Psychological Review, 98,* 54–73.

Kaplan, A. (1964). The conduct of inquiry. San Francisco: Chandler.

Lakatos, I. (1972). Falsification and the methodology of scientific research programs. In I. Lakatos and A. Musgrave (Eds.), *Criticism and the growth of knowledge* (pp. 91–196). Cambridge: Cambridge University Press.

Leventhal, H. (1970). Findings and theory in the study of fear communications. In L. Berkowitz (Ed.), *Advances in experimental social psychology* (Vol. 5, pp. 119–186). Orlando, FL: Academic Press.

Lewin, K. (1951). Formalization and progress in psychology. In D. Cartwright (Ed.), *Field theory in social science* (pp. 1–29). New York: Harper.

Lipsey, M. (1992a). Juvenile delinquency treatment: A meta-analytic inquiry in the variability of effects. In T. D. Cook, H. Cooper, D. F. Cordray, H. Hartmann, L. V. Hedges, R. J. Light, T. A. Louis, and F. Mosteller, *Meta-analysis for explanation: A casebook.* New York: Russell Sage Foundation.

Lipsey, M. (1992b). Meta-analysis in evaluation and research: Moving from description to explanation. In H. T. Chang (Ed.), *Theory driven evaluations for analyzing and developing programs and policies.* Westport, CT: Greenwood Press.

Maruyama, G. (1991). Meta-analyses relating goal structures to achievement: Findings, controversies, and impacts. *Personality and Social Psychology Bulletin, 17,* 300–305.

Marx, M. H. (1970). *Theories in contemporary psychology* (3rd ed.). New York: McGraw-Hill.

Marx, M. H., & Hillix, W. A. (1963). *Systems and theories in psychology.* New York: McGraw-Hill.

Matthews, K. A. (1988. Coronary heart disease and Type A behaviors: Update on and alternative to the Booth-Kewley and Friedman (1987) quantitative review. *Psychological Bulletin, 104,* 373–380.

McGuire, W. J. (1968). Personality and susceptibility to social influence. In E. F. Borgotta & W. W. Lambert (Eds.), *Handbook of personality theory and research.* Skokie, IL: Rand McNally.

McGuire, W. J. (1983). A contextualist theory of knowledge: Its implications for innovation and reform in psychological research. In L. Berkowitz (Ed.), *Advances in experimental social psychology* (Vol. 16, pp. 1–47). New York: Academic Press.

McGuire, W. J. (1985). Attitudes and attitude change. In G. Lindzey and E. Aronson (Eds.), *Handbook of social psychology* (Vol. 2, 3rd ed.). New York: Random House.

McGuire, W. J. (1989). A perspectivist approach to the strategic planning of programmatic scientific research. In B. Gholson, W. R. Shadish, Jr., R. A. Neimeyer, and A. C. Houts (Eds.), *Psychology of science: Contributions to meta-science* (pp. 214–245). Cambridge: Cambridge University Press.

Merton, R. K. (1949). *Social theory and social structure.* New York: Free Press.

Milgram, S. (1963). Behavioral study of obedience. *Journal of Abnormal and Social Psychology, 67,* 376.

Mill, J. S. (1874). *A system of logic, ratiocinative and inductive: Being a connected view of the principles of evidence and the methods of scientific investigation.* New York: Harper.

Miller, N., & Carlson, M. (1990). Valid theory-testing meta-analyses further question the negative state relief model of helping. *Psychological Bulletin, 107,* 215–225.

Miller, N., & Davidson-Podgorny, G. (1987). Theoretical models of intergroup relations and the use of cooperative teams as an intervention for desegregated settings. In C. Hendrick (Ed.), *Group processes and intergroup relations.* Newbury Park, CA: Sage.

Miller, N., Lee, J. Y., & Carlson, M. (1991). The validity of inferential judgments when used in theory-testing meta-analysis. *Personality and Social Psychology Bulletin, 17,* 335–343.

Miller, N., & Pollock, V. E. (in press). Meta-analysis and some science-compromising problems of social psychology. In W. Shadish (Ed.), *The social psychology of science.* New York: Oxford University Press.

Morris, J. H., Sherman, J. D., & Mansfield, E. R. (1986). Failure to detect moderating effects with ordinary least squares-moderated multiple regression: Some reasons and a remedy. *Psychological Bulletin, 99,* 282–288.

Mullen, B., Brown, R. J., & Smith, C. (1992). Ingroup bias as a function of salience, relevance, and status: An integration. *European Journal of Social Psychology, 22,* 103–122.

Mullen, B., Cooper, C., & Driskell, J. E. (1990). Jaywalking as a function of model behavior. *Personality and Social Psychology Bulletin, 16,* 320–330.

Nisbett, R. E., & Ross, L. (1980). *Human inference: Strategies and shortcomings of social judgment.* Englewood Cliffs, NJ: Prentice-Hall.

Parker, I., & Shotter, J. (1990). *Deconstructing social psychology.* London: Routledge.

Petty, R. E., & Cacioppo, J. T. (1990). Involvement and persuasion: Tradition versus integration. *Psychological Bulletin, 107,* 367–374.

Phillips, D. C. (1987). *Philosophy, science, and social inquiry.* New York: Pergamon Press.

Popper, K. (1959). *The logic of scientific discovery.* New York: Basic Books.

Popper, K. (1974). Autobiography. In P. A. Schlipp (Ed.), *The philosophy of Karl Popper.* La Salle, IL: Open Court.

Popper, K. (1976). *Unended quest.* La Salle, IL: Open Court.

Premack, S. L., & Hunter, J. E. (1988). Individual unionization decisions. *Psychological Bulletin, 103,* 223–234.

Quine, W. V. (1953). *From a logical point of view.* Cambridge, MA: Harvard University Press.

Raudenbush, S. W. (1984). Magnitude of teacher expectancy effects on pupil IQ as a function of the credibility of expectancy induction: A synthesis of findings from 18 experiments. *Journal of Educational Psychology, 76,* 85–97.

Raz, S., & Raz, N. (1990). Structural brain abnormalities in the major psychoses: A quantitative review of the evidence from computerized imaging. *Psychological Bulletin, 103,* 93–108.

Rohrlich, F. (1987). *From paradox to reality.* Cambridge: Cambridge University Press.

Rosenthal, R. (1991). Cumulating psychology: An appreciation of Donald T. Campbell. *Psychological Science, 2,* 213, 217–221.

Ross, L. D. (1977). The intuitive psychologist and his shortcomings: Distortions in the attribution process. In L. Berkowitz (Ed.), *Advances in experimental social psychology* (Vol. 10., pp. 173–220). New York: Academic Press.

Rossi, P. H. (1971). Evaluating social action programs. In F. G. Caro (Ed.), *Readings in evaluation research.* New York: Russell Sage Foundation.

Sackett, P. R., Harris, M. M., & Orr, J. M. (1986). On seeking moderator variables in the meta-analysis of correlational data: A Monte Carlo investigation of statistical power and resistance to Type I error. *Journal of Applied Psychology, 71,* 302–310.

Sanna, L. J. (1992). Self-efficacy theory: Implications for social facilitation and social loafing. *Journal of Personality and Social Psychology, 62,* 774–786.

Scher, S. J., & Cooper, J. (1989). Motivational basis of dissonance: The singular role of behavioral consequences. *Journal of Personality and Social Psychology, 56,* 899–906.

Shadish, W. R. (1992). Do family and marital psychotherapies change what people do? A meta-analysis of behavioral outcomes. In T. D. Cook, H. Cooper, D. F. Cordray, H. Hartmann, L. V. Hedges, R. J. Light, T. A. Louis, & F. Mosteller, *Meta-analysis for explanation: A casebook.* New York: Russell Sage Foundation.

Simon, H. A. (1992). What is an ''explanation'' of behavior? *Psychological Science, 3,* 150–161.

Steele, C. M. (1988). The psychology of self-affirmation: Sustaining the integrity of the self. In L. Berkowitz (Ed.), *Advances in experimental social psychology* (Vol. 21, pp. 261–302). New York: Academic Press.

Steele, C. M., & Southwick, L. (1985). Alcohol and social behavior: The psychology of drunken excess. *Journal of Personality and Social Psychology, 48,* 18–35.

Steinberg, K. K., Thacker, S. B., Smith, J., Stroup, D. F., Zack, M. M., Flanders, D., & Berkelman, R. L. (1991). A meta-analysis of the effect of estrogen replacement therapy on the risk of breast cancer. *Journal of the American Medical Association 265,* 1985–1990.

Sternberg, R. (1987). Liking vs. loving: A comparative evaluation of theories. *Psychological Bulletin, 102,* 331–345.

Sullivan, H. S. (1956). *Clinical studies in psychiatry.* New York: Norton.

Tedeschi, J. T. (1983). Social influence theory and aggression. In R. T. Geen and E. I. Donnerstein (Eds.), *Aggression: Theoretical and empirical reviews* (pp. 135–162). Orlando, FL: Academic Press.

Tedeschi, J. T., Smith, R. B., & Brown, R. C. (1974). A reinterpretation of research on aggression. *Psychological Bulletin, 81*, 540–562.

Teitelbaum, P., & Pellis, S. M. (1992). Toward a synthetic physiological psychology. *Psychological Science, 3*, 4–20.

Watson, D., & Clark, L. A. (1984). Negative affectivity: The disposition to experience aversive emotional states. *Psychological Bulletin, 96*, 465–490.

Winch, P. (1967). *The idea of a social science*. London: Routledge.

Cooper, H., and Hedges, L. V. (Eds.) 1994. *The Handbook of Research Synthesis.* New York: Russell Sage Foundation

# 30

# USING RESEARCH SYNTHESES TO PLAN FUTURE RESEARCH

**ALICE H. EAGLY**
*Purdue University*

**WENDY WOOD**
*Texas A&M University*

CONTENTS

## 1. INTRODUCTION

A quantitative synthesis of research is typically not an endpoint or final step in the investigation of a research topic. A formal synthesis rarely offers an integration that is conclusive enough to answer a question decisively. Instead, a meta-analysis more commonly serves as a way station along a sometimes winding route to answering a particular question.

Of course, a systematic integration of research findings cannot be accomplished at the beginning stage of a field's investigation and must await a body of studies addressing a hypothesis. However, research syntheses can contribute importantly at both middle and later stages of investigation. By indicating the weaknesses as well as the strengths of the existing research, a synthesis can channel future primary research in those directions that would most effectively improve the quality of empirical evidence and the adequacy of theoretical understanding. The new primary research may eventually be followed by another meta-analysis, in an interactive cycle of research and integration that develops increasingly adequate answers to research questions.

The potential for interaction between primary research and research synthesis can best be appreciated if the two forms of investigation are viewed as means for attaining a common set of goals: (a) ascertaining empirical relations among variables and (b) developing, testing, and refining theoretical explanations for these relations. With respect to establishing empirical relations, both forms of investigation seek to determine the presence and magnitude of effects. In primary research, empirical relations are examined by means of experiments, quasi-experiments, and correlational studies. Meta-analyses aggregate the findings of such efforts and thereby provide broader descriptions than a primary study can of the magnitude of an effect and its patterning across various conditions. Yet the objective of research is not typically limited to describing an effect, but includes displaying the processes that underlie it. Just as testing theories about processes lends primary research its complexity and richness, meta-analyses can also be designed to examine the plausibility of theories (see Chapter 29 and Eagly & Wood 1991).

The purpose of this chapter is to delineate the range of possible relations between research syntheses and subsequent primary research. This discussion should help investigators understand the ways in which a synthesis can provide guidance for future research. In general, scientists' perception that additional research should be carried out subsequent to a research synthesis is affected by the level of certainty that they attach to the summary's conclusions. Certainty refers to the confidence with which the scientific community accepts conclusions or the truth value they accord to them. Certainty pertains to claims about empirical relations between variables as well as to claims about theoretical explanations of these empirical relations.

For purposes of discussing the relation between meta-analyses and subsequent research, the term "certainty" is useful and has advantages over related concepts, such as "bias" or "validity," which represent the truth value of aspects of particular studies. Assessing validity in a meta-analysis is a many-sided issue; internal and external invalidity can arise from a variety of sources at the level of the underlying studies as well as at the meta-analytic, aggregative level (see Chapter 31). In general, invalidity reduces scientists' certainty about the conclusions of meta-analyses and as a consequence fosters the need for additional research. As this statement implies, the relation between invalidity and additional research is mediated by scientists' uncertainty about synthesis conclusions. Unless investigators recognize various types of invalidity and allow them to produce uncertainty, they are unlikely to proceed to additional research. In this chapter, we alert investigators to some of the meta-analytic outcomes that should influence their certainty and therefore should have implications for subsequent primary research.

Conclusions in research syntheses range from those that should be accepted with high certainty by the scientific community to those that are highly tentative and should be held with very little certainty. Although syntheses may produce conclusions of such high certainty that no further research is warranted, more often syntheses identify the issues remaining to be addressed through primary research or through new syntheses. Conclusions of extremely low certainty should emerge from research syntheses as mere suggestions or hypotheses that require additional research in order to be accepted. Between these extremes are conclusions of moderate levels of certainty that point to the need for more or less additional research.

Like the findings of primary research, results of a research synthesis require critical interpretation. The most profitable strategy to pursue in subsequent research depends on *where* the uncertainty lies in meta-analytic findings. Certainty is not attached to a whole synthesis, but rather varies with respect to the likely truth value of specific conclusions. Because a meta-analysis generally produces numerous empirical findings and various conclusions regarding the meaning of these findings, threats to validity can lower certainty with respect to any of these findings and conclusions. In particular, uncertainty may stem from lack of uniformity of the examined effect across the available studies. In such a case, a meta-analysis may not demonstrate conclusively the magnitude or even the direction of a relation between variables. Even when an effect is shown to be quite stable among the synthesized studies, uncertainty may emerge in the generalizability of the relation to other settings, subject populations, and research operations. Finally, even with well-established effects whose generalizability has been demonstrated, uncertainty can arise in the explanation for the findings. Linked to such explanatory uncertainty may be the presence of third variables that moderate main-effect findings or that serve as mediators of these effects. We consider the most promising research strategies to clarify the ambiguities represented by these several sources of uncertainty.

Although research syntheses can facilitate the development of understanding in a research area by channeling subsequent research to resolve the uncertainties that emerge, the impact of syntheses has not been uniformly beneficial. They have sometimes distorted understanding of a phenomenon and discouraged subsequent research efforts. In the last section of this chapter we discuss how meta-analyses can impede the development of knowledge by providing a false sense of certainty that an effect is already well established or well understood.

## 2. HIGH CERTAINTY IN EMPIRICAL RELATIONS: HOMOGENEOUS OUTCOMES AND WELL-SPECIFIED PREDICTIVE MODELS

An elegantly simple meta-analytic outcome that suggests high certainty in empirical relations occurs when the relation between two variables has proven to be consistent across many studies. Such an outcome allows a good estimate of the magnitude of the relation, regardless of whether that magnitude is large, small, or even null. The synthesizer would have assessed the consistency of the findings by computing one of the homogeneity tests of meta-analytic statistics (see Chapter 18). Failure to reject the hypothesis of homogeneity suggests that study findings represent a common population effect size. This high level of certainty requires that the test of homogeneity was based on a large enough body of studies to provide a statistically powerful test. Moreover, these studies should represent a range of the

conditions under which the empirical relation should obtain (e.g., different laboratories, different subject populations, different measuring instruments). With high-certainty findings, additional primary studies that replicate the synthesized studies are unnecessary because they are unlikely to yield any increment in understanding. However, as we discuss later in this chapter, even with an unambiguous demonstration of an empirical relation between variables, considerable uncertainty may be associated with the correct explanation of the relation.

### 2.1 Discrepant Findings

A slightly more complex meta-analytic outcome consisting of homogeneity after the removal of only a very small number of outlying effect sizes can also yield empirical relations that warrant high certainty. In such a situation, findings would be homogeneous, except for a few studies that produced aberrant results. Given the vagaries of human efforts in science, a very small number of discrepant outcomes should not necessarily shake one's confidence that research findings are generally consistent across studies (see Hedges 1987). Sometimes the reasons for aberrant findings cannot be discerned by synthesists and might consist, for example, of malfunctioning recording devices or misanalyzed or falsified data. Other deviant findings are easier to explain. For example, Becker and Hedges (1984) identified one study included in a synthesis of sex differences in verbal ability that had provided a standard deviation based on group means rather than individual scores. Because prior synthesists had computed an effect size based on this unusually small standard deviation, it was quite discrepant from others in the data set. In general, findings that are homogeneous except for a few outlying effect sizes also suggest that further research in the same paradigm would be redundant, especially if the causes of the discrepant findings are discernible.

A more common outcome of meta-analytic efforts is that the effect sizes included in a synthesis prove to be heterogeneous, and homogeneity is not established by removal of relatively few outlying effect sizes. In other words, studies have produced discrepant outcomes when testing the hypothesis. It is usually not appropriate merely to combine such effect sizes into a single estimate of the effect. Instead, characteristics of the studies in the sample should be evaluated to determine whether they moderate (or covary with) the effect of interest. When the systematic variability in the study findings can be satisfactorily explained merely by examining a third variable, the synthesis can still be said to have established relatively high certainty concerning the empirical relation. There would still be little need for additional research of the same kind as that included in the synthesis.

Clear outcomes of the types we have discussed were obtained in a meta-analysis by Thomas and French (1985) on sex differences in children's and adolescents' performance on various types of motor tasks. Sex differences were confirmed in their synthesis by homogeneous sets of effect sizes for some tasks (e.g., agility, flexibility, fine eye-motor coordination, throw accuracy). Yet for a number of other tasks (e.g., balance, catching, grip strength), effect sizes were inconsistent across the studies. However, moderator analyses using third variables were able to predict the effect sizes successfully. For most of these motor tasks, only one variable, subjects' age, was needed to produce a well-specified model that accounted for the variability in the effect sizes. In these cases, sex differences became larger at older ages, a nonsurprising finding. These highly certain empirical relations suggest that subsequent research examining the effects of sex on these tests of motor performance at varying age levels in similar subject populations would be unlikely to be very informative. However, as we discuss subsequently, uncertainty about Thomas and French's conclusions may arise from questions about the generalizability of these empirical relations and their correct explanation.

## 2.2 Implications for Interpreting the Magnitude of Effects

Although these relatively clear meta-analytic outcomes suggest little need for additional research of the same kind as that reviewed, they have a variety of implications for future research. The aggregated effect can provide important guidance for judging the magnitude of effects in subsequent primary studies or in meta-analyses addressing related hypotheses (Cordray & Orwin 1983). Meta-analytic findings thereby provide a context for interpreting the results of subsequent investigations by revealing whether effects obtained are smaller, typical, or larger than those that were obtained in the area in the past. For example, magnitude estimates from earlier syntheses of sex differences in social behavior (see Eagly 1987; Hall 1984) have proved very helpful in interpreting the size of sex differences displayed by subsequent meta-analyses (e.g., Eagly & Johnson 1990). Magnitude estimates can also be used to calculate power

analyses for primary data collection in the area (Cohen 1988). Once the expected effect size is known, power calculations can identify with some precision the necessary sample size to achieve statistical significance in future research using similar operations or subject samples.

## 3. THE GENERALIZABILITY OF FINDINGS OF SYNTHESES TO NEW POPULATIONS, SETTINGS, AND RESEARCH OPERATIONS

Even when a meta-analysis produces an empirical relation that is well established, high certainty should be attached to it only within the limits of the covered literature. The generalizability of the effect can be uncertain if the included primary studies share a limitation of their design, execution, or reporting. Serious limitations in the sample of studies available to a synthesist are often present and are revealed especially clearly when the attributes of the reviewed studies are presented in tables or arrayed in a systematic manner (see Chapter 28). It is important that synthesists bring this aspect of the research literature to readers' attention through such displays and discussion of their implications. Given major sample limitations, the external and construct validity of the empirical relations demonstrated by the synthesis may be compromised.

External validity refers to the generalizability of an effect to other groups of people or other settings (Cook & Campbell 1979). Meta-analyses are likely to possess poor external validity when the included studies all use the same limited subject population (e.g., undergraduate students) or are all conducted in a single setting (e.g., experimental laboratories). Construct validity refers to the validity with which generalizations can be made about higher-order constructs on the basis of research operations (Cook & Campbell 1979). Because it is rare that any one method of operationalizing a variable completely captures the meaning of the intended hypothetical concept, syntheses generally possess poor construct validity when most or all studies that are included used a particular measurement technique or a particular method of operationalizing an independent variable. The resulting meta-analytic findings may be distorted by some bias associated with this operationalization.

When uncertainty in meta-analytic conclusions arises from overrepresentation of certain types of studies in the covered literature, subsequent primary research can increase external validity by filling the gaps that have been revealed. Subsequent primary research might examine, for example, whether the effect extends to underinvestigated populations of subjects and research settings. This approach is illustrated by meta-analytic syntheses of the outcome of psychotherapy with children (Casey & Berman 1985; Weisz et al. 1987). Although positive effects of treatment have been demonstrated in these syntheses, the included studies generally examined controlled use of therapeutic techniques with (a) therapists well trained in the approach and (b) youngsters recruited specifically for the research study. Subsequent follow-up research to examine therapy outcomes in more naturalistic contexts with children actually seeking therapy yielded weaker effects of treatments, and this outcome has prompted a reevaluation of the conditions under which therapy is effective with children (Weisz & Weiss 1989).

Another example of sample limitations that lower the external validity of meta-analytic conclusions is provided by Thomas and French's synthesis of studies examining sex differences in motor performance (1985), which we noted earlier as an example of particularly well-established empirical relations. Nonetheless, the participants in these studies were young and predominantly white and middle class. Because the generalizability of the findings to other subject populations was not established (e.g., to adults, blacks, people of lower socioeconomic status), general conclusions about sex differences in motor performance should not be drawn from this meta-analysis with a very high level of certainty. Future research might therefore be directed to the understudied populations of subjects.

Subsequent research can address threats to construct validity by establishing that the effect occurs with new or underinvestigated methods of operationalizing the conceptual variables. For example, the beneficial outcome of a particular medical treatment might be established only with certain indicators, as was the case with beta-blockade drug treatment of myocardial infarction. Initial meta-analyses established the beneficial effects of drug therapy on some short-term outcomes (e.g., limitation of infarct size and reduction in ventricular arrhythmias) as well as a reduction in mortality with long-term treatment (Stampfer et al. 1982; Yusuf et al. 1985). However, strong construct validity requires that the treatment yield comparable gains on other outcome measures, such as short-term mortality rates. To examine this particular outcome, a series of randomized clinical trials was conducted with thousands of patients with suspected myocardial infarction, and short-term survival benefits were successfully demonstrated (International

Study of Infarct Survival 1986, 1988, 1990; Gruppo Italiano 1986). This new research on short-term survival thus increased the construct validity of researchers' general conclusion about the beneficial effect of the treatment.

Another instance of meta-analyses yielding conclusions of potentially low construct validity occurred with syntheses comparing men's and women's self-reports of emotional experience. Women were found to report more extreme emotions than men, including greater happiness and life satisfaction (Wood, Rhodes & Whelan 1989) as well as greater depression (Nolen-Hoeksema 1987). Because this research literature has relied exclusively on self-report ratings, it is unclear whether sex differences obtain in intensity of the underlying emotional response, in willingness to report intense emotions, or in use of the emotion rating scales. Subsequent primary research was designed to reduce uncertainty in the interpretation of the meta-analytic syntheses by examining sex differences with respect to multiple components of emotional intensity (Grossman & Wood in press). Suggesting that the self-report measures reflect intensity of underlying experience is the finding that women responded more extremely than men on physiological indicators of emotion as well as on self-reports. In this instance, subsequent research addressed the uncertainty in conceptual interpretation of the meta-analytic findings by establishing that sex differences are obtained across multiple operations of emotional experience.

## 4. MODERATORS OF MAIN-EFFECT FINDINGS

When the effect sizes integrated in a synthesis prove to be heterogeneous, characteristics of the studies in the sample can be treated as moderators of the main-effect findings. Uncertainty emerges in the empirical effects of moderator variables when the moderator or set of moderators cannot account adequately for the discrepancies between study findings or when the moderating variables are identified post hoc. We also consider the uncertainty in theoretical explanation that arises when the correct interpretation for a moderator is unclear, despite the fact that the moderator effect may be well established empirically.

### 4.1 Unexplained Variability in Study Findings and Moderators Identified Post Hoc

Significant heterogeneity in study outcomes that a synthesist cannot account for through moderator analyses suggests that the effect varies with features of the included studies that have not been identified. Unexplained discrepancies between findings threaten the construct validity of such a review's main-effect conclusion because it is unclear whether the various research operations represent a common underlying construct. Heterogeneity may also threaten statistical conclusion validity, or how accurately investigators can conclude that two variables are related (Cook & Campbell 1979). Unresolved inconsistencies between studies thus compromise the ability to detect true relations among variables. In such cases, meta-analytic findings and the conceptual interpretations for the findings should be accorded relatively low certainty.

Synthesists faced with unexplained discrepancies in effect sizes might explore an inductive approach by identifying predictors from the study outcomes themselves. For example, Hedges and Olkin (1985) suggested clustering effect sizes of similar magnitude and then evaluating the clusters of outcomes for study characteristics that might covary with the groupings. Because predictors identified post hoc present interpretational ambiguities (see subsequent discussion), the characteristics identified by this procedure are especially appropriate candidates for direct manipulation in subsequent primary research.

When substantial variability in effect sizes remains unexplained even after invoking such inductive procedures, investigators face a problematic situation. Under such circumstances, there may be few guides for how to proceed in subsequent primary research. Because such a meta-analysis demonstrates that the phenomenon in question is poorly understood, the synthesist might well caution researchers that more studies of the phenomenon would probably be unproductive unless accompanied by fresh ideas about the conditions that moderate it. Although lack of success in accounting for variability might be a disappointing outcome for a synthesist, publication of such a synthesis could inspire thoughtful analyses that yield new theories that explain discrepant study outcomes. New theories may generate novel predictors that successfully account for heterogeneity in study outcomes.

The extent to which existing research syntheses have produced main-effect findings accompanied by unexplained variability in the underlying effect sizes is largely unknown because many syntheses have not reported homogeneity statistics that evaluated the variability of the findings they included. Nor have they reported the tests of model specification for regression models or of homogeneity within categories for categorical models. These tests assess the success of the predictive models in accounting for variability in effect sizes. Often these techniques were not available or samples of studies were too small to apply such techniques meaningfully. Nonetheless, we suspect that it is rare that syntheses have been highly unsuccessful in accounting for variability in findings. By the time a body of studies is available for integration, research and theorizing have usually progressed to the point of identifying at least some of the predictors of the effect under investigation. Yet it may often be the case that variability in findings from subsets of studies within a reviewed literature cannot be accounted for adequately, and thus a phenomenon is not completely understood. For example, a synthesis of psychological techniques that prepare patients for medical procedures and pain yielded clear benefits to techniques that included both sensory information telling patients what they would feel and procedural information telling them what would happen, compared with conditions in which patients received no preparation (Suls & Wan 1989). To aid in interpreting this effect, the impact of procedures that provided only sensory information and those that provided only procedural information was compared. Although sensory information proved superior in alleviating patients' perceived pain, substantial heterogeneity was obtained in these comparisons. Therefore, it would probably not be productive to pursue similar comparisons of sensory and procedural treatments in the absence of new insight into factors controlling the effect.

Uncertainty in empirical relations also arises when moderator analyses are conducted in the absence of an adequate theoretical rationale. In meta-analytic syntheses as in primary research, analysis strategies can be derived from theoretically grounded, a priori decisions or can represent post hoc accounts of the pattern of findings obtained in the data set. Of course, the distinction between a priori predictions and post hoc accounts of serendipitous relations is often not sharp in practice, either because investigators intentionally portray post hoc findings as a priori or because they have theoretical frameworks that are flexible enough to encompass a wide range of obtained relations. Nonetheless, because moderator analyses not derived from theory can be unduly influenced by chance data patterns, statistical conclusion validity is threatened. Even though meta-analytic statistical techniques have been developed to adjust for the fact that post hoc tests capitalize on chance variability in the data (e.g., post hoc comparisons;

Hedges & Olkin 1985), less certainty should be accorded to the empirical relations established with moderators derived from post hoc tests than to those developed within an explicit theoretical framework.

## 4.2 Moderators with Ambiguous Interpretation

Even when moderators are identified a priori that successfully account for the empirical variability in study outcomes, the proper conceptual interpretation of the relation between these third variables and the effect of interest may remain in question. In such cases, low certainty must be accorded the interpretation of moderator effects, and subsequent research is necessary to clarify the appropriate theoretical explanation.

This kind of interpretative ambiguity is especially likely when moderators are identified on a between-studies basis; that is, some studies represent one level of the moderator, and other studies represent other levels. With this strategy, the moderator variable is typically an attribute of a whole research report, and subjects in the primary research have not been randomly assigned to levels of the moderator. Analyses on such "review-generated" variables (Cooper 1989) do not possess strong construct validity because the moderator variable may be confounded with other variables that covary with it.

In contrast to this between-studies strategy are within-study analyses in which two or more levels of the moderator are present in individual reviewed studies. Analyses of within-study moderators provide clearer outcomes, especially when researchers manipulated the moderators in the underlying primary studies and subjects were assigned randomly to levels of the moderator variable. Under these circumstances, effects of within-study moderators can be attributed to the manipulated variables, and interpretation can proceed with greater certainty.

A recent example of the interpretative ambiguity often associated with between-studies moderators is provided by Mullen, Johnson, and Salas's interesting meta-analytic synthesis (1991) examining the extent to which groups perform worse than individuals at brainstorming tasks. Mullen and associates found correlational evidence for four between-studies moderators of productivity losses in brainstorming groups. However, because the four factors were confounded in the sample of studies, it was difficult to evaluate the importance of any of them. Helpful with respect to this source of uncertainty is Bond and Van Leeuwen's reanalysis

of these data (1991) using multiple regression techniques. These analyses suggested that only two of the four factors could uniquely predict the performance loss in groups compared with individuals: Group size and the social context of individual performance (alone vs. others present) were the only significant moderators of performance. Nonetheless, Stroebe and Diehl (1991) further pointed out that their direct manipulations of moderators in primary research yielded findings that conflict with the between-studies correlational results of these meta-analyses. Given the higher internal validity associated with experimental findings than between-studies analyses, greater certainty should be attached to the experimental results, as Stroebe and Diehl maintained.

Sometimes it is possible to conduct analyses on both between-studies and within-study moderators in a single meta-analysis. These opportunities arise when a few studies in a literature manipulated a potential moderator and the remaining studies can be classified as possessing a particular level of that moderator. For example, some studies may have compared the effects of various dosage levels of a drug, and others may have presented a single dosage level. We recommend calculating the between-studies and within-study moderator analyses separately and comparing the findings. Comparable results across these two analysis strategies would substantially enhance the certainty accorded the empirical findings and their theoretical interpretation. When divergent results are obtained, the findings and interpretation associated with the within-study moderator analyses should be accorded greater certainty. Given the correlational nature of between-studies effects, various confounds that covaried with the moderator of interest may have worked to obscure or distort the moderator's effects in such analyses.

Even lower levels of certainty in theoretical explanation are associated with moderators that serve as proxy variables for other, causal factors. Proxy variables include publication year of the primary studies as well as attributes associated with the author of the studies. Although the empirical relation between such proxy variables and the effect of interest may be well established, its interpretation is usually not clear because the moderating variable (e.g., year, authors' gender) cannot itself be regarded as causal. For example, an effect of publication year may be a proxy for temporal changes in cultural or other contextual variables that affect the phenomenon under investigation, or for temporal changes in research techniques or reporting conventions. Effects of researchers' characteristics might reflect differences between investigators' research methods or publication practices (e.g., withholding of unfavorable data sets or inability to publish them). Although a number of effects of proxy variables have been demonstrated in meta-analytic syntheses, some with considerable empirical certainty, their interpretation is usually quite uncertain. For example, many possible explanations can be generated for the effects of publication year on sex differences in cognitive abilities: More recent studies obtained smaller sex differences in verbal performance (Hyde & Linn 1988) and math performance (Hyde, Fennema & Lamon 1990). In addition, considerable ambiguity is associated with the effects of research group that have been obtained in meta-analyses of social behavior. For example, support for Fiedler's contingency model of leadership effectiveness (1967) was marginally stronger in research by Fiedler and his associates than in research by other investigators (Strube & Garcia 1981). Similarly, support for the elaboration likelihood model of persuasion was stronger in research by the originators of the model than in research by other investigators (Johnson & Eagly 1989). Although the initial explanations of such findings are often speculative, plausible interpretations can be pursued, as we explain in the next section.

### 4.3 Strategies for Future Research Given Low Certainty about Moderators

We have argued that uncertainty can arise in moderator analyses because of instability in the obtained empirical relations or ambiguity concerning the correct conceptual interpretation of the moderator. Subsequent research can be designed to address whichever of these ambiguities weakens clarity of interpretation. Of course, when interpretation is clouded by both of these sources of ambiguity, subsequent research would need to address both concerns.

When a moderator is invoked post hoc to account for unexplained variability in the study outcomes, uncertainty arises concerning the stability of the moderator's effect, and subsequent research should focus on replication. This strategy was pursued with Eagly and Carli's unexpected finding (1981) that the proxy variable of sex of the authors of the primary research in their meta-analytic synthesis of sex differences in influenceability covaried with study outcomes. Male authorship was associated with stronger tendencies for women and girls to be more influenced than men and boys. To examine

the stability of this effect, Eagly and Carli reanalyzed the meta-analytic findings from an earlier synthesis of sex differences in the ability to decode nonverbal cues (Hall 1978). Again, authorship proved to be associated with sex difference outcomes: Male authors obtained smaller tendencies for women to be more accurate than men at decoding nonverbal cues. The authorship effects were therefore tentatively interpreted as a tendency to find or report effects flattering to one's own sex.

Interpretations given to proxy variables possess particularly low certainty because they are usually evaluated on a between-studies basis and, in addition, typically have the status of post hoc moderators. Subsequent research must demonstrate the replicability of the variable's covariation with study outcomes as well as clarify interpretation. Explaining the impact of a proxy variable can be quite difficult because a wide range of variables might be reflected in such a variable, and there may be few guides for selecting any particular candidates to pursue in subsequent research. In such cases, a promising strategy is to examine on a correlational basis the attributes of study design and analysis that are associated with the effects of the proxy variable in the meta-analytic synthesis. Applying this strategy, Eagly and Carli (1981) examined the relation between authors' sex and several characteristics of the studies in their sample, but were unsuccessful in locating a plausible mediator of their sex-of-author finding. However, Becker (1986), in a reanalysis of Eagly and Carli's findings, found methodological features of the studies (e.g., the reliability of measurement scales) that differed for male and female authors and may explain, at least in part, their discrepant results. A similar strategy was employed by Hyde, Fennema, and Lamon (1990) to clarify the effects of publication year on sex differences in math performance. Because year did not remain a significant predictor when prediction models included attributes of the subjects studied (i.e., age, math precocity) and type of math task (i.e., computation vs. problem solving), these other attributes may be responsible for the year effects. Once plausible mediators of proxy variables have been identified on a correlational basis in a meta-analysis, subsequent primary research might systematically vary these factors to examine their effects on study outcomes.

When the proxy variable that predicts study outcomes is research group, the most promising approach to explaining these findings is to demonstrate that group covaries with aspects of researchers' methods or their practices in reporting findings. In the absence of such a demonstration, an innovative procedure for disentangling discrepancies between research groups' findings entails joint design of crucial experiments by the antagonists, a procedure used by Latham, Erez, and Locke (1988) to successfully resolve conflicting findings on the effect of workers' participation on goal commitment and performance. Drawing on the spirit of scientific cooperation, the researchers who produced the discrepant findings in this area cooperated in the design and execution of experiments in order to identify critical points of divergence that accounted for the effects of research group. Especially subtle differences in methods that are not discernible from research reports can be revealed by such joint primary research.

When uncertainty arises in the conceptual interpretation of moderators, the optimal strategy for follow-up research is experimentation to manipulate the constructs that have been identified. This approach is nicely illustrated by a program of research on liking for stimuli as a function of frequency of exposure. In a meta-analysis, Bornstein (1989) examined the tendency for liking of a stimulus to increase with increased exposure to it, a phenomenon known as the "mere exposure" effect. Bornstein showed that this tendency was moderated by several factors that might reflect boredom: The effect was enhanced by brief (vs. longer) exposure durations, a limited number of (vs. many) exposures, and presentation of heterogeneous (vs. homogeneous) stimuli. Ambiguity in interpreting these moderating variables stemmed not only from the predominantly between-studies assessment of these variables, but also from the lack of any moderator that directly reflected the explanatory construct of boredom. Subsequent experimental research was designed specifically to examine whether boredom with the stimulus serves as a limiting condition for the relation between exposure and liking (Bornstein, Kale, & Cornell 1990). In these experiments, raters were grouped according to their proneness to experience boredom, and both complex, interesting stimuli and simple, boring ones were presented. As anticipated on the basis of the meta-analysis, the facilitative effects of exposure on liking held primarily for those raters not prone to boredom and for complex stimuli.

In summary, moderator variables that synthesists discover post hoc or examine on a between-studies basis can be informative, particularly in view of the scrutiny such analyses provide of relations that may not have been investigated in primary research. Nonetheless, the relatively low statistical conclusion validity that such analyses may have can yield substantial uncertainty in stability of the empirical relations, and the low construct validity that they may have can yield substantial uncertainty in theoretical accounts. Especially low levels of certainty should be associated with variables such as author sex and year of publication that serve as proxy variables for other, more proximal predictors. Conclusions about moderators that possess low empirical certainty can be clarified by replicating the moderator's impact in related meta-analyses. Moderators that possess low theoretical certainty can be clarified by examining study characteristics that covary with the moderator and by directly manipulating the moderating variables in subsequent experimentation.

## 5. MEDIATORS OF MAIN-EFFECT FINDINGS OF SYNTHESES

Meta-analytic syntheses can also be informative concerning the mediators, or causal mechanisms, underlying an effect (Eagly & Wood 1991; Chapter 29). A strong demonstration of mediation requires a closely specified set of relations between the mediator and the main-effect relation to be explained (see Baron & Kenny 1986; James & Brett 1984). A nice example of such a demonstration with meta-analytic findings is provided by Driskell and Mullen's 1990 synthesis of research testing status-based theories of interaction in small, task-performing groups. According to such theories, group members' status, or position in the group dominance hierarchy, affects their interaction with one another through its influence on members' expectations for their own and others' likely performance at the group task. That is, status affects expectations, and expectations in turn affect performance. The six studies in the synthesis provided strong support for this model. Members' status (varied through, e.g., initial task ability) affected their ratings of how well they were expected to perform, and both status and performance expectations covaried with members' performance in the group. Most important for demonstrating mediation, the relation between members' status and their performance-related behavior became "trivially weak" (p. 548) when the effect of their expectations was controlled. This pattern of findings suggests complete mediation, in which status effects on behavior were due solely to group members' expectations.

Whenever several primary studies within a literature have evaluated a common mediating process, mediator relations can be tested within a meta-analytic framework. Unfortunately, synthesists rarely find such opportunities in samples of studies that they integrate. A set of primary studies that assesses a mediating process is most likely to be found when research has been conducted within a dominant theoretical framework, as was the case for the literature on group status and performance expectations that Driskell and Mullen (1990) reviewed.

## 5.1 Mediators Yielding Conclusions of Low Certainty

It is frequently the case that only a few studies in a literature yield data concerning common mediators, and the resulting paucity of data means that only a few of the relations among mediators and the effect to be explained can be evaluated. In this circumstance, mediator findings provide only suggestive evidence for underlying mechanisms. This situation arose in a meta-analysis of the relation between self-esteem and how easily people can be influenced (Rhodes & Wood 1992). A number of studies in the synthesis assessed message recipients' recall of the persuasive arguments in the influence appeal as well as opinion change to the appeal. Lower self-esteem was associated with lesser recall as well as with lesser opinion change compared with results obtained for recipients of moderate self-esteem. People of low esteem were apparently too withdrawn and distracted to attend to and comprehend the messages and thus were not influenced by them. The parallel effects on recall and opinions provide suggestive support for models that emphasize message reception as a mediator of opinion change (e.g., McGuire 1968). However, because sufficient data were not available to examine all of the relations in the model, specifically the link between reception and influence, some uncertainty remains in the conclusion that reception of messages mediates the effects of self-esteem on opinion change. In general, the internal validity of conclusions about a mediating process is threatened to the extent that a synthesis is unable to examine the full range of relations involved in the hypothesized mediational process, and consequently the mediational model can be accepted with only a moderate level of certainty.

Even more frequently, no mediator findings from the covered studies can be synthesized at the meta-analytic level. A meta-analysis may demonstrate an empirical relation with some certainty, but the research literature may provide little direct insight into underlying processes. For example, consider the tendency for sex differences to become larger at older ages that was documented in Thomas and French's synthesis of motor task performance (1985). These investigators argued that sex differences prior to puberty were based on environmental causes (e.g., treatment, expectations, and practice opportunities that differ for boys and girls) and that physical differences in size and strength played a greater role in the sex differences obtained in adolescents. However, these causal inferences were not directly tested in their synthesis. Moreover, these assumptions about causation are not self-evident and could be contested both by biologically inclined psychologists arguing for a prepubertal influence of physical differences and by environmentally inclined psychologists arguing for a postpubertal influence of social expectations. In the absence of direct tests of the mediation of sex differences in motor performance, perhaps using variables such as prior athletic experience or reports of social expectations, synthesists could resort to more indirect methods of assessing mediating processes.

One indirect method of establishing mediation involves constructing general process models at the meta-analytic level from studies that have examined components of the process relations. For example, the effectiveness of treatment for high blood pressure might be demonstrated through a combination of two separate sets of findings—one set showing that the treatment lowers the blood pressure of hypertensive people and another set showing that lowering blood pressure reduces the occurrence of stroke among a hypertensive sample (see Grimm & Black 1991; Woolf et al. 1990). Meta-analytically constructed process models have also been used to illuminate the effects of teacher expectancies on student performance (Harris & Rosenthal 1985). The model was built on findings from two groups of studies. In one group, performance expectancies influenced the warmth of teacher-student relations and the frequency of specific types of interaction, including feedback from the teacher and opportunities for student response. A second group of studies indicated that these types of interaction with teachers affected students' scholastic performance.

In the absence of mediator data that examine the full sequence of events involved in a causal model, a meta-analytic combination of studies assessing component parts does not conclusively demonstrate that the mediating processes are related as specified in the model. Consider, for example, the findings that a medical treatment lowers blood pressure and that lower pressure is associated with reduced risk of stroke. Although these two sets of findings might be taken in combination to suggest that the treatment reduces stroke incidence, the treatment might also affect other factors associated with stroke incidence—for example, lipid levels and insulin resistance—that negate the beneficial effects of lowered blood pressure (Grimm & Black 1991). Thus, building process models at a meta-analytic level from separate tests of a model's components threatens internal validity, and such analyses cannot be interpreted with high certainty.

Another indirect method used in psychological research for evaluating mediators involves judges' coding or rating of process-relevant aspects of the synthesized studies. Process ratings are especially useful when the reviewed studies are drawn from diverse theoretical paradigms, and no single mediational process was assessed by more than a few studies. In this case process ratings may make it possible to test a general causal model across the full range of experimental paradigms that are reviewed. For example, Eagly and Steffen (1986) used process ratings to support the idea that normative beliefs concerning appropriate behavior for men and women underlie sex differences in aggression. Normative influences were estimated through judges' ratings of the likelihood that the average man and the average woman would engage in the aggressive acts in the reviewed research. When judges reported that men were especially likely to engage in aggression (compared with women), sex differences in aggressive behavior were especially large, as assessed by the effect sizes of the studies. Of course, process ratings do not directly substantiate mediating processes. Although such judgments may have been conducted with high reliability and stability and their empirical relations to effect sizes may be strong, they are not necessarily unbiased. The judgments of contemporary raters may not exactly reproduce the mediating variables in studies conducted at earlier dates (see Cialdini & Fultz 1990; Miller, Lee & Carlson 1991). For these and other reasons, judges' ratings of mediators do not yield high certainty in theoretical interpretation.

## 5.2 Strategies for Future Research Given Low Certainty about Mediators

Uncertainty concerning the empirical status of mediating processes underlying an effect is a frequent occurrence in research syntheses for the reasons we have stated. We have discussed three instances in which documentation of mediation in meta-analytic syntheses yields outcomes of insufficient certainty: when primary data are available to document only selected relations from the full mediational model, when meta-analytic mediational models are constructed from primary research that tested only subsets of the overall model, and when process ratings of the reviewed research are used to represent mediating variables. In each of these cases, the causal status of the mediator with respect to the relation of interest remains uncertain, and primary research is necessary to substantiate the process models suggested by these techniques. In addition, it is possible that evidence consistent with the proposed mediation could be found in related literatures that could also be meta-analyzed.

This strategy of initial research synthesis suggesting possible mediational models followed by primary research directly investigating causal mechanisms has been pursued in research on eyewitness facial identification. A meta-analytic synthesis by Shapiro and Penrod (1986) suggested that reinstatement of the context in which a face was initially seen facilitated subsequent recognition of the face. The mechanisms through which context had this impact could not be evaluated in the synthesis, and subsequent primary research was designed to address this issue. By experimentally varying features of the target stimulus and features of the context, follow-up research indicated that reinstatement of context enhances recognition accuracy because it functions as a memory retrieval cue (Cutler & Penrod 1988; Cutler, Penrod & Martens 1987). Context reinstatement thus had a substantial impact when few other such cues were available to assist in recognition.

In general, we advocate a two-pronged strategy to document mediational models. First, methods of evaluating the mediational process meta-analytically need to be devised and correlational analyses conducted to demonstrate that the mediator covaries as expected with the main effect of interest. Although the typical paucity of mediational data across a body of literature means that strong evidence of mediation is rarely available at a meta-analytic level, we have already noted an exceptional quantitative synthesis that obtained such evidence (Driskell & Mullen 1990). Successful demonstration of mediation occurred when the mediating process, in this case group members' expectations, accounted for the main-effect relation between members' status and their social interaction. Because mediational models claim causality, we also advocate a second step of directly manipulating the hypothesized mediating process in primary research to document its causal impact on the dependent variable. For example, a manipulation of performance expectations might provide group members with information that they are likely to perform well or poorly, and effects on social interaction could be observed (see Wood & Karten 1986). These two research strategies provide complementary evidence concerning mediation: Correlational assessment of the mediator demonstrates that it varies in the predicted manner with the relation of interest, and experimental manipulation of the mediator demonstrates its causal role. Accomplishing the correlational assessment in a meta-analysis takes advantage of this technique's ability to document main-effect relations and to suggest possible process models. Documenting causal relations in primary research, particularly in true experiments, builds on the strong internal validity of this type of research.

## 6. RESEARCH SYNTHESES THAT IMPEDE FUTURE INVESTIGATIONS

Unfortunately, research syntheses do not always facilitate the development of increasingly more valid and sophisticated answers to research questions. Meta-analyses can falsely appear to produce clear outcomes that definitively answer research questions. Conclusions that should be drawn with considerable uncertainty, because of either insufficient empirical documentation or unclear theoretical accounts, are inappropriately portrayed as highly certain. Rather than channel and direct future primary research, such a synthesis discourages subsequent investigation. To the extent that these problems occur, quantitative reviewing fails to fulfill its promise of furthering progress toward the twin goals of ascertaining empirical relations and determining valid theoretical explanations for these relations.

### 6.1 False Certainty from Incomplete Data Analysis or Inadequate Sample of Studies

The major way that quantitative syntheses can produce false certainty about the findings of primary research is by confining the analysis to the estimation of a mean effect size that describes the magnitude of the relation between two variables. Unless a synthesis also examines the homogeneity of the effect sizes that constitute the mean, it is unclear to what extent findings are consistent across the studies. The findings from syntheses that fail to estimate homogeneity are sometimes misleadingly presented as if they had adequately answered a particular question. Such presentations increase the likelihood that readers will incorrectly draw the conclusion that future

research would be redundant because it would merely produce the same answer as the reviewed research.

Instances of quantitative syntheses that aggregate relatively large samples of empirical findings but fail to examine their consistency are not uncommon. Understandably, many of these research syntheses were published at a relatively early point before techniques for evaluating the consistency of findings had been disseminated to synthesists. Quite a few early meta-analyses aggregated findings across studies only by the relatively uninformative technique of combining the probabilities (i.e., $p$ values) associated with the findings (see Chapter 15) yet featured quite confident conclusions that may have discouraged additional research.

An example of an early synthesis that failed to sufficiently consider the consistency of findings was conducted by Frieze et al. (1982) on sex differences in people's causal attributions for their own successes and failures. The synthesis presented mean effect sizes, unaccompanied by homogeneity analyses or confidence intervals. Given that the mean findings were relatively small (a result ensured by their substitution of 0.00 for effect sizes that they could not calculate), the researchers concluded that the research area might not be "fruitful" (Frieze et al. 1982, p. 341). This conclusion was modified in a subsequent reanalysis of the data set by Whitley, McHugh, and Frieze (1986), which identified considerable heterogeneity in study outcomes. Given this inconsistency across study findings, the authors very appropriately called for greater attention to moderating factors in future research on sex differences in causal explanation, stressing the importance of systematically examining situational moderators and forms of measurement. In summary, many published research syntheses have failed to stimulate subsequent primary research because the considerable uncertainty that should have been accorded to their empirical findings was not made apparent by their authors.

Another instance in which inconsistencies in the underlying literature are not satisfactorily described or resolved by a synthesis occurs when only a small number of studies have addressed a research question or only a few from a larger sample have yielded data adequate to calculate effect sizes. The resulting sample of effect sizes may be too small to provide a meaningful estimate of findings' homogeneity. In such cases, estimates of the magnitude of an effect from what are possibly heterogeneous effect sizes can still be of some use, provided that the synthesist accompanies such an analysis by an appropriately modest and cautious description of this aggregated empirical finding. The small number of effect sizes available for analysis similarly limits the statistical power that synthesists have available to examine moderators. For example, Wood, Wong, and Chachere (1991) found that they could calculate effect sizes for only 12 of the 23 studies in their meta-analysis of the effects of media violence on naturally occurring aggression during interaction with peers. Although the synthesis documented a significant increase in viewers' aggressive behavior after exposure to violent, versus nonviolent, media presentations, the effect proved to be significantly heterogeneous. Unfortunately, the small number of studies that have examined this issue curtailed the investigation of moderating conditions and thus compromised the synthesists' ability to account for variability in study outcomes.

## 6.2 False Certainty from Overinclusive Definition of Synthesis Domain

The detection of moderating conditions is also likely to be somewhat unsuccessful in syntheses that are conceptualized extremely broadly so that studies in a very wide variety of paradigms are included. Such meta-analyses often identify useful moderators, particularly those associated with the paradigms themselves (e.g., field vs. laboratory studies; child vs. adult subject populations). However, because many specific considerations may determine the size of effects within particular paradigms, it is rare that extremely broad meta-analyses show a high degree of empirical success in predicting study outcomes. In addition, the wide range of possible theoretical explanations for such diverse effects can make it difficult to generate any clear theoretical model for the findings. To achieve greater certainty, smaller, subsidiary meta-analyses examining predictors and mediators specific to each experimental paradigm would have to be conducted as well.

The problems that synthesists face when accounting for findings aggregated across diverse research paradigms is exemplified by Swim et al.'s 1989 meta-analysis on sex bias in evaluations of men's and women's behavior. Although, on the basis of a small mean effect size, these authors dismissed claims that the research in this area has shown that people are biased against women, their homogeneity analyses revealed considerable inconsistency across the studies. Yet the meta-analysis had little success in explaining this variability. When Eagly, Makhijani, and Klonsky (1992) meta-analyzed studies from one research paradigm within this large domain

(namely, experiments in which the behavior portrayed was leadership). They were considerably more successful in predicting effects across the studies. Because their hypotheses about moderating conditions stemmed largely from considerations specific to leadership studies, it is not surprising that these relations were not uncovered by Swim and collaborators' broader meta-analysis. Similarly, Eagly and Johnson's 1990 synthesis of sex differences in leadership style integrated studies from many different research paradigms. Although these authors presented homogeneity analyses and examined a large number of moderating conditions, their aggregation of studies of many types (e.g., laboratory and organizational studies) conducted in many different settings (e.g., different types of organizations, including schools, businesses, and hospitals) meant that they did not investigate many of the moderating conditions that would be important for particular subgroups of studies (e.g., those conducted in business organizations). These researchers then proceeded to meta-analyze in more detail the largest subgroup of studies in their original synthesis, those in which the leaders whose style was assessed were school principals (Eagly, Karau, & Johnson 1992).

## 7. CONCLUSION

By emphasizing the varying levels of certainty that the scientific community should accord to the conclusions of syntheses, we encourage the authors and the consumers of meta-analyses to adopt a critical stance in relation to research syntheses. Once such a stance is taken, meta-analyses cannot be regarded as the final phase of a field's consideration of a hypothesis, but as potentially helpful aids to sifting through and evaluating the available evidence. A quantitative synthesis should thus reveal the quality of the evidence with respect to a particular empirical relation, its generalizability, and its theoretical interpretation. Careful analysis of the nature of the uncertainty yielded by a synthesis can provide detailed guidance for future investigations. The mission of subsequent research should be to reduce uncertainty, so that the scientific evidence bearing on a particular hypothesis becomes more adequate. The empirical basis for an effect often needs strengthening, usually by obtaining a more complete description of the patterning of the finding across subject populations, research settings, and research methods. Frequently the theoretical basis for an effect also requires close examination, in view of the empirical evidence provided by a synthesis. New research is often needed to test theories concerning the causes even of well-established phenomena; such research usually requires the use of new designs and measuring instruments.

This chapter should encourage the authors of research syntheses to provide careful analyses of the empirical and theoretical certainty of their conclusions and to suggest needed subsequent research. Perhaps the perception that journal publication requires clear-cut findings has sometimes encouraged the authors of syntheses to announce their conclusions more confidently than their meta-analytic evidence warrants. To counter this perception, we encourage journal editors to foster appropriate exploration of uncertainty and to favor research syntheses that explore the uncertainty that should be attached to their conclusions. Careful analysis of the certainty that should be accorded to the set of conclusions produced by a meta-analysis should foster a healthy interaction between research syntheses and future primary research.

**Authors' Note**

Preparation of this chapter was aided by National Science Foundation grant No. BNS-8807495 to Alice Eagly; the chapter was completed while she was a visiting professor at the University of Tübingen, supported by a grant from the Deutsche Forschungsgemeinshaft. The authors thank Steven Karau for comments on a draft of the chapter.

## 8. REFERENCES

Baron, R. M., & Kenny, D. A. (1986). The moderator-mediator variable distinction in social psychological research: Conceptual, strategic, and statistical considerations. *Journal of Personality and Social Psychology, 51,* 1173–1182.

Becker, B. J. (1986). Influence again: An examination of reviews and studies of gender differences in social influence. In J. S. Hyde & M. C. Linn (Eds.), *The psychology of gender: Advances through meta-analysis.* Baltimore: Johns Hopkins University Press, 178–209.

Becker, B. J., & Hedges, L. V. (1984). Meta-analysis of cognitive gender differences: A comment on an analysis by Rosenthal and Rubin. *Journal of Educational Psychology, 76,* 583–587.

Bond, C. F., Jr., & Van Leeuwen, M. D. (1991). Can a part be greater than the whole? On the relationship between primary and meta-analytic evidence. *Basic and Applied Social Psychology, 12,* 33–40.

Bornstein, R. F. (1989). Exposure and affect: Overview and meta-analysis of research, 1968–1987. *Psychological Bulletin, 106,* 265–289.

Bornstein, R. F., Kale, A. R., & Cornell, K. R. (1990). Boredom as a limiting condition on the mere exposure effect. *Journal of Personality and Social Psychology, 58,* 791–800.

Casey, R. J., & Berman, J. S. (1985). The outcome of psychotherapy with children. *Psychological Bulletin, 98,* 388–400.

Cialdini, R. B., & Fultz, J. (1990). Interpreting the negative mood–helping literature via ''mega''-analysis: A contrary view. *Psychological Bulletin, 107,* 210–214.

Cohen, J. (1988). *Statistical power analysis for the behavioral sciences.* Hillsdale, NJ: Erlbaum.

Cook, T. D., & Campbell, D. T. (1979). *Quasi-experimentation: Design and analysis issues for field settings.* Chicago: Rand McNally.

Cooper, H. M. (1989). *Integrating research: A guide for literature reviews* (2nd ed.). Newbury Park, CA: Sage.

Cordray, D. S., & Orwin, R. G. (1983). Improving the quality of evidence: Interconnections among primary evaluation, secondary analysis, and quantitative synthesis. In R. H. Light (Ed.), *Evaluation studies review annual* (Vol. 8, pp. 91–119). Beverly Hills, CA: Sage.

Cutler, B. L., & Penrod, S. D. (1988). Improving the reliability of eyewitness identification: Lineup construction and presentation. *Journal of Applied Psychology, 73,* 281–290.

Cutler, B. L., Penrod, S. D., & Martens, T. K. (1987). Improving the reliability of eyewitness identification: Putting context into context. *Journal of Applied Psychology, 72,* 629–637.

Driskell, J. E., & Mullen, B. (1990). Status, expectations, and behavior: A meta-analytic review and test of the theory. *Personality and Social Psychology Bulletin, 16,* 541–553.

Eagly, A. H. (1987). *Sex differences in social behavior: A social-role interpretation.* Hillsdale, NJ: Erlbaum.

Eagly, A. H., & Carli, L. L. (1981). Sex of researchers and sex-typed communications as determinants of sex differences in influenceability: A meta-analysis of social influence studies. *Psychological Bulletin, 90,* 1–20.

Eagly, A. H., & Johnson, B. T. (1990). Gender and leadership style: A meta-analysis. *Psychological Bulletin, 108,* 233–256.

Eagly, A. H., Karau, S. J., & Johnson, B. T. (1992). Gender and leadership style among school principals: A meta-analysis. *Educational Administration Quarterly, 28,* 76–102.

Eagly, A. H., Makhijani, M. G., & Klonsky, B. G. (1992).

Gender and the evaluation of leaders: A meta-analysis. *Psychological Bulletin, 111*, 3–22.

Eagly, A. H., & Steffen, V. J. (1986). Gender and aggressive behavior: A meta-analytic review of the social psychological literature. *Psychological Bulletin, 100*, 308–330.

Eagly, A. H., & Wood, W. (1991). Explaining sex differences in social behavior: A meta-analytic perspective. *Personality and Social Psychology Bulletin, 17*, 306–315.

Fiedler, F. E. (1967). *A theory of leadership effectiveness.* New York: McGraw-Hill.

Frieze, I. H., Whitley, B. E., Jr., Hanusa, B. H., & McHugh, M. C. (1982). Assessing the theoretical models for sex differences in causal attributions for success and failure. *Sex Roles, 8*, 333–343.

Grimm, R. H., Jr., & Black, H. (1991). Workshop II—Hypertension trials and meta-analyses: Is there any value for further studies? *American Journal of Medicine, 90*(Suppl. 2A), 24S–25S.

Grossman, M., & Wood, W. (in press). Sex differences in intensity of emotional response: A social role interpretation. *Journal of Personality and Social Psychology.*

Gruppo Italiano Per Lo Studio Della Streptochinasi Nell'Infarto Miocardico [Italian Group for the Study of Streptokinase in Myocardial Infarction]. (1986). Effectiveness of intravenous thrombolytic treatment in acute myocardial infarction. *Lancet, i*, 397–401.

Hall, J. A. (1978). Gender effects in decoding nonverbal cues. *Psychological Bulletin, 85*, 845–875.

Hall, J. A. (1984). *Nonverbal sex differences: Communication accuracy and expressive style.* Baltimore: Johns Hopkins University Press.

Harris, M. J., & Rosenthal, R. (1985). Mediation of interpersonal expectancy effects: 31 meta-analyses. *Psychological Bulletin, 97*, 363–386.

Hedges, L. V. (1987). How hard is hard science, how soft is soft science? The empirical cumulativeness of research. *American Psychologist, 42*, 443–455.

Hedges, L. V., & Olkin, I. (1985). *Statistical methods for meta-analysis.* Orlando, FL: Academic Press.

Hyde, J. S., Fennema, E., & Lamon, S. H. (1990). Gender differences in mathematics performance: A meta-analysis. *Psychological Bulletin, 107*, 139–155.

Hyde, J. S., & Linn, M. C. (1988). Gender differences in verbal ability: A meta-analysis. *Psychological Bulletin, 104*, 53–69.

International Study of Infarct Survival-1. (1986). Randomized trial of intravenous atenolol among 16,027 cases of suspected acute myocardial infarction: ISIS-1. *Lancet, ii*, 57–66.

International Study of Infarct Survival-2. (1988). Collab-orative group: Randomized trial of intravenous streptokinase, oral aspirin, both, or neither among 17,187 cases of suspected acute myocardial infarction: ISIS-2. *Lancet, ii*, 349–360.

International Study of Infarct Survival. (1990). In-hospital mortality and clinical course of 20,891 patients with suspected acute myocardial infarction randomized between alteplase and streptokinase with or without heparin. *Lancet, 336*, 71–75.

James, L. R., & Brett, J. M. (1984). Mediators, moderators, and tests for mediation. *Journal of Applied Psychology, 69*, 307–321.

Johnson, B. T., & Eagly, A. H. (1989). The effects of involvement on persuasion: A meta-analysis. *Psychological Bulletin, 106*, 290–314.

Latham, G. P., Erez, M., & Locke, E. A. (1988). Resolving scientific disputes by the joint design of crucial experiments by the antagonists: Application to the Erez-Latham dispute regarding participation in goal setting. *Journal of Applied Psychology, 73*, 753–772.

McGuire, W. J. (1968). Personality and susceptibility to social influence. In E. F. Borgatta & W. W. Lambert (Eds.), *Handbook of personality theory and research* (pp. 1130–1187). Chicago: Rand McNally.

Miller, N., Lee, J., & Carlson, M. (1991). The validity of inferential judgments when used in theory-testing meta-analysis. *Personality and Social Psychology Bulletin, 17*, 335–343.

Mullen, B., Johnson, C., & Salas, E. (1991). Productivity loss in brainstorming groups: A meta-analytic integration. *Basic and Applied Social Psychology, 12*, 3–23.

Nolen-Hoeksema, S. (1987). Sex differences in unipolar depression: Evidence and theory. *Psychological Bulletin, 101*, 259–282.

Rhodes, N. D., & Wood, W. (1992). Self-esteem and intelligence affect influenceability: The mediating role of message reception. *Psychological Bulletin, 111*, 156–171.

Rosenthal, R. (1984). *Meta-analytic procedures for social research.* Beverly Hills, CA: Sage.

Shapiro, P. N., & Penrod, S. (1986). Meta-analysis of facial identification studies. *Psychological Bulletin, 100*, 139–156.

Stampfer, M. J., Goldhaber, S. Z., Yusuf, S., Peto, R., & Hennekens, C. H. (1982). Effect of intravenous streptokinase on acute myocardial infarction: Pooled results from randomized trials. *New England Journal of Medicine, 307*, 1180–1182.

Stroebe, W., & Diehl, M. (1991). You can't beat good experiments with correlational evidence: Mullen, Johnson, and Salas's meta-analytic misinterpretations. *Basic and Applied Social Psychology, 12*, 25–32.

Strube, M. J., & Garcia, J. E. (1981). A meta-analytic investigation of Fiedler's contingency model of leadership effectiveness. *Psychological Bulletin, 90,* 307–321.

Suls, J., & Wan, C. K. (1989). Effects of sensory and procedural information on coping with stressful medical procedures and pain: A meta-analysis. *Journal of Consulting and Clinical Psychology, 57,* 372–379.

Swim, J., Borgida, E., Maruyama, G., & Myers, D. G. (1989). Joan McKay versus John McKay: Do gender stereotypes bias evaluations? *Psychological Bulletin, 105,* 409–429.

Thomas, J. R., & French, K. E. (1985). Gender differences across age in motor performance: A meta-analysis. *Psychological Bulletin, 98,* 260–282.

Weisz, J. R., & Weiss, B. (1989). Assessing the effects of clinic-based psychotherapy with children and adolescents. *Journal of Consulting and Clinical Psychology, 57,* 741–746.

Weisz, J. R., Weiss, B., Alicke, M. D., & Klotz, M. L. (1987). Effectiveness of psychotherapy with children and adolescents: A meta-analysis for clinicians. *Journal of Consulting and Clinical Psychology, 55,* 542–549.

Whitley, B. E., Jr., McHugh, M. C., & Frieze, I. H. (1986). Assessing the theoretical models for sex differences in causal attributions of success and failure. In J. S. Hyde & M. C. Linn (Eds.), *The psychology of gender: Advances through meta-analysis* (pp. 102–135). Baltimore: Johns Hopkins University Press.

Wood, W. (1987). Meta-analytic review of sex differences in group performance. *Psychological Bulletin, 102,* 53–71.

Wood, W., & Karten, S. (1986). Sex differences in interaction style as a product of perceived sex differences in competence. *Journal of Personality and Social Psychology, 50,* 341–347.

Wood, W., Rhodes, N. D., & Whelan, M. (1989). Sex differences in positive well-being: A consideration of emotional style and marital status. *Psychological Bulletin, 106,* 249–264.

Wood, W., Wong, F. Y., & Chachere, J. G. (1991). Effects of media violence on viewers' aggression in unconstrained social interaction. *Psychological Bulletin, 109,* 371–383.

Woolf, S. H., Battista, R. N., Anderson, G. M., Logan, A. G., & Wang, E. (1990). Assessing the clinical effectiveness of preventive maneuvers: Analytic principles and systematic methods in reviewing evidence and developing clinical practice recommendations. *Journal of Clinical Epidemiology, 43,* 891–905.

Yusuf, S., Peto, R., Lewis, J., Collins, R., & Sleight, P. (1985). Beta blockade during and after myocardial infarction: An overview of the randomized trials. *Progress in Cardiovascular Diseases, 27,* 335–371.

# PART

# X

# SUMMARY

Cooper, H. and Hedges, L. V. (Eds.) 1994. *The Handbook of Research Synthesis.* New York: Russell Sage Foundation

# 31

# THREATS TO THE VALIDITY OF RESEARCH SYNTHESES

**GEORG E. MATT**
*San Diego State University*

**THOMAS D. COOK**
*Northwestern University*

CONTENTS

## 1. THE PROMISES OF RESEARCH SYNTHESIS

Although the list of validity threats we present is relevant to research synthesis practice, it is not definitive. All threats are empirical products. Any list of threats should change as theories of method are improved and as critical discourse about research synthesis practice accumulates. Some of the threats we discuss apply to conclusions from individual studies as well as from research syntheses. Experienced research synthesists realize that they have to correct inadequacies in individual studies before combining their results across studies (Cooper 1989). Other threats apply only to research syntheses, in that they depend on how estimates from individual studies are synthesized. Yet even these threats have higher-order analogues in general principles of research design and statistics. Thus, "publication bias" can be construed as a particular instance of the more general threat of "sampling bias." However, publication bias is one concrete example of how sampling bias may be encountered in research synthesis, and we prefer to formulate our taxonomy of individual threats in forms that are as close as possible to how research synthesists actually experience them in their practice.

Research synthesis promises to improve the quality of research conclusions in a number of different ways. One is by providing estimates of association (including causal association) that are more precise than individual studies usually permit. Combining multiple studies increases the total sample size of observations for probing a hypothesis. But these original observations may not be the units of analysis in a meta-analysis; sometimes they will be much more reliable aggregates, like a difference between group means.

Another potential benefit of research synthesis is that estimates of relationships may be less biased than those of most individual studies. The corpus of research relevant to a particular hypothesis is likely to include some studies in which the methodology is not perfect, but nonetheless outstanding. It is then possible to assign special inferential weight to studies with better methods. Moreover, subanalyses can also be made to examine how methodological quality is related to effect sizes; and having a collection of studies makes it possible to construct and defend the (difficult) argument that the magnitude of bias operating in some studies to inflate a relationship is equal to the bias operating in other studies to deflate it (Cook & Leviton 1980). While biases can also countervail within primary studies, in meta-analysis no single study needs to be unbiased. At issue is only the total bias across studies.

While associations can be of many kinds, one stands out: association that is causal in the sense that deliberately manipulating one entity will lead to variability in the other. Indeed, this was the context for which Campbell originally developed his validity threats. Our experience suggests that most meta-analytic practice is concerned with associations of this kind, leading to the hypothesis that many synthesists believe they can obtain less biased causal estimates from research syntheses than from most individual studies. As a result, we should examine the ways that causal inference is threatened because a meta-analysis is undertaken.

Most of all, though, research synthesis promises improved generalization over a single study. This superiority is of several kinds. First, research syntheses promote greater confidence in generalizations about specific populations, universes, types, classes, categories, or entities (terms we use interchangeably), irrespective of whether they describe persons, settings, times, causal agents (i.e., treatments), or effects (i.e., outcome constructs). This advantage is not a consequence of sampling theory, our most elegant and justifiable theory of generalization. Traditional sampling theory depends on selecting instances with known probability from some clearly specified population—random selection in essence. Studies entering a research synthesis rarely have samples or cases selected at random, and the studies themselves do not constitute a meaningful census or a random sample of all the studies that have been conducted (or might be conducted) to probe a particular hypothesis. However, recent advances in statistical modeling of categories with uncertain boundaries (Anderson 1991; Huttenlocher, Hedges & Duncan 1991) suggest that formal sampling models may one day be available to guide generalizations to the categories typically studied in research synthesis.

Given the current state of the art, confidence in generalization has to depend on the cases belonging to clearly specified categories. In particular, a research synthesist must ask whether the available cases have the attributes that theoretical analysis indicates are prototypical of a particular class (Rosch 1973, 1978), given the "fuzziness" of marginal details of class membership (Zadeh 1975, 1982). For example, are the persons in the studies Asian-Americans—the target population—in the sense of having ancestors that come from certain specifiable nations? Are the settings factories—the target environment—in that objects are manufactured for profit at these sites? Do the studies all occur in the 1980s—the historical period to which generalization is sought? Are the interventions instances of the more general category of "decentralized decision-making" in that all affected parties are represented in deliberations about policy? And are the outcome operations plausible measures of the higher-order construct "productivity" in the sense that a physical output is measured and related to standards about quantity or quality? Campbell (1986) has related category membership to generalization via the concept of "proximal similarity." He suggests that the cases must have an obvious similarity in surface characteristics to the target to which generalization is sought.

To Campbell (1986), however, membership in the target category is not by itself enough to justify generalization. Also required is a heterogeneity of irrelevancies. The heterogeneity of studies entering a research synthesis provides researchers with opportunities to explore whether any target categories are confounded with substantive irrelevancies. For instance: Are the Asian-Americans all Vietnamese or male? Are the factories all antiquated and producing a single product? Are the years all piled up at the beginning of the 1980s? Are the interventions biased toward cases in which decentrali-

zation is only about how to do things and not what to do? Are the particular productivity measures oriented to quantity and not quality of production? At issue is at least making sure that the samples or cases are not consistently correlated with a substantive irrelevancy. As an option for generalization, selecting proximally similar cases and probing for heterogeneity in irrelevancies is epistemologically inferior to creating a distribution at the sample level that recreates the population level within known limits of sampling error (Cook 1989). However, the former option is more feasible.

Research synthesis can also promote another kind of generalization based on probing the robustness of a particular relationship. Meta-analytic study of almost any relationship is likely to reveal primary studies with their own unique populations of persons, their own categories of setting, their own time period, and their own theoretical descriptions of what a treatment or outcome class is and how it should be manipulated or measured. Here, the issue is not to generalize to a particular population. Instead, it is probing how well a relationship generalizes across different populations. Does a particular relationship hold with persons from different ethnic, class, or age backgrounds; in settings that vary considerably in characteristics that might be expected to influence the outcome, and so on? When a relationship is not robust, the analyst seeks to specify some of the contingencies on which its appearance depends. Of particular importance is identifying moderator variables that have specific theory and policy importance because they nullify or reverse the sign of a relationship as opposed to merely change its magnitude.

The discussion of generalization above deals only with problems in which the sampling base contains instances that belong in specifiable categories. But generalization is also involved when we seek to extrapolate beyond the database in order to draw conclusions about unsampled populations (Cronbach 1982). This is a difficult enterprise, but here, too, meta-analysis has considerable advantages over single studies. One practical basis for extrapolation is when a relationship is demonstrably robust across a wide range of persons, settings, and times and the analyst is willing to induce from this broad range that it is likely to hold in other as-yet-unstudied circumstances. Of course, conceptual examination of these circumstances is also required to make sure that they are not characterized by specific factors that theory suggests will modify the relationship.

Extrapolating from cause and effect constructs to different causes and effects is even more difficult. It is probably most feasible in the time-honored mode of extrapolation whereby researchers seek to identify the process causally mediating a relationship. Scientists seek to specify the causal powers that generate observed relationships between variables under the assumption that, once identified, they can often be set in motion by different causal agents than those studied to date. Indeed, the rationale offered to the general public for its support of basic science is exactly that: Processes will be discovered that can be set in motion in many practical ways and that will therefore be viable across a wide range of persons, settings, and times other than those in which the relationship was discovered or has been probed to date. The crucial issue then becomes: What are the obstacles (i.e., ''threats'') to using research synthesis for extrapolating findings through identifying the causal mediating (i.e., ''explanatory'') mechanisms that occur after one variable has changed and before another has responded? This is a particularly difficult issue because explicit examples of causal explanation are rare in meta-analysis. There are some, though, and they are becoming more frequent (e.g., Becker 1992; Harris & Rosenthal 1985; Premack & Hunter 1988; Shadish & Sweeney 1991). There are even some general discussions of meta-analysis and causal mediation (e.g., Chapter 23; Cook 1989; Cook et al. 1992).

The structure of this chapter follows from the benefits that research synthesis promises us. In section 2 we discuss threats that apply to meta-analyses that seek only to describe the degree of association between two variables. In section 3 we discuss threats to the inferences that the nature of the relationship is causal in the ''manipulability'' or ''activity'' theory sense (Collingwood 1940; Gasking 1955; Whitbeck 1977). In section 4 we turn our attention to generalization, beginning with those validity threats that apply when generalizing to particular target populations, constructs, categories, and so on. Then we examine the threats pertinent to analyses of potential moderator variables from which conclusions are drawn about empirical robustness and causal contingency (Mackie 1974). Finally, we examine threats that uniquely apply to research that seeks to promote extrapolation to unstudied populations through identifying more general causal mediating processes. Fewer threats are noted in the later sections. This is because we emphasize only the unique threats; all threats discussed earlier under different section headings also apply to the later tasks.

**Table 31.1 Threats to Inferences About the Existence of a Relationship Between Treatment and Outcome Classes**

1. Unreliability in primary studies
2. The restriction of range in primary studies
3. Missing effect sizes in primary studies
4. The unreliability of codings in meta-analyses
5. Capitalizing on chance in meta-analyses
6. Bias in transforming effect sizes
7. The lack of statistical independence among effect sizes
8. The failure to weight study-level effect sizes proportional to their precision
9. The underjustified use of fixed or random effects models
10. The lack of statistical power

## 2. THREATS TO INFERENCES ABOUT THE EXISTENCE OF A RELATIONSHIP BETWEEN TREATMENT AND OUTCOME CLASSES

The following threats deal with issues that may lead a research synthesist to draw erroneous conclusions about the existence of a relationship between a class of independent variables (i.e., ''treatments'') and a class of dependent variables (i.e., ''outcomes''). In the language of statistical hypothesis testing, these threats may lead to Type I or Type II errors because of deficiencies in either the primary studies or the meta-analytic review process. A single threat in a single study is not likely to jeopardize meta-analytic conclusions in any meaningful way. More critical is whether the same source of bias operates across all or most of the studies being reviewed or whether different sources of bias fail to cancel each other out across studies and so lead to one direction of bias predominating—say, to inflate estimates of relationship. It is the need to rule out these possibilities that leads to the list of validity threats that follows (see Table 31.1 for an overview).

### 2.1 Unreliability in Primary Studies

Unreliability in implementing or measuring variables contributes random error to the within-group variability of a primary study, thereby attenuating effect size estimates not only within such a study but also when studies are aggregated meta-analytically.

Some meta-analysts have proposed that correction formulas should be used to adjust effect estimates and their standard errors (Hunter & Schmidt 1990; Rosenthal 1984; Wolf 1990; also Chapters 16 and 21). Attenuation corrections may be used to provide estimates under the assumption that interventions were consistently implemented and outcomes measured without error. They may also be used to make the degree of attentuation constant across studies. Unfortunately, the implementation of interventions is often not well understood and is rarely documented in primary studies. The reliability of outcome measures is theoretically better understood, but not all primary researchers report reliability estimates. Such *practical* limitations impede comprehensive attempts to correct individual effect size estimates and force some meta-analysts to generate (untested) assumptions about what the reliability would have been in a particular study had it been assessed.

## 2.2 The Restriction of Range in Primary Studies

When the range of an outcome measure is restricted in a primary study, it attenuates all correlation coefficients involving this measure. However, the range restriction may influence other effect size measures differently. For instance, in randomized trials or quasi-experiments blocking or matching will reduce both within-group variability and range. But by decreasing the denominator of the effect size estimate, *d*, the blocking also increases effect sizes. When such design characteristics operate, Kulik and Kulik (1986) refer to the resulting effect sizes as operative rather than interpretable. Aggregating such operative effect sizes across studies may influence average effect estimates and their standard errors.

Meta-analysts have suggested correction formulas to adjust mean correlation effect estimates and their standard error for attenuation due to range restriction (see Chapters 16 and 21). If valid estimates of the population range or variance are available, such corrections provide estimates of the magnitude of the correlation that would be observed in a population with that variance.

## 2.3 Missing Effect Sizes in Primary Studies

One way of capitalizing on chance in primary studies is by conducting multiple tests without controlling for inflation of Type I error rate. But since meta-analysts are more interested in the magnitude of effects than their statistical significance, the failure to adjust the Type I error rate in primary studies is not necessarily a problem in meta-analyses. However, if researchers in primary studies capitalize on chance and fail to report statistically nonsignificant findings, meta-analytic findings may be biased upward.

To prevent this bias, it is desirable to code the most complete available documents (e.g., dissertations and technical reports rather than published articles) and to contact study authors to obtain information not available in a research report, as Premack and Hunter (1988) and Shadish (1992) did with some success. However, this strategy is not always feasible, especially if the authors cannot be located or they have discarded the relevant information. In these cases, meta-analysts need to pursue other strategies. One is to explore how missing data might have affected their findings by examining whether studies with little or no missing data yield comparable findings to studies with more missing data or missing data patterned in a particular way.

Another strategy is to pursue imputation strategies discussed in Chapter 12. However, all imputation strategies require assumptions. When these assumptions cannot be convincingly justified, the validity of meta-analytic inferences has to be questioned. For example, in early meta-analyses of the psychotherapy outcome literature, it was assumed that the most likely estimate for a missing effect size was zero. This assumption was based on the presumption that researchers failed to report outcomes only if they did not differ from zero and were statistically nonsignificant. Although this assumption has never been comprehensively tested, Shapiro and Shapiro (1982) coded 540 unreported effect sizes as zero and then added them to 1,828 reported effects. This reduced the average effect from .93 to .72. But there may be other reasons why effects sizes are not reported, for instance when they are negative, or when they are positive but associated with unreliable measures. At issue then is the justification for the bases that meta-analysts offer for the values to impute. In Chapter 12, Pigott also discusses several more complex model-based estimation strategies under missing data (see also Rubin 1987; Little & Rubin 1987).

## 2.4 The Unreliability of Codings in Meta-Analyses

Meta-analyses contribute sources of unreliability in addition to those in primary studies. All the data synthesized in a meta-analysis are collected through a coding process susceptible to human error. Unreliability in the coding process adds random variation to the observations, increasing estimates of standard error and attenuating correlations among effect size estimates and study characteristics. Several strategies for controlling and reducing error in codings are discussed in Chapter 11, including pilot testing of the coding protocol, comprehensive coder training, coder expertise in the substantive areas covered by the coding system, consulting external literature, contacting primary authors, reliability assessments, confidence ratings for individual codings, and sensitivity analyses.

## 2.5 Capitalizing on Chance in Meta-Analyses

There are three major ways in which meta-analyses may capitalize on chance. First, a publication bias may exist such that studies with statistically significant findings in support of a study's hypotheses are more likely to be submitted for publication. Indeed, Greenwald (1975), Rosenthal (1979), and others have argued that the studies published in the behavioral and social sciences are likely to be a biased sample of all the studies actually carried out (see also Chapter 25). An extension of this bias may operate even among published studies if those that are easier to identify and retrieve have different effect sizes than other studies. This availability bias can arise because of the greater visibility of studies that appear in "major" publications, if the publication source is well abstracted by the major referencing services, if the authors are well connected in the professional networks, and if the paper's title or abstract contains keywords relevant for a particular meta-analysis. Thus, the unsuccessful replication by an unknown assistant professor may have been rejected in a "major" journal, however appropriate it might have been for it to be read at a conference or to appear in a less well-known publication.

The chapters on scientific communication (Chapter 4), reference databases (Chapter 5), registers and bibliographies (Chapter 6), publication bias (Chapter 25), and fugitive literature (Chapter 7) provide many suggestions for dealing with publication bias. We would like to stress three of them:

1. Strenuous attempts should be made to find studies that are unpublished or are otherwise difficult to retrieve.

2. Separate effect size estimates should be obtained for published and unpublished studies, and for studies that varied in how difficult they were to identify and locate.

3. If the evidence indicates that effect estimates depend on publication history, the likely consequences of this bias should be assessed using Rosenthal's 1979 fail-safe number or Hedges's 1984 worst case scenario of censored retrieval.

A second way in which meta-analysts may capitalize on chance is by analyzing the selection of effect sizes within studies. Research reports frequently present more than one estimate, especially when there are multiple outcome measures, multiple treatment and control groups, and multiple delayed time points for assessment. Not all of these effect estimates may be relevant for a particular topic, and some of the relevant ones may be more important than others. Meta-analysts must decide which effect estimates should be selected to enter the meta-analysis. Bias occurs when effect estimates are selected that are just as substantively relevant as those not selected but that differ from them in average effect size. Matt (1989) discovered this when three independent coders recoded a subsample of the studies in Smith, Glass, and Miller's meta-analysis of the benefits of psychotherapy (1980). Following what seemed to be their rules for selecting and calculating effect estimates, the three independent recoders extracted almost three times as many effect estimates and their mean effect size was approximately .50 compared with the .90 from Smith, Glass, and Miller's original codings. In each meta-analysis rules should clearly indicate which effect estimates to include or exclude. If several plausible rules are identified, it is important to examine empirically whether they lead to the same results. While it may be relatively easy to specify such rules, implementing them in a reliable and valid way is another question. Hence, coders should also be trained in identifying relevant effect sizes within studies, and data analyses should explore for possible coder differences in results.

A third way in which meta-analysts may capitalize on chance is by conducting a large number of statistical tests without adequately controlling for Type I error. Typically, meta-analysts conduct many tests as they probe the dependence of an effect size on methodological and substantive characteristics. Traditionally, Type I error is set at a fixed level (e.g., $\alpha = .05$) and controlled simultaneously for a set of statistical tests. However, the larger the number of tests to be controlled simultaneously, the lower is the statistical power of the test. Hedges (1990) points out that there is a limit to the number of tests that can be supported with sufficient statistical power by a given collection of studies. If the number of tests relative to the number of independent effect sizes is small, research synthesists are better off to test only an a priori specified subset of possible hypotheses.

## 2.6 Bias in Transforming Effect Sizes

Meta-analyses require that findings from primary studies be transformed into a common metric such as a correlation coefficient, a standardized mean difference, or standard normal deviate (see Chapter 16). Because studies differ in the type of quantitative information they provide about intervention effects, transformation rules were developed to derive common effect size estimates from many different metrics. Bias results if some types of transformation lead to systematically different estimates of average effect size or standard error than other types.

The best understood case of transformation bias concerns the situation in which probability levels are aggregated across studies and some of these levels have been truncated (Rosenthal 1990; Wolf 1990). For instance, a study might report that a group difference was statistically significant at $p < .05$, failing to specify the exact probability level. Another case of potential bias involves probit transformations, which are commonly used to convert dichotomous outcome information (e.g., improved vs. not improved; convicted vs. not convicted) into a continuous effect size metric. Probit transformations may inflate effect size estimates if the distribution of the continuous variable assumed to underlie the reported dichotomous outcome is nonnormal (Glass, McGaw, & Smith 1981). Moreover, probit-based effect size estimates are much more uncertain than estimates computed directly from means of the continuous variable (see Chapter 16). Whenever possible, meta-analysts are advised to calculate effect sizes directly from means, standard deviations, or the like rather than from such approximations as truncated $p$ levels or proportions improved. This will be possible for many studies, though not all. When it is not possible, our limited understanding of approximate effect sizes suggests that meta-analysts should empirically examine whether estimates differ by type of effect size transformation.

## 2.7 The Lack of Statistical Independence Among Effect Sizes

Stochastic dependencies among effect sizes may influence average effect estimates and their precision (see Chapter 22). Effect size estimates entering into a meta-analysis may lack statistical independence for at least four reasons (Hedges 1990):

1. Different effect size estimates may be calculated on the same respondents using different measures.

2. Effect sizes may be calculated by comparing different interventions with a single control group, or different control groups with a single intervention group.

3. Different samples may be used in the same study to calculate an effect estimate for each sample.

4. A series of studies may be conducted by the same research team resulting in nonindependent results.

Chapters 16 and 22 discuss several approaches to dealing with such dependencies. The simplest involves analyzing for each study only one of the set of possible correlated effects (e.g., the mean or median of all effects, a randomly selected effect estimate, or the most theoretically relevant estimate). This strategy is conservative and does not take account of all the available data. Hedges and Olkin (1985) developed a multivariate statistical framework in which dependencies can be directly modeled (see also Chapters 2 and 3; and Raudenbush, Becker, & Kalaian 1988; Rosenthal & Rubin 1986). This framework allows one, for instance, to combine correlated effect sizes to get a single effect size estimate or to combine vectors of effect sizes measured on different variables to estimate an ensemble of correlated effects. These multivariate models are more complex than the previously discussed univariate techniques and require estimates of the covariance structure among the correlated effect sizes. These may be difficult, if not impossible, to obtain in part because of missing information in primary studies.

## 2.8 The Failure to Weight Study-Level Effect Sizes Proportional to Their Precision

Even if one obtains unbiased effect estimates within a study, simply averaging them may yield biased average effect estimates and incorrect sampling errors if the effect sizes from different studies vary in precision (i.e., have different standard errors; see Chapter 18). Therefore, each study-level effect size should be weighted proportional to its precision, giving more weight to the more precise estimates. Because precision is largely a function of a study's sample size, weighting each study-level effect size according to the inverse of its sampling variance (Hedges & Olkin 1985) gives more weight to studies with larger samples.

## 2.9 The Underjustified Use of Fixed or Random Effects Models

For the statistical analysis of effect sizes, Hedges and Olkin (1985) distinguish between postulating a model with fixed effects and one with random effects. The fixed effects model assumes in its simplest form that all studies have a common but unknown effect size and that estimates of this population value differ only as a result of sampling variability. Thus, each realization of a treatment is considered to be an instance randomly drawn from the population of treatment effects. Homogeneity tests provide one way of determining whether the observed variability among effect size estimates is reasonably consistent with the model of a single fixed effect size across studies. In the random effects model, each treatment is assumed to have its own unique underlying effect and to be a sample realization from a universe of related but distinct treatments. Under the random effects model, the effects of a sample of treatments are best represented as a distribution of true effects rather than as a point estimate. The two models have different implications for the analysis and interpretation of effect size estimates (see Chapters 19 and 20). For instance, in the fixed effects model the average effect estimate and its sampling error are meaningful indices of overall treatment efficacy, whereas in the random effects model the average effect estimate is not very meaningful without a measure of the variation in the true effect of the treatment(s).

The decision about whether to assume a fixed or random effects model is primarily influenced by the assumptions that analysts make about the underlying processes generating an effect. Only secondarily is the decision influenced by the heterogeneity observed in the data and by the results of a homogeneity test. To assume a fixed model seems more reasonable if the hypothesis of homogeneity is not rejected, and no third variables can be adduced that may have caused the consistency. However, if theory suggests a fixed population effect but a homogeneity test indicates that the observed variability exceeds what is expected based on sampling error alone, two possible interpretations follow. One is that the assumption of a fixed population is wrong and that a random effects model provides a more adequate rep-

**Table 31.2 Threats to Inferences About the Causal Relationship Between Treatment and Outcome Classes**

1. The failure to assign at random
2. Deficiencies in the implementation of treatment contrasts
3. Confounding levels of a moderator variable with substantively irrelevant study characteristics
4. The misspecification of causal mediating relationships

resentation of the data. The second is that the fixed effects model is true but variables responsible for the increased variability are not known or adequately modeled. Thus, there is no simple indicator of which model is correct (see Chapter 3). However, it is useful to examine as critically as possible all the substantive theoretical reasons for inferring a fixed effects model over a random effects model, particularly when the homogeneity assumption is rejected, as it frequently is.

## 2.10 Lack of Statistical Power

Compared with statistical analyses in primary studies, statistical power will typically be much higher in meta-analyses, particularly when meta-analysts are interested only in estimating the average effect of a broad class of interventions. But some meta-analysts do have small samples of estimates, and most meta-analysts are interested in examining effect sizes for subclasses of treatments and outcomes, different types of settings, and different subpopulations. In these last cases, the small number of studies and the large number of statistical tests reduce statistical power. The meta-analyst then has to decide which trade-off to make between the number of statistical tests and the statistical power of these tests.

## 3. THREATS TO INFERENCES ABOUT THE CAUSAL RELATIONSHIP BETWEEN TREATMENT AND OUTCOME CLASSES

The foregoing discussion was about threats to any type of claim about the association of two variables. Whenever a reliable association between independent and dependent variables is presumed to be causal, some *additional* threats need to be considered (see Table 31.2 for an overview). In this regard, inferences about the possible causal nature of a treatment-outcome relationship are not necessarily jeopardized by deficiencies in primary studies, for all the individual sources of bias may cancel each other out exactly—at least in theory. A plausible threat arises only if the deficiencies within each study combine across studies to create a predominant direction of bias. In the following discussion, we distinguish among three groups of threats to valid inference about causality according to the three major types of causal relationships outlined in the introduction—that is, a simple bivariate descriptive causal relationship, a causal moderator relationship, and a causal mediating relationship.

## 3.1 The Failure to Assign at Random

Questions about descriptive bivariate causal relationships are among the most frequently examined in meta-analysis. They include questions such as: Do juvenile delinquency interventions reduce recidivism? Does psychotherapy influence mental health? Do early childhood intervention programs influence cognitive development? For these types of causal questions, the failure to assign units to treatments at random (or with some other perfectly known assignment system) may jeopardize meta-analytic conclusions because it is likely to result in a predominant direction of bias across primary studies.

In primary studies, ambiguity about the direction of causality and ambiguity about third-variable alternative explanations provide the major threats. The direction of causality issue is minor in experimental and quasi-experimental studies in which knowledge about the temporal sequence from manipulation to effect measurement is usually available. However, even in this situation a variety of third-variable explanations can still jeopardize causal inference. For instance, selection threats are pervasive in quasi-experimental studies of early childhood interventions and juvenile delinquency, and those participating in programs are said to be the more disadvantaged and likely to mature at different rates than those in control groups (Campbell & Boruch 1975). Indeed, a higher level of initial economic disadvantage is a precondition for entry into some early childhood programs.

An obvious way to deal with possibilities like this is to examine separately those studies with random assignment, if any are available. Assuming their methodological quality (see next threat), it is possible to contrast estimates from randomized experiments and lesser designs, though randomized experiments and quasi-experiments sometimes result in similar estimates (e.g., Lipsey 1992; Smith, Glass, & Miller 1980; Wittmann & Matt 1986). A second strategy involves making as-

sumptions about differences in design quality and rating studies accordingly. Then, adjustments can be made to estimates based on the quality of design used. The problem here, of course, is justifying the hierarchy of designs developed and the weights attached to each (see Chapter 8 for a full discussion).

## 3.2 Deficiencies in the Implementation of Treatment Contrasts

Random assignment of subjects to different experimental conditions assures the initial comparability between groups within known limits of sampling error. However, outside of controlled laboratories, random assignment is often difficult to implement; and even if successfully implemented, it does not ensure that comparability between groups is maintained beyond the initial assignment. Even the most carefully designed randomized experiments and quasi-experiments are not immune to implementation problems, such as differential attrition and diffusion or imitation of treatments. If the reviewed studies share deficiencies of implementation, a predominant bias may result when studies are combined. Deficiencies of implementation have been invoked to explain why effect estimates based on randomized experiments do not differ from those of quasi-experiments in many meta-analyses (e.g., Lipsey 1992; Smith, Glass & Miller 1980; Wittmann & Matt 1986). It may also be that the quasi-experiments were less biased than it seemed, or that, across all the quasi-experiments examined, the biases in one direction completely canceled out the biases in the other direction. However, there are instances of clear design effects resulting after random assignment had been initially implemented. For instance, Lipsey's meta-analysis of juvenile delinquency interventions (1992) found that differential attrition in randomized experiments and certain types of nonequivalence in quasi-experiments (e.g., different proportions of men in treatment and control groups) were associated with different effect sizes. The first suggests that the more amenable juveniles might have dropped out of treatment groups and/or the more delinquent juveniles out of control groups. The net effect is a potential bias.

## 3.3 Confounding Levels of a Moderator Variable with Substantively Irrelevant Study Characteristics

Moderator variables condition causal relationships by specifying how an outcome is related to different variants of an intervention, to different dosage levels, to different classes of outcomes, and to different types of settings and populations. Moderators can change the magnitude or the sign of a causal effect, as when a meta-analysis suggests that persuasive communications change attitudes more with girls than boys or that school segregation decreases academic achievement in schools that are juridically desegregated but improves it in schools that voluntarily desegregate. All moderator variables imply a statistical interaction and identify those factors that lead to cause-effect relationships of different sizes.

Threats to valid inference about the causal moderating role of a variable arise if substantively irrelevant factors are differentially associated with each level or category of the moderator variable under analysis. If the moderator variable (e.g., voluntary vs. court-ordered desegregation) is confounded with characteristics of the design, setting, or population (e.g., parent educational attainment), differences in the size or direction of a treatment effect brought about by the moderator cannot be distinguished from differential effects brought about by the potentially confounding variable.

There are two major strategies for dealing with this possibility. First, meta- analysts may be able to examine within-study comparisons of the moderator effect since they are obviously not prone to between-studies confounds. For instance, if the moderating role of treatment types A, B, and C is at stake, a meta-analysis can be conducted of all the studies with internal comparisons of treatment types A, B, and C (e.g., Shapiro & Shapiro 1982). Or if the moderating role of subject gender is of interest, inferences about gender differences might depend on within-study contrasts rather than on comparing studies with only males or females or on constructing a study-specific variable representing the percentage of males. A meta-analysis of within-study contrasts of the moderator effect provides an elegant approach to coping with confounding threats when examining hypotheses about moderator variables.

Second, statistical modeling may be a possible strategy. Shadish (1992) has illustrated how confounding variables can be statistically modeled by including higher-order interaction terms into meta-analytic regression models. If the confounding influences are confirmed because of a statistically reliable interaction of a treatment with, for instance, setting types, then follow-up tests can be performed to determine whether the moderator still exerts its influence after controlling for the setting variable.

## 3.4 The Misspecification of Causal Mediating Relationships

Mediator variables transmit a cause-effect relationship in the sense that they are consequences of a more distal manipulated cause and are also causes of a more distal measured effect. Mediating processes are typically invoked to explain a cause-effect connection and often involve more than one variable. That is, a *chain* of causal variables is used to describe the process set off by the agent. Few meta-analyses of mediating processes exist, and those that do utilize quite different strategies. Harris and Rosenthal's 1985 meta-analysis of the mediation of interpersonal expectancy effects used those available experimental studies that had information on at least one of the four mediational links abstracted from relevant substantive theory and never tested together in any individual study. Premack and Hunter's 1988 meta-analysis of mediation processes underlying individual decisions to form a trade union relied on combining correlation matrices from different studies on subsets of variables believed to mediate a cause-effect relationship. The entire mediation model had not been probed in any individual study. Becker's 1992 meta-analysis relied on the collection of individual correlations or correlation matrices to generate a combined correlation matrix. That is, individual studies may contribute evidence for one or more of the different causal links postulated in the mediational model. All these approaches examine mediational processes in which the data about links between variables come from within study comparisons. However, a fourth mediational approach infers causal links from between-studies comparisons. Shadish's 1992 research (also see Shadish & Sweeney 1991) on the mediation of the effects of therapeutic orientation on treatment effectiveness is a salient example of this.

While the four approaches differ considerably, they all struggle with the same practical problem—how to test mediational models involving multiple causal connections when only a few studies are available in which all the connections have been examined within the same study. A major source of threats to the meta-analytic study of mediation processes arises when the different mediational links are supported by different quantity and quality of evidence, perhaps because of excessive missing data on some mediational links, the operation of a predominant direction of bias for some other mediational links, or publication biases involving yet other parts of the mediational model.

On the basis of the few available meta-analyses of

causal mediational processes, it seems reasonable at this time to hypothesize that missing data are likely to be the most pervasive reason for misspecifying causal models (Cook et al. 1992). Missing data may lead the meta-analyst to omit important mediational links from the model that is actually tested and may also prevent consideration of alternative plausible models. While there are many substantive areas in which large numbers of studies probe a particular descriptive causal relationship, there are many fewer areas in which large numbers of studies provide a broad range of information on mediational processes, and even fewer in which two or more causal mediating models are directly compared. There are many reasons for these deficiencies. Process models are derived from substantive theory, and these theories change over time as they are improved or as new theories emerge. Obviously, the novel constructs in today's theories are not likely to have been measured well in past work. Moreover, today's researchers are reluctant to measure constructs from past theories that are now out of fashion or obsolete. Thus, the dynamism of theory development does not fit well the meta-analytic requirement for a stable set of mediating constructs or the simultaneous comparison of several competing substantive theories. Another relevant factor is that even if a large number of mediational variables have been measured, they are often measured less well and documented less thoroughly than are measures of cause and effect constructs. Measures of mediating variables are given less attention and are sometimes not analyzed unless a molar causal relationship has been established. Given the pressure to publish findings in timely fashion and to write succinct rather than comprehensive reports, the examination of mediating processes is often postponed, limited to selected findings, or based on inferior measures.

The consequences of and solutions to problems of misspecification are well documented in the statistical and methodological literature on multivariate causal models in primary studies (e.g., Bollen 1989; Glymour et al. 1987). However, the meta-analytic context in which these threats arise limits traditional solutions to these problems, and not much can be done about missing data in meta-analyses. Becker's study (1992) provides an example for what we expect is typical in many other fields. The model she wanted to study evolved from Eccles's model of social and psychological factors in achievement behavior (Eccles et al. 1983). It involves some 11 constructs, so that a complete test of the model would require information on 55 intercorrelations (i.e.,

potential mediating links). Of the 39 independent studies included in the review, evidence could be obtained for only 20 of the 55 intercorrelations, and the number of samples providing evidence for these 20 interrelations varied from 2 to 100 (median = 8). Nonetheless, Becker was able to examine several relevant submodels from Eccles's model, which can be a valuable addition to the literature.

## 4. THREATS TO GENERALIZED INFERENCES

Meta-analyses have the potential to generate findings that are much more generalizable than findings from single studies. Following Cronbach (1982) and Campbell and Stanley (1963), we consider generalizations to refer to universes of persons, treatments, outcomes, settings, and times. Generalized inferences about *classes* of persons, treatments, outcomes, settings, and times from which the reviewed studies were sampled are desired in all meta-analyses. These are the generalizations that meta-analysts like to make about, for instance, the effects of homework (the treatment class) on achievement (the outcome class) among 8-to-12-year-olds (the target population) in private schools (the target setting class) during the 1980s (the target time). To achieve such generalization, the meta-analyst must use studies that differ in the samples, instances, or cases of homework, of outcome measures, of student age and background, and of different private schools during the entire period between 1980 and 1989.

The data sources are the same when examining generalization *across universes*. For instance, are gender differences in aggression consistent across age groups and across types of aggressive behaviors (e.g., physical, verbal, fantasy), and are they the same in the 1980s as in the 1970s and 1960s? At issue here, of course, are moderator variables.

However, many consumers of meta-analyses are interested in the generalizability of findings *beyond the universes* of persons, treatments, outcomes, and settings for which data are available. For example: Can the effects of psychotherapy on mental health observed only in university settings be generalized to private practice settings and community mental health centers? Are the effects of school desegregation observed only in the 1960s and 1970s generalizable to the 1990s? In each of these examples, the issue is how one can justify inferences to these novel universes of persons, treatments, outcomes, settings, and times on the basis of findings in other universes.

**Table 31.3 Threats to Generalized Inferences**

1. Unknown sampling probabilities associated with the set of persons, settings, treatments, outcomes, and times entering a meta-analysis
2. The underrepresentation of prototypical attributes
3. The failure to test for heterogeneity in effect sizes
4. The lack of statistical power for studying disaggregated groups
5. The restricted heterogeneity of substantively irrelevant characteristics
6. The confounding of subclasses with substantively irrelevant characteristics
7. The restricted heterogeneity in classes

---

Generalizing on the basis of samples is most warranted when formal statistical sampling procedures have been used to draw the particular instances studied. Then, the sample matches the population on all attributes (measured and unmeasured) within known limits of sampling error. This entails, in the example above, assuming that the samples of homework, achievement measures, children, private schools, and years represented in the studies in the meta-analysis constitute random samples from whatever universes were specified in the guiding research question. However, this assumption cannot be tested, and in meta-analyses it is not clear how the sampled instances came to be chosen.

Nevertheless, Cook (1989) argues that generalized inferences about persons, treatments, outcomes, and settings can be *tentatively* justified even in the absence of random sampling. He discusses several principles for doing this. The first is based on identifying the prototypical, identity-inferring elements (Rosch 1973, 1978) of the target persons, settings, causes, and effects and then examining or assuming that they are likely to be better represented in a sample of studies than in any one study. The case can then be made that the sample and population are "proximally similar" (Campbell 1986). Moreover, each individual study's setting, population, measure, and treatments are likely to have unique components that are not part of the target class, making these heterogeneous irrelevancies (Campbell & Fiske 1959). Meta-analysis provides a wider range of such irrelevancies than any single study, and hence promotes the possibility of examining whether effects depend on such irrelevancies rather than on the target universe or class. The second principle for generalizing when random selection cannot be assumed is empirical interpolation and extrapolation—for example, generalizing to patients aged 30–40, given that patients aged 20–30 and 40–60 were examined; or generalizing to phobias A and B, given that phobias C, D, E, and F have been studied. Below are some threats related to the different types of generalized inference desired in meta-analyses (see Table 31.3 for an overview.).

## 4.1 Unknown Sampling Probabilities Associated with the Set of Persons, Settings, Treatments, Outcomes, and Times Entering a Meta-Analysis

As compelling as sampling theory is, we can rarely assume that the instances represented in a meta-analysis were randomly selected from the population of persons, settings, treatments, and outcomes to which generalization is desired. Even if there are random samples at the individual study level—which is itself rare—it is rarely feasible to assume that the studies entering into a meta-analysis constitute a formally representative sample of all such possible study-specific populations. The samples entering primary studies are chosen for proximal similarity and convenience rather than for reasons of formal sampling theory, and the studies containing these samples have an unknown relationship to all the studies that have been completed and that might be done on a particular topic.

## 4.2 The Underrepresentation of Prototypical Attributes

To demonstrate proximal similarity between a sample and its referent universe requires matching theoretically derived prototypical elements of the universe with the elements of the studies at hand. For instance, school desegregation can be explicated to have as its most prototypical element the education of children from mixed racial backgrounds within the same school building for "many" years. A meta-analysis in which none of the studies has desegregation implemented for more than three years might not therefore constitute school desegregation as widely understood, the more so if the studies under review were themselves biased toward examining the first year of desegregation rather than three years (Cook 1984). In a similar vein, any meta-analysis predicated on examining individual children's performance both before and after school desegregation would necessarily have to involve children who had switched from segregated to desegregated schools. Yet school desegregation can be explicated to have as another prototypical element that racial desegregation is the norm; that is, there is no other viable alternative and so no possibility of going from a segregated to a desegregated school. This aspect of the definition would be lost in any research synthesis that underrepresented situations in which children had never known any state other than attending a desegregated school.

The obvious solution to this threat is a thorough and explicit theoretical analysis of the key populations or classes to which generalization is sought, mindful of the reality that not all theorists will (or should) agree. In generalizing to target causal treatment and effects, it has long been traditional to rely on such theoretical analyses to select instances rather than to rely on randomly sampling treatment variants or outcome measures from some exhaustive pool (Cronbach et al. 1972). At issue in meta-analysis is following the same sampling strategy for persons, settings, and times and then applying the analysis to the sample of studies judged to be relevant to answering a particular research question.

## 4.3 The Failure to Test for Heterogeneity in Effect Sizes

Combining effect estimates across studies is reasonable only if the studies share a common population effect size, $\theta$. A statistical test for homogeneity has been developed (Hedges 1982; Rosenthal & Rubin 1982) to determine whether the variability in effect size estimates exceeds that expected from sampling error alone. If the statistical null hypothesis of homogeneous effect sizes is not rejected, it is assumed that a single population effect size fits the data adequately and that the weighted mean effect size $\bar{T}$ provides an adequate estimate of the population effect size $\theta$. If the hypothesis is rejected, the implication is that subclasses of studies exist which differ in effect size. This begins the search to identify the nature of such subclasses. Hence, heterogeneity tests play an important role in examining the robustness of a relationship and in initiating the search for factors that might moderate the relationship. The failure to test for heterogeneity may result in lumping into one category manifestly different subclasses of persons, treatments, outcomes, settings, or times. This problem is frequently referred to as the apples and oranges problem of meta-analysis. However, Glass (1978; also see Smith, Glass, & Miller 1980) and Rosenthal (1990) have both argued that apples and oranges should indeed be mixed if the interest is in generalizing to such higher-order characteristics as fruit or whatever else inheres in an array of

different treatments, outcomes, settings, persons, and times. We should indeed be willing to combine studies if different sample characteristics yield comparable results in reviews. In this context, the heterogeneity test indicates when studies yield such different results that average effect sizes need to be disaggregated through blocking on study characteristics that might explain the mean differences in effect size.

Coping with this threat is relatively simple, and homogeneity tests have to become standard both as a means of identifying the most parsimonious statistical model to describe the data and as a means of testing model specification (see Chapter 19). However, the likelihood of design flaws in primary studies and of publication biases and the like makes the interpretation of homogeneity tests more complex (Hedges & Becker 1986). If all the studies being meta-analyzed share the same flaw, or if studies with zero and negative effects are less likely to be published, then a consistent bias results across studies and can make the effect sizes appear more consistent than they really are. Failure to reject the null hypothesis that observed effect sizes are a sample realization of the same population effect does not prove it. Conversely, if all the studies have different design flaws, effect sizes could be heterogeneous even though they actually share the same population effect. Obviously, the causes of heterogeneity that are of greatest interest are of a substantive rather than a methodological nature. Consequently, it is useful to differentiate between homogeneity tests conducted before and after the assumption has been defended that all study-level differences in methodological irrelevancies have been accounted for. We will return to this issue later, and for now it is important to note only that early analyses of design characteristics should always be carried out to help identify design features that may inflate estimates of heterogeneity.

## 4.4 The Lack of Statistical Power for Studying Disaggregated Groups

If there is evidence that effect sizes are moderated by substantive variables of interest, highly aggregated classes of treatments, outcomes, persons, or settings can be disaggregated to examine the conditions under which an effect changes in sign or magnitude. Such subgroup analyses rely on a smaller number of studies than main-effect analyses and may involve additional statistical tests, lowering the statistical power for the subanalyses in question. Large samples mitigate against this problem, as do statistical tests adjusted to take into account the number of tests made. But even more useful—though less often feasible—are analyses based on aggregating within-study estimates of consequences of particular moderator variables.

## 4.5 The Restricted Heterogeneity of Substantively Irrelevant Characteristics

Even if prototypical attributes of a universe are represented in the reviewed studies, a threat arises if a meta-analysis cannot demonstrate that the generalized inference holds across substantively irrelevant characteristics. For instance, if the reviewed studies were conducted by just one research team, relied on voluntary participation by students, or depended on teachers being highly motivated, the threat would then arise that all conclusions about the general effectiveness of homework are confounded with substantively irrelevant aspects of the research context. To give an even more concrete example, if private schools are explicated to be those where school expenses come from student fees, donations, and the proceeds on endowments (rather than from taxes), it is irrelevant whether the schools are parochial or nonparochial; Catholic, Jewish, Protestant, or Muslim; military schools or elite academic schools. To generalize to private schools in the abstract requires being able to show that relationships are not limited to one or a few of these contexts—say parochial or military schools.

Limited heterogeneity in substantively irrelevant variables will also impede the transfer of findings to new universes because it hinders the ability to demonstrate the robustness of a causal relationship across substantive irrelevancies of design, implementation, or measurement method. The wider the range and the larger the number of substantively irrelevant aspects across which a finding is robust, and the better moderating influences are understood, the stronger is the belief that the finding will also hold under the influence of not yet examined contextual irrelevancies.

## 4.6 The Confounding of Subclasses with Substantively Irrelevant Characteristics

Even if substantively irrelevant aspects are heterogeneous across studies, the possibility arises that subclasses of treatments, outcomes, settings, persons, or times are confounded with substantively irrelevant char-

acteristics of studies. This happened in a meta-analysis of psychotherapy outcomes in which differences in treatment effects were observed across different types of psychotherapy, but psychotherapy types were confounded with such substantively irrelevant research design features as the way psychotherapy outcomes were assessed (Wittmann & Matt 1986). This impedes the ability to identify treatment type as a characteristic that moderates intervention effects.

There are two major strategies for dealing with such confounding. First, meta-analysts may be able to examine within-study comparisons of the moderator effect since they are obviously not prone to between-studies confounds. Second, statistical modeling of the confounding threats may be possible. Thus, when Wittmann and Matt (1983) statistically controlled for differences in research design using hierarchical regression analysis, the type of psychotherapy no longer moderated the treatment effect. To eliminate the biases due to pretest nonequivalence, attrition, sample size, type of control group, and type of outcome measure, Lipsey (1992) used a weighted hierarchical regression analysis, first partialing out the variance in effect size due to method characteristics and then examining the incremental contribution of treatment characteristics. The critical question in statistically controlling for sources of nonequivalence between studies with different moderator variable characteristics is whether all relevant differences have been measured and their influence adequately modeled. Lipsey makes a convincing case that he was able to control for most of the irrelevant between-studies differences because only 11 percent of the total variance to be explained was left unaccounted for after sampling error, measurement error, method characteristics, and treatment characteristics were taken into account.

## 4.7 Restricted Heterogeneity in Classes of Persons, Treatments, Outcomes, Settings, and Times

Inferences about the robustness of a relationship and the conditions moderating its magnitude and direction are facilitated if the relationship can be studied for a large number and a wide range of persons, treatments, outcomes, settings, and times. This is the single most important potential strength of research syntheses over individual studies. While meta-analyses of standardized treatments and specifically designated outcomes, populations, and settings may increase the precision of some effect size estimates, such restrictions hamper our ability to better understand the conditions under which such relationships can and cannot be observed. Rather than limiting a research synthesis of a single facet of the universe of interest or lumping together a heterogeneous set of facets, we encourage meta-analysts—sample sizes permitting—to explicitly represent and take advantage of such heterogeneities.

Such advice has implications for those observers who have suggested that causal inferences in general—and causal moderator inferences in particular—could be enhanced if research synthesists relied only on studies with superior methodology, particularly randomized experiments with standardized treatments, manifestly valid outcomes, and clearly designated settings and populations (see Chalmers et al. 1988; Slavin 1986). Such a strategy appears to be useful in areas in which research is fairly standardized. However, other limitations arise because this standardization limits the heterogeneity in research designs, treatment implementations, outcome measures, recruitment strategies, subject characteristics, and the like. Hence, it is not possible to examine empirically the robustness of a particular effect that has been obtained in a restricted, standardized context.

Meta-analysis has the potential to increase one's confidence in generalizations to new universes if findings are robust across a wide range and a large number of different universes. The more robust the findings and the more heterogeneous the populations, settings, treatments, outcomes, and times in which they were observed, the greater is the belief that similar findings will be observed beyond the populations studied. If the evidence for stubborn empirical robustness can be augmented by evidence for causal moderating conditions, the novel universes in which a causal relationship is expected to hold can be even better identified.

The logical weakness of this argument lies in its inductive basis. The fact that psycho-educational interventions with adult surgical patients have consistently shown earlier release from the hospital across a broad range of major and minor surgeries and across a wide range of respondents and of treatment providers throughout the 1960s, 1970s, and 1980s (Devine 1992) cannot logically guarantee that the same effect will hold for as yet unstudied surgeries, and in the future. However, the robustness of the relationship does strengthen the belief that psycho-educational interventions will have beneficial effects with new groups of patients and with novel surgeries in the near future. Homogeneous populations, treatments, outcomes, settings, and times limit the examination of causal contingencies and robustness and,

consequently, impede inferences about the transfer of findings to novel contexts.

## 5. CONCLUSION

We have attempted to present a series of threats to the validity of the types of conclusions most often drawn from research syntheses. Some threats speak to problems in drawing inferences about simple bivariate relationships, others to descriptive causal inferences, and yet others to more explanatory inferences based on identifying factors that moderate or mediate particular relationships. The threats we have presented are in large measure a summary of what other scholars have identified since Glass's pioneering work (Glass 1976, 1978; Smith & Glass 1977). We can expect the list to change at the margin as new threats are identified, current ones are seen as less relevant than we now think, and meta-analysis is put to new purposes.

We have also pointed to some of the tasks facing research synthesists in the next decade. One is to model substantively irrelevant study factors when examining moderator variables, because it will not always be possible to rule out such factors using within-study comparisons. A related task is to construct a viable new theory of generalization because our most elegant theory of generalization—formal sampling theory—is rarely practical in research synthesis. Yet it is precisely in the realm of generalization and the specification of causal contingencies that research synthesis promises to have its strongest impact. In this chapter, we have constructed one justification in terms of purposive selection for both prototypical elements and heterogeneous irrelevancies, but this and other approaches should be explored in the future.

Another issue for the future has to be the extension of research synthesis into areas in which causal mediation is at issue. In our judgment, it will be difficult to use meta-analysis for explanatory purposes as fine as identifying mediating processes. This is not for reasons intrinsic to meta-analysis, but because measurement of potential mediating variables tends to be sporadic and of low quality across studies. For research synthesis to become a widely used approach in investigating causal mediation, there will have to be changes in how primary studies are designed, conducted, and published. While it is not realistic to expect such changes in the short run, a long-term goal should be to encourage primary research with mediational measures taken from a number of different substantive theories and to encourage the greater availability of research reports that present correlation matrices among all the potential mediating variables.

# 6. REFERENCES

Anderson, J. R. (1991). The adaptive nature of human categorization. *Psychological Review, 98,* 409–429.

Becker, B. J. (1992). Models of science achievement: Forces affecting male and female performance in school science. In T. D. Cook, H. Cooper, D. S. Cordray, H., Hartmann, L. V. Hedges, R. J. Light, T. A. Louis, & F. Mosteller (Eds.), *Meta-analysis for explanation: A casebook* (pp. 209–281). New York: Russell Sage Foundation.

Bollen, K. A. (1989). *Structural equations with latent variables.* New York: Wiley.

Campbell, D. T. (1957). Factors relevant to the validity of experiments in social settings. *Psychological Bulletin, 54,* 297–312.

Campbell, D. T. (1986). Relabeling internal and external validity for applied social scientists. In W. M. K. Trochim (Ed.), *Advances in quasi-experimental design and analysis* (New Directions in Program Evaluation No. 31, pp. 67–77). San Francisco: Jossey-Bass.

Campbell, D. T., & Boruch, R. F. (1975). Making the case for randomized assignment to treatments by considering the alternatives: Six ways in which quasi-experimental evaluations tend to underestimate effects. In C. A. Bennett & A. A. Lumsdaine (Eds.), *Evaluation and experience: Some critical issues in assessing social programs* (pp. 195–296). New York: Academic Press.

Campbell, D. T., & Fiske, D. W. (1959). Convergent and discriminant validation by the multitrait-multimethod matrix. *Psychological Bulletin, 56,* 81–105.

Campbell, D. T., & Stanley, J. C. (1963). Experimental and quasi-experimental designs for research on teaching. In N. L. Gage (Ed.), *Handbook of research on teaching* (pp. 171–246). Chicago: Rand McNally.

Chalmers, T. C., Berrier, J., Hewitt, P., Berlin, J., Reitman, D., Nagalingam, R., & Sacks, H. (1988). Meta-analysis of randomized controlled trials as a method of estimating rare complications of non-steroid anti-inflammatory drug therapy. *Alimentary and Pharmacological Therapy, 2S,* 9–26.

Collingwood, R. G. (1940). *An essay on meta-physics.* Oxford: Clarendon Press.

Cook, T. D. (1984). What have black children gained academically from school integration? Examination of the meta-analytic evidence. In T. D. Cook, D. Armor, R. Crain, N. Miller, W. Stephan, H. Walberg, & P. Wortman (Eds.), *School desegregation and black achievement.* Unpublished report. Washington, DC: National Institute of Education. (ERIC No. ED 241 671)

Cook, T. D. (1989). The generalization of causal connections: Multiple theories in search of clear practice. In L. Sechrest, E. Perrin, & J. Bunker (Eds.), *Research methodology: Strengthening causal interpretations of nonexperimental data.* Washington, DC: U.S. Department of Health and Human Services. (DHHS Publication No. (PHS) 90-3454)

Cook, T. D., & Campbell, D. T. (1979). *Quasi-experimentation: Design and analysis issues for field settings.* Chicago: Rand McNally.

Cook, T. D., Cooper, H., Cordray, D. S., Hartmann, H., Hedges, L. V., Light, R. J., Louis, T. A., & Mosteller, F. (1992). *Meta-analysis for explanation: A casebook.* New York: Russell Sage Foundation.

Cook, T. D., & Leviton, L. (1980). Reviewing the literature: A comparison of traditional methods with meta-analysis. *Journal of Personality, 48,* 449–472.

Cooper, H. M. (1989). *Integrating research: A guide for literature reviews* (2nd ed.). Newbury Park, CA: Sage.

Cronbach, L. J. (1982). *Designing evaluation of educational and social programs.* San Francisco: Jossey-Bass.

Cronbach, L. J., Gleser, G. C., Nanda, H., & Rajaratnam, N. (1972). *Dependability of behavioral measurements.* New York: Wiley.

Devine, E. C. (1992). Effects of psychoeducational care with adult surgical patients: A theory-probing meta-analysis of intervention studies. In T. D. Cook, H. Cooper, D. S. Cordray, H. Hartman, L. V. Hedges, R. J. Light, T. A. Louis, & F. Mosteller, *Meta-analysis for explanation: A casebook* (pp. 35–82). New York: Russell Sage Foundation.

Eccles (Parsons), J., Adler, T. F., Futterman, R., Goff, S. B. Kaczala, C. M., Meece, J. L., & Midgley, C. (1983). Expectations, values, and academic behaviors. In J. T. Spence (Ed.), *Perspectives on achievement and achievement motivation.* San Francisco: Freeman.

Gasking, D. (1955). Causation and recipes. *Mind, 64,* 479–487.

Glass, G. V. (1976). Primary, secondary, and meta-analysis. *Educational Researcher, 5,* 3–8.

Glass, G. V. (1978). Integrating findings: The meta-analysis of research. *Review of Research in Education, 5,* 351–379.

Glass, G. V., McGaw, B., & Smith, M. L. (1981). *Meta-analysis in social research.* Beverly Hills, CA: Sage.

Glymour, C., Scheines, R., Spirtes, K., & Kelly, K.

(1987). *Discovering causal structures: Artificial intelligence, philosophy of science, and statistical modeling.* Orlando, FL: Academic Press.

Greenwald, A. G. (1975). Consequences of prejudice against the null hypothesis. *Psychological Bulletin, 82,* 1–20.

Harris, M. J., & Rosenthal, R. R. (1985). Mediation of interpersonal expectancy effects: 31 meta-analyses. *Psychological Bulletin, 97,* 363–386.

Hedges, L. V. (1981). Distribution theory for Glass's estimator of effect size and related estimators. *Journal of Educational Statistics, 6,* 107–128.

Hedges, L. V. (1982). Estimating effect size from a series of independent experiments. *Psychological Bulletin, 92,* 490–99.

Hedges, L. V. (1984). Estimation of effect size under nonrandom sampling: The effects of censoring studies yielding statistically insignificant mean differences. *Journal of Educational Statistics, 9,* 61–85.

Hedges, L. V. (1990). Directions for future methodology. In K. W. Wachter & M. L. Straf (Eds.), *The future of meta-analysis* (pp. 11–26). New York: Russell Sage Foundation.

Hedges, L. V., & Becker, B. J. (1986). Statistical methods in the meta-analysis of research on gender differences. In J. S. Hyde & M. C. Linn (Eds.), *The psychology of gender: Advances through meta-analysis* (pp. 14–50). Baltimore: Johns Hopkins University Press.

Hedges, L. V., & Olkin, I. (1985). *Statistical methods for meta-analysis.* Orlando, FL: Academic Press.

Hunter, J. E., & Schmidt, F. L. (1990). *Methods of meta-analysis: Correcting error and bias in research findings.* Newbury Park: Sage.

Huttenlocher, J., Hedges, L. V., & Duncan, S. (1991). Categories and particulars: Prototype effects in estimating spatial location. *Psychological Review, 98,* 352–376.

Kulik, J. A., & Kulik, C. L. C. (1986, April). *Operative and interpretable effect sizes in meta-analysis.* Paper presented at the annual meeting of the American Educational Research Association, San Francisco. (ERIC No. ED 276529).

Lipsey, M. W. (1992). Juvenile delinquency treatment: A meta-analytic inquiry into the variability of effects. In T. D. Cook, H. Cooper, D. S. Cordray, H. Hartmann, L. V. Hedges, R. J. Light, T. A. Louis, & F. Mosteller, *Meta-analysis for explanation: A casebook* (pp. 83–127). New York: Russell Sage Foundation.

Little, R. J. A., & Rubin, D. B. (1987). *Statistical analysis with missing data.* New York: Wiley.

Mackie, J. L. (1974). *The cement of the universe: A study of causation.* Oxford: Oxford University Press.

Matt, G. E. (1989). Decision rules for selecting effect sizes in meta-analysis: A review and reanalysis of psychotherapy outcome studies. *Psychological Bulletin, 105,* 106–115.

Premack, S. L., & Hunter, J. E. (1988). Individual unionization decisions. *Psychological Bulletin, 103,* 223–234.

Raudenbush, S. W., Becker, B. J., & Kalaian, H. (1988). Modeling multivariate effect sizes. *Psychological Bulletin, 103,* 111–120.

Rosch, E. (1973). Natural categories. *Cognitive Psychology, 4,* 328–350.

Rosch, E. (1978). Principles in categorization. In E. Rosch & B. B. Lloyd (Eds.), *Cognition and categorization.* Hillsdale, NJ: Erlbaum.

Rosenthal, R. (1979). The "file-drawer problem" and tolerance for null results. *Psychological Bulletin, 86,* 638–641.

Rosenthal, R. (1984). *Meta-analytic procedures for social research.* Beverly Hills, CA: Sage.

Rosenthal, R. (1990). An evaluation of procedure and results. In K. W. Wachter & M. L. Straf (Eds.), *The future of meta-analysis* (pp. 123–133). New York: Russell Sage Foundation.

Rosenthal, R., & Rubin, D. B. (1982). Comparing effect sizes of independent studies. *Psychological Bulletin, 85,* 185–193.

Rosenthal, R., & Rubin, D. B. (1986). Meta-analytic procedures for combining studies with multiple effect sizes. *Psychological Bulletin, 99,* 400–406.

Rubin, D. B. (1987). *Multiple imputation for nonresponse in surveys.* New York: Wiley.

Shadish, W. R., Jr. (1992). Do family and marital psychotherapies change what people do? A meta-analysis of behavioral outcomes. In T. D. Cook, H. Cooper, D. S. Cordray, H. Hartman, L. V. Hedges, R. J. Light, T. A. Louis, & F. Mosteller, *Meta-analysis for explanation: A casebook* (pp. 129–208). New York: Russell Sage Foundation.

Shadish, W. R., Jr., & Sweeney, R. B. (1991). Mediators and moderators in meta-analysis: There's a reason we don't let dodo birds tell us which psychotherapies should have prizes. *Journal of Consulting and Clinical Psychology, 59,* 883–893.

Shapiro, D. A., & Shapiro, D. (1982). Meta-analysis of comparative therapy outcome studies: A replication and refinement. *Psychological Bulletin, 92,* 581–604.

Slavin, R. E. (1986). Best-evidence synthesis: An alternative to meta-analytic and traditional reviews. *Educational Researchers, 15,* 5–11.

Smith, M. L., & Glass, G. V. (1977). Meta-analysis of

psychotherapy outcome studies. *American Psychologist, 32,* 752–760.

Smith, M. L., Glass, G. V., & Miller, T. I. (1980). *The benefits of psychotherapy.* Baltimore: Johns Hopkins University Press.

Whitbeck, C. (1977). Causation in medicine: The disease entity model. *Philosophy of Science, 44,* 619–637.

Wittmann, W. W., & Matt, G. E. (1986). Meta-Analyse als Integration von Forschungsergebnissen am Beispiel deutschsprachiger Arbeiten zur Effektivität von Psychotherapie [Integration of German-language psychotherapy outcome studies through meta-analysis.]. *Psychologische Rundschau, 37,* 20–40.

Wolf, I. M. (1990). Methodological observations on bias. In K. W. Wachter & M. L. Straf (Eds.), *The future of meta-analysis* (pp. 139–151). New York: Russell Sage Foundation.

Zadeh, L. A. (1975). Fuzzy logic and approximate reasoning. *Synthese, 30,* 407–428.

Zadeh, L. A. (1982). A note on prototype theory and fuzzy sets. *Cognition, 12,* 291–297.

Cooper, H., and Hedges, L. V. (Eds.) 1994. *The Handbook of Research Synthesis.* New York: Russell Sage Foundation

# 32

# POTENTIALS AND LIMITATIONS OF RESEARCH SYNTHESIS

**HARRIS COOPER**
*University of Missouri*

**LARRY V. HEDGES**
*University of Chicago*

CONTENTS

## 1. INTRODUCTION

We suspect that readers of this volume reacted to it in one of two distinct ways: They may have been overwhelmed by the number and complexity of the issues that face a research synthesist; alternatively, they may have been delighted to have available a manual to help them through the synthesis process. We further suspect that which reaction was experienced depended on whether the book was read while thinking about or while actually performing a synthesis. In the abstract, the concerns raised in this handbook must seem daunting. Concretely however, research syntheses have been carried out for decades and will be for decades to come, and the problems encountered in their conduct do not really go away when they are ignored. Knowledge builders need a construction manual to accompany their blueprints and bricks.

Further, there is no reason to believe that carrying out a sound research synthesis is any more complex than carrying out sound primary research. The analogies between synthesis and survey research, content analysis, or even quasi-experimentation fit too well for this not to be the case. Certainly, each type of research has its unique characteristics. Still, when research synthesis procedures have become as familiar as primary research procedures much of what now seems overwhelming will come to be viewed as difficult, but manageable.

Likewise, expectations will change. Today, we do not expect a primary study to provide unequivocal answers to research questions, nor do we expect it to be performed without flaw. Research syntheses are the same. The perfect synthesis does not and never will exist. Synthesists who set standards that require them to implement all of the most rigorous techniques described in this book are bound to be disappointed. Time and other resources (not to mention the logic of discovery) will prevent such an accomplishment. The synthesist, like the primary researcher, must balance methodological rigor against practical feasibility.

In the remainder of this chapter, we will revisit some of the major issues that have emerged from the preceding pages. We will state once more some unique contributions that research synthesis can make to our understanding of scientific evidence. We will suggest a few limitations. Also, from our own reading of this handbook, we will identify several recurring or emerging issues in research synthesis methodology. Finally, we will briefly share some perspectives on what makes a knowledge synthesis of any kind, not just a research synthesis, most valuable to its readership.

## 2. UNIQUE CONTRIBUTIONS OF RESEARCH SYNTHESIS

### 2.1 Increased Precision and Reliability

Some comparisons were made above between primary research and research synthesis. It was suggested that the two forms of study had much in common. In contrast, when we compare research synthesis as described in this handbook with research synthesis as it was practiced prior to the popularization of meta-analytic techniques (and is still practiced in some quarters today), it is the dissimilarities that capture attention. Perhaps most striking are the improvements in precision and reliability that new techniques have made possible.

Precision in literature searches has been improved dramatically by the procedures described herein. Yesterday's synthesist attempted to uncover a literature by examining a small journal network and making a few phone calls. This strategy cannot suffice today. The proliferation of journals and the increase in the sheer quantity of research renders the old strategy inadequate. Today, the computer revolution in information science and the emergence of research registries mean that a synthesist can reach into thousands of journals and individual researcher's data files. While the present process is far from perfect, it is an enormous improvement over past practice.

The coding of studies and their evaluation for quality have also come a long way. The old process was rife with potential bias. In 1976, Glass wrote:

> A common method for integrating several studies with inconsistent findings is to carp on the design or analysis deficiencies of all but a few studies—those remaining frequently being one's own work or that of one's students and friends—and then advancing the one or two "acceptable" studies as the truth of the matter. (p. 4)

Today, research synthesists code their studies with considerably more care to avoid bias. Explicit, well-defined coding frames are used by multiple coders. Judgments about quality of research are sometimes eschewed entirely, allowing the data to determine if research design influences study outcomes.

Finally, the process of integrating and contrasting primary study results has taken a quantum leap forward. Gone are the days when a vote count of results decided an issue. It is no longer acceptable to string together paragraph descriptions of studies, with details of significance tests, and then conclude that "the data are inconsistent but appear to indicate. . . ." Today's synthesist can provide (a) confidence intervals around effect size estimates (b) for separate parts of a literature distinguished by both methodological and theoretical criteria (c) calculated several different ways using different assumptions about the adequacy of the literature search and coding scheme, and alternative statistical models.

These are only a few of the ways that the precision and reliability of current syntheses outstrip those of their predecessors. The increases in precision and reliability that a synthesist can achieve when a body of literature grows from 2 to 20 to 200 studies were squandered with yesterday's methods.

## 2.2 Testing Generalization and Moderating Influences

Current methods not only capitalize on accumulating evidence by making estimates more precise, but they also permit the testing of hypotheses that may have never been tested in primary studies. This advantage is most evident when the objective of the synthesist is to establish the generality or specificity of results. The ability of a synthesis to test whether a finding applies across settings, times, people, and researchers surpasses by far the ability of most primary studies. However, for yesterday's synthesist, the variation among studies was a nuisance; it clouded interpretation. The old methods of synthesis were handicapped severely when it came to judgments of whether a set of studies revealed consistent results and, if not, what might account for the inconsistency. Yesterday's synthesist often chose the wrong datum (significance tests rather than effect sizes) and the wrong evaluation criteria (implicit cognitive algebra rather than formal statistical test) on which to base these judgments. For today's synthesist, variety is the spice of life. The methods described in this handbook make such analyses routine. When the outcomes of studies prove too discrepant to support a claim that one underlying result describes them all, current techniques provide the synthesist with a way of systematically search-

ing for moderating influences, using consistent and explicit rules of evidence.

## 2.3 Asking Questions About the Scientific Enterprise

Finally, the practice of research synthesis permits scientists to study their own enterprise. Questions can be asked about trends in research over time, trends in both results and how research is carried out. For example, Ottenbacher and Cooper (1984) examined the effects of special versus regular class placement on the social adjustment of mentally retarded children. The found that studies of social adjustment conducted after 1968, when "mainstreaming" became the law, favored regular class placement, whereas studies prior to 1968 favored special classes.

Synthesists often uncover results that raise interesting questions about the relationship between research and the general societal atmosphere in which it takes place. By facilitating this form of self-analysis, current synthesis methods can be used to advance not only particular problem areas but also entire disciplines, by addressing more general questions in the psychology and sociology of science.

## 3. LIMITATIONS OF RESEARCH SYNTHESES

### 3.1 The Correlational Nature of Review Evidence

Research syntheses have limitations as well. Among the most critical is the correlational nature of review-generated evidence. Cooper (1982) introduced the terms "study-generated evidence" and "review-generated evidence" to distinguish between two types of evidence that appear in research syntheses. Study-generated evidence appears when individual studies contain results that directly test the relation under consideration. Suppose that each study in a set of studies experimentally manipulates an independent variable by randomly assigning subjects to conditions (say, whether heart patients take aspirin or whether students do homework). Then, a cumulative accounting of these studies permits the synthesist to make statements about causal relations with dependent variables. If the antecedent variable of interest is not manipulated (i.e., subjects are simply asked, "Do you take aspirin?" or "Do you do homework?''), then causal inferences are not permissible by either the primary researcher or the synthesist.

Review-generated evidence appears when the results of studies using different procedures to test the same hypothesis are compared. Suppose that half of all homework studies occurred in math classes and half in English classes. Suppose further that homework was found to improve achievement in math studies only. The synthesist cannot claim a causal link between subject matter and the effect of homework. This inference is not permissible because subject matter was not randomly assigned to studies and, therefore, confounds might exist. For example, math studies might have been conducted in high schools or might have used standardized tests, whereas English studies might have used elementary schools or teacher grades.

Specific confounds can be controlled statistically at the level of review-generated evidence, but the result can never lead to the same confidence in inferences produced by study-generated evidence from investigations employing random assignment. This is an inherent limitation of research syntheses. It also provides the synthesist with a fruitful source of suggestions concerning directions for future primary research.

## 3.2 The Post Hoc Nature of Synthesis Tests

It is almost always the case that researchers interested in conducting syntheses set upon the process with some, if not considerable, knowledge of the empirical data base they are about to summarize. They begin with a good notion of what the literature says about which interventions work, which moderators operate, and which explanatory variables are helpful. This being the case, the synthesist cannot state a hypothesis so derived and then also conclude that the same evidence supports the hypothesis. As Wachter and Straf (1990) pointed out, once data have been used to develop a theory, the same data cannot be used to test it. Synthesists who wish to test specific, a priori hypotheses in meta-analysis must go to extra lengths to convince their audience that the generation of the hypothesis and the data used to test it are truly independent.

## 3.3 The Need for New Primary Research

Each of the above limitations serves to underscore an obvious point: A research synthesis should never be considered a replacement for new primary research. Primary research and its synthesis are complementary

parts of a common process; they are not competing alternatives. The additional precision and reliability brought to syntheses by the procedures described in this text do not make research integrations substitutes for new data-gathering efforts. Instead, they help to ensure that the next wave of primary research is sent off in the most illuminating direction. A synthesis that concludes a problem is solved, that no future research is needed, should be deemed a failure. Even the best architects can see how the structures they have built can be improved.

## 4. EMERGING DEVELOPMENTS IN RESEARCH SYNTHESIS METHODOLOGY

### 4.1 Improving the Research Synthesis Databases

Two problems that confront research synthesists recurred throughout this text. They concern (a) the comprehensiveness of literature searches, especially as searches are influenced by publication bias, and (b) missing data in research reports. While each of these issues was treated in its own chapter, many authors felt the need to consider their impact in the context of other tasks carried out by the synthesist. The correspondence between the studies that can be accessed by the synthesist and the target population of studies is an issue in data collection, analysis, and interpretation. Missing data is an issue in data coding, analysis, and interpretation.

There is little need to reiterate the frustration that synthesists feel when they contemplate the possible biases in their conclusions caused by studies and results they cannot retrieve. Instead, when we consider the next generation of improvements in research synthesis procedures, we should look for ways to restructure the scientific information delivery systems so that more of the needed information becomes available to the research synthesist.

First, therefore, meta-analysts should call for an upgrading of standards for reporting of primary research results in professional journals. Journals need to make space for authors to report the means and standard deviations for all conditions, for the reliability of measures (and for full texts of measures when they are not previously published), and for range restrictions in samples. Further, as primary statistical analyses become more complex, the requirements of adequate reporting will become more burdensome. While means and standard deviations are sufficient for simple analyses, full correlation matrices (or even separate correlation matrices for each of several groups studied) may also be required for adequate reporting of multivariate analyses. Reporting this detailed information in journals is less feasible since it would require even more journal space. Yet primary analyses are not fully interpretable (and synthesis is certainly not possible) without them. Therefore, meta-analysts need some system whereby authors submit extended results sections along with their manuscripts and these sections are made available on request.

Journal reporting standards, however, are only a stopgap measure for addressing the problem of missing data, not publication bias. There are hints at some more comprehensive solutions. One answer may involve the continued development of research registers. Because research registers attempt to catalog investigations when they are initiated rather than when they are complete, they represent a unique opportunity for overcoming publication bias. In addition, they may be able to provide meta-analysts with more thorough reports of study results.

Of course, registers are not a panacea. Registers are helpful only if the researchers who register their studies keep and make available the results of their studies to synthesists who request them. Thus, we need professional standards that promote this level of sharing of even unpublished research findings. Also, registers will not be able to surmount problems in reporting format that make different study results incommensurable. Finally, they cannot tell a primary researcher which hypothesis to test so that their results are relevant to future synthesis topics.

Still, forward-looking researchers and funding agencies would be well advised to look toward the development of research registers as one of the most effective means for fostering knowledge accumulation. Given the pervasiveness of the publication bias and missing data problems, registers seem to hold considerable promise for alleviating these difficulties, even if they are only a partial solution.

## 4.2 Improving Analytic Procedures

Many aspects of analytic procedures in research synthesis have undergone rapid development in the last two decades. However, there are still many areas in which the development of new statistical methods or the adaptation of methods used elsewhere are needed. Perhaps as important as the addition of new methods is the wise use of the considerable repertoire of analytic methods already available to the research synthesist. We mention here a few analytic issues that arise repeatedly throughout this handbook. The first two relate to the database problems just mentioned.

**4.2.1 Missing data** Perhaps the most pervasive practical problem in research synthesis is that of missing data, which obviously influences any statistical analyses. While missing data as a general problem was addressed directly in Chapter 12, and the special case of missing data due to publication bias was addressed in Chapter 25, the problems created by missing data arose implicitly in many chapters of this handbook. For example, the prevalence of missing data on moderator and mediating variables influences the degree to which the problems investigated by a synthesis can be formulated. Missing data influences the data collection stage of a research synthesis by affecting the potential representativeness of studies in which complete data are available. It also affects coding certainty and reliability in studies with partially complete information. Missing data proves an especially pernicious problem as research syntheses turn to increasingly sophisticated analytic methods to handle dependencies and multivariate causal models as described in Chapter 23.

We believe that one of the most important emerging areas in research synthesis is the development of analytic methods to better handle missing data. Much of this work will likely be in the form of adapting methods that have been developed in other areas of statistics to the special requirements of research synthesis. These methods will produce more accurate analyses when data are not missing completely at random (i.e., are not a random sample of all data), but are well enough related to observed study characteristics that they can be predicted reasonably well with a model based on data that *are* observed. The methods discussed in Chapter 12, the EM algorithm-based methods discussed in section 3.6.2 of Chapter 23, and those discussed by Little and Rubin (1987) and Rubin (1987) are of this type.

**4.2.2 Publication bias** Publication bias is a form of missing data that is less easy to address via analytic approaches. We expect that there will be progress in the development of analytic models of publication bias and its correction by analytic means. The beginnings of these analytic methodologies were discussed in Chapter 25.

While these emerging methods are promising, even their most enthusiastic advocates suggest that it is better not to have to correct for publication bias in the first place. Thus, the best remedy for publication bias is the development of invariant sampling frames that would arise through research registers. This nonanalytic development in methodology could be a better substitute for improved statistical corrections in areas in which it is feasible.

**4.2.3 Fixed versus random effects models** The contrast between fixed and random effects models has been drawn repeatedly—directly in Chapters 3, 18–20, and 23; indirectly in Chapters 21, 24, and 26; and implicitly in Chapters 12 and 25. The issues in choosing between fixed and random effects models are subtle, and sound choices often involve a considerable amount of subjective judgment. In all but the most extreme cases, reasonable and intelligent people might disagree about their choices of modeling strategy. However, there is much agreement about criteria that might be used in these judgments.

The criterion offered in Chapter 3 (and reiterated in Chapter 31) for the choice between fixed and random effects models is conceptual. Meta-analysts should choose random effects models if they think of studies as different from one another in ways too complex to capture by a few simple study characteristics. If the object of the analysis is to make inferences about a universe of such diverse studies, then the random effects approach is conceptually sensible. Synthesists should choose fixed effects models if they believe that the important variation in effects is a consequence of a small number of study characteristics. In the fixed effects analysis the object is to draw inferences about studies with similar characteristics.

A practical criterion for choosing between fixed and random effects models is offered in Chapters 18, 19, and 23—namely, the criterion of empirical adequacy of the fixed effects model. In each of these chapters, the authors refer to tests of homogeneity, model specification, or goodness of fit of the fixed effects model. These tests essentially compare the observed (residual) variation of effect size estimates with the amount that would be expected if the fixed effects model fit the parameter values *exactly*. All of the authors argued that the use of fixed effects models was more difficult to justify when tests of model specification showed substantial variation in effect sizes that was not explained by the fixed effects model as specified. Conversely, fixed effects models were easier to justify when tests of model specification showed no excess (residual) variation. As noted in section 2.9 of Chapter 31, this empirical criterion, while important, is secondary to the theoretical consideration of how best to conceive the inference.

Some authors prefer the use of fixed effects models under almost any circumstances, regarding unexplained variation in effect size parameters as seriously compromising the certainty of inferences drawn from a synthesis (see Peto 1987; or section 4.1 of Chapter 30).

Other authors advocate essentially a random effects approach under all circumstances. The random effects model underlies all of the methods discussed in Chapter 21, and it is consistent with the Bayesian methods discussed in Chapter 26. In both cases the implicit argument was conceptual, namely, that studies constituted exchangeable units from some universe of similar studies. In both cases the object was to discover the mean and variance of effect size parameters associated with this universe.

One difference in the interpretation used in these two chapters is that the Bayesian interpretation of random effects models draws on the idea that between-studies variation can be conceived as uncertainty about the effect size parameter (see section 2.2. of Chapter 20). This interpretation of random effects models was also used in the treatment of synthetic regression models in section 3.8.2 of Chapter 23, where the use of a random effects model was explicitly referred to as adding a between-studies component of uncertainty to the analysis.

Yet another empirical criterion that was offered in Chapter 20 was based on the number of studies. Random effects analyses involve inferences from a sample of studies to a universe of studies. The precision of such inferences depends, in part, on the sample size—the number of studies available. Fixed effects models were advocated when the number of studies is small—too small for meaningful inferences from the sample of studies to a universe of studies. Random effects models were advocated when the number of studies is large enough to support such inferences. The reason for choosing random effects models (when empirically feasible) was conceptual—the belief that study effect sizes would be different across studies and that those differences would be controlled by a large number of unpredictable influences.

Thus, although there are differences among the details of the criteria given, the positions of these authors reflect a consensus on criteria. Conceptual criteria would be applied first, with the model chosen according to the goals of the inference. Only after considering the object of the inference would empirical criteria influence modeling strategy, perhaps by forcing a reformulation of the question to be addressed in the synthesis. The empirical finding of persistent heterogeneity among the effect sizes might force reconsideration of the choice of a fixed effects analysis. Similarly, the ambition to employ a random effects approach to draw inferences about a broad universe of studies might need to be reconsidered if the collection of empirical research results was too small for meaningful inference, to be replaced by fixed effects comparisons among particular studies.

A particularly interesting area of development is the use of random effects models to estimate the results of populations of studies that may not be identical in composition to the study sample (see U.S. General Accounting Office 1992). For example, in medical research, the patients (or doctors or clinics) selected to participate in clinical trials are typically not representative of the general patient population. Although the studies as conducted may be perfectly adequate for assessing whether a new treatment can produce treatment effects that are different from zero, they may not give a representative sample for assessing the likely effect in the nation if the new treatment became the standard. Simply extrapolating from the results of the studies conducted would not be warranted if the treatment was less effective with older or sicker patients than were typically included in the trials. Efforts to use information about systematic variation in effect sizes to predict the impact on the nation if a new medical treatment (or any other innovation) were adopted are an exciting application of research synthesis.

**4.2.4 Bayesian methods** Research synthesis, like any scientific endeavor, has many subjective aspects. Bayesian statistical analyses, designed to formally incorporate subjective knowledge and its uncertainty, have become increasingly important in many areas of applied statistics, and we expect research synthesis to be no exception. Chapter 26 provided only a brief introduction to how Beyesian methods might be used to incorporate subjective notions into a research synthesis. As quantitative research syntheses are more widely used, we expect to see a concomitant development of Bayesian methods suited to particular applications. One advantage to Bayesian methods is that potentially they can be adapted to combine hard data on some aspects of a problem with subjective assessments concerning other aspects of the problem about which there are no hard data. One such situation arises when the inference that is desired depends on several links in a causal chain, but not all of the links have been subjected to quanti-

tative empirical research (see Eddy, Hasselblad & Schacter 1992).

**4.2.5 Causal modeling in research synthesis** Causal modeling is destined to become more important in research synthesis for two reasons. First, the use of multivariate causal models in primary research will necessitate their greater use in research synthesis. Second, as research synthesists strive for greater explanation, it seems likely that they will turn to causal explanatory models whether or not they have been used in the underlying primary research literature (see Cook et al. 1992). The basic methodology for the meta-analysis of models is given in Chapter 23, and we expect the work given there to be the basis of many syntheses designed to probe causal explanations in future research syntheses.

A different and entirely new aspect of this methodology is that it has been used to examine the generalizability of research findings over facets that constitute differences in study characteristics (Becker, in press). For example, the method has been used to estimate the contribution of between-measures variation to the overall uncertainty (standard error) of the relationship or partial relationships between variables. This application of models in synthesis is exciting because it provides a mechanism for evaluating quantitatively the effect of construct breadth on generalizability of research results. Because broader constructs (those admitting a more diverse collection of operations) will typically lead to more between-studies variation associated with between-operations variation, syntheses based on broader constructs will typically be associated with greater overall uncertainty. However, broader constructs will have a larger range of application. Quantitative analyses of generalizability provide a means not only of understanding the body of research that is synthesized, but also of planning the measurement strategy of future research studies to ensure adequate generalizability across the constructs that are of interest.

## 5. CRITERIA FOR JUDGING REVIEW QUALITY

In discussing several meta-analyses of the desegregation literature, Wachter and Straf (1990) pointed out that sophisticated literature searching procedures, data quality controls, and statistical techniques can bring a research synthesist only so far. Eventually, Wachter wrote, ''there doesn't seem to be a big role in this kind of work for much intelligent statistics, as opposed to much wise thought'' (p. 182).

In the previous chapter, Matt and Cook began the process of extracting wisdom from technique. They attempted to help synthesists take the broad view of their work, to hold it up to standard that begin answering the question, "What have I learned?"

Strike and Posner (1983) addressed questions similar to Cook and Matt, but did so for knowledge syntheses in general, not just research syntheses. Their standards were more abstract. They suggested that a valuable knowledge synthesis must have both intellectual quality and practical utility. A synthesis should clarify and resolve issues in a literature rather than obscure them. It should result in a progressive paradigm shift, meaning that it brings (a) to a theory greater explanatory power, (b) to a practical program expanded scope of application, and (c) to future primary research an increased capacity to pursue unsolved problems. Always, a knowledge synthesis should answer the question asked; readers should be provided a sense of closure.

In fact, readers have their own criteria for what makes a good synthesis. Cooper (1986) asked post-master's graduate students to read the same desegregation meta-analyses commented on by Wachter and Straf (1990) and to evaluate five separate aspects of the papers. The results revealed that readers' judgments were highly intercorrelated: Syntheses perceived as superior on one dimension were also perceived as superior on other dimensions. Further, the best predictor of readers' quality judgments was their confidence in their ability to interpret the review. Syntheses seen as more interpretable were given higher quality ratings. Readers were also asked to provide open-ended comments on papers, which were subjected to an informal content analysis. The dimensions that readers mentioned most frequently were (a) organization, (b) writing style, (c) clarity of focus, (d) use of citations, (e) attention to variable definitions, (f) attention to study methodology, and (g) manuscript preparation.

Finally, the criteria for quality syntheses can vary with the needs of the reader. Cozzens (1981) found that readers using reviews to follow developments within their area of expertise valued comprehensiveness and did not consider the reputation of the author important. However, if the synthesis was outside the reader's area, the expertise of the author was important, as was brevity.

In sum then, Wachter and Straf (1990) were correct in re-emphasizing the importance of wisdom in research integration. Wisdom is essential to any scientific enterprise, but wisdom starts with sound procedure. Synthesists must consider a wide range of technical issues as they piece together a research domain. This handbook is meant to help research synthesists build well-supported knowledge structures. But structural integrity is a minimum criterion for a synthesis to lead to scientific progress. A more general kind of design wisdom is also needed to build knowledge structures that people want to view, visit, and, ultimately, live within.

## 6. REFERENCES

Becker, B. J. (in press). The generalizability of empirical research results. In C. Benbow and D. Lubinsky (Eds.), *From psychometrics to giftedness: Papers in honor of Julian Stanley.*

Cook, T. D., Cooper, H., Cordray, D. S., Hartmann, H., Hedges, L. V., Light, R. J., Louis, T. A., & Mosteller, F. (1992). *Meta-analysis for explanation: A casebook.* New York: Russell Sage Foundation.

Cooper, H. (1982). Scientific guidelines for conducting integrative research reviews. *Review of Educational Research, 52,* 291–302.

Cooper, H. (1986). On the social psychology of using integrative research reviews: The case of desegregation and black achievement. In R. Feldman (Ed.), *The social psychology of education.* Cambridge: Cambridge University Press.

Cozzens, S. (1981). *Users requirements for scientific reviews.* (Grant Report No. IST-7821947). Washington, DC: National Science Foundation.

Eddy, D. M., Hasselblad, V., & Schacter, R. (1992). *Meta-analysis by the confidence interval approach.* San Diego: Academic Press.

Glass, G. V. (1976). Primary, secondary, and meta-analysis of research. *Educational Researcher, 5,* 3–8.

Little, R. J. A., & Rubin, D. B. (1987). *Statistical analysis with missing data.* New York: Wiley.

Ottenbacher, K., & Cooper, H. (1984). The effects of class placement on the social adjustment of mentally retarded children. *Journal of Research and Development in Education, 17,* 1–14.

Peto, R. (1987). Why do we need systematic overviews of randomized trials (with discussion). *Statistics in Medicine, 6,* 233–244.

Rubin, D. B. (1987). *Multiple imputation for nonresponse in surveys.* New York: Wiley.

Strike, K., & Posner, G. (1983). Types of syntheses and their criteria. In S. Ward & L. Reed (Eds.), *Knowledge* structure and use: Implications for synthesis and interpretation. Philadelphia: Temple University Press.

U.S. General Accounting Office. (1992). *Cross design synthesis: A new strategy for medical effectiveness research*. Washington, DC: U.S. General Accounting Office. (GAO/PEMD No. 92-18).

Wachter, K. W. & Straf, M. L. (Eds.). (1990). *The future of meta-analysis*. New York: Russell Sage Foundation.

# GLOSSARY

**A Posteriori Tests**   Tests that are conducted after examination of study results. Used to explore patterns that seem to be emerging in the data. The same as *Post hoc tests*.

**A Priori Tests**   Tests that are planned before the examination of the results of the studies under analysis. The same as *Planned tests*.

**Acceptability**   The use of internal and statistical conclusion validity for selecting which relevant studies to include in a synthesis.

**Across-Studies Correlations**   Correlations between variables defined in meta-analysis at the study level, for example, the correlation across studies of their effect size estimates involving attitude and behavioral measures.

**Agreement Rate**   The most widely used index of interrater reliability in research synthesis. Defined as the number of observations agreed on divided by the total number of observations. Also called ''percentage agreement.''

**Analysis of Variance**   A statistical analysis procedure that tests for differences among means of grouped observations by comparing variation within and between groups of observations.

**Apples and Oranges Problem**   A metaphor for studies that appear related, but are actually measuring different things. A label sometimes given as a criticism of meta-analysis because meta-analysis combines studies that may have differing methods and operational definitions of the variables involved in the calculation of the effect sizes.

**Arcsin Transformation**   A transformation that makes equal differences between proportions equally detectable. The arcsin transformation of a proportion $p$ is $\sin^{-1}(\sqrt{p})$.

**Artifact Correction**   The modification of an estimate of effect size (usually by an artifact multiplier) to correct for the effects of an artifact.

**Artifact Distribution**   A distribution of values for a particular artifact multiplier derived from a particular research literature.

**Artifact Multiplier**   The factor by which a statistical or measurement artifact changes the expected observed value of a statistic.

**Artifacts**   Statistical and measurement imperfections that cause observed statistics to depart from the population (parameter) values the researcher intends to estimate.

**Artificial Dichotomization**   The arbitrary division of scores on a measure of a continuous variable into two categories.

**Attenuation**   A reduction in the expected value of a statistic due to the operation of a statistical or measurement artifact.

**Back-to-Back Stem-and-Leaf Displays**   Two or more stem-and-leaf displays arrayed on the same scale. Useful for comparing the center, spread, and shape of two or more distributions.

**Bare-Bones Meta-Analysis**   A meta-analysis that corrects for only the effects of sampling error.

**Baseline Estimate of Random Effects Variance**   An estimate of the random effects variance in a model without between-studies predictors; a model in which each true effect size is viewed as equal to the grand mean plus a random effect.

**Bayes Factor**   The amount that prior odds are changed by the data in a Bayesian calculation of the posterior odds.

**Bayes Posterior Coverage**   A Bayesian analogue to the confidence interval.

**Bayesian Analysis** An approach that incorporates a prior distribution to express uncertainty about population parameter values.

**Bayes's Theorem** A method of incorporating data into a prior distribution to obtain a posterior distribution.

**BESD** See **Binomial Effect Size Display.**

**Between-Studies Moderators** Third variables or sets of variables that affect the direction or magnitude of relations between other variables. Identified on a between-studies basis when some reviewed studies represent one level of the moderator and other studies represent other levels. See **Within-Study Moderators.**

**Between-Studies Predictors** Measured characteristics of studies hypothesized to affect true effect sizes.

**Between-Studies Sample Size** The number of studies in a meta-analysis.

**Bibliographic Database** A machine-readable file of information about documents. Most often consists of bibliographic citations, although some databases provide abstracts or summaries of a document's contents, the sponsoring institutions, list of terms reflecting the document's contents, and so on. Typically can be searched using a variety of fields (e.g., author's name, keywords in title, year of publication, sponsoring agency).

**Bibliographic Search** An exploration of the published literature for reports of interest. Typically conducted by scanning periodicals, paper indexes, and reference lists of selected articles (a ''hand'' search) or by means of computer-based software that accesses existing listings of references or bibliographic databases (''electronic search''). See **MEDLINE.**

**Binomial Effect Size Display (BESD)** An alternative procedure for displaying a correlation *(r)* of any given magnitude.

**Birge Ratio** The ratio of certain chi-square statistics (used in tests for heterogeneity of effects, model fit, or that variance components are zero) to their degrees of freedom. Used as an index of heterogeneity or lack of fit. Has an expected value of one under correct model specification or when the between-studies variance component is zero.

**Blocking** Subdividing sampling units to increase precision and/or permit the investigation of moderator variables.

**Box Plot** See **Schematic Plot.**

**Breslow-Day Test** A test for the homogeneity of odds ratios.

**Buck's Method** A method for analysis of data with missing observations suggested by Buck (1960), which fills in values for missing observations using fitted values from a linear regression. Cases observing all variables are used to estimate a series of regression equations for predicting values for missing observations.

**Case-Control Study** A study design, popular in epidemiology, in which the association between exposure to a hypothesized risk factor and the occurrence of illness is determined by sampling cases and noncases (the controls) and estimating the fractions that had been exposed.

**Categorical (Grouping) Variable** A variable that can take on a finite number of values used to define groups of studies.

**CD-ROM (Compact Disk–Read Only Memory)** A computer storage medium. In the library context, a CD-ROM can contain a database of information that may be searched using appropriate computer search software, either on a personal computer or a computer linked to a network.

**Certainty** The confidence with which the scientific community accepts research conclusions, reflecting the truth value accorded to conclusions.

**Citation Search** A literature search based on reference lists.

**Classical Analysis** An analysis that assumes that parameter values are fixed, unknown constants and that the data contain all the information about these paramters.

**Clinical Trial** An experimental study designed to test the safety or efficacy of a specified intervention. In medicine, usually conducted in a setting where the intervention is compared with a placebo or standard care.

**Code Book** A document that describes objectives and procedures for a research synthesis and includes definitions of important constructs, descriptions of coded items and corresponding coding conventions, an outline of the overall coding process, and a specification of the organization of forms. See also **Data Coding Protocol.**

**Coded Item** A feature of a study that a meta-analyst chooses to code for a research synthesis. Major categories of typically coded items deal with effect size, study identification, methodology, setting, subjects, and treatment.

**Coder** A person who reads and extracts information from research reports. One or more coders are assigned to any research synthesis and multiple coders may be assigned to the coding of important item(s).

**Coder Reliability** The equivalence with which coders extract information from research reports.

**Coder Training** A process of describing and practicing the coding of studies. Modifications of coding forms, coding conventions, and a code book may occur during the training process.

**Coding Conventions** Specific methods used to transform information in research reports into numerical form. A primary criterion for choosing such conventions is to retain as much of the original information as possible.

**Coding Forms** The physical records of coded items extracted from a research report. The forms, and items on them, are organized to assist coders and data entry personnel.

**Combined Probability** The significance level that arises from the application of a combined significance test.

**Combined Significance Test** One of a collection of statistical procedures that are intended to test the null hypothesis that all studies in a series have population (effect size) parameters equal to zero.

**Combining Results** Putting effect sizes on a common metric (e.g., $r$ or $d$) and calculating measures of location (e.g., mean, median) or combining tests of significance.

**Comparative Study** A study in which two or more groups of individuals are compared. The groups may involve different participants, such as when the two groups of patients receive two different treatments, or the same group being tested or administered treatment at two separate times, such as when two diagnostic tests that measure the same parameter are administered at separate times to the same group.

**Comparisons** Linear combinations of means (of effect sizes), often used in the investigation of patterns of differences among three or more means (of effect sizes). The same as **Contrasts.**

**Complete Case Analysis** A method for analysis of data with missing observations, which uses only cases that observe all variables in the model under investigation.

**Compound Model** A repeated sampling from both the prior and sampling distributions. See **Hyperprior Distribution.**

**Conceptual Redundancy Rule** A coding rule that excludes effect sizes based on conceptually redundant outcome measures even if they are not operationally identical.

**Conditional Distribution** The sampling distribution of a statistic (such as an effect size estimate) when a parameter of interest (such as the effect size parameter) is held constant.

**Conditional Exchangeability of Study Effect Sizes** A property of a set of studies that applies when the investigator has no a priori reason to expect the true effect size of any study to exceed the true effect size of any other study in the set, given that the two studies share certain identifiable characteristics.

**Conditional Variance, $v_i$** The variance of an effect size estimate given a fixed effect size parameter. The same as **Estimation Variance.**

**Confidence Interval (CI)** The interval within which population parameters are expected to lie.

**Confidence Ratings** A method for coders to directly rate their confidence level in the accuracy, completeness, and so on, of the data being extracted from primary studies. Can establish a mechanism for discerning high-quality from lesser-quality information in the conduct of subsequent analyses.

**Construct Validity** The extent to which generalizations can be made about higher-order constructs on the basis of research operations. The correlation in the reference population between true scores on a measurement scale and the actual construct the scale is intended to measure.

**Contrast Coefficients** The coefficients of the linear combination that defines the contrast; that is, the numbers that are multiplied times each mean before the products are added together to compute the value of the contrast.

**Contrasts** Linear combinations of means (of effect sizes), often used in the investigation of patterns of differences among three or more means (of effect sizes). The same as **Comparisons.**

**Controlled Vocabulary** The standardized terminology defined by an indexing or abstracting service, or database producer, for use in describing the subject contents of materials contained within the file. Typically defined in a database or index/abstract thesaurus.

**Correlation Coefficient** The sample statistic $r$, population parameter $\rho$. A standard index of linear relationship defined as the mean of the products of corresponding $Z$ scores. See also **Z-Transformed Correlation Coefficient.**

**Correlation Matrix** A matrix (rectangular listing arrangement) of the zero-order correlations among a set of $p$ variables. The diagonal elements of the correlation matrix equal one because they represent the correlation of each variable with itself. Within a single study the off-diagonal elements are denoted $r_{ij}$, for $i, j, = 1$ to $p$, $i \neq j$. The correlation $r_{ij}$ is the correlation between variables $i$ and $j$.

**Cross-Product Ratio** See **Odds Ratio.**

**Data Coding** The process of obtaining data. In meta-analysis it consists of reading studies and recording relevant information on data collection forms.

**Data Coding Protocol** A manual of instruction for data coders, which explains how to code data items, how to handle exceptions, and when to consult the project manager to resolve unexpected situations. See also **Code Book.**

**Data Entry** The process of transferring information from

data collection forms into a database, requiring clerical skills.

**Data Entry System** A statistical program that permits data to be entered in a series of computer screens designed to resemble a paper data collection form.

**Data Extraction Bias** The bias in the process of collecting and recording data from primary studies included in the research synthesis.

**Data Manager** A person who is responsible for a database system, particularly for defining the rules by which data are accessed and stored.

**Data Reduction** The process of combining data items in a database to produce a cases-by-variables file for statistical analysis.

**Database Management System** A set of computer programs that facilitates the creation and maintenance of a database and the analysis of data in the database.

**Density Function** A mathematical function that defines the probability of occurrence of values of a random variable.

**Deconstructionism** A philosophical view that seeks to reveal the hidden social and political processes underlying a text or any area of study—teasing out its strategically neglected aspects in an attempt to understand its hidden presuppositions.

**Descriptive Analysis** Descriptive statistics that characterize the results and attributes of a collection of research studies in an synthesis.

**Descriptors** Subject headings designed to name salient concepts in a work rather than to characterize it as a whole. Combined at the time of a literature search to express a researcher's interests. See also **Thesaurus.**

**Difference Between Proportions** The sample statistic $D$, population parameter $\Delta$. Computed as $D = p_1 - p_2$, where $p$ is a proportion.

**d-Indices** A family of effect size estimates all based on the difference between two means divided by an estimate of the standard deviation of individual measurements.

**Directory Database** A machine-readable file that consists of information about people, organizations, or services.

**Disattenuation** A correction that removes the effects of attenuation. See **Attenuation.**

**Duhem-Quine Thesis** The idea emphasized first by P. Duhem and subsequently by W. Quine that a scientific theory must ultimately withstand the test of experience. When negative evidence bearing on the theory is obtained, it will be necessary to modify the theory, but such modification can be made within any part of it so long as the theory, as a whole, continues to provide an internally consistent and coherent account. The result is that theories are relatively invulnerable to disconfirming evidence.

**Effect Size** The sample statistic $T$, population parameter $\theta$. A generic term that refers to the magnitude of an effect or more generally the size of the relation between two variables. Special cases include standardized mean difference, correlation coefficient, odds ratio, or the raw mean difference.

**Effect Size Items (Coding)** Items related to an effect size. Can include the nature and reliability of outcome and predictor measures, sample size(s), means and standard deviations, and indices of association.

**Electronic Network** A communication system that uses transmission channels (telephone lines, optical fiber, or coaxial cable) and computer hardware and software.

**Eligibility Criteria** Conditions that must be met by a primary study in order for it to be included in the research synthesis. Also called "inclusion criteria."

**EM Algorithm** An iterative estimation procedure that cycles between estimation of the posterior expectation (E) of a random variable (or collection of variables) and the maximization (M) of its posterior likelihood. Useful for maximum likelihood estimation with missing data.

**Emic** An account of an event that is provided by a participant who has an internal perspective of it, as contrasted with **Etic,** in which the account is provided by a participant who has an external perspective (and so does not share the same context or frame of reference of participants in the situation).

**Empirical Bayes Analysis** An analysis in which the data are used to estimate parameters of the Bayes prior distribution.

**Endpoint** In medical studies, the time at which a measurement of the outcome variable is made, or the variable itself. For example, a study that measures survival rate six months after an operation is said to have an endpoint at six months post operation.

**End-User Search System** An automated information-retrieval system that allows one to search for information without extensive training or documentation. Intended for those with a modicum of training, these retrieval systems are often menu-driven (allowing one to choose functions and files from a selection menu) or dependent on commands utilizing common-language commands.

**Epidemiology** The biomedical specialty that studies the distributions and causes of illness in human populations.

**Error of Measurement** Random errors in the scores produced by a measuring instrument.

**Estimation Variance, $v_i$** The variance of the effect size estimator given a fixed true effect size. The same as **Conditional Variance.**

**Estimator of Effect Size, $T_i$** The estimator of the true effect size based on collecting a sample of data.

**Ethics Committees** See **Institutional Review Boards.**

**Etic** See **Emic.**

**Exclusion Criteria** See **Ineligibility Criteria.**

**Experimental Units** The smallest division of the experimental (or observational) material such that any two units may receive different treatments.

**Exploratory Data Analysis** A data analysis that focuses on description rather than inference. Supplements numerical summaries with visual displays.

**External Validity** The value of a study or set of studies for generalizing to individuals, settings, or procedures. Studies with high external validity can be generalized to a larger number of individuals, settings, or procedures than can studies with lower external validity. Largely determined by the sampling of individuals, settings, or procedures employed in the investigations from which generalizations are to be drawn.

**Extrinsic Factors** The characteristics of research other than the phenomenon under investigation or the methods used to study that phenomenon, for example, the date of publication and the gender of the author.

**File-Drawer Problem** The situation in which study results go unreported (and thus are left in file drawers) when tests of hypotheses do not show statistically significant results.

**Fixed Effects** Effects (effects sizes or components of a model for effect size parameters) that are unknown constants. Compare with **Random Effects.**

**Fixed Effects Model** A statistical model which stipulates that the units of one or more of the factors under analysis (studies, in a meta-analysis) are the ones of interest, and thus constitute the entire population of units. Only within-study sampling error is taken to influence the uncertainty of the results of the meta-analysis. Compare with **Random Effects Models.**

**Flat File** In data management, a file that constitutes a collection of records of the same type that do not contain repeating items. Can be represented by a two-dimensional array of data items, that is, a cases-by-variables data matrix.

**Footnote Chasing** A technique for discovering relevant documents by tracing authors' footnotes (more broadly, their references) to earlier documents. Also known as the "ancestry approach." See also **Forward Citation Searching.**

**Formal Methods of Retrieval** The retrieval of articles and papers using published abstracts and indexes, popular computer-readable databases, and literature reviews.

**Forward Citation Searching** A way of discovering relevant documents by looking up a known document in a citation index and finding the later documents that have cited it. See also **Footnote Chasing.**

**Fourfold Table** A table that reports data concerning the relationship between two dichotomous factors. See **Odds Ratio, Log Odds Ratio,** and **Rate Difference.**

**Free-Text Search** A search that is not dependent on a controlled vocabulary, or predefined list of subject headings, to represent the topic or concept needed. The query of a computerized bibliographic database that scans the entire record for each entry, including the title and abstract, to identify relevant references using terms that may be absent from the controlled vocabulary of the database. Also called "natural language search."

**Fugitive Literature** Papers or articles produced in small quantities, not widely distributed, and often not listed in commonly used abstracts and indexes.

**Full-Text Database** A machine-readable file that consists of citations or bibliographic references, as well as the complete text of documents.

**Funnel Plot** A graphic display of sample size plotted versus effect size. When many studies come from the same population, each estimating the same underlying parameter, the graph should resemble a funnel with a single spout. Also called a "funnel graph."

**Gaussian Distribution** Data distributed according to the normal or "bell-shaped" curve.

**Generalized Least Squares (GLS) Estimation** An estimation procedure similar to the more familiar ordinary least squares method. A sum of squared deviations between parameters and data is minimized, but GLS allows the data points for which parameters are being estimated to have unequal population variances and nonzero covariances (i.e., to be dependent).

**Hermeneutics** The discipline of systematic interpretation and explanation achieved through the study of literary material and, more recently, through the study of human actions and cultures (includes the intrusion of the human interpreter's biases in the process).

**Heterogeneity** In research synthesis, the variability of a collection of sizes of effects. Available tests enable the synthesist to ascertain whether a given collection is more heterogeneous than would be expected on the basis of sampling variation alone.

**Heterogeneity/Homogeneity of Classes.** The range/similarity of classes of persons, treatments, outcomes, settings, and times included in the studies that have been reviewed.

**High-Inference Codings** Codings for which the coder must rate or otherwise evaluate the methodology or phenomenology of a study on dimensions or scales—for example, of how anxiety-provoking an experimental situation is. Low- and high-inference codings constitute a continuum of coder inference, not discrete categories.

**Homogeneity Test** A test that effect size estimates exhibit greater variability than would be expected if their corresponding effect size parameters were identical.

**Hyperprior Distribution** A distribution of parameters of the Bayes prior distribution. See also **Compound Model.**

**Identification Items (Coding)** The category of coded items that document the research reports that are synthesized. Author, coder, country, and year and source of publication are typical items.

**Ignorable Response Mechanism** A term that describes reasons for missing observations in a data set. A response mechanism is considered ignorable if the reasons for missing data are either (a) completely unrelated to any variables in the data set (as if the observations are deleted at random) or (b) related to completely observed variables that are included in the model.

**Inclusion Criteria** See **Eligibility Criteria.**

**Inductive Fallacy** Erroneous reasoning engendered by the form "all observed $X$'s possess property $Y$; thus, all $X$'s possess $Y$."

**Ineligibility Criteria** Conditions or characteristics that render a primary study ineligible for inclusion in the research synthesis. The same as **Exclusion Criteria.**

**Informal Methods of Retrieval** Information gathering through informal means, for example, letters of request for reprints, or membership in an invisible college.

**Information Broker** A professional who provides literature searches and document delivery services for a fee.

**Informative or Non-Informative Prior Distribution** A prior distribution that incorporates (or does not incorporate) prior information about the parameter to be estimated in the Bayes analysis.

**Institutional Review Boards** Committees that are formed by hospitals or other institutions that conduct research and that review research protocols involving humans in order to determine the safety and ethical nature of the proposed study. Typically, in the United States, institutional review boards require that (a) studies conform to general ethical principles set forth in the Nuremberg Code of 1949 and the World Medical Association Declaration of Helsinki of 1964 and 1975 and that (b) participants or their surrogates provide informed consent to inclusion in the research. Also called "ethics committees."

**Instrumentalism** A philosophical view that scientific theories or their concepts and measures have no necessary relation to external reality.

**Intercoder Correlation** An index of interrater reliability for continuous variables, based on the Pearson correlation coefficient. Used in research synthesis to estimate interrater reliability, analogous to its use in education to estimate test reliabilities when parallel test forms are available.

**Interim Report** A report written on completion of a portion of a study. A series of interim reports may be generated during the course of a single study.

**Internal Validity** The value of a study or set of studies for concluding that a causal relationship exists between variables, that is, that one variable affects another. Studies with high internal validity provide a strong basis for making a causal inference. Largely determined by the control of alternative variables that could explain relationships found within a study.

**Interrater Reliability** The extent to which different raters rating the same studies assign the same rating to coded variables.

**Intraclass Correlation** A family of indices of interrater reliability for continuous variables, computed as the ratio of the variance of interest over the sum of the variance of interest plus error. Permits the researcher to choose whether or not to include the between-raters variance in the error term and, more generally, to isolate different sources of variation in the measurement and to estimate their magnitude using the analysis of variance.

**Invisible College** A network of scientists or colleagues involved in a particular research area who share scientific information through personal communication.

**Jackknife** An algorithm for reducing the bias, if any, in an estimator and for estimating its standard error.

**Kappa** A versatile family of indices of interrater reliability for categorical data, defined as the proportion of the best possible improvement over chance that is actually obtained by the raters. Generally superior to other indices designed to remove the effects of chance agreement, kappa is a "true" reliability statistic that in large samples is equivalent to the intraclass correlation coefficient.

**Large-Sample Approximation** The statistical theory that is valid when each (every) study has a "large" (within-study) sample size. The exact number of cases required to qualify as large depends on the effect size index used.

In meta-analysis, most statistical theory is based on large-sample approximations.

**Log Odds**    See **Logit.**

**Log Odds Ratio**    The sample statistic $l$, population parameter $\lambda$. Computed as the natural logarithm of the odds ratio $\ln(o)$. See **Fourfold table.**

**Logistic Regression**    A statistical model in which the logit of a probability is postulated to be a linear function of a set of independent variables.

**Logit**    The logarithm of the odds value associated with a probability. If $\Pi$ is a probability, its logit is $\ln[\Pi/(1 - \Pi)]$, where ln denotes natural logarithm.

**Logit Transformation**    A transformation commonly used with proportions or other numbers that have values between zero and one. The logit is the logarithmic transformation of the ratio $[p/(1 - p)]$, that is, $\ln[p/(1 - p)]$.

**Low-Inference Codings**    Codings for which little or no judgment is required on the coder's part—for example, year of publication, sex of author, and number of items on a measuring instrument. High- and low-inference codings constitute a continuum of coder inference, not discrete categories.

**Mantel-Haenszel Statistics**    A set of statistics for combining odds ratios and testing the significance of the resulting average odds ratio.

**Marginal Distribution**    The distribution of a statistic (such as an effect size estimate) when relevant parameters (such as the effect size parameter) are allowed to vary according to the prior distribution.

**Marker Variables**    Study characteristics that may be associated with research practices, but do not themselves plausibly exercise direct influence on study results, for example, publication source.

**Matching**    A research strategy in which subjects are grouped into sets such that the subjects within a set are similar on characteristics expected to be associated with the variables under study.

**Maximum Likelihood Methods for Missing Data**    Methods for analysis of data with missing observations that provide maximum likelihood estimates of model parameters.

**Mean of the Random Effects, $\mu_\theta$**    The mean of the true effect sizes in a random effects model.

**Mediating Variable**    Third variables or sets of variables that provide a causal account of the mechanisms underlying the relationship between other variables. Transmits a cause-effect relationship in the sense that it is a consequence of a more distal cause and a cause of more distal measured effects.

**MEDLINE**    An acronym for MEDLARS on Line. (MEDLARS is an acronym for Medical Literature Analysis and Retrieval System and comprises 18 databases.) The most frequently used electronic bibliographic database within MEDLARS, it contains more than 6 million citations from over 3,300 selected medical and scientific journals from 1966 to the present. Compiled by the National Library of Medicine. The paper version of MEDLINE is *Index Medicus*.

**MeSH Medical Subject Heading(s)**    The controlled vocabulary index created by the National Library of Medicine to index published articles listed in *Index Medicus* and MEDLINE. It contains approximately 15,000 terms.

**Meta-Analysis**    The statistical analysis of a collection of analysis results from individual studies for the purpose of integrating the findings.

**Method of Maximum Likelihood**    A method of statistical estimation in which one chooses as the point estimates of a set of parameters values that maximize the likelihood of observing the data in a sample.

**Method of Moments**    A method of statistical estimation in which the sample moments are equated to their expectations and the resulting set of equations solved for the parameters of interest.

**Methodology Items (Coding)**    Items related to the general conduct of a study. They portray research design, details of sampling, and presence and absence of threats to validity. Ratings of study quality are considered methodology items.

**Metrics of Measurement**    The indices used to quantify variables and the relationships between variables.

**Missing at Random**    Observations that are missing for reasons related to completely observed variables that are included in the model.

**Missing Completely at Random**    Observations that are missing for reasons unrelated to any variables in the data. Missing observations occur as if they were deleted at random.

**Missing Data**    Data representing either study outcomes or study characteristics that are unavailable to the reviewer. Data may be missing for a number of reasons; they may not have been reported because of space limitations or nonsignificant results, or the primary research study may not have measured a variable of interest.

**Moderator Variable**    Any factor that influences the size of a particular relationship and is itself not a consequence of the relationship.

**Multinomial Distribution**    A probability distribution associated with the independent classifications of a sample of subjects into a series of mutually exclusive and exhaustive categories. When the number of categories is two, the distribution is the binomial distribution.

**Multiple-Endpoint Studies**    Studies that measure the outcome on the same subject at different points in time.

**Multiple Imputation**    A method for analysis of data with missing observations, which involves deriving several possible substitutes for each missing observation based on models for the reasons for the missing data.

**Multiple Operationalization**    Implementing a theoretical or abstract term by using several different types of empirical procedures or instruments.

**Nonignorable Response Mechanism**    A term that describes observations that are missing for reasons related to unobserved variables. Occurs when observations are missing because of their unknown values or because of other unknown variables.

**Nonparametric Statistical Procedures**    Statistical procedures (tests or estimators) whose distributions do not require knowledge of the functional form of the probability distribution of the data. Also called ''distribution-free statistics.''

**Normal Deviate**    The location on a standard normal curve given in $Z$-score form.

**Normal Distribution**    A bell-shaped curve that is completely described by its mean and standard deviation.

**Odds Ratio**    The sample statistic $o$, population parameter $\omega$. Odds ratios compare odds values for two groups of people. When the odds ratio equals one, the event is equally likely to occur for both groups, and when it is greater than one, the event is more likely to occur for the group represented in the numerator. Useful for describing the results of studies that employ categorical outcomes. The ratio of two odds values. See **Fourfold Table.**

**Odds Value**    A probability divided by its complement. If $\Pi$ is a probability, its associated odds value is $\Pi(1 - \Pi)$.

**Omnibus Tests of Significance**    Significance tests that address unfocused questions, as in $F$ tests with more than 1 degree of freedom $(df)$ for the numerator or in chi-square tests with more than 1 $df$.

**One-Sided Combination Problem**    A test of the null hypothesis that each of a series of parameters equals zero versus the alternative model that one or more populations has a positive parameter value.

**Ontology**    The discipline that investigates the nature and properties of being.

**Operational Definition**    A definition of a concept that relates the concept to observable events.

**Operational Effect Size**    The effect size actually estimated in the study as it is conducted; for example, the (attenuated) effect size computed using an unreliable outcome measure. Compare with **Theoretical Effect Size.**

**Overdispersion**    A larger than expected variance.

**p Value**    The probability associated with a statistical hypothesis test. The $p$ value is the probability of obtaining a particular sample result (statistic), given the hypothesis that only variation due to random sampling causes the observed result to deviate from the hypothesized parameter value.

**p Value Summary**    See **Combined Significance Test.**

**Parallel Randomized Experiments**    A set of randomized experiments testing the same hypothesis about the relationship between treatments (independent variables) and outcomes (dependent variables).

**Parallel Schematic Plots**    See **Side-by-Side Schematic Plots.**

**Parameter**    The population value of a statistic.

**Pearson Correlation**    See **Correlation Coefficient.**

**Peer Review**    The review of research by an investigator's peers, usually conducted at the request of a journal editor prior to publication of the research and for purposes of evaluation to ensure that the research meets generally accepted standards of the research community.

**Phi Coefficient**    The product moment correlation coefficient between a pair of binary random variables (each coded, for simplicity, as 0 or 1).

**Placebo**    A pseudo-treatment administered to subjects in a control group.

**Planned Tests**    Tests that are planned before the examination of the results of the studies under analysis. The same as **A Priori Tests.**

**Pooling Results**    Using data or results from several primary studies to compute a combined significance test or estimate.

**Positivism**    The use of scientific methods to increase knowledge, but with a variety of connotations. *Logical* positivism refers to the notion that empirical verification is necessary to establish meaning. *Post*-positivism emphasizes the tenuousness of the scientific method and the difficulties in the positivist position.

**Post Hoc Tests**    Tests that are conducted after examination of study results to explore patterns that seem to be emerging in the data. The same as **A Posteriori Tests.**

**Posterior Distribution**    An updated prior distribution that incorporates observed data (also posterior mean, posterior variance, etc.).

**Power**    The probability that a statistical test rejects a false null hypothesis, given that a particular identified alternative is true.

**Power Analysis**   A statistical analysis that estimates the likelihood of obtaining a statistically significant relation between variables, given various sample sizes and true relations of certain magnitude.

**Precision**   A measure used in evaluating literature searches. The ratio of documents retrieved and deemed relevant to total documents retrieved. See **Recall.**

**Precision of Estimation**   The inverse of the variance of an estimator.

**Primary Study**   A report of original research, usually published in a technical journal or appearing as a thesis or dissertation; refers to the original research reports collected for a research synthesis.

**Prior Distribution**   An expression of the uncertainty of parameter values as a statistical distribution before observing the data (also prior mean, prior variance, etc.).

**Prior Odds**   The relative prior likelihood of pairs of parameter values.

**Process Items (Coding)**   Coded items that pertain to behaviors and dispositions of coders during coding. Coding time and rating of confidence with respect to an individual item are important items in this category.

**Process Ratings**   A technique for identifying mediators that involves judges' coding of the process-relevant aspects of reviewed studies.

**Proportion of Effect Size Variance Explained**   The ratio of the reduction of random effects variance to the baseline random effects variance.

**Prospective Registration**   The compilation and collation of initiated research projects while they are still ongoing. See also **Retrospective Registration.**

**Prospective Study**   A study design in epidemiology in which the association between exposure to a hypothesized risk factor and the occurrence of illness is determined by sampling exposed and unexposed subjects and estimating the proportions who develop the illness under study.

**Proximal Similarity**   The similarity in manifest characteristics (e.g., prototypical attributes) between samples of persons, treatments, outcomes, settings, and times and their corresponding universes.

**Proxy Variables**   Variables, such as year of study publication, that serve as surrogates for the true, causal variables, such as developments in research methods or changes in data-reporting practices.

**Publication Bias**   A selection bias in the published literature such that publication of research depends on the nature and direction of the study results (e.g., statistically significant findings).

**Quasi-Formal Methods of Retrieval**   Information gathering that is formal to some degree, for example, heard in a formal paper presentation or read in an electronic journal.

**Random Effect in a Regression Model for Predicting Effect Size**   The deviation of a study's $i$'s true effect size from the value predicted on the basis of the regression model.

**Random Effects**   Effects that are assumed to be sampled from a distribution of effects. Compare with *Fixed Effects*.

**Random Effects Model**   A statistical model in which both within-study sampling error and between-studies variation are included in the assessment of the uncertainty of the results of the meta-analysis. Compare with **Fixed Effects Models.**

**Random Effects Variance (Component), $\sigma_\theta^2$**   A variance of the true effect size viewed as either (a) the variance of true effect sizes in a population of studies from which the synthesized studies constitute a random sample or (b) the degree of the investigator's uncertainty about the proposition that the true effect size of a particular study is near a predicted value.

**Randomization**   The allocation of individuals, communities, groups, or other units of study to an experimental intervention, using a method that assures that assignment to any particular group is by chance.

**Range Restriction**   A reduction in the standard deviation or variance of a variable stemming from partial or total systematic exclusion of scores in particular ranges of the reference population score distribution.

**Rank Correlation Test**   A nonparametric statistical test in which the correlation between two factors is assessed by comparing the ranking of the two samples.

**Rate Difference**   See **Difference Between Proportions** and **Fourfold Table.**

**Rate Ratio**   The ratio of two probabilities of occurrence of an unwanted outcome. If $\Pi_1$ and $\Pi_2$ are the probabilities in two populations, the rate ratio is equal to $\Pi_1/\Pi_2$.

**Raw Mean Difference**   The sample statistic $T$, population parameter $\theta$. Computed as $T = X^t - X^c$, where $X^t$ is the mean of the treatment group on some variable and $X^c$ is the mean of the control group on that variable.

**Realism**   A philosophical view that an objective reality exists independent of our perceptions and that scientific theories provide an isomorphic map of this external world.

**Recall**   A measure used in evaluating literature searches. The ratio of relevant documents retrieved to total documents deemed relevant in a collection. See **Precision.**

**Reduction of Random Effects Variance**   The difference between the baseline and the residual random effects variance.

**Reductionism**   The view that one branch of science can

be explained by another that provides a finer-grained, or smaller unit of analysis, account of the phenomena (e.g., the notion that chemistry can be "reduced" to physics).

**Relational Database**  A database that consists of a collection of flat files. Records in different flat files are linked by means of one or more key variables.

**Relative Risk**  See **Rate Ratio.**

**Relevance**  The use of construct and external validity as entry criteria for selecting studies for a synthesis.

**Reliability**  The proportion of the observed variance of scores of a measuring scale that is not due to the variance of random measurement errors; the proportion of observed variance of scores that is due to variance of true scores.

**Replication**  The repetition of a previously conducted study.

**Research Quality**  Factors such as the design or design features that affect the validity of a study or a set of studies.

**Research Register**  A database of research studies, planned, active and/or completed, usually oriented around a common feature of the studies such as subject matter, funding source, or design.

**Research Synthesis With a Balanced Design**  A synthesis in which the estimation variance $v_i$ for every study is identical, that is, $v_i = v$, $i = 1, \ldots, k$.

**Research Synthesis with an Unbalanced Design**  A synthesis in which the estimation variances of the studies are not all identical.

**Residual Random Effects Variance**  The residual variance of the true random effects after taking into account a set of between-studies predictors.

**Response Mechanism**  The mechanism that determines whether or not a variable is observed. A formal way to refer to the reasons for missing observations.

**Retrieved Studies**  Primary studies identified in the literature search phase of a research synthesis and whose research report is obtained in full by the research synthesis investigators.

**Retrospective Registration**  The compilation and collation of initiated research projects that have been completed. This process can include compiling bibliographies of published reports of studies. See also **Prospective Registration.**

**r-Indices**  A family of effect size estimates, all based on the Pearson correlation coefficient, between pairs of variables. See **Correlation Coefficient.**

**Risk Ratio**  See **Rate Ratio.**

**Robust Methods**  Techniques that are not overly sensitive to the choice of a prior or sampling distribution or to outliers in the data.

**Robustness**  Consistency in sign and/or magnitude of ef-

fect size for studies involving different classes of persons, treatments, settings, outcomes, or times.

**Samples**  Constituents or members of a universe, class, population, category, type, or entity.

**Sampling Error**  The difference between an effect size estimate and the population parameter that it estimates.

**Schematic Plot**  A graphic display of a variable's distribution. A center "box" indicates where the middle 50 percent of the data points fall, a crossbar in the middle of the box indicates the distribution's sample median, and "whiskers" indicate the maximum and minimum values. Also called a "box plot."

**Search Strategy**  The algorithm used in an electronic bibliographic search to identify relevant citations. Within a given bibliographic database, a controlled vocabulary is usually used to index all articles. The individual performing a search probes the database for all articles that are indexed under specified terms in the vocabulary or that include specified words in their text.

**Selection Bias**  An error produced by systematic differences between individuals, entities, or studies selected for analysis and those not selected.

**Sensitivity Analysis**  An analysis used to determine how sensitive the conclusions of the analysis are to the choice of the assumed prior distribution of effect sizes and other modeling assumptions.

**Setting Items (Coding)**  Coded items that describe general conditions associated with a study. Possible items include scope of sampling, involvement of special populations, and other attributes of a milieu, such as the socioeconomic level of a community.

**75 Percent Rule**  A rule of thumb that assumes that if 75 percent of the variability of between effect size estimates is due to quantified artifacts, the remaining 25 percent is probably due to artifacts that could not be quantified and corrected for.

**Side-by-Side Schematic Plots (Parallel Schematic Plots)**  Two or more schematic plots arrayed on the same scale. Useful for comparing the center, spread, and shape of two or more distributions.

**Signal-to-Noise Ratio**  Any of the many indices of information in which how much is known is divided by what is not known.

**Significance Level**  See **p Value.**

**Significance Test**  A statistical test that gives evidence about the plausibility of the hypothesis of no relationship between variables.

**Significance-Level Summary**  See **Combined Significance Test.**

**Simultaneous Test Procedure**  A method of statistical

testing that controls the probability of *at least one* Type I error in a group of tests (e.g., tests for a set of contrasts), usually called the simultaneous significance level of the tests.

**Single-Value Imputation**   Methods for analysis of data with missing observations, which involve substituting single values for missing observations. Filling in the complete case mean value for every missing observation or using Buck's method are examples of single-value imputation.

**Size of Study Index**   Any of the many measures of the effective size of an investigation, for example, $N$, $\sqrt{N}$, $df$, $\sqrt{df}$, $df_{error}/df_{means}$.

**Spreadsheet**.   Computer software that permits entry of data into a matrix (spreadsheet). Spreadsheets provide a variety of data manipulations, but are generally not the most convenient way to implement meta-analysis.

**Standardized Mean Difference**   The sample statistic $d$, population parameter $\delta$. Computed as the raw mean difference divided by an estimate of the within-group standard deviation. See also **d-Indices.**

**Statistical Conclusion Validity**   The degree of accuracy with which researchers can conclude that two variables are related.

**Statistical Database**   A machine-readable file that contains numeric information.

**Statistical Power**   See **Power.**

**Stem-and-Leaf Display**   A histogram in which the data values themselves are used to characterize the distribution of a variable. Useful for describing the center, spread, and shape of a distribution.

**Study Descriptors**   Coded variables that describe the characteristics of research studies other than their results or outcomes—for example, the nature of the research designs and procedures used, attributes of the subject sample, and features of the setting, personnel, activities, and circumstances involved.

**Study Protocol**   A written document that defines the concepts used in the research and that describes study procedures in as much detail as possible before the research begins.

**Subject Items (Coding)**   The items related to specific characteristics of the sample(s) used in a study. They describe demographic, cognitive, personality, and other attributes measured and reported for the subjects.

**Subject Subsamples**   Groupings of a subject sample by some characteristic—for example, gender or research site.

**Substantive Factors**   Characteristics of research studies that represent aspects of the phenomenon under investi-

gation—for example, the nature of the treatment conditions applied and the personal characteristics of the subjects treated.

**Substantively   Irrelevant   Study   Characteristics**   Characteristics of studies that are irrelevant to the major hypotheses under study, but are inevitably incorporated into research operations to make them feasible. The analyst's goal is to show that tests of the hypothesis are not confounded with such substantive irrelevancies.

**Synthetic Correlation Matrix**   A matrix of correlations, each synthesized from one or more studies.

**Systematic Artifacts**   Statistical and measurement imperfections that bias observed statistics (statistical estimates) in a systematic direction, either upward or downward. See *Artifacts.*

**Technical Report**   A scientific paper or article recording current findings from a research project.

**Test of Significance**   See **Significance Test.**

**Theoretical Effect Size**   The effect size that would be obtained in a study that differs in some theoretically defined way from one that is actually conducted. Typically, theoretical effect sizes are estimated from operational effect sizes with the aid of auxiliary information about study designs or measurement methods. For example, the (disattenuated) correlation coefficient corrected for the effects of measurement unreliability is a theoretical effect size. Compare with **Operational Effect Size.**

**Theory Testing**   The empirical validation of hypothesized relationships, which may involve the validation of a single relationship between two variables or a network of relationships between several variables. Often validation depends on observing consequences implied by, but far removed from, the basic elements of the theory.

**Thesaurus**   A list of terms authorized by subject experts for indexing a large literature, which enables searchers to define their research interests in standardized language. Differentiates homonyms and controls synonyms by mapping nonauthorized terms to their preferred equivalents and defines and shows interrelationships among authorized terms, which are often called ''descriptors.'' The source of controlled vocabulary for a database or print index/ abstract, for example, *Thesaurus of Psychological Index Terms.*

**Threat to Validity**   A likely source of bias, alternative explanation, or ''plausible rival hypothesis'' for the research findings.

**Tolerance Interval**   The interval within which sample statistics are expected to lie.

**Total Variance of an Effect Size Estimate, $v_i^* = \sigma_{\hat{\theta}}^2 + v_i$**   The sum of the random effects variance and the estimation variance. The same as **Unconditional Variance.**

**Transformation**   The application of some arithmetic principle to a set of observations to convert the scale of measurement to one with more desirable characteristics—for example, normality, homogeneity, or linearity.

**Treatment Items (Coding)**   Items that document the nature of treatments and other interventions. Items that describe specific elements of treatments, duration of treatments, and theoretical bases for treatments are all possibilities.

**Treatment-by-Studies Interaction**   The varying effect of a treatment across different studies; equivalently, the effect of moderators on the true effect size in a set of studies of treatment efficacy.

**True Effect Size $\Theta_i$**   The effect magnitude that an investigator seeks to estimate when planning a study.

**Type A, B, and C Meta-Analyses**   Three types of meta-analyses with increasingly complex goals. *Type A:* aggregation of study-level evidence and ruling out of rival methodological interpretations. *Type B:* in addition to achieving Type A goals, assessment of differentiation and generalization, by employing tests of moderators and mediators proposed in prior primary research. *Type C:* in addition to achieving Type A and Type B goals, test of moderating or mediating role of new theoretical concepts not involved in prior primary research.

**Unconditional Variance, $v_i^* = \sigma_\theta^2 + v_i$**   The sum of the random effects variance and the estimation variance. The same as **Total Variance of an Effect Size Estimate.**

**Unit of Analysis**   In research synthesis, the study unit that contributes to the calculation of an effect size within a study. The unit may be a single individual or an aggregate of individuals, like a classroom or dyad.

**Universe**   The population (or hyperpopulation) of studies to which one wishes to generalize. Higher-order constructs referring to persons, settings, times, treatments (i.e., causal agents), and effects (i.e., outcomes constructs), which are the conceptual referents for inferences about association, the causal nature of the association, or generalization.

**Unpublished Literature**   Papers or articles not made available to the public through the action of a publisher.

**Unsystematic Artifacts**   Statistical imperfections, such as sampling error, which cause statistical estimates to depart randomly from the population parameters that a researcher intends to estimate. See **Artifacts.**

**Validity Threat**   Plausible reasons for drawing false conclusions about the association between a class of treatments and a class of outcomes, about the causal nature of their association, and about the generalization of the association.

**Variance Components**   The sources into which the variance (of effect sizes) is partitioned. Also, the random variables whose variances are the summands for the total variance.

**Variance-Covariance Matrix**   A matrix (rectangular listing arrangement) that contains the variances and covariances for a set of $p$ variables. Within a single study the diagonal elements of the covariance matrix are the variances $S_{ii}^2$ for variables $i = 1$ to $p$. The covariances $S_{ij}$ for $i, j = 1$ to $p$, $i \neq j$, are the off-diagonal elements of the matrix.

**Vote-counting**   A method of making a decision about a null hypothesis for a series of studies based only on counts of significant and nonsignificant study results.

**Weighted Least Squares Regression in Research Synthesis**   A technique for estimating the parameters of a multiple regression model wherein each study's contribution to the sum of products of the measured variables is weighted by the precision of that study's effect size estimator.

**Within-Study Moderators**   Third variables or sets of variables that affect the direction or magnitude of relations between other variables. Moderators are identified on a within-study basis when two or more levels of the moderator are present in individual reviewed studies. See **Between-Studies Moderators.**

**Within-Study Sample Size**   The number of units within a primary study.

**Z-Transformed Correlation Coefficient**   The sample statistic $z$, population parameter $\zeta$. The Fisher Z transformation of a correlation $r$ is $.5 \ln[(1 + r)/(1 - r)].1$.

# APPENDIX A

# Data Sets

Three data sets have been used repeatedly throughout this handbook. This appendix provides brief descriptions of the data sets, references for the research studies that reported the primary data analyses, and integrative research reviews that examined the studies.

## 1. DATA SET I: Studies of Gender Differences in Conformity Using the Fictitious Norm Group Paradigm

Eagly and Carli (1981) conducted a comprehensive review of experimental studies of gender differences in conformity. The studies in this data set are a portion of the studies that Eagly and Carli examined, the studies that they called "other conformity studies." Because all of these studies use an experimental paradigm involving a nonexistent norm group, we call them "fictitious norm group" studies.

These studies measure conformity by examining the effect of knowledge of other people's responses on an individual's response. Typically, an experimental subject is presented with an opportunity to respond to a question of opinion. Before responding, the individual is shown some "data" on the responses of other individuals. The "data" are manipulated by the experimenters, and the "other individuals" are the fictitious norm group. For example, the subject might be asked for an opinion on a work of art and told that 75 percent of Harvard undergraduates liked the work "a great deal."

Several methodological characteristics of studies that might mediate the gender difference in conformity were examined by Eagly and Carli (1981) and by Becker (1986). Two of them are reported here: the percentage of male authors and the number of items on the instrument used to measure conformity. Eagly and Carli reasoned that male experimenters might engage in sex-typed communication that transmitted a subtle message to female subjects to conform. Consequently, studies with a large percentage of male experimenters would obtain a higher level of conformity from female subjects. Becker reasoned that the number of items on the measure of conformity might be related to effect size for two reasons: Because each item is a stimulus to conform, instruments with a larger number of items produce a greater press to conform; instruments with a larger number of items would also tend to be more reliable, and hence they would be subject to less attenuation due to measurement unreliability.

A summary of the ten studies and the effect size estimates calculated by Eagly and Carli, and in some cases recalculated by Becker, is given in Table A.1. The effect size is the standardized difference between the mean for males and that for females, and a positive value implies that females are more conforming than males. The total sample size (the sum of the male and female sample sizes), the percentage of male authors, and the number of items on the outcome measure are also given.

## 2. DATA SET II: Studies of the Effects of Teacher Expectancy on Pupil IQ

Raudenbush (1984) reviewed randomized experiments on the effects of teacher expectancy on pupil IQ (see

### Table A.1 Data Set I: Studies of Gender Differences in Conformity

| Study | Total Sample Size | Effect Size Estimate | Male Authors (%) | Items (n) |
|---|---|---|---|---|
| King 1959 | 254 | .35 | 100 | 38 |
| Wyer 1966 | 80 | .37 | 100 | 5 |
| Wyer 1967 | 125 | −.06 | 100 | 5 |
| Sampson & Hancock 1967 | 191 | −.30 | 50 | 2 |
| Sistrunk 1971 | 64 | .69 | 100 | 30 |
| Sistrunk & McDavid 1967 [1] | 90 | .40 | 100 | 45 |
| Sistrunk & McDavid 1967 [4] | 60 | .47 | 100 | 45 |
| Sistrunk 1972 | 20 | .81 | 100 | 45 |
| Feldman-Summers et al. 1977 [1] | 141 | −.33 | 25 | 2 |
| Feldman-Summers et al. 1977 [2] | 119 | .07 | 25 | 2 |

NOTE: These data are from Eagly and Carli (1981) and Becker (1986).

also Raudenbush & Bryk 1985). The experiments usually involve the researcher administering a test to a sample of students. A randomly selected portion of the students (the treatment group) are identified to their teachers as "likely to experience substantial intellectual growth." All students are tested again, and the standardized difference between the mean treatment group and that of the other students is the effect size. The theory underlying the treatment is that the identification of students as showing promise of exceptional growth changes teacher expectations about those students, which may in turn effect outcomes such as intelligence (possibly through intermediate variables). Raudenbush (1984) proposed that an important characteristic of studies that

### Table A.2 Data Set II: Studies of the Effects of Teacher Expectancy on Pupil IQ

| Study | Estimated Weeks of Teacher-Student Contact Prior to Expectancy Induction | d | Standard Error |
|---|---|---|---|
| Rosenthal et al. 1974 | 2 | .03 | .125 |
| Conn et al. 1968 | 21 | .12 | .147 |
| Jose & Cody 1971 | 19 | −.14 | .167 |
| Pellegrini & Hicks 1972 [1] | 0 | 1.18 | .373 |
| Pellegrini & Hicks 1972 [2] | 0 | .26 | .369 |
| Evans & Rosenthal 1968 | 3 | −.06 | .103 |
| Fielder et al. 1971 | 17 | −.02 | .103 |
| Claiborn 1969 | 24 | −.32 | .220 |
| Kester 1969 | 0 | .27 | .164 |
| Maxwell 1970 | 1 | .80 | .251 |
| Carter 1970 | 0 | .54 | .302 |
| Flowers 1966 | 0 | .18 | .223 |
| Keshock 1970 | 1 | −.02 | .289 |
| Henrikson 1970 | 2 | .23 | .290 |
| Fine 1972 | 17 | −.18 | .159 |
| Greiger 1970 | 5 | −.06 | .167 |
| Rosenthal & Jacobson 1968 | 1 | .30 | .139 |
| Fleming & Anttonen 1971 | 2 | .07 | .094 |
| Ginsburg 1970 | 7 | −.07 | .174 |

NOTE: These data are from Raudenbush and Bryk (1985); see also Raudenbush (1984).

was likely to be related to effect size was the amount of contact that teachers had with the students prior to the attempt to change expectations. He reasoned that teachers who had more contact would have already formed more stable expectations of students—expectations that would prove more difficult to change via the experimental treatment. A summary of the studies and their effect sizes is given in Table A.2. The effect size is the standardized difference between the means of the expectancy group and the control group on an intelligence test. Positive values of the effect size imply a higher mean score for the experimental (high-expectancy) group.

## 3.  DATA SET III: Validity Studies Correlating Student Ratings of the Instructor with Student Achievement

Cohen (1981, 1983) reviewed studies of the validity of student ratings of instructors. The studies were usually conducted in multisection courses in which the sections had different instructors but all sections used a common

final examination. The index of validity was a correlation coefficient (a partial correlation coefficient, controlling for a measure of student ability) between the section mean instructor ratings and the section mean examination score. Thus, the effective sample size was the number of sections. Table A.3 gives the effect size (product moment correlation coefficient) and a summary of each study with a sample size of ten or greater.

## 4.  REFERENCES

Becker, B. J. (1986). Influence again. In J. S. Hyde and M. L. Linn (Eds.), *The psychology of gender: Progress through meta-analysis.* Baltimore: Johns Hopkins University Press.

Cohen, P. A. (1981). Student ratings of instruction and student achievement: A meta-analysis of multisection validity studies. *Review of Educational Research, 51,* 281–309.

Cohen, P. A. (1983). Comment on ''A selective review of the validity of student ratings of teaching.'' *Journal of Higher Education, 54,* 449–458.

**Table A.3  Data Set III: Validity Studies Correlating Student Ratings of the Instructor with Student Achievement**

| Study | Sample | Ability Control | $n$[a] | $r$ |
|---|---|---|---|---|
| Bolton et al. 1979 | General psychology | Random assignment | 10 | .68 |
| Bryson 1974 | College algebra | CIAT pretest | 20 | .56 |
| Centra 1977 [1] | General biology | ⎰ Final exam for prior | 13 | .23 |
| Centra 1977 [2] | General psychology | ⎱ semester of same course | 22 | .64 |
| Crooks & Smock 1974 | General physics | Math pretest | 28 | .49 |
| Doyle & Crichton 1978 | Introductory communications | PSAT verbal score | 12 | −.04 |
| Doyle & Whitely 1974 | Beginning French aptitude test | Minnesota Scholastic | 12 | .49 |
| Elliot 1950 | General chemistry | College entrance exam scores | 36 | .33 |
| Ellis & Richard 1977 | General psychology | Random assignment | 19 | .58 |
| Frey, Leonard & Beatty 1975 | Introductory calculus | SAT math scores | 12 | .18 |
| Greenwood et al. 1976 | Analytic geometry and calculus | Achievement pretest | 36 | −.11 |
| Hoffman 1978 | Introductory math | SAT math scores | 75 | .27 |
| McKeachie et al. 1971 | General psychology | Intelligence test scores | 33 | .26 |
| Marsh et al. 1956 | Aircraft mechanics | Hydraulics pretest | 121 | .40 |
| Remmer et al. 1949 | General chemistry | Orientation test scores | 37 | .49 |
| Sullivan & Skanes 1974 [1] | First-year science | Random assignment | 14 | .51 |
| Sullivan & Skanes 1974 [2] | Introductory psychology | Random assignment | 40 | .40 |
| Sullivan & Skanes 1974 [3] | First-year math | Random assignment | 16 | .34 |
| Sullivan & Skanes 1974 [4] | First-year biology | Random assignment | 14 | .42 |
| Wherry 1952 | Introductory psychology | Ability scores | 20 | .16 |

NOTE: These data are from Cohen (1983); studies with sample sizes less than ten were excluded.
[a] Number of sections.

Eagly, A. H., & Carli, L. L. (1981). Sex of researchers and sex typed communication as determinants of sex differences in influenceability: A meta-analysis of social influence studies. *Psychological Bulletin, 90,* 1–20.

Raudenbush, S. W. (1984). Magnitude of teacher expectancy effects on pupil IQ as a function of the credibility of expectancy induction: A synthesis of findings from 18 experiments. *Journal of Educational Psychology, 76,* 85–97.

Raudenbush, S. W., & Bryk, A. S. (1985). Empirical Bayes meta-analysis. *Journal of Educational Statistics, 10,* 75–98.

## 4.1   Data Set I: Studies Reporting Primary Results

Feldman-Summers, S., Montano, D. E., Kasprzyk, D., & Wagner, B. (1977). *Influence when competing views are gender related: Sex as credibility.* Unpublished manuscript, University of Washington.

King, B. T. (1959). Relationships between susceptibility to opinion change and child rearing practices In C. I. Hovland and I. L. Janis (Eds.), (pp. 207–221). *Personality and persuasibility* New Haven: Yale University Press.

Sampson, E. E., & Hancock, F. T. (1967). An examination of the relationship between ordinal position, personality, and conformity. *Journal of Personality and Social Psychology, 5,* 398–407.

Sistrunk, F. (1971). Negro-white comparisons in social conformity. *Journal of Social Psychology, 85,* 77–85.

Sistrunk, F. (1972). Masculinity-femininity and conformity. *Journal of Social Psychology, 87,* 161–162.

Sistrunk, F., & McDavid, J. W. (1971). Sex variable in conformity behavior. *Journal of Personality and Social Psychology, 17,* 200–207.

Wyer, R. S., Jr. (1966). Effects of incentive to perform well, group attraction, and group acceptance on conformity in a judgmental task. *Journal of Personality and Social Psychology, 4,* 21–26.

Wyer, R. S., Jr. (1967). Behavioral correlates of academic achievement: Conformity under achievement-affiliation-incentive conditions. *Journal of Personality and Social Psychology, 6,* 255–263.

## 4.2   Data Set II: Studies Reporting Primary Results

Carter, D. L. (1971). The effect of teacher expectations on the self-esteem and academic performance of seventh grade students (Doctoral dissertation, University of Tennessee, 1970). *Dissertation Abstracts International, 31,* 4539-A. (University Microfilms No. 7107612)

Claiborn,W. (1969). Expectancy effects in the classroom: A failure to replicate. *Journal of Educational Psychology, 60,* 377–383.

Conn, L. K., Edwards, C. N., Rosenthal, R., & Crowne, D. (1968). Perception of emotion and response to teachers' expectancy by elementary school children. *Psychological Reports, 22,* 27–34.

Evans, J., & Rosenthal, R. (1969). Interpersonal self-fulfilling prophecies: Further extrapolations from the laboratory to the classroom. *Proceedings of the 77th Annual Convention of the American Psychological Association, 4,* 371–372.

Fielder, W. R., Cohen, R. D., & Feeney, S. (1971). An attempt to replicate the teacher expectancy effect. *Psychological Reports, 29,* 1223–1228.

Fine, L. (1972). The effects of positive teacher expectancy on the reading achievement of pupils in grade two (Doctoral dissertation, Temple University, 1972). *Dissertation Abstracts International, 33,* 1510-A. (University Microfilms No. 7227180)

Fleming, E., & Anttonen, R. (1971). Teacher expectancy or my fair lady. *American Educational Research Journal, 8,* 241–252.

Flowers, C. E. (1966). Effects of an arbitrary accelerated group placement on the tested academic achievement of educationally disadvantaged students (Doctoral dissertation, Columbia University, 1966). *Dissertation Abstracts International, 27,* 991-A. (University Microfilms, No. 6610288)

Ginsburg, R. E. (1971). An examination of the relationship between teacher expectations and student performance on a test of intellectual functioning (Doctoral dissertation, University of Utah, 1970). *Dissertation Abstracts International, 31,* 3337-A. (University Microfilms No. 710922)

Grieger, R. M., II. (1971). The effects of teacher expectancies on the intelligence of students and the behaviors of teachers (Doctoral dissertation, Ohio State University, 1970). *Dissertation Abstracts International, 31,* 3338-A. (University Microfilms No. 710922)

Henrikson, H. A. (1971). An investigation of the influence of teacher expectation upon the intellectual and academic performance of disadvantaged children (Doctoral dissertation, University of Illinois, Urbana-Champaign, 1970). *Dissertation Abstracts International, 31,* 6278-A. (University Microfilms No. 7114791)

Jose, J., & Cody, J. (1971). Teacher-pupil interaction as it relates to attempted changes in teacher expectancy of academic ability achievement. *American Educational Research Journal, 8,* 39–49.

Keshock, J. D. (1971). An investigation of the effects of the expectancy phenomenon upon the intelligence, achievement, and motivation of inner-city elementary school children (Doctoral dissertation, Case Western Reserve, 1970). *Dissertation Abstracts International, 32,* 243-A. (University Microfilms No. 7119010)

Kester, S. W. (1969). The communication of teacher expectations and their effects on the achievement and attitudes of secondary school pupils (Doctoral dissertation, University of Oklahoma, 1969). *Dissertation Abstracts International, 30,* 1434-A. (University Microfilms No. 6917653)

Maxwell, M. L. (1971). A study of the effects of teachers' expectations on the IQ and academic performance of children (Doctoral dissertation, Case Western Reserve, 1970). *Dissertation Abstracts International, 31,* 3345-A. (University Microfilms No. 7101725)

Pellegrini, R., & Hicks, R. (1972). Prophecy effects and tutorial instruction for the disadvantaged child. *American Educational Research Journal, 9,* 413–419.

Rosenthal, R., Baratz, S., & Hall, C. M. (1974). Teacher behavior, teacher expectations, and gains in pupils' rated creativity. *Journal of Genetic Psychology, 124,* 115–121.

Rosenthal, R., & Jacobson, L. (1968). *Pygmalion in the classroom.* New York: Holt, Rinehart & Winston.

## 4.3 Data Set III: Studies Reporting Primary Results

Bolton, B., Bonge, D., & Marr, J. (1979). Ratings of instruction, examination performance, and subsequent enrollment in psychology courses. *Teaching of Psychology, 6,* 82–85.

Bryson, R. (1974). Teacher evaluations and student learning: A reexamination. *Journal of Educational Research, 68,* 12–14.

Centra, J. A. (1977). Student ratings of instruction and their relationship to student learning. *American Educational Research Journal, 14,* 17–24.

Crooks, T. J., & Smock, H. R. (1974). Student ratings of

instructors related to student achievement. Urbana: University of Illinois, Office of Instructional Resources.

Doyle, K. O., & Crichton, L. I. (1978). Student, peer, and self-evaluations of college instructors. *Journal of Educational Psychology, 70,* 815–826.

Doyle, K. O., & Whitely, S. E. (1974). Student ratings as criteria for effective teaching. *American Educational Research Journal, 11,* 259–274.

Elliott, D. N. (1950). Characteristics and relationships of various criteria of college and university teaching. *Purdue University Studies in Higher Education, 70,* 5–61.

Ellis, N. R., & Rickard, H. C. (1977). Evaluating the teaching of introductory psychology. *Teaching of Psychology, 4,* 128–132.

Frey, P. W., Leonard, D. W., & Beatty, W. W. (1975). Student ratings of instruction: Validation research. *American Educational Research Journal, 12,* 435–447.

Greenwood, G. E. Hazelton, A., Smith, A. B., & Ware, W. B. (1976). A study of the validity of four types of student ratings of college teaching assessed on a criterion of student achievement gains. *Research in Higher Education, 5,* 171–178.

Hoffman, R. G. (1978). Variables affecting university student ratings of instructor behavior. *American Educational Research Journal, 15,* 287–299.

McKeachie, W. J., Lin, Y. G., & Mann, W. (1971). Student ratings of teacher effectiveness: Validity studies. *American Educational Research Journal, 8,* 435–445.

Morsh, J. E., Burgess, G. G., & Smith, P. N. (1956). Student achievement as a measure of instructor effectiveness. *Journal of Educational Psychology, 47,* 79–88.

Remmers, H. H., Martin, F. D., & Elliott, D. N. (1949). Are students ratings of instructors related to their grades? *Purdue University Studies in Higher Education, 66,* 17–26.

Sullivan, A. M., & Skanes, G. R. (1974). Validity of student evaluation of teaching and the characteristics of successful instructors. *Journal of Educational Psychology, 66,* 584–590.

Wherry, R. J. (1952). *Control of bias in ratings* (PRS Reports Nos. 914, 915 919, 920, and 921). Washington, DC: Department of the Army, Adjutant General's Office.

# APPENDIX B

# Tables

**Table B.1 Probability that a Standard Normal Deviate Exceeds Z**

| Z | Second Digit of Z | | | | | | | | | |
|---|---|---|---|---|---|---|---|---|---|---|
| | .00 | .01 | .02 | .03 | .04 | .05 | .06 | .07 | .08 | .09 |
| .0 | .5000 | .4960 | .4920 | .4880 | .4840 | .4801 | .4761 | .4721 | .4681 | .4641 |
| .1 | .4602 | .4562 | .4522 | .4483 | .4443 | .4404 | .4364 | .4325 | .4286 | .4247 |
| .2 | .4207 | .4168 | .4129 | .4090 | .4052 | .4013 | .3974 | .3936 | .3897 | .3859 |
| .3 | .3821 | .3783 | .3745 | .3707 | .3669 | .3632 | .3594 | .3557 | .3520 | .3483 |
| .4 | .3446 | .3409 | .3372 | .3336 | .3300 | .3264 | .3228 | .3192 | .3156 | .3121 |
| .5 | .3085 | .3050 | .3015 | .2981 | .2946 | .2912 | .2877 | .2843 | .2810 | .2776 |
| .6 | .2743 | .2709 | .2676 | .2643 | .2611 | .2578 | .2546 | .2514 | .2483 | .2451 |
| .7 | .2420 | .2389 | .2358 | .2327 | .2296 | .2266 | .2236 | .2206 | .2177 | .2148 |
| .8 | .2119 | .2090 | .2061 | .2033 | .2005 | .1977 | .1949 | .1922 | .1894 | .1867 |
| .9 | .1841 | .1814 | .1788 | .1762 | .1736 | .1711 | .1685 | .1660 | .1635 | .1611 |
| 1.0 | .1587 | .1562 | .1539 | .1515 | .1492 | .1469 | .1446 | .1423 | .1401 | .1379 |
| 1.1 | .1357 | .1335 | .1314 | .1292 | .1271 | .1251 | .1230 | .1210 | .1190 | .1170 |
| 1.2 | .1151 | .1131 | .1112 | .1093 | .1075 | .1056 | .1038 | .1020 | .1003 | .0985 |
| 1.3 | .0968 | .0951 | .0934 | .0918 | .0901 | .0885 | .0869 | .0853 | .0838 | .0823 |
| 1.4 | .0808 | .0793 | .0778 | .0764 | .0749 | .0735 | .0721 | .0708 | .0694 | .0681 |
| 1.5 | .0668 | .0655 | .0643 | .0630 | .0618 | .0606 | .0594 | .0582 | .0571 | .0559 |
| 1.6 | .0548 | .0537 | .0526 | .0516 | .0505 | .0495 | .0485 | .0475 | .0465 | .0455 |
| 1.7 | .0446 | .0436 | .0427 | .0418 | .0409 | .0401 | .0392 | .0384 | .0375 | .0367 |
| 1.8 | .0359 | .0351 | .0344 | .0336 | .0329 | .0322 | .0314 | .0307 | .0301 | .0294 |
| 1.9 | .0287 | .0281 | .0274 | .0268 | .0262 | .0256 | .0250 | .0244 | .0239 | .0233 |
| 2.0 | .0228 | .0222 | .0217 | .0212 | .0207 | .0202 | .0197 | .0192 | .0188 | .0183 |
| 2.1 | .0179 | .0174 | .0170 | .0166 | .0162 | .0158 | .0154 | .0150 | .0146 | .0143 |
| 2.2 | .0139 | .0136 | .0132 | .0129 | .0125 | .0122 | .0119 | .0116 | .0113 | .0110 |
| 2.3 | .0107 | .0104 | .0102 | .0099 | .0096 | .0094 | .0091 | .0089 | .0087 | .0084 |
| 2.4 | .0082 | .0080 | .0078 | .0075 | .0073 | .0071 | .0069 | .0068 | .0066 | .0064 |
| 2.5 | .0062 | .0060 | .0059 | .0057 | .0055 | .0054 | .0052 | .0051 | .0049 | .0048 |
| 2.6 | .0047 | .0045 | .0044 | .0043 | .0041 | .0040 | .0039 | .0038 | .0037 | .0036 |
| 2.7 | .0035 | .0034 | .0033 | .0032 | .0031 | .0030 | .0029 | .0028 | .0027 | .0026 |
| 2.8 | .0026 | .0025 | .0024 | .0023 | .0023 | .0022 | .0021 | .0021 | .0020 | .0019 |
| 2.9 | .0019 | .0018 | .0018 | .0017 | .0016 | .0016 | .0015 | .0015 | .0014 | .0014 |
| 3.0 | .0013 | .0013 | .0013 | .0012 | .0012 | .0011 | .0011 | .0011 | .0010 | .0010 |
| 3.1 | .0010 | .0009 | .0009 | .0009 | .0008 | .0008 | .0008 | .0008 | .0007 | .0007 |
| 3.2 | .0007 | | | | | | | | | |
| 3.3 | .0005 | | | | | | | | | |
| 3.4 | .0003 | | | | | | | | | |
| 3.5 | .00023 | | | | | | | | | |
| 3.6 | .00016 | | | | | | | | | |
| 3.7 | .00011 | | | | | | | | | |
| 3.8 | .00007 | | | | | | | | | |
| 3.9 | .00005 | | | | | | | | | |
| 4.0 | .00003 | | | | | | | | | |

SOURCE: Reproduced from S. Siegel, *Nonparametric Statistics* (New York: McGraw-Hill, 1956), p. 247, with the permission of the publisher.

### Table B.2  Critical Values of the Chi-Square Distribution

| Degrees of Freedom | Left Tail Area | | | | | | |
|---|---|---|---|---|---|---|---|
| | 0.50 | 0.75 | 0.90 | 0.95 | 0.975 | 0.99 | 0.995 |
| 1 | 0.4549 | 1.323 | 2.706 | 3.841 | 5.025 | 6.635 | 7.879 |
| 2 | 1.386 | 2.773 | 4.605 | 5.991 | 7.378 | 9.210 | 10.60 |
| 3 | 2.366 | 4.108 | 6.251 | 7.815 | 9.348 | 11.34 | 12.84 |
| 4 | 3.357 | 5.385 | 7.779 | 9.488 | 11.14 | 13.28 | 14.86 |
| 5 | 4.351 | 6.626 | 9.236 | 11.07 | 12.83 | 15.09 | 16.75 |
| 6 | 5.348 | 7.841 | 10.64 | 12.59 | 14.45 | 16.81 | 18.55 |
| 7 | 6.346 | 9.037 | 12.02 | 14.07 | 16.01 | 18.48 | 20.28 |
| 8 | 7.344 | 10.22 | 13.36 | 15.51 | 17.53 | 20.09 | 21.95 |
| 9 | 8.343 | 11.39 | 14.68 | 16.92 | 19.02 | 21.67 | 23.59 |
| 10 | 9.342 | 12.55 | 15.99 | 18.31 | 20.48 | 23.21 | 25.19 |
| 11 | 10.34 | 13.70 | 17.28 | 19.68 | 21.92 | 24.72 | 26.76 |
| 12 | 11.34 | 14.85 | 18.55 | 21.03 | 23.34 | 26.22 | 28.30 |
| 13 | 12.34 | 15.98 | 19.81 | 22.36 | 24.74 | 27.69 | 29.82 |
| 14 | 13.34 | 17.12 | 21.06 | 23.68 | 26.12 | 29.14 | 31.32 |
| 15 | 14.34 | 18.25 | 22.31 | 25.00 | 27.49 | 30.58 | 32.80 |
| 16 | 15.34 | 19.37 | 23.54 | 26.30 | 28.85 | 32.00 | 34.27 |
| 17 | 16.34 | 20.49 | 24.77 | 27.59 | 30.19 | 33.41 | 35.72 |
| 18 | 17.34 | 21.60 | 25.99 | 28.87 | 31.53 | 34.81 | 37.16 |
| 19 | 18.34 | 22.72 | 27.20 | 30.14 | 32.85 | 36.19 | 38.58 |
| 20 | 19.34 | 23.83 | 28.41 | 31.41 | 34.17 | 37.57 | 40.00 |
| 21 | 20.34 | 24.93 | 29.62 | 32.67 | 35.48 | 38.93 | 41.40 |
| 22 | 21.34 | 26.04 | 30.81 | 33.92 | 36.78 | 40.29 | 42.80 |
| 23 | 22.34 | 27.14 | 32.01 | 35.17 | 38.08 | 41.64 | 44.18 |
| 24 | 23.34 | 28.24 | 33.20 | 36.42 | 39.36 | 42.98 | 45.56 |
| 25 | 24.34 | 29.34 | 34.38 | 37.65 | 40.65 | 44.31 | 46.93 |
| 26 | 25.34 | 30.43 | 35.56 | 38.89 | 41.92 | 45.64 | 48.29 |
| 27 | 26.34 | 31.53 | 36.74 | 40.11 | 43.19 | 46.96 | 49.64 |
| 28 | 27.34 | 32.62 | 37.92 | 41.34 | 44.46 | 48.28 | 50.99 |
| 29 | 28.34 | 33.71 | 39.09 | 42.56 | 45.72 | 49.59 | 52.34 |
| 30 | 29.34 | 34.80 | 40.26 | 43.77 | 46.98 | 50.89 | 53.67 |
| 31 | 30.34 | 35.89 | 41.42 | 44.99 | 48.23 | 52.19 | 55.00 |
| 32 | 31.34 | 36.97 | 42.58 | 46.19 | 49.48 | 53.49 | 56.33 |
| 33 | 32.34 | 38.06 | 43.75 | 47.40 | 50.73 | 54.78 | 57.65 |
| 34 | 33.34 | 39.14 | 44.90 | 48.60 | 51.97 | 56.06 | 58.96 |
| 35 | 34.34 | 40.22 | 46.06 | 49.80 | 53.20 | 57.34 | 60.27 |
| 36 | 35.34 | 41.30 | 47.21 | 51.00 | 54.44 | 58.62 | 61.58 |
| 37 | 36.34 | 42.38 | 48.36 | 52.19 | 55.67 | 59.89 | 62.88 |
| 38 | 37.34 | 43.46 | 49.51 | 53.38 | 56.90 | 61.16 | 64.18 |
| 39 | 38.34 | 44.54 | 50.66 | 54.57 | 58.12 | 62.43 | 65.48 |
| 40 | 39.34 | 45.62 | 51.81 | 55.76 | 59.34 | 63.69 | 66.77 |
| 50 | 49.33 | 56.33 | 63.17 | 67.50 | 71.42 | 76.15 | 79.49 |
| 60 | 59.33 | 66.98 | 74.40 | 79.08 | 83.30 | 88.38 | 91.95 |
| 70 | 69.33 | 77.58 | 85.53 | 90.53 | 95.02 | 100.4 | 104.2 |
| 80 | 79.33 | 88.13 | 96.58 | 101.9 | 106.6 | 112.3 | 116.3 |
| 90 | 89.33 | 98.65 | 107.6 | 113.1 | 118.1 | 124.1 | 128.3 |

APPENDIX B

### Table B.2 (continued)

| Degrees of Freedom | Left Tail Area | | | | | | |
|---|---|---|---|---|---|---|---|
| | 0.50 | 0.75 | 0.90 | 0.95 | 0.975 | 0.99 | 0.995 |
| 100 | 99.33 | 109.1 | 118.5 | 124.3 | 129.6 | 135.8 | 140.2 |
| 110 | 109.3 | 119.6 | 129.4 | 135.5 | 140.9 | 147.4 | 151.9 |
| 120 | 119.3 | 130.1 | 140.2 | 146.6 | 152.2 | 159.0 | 163.6 |
| 130 | 129.3 | 140.5 | 151.0 | 157.6 | 163.5 | 170.4 | 175.3 |
| 140 | 139.3 | 150.9 | 161.8 | 168.6 | 174.6 | 181.8 | 186.8 |
| 150 | 149.3 | 161.3 | 172.6 | 179.6 | 185.8 | 193.2 | 198.4 |
| 160 | 159.3 | 171.7 | 183.3 | 190.5 | 196.9 | 204.5 | 209.8 |
| 170 | 169.3 | 182.0 | 194.0 | 201.4 | 208.0 | 215.8 | 221.2 |
| 180 | 179.3 | 192.4 | 204.7 | 212.3 | 219.0 | 227.1 | 232.6 |
| 190 | 189.3 | 202.8 | 215.4 | 223.2 | 230.1 | 238.3 | 244.0 |
| 200 | 199.3 | 213.1 | 226.0 | 234.0 | 241.1 | 249.4 | 255.3 |

SOURCE: Reprinted from L. V. Hedges and I. Olkin, *Statistical Methods for Meta-Analysis* (New York: Academic Press, 1985), with permission of the publisher.

### Table B.3 Fisher's z Transformation of r

| r | Second Digit of r | | | | | | | | | |
|---|---|---|---|---|---|---|---|---|---|---|
| | .00 | .01 | .02 | .03 | .04 | .05 | .06 | .07 | .08 | .09 |
| .0 | .000 | .010 | .020 | .030 | .040 | .050 | .060 | .070 | .080 | .090 |
| .1 | .100 | .110 | .121 | .131 | .141 | .151 | .161 | .172 | .182 | .192 |
| .2 | .203 | .213 | .224 | .234 | .245 | .255 | .266 | .277 | .288 | .299 |
| .3 | .310 | .321 | .332 | .343 | .354 | .365 | .377 | .388 | .400 | .412 |
| .4 | .424 | .436 | .448 | .460 | .472 | .485 | .497 | .510 | .523 | .536 |
| .5 | .549 | .563 | .576 | .590 | .604 | .618 | .633 | .648 | .662 | .678 |
| .6 | .693 | .709 | .725 | .741 | .758 | .775 | .793 | .811 | .829 | .848 |
| .7 | .867 | .887 | .908 | .929 | .950 | .973 | .996 | 1.020 | 1.045 | 1.071 |
| .8 | 1.099 | 1.127 | 1.157 | 1.188 | 1.221 | 1.256 | 1.293 | 1.333 | 1.376 | 1.422 |

| r | Third Digit of r | | | | | | | | | |
|---|---|---|---|---|---|---|---|---|---|---|
| | .000 | .001 | .002 | .003 | .004 | .005 | .006 | .007 | .008 | .009 |
| .90 | 1.472 | 1.478 | 1.483 | 1.488 | 1.494 | 1.499 | 1.505 | 1.510 | 1.516 | 1.522 |
| .91 | 1.528 | 1.533 | 1.539 | 1.545 | 1.551 | 1.557 | 1.564 | 1.570 | 1.576 | 1.583 |
| .92 | 1.589 | 1.596 | 1.602 | 1.609 | 1.616 | 1.623 | 1.630 | 1.637 | 1.644 | 1.651 |
| .93 | 1.658 | 1.666 | 1.673 | 1.681 | 1.689 | 1.697 | 1.705 | 1.713 | 1.721 | 1.730 |
| .94 | 1.738 | 1.747 | 1.756 | 1.764 | 1.774 | 1.783 | 1.792 | 1.802 | 1.812 | 1.822 |
| .95 | 1.832 | 1.842 | 1.853 | 1.863 | 1.874 | 1.886 | 1.897 | 1.909 | 1.921 | 1.933 |
| .96 | 1.946 | 1.959 | 1.972 | 1.986 | 2.000 | 2.014 | 2.029 | 2.044 | 2.060 | 2.076 |
| .97 | 2.092 | 2.109 | 2.127 | 2.146 | 2.165 | 2.185 | 2.205 | 2.227 | 2.249 | 2.273 |
| .98 | 2.298 | 2.323 | 2.351 | 2.380 | 2.410 | 2.443 | 2.477 | 2.515 | 2.555 | 2.599 |
| .99 | 2.646 | 2.700 | 2.759 | 2.826 | 2.903 | 2.994 | 3.106 | 3.250 | 3.453 | 3.800 |

SOURCE: Reprinted from G. W. Snedecor and W. G. Cochran, *Statistical Methods,* 7th ed. (Ames: Iowa State University Press, 1980), with permission of the publisher.

NOTE: $z$ is obtained as $\frac{1}{2} \ln_e \frac{1+r}{1-r}$.

# INDEX

Page numbers in **boldface** refer to figures, illustrations, and tables.